New Perspectives on

HTML, XHTML, and Dynamic HTML

4th Edition

Comprehensive

New Perspectives on

HTML, XHTML, and Dynamic HTML

4th Edition

Comprehensive

Patrick Carey

COURSE TECHNOLOGY
CENGAGE Learning™

Australia • Brazil • Japan • Korea • Mexico • Singapore • Spain • United Kingdom • United States

COURSE TECHNOLOGY
CENGAGE Learning™

New Perspectives on HTML, XHTML, and Dynamic HTML, 4th Edition—Comprehensive

Vice President, Publisher: Nicole Jones Pinard

Executive Editor: Marie L. Lee

Senior Product Manager: Kathy Finnegan

Associate Acquisitions Editor: Brandi Shailer

Associate Product Manager: Leigh Robbins

Editorial Assistant: Julia Leroux-Lindsey

Director of Marketing: Cheryl Costantini

Marketing Manager: Ryan DeGrote

Marketing Coordinator: Kristen Panciocco

Developmental Editors: Mary Kemper, Robin M. Romer

Senior Content Project Manager: Jennifer Goguen McGrail

Composition: GEX Publishing Services

Text Designer: Steve Deschene

Art Director: Marissa Falco

Cover Designer: Elizabeth Paquin

Cover Art: Bill Brown

Copyeditor: Suzanne Huizenga

Proofreader: Kathy Orrino

Indexer: Alexandra Nickerson

For product information and technology assistance, contact us at
Cengage Learning Customer & Sales Support, 1-800-354-9706

For permission to use material from this text or product, submit all requests online at **cengage.com/permissions**
Further permissions questions can be emailed to
permissionrequest@cengage.com

ISBN-13: 978-1-4239-2543-9

ISBN-10: 1-4239-2543-2

Course Technology
20 Channel Center Street
Boston, Massachusetts 02210
USA

Cengage Learning is a leading provider of customized learning solutions with office locations around the globe, including Singapore, the United Kingdom, Australia, Mexico, Brazil, and Japan. Locate your local office at:
international.cengage.com/region

Cengage Learning products are represented in Canada by Nelson Education, Ltd.

To learn more about Course Technology, visit **www.cengage.com/coursetechnology**
To learn more about Cengage Learning, visit **www.cengage.com**

Purchase any of our products at your local college store or at our preferred online store **www.ichapters.com**

Printed in the United States of America
3 4 5 6 7 8 9 13 12 11 10

Preface

The New Perspectives Series' critical-thinking, problem-solving approach is the ideal way to prepare students to transcend point-and-click skills and take advantage of all that the World Wide Web has to offer.

Our goal in developing the New Perspectives Series was to create books that give students the software concepts and practical skills they need to succeed beyond the classroom. With this new edition, we've updated our proven case-based pedagogy with more practical content to make learning skills more meaningful to students.

With the New Perspectives Series, students understand *why* they are learning *what* they are learning, and are fully prepared to apply their skills to real-life situations.

"This text is filled with excellent explanations and activities. My students vary in their abilities, and this text covers exactly what they need in a logical, incremental fashion. It's a great reference book that students will find useful for years."
—Kenneth Wade
Champlain College

About This Book

This book provides complete coverage of HTML and XHTML, and includes the following:

- Up-to-date coverage of using HTML and XHTML to create and design Web sites
- Instruction on using CSS to create styles that enhance Web page design and layout, including table and print styles
- Expanded and in-depth coverage of embedding multimedia content; using JavaScript to create Web sites with dynamic content and styles; creating Web forms; and using JavaScript to provide client-side form validation
- Reinforcement of code compliance with strict applications of HTML and XHTML and compliance with Section 508 accessibility guidelines
- Web demos, which give students an interactive approach to learning HTML, XHTML, CSS, and JavaScript
- An Online Companion, which provides supplemental information related to the content of each tutorial as well as access to the student data files
- Updated business case scenarios throughout, which provide a rich and realistic context for students to apply the concepts and skills presented

System Requirements

This book assumes that students have an Internet connection, a text editor, and a current Web browser that supports HTML 4.0 and XHTML 1.1 standards. The following is a list of the most recent versions of the major browsers at the time this text was published: Windows—Firefox 2.0, Internet Explorer 7.0, Opera 9.25, and Safari 3.0; Macintosh—Safari 3.0. All Web browsers interpret HTML and CSS code in slightly different ways. It is highly recommend that students have several different browsers installed on their systems, for comparison purposes. Students might also want to run older versions of these browsers to highlight compatibility issues, but the code in this book is designed to support those browser versions. The screenshots in this book were produced using Internet Explorer 7.0 running on Windows Vista, unless otherwise noted. If students are using a different browser or operating system, their screens will vary slightly from those shown in the book; this does not present any problems for students in completing the tutorials.

"The New Perspectives Series approach, which combines definition and real-world application of content, makes it an easy choice for me when selecting textbooks. I am able to teach concepts that students can immediately apply."
—Brian Morgan
Marshall University

The New Perspectives Approach

Context
Each tutorial begins with a problem presented in a "real-world" case that is meaningful to students. The case sets the scene to help students understand what they will do in the tutorial.

Hands-on Approach
Each tutorial is divided into manageable sessions that combine reading and hands-on, step-by-step work. Colorful screenshots help guide students through the steps. **Trouble?** tips anticipate common mistakes or problems to help students stay on track and continue with the tutorial.

InSight

InSight Boxes
New for this edition! InSight boxes offer expert advice and best practices to help students better understand how to work with HTML, XHTML, and Dynamic HTML. With the information provided in the InSight boxes, students achieve a deeper understanding of the concepts behind the features and skills presented.

Tip

Margin Tips
New for this edition! Margin Tips provide helpful hints and shortcuts for more efficient use of HTML, XHTML, and Dynamic HTML. The Tips appear in the margin at key points throughout each tutorial, giving students extra information when and where they need it.

Reality Check

Reality Checks
New for this edition! Comprehensive, open-ended Reality Check exercises give students the opportunity to practice skills by completing practical, real-world tasks, such as creating a personal Web site and creating and posting an online resume.

Review

In New Perspectives, retention is a key component to learning. At the end of each session, a series of Quick Check questions helps students test their understanding of the concepts before moving on. Each tutorial also contains an end-of-tutorial summary and a list of key terms for further reinforcement.

Apply

Assessment
Engaging and challenging Review Assignments and Case Problems have always been a hallmark feature of the New Perspectives Series. Colorful icons and brief descriptions accompany the exercises, making it easy to understand, at a glance, both the goal and level of challenge a particular assignment holds.

Reference Window

Reference
While contextual learning is excellent for retention, there are times when students will want a high-level understanding of how to accomplish a task. Within each tutorial, Reference Windows appear before a set of steps to provide a succinct summary and preview of how to perform a task. In addition, each book includes a combination Glossary/Index to promote easy reference of material.

www.cengage.com/ct/newperspectives

Our Complete System of Instruction

Brief
Introductory
Comprehensive

Coverage To Meet Your Needs

Whether you're looking for just a small amount of coverage or enough to fill a semester-long class, we can provide you with a textbook that meets your needs.

- Brief books typically cover the essential skills in just 2 to 4 tutorials.
- Introductory books build and expand on those skills and contain an average of 5 to 8 tutorials.
- Comprehensive books are great for a full-semester class, and contain 9 to 12+ tutorials.

So if the book you're holding does not provide the right amount of coverage for you, there's probably another offering available. Visit our Web site or contact your Course Technology sales representative to find out what else we offer.

Online Companion

This book has an accompanying Online Companion Web site designed to enhance learning. This Web site, www.course.com/np/dhtml4, includes the following:

- Supplemental information tied directly to the content of each tutorial, for further student exploration and reference
- Student Data Files needed to complete the tutorials and end-of-tutorial exercises

COURSECASTS

CourseCasts – Learning on the Go. Always available...always relevant.

Want to keep up with the latest technology trends relevant to you? Visit our site to find a library of podcasts, CourseCasts, featuring a "CourseCast of the Week," and download them to your mp3 player at http://coursecasts.course.com.

Ken Baldauf, host of CourseCasts, is a faculty member of the Florida State University Computer Science Department where he is responsible for teaching technology classes to thousands of FSU students each year. Ken is an expert in the latest technology trends; he gathers and sorts through the most pertinent news and information for CourseCasts so your students can spend their time enjoying technology, rather than trying to figure it out. Open or close your lecture with a discussion based on the latest CourseCast.

Visit us at http://coursecasts.course.com to learn on the go!

Instructor Resources

We offer more than just a book. We have all the tools you need to enhance your lectures, check students' work, and generate exams in a new, easier-to-use and completely revised package. This book's Instructor's Manual, ExamView testbank, PowerPoint presentations, data files, solution files, figure files, and a sample syllabus are all available on a single CD-ROM or for downloading at http://www.cengage.com/coursetechnology.

Skills Assessment and Training

SAM 2007 helps bridge the gap between the classroom and the real world by allowing students to train and test on important computer skills in an active, hands-on environment. SAM 2007's easy-to-use system includes powerful interactive exams, training or projects on critical applications such as Word, Excel, Access, PowerPoint, Outlook, Windows, the Internet, and much more. SAM simulates the application environment, allowing students to demonstrate their knowledge and think through the skills by performing real-world tasks. Powerful administrative options allow instructors to schedule exams and assignments, secure tests, and run reports with almost limitless flexibility.

Blackboard

Online Content

Blackboard is the leading distance learning solution provider and class-management platform today. Course Technology has partnered with Blackboard to bring you premium online content. Content for use with *New Perspectives on HTML, XHTML, and Dynamic HTML, 4th Edition, Comprehensive* is available in a Blackboard Course Cartridge and may include topic reviews, case projects, review questions, test banks, practice tests, custom syllabi, and more. Course Technology also has solutions for several other learning management systems. Please visit http://www.cengage.com/coursetechnology today to see what's available for this title.

Acknowledgments

I would like to thank the people who worked so hard to make this book possible. Special thanks to my developmental editors, Mary Kemper and Robin Romer, for their hard work and valuable insights, and to my Product Manager, Kathy Finnegan, who has worked tirelessly in overseeing this project and made my task so much easier with her enthusiasm and good humor. Other people at Course Technology who deserve credit are Marie Lee, Executive Editor; Brandi Shailer, Associate Acquisitions Editor; Leigh Robbins, Associate Product Manager; Julia Leroux-Lindsey, Editorial Assistant; Jennifer Goguen McGrail, Senior Content Project Manager; Christian Kunciw, Manuscript Quality Assurance (MQA) Supervisor; and John Freitas, Serge Palladino, Danielle Shaw, Teresa Storch, and Susan Whalen, MQA testers.

Feedback is an important part of writing any book, and thanks go to the following reviewers for their helpful ideas and comments: Sally Catlin, Indiana University—Purdue University Indianapolis; Heith Hennel, Valencia Community College; Diana Kokoska, University of Maine; Angela McFarland, B.T. Washington High School, Escambia; Brian Morgan, Marshall University; James Papademas, DeVry University Chicago; and Luke Papademas, DeVry University Chicago. My thanks as well to the members of the New Perspectives HTML Advisory Board for their insights and suggestions for this new edition: Lisa Macon, Valencia Community College; Don Mangione, Baker College of Muskegon; Chuck Riden, Arizona State University; and Kenneth Wade, Champlain College.

Writing a book is like giving birth and I have the stretch marks to prove it, so I want to thank my wife Joan for her love, encouragement, and patience. This book is dedicated to my six children: Catherine, Stephen, Michael, Peter, Thomas, and John.

– Patrick Carey

Brief Contents

Table of Contents

Objectives

Session 1.1
- Learn the history of the Web and HTML
- Describe HTML standards and specifications
- Understand HTML elements and markup tags
- Create the basic structure of an HTML file
- Insert an HTML comment

Session 1.2
- Work with block-level elements
- Create ordered, unordered, and definition lists
- Work with inline elements
- Understand the div and span elements

Session 1.3
- Add attributes to HTML elements
- Format page content using the style attribute
- Mark empty elements with one-sided tags
- Add an inline image to a Web page
- Work with character sets and codes

Developing a Web Page

Creating a Product Page for a Startup Company

Case | Dave's Devil Sticks

Dave Vinet is a machinist in Auburn, Maine. In his spare time, Dave builds and juggles devil sticks—juggling props used in circuses and by street performers. In recent years, he has made customized sticks for his friends and colleagues. Encouraged by their enthusiasm for his work, Dave has decided to start a business called Dave's Devil Sticks. So far his customers have come through word of mouth; now Dave wants to advertise his business on the Web. To do that, Dave needs to create a Web page that describes his company and its products. He has the text describing his company in a flyer that he hands out at juggling conventions. He has also contacted a graphic artist to design a logo. He wants to use this material in his Web page.

He has come to you for help in designing a Web page and writing the code. He wants the Web page to contain the same information and graphics contained in his flyer. To create Dave's Web page, you'll have to learn how to work with HTML, the markup language used to create documents on the World Wide Web.

Starting Data Files

Tutorial.01 →

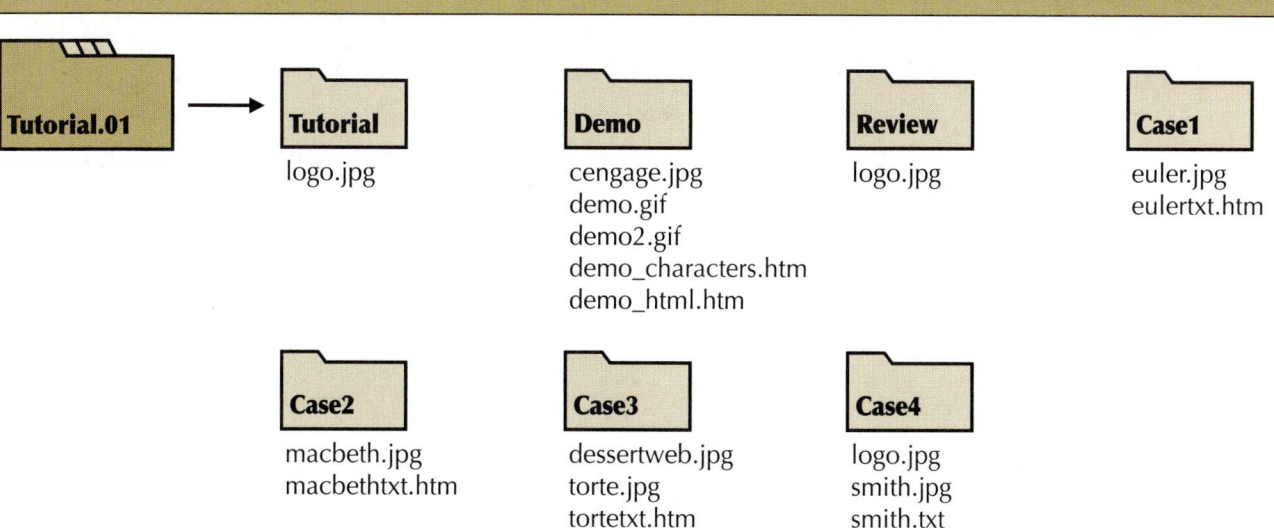

Tutorial
logo.jpg

Demo
cengage.jpg
demo.gif
demo2.gif
demo_characters.htm
demo_html.htm

Review
logo.jpg

Case1
euler.jpg
eulertxt.htm

Case2
macbeth.jpg
macbethtxt.htm

Case3
dessertweb.jpg
torte.jpg
tortetxt.htm

Case4
logo.jpg
smith.jpg
smith.txt

Session 1.1

Exploring the History of the World Wide Web

Before you start creating a Web page for Dave, it's helpful to first look at the history of the Web and how HTML was developed. You'll start by reviewing networks.

Networks

A **network** is a structure that links several points called **nodes** allowing for the sharing of information and services. For computer networks, each node is a device such as a computer or a printer or a scanner, capable of sending and receiving data electronically over the network. A computer node is also called a **host** to distinguish it from other node devices.

As the network operates, nodes are either providing data to other nodes on the network or requesting data. A node that provides information or a service is called a **server**. For example, a **print server** is a network node that provides printing services to the network; a **file server** is a node that provides storage space for saving and retrieving files. A computer or other device that requests services from a server is called a **client**. Networks can follow several different designs. One of the most commonly used designs is the **client-server network** in which several clients access information provided by one or more servers. You might be using such a network to access your data files for this tutorial.

Networks can also be classified based on the range they cover. A network confined to a small geographic area, such as within a building or department, is referred to as a **local area network** or **LAN**. A network that covers a wider area, such as several buildings or cities, is called a **wide area network** or **WAN**. Wide area networks typically consist of two or more local area networks connected together.

The largest WAN is the Internet. The origins of the Internet can be traced backed to a WAN called the **ARPANET**, which started with two network nodes located at UCLA and Stanford connected by a single phone line. Today, the **Internet** has grown to an uncountable number of nodes involving computers, cell phones, PDAs, MP3 players, gaming systems, and television stations. The physical structure of the Internet uses fiber-optic cables, satellites, phone lines, wireless access points, and other telecommunications media, enabling a world-wide community to communicate and share information. See Figure 1-1. It is within this expansive network that Dave wants to advertise his devil sticks business.

Figure 1-1 **Structure of the Internet**

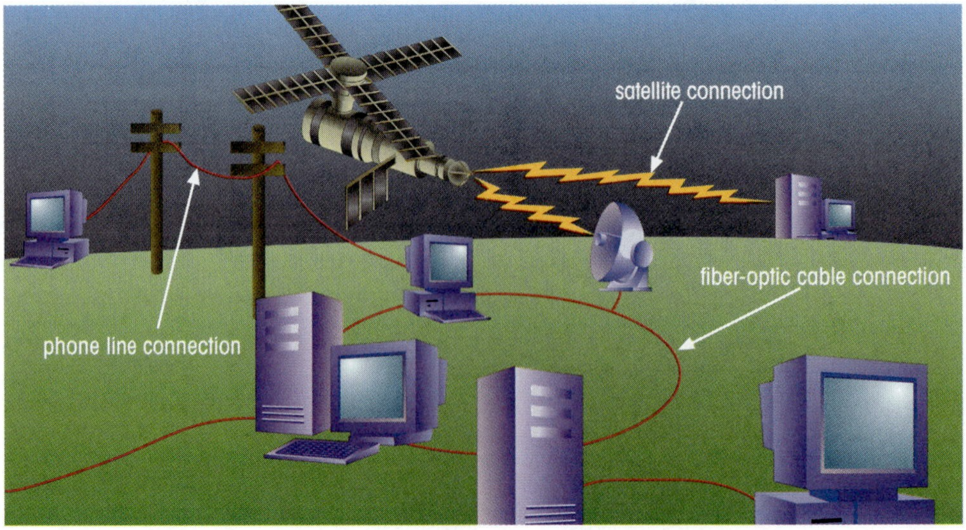

Locating Information on a Network

One of the biggest obstacles to effectively using a network is not mechanical—it's the human element. Users must be able to easily navigate the network and locate the information and services they need. Most of the early Internet tools required users to master a bewildering array of terms, acronyms, and commands. Because network users had to be well versed in computers and network technology, Internet use was limited to universities and departments of the government. To make the Internet accessible to the general public, it needed a simpler interface. This interface proved to be the World Wide Web.

The foundations for the **World Wide Web**, or the **Web** for short, were laid in 1989 by Timothy Berners-Lee and other researchers at the CERN nuclear research facility near Geneva, Switzerland. They needed an information system that would make it easy for their researchers to locate and share data with minimal training and support. To meet this need, they developed a system of hypertext documents that enabled users to easily navigate from one topic to another. **Hypertext** is a method of organization in which information is not presented linearly, but in whatever order is requested by the user. For example, if you read the operating manual for your car starting with page 1 and proceeding to the end, you are processing the information linearly and in the order determined by the manual's author. A hypertext approach would place the same information in a series of smaller documents, with each document dedicated to a single topic, allowing you—and not the author—to choose the order and selection of topics you'll view.

The key to hypertext is the use of **links**, which are the elements in a hypertext document that allow you to jump from one topic or document to another, usually by clicking a mouse button. Hypertext is ideally suited to use with networks because the end user does not need to know where a particular document, information source, or service is located—he or she only needs to know how to activate the link. In the case of an expansive network like the Internet, documents can be located anywhere in the world; but that is largely unseen by the user because of the hypertext structure. The fact that the Internet and the World Wide Web are synonymous in many users' minds is a testament to the success of the hypertext approach.

The original Web supported only textual documents, but the use of hypertext links has expanded through the years to encompass information in any form, including video, sound, interactive programs, conferencing, and online gaming. While the Web has greatly expanded to include these services, the basic foundation is still the same: a collection of interconnected documents linked through the use of hypertext.

Web Pages and Web Servers

Each document on the World Wide Web is referred to as a **Web page**. Web pages are stored on **Web servers**, which are computers that make Web pages available to any device connected to the Internet. To view a Web page, the end user's device needs a software program called a **Web browser**, which retrieves the page from the Web server and renders it on the user's computer or other device. See Figure 1-2.

Figure 1-2 **Using a browser to view a Web document from a Web server**

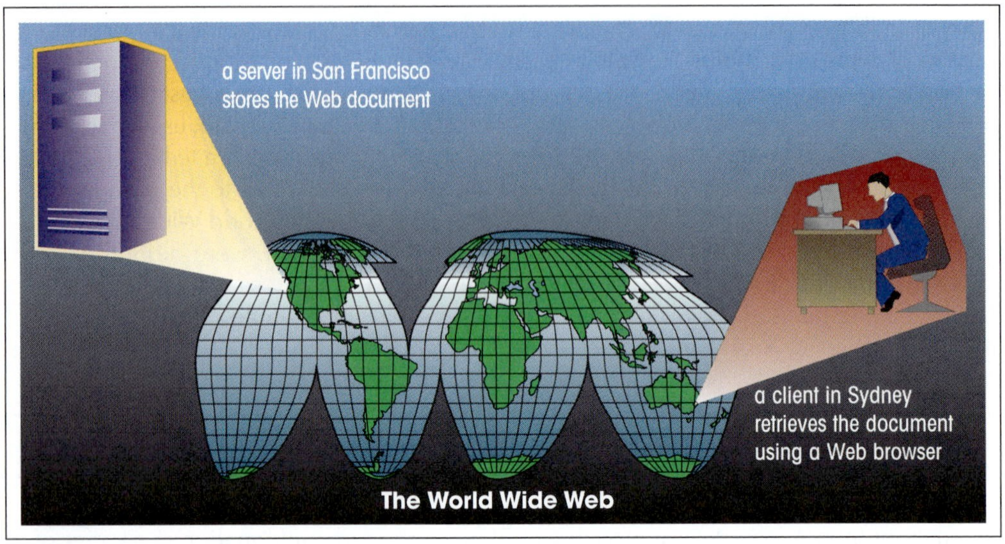

The earliest browsers, known as **text-based browsers**, were limited to displaying only text. Today's browsers are capable of displaying text, images, video, sound, and animations. In the early days of the Internet, Web browsing was limited to computers. Now browsers are installed on cell phones, PDAs (personal digital assistants), MP3 players, and gaming systems. How does a Web page work with so many combinations of browsers and clients and devices? To understand, you need to look at how Web pages are created.

Introducing HTML

A Web page is actually a text file written in **Hypertext Markup Language** or **HTML**. We've already discussed hypertext, but what is a markup language? A **markup language** is a language that describes the content and structure of a document. If this tutorial were written using a markup language, the language would identify the parts of the document, indicating which sections correspond to paragraphs, figure captions, tables, page headings, and so forth.

There are several things that HTML is not. While Web pages often contain interactive programs, HTML is not a programming language. In addition, while HTML can describe the content of a document, it is not a formatting language because it does not necessarily describe how content should be rendered. This is a necessary facet of HTML: the Web page author has no control over what device is used to view the Web page, so the browser—not the HTML—determines how the Web page will look. The end user might be using a large-screen television monitor, a cell phone, or even a device that renders Web pages in Braille or in aural speech.

If you want to format your document, the preferred method is to use styles. **Styles** are formatting rules written in a separate language from HTML telling the browser how to render each element for particular devices. A Web page author can write a style that displays page headings one way for computer monitors and another way for printed output. You'll explore some basic styles as you create your first Web pages.

The History of HTML

HTML evolved as the Web itself evolved. Thus in order to fully appreciate the nuances of HTML, it's a good idea to review the language's history. The first popular markup language was the **Standard Generalized Markup Language** (**SGML**). Introduced in the 1980s, SGML is device- and system-independent, meaning that it can be applied to almost any type of document stored in almost any format. While powerful, SGML is also quite complex; and for this reason SGML is limited to those organizations that can afford the cost and overhead of maintaining complex SGML environments. However, SGML can also be used to create other markup languages that are tailored to specific tasks and are simpler to use and maintain. HTML is one of the languages created with SGML.

In the early years after HTML was created, no single organization was responsible for the language. Web developers were free to define and modify HTML in whatever ways they thought best. Eventually, competing browsers, seeking to dominate the market, added new features called **extensions** to the language. The two major browsers during the 1990s, Netscape Navigator and Microsoft Internet Explorer, added the most extensions to HTML. Netscape provided an extension to add background sounds to documents, while Internet Explorer added an extension to provide marquee-style text that would scroll automatically across the page. These extensions and others provided Web page authors with more options, but at the expense of complicating Web page development. A Web page that took advantage of extensions might work in one browser but not in another.

Thus Web page authors faced the challenge of determining which browser or browser version supported a particular extension, and they had to create a workaround for browsers that did not. By adding this layer of complexity to Web design, extensions, while often useful, diminished the promise of simplicity that made HTML so attractive in the first place.

Ultimately, a group of Web developers, programmers, and authors called the **World Wide Web Consortium**, or the **W3C**, created a set of standards or specifications that all browser manufacturers were to follow. The W3C has no enforcement power; but because a uniform language is in everyone's best interest, the W3C's recommendations are usually followed, though not always right away. The W3C also provides online tutorials, documentation, and quizzes that you can use to test your knowledge of HTML and other languages. For more information on the W3C and the services it offers, see its Web site at *www.w3c.org*.

Figure 1-3 summarizes the various versions of HTML that the W3C has released over the past decade. While you may not grasp all of the details of these versions yet, it's important to understand that HTML doesn't come in only one version.

Figure 1-3 **History of HTML and XHTML**

Version	Date of Release	Description
HTML 1.0	1989	The first public version of HTML which included browser support for inline images and text controls.
HTML 2.0	1995	The first version supported by all graphical browsers. It introduced interactive form elements such as option buttons and text boxes. A document written to the HTML 2.0 specification is compatible with almost all browsers on the World Wide Web.
HTML 3.0	1996	A proposed replacement for HTML 2.0 that was never widely adopted.
HTML 3.2	1997	This version included additional support for creating and formatting tables and expanded the options for interactive form elements. It also supported limited programming using scripts.
HTML 4.01	1999	This version added support for style sheets to give Web designers greater control over page layout. It added new features to tables and forms and provided support for international features. This version also expanded HTML's scripting capability and added increased support for multimedia elements.
HTML 5.0	not yet released	This version supports elements that reflect current Web usage, including elements for Web site navigation and indexing for use with search engines. This version also removes support for purely presentational elements because those effects can be better handled with styles.
XHTML 1.0	2001	This version is a reformulation of HTML 4.01 in XML and combines the strength of HTML 4.0 with the power of XML. XHTML brings the rigor of XML to Web pages and provides standards for more robust Web content on a wide range of browser platforms.
XHTML 1.1	2002	A minor update to XHTML 1.0 that allows for modularity and simplifies writing extensions to the language.
XHTML 2.0	not yet released	The latest version, designed to remove most of the presentational features left in HTML. XHTML 2.0 is not backward compatible with XHTML 1.1.
XHTML 5.0	not yet released	A version of HTML 5.0 written under the specifications of XML, unlike XHTML 2.0, XHTML 5.0 will be backward-compatible with XHTML 1.1.

Tip

You can learn more about deprecated features by examining the documentation available at the W3C Web site and by viewing the source code of various pages on the Web.

When you work with HTML, you should keep in mind not only what the W3C has recommended, but also what HTML features the browser market actually supports. This might mean dealing with a collection of approaches: some browsers are new and meet the latest W3C specifications, while some are older but still widely supported. Older features of HTML are often **deprecated**, or phased out, by the W3C. While deprecated features might not be supported in current or future browsers, that doesn't mean that you won't encounter them—indeed, if you are supporting older browsers that recognize only early versions of HTML, you might need to use them. Because it's hard to predict how quickly deprecated features will disappear from common usage, it's crucial to be familiar with them.

Current Web developers are increasingly using **XML** (**Extensible Markup Language**), a language for creating markup languages, like SGML, but without SGML's complexity and overhead. Using XML, developers can create documents that obey specific rules for their content and structure. This is in contrast with a language like HTML, which supported a wide variety of rules but did not include a mechanism for enforcing those rules.

Indeed, one of the markup languages created with XML is **XHTML** (**Extensible Hypertext Markup Language**), a stricter version of HTML. XHTML is designed to confront some of the problems associated with the various competing versions of HTML and to better integrate HTML with other markup languages like XML. The current version of XHTML is XHTML 1.1, which is mostly (but still not completely) supported by all browsers. Because XHTML is an XML version of HTML, most of what you learn about HTML can be applied to XHTML.

Another version of XHTML, **XHTML 2.0**, is still in the draft stage and has proved to be controversial because it is not backward-compatible with earlier versions of HTML and XHTML. In response to this controversy, another working draft of HTML called **HTML 5.0** is being developed. It provides greater support for emerging online technology while still providing support for older browsers. HTML 5 is also being developed under the XML specifications as **XHTML 5.0**. At the time of this writing, none of these versions has moved beyond the development stage nor has been adopted by the major browsers. This book discusses the syntax of HTML 4.01 and XHTML 1.1, but also brings in deprecated features and browser-supported extensions where appropriate.

Writing HTML Code | InSight

Part of writing good HTML code is being aware of the requirements of various browsers and devices as well as understanding the different versions of the language. Here are a few guidelines for writing good HTML code:

- Become well versed in the history of HTML and the various versions of HTML and XHTML. Unlike other languages, HTML's history does impact how you write your code.
- Know your market. Do you have to support older browsers, or have your clients standardized on one particular browser or browser version? Will your Web pages be viewed on a single device like a computer, or do you have to support a variety of devices?
- Test your code on several different browsers and browser versions. Don't assume that if your page works in one browser it will work on other browsers or even on earlier versions of the same browser. Also check on the speed of the connection. A large file that performs well under a high-speed connection might be unusable under a dial-up connection.
- Read the documentation on the different versions of HTML and XHTML at the W3C Web site and review the latest developments in new versions of the languages.

In general, any HTML code that you write should be compatible with the current versions of the following browsers: Internet Explorer (Windows), Firefox (Windows and Macintosh), Netscape Navigator (Windows), Opera (Windows), and Safari (Macintosh).

Tools for Creating HTML Documents

Because HTML documents are simple text files, you can create them with nothing more than a basic text editor such as Windows Notepad. Specialized HTML authoring programs, known as HTML converters and HTML editors, are also available to perform some of the rote work of document creation. An **HTML converter** is a program that translates text written in another language into HTML code. You can create the source document with a word processor such as Microsoft Word, and then use the converter to save the document as an HTML file. Converters free you from the laborious task of typing HTML code; and because the conversion is automated, you usually do not have to worry about introducing coding errors into your document. However, converters tend to create large and complicated HTML files resulting in "bloated" code, which is more difficult to edit if you need to make changes. So while a converter can speed up Web page development, you will probably still have to invest time in cleaning up the code.

An **HTML editor** is a program that helps you create an HTML file by inserting HTML codes for you as you work. HTML editors can save you a lot of time and can help you work more efficiently. Their advantages and limitations are similar to those of HTML converters. Like converters, HTML editors allow you to set up a Web page quickly, but you will still have to work directly with the underlying HTML code to create a finished product.

Creating an HTML Document

Now that you've had a chance to explore some of the history of the Web and HTML's role in its development, you are ready to work on the Web page for Dave's Devil Sticks. It's always a good idea to plan your Web page before you start coding it. You can do this by drawing a sketch or by creating a sample document using a word processor. The preparatory work can weed out errors or point to potential problems. In this case, Dave has already drawn up a flyer he's passed out at juggling and circus conventions. The handout provides information about Dave's company and his products. Figure 1-4 shows Dave's current flyer.

Figure 1-4 **Elements of the Dave's Devil Sticks flyer**

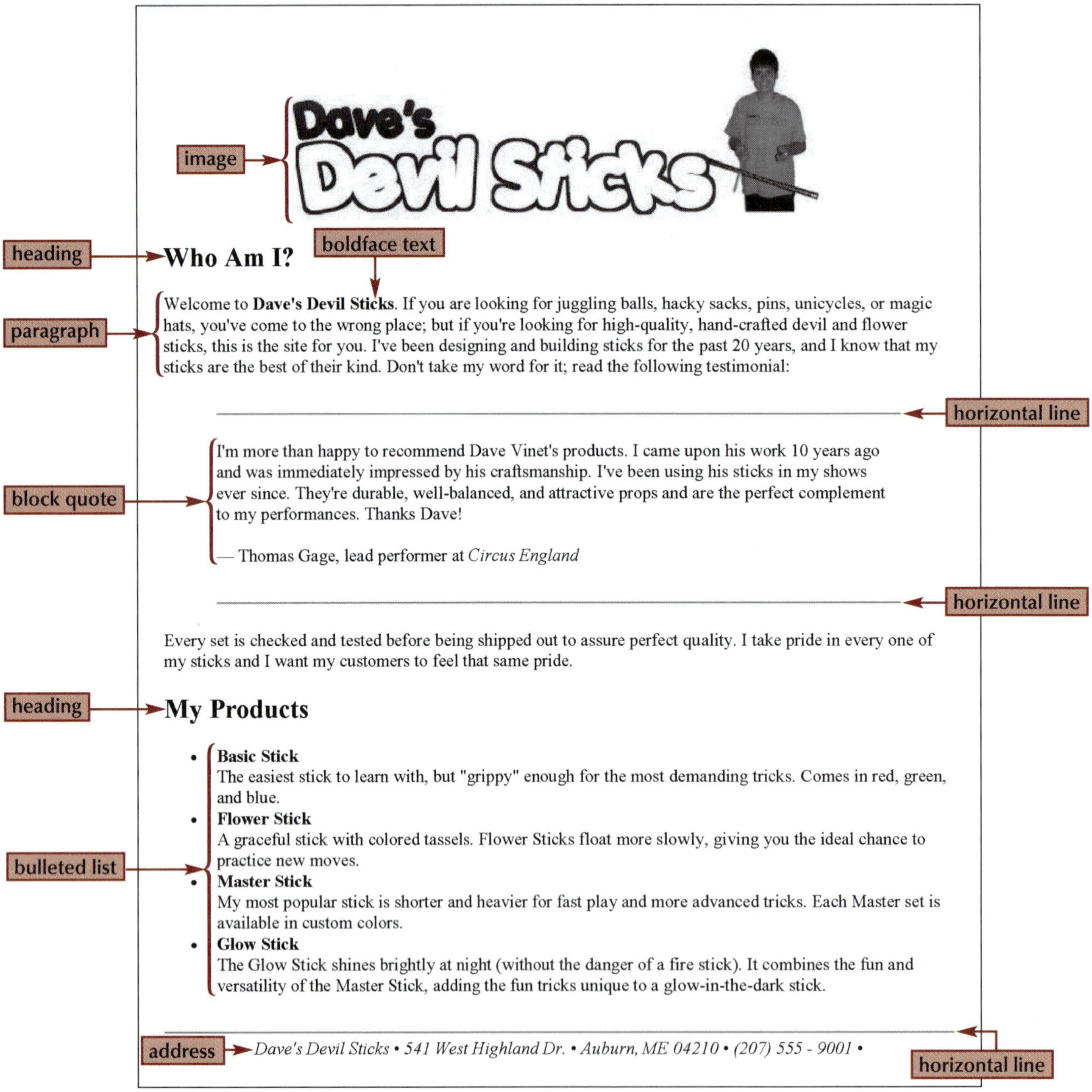

Dave's Devil Sticks

Who Am I?

Welcome to **Dave's Devil Sticks**. If you are looking for juggling balls, hacky sacks, pins, unicycles, or magic hats, you've come to the wrong place; but if you're looking for high-quality, hand-crafted devil and flower sticks, this is the site for you. I've been designing and building sticks for the past 20 years, and I know that my sticks are the best of their kind. Don't take my word for it; read the following testimonial:

> I'm more than happy to recommend Dave Vinet's products. I came upon his work 10 years ago and was immediately impressed by his craftsmanship. I've been using his sticks in my shows ever since. They're durable, well-balanced, and attractive props and are the perfect complement to my performances. Thanks Dave!
>
> — Thomas Gage, lead performer at *Circus England*

Every set is checked and tested before being shipped out to assure perfect quality. I take pride in every one of my sticks and I want my customers to feel that same pride.

My Products

- **Basic Stick**
  The easiest stick to learn with, but "grippy" enough for the most demanding tricks. Comes in red, green, and blue.
- **Flower Stick**
  A graceful stick with colored tassels. Flower Sticks float more slowly, giving you the ideal chance to practice new moves.
- **Master Stick**
  My most popular stick is shorter and heavier for fast play and more advanced tricks. Each Master set is available in custom colors.
- **Glow Stick**
  The Glow Stick shines brightly at night (without the danger of a fire stick). It combines the fun and versatility of the Master Stick, adding the fun tricks unique to a glow-in-the-dark stick.

Dave's Devil Sticks • 541 West Highland Dr. • Auburn, ME 04210 • (207) 555 - 9001 •

When you sketch a sample document, it is a good idea to identify the document's various elements. An **element** is a distinct object in the document, like a paragraph, a heading, or the page's title. Even the whole document is considered an element. Dave's flyer includes several elements: an image displays his company's logo, several headings break his flyer into sections, the text in his flyer is laid out in paragraphs, a bulleted list describes his products, and the address of his company is at the bottom of the flyer. Note that some elements are marked by their appearance in the text. For example, the name of his company is displayed in boldface text at the top of the flyer to set it off from other text in the opening paragraph. Italics are also used in several locations on the page. As you recreate this flyer as a Web page, you should periodically refer to Figure 1-4.

Marking Elements with Tags

The core building block of HTML is the **tag**, which marks the presence of an element. If the element contains content such as text or another element, it is marked using a **two-sided tag** in which an **opening tag** indicates the beginning of the content and a **closing tag** indicates the content's end. The syntax of a two-sided tag is:

```
<element>content</element>
```

where *element* is the name of the element and *content* is any content contained within the element. For example, the following code is used to mark a paragraph element within a document:

```
<p>Welcome to Dave's Devil Sticks.</p>
```

In this example, the <p> tag marks the beginning of the paragraph, the text "Welcome to Dave's Devil Sticks." constitutes the content of the paragraph element and the </p> tag marks the end of the paragraph.

Note that an "element" is an object in the Web document, and a "tag" is the part of the HTML code that marks the element. So you would mark a paragraph element in a document by enclosing the paragraph content within opening and closing paragraph tags.

Elements can also contain other elements. For example, the paragraph tags in the following code

```
<p>Welcome to <b>Dave's Devil Sticks</b>.</p>
```

enclose both the text of the paragraph as well as another set of tags <b> ... </b> that are used to mark content that should be treated by the browser as boldface text. Note that the <b> tags have to be completely enclosed or nested within the <p> tags. It's improper syntax to have tags overlap as in the following code sample:

```
<p>Welcome to <b>Dave's Devil Sticks.</p></b>
```

In this example, the closing </b> tag is placed *after* the closing </p> tag, which is improper because the boldface text marked with these tags must be completely enclosed *within* the paragraph.

The Structure of an HTML Document

All documents written in a markup language need to have a **root element** that contains all of the elements used in the document. For HTML documents, the root element is marked using the <html> tag as follows

```
<html>
 document content
</html>
```

where *document content* is the content of the entire document, including all other elements. The presence of the opening <html> tag in the first line of the file tells any device reading the document that this file is written in HTML. The closing </html> tag signals the end of the document and should not be followed by any other content or markup tags.

Tip

Enter your tags using all lowercase letters. For example, use <html> rather than <HTML>. While many browsers accept uppercase tag names, XHTML code requires tag names to be lowercase.

Web pages are divided into two main sections: a head and a body. The **head element** contains information about the document—for example, the document's title or a list of keywords that would aid a search engine on the Web identifying this document for other users. The **body element** contains all of the content that will appear on the Web page. Taken together, the syntax of the entire HTML file including the head and body elements is

```
<html>
   <head>
      head content
   </head>
   <body>
      body content
   </body>
</html>
```

where *head content* and *body content* are the content you want to place within the document's head and body. Note that the body element is always placed after the head element and that no other elements can be placed between the html, head, and body elements.

Reference Window | Creating the Basic Structure of an HTML Document

- Enter the following HTML tags

```
<html>
   <head>
      head content
   </head>
   <body>
      body content
   </body>
</html>
```

  where *head content* and *body content* are the content you want to place within the document's head and body.
- To specify the page title, enter the following tag within the head section

```
<title>content</title>
```

  where *content* is the text of the Web page title.

Now that you've learned about the basic structure of an HTML file, you can start writing the HTML code for Dave's Web page.

To create the basic structure of an HTML document:

1. Start your text editor, opening it to a blank document.

   Trouble? If you don't know how to start or use your text editor, ask your instructor or technical support person for help.

2. Type the following lines of code in your document. Press the **Enter** key after each line. Press the **Enter** key twice for a blank line between lines of code. See Figure 1-5.

```
<html>

<head>
</head>

<body>
</body>

</html>
```

Basic structure of an HTML document — Figure 1-5

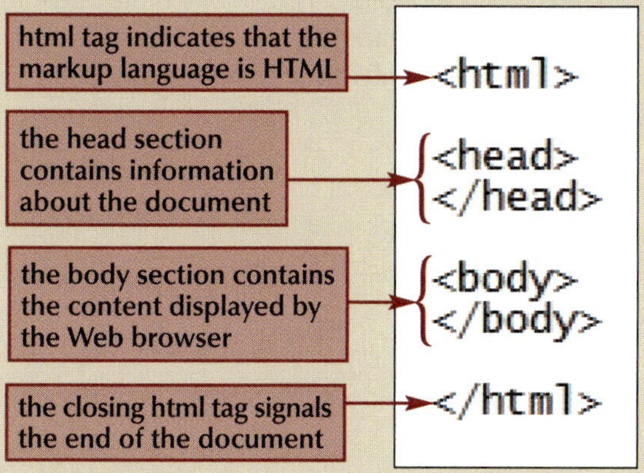

3. Save the file as **dave.htm** in the tutorial.01\tutorial folder included with your Data Files.

   Trouble? If you are using the Windows Notepad text editor to create your HTML file, make sure you don't save the file with the extension .txt, which is the default file extension for Notepad. Instead, make sure you save the file with the file extension .htm or .html. Using the incorrect file extension might make the file unreadable to Web browsers, which require file extensions of .htm or .html.

Tip

To make it easier to link to your Web pages, follow the Internet convention in which HTML filenames and folder names use only lowercase letters with no spaces.

InSight | Converting an HTML Document into XHTML

There is considerable overlap between HTML and XHTML. You can quickly change an HTML document into an XHTML document just by altering the first three lines of code. To convert an HTML file into an XHTML file, replace the opening <html> tag with the following three lines of code:

```
<?xml version="1.0" encoding="UTF-8" standalone="no" ?>
<!DOCTYPE html PUBLIC "-//W3C//DTD XHTML 1.0 Strict//EN"
  "http://www.w3.org/TR/xhtml1/DTD/xhtml1-strict.dtd">
<html xmlns="http://www.w3.org/1999/xhtml">
```

Each line has an important role in converting the HTML document into XHTML. XHTML documents are written in XML, so the first line notifies the browser that the document is an XML file. The version number—1.0—tells the browser that the file is written in XML 1.0.

XHTML files differ from HTML files in that XHTML files have to be tested against a set of rules that define exactly which markup tags are allowed and how they can be used. To reference the set of rules, you have to include a DOCTYPE declaration in the second line of the file, indicating the collection of rules to be used. XHTML documents can be tested against several different rules. The code sample above assumes a strict interpretation of the rules is being enforced.

The third line of the file contains the opening <html> tag. In XHTML, the <html> tag must include what is known as a namespace declaration indicating that any markup tags in the document should, by default, be considered part of the XHTML language. This is necessary because XML documents can contain a mixture of several different markup languages and there must be a way of defining the default language of the document.

With these three lines in place, browsers recognize the file as an XHTML rather than an HTML document. After these three lines, there is little difference between the code in an HTML file and in an XHTML file.

Defining the Page Title

One of the elements you can add to the document head is the document title. The syntax of the document title is

```
<title>document title</title>
```

where *document title* is the text of the document title. The document title is not displayed within the page, but is usually displayed in the browser's title bar. The document title is also used by search engines like Google or Yahoo! to report on the contents of the file.

To add a title to a Web page:

1. Click at the end of the <head> tag, and then press the **Enter** key to insert a new line in your text editor.
2. Press the **Spacebar** three times to indent the new line of code, and then type **<title>Dave's Devil Sticks</title>** as shown in Figure 1-6.

Tip

Indent your markup tags and insert extra blank spaces as shown in this book to make your code easier to read. It does not affect how the page is rendered by the browser.

Figure 1-6 Defining the page title

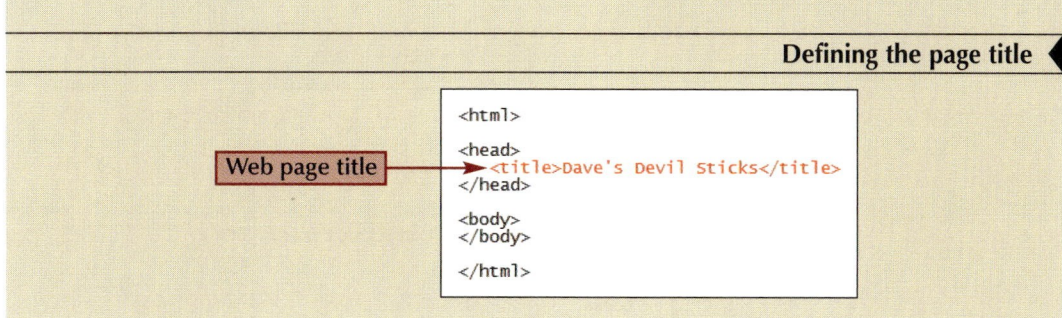

Web page title

```
<html>

<head>
  <title>Dave's Devil Sticks</title>
</head>

<body>
</body>

</html>
```

Adding Comments

As you create a Web page, you might want to add notes or comments about your code. These comments might include the name of the document's author and the date the document was created. Such notes are not intended to be displayed by the browser, but are instead used to help explain your code to yourself and others. To add notes or comments, insert a **comment tag** with the syntax

```
<!-- comment -->
```

where *comment* is the text of the comment or note. For example, the following code inserts a comment describing the page you'll create for Dave's business:

```
<!-- Page created for Dave Vinet's devil stick business -->
```

A comment can also be spread out over several lines as follows:

```
<!-- Dave's Devil Sticks
     A Web page created for Dave Vinet -->
```

Because they are ignored by the browser, comments can be added anywhere within the HTML document.

Adding an HTML Comment | Reference Window

- To insert an HTML comment anywhere within your document, enter
  ```
  <!-- comment -->
  ```
  where *comment* is the text of the HTML comment.

You'll add a comment to the head of Dave's file indicating its purpose, author, and date created.

To add a comment to Dave's file:

1. Click at the end of the <head> tag, and then press the **Enter** key to insert a new line directly above the title element you've just entered.
2. Type the following lines of code, as shown in Figure 1-7

   ```
   <!-- Dave's Devil Sticks
        Author: your name
        Date:   the date
   -->
   ```

   where *your name* is your name and *the date* is the current date.

Figure 1-7 Adding a comment tag

multiline comment

```
<html>

<head>
<!-- Dave's Devil Sticks
     Author: David Vinet
     Date:   3/1/2011
-->
   <title>Dave's Devil Sticks</title>
</head>

<body>
</body>

</html>
```

Displaying an HTML File

As you continue modifying the HTML code, you should occasionally view the page with your Web browser to verify that you have not introduced any errors. You might even want to view the results using different browsers to check for compatibility. In this book Web pages are displayed using the Windows Internet Explorer 7.0 browser. Be aware that if you are using a different browser or a different operating system, you might see slight differences in the layout and appearance of the page.

To view Dave's Web page:

1. Save your changes to the **dave.htm** file.
2. Start your Web browser. You do not need to be connected to the Internet to view local files stored on your computer.

   Trouble? If you start your browser and are not connected to the Internet, you might get a warning message. Click the OK button to ignore the message and continue.
3. After your browser loads its home page, open the **dave.htm** file from the tutorial.01\tutorial folder.

   Trouble? If you're not sure how to open a local file with your browser, check for an Open or Open File command under the browser's File menu. If you are still having problems accessing the dave.htm file, talk to your instructor or technical resource person.

   Your browser displays the Web page shown in Figure 1-8. Note that the page title appears in the browser's title bar; and if your browser supports tabs, it also appears in the tab title. The page itself is empty because you have not yet added any content to the body element.

Figure 1-8 Viewing a page title in the browser window

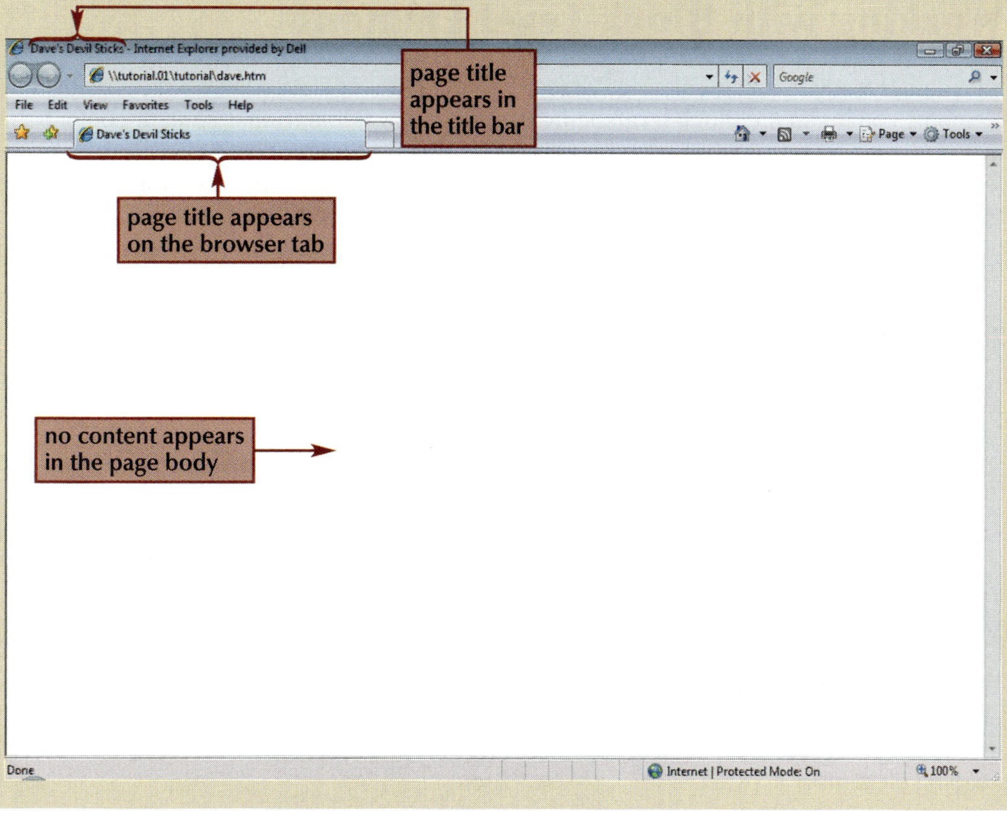

You've completed the head section of the HTML document. In the next session, you'll define the elements that are displayed in the body section. For now, you can close your files and Web browser if you want to take a break before starting the next session.

Session 1.1 Quick Check | Review

1. What is a hypertext document?
2. What is a Web server? What is a Web browser? Describe how they work together.
3. How do HTML documents differ from documents created with a word processor such as Word or WordPerfect?
4. What is a deprecated feature?
5. What element do you use to mark the beginning and end of an HTML document?
6. What code would you enter in your document to set the page title to "Technical Support"? Where would you enter this code?
7. Specify the code needed to add the comment "Page Updated on 4/15/2011" to an HTML file.
8. What error was made in the following HTML code?:

```
<head>
   <title>Customer Comments Form
   </head>
</title>
```

Session 1.2

Working with Block-Level Elements

You're now ready to begin entering content into the body of Dave's Web page. The first elements you'll add are **block-level elements**, which are elements that contain content that is viewed as a distinct block within the Web page. When rendered visually, block-level elements start on a new line in the document. Paragraphs are one example of a block-level element. To explore block-level and other HTML elements, a demo page has been prepared for you.

To open the HTML Tags demo page:

1. Use your browser to open the **demo_html.htm** file from the tutorial.01\demo folder.
2. If your browser prompts you to allow code on the Web page to be run, click the **OK** button.

Working with Headings

The first block-level elements you'll explore are heading elements. **Heading elements** are elements that contain the text of main headings on the Web page. They are often used for introducing new topics or dividing the page into topical sections. The syntax to mark a heading element is

```
<hn>content</hn>
```

where *n* is an integer from 1 to 6. Content marked with the <h1> tag is considered a major heading and is usually displayed in large bold text. Content marked with <h2> down to <h6> tags is used for subheadings and is usually displayed in progressively smaller bold text. To see how these headings appear on your computer, use the demo page.

Reference Window | Marking Block-Level Elements

- To mark a heading, enter
  `<hn>content</hn>`
  where *n* is an integer from 1 to 6 and *content* is the text of heading.
- To mark a paragraph, enter
  `<p>content</p>`
- To mark a block quote, enter
  `<blockquote>content</blockquote>`
- To mark a generic block-level element, enter
  `<div>content</div>`

To view heading elements:

1. Click in the blue box on the bottom left of the demo page, type **<h1>Dave's Devil Sticks</h1>** and then press the **Enter** key to go to a new line.
2. Type **<h2>Auburn, ME 04210</h2>**.

3. Click the **Preview Code** button located below the blue code window. Your browser displays a preview of how this code would appear in your Web browser (see Figure 1-9).

Figure 1-9 **Marking an h1 and h2 element**

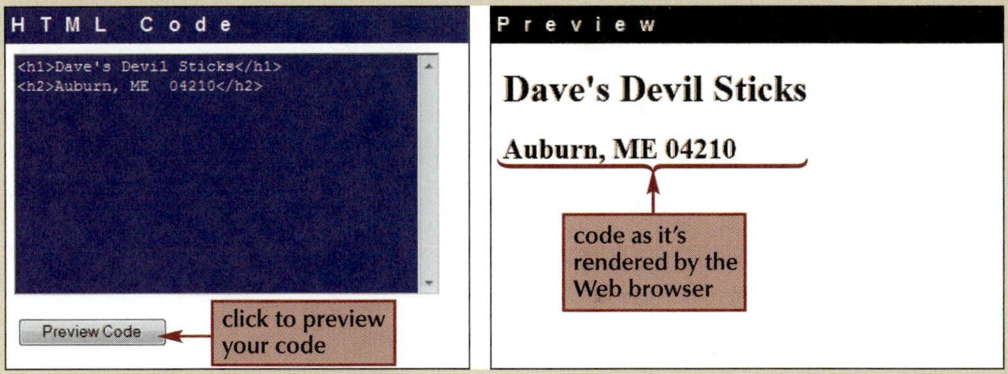

Trouble? If you are using a browser other than Internet Explorer 7.0 running on Windows Vista, your screen might look slightly different from that shown in Figure 1-9.

4. To see how an h3 heading would look, change the opening and closing tags for the store's city and state information from <h2> and </h2> to **<h3>** and **</h3>**. Click the **Preview Code** button again.

   Your browser renders the code again, this time with the city and state information displayed in a smaller font. If you continued to change the heading element from h2 down to h6, you would see the text in the Preview box get progressively smaller.

It's important not to treat markup tags as simply a way of formatting the Web page. The h1 through h6 elements are used to identify headings, but the exact appearance of these headings depends on the browser and the device being used. Remember that the headings might not even be displayed visually. A browser that renders content aurally might convey an h1 heading using increased volume preceded by an extended pause.

Now that you've seen how to mark page headings, you can add some to Dave's Web page. Dave has three headings he wants to add to his document. The first is an h1 heading that will contain the company's name. The other two are h2 headings that preface two different sections of the document: one titled "Who Am I?" and the other titled "My Products."

To add headings to Dave's document:

1. Return to the **dave.htm** file in your text editor.
2. Between the opening and closing <body> tags, insert the following code:

```
<h1>Dave's Devil Sticks</h1>
<h2>Who Am I?</h2>
<h2>My Products</h2>
```

   Indent your code to make it easy to read, as shown in Figure 1-10.

Figure 1-10 Adding <h1> and <h2> markup tags

```
<body>
   <h1>Dave's Devil Sticks</h1>
   <h2>Who Am I?</h2>
   <h2>My Products</h2>
</body>
```

3. Save your changes to the file, and then reload or refresh the **dave.htm** file in your Web browser. Figure 1-11 shows the revised Web page.

Figure 1-11 Headings on the Web page

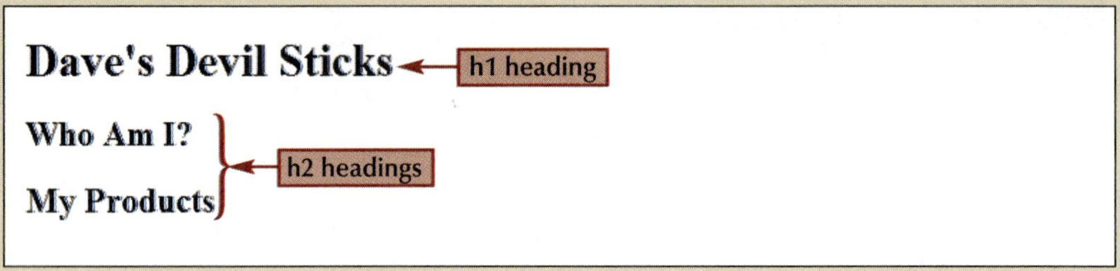

The next block-level elements you'll add are paragraphs about Dave's company and its wares.

Marking Paragraph Elements

As you saw earlier, you can mark a paragraph element using the <p> tag

```
<p>content</p>
```

where *content* is the content of the paragraph. When rendered in a browser, paragraphs are started on a new line. In older HTML code, you might occasionally see paragraphs marked with only the opening <p> tag but without a closing tag. In those situations, the <p> tag marks the start of each new paragraph. While this convention is still accepted by many browsers, it does violate HTML's syntax rules; if you want XHTML-compliant code, you must include the closing tags.

To add two paragraphs to Dave's Web page:

1. Return to the **dave.htm** file in your text editor.
2. Directly below the Who Am I? h2 heading, insert a new line, and then type the following code, as shown in Figure 1-12:

```
<p>Welcome to Dave's Devil Sticks. If you are looking for juggling
balls, hacky sacks, pins, unicycles, or magic hats, you've come
to the wrong place; but if you're looking for high-quality,
hand-crafted devil and flower sticks, this is the site for you.
I've been designing and building sticks for the past 20 years,
and I know that my sticks are the best of their kind.</p>

<p>Every set is checked and tested before being shipped out to
 assure perfect quality. I take pride in every one of my sticks
 and I want my customers to feel that same pride.</p>
```

Figure 1-12 Marking paragraph elements

```
<body>
   <h1>Dave's Devil Sticks</h1>
   <h2>Who Am I?</h2>
   <p>Welcome to Dave's Devil Sticks. If you are looking for juggling balls,
      hacky sacks, pins, unicycles, or magic hats, you've come to the wrong
      place; but if you're looking for high-quality, hand-crafted devil and
      flower sticks, this is the site for you. I've been designing and building
      sticks for the past 20 years, and I know that my sticks are the best of
      their kind.</p>

   <p>Every set is checked and tested before being shipped out to assure perfect
      quality. I take pride in every one of my sticks and I want my customers to
      feel that same pride.</p>

   <h2>My Products</h2>
</body>
```

paragraphs

Trouble? Don't worry if your lines do not wrap at the same locations shown in Figure 1-12. As you'll see shortly, line wrap in the HTML code does not affect how the page is rendered by the browser.

3. Save your changes to the file and then refresh the **dave.htm** file in your Web browser. Figure 1-13 shows the new paragraphs added to the Web page.

Figure 1-13 Paragraphs added to Dave's Web page

Dave's Devil Sticks
Who Am I?
Welcome to Dave's Devil Sticks. If you are looking for juggling balls, hacky sacks, pins, unicycles, or magic hats, you've come to the wrong place; but if you're looking for high-quality, hand-crafted devil and flower sticks, this is the site for you. I've been designing and building sticks for the past 20 years, and I know that my sticks are the best of their kind.
Every set is checked and tested before being shipped out to assure perfect quality. I take pride in every one of my sticks and I want my customers to feel that same pride.
My Products
paragraphs

White Space and HTML

If you compare the paragraph text from the HTML code in Figure 1-12 to the way it's rendered on the Web page in Figure 1-13, you'll notice that the line returns in the code are not reflected in the Web page. When the browser renders HTML code, it ignores the presence of white space within the HTML text file. **White space** consists of blank spaces, tabs, and line breaks. As far as the browser is concerned, there is no difference between a blank space, a tab, or a line break. To explore this issue further, you'll experiment with the HTML demo page.

To explore how white space is treated by the Web browser:

1. Return to the **demo_html.htm** file in your Web browser.
2. Delete the HTML code in the left box and replace it with the following:

```
<p>Dave's Devil Sticks</p>

<p>Dave's                    Devil                     Sticks</p>

<p>Dave's
  Devil
  Sticks</p>
```

3. Click the **Preview Code** button. Figure 1-14 shows how the browser renders the three paragraphs of code.

Figure 1-14 Viewing the effects of white space on HTML code

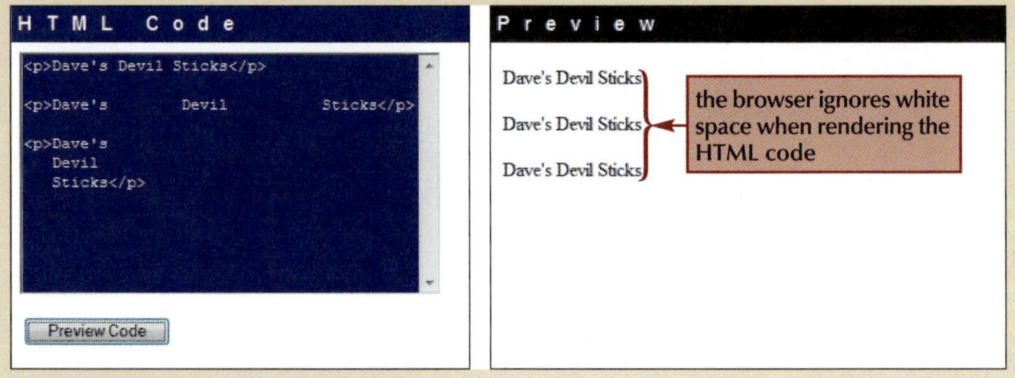

Tip

To force the browser to retain the extra blank spaces, tabs, and line breaks from your HTML code, enclose the white space within a set of opening and closing <pre> tags.

Each paragraph is rendered exactly the same by the browser. Notice that even adding blank spaces within the paragraph does not change the appearance of the text. This is because the browser ignores extra blank spaces. Consequently, you are free to use white space however you wish as you lay out the HTML code to make it easier for you to read—without impacting the appearance of the Web page.

Marking a Block Quote

The next element that Dave wants you to enter into his document is a quote from a satisfied customer. Dave wants the quote, shown earlier in Figure 1-4, to be indented from the surrounding paragraphs to make it stand out more. However, as you just saw, any indenting you do in the HTML file will be ignored by the browser. So how do you achieve this effect? Remember that HTML is used to mark up document content, and so you need a markup tag that identifies quoted material. The syntax for marking an extended quote is

```
<blockquote>content</blockquote>
```

where *content* is the text of the quote. Most browsers will by default indent block quotes on the Web page, so you'll still achieve the visual effect that Dave wants. Note that some browsers might display block quotes differently, and the only way to ensure that block quotes are always indented is by using styles. You'll explore how to apply styles shortly.

To create a block quote:

1. Return to the **dave.htm** file in your text editor.
2. At the end of the first paragraph, directly *before* the closing </p> tag, insert a space and then type the following text:

   ```
   Don't take my word for it; read the following testimonial:
   ```

3. Between the closing </p> tag from the first paragraph and the opening <p> tag of the second paragraph, insert the following code, as shown in Figure 1-15:

   ```
   <blockquote>

     <p>I'm more than happy to recommend Dave Vinet's products. I came
     upon his work 10 years ago and was immediately impressed by his
     craftsmanship. I've been using his sticks in my shows ever since.
     They're durable, well-balanced, and attractive props and are
     the perfect complement to my performances. Thanks Dave!</p>

     <p>Thomas Gage, lead performer at Circus England</p>

   </blockquote>
   ```

Figure 1-15 Marking a block quote

```
<p>Welcome to Dave's Devil Sticks. If you are looking for juggling balls,
   hacky sacks, pins, unicycles, or magic hats, you've come to the wrong
   place; but if you're looking for high-quality, hand-crafted devil and
   flower sticks, this is the site for you. I've been designing and building
   sticks for the past 20 years, and I know that my sticks are the best of
   their kind. Don't take my word for it; read the following testimonial:</p>

<blockquote>
   <p>I'm more than happy to recommend Dave Vinet's products. I came upon his
      work 10 years ago and was immediately impressed by his craftsmanship.
      I've been using his sticks in my shows ever since. They're durable,
      well-balanced, and attractive props and are the perfect complement to
      my performances. Thanks Dave!</p>

   <p>Thomas Gage, lead performer at Circus England</p>
</blockquote>

<p>Every set is checked and tested before being shipped out to assure perfect
   quality. I take pride in every one of my sticks and I want my customers to
   feel that same pride.</p>
```

block quote

4. Save your changes to the file, and then reload **dave.htm** in your Web browser. Figure 1-16 shows the revised page with the quoted material.

Figure 1-16 Dave's Web page with customer comment

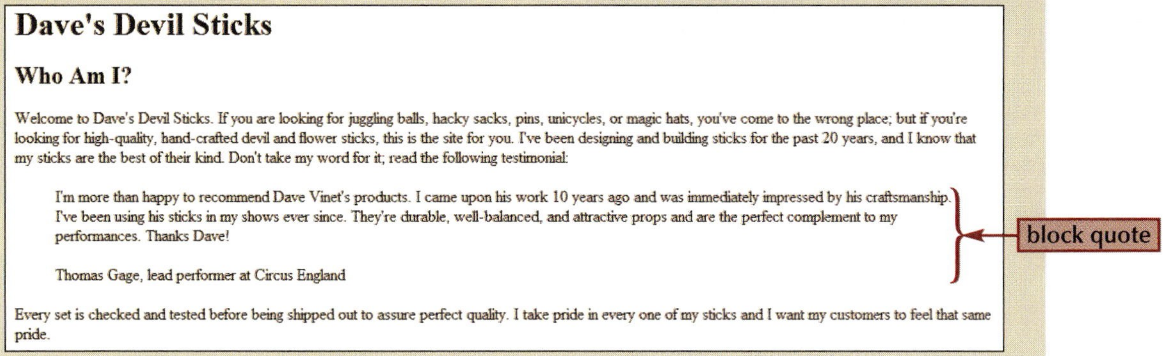
Dave's Devil Sticks
Who Am I?
Welcome to Dave's Devil Sticks. If you are looking for juggling balls, hacky sacks, pins, unicycles, or magic hats, you've come to the wrong place; but if you're looking for high-quality, hand-crafted devil and flower sticks, this is the site for you. I've been designing and building sticks for the past 20 years, and I know that my sticks are the best of their kind. Don't take my word for it; read the following testimonial:
I'm more than happy to recommend Dave Vinet's products. I came upon his work 10 years ago and was immediately impressed by his craftsmanship. I've been using his sticks in my shows ever since. They're durable, well-balanced, and attractive props and are the perfect complement to my performances. Thanks Dave!
Thomas Gage, lead performer at Circus England
Every set is checked and tested before being shipped out to assure perfect quality. I take pride in every one of my sticks and I want my customers to feel that same pride.
block quote

Note that the customer quote also included two paragraph elements nested within the blockquote element. The indentation applied by the browser to the block quote was also applied to any content within that element, so those paragraphs were indented even though browsers do not indent paragraphs by default.

Marking a List

Dave has a list of products that he wants to display on his Web page. This information is presented on his flyer as a bulleted list. He wants something similar on the Web site. HTML supports three kinds of lists: ordered, unordered, and definition.

Ordered Lists

Use an **ordered list** for items that must appear in a numeric order. The beginning of an ordered list is marked by the <ol> (ordered list) tag. Each item within that ordered list is subsequently marked using the <li> (list item) tag. The syntax of an ordered list is therefore

```
<ol>
   <li>item1</li>
   <li>item2</li>
...
</ol>
```

where *item1*, *item2*, and so forth are the items in the list. To explore creating an ordered list, return to the HTML demo page.

To create an ordered list:

1. Return to the **demo_html.htm** file in your Web browser.
2. Delete the HTML code in the left box and replace it with the following:

```
<ol>
   <li>First Item</li>
   <li>Second Item</li>
   <li>Third Item</li>
</ol>
```

3. Click the **Preview Code** button. Figure 1-17 shows how the browser renders the ordered list contents.

Figure 1-17 **Viewing an ordered list**

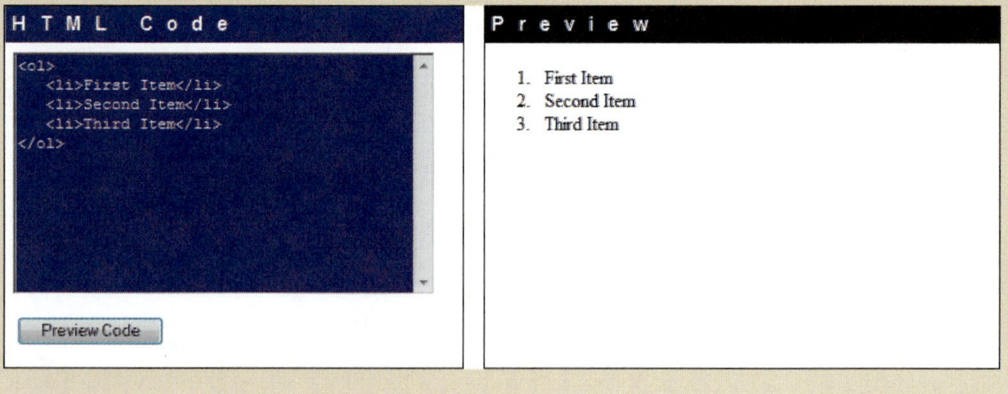

By default, entries in an ordered list are numbered, with the numbers supplied automatically by the browser.

Unordered Lists

To mark a list in which the items do not need to occur in any special order, create an **unordered list**. The structure of ordered and unordered lists is the same, except that the list contents are contained with a set of <ul> (unordered list) tags:

```
<ul>
   <li>item1</li>
   <li>item2</li>
...
</ul>
```

Try creating an unordered list with the demo page.

To create an unordered list:

1. Delete the HTML code in the left box and replace it with the following:

```
<ul>
   <li>Basic Stick</li>
   <li>Flower Stick</li>
   <li>Master Stick</li>
   <li>Glow Stick</li>
</ul>
```

2. Click the **Preview Code** button. Figure 1-18 shows how the browser renders the unordered list.

Figure 1-18 Viewing an unordered list

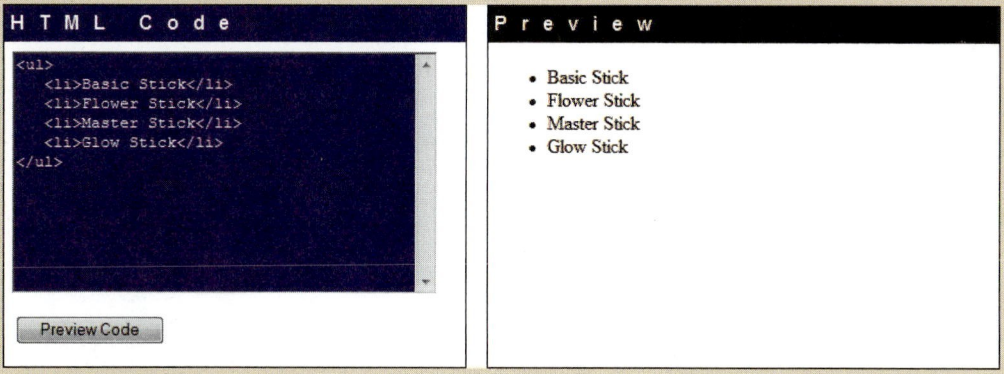

Trouble? On some browsers, the list appears with diamond shapes rather than circular bullets.

By default, unordered lists appear as bulleted lists. The exact bullet marker depends on the browser. Most browsers use a filled-in circle.

Reference Window | Marking Lists

- To mark an ordered list, enter

```
<ol>
    <li>item1</li>
    <li>item2</li>
...
</ol>
```

  where *item1*, *item2*, and so forth are the items in the list.
- To mark an unordered list, use

```
<ul>
    <li>item1</li>
    <li>item2</li>
...
</ul>
```

- To mark a definition list, use

```
<dl>
    <dt>term1</dt>
    <dd>description1</dd>
    <dt>term2</dt>
    <dd>description2a</dd>
    <dd>description2b</dd>
...
</dl>
```

  where *term1*, *term2*, etc. are the terms in the list and *description1*, *description2a*, *description2b*, etc. are the descriptions associated with each term.

Nesting Lists

You can place one list inside of another to create several levels of list items. The top level of the nested list contains the major items, with each sublevel containing items of lesser importance. Most browsers differentiate the various levels by using a different list symbol. Use the demo page to see how this works with unordered lists.

To create an unordered list:

1. Click at the end of the <li>Basic Stick</li> line, and then press the **Enter** key to insert a new blank line.
2. Insert the following code between the <li>Basic Stick</li> and <li>Flower Stick</li> lines:

```
<ul>
    <li>Red</li>
    <li>Blue</li>
    <li>Green</li>
</ul>
```

3. Click the **Preview Code** button. Figure 1-19 shows the result of creating a nested list.

Figure 1-19 Viewing a nested list

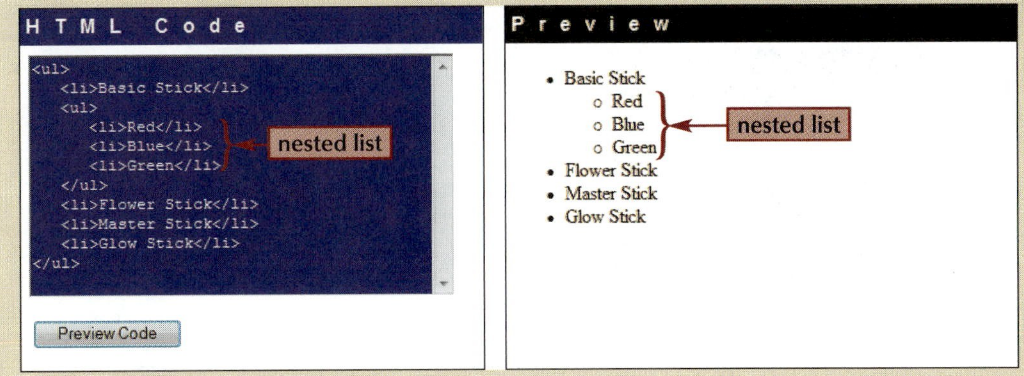

Trouble? Depending on your browser, the sublist of basic stick colors might appear with solid bullets rather than open circles.

The lower level of items is displayed using an open circle as the list bullet and indented on the page. Once again, the exact choice of formatting a nested list is left to the browser at this point. As you continue your study of HTML you'll learn how to specify the appearance of nested lists using styles.

Definition Lists

A third type of list is the **definition list**, which contains a list of terms, each followed by the term's description. The syntax for creating a definition list is

```
<dl>
   <dt>term1</dt>
   <dd>description1</dd>
   <dt>term2</dt>
   <dd>description2a</dd>
   <dd>description2b</dd>
...
</dl>
```

where *term1*, *term2*, etc. are the terms in the list and *description1*, *description2a*, *description2b*, etc. are the descriptions associated with each term. Note that definition lists must follow a specified order, with each dt (definition term) element followed by one or more dd (definition description) elements.

To create a definition list:

1. Replace the code in the left box of the HTML demo page with:

```
<dl>
   <dt>Basic Stick</dt>
   <dd>Easiest stick to learn</dd>
   <dt>Flower Stick</dt>
   <dd>A graceful stick with tassels</dd>
   <dt>Master Stick</dt>
   <dd>Our most popular stick</dd>
</dl>
```

2. Click the **Preview Code** button. Figure 1-20 shows the appearance of the definition list in the browser.

Figure 1-20 Viewing a definition list

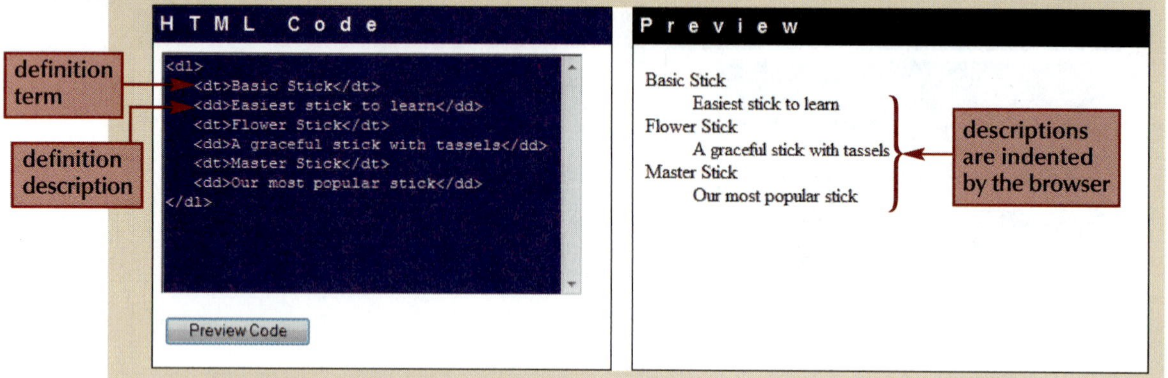

> **Tip**
>
> Definition lists can also mark dialogs, with each dt element naming a speaker, and each dd element containing the speaker's words. For long speeches, use multiple dd elements per speaker to break the speaker's words into separate blocks.

The demo page shows each term followed by a description that is placed in a new block below the term and indented on the page. If you had included multiple dd elements, each description would have been contained within its own block and indented.

Now that you've experimented with the three types of HTML lists, you'll add an unordered list of products to Dave's Web page. By default, the product names will appear as a bulleted list.

To add an unordered list to Dave's Web page:

1. Return to the **dave.htm** file in your text editor.
2. Directly below the <h2>My Products</h2> heading, insert the following code, as shown in Figure 1-21:

```
<ul>
   <li>Basic Stick</li>
   <li>Flower Stick</li>
   <li>Master Stick</li>
   <li>Glow Stick</li>
</ul>
```

Figure 1-21 Adding an unordered list

```
  <h2>My Products</h2>
  <ul>
     <li>Basic Stick</li>
     <li>Flower Stick</li>
     <li>Master Stick</li>
     <li>Glow Stick</li>
  </ul>
</body>
```

3. Save your changes to the file, and then refresh the **dave.htm** file in your Web browser. As shown in Figure 1-22, the list of products appears as a bulleted list at the bottom of the page.

Figure 1-22 Product list on Dave's Web page

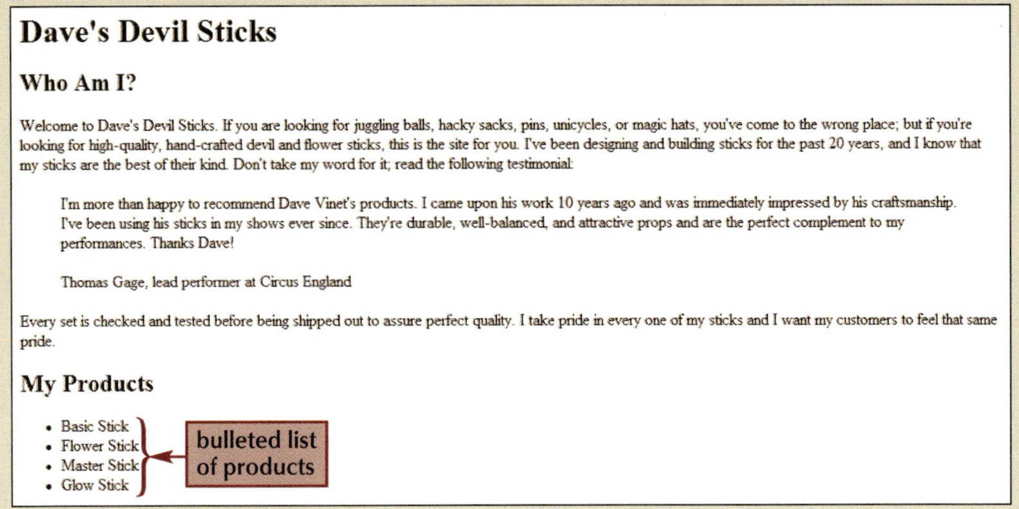

Dave's Devil Sticks

Who Am I?

Welcome to Dave's Devil Sticks. If you are looking for juggling balls, hacky sacks, pins, unicycles, or magic hats, you've come to the wrong place; but if you're looking for high-quality, hand-crafted devil and flower sticks, this is the site for you. I've been designing and building sticks for the past 20 years, and I know that my sticks are the best of their kind. Don't take my word for it; read the following testimonial:

> I'm more than happy to recommend Dave Vinet's products. I came upon his work 10 years ago and was immediately impressed by his craftsmanship. I've been using his sticks in my shows ever since. They're durable, well-balanced, and attractive props and are the perfect complement to my performances. Thanks Dave!
>
> Thomas Gage, lead performer at Circus England

Every set is checked and tested before being shipped out to assure perfect quality. I take pride in every one of my sticks and I want my customers to feel that same pride.

My Products

- Basic Stick
- Flower Stick
- Master Stick
- Glow Stick

Exploring Other Block-Level Elements

HTML supports several other block-level elements you'll find useful. Dave wants to display the company's address at the bottom of the body of his page. Contact information like addresses can be marked using the <address> tag

```
<address>content</address>
```

where *content* is the contact information. Most browsers render addresses in italics, and some also indent or right-justify addresses. You'll use the address element to display the address of Dave's company.

To add an address to the bottom of Dave's Web page:

1. Return to the **dave.htm** file in your text editor.
2. Directly above the </body> tag, insert the following code, as shown in Figure 1-23:

```
<address>Dave's Devil Sticks
         541 West Highland Dr.
         Auburn, ME 04210
        (207) 555 - 9001
</address>
```

Figure 1-23 Adding an address element

```
    <address>Dave's Devil Sticks
             541 West Highland Dr.
             Auburn, ME 04210
             (207) 555 - 9001
    </address>
</body>

</html>
```

3. Save your changes to the file, and then refresh **dave.htm** in your Web browser. Figure 1-24 shows the revised page with the address text.

Figure 1-24 Address text on Dave's Web page

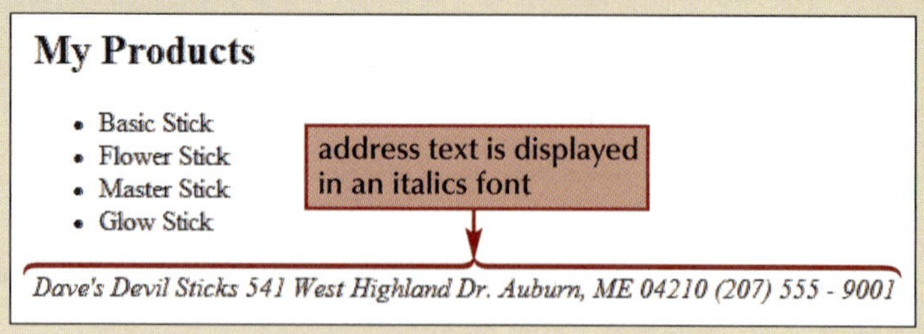

The address text appears in italics at the bottom of the page. Note that the company name, street address, city, state, and phone number all appear to run together. Remember that the browser ignores the occurrence of line breaks, tabs, and other white space in your text document. In the next session, you'll learn how to make this text more readable. For now, you'll leave the address text as it is.

At this point, you're done adding block-level elements to Dave's Web page. Figure 1-25 summarizes the properties and uses of HTML's block-level elements, including information on some block-level elements you did not add to Dave's document.

Figure 1-25 Block-level elements

Block-Level Element	Marks	Usual Visual Appearance
`<address> ... </address>`	Contact information	*Italicized text*
`<blockquote> ... </blockquote>`	An extended quotation	Plain text indented from the left and right
`<center> ... </center>`	Text horizontally centered with the block (**deprecated**)	Plain text, centered
`<dd> ... </dd>`	A definition description	Plain text
`<dir> ... </dir>`	A multicolumn directory list (**deprecated**)	Plain text
`<div> ... </div>`	A generic block-level element	Plain text
`<dl> ... </dl>`	A definition list	Plain text
`<dt> ... </dt>`	A definition term from a definition list	Plain text
`<hn> ... </hn>`	A heading where *n* is a value from 1 to 6 with h1 as the most prominent heading and h6 the least prominent	**Boldfaced text of various font sizes**
`<li> ... </li>`	A list item from an ordered or unordered list	Bulleted or numbered text
`<menu> ... </menu>`	A single column menu list (**deprecated**)	Plain text
`<ol> ... </ol>`	An ordered list	Plain text
`<p> ... </p>`	A paragraph	Plain text
`<pre> ... </pre>`	Preformatted text, retaining all white space and special characters	`Fixed width text`
`<ul> ... </ul>`	An unordered list	Plain text

Working with Inline Elements

Block-level elements place their content starting on a new line within the page. Another type of element is an **inline element**, which marks a section of text within a block-level element. If you think of a block-level element as a paragraph, an inline element is like a phrase or a collection of characters within that paragraph. Inline elements do not start out on a new line or block, but instead flow "in-line" with the rest of the characters in the block.

Character Formatting Elements

Inline elements are often used to format characters and words. For example, you can use an inline element to make a name or title appear in **boldface** letters or *italics*. Inline elements used in this fashion are referred to as **character formatting elements**. Figure 1-26 describes some of the inline elements supported by HTML.

Figure 1-26 Inline elements

Inline Element	Marks	Usual Visual Appearance
`<abbr> ... </abbr>`	An abbreviation	Plain text
`<acronym> .. </acronym>`	An acronym	Plain text
`<b> ... </b>`	Boldfaced text	**Boldfaced text**
`<big> ... </big>`	Big text	Larger text
`<cite> ... </cite>`	A citation	*Italicized text*
`<code> ... </code>`	Program code	`Fixed width text`
`<del> ... </del>`	Deleted text	~~Strikethrough text~~
`<dfn> ... </dfn>`	A definition term	*Italicized text*
`<em> ... </em>`	Emphasized content	*Italicized text*
`<i> ... </i>`	Italicized text	*Italicized text*
`<ins> ... </ins>`	Inserted text	Underlined text
`<kbd> ... </kbd>`	Keyboard-style text	`Fixed width text`
`<q> ... </q>`	Quoted text	"Quoted text"
`<s> ... </s>`	Strikethrough text (**Deprecated**)	~~Strikethrough text~~
`<samp> ... </samp>`	Sample computer code	`Fixed width text`
`<small> ... </small>`	Small text	Smaller text
`<span> ... </span>`	A generic inline element	Plain text
`<strike> ... </strike>`	Strikethrough text (**Deprecated**)	~~Strikethrough text~~
`<strong> ... </strong>`	Strongly emphasized content	**Boldfaced text**
`<sub> ... </sub>`	Subscripted text	Subscripted text
`<sup> ... </sup>`	Superscripted text	Superscripted text
`<tt> ... </tt>`	Teletype text	`Fixed width text`
`<u> ... </u>`	Underlined text (**Deprecated**)	Underlined text
`<var> ... </var>`	Programming variables	*Italicized text*

To see how to use inline elements in conjunction with block-level elements, you'll return to the HTML demo page.

To explore the use of inline elements:

1. Return to the **demo_html.htm** file in your Web browser.
2. In the left box, enter the HTML code:

```
<p>Welcome to Dave's Devil Sticks, owned and operated by David
Vinet.</p>
```

3. Click the **Preview Code** button to display this paragraph in the Preview box.

   To mark "Dave's Devil Sticks" as boldface text, you can enclose that phrase within a set of <b> tags.

4. Insert a **<b>** tag directly before the word "Dave's" in the box on the left. Insert the closing **</b>** tag directly after the word "Sticks." Click the **Preview Code** button to confirm that "Dave's Devil Sticks" is now displayed in bold.

   You can use the <i> tag to mark italicized text. Try this now by enclosing "David Vinet" within a set of <i> tags.

5. Insert an **<i>** tag directly before the word "David" and insert the closing **</i>** tag directly after "Vinet". Click the **Preview Code** button to view the revised code. Figure 1-27 shows the result of applying the <b> and <i> tags to the paragraph text.

Figure 1-27 Using the <b> and <i> tags

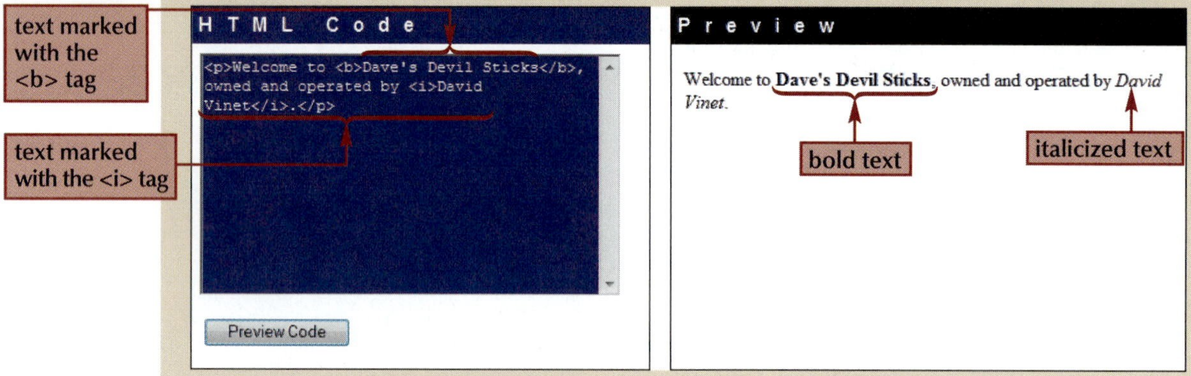

6. Close the HTML demo page.

You can nest inline elements to mark text with more than one character-formatting element. The code

```
<p>Welcome to <b><i>Dave's Devil Sticks</i></b>.</p>
```

displays "Dave's Devil Sticks" in a ***bold italic*** font.

Dave wants to use the <b> and <i> tags in several locations in his document. He wants to display the name of his company and the names of all of his devil stick products in bold. He would also like to display the name of the juggling troupe, *Circus England*, in italics. Make these changes to his document now.

Marking Inline Elements

| Reference Window

- To mark boldface text, enter
  <b>*content*</b>
  where *content* is the text to be displayed in boldface.
- To mark italicized text, use
  <i>*content*</i>
- To mark text with a generic inline element, use
  <span>*content*</span>

To mark boldface and italicized text:

1. Return to the **dave.htm** file in your text editor.
2. Go to the first paragraph of the body section and enclose the text "Dave's Devil Sticks" within a set of opening and closing <b> tags.
3. Go to the second paragraph within the blockquote element and enclose the text "Circus England" within a set of opening and closing <i> tags.
4. Go to the unordered list and enclose each product item within a set of opening and closing <b> tags. Nest the <b> tags within the <li> tags. Figure 1-28 highlights the revised code of Dave's document.

Figure 1-28 Marking bold and italicized text

```
<body>
   <h1>Dave's Devil Sticks</h1>
   <h2>Who Am I?</h2>
   <p>Welcome to <b>Dave's Devil Sticks</b>. If you are looking for juggling balls,
      hacky sacks, pins, unicycles, or magic hats, you've come to the wrong
      place; but if you're looking for high-quality, hand-crafted devil and
      flower sticks, this is the site for you. I've been designing and building
      sticks for the past 20 years, and I know that my sticks are the best of
      their kind. Don't take my word for it; read the following testimonial:</p>

   <blockquote>
      <p>I'm more than happy to recommend Dave Vinet's products. I came upon his
         work 10 years ago and was immediately impressed by his craftsmanship.
         I've been using his sticks in my shows ever since. They're durable,
         well-balanced, and attractive props and are the perfect complement to
         my performances. Thanks Dave!</p>

      <p>Thomas Gage, lead performer at <i>Circus England</i></p>
   </blockquote>

   <p>Every set is checked and tested before being shipped out to assure perfect
      quality. I take pride in every one of my sticks and I want my customers to
      feel that same pride.</p>

   <h2>My Products</h2>
   <ul>
      <li><b>Basic Stick</b></li>
      <li><b>Flower Stick</b></li>
      <li><b>Master Stick</b></li>
      <li><b>Glow Stick</b></li>
   </ul>

   <address>Dave's Devil Sticks
         541 West Highland Dr.
         Auburn, ME 04210
         (207) 555 - 9001
   </address>
</body>
```

5. Save your changes to the file.
6. Refresh the **dave.htm** file in your Web browser. Figure 1-29 shows the revised appearance of the Web page.

Figure 1-29 Dave's revised Web page

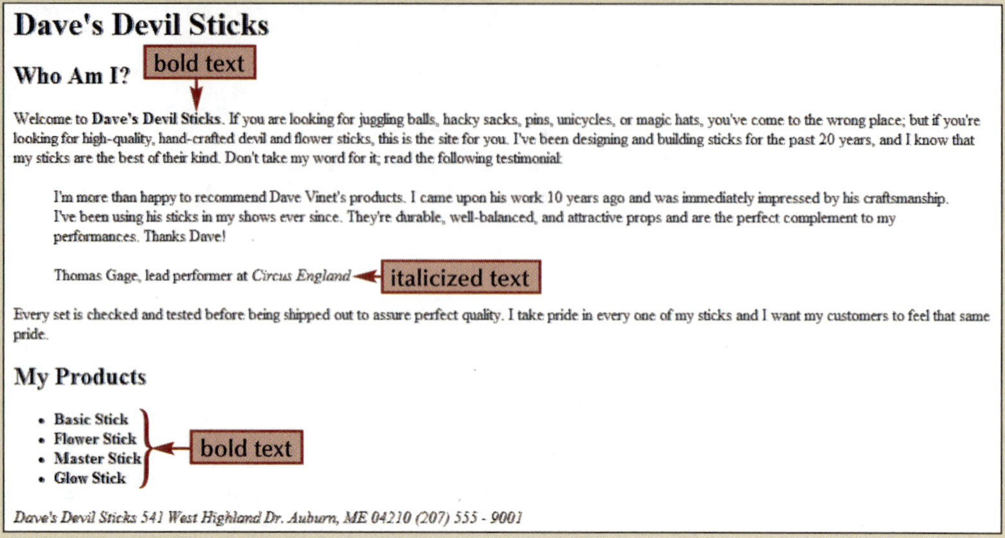
Dave's Devil Sticks
Who Am I?
bold text
Welcome to Dave's Devil Sticks. If you are looking for juggling balls, hacky sacks, pins, unicycles, or magic hats, you've come to the wrong place; but if you're looking for high-quality, hand-crafted devil and flower sticks, this is the site for you. I've been designing and building sticks for the past 20 years, and I know that my sticks are the best of their kind. Don't take my word for it; read the following testimonial:
I'm more than happy to recommend Dave Vinet's products. I came upon his work 10 years ago and was immediately impressed by his craftsmanship. I've been using his sticks in my shows ever since. They're durable, well-balanced, and attractive props and are the perfect complement to my performances. Thanks Dave!
Thomas Gage, lead performer at Circus England
italicized text
Every set is checked and tested before being shipped out to assure perfect quality. I take pride in every one of my sticks and I want my customers to feel that same pride.
My Products
Basic Stick
Flower Stick
Master Stick
Glow Stick
bold text
Dave's Devil Sticks 541 West Highland Dr. Auburn, ME 04210 (207) 555 - 9001

7. If you want to take a break before starting the next session, you can close your browser and any open files now.

Using the Generic Elements: div and span

Most of the block-level and inline elements you've examined have a specific meaning or purpose in your document. Sometimes you will want an element that represents a text block or a string of inline text without it having any other meaning. HTML supports two types of generic elements: div and span. The div element is used to mark general block-level content and has the syntax

```
<div>content</div>
```

The span element, used to mark general inline content, has the syntax

```
<span>content</span>
```

Browsers recognize both elements but do not assign any default format to content marked with those elements. Web authors like using the div and span elements because they know they can completely control the appearance of the content through the use of styles. This is not the case with elements such as addresses or headings, which have default formats assigned to them by the Web browser.

Logical Elements vs. Physical Elements | InSight

As you learn more HTML, you'll notice some overlap in how certain elements are displayed by the browser. To display italicized text, you could use the <dfn>, <em>, <i>, or <var> tags, or if you want to italicize an entire block of text, you could use the <address> tag. It's important to distinguish between how a browser displays an element and the element's purpose in the document. Page elements can be organized into two types: logical elements and physical elements. A logical element, marked with tags like <cite> or <code>, describes the nature of the enclosed content but not necessarily how that content should appear. A physical element, on the other hand, marked with tags like <b> or <i>, describes how content should appear but doesn't indicate the content's nature.

While it can be tempting to use logical and physical elements interchangeably, your HTML code benefits in several ways when you respect the distinction. For one, different browsers can and do display logical elements differently. For example, both Netscape's browser and Internet Explorer display text marked with the <cite> tag in italics, but the text-based browser Lynx displays the citation text using a fixed width font. An aural browser that doesn't render pages visually might increase the volume when it encounters cited text. In addition, Web programmers can also use logical elements to extract information from a page. For example, a program could automatically generate a bibliography from all of the citations listed within a Web site.

In general, you should use a logical element that accurately describes the enclosed content whenever possible, letting the browser determine the appearance based on its function, and use physical elements only for general content.

You're finished working with block-level elements and inline elements. In the next session you'll learn how to add images to the document as well as how to use styles to control the appearance of your Web pages.

Session 1.2 Quick Check | Review

1. What is the difference between a block-level element and an inline element?
2. If you want to add an extra blank line between paragraphs on your Web page, why can't you simply add an extra blank line to the HTML file?
3. Specify the code to mark the main heading on your Web page.
4. Specify the tag to mark an extended quotation. How would that quotation be rendered in most visual browsers?
5. Specify the code you would use to display the seasons of the year (Winter, Spring, Summer, and Fall) as an unordered list.
6. The following is a dialog from Shakespeare's *Hamlet*. Indicate how you would use a definition list to mark up this text, distinguishing between the speaker and the lines spoken.

   HAMLET

   There's ne'er a villain dwelling in all Denmark; but he's an arrant knave.

   HORATIO

   There needs no ghost, my lord, come from the grave to tell us this.
7. What code would you enter to display the following text as a paragraph in your Web page? Include both the block-level and inline element tags.

   Hamlet, a play by William Shakespeare.
8. What are the two generic page elements?

Session 1.3

Using Element Attributes

So far you've used markup tags only to create Dave's Web page. However, many markup tags contain **attributes** that control the use, behavior, and in some cases the appearance of elements in the document. You apply an attribute to an element by adding it to the element's markup tag using the syntax

```
<element attribute1="value1" attribute2="value2" ...>content</element>
```

where *attribute1*, *attribute2*, etc. are the names of attributes associated with the element and *value1*, *value2*, etc. are the values of those attributes. You can list attributes in any order, but you must separate them from one another with white space.

One attribute that is associated with most elements is the id attribute, which uniquely identifies the element in the Web page. The following code assigns the id value of "mainhead" to the h1 heading "Dave's Devil Sticks," distinguishing it from other h1 headings that might exist in the document:

```
<h1 id="mainhead">Dave's Devil Sticks</h1>
```

You'll learn more about the id attribute in the next tutorial. For a list of attributes associated with each element, you can also refer to the appendices.

Tip

Attribute names should be entered in lowercase letters to be completely compliant with the syntax rules of XHTML. Attribute values must be enclosed within single or double quotation marks.

Reference Window | Adding an Attribute to an Element

- To add an element attribute, enter
  ```
  <element attribute1="value1" attribute2="value2" ...>content
  </element>
  ```
  where *attribute1*, *attribute2*, etc. are the names of attributes associated with the element and *value1*, *value2*, etc. are the values of those attributes.

The Style Attribute

Another important attribute is the style attribute. As you've seen, an element's appearance on the Web page is determined by the browser. If you want to change how the browser displays an element, you can use the style attribute. The syntax of the style attribute is

```
<element style="rules" ...>content</element>
```

where *rules* is a set of style rules. Style rules are entered by specifying a style name followed by a colon and then a style value. You can have multiple style rules with each style name/value pair, separated from each other by a semicolon. The general form of the style attribute is therefore

```
style="name1:value1; name2:value2; ..."
```

where *name1*, *name2*, etc. are style names and *value1*, *value2* and so forth are the values of those styles.

As you proceed in your study of HTML you'll learn more about styles and how to apply them. For now you'll focus only on a few basic ones. The first is a style to align text. As you may have noticed, Web page text is usually aligned with the page's left margin. To choose a different alignment, you can apply the following text-align style to the element

```
style="text-align: alignment"
```

where *alignment* is left, right, center, or justify. For example, to center an h1 heading, you would enter the following markup tag:

```
<h1 style="text-align: center"> ... </h1>
```

A second style you'll explore defines the text color used in an element. Most browsers display text in a black font. To apply a different text color, use

```
style="color: color"
```

where *color* is a color name such as red, blue, green, and so forth. Applying the following attribute to an h1 heading causes the browser to render the heading text in a red font:

```
<h1 style="color: red"> ... </h1>
```

You can both center the text and change its font color to red by combining the two styles in one style attribute:

```
<h1 style="text-align: center; color: red"> ... </h1>
```

Applying the Style Attribute | Reference Window

- To add the style attribute, in the opening tag enter
  `style="name1:value1; name2:value2; ..."`
  where *name1*, *name2*, etc. are style names and *value1*, *value2* and so forth are the values of those styles.
- To center text horizontally, use
  `style="text-align: alignment"`
  where *alignment* is left, right, center, or justify.
- To set the font color, use
  `style="color: color"`
  where *color* is a color name.

To explore how to apply these two styles to a page element, you'll return to the HTML demo page.

To explore the style attribute:

1. Return to the **demo_html.htm** file in your Web browser.
2. Enter the following code in the left box, and then click the **Preview Code** button:

   ```
   <h1>Dave's Devil Sticks</h1>
   ```

   The demo page displays Dave's Devil Sticks as an h1 heading in the Preview box. Now you'll change the font color to red and center this heading in the box.

3. Within the opening <h1> tag, insert a space after "h1," and then type the attribute

   ```
   style="text-align: center; color: red"
   ```

4. Click the **Preview Code** button. As shown in Figure 1-30, the h1 heading is now centered and displayed in a red font.

Figure 1-30 Applying styles to an element

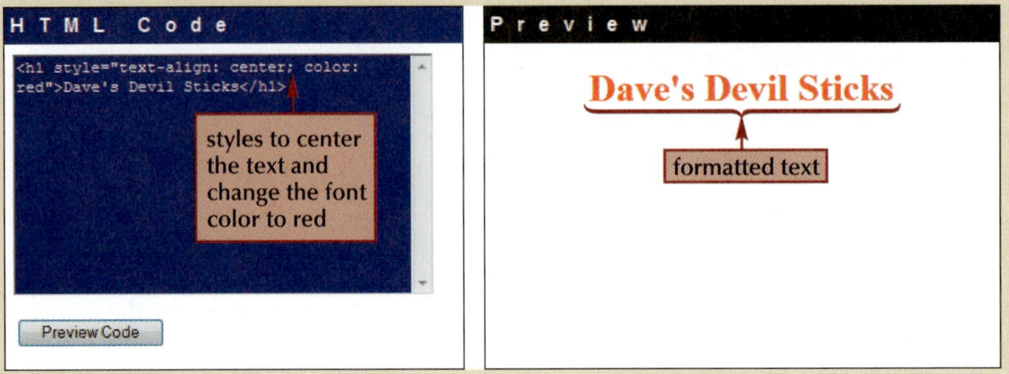

5. Continue exploring the text-align and color styles by creating headings right-aligned or centered in a blue, green, and gray-colored text.
6. Close the HTML demo page when you are finished exploring these two styles.

Dave has had a chance to examine your progress on his Web page and suggests that you center the address text at the bottom of the page. Now that you've explored the uses of the style attribute, you can make this change to his document.

To apply a style to the address element:

1. Return to the **dave.htm** file in your text editor.
2. Locate the address element at the bottom of the file and insert the following style attribute, as shown in Figure 1-31:

   ```
   style="text-align: center"
   ```

Figure 1-31 Apply the text-align style to an address

```
   <address style="text-align: center">Dave's Devil Sticks
            541 West Highland Dr.
            Auburn, ME 04210
            (207) 555 - 9001
   </address>
</body>

</html>
```

3. Save your changes to the file and refresh the **dave.htm** file in your Web browser. Verify that the address text is centered horizontally at the bottom of the page.

Presentational Attributes

You learned in the first session that early versions of HTML were used mostly by scientists and researchers. HTML was intended to be a language that described the structure but not necessarily the appearance of documents. Scientists and researchers didn't need flashy graphics, various fonts, or even much color on a page. The earliest Web pages weren't fancy and did not require much from the browsers that displayed them. This changed as the Web became more popular and attracted the attention of graphic designers and artists.

One way that HTML changed to accommodate this new class of users was to introduce **presentational attributes**, which are attributes that specifically describe how any element should be rendered. Rather than using styles, early versions of HTML would align text using the align attribute

```
<element align="alignment">content</element>
```

where *alignment* is either left, right, center, or justify. Thus to center an h1 heading you could use either of the following:

```
<h1 style="text-align: center">Dave's Devil Sticks</h1>
```

or

```
<h1 align="center">Dave's Devil Sticks</h1>
```

Almost all presentational attributes are now deprecated in favor of styles, but you will still see them used. Many HTML editors and converters use presentational attributes in place of styles. Even though using a deprecated attribute like align will probably not cause your Web page to fail, you should still use styles because that will ensure compatibility with future browser versions and with XHTML.

Working with Empty Elements

As he examines your work on the Web page, Dave notices that the product list you created in the last session lacks descriptions of the items. Dave wants you to take the information from his original flyer and add it to the Web page.

To add a description of each item in the product list:

1. Return to the **dave.htm** file in your text editor.
2. Locate the first closing </b> tag in the unordered list directly after the text "Basic Stick." Press the **Enter** key and type the following text, indenting it to make the code easier to read:

   ```
   The easiest stick to learn with, but "grippy" enough for the most
   demanding tricks. Comes in red, green, and blue.
   ```

3. Insert the following description for the Flower Stick, directly after the closing </b> tag for that product name:

   ```
   A graceful stick with colored tassels. Flower Sticks float more
   slowly, giving you the ideal chance to practice new moves.
   ```

4. Add the following description for the Master Stick after the closing </b> tag:

   ```
   My most popular stick is shorter and heavier for fast play and more
   advanced tricks. Each Master set is available in custom colors.
   ```

5. Finally, add the following description for the Glow Stick:

```
The Glow Stick shines brightly at night (without the danger of a fire
stick). It combines the fun and versatility of the Master Stick,
adding the fun tricks unique to a glow-in-the-dark stick.
```

Figure 1-32 highlights the newly added product descriptions.

Figure 1-32 **Adding product descriptions**

```
<h2>My Products</h2>
<ul>
   <li><b>Basic Stick</b>
         The easiest stick to learn with, but "grippy" enough for the most demanding
         tricks. Comes in red, green, and blue.</li>
   <li><b>Flower Stick</b>
         A graceful stick with colored tassels. Flower Sticks float more slowly, giving
         you the ideal chance to practice new moves.</li>
   <li><b>Master Stick</b>
         My most popular stick is shorter and heavier for fast play and more advanced
         tricks. Each Master set is available in custom colors.</li>
   <li><b>Glow Stick</b>
         The Glow Stick shines brightly at night (without the danger of a fire stick).
         It combines the fun and versatility of the Master Stick, adding the fun tricks
         unique to a glow-in-the-dark stick.</li>
</ul>
```

6. Save your changes to the file and then refresh the **dave.htm** file in your Web browser. Figure 1-33 shows the new product descriptions as they appear in the browser.

Figure 1-33 **Product descriptions on the Web page**

My Products

- **Basic Stick** The easiest stick to learn with, but "grippy" enough for the most demanding tricks. Comes in red, green, and blue.
- **Flower Stick** A graceful stick with colored tassels. Flower Sticks float more slowly, giving you the ideal chance to practice new moves.
- **Master Stick** My most popular stick is shorter and heavier for fast play and more advanced tricks. Each Master set is available in custom colors.
- **Glow Stick** The Glow Stick shines brightly at night (without the danger of a fire stick). It combines the fun and versatility of the Master Stick, adding the fun tricks unique to a glow-in-the-dark stick.

Dave thinks the revised product list is difficult to read and suggests that you place the descriptions on a new line directly below the product name. To do that you'll have to insert a line break into the Web page. The line break element is an example of an **empty element** because it contains no content. Empty elements appear in code as **one-sided tags** using

```
<element />
```

where *element* is the name of the empty element. As with other markup tags, one-sided tags can also contain attributes that define how the element is used in the document. The one-sided tag to mark a line break is

```
<br />
```

Line breaks need to be placed within block-level elements such as paragraphs or headings. Some browsers accept line breaks placed anywhere within the body of the Web page, but this is not good coding technique. XHTML in particular will reject code in which an inline element like the br element is not placed within a block-level element.

Use the br element now to mark a line break between the names and descriptions in Dave's product list.

To create line breaks between the product names and descriptions:

1. Return to the **dave.htm** file in your text editor.
2. Insert a **
** tag directly after the closing </b> tag for the Basic Stick product description.
3. Add a **
** tag after the closing </b> tag for each of the remaining three product names. Figure 1-34 shows the revised HTML code.

Figure 1-34 Adding line breaks to the Web page

```
<h2>My Products</h2>
<ul>
   <li><b>Basic Stick</b><br />
         The easiest stick to learn with, but "grippy" enough for the most demanding
         tricks. Comes in red, green, and blue.</li>
   <li><b>Flower Stick</b><br />
         A graceful stick with colored tassels. Flower Sticks float more slowly, giving
         you the ideal chance to practice new moves.</li>
   <li><b>Master Stick</b><br />
         My most popular stick is shorter and heavier for fast play and more advanced
         tricks. Each Master set is available in custom colors.</li>
   <li><b>Glow Stick</b><br />
         The Glow Stick shines brightly at night (without the danger of a fire stick).
         It combines the fun and versatility of the Master Stick, adding the fun tricks
         unique to a glow-in-the-dark stick.</li>
</ul>
```

forces the browser to insert a line break before rendering the next line of text

4. Save your changes to the file and then refresh the Web page in your browser. Verify that each of the four product descriptions is displayed on a new line directly below the product name.

Marking a Horizontal Rule

Another useful empty element is the hr or horizontal rule element, which places a horizontal line across the Web page. The syntax of the hr element is

```
<hr />
```

The exact appearance of the horizontal rule is left to the browser. Most browsers display a gray-shaded line a few pixels in height. Horizontal rules are considered block-level elements because they are displayed starting on a new line in the Web page. The hr element can be nested either within the <body> tag, in which case the horizontal rule will extend across the width of the Web page, or within a blockquote element, in which case the horizontal rule will be indented like other contents of the block quote.

Horizontal rules are useful in breaking up a long Web page into topical sections. Dave suggests that you place a horizontal rule above and one below the customer quotation and a third at the bottom of the page directly above the company address.

To create three horizontal rules:

1. Return to the **dave.htm** file in your text editor.
2. Directly below the opening <blockquote> tag, press the **Enter** key to insert a blank line, and then insert an **<hr />** tag.
3. Insert one **<hr />** tag directly above the closing </blockquote> tag and another above the opening <address> tag. Figure 1-35 highlights the revised code.

Figure 1-35 Marking horizontal rules with the <hr /> tag

```
<blockquote>
   <hr />
   <p>I'm more than happy to recommend Dave Vinet's products. I came upon his
      work 10 years ago and was immediately impressed by his craftsmanship.
      I've been using his sticks in my shows ever since. They're durable,
      well-balanced, and attractive props and are the perfect complement to
      my performances. Thanks Dave!</p>

   <p>Thomas Gage, lead performer at <i>Circus England</i></p>
   <hr />
</blockquote>

<p>Every set is checked and tested before being shipped out to assure perfect
   quality. I take pride in every one of my sticks and I want my customers to
   feel that same pride.</p>

<h2>My Products</h2>
<ul>
   <li><b>Basic Stick</b><br />
         The easiest stick to learn with, but "grippy" enough for the most demanding
         tricks. Comes in red, green, and blue.</li>
   <li><b>Flower Stick</b><br />
         A graceful stick with colored tassels. Flower Sticks float more slowly, giving
         you the ideal chance to practice new moves.</li>
   <li><b>Master Stick</b><br />
         My most popular stick is shorter and heavier for fast play and more advanced
         tricks. Each Master set is available in custom colors.</li>
   <li><b>Glow Stick</b><br />
         The Glow Stick shines brightly at night (without the danger of a fire stick).
         It combines the fun and versatility of the Master Stick, adding the fun tricks
         unique to a glow-in-the-dark stick.</li>
</ul>

<hr />

<address style="text-align: center">Dave's Devil Sticks
         541 West Highland Dr.
         Auburn, ME 04210
         (207) 555 - 9001
</address>
</body>
```

4. Save your changes to the file and then refresh the Web page in your browser. As shown in Figure 1-36, three horizontal rules have been added to the document, visually breaking the Web page into sections.

Figure 1-36 Adding horizontal rules to the Web page

Dave's Devil Sticks
Who Am I?
Welcome to Dave's Devil Sticks. If you are looking for juggling balls, hacky sacks, pins, unicycles, or magic hats, you've come to the wrong place; but if you're looking for high-quality, hand-crafted devil and flower sticks, this is the site for you. I've been designing and building sticks for the past 20 years, and I know that my sticks are the best of their kind. Don't take my word for it; read the following testimonial:
I'm more than happy to recommend Dave Vinet's products. I came upon his work 10 years ago and was immediately impressed by his craftsmanship. I've been using his sticks in my shows ever since. They're durable, well-balanced, and attractive props and are the perfect complement to my performances. Thanks Dave!
Thomas Gage, lead performer at Circus England
Every set is checked and tested before being shipped out to assure perfect quality. I take pride in every one of my sticks and I want my customers to feel that same pride.
My Products
Basic Stick
The easiest stick to learn with, but "grippy" enough for the most demanding tricks. Comes in red, green, and blue.
Flower Stick
A graceful stick with colored tassels. Flower Sticks float more slowly, giving you the ideal chance to practice new moves.
Master Stick
My most popular stick is shorter and heavier for fast play and more advanced tricks. Each Master set is available in custom colors.
Glow Stick
The Glow Stick shines brightly at night (without the danger of a fire stick). It combines the fun and versatility of the Master Stick, adding the fun tricks unique to a glow-in-the-dark stick.
Dave's Devil Sticks 541 West Highland Dr. Auburn, ME 04210 (207) 555 - 9001

You show the revised page to Dave and he's pleased with the addition of the horizontal rules. They have made the text easier to read and have nicely highlighted Thomas Gage's tribute.

Inserting an Inline Image

Dave wants you to replace the name of the company with the company logo centered at the top of the page. Because HTML files are simple text files, nontextual content like graphics must be stored in separate files, which are then loaded by the browser as it renders the page. The location of the graphic is marked as an **inline image** using the one-sided tag

```
<img src="file" alt="text" />
```

where *file* is the name of the graphic image file and *text* is text displayed by the browser in place of the graphic image. In this tutorial, you'll assume that the graphic image file is located in the same folder as the Web page, so you don't have to specify the location of the file. In the next tutorial, you'll learn how to reference files placed in other folders or locations on the Web.

As the name implies, inline images are another example of an inline element and thus must be placed within a block-level element such as a heading or a paragraph. Inline images are most widely stored in one of two formats: GIF (Graphics Interchange Format) or JPEG (Joint Photographic Experts Group). You can use an image editing application such as Adobe Photoshop to convert images to either of these two formats. Dave has already created such a graphic and stored it with the filename **logo.jpg**, located in the tutorial.01\tutorial folder included with your Data Files.

Tip

Always include alternate text for inline images. The alt attribute is required in XHTML code and is highly recommended as a way of accommodating users running nonvisual Web browsers.

Marking Empty Elements | Reference Window

- To mark a line break, use
  ```
  <br />
  ```
- To mark a horizontal rule, use
  ```
  <hr />
  ```
- To mark an inline image, use
  ```
  <img src="file" alt="text" />
  ```
  where *file* is the name of the graphic image file and *text* is text displayed by the browser in place of the graphic image.

To insert Dave's logo centered at the top of the page:

1. Return to the **dave.htm** file in your text editor.
2. Go to the h1 heading element at the top of the body section and insert the following attribute into the opening <h1> tag:
   ```
   style="text-align: center"
   ```
3. Delete the text **Dave's Devil Sticks** from between the opening and closing <h1> tags and replace it with
   ```
   <img src="logo.jpg" alt="Dave's Devil Sticks" />
   ```
   Figure 1-37 shows the revised code in the **dave.htm** file.

Figure 1-37 **Adding an inline image to a Web page**

center the contents of the h1 element

inline image element

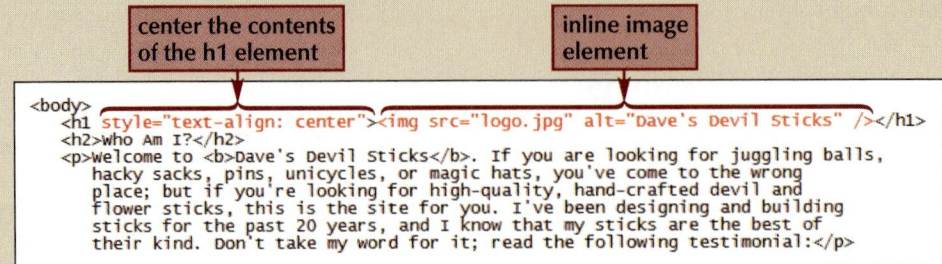

```
<body>
   <h1 style="text-align: center"><img src="logo.jpg" alt="Dave's Devil Sticks" /></h1>
   <h2>Who Am I?</h2>
   <p>Welcome to <b>Dave's Devil Sticks</b>. If you are looking for juggling balls,
      hacky sacks, pins, unicycles, or magic hats, you've come to the wrong
      place; but if you're looking for high-quality, hand-crafted devil and
      flower sticks, this is the site for you. I've been designing and building
      sticks for the past 20 years, and I know that my sticks are the best of
      their kind. Don't take my word for it; read the following testimonial:</p>
```

4. Save your changes to the file, and then refresh the Web page in your browser. Figure 1-38 shows the new heading with the logo centered across the page.

Figure 1-38 **Viewing Dave's logo**

logo centered on page
Dave's Devil Sticks
Who Am I?
Welcome to Dave's Devil Sticks. If you are looking for juggling balls, hacky sacks, pins, unicycles, or magic hats, you've come to the wrong place; but if you're looking for high-quality, hand-crafted devil and flower sticks, this is the site for you. I've been designing and building sticks for the past 20 years, and I know that my sticks are the best of their kind. Don't take my word for it; read the following testimonial:

Working with Character Sets and Special Characters

Dave likes the work you've done so far on the Web page. He has only one remaining concern: he feels that the address information at the bottom of the page is difficult to read and would like you to add a solid circular marker separating the different sections of the address. However, this marker is not represented by any keys on your keyboard. How then do you insert this symbol into the Web page?

Character Sets

To add dots to Dave's address, you must reference a symbol that your browser will be able to display but is not found on your keyboard. This is done by using a collection of characters and symbols called a **character set**. Character sets come in a wide variety of sizes, based on the number of symbols required for communication in the chosen language. For English, no more than about 127 characters are needed to represent all of the upper- and lowercase letters, numbers, punctuation marks, spaces, and special typing symbols in the English language. Other languages, such as Japanese or Chinese, require character sets containing thousands of symbols.

Each character set has a name. The character set representing the alphabet of English characters is called **ASCII** (**American Standard Code for Information Interchange**). A more extended character set called **Latin-1** or the **ISO 8859-1** character set supports 255 characters and can be used by most languages that employ the Latin alphabet, including English, French, Spanish, and Italian. The most extended character set is **Unicode**, which can be used for any of the world's languages, supporting up to 65,536 symbols. The most commonly used character set on the Web is **UTF-8**, which is a compressed version of Unicode and is probably the default character set assumed by your browser. You can learn more about character sets by visiting the W3C Web site and the Web site for the Internet Assigned Numbers Authority at *www.iana.org*.

Numeric Character References

To store a character set, browsers need to associate each symbol with a number in a process called **character encoding**. The number is called the **numeric character reference**. For example, the copyright symbol © from the UTF-8 character set has the number 169. If you know the numeric reference, you can insert the number directly into your code to display the symbol. The syntax to insert a numeric character reference is

```
&#code;
```

where *code* is the reference number. Thus to display the © symbol in your Web page, you would enter

```
&#169;
```

into your HTML file. To render a numeric character reference correctly, the browser needs to know the character set and encoding being used in the Web page. This information is typically sent by the Web server as it transfers the HTML page to the browser; and unless you are working with specialized international documents, you usually do not have to worry about specifying the character set for the browser.

Character Entity References

Another way to insert a special symbol is to use a **character entity reference**, in which a short memorable name is used in place of the numeric character reference. The syntax to insert a character entity reference is

```
&char;
```

where *char* is the character's name. The character entity reference for the copyright symbol is "copy," so to display the © symbol in your Web page you could also insert

```
&copy;
```

into your HTML code. One of the advantages of character entity references is that browsers can use them without knowing the character set or encoding. A disadvantage is that older browsers might not recognize the character entity reference and will thus display the reference name but not the symbol it represents.

Reference Window | Inserting Character Codes

- To insert a character based on a numeric character reference, use
```
&#code;
```
where *code* is the character code number.
- To insert a character based on the character entity reference, use
```
&char;
```
where *char* is the name assigned to the character.
- To insert a nonbreaking space, use
```
 
```
- To insert the < symbol, use
```
&lt;
```
- To insert the > symbol, use
```
&gt;
```

To explore various numeric character references and character entity references, you can view a demo page supplied with your Data Files.

To view the demo page:

1. Use your Web browser to open the **demo_characters.htm** file from the tutorial.01\demo data folder.
2. Type **£** in the input box at the top of the page, and then click the **Show** button. The Web browser displays the £ symbol in the ivory-colored box below. As you can see, to display the British pound symbol (£), you can use the &#163 numeric character reference.
3. Now try to display a special symbol using a character entity reference. Replace the value in the input box with **®** and then click the **Show** button. The browser now displays the ® symbol, which is the symbol for registered trademarks.

   You can view a collection of numeric character references and character entity references by selecting a table from the list box on the page.
4. Verify that General Symbols is displayed in the selection list box, and then click the **Show Table** button. As shown in Figure 1-39, the browser displays a list of 35 symbols with the character entity reference and numeric references displayed beneath each symbol.

HTML characters demo page

Figure 1-39

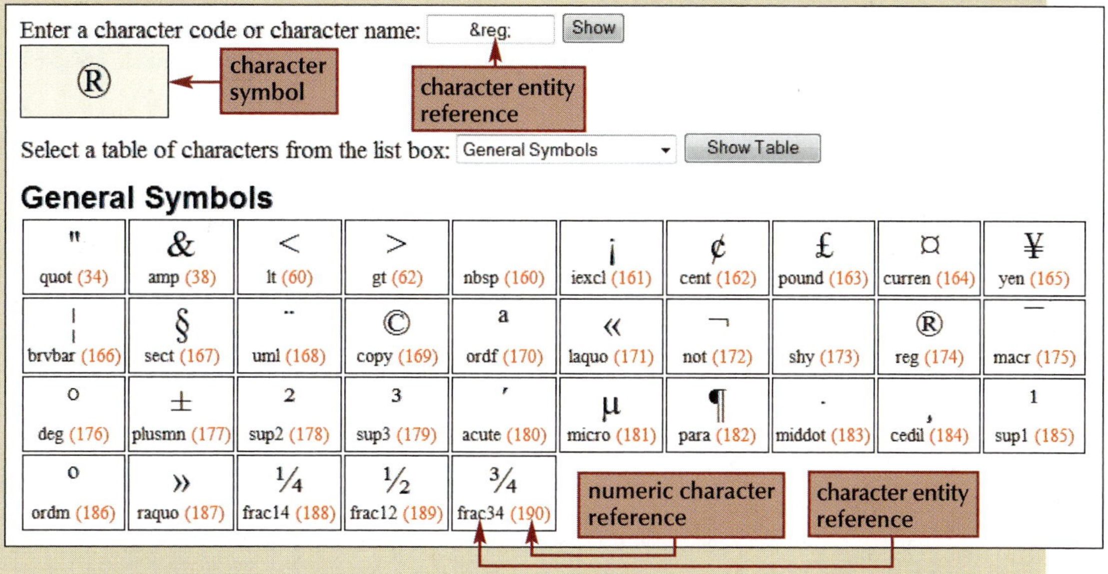

5. Take some time to explore the variety of numeric references and character entity references supported by your browser. Close the demo when you're finished, but leave your browser open.

Special Characters

One use of character codes is to insert text about HTML itself. For example, if you want your Web page to describe the use of the <h1> tag, you cannot simply type

```
The <h1> tag is used to mark h1 headings.
```

because the browser will interpret the <h1> text as marking the beginning of an h1 heading! Instead, you have to use the < and > entity references to insert the < and > symbols. The text would then be

```
The &lt;h1&gt; tag is used to mark h1 headings.
```

Another use of character codes is to add extra spaces to your Web page. Remember that browsers ignore extra blank spaces in the HTML file. To insert additional spaces, use the   entity reference ("nbsp" stands for nonbreaking space), which forces the browser to insert extra spaces.

On Dave's Web page, you decide to use the bullet symbol to break up the address text into sections. The symbol has the numeric character code value of 8226 and the entity character reference name "bull." Dave suggests you also add a long horizontal line called an em-dash to mark Thomas Gage's name as the author of the recommendation for Dave's business. The character code and entity reference for an em-dash are 8212 and "mdash," respectively.

Tip

Use the   character entity reference to fine-tune the layout of your documents by adding extra blank spaces to your text.

To add bullets and an em-dash to Dave's Web page:

1. Return to the **dave.htm** file in your text editor.
2. Locate the paragraph within the blockquote element containing the name of Thomas Gage. Directly after the opening <p> tag, insert the following numeric character code, followed by a space:

   ```
   &#8212;
   ```

3. Scroll down to the address element at the bottom of the file. At the end of each line within the address element (except the last line), insert a space and then type the **•** character entity reference. Figure 1-40 highlights the newly added code in the file.

Figure 1-40 Adding character references to the HTML file

```
<blockquote>
   <hr />
   <p>I'm more than happy to recommend Dave Vinet's products. I came upon his
      work 10 years ago and was immediately impressed by his craftsmanship.
      I've been using his sticks in my shows ever since. They're durable,
      well-balanced, and attractive props and are the perfect complement to
      my performances. Thanks Dave!</p>

   <p>&#8212; Thomas Gage, lead performer at <i>Circus England</i></p>
   <hr />
</blockquote>

<p>Every set is checked and tested before being shipped out to assure perfect
   quality. I take pride in every one of my sticks and I want my customers to
   feel that same pride.</p>

<h2>My Products</h2>
<ul>
   <li><b>Basic Stick</b><br />
          The easiest stick to learn with, but "grippy" enough for the most demanding
          tricks. Comes in red, green, and blue.</li>
   <li><b>Flower Stick</b><br />
          A graceful stick with colored tassels. Flower Sticks float more slowly, giving
          you the ideal chance to practice new moves.</li>
   <li><b>Master Stick</b><br />
          My most popular stick is shorter and heavier for fast play and more advanced
          tricks. Each Master set is available in custom colors.</li>
   <li><b>Glow Stick</b><br />
          The Glow Stick shines brightly at night (without the danger of a fire stick).
          It combines the fun and versatility of the Master Stick, adding the fun tricks
          unique to a glow-in-the-dark stick.</li>
</ul>

<hr />

<address style="text-align: center">Dave's Devil Sticks &bull;
         541 West Highland Dr. &bull;
         Auburn, ME 04210 &bull;
         (207) 555 - 9001 &bull;
</address>
</body>
```

numeric character reference

character entity reference

4. Close the file, saving your changes.
5. Refresh the **dave.htm** file in your Web browser. Figure 1-41 shows the final version of Dave's Web page.

Figure 1-41 Dave's completed Web page

Who Am I?

Welcome to **Dave's Devil Sticks**. If you are looking for juggling balls, hacky sacks, pins, unicycles, or magic hats, you've come to the wrong place; but if you're looking for high-quality, hand-crafted devil and flower sticks, this is the site for you. I've been designing and building sticks for the past 20 years, and I know that my sticks are the best of their kind. Don't take my word for it; read the following testimonial:

> I'm more than happy to recommend Dave Vinet's products. I came upon his work 10 years ago and was immediately impressed by his craftsmanship. I've been using his sticks in my shows ever since. They're durable, well-balanced, and attractive props and are the perfect complement to my performances. Thanks Dave!
>
> — Thomas Gage, lead performer at *Circus England*

Every set is checked and tested before being shipped out to assure perfect quality. I take pride in every one of my sticks and I want my customers to feel that same pride.

My Products

- **Basic Stick**
  The easiest stick to learn with, but "grippy" enough for the most demanding tricks. Comes in red, green, and blue.
- **Flower Stick**
  A graceful stick with colored tassels. Flower Sticks float more slowly, giving you the ideal chance to practice new moves.
- **Master Stick**
  My most popular stick is shorter and heavier for fast play and more advanced tricks. Each Master set is available in custom colors.
- **Glow Stick**
  The Glow Stick shines brightly at night (without the danger of a fire stick). It combines the fun and versatility of the Master Stick, adding the fun tricks unique to a glow-in-the-dark stick.

Dave's Devil Sticks • 541 West Highland Dr. • Auburn, ME 04210 • (207) 555 - 9001 •

6. If you plan on taking a break before working on the end of tutorial problems, you can close your Web browser and any other open files or programs.

You show the completed Web page to Dave. He's pleased that you were able to duplicate much of what was on his original flyer. As you and Dave grow in your understanding of HTML and the Web, you'll add more pages to his site; but for now, this is a good start on giving him a presence on the Internet.

InSight | Publishing Your Page on the Web

Once you've completed your Web page, your next step is to research ways of getting it on the Web. You first need to find a Web server to host the page. Some of the issues you'll need to consider are how much you want to pay, how much space you need, and how important it is for you to have a highly trafficked Web site. You might first look toward the company that provides your Internet access. Most **ISPs** (**Internet Service Providers**) offer space on their Web server as part of their regular service or for a small fee. However, they usually limit the amount of space available to you, unless you pay an extra fee to host a larger site. There are also free Web hosts, which provide space on servers for personal or noncommercial use. Once again, the amount of space you get is limited. Free Web hosting services make their money from selling advertising space on your site, so you should be prepared to act as a billboard in return for space on their server.

Web sites are identified by their domain names. If you're planning to create a commercial site to advertise a product or service, you want the domain name to reflect your business. Free Web hosts usually include their names in your Web address. Thus instead of having a Web address like

davesdevilsticks.com

you might have something like

freewebhosting.net/members/~davesdevilsticks.html

If you're running a site for personal use, this might not be a problem—but it would look unprofessional on a commercial site. If you are planning a commercial site and simply want to advertise your product by publishing an online brochure, you can usually find an inexpensive host and pay a nominal yearly fee to reserve a Web address that reflects your company's name. On the other hand, if you intend to run an e-commerce site where users can purchase products online, you will need to invest in software and storage space to manage customer orders and inventory. You will also need to invest in getting your Web site noticed in the increasingly crowded Internet market. Commercial pages require careful planning and good design so that the investment in publishing the site is not wasted.

Review | Session 1.3 Quick Check

1. Specify the code you would enter to display the text "Product List" as an h2 heading, centered horizontally on the page.
2. What is a presentational attribute? What is a reason for using presentational attributes? What is a reason for avoiding them?
3. Specify the code you would enter to mark the text "Hamlet by William Shakespeare" as a centered h1 heading with a line break after the word "Hamlet."
4. You want to add the graphic file portrait.gif to your Web page as an inline image. For nonvisual browsers, your page should display the text "David Vinet" in place of the image. Specify the code to do this.
5. What is ISO-8859-1?
6. The trademark symbol ™ has the Unicode number 8482. How would you enter this symbol into your Web page?
7. The Greek letter b has the character entity name of "beta." How would you enter this symbol into your Web page?
8. Specify the code you would enter to add three consecutive blank spaces to your Web page.
9. Specify the code you would enter to display the text "<h2>Hamlet</h2>" on your Web page.

Tutorial Summary | Review

In this tutorial you learned how to create a basic Web page using HTML. The tutorial began by examining concepts and history surrounding networks and the development of the World Wide Web. It then explored the history of HTML, explaining how the development of HTML was a key component in the development of the Web. The first session concluded with the creation of a simple Web page consisting only of the page head. Work on designing the page body began in the second session by first exploring how to mark block-level elements. The discussion of block-level elements included work with headings, paragraphs, block quotes, and lists. The second session concluded with coverage of inline elements and discussed the issue of physical elements versus logical elements. The third session began by exploring element attributes, showing how to use the style attribute to center the contents of a block-level element. Because Web pages often need to display nontextual content, the third session then examined how to use empty elements such as line breaks, horizontal rules, and inline images. The session and the tutorial concluded by discussing character sets and explored how to insert special character symbols into a Web page.

Key Terms

ARPANET
ASCII
attribute
block-level element
body element
character encoding
character entity reference
character formatting element
character set
client
client-server network
closing tag
comment tag
definition list
deprecated
element
empty element
Extensible Hypertext Markup Language
Extensible Markup Language
extensions
file server
head element
heading element
host
HTML
HTML 5.0
HTML converter
HTML editor
hypertext
Hypertext Markup Language
inline element
inline image
Internet Service Provider
ISO-8859-1
ISP
LAN
Latin-1
link
local area network
logical element
markup language
network
node
numeric character reference
one-sided tag
opening tag
ordered list
physical element
presentational attribute
print server
root element
server
SGML
Standard Generalized Markup Language
style
tag
text-based browser
two-sided tag
Unicode
unordered list
UTF-8
W3C
WAN
Web
Web browser
Web page
Web server
white space
wide area network
World Wide Web
World Wide Web Consortium
XHTML
XHTML 2.0
XHTML 5.0
XML

Practice | Review Assignments

Practice the skills you learned in the tutorial using the same case scenario.

Data File needed for the Review Assignments: logo.jpg

Dave has found a host for his Web page and has published the document you helped him create on the Internet. He wants to start adding more pages to his Web site. He's come to you for help in creating a page describing his basic stick. He's already written the text for the Web page; he needs you to translate that text into HTML code. Figure 1-42 shows a preview of the page you'll create for Dave.

Figure 1-42

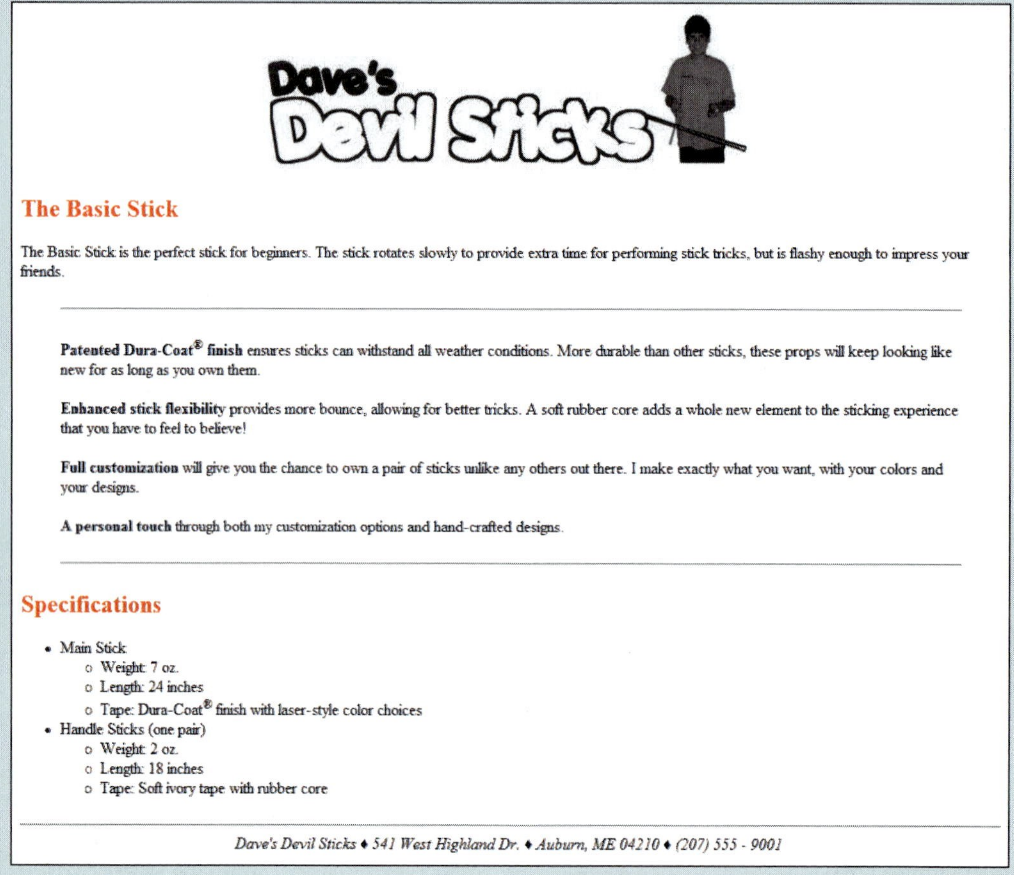
Dave's
Devil Sticks
The Basic Stick
The Basic Stick is the perfect stick for beginners. The stick rotates slowly to provide extra time for performing stick tricks, but is flashy enough to impress your friends.
Patented Dura-Coat® finish ensures sticks can withstand all weather conditions. More durable than other sticks, these props will keep looking like new for as long as you own them.
Enhanced stick flexibility provides more bounce, allowing for better tricks. A soft rubber core adds a whole new element to the sticking experience that you have to feel to believe!
Full customization will give you the chance to own a pair of sticks unlike any others out there. I make exactly what you want, with your colors and your designs.
A personal touch through both my customization options and hand-crafted designs.
Specifications
Main Stick
Weight: 7 oz.
Length: 24 inches
Tape: Dura-Coat® finish with laser-style color choices
Handle Sticks (one pair)
Weight: 2 oz.
Length: 18 inches
Tape: Soft ivory tape with rubber core
Dave's Devil Sticks ♦ 541 West Highland Dr. ♦ Auburn, ME 04210 ♦ (207) 555 - 9001

Complete the following:

1. Use your text editor to create a new file named **basic.htm**, and save it in the tutorial.01\review folder included with your Data Files.
2. Within the basic.htm file, insert the structure of the HTML file, including the head and body sections.
3. Within the head section, insert a comment containing

   Dave's Devil Sticks

   Basic Stick

   Author: ***your name***

   Date: ***the date***

   where *your name* is your name and *the date* is the current date.

4. Add the page title **Basic Sticks** to the head section.
5. Within the body section, insert an h1 heading centered horizontally on the page and containing the inline image file **logo.jpg**, located in the tutorial.01\review folder included with your Data Files. Specify the following alternate text for the image: **Dave's Devil Sticks: The Basic Stick**.
6. Add two h2 headings containing the text **The Basic Stick** and **Specifications**. Set the font color of the heading 2 text to red.
7. Directly below the first h2 heading, insert a paragraph containing the text: **The Basic Stick is the perfect stick for beginners. The stick rotates slowly to provide extra time for performing stick tricks, but is flashy enough to impress your friends.**
8. Directly below the paragraph but above the second h2 heading, insert a block quote that contains the following:
    a. Place a horizontal rule at the top and the bottom of the block quote.
    b. Between the two horizontal rules, insert the following four paragraphs:
    Patented Dura-Coat finish ensures sticks can withstand all weather conditions. More durable than other sticks, these props will keep looking like new for as long as you own them.
    Enhanced stick flexibility provides more bounce, allowing for better tricks. A soft rubber core adds a whole new element to the sticking experience that you have to feel to believe!
    Full customization will give you the chance to own a pair of sticks unlike any others out there. I make exactly what you want, with your colors and your designs.
    A personal touch through both my customization options and hand-crafted designs.
    c. Change the first few words of each of the four paragraphs to a bold font, as indicated in Figure 1-42.
9. Directly below the second h2 heading, insert an unordered list. The list should contain two items: **Main Stick** and **Handle Sticks (one pair)**.
10. Directly below the Main Stick list item, insert an unordered list containing the following items:
    Weight: 7 oz.
    Length: 24 inches
    Tape: Dura-Coat finish with laser-style color choices
11. Directly below the Handle Sticks (one pair) list item, insert an unordered list containing:
    Weight: 2 oz.
    Length: 18 inches
    Tape: Soft ivory tape with rubber core
12. Locate the two occurrences of "Dura-Coat" in the document. Directly after the word "Dura-Coat," insert the registered trademark symbol ®. The character entity name of the ® symbol is "reg." Display the ® symbol as a superscript by placing the character within the sup inline element.
13. At the bottom of the body section, insert the company's address:
    Dave's Devil Sticks
    541 West Highland Dr.
    Auburn, ME 04210
    (207) 555 - 9001

14. Center the address on the page.
15. Separate the different sections of the address using a solid diamond ♦ (character code 9830).
16. Add a horizontal rule directly above the address element.
17. Save your changes to the file, and then open it in your Web browser to verify that the content and layout are correct.
18. Submit your completed files to your instructor.

Apply | Case Problem 1

Apply your knowledge of HTML to create a Web page for a mathematics department at a university.

Data Files needed for this Case Problem: euler.jpg and eulertxt.htm

Mathematics Department, Coastal University Professor Lauren Coe of the Mathematics Department of Coastal University in Anderson, South Carolina, is preparing material for a course on the history of mathematics. As part of the course, she has written biographies of famous mathematicians. Lauren would like you to use content she's already written to create Web pages that students can access on Coastal University's Web server. You'll create the first one in this exercise. Figure 1-43 shows a preview of this page, which profiles the mathematician Leonhard Euler.

Figure 1-43

Leonhard Euler (1707-1783)

The greatest mathematician of the eighteenth century, **Leonhard Euler** was born in Basel, Switzerland. There, he studied under another giant of mathematics, **Jean Bernoulli**. In 1731 Euler became a professor of physics and mathematics at St. Petersburg Academy of Sciences. Euler was the most prolific mathematician of all time, publishing over *800 different books and papers*. His influence was felt in physics and astronomy as well. Euler's work on mathematical analysis, *Introductio in analysin infinitorum* (1748) remained a standard textbook for well over a century. For the princess of Anhalt-Dessau he wrote *Lettres à une princesse d'Allemagne* (1768-1772), giving a clear non-technical outline of the main physical theories of the time.

One can hardly do math without copying Euler. Notations still in use today, such as e and π, were introduced in Euler's writings. He is perhaps best known for his research into mathematical analysis. Euler's formula

$$\cos(x) + i\sin(x) = e^{(ix)}$$

demonstrates the relationship between algebra, complex analysis, and trigonometry. From this equation, it's easy to derive the equation

$$e^{(\pi i)} + 1 = 0$$

which relates the fundamental constants: 0, 1, π, e, and i in a single beautiful and elegant statement.

Leonhard Euler died in 1783, leaving behind a legacy perhaps unmatched, and certainly unsurpassed, in the annals of mathematics.

Math 895: The History of Mathematics

Complete the following:

1. Open the **eulertxt.htm** file from the tutorial.01\case1 folder included with your Data Files. Save the file as **euler.htm** in the same folder.

2. Add opening and closing <html> tags to the file. Insert a head section and enclose Lauren's text on Euler within a body element.
3. Within the head section, insert a comment containing
   History of Math 895: Leonhard Euler
   Author: ***your name***
   Date: ***the date***
   where *your name* is your name and *the date* is the current date.
4. Add the page title **History of Math 895: Leonhard Euler** to the head section.
5. Directly below the opening <body> tag, insert a paragraph containing the inline image file **euler.jpg**, located in the tutorial.01\case1 folder included with your Data Files. Specify "Portrait of Leonhard Euler" as the alternative text.
6. Mark the next line containing "Leonhard Euler (1707 - 1783)" as an h1 heading.
7. Mark the five blocks of text describing Euler's life as paragraphs.
8. Mark the two equations as block quotes. Change the font color of the two block quotes to red.
9. Mark the name of the course title at the bottom of the file as an address.
10. Insert horizontal rules directly above the h1 heading and the address element.

EXPLORE

11. Within the first paragraph, display the names "Leonhard Euler" and "Jean Bernoulli" in boldface. Mark the phrase "800 different books and papers" as emphasized text using the em element. Mark the phrase "Introduction in analysin infinitorum" as a citation.
12. In the phrase, "Lettres a une princesse d'Allemagne" replace the one-letter word a with à (the character entity name is "agrave"). Mark the entire publication as a citation.
13. In the second paragraph, italicize the notation for e and replace "pi" with the character π (the character name is "pi").
14. In the first equation, italicize the letters *e*, *x*, and *i* (but do not italicize the "i" in "sin"). Display the term (*ix*) as a superscript.
15. In the second equation, replace "pi" with the character π. Italicize the letter *e* and *i*. Display (π*i*) as a superscript.
16. In the last paragraph, italicize the notations for *e* and *i* and replace "pi" with π.
17. Save your changes to the file, and then verify that the page appears correctly in your Web browser.
18. Submit your completed files to your instructor.

Apply | Case Problem 2

Apply your knowledge of HTML to create a page showing text from a scene of a Shakespeare play.

Data Files needed for this Case Problem: macbeth.jpg and macbethtxt.htm

Mansfield Classical Theatre Steve Karls is the director of Mansfield Classical Theatre, a theatre company for young people located in Mansfield, Ohio. This summer the company is planning to perform the Shakespeare play *Macbeth*. Steve wants to put the text of the play on the company's Web site and has asked for your help in designing and completing the Web page. Steve wants to have a separate page for each scene from the play. A preview of the page you'll create for Act I, Scene 1 is shown in Figure 1-44. Steve has already typed the text of the scene. He needs you to supply the HTML code.

Figure 1-44

Macbeth

ACT I

SCENE 1.

Summary A thunderstorm approaches and three witches convene. They agree to confront the great Scot general Macbeth upon his victorious return from a war between Scotland and Norway. Soon, heroic Macbeth will receive the title of Thane of Cawdor from King Duncan. However, Macbeth learns from the witches that he is fated for greater things and he will be led down to the path of destruction by his unquenchable ambition.

A desert place.

Thunder and lightning. Enter three Witches.

First Witch
    When shall we three meet again
    In thunder, lightning, or in rain?
Second Witch
    When the hurlyburly's done,
    When the battle's lost and won.
Third Witch
    That will be ere the set of sun.
First Witch
    Where the place?
Second Witch
    Upon the heath.
Third Witch
    There to meet with Macbeth.
First Witch
    I come, Graymalkin!
Second Witch
    Paddock calls.
Third Witch
    Anon.
ALL
    Fair is foul, and foul is fair:
    Hover through the fog and filthy air.

Exeunt

Go to Scene 2 ⇒

Text provided by Online Shakespeare

Complete the following:

1. Open the **macbethtxt.htm** file from the tutorial.01\case2 folder included with your Data Files. Save the file as **macbeth.htm** in the same folder.
2. Enclose the entire Macbeth text within the structure of an HTML document.
3. Within the head section, insert a comment containing the following text:
   Macbeth: Act I, Scene 1
   Author: ***your name***
   Date: ***the date***
4. Add the page title **Macbeth: Act I, Scene 1** to the head section.
5. Directly below the opening <body> tag, insert an h1 heading containing the inline image file **macbeth.jpg** (located in the tutorial.01\case2 folder included with your Data Files) with **Macbeth** as the alternate text for nonvisual browsers. Add a horizontal rule directly below the h1 heading.
6. Mark the text "ACT I" as an h2 heading. Mark "SCENE 1." as an h3 heading.

7. Mark the summary of the scene as a paragraph. Display the word "Summary" in bold.
8. In the text of the play, mark the descriptions of setting, scene, and exits as separate paragraphs, and italicize the text, as shown in Figure 1-44.

EXPLORE

9. Mark the dialog as a definition list, with each character's name marked as a definition term and each speech marked as a definition description. Where the speech goes over one line, use a line break to keep the speech on separate lines, as shown in the figure.
10. Directly below the Exeunt paragraph, insert the line **Go to Scene 2**. Mark this line as a div element and align it with the right page margin. (Steve will mark this as a link later.) At the end of the line, insert a right arrow character using the 8658 character number. Add horizontal rules directly above and below this statement.

EXPLORE

11. Mark the line "Text provided by Online Shakespeare" as a paragraph, with the text itself marked with the cite element. Align the text with the right page margin.
12. Save your changes to the file, and then confirm the layout and content of the page in your Web browser.
13. Submit the completed files to your instructor.

Challenge | Case Problem 3

Explore how to use HTML to create a recipe page.

Data Files needed for this Case Problem: dessertweb.jpg, torte.jpg, and tortetxt.htm

dessertWEB Amy Wu wants to take her love of cooking and sharing recipes to the World Wide Web. She's interested in creating a new Web site called *dessertWEB* where other cooks can submit and review dessert recipes. Each page within her site will have a photo and description of the dessert, the ingredients, the cooking directions, and a list of reviews. Each recipe will be rated on a 5-star scale. She already has information on one recipe: Apple Bavarian Torte. She's asked for your help in creating a Web page from the data she's collected. A preview of the completed page is shown in Figure 1-45.

Figure 1-45

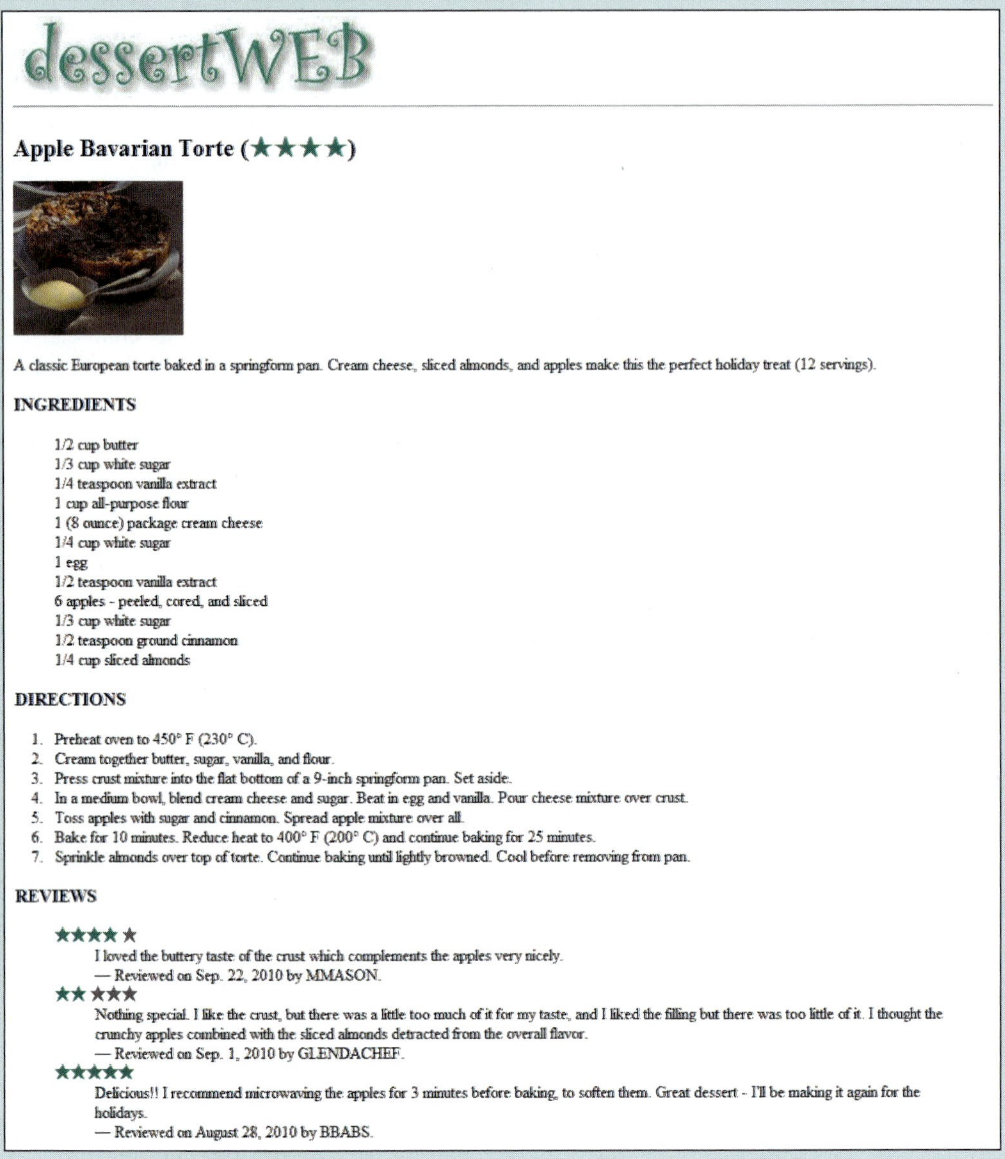
dessertWEB

Apple Bavarian Torte (★★★★)

A classic European torte baked in a springform pan. Cream cheese, sliced almonds, and apples make this the perfect holiday treat (12 servings).

INGREDIENTS

1/2 cup butter
1/3 cup white sugar
1/4 teaspoon vanilla extract
1 cup all-purpose flour
1 (8 ounce) package cream cheese
1/4 cup white sugar
1 egg
1/2 teaspoon vanilla extract
6 apples - peeled, cored, and sliced
1/3 cup white sugar
1/2 teaspoon ground cinnamon
1/4 cup sliced almonds

DIRECTIONS

1. Preheat oven to 450° F (230° C).
2. Cream together butter, sugar, vanilla, and flour.
3. Press crust mixture into the flat bottom of a 9-inch springform pan. Set aside.
4. In a medium bowl, blend cream cheese and sugar. Beat in egg and vanilla. Pour cheese mixture over crust.
5. Toss apples with sugar and cinnamon. Spread apple mixture over all.
6. Bake for 10 minutes. Reduce heat to 400° F (200° C) and continue baking for 25 minutes.
7. Sprinkle almonds over top of torte. Continue baking until lightly browned. Cool before removing from pan.

REVIEWS

★★★★★
I loved the buttery taste of the crust which complements the apples very nicely.
— Reviewed on Sep. 22, 2010 by MMASON.
★★★★★
Nothing special. I like the crust, but there was a little too much of it for my taste, and I liked the filling but there was too little of it. I thought the crunchy apples combined with the sliced almonds detracted from the overall flavor.
— Reviewed on Sep. 1, 2010 by GLENDACHEF.
★★★★★
Delicious!! I recommend microwaving the apples for 3 minutes before baking, to soften them. Great dessert - I'll be making it again for the holidays.
— Reviewed on August 28, 2010 by BBABS.

Complete the following:

1. Open the **tortetxt.htm** file from the tutorial.01\case3 folder included with your Data Files. Save the file as **torte.htm** in the same folder.
2. Add the structure of an HTML document around the recipe text. Within the head section, insert a comment containing the following text:
   Apple Bavarian Torte
   Author: ***your name***
   Date: ***the date***
3. Add the page title **Apple Bavarian Torte Recipe** to the head section.
4. Directly below the opening <body> tag, insert a div element containing the inline image **dessertweb.jpg** located in the tutorial.01\case3 folder included with your Data Files. Specify the alternative text **dessertWEB**. Insert a horizontal rule directly below the div element.

5. Mark the text "Apple Bavarian Torte" as an h2 heading.

EXPLORE

6. Change the text "(4 stars)" to a set of 4 star symbols (character number 9733). Enclose the star symbols in a span element, setting the font color to teal.
7. Directly below the h2 heading, insert another div element containing the inline image **torte.jpg**, located in the tutorial.01\case3 folder included with your Data Files. Specify the alternative text **Torte image**.
8. Mark the description of the dessert as a paragraph.
9. Mark "INGREDIENTS," "DIRECTIONS," and "REVIEWS" as h3 headings.
10. Enclose the list of ingredients in a block quote. Add line breaks after each item in the list.

EXPLORE

11. Mark the list of directions as an ordered list, with each direction a separate item in the list. Replace the word "degrees" with the degree symbol (character name deg).
12. Enclose the list of reviews in a block quote. Turn the list into a definition list. Mark up the definition list as follows:

EXPLORE

    a. The definition term is the number of stars assigned by each reviewer. Change the number of stars in the text file to star symbols (character number 9733). Amy wants you to display 5 stars for each review with the number of stars displayed in a teal font matching the stars given by the reviewer and the remaining stars displayed in a gray font. Use the span element to enclose the two different groups of stars.
    b. There are two definition descriptions for each review. The first encloses the text of the review. The second encloses the date of the review and the name of the reviewer.
    c. Insert an em-dash (character name "mdash") before the word "Reviewed" in each of the reviews.
13. Save your changes to the file, and then verify the layout and content of the page in your Web browser.
14. Submit the completed files to your instructor.

Create | Case Problem 4

Test your knowledge of HTML and use your creativity to design a Web page for an exercise equipment company.

Data Files needed for this Case Problem: logo.jpg, smith.jpg, and smith.txt

Body Systems Body Systems is a leading manufacturer of home gyms. The company recently hired you to assist in developing its Web site. Your first task is to create a Web page for the LSM400, a popular weight machine sold by the company. You've been given a text file describing the features of the LSM400. You've also received two image files: one of the company's logo and one of the LSM400. You are free to supplement these files with any other resources available to you. You are responsible for the page's content and appearance.

Complete the following:

1. Create a new HTML file named **smith.htm** and save it in the tutorial.01\case4 folder included with your Data Files.
2. Add a comment to the head section of the document describing the document's content and containing your name and the date.
3. Add an appropriate page title to the document.

4. Use the contents of the **smith.txt** document (located in the tutorial.01\case4 folder) as the basis of the text in the Web page. Include at least one example of each of the following:
   - a heading
   - a paragraph
   - an ordered or unordered list
   - an inline element
   - an inline image
   - a horizontal rule
   - a special character
   - an element attribute
5. Structure your HTML code so that it will be easy for others to read and understand.
6. Save your changes to the file, and then open it in your Web browser to verify that it is readable and attractive.
7. Submit your completed files to your instructor.

Review | Quick Check Answers

Session 1.1

1. A hypertext document is an electronic file containing elements that users can select, usually by clicking a mouse, to open other documents.
2. A Web server is a computer on a network that stores a Web site and makes it available to clients. Users access the Web site by running a program called a Web browser on their computers.
3. HTML documents do not exactly specify the appearance of a document; rather they describe the purpose of various elements in the document and leave it to the Web browser to determine the final appearance. A word processor like Microsoft Word exactly specifies the appearance of each document element.
4. Deprecated features are those features that are being phased out by the W3C and might not be supported by future browsers.
5. The html element.
6. In the head section of the document you would enter the code `<title>Technical Support</title>`
7. `<!-- Page Updated on 4/15/2011 -->`
8. The title element was not properly nested within the head element.

Session 1.2

1. Block-level elements contain content that is displayed in a separate section within the page, such as a paragraph or a heading. An inline element is part of the same block as its surrounding content—for example, individual words or phrases within a paragraph.
2. Web browsers will strip out extra occurrences of white space and thus will ignore the extra blank line.
3. `<h1>`*content*`</h1>`
4. Use the blockquote element. Most browsers indent blockquote text.

5.
```
<ul>
   <li>Winter</li>
   <li>Spring</li>
   <li>Summer</li>
   <li>Fall</li>
</ul>
```

6.
```
<dl>
   <dt>HAMLET</dt>
   <dd> There's ne'er a villain dwelling in all Denmark; but he's
an arrant knave.</dd>
   <dt>HORATIO</dt>
   <dd> There needs no ghost, my lord, come from the grave to tell
us this.</dd>
</dl>
```

7.
```
<p><i>Hamlet</i>, a play by William Shakespeare</p>
```

8. div and span

Session 1.3

1.
```
<h2 style="text-align: center">Product List</h2>
```

2. Presentational attributes are HTML attributes that exactly specify how the browser should render an HTML element. Most presentational attributes have been deprecated, replaced by styles. You should use presentational attributes when you need to support older browsers.

3.
```
<h1 style="text-align: center">Hamlet<br /> by William
Shakespeare</h1>
```

4.
```
<img src="portrait.gif" alt="David Vinet" />
```

5. ISO-8859-1 is a character set that supports 255 characters and can be used by most languages that use the Latin alphabet.

6.
```
&#8482;
```

7.
```
&beta;
```

8.
```
   
```

9.
```
&lt;h2&gt;Hamlet&lt;/h2&gt;
```

Ending Data Files

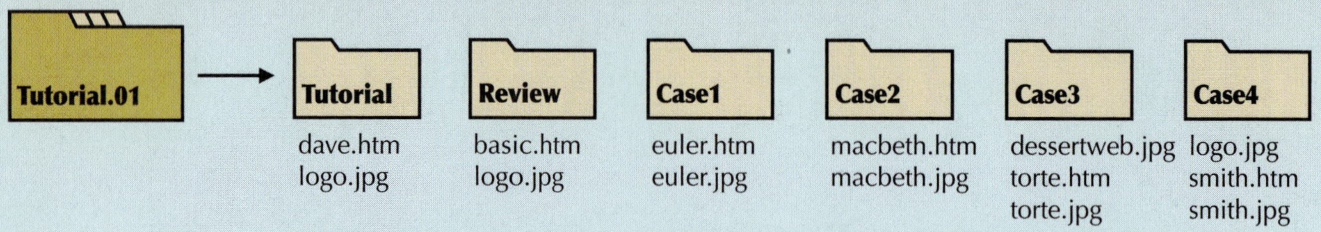

Objectives

Session 2.1
- Storyboard various Web site structures
- Create links documents in a Web site
- Understand relative and absolute folder paths
- Work with the base element

Session 2.2
- Mark a location with the id attribute
- Create a link to an id
- Mark an image as a link
- Create an image map
- Remove an image border

Session 2.3
- Understand URLs
- Link to a site on the Web
- Link to an e-mail address
- Work with hypertext attributes
- Work with metadata

Developing a Web Site

Creating a Web Site for Digital Photography Enthusiasts

Case | CAMshots

Gerry Hayward is an amateur photographer and digital camera enthusiast. He's decided to create a Web site named CAMshots, where he can offer advice and information to people who are just getting started with digital photography or who are long-time hobbyists like himself and are looking to share tips and ideas. Gerry's Web site will contain several pages, with each page dedicated to a particular topic. He has created a few pages for the Web site, but he hasn't linked them together. He has asked your help in designing his site. You'll start with only a few pages and then Gerry can build on your work as he adds more information to the site.

Starting Data Files

Tutorial.02 →

Tutorial
glosstxt.htm
hometxt.htm
tipstxt.htm
+ 3 graphic files

Demo
demo_mailto.htm
+ 3 graphic files

Review
childtxt.htm
contesttxt.htm
flowertxt.htm
scenictxt.htm
+ 22 graphic files

Case1
colleges.txt
uwlisttxt.htm
+ 1 graphic file

Case2
hometxt.htm
slide1txt.htm
slide2txt.htm
slide3txt.htm
slide4txt.htm
slide5txt.htm
slide6txt.htm
+ 18 graphic files

Case3
classtxt.htm
hometxt.htm
indextxt.htm
memtxt.htm
+ 1 graphic file

Case4
characters.txt
notes.txt
tempest.txt
+ 1 graphic file

Session 2.1

Exploring Web Site Structures

You meet with Gerry to discuss his plans for the CAMshots Web site. Gerry has already created a prototype for the Web site. He's created three Web pages: one page is the site's home page and contains general information about CAMshots; the second page contains tips about digital photography; and the third page contains a partial glossary of photographic terms. The pages are not complete, nor are they linked to one another. You'll begin your work for Gerry by viewing these files in your text editor and browser.

To view Gerry's Web pages:

1. Start your text editor, and then one at a time, open the **hometxt.htm**, **tipstxt.htm**, and **glosstxt.htm** files, located in the tutorial.02\tutorial folder included with your Data Files.
2. Within each file, go to the comment section at top of the file and add ***your name*** and ***the date*** in the space provided.
3. Save the files as **home.htm**, **tips.htm**, and **glossary.htm**, respectively, in the tutorial.02\tutorial folder.
4. Take some time reviewing the HTML code within each document so that you understand the structure and content of the files.
5. Start your Web browser, and then one at a time, open the **home.htm, tips.htm,** and **glossary.htm** files. Figure 2-1 shows the current layout and appearance of Gerry's three Web pages.

Figure 2-1 Pages in the CAMshots Web site

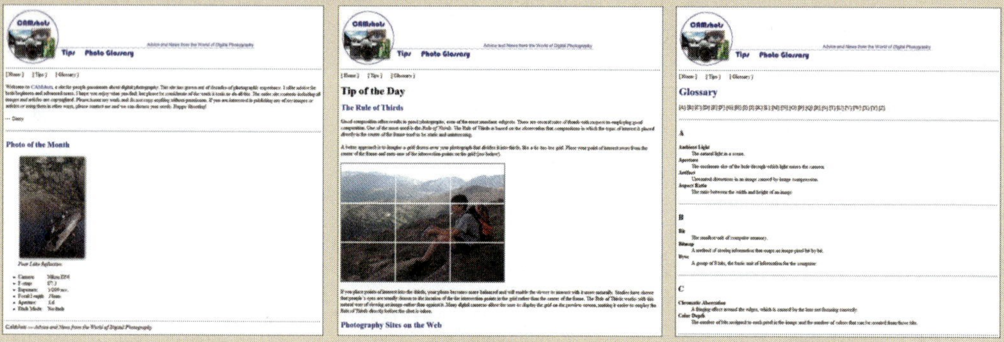

home.htm — the CAMshots home page | tips.htm — the CAMshots tip of the day | glossary.htm — a partial glossary of photography terminology

Gerry wants to create links among the three pages so that users can easily navigate from one page to another. Before you write code for the links, it's worthwhile to map out exactly how you want the pages to relate to each other, using a technique known as storyboarding. A **storyboard** is a diagram of a Web site's structure, showing all the pages in the site and indicating how they are linked together. Because Web sites use a variety of structures, it's important to storyboard your Web site before you start creating your pages. This helps you determine which structure works best for the type of information your site contains. A well-designed structure ensures that users will able to navigate the site without getting lost or missing important information.

Every Web site starts with a single **home page** that acts as a focal point for the Web site. It is usually the first page that users see. Starting from the home page, you add the links to other pages in the site, creating the site's overall structure. The Web sites you commonly encounter as you navigate the Web use one of several different Web structures. Examine some of these structures to help you decide how to design your own sites.

Linear Structures

If you wanted to create an online version of a famous play, like Shakespeare's *Hamlet*, one method would be to link the individual scenes of the play in a long chain. Figure 2-2 shows the storyboard for this type of **linear structure**, in which each page is linked with the pages that follow and precede it. Readers navigate this structure by moving forward and backward through the pages, much as they might move forward and backward through the pages of a book.

A linear structure **Figure 2-2**

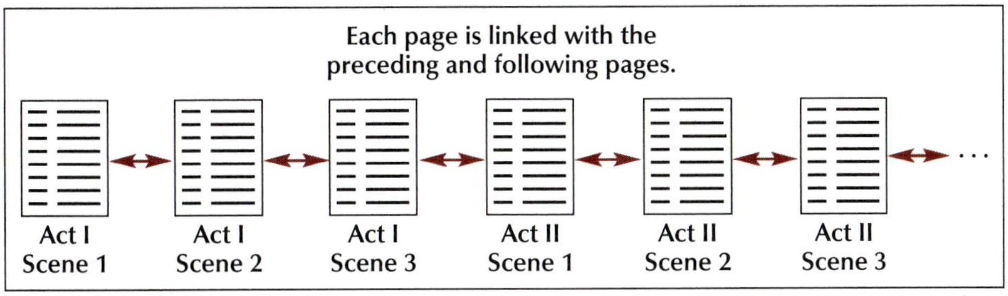

Linear structures work for Web sites with a clearly defined order of pages that are small in size. However, they can be difficult to work with as the chain of pages increases in length. An additional problem is that in a linear structure you move farther and farther away from the home page as you progress through the site. Because home pages often contain important general information about the site and its author, this is usually not the best design technique.

You can modify this structure to make it easier for users to return immediately to the home page or other main pages. Figure 2-3 shows this online play with an **augmented linear structure**, in which each page contains an additional link back to the opening page of each act.

An augmented linear structure **Figure 2-3**

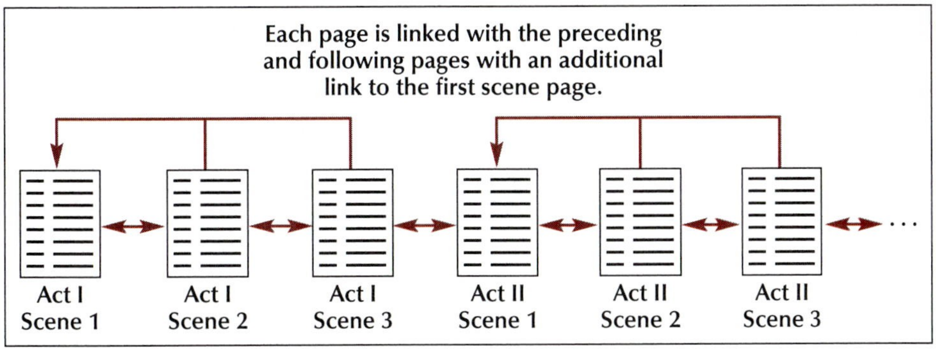

Hierarchical Structures

Another popular structure is the **hierarchical structure**, in which the pages are linked going from the home page down to pages dedicated to specific topics. Those pages, in turn, can be linked to even more specific topics. So, a hierarchical structure allows users to easily move from general to specific and back again. In the case of the online play, you can link an introductory page containing general information about the play to pages that describe each of the play's acts, and within each act you can include links to individual scenes. See Figure 2-4. With this structure, a user can move quickly to a specific scene within the page, bypassing the need to move through each scene in the play.

Figure 2-4 **A hierarchical structure**

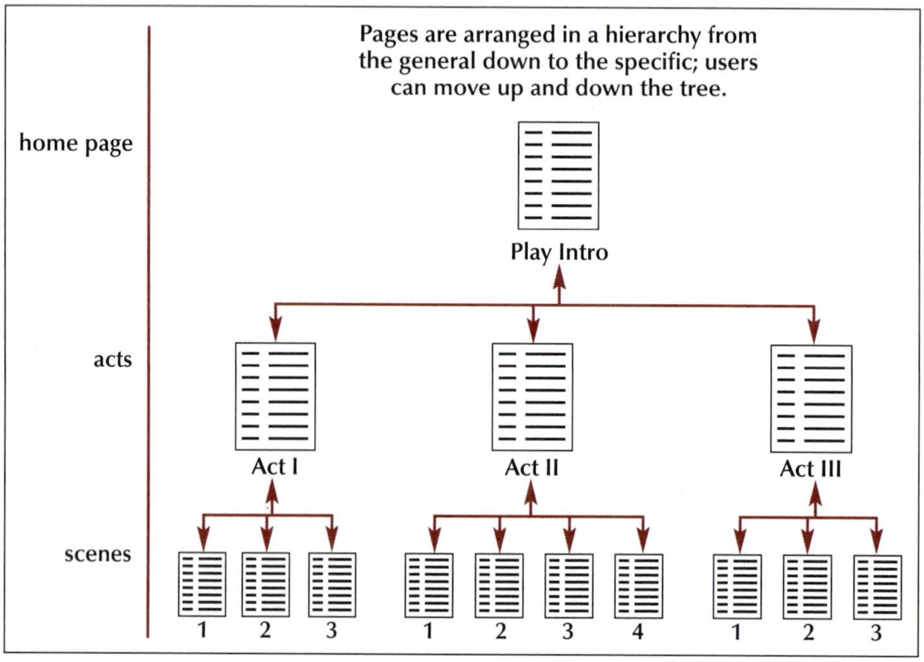

Mixed Structures

With larger and more complex Web sites, you often need to use a combination of structures. Figure 2-5 shows the online play using a mixture of the three main structures. The overall form is hierarchical, as users can move from a general introduction down to individual scenes; however, users can also move through the site in a linear fashion, going from act to act and scene to scene. Finally, each individual scene contains a link to the home page, allowing users to jump to the top of the hierarchy without moving through the different levels.

Figure 2-5 A mixed structure

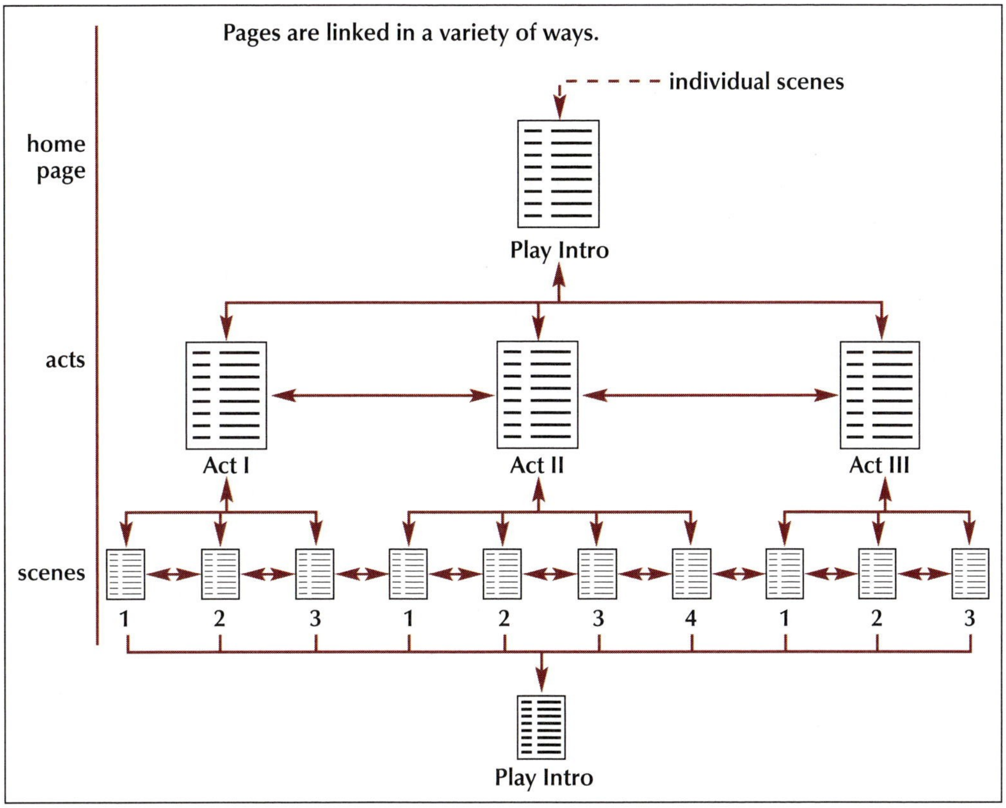

As these examples show, a little foresight can go a long way toward making your Web site easier to use. Also keep in mind that search results from a Web search engine such as Google or Yahoo! can point users to any page in your Web site—not just your home page—so they will need to quickly understand what your site contains and how to navigate it. At a minimum, each page should contain a link to the site's home page or to the relevant main topic page. In some cases, you might want to supply your users with a **site index**, which is a page containing an outline of the entire site and its contents. Unstructured Web sites can be difficult and frustrating to use. Consider the storyboard of the site displayed in Figure 2-6.

Figure 2-6 **Web site with no coherent structure**

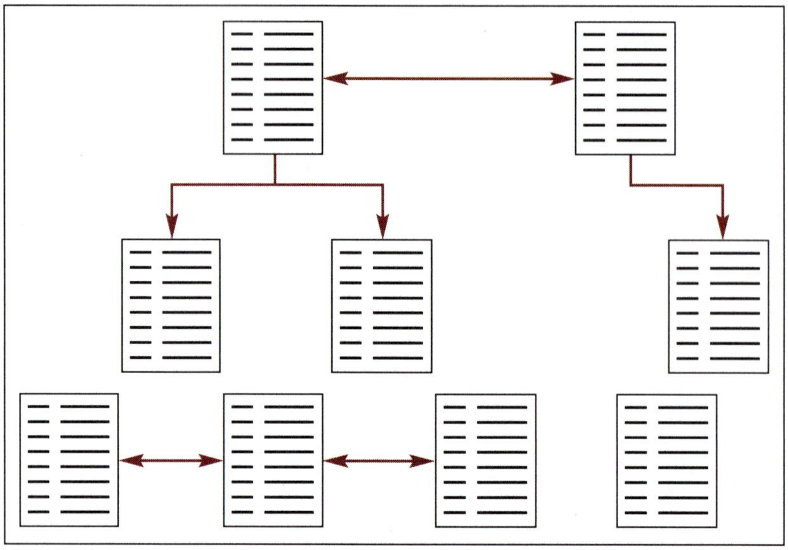

This confusing structure makes it difficult for users to grasp the site's contents and scope. The user might not even be aware of the presence of some pages because there are no connecting links, and some of the links only point in one direction. The Web is a competitive place; studies have shown that users who don't see how to get what they want within the first few seconds often leave a Web site. How long would a user spend on a site like the one shown in Figure 2-6?

Protected Structures

Sections of most commercial Web sites are off-limits except to subscribers and registered customers. As shown in Figure 2-7, these sites have a password-protected Web page that users must go through to get to the off-limits areas. The same Web site design principles apply to the protected section as the regular, open section of the site.

Figure 2-7 **A protected structure**

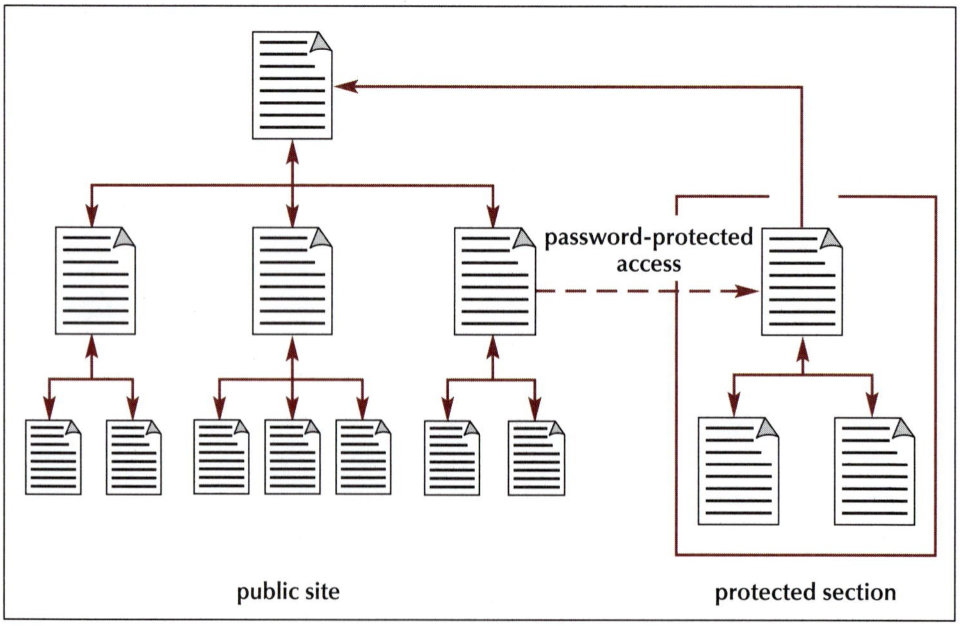

Storyboarding a protected structure is particularly important to ensure that no unmonitored "back doors" to the protected area are allowed in the site design.

Creating a Hypertext Link

Gerry wants his site visitors to be able to move effortlessly among the three documents he's created. To do that, you'll link each page to the other two pages. Figure 2-8 provides the storyboard for the simple structure you have in mind.

Storyboard for the CAMshots Web site **Figure 2-8**

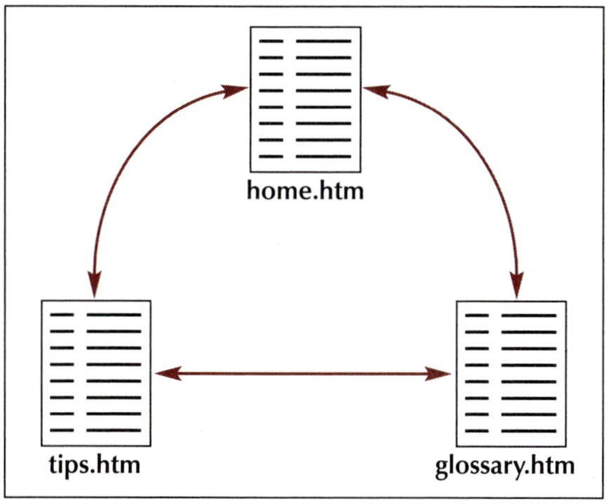

To create these links, you have to add hypertext links to each of the three documents. Hypertext links are created by enclosing some document content with a set of opening and closing <a> tags. The general syntax to create a hypertext link is

```
<a href="reference">content</a>
```

where *reference* is the location being linked to and *content* is the document content that is being marked as a link. The *reference* value can be a page on the World Wide Web, a local file, an e-mail address, or a network server. For example, to create a hypertext link to the tips.htm file, you could enter the following code:

```
<a href="tips.htm">Photography Tips</a>
```

This code marks the text "Photography Tips" as a hypertext link. When rendered by the browser, the words "Photography Tips" will be underlined, providing a visual clue to the user that the text is linked to another document. If the user clicks the text with a mouse, the browser will load the linked document (tips.htm).

Filenames are case sensitive on some operating systems, including the UNIX and Macintosh operating systems. Web servers running on those systems differentiate between a file named tips.htm and Tips.htm. For this reason, you might find that links you create on your computer do not work when you transfer your files to a Web server. To avoid this problem, the current standard is to always use lowercase filenames for all Web site files and to avoid using special characters such as blanks and slashes (/).

> **Tip**
> Keep your filenames short so that users are less apt to make a typing error when accessing your Web site.

At the top of the home.htm, tips.htm, and glossary.htm files, Gerry has already entered the names of each of his three documents. Your first task is to mark these names as hypertext links to each of Gerry's three files. You'll start with the names in the home.htm file.

Reference Window | Marking a Hypertext Link

- To mark content as hypertext, use
  `<a href="reference">content</a>`
  where *reference* is the location being linked to and *content* is the document content that is being marked as a link.

To create a hypertext link to a document:

1. Return to the **home.htm** file in your text editor and locate the second div element at the top of the file.
2. Mark the text "Home" as a hypertext link using a set of <a> tags as follows:
   ```
   <a href="home.htm">Home</a>
   ```
3. Mark the text "Tips" as a hypertext link using the following code:
   ```
   <a href="tips.htm">Tips</a>
   ```
4. Mark the text "Glossary" as a hypertext link as follows:
   ```
   <a href="glossary.htm">Glossary</a>
   ```
   Figure 2-9 highlights the revised text in the home.htm file.

Figure 2-9 Marking hypertext links in the home.htm file

```
<body>
   <div>
      <img src="camshots.jpg" alt="CAMshots" />
   </div>
   <hr />

   <div>
      [ <a href="home.htm">Home</a> ]
           
      [ <a href="tips.htm">Tips</a>  ]
           
      [ <a href="glossary.htm">Glossary</a>  ]
   </div>
```

5. Save your changes to the file.
6. The two other files have the same headings at the top of the document. Go to the **tips.htm** file in your text editor and repeat Steps 2 through 5 for the Home, Tips, and Glossary titles at the top of that file.
7. Go to the **glossary.htm** file in your text editor and repeat Steps 2 through 5 to mark the titles in that document as hypertext links as well.

   Now that you've added hypertext links to each of the three documents, test those links in your browser.

8. Reload or refresh the **home.htm** file in your Web browser. As indicated in Figure 2-10, the titles at the top of the page should now be underlined, providing visual evidence that these words are treated as hypertext links.

Hypertext links in the home page **Figure 2-10**

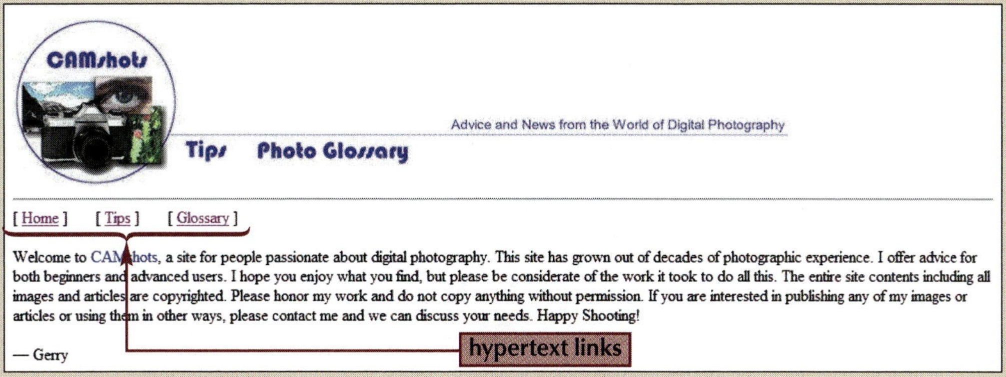

9. Click the **Tips** link from the list of page names. Verify that the browser loads and displays the Tips page.
10. Click the **Glossary** link. Verify that the Glossary page is opened by the browser.
11. Continue to click the hypertext links from the list, confirming that you can jump from any of the three pages to each of the other two pages.

    Trouble? If the links do not work, check the spelling of the filenames in the href attributes of the <a> tags. Because some Web servers require you to match capitalization in a filename, you should verify this in your attributes as well.

Specifying a Folder Path

In the links you've just created, you specified only the filename and not the location of the file. When you specify only the filename, the browser searches for the file in the same folder as the document containing the hypertext link; however, large Web sites containing hundreds of documents often place those documents in separate folders to make them easier to manage.

As Gerry adds more files to his Web site, he will probably want to use folders to organize the files. Figure 2-11 shows a preview of how Gerry might employ those folders. In this case, the topmost folder is named camshots. Gerry has placed some of his HTML files within the pages folder, which he has then divided into three subfolders named tips, glossary, and articles. He has also created separate folders for the images and video clips used on his Web site. Figure 2-11 displays the location of four HTML files named index.htm, tips1.htm, tips2.htm, and glossary.htm.

Figure 2-11 **A sample folder structure**

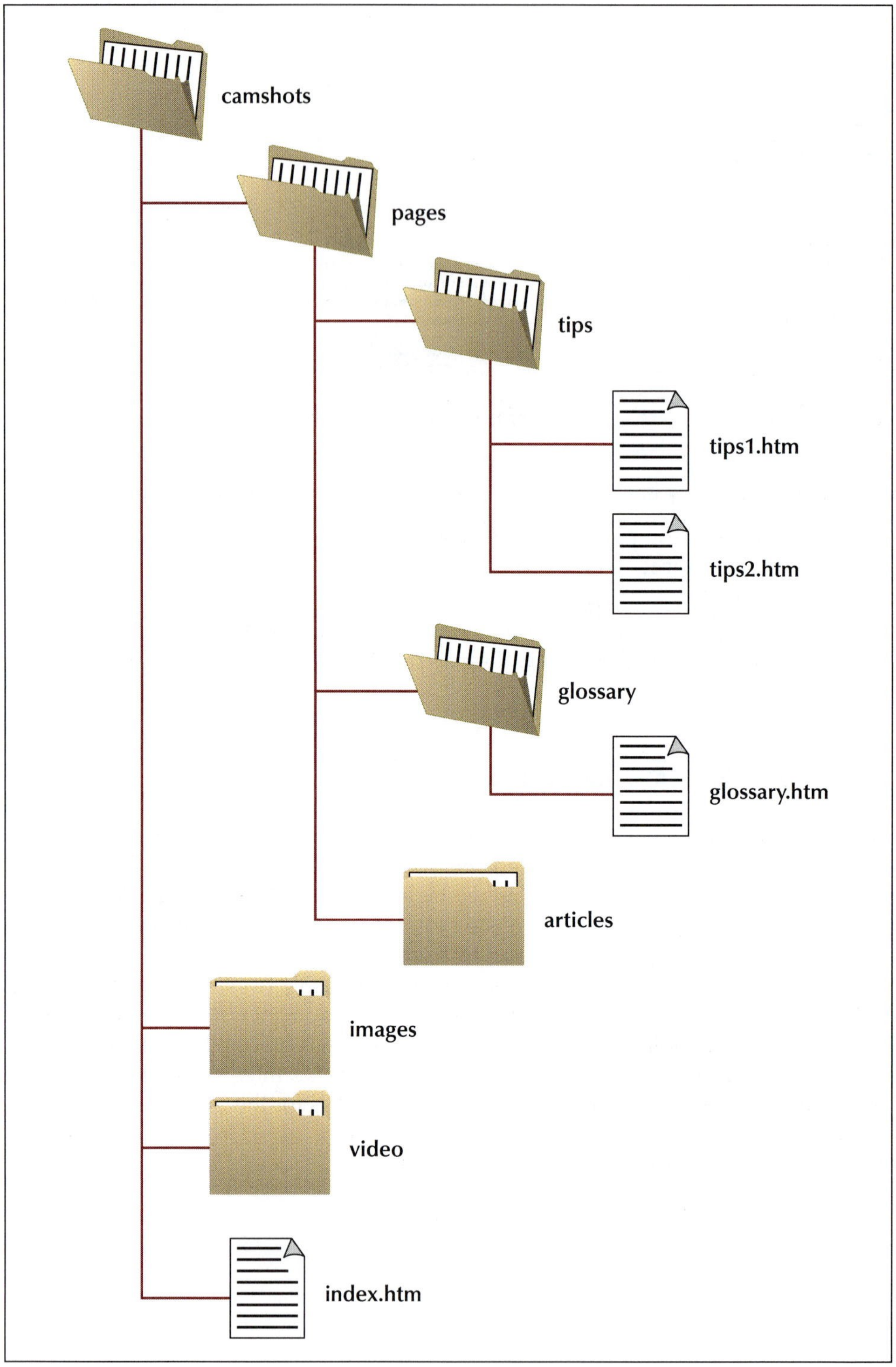

To create a link to a file located in a different folder than the current document, you must specify the file's location, or **path**, so that browsers can find it. HTML supports two kinds of paths: absolute and relative.

Absolute Paths

An **absolute path** specifies a file's precise location within a computer's entire folder structure. Absolute pathnames employ the syntax

/folder1/folder2/folder3/file

where *folder1* is the topmost folder in the computer's folder tree, followed by *folder2*, *folder3*, and so forth, down to the file you want to link to. Figure 2-12 shows how you would express absolute paths to the four files listed in Figure 2-11.

Tip

To make your Web site easier to maintain, organize your folders to match the organization of the pages on the Web site and group images and other media files within folders separate from your HTML files.

Figure 2-12 Absolute paths

Absolute Path	Interpretation
/camshots/pages/tips/tips1.htm	The tips1.htm file located in the pages/tips subfolder
/camshots/pages/tips/tips2.htm	The tips2.htm file located in the pages/tips subfolder
/camshots/pages/glossary/glossary.htm	The glossary.htm file located in the pages/glossary subfolder
/camshots/index.htm	The index.htm file located in the camshots folder

If files are located on different drives as well as in different folders, you must include the drive letter in the form

/drive|/folder1/folder2/folder3/file

where *drive* is the letter assigned to the drive. For example, the tips1.htm file located on drive C in the /camshots/pages/tips folder would have the absolute path:

```
/C|/camshots/pages/tips/tips1.htm
```

Remember that you don't have to include a drive letter if the destination document is located on the same drive as the document containing the link.

Relative Paths

When many folders and subfolders are involved, absolute pathnames can be cumbersome and confusing. For that reason, most Web designers prefer to use relative paths. A **relative path** specifies a file's location in relation to the location of the current document. If the file is in the same location as the current document, the relative path is simply the filename. If the file is in a subfolder of the current document, include the name of the subfolder without the forward slash in the form

folder/file

where *folder* is the name of the subfolder. To go farther down the folder tree to other subfolders, include those in the relative path separated by forward slashes, i.e.

folder1/folder2/folder3/file

where *folder1*, *folder2*, *folder3*, and so forth are subfolders of the current folder. Finally, a relative path can go up the folder tree by starting the pathname with a double period (..) followed by a forward slash and the name of the file. The path

../file

references the *file* document located in the parent folder of the current document. To reference a different folder on the same level of the folder tree, known as a **sibling folder**, you move up the folder tree using the double period (..) and then down using the name of the sibling folder. The general syntax is

../*folder*/*file*

where *folder* is the name of the sibling folder. Figure 2-13 shows the relative paths to the six files in the tree from Figure 2-11, starting from the camshots/pages/tips subfolder.

Figure 2-13 Relative paths

Relative Path from the /camshots/pages/tips Subfolder	Interpretation
tips1.htm	The tips1.htm file located in the current folder
tips2.htm	The tips2.htm file located in the current folder
../glossary/glossary.htm	The glossary.htm file located in the sibling glossary folder
../../index.htm	The index.htm file located in the parent camshots folder

Tip

You can reference the current folder using a single period (.) character.

You should almost always use relative paths in your links. If you have to move your files to a different computer or server, you can move the entire folder structure without having to change the relative pathnames you created. If you use absolute pathnames, you will probably have to revise each link to reflect the new location of the folder tree on the computer.

Changing the Base

As you've just seen, a browser resolves relative pathnames based on the location of the current document. You can change this behavior by specifying a different base or starting location for all relative paths. The code to specify a different base is

```
<base href="path" />
```

where *path* is the folder location that you want the browser to use when resolving relative paths in the current document. The base element has to be added to the head section of the HTML file and will be applied to all hypertext links found within the document.

Reference Window | Using the Base Element to Set the Default Location of Relative Paths

- To set the default location for a relative path, add the element
  `<base href="path" />`
  to the document head, where *path* is the folder location that you want the browser to use when resolving relative paths in the current document.

The base element is useful when a single document is moved to a new folder. Rather than rewriting all of the relative paths to reflect the document's new location, the base element redirects browsers to the document's old location, allowing any relative paths to be resolved as they were before.

Managing Your Web Site | InSight

Web sites can quickly grow from a couple of pages to dozens or hundreds of pages. As the size of the site increases, it becomes more difficult to get a clear picture of the site's structure and content. Imagine deleting or moving a file in a Web site that contains dozens of folders and hundreds of files. Can you easily project the effect of this change? Will all of your hypertext links still work after you move or delete the file?

To effectively manage a Web site, you should follow a few important rules. The first is to be consistent in how you structure the site. If you decide to collect all image files in one folder, you should follow that rule as you add more pages and images. Web sites are more likely to break down if files and folders are scattered throughout the server without a consistent rule or pattern. Decide on a structure early on and stick with it.

The second rule is to create a folder structure that matches the structure of the Web site itself. If the pages can be easily categorized into different groups, that grouping should also be reflected in the grouping of the subfolders. The names you assign to your files and folder should also reflect their use on the Web site. This makes it easier for you to predict how modifying a file or folder will impact other pages on the site.

Finally, you should document your work by adding comments to each new Web page. Comments are useful not only for colleagues who may be working on the site, but also for the author who has to revisit those files months or even years after creating them. The comments should include:

- The page's filename and location
- The page's author and the date the page was initially created
- A list of any supporting files used in the document, such as image and audio files
- A list of the files and their locations that link to the page
- A list of the files and their locations that the page links to

By following these rules, you can reduce a lot of the headaches associated with maintaining a large and complicated Web site.

You've completed your initial work linking the three files in Gerry's Web site. In the next session, you'll learn how to work with hypertext links that point to locations within files. If you want to take a break before starting the next session, you can close your files and your Web browser now.

Session 2.1 Quick Check | Review

1. What is storyboarding? Why is it important in creating a Web page system?
2. What is a linear structure? What is a hierarchical structure?
3. What code would you enter to link the text "Sports Info" to the sports.htm file? Assume that the current document and sports.htm are in the same folder.
4. What's the difference between an absolute path and a relative path?
5. Refer to Figure 2-11. If the current file is in the camshots/pages/glossary folder, what are the relative paths for the four files listed in the folder tree?
6. What is the purpose of the base element?

Session 2.2

Tip

In general, Web pages should not span more than one or two screen heights. Studies show that long Web pages are often skipped by busy users.

Linking to Locations within Documents

Gerry likes the links you've created in the last session and would like you to add some more links to the Glossary page. Recall that the Glossary page contains a list of digital photography terms. The page is very long, requiring users to scroll through the document to find a term of interest. At the top of the page Gerry has listed the letters A through Z. Gerry wants to give users the ability to jump to a specific section of the document by clicking a letter from the list. See Figure 2-14.

Figure 2-14 Jumping to a location within a Web page

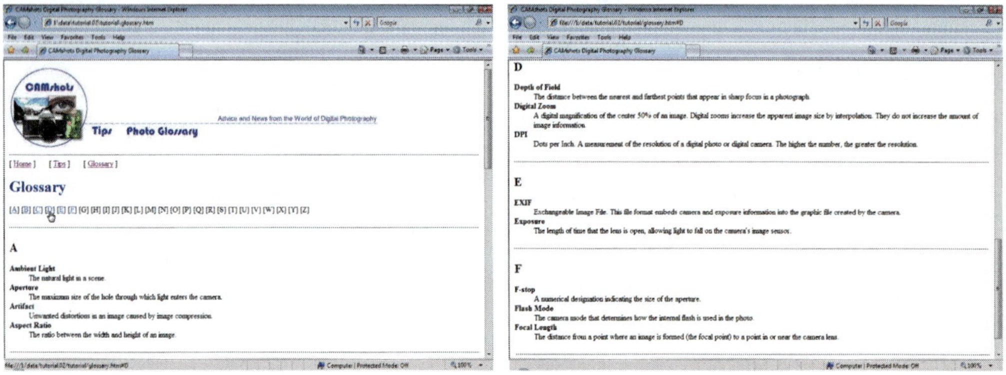

clicking the letter D from the alphabetical list ...

...jumps the user to the D section of the glossary

Using the id Attribute

To jump to a specific location within a document, you first need to mark that location. One way of doing this is to add an id attribute to an element at that location in the document. The syntax of the id attribute is

```
id="id"
```

where *id* is the value of the element id. For example, the following code marks the h2 element with an id value of H:

```
<h2 id="H">H</h2>
```

Note that id names must be unique. If you assign the same id name to more than one element on your Web page, the browser uses the first occurrence of the id name. XHTML documents will be rejected if they contain elements with duplicate ids. Id names are not case sensitive, so browsers do not differentiate between ids named top and TOP.

Reference Window | Defining an Element id

- To define the id of a specific element in a Web document, use the attribute
  `id="`*`id`*`"`
  where *id* is the value of the element id.

The Glossary page has only a partial list of the photography terms that Gerry will eventually add to his Web site. For now, you'll only mark sections in the glossary corresponding to the letters A through F.

To add the id attribute to h2 headings:

1. Return to the **glossary.htm** file in your text editor.
2. Scroll down the file and locate the h2 heading for the letter A. Within the opening <h2> tag, insert the following attribute:

   ```
   id="A"
   ```

3. Locate the h2 heading for the letter B and insert the following attribute in the opening <h2> tag:

   ```
   id="B"
   ```

   Figure 2-15 highlights the revised code.

Figure 2-15 Adding the id attribute to h2 headings

```
<hr />
<h2 id="A">A</h2>
<dl>
   <dt><b>Ambient Light</b></dt>
   <dd>The natural light in a scene.</dd>
   <dt><b>Aperture</b></dt>
   <dd>The maximum size of the hole through which light enters the camera.</dd>
   <dt><b>Artifact</b></dt>
   <dd>Unwanted distortions in an image caused by image compression.</dd>
   <dt><b>Aspect Ratio</b></dt>
   <dd>The ratio between the width and height of an image.</dd>
</dl>

<hr />
<h2 id="B">B</h2>
<dl>
   <dt><b>Bit</b></dt>
   <dd>The smallest unit of computer memory.</dd>
   <dt><b>Bitmap</b></dt>
   <dd>A method of storing information that maps an image pixel bit by bit.</dd>
   <dt><b>Byte</b></dt>
   <dd>A group of 8 bits, the basic unit of information for the computer.</dd>
</dl>
```

4. Continue going down the file, adding id attributes to the opening <h2> heading tags for C, D, E, and F corresponding to the letters of those headings.

For longer documents like the Glossary page, it's also helpful to the reader to be able to jump directly from the bottom of a long page to the top of the page rather than having to scroll back up. With that in mind, you'll also add an id attribute marking the element at the top of the page.

To mark the top of the page:

1. Scroll up the **glossary.htm** file in your text editor and locate the div element directly below the opening <body> tag.
2. Insert the following attribute within the opening <div> tag, as shown in Figure 2-16:

   ```
   id="top"
   ```

Figure 2-16 Adding an id attribute to the div element

```
<body>
   <div id="top">
      <img src="camshots.jpg" alt="CAMshots" />
   </div>
   <hr />
```

Linking to an id

Once you've marked an element using the id attribute, you can create a hypertext link to that element using the hypertext link

```
<a href="#id">content</a>
```

where *id* is the value of the id attribute of the element. For example, to create a link to the h2 heading for the letter A in the glossary document, you would enter the following code:

```
<a href="#A">A</a>
```

Use this code to change the entries on the Glossary page to hypertext links pointing to the section of the glossary corresponding to the selected letter.

To change the list of letters to hypertext links:

1. Locate the letter A in the list of letters at the top of the **glossary.htm** file.
2. After the [character, insert the following opening tag:

   ```
   <a href="#A">
   ```

3. Between the letter A and the] character, insert closing **</a>** tag. Figure 2-17 shows the revised code.

Figure 2-17 **Creating a hypertext link for "A"**

```
<h1 style="color: teal">Glossary</h1>
<p>
   [<a href="#A">A</a>] [B] [C]
   [D] [E] [F]
   [G] [H] [I]
   [J] [K] [L]
   [M] [N] [O]
   [P] [Q] [R]
   [S] [T] [U]
   [V] [W] [X]
   [Y] [Z]
</p>
```

4. Mark the letters B through F in the list as hypertext links pointing to the appropriate h2 headings in the document. Figure 2-18 shows the revised code for the list of letters.

Figure 2-18 **Hypertext links for the list of letters**

```
<h1 style="color: teal">Glossary</h1>
<p>
   [<a href="#A">A</a>] [<a href="#B">B</a>] [<a href="#C">C</a>]
   [<a href="#D">D</a>] [<a href="#E">E</a>] [<a href="#F">F</a>]
   [G] [H] [I]
   [J] [K] [L]
   [M] [N] [O]
   [P] [Q] [R]
   [S] [T] [U]
   [V] [W] [X]
   [Y] [Z]
</p>
```

Gerry also wants you to create a hypertext link at the bottom of the file that points to the top (using the id attribute you created in the last set of steps).

5. Scroll to the bottom of the file and locate the text "Return to Top."
6. Mark the text as hypertext, pointing to the element with an id value of top. See Figure 2-19.

Figure 2-19 Hypertext link to return to the top of the document

```
<hr />
<div><a href="#top">Return to Top</a> &#8657;</div>
<hr />
<address>
   CAMshots &#8250;&#8250;&#8250; Tips and News from the World of Digital Photography
</address>
```

7. Save your changes to the file and then reload or refresh the **glossary.htm** file in your Web browser.
8. As shown in Figure 2-20, the letters A through F in the alphabetic list are displayed as hypertext links. Click the link for **F** and verify that you jump down to the end of the document, where the photographic terms starting with the letter F are listed.

Figure 2-20 Hypertext links in the glossary page

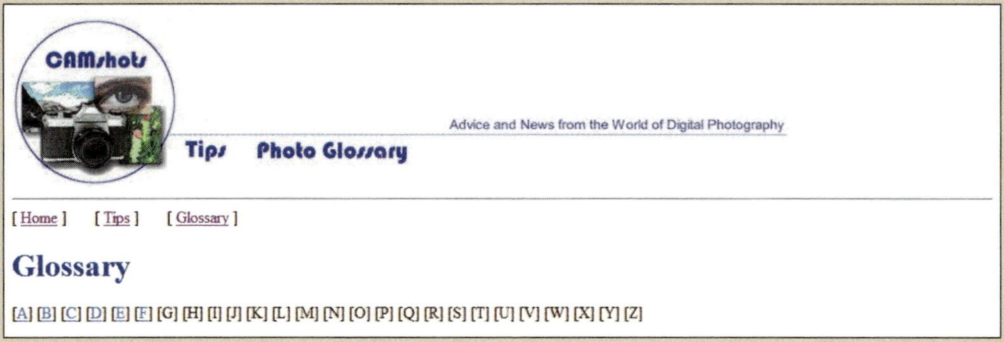

9. Click the **Return to Top** hypertext link and verify that you jump back to the top of the document.
10. Click the other links within the document and verify that you jump to the correct sections of the glossary.

    Trouble? The browser cannot scroll farther than the end of the page. So, you might not see any difference between jumping to the E section of the glossary and jumping to the F section.

InSight | **Working with Anchors**

Early browser versions might not support the use of the id attribute as a way of marking document elements. These early browser versions instead used anchors or bookmarks to mark document locations. The syntax of the anchor element is

```
<a name="anchor">content</a>
```

where *anchor* is the name of the anchor that marks the location of the document *content*. For example, to mark the h2 heading with an anchor of "A," you would enter the following code:

```
<h2><a name="A">A</a></h2>
```

Marking a location with an anchor does not change your document's appearance in any way; it merely creates a destination within your document.

You use the same syntax to link to locations marked with an anchor as you would with locations marked with id attributes. To link to the above anchor, you could use the following code:

```
<a href="#A">A</a>
```

The use of anchors is a deprecated feature of HTML and is not supported in strict applications of XHTML, but you will still see anchors used in older code and in code generated by HTML editors and converters.

Creating Links between Documents

Gerry knows that the glossary will be one of the most useful parts of his Web site, especially for novice photographers. However, he's also aware that most people do not read through glossaries. He would like to create links from the words he uses in his articles to glossary entries so that readers of his articles can quickly access definitions for terms they don't understand. His articles are not on the same page as his Glossary page, so he will have to create a link between those pages and specific glossary entries.

To create a link to a specific location in another file, enter the code

```
<a href="reference#id">content</a>
```

where *reference* is a reference to an HTML or XHTML file and *id* is the id of an element marked within that file. For example, the code

```
<a href="glossary.htm#D">"D" terms in the Glossary</a>
```

creates a hypertext link to the D section in the glossary.htm file. This assumes that the glossary.htm file is located in the same folder as the document containing the hypertext link. If not, you have to include either the absolute or relative path information along with the filename, as described in the last session.

Reference Window | **Linking to an id**

- To link to a specific location within the current file, use
  ```
  <a href="#id">content</a>
  ```
  where *id* is the id value of an element within the document.
- To link to a specific location in another file, use
  ```
  <a href="reference#id">content</a>
  ```
  where *reference* is a reference to an external file and *id* is the id value of an element in that file.

On Gerry's home page, he wants to showcase a Photo of the Month, displaying a photo that his readers might find interesting or useful in their own work. Along with the photo, he has included the digital camera settings used in taking the photo. Many of the camera settings are described on the Glossary page. Gerry suggests that you create a link between the setting name and the glossary entry. The five entries he wants to link to are: F-stop, Exposure, Focal Length, Aperture, and Flash Mode. Your first step is to mark these entries in the glossary using the id attribute.

To mark the glossary entries:

1. Return to the **glossary.htm** file in your text editor.
2. Scroll down the file and locate the Aperture definition term.
3. As shown in Figure 2-21, within the opening <dt> tag, insert the attribute

   id="aperture"

Figure 2-21 **Inserting an id attribute**

```
<hr />
<h2 id="A">A</h2>
<dl>
   <dt><b>Ambient Light</b></dt>
   <dd>The natural light in a scene.</dd>
   <dt id="aperture"><b>Aperture</b></dt>
   <dd>The maximum size of the hole through which light enters the camera.</dd>
   <dt><b>Artifact</b></dt>
   <dd>Unwanted distortions in an image caused by image compression.</dd>
   <dt><b>Aspect Ratio</b></dt>
   <dd>The ratio between the width and height of an image.</dd>
</dl>
```

4. Scroll down the file and locate the Exposure definition term.
5. Within the opening <dt> tag, insert the following attribute:

   id="exposure"

6. Go to the F section of the glossary and mark the terms with the following ids:

   F-stop with the id f-stop

   Flash Mode with the id flash_mode

   Focal Length with the id focal_length

7. Save your changes to the **glossary.htm** file.

Next you'll go to the Home page and create links from these terms in the Photo of the Month description to their entries on the Glossary page.

To create links to the glossary entries:

1. Open the **home.htm** file in your text editor.
2. Scroll down the file and locate the F-stop term from the unordered list.
3. Mark "F-stop" as a hypertext link using the following code:

   <a href="glossary.htm#f-stop">F-stop</a>

4. Mark "Exposure" as a hypertext link with:

   <a href="glossary.htm#exposure">Exposure</a>

5. Mark the remaining three entries in the unordered list as hypertext pointing to their corresponding entries on the Glossary page. Figure 2-22 highlights the revised code in the file.

Figure 2-22 Linking to a location within another document

```
      <i>Pear Lake Reflection</i></blockquote>
<ul>
   <li>Camera:
              
      Nikon D50</li>
   <li><a href="glossary.htm#f-stop">F-stop</a>:
                
      f/7.1</li>
   <li><a href="glossary.htm#exposure">Exposure</a>:
            
      1/200 sec.</li>
   <li><a href="glossary.htm#focal_length">Focal Length</a>:
       
      18mm</li>
   <li><a href="glossary.htm#aperture">Aperture</a>:
             
      3.6</li>
   <li><a href="glossary.htm#flash_mode">Flash Mode</a>:
          No flash</li>
</ul>
```

document file

element id

6. Save your changes to the file.

7. Refresh the **home.htm** file in your Web browser. As shown in Figure 2-23, the settings from the Photo of the Month description are now displayed as hypertext links.

Figure 2-23 Linked photography terms

8. Click the **F-stop** hypertext link and verify that you jump to the Glossary page with the F-stop entry displayed in the browser window.

9. Return to the **CAMshots home page** and click the hypertext links for the other terms in the list of photo settings, verifying that you jump to the section of the glossary that displays that term's definition.

Working with Linked Images and Image Maps

A standard practice on the Web is to turn the Web site's logo into a hypertext link pointing to the home page. This gives users a quick reference point to the home page rather than searching for a link to the home page. To mark an inline image as a hypertext link, you enclose the <img> tag within a set of <a> tags as follows:

```
<a href="reference"><img src="file" alt="text" /></a>
```

Once the image has been linked, clicking anywhere within the image jumps the user to the linked file.

> **Tip**
>
> Always include alternative text for your linked images to allow nongraphical browsers to display a text link in place of the linked image.

Introducing Image Maps

When you mark an inline image as a hypertext link, the entire image is linked to the same destination file; however, HTML also allows you to divide an image into different zones, or **hotspots,** each linked to a different destination. Therefore, a single inline image can be linked to several locations. Gerry is interested in doing this with the CAMshots logo. He would like you to create hotspots for the logo so that if the user clicks anywhere within the CAMshots circle on the left side of the logo, the user jumps to the Home page, while clicking either Tips or Photo Glossary in the logo takes the user to the Tips page or the Glossary page. See Figure 2-24.

Figure 2-24 Hotspots within the CAMshots logo

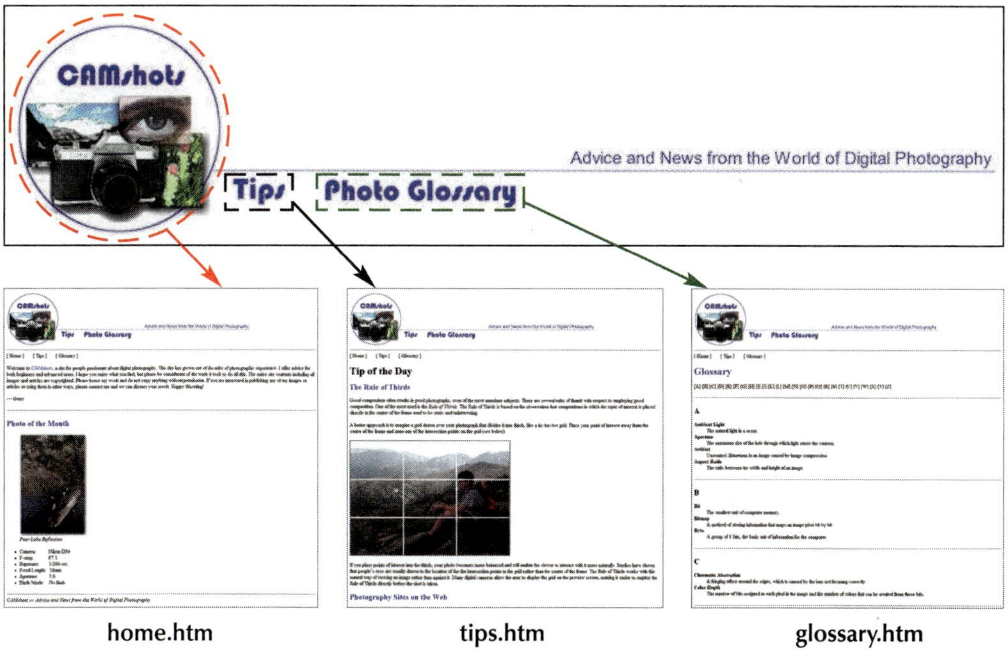

To define these hotspots, you create an **image map** that matches a specified region of the inline image to a specific destination. HTML supports two kinds of image maps: client-side image maps and server-side image maps. You'll first study how to create a client-side image map.

Client-Side Image Maps

A **client-side image map** is an image map that is handled entirely by the Web browser running on the user's computer. Client-side image maps are defined with the map element

```
<map id="map" name="map">
   hotspots
</map>
```

where *map* is the name of the image map and *hotspots* are the locations of the hotspots within the image. Each image map has to be given an id and a name. You have to include both attributes, setting them to the same value, because HTML code requires the name attribute and XHTML requires the id attribute. As long as you include both, your code will work under all browsers. For example, the following code creates a map element named logomap:

```
<map id="logomap" name="logomap">
...
</map>
```

Map elements can be placed anywhere within the body of the Web page because they are not actually displayed by the browser, but used as references for mapping hotspots to inline images. The common practice is to place the map element below the inline image.

Defining Hotspots

The individual hotspots are defined using the area element

```
<area shape="shape" coords="coordinates" href="reference" alt="text" />
```

where *shape* is the shape of the hotspot region, *coordinates* are the list of points that define the boundaries of the region, *reference* is the file or location that the hotspot is linked to, and *text* is alternate text displayed for nongraphical browsers. Hotspots can be created in the shape of rectangles, circles, or polygons (multisided figures). So, the shape attribute can have the value rect for a rectangular hotspot, "circle" for a circular hotspot, and "poly" for a polygonal or multisided hotspot. A fourth shape option is "default," representing the remaining area of the inline image not covered by hotspots. There is no limit to the number of area elements you can add to an image map. Hotspots can also overlap. If they do and the user clicks an overlapping area, the browser opens the link of the first hotspot defined in the map.

Hotspot coordinates are measured in **pixels**, which are the smallest unit or dot in a digital image or display. Your computer monitor might have a size of 1024 x 768 pixels, which means that the display is 1024 dots wide by 768 dots tall. The CAMshots logo that Gerry uses in his Web site has a dimension of 778 pixels wide by 164 pixels tall. When used with the coords attribute of the area element, the pixel values exactly define the location and size of the hotspot region.

Each hotspot shape has a different set of coordinates that define it. To define a rectangular hotspot, enter

```
<area shape="rect" coords="x1, y1, x2, y2" ... />
```

where *x1, y1* are the coordinates of the upper-left corner of the rectangle and *x2, y2* are the coordinates of the rectangle's lower-right corner. Figure 2-25 shows the coordinates of the rectangular region surrounding the Photo Glossary hotspot.

Figure 2-25 Rectangular hotspot and area element

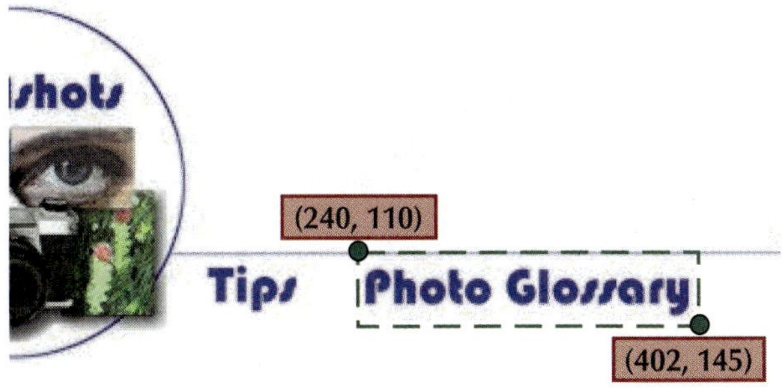


```
<area shape="rect" coords="240, 110, 402, 145" />
```

The upper-left corner of the rectangle has the coordinates (240, 110). The lower-right corner is found at the coordinates (402, 145). Coordinates are always expressed relative to the image's top-left corner. A coordinate of (240, 110) refers to a point that is 240 pixels to the right and 110 pixels down from the image's top-left corner.

Circular hotspots are defined using the area element

```
<area shape="circle" coords="x, y, r" ... />
```

where *x* and *y* are the coordinates of the center of the circle and *r* is the circle's radius. Figure 2-26 shows the coordinates for a circular hotspot around the CAMshots image from the Web site logo. The center of the circle is located at the coordinates (82, 78) and the circle has a radius of 80 pixels.

Figure 2-26 Circular hotspot and area element

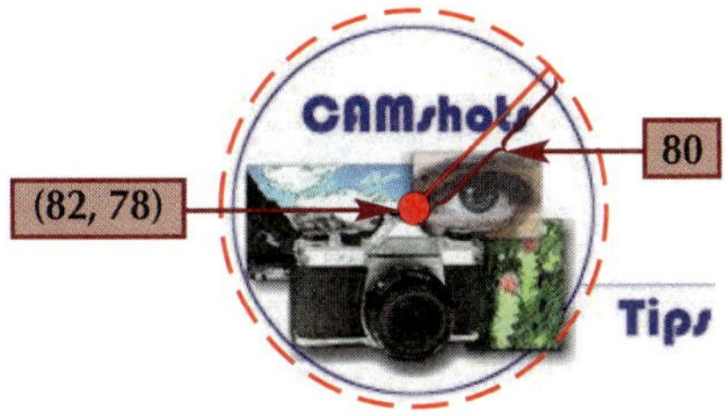


```
<area shape="circle" coords="82, 78, 80" />
```

Polygonal hotspots are defined with

```
<area shape="poly" coords="x1, y1, x2, y2, x3, y3, ..." ... />
```

where (*x1*, *y1*), (*x2*, *y2*), (*x3*, *y3*) and so forth define the coordinates of each corner in the multisided shape. Figure 2-27 shows the coordinates for a triangular-shaped hotspot with corners at (30, 142), (76, 80), and (110, 142). With polygonal hotspots, you can create a wide variety of shapes as long you know the coordinates of each corner.

Figure 2-27 **Polygonal hotspot and area element**

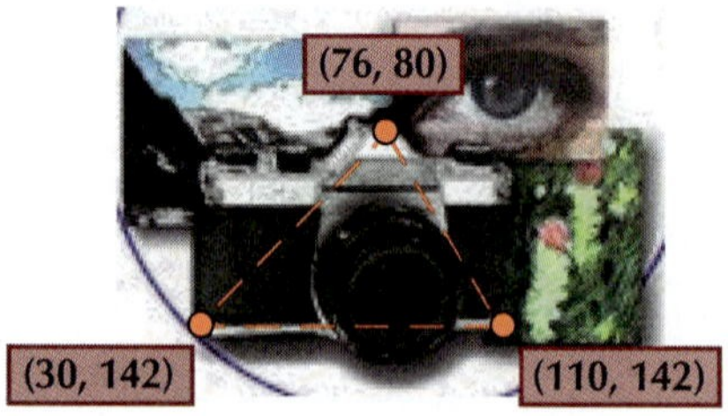


```
<area shape="poly" coords="30, 142, 76, 80, 110, 142" />
```

Finally, to define the default hotspot for the image use

```
<area shape="default" coords="0, 0, x, y" ... />
```

where *x* is the width of the inline image in pixels and *y* is the image's height. Any spot in the inline image that is not covered by another hotspot will activate the default hotspot link.

To determine the coordinates of a hotspot, you can use either a graphics program such as Adobe Photoshop or image map software that automatically generates the HTML code for the hotspots you define.

In this case, assume that Gerry has already determined the coordinates for the hotspots in his image map and provided them for you. He has three hotspots that he wants you to create, shown earlier in Figure 2-24. The first is a circular hotspot linked to the home.htm file, centered at the point (82, 78) and having a radius of 80 pixels. The second is a rectangular hotspot, linked to the tips.htm file with corners at (168, 110) and (225, 145). The third is also rectangular, linked to the glossary.htm file with corners at (240, 110) and (402, 145). You do not have to create a polygonal hotspot.

You'll name the image map containing these hotspots logomap.

To create an image map:

1. Return to **home.htm** file in your text editor.
2. Directly below the <img> tag for the CAMshots inline image, insert the following map element:

```
<map id="logomap" name="logomap">
</map>
```

3. Within the map element, insert a circular hotspot that points to the home.htm file using the following area element:

```
<area shape="circle" coords="82, 78, 80"
      href="home.htm" alt="Home" />
```

4. Directly below the <area> tag for the circular hotspot, insert the following two rectangular hotspots pointing to the tips.htm and glossary.htm files:

```
<area shape="rect" coords="168, 110, 225, 145"
      href="tips.htm" alt="Tips" />
<area shape="rect" coords="240, 110, 402, 145"
      href="glossary.htm" alt="Glossary" />
```

Figure 2-28 highlights the new code in the file.

Figure 2-28 Creating an image map

hotspots

```
<body>
   <div>
      <img src="camshots.jpg" alt="CAMshots" />
      <map id="logomap" name="logomap">
         <area shape="circle" coords="82, 78, 80"
               href="home.htm" alt="Home" />
         <area shape="rect" coords="168, 110, 225, 145"
               href="tips.htm" alt="Tips" />
         <area shape="rect" coords="240, 110, 402, 145"
               href="glossary.htm" alt="Glossary" />
      </map>
   </div>
   <hr />
```

5. Save your changes to the file.

Creating a Client-Side Image Map | Reference Window

- To create a client-side image map, insert the map element
  ```
  <map name="map" id="map">
    hotspots
  </map>
  ```
  anywhere within the Web page body, where *map* is the name and id of the image map and *hotspots* is a list of hotspot areas defined within the image map.
- To add a hotspot to the image map, place the element
  ```
  <area shape="shape" coords="coordinates" href="reference"
  alt="text" />
  ```
  within the map element, where *shape* is the shape of the hotspot region, *coordinates* are the list of points that define the boundaries of the region, *reference* is the file or location that the hotspot is linked to, and *text* is alternate text displayed for nongraphical browsers.
- To define a rectangular-shaped hotspot, use the area element
  ```
  <area shape="rect" coords="x1, y1, x2, y2" ... />
  ```
  where x1, y1 are the coordinates of the upper-left corner of the rectangle and x2, y2 are the coordinates of the rectangle's lower-right corner.
- To define a circular hotspot, use
  ```
  <area shape="circle" coords="x, y, r" ... />
  ```
  where *x* and *y* are the coordinates of the center of the circle and *r* is the circle's radius.
- To define a polygonal hotspot, use
  ```
  <area shape="poly" coords="x1, y1, x2, y2, x3, y3, ..." ... />
  ```
  where (*x1*, *y1*), (*x2*, *y2*), (*x3*, *y3*), and so forth define the coordinates of each corner in the multisided shape.
- To define the default hotspot, use
  ```
  <area shape="default" coords="0, 0, x, y" ... />
  ```
  where *x* is the width of the inline image in pixels and *y* is the height in pixels.
- To apply an image map to an inline image, add the usemap attribute
  ```
  <img src="file" alt="text" usemap="#map" />
  ```
  to the img element, where *map* is the name or id of the map element.

Now that you've defined the image map, your next task is to apply the map to the CAMshots logo.

Applying an Image Map

To apply an image map to an image, add the usemap attribute to the inline image's <img> tag. The syntax is

```
<img src="file" alt="text" usemap="#map" />
```

where *map* is the id or name of the map element. If you place the map element in a separate file, you can reference it using the code

```
<img src="file" alt="text" usemap="reference#map" />
```

where *reference* is a reference to an HTML or XHTML file containing the map element. Unfortunately, most browsers do not support this option, so you should always place the image map in the same file as the inline image. You'll apply the logomap to the CAMshots logo and then test it on your Web browser.

To apply the logomap image map:

1. Add the following attribute to the <img> tag for the CAMshots logo, as shown in Figure 2-29.

   ```
   usemap="#logomap"
   ```

Figure 2-29 Applying an image map

```
<body>
   <div>
      <img src="camshots.jpg" alt="CAMshots" usemap="#logomap" />
      <map id="logomap" name="logomap">
         <area shape="circle" coords="82, 78, 80"
               href="home.htm" alt="Home" />
         <area shape="rect" coords="168, 110, 225, 145"
               href="tips.htm" alt="Tips" />
         <area shape="rect" coords="240, 110, 402, 145"
               href="glossary.htm" alt="Glossary" />
      </map>
   </div>
   <hr />
```

imagemap

map element name or id

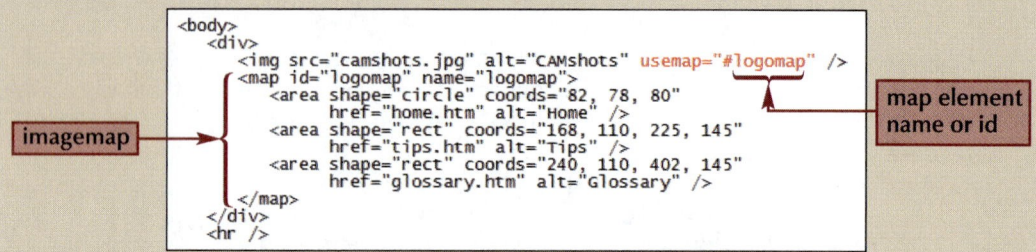

2. Save your changes to the file and reload or refresh the **home.htm** file in your Web browser.

   Trouble? Depending on your browser, you might see a border around the CAMshots logo, which you can ignore for now. You'll remove it shortly.

3. Click anywhere within the word **Tips** in the logo image and verify that the browser opens the Tips page.

4. Return to the home page and click anywhere within the word **Photo Glossary** to verify that the browser opens the Glossary page.

Tip

If you need to be compatible with older browsers, use the attribute border="0" in place of the border-width style. Note that the border attribute has been deprecated and is not supported in strict applications of XHTML.

After changing the logo to a hypertext link, you may have noticed that you have added a border around the image. Hypertext links are usually underlined in the Web page; but with inline images, the image is displayed with a lined border. Gerry would prefer not to have a border because he feels that it detracts from the logo's appearance. He asks if you can remove the border but still keep the logo functioning as a hypertext link.

To remove the border, you can apply a border-width style to the inline image. By setting the width of the border to zero, you will effectively remove it from the logo. The style attribute to change the width of a border is

```
style="border-width: 0"
```

Removing the Border from an Inline Image | Reference Window

- To remove a border from an inline image, add the following attribute to the <img> tag:
  `style="border-width: 0"`

Use the border-width style to remove the border from the CAMshots logo on the three pages of Gerry's Web site.

To set the border width of the CAMshots logo to 0:

1. Return to the **home.htm** file in your text editor.
2. Add the following style attribute to the <img> tag for the logo inline image, as shown in Figure 2-30.

   `style="border-width: 0"`

Figure 2-30 **Removing an inline image border**

```
<body>
   <div>
      <img src="camshots.jpg" alt="CAMshots" usemap="#logomap" style="border-width: 0" />
      <map id="logomap" name="logomap">
         <area shape="circle" coords="82, 78, 80"
               href="home.htm" alt="Home" />
         <area shape="rect" coords="168, 110, 225, 145"
               href="tips.htm" alt="Tips" />
         <area shape="rect" coords="240, 110, 402, 145"
               href="glossary.htm" alt="Glossary" />
      </map>
   </div>
   <hr />
```

set the width of the image border to 0

3. Save your changes to the file.
4. Reload the **home.htm** file in your browser and verify that the border has been removed from the image.

Now that you've created an image map for the logo on the home page, you can create similar image maps for the logos on the Tips and Glossary pages.

To add image maps to the other Web pages:

1. Return to the **tips.htm** file in your text editor.
2. Replace the code within the div element for the logo image with the code shown earlier in Figure 2-30. (Hint: You can use the copy and paste feature of your text editor to copy the code from the home.htm file into the tips.htm file.)
3. Save your changes to the file.
4. Go to the **glossary.htm** file in your text editor.
5. As you did for the tips.htm file, replace the code within the div element for the logo image with the code from the home.htm file. Save your changes to the file.
6. Return to the **home.htm** file in your Web browser and verify that you can switch among the three Web pages by clicking the hotspots in the CAMshots logo.
7. If you want to take a break before starting the next session, close your files and programs now.

Server-Side Image Maps

The other type of image map you might encounter on the Web is a **server-side image map**, which is stored on the Web server rather than entered into the HTML code of the Web page. When you click a hotspot on a server-side image map, the coordinates of the mouse click are sent to the server, which activates the corresponding link, downloading the page to your Web browser.

The server-side image map was the original HTML standard and is still supported on the Web. However, this map has some limitations compared to client-side image maps. Because the map is located on the server, you cannot test your Web page without server access. Also, server-side image maps might be slower because information must be sent to the server with each mouse click. Finally, unlike client-side image maps, server-side image maps require the use of a mouse. This makes them unsuitable for users with disabilities or users running nongraphical browsers.

To create a server-side image map, enclose the inline image with a hypertext link such as

```
<a href="map">
   <img src="file" alt="text" ismap="ismap" />
</a>
```

where *map* is the name of a program or file running on the Web server that will handle the image map. The ismap attribute tells the Web browser to treat the inline image as an image map.

At this time, you do not foresee a need to use a server-side image map in the CAMshots Web site. In any future projects, you'll continue to work with client-side maps.

InSight | Writing Effective Hypertext Links

To make it easier for users to navigate your Web site, you should follow a few key design tips. Write the text of your hypertext links so that they tell the reader exactly what type of document the link points to. For example, the link text

Click here for more information.

doesn't tell the user what type of document will appear when "here" is clicked. In the place of phrases like "click here," use descriptive link text such as:

For more information, view a list of frequently asked questions.

If the link points to a non-HTML file, such as a PDF document, include that information in the link text. If the linked document is extremely large and will take a while to download to the user's computer, include that information in your link text so that users can decide whether or not to initiate the transfer. The following link text informs users of the size of the video clip before they initiate the link:

Download the video clip (16 MB).

Make your link text easy to locate. Because most browsers underline hypertext links, don't use underlining for other text elements; use italic or boldface fonts instead. Users should never be confused about what is a link and what is not. Also, if you apply a color to your text, do not choose colors that will make the linked text harder to pick out against the Web page background.

Gerry is pleased with the progress you've made on his Web site. Adding the links to the glossary and within the CAMshots logo has made his site easier to navigate. However, there are many other sources of information about digital photography and digital cameras that Gerry wants to make available to his readers. In the next session you'll examine how to create links between his Web site and other sites on the World Wide Web.

Session 2.2 Quick Check | Review

1. Specify the code for marking the text "CAMshots FAQ" as an h2 heading with the id "faq."
2. Specify the code for marking the text "Read our FAQ" as hypertext linked to an element in the current document with the id "faq."
3. Specify the code for marking the text "Read our FAQ" as a hypertext link, pointing to an element with the id "faq" in the help.htm file. Assume that help.htm lies in the same folder as the current document.
4. Specify the code for placing an anchor with the name "faq" within the h2 heading "CAMshots FAQ."
5. For marking locations within a Web page, what is one advantage of using anchors rather than the id attribute? What is one disadvantage?
6. The CAMmap image map has a circular hotspot centered at the point (50, 75) with a radius of 40 pixels pointing to the faq.htm file. Specify the code to create this map element with that circular hotspot.
7. An inline image based on the logo.jpg file with the alternative text "CAMshots" needs to use the CAMmap image map. Specify the code to apply the image map to the image.
8. What attribute do you add to the inline image from the previous question to remove its border?

Session 2.3

Linking to Resources on the Internet

Gerry has a final set of tasks for you. In the tips.htm file, he has listed some of the Web sites he finds useful in his study of photography. He would like to change the entries in this list to hypertext links that his readers can click to quickly access the sites.

Introducing URLs

To create a link to a resource on the Internet, you need to know its URL. A **URL**, or **Uniform Resource Locator**, specifies the precise location of a resource on the Internet. Examples of URLs include *www.whitehouse.gov*, the home page of the President of the United States, and *www.w3.org*, the home page of the World Wide Web consortium. All URLs share the common form

> **Tip**
>
> Because URLs cannot contain blank spaces, avoid blank spaces in Web site file and folder names.

```
scheme:location
```

where *scheme* indicates the type of resource referenced by the URL and *location* is the location of that resource. For Web pages, the location refers to the location of the HTML file; but for other resources, the location might simply be the name of the resource. For example, a link to an e-mail account has the e-mail address as the resource.

The name of the scheme is taken from the protocol used to access the resource. A **protocol** is a set of rules defining how information is passed between two devices. Your Web browser communicates with Web servers using the **Hypertext Transfer Protocol** or **HTTP**. Therefore, the URLs for all Web pages must start with the http scheme. This tells the browser to use http when it tries to access the Web page. Other Internet resources, described in Figure 2-31, use different communication protocols and have different scheme names.

Figure 2-31 Internet protocols

Protocol	Used To
file	access documents stored locally on a user's computer
ftp	access documents stored on an FTP server
gopher	access documents stored on a gopher server
http	access Web pages stored on the World Wide Web
https	access Web pages over a secure encrypted connection
mailto	open a user's e-mail client and address a new message
news	connect to a Usenet newsgroup
telnet	open a telnet connection to a specific server
wais	connect to a Wide Area Information Server database

Linking to a Web Site

The URL for a Web page has the general form

```
http://server/path/filename#id
```

where *server* is the name of the Web server, *path* is the path to the file on that server, *filename* is the name of the file, and if necessary, *id* is the name of an id or anchor within the file. A Web page URL can also contain specific programming instructions for a browser to send to the Web server (a topic beyond the scope of this tutorial). Figure 2-32 shows the URL for a sample Web page with all of the parts identified.

Figure 2-32 Parts of a URL

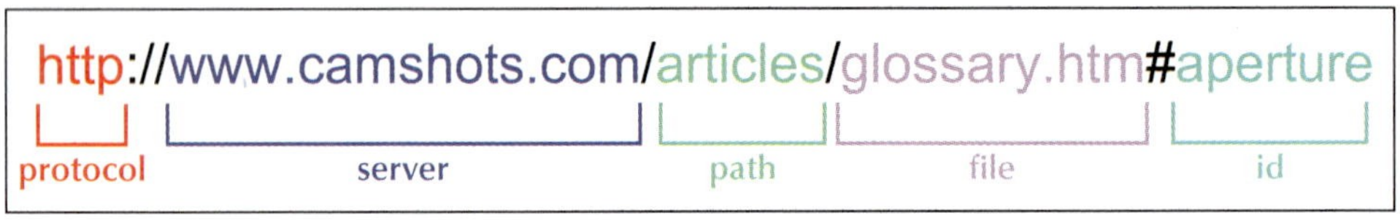

You might have noticed that a URL like *http://www.camshots.com* doesn't include any pathname or filename. If a URL doesn't specify a path, then it indicates the topmost folder in the server's directory tree. If a URL doesn't specify a filename, the server will return to the default home page. Many servers use index.html as the filename for the default home page, so a URL like *http://www.camshots.com/index.html* would be equivalent to *http://www.camshots.com*.

Understanding Domain Names | InSight

The server name portion of the URL is also called the **domain name**. By studying the domain name you learn about the server hosting the Web site. Each domain name contains a hierarchy of names separated by periods (.), with the topmost level appearing at the end. The top level, called an **extension**, indicates the general audience supported by the Web server. For example, .edu is the extension reserved for educational institutions, .gov is used for agencies of the United States government, and .com is used for commercial sites or general-use sites.

The next lower level appearing before the extension displays the name of the individual or organization hosting the site. A domain name like camshots.com indicates a commercial or general use site owned by CAMshots. To avoid duplicating domain names, the two top-most levels of the domain have to be registered with the IANA (Internet Assigned Numbers Authority) before they can be used. You can usually register your domain name through your Internet Service Provider. Be aware that you will have to pay an annual fee to keep the domain name.

The lowest levels of the domain, which appear farthest to the left in the domain name, are assigned by the individual or company hosting the site. Large Web sites involving hundreds of pages typically divide their domain names into several levels. For example, a large company like Microsoft might have one domain name for file downloads—*downloads.microsoft.com*—and another for customer service—*service.microsoft.com*. Finally, the lowest level of the domain, the first part of the domain name, displays the name of the hard drive or resource storing the Web site files. Many companies have standardized on using "www" as the name of the lowest level in their domain.

Gerry has listed four Web pages that he wants his readers to be able to access. He's provided you with the URLs for these pages, which are shown in Figure 2-33.

Web site URLs **Figure 2-33**

Web Site	URL
Apogee Photo	http://www.apogeephoto.com
Outdoor Photographer	http://www.outdoorphotographer.com
PCPhoto	http://www.pcphotomag.com
Popular Photography and Imaging	http://www.popphoto.com

To create a link to these Web sites from your document, you need to mark some text as a hypertext link, using the URL of the Web site as the value of the href attribute. So to link the text "Apogee Photo" to the Apogee Photo Web site, you would enter the following code:

```
<a href="http://www.apogeephoto.com">Apogee Photo</a>
```

Use the information that Gerry has given you to create links to all four of the Web sites listed on his tips page.

To create links to sites on the Web:

1. Return to the **tips.htm** file in your text editor.
2. Scroll to the bottom of the file and locate the definition list containing the list of Web sites.

3. Mark the entry for Apogee Photo as a hypertext link using the following code:

```
<a href="http://www.apogeephoto.com">Apogee Photo</a>
```

4. Mark the remaining three entries in the list as hypertext links pointing to each company's Web site. Figure 2-34 highlights the revised code in the file.

Figure 2-34 Linking to sites on the Web

```
<h2 style="color: blue">Photography Sites on the Web</h2>
<p>The Web is an excellent resource for articles on photography and digital cameras.
   Here are a few of my favorites.</p>
<dl>
   <dt>&#9758; <a href="http://www.apogeephoto.com">Apogee Photo</a></dt>
   <dd>An established online photography magazine with articles by top pros,
       discussion forums, workshops, and more.</dd>
   <dt>&#9758; <a href="http://www.outdoorphotographer.com">Outdoor Photographer</a></dt>
   <dd>The premier magazine for outdoor photography. The site includes extensive tips
       on photographing wildlife, action sports,
       scenic vistas, and travel sites.</dd>
   <dt>&#9758; <a href="http://www.pcphotomag.com">PCPhoto</a></dt>
   <dd>An excellent site for novices and professionals with informative reviews and
       buying guides for the latest equipment and software.</dd>
   <dt>&#9758; <a href="http://www.popphoto.com">Popular Photography and Imaging</a></dt>
   <dd>A useful and informative site with articles from the long-established
       magazine of professional and amateur photographers.</dd>
</dl>
```

5. Save your changes to the file.

6. Reload or refresh the **tips.htm** file in your Web browser. Figure 2-35 shows the revised list with each entry appearing as a hypertext link.

Figure 2-35 Links on the tips page

Photography Sites on the Web

The Web is an excellent resource for articles on photography and digital cameras. Here are a few of my favorites.

☞ Apogee Photo
  An established online photography magazine with articles by top pros, discussion forums, workshops, and more.
☞ Outdoor Photographer
  The premier magazine for outdoor photography. The site includes extensive tips on photographing wildlife, action sports, scenic vistas, and travel sites.
☞ PCPhoto
  An excellent site for novices and professionals with informative reviews and buying guides for the latest equipment and software.
☞ Popular Photography and Imaging
  A useful and informative site with articles from the long-established magazine of professional and amateur photographers.

7. Click each of the links on the page and verify that the appropriate Web site opens.

Trouble? To open these sites, you must be connected to the Internet. If you are still having problems, compare your code to the URLs listed in Figure 2-34 to confirm that you have not made a typing error. Also keep in mind that because the Web is constantly changing, the Web sites for some of these links might have changed, or a site might have been removed since this book was published.

Web pages are only one type of resource that you can link to. Before continuing work on the CAMshots Web site, you should explore how to access some of these other resources.

Linking to FTP Servers

Another method of storing and sharing files on the Internet is through FTP servers. **FTP servers** are file servers that act like file cabinets in which users can store and retrieve data files, much as they store and retrieve files from their own computer. FTP servers transfer information using a communications protocol called **File Transfer Protocol**, or **FTP** for short. The URL to access an FTP server follows the general format

```
ftp://server/path/
```

where *server* is the name of the FTP server and *path* is the folder path on the server that contains the files you want to access. When you access the FTP site, you can navigate through its folder tree as you would navigate the folders on your own hard disk. Figure 2-36 shows how someone can use Internet Explorer to view the FTP site and how the site appears as a collection of folders that can be opened and viewed.

FTP site appearing in the browser and in Windows Explorer **Figure 2-36**

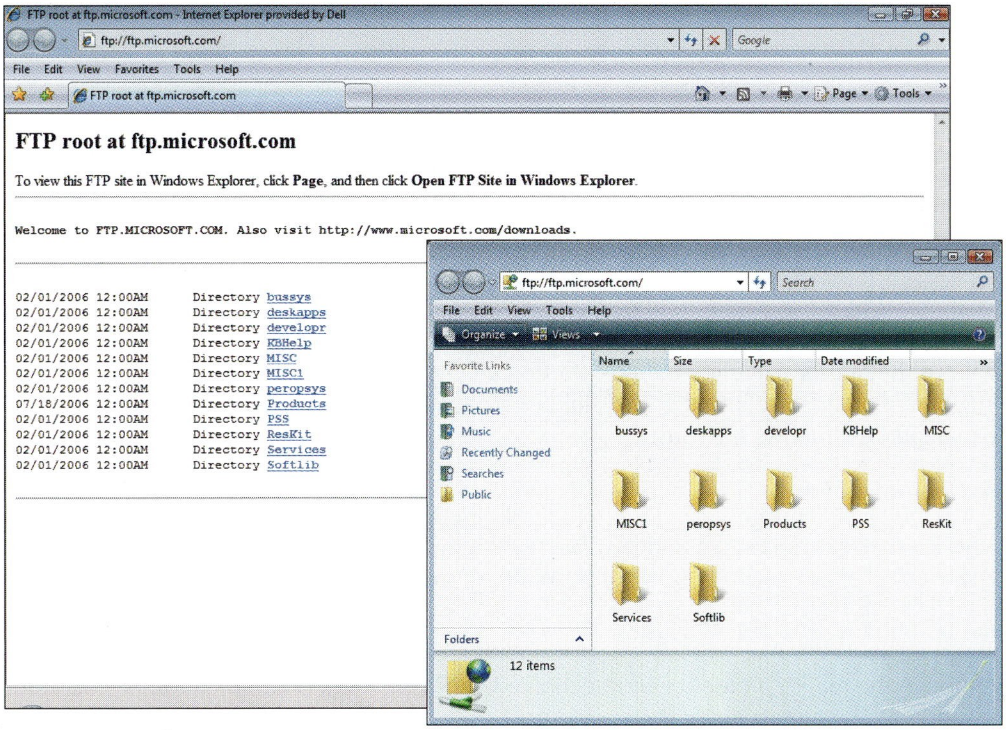

FTP servers require each user to enter a password and a username to gain access to the server's files. The standard username is anonymous and requires no password. Your browser supplies this information automatically, so in most situations you don't have to worry about passwords and usernames. However, some FTP servers do not allow anonymous access. In these cases, either your browser prompts you for the username and the password, or you can supply a username and password within the URL using the format

```
ftp://username:password@server/path
```

where *username* and *password* are a username and password that the FTP server recognizes. It is generally *not* a good idea, however, to include usernames and passwords in URLs, as it can allow others to view your sensitive login information. It's better to let the browser send this information or to use a special program called an **FTP client**, which can encrypt or hide this information during transmission.

Linking to a Local File

HTML is a very useful language for creating collections of linked documents. Many software developers have chosen to distribute their online help in the form of HTML files. The Web site for their help files then exist locally on the user's computer or network. If the Web site needs to reference local files (as opposed to files on the Internet or another wide area network), the URL needs to reflect this fact. The URL for a local file has the general form

```
file://server/path/filename
```

where *server* is the name of the local network server, *path* is the path on that server to the file, and *filename* is the name of the file. If you're accessing a file from your own computer, the server name can be omitted and replaced by an extra slash (/). So, a file from the documents/articles folder might have the URL:

```
file:///documents/articles/tips.htm
```

If the file is on a different disk within your computer, the hard drive letter would be included in the URL as follows:

```
file://D:/documents/articles/tips.htm
```

Unlike the other URLs you've examined, the "file" scheme in this URL does not imply any particular communication protocol; instead, the browser retrieves the document using whatever method is the local standard for the type of file specified in the URL.

Linking to an E-Mail Address

Many Web sites use e-mail to allow users to communicate with a site's owner, sales representative, or technical support staff. You can turn an e-mail address into a hypertext link, so that a user can click the link starting an e-mail program and automatically inserting the e-mail address into the "To" field of a new outgoing message. The URL for an e-mail address follows the form

```
mailto:address
```

where *address* is the e-mail address. To create a hypertext link to the e-mail address ghayward@camshots.com, you could use the following URL:

```
mailto:ghayward@camshots.com
```

Tip

To link to more than one e-mail address, add the addresses to the mailto link in a comma-separated list.

Although the mailto protocol is not technically an approved communication protocol, it is supported by almost every Web browser.

The mailto protocol also allows you to add information to the e-mail, including the subject line and the text of the message body. To add this information to the link, you use the form

```
mailto:address?header1=value1&header2=value2& ...
```

where *header1*, *header2*, etc. are different e-mail headers and *value1*, *value2*, and so on are the values of the headers. So to create the e-mail message

```
TO: ghayward@camshots.com
SUBJECT: Test
BODY: This is a test message
```

you would use the following URL:

```
mailto:ghayward@camshots.com?Subject=Test&Body=This%20is%20a%20test%20message
```

Notice that the spaces in the message body "This is a test message" have been replaced with %20 characters. This is necessary because URLs cannot contain blank spaces. To preserve information about blank spaces, URLs use **escape characters**, which are symbols that represent characters including nonprintable characters such as spaces, tabs, and line feeds. Escape characters use many of the same values as HTML character codes, though the syntax of escape characters is different. So, when the browser receives the following character string in a URL such as

```
This%20is%20a%20test%20message
```

it interprets the %20 escape character as a blank space and resolves the string as

```
This is a test message
```

Figure 2-37 lists some of the escape characters that can be used in any URL in place of printable or nonprintable characters.

Escape character codes **Figure 2-37**

<table>
<tr><th>Escape Character Code</th><th>Character</th><th>Escape Character Code</th><th>Character</th></tr>
<tr><td>%20</td><td>space</td><td>%5B</td><td>[</td></tr>
<tr><td>%0D%0A</td><td>new line</td><td>%5D</td><td>]</td></tr>
<tr><td>%3C</td><td><</td><td>%60</td><td>`</td></tr>
<tr><td>%3E</td><td>></td><td>%3B</td><td>;</td></tr>
<tr><td>%23</td><td>#</td><td>%2F</td><td>/</td></tr>
<tr><td>%25</td><td>%</td><td>%3F</td><td>?</td></tr>
<tr><td>%7B</td><td>{</td><td>%3A</td><td>:</td></tr>
<tr><td>%7D</td><td>}</td><td>%40</td><td>@</td></tr>
<tr><td>%7C</td><td>|</td><td>%3D</td><td>=</td></tr>
<tr><td>%5C</td><td>\</td><td>%26</td><td>&</td></tr>
<tr><td>%5E</td><td>^</td><td>%24</td><td>$</td></tr>
<tr><td>%7E</td><td>~</td><td></td><td></td></tr>
</table>

To further explore how to convert an e-mail message into a URL, you can experiment with a demo page.

To view the e-mail demo:

1. Use your Web browser to open the **demo_mailto.htm** file from the tutorial.02\demo folder included with your Data Files.
2. Scroll down the page, and in the TO: input box, enter the e-mail address **ghayward@camshots.com**.
3. Type **CAMshots Message** in the SUBJECT input box.
4. Type the following in the BODY input box:

   ```
   This is a message generated by the CAMshots Web site for
   Gerry Hayward.
   ```

5. Click the **Generate URL** button to create the URL for this e-mail message.

   As shown in Figure 2-38, the demo page generates the URL for the e-mail message. All of the blank spaces in the mail message have been replaced with the %20 escape character.

Figure 2-38 Converting an e-mail message to a URL

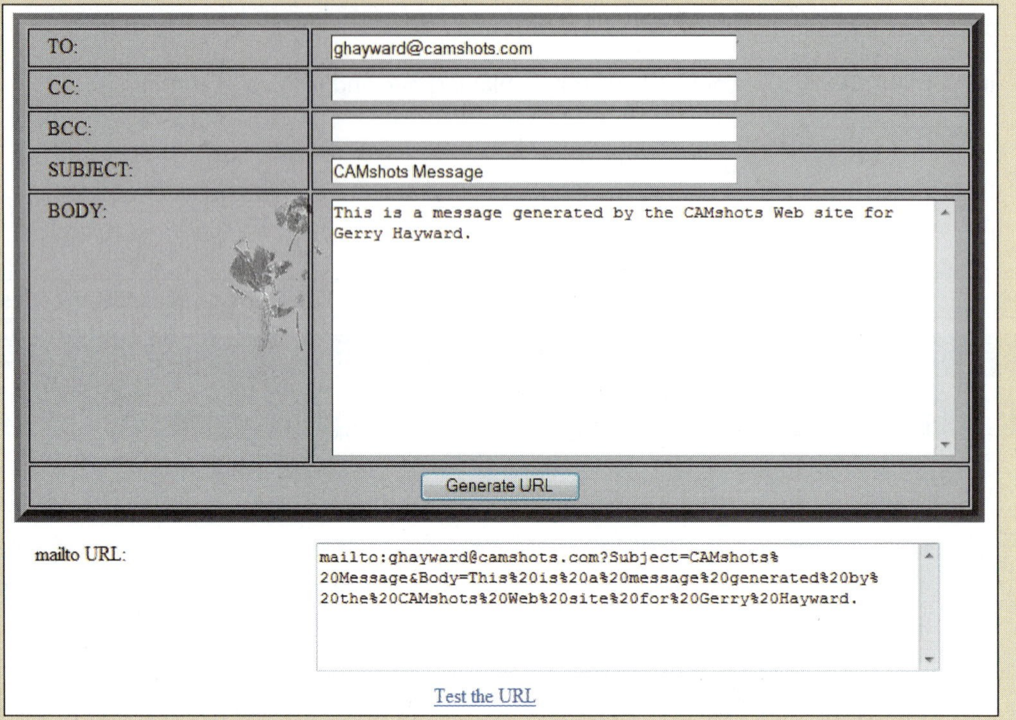

6. Click the **Test the URL** button at the bottom of the page. As shown in Figure 2-39, the browser opens the user's e-mail program, with the e-mail fields already filled in, based on the text of the URL.

Figure 2-39 E-mail message generated by the hypertext link

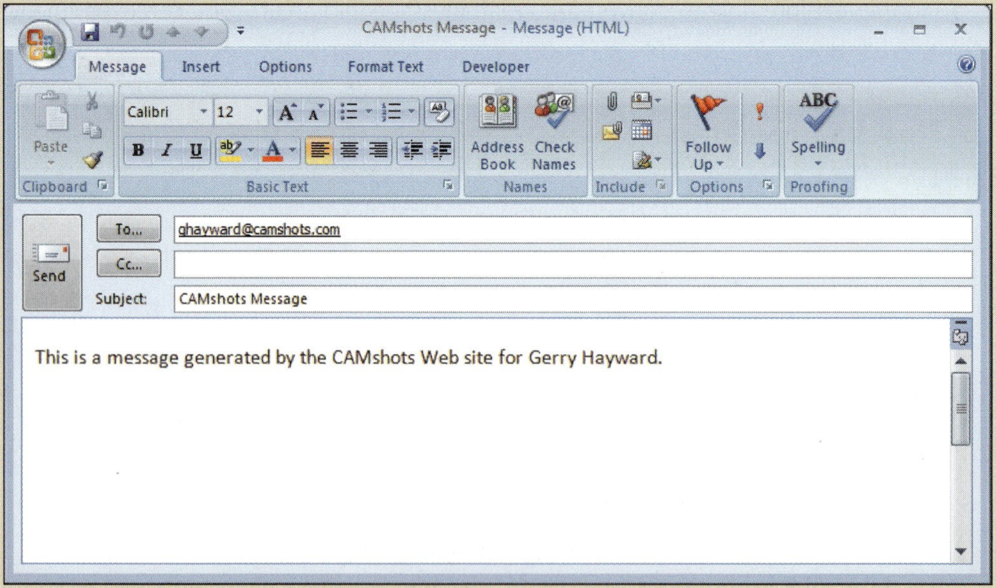

Trouble? Your e-mail window might look different depending on the e-mail program installed on your computer. If you do not have access to an e-mail program, you might not see any result or you might receive an error message after clicking the Test the URL button.

7. Close the message window without saving the message.
8. Continue experimenting with the demo page, exploring the effects of different e-mail messages on the URL text. Close the demo page when you are finished.

Gerry wants you to add to a link to his e-mail address on the CAMshots home page. This gives people who read his site the ability to contact him with additional questions or ideas.

To link to an e-mail address on Gerry's home page:

1. Return to the **home.htm** file in your text editor.
2. Go to the first paragraph and locate the text "contact me."
3. Mark "contact me" as a hypertext link using the following code, as shown in Figure 2-40:

```
<a href="mailto:ghayward@camshots.com?subject=CAMshots%20Message">
   contact me
</a>
```

Figure 2-40 Adding an e-mail link to the CAMshots home page

```
<p>Welcome to <span style="color: blue">CAMshots</span>, a site for people passionate about
   digital photography. This site has grown out of decades of photographic experience.
   I offer advice for both beginners and advanced users. I hope you enjoy what you find,
   but please be considerate of the work it took to do all this.
   The entire site contents including all images and articles are copyrighted.
   Please honor my work and do not copy anything without permission. If you are
   interested in publishing any of my images or articles or using them in other ways,
   please <a href="mailto:ghayward@camshots.com?subject=CAMshots%20Message">contact me</a>
   and we can discuss your needs. Happy Shooting!</p>
<p>&mdash; Gerry</p>
```

4. Save your changes to the file.
5. Refresh the **home.htm** file in your browser. Verify that the text "contact me" in the opening paragraph now appears as a hypertext link.
6. Click **contact me** and verify that your e-mail program displays a message with ghayward@camshots.com as the recipient and CAMshots Message as the subject.
7. Close your message window without saving the message.

InSight | **E-Mail Links and Spam**

Use caution when adding e-mail links to your Web site. While it may make it more convenient for users to contact you, it also might make you more vulnerable to spam. **Spam** is unsolicited e-mail sent to large numbers of people, promoting products, services, and in some cases inappropriate Web sites. Spammers create their e-mail lists by scanning discussion groups, stealing Internet mailing lists, and using programs called **e-mail harvesters** to scan HTML code for the e-mail addresses contained in mailto URLs. Many Web developers have removed e-mail links from their Web sites in order to foil these harvesters, replacing the links with Web forms that submit e-mail requests to a secure server. If you need to include an e-mail address on your Web page, you can take a few steps to reduce your exposure to spammers:

- Replace the text of the e-mail addresses with inline images that are more difficult for e-mail harvesters to read.
- Write a program to scramble any e-mail addresses in the HTML code, unscrambling the e-mail address only when it is clicked by the user.
- Replace the characters of the e-mail address with escape characters. For example, you can replace the "@" symbol with the escape sequence %40.

There is no quick and easy solution to this problem. Fighting spammers is an ongoing battle, and they have proved very resourceful in overcoming some of the defenses people have created. As you develop your Web site, you should carefully consider how to handle e-mail addresses and review the most current methods for safeguarding that information.

Reference Window | **Linking to Various Interent Resources**

- The URL for a Web page has the form
  `http://`*`server/path/filename#id`*
  where *server* is the name of the Web server, *path* is the path to a file on that server, *filename* is the name of the file, and if necessary *id* is the name of an id or anchor within the file.
- The URL for an FTP site has the form
  `ftp://`*`server/path/filename`*
  where *server* is the name of the FTP server, *path* is the folder path, and *filename* is the name of the file.
- The URL for an e-mail address has the form
  `mailto:`*`address?header1=value1&header2=value2& ...`*
  where *address* is the e-mail address; *header1*, *header2*, etc. are different e-mail headers; and *value1*, *value2*, and so on are the values of the headers.
- The URL to reference a local file has the form
  `file://`*`server/path/filename`*
  where *server* is the name of the local server or computer, *path* is the path to the file on that server, and *filename* is the name of the file. If you are accessing a file on your own computer, the server name is replaced by a third slash (/).

Tip

All of the hypertext attributes applied to the <a> tag can also be applied to the <area> tags within your image maps.

Working with Hypertext Attributes

HTML provides several attributes to control the behavior and appearance of your links. Gerry suggests that you study a few of these to see whether they would be effective in his Web site.

Opening a Secondary Window or Tab

By default, each page you open replaces the contents of the current page in the browser window. This means that when Gerry's readers click on one of the four external links listed on the tips page, they leave the CAMshots Web site. To return to the Web site, users would have to click their browser's Back button.

Gerry wants his Web site to stay open when a user clicks one of the links to the external Web sites. Most browsers allow users to open multiple browser windows or multiple tabs within the same browser window. Gerry suggests that links to external sites be opened in a second browser window or tab. He wants these external sites to be displayed in a second browser window or tab. This arrangement allows continual access to his Web site, even as users are browsing other sites.

To force a document to appear in a new window or tab, add the target attribute to the <a> tag. The general syntax is

```
<a href="url" target="window">content</a>
```

where *window* is a name assigned to the new browser window or browser tab. The value you use for the target attribute doesn't affect the appearance or content of the page being opened; the target simply identifies the different windows or tabs that are currently open. You can choose any name you wish for the target. If several links have the same target name, they all open in the same location, replacing the previous content. HTML also supports several special target names, described in Figure 2-41.

Figure 2-41 Target names for browser windows and tabs

Target Name	Description
target	Opens the link in a new window or tab named *target*
_blank	Opens the link in a new, unnamed window or tab
_self	Opens the link in the current browser window or tab

Whether the new page is opened in a tab or in a browser window is determined by the browser settings. It cannot be set by the HTML code.

Opening a Link in a New Window or Tab

| Reference Window

- To open a link in a new browser window or browser tab, add the attribute
  `target="window"`
  to the <a> tag, where *window* is a name assigned to the new browser window or tab.

Gerry suggests that all of the external links from his page be opened in a browser window or tab identified with the target name "new."

To specify a link target:

1. Return to the **tips.htm** file in your text editor.
2. Scroll to the bottom of the file and locate the four links to the external Web sites.
3. Within each of the opening <a> tags, insert the following attribute, as shown in Figure 2-42.

   ```
   target="new"
   ```

Figure 2-42 Setting a target for a hyperlink

```
<h2 style="color: blue">Photography Sites on the Web</h2>
<p>The Web is an excellent resource for articles on photography and digital cameras.
   Here are a few of my favorites.</p>
<dl>
   <dt>&#9758; <a href="http://www.apogeephoto.com" target="new">Apogee Photo</a></dt>
   <dd>An established online photography magazine with articles by top pros,
       discussion forums, workshops, and more.</dd>
   <dt>&#9758; <a href="http://www.outdoorphotographer.com" target="new">Outdoor Photographer</a></dt>
   <dd>The premier magazine for outdoor photography. The site includes extensive tips
       on photographing wildlife, action sports,
       scenic vistas, and travel sites.</dd>
   <dt>&#9758; <a href="http://www.pcphotomag.com" target="new">PCPhoto</a></dt>
   <dd>An excellent site for novices and professionals with informative reviews and
       buying guides for the latest equipment and software.</dd>
   <dt>&#9758; <a href="http://www.popphoto.com" target="new">Popular Photography and Imaging</a></dt>
   <dd>A useful and informative site with articles from the long-established
       magazine of professional and amateur photographers.</dd>
</dl>
```

4. Save your changes to the file.
5. Refresh the **tips.htm** file in your browser. Click each of the four links to external Web sites and verify that each opens in the same new browser window or tab.
6. Close the secondary browser window or tab.

Tip

To force all hypertext links in your page to open in the same target, add the target attribute to a base element located in the document's header.

You should use the target attribute sparingly in your Web site. Creating secondary windows can clutter up the user's desktop. Also, because the page is placed in a new window, users cannot use the Back button to return to the previous page in that window; they must click the browser's program button or the tab for the original Web site. This confuses some users and annoys others. Many Web designers now advocate not using the target attribute at all, leaving the choice of opening a link in a new tab or window to the user. Note that the target attribute is not supported in strict XHTML-compliant code.

Creating a Tooltip

If you want to provide additional information about a link on your Web page, you can add a tooltip to the link. A **tooltip** is descriptive text that appears when a user positions the mouse pointer over a link. Figure 2-43 shows an example of a tooltip applied to one of Gerry's links.

Figure 2-43 Viewing a tooltip

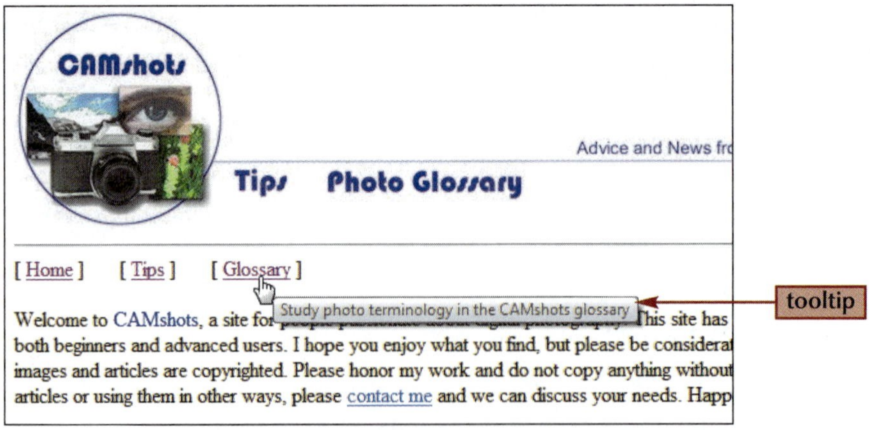

To create the tooltip, add the title attribute to the opening <a> tag in the form

```
<a href="url" title="text">content</a>
```

where *text* is the text that appears in the tooltip. To create the tooltip shown in Figure 2-43, you would enter the following HTML code:

```
<a href="glossary.htm"
   title="Study photo terminology in the CAMshots glossary">
   Glossary
</a>
```

Note that because some browsers do not support this feature, you should not place crucial information in a tooltip.

Creating a Semantic Link

The text of a hypertext link should always describe the type of document that will be called up by the link. You can also use the rel and rev attributes to add information about the link. The rel attribute describes the relation of the current document to the linked document. For example, in the link to the Glossary page, Gerry could insert the following rel attribute:

```
<a href="glossary.htm" rel="glossary">Glossary</a>
```

The rev attribute describes the reverse relationship: how the linked document views the current document. For example, if you're linking to the Glossary page from the home page, the reverse relation is "home" (because that is how the Glossary page views the home page). The HTML code would be:

```
<a href="glossary.htm" rel="glossary" rev="home">Glossary</a>
```

Links containing the rel and rev attributes are called **semantic links** because the tag contains information about the relationship between the link and its destination. This information is not designed for the user, but for the browser. A browser could display all hypertext links marked having a rel value of glossary with a special icon. The browser could also collect all of the hypertext links within the Web page and place them within a customized toolbar. Few browsers currently take advantage of these attributes, but future browsers may do so.

Although rel and rev are not limited to a fixed set of attribute values, the specifications for HTML and XHTML include a proposed list of rel and rev names. Figure 2-44 shows some of these proposed relationship values.

Figure 2-44 **Link relations for the rel and rev attributes**

Link Relation	Description
alternate	A substitute version of the current document, perhaps in a different language or in a different medium
appendix	An appendix
bookmark	A bookmark in a collection of documents
chapter	A document serving as a chapter in a collection of documents
contents	A table of contents
copyright	A copyright statement
glossary	A glossary
help	A help document
index	An index
next	The next document in a linear sequence of documents
prev	The previous document in a linear sequence of documents
section	A document serving as a section in a collection of documents
start	The first document in a collection of documents
top	The Web site's home page
stylesheet	An external style sheet
subsection	A document serving as a subsection in a collection of documents

At this point, Gerry decides against using the rel and rev attributes on his Web site. However, he'll keep them in mind as an option as his Web site expands in size and complexity.

Using the Link Element

Another way to add a hypertext link to your document is to add a link element to the document's head. Link elements are created using the one-sided tag

```
<link href="url" rel="text" rev="text" target="window" />
```

where the *href*, *rel*, *rev*, and *target* attributes serve the same purpose as in the <a> tag. For example, to use the link element to create semantic links to the three pages of Gerry's Web site, you could add the following link elements to the heading of each document:

```
<link rel="top" href="home.htm" />
<link rel="help" href="tips.htm" />
<link rel="glossary" href="glossary.htm" />
```

Because they are placed within a document's head, link elements do not appear as part of the Web page. Instead, if the browser supports them, link elements are displayed in a browser toolbar. Figure 2-45 shows how the three link elements described above would appear in the Opera's Navigation toolbar. If you click an entry on the toolbar, the browser loads the referenced page.

Figure 2-45 Navigation toolbar in Opera

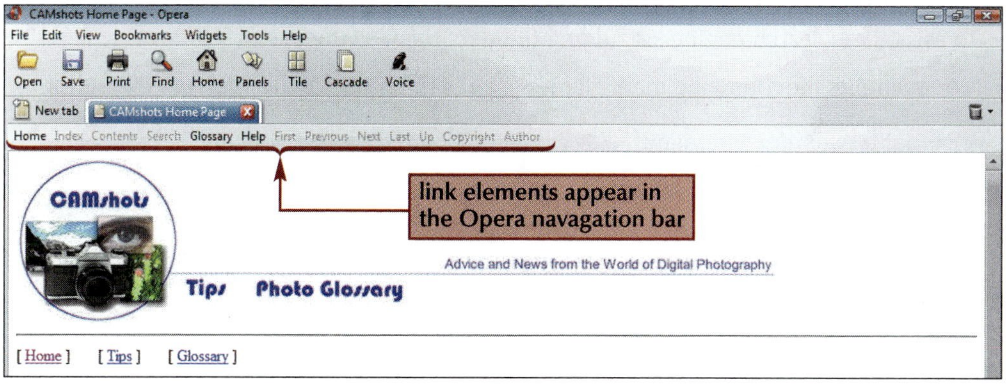

The advantage of the link element is that it places the list of links outside of the Web page, freeing up page space for other content. Also, because the links appear in a browser toolbar, they are always easily accessible to users. Currently, Opera is one of the few browsers with built-in support for the link element. Third party software exists to provide this support for Internet Explorer and Firefox. Because no single list of relationship names is widely accepted, you must check with each browser's documentation to find out what relationship names it supports. Until link elements are embraced by more browsers, you should use them only if you duplicate that information elsewhere on the page.

Working with Metadata

Gerry is happy with the work you've done on the design for his CAMshots Web site. Now he wants to start working on getting the site noticed. When someone searches for "digital photography tips" or "camera buying guide," will they find Gerry's Web site? There are thousands of photography sites on the Web. Gerry knows he needs to add a few extra touches to his home page to make it more likely that the site will be picked up by major search engines such as Yahoo! and Google.

Optimizing a Web site for search engines can be a long and involved process. For the best results, Web authors often turn to companies that specialize in making sites appear more prominently in search engines. CAMshots is a hobby site and Gerry does not want to invest any money in improving the site's visibility, but he would like to do a few simple things that would help.

Using the Meta Element

To be noticed on the Web, a site needs to include information about itself so the search engines can read it and add the site to their search indices. Information about the site is called **metadata**. You can add metadata to your Web pages by adding a meta element to the head section of the document. The syntax of the meta element is

```
<meta name="text" content="text" scheme="text" http-equiv="text" />
```

where the name attribute specifies the type of metadata, the content attribute stores the metadata value, the scheme attribute defines the metadata format, and the http-equiv attribute is used to attach metadata or commands to the communication stream between the Web server and the browser. There are three uses of the meta element:

- To store information about the document that can be read by the author, other users, or the Web server.

- To control how the browser handles the document, including forcing the browser to automatically refresh the page at timed intervals.
- To assist Web search engines in adding the document to their search index.

For example, the following meta element stores the name of the Web page's author:

```
<meta name="author" content="Gerry Hayward" />
```

Tip

Avoid generic and vague descriptions of your Web site. Instead, to attract a specific target audience to your site, use descriptions and keywords that will show how your Web site is different from others.

For search engines, you should include metadata describing the site and the topics it covers. This is done by adding a meta element containing the site description and another meta element with a list of keywords. The following two elements would summarize the CAMshots Web site for any search engines running on the Web:

```
<meta name="description" content="CAMshots provides advice on digital
cameras and photography" />
<meta name="keywords" content="photography, cameras, digital imaging" />
```

Figure 2-46 lists some other examples of metadata that you can use to describe your document.

Figure 2-46 Metadata

Meta Name	Example	Description
author	`<meta name="author" content="Gerry Hayward" />`	Supplies the name of the document author
classification	`<meta name="classification" content="photography" />`	Classifies the document
copyright	`<meta name="copyright" content="© 2011 CAMshots" />`	Provides a copyright statement
description	`<meta name="description" content="Digital photography and advice" />`	Provides a description of the document
generator	`<meta name="generator" content="Dreamweaver" />`	Indicates the name of the program that created the HTML code for the document
keywords	`<meta name="keywords" content="photography,cameras, digital" />`	Provides a list of keywords describing the document
owner	`<meta name="owner" content="CAMshots" />`	Indicates the owner of the document
rating	`<meta name="rating" content="general" />`	Provides a rating of the document in terms of its suitability for minors
reply-to	`<meta name="reply-to" content="ghayward@camshots.com (G. Hayward)" />`	Supplies a contact e-mail address and name for the document

In recent years, search engines have become more sophisticated in evaluating Web sites. In the process, the meta element has decreased in importance. However, it is still used by search engines when adding a site to their indexes. Because adding metadata requires very little effort, you should still include meta elements in your Web documents.

Working with Metadata | Reference Window

- To document the contents of your Web page, use the meta element
```
<meta name="text" content="text" />
```
where the name attribute specifies the type of metadata and the content attribute stores the metadata value.
- To add metadata or a command to the communication stream between the Web server and Web browser, use
```
<meta http-equiv="text" content="text" />
```
where the http-equiv attribute specifies the type of data or command attached to the communication stream and the content attribute specifies the data value or command.

Having discussed metadata issues with Gerry, he asks that you include a few meta elements to describe his new site.

To add metadata to Gerry's document:

1. Return to the **home.htm** file in your text editor.
2. Directly below the opening <head> tag, insert the following meta elements, as shown in Figure 2-47:
```
<meta name="author" content="your name" />
<meta name="description" content="A site for sharing information on
           digital photography and cameras" />
<meta name="keywords" content="photography, cameras, digital
imaging" />
```

Adding meta elements to the CAMshots home page | **Figure 2-47**

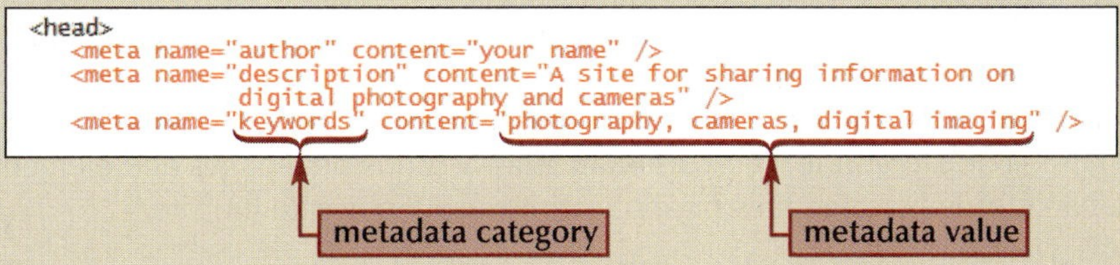

3. Close the file, saving your changes.

Applying Metadata to the Communication Stream

Describing your document is not the only use of the meta element. As you learned earlier, servers transmit Web pages using a communication protocol called HTTP. You can add information and commands to this communication stream with the meta element's http-equiv attribute. One common use of the http-equiv attribute is to force the browser to refresh the Web page at timed intervals, which is useful for Web sites that publish scoreboards or stock tickers. For example, to automatically refresh the Web page every 60 seconds, you would apply the following meta element:

```
<meta http-equiv="refresh" content="60" />
```

Another use of the meta element is to redirect the browser from the current document to a new document. This might prove useful to Gerry someday if he changes the URL of his site's home page. As his readers get accustomed to the new Web address, he can keep the old address online, automatically redirecting readers to the new site. The meta element to perform an automatic redirect has the general form

```
<meta http-equiv="refresh" content="sec;url=url" />
```

where *sec* is the time in seconds before the browser redirects the user and *url* is the URL of the new site. To redirect users after five seconds to the Web page at *http://www.camshots.com*, you could enter the following meta element:

```
<meta http-equiv="refresh" content="5;url=www.camshots.com" />
```

> **Tip**
> When redirecting a Web site to a new URL, always include text notifying the user that the page is being redirected. This avoids confusion and provides users several seconds to read the text.

Another use of the http-equiv attribute is to specify the character set used by the document. (For a discussion of character sets, see Tutorial 1.) This is particularly useful for international documents in which the browser might need to know the character set being used to correctly interpret the document. The syntax to specify the character set for an HTML document is

```
<meta http-equiv="Content-Type" content="text/html;charset=char-set" />
```

where *char-set* is the character set used by the document. So to indicate that the browser uses the ISO-8859-1 character set, you would include the following meta element in the document's header:

```
<meta http-equiv="Content-Type" content="text/html;charset=ISO-
8859-1" />
```

With the Web expanding its international presence, many Web developers advocate always including metadata about the character set so there is no ambiguity in the interpretation of the character encoding used in the document.

At this point, Gerry does not need to use the meta element to send data or commands through the HTTP communication protocol. However, he will keep this option in mind if moves the site to a new address.

Gerry is happy with the Web site you've started. He'll continue to work on the site and will come back to you for more assistance as he adds new pages and elements. For now you can close any open files or applications used to create the site.

Review | Session 2.3 Quick Check

1. What are the five parts of a URL?
2. Specify the code to link the text "White House" to the URL *http://www.whitehouse.gov*, with the destination document displayed in a new unnamed browser window.
3. Specify the code to link the text "Washington" to the FTP server at *ftp.uwash.edu*.
4. Specify the code to link the text "President" to the e-mail address *president@whitehouse.gov*.
5. What attribute would you add to a hypertext link to display the popup title "Tour the White House"?
6. What attribute would you add to a link specifying that the destination is the next page in a linear sequence of documents?
7. Specify the code to add the description "United States Office of the President" as metadata to a document.
8. Specify the code to automatically refresh the document every 5 minutes.

Tutorial Summary | Review

In this tutorial you explored some of the issues involved in creating a Web site with several linked pages. The first session began with an overview of storyboarding as a tool for designing and maintaining complex Web site structures. The session then turned to creating a simple Web site involving three Web pages linked together with the <a> tag element. The second session focused on creating links to locations within documents, first examining how to mark a location by using the id attribute and the anchor element. It then covered how to create links to these locations from within the same document and from within another document. The second session concluded by examining how to use inline images and image maps to create links to several documents. The third session expanded the discussion of hypertext by showing how to create links to sites on the World Wide Web and non-Web locations, including FTP sites and e-mail addresses. The third session then examined how to set different hypertext attributes to control how the browser displays and reacts to hypertext links. The session and the tutorial concluded by discussing the uses of the meta element for conveying information to Web search engines.

Key Terms

absolute path
augmented linear structure
client-side image map
domain name
e-mail harvester
escape characters
extension
File Transfer Protocol
FTP
FTP server
hierarchical structure
home page
hotspot
HTTP
Hypertext Transfer Protocol
image map
linear structure
metadata
mixed structure
protected structure
protocol
relative path
semantic link
server-side image map
sibling folder
site index
spam
storyboard
tooltip
Uniform Resource Locator
URL

Practice | Review Assignments

Practice the skills you learned in the tutorial using the same case scenario.

Data Files needed for the Review Assignments: child1.jpg - child3.jpg, childtxt.htm, contest0.jpg - contest3.jpg, contesttxt.htm, flower1.jpg - flower3.jpg, flowertxt.htm, scenic1.jpg - scenic3.jpg, scenictxt.htm, and thumb1.jpg - thumb9.jpg

Gerry has been working on the CAMshots Web site for a while. During that time, the site has grown in popularity with amateur photographers. Gerry wants to host a monthly photo contest to highlight the work of his colleagues. Each month Gerry will pick the three best photos from different photo categories. He's asked for your help in creating the collection of Web pages highlighting the winning entries. Gerry has already created four pages. The first page contains information about the photo contest; the next three pages contain the winning entries for child photos, scenic photos, and flower photos. Although Gerry has already entered much of the page content, he needs you to work on creating the links between and within each page. Figure 2-48 shows a preview of the photo contest's home page.

Figure 2-48

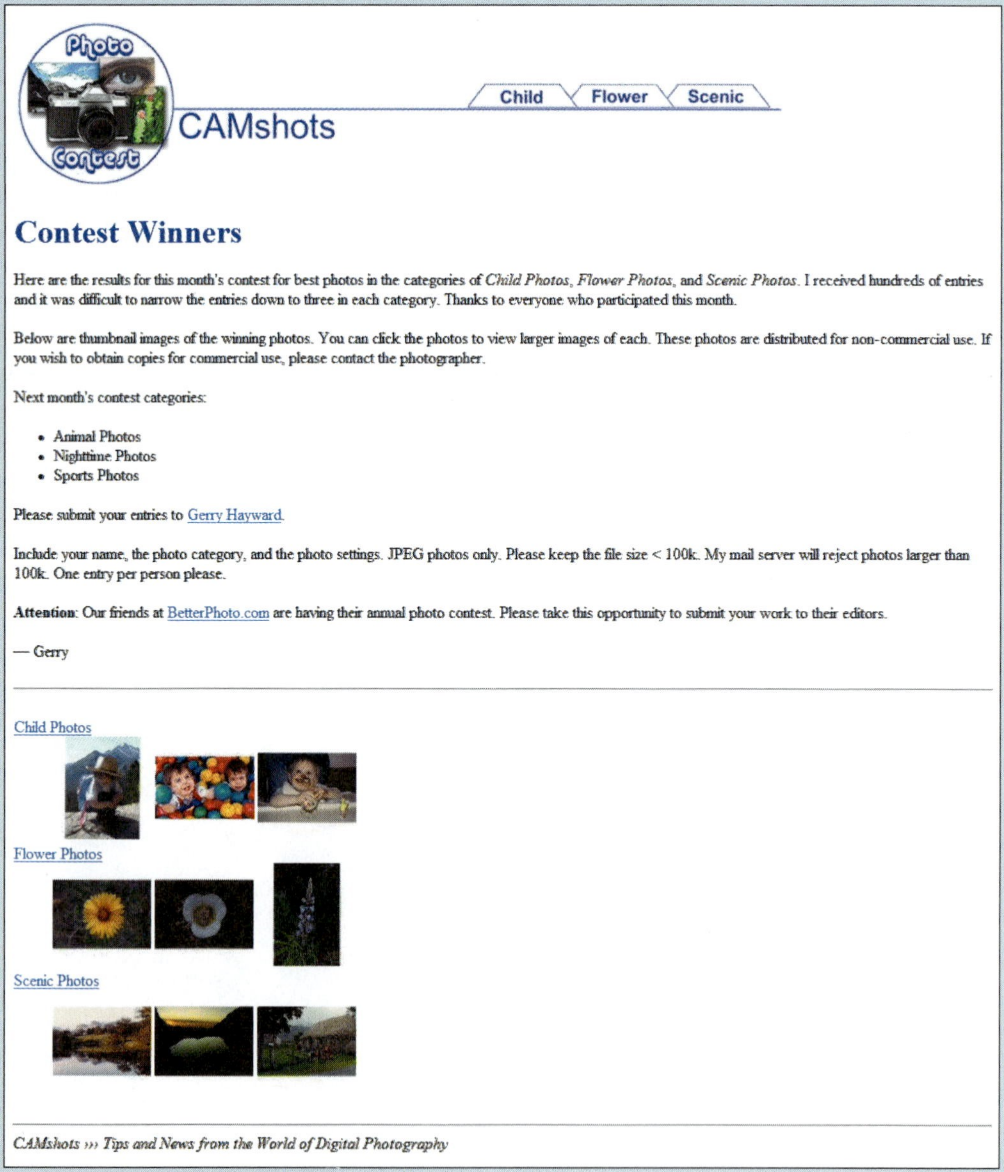
Photo
Contest
CAMshots
Child
Flower
Scenic
Contest Winners
Here are the results for this month's contest for best photos in the categories of Child Photos, Flower Photos, and Scenic Photos. I received hundreds of entries and it was difficult to narrow the entries down to three in each category. Thanks to everyone who participated this month.
Below are thumbnail images of the winning photos. You can click the photos to view larger images of each. These photos are distributed for non-commercial use. If you wish to obtain copies for commercial use, please contact the photographer.
Next month's contest categories:
Animal Photos
Nighttime Photos
Sports Photos
Please submit your entries to Gerry Hayward.
Include your name, the photo category, and the photo settings. JPEG photos only. Please keep the file size < 100k. My mail server will reject photos larger than 100k. One entry per person please.
Attention: Our friends at BetterPhoto.com are having their annual photo contest. Please take this opportunity to submit your work to their editors.
— Gerry
Child Photos
Flower Photos
Scenic Photos
CAMshots ››› Tips and News from the World of Digital Photography

Complete the following:

1. Use your text editor to open the **contesttxt.htm**, **childtxt.htm**, **scenictxt.htm**, and **flowertxt.htm** files from the tutorial.02\review folder included with your Data Files. Enter ***your name*** and ***the date*** within each file, and then save them as **contest.htm**, **child.htm**, **scenic.htm**, and **flower.htm**, respectively, in the same folder.
2. Go to the **child.htm** file in your text editor. Locate the inline image within the first div element at the top of the file. Directly below the inline image insert an image map with the following properties:
   - Set the id and name of the image map to contestmap.
   - Add a polygonal hotspot pointing to the child.htm file containing the points (457, 84), (474, 63), (549, 63), and (566, 84). Specify "Child Photos" as the alternate text for the hotspot.
   - Add a polygonal hotspot pointing to the flower.htm file containing the points (554, 84), (571, 63), (646, 63), and (663, 84). Specify "Flower Photos" as the alternate text for the hotspot.
   - Add a polygonal hotspot pointing to the scenic.htm file containing the points (651, 84), (668, 63), (743, 63), and (760, 84). Specify "Scenic Photos" as the alternate text for the hotspot.
   - Add a circular hotspot pointing to the contest.htm file centered at the point (82, 82) and having a radius of 78 pixels. Specify "Contest Results" as the alternate text for the hotspot.
3. Apply the contestmap image map to the logo image at the top of the page. Set the width of the border to 0.
4. Locate the three h2 elements naming the three child photo winners. Assign the h2 elements the ids child1, child2, and child3, respectively.
5. Save your changes to the **child.htm** file.
6. Go to the **scenic.htm** file in your text editor. Repeat Steps 2 and 3 for the logo image at the top of the page.
7. Assign the ids scenic1, scenic2, and scenic3 to the three h2 elements located farther down in the file. Save your changes to the document.
8. Go to the **flower.htm** file in your text editor and repeat the same edits you applied to the child.htm and scenic.htm files. Assign the ids flower1 through flower3 to the three h2 headings located at the bottom of the document. Save your changes.
9. Go to the **contest.htm** file in your text editor. Repeat Steps 2 and 3 for the logo image at the top of the page.
10. Scroll to the definition list at the bottom of the file. Mark the definition term "Child Photos" as a hypertext link pointing to the child.htm file. Mark the definition term "Flower Photos" as a link to the flower.htm file. Mark the term "Scenic Photos" as a link to the scenic.htm file.
11. Following each definition term is a definition description containing three thumbnail images of the winning photos. Mark the nine thumbnail images as hypertext links pointing to the larger images (contained in the child.htm, flower.htm, and scenic.htm files). For example, mark the first child photo (thumb1.jpg) as a hypertext link pointing to the h2 element with the id child1 in the child.htm file. Set the border width of each of the nine thumbnail images to 0.
12. Scroll up and locate the fourth paragraph. Mark the text "Gerry Hayward" as a hypertext link to an e-mail message sent to *ghayward@camshots.com* with the subject line "Photo Contest."

13. Go to the sixth paragraph and mark the text "BetterPhoto.com" as a hypertext link pointing to the URL *http://www.betterphoto.com*. Set the attribute of the link so that it opens in a new browser window or tab.
14. Save your changes to the **contest.htm** file.
15. Open **contest.htm** in your Web browser. Verify that the e-mail link opens a new mail message window with the subject line "Photo Contest." Verify that the link to BetterPhoto.com opens that Web site in a new browser window or tab. Verify that the three links to the photo pages are connected to the child.htm, scenic.htm, and flower.htm files. Finally, click each of the nine thumbnail images at the bottom of the page and verify that they connect to the larger image of the photo.
16. Open **child.htm** in your Web browser. Verify that the Scenic Photos link at the top of the page is connected to the scenic.htm file. Navigate forward and backward through the three photo pages by clicking the links at the top of each page. Verify that on each page you can return to the contest page by clicking the contest logo.
17. Submit your completed files to your instructor.

Apply | Case Problem 1

Apply your knowledge of hypertext links to create a directory of universities and colleges.

Data Files needed for this Case Problem: colleges.txt, highered.jpg, and uwlisttxt.htm

HigherEd Adella Coronel is a guidance counselor for Eagle High School in Waunakee, Wisconsin. She wants to take her interest in helping students choose colleges to the Web by starting a Web site called *HigherEd*. She's come to you for help in creating the site. The first page she wants to create is a simple directory of Wisconsin colleges and universities. She's created the list of schools, but has not yet marked the entries in the list as hypertext links. Also, the list is very long, so she has broken it down into three categories: private colleges and universities, technical colleges, and public universities. Because of the length of the page, she wants to include hypertext links that allow students to jump down to a specific college category. Figure 2-49 shows a preview of the page you'll create for Adella.

Figure 2-49

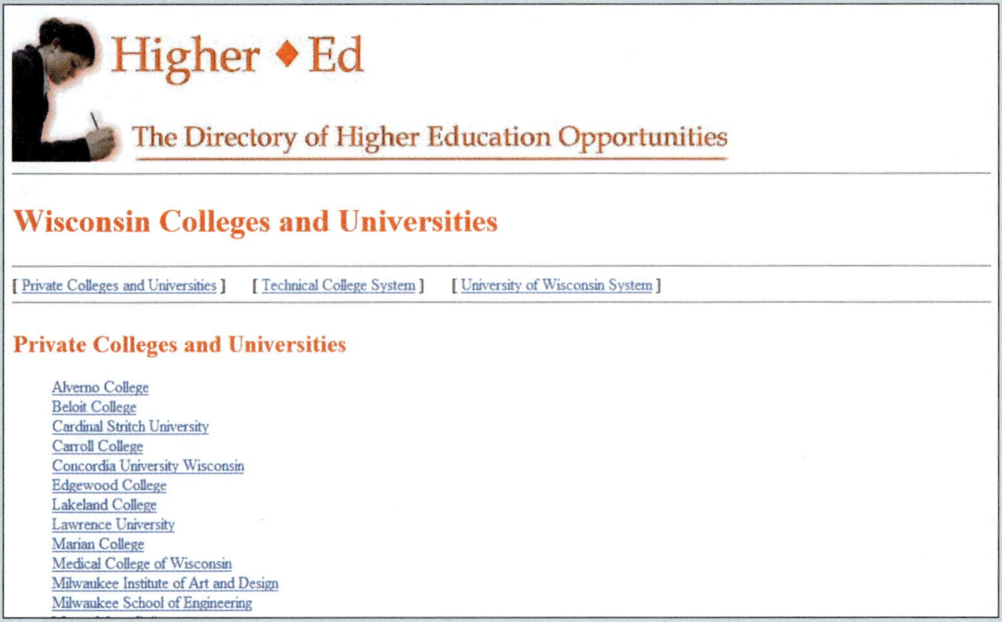
Higher ♦ Ed
The Directory of Higher Education Opportunities
Wisconsin Colleges and Universities
[Private Colleges and Universities] [Technical College System] [University of Wisconsin System]
Private Colleges and Universities
Alverno College
Beloit College
Cardinal Stritch University
Carroll College
Concordia University Wisconsin
Edgewood College
Lakeland College
Lawrence University
Marian College
Medical College of Wisconsin
Milwaukee Institute of Art and Design
Milwaukee School of Engineering

Complete the following:

1. In your text editor, open the **uwlisttxt.htm** file from the tutorial.02\case1 folder included with your Data Files. Enter ***your name*** and ***the date*** in the comment section of the file. Save the file as **uwlist.htm** in the same folder.
2. Mark each of the school entries on the page as a hypertext link. Use the URLs provided in the colleges.txt file. (Hint: Use the copy and paste feature of your text editor to efficiently copy and paste the URL text.)

EXPLORE

3. Adella wants the links to the school Web sites to appear in a new tab or window. Because there are so many links on the page, add a base element to the document header specifying that all links will open by default in a new browser window or tab named "collegeWin."
4. Add the id names "private," "technical," and "public" to the three h2 headings that categorize the list of schools.
5. Create hyperlinks from the entries in the category list at the top of the page to the three headings.

EXPLORE

6. For each of the hypertext links you marked in Step 5, set the link to open in the current browser window and not in a new browser window or tab.
7. Save your changes to the file.
8. Open **uwlist.htm** in your Web browser and verify that the school links all open in the same browser window or tab and that the links within the document to the different school categories bring the user to those locations on the page but not in a new window tab.
9. Submit your completed files to your instructor.

Apply | Case Problem 2

Apply your knowledge of HTML to create a slide show Web site.

Data Files needed for this Case Problem: back.jpg, end.jpg, fiddler.jpg, forward.jpg, home.jpg, hometxt.htm, slide1.jpg - slide6.jpg, slide1txt.htm - slide6txt.htm, start.jpg, and thumb1.jpg - thumb6.jpg

Lakewood School Tasha Juroszek is a forensics teacher at Lakewood School, a small private school in Moultrie, Georgia. Tasha has just finished directing her students in *Fiddler on the Roof Jr.* and wants to place a slide show of the performances on the Web. She has already designed the layout and content of the pages, but needs help to finish the slide show. She has asked you to add hypertext links between the slide pages and the site's home page. Figure 2-50 shows a preview of one of the slide pages on the Web site.

Figure 2-50

Complete the following:

1. Use your text editor to open the **hometxt.htm**, and **slide1txt.htm** through **slide6txt.htm** files from the tutorial.02\case2 folder included with your Data Files. Enter ***your name*** and ***the date*** in the comment section of each file. Save the files as **home.htm** and **slide1.htm** through **slide6.htm,** respectively.
2. Return to the **slide1.htm** file in your text editor. At the top of the page are five buttons used to navigate through the slide show. Locate the inline image for the home button (home.jpg) and mark it as a hypertext link pointing to the home.htm file.

3. There are six slides in Tasha's slide show. Mark the start button as a hypertext link pointing to the slide1.htm file. Mark the end button as a link to the slide6.htm file. Link the back button to slide1.htm, the first slide in the show. Link the forward button to the slide2.htm file.
4. Directly below the slide show buttons are thumbnail images of the six slides. Link each thumbnail image to its slide page.
5. Set the border width of each linked image to 0, *except* the thumbnail image for slide1. Set the border width of that thumbnail to 5.
6. Save your changes to the file.

EXPLORE

7. Repeat Steps 2 through 6 for the five remaining slide pages. Within each page, set the navigation buttons to go back and forth through the slide show. For the slide6.htm file, the forward button should point to the slide6.htm file since it is the last slide in the show. The border width of each linked image should be set to 0 *except* the border width of the current slide, which should be set to 5.
8. Go to the **home.htm** file in your text editor. Go to the second paragraph and mark the text "slide show" as a hypertext link pointing to the slide1.htm file.

EXPLORE

9. Go to the end of the second paragraph and mark the phrase "contact me" as a hypertext link pointing to the following e-mail message:
   TO: tashajur@lakewood.edu
   SUBJECT: Photo CD
   BODY: Please send me a copy of the photos.
10. Save your changes to the file.
11. Load the **home.htm** file in your Web browser. Test the links in the Web site and verify that they work correctly.
12. Submit your completed files to your instructor.

Challenge | Case Problem 3

Broaden your knowledge of HTML by exploring how to use anchors and pop-up titles in a Web site for a health club.

Data Files needed for this Case Problem: classtxt.htm, diamond.jpg, hometxt.htm, indextxt.htm, and memtxt.htm

Diamond Health Club, Inc. You work for Diamond Health Club, a health club in Boise, Idaho that has been serving active families for 25 years. The director, Karen Padilla, has asked you to help work on their Web site. The site contains three pages: the home page describing the club, a page listing classes offered, and a page describing the various membership options. You need to add links within the main page and add other links connecting the pages. Because this Web site will need to support older browsers, you will have to use the anchor tag to mark specific locations in the three documents. Karen would also like you to create pop-up titles for some of the links in the site to supply additional information about the links to the users.

Finally, this new site will replace the old company Web site. Karen wants to keep the old Web site address and redirect users automatically to the new home page. She wants you to insert the code required to do this.

Figure 2-51 shows a preview of the completed home page.

Figure 2-51

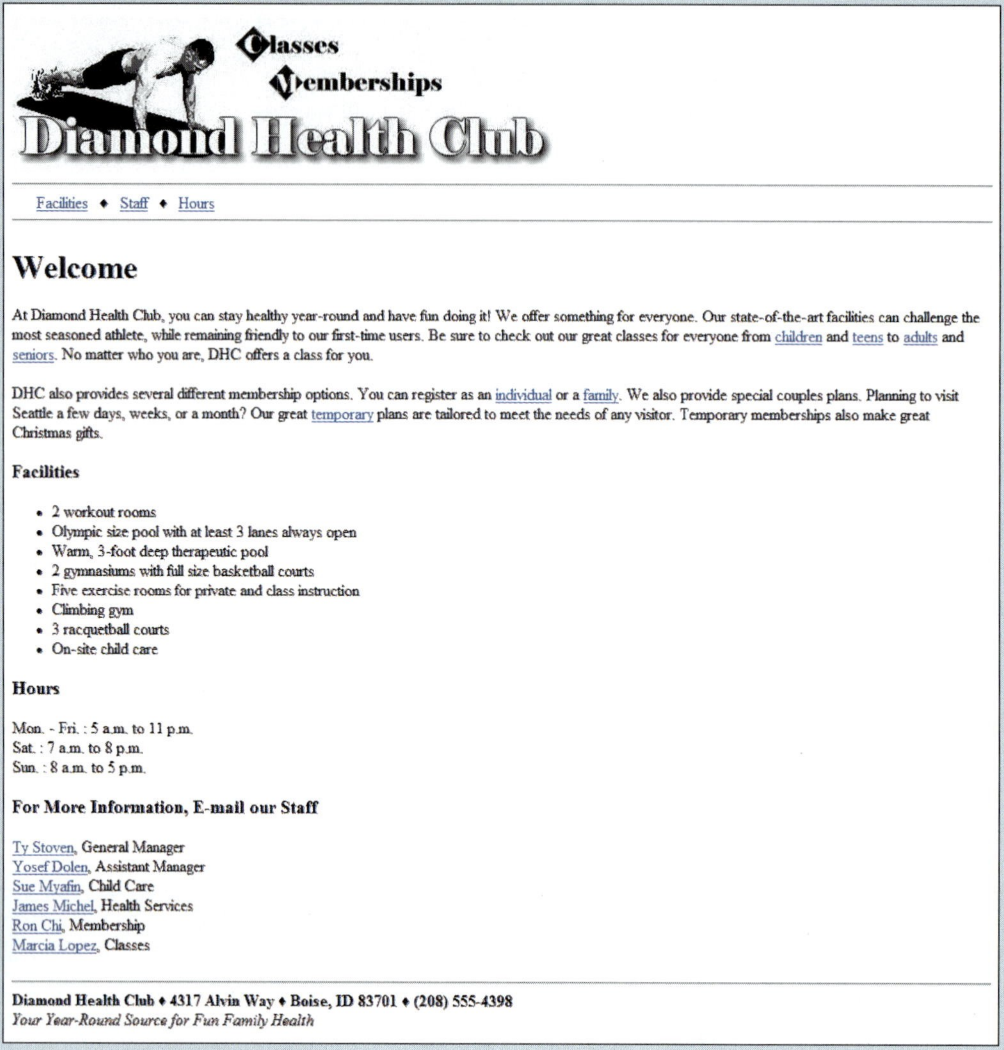

Classes
Memberships
Diamond Health Club
Facilities ♦ Staff ♦ Hours
Welcome
At Diamond Health Club, you can stay healthy year-round and have fun doing it! We offer something for everyone. Our state-of-the-art facilities can challenge the most seasoned athlete, while remaining friendly to our first-time users. Be sure to check out our great classes for everyone from children and teens to adults and seniors. No matter who you are, DHC offers a class for you.
DHC also provides several different membership options. You can register as an individual or a family. We also provide special couples plans. Planning to visit Seattle a few days, weeks, or a month? Our great temporary plans are tailored to meet the needs of any visitor. Temporary memberships also make great Christmas gifts.
Facilities
2 workout rooms
Olympic size pool with at least 3 lanes always open
Warm, 3-foot deep therapeutic pool
2 gymnasiums with full size basketball courts
Five exercise rooms for private and class instruction
Climbing gym
3 racquetball courts
On-site child care
Hours
Mon. - Fri. : 5 a.m. to 11 p.m.
Sat. : 7 a.m. to 8 p.m.
Sun. : 8 a.m. to 5 p.m.
For More Information, E-mail our Staff
Ty Stoven, General Manager
Yosef Dolen, Assistant Manager
Sue Myafin, Child Care
James Michel, Health Services
Ron Chi, Membership
Marcia Lopez, Classes
Diamond Health Club ♦ 4317 Alvin Way ♦ Boise, ID 83701 ♦ (208) 555-4398
Your Year-Round Source for Fun Family Health

Complete the following:

1. Use your text editor to open the **hometxt.htm**, **indextxt.htm**, **classtxt.htm**, and **memtxt.htm** files from the tutorial.02\case3 folder included with your Data Files. Enter ***your name*** and ***the date*** in the comment section of each file. Save the files as **home.htm**, **index.htm**, **classes.htm**, and **members.htm** respectively.

EXPLORE

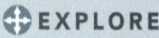

2. Go to the **index.htm** file. Use the <a> tag to add the anchor names fac, hours, and staff to the h3 headings "Facilities," "Hours," and "For More Information, E-mail our Staff."

EXPLORE

3. Scroll up to the top of the file. Below the logo image at the top of the page, add an image map with the following properties:
   - Give the image map a name and id of diamondmap.
   - Create a rectangular hotspot with the coordinates (225, 7) and (333, 40). Point the hotspot to the classes.htm file with the alternate text "Classes." Add the tooltip "View our classes."

- Create a rectangular hotspot with the coordinates (258, 44) and (437, 82). Point the hotspot to the members.htm file with the alternate text "Memberships." Add the tooltip "View our membership options."
- Create a default hotspot for the inline image. (*Hint:* the image is 548 pixels wide and 150 pixels tall.) Point the default hotspot to the index.htm file with the alternate text "Home Page." Add the tooltip "Return to the Home Page."

4. Apply the diamondmap hotspot to the logo image. Remove the border around the inline image.
5. In the list at the top of the page, mark "Facilities" as a link pointing to the fac anchor within the index.htm document. Mark "Staff" as a link pointing to the staff anchor within the index.htm file. Mark "Hours" as a link pointing to the hours anchor within the index.htm file.

EXPLORE

6. Add the tooltip "Learn more about our facilities" to the Facilities link. Add the tooltip "Meet the DHC staff" to the Staff link. Add the tooltip "View the DHC hours of operation" to the Hours link.
7. Go to the staff list at the bottom of the page. Format each name as a link that points to the individual's e-mail address. The e-mail addresses are:

Ty Stoven:	tstoven@dmond-health.com
Yosef Dolen:	ydolen@dmond-health.com
Sue Myafin:	smyafin@dmond-health.com
James Michel:	jmichel@dmond-health.com
Ron Chi:	rchi@dmond-health.com
Marcia Lopez:	mlopez@dmond-health.com

8. Save your changes to the file.
9. Go to the **members.htm** file in your text editor and repeat Steps 3 through 6.
10. Use the <a> tag to add anchors named "ind" to the "Individual memberships" h3 heading, "fam" to the "Family memberships" h3 heading, and "temp" to the "Temporary memberships" h3 heading.
11. Format the phrase "e-mail Ron Chi" in the first paragraph as a link pointing to Ron Chi's e-mail address. Save your changes to the file.
12. Go to the **classes.htm** file in your text editor and repeat Steps 3 through 6 for the entries at the top of that page.
13. Use the <a> tag to add the following anchors to h3 headings in the file: "senior" for "Senior Classes," "adult" for "Adult Classes," "teen" for "Teen Classes," and "child" for "Children's Classes."
14. Format the phrase "e-mail Marcia Lopez" in the first paragraph as a link pointing to Marcia Lopez's e-mail address. Save your changes to the file.
15. Return to the **index.htm** file in your text editor. Within the first paragraph, link the word "children" to the child anchor in the classes.htm file. Link the word "teens" to the teen anchor in the classes.htm file. Link the word "adults" to the adult anchor in classes.htm. Finally, link "seniors" to the senior anchor in classes.htm.
16. Within the second paragraph of index.htm, link the word "individual" to the ind anchor in the members.htm file. Link the word "family" to the fam anchor in members.htm. Finally, link the first occurrence of the word "temporary" to the temp anchor in members.htm.

17. Go to the head section of the document and add the following metadata directly below the opening <head> tag:
    - The description: "The Diamond Health Club is your year-round source for fun family health."
    - The keywords: health club, exercise, family, seattle
18. Save your changes to the file.

EXPLORE

19. Go to the **home.htm** file in your text editor. Within the head section, insert a meta element to redirect the browser to the index.htm file after a 5 second delay.
20. Mark the phrase "this link to our new Web site" as a hypertext link pointing to the index.htm file. Save your changes to the file.
21. Open the **home.htm** file in your Web browser. Verify that the browser loads the index.htm file after a 5 second delay.
22. Once the index.htm file is loaded, verify that all of your links work correctly, including the links that point to sections within documents and the links within the image map. Verify that tooltips appear as you move your mouse pointer over the links at the top of each page. (Note: Internet Explorer does not currently support tooltips found within image map hotspots.)
23. Submit your completed files to your instructor.

Create | Case Problem 4

Test your knowledge of HTML and use your creativity to design a Web site documenting a Shakespeare play.

Data Files needed for this Case Problem: characters.txt, notes.txt, tempest.jpg, and tempest.txt

Mansfield Classical Theatre Steve Karls continues to work as the director of Mansfield Classical Theatre in Mansfield, Ohio. The next production he plans to direct is *The Tempest*. Steve wants to put the text of this play on the Web, but he also wants to augment the dialog of the play with notes and commentary. However, he doesn't want his commentary to get in the way of a straight-through reading of the text, so he has hit on the idea of linking his commentary to key phrases in the dialog. Steve has created text files containing an excerpt from *The Tempest* as well as his commentary and other supporting documents. He would like you to take his raw material and create a collection of linked pages.

Complete the following:

1. Create HTML files named **tempest.htm**, **commentary.htm**, and **cast.htm** and save them in the tutorial.02\case4 folder included with your Data Files. Add comment tags to the head section of each document containing ***your name*** and ***the date***. Add an appropriate page title to each document.
2. Using the contents of the tempest.txt, notes.txt, and characters.txt text files, create the body of the three Web pages in Steve's Web site. The design of these pages is left to your imagination and skill. Make the pages easy to read and visually interesting. You can supplement the material on the page with appropriate material you find on your own.
3. Use the **tempest.jpg** file as a logo for the page. Create an image map from the logo pointing to the tempest.htm, commentary.htm, and cast.htm files. The three rectangular boxes on the logo have the following coordinates for their upper-left and lower-right corners:
    - The Play: (228, 139) (345, 173)
    - Commentary: (359, 139) (508, 173)
    - The Cast: (520, 139) (638, 173)

   Use this image map in all three of the Web pages from this Web site.

4. Create links between the dialog on the play page and the notes on the commentary page. The notes contain line numbers to aid you in linking each line of dialog to the appropriate note.
5. Create a link between the first appearances of each character's name from the tempest.htm page with the character's description on the cast.htm page.
6. Include a link to Steve Karl's e-mail address on the tempest.htm page. Steve's e-mail address is *stevekarls@mansfieldct.com*. E-mail sent to Steve's account from this Web page should have the subject line "Comments on the Tempest."
7. Add appropriate meta elements to each of the three pages documenting the page's contents and purpose.
8. Search the Web for sites that would provide additional material about the play. Add links to these pages on the tempest.htm page. The links should open in a new browser window or tab.
9. Submit your completed files to your instructor.

Review | Quick Check Answers

Session 2.1

1. Storyboarding is the process of diagramming a series of related Web pages, taking care to identify all links among the various pages. Storyboarding is an important tool in creating Web sites that are easy to navigate and understand.
2. A linear structure is one in which Web pages are linked from one to another in a direct chain. Users can go to the previous page or the next page in the chain, but not to a page in a different section of the chain. A hierarchical structure is one in which Web pages are linked from general to specific topics. Users can move up and down the hierarchy tree.
3. `<a href="sports.htm">Sports Info</a>`
4. An absolute path indicates the location of the file based on its placement in the computer. A relative path indicates the location of the file relative to the location of the current document.
5. glossary.htm
   ../tips/tips1.htm
   ../tips/tips2.htm
   ../../index.htm
6. The base element specifies the default location that the browser should use to resolve all relative paths.

Session 2.2

1. `<h2 id="faq">CAMshots FAQ</h2>`
2. `<a href="#faq">Read our FAQ</a>`
3. `<a href="help.htm#faq">Read our FAQ</a>`
4. `<h2><a name="faq">CAMshots FAQ</a></h2>`
5. Anchors are supported by older browsers. Some older browsers do not support using the id attribute to mark a location in a document. However, use of anchor tags has been deprecated, so it is not supported in strict applications of XHTML. Also, because it is deprecated, use of the anchor tag may be phased out in future browser releases.

6.
```
<map name="CAMmap" id="CAMmap">
   <area shape="circle" coords="50, 75, 40" href="faq.htm" />
</map>
```

7.
```
<img src="logo.jpg" alt="CAMshots" usemap="#CAMmap"/>
```

8.
```
style="border-width: 0"
```

Session 2.3

1. The protocol, the hostname, the folder name, the filename, and the anchor name or id.

2.
```
<a href="http://www.whitehouse.gov target="_blank">White House</a>
```

3.
```
<a href="ftp://ftp.uwash.edu">Washington</a>
```

4.
```
<a href="mailto:president@whitehouse.gov">President</a>
```

5.
```
title="Tour the White House"
```

6.
```
rel="next"
```

7.
```
<meta name="description" content=" United States Office of the
President" />
```

8.
```
<meta http-equiv="refresh" content="300" />
```

Ending Data Files

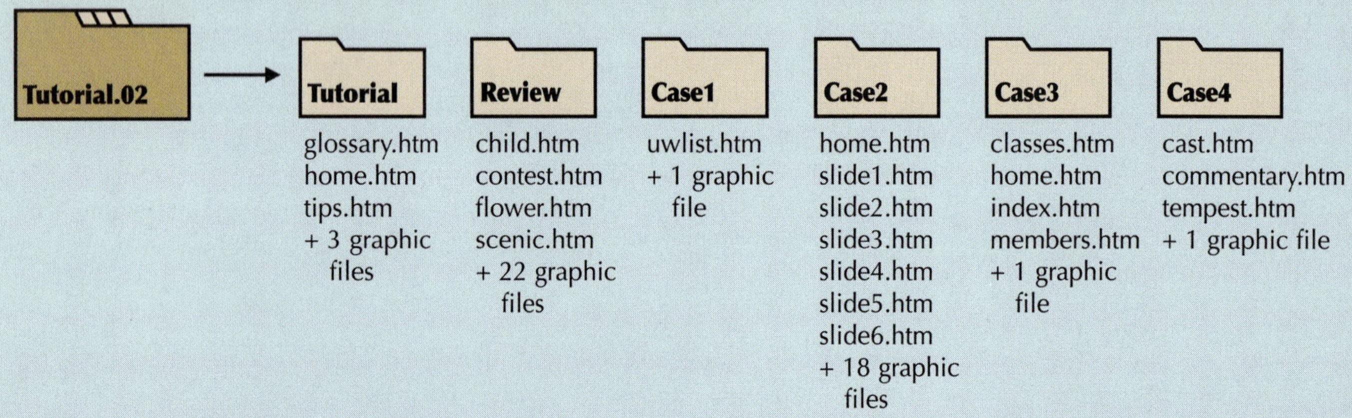

Reality Check

The Web has become an important medium for advertising products and one's self. By making your resume available online, you can quickly get prospective employers information they need to make a hiring decision. There are many sites that will assist you in writing and posting your resume. They will also, for a fee, present your online resume to employers in your chosen field. Assuming you don't want to pay to use such a site, you can also create your own Web site containing your employment history and talents. In this exercise, you'll use the skills and tasks you learned in Tutorials 1 and 2 to design your own Web site and create an online resume.

1. Collect material on yourself that would be useful in an online resume. You should include material for a page on your employment history, talents and special interests, a general biography, and a summary of the main points of your resume.
2. Create a storyboard outlining the pages on your Web site. Clearly indicate the links between the pages. Make sure that your site is easy to navigate no matter which page the user starts on.
3. Collect or create graphical image files to make your site interesting to the viewer. If you obtain graphics from the Web, be sure to follow all copyright restrictions on the material.
4. Start designing your site's home page. It should include an interesting and helpful logo. The home page should be brief and to the point, summarizing the main features of your resume. Its height should not be greater than two screens.
5. Add other pages containing more detailed information. Each page should have a basic theme and topic. The pages should follow a unified theme and design.
6. Use boldface fonts and italics to highlight important ideas. Do not overuse these page elements; doing so can distract from your page's readability rather than enhancing it.
7. Use numbered and bulleted lists to list the main points in your resume.
8. Use block quotes to highlight recommendations from colleagues and former employers.
9. Use horizontal rules to divide longer pages into topical sections.
10. If there are sites on the Web that would be relevant to your online resume (such as the Web sites of former or current employers), include links to those sites.
11. Include a link to your e-mail address. Write the e-mail address link so that it automatically adds an appropriate subject line to the e-mail message.
12. Save your completed Web site and present it to your instructor.

Objectives

Session 3.1
- Review the history and concepts of CSS
- Explore inline styles, embedded styles, and external style sheets
- Understand style precedence and style inheritance
- Understand the CSS use of color

Session 3.2
- Explore CSS styles for fonts and text
- Review and compare different image formats
- Display an animated graphic
- Apply a background image to an element

Session 3.3
- Float elements on a Web page
- Explore the properties of the box model
- Apply border styles to an element

Working with Cascading Style Sheets

Designing a Web Site

Case | Sunny Acres

Tammy Nielsen and her husband Brent live and work at Sunny Acres, a 200-acre farm near Council Bluffs, Iowa. Over the past 25 years, the Nielsen family has expanded the farm's operations to include a farm shop, which sells fresh produce, baked goods, jams and jellies, and gifts; a pick-your-own garden, which operates from May through October and offers great produce at discounted prices; a petting barn, with over 100 animals and the opportunity to bottle-feed the baby animals; a corn maze, with over 4 miles of twisting trails through harvested corn fields; and a Halloween Festival featuring the corn maze haunted with dozens of spooks and tricks. The farm also hosts special holiday events during the winter.

Tammy created a Web site for Sunny Acres several years ago to make information about the farm easily accessible to her current customers. The Web site has become outdated, so Tammy would like to enliven it with a new design. She also wants to catch the attention of new customers via the Web. She has several pictures she wants to use on the Web site and has ideas for the look and feel of each Web page. Tammy's knowledge of HTML and Web styles is limited, so she's come to you for help in creating a new look for the Sunny Acres Web site.

Starting Data Files

Tutorial.03 →

Tutorial
farmtxt.css
haunttxt.htm
hometxt.htm
indextxt.htm
mazetxt.htm
pettingtxt.htm
producetxt.htm
+ 9 graphic files

Demo
demo_color_names.htm
demo_css.htm
demo_safety_palette.htm
+ 3 graphic files

Review
holidaytxt.htm
sunnytxt.css
+ 3 graphic files

Case1
algo.htm
crypttxt.htm
enigma.htm
history.htm
public.htm
single.htm
+ 5 graphic files

Case2
bmtourtxt.htm
wheelstxt.css
+ 4 graphic files

Case3
centertxt.css
kingtxt.htm
+ 7 graphic files

Case4
casttxt.htm
hebtxt.htm
hightxt.htm
lakestxt.htm
+ 6 graphic files

Session 3.1

Introducing CSS

You and Tammy have recently discussed the work she wants done on the new Web site. She's already entered the content for six pages of the Web site. The six pages are:

- index.htm—the page that users see when first accessing the site, currently blank
- home.htm—the home page, describing the operations and events sponsored by the farm
- maze.htm—a page describing the farm's corn maze
- haunted.htm—a page describing the farm's annual Halloween Festival and haunted maze
- petting.htm—a page describing the farm's petting barn
- produce.htm—a page describing the Sunny Acres farm shop and the pick-your-own produce garden

Figure 3-1 shows the links among these sites in the Sunny Acres storyboard. Open these files now in your text editor and browser.

Figure 3-1 Storyboard of the Sunny Acres Web site

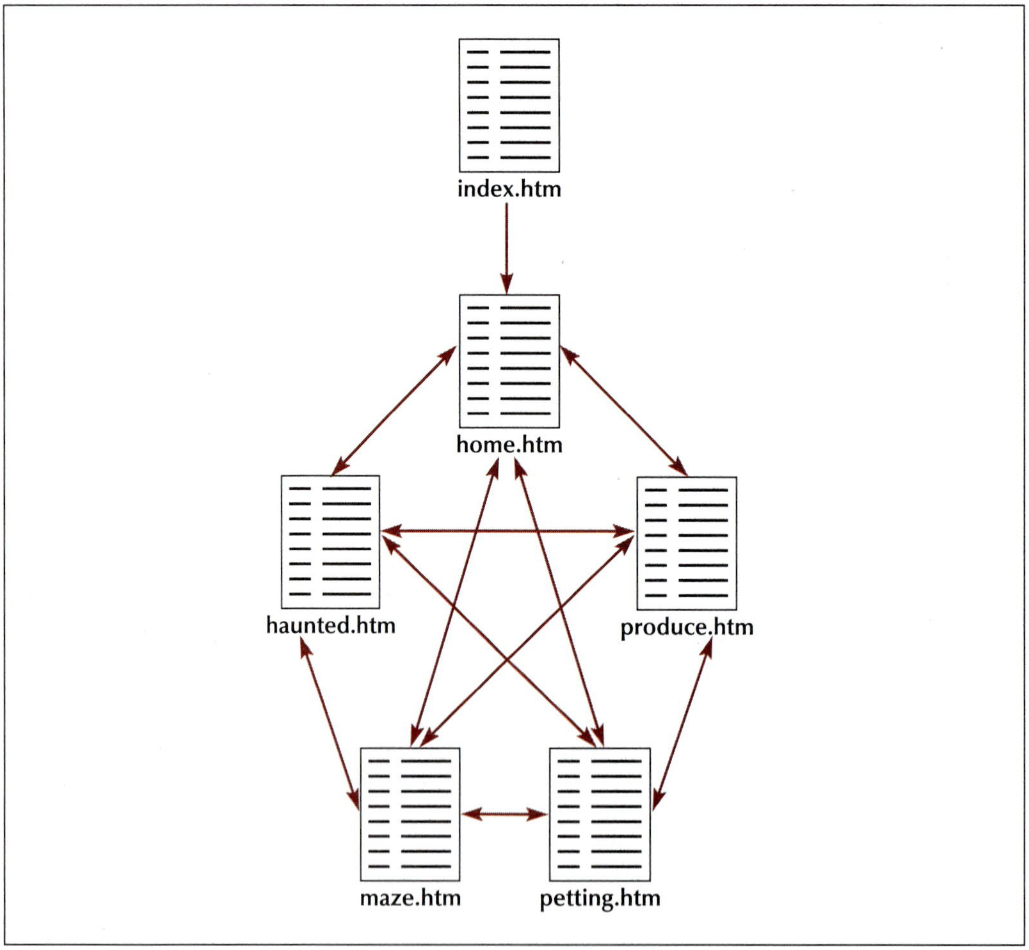

To view the Sunny Acres Web pages:

1. Use your text editor to open the **haunttxt.htm**, **hometxt.htm**, **indextxt.htm**, **mazetxt.htm**, **pettingtxt.htm**, and **producetxt.htm** files, located in the tutorial.03\tutorial folder included with your Data Files. Within each file, go to the comment section at top of the file and add ***your name*** and ***the date*** in the space provided. Save the files as **haunted.htm**, **home.htm**, **index.htm**, **maze.htm**, **petting.htm**, and **produce.htm**, respectively, in the same folder.
2. Take some time to review the HTML code within each document so that you understand the structure and content of the files.
3. Open the **home.htm** file in your Web browser, and then click the links at the top of the page to view the current appearance of the haunted.htm, maze.htm, petting.htm, and produce.htm files. Figure 3-2 shows the current layout and appearance of the Sunny Acres home page. Note that currently the index.htm file does not have any page content. You'll add that later in this tutorial.

Figure 3-2 **Initial Sunny Acres home page**

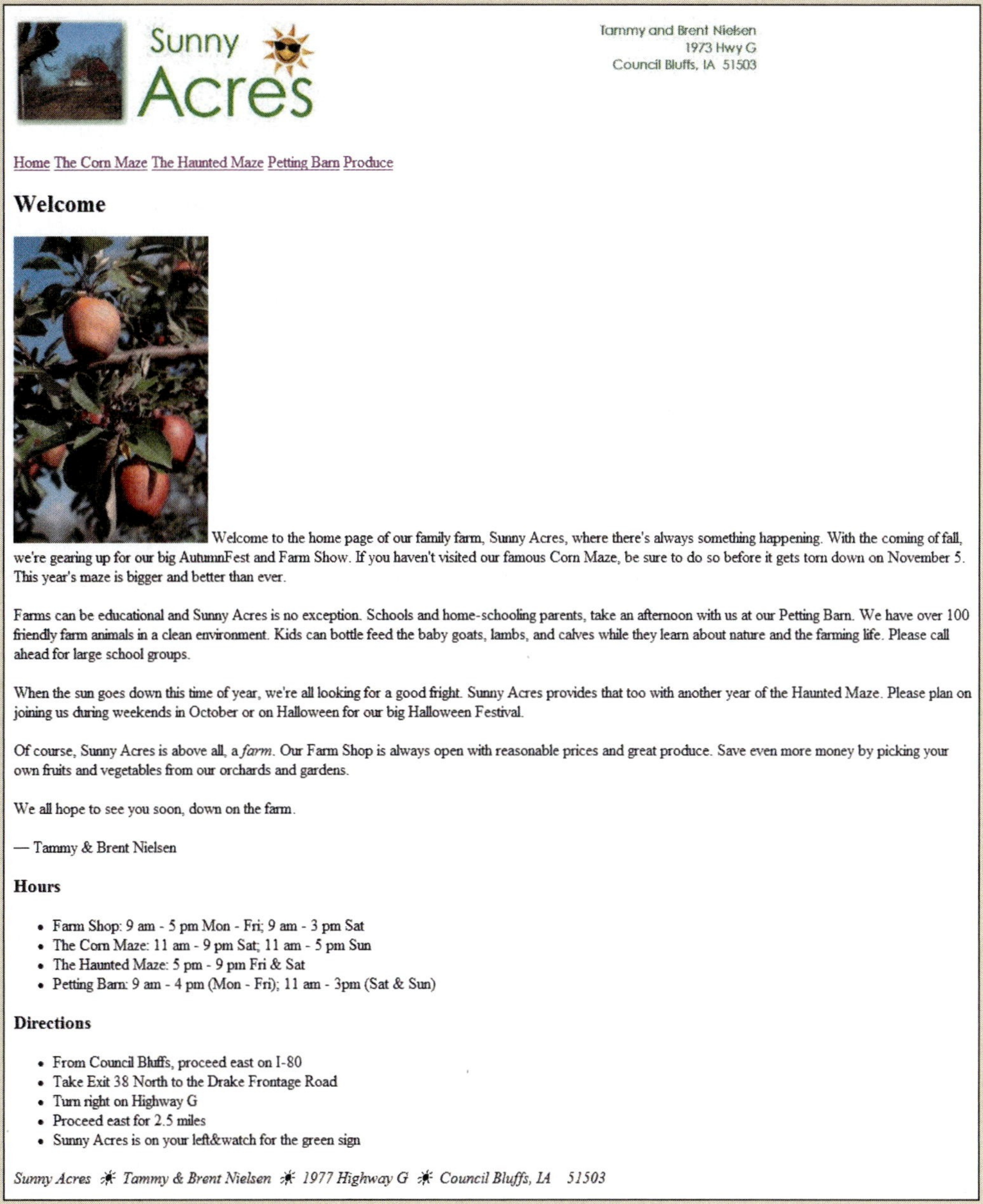
Sunny Acres
Tammy and Brent Nielsen
1973 Hwy G
Council Bluffs, IA 51503
Home The Corn Maze The Haunted Maze Petting Barn Produce
Welcome
Welcome to the home page of our family farm, Sunny Acres, where there's always something happening. With the coming of fall, we're gearing up for our big AutumnFest and Farm Show. If you haven't visited our famous Corn Maze, be sure to do so before it gets torn down on November 5. This year's maze is bigger and better than ever.
Farms can be educational and Sunny Acres is no exception. Schools and home-schooling parents, take an afternoon with us at our Petting Barn. We have over 100 friendly farm animals in a clean environment. Kids can bottle feed the baby goats, lambs, and calves while they learn about nature and the farming life. Please call ahead for large school groups.
When the sun goes down this time of year, we're all looking for a good fright. Sunny Acres provides that too with another year of the Haunted Maze. Please plan on joining us during weekends in October or on Halloween for our big Halloween Festival.
Of course, Sunny Acres is above all, a *farm*. Our Farm Shop is always open with reasonable prices and great produce. Save even more money by picking your own fruits and vegetables from our orchards and gardens.
We all hope to see you soon, down on the farm.
— Tammy & Brent Nielsen
Hours
• Farm Shop: 9 am - 5 pm Mon - Fri; 9 am - 3 pm Sat
• The Corn Maze: 11 am - 9 pm Sat; 11 am - 5 pm Sun
• The Haunted Maze: 5 pm - 9 pm Fri & Sat
• Petting Barn: 9 am - 4 pm (Mon - Fri); 11 am - 3pm (Sat & Sun)
Directions
• From Council Bluffs, proceed east on I-80
• Take Exit 38 North to the Drake Frontage Road
• Turn right on Highway G
• Proceed east for 2.5 miles
• Sunny Acres is on your left&watch for the green sign
Sunny Acres ☀ Tammy & Brent Nielsen ☀ 1977 Highway G ☀ Council Bluffs, IA 51503

The home page has all of the content that Tammy needs, but its design needs work. In Figure 3-3 she sketches how she would like the home page to appear.

Figure 3-3 **Proposed design for the Sunny Acres home page**

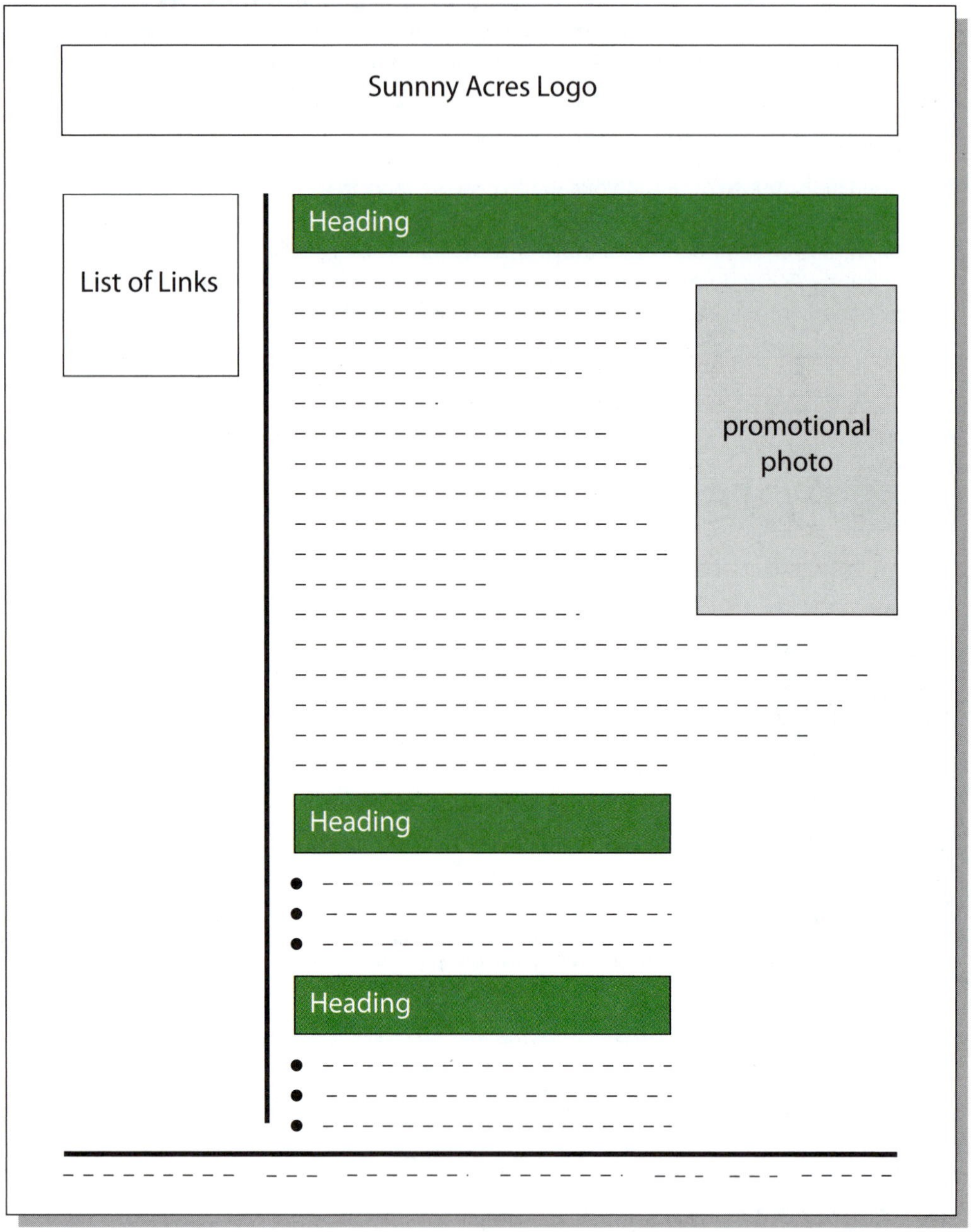

To apply this design not just to the Sunny Acres home page but also to the other pages on the Sunny Acres Web site, you'll create a page design using style sheets.

The History of CSS

A **style sheet** is a set of declarations describing the layout and appearance of a document. As you learned in Tutorial 1, HTML specifies a document's content and structure but not necessarily its appearance. To create a document design, you have to work in a different language. Several style sheet languages exist, but the most commonly used on the Web by far is the **Cascading Style Sheets** language, also known as **CSS**. You've actually been using CSS since Tutorial 1, when you used the style attribute. While the style attribute is part of the specifications for HTML and XHTML, the text of the attribute value is written in the CSS language.

Like HTML and XHTML, the specifications for CSS are maintained by the World Wide Web Consortium (W3C); and like those languages, several versions of CSS exist with varying levels of browser support. The first version of CSS, called **CSS1**, was introduced in 1996, but it was not fully implemented by any browser for another three years. CSS1 introduced styles for the following document features:

- *Fonts*: Setting font size, type, and other properties
- *Text*: Controlling text alignment and applying decorative elements such as underlining, italics, and capitalization
- *Color*: Specifying background and foreground colors of various page elements
- *Backgrounds*: Setting the background image for an element
- *Block-level elements*: Setting the margins, internal space, and borders of block-level elements

The second version of CSS, **CSS2**, was introduced in 1998. It expanded the language to support styles for:

- *Positioning*: Placing elements at specific locations on the page
- *Visual formatting*: Clipping and hiding element content
- *Media types*: Creating styles for various output devices, including printed media and aural devices
- *Interfaces*: Controlling the appearance and behavior of browser features such as scroll bars and mouse cursors

An update to CSS2, **CSS 2.1,** was introduced by the W3C in April 2002. Although the update did not add any new features to the language, it cleaned up minor errors that were introduced in the original specification. Even as browsers are implementing all of the features of CSS2, the W3C has pressed forward to the next version, **CSS3**. Still in development as of this writing, CSS3 will add styles for:

- *User interfaces*: Adding dynamic and interactive features
- *Accessibility*: Supporting users with disabilities and other special needs
- *Columnar layout*: Giving Web authors more page layout options
- *International features*: Providing support for a wide variety of languages and typefaces
- *Mobile devices*: Supporting the device requirements of PDAs and cell phones
- *Scalable vector graphics*: Making it easier for Web authors to add graphic elements to their Web pages

CSS3 will break up all of the style sheet specifications into individual modules. This approach should make it easier for developers of Web browsers to create products that support only those parts of CSS that are relevant to their products. For example, an aural browser might not need to support the CSS styles associated with printed media, so the browser's developers would need to concentrate only on the CSS3 modules that deal with aural properties. This CSS revision promises to make browser development easier; and the resulting browser products will therefore be more efficient and compact.

As with HTML, the usefulness of style sheets depends on the support of the browser community. Currently, CSS 2.1 enjoys good browser support—though there are some important differences between the major browsers that you'll explore later in this tutorial. As always, a Web page designer needs to be aware of compatibility issues that arise not just among different versions of CSS, but also among different versions of the same browser.

Applying a Style Sheet

You can apply styles to a Web site in three ways: with inline styles, with an embedded style sheet, and with an external style sheet. Each approach has its own advantages and disadvantages; you'll probably use some combination of all three in developing your Web sites. Tammy suggests that you explore each approach.

Using Inline Styles

An **inline style** is a style that is applied directly to an element through the use of the following style attribute

```
style = "style1: value1; style2: value2; style3: value3; ..."
```

where *style1*, *style2*, *style3*, and so forth are the names of the style properties, and *value1*, *value2*, *value3*, and so on are the values associated with each style property. So to center an h1 heading and display it in a red font, add the following inline style to the opening <h1> tag:

```
<h1 style="text-align: center; color: red">Sunny Acres</h1>
```

Inline styles are easy to interpret because they are applied directly to the elements they affect. However, this also makes them cumbersome. For example, if you wanted to use inline styles to make all of your headings the same font color, you would have to locate all of the h1 through h6 elements on the Web site and apply the same color style to them. This would be no small task on a large Web site containing hundreds of headings spread out among dozens of Web pages.

In addition, some developers point out that inline styles aren't consistent with the goal of separating content from style. After all, there is arguably little difference between using the inline style

```
<h1 style="text-align: center"> ... </h1>
```

and the deprecated align attribute

```
<h1 align="right"> ... </h1>
```

One goal of style sheets is to separate the development of a document's style from the development of its content. Ideally, the HTML code and CSS styles should be separate so that one person could work on content using HTML and another on design using CSS. This isn't possible with inline styles.

Using an Embedded Style Sheet

The power of style sheets becomes evident when you move style definitions away from document content. One way of doing this is to collect all of the styles used in the document in an **embedded style sheet** that is placed in the head section of the document. Embedded style sheets are created using the style element

```
<style type="text/css">
   style declarations
</style>
```

where *style declarations* are the declarations of the various styles to be applied to elements in the current document. Each style declaration has the syntax

```
selector {style1: value1; style2: value2; style3: value3; ...}
```

where *selector* identifies an element or elements within the document and the *style*: *value* pairs follow the same syntax that you've been using with inline styles. So to display all of the h1 headings in the documents in centered red text, add the following embedded style to the document head:

```
<style type="text/css">
   h1 {text-align: center; color: red}
</style>
```

You can apply the same style to several elements by entering the elements in a comma-separated list before the list of style properties. The following embedded style applies the centered-red font style to all of the h1 and h2 headings in the current document:

```
<style type="text/css">
   h1, h2 {text-align: center; color: red}
</style>
```

To see how to create and apply an embedded style, add one now to the home.htm file, setting the font color of all h2 and h3 headings in the document to green.

To apply an embedded style to Tammy's home page:

1. Return to the **home.htm** file in your text editor.
2. Directly above the closing </head> tag, insert the following embedded style, as shown in Figure 3-4:

```
<style type="text/css">
   h2, h3 {color: green}
</style>
```

Figure 3-4

Creating an embedded style sheet

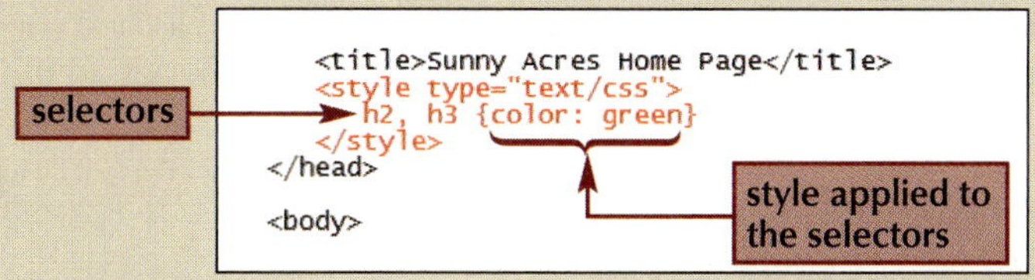

3. Save your changes to the file and refresh the **home.htm** file in your Web browser. The Welcome heading (an h2 element) and the Hours and Directions headings (both h3 elements) should now be displayed in a green font.

Styles from an embedded style sheet are applied to each of the elements listed in the style declaration—unless one of those elements has an inline style. In the case of conflicts, an inline style takes precedence over an embedded style sheet.

Using an External Style Sheet

Note that an embedded style sheet is limited to the page elements of the current document. If you wanted to use embedded styles to apply a style to an entire Web site, you would have to repeat the styles in the head section of each document. For a large Web site with many documents, this would be a cumbersome and error-prone process. Instead, you can place the style declarations in an external style sheet. An **external style sheet** is a text file that contains style declarations. The file can then be linked to any or all pages on the Web site, allowing the same styles to be applied to the entire site. The filename extension indicates the language of the style sheet. The extension for CSS style sheets is .css. An external style sheet looks like a list of embedded styles, except that the style declarations are not enclosed within opening and closing <style> tags. The following style declaration in an external style sheet

```
h1 {text-align: center; color: red}
```

would cause all Web pages linked to that style sheet to have their h1 headings displayed in centered red text. The great advantage of external style sheets is that you can create and change the style for an entire Web site by modifying one style sheet rather than editing the code of dozens of Web pages.

Adding Style Comments

Tip

Style comments can also be added to embedded style sheets as long as they are placed between the opening and closing <style> tags.

Style sheets can be as long and complicated as HTML files. To help others interpret your style sheet code, you should document the content and purpose of the style sheet using style sheet comments. The syntax to add a style sheet comment is

```
/* comment */
```

where *comment* is the text of the comment. CSS ignores the presence of whitespace, so as with HTML code, you can place style comments and style text on several lines to make your document easier to read. For example, the following style comment extends over four lines in the style sheet:

```
/*
   Sunny Acres
   Style Sheet
*/
```

Tammy would like you to use an external style sheet for the design of her Sunny Acres Web site. She has provided a text file with the main structure of a style sheet already entered. She'd like you to start by adding a style to center the text of all the address elements.

To create an external style sheet:

1. Use your text editor to open the **farmtxt.css** file from the tutorial.03\tutorial folder included with your Data Files. Enter ***your name*** and ***the date*** in the comment section at the top of the file.
2. Below the comment section, insert the following style declaration. Figure 3-5 shows the completed style sheet.

```
address {text-align: center}
```

Creating an external style sheet **Figure 3-5**

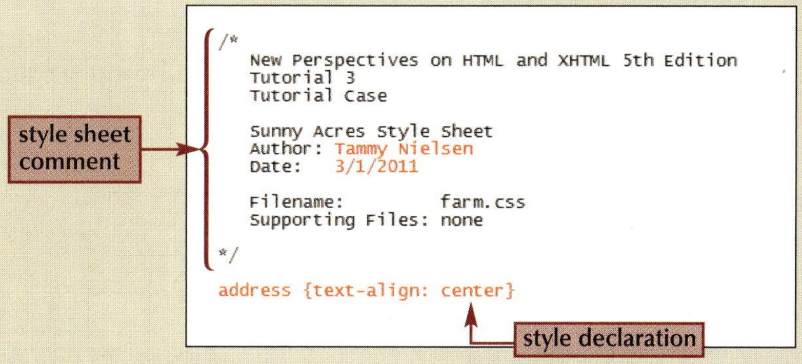
/*
New Perspectives on HTML and XHTML 5th Edition
Tutorial 3
Tutorial Case
Sunny Acres Style Sheet
Author: Tammy Nielsen
Date: 3/1/2011
Filename: farm.css
Supporting Files: none
*/
address {text-align: center}
style sheet comment
style declaration

3. Save the file as **farm.css** to the tutorial.03\tutorial folder.

To apply this style to Tammy's document, you have to create a link between the home.htm file and the farm.css style sheet.

Linking to an External Style Sheet

You create a link between Web pages and external style sheets using the same link element discussed in Tutorial 2. The code to create a style sheet link is

```
<link href="url" rel="stylesheet" type="text/css" />
```

where *url* is the URL of the external style sheet. As with the link elements discussed in Tutorial 2, link elements used for style sheets must be placed in the head section of the Web page document. For example, to create a link to a styles.css style sheet, you would insert the following element into the head section of the HTML file:

```
<link href="styles.css" rel="stylesheet" type="text/css" />
```

The URL in the href attribute is interpreted in the same way as URLs for linked Web pages. In this case, you assume that the styles.css file is located in the same folder as the current document because no additional path information has been provided.

Applying a Style | Reference Window

- To apply an inline style to a page element, insert the HTML attribute
  ```
  style="style1: value1; style2: value2; style3: value3; ..."
  ```
  where *style1*, *style2*, *style3*, and so on are the names of the style properties, and *value1*, *value2*, *value3*, and so on are the values associated with each style property.
- To apply an embedded style sheet to a Web page, add to the document's head
  ```
  <style type="text/css">
    style declarations
  </style>
  ```
  where *style declarations* are lists of styles in the form
  ```
  selector {style1: value1; style2: value2; style3: value3; ...}
  ```
  with *selector* identifying the element or elements within that document receiving the style.
- To apply an external style sheet, use your text editor to create a text file containing style declarations. Use the .css filename extension. To link to the external style sheet, add
  ```
  <link href="url" rel="stylesheet" type="text/css" />
  ```
  to the document head, where *url* is the URL of the external style sheet.

You'll use the link element to create a link between Tammy's home.htm file and the farm.css style sheet.

To link the farm.css external style sheet to Tammy's home page:

1. Return to the **home.htm** file in your text editor.
2. Between the closing </style> tag and the closing </head> tag, insert the following link element, as shown in Figure 3-6:

```
<link href="farm.css" rel="stylesheet" type="text/css" />
```

Figure 3-6 Linking to an external style sheet

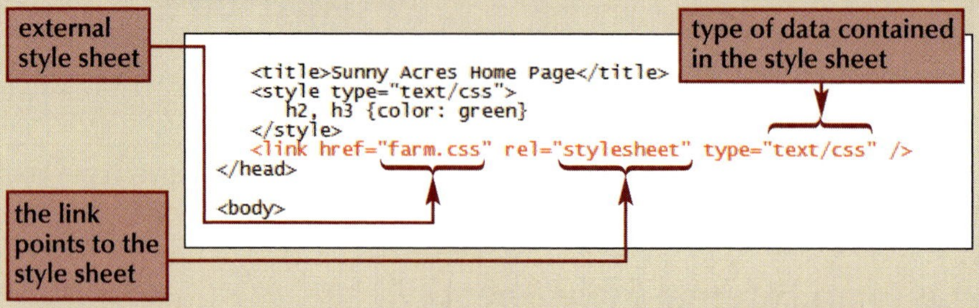

3. Save your changes to the file and then reload or refresh the **home.htm** file in your Web browser.
4. Scroll to the bottom of the page and confirm that the address text for the Sunny Acres farm is now centered horizontally on the page.

InSight | Importing Style Sheets

On large Web sites that involve hundreds of pages, you might decide to use different styles for different groups of pages to give a visual cue to users about where they are on the site. One way of organizing these different styles is to break them into smaller, more manageable units. The different style sheets can then be imported into a single sheet. To import a style sheet, add the following statement to either an embedded style sheet or an external style sheet file

```
@import url(url)
```

where (*url*) is the URL of an external style sheet file. For example, a company might have one style sheet named company.css that contains basic styles used in all Web pages and another style sheet named support.css that only applies to Web pages containing technical support information. The following embedded style sheet imports both files:

```
<style type="text/css">
   @import url(company.css)
   @import url(support.css)
</style>
```

The @import statement must always come before any other style declarations in the embedded or external style sheet. When the browser encounters the @import statement, it imports the content of the style sheet file directly into current style sheet, much as if you had typed the style declarations yourself.

Setting up Alternate Style Sheets

Many browsers allow Web pages to support alternative style sheets. This is particularly useful in situations with users who have special needs (such as a need for large text with highly contrasting colors). To support these users, you can create an alternate style sheet with the link element

```
<link href="url1" rel="alternate stylesheet"
      type="text/css" title="title1" />
<link href="url2" rel="alternate stylesheet"
      type="text/css" title="title2" />
```

where *url1*, *url2*, and so forth are the URLs of the style sheet files, and *title1*, *title2*, etc. are the titles of the alternate style sheets. For example, the following HTML code creates links to two style sheets named Large Text and Regular Text:

```
<link href="large.css" rel="alternate stylesheet" type="text/css"
      title="Large Text" />
<link href="regular.css" rel="alternate stylesheet" type="text/css"
      title="Regular Text" />
```

Browsers that support alternate style sheets provide a menu option for the user to select which style sheet to apply. Figure 3-7 shows how users could choose between the Large Text and the Regular Text style sheets under the Firefox browser.

Choosing between alternate style sheets in Firefox **Figure 3-7**

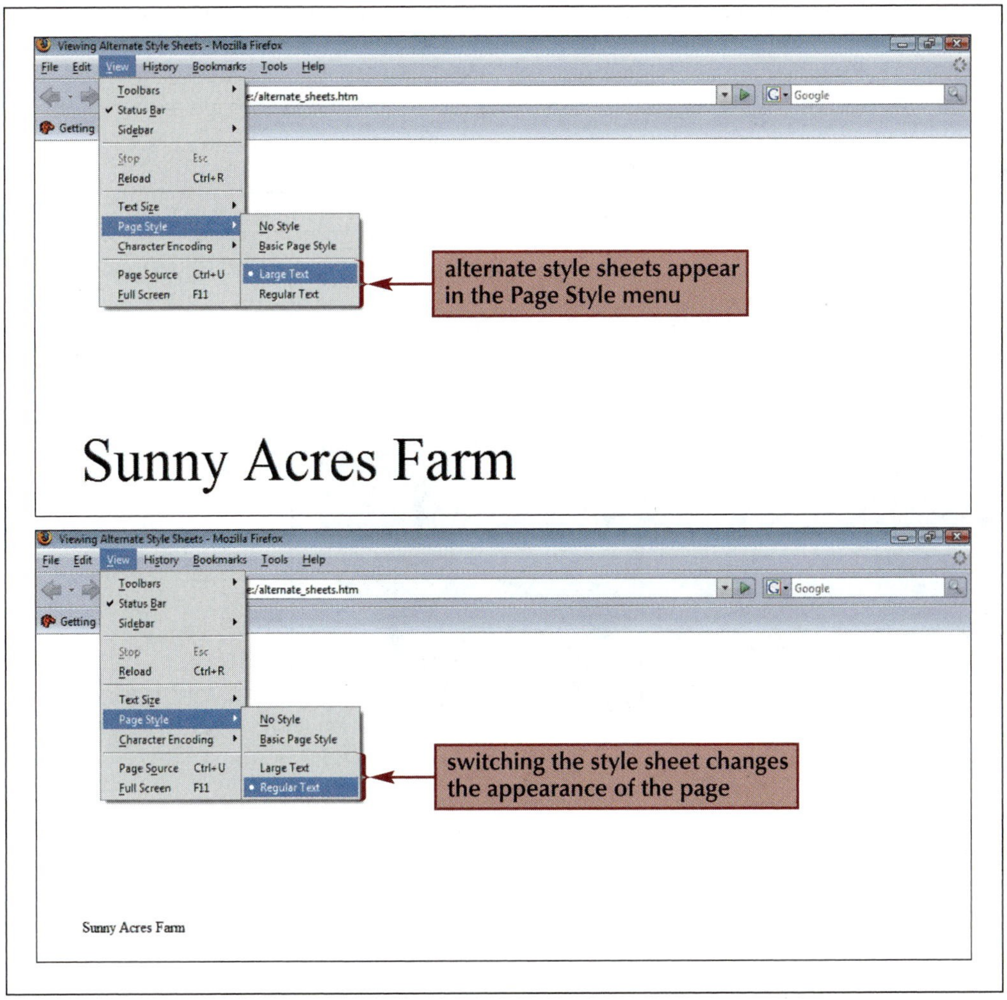

Among the major browsers, currently Netscape, Firefox, Opera, and Safari support alternate style sheets. At the time of this writing, Internet Explorer supports them only if a specialized add-in program is installed on the user's computer. Tammy wants you to be aware of alternate style sheets for the future; but for now, you will not be specifying alternate style sheets for the Sunny Acres Web site.

Understanding Cascading Order

With so many ways of applying styles to a Web site, you might wonder which style is ultimately used by the browser when the page is rendered. For example, consider a Web page that is linked to an external style sheet that sets all h1 elements in bold, red font. But the author also has an inline style for one of the h1 elements specifying centered blue font. Furthermore, the browser specifies that all h1 elements are rendered in a regular black font that is not centered on the page. Which style rule is ultimately applied to the page? To answer that question, you have to examine the principals of style precedence and style inheritance.

Style Precedence

Style precedence is the rule that determines which style is applied when one or more styles conflict. The general rule is that in the case of conflict, the more specific style has precedence over the more general style.

As shown in Figure 3-8, the most general style is the one that is built into the Web browser. Each browser has an internal style sheet that it uses for rendering page elements. The reason that most browsers indent block quotes or display h1 headings in a large font is that they are applying an internal style sheet that governs how those elements are rendered. Unless a different style is specified by the Web page author or the user viewing the page, these browser styles are used.

Figure 3-8 Levels of style precedence

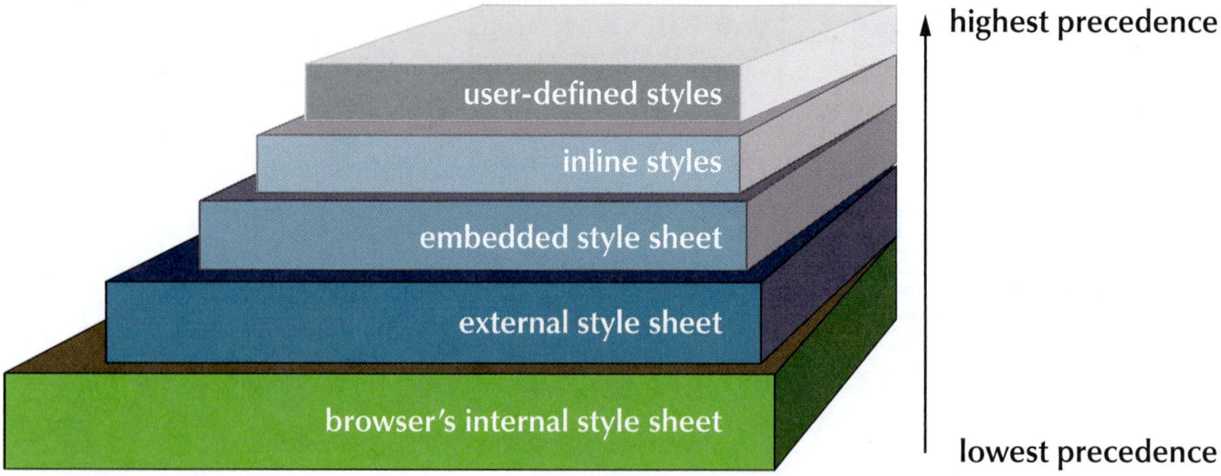

The next three levels of styles are those defined by the Web site author. The first are styles defined in an external style sheet. When linked to a Web page, those styles will have precedence over the browser's built-in styles. In the same way, an embedded style sheet applied to a specific Web page has precedence over external style sheets. Finally, inline styles applied to specific elements within a Web page have precedence over the styles defined in the embedded style sheet.

The highest level of style rules includes those defined by the user of the Web page. Most browsers allow users to modify the style sheets used by the browser and the Web page. For example, the Accessibility dialog box in Internet Explorer shown in Figure 3-9 is often used by people with disabilities to set up style sheets that meet specific needs. These user-defined styles take precedence over the browser's internal styles and any styles specified by the Web page author.

Tip

View your Web pages without the style sheets to ensure that the page is still readable even when your style sheets are not adopted by the user. The ability to understand page content should not depend on the ability to access your style sheet.

Accessibility dialog box in Internet Explorer | **Figure 3-9**

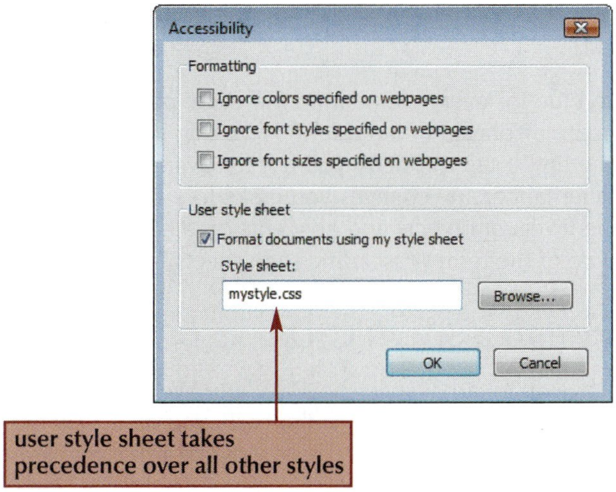

When conflicting styles are on the same level, the one declared last has precedence. For example, the following embedded style sheet

```
<style type="text/css">
   h1 {color: orange; text-align: center}
   h1 {color: blue}
</style>
```

results in h1 headings displayed in centered blue text. The text is blue because the second style declaration has precedence over the first. However, the text is still centered because the second style declaration did not alter the text-align style, so the text-align setting from the first style declaration is still in force.

You can override the precedence rules by adding the !important property to a style declaration. The style sheet

```
<style type="text/css">
 h1 {color: orange !important }
 h1 {color: blue; text-align: center }
</style>
```

results in h1 headings rendered in centered orange text because the orange style is given a higher weight than the blue style even though the blue style is declared last. The !important property is useful in situations where you want to ensure that a particular style is always enforced regardless of its location in the order of precedence.

Note that even with the !important property, any styles you specify can still be overridden by users who set up their own style sheets with their browsers.

Style Inheritance

Where there is no conflict, styles are passed down from the more general levels to the more specific in what is known as **style inheritance**. When you use an external style sheet to set the font color of h1 headings to blue, that color is assumed in all other h1 heading styles unless a different color is specified. This is also true for page elements that are nested within other page elements. For example, to set the font color of every element on the page to blue, you could enter the following style declaration:

```
body {color: blue}
```

Every element nested within the body element (that is, every element on the page) would inherit this style. This means that every h1 heading, every paragraph, every numbered list, and so forth would be displayed in blue text. To override style inheritance, you specify an alternate style for one of the descendant elements of the parent. The styles

```
body {color: blue}
p    {color: red}
```

set the text color to blue for every element on the page; paragraphs and elements contained within them are displayed in a red font. Note that you can override style inheritance using the same !important property you use for overriding style precedence.

Through style inheritance, any changes you make to a style sheet will automatically be passed down the levels of objects and elements on the Web site. This cascade of style changes is the source of the term "cascading style sheets."

Applying a Style to a Specific ID

Sometimes you'll have an external style sheet for your Web site, but will still want to apply a style to a specific element. If that is the case, you can mark the element with the id attribute, as discussed in Tutorial 2. To create a style for that marked element, apply the style declaration

```
#id {style rule}
```

where *id* is the value of the element's id attribute and *style rule* stands for the styles applied to that specific element. For example, if you have the h2 element

```
<h2 id="subtitle">A Fun Family Farm</h2>
```

in your code, you can set the font color to red using the following style:

```
#subtitle {color: red}
```

You do the same with an inline style, but using the id attribute has the advantage of moving the style declaration out of the HTML file, where it can be more easily maintained and revised.

Reference Window | Applying a Style to an ID

- To apply a style to an element marked with a specific id value, use the declaration
  `#id {style rule}`
  where *id* is the value of the element's id attribute and *style rule* stands for the styles applied to that specific element.

You'll create styles for specific element ids later in this tutorial.

Working with Color in HTML and CSS

Now that you've seen how embedded and external style sheets work, you'll begin exploring various aspects of the CSS language. You'll start by examining how to work with color. If you've worked with graphics software, you've probably made your color choices without much difficulty due to the graphical interfaces that those applications employ. Graphical interfaces, known as WYSIWYG (what you see is what you get), allow you to select colors visually. Specifying a color with CSS is somewhat less intuitive because CSSis a text-based language and requires you to define your colors in textual terms. This can be done by specifying either a color value or a color name.

Color Values

A **color value** is a numerical expression that precisely describes a color. To better understand how numbers can represent colors, it helps to review some of the basic principles of color theory and how they relate to the colors that your monitor displays.

White light is made up of three primary colors (red, green, and blue) mixed at equal intensities. By adding two of the three primary colors you can generate a trio of complementary colors: yellow, magenta, and cyan, as shown Figure 3-10.

Figure 3-10 **Primary color model for light**

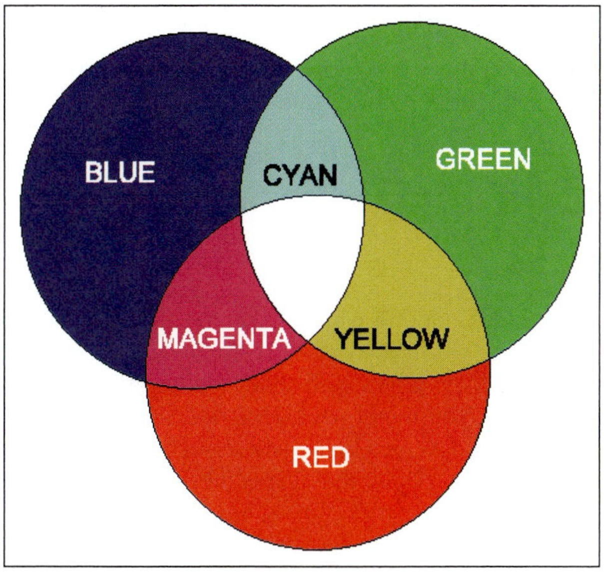

To generate a wider range of colors, you simply vary the intensity of the red, green, and blue light. For example, orange is created from a high intensity of red light, a moderate intensity of green light, and an absence of blue light. Your computer monitor generates colors by emitting red, green, and blue light at different intensities. CSS represents these intensities mathematically. Each color is represented by a triplet of numbers called an **RGB triplet**, whose values are based on the strength of its red, green, and blue components. This triplet has the form

```
rgb(red, green, blue)
```

where *red*, *green*, and *blue* are the intensity values of the red, green, and blue components. The intensity values range from 0 (absence of color) to 255 (highest intensity). For example, the RGB triplet for white is (255, 255, 255), indicating that red, green, and blue are equally mixed at the highest intensity. Orange has the triplet (255, 165, 0) which means it results from a mixture of high-intensity red, moderate-intensity green, and no blue. You can also enter each component value as a percentage, with 100% representing the highest intensity. In this form, you specify the color orange with

```
rgb(100%, 65%, 0%)
```

The percentage form is less commonly used than RGB values. RGB triplets can specify 256^3 (16.7 million) possible colors, which is more colors than the human eye can distinguish.

Originally, HTML required that color values be entered using the hexadecimal system. A **hexadecimal** is a number expressed in the base 16 numbering system rather than in the base 10 form you use every day. In base 10 counting, you use combinations of 10 characters (0 through 9) to represent numerical values. The hexadecimal system includes six extra characters: A (for 10), B (for 11), C (for 12), D (for 13), E (for 14), and F (for 15). For values above 15, you use a combination of those 16 characters. Therefore, to represent a number in hexadecimal terms, you convert the value to multiples of 16, plus a remainder. For example, 16 is equal to (16 × 1) + 0, so its hexadecimal representation is 10. A value of 21 is equal to (16 × 1) + 5, for a hexadecimal representation of 15. The number 255 is equal to (16 × 15) + 15, or FF in hexadecimal format (remember that F = 15 in hexadecimal). In the case of the number 255, the first F represents the number of times 16 goes into 255 (which is 15), and the second F represents the remainder of 15. A color value represented as a hexadecimal number has the form

```
#redgreenblue
```

where *red*, *green*, and *blue* are the hexadecimal values of the red, green, and blue components. Therefore, the color yellow could be represented either by the RGB triplet

```
rgb(255,255,0)
```

or in the hexadecimal form

```
#FFFF00
```

At this point, you might be wondering whether you have to become a math major before you can start adding color to your Web pages! Fortunately, this is not the case. You can specify most colors on your Web pages with styles that use RGB triplets rather than the hexadecimal form. However, you might see HTML or CSS code that sets a color value to something like #FFA500, and now you know where such a representation comes from—even if you can't tell at a glance that it specifies the color orange.

Using Color Names

If you don't want to use color values, you can also specify colors by name. HTML and XHTML support 16 basic color names. These color names are also supported by CSS 2.1, with the addition of orange to make 17 color names. The 17 color names and their RGB and hexadecimal color values are shown in Figure 3-11.

Figure 3-11 The 17 basic color names from CSS 2.1

Color Name	RGB Triplet	Hexadecimal	Color Name	RGB Triplet	Hexadecimal
Aqua	(0, 255, 255)	00FFFF	Olive	(128, 128, 0)	808000
Black	(0, 0, 0)	000000	Orange	(255, 165, 0)	FFA500
Blue	(0, 0, 255)	0000FF	Purple	(128, 0, 128)	800080
Fuchsia	(255, 0, 255)	FF00FF	Red	(255, 0, 0)	FF0000
Gray	(128, 128, 128)	808080	Silver	(192, 192, 192)	C0C0C0
Green	(0, 128, 0)	008000	Teal	(0, 128, 128)	008080
Lime	(0, 255, 0)	00FF00	White	(255, 255, 255)	FFFFFF
Maroon	(128, 0, 0)	800000	Yellow	(255, 255, 0)	FFFF00
Navy	(0, 0, 128)	000080			

Seventeen colors are not a lot, so most browsers support an extended list of 140 color names, including such colors as crimson, khaki, and peachpuff. Although this extended color list is not part of the specifications for either HTML or CSS, most browsers support it. You can view these color names in a demo page.

To view the extended list of color names:

1. Use your browser to open the **demo_color_names.htm** file from the tutorial.03\demo folder included with your Data Files.
2. As shown in Figure 3-12, the demo page displays the list of 140 color names along with their color values expressed both as RGB triplets and in hexadecimal form. The 17 color names supported by CSS 2.1 are highlighted in the table.

Figure 3-12 A partial list of extended color names

Sample	Name	RGB	Hexadecimal
	aliceblue	(240,248,255)	#F0F8FF
	antiquewhite	(250,235,215)	#FAEBD7
	aqua	**(0,255,255)**	**#00FFFF**
	aquamarine	(127,255,212)	#7FFFD4
	azure	(240,255,255)	#F0FFFF
	beige	(245,245,220)	#F5F5DC
	bisque	(255,228,196)	#FFE4C4
	black	**(0,0,0)**	**#000000**
	blanchedalmond	(255,235,205)	#FFEBCD
	blue	**(0,0,255)**	**#0000FF**
	blueviolet	(138,43,226)	#8A2BE2
	brown	(165,42,42)	#A52A2A
	burlywood	(222,184,135)	#DEB887

3. Close the page when you are finished reviewing the extended color names list.

Depending on the design requirements of your site, you might sometimes need to use color values to get exactly the right color. However, if you know the general color that you need, you can usually enter the color name without having to look up its RGB value.

Defining Text and Background Colors

Tip

About 8% of all men and 0.5% of all women have some form of color blindness. Because red-green color blindness is the most common form of color impairment, you should avoid using red text on a green background or green text on a red background.

Now that you've studied how to specify a color in HTML and CSS, you can start applying it to the elements of Tammy's Web pages. CSS supports styles to define the text and background color for each element on your page. You've already worked with the color style to define text color. The style to define the background color is

```
background-color: color
```

where *color* is either a color value or a color name. If you do not define an element's color, it takes the color of the element that contains it. For example, if you specify red text on a gray background for the Web page body, all elements within the page inherit that color combination unless you specify different styles for specific elements.

Reference Window | Setting the Background Color

- To set the background color of an element, use
  `background-color: color`
  where *color* is a color name or a color value.

Tammy wants each of her pages to have a slightly different color theme. For the home page, she wants a white page background, and she wants the heading text to appear in white text on a dark green background. Although most browsers assume a white background by default, it's a good idea to make this explicit in case a browser has a differentsetting. You'll add to this style to the farm.css external style sheet because you'll eventually apply this to the entire Sunny Acres Web site. For the background color of the heading, you'll use the value

```
rgb(0, 154, 0)
```

You'll add this to an embedded style sheet in the home.htm file because Tammy doesn't intend to use the same heading background on her other pages.

To set the text and background colors on Tammy's home page:

1. Return to the **home.htm** file in your text editor.
2. As shown in Figure 3-13, change the style for h2 and h3 headings to:

```
h2, h3 {color: white; background-color: rgb(0, 154, 0)}
```

Figure 3-13 Specifying text color and background colors

```
   <title>Sunny Acres Home Page</title>
   <style type="text/css">
      h2, h3 {color: white; background-color: rgb(0, 154, 0)}
   </style>
   <link href="farm.css" rel="stylesheet" type="text/css" />
</head>
```

3. Save your changes to the file.
4. Return to the **farm.css** file in your text editor.
5. As shown in Figure 3-14, above the style declaration for the address element, insert the following style:

```
body {background-color: white}
```

Setting the background color for the page body — **Figure 3-14**

```
body    {background-color: white}
address {text-align: center}
```

6. Save your changes to the file.
7. Reload the **home.htm** file in your Web browser. As shown in Figure 3-15, the h2 and h3 heading text should now appear as white text on a dark green background.

Formatted heading — **Figure 3-15**

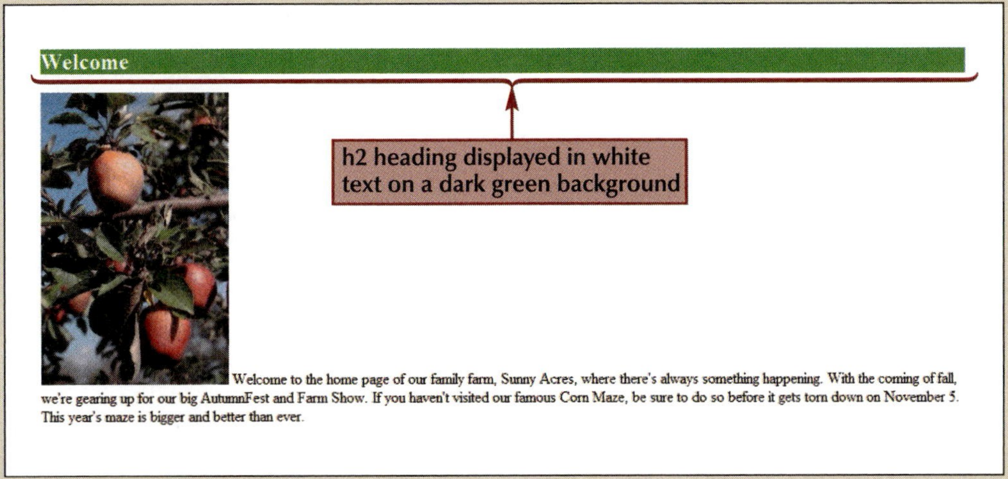
Welcome
h2 heading displayed in white text on a dark green background
Welcome to the home page of our family farm, Sunny Acres, where there's always something happening. With the coming of fall, we're gearing up for our big AutumnFest and Farm Show. If you haven't visited our famous Corn Maze, be sure to do so before it gets torn down on November 5. This year's maze is bigger and better than ever.

8. If you want to take a break before starting the next session, you can close your files and applications now.

Deprecated Approaches to Color | InSight

CSS was not part of the original HTML specifications. If you need to work with older HTML code or need to support older browser versions, you might need to use several deprecated attributes such as bgcolor and text. Both attributes require you to enter either the hexadecimal color value or a recognized color name. You use the bgcolor attribute in the <body> tag to define the background color for an entire page. To define the text color for the entire page, use the text attribute. For example, the following code changes the page background to yellow and the page's text color to sky blue with the hexadecimal value 99CCFF:

```
<body bgcolor="yellow" text="#99CCFF">
```

If you need to color a section of text on your page, enclose the text within the two-sided <font> tag. The <font> tag is a deprecated element that supports several design attributes. Among those supported is the color attribute, which you can use to specify a color name or a hexadecimal color value. For example, the following HTML code sets the text color of an h1 heading to green:

```
<h1><font color="green">Sunny Acres</font></h1>
```

Note that the bgcolor and text attributes and the font element are not part of XHTML and will be rejected by documents that require a strict application of XHTML standards.

You show Tammy the work you've done on colors. She's pleased with the ease of CSS to modify the design and appearance of elements on the Sunny Acres home page. In the next session, you'll continue to explore CSS styles, focusing on text and image styles.

Review | **Session 3.1 Quick Check**

1. What are inline styles, embedded styles, and external style sheets? Which would you use to create a design for an entire Web site?
2. Specify the code to enter the following comment into a CSS file:

   ```
   Sunny Acres Style Sheet
   ```
3. Specify the code to set the text color of every paragraph element within the Web page to red.
4. If a style sheet has the following declarations, how will address text be rendered by the browser?:

   ```
   address {color: red; text-align: left}
   address {color: blue}
   ```
5. If a style sheet has the following declarations, how will paragraph text be rendered by the browser?:

   ```
   body {background-color: ivory}
   p    {color: red}
   ```
6. What property do you add to a style to override style precedence and style inheritance?
7. Specify the style to display block quote text in a color with a red intensity of 221, a green intensity of 128, and a blue intensity of 0.

Session 3.2

Working with Fonts and Text Styles

Tammy has noticed that all of the text on her pages is displayed in the same typeface. She'd like to see more variety in the page fonts. To modify the text, you'll work with the CSS text and font styles.

Choosing a Font

By default, browsers display Web page text in a single font—usually Times New Roman. You can specify a different font for any page element using the style

```
font-family: fonts
```

where *fonts* is a comma-separated list of fonts that the browser can use in any element. Font names can be either specific or generic. A **specific font** is a font that is actually installed on a user's computer; examples are Times New Roman, Arial, and Garamond. A **generic font** is a name for a grouping of fonts that share a similar appearance. Browsers recognize five generic font groups: serif, sans-serif, monospace, cursive, and fantasy. Figure 3-16 shows examples of each.

Figure 3-16 Generic fonts

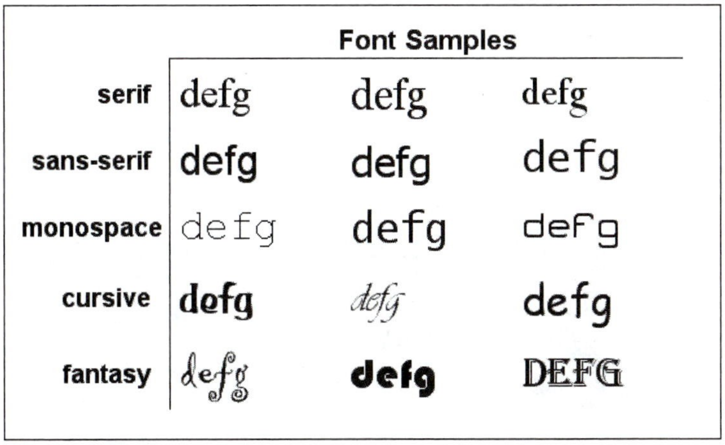

Note that within a font family, the actual appearance of the text might vary widely and you cannot be sure which font a given user's browser will use. For this reason, CSS allows you to specify a list of specific fonts along with a generic font. You list the specific fonts first, in order of preference, and then end the list with the generic font. If the browser cannot find any of the specific fonts listed, it uses the generic font. For example, to specify a sans-serif font, you could enter the following style:

```
font-family: Arial, Helvetica, 'Trebuchet MS', sans-serif
```

This style tells the browser to first look for the Arial font; if Arial is not available, the browser looks for Helvetica, and then Trebuchet MS. If none of those fonts is available, the browser uses a generic sans-serif font. Note that font names containing one or more blank spaces (such as Trebuchet MS) must be enclosed within single or double quotes.

To see how the generic fonts appear on your browser, you can use a demo page on text styles.

To use the demo to view your browser's generic fonts:

1. Use your Web browser to open the **demo_css.htm** file from the tutorial.03\demo folder included with your Data Files.

   The demo page contains a collection of text styles you'll explore in this session. You can select a text style value from the drop-down lists on the left side of the demo. You can specify the text to apply the style to in the top-right box. The style as applied to the sample text appears in the middle box. The CSS code for the style appears in the bottom-right box. You press the Tab key to apply the style.

2. Click the top-right corner box, select and delete the text "Enter sample text here" and type **Sunny Acres**, press the **Enter** key, and then type **Corn Maze**. Press the **Tab** key to display this text in the Preview box.

3. In the three color input boxes, enter the RGB value

   ```
   rgb(255, 255, 255)
   ```

   and in the three background-color input boxes, enter

   ```
   rgb(153, 102, 102)
   ```

   and then press the **Tab** key.

4. Select **sans-serif** from the font-family list box. As shown in Figure 3-17, the demo page shows the effect of the styles applied to the sample text. The CSS code for these styles is shown in the Style box.

Figure 3-17 Viewing the sans-serif font

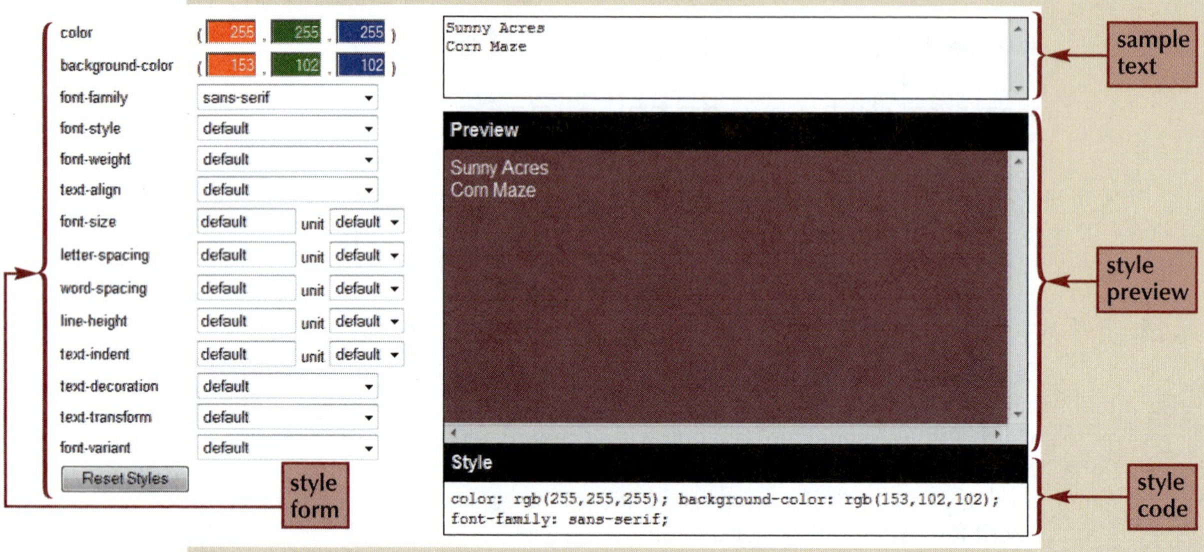

Tip

Including too many font styles can make your page difficult to read. Don't use more than two or three fonts within a single page.

If you think users will want to print your Web pages, be aware that the general rule is to use sans-serif fonts for headlines and serif fonts for body text. For computer monitors, which have lower resolutions than printed material, the general rule is to use sans-serif fonts for headlines and body text, leaving serif fonts for special effects and large text. Tammy expects that her Web page will only be viewed on computer monitors, so you'll use a sans-serif font for all of the body text. You'll do this in the farm.css external style sheet so it can be applied to all pages on the site.

To apply a sans-serif font to the body text in Tammy's external style sheet:

1. Return to the **farm.css** file in your text editor.
2. Add the style

   ```
   font-family: Arial, Helvetica, sans-serif
   ```

   to the style declaration for the body element. Be sure to use a semicolon to separate this new style from the background-color style. Figure 3-18 shows the revised code.

Figure 3-18 Setting the font-family style for the body text

```
body    {background-color: white; font-family: Arial, Helvetica, sans-serif}
address {text-align: center}
```

3. Save your changes to the file and then reload the **home.htm** file in your Web browser. As shown in Figure 3-19, all of the body text in the Web page should now be displayed in a sans-serif font.

Figure 3-19 Body text in a sans-serif font

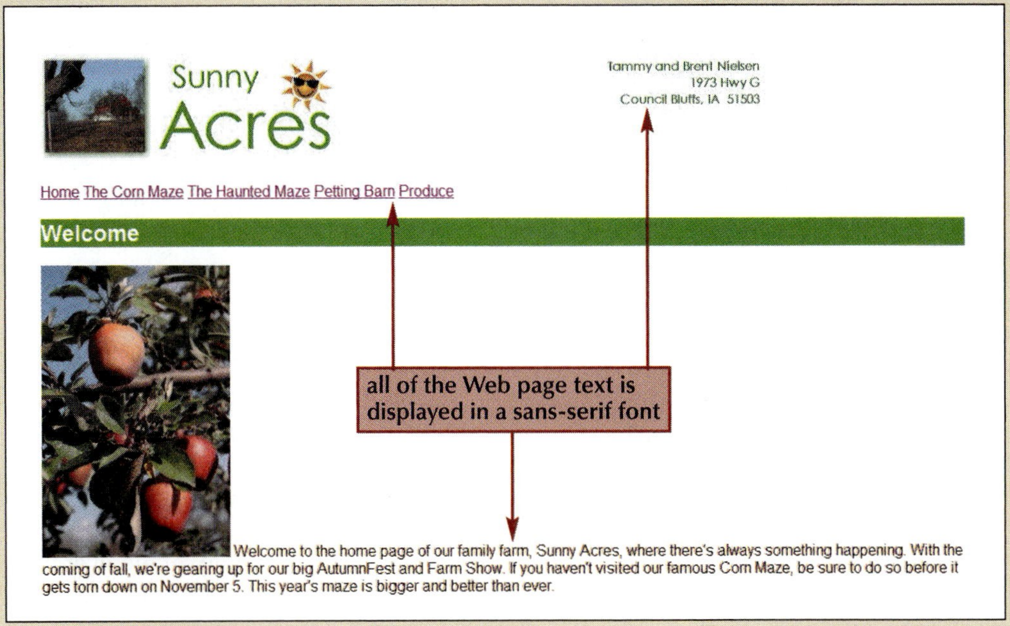
Sunny Acres
Tammy and Brent Nielsen
1973 Hwy G
Council Bluffs, IA 51503
Home The Corn Maze The Haunted Maze Petting Barn Produce
Welcome
all of the Web page text is displayed in a sans-serif font
Welcome to the home page of our family farm, Sunny Acres, where there's always something happening. With the coming of fall, we're gearing up for our big AutumnFest and Farm Show. If you haven't visited our famous Corn Maze, be sure to do so before it gets torn down on November 5. This year's maze is bigger and better than ever.

Note that the sans-serif font is applied to all page elements on the Sunny Acres home page. This is because you applied the style to the body element, and so it cascades through all the elements on the page.

Setting the Font Size

Tammy would like the Welcome heading on her home page to be displayed in slightly larger text than the rest of her site. The style to change the font size of the text within an element is

```
font-size: length
```

where *length* is a length measurement. Lengths can be specified in four different ways:

- with a unit of measurement
- with a keyword description
- as a percentage of the size of the containing element
- with a keyword expressing the size relative to the size of the containing element

If you choose to specify lengths using measurement units, you can use absolute units or relative units. Because absolute and relative units appear in several styles, it's worthwhile to spend some time understanding them. **Absolute units** are units that are fixed in size regardless of the device rendering the Web page and are specified in one of five standard units of measurement: mm (millimeters), cm (centimeters), in (inches), pt (points), and pc (picas). The points and picas measurements might not be as familiar to you as inches, millimeters, and centimeters. For comparison, there are 72 points in an inch, 12 points in a pica, and 6 picas in an inch. Size values for any of these measurements can be whole numbers (0, 1, 2 ...) or decimals (0.5, 1.6, 3.9 ...). For example, ifyou want your text to be 1/2 inch in size, you can use any of the following styles (note that you should not insert a space between the size value and the unit abbreviation):

```
font-size: 0.5in
font-size: 36pt
font-size: 3pc
```

Tip

Use absolute units only when you can predict or can fix the size and dimensions of the output device.

Absolute measurements are appropriate when you know the physical properties of the output device and want to fix the size to a specific value. Of course this is not often the case with Web pages because they can be displayed on a variety of devices, monitor sizes, and resolutions. This is one of the fundamental differences between Web page design and print design (in which you usually know the size and properties of the paper).

To cope with a wide variety of output devices and sizes, many Web page designers opt to use **relative units**, which are expressed relative to the size of other objects within the Web page. One commonly used relative unit is the **em unit**. The exact meaning of the em unit depends on its use in the style sheet. If the em unit is used for setting font size, it expresses the size relative to the font size of the parent element. For an h1 heading, the parent element is the Web page body. So the style

```
h1 {font-size: 2em}
```

sets the font size of h1 headings to twice the font size of body text. If the browser has been configured to display body text in a 12-point font, this style will cause h1 headings to be displayed in a 24-point font. On the other hand, if the h1 heading is nested within another element such as a blockquote element or div element, then the size of the h1 heading will be twice the size of text in that containing element. Context is important when interpreting the effect of the em unit.

When used for sizing objects other than fonts, the em unit is equal to a little over the width of the capital letter "M" in the font size of the current element. The style

```
h1 {width: 20em}
```

sets the width of the h1 heading to a little over the width of 20 capital Ms. Of course, the actual size of the Ms depends on the font used in the h1 heading. Because capital Ms take up the most width of any character, another way to think of the em unit is as about the length of two characters. The above style would fit about 40 characters of text in the h1 heading.

One of the great advantages of relative units like the em unit is that they can make your page **scalable**, allowing the page to be rendered the same way no matter what font size is used by the browser. For example, one user with a large monitor might have body text set to 18 points, while another user with a smaller monitor might have body text setto 10 points. Regardless of the size of the monitor, your heading text should be about 50% larger than the body text. Setting the font size of h1 headings to 1.5 em ensures that they are sized appropriately.

Another relative unit is the percentage. Like the em unit, percentages have one meaning when used for font sizes and another meaning when used to size other objects. When used for font sizes, the percentages are based on the font size of the parent element. The style

```
h1 {font-size: 200%}
```

sets the font size of h1 headings to be 200% or twice that of body text. When used to set the size of other objects, the percentage refers to the width of the parent element. So the style

```
h1 {width: 50%}
```

sets the width of the h1 heading to be 50% or half that of the body text. You'll learn more about the width style later in this tutorial.

The final unit of measurement used in Web pages is the pixel, which represents a single dot on the output device.

Be aware that the exact size of a pixel depends on the output device. Different devices have different resolutions, which are typically expressed in terms of dots per inch or dpi. For example, a 600 dpi printer has six times more pixels per inch than a typical computer monitor.

Finally, you can express font sizes using seven descriptive keywords: xx-small, x-small, small, medium, large, x-large, or xx-large. Each browser is configured to display text at a particular size for each of these keywords, but the exact size is determined by the browser's internal style sheet. You can also use the relative keywords larger and smaller to make a font one size larger or smaller than the surrounding text. For example, the following set of styles causes the body text to be displayed in a small font, while h2 text is displayed in a font one size larger (medium in this case):

```
body {font-size: small}
h2 {font-size: larger}
```

Tammy suggests that you make the h2 headings twice the size of body text. You'll add this style to the external style sheet because you want to eventually apply it to her entire Web site.

To set the font size of h2 headings in Tammy's external style sheet:

1. Return to the **farm.css** file in your text editor.
2. Directly below the style for the body element, insert the following style, as shown in Figure 3-20:

   ```
   h2 {font-size: 2em}
   ```

Figure 3-20 Setting the font size of h2 headings

```
body    {background-color: white; font-family: Arial, Helvetica, sans-serif}
h2      {font-size: 2em}
address {text-align: center}
```

h2 headings will be twice the size of body text

3. Save your changes to the file and then reload the **home.htm** file in your Web browser. Verify that the font size used for the h2 heading at the top of the page is larger than before.

InSight | The 62.5% Hack

Web designers often have to work in both the em and pixel units of measure. Trying to translate between the two measuring units can be a challenge. One popular approach to defining sizes on a Web page is the so-called 62.5% hack. The idea, introduced by Richard Rutter in his Web design blog called Clagnut, is to define the default font size of the body text in a Web page as 62.5% of the width of the Web page using the following style:

```
body {font-size: 62.5%}
```

The reasoning behind the 62.5% hack is that most Web browsers display body text in a medium font, with the text at a height of 16 pixels. Taking 62.5% of this value assigns the value of 1 em to 10 pixels for body text. With these numbers, you can easily translate between the em unit and the pixel unit. The width of an element can be set to either 100 pixels or its equivalent of 10 em.

You have to be careful when using the 62.5% hack because the value of the em unit depends on its context in the document. As you nest one element within another, the em unit is expressed relative to the font size of the parent element. Several sites on the Web provide em calculators, making it easier for you to track the changing values of the em unit as you drill down through a series of nested elements.

Despite the complication with nesting, the 62.5% hack has become so popular with Web designers that it is considered a standard tool for designing challenging and visually interesting Web pages.

Controlling Spacing and Indentation

Tammy thinks that the text for the Welcome heading looks too crowded. She's wondering if you can spread it out more across the width of the page. She also would like to see more space between the first letter, "W," and the left edge of the green background.

CSS supports styles that allow you to perform some basic typographic tasks, such as kerning and tracking. **Kerning** refers to the amount of space between characters, while **tracking** refers to the amount of space between words. The styles to control an element's kerning and tracking are

```
letter-spacing: value
word-spacing: value
```

where *value* is the size of space between individual letters or words. You specify these sizes with the same units that you use for font sizing. As with font sizes, the default unit of length for kerning and tracking is the pixel (px). The default value for both kerning and tracking is 0 pixels. A positive value increases the letter and word spacing. A negative value reduces the space between letters and words. If you choose to make your pages scalable for a variety of devices and resolutions, you will want to express kerning and tracking values as percentages or in em units.

To see how modifying these values can affect the appearance of your text, return to the CSS styles demo page.

To use the demo to explore kerning and tracking styles:

1. Return to the **css_demo.htm** file in your Web browser.
2. Enter **2** in the font-size input box, and then select **em** from the corresponding unit drop-down list.
3. Select **center** from the text-align list box.

4. Enter **0.3** in the letter-spacing input box and **em** from the corresponding drop-down list. Press the **Tab** key.

5. Enter **0.8** in the word-spacing input box and **em** from the corresponding drop-down list. Press the **Tab** key. Figure 3-21 shows the revised appearance of the text after applying the letter-spacing and word-spacing styles.

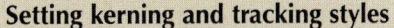

Figure 3-21 **Setting kerning and tracking styles**

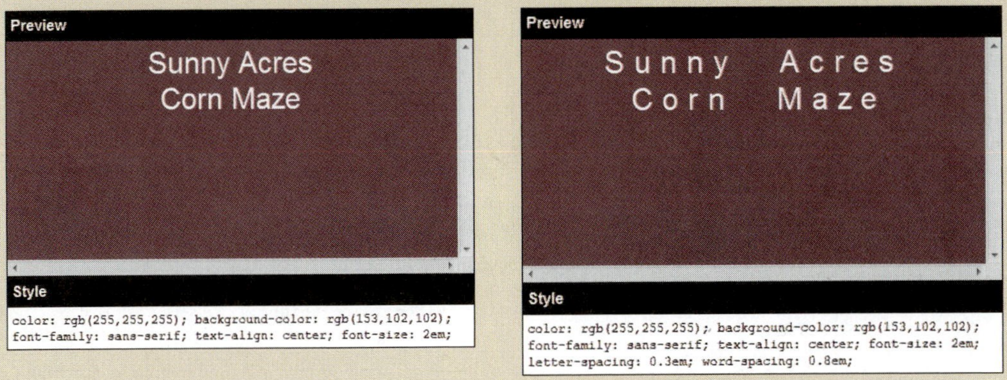

default kerning and tracking | kerning set to 0.3 em, tracking set to 0.8 em

Another typographic feature that you can set is **leading**, which is the space between lines of text. The style to set the leading for the text within an element is

```
line-height: length
```

where *length* is a specific length or a percentage of the font size of the text on those lines. If no unit is specified, most browsers interpret the number to represent the ratio of the line height to the font size. The standard ratio is 1.2:1, which means that the line height is usually 1.2 times the font size. On the other hand, the style

```
p {line-height: 2}
```

makes all paragraphs double-spaced. A common technique is to create multiline titles with large fonts and small line heights in order to give title text more impact. Use the demo page to see how this works.

To use the demo to explore leading styles:

1. Enter **0.75** in the line-height input box, and then select **em** from the corresponding unit drop-down list.

2. Press the **Tab** key to apply the line-height style. Figure 3-22 shows the revised appearance of the text.

Figure 3-22 **Setting the line-height style**

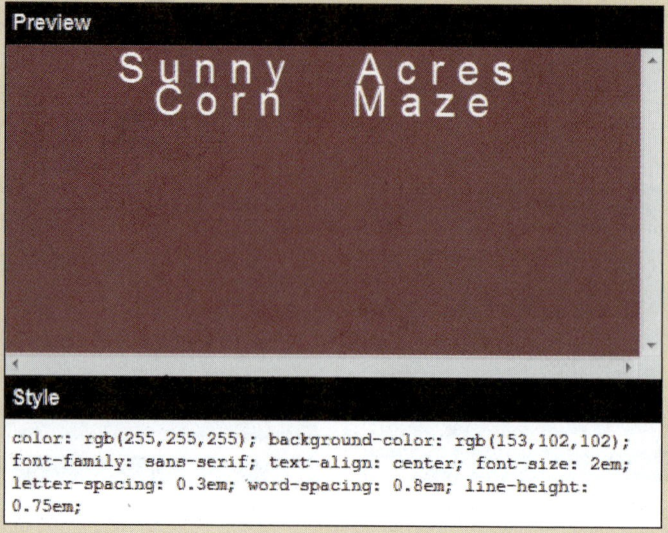

line height set to 0.75 em

An additional way to control text spacing is to set the indentation for the first line of a block of text. The style is

```
text-indent: value
```

where *value* is a length expressed in absolute or relative units or as a percentage of the width of the text block. For example, an indentation value of 5% indents the first line by 5% of the width of the block. The indentation value can also be negative, extending the first line to the left of the text block to create a **hanging indent**.

Reference Window | Setting the Font Face and Sizes

- To define the font face, use the style property
  `font-family: fonts`
  where *fonts* is a comma-separated list of fonts that the browser can use with the element. List specific fonts first and complete the list with a generic font.
- To set the font size, use
  `font-size: length`
  where *length* is a CSS unit of length in either relative or absolute units.
- To set the kerning (the space between letters), use
  `letter-spacing: length`
- To set the tracking (the space between words), use
  `word-spacing: length`

Now you can use what you've learned about spacing to make the changes that Tammy has suggested. To make her heading text more spread out, you'll set the kerning of the h2 elements to 0.4 em. You'll also set the indentation to 1 em, moving the text of all h2 headings to the left.

To change the spacing of the h2 headings in Tammy's external style sheet:

1. Return to the **farm.css** style sheet in your text editor.
2. Add the following attributes to the h2 style as shown in Figure 3-23. Be sure to separate each attribute with a semicolon.

```
letter-spacing: 0.4em; text-indent: 1em
```

Figure 3-23 Applying the letter-spacing and text-indent styles to h2 headings

```
body    {background-color: white; font-family: Arial, Helvetica, sans-serif}
h2      {font-size: 2em; letter-spacing: 0.4em; text-indent: 1em }
address {text-align: center}
```

3. Save your changes to the file and then refresh the Sunny Acres home page in your Web browser. Figure 3-24 shows the revised appearance of the h2 heading on that page.

Figure 3-24 Formatted h2 heading

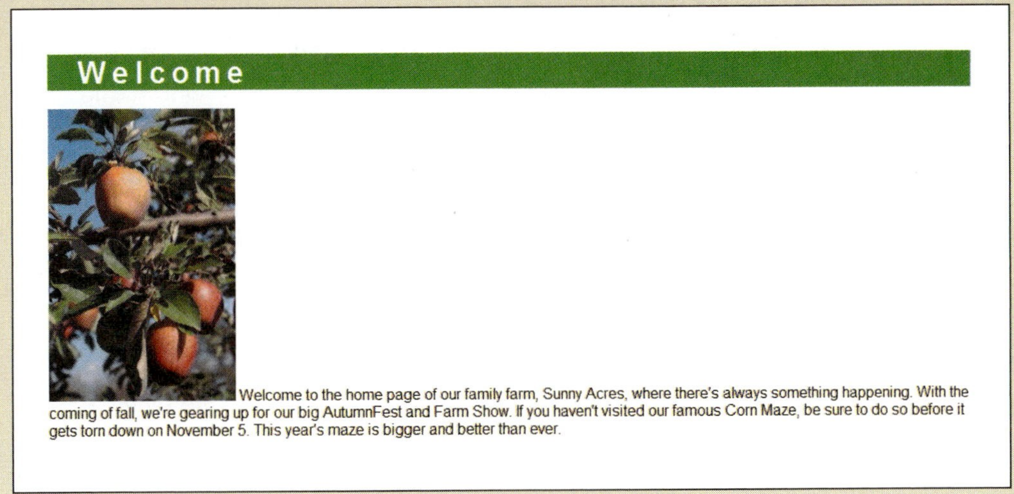
Welcome
Welcome to the home page of our family farm, Sunny Acres, where there's always something happening. With the coming of fall, we're gearing up for our big AutumnFest and Farm Show. If you haven't visited our famous Corn Maze, be sure to do so before it gets torn down on November 5. This year's maze is bigger and better than ever.

By increasing the kerning in the h2 heading, you've made the text appear less crowded, making it easier to read.

Applying Font Features

As you saw in the first tutorial, browsers often apply default font styles to particular types of elements. Text marked with an <address> tag, for example, usually appears in italics. This is handy when you don't have a specific design in mind for your text. However, you can also choose a specific font style, such as italics, bold, underline, and so forth. You can specify font styles using the style

```
font-style: type
```

where *type* is normal, italic, or oblique. The italic and oblique styles are similar in appearance, but might differ subtly depending on the font in use.

You have also seen that browsers render certain elements in heavier fonts. For example, most browsers render headings in a boldfaced font. You can specify the font weight for any page element using the style

```
font-weight: weight
```

where *weight* is the level of bold formatting applied to the text. You express weights as values ranging from 100 to 900, in increments of 100. In practice, however, most browsers cannot render nine different font weights. For practical purposes, you can assume that 400 represents normal (unbolded) text, 700 is bold text, and 900 represents heavy bold text. You can also use the keywords normal or bold in place of a weight value, or you can express the font weight relative to the containing element, using the keywords bolder or lighter.

Another style you can use to change the appearance of your text is

> **Tip**
>
> You can remove underlining from hypertext links by setting the text-decoration style to none.

```
text-decoration: type
```

where *type* is none (for no decoration), underline, overline, line-through, or blink (to create blinking text). You can apply several decorative features to the same element by listing them as part of the text-decoration style. For example, the style

```
text-decoration: underline overline
```

places a line under and over the text in the element. Note that the text-decoration style cannot be applied to nontextual elements, such as inline images.

To control the case of the text within an element, use the style

```
text-transform: type
```

where *type* is capitalize, uppercase, lowercase, or none (to make no changes to the text case). For example, if you want to capitalize the first letter of each word in the element, you could use the style

```
text-transform: capitalize
```

Finally, you can display text in uppercase letters and a small font using the style

```
font-variant: type
```

where *type* is normal (the default) or small caps (small capital letters). Small caps are often used in legal documents, such as software agreements, in which the capital letters indicate the importance of a phrase or point, but the text is made small so as to not detract from other elements in the document.

Setting Font and Text Appearance | Reference Window

- To specify the font style, use
  `font-style: type`
  where *type* is normal, italic, or oblique.
- To specify the font weight, use
  `font-weight: type`
  where *type* is normal, bold, bolder, light, lighter, or a font weight value.
- To specify a text decoration, use
  `text-decoration: type`
  where *type* is none, underline, overline, line-through, or blink.
- To transform the text, use
  `text-transform: type`
  where *type* is capitalize, uppercase, lowercase, or none.
- To display a font variant of the text, use
  `font-variant: type`
  where *type* is normal or small-caps.

To see the impact of these styles, return to the demo page.

To use the demo to view the various font styles:

1. Return to the **CSS demo page** in your Web browser.
2. Select **bold** from the font-weight list box.
3. Select **small-caps** from the font-variant list box. Figure 3-25 shows the impact of applying the font-weight and font-variant styles.

Figure 3-25 Applying the font-weight and font-variant styles

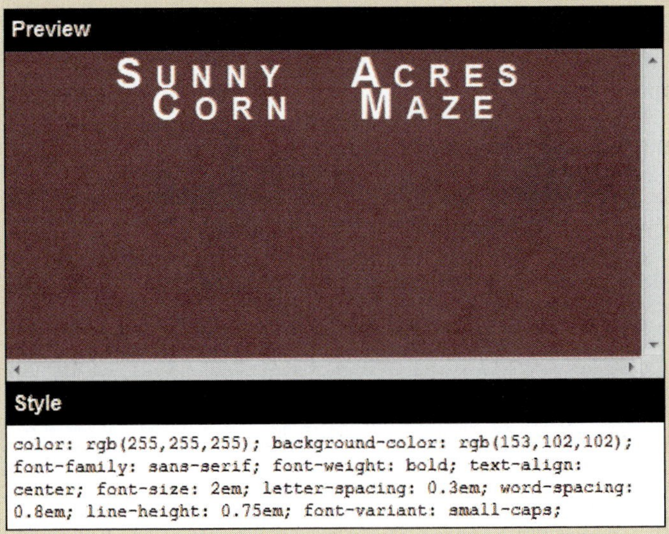

4. You've completed your work with the CSS demo page. You can continue to explore different CSS font and text styles or close the demo Web page now.

Aligning Text Vertically

In Tutorial 1, you learned how to align text horizontally using the text-align style. You can also vertically align inline elements within the content of the surrounding block. The style for setting vertical alignment is

```
vertical-align: type
```

where *type* is one of the keywords described in Figure 3-26.

Figure 3-26 **Values of the vertical-align style**

Value	Description
baseline	Aligns the element with the bottom of lowercase letters in surrounding text (the default)
bottom	Aligns the bottom of the element with the bottom of the lowest element in surrounding content
middle	Aligns the middle of the element with the middle of the surrounding content
sub	Subscripts the element
super	Superscripts the element
text-bottom	Aligns the bottom of the element with the bottom of the font of the surrounding content
text-top	Aligns the top of the element with the top of the font of the surrounding content
top	Aligns the top of the element with the top of the tallest object in the surrounding content

Instead of using keywords, you can specify a length or a percentage for the element to be aligned relative to the surrounding content. A positive value moves the element up and a negative value lowers the element. For example, the style

```
vertical-align: 50%
```

raises the element by half of the line height of the surrounding content, while the style

```
vertical-align: -100%
```

drops the element an entire line height below the baseline of the current line.

Combining All Text Formatting in a Single Style

You've learned a lot of different text and font styles. You can combine most of them into a single declaration, using the style

```
font: font-style font-variant font-weight font-size/line-height
font-family
```

where *font-style* is the font's style, *font-variant* is the font variant, *font-weight* is the weight of the font, *font-size* is the size of the font, *line-height* is the height of each line, and *font-family* is the font face. For example, the style

```
font: italic small-caps bold 16pt/24pt Arial, sans-serif
```

displays the text of the element in italics, bold, and small capital letters in Arial or another sans-serif font, with a font size of 16pt and spacing between the lines of 24pt. You do not have to include all of the properties of the font style; the only required properties are size and font-family. A browser assumes the default value for any omitted property. However, you must place any properties that you do include in the order indicated above.

Tammy thinks that the size of the address text at the bottom of the page is too large, and would like it in a smaller, non-italics, small caps, sans-serif font. You should modify the style for the address element in the farm.css style sheet so that Tammy can apply the style to any page on her Web site.

To change the style of the address element in Tammy's external style sheet:

1. Return to the **farm.css** file in your text editor.
2. Within the style declaration for the address element, add the following style attributes. See Figure 3-27.

```
font: normal small-caps 0.8em sans-serif
```

Applying the font style to the address element — Figure 3-27

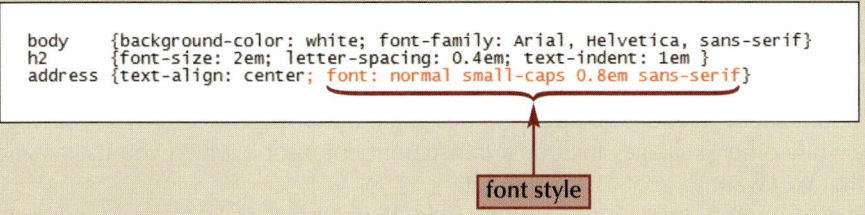

```
body    {background-color: white; font-family: Arial, Helvetica, sans-serif}
h2      {font-size: 2em; letter-spacing: 0.4em; text-indent: 1em }
address {text-align: center; font: normal small-caps 0.8em sans-serif}
```

font style

3. Save your changes to the file.
4. Refresh the **home.htm** file in your Web browser. Scroll to the bottom of the page and verify that the style of the address element has been changed as shown in Figure 3-28.

Formatted address text — Figure 3-28

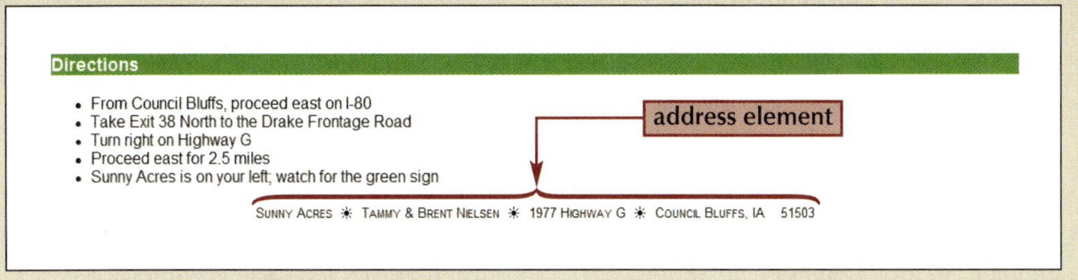
Directions
From Council Bluffs, proceed east on I-80
Take Exit 38 North to the Drake Frontage Road
Turn right on Highway G
Proceed east for 2.5 miles
Sunny Acres is on your left; watch for the green sign
address element
Sunny Acres * Tammy & Brent Nielsen * 1977 Highway G * Council Bluffs, IA 51503

Tammy likes the way the fonts appear on her Web site. She especially likes the fact that because these changes were made in a CSS style sheet, she can apply the styles to any Web page she adds to the site in the future.

Working with Images

Tammy wants you to turn your attention to her Web site's graphic images. Graphic images can greatly increase the size of the Web page so you must balance the goal of creating an interesting and attractive page against the need to keep the size of your page and its supporting files small. Many users will turn away from Web pages that take a long time to load.

Web browsers support three graphic formats: GIF, JPEG, and PNG. Each file format has its advantages and disadvantages, and you will probably use a combination of all three formats in your Web page designs. First, you'll look at the advantages and disadvantages of using GIF image files.

Working with GIF Images

GIF (**Graphics Interchange Format**) is a common image format first developed for the CompuServe online information service. GIF files are limited to 256 colors, so they are most often used for graphics requiring fewer colors, such as clip art images, line art, logos, and icons. Images that require more color depth, such as photographs, can appear grainy when saved as GIF files. GIF image files can be large. One way to reduce the size of a GIF is to reduce the number of colors in its color palette. For example, if an image contains only 32 different colors, you can use an image editing program to reduce the palette to those 32 colors, resulting in a smaller image file that loads faster.

Another feature of GIFs is their ability to use transparent colors. A **transparent color** is a color that is not displayed when the image is viewed in an application. In place of the transparent color, a browser displays whatever is on the page background. The process by which you create a transparent color depends on the graphics software you are using. Many applications include the option to designate a transparent color when saving an image, while other packages include a transparent color tool, which you use to select the color that you want to treat as transparent.

GIFs also support animation. An **animated GIF** is composed of several images that are displayed one after the other, creating the illusion of motion. There are many online collections of animated GIFs on the Web. You can also create your own with animated GIF software, which allows you to control the rate at which an animation plays (as measured by frames per second) and to determine the number of times the animation repeats before stopping (or to set it to repeat without stopping).

Animated GIFs are a mixed blessing. They make a Web page appear more dynamic, but they are larger than static GIF files, so using them can slow down the loading of a Web page. Also, as with all formatting features, you should be careful not to overuse animated images. Animated GIFs can quickly irritate users once the novelty wears off, especially because there is no way for users to turn them off! Finally, keep in mind that like static GIF files, animated GIFs are limited to 256 colors.

One of the pages Tammy is planning for the Sunny Acres Web site is the index.htm file, which acts as a splash screen. A **splash screen** is a Web page containing interesting animation or graphics that introduces a Web site. Tammy suggests that you use an animated GIF for her splash screen. You've located a fun animated GIF of a scarecrow and another GIF that contains the Sunny Acres logo. You'll add both of these graphics as inline images to the index.htm file.

To insert GIF files into the splash screen page:

1. Open the **index.htm** file in your text editor.
2. Within the div element, insert the following inline image for the Sunny Acres logo:

```
<img src="salogo.gif" alt="Sunny Acres" /><br />
```

3. Tammy wants the animated GIF to also function as a hypertext link, pointing to the home.htm file. As shown in Figure 3-29, insert the following linked graphic directly below the Sunny Acres logo:

```
<a href="home.htm">
 <img src="scarecrow.gif" alt="animated GIF"
      style="border-width: 0" />
</a>
```

Inserting GIF images **Figure 3-29**

```
<body>
   <div style="text-align: center">
      <img src="salogo.gif" alt="Sunny Acres" /><br />
      <a href="home.htm"><img src="scarecrow.gif" alt="animated GIF" style="border-width: 0" /></a>
   </div>
</body>
```

4. Save your changes to the file and then open the **index.htm** file in your Web browser. As shown in Figure 3-30, an animated scarecrow appears on the Web page directly below the Sunny Acres logo.

Sunny Acres splash screen **Figure 3-30**

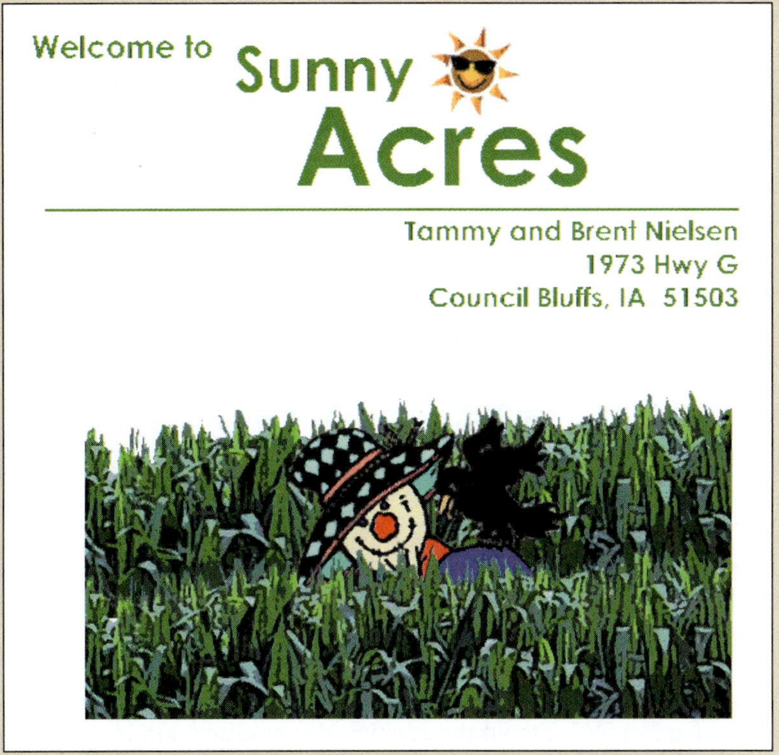

JPEG Images

The other main image file format for Web pages is JPEG. **JPEG** stands for **Joint Photographic Experts Group**. JPEGs differ from GIFs in several ways. In the JPEG format, you can create images that use all 16.7 million colors available in the color palette. Because of this, JPEG files are most often used for photographs and other images that cover a wide spectrum of color. In addition, despite the fact that JPEGs use the full color palette, the image compression algorithm used by JPEG files yields image files that are usually (though not always) smaller than their GIF counterparts. (Note that in some situations, though, the GIF format creates a smaller and better-looking image—for example, when an image contains large sections covered with a single color.) You can set the amount of compression applied to JPEGs in your imaging editing software, allowing you to balance the desire for a high-quality image versus the need to keep images compact.

As a general rule, you should use JPEGs for photos and use GIFs for illustrations that involve only a few colors. All of the photos on the Sunny Acres Web site are in JPEG format. Note that JPEGs do not support animation or transparent colors.

PNG Images

A third graphic format gaining wider acceptance is the **Portable Network Graphics** or **PNG** format. PNG files include most of the same features as GIFs (including animation and transparency) but also provide file compression and the full 16.7 million colors available with JPEGs. You can also designate several transparent colors in a PNG file, rather than the single color that GIFs support. The only problem with the PNG format is that older browsers do not support it. This is becoming less of a problem as time goes by. Figure 3-31 summarizes the features of the three major graphics formats on the Web.

Figure 3-31 **Comparison of Web graphic formats**

Feature	GIF	JPEG	PNG
Color resolution	256	16.7 million	16.7 million
Useful for line art	Yes	No	Yes
Useful for photographs	No	Yes	Yes
Interlacing/progressive encoding	Yes	Yes	Yes
Compressible	Yes	Yes	Yes
Transparent colors	Yes (1)	No	Yes (multiple)
Supported by older browsers	Yes	Yes	No

InSight | **Other Image Formats**

The GIF, JPEG, and PNG formats are not the only ways to add graphic images and animation to your Web site. The World Wide Web Consortium (W3C) promotes the **Scalable Vector Graphics** (**SVG**) specification, which is a graphic format written with XML that you can use to create line art composed of straight lines and curves. SVG also supports animation, and it can be used with programmable scripts that control the behavior and appearance of the animation. Because SVG files are written in XML, they are transferred as simple text files, allowing the application to interpret the SVG commands and render the graphic. Most browsers do not support SVG without the addition of specialized add-in programs.

Another popular approach is to use the Flash software program from Macromedia. You can use Flash to create interactive animations, scalable graphics, animated logos, and navigation controls for a Web site. To view a Flash animation, users must have the Flash player installed on their computers. Users can download and install the player for free, and are generally prompted to do this the first time they open a Web page that uses Flash. Flash players are available for all browsers and operating systems, so Flash is a safe and well supported method of creating animated effects and specialized graphics.

Setting the Image Size

By default, browsers display an image at its saved size. You can specify a different size by adding the HTML attributes

```
width="value" height="value"
```

to the <img /> tag, where the width and height values represent the dimensions of the image in pixels.

Changing an image's dimensions within the browser does not affect the file size. If you want to decrease the file size of an image, you should do so using an image editing application so that the image's file size is reduced in addition to its dimensions. Because of the way that browsers work with inline images, it is a good idea to specify the height and width of an image even if you're not trying to change its dimensions. When a browser encounters an inline image, it calculates the image size and then uses this information to lay out the page. If you include the dimensions of the image, the browser does not have to perform that calculation, reducing the time required to render the page. You can obtain the height and width of an image as measured in pixels using an image editing application such as Adobe Photoshop, or by viewing the properties of the graphic file in your computer's operating system.

Tip

You can also set the image dimensions using the CSS width and height styles.

The salogo.gif image is 599 pixels wide by 223 pixels high. The animated scarecrow graphic is 500 pixels wide by 300 pixels high. You decide to specify these dimensions in the HTML code of the index.htm file so that browsers won't have to calculate the images' dimensions when loading the page.

To set the dimensions for Tammy's splash screen images:

1. Return to the **index.htm** file in your text editor.
2. Within the <img> tag for the Sunny Acres logo, add the following attributes:

   ```
   width="599" height="223"
   ```

3. Within the <img> tag for the animated scarecrow graphic, add the following attributes:

   ```
   width="500" height="300"
   ```

   Place the attributes on a new line to make your HTML code easier to read. Figure 3-32 shows the revised code for the index.htm file.

Figure 3-32 Specifying image width and height

```
<body>
   <div style="text-align: center">
      <img src="salogo.gif" alt="Sunny Acres" width="599" height="223" /><br />
      <a href="home.htm"><img src="scarecrow.gif" alt="animated GIF"
                             width="500" height="300" style="border-width: 0" /></a>
   </div>
</body>
```

Formatting Backgrounds

Tammy has one more suggestion for the splash screen page. She would like you to change the background from its plain white color to the image shown in Figure 3-33.

Figure 3-33 Tammy's proposed background image

You can add a background image to any element. The style to apply a background image to an element is

```
background-image: url(url)
```

where (*url*) defines the name and location of the image file. When a browser loads the background image, it repeats the image in both the vertical and the horizontal directions until the background of the entire element is filled. This process is known as **tiling** because of its similarity to the process of filling up a floor or other surface with tiles. Let's see how Tammy's image looks in the splash screen page by adding it as a background for the entire page body. The image is saved as background.jpg.

To add a background image to the body element of Tammy's splash screen:

1. Within the opening <body> tag, insert the following style attribute, as shown in Figure 3-34:

```
style="background-image: url(background.jpg)"
```

Figure 3-34 Setting the background image for the page body

```
<body style="background-image: url(background.jpg)">
   <div style="text-align: center">
      <img src="salogo.gif" alt="Sunny Acres" width="599" height="223" /><br />
      <a href="home.htm"><img src="scarecrow.gif" alt="animated GIF"
                         width="500" height="300" style="border-width: 0" /></a>
   </div>
</body>
```

2. Close the file, saving your changes.

3. Reload the **index.htm** file in your Web browser. Verify that the Web page has the tiled background image shown in Figure 3-35.

Figure 3-35 Final splash screen page

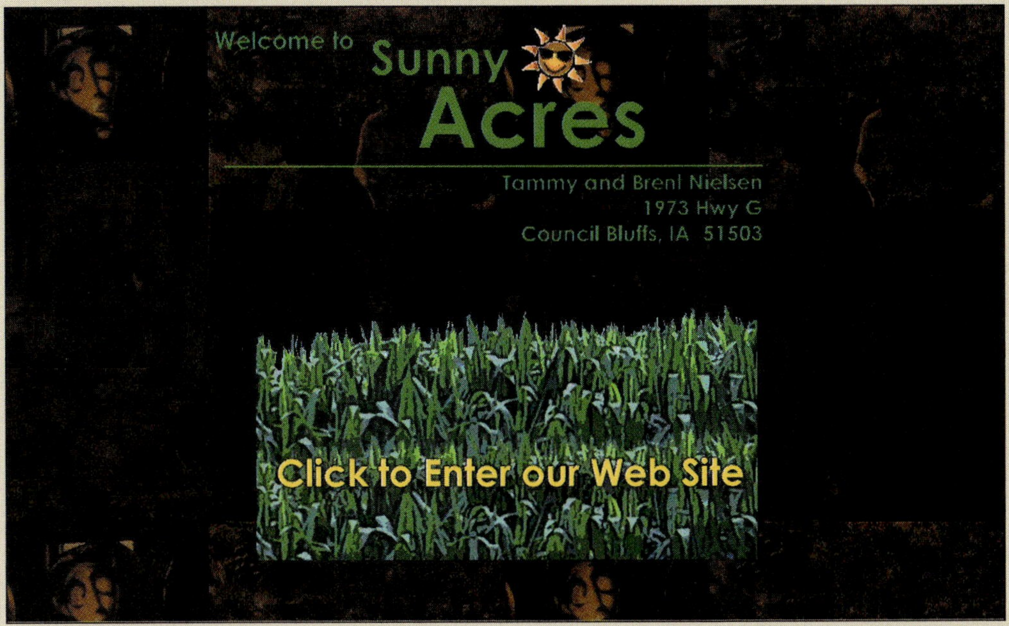

Tip

When using splash screens, include a meta element that automatically redirects the user to the site's home page after a few seconds have passed.

Note that both of the GIF images on this page employ a transparent color. This allows you to see the tiled background image behind the logo and the animated scarecrow graphic.

4. If you want to take a break before starting the next session, close any open files or applications now.

Background Image Options

By default, background images are tiled both horizontally and vertically until the entire background of the element is filled up. You can specify the direction of the tiling using the style

```
background-repeat: type
```

where *type* is repeat (the default), repeat-x, repeat-y, or no-repeat. Figure 3-36 describes each of the repeat types and Figure 3-37 shows examples of the style values.

Figure 3-36 Values of the background-repeat style

Value	Description
repeat	The image is tiled both horizontally and vertically until the entire background of the element is covered
repeat-x	The image is tiled only horizontally across the width of the element
repeat-y	The image is tiled only vertically across the height of the element
no-repeat	The image is not repeated at all

Figure 3-37 Tiling the background image

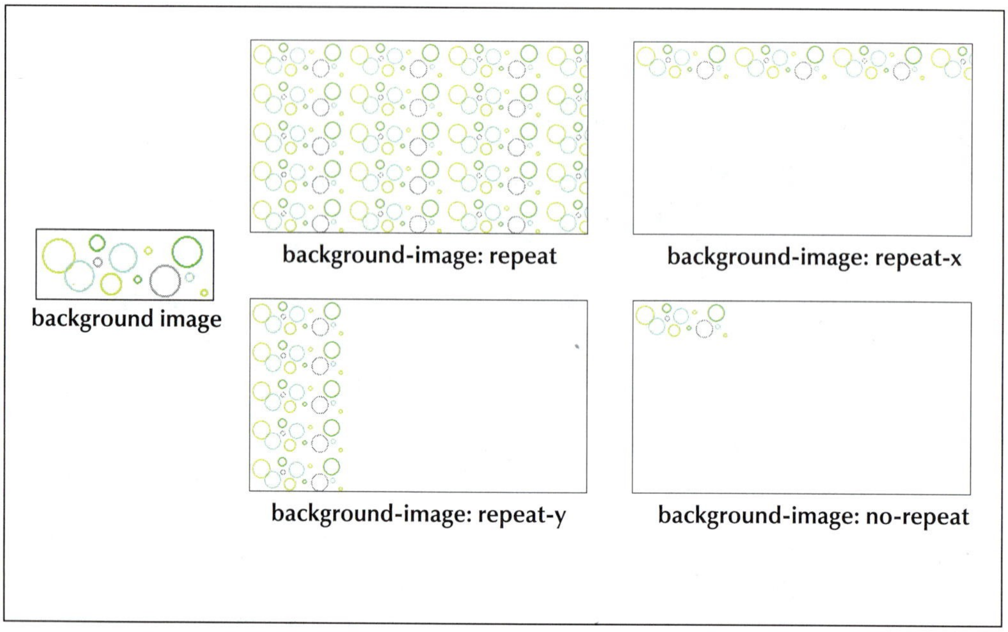

Browsers initially place a background image in an element's upper-left corner; and then if the code specifies tiling, the image is repeated from there. You can change the initial position of a background image using the style

```
background-position: horizontal vertical
```

where *horizontal* is the horizontal position of the image and *vertical* is its vertical position. You can specify a position as the distance from the top-left corner of the element, as a percentage of the element's width or height, or with a keyword. Keyword options are top, center, or bottom for vertical position, and left, center, or right for horizontal placement. For example, the style

```
background-position: 10% 20%
```

specifies an initial position for the background image 10% to the right and 20% down from the upper-left corner of the element. The style

```
background-position: right bottom
```

places the background image at the lower-right corner of the element. If you include only one position value, the browser applies that value to the horizontal position and vertically centers the image. So the style

```
background-position: 30px
```

places the background image 30 pixels to the right of the element's left border and centers it vertically.

By default, a background image moves along with its element as a user scrolls through a page. You can change this using the style

```
background-attachment: type
```

where *type* is either scroll or fixed. Scroll (the default) scrolls the image along with the element, while fixed places the image in a fixed place in the browser's display window, preventing it from moving even if the user scrolls down through the Web page. Fixed background images are often used to create the effect of a watermark, which is a translucent graphic impressed into the very fabric of paper, often found on specialized stationery.

The Background Style

Like the font style discussed in earlier in this session, you can combine the various background styles into the following single style

```
background: color url(url) repeat attachment horizontal vertical
```

where *color*, (*url*), *repeat*, *attachment*, *horizontal*, and *vertical* are the values for the background style attributes that set the background color and control the placement and tiling of a background image. For example, the style

```
background: yellow url(logo.gif) no-repeat fixed center center
```

creates a yellow background on which the image file logo.gif is displayed. The image file is not tiled across the background, but is instead fixed in the horizontal and vertical center. You do not have to enter all of the values of the background style. However, those values that you do specify should follow the order indicated by the syntax to avoid unpredictable results.

Setting the Background Style | Reference Window

- To set the background style of an element, use
  `background color url(url) repeat attachment horizontal vertical`
  where *color* is a color name or a color value, (*url*) is the URL of the background image file, *repeat* specifies how the background image is tiled across the background (repeat, repeat-x, repeat-y, or no-repeat), *attachment* specifies whether the image scrolls with the Web page (scroll or fixed), and *horizontal* and *vertical* specify the initial position of the tiled background image.

You've completed your work with styles for the text and graphic images on the Sunny Acres Web site. You still have work to do to make the page layout interesting and attractive. In the next session you'll work with styles for block-level elements and lists.

Session 3.2 Quick Check | Review

1. Specify the style declaration to display all code elements in the Courier New font; and if that font is unavailable, use a monospace font.
2. If the font size of blockquote element text is set to 12 points, what will be the size of h2 headings nested within a blockquote if the following style declaration is applied to the Web page?

```
h2 {font-size: 1.5em}
```

3. Specify the style declaration to display all h3 headings with both an overline and an underline.
4. Specify the style declaration to set the kerning of address text to 0.5 em and tracking to 0.9 em.
5. Specify the style declaration to display the text of all definition term elements in uppercase letters.
6. Which graphic image format should you use for photographic images—GIF or JPEG—and why?
7. What attributes do you add to the <img /> tag to set the size of the image to 200 pixels wide by 100 pixels high?
8. Specify the style to use the image file mark.jpg as the background image for all blockquote elements. Fix the image at the top left of the block quote with no tiling.

Session 3.3

Floating an Element

Tammy wants you to return to work on her home page. She notices that the inline image below the Welcome heading forces a large space between the heading and the following paragraph (see Figure 3-24 from the last session). She would like the image placed alongside the right margin and the paragraph text to wrap around it. You can do this by floating the inline image.

Floating an element like an inline image causes the element to move out of the normal document flow on the page, moving to a position along the left or right margins of the parent element. The other elements on the Web page that are not floated are then moved up to occupy the position previously occupied by the floating element. Figure 3-38 shows a diagram of an element that is floated along the right margin of the page body.

Figure 3-38 **Floating an element**

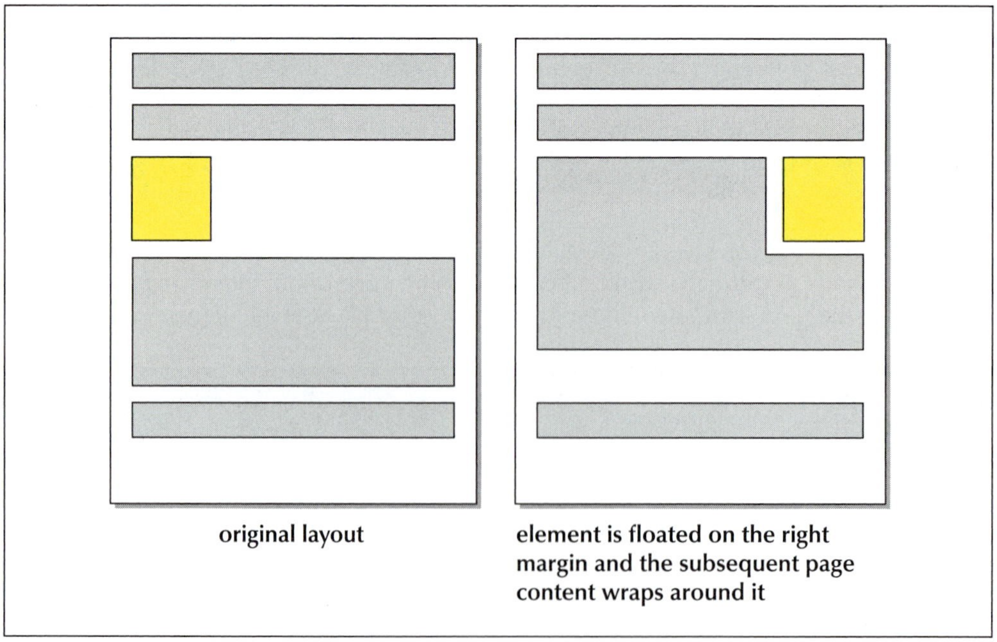

To float an element, apply the style

```
float: position
```

where *position* is none (the default to turn off floating), left, or right. Most page elements can be floated. You can also stack floating elements to create a column effect in your page layout, as in Figure 3-39.

Figure 3-39 Floating multiple elements to create columns

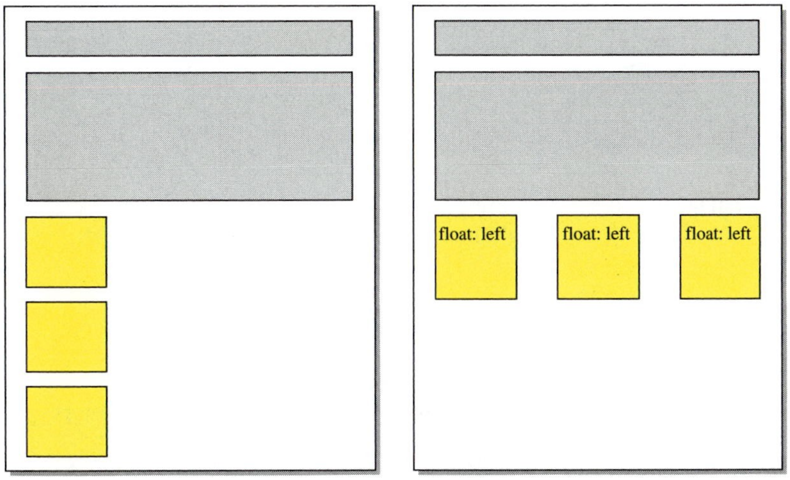

original layout

each element is floated on the left margin, causing the elements to stack up, mimicking three columns

Sometimes you will want to prevent an object from wrapping around a floating element. For example, you might not want headings to wrap around inline images. To prevent an element from wrapping, apply the clear style

```
clear: position
```

where *position* is none (the default), left, right, or both. For example, the style declaration

```
clear: right
```

causes the element not to be displayed until the right margin of the parent element is clear of floating objects. See Figure 3-40.

Figure 3-40 Using the clear style

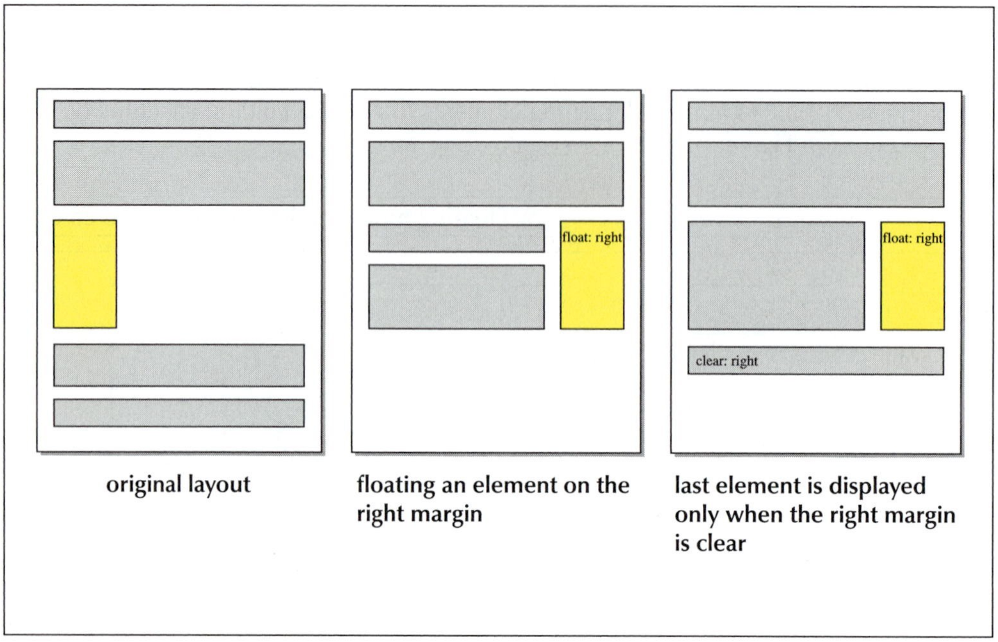

Reference Window | Floating an Element

- To float an element, use the style
  `float: position`
  where *position* is none (to turn off floating), left or right.
- To display an element clear of a floating element, use the style
  `clear: position`
  where *position* is none, left, right, or both.

Tammy wants you to use what you've learned about the floating style to float the inline image from the home page on the right margin of the paragraph that contains it. You could add the float style as an inline style directly to the <img> tag for the image, but Tammy has similar promotional photos on several of the pages from her Web site. She has given each promotional photo the id promoimage. Recall from the first session that you can create style declarations for elements based on their id values. This means you can use the farm.css style sheet to float all of these images with the following style declaration:

```
#promoimage {float: right}
```

Tammy wants you to add this style to the farm.css style sheet.

To float the promotional images on the Sunny Acres Web site:

1. Return to the **farm.css** style sheet in your text editor.
2. At the bottom of the file, add the following style as shown in Figure 3-41:

```
#promoimage {float: right}
```

Figure 3-41 Applying the float style

```
body    {background-color: white; font-family: Arial, Helvetica, sans-serif}
h2      {font-size: 2em; letter-spacing: 0.4em; text-indent: 1em }
address {text-align: center; font: normal small-caps 0.8em sans-serif}

#promoimage {float: right}
```

id of promotional images (points to `#promoimage`)

float the image on the right margin (points to `{float: right}`)

Tip

The float style floats the object on the margin of the parent element, not necessarily the margin of the Web page.

3. Save your changes to the file.
4. Refresh the **home.htm** file in your Web browser. As shown in Figure 3-42, the promotional inline image is now floated on the right margin of the first paragraph. The subsequent page content flows around the image.

Figure 3-42 Floating the image on the paragraph's right margin

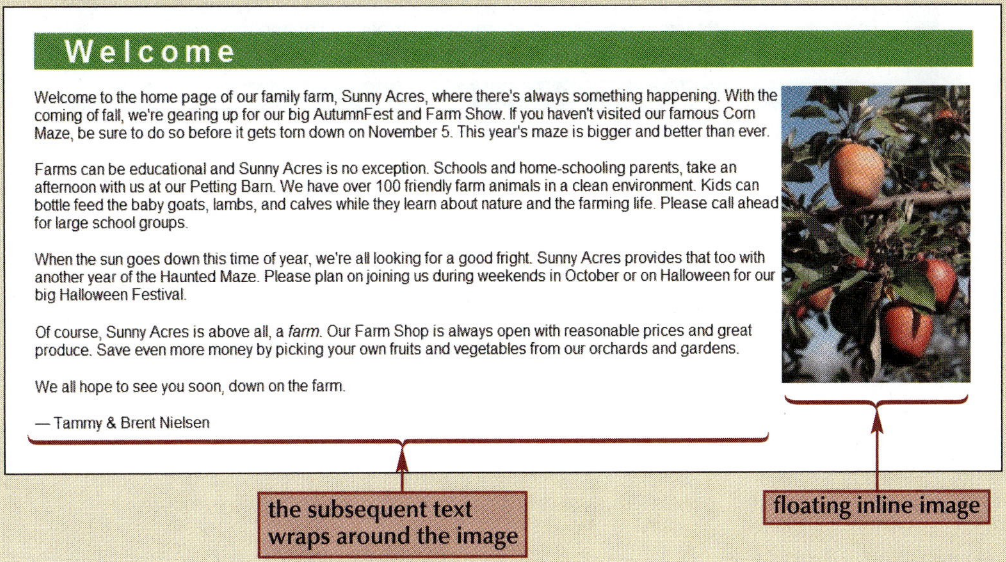
Welcome
Welcome to the home page of our family farm, Sunny Acres, where there's always something happening. With the coming of fall, we're gearing up for our big AutumnFest and Farm Show. If you haven't visited our famous Corn Maze, be sure to do so before it gets torn down on November 5. This year's maze is bigger and better than ever.
Farms can be educational and Sunny Acres is no exception. Schools and home-schooling parents, take an afternoon with us at our Petting Barn. We have over 100 friendly farm animals in a clean environment. Kids can bottle feed the baby goats, lambs, and calves while they learn about nature and the farming life. Please call ahead for large school groups.
When the sun goes down this time of year, we're all looking for a good fright. Sunny Acres provides that too with another year of the Haunted Maze. Please plan on joining us during weekends in October or on Halloween for our big Halloween Festival.
Of course, Sunny Acres is above all, a farm. Our Farm Shop is always open with reasonable prices and great produce. Save even more money by picking your own fruits and vegetables from our orchards and gardens.
We all hope to see you soon, down on the farm.
— Tammy & Brent Nielsen
the subsequent text wraps around the image
floating inline image

In older HTML code, you might see inline images floated using the align attribute. The general syntax of the align attribute is

```
<img align="position" ... />
```

where *position* is left or right. Note that the align attribute has been deprecated and is not supported in strict applications of XHTML.

Working with the Box Model

Floating the promotional image improved the appearance of the page. Tammy wants you to work with the size and placement of other elements on the page such as the heading and address elements. She wants a page layout that is easy to read and attractive to the eye.

A study of the technique of Web page layout starts with an appreciation of the CSS box model. The **box model** describes the structure of page elements as they are laid out on the Web page. In the box model, each element is composed of the four sections shown in Figure 3-43:

- the **margin** between the element and other page content
- the **border** of the box containing the element content
- the **padding** between the element's content and the box border
- the **content** of the element itself

Figure 3-43 **The box model**

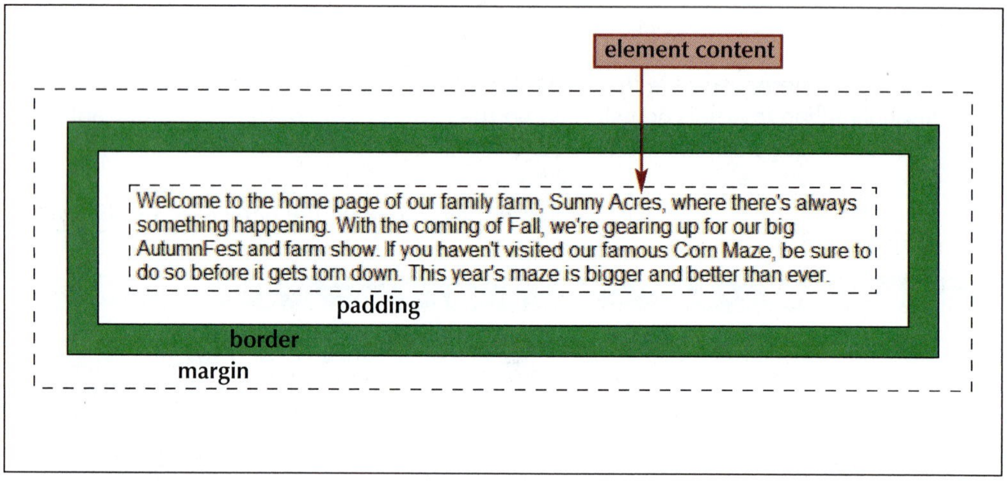
element content
Welcome to the home page of our family farm, Sunny Acres, where there's always something happening. With the coming of Fall, we're gearing up for our big AutumnFest and farm show. If you haven't visited our famous Corn Maze, be sure to do so before it gets torn down. This year's maze is bigger and better than ever.
padding
border
margin

The size and appearance of these four sections determine how the element is displayed by the browser and play an important role in determining the layout of the elements on the Web page. Start exploring the box model by examining how to set the margins around an element.

Margin Styles

CSS supports several styles to set the element margin. The following four styles

```
margin-top: length
margin-right: length
margin-bottom: length
margin-left: length
```

set the sizes of the top, right, bottom, and left margins. Here *length* is a length expressed in one of the CSS units of measure discussed in the last session. You can also use the keyword auto, which leaves it to the browser to determine the margin size. The style declaration

```
h1 {margin-top: 10px; margin-right: 20px; margin-bottom: 10px;
    margin-left: 20px}
```

creates margins of 10 pixels above and below the h1 heading and margins of 20 pixels to the left and right of the heading.

These four margin styles can be combined into the single style

```
margin: top right bottom left
```

where *top, right, bottom,* and *left* are the sizes of the top, right, bottom, and left margins. (To help remember this order, think of moving clockwise around the element, starting with the top margin.) The style

```
h1 {margin: 10px 20px 10px 20px}
```

applies an identical set of margins to the longer style described above.

You don't have to supply values for all of the margins. If you specify only three values, they are applied to the top, right, and bottom margins. If you specify only two values, they're applied to the top and bottom margins. If you specify only a single value, a browser applies that value to all four margins. So the style

Tip

You can overlap page elements by specifying negative values for the margins.

```
h1 {margin: 10px 20px}
```

applies a 10-pixel margin above and below the h1 heading and a 20-pixel margin to the left and right. The style

```
h1 {margin: 10px}
```

creates a 10-pixel margin around the entire heading.

One of the changes that Tammy suggested is to add more space between the promotional image and the surrounding text. She thinks that the text is too tight around the image and suggests that you set a 1-em margin below and to the left of the image. The top margin and the right margin can be set to 0 em units. Remember that you are making these changes to the CSS style sheet so that Tammy can apply them to any image she marks with the promotional id.

To set the margins around the promotional image in Tammy's external style sheet:

1. Return to the **farm.css** style sheet in your text editor.
2. Add the following margin style to the style declaration for the promotional image, as shown in Figure 3-44:

   `margin: 0em 0em 1em 1em`

Figure 3-44 Setting margins around the promotional images

```
body    {background-color: white; font-family: Arial, Helvetica, sans-serif}
h2      {font-size: 2em; letter-spacing: 0.4em; text-indent: 1em }
address {text-align: center; font: normal small-caps 0.8em sans-serif}

#promoimage {float: right; margin: 0em 0em 1em 1em}
```

3. Save your changes to the file.
4. Reload the **home.htm** file in your Web browser. Verify that the margin to the left and below the promotional image has been increased slightly.

The margin styles can also be applied to the body element. By setting the margin around the page body to 0, you can remove the extra space many browsers insert by default between the page content and the edge of the browser window.

Padding Styles

The styles for the size of the padding in the box model are similar to the margin styles. The following four styles set the size of the padding above, to the right, below, and to the left of the element content:

```
padding-top: length
padding-right: length
padding-bottom: length
padding-left: length
```

You can also combine these four styles in a single padding style

```
padding: top right bottom left
```

where *top*, *right*, *bottom*, and *left* are the padding sizes around the element content. As with the margin style, you can specify any or all of the four padding values. When you specify a single value, it is applied to all four padding values. The style

```
h1 {padding: 5px}
```

sets the padding space around the h1 heading content to 5 pixels in each direction. By default, elements have no padding. The space between elements such as between adjacent paragraphs is set by the margins alone.

Reference Window | Setting Margin and Padding Space in the Box Model

- To set the margin space around an element, use
  `margin: length`
  where *length* is the size of the margin using one of the CSS units of measure.
- To set the padding space within an element, use
  `padding: length`
- To set a margin or padding for one side of the box model only, specify the direction (top, right, bottom, or left). For example, use
  `margin-right: length`
  to set the length of the right margin.

Border Styles

CSS supports three types of styles for the box model border. You can set the border width, the border color, or the border style. As with the margin and padding styles, there are styles that affect the top, right, bottom, and left borders or all borders at once. To define the width of the border, use

```
border-top-width: length
border-right-width: length
border-bottom-width: length
border-left-width: length
```

or the following single border-width style for setting the width for any or all of the borders:

```
border-width: top right bottom left
```

You've already worked with the border-width style in Tutorial 2, where you used it to remove the border around a linked image. The style

```
img {border-width: 0px}
```

could be used to remove the borders around all of the inline images on the Web page or Web site. Border widths can also be expressed using the keywords thin, medium, or thick. The exact meaning of these sizes depends on the browser.

The next set of styles set the color of the border (if one exists) around an element. These styles are

```
border-top-color: color
border-right-color: color
border-bottom-color: color
border-left-color: color
border-color: top right bottom left
```

where *color* is a color name, color value, or the keyword transparent to create an invisible border. For example, the following style adds a 4-pixel red border directly above the address element:

```
address {border-top-width: 4px; border-top-color: red}
```

If you don't specify a color, the browser uses the text color of the element within the box.

The final border style defines the border design. The five border styles are

```
border-top-style: type
border-right-style: type
border-bottom-style: type
border-left-style: type
border-style: top right bottom left
```

where *type* is one of the nine border style displayed in Figure 3-45.

Tip

You can create the illusion of a drop shadow by adding borders of different thicknesses around the element. Try border styles such as `border-width: 1px 4px 4px 1px` to create this effect.

Figure 3-45 Border style designs

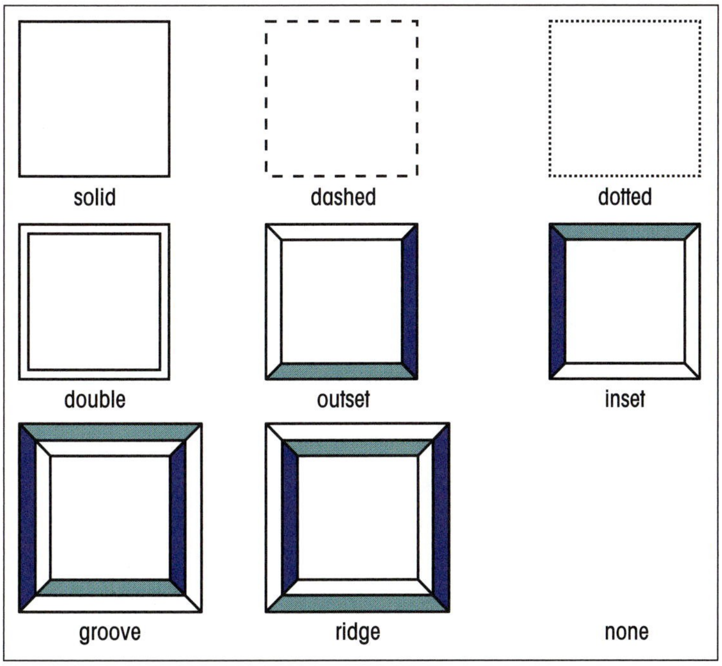

For example, to place a double border below an element, use the style:

```
border-style-bottom: double.
```

All of the border styles discussed above can be combined into a single style that defines each or all of the borders around the element. The syntax of these border styles is

```
border-top: width style color
border-right: width style color
border-bottom: width style color
border-left: width style color
border: width style color
```

where *width* is the width of the border, *style* is the style of the border, and *color* is the border color. The three properties must be entered in that order. For example, the style

```
h1 {border: 2px solid blue}
```

adds a 2-pixel wide solid blue border around every h1 heading.

Reference Window | Setting Border Styles in the Box Model

- To set the border width, use
  `border-width: length`
  where *length* is the width of the border using one of the CSS units of measure.
- To set the border color, use
  `border-color: color`
  where *color* is a color name or value.
- To set the border design, use
  `border-style: type`
  where *type* is none, solid, dashed, dotted, double, outset, inset, groove, or ridge.
- To set all of the border options in one style, use
  `border: length color type`
  in that order.

Having discussed the wide varieties of border styles with Tammy, she suggests you add a top border to the address element on the Sunny Acres home page. She thinks a double green border 0.5 em in height would look good. To keep the border from crowding the address text, you'll increase the padding between the text and the border to 1 em.

To create a border for the address element in Tammy's external style sheet:

1. Return to the **farm.css** style sheet in your text editor.
2. Add the following styles to the address element as shown in Figure 3-46. Place the styles on a new line to make your code easier to read. Be sure to separate all styles with a semicolon.

```
border-top: 0.5em double green; padding-top: 1em
```

Figure 3-46 Using the border-top and padding-top styles

```
body    {background-color: white; font-family: Arial, Helvetica, sans-serif}
h2      {font-size: 2em; letter-spacing: 0.4em; text-indent: 1em }
address {text-align: center; font: normal small-caps 0.8em sans-serif;
         border-top: 0.5em double green; padding-top: 1em}

#promoimage {float: right; margin: 0em 0em 1em 1em}
```

3. Save your changes to the file.
4. Reload the **home.htm** file in your Web browser. Scroll to the bottom of the page and verify that a double green border has been added to the top of the address element, as shown in Figure 3-47.

Figure 3-47 Adding a double top border to the address element

Hours
Farm Shop: 9 am - 5 pm Mon - Fri; 9 am - 3 pm Sat
The Corn Maze: 11 am - 9 pm Sat; 11 am - 5 pm Sun
The Haunted Maze: 5 pm - 9 pm Fri & Sat
Petting Barn: 9 am - 4 pm (Mon - Fri); 11 am - 3pm (Sat & Sun)
Directions
From Council Bluffs, proceed east on I-80
Take Exit 38 North to the Drake Frontage Road
Turn right on Highway G
Proceed east for 2.5 miles
Sunny Acres is on your left; watch for the green sign
Sunny Acres ☀ Tammy & Brent Nielsen ☀ 1977 Highway G ☀ Council Bluffs, IA 51503

Because of their flexibility, border styles are usually applied in place of the hr (horizontal rule) element discussed in Tutorial 1 as a way of creating section breaks on Web pages.

Width and Height Styles

The final aspect of the box model that can be controlled with CSS styles is the box's width and height. The default width and height are determined by the browser. For inline elements, the width is the width of the element content and the height is the height of a single line. Block-level elements extend across the width of their parent element with a height that expands to meet the content enclosed within the block. So a heading element will have a width than spans the width of the Web page. If the heading is nested within a blockquote element, its width will span the width of the blockquote, and so on. You can set a different width using the style

```
width: value
```

where *value* is the width of the content expressed in one of the CSS units of measure discussed in the last session. According to the CSS specifications, the width value does not take into account the size of the margins, padding space, or borders. It applies only to the actual content of the element. Most browsers follow the CSS specifications, except Internet Explorer. With Internet Explorer, the width style value is applied to element content, padding, and borders. This means that if you are using the box model for page layout, you can end up with different layouts under different browsers. For example, the style declaration

```
p {width: 500px; padding: padding: 30px; border: 10px solid green}
```

results in a paragraph that is 500 pixels wide under Internet Explorer with 420 pixels reserved for the width of the element content. Under other browsers that follow the CSS specifications (such as Firefox, Opera, and Safari), the element content is 500 pixels wide and the width of the entire box (including the padding and borders) is 580 pixels. See Figure 3-48.

Figure 3-48 **Interpretations of the box model width style**

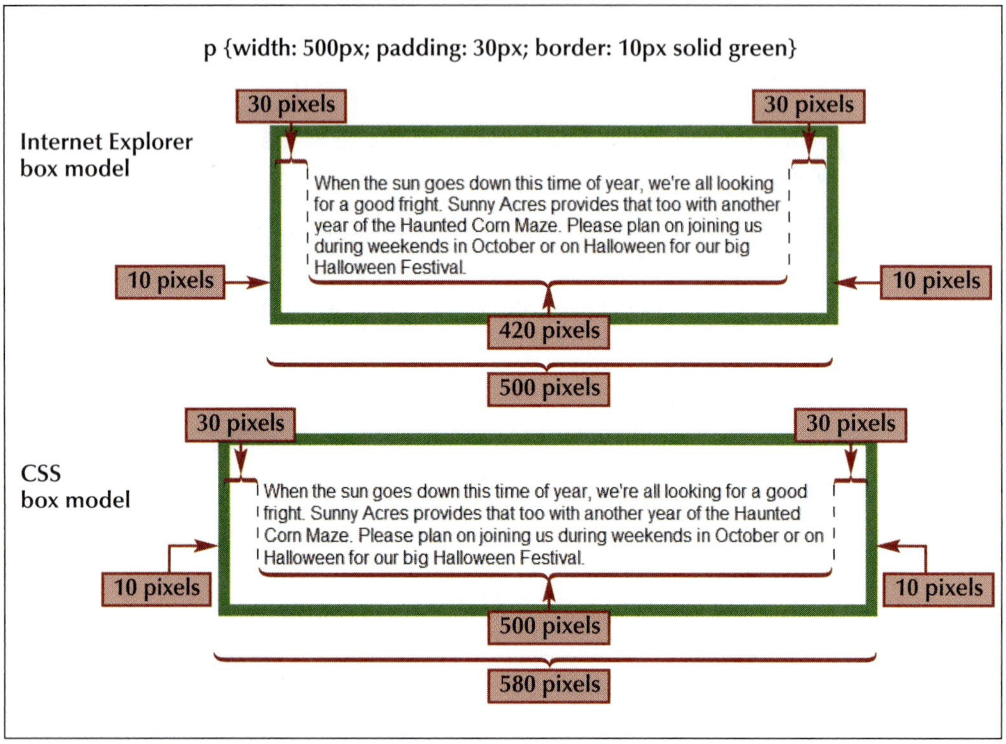
p {width: 500px; padding: 30px; border: 10px solid green}
Internet Explorer box model
30 pixels
30 pixels
When the sun goes down this time of year, we're all looking for a good fright. Sunny Acres provides that too with another year of the Haunted Corn Maze. Please plan on joining us during weekends in October or on Halloween for our big Halloween Festival.
10 pixels
10 pixels
420 pixels
500 pixels
CSS box model
30 pixels
30 pixels
When the sun goes down this time of year, we're all looking for a good fright. Sunny Acres provides that too with another year of the Haunted Corn Maze. Please plan on joining us during weekends in October or on Halloween for our big Halloween Festival.
10 pixels
10 pixels
500 pixels
580 pixels

There are several ways of reconciling these interpretations of the box model that we'll discuss later. For now, you should simply be aware that this is an ongoing concern for designers trying to do precise Web page layout.

Quirks Mode and Standards Mode | InSight

Internet Explorer has two modes it can work in. One is **quirks mode**, in which the browser applies the Internet Explorer interpretation of the box model and other features of CSS. However, starting with Internet Explorer 6, you can force the IE browser to adopt the CSS interpretation of the box model styles by putting it into **standards mode**. This is done by changing the code of your Web page from HTML to XHTML by replacing the opening <html> tag with the following three lines:

```
<?xml version="1.0" encoding="UTF-8" standalone="no" ?>

<!DOCTYPE html PUBLIC "-//W3C//DTD XHTML 1.0 Strict//EN"
  "http://www.w3.org/TR/xhtml1/DTD/xhtml11-strict.dtd">

<html xmlns="http://www.w3.org/1999/xhtml">
```

When the IE browser encounters these lines, it interprets all CSS styles in accord with a strict interpretation of the CSS guidelines. Standards mode also enforces other aspects of the CSS specifications; so to be more compliant with CSS, you should use the three lines of code above to put the IE browser in standards mode. By default, Internet Explorer works in quirks mode, which is often necessary to support older HTML and CSS code written before the CSS 2.1 standards were introduced.

As long as you are not doing exact Web page design in which the difference of a few pixels can render your page unreadable, you can work in either standards or quirks mode. However, as you gain confidence in Web design and attempt more intricate layouts, you might find a need to work in standards mode. Note that all browsers, not just Internet Explorer, support a standards mode and quirks mode. You can learn more by reading the browser's technical documentation or by doing a Web search on the differences between quirks and standards models.

To set the height of the element content, use the height style

```
height: value
```

where *value* is the height of the content expressed in CSS units of measure. If you set a height value that is insufficient to display all of the element content, the browser will ignore the height value and still expand the height of the box. There are styles to override this behavior that you explore in Tutorial 4.

Setting the Width and Height in the Box Model | Reference Window

- To set the box model width, use
  `width: length`
  where *length* is the width of the box content in one of the CSS units of measure. (Note that Internet Explorer applies the width value to the box model content, padding space, and border.)
- To set the box model height, use
  `height: length`
  where *length* is the height of the box content in one of the CSS units of measure.

Tammy doesn't like the appearance of h3 headings on the home page shown earlier in Figure 3-47. The headings identify two subsections of the document: one for the hours the farm is open and the other for directions to the farm. Currently the two headings extend across the width of the Web page. Tammy suggests that the headings would look better if they were about the same width as the text of the bulleted lists they introduce. You'll also increase the size of the left padding to offset the text a few spaces from the box's left border. You'll apply this style to other h3 headings on the Sunny Acres Web site, so you'll add the style to the farm.css external style sheet.

To set the style of the h3 headings in Tammy's external style sheet:

1. Return to the **farm.css** style sheet in your text editor.
2. Insert the following style directly below the style for the h2 heading, as shown in Figure 3-49:

```
h3 {width: 20em; padding-left: 1em}
```

Figure 3-49 Setting the width and left padding of the h3 element

```
body    {background-color: white; font-family: Arial, Helvetica, sans-serif}
h2      {font-size: 2em; letter-spacing: 0.4em; text-indent: 1em }
h3      {width: 20em; padding-left: 1em}
address {text-align: center; font: normal small-caps 0.8em sans-serif;
         border-top: 0.5em double green; padding-top: 1em}

#promoimage {float: right; margin: 0em 0em 1em 1em}
```

3. Save your changes to the file.
4. Reload the **home.htm** file in your Web browser. Figure 3-50 shows the revised appearance of the two h3 headings.

Figure 3-50 Reformatted h3 headings

Hours
Farm Shop: 9 am - 5 pm Mon - Fri; 9 am - 3 pm Sat
The Corn Maze: 11 am - 9 pm Sat; 11 am - 5 pm Sun
The Haunted Maze: 5 pm - 9 pm Fri & Sat
Petting Barn: 9 am - 4 pm (Mon - Fri); 11 am - 3pm (Sat & Sun)
Directions
From Council Bluffs, proceed east on I-80
Take Exit 38 North to the Drake Frontage Road
Turn right on Highway G
Proceed east for 2.5 miles
Sunny Acres is on your left; watch for the green sign

Controlling Page Layout with div Containers

Tammy is pleased with the layout of the Sunny Acres home page. But when she displayed it on her laptop's wide-screen monitor, she expressed concern about the text that extends across the screen. Studies show that text gets more difficult to read as the length of the line extends beyond about 30 to 50 characters per line. A page layout like that shown in Figure 3-51 is difficult enough to read that many people will skip over it.

Figure 3-51 Page layout on a wide-screen monitor

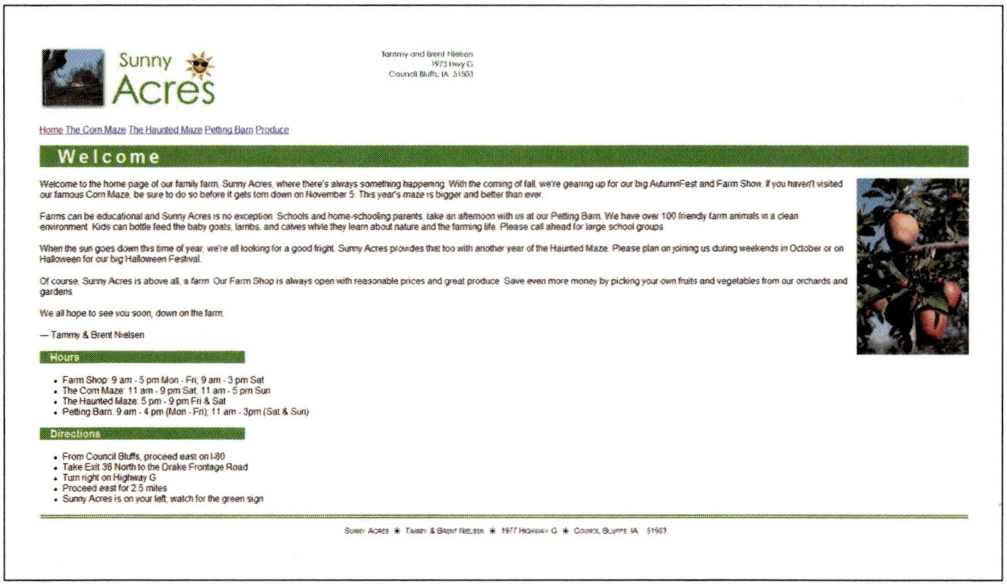

Tammy wants you to modify the page layout so that the length of the line is always kept within an acceptable limit under any monitor resolution. To do that, you'll use the style associated with the box model to set the width and margins of the different sections of the page. The technique involves placing different sections of the page within div elements called **div containers**, which you can then resize and float to create different page layouts. Recall that the div element is a generic block-level element. Browsers do not have default styles for the element's padding, border, margins, or width, so you can set all of these with your style sheet without worrying about conflicts with the browser's default settings.

The first div container that you'll add to the Sunny Acres home page will enclose the entire page content. You'll give this div container the id, outer.

To create the outer div container on Tammy's home page:

1. Open the **home.htm** file with your text editor.
2. Directly below the opening <body> tag, insert the following:

```
<div id="outer">
```

3. Scroll down to the bottom of the file. Directly above the closing </body> tag, insert the following:

```
</div>
```

Figure 3-52 highlights the newly added code.

Figure 3-52 Adding the outer div container

```
<body>

<div id="outer">
   <h1><img src="salogo.jpg" alt="Sunny Acres" /></h1>
   <div id="links">
      <a href="home.htm">Home</a>
      <a href="maze.htm">The Corn Maze</a>
      <a href="haunted.htm">The Haunted Maze</a>
      <a href="petting.htm">Petting Barn</a>
      <a href="produce.htm">Produce</a>
   </div>

   <h2>Welcome</h2>

   <address>
      Sunny Acres  &#9728; 
      Tammy &amp; Brent Nielsen  &#9728; 
      1977 Highway G  &#9728; 
      Council Bluffs, IA    51503
   </address>

</div>
</body>
```

4. Save your changes to the file.

Now that you've enclosed the page content within a div container, you can specify the width of the content. Rather than letting the content extend across the width of the browser window, you'll set the width to 50 em.

To set the width of the outer div container:

1. Return to the **farm.css** style sheet in your text editor.
2. Add the following style to the bottom of the file, as shown in Figure 3-53:

```
#outer {width: 50em}
```

Figure 3-53 Setting the width of the outer div container

```
body    {background-color: white; font-family: Arial, Helvetica, sans-serif}
h2      {font-size: 2em; letter-spacing: 0.4em; text-indent: 1em }
h3      {width: 20em; padding-left: 1em}
address {text-align: center; font: normal small-caps 0.8em sans-serif;
         border-top: 0.5em double green; padding-top: 1em}

#promoimage {float: right; margin: 0em 0em 1em 1em}
#outer      {width: 50em}
```

3. Save your changes to the file, and then reload **home.htm** in your Web browser. Verify that the width of the page content has been changed.

Note that by setting the width of the outer div container to 50 em, you've set the width to a defined size. Most monitors can fit this size; but if the user is using a smaller monitor, it's possible that the page width will extend beyond the browser window. If that is the case, the user will have to scroll horizontally through the browser window to view the entire page text. This is considered bad design, so you should test your Web pages on a variety of devices and resolutions to ensure this doesn't happen. Setting a page width is often a balancing act between competing needs.

Tip

You can set the page width by applying the width style to the body element.

Tammy has included a list of links at the top of the home page. She would like to display these links to the left of the Sunny Acres introduction. The links have been placed in a div container of their own with the id named links, so you can apply the following styles to the links div container:

- float it on the left margin of the outer div container
- set the width to 10 em
- set the background color to white
- add an outset border 0.5 em in width

You'll add this style declaration to the farm.css external style sheet so that Tammy can use it throughout her Web site.

To set the style for the list of links:

1. Return to the **farm.css** style sheet in your text editor.
2. As shown in Figure 3-54, add the following style:

```
#links {float: left; width: 10em; background-color: white;
        border-style: outset; border-width: 0.5em}
```

Figure 3-54 Setting the style of the links div container

```
#promoimage {float: right; margin: 0em 0em 1em 1em}
#outer      {width: 50em}
#links      {float: left; width: 10em; background-color: white;
             border-style: outset; border-width: 0.5em}
```

3. Save your changes to the file, and then reload **home.htm** in your Web browser. Figure 3-55 shows the revised appearance of the Sunny Acres home page.

Figure 3-55 List of links floated on the left margin

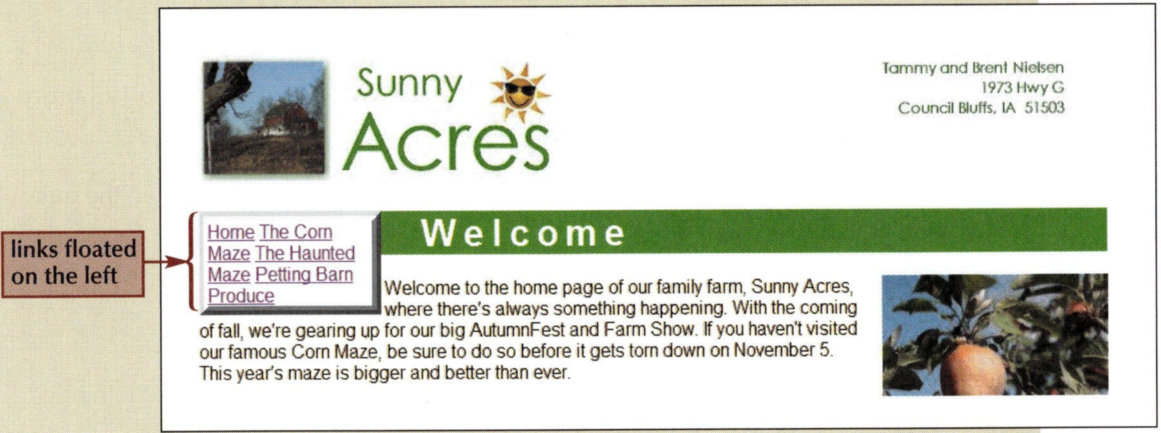
links floated on the left
Sunny Acres
Tammy and Brent Nielsen
1973 Hwy G
Council Bluffs, IA 51503
Home The Corn Maze The Haunted Maze Petting Barn Produce
Welcome
Welcome to the home page of our family farm, Sunny Acres, where there's always something happening. With the coming of fall, we're gearing up for our big AutumnFest and Farm Show. If you haven't visited our famous Corn Maze, be sure to do so before it gets torn down on November 5. This year's maze is bigger and better than ever.

Floating the list of links on the left page margin has saved some vertical space, but the layout is not attractive. Tammy thinks it would look much better if the welcoming text did not wrap around the links box, but instead was placed in a separate column. You can do this by enclosing the welcoming text within a div container of its own and then setting the left margin large enough to clear the links box.

To create the div container:

1. Return to the **home.htm** file in your text editor.
2. Directly above the opening <h2> tag for the Welcome title, insert:

   ```
   <div id="inner">
   ```

3. Scroll down the file and directly above the opening <address> tag, insert:

   ```
   </div>
   ```

   Figure 3-56 highlights the revised text.

Figure 3-56 Adding the inner div container

```
<div id="inner">
<h2>Welcome</h2>
<p>
   <img src="photo1.jpg" alt="home page photo" id="promoimage" />
   Welcome to the home page of our family farm,
   Sunny Acres, where there's always something
   happening. With the coming of fall, we're gearing up for our big AutumnFest
   and Farm Show. If you haven't visited our famous Corn Maze, be sure to do
   so before it gets torn down on November 5. This year's maze is bigger and
   better than ever.
</p>
```

```
   <h3>Directions</h3>
   <ul>
      <li>From Council Bluffs, proceed east on I-80</li>
      <li>Take Exit 38 North to the Drake Frontage Road</li>
      <li>Turn right on Highway G</li>
      <li>Proceed east for 2.5 miles</li>
      <li>Sunny Acres is on your left; watch for the green sign</li>
   </ul>
   </div>
```

4. Save your changes to the file.

Now you can set the styles for the inner div container. To separate the text in the inner div container from the links box, you'll apply styles to:

- set the left margin to 12 em
- display a solid green border 0.1 em wide on the left side of the container
- set the left padding to 1 em

You want to add this style to the farm.css style sheet so that Tammy can use it in any of her pages.

To create a style for the inner div container:

1. Return to the **farm.css** style sheet in your text editor.
2. Add the following style, as shown in Figure 3-57:

```
#inner {margin-left: 12em; padding-left: 1em;
        border-left: 0.1em solid green}
```

Figure 3-57 **Setting the style of the inner div container**

```
#promoimage {float: right; margin: 0em 0em 1em 1em}
#outer      {width: 50em}
#links      {float: left; width: 10em; background-color: white;
             border-style: outset; border-width: 0.5em}
#inner      {margin-left: 12em; padding-left: 1em;
             border-left: 0.1em solid green}
```

3. Save your changes to the file and then reload or refresh **home.htm** in your Web browser. Figure 3-58 shows the revised layout of the Sunny Acres home page.

Figure 3-58 **Layout of the inner div container**

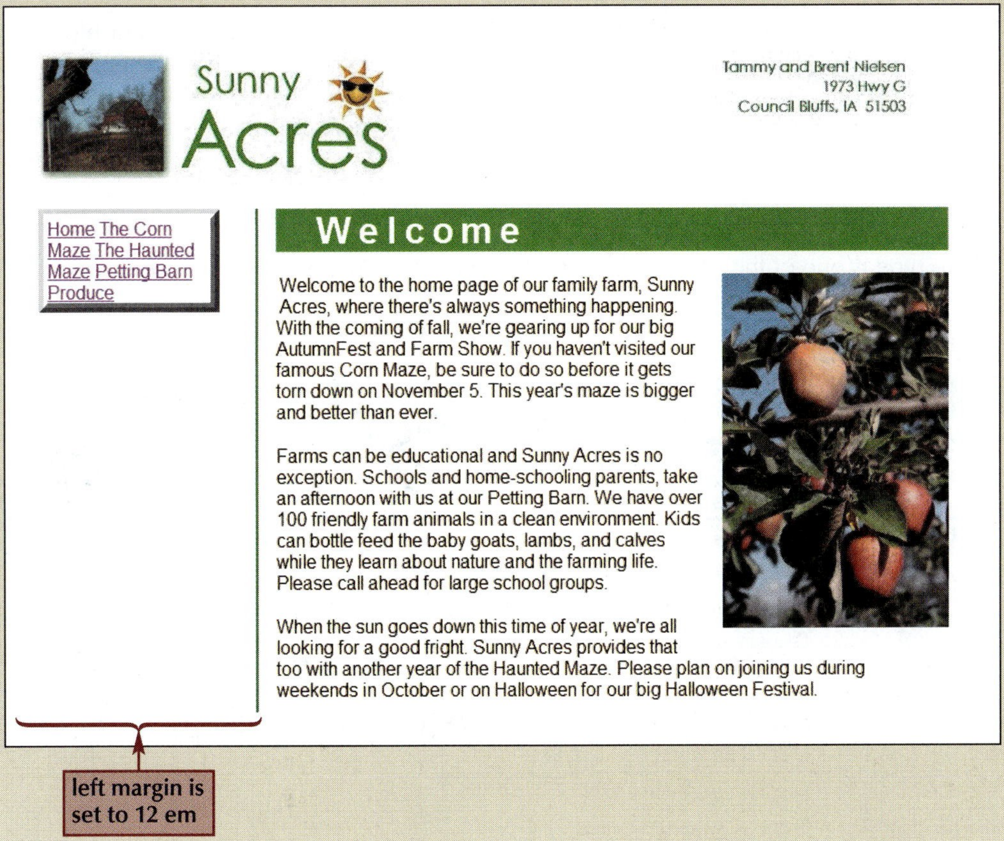
Sunny Acres
Tammy and Brent Nielsen
1973 Hwy G
Council Bluffs, IA 51503
Home The Corn Maze The Haunted Maze Petting Barn Produce
Welcome
Welcome to the home page of our family farm, Sunny Acres, where there's always something happening. With the coming of fall, we're gearing up for our big AutumnFest and Farm Show. If you haven't visited our famous Corn Maze, be sure to do so before it gets torn down on November 5. This year's maze is bigger and better than ever.
Farms can be educational and Sunny Acres is no exception. Schools and home-schooling parents, take an afternoon with us at our Petting Barn. We have over 100 friendly farm animals in a clean environment. Kids can bottle feed the baby goats, lambs, and calves while they learn about nature and the farming life. Please call ahead for large school groups.
When the sun goes down this time of year, we're all looking for a good fright. Sunny Acres provides that too with another year of the Haunted Maze. Please plan on joining us during weekends in October or on Halloween for our big Halloween Festival.
left margin is set to 12 em

The page looks much better with the two div containers separating the content on the home page.

InSight | **The Box Model and Nested div Containers**

One source of page layout conflicts come from the different ways browsers apply the padding space. One way to avoid this problem is to set the padding space to 0 and only use the margin style with nested div containers. For example, if you need to set the padding space around your paragraphs to 10 pixels, but you worry that this will adversely affect the layout for IE users, place the paragraph in a div container and set the margin around the paragraph to 10 pixels. Because margins are interpreted the same way by all browsers, you will find that the paragraph's width will be the same under the IE box model and the CSS box model.

Setting the Display Style

Tammy likes the revised page layout but still finds the list of links difficult to read. She thinks it would be better if each link were on a separate line. You could fix this by enclosing each link within its own paragraph or by inserting a line break between each link. However, Tammy wants to move as much of the formatting into style sheets as she can, rather than making these changes to document content. She also might want to explore different layouts in the future—for example, laying out the links horizontally at the top of the page—and doesn't want to have to remove paragraph tags or line breaks if she does that.

As you've seen, most page elements are classified as either inline elements or block-level elements. Browsers treat links as inline elements, which is why all of the entries in the links list run together on a single line. You can use CSS to change the display style applied to any element, allowing you to make inline elements appear as block-level elements and vice versa. The syntax of the display style is

```
display: type
```

where *type* is one of the CSS display types described in Figure 3-59.

Figure 3-59 **Values of the display style**

Display	Description
block	Display as a block-level element
inline	Display as an inline element
inline-block	Display as an inline element with some of the properties of a block (much like an inline image or frame)
inherit	Inherit the display property of the element's parent
list-item	Display as a list item
none	Do not display the element
run-in	Display as either an inline or block-level element depending on the context (CSS2)
table	Display as a block-level table
inline-table	Display as an inline table
table-caption	Treat as a table caption
table-cell	Treat as a table cell
table-column	Treat as a table column
table-column-group	Treat as a group of table columns
table-footer-group	Treat as a group of table footer rows
table-header-group	Treat as a group of table header rows
table-row	Treat as a table row
table-row-group	Treat as a group of table rows

To display all hypertext links as block-level elements rather than inline elements, apply the following style

```
a {display: block}
```

which has the same effect on page layout as turning the hypertext link into a generic div element.

Setting the Display Style

| Reference Window

- To set the display style of an element, use
  `display: type`
  where *type* is the type of display. Use inline for inline elements and block for block-level elements.

You'll add this style to the farm.css style sheet. You'll also set the margin around each of the hypertext links to 0.1 em to provide more space between the links and the links box.

To set the display style for the links container:

1. Return to the **farm.css** file in your text editor.
2. As shown in Figure 3-60, add the following style:

```
a {display: block; margin: 0.3em}
```

The final farm.css style sheet

Figure 3-60

```
body    {background-color: white; font-family: Arial, Helvetica, sans-serif}
h2      {font-size: 2em; letter-spacing: 0.4em; text-indent: 1em }
h3      {width: 20em; padding-left: 1em}
address {text-align: center; font: normal small-caps 0.8em sans-serif;
         border-top: 0.5em double green; padding-top: 1em}
a       {display: block; margin: 0.3em}

#promoimage {float: right; margin: 0em 0em 1em 1em}
#outer      {width: 50em}
#links      {float: left; width: 10em; background-color: white;
             border-style: outset; border-width: 0.5em}
#inner      {margin-left: 12em; padding-left: 1em;
             border-left: 0.1em solid green}
```

3. Save your changes to the file and then refresh **home.htm** in your Web browser. Figure 3-61 shows the final layout of the entire Sunny Acres home page.

Figure 3-61 **The final layout of the Sunny Acres home page**

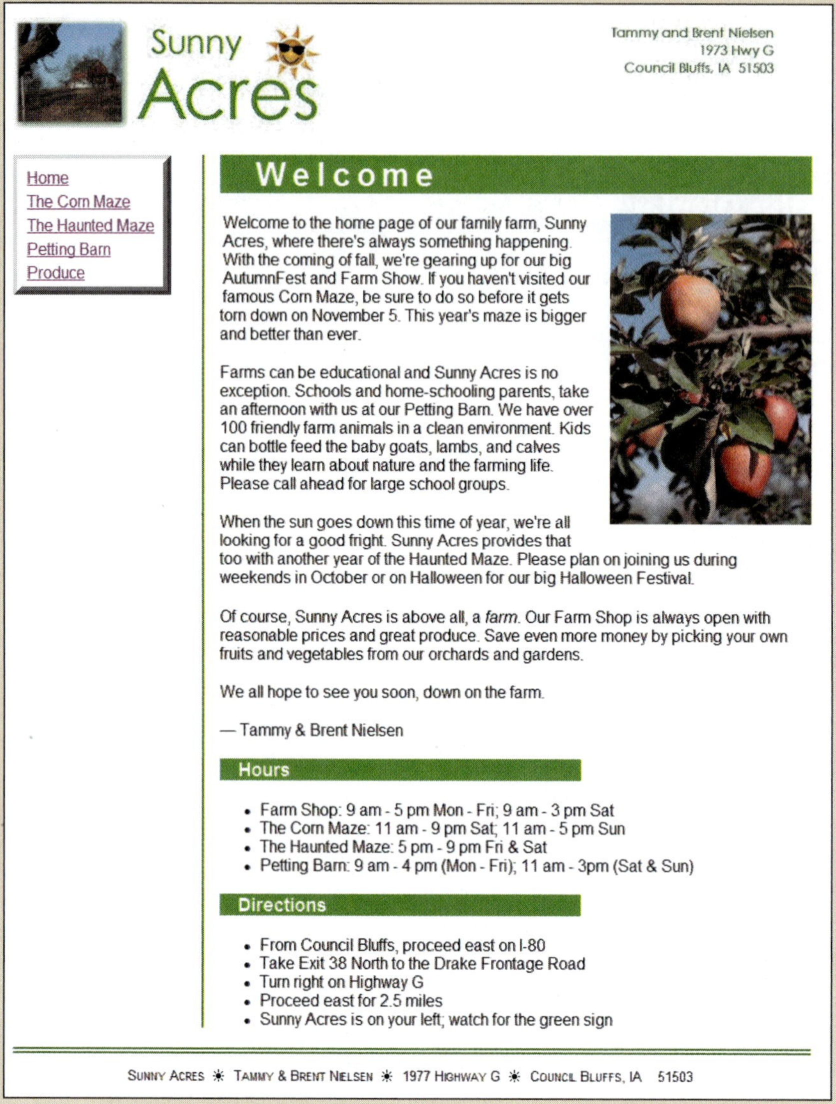
Sunny Acres
Tammy and Brent Nielsen
1973 Hwy G
Council Bluffs, IA 51503
Home
The Corn Maze
The Haunted Maze
Petting Barn
Produce
Welcome
Welcome to the home page of our family farm, Sunny Acres, where there's always something happening. With the coming of fall, we're gearing up for our big AutumnFest and Farm Show. If you haven't visited our famous Corn Maze, be sure to do so before it gets torn down on November 5. This year's maze is bigger and better than ever.
Farms can be educational and Sunny Acres is no exception. Schools and home-schooling parents, take an afternoon with us at our Petting Barn. We have over 100 friendly farm animals in a clean environment. Kids can bottle feed the baby goats, lambs, and calves while they learn about nature and the farming life. Please call ahead for large school groups.
When the sun goes down this time of year, we're all looking for a good fright. Sunny Acres provides that too with another year of the Haunted Maze. Please plan on joining us during weekends in October or on Halloween for our big Halloween Festival.
Of course, Sunny Acres is above all, a farm. Our Farm Shop is always open with reasonable prices and great produce. Save even more money by picking your own fruits and vegetables from our orchards and gardens.
We all hope to see you soon, down on the farm.
— Tammy & Brent Nielsen
Hours
Farm Shop: 9 am - 5 pm Mon - Fri; 9 am - 3 pm Sat
The Corn Maze: 11 am - 9 pm Sat; 11 am - 5 pm Sun
The Haunted Maze: 5 pm - 9 pm Fri & Sat
Petting Barn: 9 am - 4 pm (Mon - Fri); 11 am - 3pm (Sat & Sun)
Directions
From Council Bluffs, proceed east on I-80
Take Exit 38 North to the Drake Frontage Road
Turn right on Highway G
Proceed east for 2.5 miles
Sunny Acres is on your left; watch for the green sign
SUNNY ACRES ☀ TAMMY & BRENT NIELSEN ☀ 1977 HIGHWAY G ☀ COUNCIL BLUFFS, IA 51503

Compared to the initial design of this page shown earlier in Figure 3-2, you've improved the appearance of the page and made it easier to read. There are four other pages on the Sunny Acres Web site that you haven't yet formatted. However, they share a common document structure with the home page, so you can apply the same style rules you've created for the home.htm file to those files. This is why external style sheets are so powerful: You can apply the same styles to many pages without having to duplicate your work.

Tammy wants those other pages to have slightly different color schemes, so you'll have to apply some embedded styles to each of them. They already have the outer and inner div containers, so you will not have to add those elements to the files.

To apply Tammy's external style sheet to the rest of the pages on her Web site:

1. Open the **haunted.htm** file from the tutorial.03\tutorial folder included with your Data Files.
2. Directly above the closing </head> tag, insert the following code, as shown in Figure 3-62:

```
<style type="text/css">
   h2, h3 {color: white; background-color: black}
</style>
<link href="farm.css" rel="stylesheet" type="text/css" />
```

Figure 3-62 Applying the style sheet to the haunted.htm file

```
   <title>Sunny Acres Haunted Maze</title>
   <style type="text/css">
      h2, h3 {color: white; background-color: black}
   </style>
   <link href="farm.css" rel="stylesheet" type="text/css" />
</head>
```

3. Close the file, saving your changes.
4. Open the **maze.htm** file and repeat Steps 2 and 3, using a background color value of (200, 105, 0).
5. Open the **petting.htm** file and repeat Steps 2 and 3, using a background color of blue.
6. Open the **produce.htm** file and repeat Steps 2 and 3, using a background color of red.
7. Return to the Sunny Acres home page in your Web browser, and then click the links in the links box to view the appearance of the other four Web pages to verify that you've applied a uniform design to the Web site. Figure 3-63 shows the appearance of each of the four other pages.

Figure 3-63 Revised design of the Sunny Acres Web site

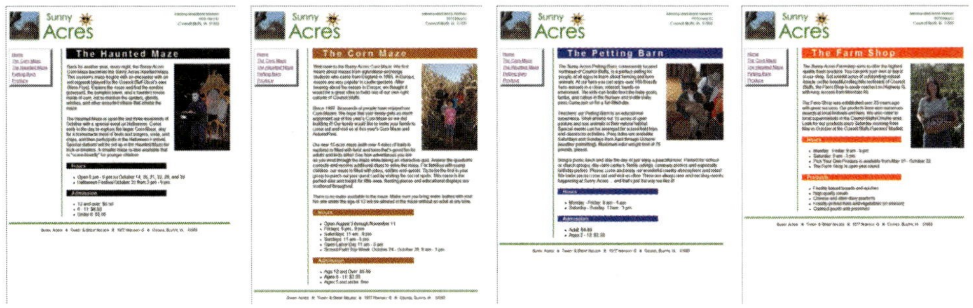

haunted.htm | maze.htm | petting.htm | produce.htm

8. Close any remaining open files or applications.

You've completed your work on the Sunny Acres Web site. Through the use of style sheets, you've managed to create a common look and feel for all of Tammy's Web pages. Style sheets also speeded up the development time as you were able to apply previously created style sheets to other pages on the site. Finally, if you or Tammy decide to make a change to the site's design style, you can make your modifications to the farm.css style sheet and have your revisions instantly applied to all of the Web site pages. Tammy will continue to work with the Web site, adding new material and making other design decisions.

Review | Session 3.3 Quick Check

1. An inline image has the id photoImage. Specify the style declaration you would enter to float this inline image on the left margin.
2. Specify the style declaration to set the right and bottom margins of the photoImage inline image to 5 pixels each.
3. You want your paragraphs to have a padding space above and below the paragraph equal to 10 pixels. Specify the style declaration to do this.
4. You want your block quotes to have a 20-pixel left margin and to have a solid gray 4-pixel-wide left border. Specify the style declaration to do this.
5. You want the h1 heading with the mainHeading id to be displayed in a green font with a double green border 8 pixels wide. Specify the style declaration to do this.
6. Describe the difference between how Internet Explorer and CSS calculate element widths under the box model.
7. By default, images are displayed as inline elements. Specify the style declaration you would enter to display all inline images as block-level elements.

Tutorial Summary | Review

In this tutorial, you learned how to use the CSS language to create and apply style sheets. In the first session, you learned how to apply inline styles, embedded styles, and external style sheets. You also explored the parts of style declarations and saw how they relate to elements within Web page documents. The first session concluded by examining how both foreground and background color can be described and rendered under CSS and HTML. In the second session, you began by working with the different CSS styles associated with text and fonts. You also learned about several different measuring units that can be applied to font sizes and letter, word, and line spacing. The second session also provided an overview of different image types supported by most browsers and showed how to use these images to create animated graphics and wallpaper-style backgrounds. The final session began by looking at how to float elements within a Web page layout. You then explored the box model, showing how to define an element's internal and external space. The session also showed how to add borders to any page element. The session concluded by looking at div containers, showing how they can be used as tools to create dynamic and interesting page layouts.

Key Terms

absolute unit
animated GIF
box model
Cascading Style Sheets
color value
CSS
CSS2
CSS 2.1
CSS3
div container
em unit
embedded style sheet
external style sheet
Flash
floating
generic font
GIF
Graphics Interchange Format
hanging indent
hexadecimal
inline style
Joint Photographic Experts Group
JPEG
kerning
leading
margin
padding
PNG
Portable Network Graphics
quirks mode
relative unit
RGB triplet
scalable
Scalable Vector Graphics
specific font
splash screen
standards mode
style inheritance
style precedence
style sheet
SVG
tiling
tracking
transparent color

Practice | Review Assignments

Practice the skills you learned in the tutorial using the same case scenario.

Data Files needed for the Review Assignments: greenbar.jpg, holiday.jpg, holidaytxt.htm, salogo.jpg, and sunnytxt.css

Tammy has been working with the Web site you designed. She's returned to you for help with another Web page. The Sunny Acres farm is planning a festival called *Holiday on the Farm* to bring people to Sunny Acres during the months of November and December. They're planning to offer sleigh rides, sledding (weather permitting), and a visit with Santa Claus. Tammy has already created the content for this page and located a few graphics she wants you to use. One is the Sunny Acres logo that she's placed at the top of the page. Another is a promotional photo that she wants placed in a box floated on the right margin of the Web page. The third graphic displays a green bar that Tammy wants to tile as a background. A preview of the page you'll create for Tammy is shown in Figure 3-64.

Figure 3-64

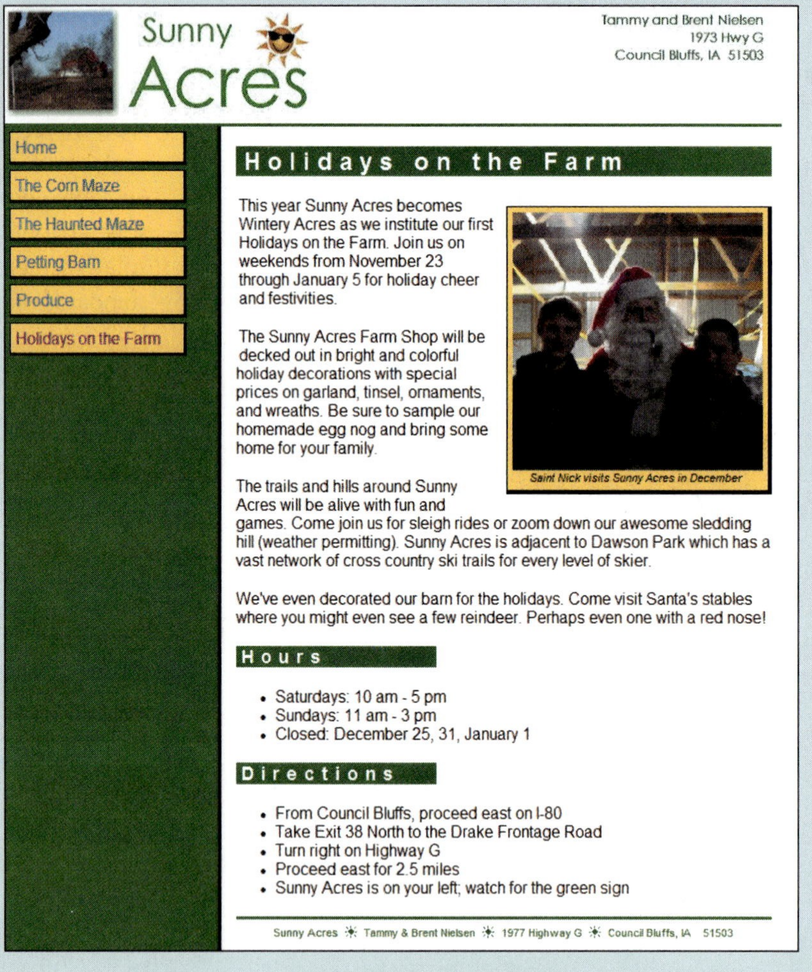

Complete the following:

1. Use your text editor to open the **holidaytxt.htm** and **sunnytxt.css** files from the tutorial.03\review folder included with your Data Files. Enter ***your name*** and ***the date*** in the comment section within each file and save them as **holiday.htm** and **sunny.css**, respectively, in the same folder. Take some time to review the content and appearance of the holiday.htm file in your text editor and Web browser.
2. Go to the holiday.htm file in your text editor. Add a div container named outer that encloses the entire page content within the opening and closing <body> tags.
3. Add a second div container named inner that encloses the page content from the h2 heading down to the address element.
4. Locate the photo inline image. Set the width and height of this image to 250 pixels.
5. Link the **holiday.htm** file to the **sunny.css** style sheet. Close the file, saving your changes.
6. Return to the **sunny.css** file in your text editor. Add the following style for the page body:
    - Set the margin to 0 pixels.
    - Set the default font face to Arial, Helvetica, or the generic sans-serif font.
    - Change the background color to white and display the background image file **greenbar.jpg** tiled in the vertical direction only starting from the top left corner of the page.
7. Display the h1 headings with a 3-pixel-wide solid green bottom border and a margin of 0 pixels.
8. Display the h2 and h3 headings in white text on a green background. Set the left padding to 5 pixels and the kerning to 7 pixels. Set the width of the h3 headings to 200 pixels.
9. Display the address text in an 8-point normal green font. Center the address text with a top padding of 5 pixels. Add a 3-pixel solid green border to the top of the address text.
10. Set the width of the outer div container to 770 pixels.
11. Set the left margin of the inner div container to 225 pixels. Set the left padding of the inner div container to 10 pixels.
12. The holiday.htm file contains the photobox paragraph, which displays the photo inline image followed by a caption for the image. Apply the following styles to the photobox paragraph:
    - Float the paragraph on the right margin.
    - Center the text horizontally within the box.
    - Display the text in an 8-point italic font.
    - Change the background color to the value (255, 215, 71).
    - Add a 10-pixel margin to the top of, below, and to the left of the box, and set the right margin to 0 pixels.
    - Add a solid black border that is 1 pixel wide on the box's top and left, and 4 pixels wide on the right and bottom.
13. Display the photo image within the photobox paragraph as a block-level element.
14. Tammy has placed a list of links within the links div container. Float this container on the left margin.
15. Display all hypertext links using the following styles:
    - Remove any underlining from the hypertext links by setting the text decoration to none.

- Display each link as a block-level element 180 pixels wide with a 5-pixel margin and 5 pixels of internal padding.
- Set the background to the color value (255, 215, 71).
- Add a solid black border that is 1 pixel wide on the top and left, and 3 pixels wide on the right and bottom.

16. Save your changes to the file and then open the **holiday.htm** file in your Web browser. Verify that the page layout appears similar to that shown in Figure 3-64. Note that Figure 3-64 displays the page as rendered by the Internet Explorer browser; you will see some slight differences under other Web browsers.
17. Submit your completed files to your instructor.

Apply | Case Problem 1

Apply your knowledge of hypertext links to create a Web page for the International Cryptographic Institute.

Data Files needed for this Case Problem: algo.htm, back1.gif, back2.gif, crypttxt.htm, enigma.htm, history.htm, locks.jpg, logo.gif, public.htm, scytale.gif, and single.htm

International Cryptographic Institute Sela Dawes is the media representative for the ICI, the International Cryptographic Institute. The ICI is an organization of cryptographers who study the science and mathematics of secret codes, encrypted messages, and code breaking. Part of the ICI's mission is to inform the public about cryptography and data security. Sela has asked you to work on a Web site containing information about cryptography for use by high school science and math teachers. She wants the design to be visually interesting in order to help draw students into the material. Figure 3-65 shows a preview of your design.

Figure 3-65

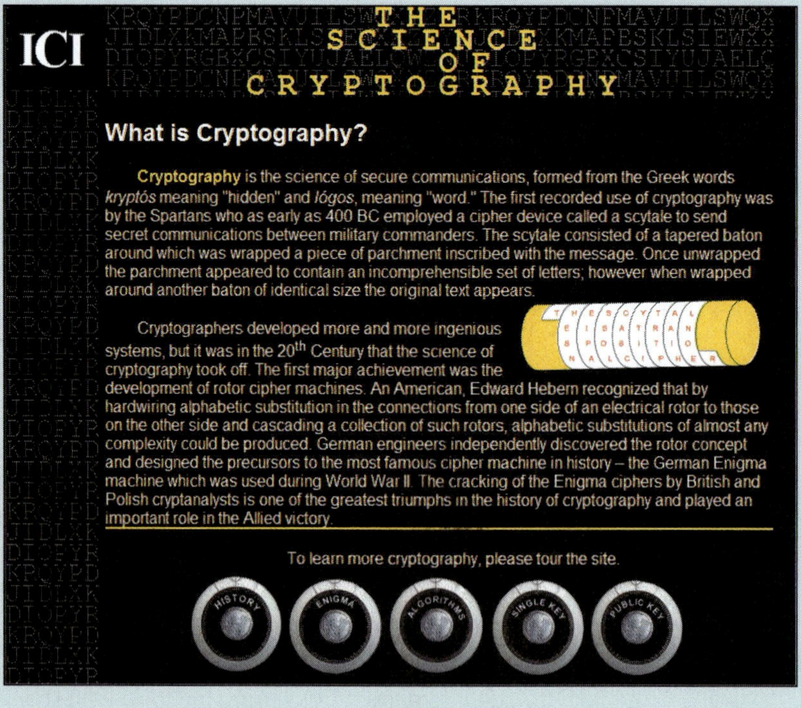

Complete the following:

1. In your text editor, open **crypttxt.htm** from the tutorial.03\case1 folder included with your Data Files. Enter ***your name*** and ***the date*** in the comment section of the file. Save the file as **crypt.htm** in the same folder.
2. Add a div container covering the page content from the h1 heading through the end of the third paragraph. Give the div element the id pageContent.
3. Add an embedded style sheet to the head section of the document. With the style sheet, create the following style for the page body:
   - Set the background color to black and the text color to white.
   - Use the file **back1.gif** as a background image tiled in the vertical direction only.
   - Sets the margin to 0 pixels.
4. Apply the following styles to the pageContent div container:
   - Set the width to 670 pixels and the left margin to 100 pixels.
   - Set the default font to Arial, Helvetica, or sans-serif.
5. Apply the following styles to the h1 element:
   - Set the font family to Courier New or monospace.
   - Set the font size to 24 points, the kerning to 10 points, and the leading to 0.7 points.
   - Center the text of the h1 heading horizontally.
   - Change the font color to yellow.
   - Use **back2.gif** as the background image.
   - Set the margin to 0 pixels.
6. Create a style to display bold text in a yellow font.
7. Create a style to indent paragraphs by 2 em units.
8. Locate the inline image for the **logo.gif** file. Set the width and height for the image to 95 pixels wide by 78 pixels high. Float the image on the left page margin.
9. Locate the **scytale.gif** image. Set the dimensions to 250 pixels wide by 69 pixels high. Float the image on the right margin.
10. Use an inline style to add a 2-pixel solid yellow border to the bottom of the second paragraph. Change the bottom padding of the paragraph to 10 pixels.
11. Use an inline style to center the contents of the third paragraph.
12. Locate the **locks.jpg** inline image and set the dimensions of the image to 510 pixels wide by 110 pixels high.
13. Directly below the locks.jpg inline image, create an image map with the name and id, locks. Add the following hotspots to the image map:
    - A circular hotspot linked to history.htm centered at the coordinate (52, 52) with a radius of 43 pixels; the alternate text should be "History"
    - A circular hotspot with a radius of 43 pixels located at the coordinate (155, 52); link the hotspot to enigma.htm and set the alternate text to "Enigma"
    - A circular hotspot with a radius of 43 pixels located at the coordinate (255, 52); link the hotspot to algo.htm and set the alternate text to "Algorithms"
    - A circular hotspot with a radius of 43 pixels located at the coordinate (355, 52); link the hotspot to single.htm and set the alternate text to "Single Key"
    - A circular hotspot with a radius of 43 pixels located at the coordinate (455, 52); link the hotspot to public.htm and set the alternate text to "Public Key"
14. Apply the locks image map to the **locks.jpg** inline image. Use an inline style to remove the border around the inline image.

15. Save your changes to the file. Load **crypt.htm** in your Web browser. Verify that the layout appears similar to that shown in Figure 3-65 and that the image map hotspots open the appropriate pages on your Web site.
16. Submit your completed files to your instructor.

Apply | Case Problem 2

Apply your knowledge of CSS to create a three-column layout for a bike touring company.

Data Files needed for this Case Problem: block.jpg, bmtourtxt.htm, body.jpg, h1back.jpg, h1title.gif, and wheelstxt.css

Mountain Wheels Adriana and Ivan Turchenko are the co-owners of Mountain Wheels, a bike shop and touring agency in Littleton, Colorado. One of their most popular tours is the Bike the Mountains Tour, a six-day excursion over some of the highest roads in Colorado. Adriana wants to update the company's Web site, providing more information about the Bike the Mountains Tour. She envisions a three-column layout with a list of links in the first column and descriptive text in the second and third columns. She has asked for your help in working up a design. As a first step, you'll design the page containing the tour's itinerary. Adriana has already created all of the page content and provided all of the graphics needed for page backgrounds. She needs your help in working with the CSS. Figure 3-66 shows a preview of the Web page you'll create.

Figure 3-66

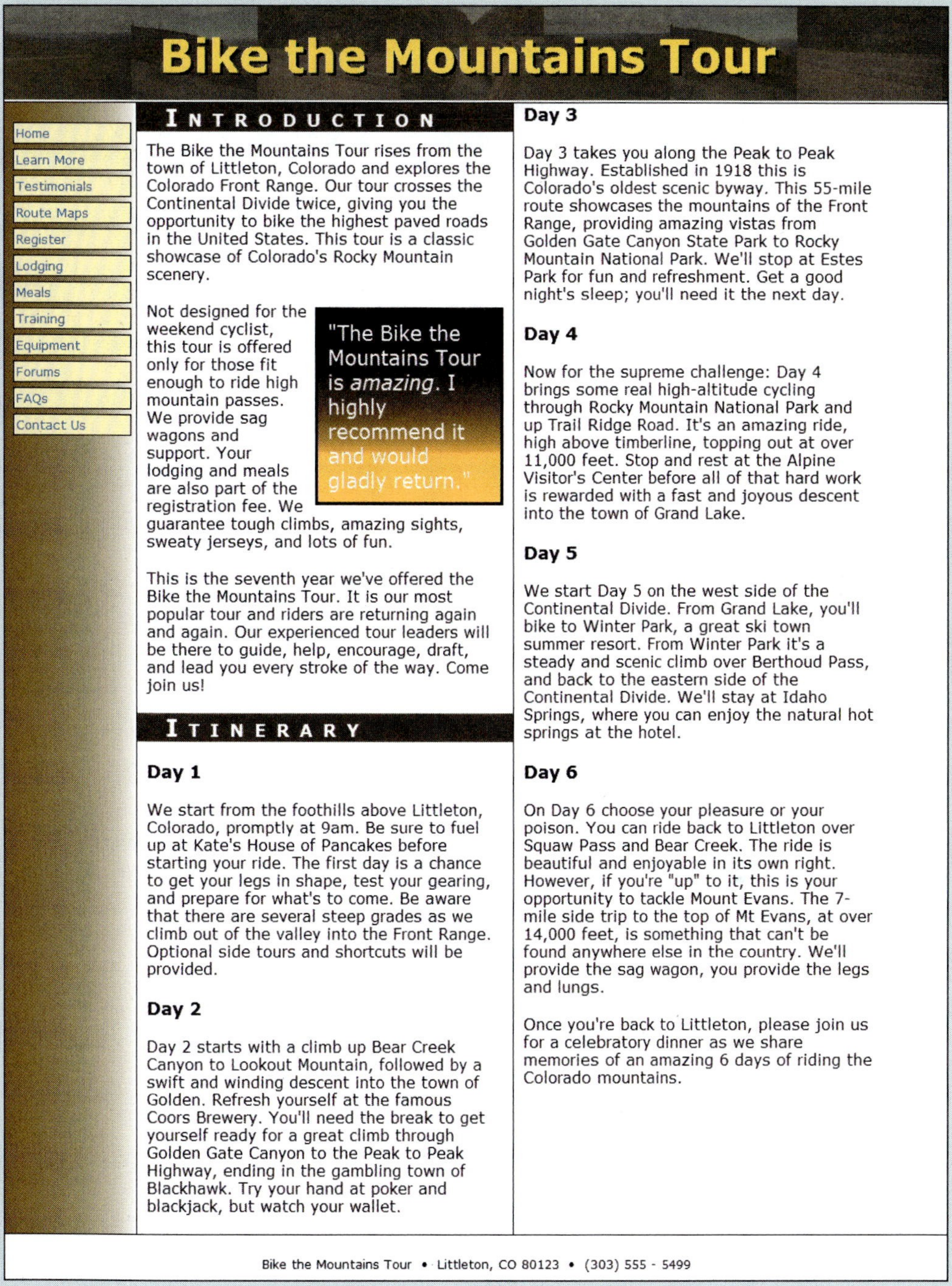
Bike the Mountains Tour
Home
Learn More
Testimonials
Route Maps
Register
Lodging
Meals
Training
Equipment
Forums
FAQs
Contact Us
INTRODUCTION
The Bike the Mountains Tour rises from the town of Littleton, Colorado and explores the Colorado Front Range. Our tour crosses the Continental Divide twice, giving you the opportunity to bike the highest paved roads in the United States. This tour is a classic showcase of Colorado's Rocky Mountain scenery.
Not designed for the weekend cyclist, this tour is offered only for those fit enough to ride high mountain passes. We provide sag wagons and support. Your lodging and meals are also part of the registration fee. We guarantee tough climbs, amazing sights, sweaty jerseys, and lots of fun.
"The Bike the Mountains Tour is amazing. I highly recommend it and would gladly return."
This is the seventh year we've offered the Bike the Mountains Tour. It is our most popular tour and riders are returning again and again. Our experienced tour leaders will be there to guide, help, encourage, draft, and lead you every stroke of the way. Come join us!
ITINERARY
Day 1
We start from the foothills above Littleton, Colorado, promptly at 9am. Be sure to fuel up at Kate's House of Pancakes before starting your ride. The first day is a chance to get your legs in shape, test your gearing, and prepare for what's to come. Be aware that there are several steep grades as we climb out of the valley into the Front Range. Optional side tours and shortcuts will be provided.
Day 2
Day 2 starts with a climb up Bear Creek Canyon to Lookout Mountain, followed by a swift and winding descent into the town of Golden. Refresh yourself at the famous Coors Brewery. You'll need the break to get yourself ready for a great climb through Golden Gate Canyon to the Peak to Peak Highway, ending in the gambling town of Blackhawk. Try your hand at poker and blackjack, but watch your wallet.
Day 3
Day 3 takes you along the Peak to Peak Highway. Established in 1918 this is Colorado's oldest scenic byway. This 55-mile route showcases the mountains of the Front Range, providing amazing vistas from Golden Gate Canyon State Park to Rocky Mountain National Park. We'll stop at Estes Park for fun and refreshment. Get a good night's sleep; you'll need it the next day.
Day 4
Now for the supreme challenge: Day 4 brings some real high-altitude cycling through Rocky Mountain National Park and up Trail Ridge Road. It's an amazing ride, high above timberline, topping out at over 11,000 feet. Stop and rest at the Alpine Visitor's Center before all of that hard work is rewarded with a fast and joyous descent into the town of Grand Lake.
Day 5
We start Day 5 on the west side of the Continental Divide. From Grand Lake, you'll bike to Winter Park, a great ski town summer resort. From Winter Park it's a steady and scenic climb over Berthoud Pass, and back to the eastern side of the Continental Divide. We'll stay at Idaho Springs, where you can enjoy the natural hot springs at the hotel.
Day 6
On Day 6 choose your pleasure or your poison. You can ride back to Littleton over Squaw Pass and Bear Creek. The ride is beautiful and enjoyable in its own right. However, if you're "up" to it, this is your opportunity to tackle Mount Evans. The 7-mile side trip to the top of Mt Evans, at over 14,000 feet, is something that can't be found anywhere else in the country. We'll provide the sag wagon, you provide the legs and lungs.
Once you're back to Littleton, please join us for a celebratory dinner as we share memories of an amazing 6 days of riding the Colorado mountains.
Bike the Mountains Tour • Littleton, CO 80123 • (303) 555 - 5499

Complete the following:

1. In your text editor, open **bmtourtxt.htm** and **wheelstxt.css** from the tutorial.03\case2 folder included with your Data Files. Enter ***your name*** and ***the date*** in the comment section of each file. Save the files as **bmtour.htm** and **wheels.css** in the same folder.

2. Review the contents and current layout of the **bmtour.htm** file in your text editor and browser. Create three div containers for the three columns that Adriana wants to use in her proposed page layout. To create the three div containers:
   - Locate the div container for the list of links at the top of the file. Give this div element the id, column1.
   - Enclose the page content starting with the h2 Introduction heading through the paragraph describing the Day 2 activities of the tour in another div container. Give this div element the id, column2.
   - Enclose the page content starting with the Day 3 heading through the last paragraph describing the Day 6 activities in a div element with the id, column3.
3. Within the head section, create a link to the external style sheet, **wheels.css**. Save your changes to the **bmtour.htm** file.
4. Go to the **wheels.css** style sheet in your text editor. Create a style for the page body containing the following style rules:
   - Set the font family to Verdana, Helvetica, or sans-serif.
   - Set the margin size to 0 pixels.
   - Set the background color to white and add a background image using the body.jpg file tiled in the vertical direction.
5. Create the following style for the first column in the layout of the **bmtour.htm** file:
   - Set the width to 140 pixels. Set the left padding to 10 pixels and the top padding to 20 pixels.
   - Float the column on the left page margin.
6. Create the following style for the second column of the **bmtour.htm** file:
   - Set the width to 40% of the width of the page body.
   - Float the column on the left margin.
   - Add a 1-pixel-wide solid black border to the left and right of the column.
7. Set the width of the third column to 40% of the width of the page body and also float this column on the left.
8. Create the following style for the h1 heading:
   - Center the contents of the heading, setting the height to 100 pixels and the margin to 0 pixels.
   - Set the background color to white with the file h1back.jpg as the background image, tiled in the horizontal direction.
   - Add a 1-pixel-wide solid black bottom border.
9. Create the following style for the h2 headings:
   - Indent the text 30 pixels.
   - Set the font color to white and the background to the color value (108, 87, 12).
   - Set the kerning to 8 points and the margin to 0 pixels.
   - Display the text in small caps.
10. Set the left margin of h3 headings to 10 pixels.
11. Set the margins of all paragraphs to 10 pixels on the top and left and 20 pixels on the right and bottom.
12. Apply the following styles to blockquote elements on the page:
    - Set the width of every blockquote element to 200 pixels with 10 pixels of padding.
    - Display the text in a 16-point white font.
    - Add a 3-pixel-wide solid black border.

- Change the background color to the value (255, 204, 0) with the image file **block.jpg** as the background, tiled in the horizontal direction.
- Set the margins around the blockquote to 5 pixels, except for the right margin, which should be set to 10 pixels.
- Float the blockquote on the right margin.

13. Apply the following styles to hypertext elements:
    - Display hypertext elements as block-level elements with 2 pixels of padding.
    - Set the top, right, and bottom margins to 5 pixels. Set the left margin to 0 pixels.
    - Set the font size to 10 points.
    - Remove underlining from the hypertext links by setting the text decoration to none.
    - Add a 1-pixel-wide solid black border.
    - Change the background color to the value (255, 255, 192).
14. Apply the following styles to the address element:
    - Center the address text.
    - Display the text in a 10-point normal font (no italics).
    - Set the background color to white.
    - Set the padding size to 10 pixels and add a 1-pixel-wide solid black top border.
    - EXPLORE — Display the address only when both margins are clear of floating elements.
15. Save your changes to the file.
16. Open the **bmtour.htm** file in your Web browser. Verify that the layout resembles that shown in Figure 3-66.
17. EXPLORE — Try to locate a wide screen monitor and view the Web page under that monitor's resolution. What aspect of your style sheet allowed the columns to be resized to fit the increased width of the monitor? This type of page layout is called a fluid or liquid layout. Explain why.
18. Submit your completed files to your instructor.

Challenge | Case Problem 3

Broaden your knowledge of CSS and HTML by creating an image with an irregular text wrap.

Data Files needed for this Case Problem: banner.jpg, king1.gif – king6.gif, kingtxt.htm, and centertxt.css

Center for Diversity Stewart Tompkins is the project coordinator for the Midwest University Center for Diversity. He is currently working on a Web site titled The Voices of Civil Rights, containing Web pages with extended quotes from civil rights leaders of the past and present. He has asked you to help develop a design for the pages in the series. He has given you the text for one of the pages, which is about Dr. Martin Luther King, Jr.

Stewart has supplied a photo of Dr. King that he would like you to include on the page. He has seen how text can be made to wrap irregularly around a photo in graphic design software, and he wonders if you can do the same thing on a Web page. Although you cannot use this same technique with page elements, which are always rectangular, you can break a single image into a series of rectangles of different sizes. When the text wraps around these stacked rectangles, they provide the appearance of a single image with an irregular line wrap. Stewart asks you to try this with his Dr. King photo. Figure 3-67 shows a preview of the page you'll create. Note how the right margin of the text seems to wrap around Dr. King's image along a diagonal line, rather than a vertical one.

Figure 3-67

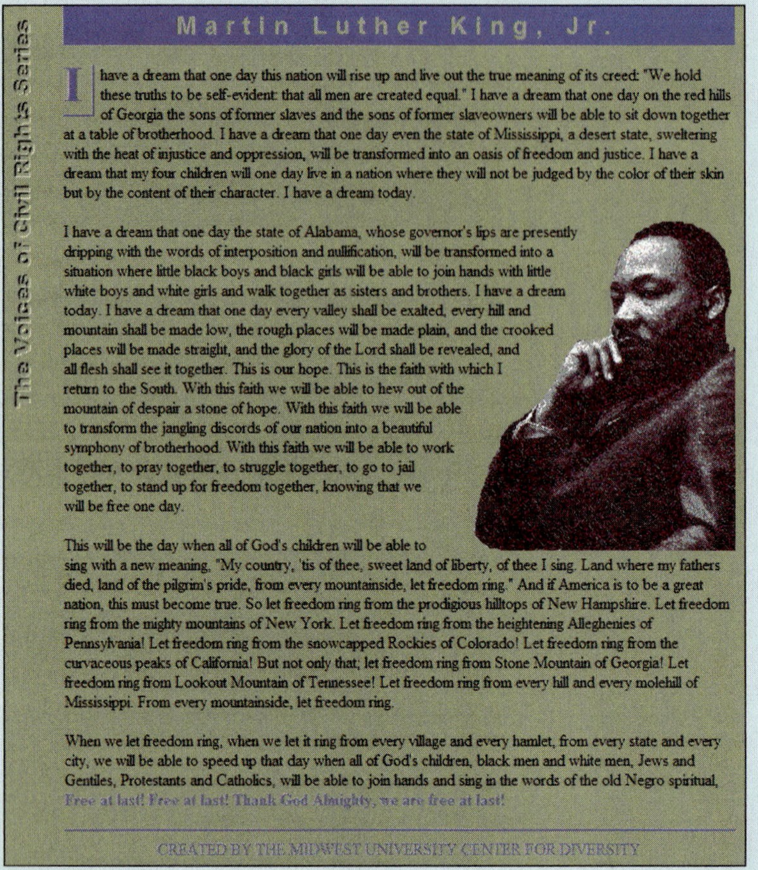

Complete the following:

1. In your text editor, open the **kingtxt.htm** and **centertxt.css** files from the tutorial.03\case3 folder included with your Data Files. Enter ***your name*** and ***the date*** in the comment section of each file. Save the files as **king.htm** and **center.css** in the same folder. Take some time to study the content and layout of the king.htm file as it appears in your text editor and Web browser.
2. Return to the **king.htm** file in your text editor. Directly below the opening <body> tag, insert a div element with the id banner. Within the div element, insert an inline image for the **banner.jpg** graphic file. Give the inline image the id, bannerImage, and specify the alternate text "The Voices of Civil Rights Series."
3. Enclose the rest of the page content, starting with the h1 heading at the top of the page through the address at the bottom of the file, in a div element with the id, pageContent.
4. Save your changes to the file.
5. In your text editor, go to the **center.css** file. Create a style for the body element that sets the font color to black, the background color to the value (204, 204, 153), and the margin to 0 em.
6. Float the banner div container on the left page margin.
7. Set the width of the pageContent div container to 42 em and the left margin to 4 em.
8. Apply the following styles to h1 headings:
   - Set the font face to Arial, Helvetica, or sans-serif.

- Set the font size to 1.5 em and the kerning to 0.5 em. Center the h1 heading text.
- Set the padding to 0.2 em.
- Set the font color to the value (204, 204, 153) and the background color to the value (102, 102, 204).

9. Display text marked as an em element in a normal bold font. Set the font color to the value (102, 102, 204).
10. Apply the following styles to the address element:
    - Set the font style to normal to remove the default italics style.
    - Display the text in uppercase letters. Set the font color to (102, 102, 204).
    - Center the address text.
    - Set the padding to 0.5 em.
    - Add a solid top border 0.1 em wide in the color value (102, 102, 204).
11. Save your changes to the **center.css** style sheet.
12. Return to the **king.htm** file in your text editor. Add a link to the center.css to the head of the document.

EXPLORE

13. Stewart wants the opening word from Dr. King's speech to appear as a drop cap. To create this effect, enclose the word in a span element and apply the following inline styles:
    - Float the span element on the left paragraph margin.
    - Set the font weight to bold and the font size to 3 em.
    - Set the font color to the value (102, 102, 240).
    - Set the line height to 0.8 em.
    - Add a solid border 0.05 em wide with the color value (102, 102, 204) to the right and bottom edge of the span element.
    - Set the bottom and right padding to 0.2 em.
    - Set the right margin to 0.2 em.

EXPLORE

14. To create an irregular line wrap around the image, you have to break the image into several files and then stack them on the left or right margin, displaying an image only when the margin is clear of the previous image. To remove the seams between the images, you have to set the top and bottom margins to 0. The Dr. Martin Luther King, Jr. graphic has been broken into six files for you. To stack them:
    - Directly below the first paragraph, insert a div element containing six inline images for the graphic files **king1.gif** through **king6.gif**. For each image, set the alternate text to an empty text string.
    - Use inline styles to set the width of the six inline images to the following values: king1.gif = 6.7 em, king2.gif = 7.85 em, king3.gif = 11.45 em, king4.gif = 14.25 em, king5.gif = 15.5 em, king6.gif = 16.6 em.
15. Scroll to the top of the file and add an embedded style sheet to the head section of the document.
16. Within the embedded style sheet, create the following styles for inline images in the document:
    - Float the images on the right margin.
    - Set the clear style so that the image is only displayed when the right margin is clear of other floating images.
    - Set the left margin to 2 em and the other margins to 0 em.
17. Directly below the style you just created, add the following styles for the inline image with the bannerImage id:
    - Set the width to 3.5 em.

- Set the value of the float style to none (to prevent this inline image from floating on the page).
- Set the margin to 0 em.

18. Save your changes to the file. Open the **king.htm** file in your Web browser and verify that it resembles the layout shown in Figure 3-67. Verify that the first letter in the speech appears as a drop cap and that the image of Dr. King is surrounded by an irregular line wrap with no seams appearing between the six stacked images.

EXPLORE

19. Using Firefox or another browser that allows the user to increase and decrease the browser's default font size, increase and decrease the font size on the Dr. King Web page. What happens to the size of the images and the general appearance of the page layout? This type of design is called an elastic layout. Can you see why? How did choosing the em unit to size the page elements and the graphic images create this effect?
20. Submit your completed files to your instructor.

Create | Case Problem 4

Test your knowledge of CSS and HTML by creating a design for a Scottish touring company's Web site.

Data Files needed for this Case Problem: castles.jpg, casttxt.htm, Hebrides.jpg, hebtxt.htm, highland.jpg, hightxt.htm, lake.jpg, lakestxt.htm, parch.jpg, and tslogo.gif

Travel Scotland! Fiona Henderson is the owner of *Travel Scotland!*, a touring company specializing in guided tours of Scotland. She's come to you for help in creating a design for the *Travel Scotland!* Web site. Fiona has four Web pages describing four of the company's tours. She's already inserted the content and gathered some graphic images to supplement her text. She wants you to take her unformatted Web pages and create an interesting design and layout.

Complete the following:

1. In your text editor, open the **casttxt.htm**, **hebtxt.htm**, **hightxt.htm**, and **lakestxt.htm** from the tutorial.03\case4 folder included with your Data Files. Enter ***your name*** and ***the date*** in the comment section of each file. Save the files as **castles.htm**, **hebrides.htm**, **highland.htm**, and **lakes.htm** in the same folder. Take some time to study the content of these four files. You are free to supplement the content of these Web pages with additional material you find on your own. You may also edit the HTML tags and attributes within these pages if they help you achieve your final design.
2. Use your text editor to create an external style sheet named **ts.css**, placed in the tutorial.03\case4 folder. Add a comment section to the style sheet containing ***your name***, ***the date***, a description of the style sheet, and its purpose in the Web site.
3. Add styles to the ts.css style sheet that you'll apply to the four pages on the *Travel Scotland!* Web site. The design of the Web site is up to you, but it should include at least one example of each of the following:
   - A style that modifies the text and background colors of page elements
   - A style that modifies the font size, face, and appearance of element text
   - A style that defines an element's padding and margins, distinctly different in at least two directions
   - A style to define the border appearance of an element
   - A style that floats an inline image or element
   - A style that adds a background image to an element
   - A style applied to a div container identified by an id value

4. Each of the four Web pages should have a slightly different appearance. Add an embedded style sheet to each file that provides a slightly different color scheme for each Web page.
5. Link your Web pages to your style sheet, and then test your Web page under a variety of browsers and monitor resolutions. Correct any problems that arise from those differing environments.
6. Submit your completed files to your instructor.

Review | Quick Check Answers

Session 3.1

1. Inline styles are styles applied directly to an element through the use of the style attribute in the element's tag. Embedded styles are styles placed in the head section of a document and apply to elements within that document. External style sheets are files separate from the document and can be applied to any document on a Web site. External style sheets are best for setting the styles of an entire Web site.
2. `/* Sunny Acres Style Sheet */`
3. `p {color: red}`
4. As left-aligned blue text
5. In red text with an ivory-color background
6. `!important`
7. `blockquote {color: rgb(221, 128, 0)}`

Session 3.2

1. `code {font-family: Courier New, monospace}`
2. 18 points
3. `h3 {text-decoration: overline underline}`
4. `address {letter-spacing: 0.5em; word-spacing: 0.9em}`
5. `dt {text-transform: uppercase}`
6. JPEG because the JPEG format supports a much larger color palette, while GIFs are limited to 256 colors and so will not display photographic images without dithering the colors.
7. `width = "200" height = "100"`
8.
```
blockquote {background-image: url(mark.jpg);
            background-repeat: no-repeat;
            background-position: left top;
            background-attachment: fixed}
```

Session 3.3

1. `#photoImage {float: left}`
2. `#photoImage {margin-right: 5px; margin-bottom: 5px}`
3. `p {padding-top: 10px; padding-bottom: 10px}`
4. `blockquote {margin-left: 20px; border-left: 4px solid gray}`
5. `#mainHeading {color: green; border: 8px double green}`
6. Internet Explorer applies the width property to the entire box, including the padding and border spaces. The CSS box model applies the width property to the content of the box, but not to the padding and margins.
7. `img {display: block}`

Ending Data Files

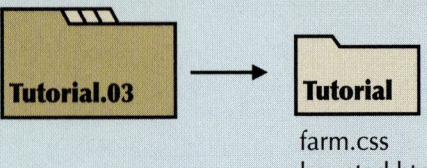

Tutorial.03 →

Tutorial
farm.css
haunted.htm
home.htm
index.htm
maze.htm
petting.htm
produce.htm
+ 9 graphic files

Review
holiday.htm
sunny.css
+ 3 graphic files

Case1
algo.htm
crypt.htm
enigma.htm
history.htm
public.htm
single.htm
+ 5 graphic files

Case2
bmtour.htm
wheels.css
+ 4 graphic files

Case3
center.css
king.htm
+ 7 graphic files

Case4
castles.htm
hebrides.htm
highland.htm
lakes.htm
ts.css
+ 6 graphic files

Tutorial 4

Objectives

Session 4.1
- Work with CSS selectors
- Create styles for lists
- Create and apply class styles
- Create a rollover effect
- Create a drop cap using a pseudo-element

Session 4.2
- Manage page layout with CSS
- Work with overflow and clipping styles
- Create stacked objects

Session 4.3
- Apply styles to various media
- Hide elements from printing
- Create and apply printer styles
- Create and prohibit page breaks for printing

Creating Special Effects with CSS

Adding Advanced Styles to a Web Site

Case | Online Scrapbooks

Scrapbooking is the popular hobby of creating albums containing photos, memorabilia, writing, and other embellishments. This hobby has become a multimillion-dollar industry with companies that specialize in scrapbooking supplies and support. One of these companies is Online Scrapbooks.

Kathy Pridham, who leads the Web development team at Online Scrapbooks, has hired you to work on the style for the new company's Web site. The Web site's home page will have information on how to get started in scrapbooking and links to other pages that contain a wide variety of information. Because the Web site will have so many pages, Kathy is using Cascading Style Sheets to manage the layout, design, and function of the pages. She has a style sheet providing the site's basic layout and design. She would like you to add features such as graphical bullets, rollover effects, and drop caps. To make those enhancements, you'll need to use some of the special features supported by CSS.

Kathy knows that many users want to access the Web site from mobile devices, while others want to be able to print some of the site's contents. She wants the site to work with any kind of output, including mobile devices and printed output.

Starting Data Files

Tutorial.04 →

Tutorial
printtxt.css
samptxt.htm
scrapstxt.css
starttxt.htm
+ 4 graphic files

Demo
demo_positioning.htm
+ 5 graphic files

Review
gallerytxt.htm
printertxt.css
screentxt.css
+ 7 graphics files

Case1
h01txt.htm-h18txt.htm
printtxt.css
willettxt.css
+ 21 graphic files

Case2
cwpagetxt.htm
cwtxt.css
+ 2 graphic files

Case3
longstxt.htm
+ 11 graphic files

Case4
bizetbio.txt
bizetlist.txt
mozartbio.txt
mozartlist.txt
puccinibio.txt
puccinilist.txt
verdibio.txt
verdilist.txt
wagnerbio.txt
wagnerlist.txt
+ 5 graphic files

Session 4.1

Working with Selector Patterns

Kathy has already created a basic Web page describing how to get started in scrapbooking. She's written an article and created the basic Web page layout using an external style sheet. She's provided you with her HTML document, her graphic files, and her style sheet to study. Kathy suggests that this Web page would be a good place to start in your task of enhancing her basic design.

To view Kathy's data files:

1. In your text editor, open the **starttxt.htm** and **scrapstxt.css** files, located in the tutorial.04\tutorial folder included with your Data Files. Within the comment section at the top of each file, add ***your name*** and ***the date*** in the space provided. Save the files as **start.htm** and **scraps.css**, respectively, in the same folder.
2. Take some time to review the code in both the external style sheet file and the HTML document. Note how the CSS styles are applied to specific elements in the start.htm file to create an interesting layout and design.
3. Open **start.htm** in your Web browser. Figure 4-1 shows the current appearance of the start.htm file.

Figure 4-1 Initial design for the Getting Started page

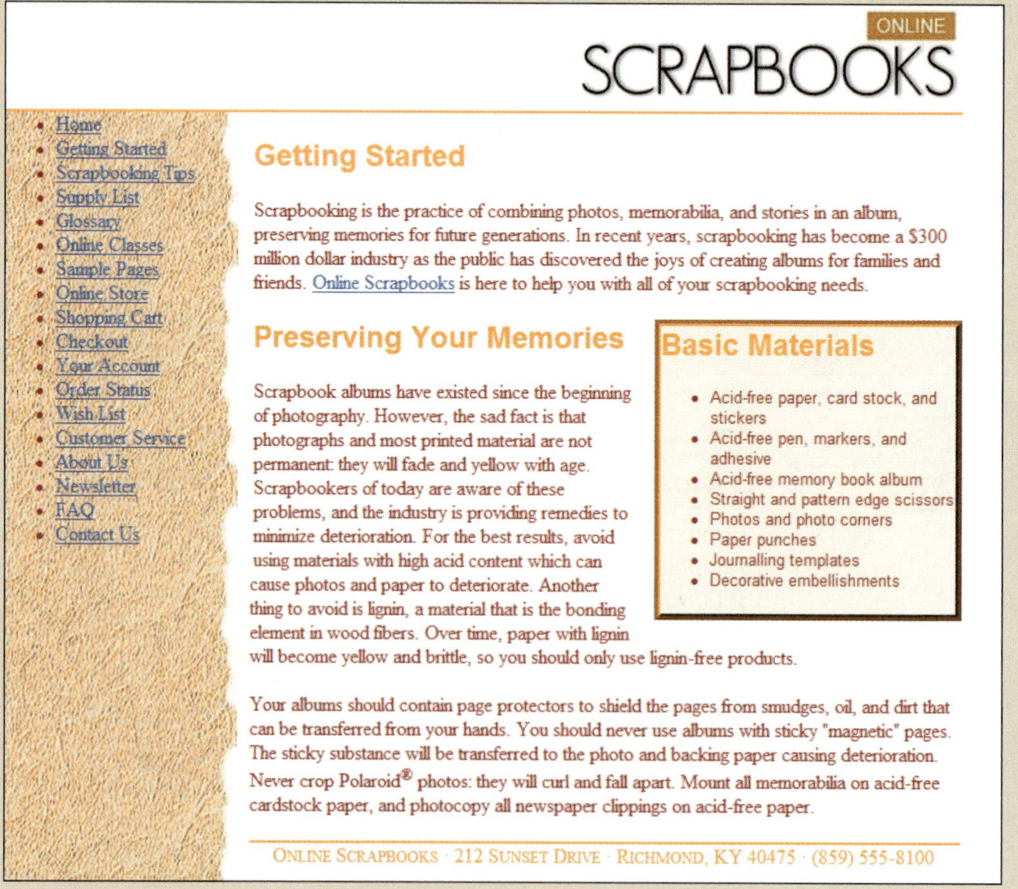
ONLINE
SCRAPBOOKS
Home
Getting Started
Scrapbooking Tips
Supply List
Glossary
Online Classes
Sample Pages
Online Store
Shopping Cart
Checkout
Your Account
Order Status
Wish List
Customer Service
About Us
Newsletter
FAQ
Contact Us
Getting Started
Scrapbooking is the practice of combining photos, memorabilia, and stories in an album, preserving memories for future generations. In recent years, scrapbooking has become a $300 million dollar industry as the public has discovered the joys of creating albums for families and friends. Online Scrapbooks is here to help you with all of your scrapbooking needs.
Preserving Your Memories
Scrapbook albums have existed since the beginning of photography. However, the sad fact is that photographs and most printed material are not permanent: they will fade and yellow with age. Scrapbookers of today are aware of these problems, and the industry is providing remedies to minimize deterioration. For the best results, avoid using materials with high acid content which can cause photos and paper to deteriorate. Another thing to avoid is lignin, a material that is the bonding element in wood fibers. Over time, paper with lignin will become yellow and brittle, so you should only use lignin-free products.
Basic Materials
Acid-free paper, card stock, and stickers
Acid-free pen, markers, and adhesive
Acid-free memory book album
Straight and pattern edge scissors
Photos and photo corners
Paper punches
Journalling templates
Decorative embellishments
Your albums should contain page protectors to shield the pages from smudges, oil, and dirt that can be transferred from your hands. You should never use albums with sticky "magnetic" pages. The sticky substance will be transferred to the photo and backing paper causing deterioration. Never crop Polaroid® photos: they will curl and fall apart. Mount all memorabilia on acid-free cardstock paper, and photocopy all newspaper clippings on acid-free paper.
ONLINE SCRAPBOOKS · 212 SUNSET DRIVE · RICHMOND, KY 40475 · (859) 555-8100

As you can see from Figure 4-1, Kathy has applied a layout in which the list of links floats on the left page margin and a box describing basic scrapbooking materials floats on the right margin. There is one main heading marked as an h1 element displayed at the top of page, providing a logo with the company name.

The three other headings—Getting Started, Preserving Your Memories, and Basic Materials—are marked as h2 elements. Kathy wants to apply a slightly different format to the Basic Materials h2 heading than the one applied to the Getting Started and Preserving Your Memories h2 headings. One way of applying a specific format to this heading is through the use of an id attribute. However, Kathy doesn't want to maintain a list of id values for all the various elements on her Web page. Instead, she would like to create styles for elements based on their location or their use in the document. She asks if this can be done with CSS.

Contextual Selectors

So far, the only styles you've worked with are ones in which the style selector references either an element (or a group of elements) or an element identified by an id. For example, the style

```
b {color: blue}
```

displays all boldface text in a blue font. What would you do, however, if you didn't want every example of boldface text to be displayed in a blue font? What if you wanted this style applied only to boldface text located within an ordered or unordered list?

Recall that on a Web page, elements are nested within other elements, forming a hierarchical tree structure. The top element on the Web page is the body element because it contains all of the content appearing in the page. From this top element, other elements descend. Figure 4-2 shows an example of such a tree structure for a Web page consisting of a few headings, a couple of paragraphs, some boldface elements, and a span element nested within a paragraph.

Figure 4-2 **A sample tree hierarchy of page elements**

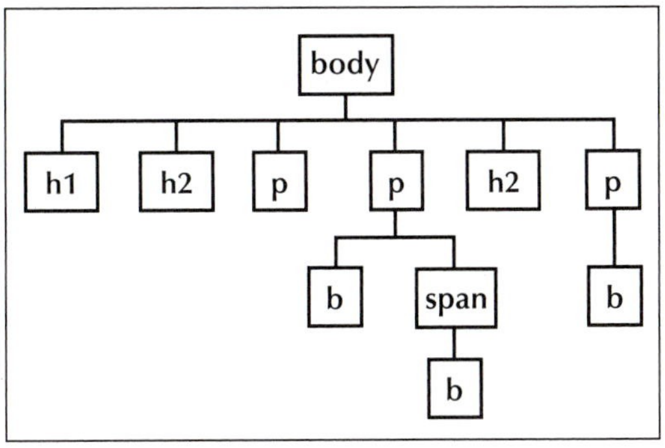

To take advantage of this tree structure, CSS allows you to create **contextual selectors** that express the location of an element within the hierarchy of elements. The general syntax of a contextual selector has the form

```
parent descendant {styles}
```

where *parent* is the parent element, *descendant* is a descendant of the parent, and *styles* are the styles to be applied to the descendant element. To apply a blue color only to boldface text found in lists, you would use the style:

```
li b {color: blue}
```

In this case, li is the parent element and b is the descendant element (because it is contained within the list item). Any bold element not nested within a list element is not affected by this style. Note that the descendant element does not have to be a direct child of the parent element; it can appear several levels below the parent element in hierarchy. For example in the code

```
<li>
   <span><b>Special</b>Orders</span> this month!
</li>
```

the bold element is a descendant of the list item, but it is a direct child only of the span element. So the word "Special" would appear in a bold font if the above style is applied to the document. Contextual selectors can be grouped with other selectors. The following style applies a blue font to h2 headings and to boldface list items, but nowhere else:

```
li b, h2 {color: blue}
```

Contextual selectors can also be applied with elements marked with a specific id. The style

```
#notes b {color: blue}
```

displays bold text in a blue font if it is nested within an element with an id of notes.

The parent/descendant form is only one example of a contextual selector. Figure 4-3 describes some of the other contextual forms supported by CSS.

Figure 4-3 **Contextual selectors**

Selector	Description
*	Matches any element in the hierarchy
e	Matches any element, *e*, in the hierarchy
e1, *e2*, *e3*, ...	Matches the group of elements: *e1*, *e2*, *e3*, ...
e *f*	Matches any element, *f*, that is a descendant of an element, e
e > *f*	Matches any element, *f*, that is a direct child of an element, e
e + *f*	Matches any element, *f*, that is immediately preceded by a sibling element, e

For example, the style

```
* {color: blue}
```

causes *all* of the elements in the document to appear in a blue font. On the other hand, the style

```
p > b {color: blue}
```

applies the blue font only to boldface text that is contained within a paragraph element as a child of that element and not any descendent. Figure 4-4 provides additional examples of how to select different elements of the Web page document based on the expression in the contextual selector. Selected elements are highlighted in red for each pattern. Remember that because of style inheritance, any style applied to an element is passed down the document tree. So a style applied to a paragraph element is automatically passed down to elements contained within that paragraph unless it conflicts with a more specific style.

Figure 4-4 Simple and contextual selectors

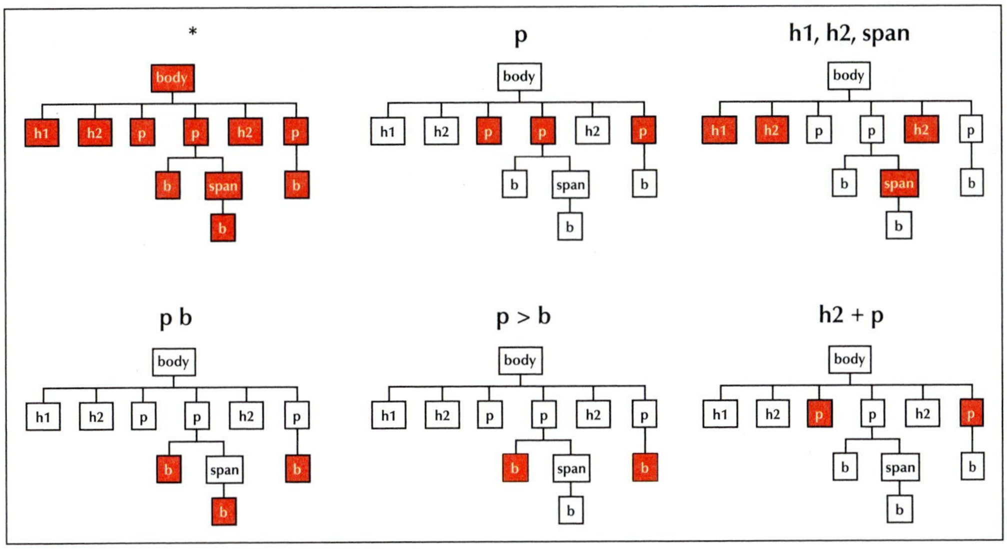

Although the contextual selectors listed in Figure 4-3 are part of the specifications for CSS2, they are not well supported by earlier versions of the Internet Explorer browser. In particular, the *e* > *f* and *e* + *f* contextual selectors should be used with caution if you need to support Internet Explorer. Other browsers, including Firefox, Opera, and Safari, do support all of the contextual selectors described in Figure 4-3.

Tip

Each browser has built-in margin and padding values for different page elements. You can ensure that your own values have precedence by applying the style declaration `* {margin: 0; padding: 0}` to "erase" all of the default margin and padding settings.

Attribute Selectors

On occasion you might also need to select elements based on their attribute values. For example, if you want to display link text in a blue font, you might use the following declaration:

```
a {color: blue}
```

However, this declaration makes no distinction between <a> tags used to mark links and <a> tags used to mark document anchors (for a discussion of anchors, see Tutorial 2). HTML makes this distinction based on the presence or absence of the href attribute. To select an element based on the element's attributes, you can create an **attribute selector** that has the form

```
element[att] {styles}
```

where *element* is a page element, *att* is the name of an attribute associated with the element, and *styles* are the styles applied to the element. The declaration

```
a[href] {color: blue}
```

applies the blue font color style only to link elements that contain an href attribute. Any <a> tag used to mark anchors would not contain the href attribute, and therefore would not be affected by this style. Figure 4-5 describes some of the other attribute selectors supported by CSS.

Figure 4-5 **Attribute selectors**

Selector	Description	Example	Interpretation
`elem[att]`	The element contains the *att* attribute	`a[href]`	Matches hypertext elements containing the href attribute
`elem[att="val"]`	The element's *att* attribute equals *val*	`a[href="gloss.htm"]`	Matches hypertext elements whose href attribute equals "gloss.htm"
`elem[att~="val"]`	The element's *att* attribute value is a space-separated list of words, one of which is exactly *val*	`a[rel~="glossary"]`	Matches hypertext elements whose rel attribute contains the word "glossary"
`elem[att|="val"]`	The element's *att* attribute value is a hyphen-separated list of words beginning with *val*	`p[id|="first"]`	Matches paragraphs whose id attribute starts with the word "first" in a hyphen-separated list of words
`elem[att^="val"]`	The element's *att* attribute begins with *val* (CSS3)	`a[rel^="prev"]`	Matches hypertext elements whose rel attribute begins with "prev"
`elem[att$="val"]`	The element's *att* attribute ends with *val* (CSS3)	`a[href$="org"]`	Matches hypertext elements whose href attribute ends with "org"
`elem[att*="val"]`	The element's *att* attribute contains the value *val* (CSS3)	`a[href*="faq"]`	Matches hypertext elements whose href attribute contains the text string "faq"

Browser support for attribute selectors is mixed. For this reason, you should use attribute selectors with caution. Note that some of the attribute selectors listed in Figure 4-5 are part of the proposed specifications for CSS3 and have scattered browser support at the present time. As with contextual selectors, attribute selectors enjoy good support from Firefox, Opera, and Safari, but poor support from Internet Explorer. IE does support attribute and contextual selectors if you write your HTML code to put Internet Explorer into standards mode (for a discussion of standards mode, see Tutorial 3).

Using Selector Patterns | Reference Window

- To apply a style to all elements in the document, use the * selector.
- To apply a style to a single element, use the *e* selector, where *e* is the name of the element.
- To apply a selector to a descendant element, *f*, use the *e f* selector, where *e* is the name of the parent element and *f* is an element nested within the parent.
- To apply a selector to a child element, *f*, use the *e* > *f* selector, where *e* is the name of a parent element and *f* is an element that is a direct child of the parent.
- To apply a selector to a sibling element, use the *e* + *f* selector, where *e* and *f* are siblings and *f* immediately follows *e* in the document tree.

Applying a Selector Pattern

After discussing how to use selector patterns, you and Kathy decide to apply them to her Getting Started document. You decide to create a style for the h2 heading in the Basic Materials box so that you can use the style in similar boxes on other pages in the Online Scrapbooking site. You'll center this heading, change the background color to white, reduce the top margin to 0 pixels, and add a solid orange border to the bottom of the element. Because this heading appears within a div element that is identified with an id value of pullout, you'll add the following style to the style sheet:

```
#pullout h2 {text-align: center; background-color: white; margin-top:
 0px;
             border-bottom: 2px solid orange}
```

Add this style declaration to the scraps.css file.

To add a contextual selector to the style sheet:

1. Go to the **scraps.css** file in your text editor.
2. Directly below the style for the #pullout selector, insert the following style, as shown in Figure 4-6:

```
#pullout h2 {text-align: center; background-color: white;
             margin-top: 0px; border-bottom: 2px solid orange}
```

Figure 4-6 Using a contextual selector

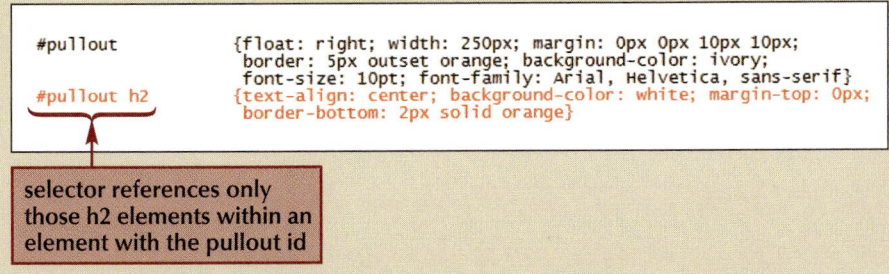

```
#pullout          {float: right; width: 250px; margin: 0px 0px 10px 10px;
                   border: 5px outset orange; background-color: ivory;
                   font-size: 10pt; font-family: Arial, Helvetica, sans-serif}
#pullout h2       {text-align: center; background-color: white; margin-top: 0px;
                   border-bottom: 2px solid orange}
```

selector references only those h2 elements within an element with the pullout id

3. Save your changes to the file and then reload **start.htm** in your Web browser. Figure 4-7 shows the revised appearance of the document.

Figure 4-7 Applying a style to a nested h2 element

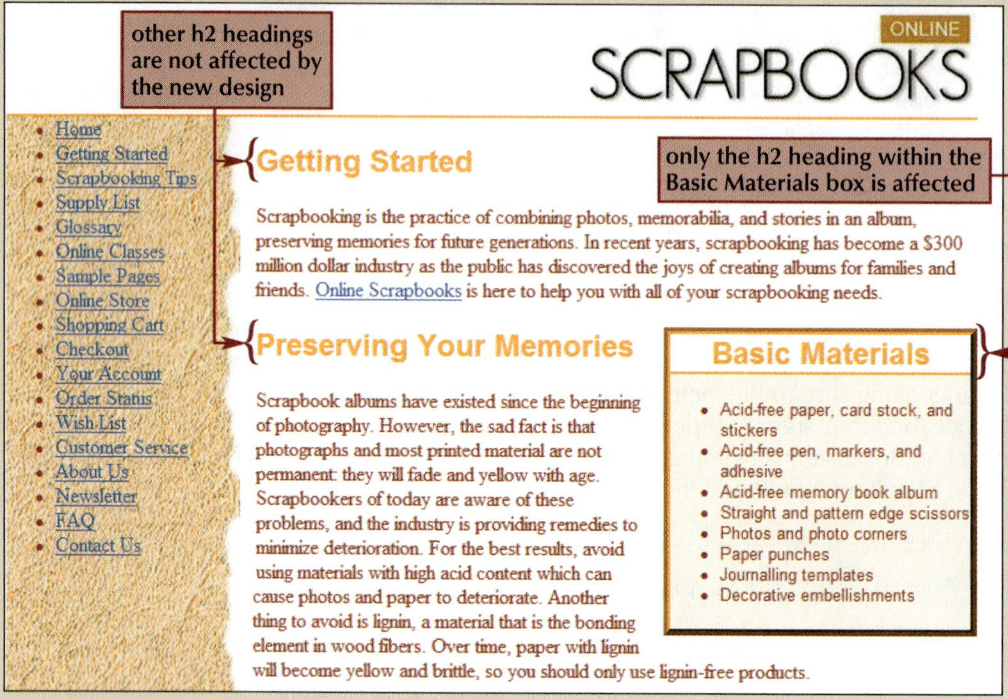
other h2 headings are not affected by the new design
ONLINE
SCRAPBOOKS
Home
Getting Started
Scrapbooking Tips
Supply List
Glossary
Online Classes
Sample Pages
Online Store
Shopping Cart
Checkout
Your Account
Order Status
Wish List
Customer Service
About Us
Newsletter
FAQ
Contact Us
Getting Started
only the h2 heading within the Basic Materials box is affected
Scrapbooking is the practice of combining photos, memorabilia, and stories in an album, preserving memories for future generations. In recent years, scrapbooking has become a $300 million dollar industry as the public has discovered the joys of creating albums for families and friends. Online Scrapbooks is here to help you with all of your scrapbooking needs.
Preserving Your Memories
Basic Materials
Acid-free paper, card stock, and stickers
Acid-free pen, markers, and adhesive
Acid-free memory book album
Straight and pattern edge scissors
Photos and photo corners
Paper punches
Journalling templates
Decorative embellishments
Scrapbook albums have existed since the beginning of photography. However, the sad fact is that photographs and most printed material are not permanent: they will fade and yellow with age. Scrapbookers of today are aware of these problems, and the industry is providing remedies to minimize deterioration. For the best results, avoid using materials with high acid content which can cause photos and paper to deteriorate. Another thing to avoid is lignin, a material that is the bonding element in wood fibers. Over time, paper with lignin will become yellow and brittle, so you should only use lignin-free products.

As shown in Figure 4-7, the appearance of the h2 element nested within the Basic Materials box has been modified under the new style, but h2 elements located elsewhere in the document retain their original appearance.

Conditional Comments and Internet Explorer | InSight

Several versions of the Internet Explorer browser don't follow all of the CSS specifications for selectors and styles. You can correct many of the incompatibilities by converting your HTML code to XHTML and putting IE into standards mode rather than quirks mode. However, this might not work for older versions of Internet Explorer, such as IE5 and even IE6. For those browser versions, you can use **conditional comments** that allow you to apply different HTML code for different versions of Internet Explorer. The general syntax of a conditional comment is

```
<!--[if condition IE version]><!-->
   HTML code
<!--<![endif]-->
```

where *condition* is a condition that is either true or false, *version* is the version number of an IE browser, and *HTML code* is code that will be run if *condition* is true. For example, the code

```
<!--[if lt IE 6]><!-->
   <link rel="stylesheet" type="text/css" href="old.css" />
<!--<![endif]-->
```

links the Web page to the old.css style sheet file, but only if the browser version in use is older than Internet Explorer 6. In this case, the *condition* value is lt for "less than." Other *condition* values include lte (less than or equal to), gt (greater than), gte (greater than or equal to), and ! (not equal to). If you specify no *condition* value, the *HTML code* will be run only for the specified version of Internet Explorer. You can also leave off the version number to apply the HTML code to Internet Explorer but not to other browsers. So the code

```
<!--[if IE]><!-->
   <link rel="stylesheet" type="text/css" href="ie_styles.css" />
<!--<![endif]-->
```

links the file to the ie_styles.css style sheet file, but only if Internet Explorer is being used.

Conditional comments are one of the best ways you can tailor your HTML code to match the capabilities of different versions of Internet Explorer and other browsers.

Applying Styles to Lists

Kathy has her Web page links in an unordered list that is displayed in a box floated on the left page margin. Like all unordered lists, the browser displays the items in this list with bullet markers. Kathy would like to remove the bullet markers from this list. To remove the markers you can apply one of the many CSS list styles.

Choosing a List Style Type

To specify the list marker displayed by the browser, you can apply the style

```
list-style-type: type
```

where *type* is one of the markers shown in Figure 4-8.

Figure 4-8 **List style types**

list-style-type	Marker (s)
disc	●
circle	○
square	□
decimal	1, 2, 3, 4, ...
decimal-leading-zero	01, 02, 03, 04, ...
lower-roman	i, ii, iii, iv, ...
upper-roman	I, II, III, IV, ...
lower-alpha	a, b, c, d, ...
upper-alpha	A, B, C, D, ...
none	no marker displayed

For example, to create a list with alphabetical markers such as

A. Home
B. Getting Started
C. Scrapbooking Tips
D. Supply List

you would apply the following list style to the ol list element:

```
ol {list-style-type: upper-alpha}
```

List style types can be used with contextual selectors to create an outline style for several levels of nested lists. Figure 4-9 shows an example in which several levels of list style markers are used in formatting an outline. Note that each marker style is determined by the location of each ordered list within the levels of the outline. The top level is displayed with uppercase Roman numerals; the bottom level, nested within three other ordered lists, uses lowercase letters for markers.

Creating an outline style **Figure 4-9**

```
ol          {list-style-type: upper-roman}
ol ol       {list-style-type: upper-alpha}
ol ol ol    {list-style-type: decimal    }
ol ol ol ol {list-style-type: lower-alpha}
```

styles

```
<ol>
   <li>Main Point 1</li>

   <ol>
      <li>Subpoint 1</li>
      <li>Subpoint 2</li>

      <ol>
         <li>Item 1</li>
         <li>Item 2</li>

         <ol>
            <li>Subitem 1</li>
            <li>Subitem 2</li>
         </ol>

         <li>Item 3</li>
      </ol>

      <li>Subpoint 3</li>
   </ol>

   <li>Main Point 2</li>
   <li>Main Point 3</li>
</ol>
```

HTML code

```
I.   Main Point 1
     A. Subpoint 1
     B. Subpoint 2
        1. Item 1
        2. Item 2
           a. Subitem 1
           b. Subitem 2
        3. Item 3
     C. Subpoint 3
II.  Main Point 2
III. Main Point 3
```

text as rendered by browser

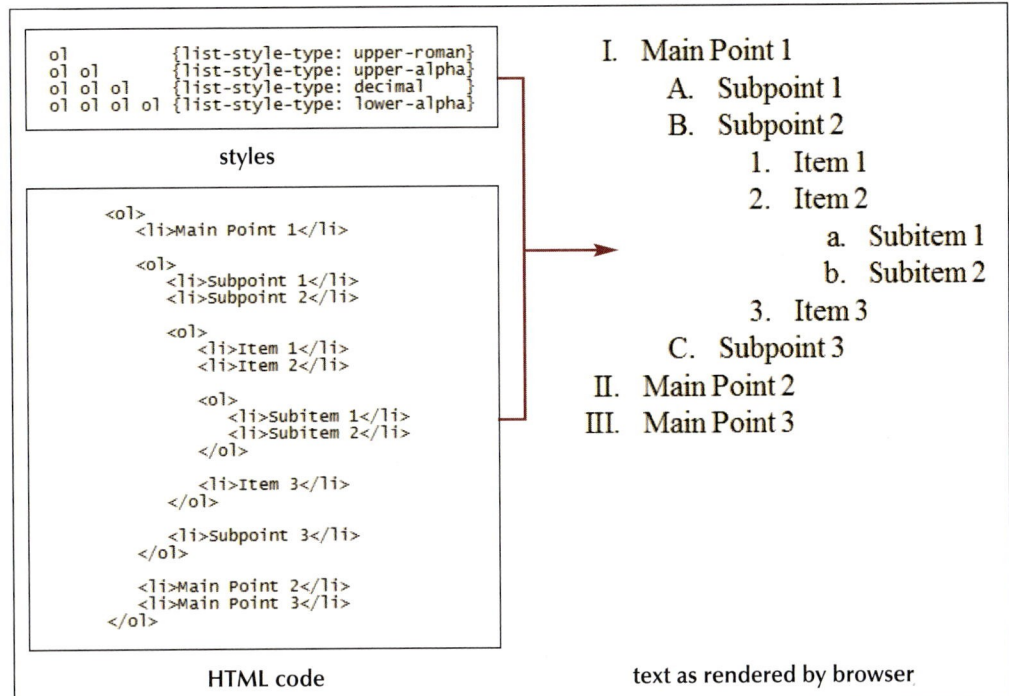

If you don't find the marker you want from the list-style-type style, you can supply your own in a graphic image file. To use a graphic image for the list marker, use the style

```
list-style-image: url(url)
```

where (*url*) is the URL of the graphic image file. The style

```
ul {list-style-image: url(redball.gif) }
```

displays items in an unordered list marked with the graphic image in the redball.gif file.

Kathy wants her list of links to appear without any bullet marker, but she wants the list of basic materials to appear with a bullet marker based on one of her graphic image files. She suggests that you use both the list-style-type and list-style-image attributes to modify the appearance of the two lists. To differentiate between the two lists, you'll use contextual selectors. The list of links is an unordered list nested within a div container with the id named links, while the list of basic materials is nested within the pullout div box.

To apply a list style to Kathy's list of links:

1. Return to the **scraps.css** file in your text editor.
2. Directly below the style for the #links selector, enter:

   ```
   #links ul   {list-style-type: none}
   ```

3. Directly below the style for the #pullout h2 selector, enter:

   ```
   #pullout ul {list-style-image: url(bullet.jpg)}
   ```

   Figure 4-10 shows the revised code in the style sheet.

Figure 4-10 Setting the style of the list marker

```
body        {margin: 0px; color: brown;
             background: white url(back.jpg) repeat-y}
h1, h2, h3  {font-family: Arial, Helvetica, sans-serif; color: orange}
h1          {border-bottom: 2px solid orange; background-color: white; margin: 0px; padding: 0px}
ul          {margin-top:0px}

#outer_container    {width: 780px}
#head               {text-align: right}

#links              {float: left; width: 200px}
#links ul           {list-style-type: none}

#article            {margin-left: 200px}

#pullout            {float: right; width: 250px; margin: 0px 0px 10px 10px;
                     border: 5px outset orange; background-color: ivory;
                     font-size: 10pt; font-family: Arial, Helvetica, sans-serif}
#pullout h2         {text-align: center; background-color: white; margin-top: 0px;
                     border-bottom: 2px solid orange}
#pullout ul         {list-style-image: url(bullet.jpg)}

address             {text-align: center; font-style: normal; font-variant: small-caps;
                     border-top: 2px solid orange; color: orange}
```

no marker is used with the list

the graphic file bullet.jpg is used for the list marker

4. Save your changes to the file, and then refresh **start.htm** in your Web browser. Figure 4-11 shows the revised appearance of the two lists in the document.

Figure 4-11 Formatted lists

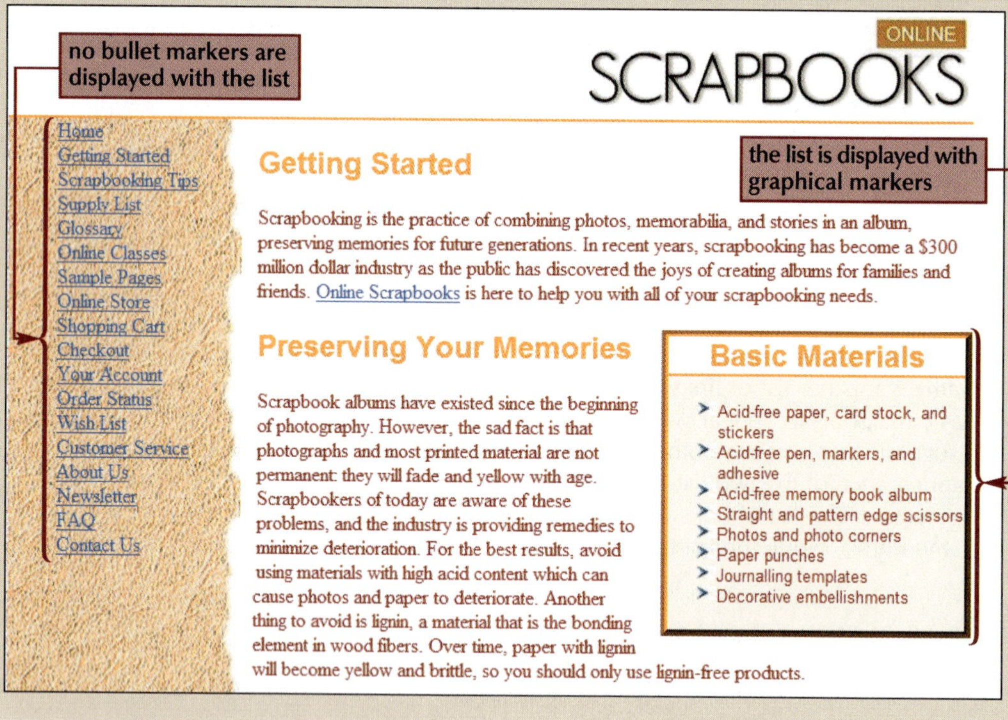
no bullet markers are displayed with the list
ONLINE
SCRAPBOOKS
Home
Getting Started
Scrapbooking Tips
Supply List
Glossary
Online Classes
Sample Pages
Online Store
Shopping Cart
Checkout
Your Account
Order Status
Wish List
Customer Service
About Us
Newsletter
FAQ
Contact Us
Getting Started
the list is displayed with graphical markers
Scrapbooking is the practice of combining photos, memorabilia, and stories in an album, preserving memories for future generations. In recent years, scrapbooking has become a $300 million dollar industry as the public has discovered the joys of creating albums for families and friends. Online Scrapbooks is here to help you with all of your scrapbooking needs.
Preserving Your Memories
Scrapbook albums have existed since the beginning of photography. However, the sad fact is that photographs and most printed material are not permanent: they will fade and yellow with age. Scrapbookers of today are aware of these problems, and the industry is providing remedies to minimize deterioration. For the best results, avoid using materials with high acid content which can cause photos and paper to deteriorate. Another thing to avoid is lignin, a material that is the bonding element in wood fibers. Over time, paper with lignin will become yellow and brittle, so you should only use lignin-free products.
Basic Materials
Acid-free paper, card stock, and stickers
Acid-free pen, markers, and adhesive
Acid-free memory book album
Straight and pattern edge scissors
Photos and photo corners
Paper punches
Journalling templates
Decorative embellishments

Tip

Web browsers always place bullets to the left of the list text. To create a right-side bullet marker, add a background image containing the marker symbol to each list item, placing the image on the right border of the list element.

The bullet markers have been removed from the list of links and have been replaced by blue arrows in the Basic Materials list.

Defining the List Position and Layout

Kathy likes the revised markers, but she thinks there's too much empty space to the left of the lists. She would like you to modify the layout to remove the extra space. As you learned in Tutorial 1, each list is treated as a block-level element. By default, most browsers place the list marker to the left of this block, lining up the markers with each list item. You can change this default behavior by using the style

```
list-style-position: position
```

where *position* is either "outside" (the default) or "inside." Placing the marker inside of the block causes the list text to flow around the marker. Figure 4-12 shows how the list-style-position affects the appearance of a bulleted list.

Figure 4-12 **Formatted lists**

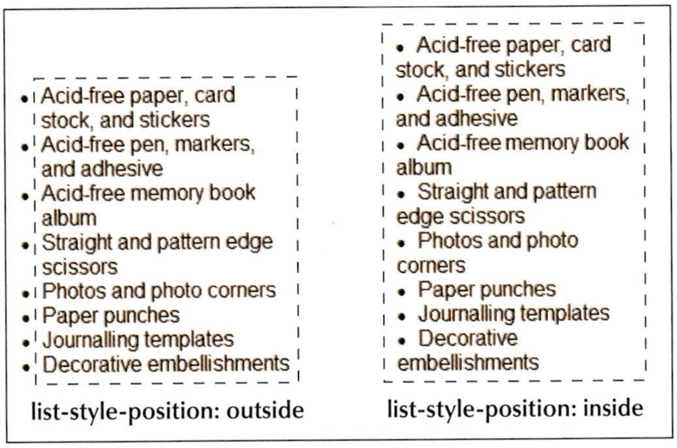

By specifying "inside" for the list-style-position value, you force both the list text and the list marker to be displayed inside of the block. With the addition of the list marker, you will have less space available for the list text.

When a browser renders a list, it offsets the list text a certain distance from the bullet marker. At this time there is no style for specifying the space between the list marker and the list text. The browser also indents the entire list a certain distance from other elements on the page. There is no commonly accepted value for the length that the entire list is indented. Browsers indent lists by setting a value for either the list's left margin or left padding. Firefox indents the list by setting the left padding value, while Opera and Internet Explorer set the size of the left margin. So to have a consistent layout across all browsers, you need to set a value for both the left padding and the left margin.

The internal style sheets for Explorer and Opera set the left margin size to 40 pixels or about 2.5 em and set the left padding space to 0 pixels. Firefox's internal style sheet does the opposite, setting the size of the left margin to 0 pixels and the left padding space to 40 pixels or 2.5 em. So if you want to reduce the indent applied by the browser, you should choose a style that reduces the sum of the left margin and left padding spaces to less than 40 pixels or 2.5 em. Finding the right combination of left padding and left margin values is often a matter of trial and error; you'll have to test your choices under different browsers and different resolutions.

Reference Window | Applying List Styles

- To define appearance of the list marker, use the style
  `list-style-type: type`
  where *type* is disc, circle, square, decimal, decimal-leading-zero, lower-roman, upper-roman, lower-alpha, upper-alpha, or none.
- To insert a graphic image as a list marker, use the style
  `list-style-image: url(url)`
  where (*url*) is the URL of the graphic image file.
- To set the position of the list marker, use the style
  `list-style-position: position`
  where *position* is inside or outside.
- To define all of the list style properties in a single style, use
  `list-style: type url(url) position`

After some work, you decide to indent Kathy's list of links by 15 pixels and the Basic Materials list by 25 pixels. You'll add these styles to the scraps.css external style sheet.

To change the margins and padding for the two lists:

1. Return to the **scraps.css** file in your text editor.
2. Add the following style to the style declaration for the #links ul selector:

   ```
   margin-left: 15px; padding-left: 0px
   ```
3. Add the following to the style declaration for the #pullout ul selector:

   ```
   margin-left: 25px; padding-left: 0px
   ```

   Figure 4-13 shows the revised style code.

Figure 4-13 Setting the spacing within the lists

```
#outer_container    {width: 780px}
#head               {text-align: right}

#links              {float: left; width: 200px}
#links ul           {list-style-type: none; margin-left: 15px; padding-left: 0px}

#article            {margin-left: 200px}

#pullout            {float: right; width: 250px; margin: 0px 0px 10px 10px;
                     border: 5px outset orange; background-color: ivory;
                     font-size: 10pt; font-family: Arial, Helvetica, sans-serif}
#pullout h2         {text-align: center; background-color: white; margin-top: 0px;
                     border-bottom: 2px solid orange}
#pullout ul         {list-style-image: url(bullet.jpg); margin-left: 25px; padding-left: 0px}

address             {text-align: center; font-style: normal; font-variant: small-caps;
                     border-top: 2px solid orange; color: orange}
```

4. Save your changes to the file, and then reload or refresh **start.htm** in your Web browser. Verify that both lists moved slightly to the left as a result of the reduced left margin and left padding values in the scraps.css style sheet.

You can combine all of the CSS styles for lists into a single style attribute. The syntax of this combined style is

```
list-style: type url(url) position
```

where *type* is one of the CSS marker types, (*url*) is the location of a graphic file containing a marker image, and *position* is the position of the list markers relative to the containing box.

Nongraphical browsers use the marker defined by the *type* value, while graphical browsers use the image from the graphic file. For example, the style

```
ul {list-style: circle url(dot.gif) inside}
```

displays unordered lists using the marker stored in the dot.gif file; unless a nongraphical browser is displaying the page, in which case the circle marker is applied. In both cases, the marker will be displayed on the inside of the box surrounding the list.

Tip

You can change a vertical list into a horizontal list by changing the display style of the list elements to inline.

Working with Classes

The list of links on the Getting Started page covers three main areas: pages that teach scrapbooking, pages that sell products, and pages that provide information about the company. Although Kathy has ordered the links by area, the sections are not separated visually on the rendered page. Kathy suggests that you increase the space between the three groups so it's clear where one group ends and another starts. One method for doing this is to mark the first link in each group, and then to increase the size of the margin above those links. You can mark those links using the class attribute. The class attribute is used when you want to identify elements that share a common characteristic. It has the syntax

```
<elem class="class"> ... </elem>
```

where *elem* is an element in the body of the Web page and *class* is a name that identifies the class of objects to which the element belongs. The HTML code

```
<h2 class="subtitle">Getting Started</h2>
<h2 class="subtitle">Preserving Your Memories</h2>
```

marks both of the h2 headings—Getting Started and Preserving Your Memories—as belonging to the subtitle class. Note that unlike the id attribute, several elements can share the same class value. The class values need not be assigned to the same type of element. You can, for example, also mark h3 headings and address elements as belonging to the subtitle class if it suits your purpose. Also, unlike the id attribute, you can place several class values in a space-separated list in the class attribute. The h2 element

```
<h2 class="subtitle mainpage">Preserving Your Memories</h2>
```

belongs to both the subtitle and the mainpage classes.

The advantage of the class attribute is that you can use it to assign the same style to multiple elements sharing the same class value. The selector for the class attribute is

```
.class {styles}
```

where *class* is the name of the class and *styles* are the styles applied to that class of element. So to display all elements belonging to the subtitle class in a blue font, you could apply the following style:

```
.subtitle {color: blue}
```

Because the same class name can be used with elements of different types, you might need to specify exactly which elements of a particular class receive a defined style. This is done using the selector

```
elem.class {styles}
```

where *elem* is the element and *class* is the class. The style

```
h2.subtitle {color: blue}
```

applies a blue font to elements of the subtitle class, but only if they are h2 headings. You can also use class selectors with other selectors in more complicated expressions. The style

```
blockquote h2.subtitle {color: blue}
```

applies the blue font color only to h2 headings of the subtitle class nested within a blockquote element.

Reference Window | Applying a Style to an Element Class

- To assign an element to a class, add the attribute
  `class="class"`
  to the element's markup tag, where *class* is the name of the class.
- To apply a style to a class of elements, use the selector
  `.class`
  where *class* is the name of the class.
- To apply a style to an element of a particular class, use the selector
  `elem.class`
  where *elem* is the name of the element and *class* is the name of the class.

Now that you've seen how to create and apply a style to an element class, you can create a style for the list of links on the Getting Started page. The three links that indicate the start of a new link group are named Home, Online Store, and About Us. You need to mark these as belonging to the newGroup class and then apply a style that increases the top margin of these elements.

To create a style for a class of elements:

1. Go to the **start.htm** file in your text editor.
2. Locate the div element containing the list of links, and then insert the attribute

   ```
   class="newGroup"
   ```

   in the opening <li> tag for the Home, Online Store, and About Us links. See Figure 4-14.

Figure 4-14 **Inserting the class attribute**

```
<div id="links">
   <ul>
      <li class="newGroup"><a href="#">Home</a></li>
      <li><a href="#">Getting Started</a></li>
      <li><a href="#">Scrapbooking Tips</a></li>
      <li><a href="#">Supply List</a></li>
      <li><a href="#">Glossary</a></li>
      <li><a href="#">Online Classes</a></li>
      <li><a href="#">Sample Pages</a></li>
      <li class="newGroup"><a href="#">Online Store</a></li>
      <li><a href="#">Shopping Cart</a></li>
      <li><a href="#">Checkout</a></li>
      <li><a href="#">Your Account</a></li>
      <li><a href="#">Order Status</a></li>
      <li><a href="#">Wish List</a></li>
      <li><a href="#">Customer Service</a></li>
      <li class="newGroup"><a href="#">About Us</a></li>
      <li><a href="#">Newsletter</a></li>
      <li><a href="#">FAQ</a></li>
      <li><a href="#">Contact Us</a></li>
   </ul>
</div>
```

3. Save your changes to the file.

   Next you'll go to the style sheet and create a style for the class of newGroup elements.

4. Return to the **scraps.css** file in your text editor. Directly below the style for the #links ul selector, insert the following style:

   #links li.newGroup {margin-top: 15px}

   Note that the selector includes both the element name and the class name to make it clear that elements receive the margin-top style. Figure 4-15 shows the revised style code.

Figure 4-15 **Defining a style for the newGroup class**

```
#links           {float: left; width: 200px}
#links ul        {list-style-type: none; margin-left: 15px; padding-left: 0px}
#links li.newGroup {margin-top: 15px}
```

5. Save your changes to the file and then refresh **start.htm** in your Web browser. As shown in Figure 4-16, the list of links is now divided into three topical areas.

Figure 4-16 **Links list separated into groups**

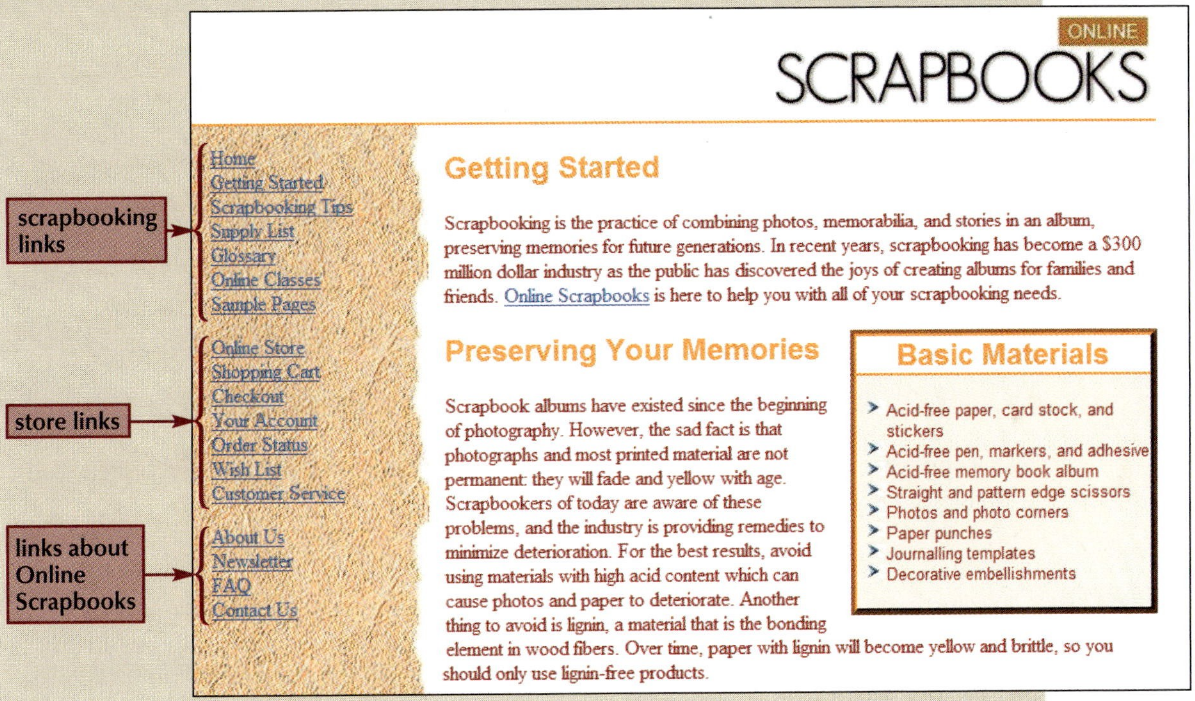

ONLINE
SCRAPBOOKS
scrapbooking links
store links
links about Online Scrapbooks
Home
Getting Started
Scrapbooking Tips
Supply List
Glossary
Online Classes
Sample Pages
Online Store
Shopping Cart
Checkout
Your Account
Order Status
Wish List
Customer Service
About Us
Newsletter
FAQ
Contact Us
Getting Started
Scrapbooking is the practice of combining photos, memorabilia, and stories in an album, preserving memories for future generations. In recent years, scrapbooking has become a $300 million dollar industry as the public has discovered the joys of creating albums for families and friends. Online Scrapbooks is here to help you with all of your scrapbooking needs.
Preserving Your Memories
Scrapbook albums have existed since the beginning of photography. However, the sad fact is that photographs and most printed material are not permanent: they will fade and yellow with age. Scrapbookers of today are aware of these problems, and the industry is providing remedies to minimize deterioration. For the best results, avoid using materials with high acid content which can cause photos and paper to deteriorate. Another thing to avoid is lignin, a material that is the bonding element in wood fibers. Over time, paper with lignin will become yellow and brittle, so you should only use lignin-free products.
Basic Materials
Acid-free paper, card stock, and stickers
Acid-free pen, markers, and adhesive
Acid-free memory book album
Straight and pattern edge scissors
Photos and photo corners
Paper punches
Journalling templates
Decorative embellishments

Kathy likes the layout of the list of links. Now she wants to focus on some design elements to enhance the user's interaction with those links.

Using Pseudo-Classes and Pseudo-Elements

Although she realizes that most browsers underline linked text by default, Kathy thinks that a large block of underlined text is difficult to read. She's seen sites in which links are underlined only when the mouse pointer hovers over the linked text. This type of effect is called a **rollover effect** because it is applied only when a user "rolls" the mouse pointer over an element. She would like you to make underlining a rollover effect for the list of links.

Creating a Link Rollover

Rollover effects for links can be created using pseudo-classes. A **pseudo-class** is a classification of an element based on its current status, position, or use in the document. For example, one pseudo-class indicates whether a link has been previously visited by the user. Another pseudo-class indicates whether a link is currently being activated or clicked. To create a style for a pseudo-class, use the style

```
selector:pseudo-class {styles}
```

where *selector* is an element or group of elements within a document, *pseudo-class* is the name of a pseudo-class, and *styles* are the styles you want to apply. Figure 4-17 lists some of the pseudo-classes supported by CSS.

Figure 4-17 **Pseudo-classes**

Pseudo-class	Description	Example
link	The link has not yet been visited by the user	`a:link {color: red}`
visited	The link has been visited by the user	`a:visited {color: green}`
active	The link is in the process of being activated by the user	`a:active {color: yellow}`
hover	The mouse pointer is hovering over the link	`a:hover {color: blue}`
focus	The element has received the focus of the keyboard or mouse pointer	`input.focus {background-color: yellow}`
first-child	The element is the first child of its parent	`p:first-child {text-indent: 0}`
lang	Specifies the language to be used with the element	`q:lang(FR) {quotes: '<<' '>>'}`

If you want the font color of your links to change to red after they've been visited, you could use the following style declaration:

```
a:visited {color: red}
```

Tip

You can achieve interesting rollover effects by having the browser change the background image or background color of the hypertext link.

In some cases, two or more pseudo-classes can apply to the same element—for example, a link can be both previously visited and hovered over. In such situations, the standard cascading rules apply: the pseudo-class that is listed last in the style sheet will be applied to the element. For this reason, you should enter the hypertext pseudo-classes in an order that reflects how users interact with hypertext links. The link pseudo-class should come first, followed by the visited class, the hover class, and finally the active class. The link pseudo-class comes first because it represents a hypertext link that has not yet been visited or even clicked by the user. The visited pseudo-class comes next, for the link that has been previously visited or clicked. The hover pseudo-class comes next, for the situation in which the user has once again moved the mouse pointer over the hypertext link before clicking the link. The active pseudo-class is last, representing the exact instant in which the link is clicked by the user.

Creating a Hypertext Rollover

| Reference Window

- To create a rollover for a hypertext link, apply these styles to the link element

```
a:link    {styles}
a:visited {styles}
a:hover   {styles}
a:active  {styles}
```

where *styles* are the CSS styles applied to hypertext links that have not been visited (link), already visited (visited), have the mouse pointer over them (hover), or are actively being clicked (active).

Kathy wants to remove the underlining from all of the links on her Getting Started page. If the mouse pointer is hovering over a link, however, she wants the link text to appear in a black font and underlined. The style declarations to remove the underlining and to create this rollover effect are:

```
#links a:link {text-decoration: none}
#links a:visited {text-decoration: none}
#links a:hover {color: black; text-decoration: underline}
#links a:active {text-decoration: none}
```

Add these styles now to the scraps.css style sheet.

To create a rollover effect for hypertext links:

1. Return to the **scraps.css** file in your text editor.
2. Directly below the style for the #links li.newGroup selector, insert the following style declarations, as shown in Figure 4-18:

```
#links a:link {text-decoration: none}
#links a:visited {text-decoration: none}
#links a:hover {color: black; text-decoration: underline}
#links a:active {text-decoration: none}
```

Using pseudo-classes in a selector

Figure 4-18

```
#links            {float: left; width: 200px}
#links ul         {list-style-type: none; margin-left: 15px; padding-left: 0px}
#links li.newGroup {margin-top: 15px}
#links a:link     {text-decoration: none}
#links a:visited  {text-decoration: none}
#links a:hover    {color: black; text-decoration: underline}
#links a:active   {text-decoration: none}
```

3. Save your changes to the file, and then refresh the **start.htm** file in your Web browser.
4. Verify that the links in the list of links are no longer underlined (because you have set the text-decoration style to have a value of none).
5. Hover your mouse pointer over a link in the list and verify that when the mouse pointer hovers over the link, it appears in a black font and is underlined. See Figure 4-19.

Figure 4-19 Viewing a rollover effect

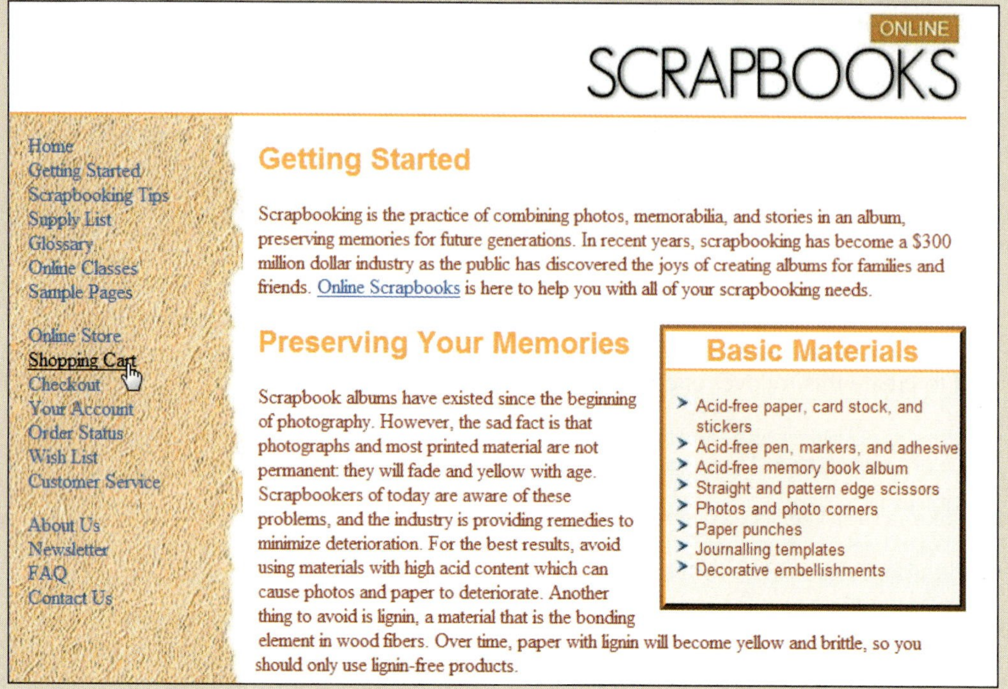
ONLINE
SCRAPBOOKS
Home
Getting Started
Scrapbooking Tips
Supply List
Glossary
Online Classes
Sample Pages
Online Store
Shopping Cart
Checkout
Your Account
Order Status
Wish List
Customer Service
About Us
Newsletter
FAQ
Contact Us
Getting Started
Scrapbooking is the practice of combining photos, memorabilia, and stories in an album, preserving memories for future generations. In recent years, scrapbooking has become a $300 million dollar industry as the public has discovered the joys of creating albums for families and friends. Online Scrapbooks is here to help you with all of your scrapbooking needs.
Preserving Your Memories
Scrapbook albums have existed since the beginning of photography. However, the sad fact is that photographs and most printed material are not permanent: they will fade and yellow with age. Scrapbookers of today are aware of these problems, and the industry is providing remedies to minimize deterioration. For the best results, avoid using materials with high acid content which can cause photos and paper to deteriorate. Another thing to avoid is lignin, a material that is the bonding element in wood fibers. Over time, paper with lignin will become yellow and brittle, so you should only use lignin-free products.
Basic Materials
Acid-free paper, card stock, and stickers
Acid-free pen, markers, and adhesive
Acid-free memory book album
Straight and pattern edge scissors
Photos and photo corners
Paper punches
Journalling templates
Decorative embellishments

InSight | Presentational Attributes for Hypertext Links

Earlier versions of HTML did not include support for the link, visited, and active pseudo-classes. If a Web page author wanted to change the color of a hypertext link, he or she would have to add to the page's <body> tag the attributes

```
<body link="color" vlink="color" alink="color">
```

where the link attribute specifies the color of unvisited links, the vlink attribute specifies the color of visited links, and the alink attribute specifies the color of active links. Colors had to be entered either as a supported color name or as a hexadecimal color value. There is no HTML attribute for creating a rollover effect, so for older browsers you would have to use CSS (if it was supported) or a programming language such as JavaScript to display rollovers.

The link, vlink, and alink attributes have been deprecated and are not supported by strictly compliant XHTML code, but you might still see them used in the code of older Web pages.

Creating a Drop Cap

Kathy has a few more formatting changes she would like you to make to the Getting Started page. She wants you to add the following effects to the first paragraph on the page:

- The first line should be displayed in a small caps style.
- The first letter should be increased in size and displayed as a drop cap.

So far all of our selectors have been based on elements that exist somewhere in the document hierarchy. We can also define selectors based on **pseudo-elements** that are not part of the document tree, but instead are abstracted from what we know of an element's content, use, or position in the document. For example, a paragraph element is part of the document tree and is marked with the <p> tag, but the first line of that paragraph is not—there is no "first line" element even though people intuitively know what page content corresponds to the paragraph's first line. CSS's support for pseudo-elements enables you to create styles for objects such as a paragraph's first line.

The selector for a pseudo-element is similar to what we use for a pseudo-class. The syntax of the pseudo-element selector is

```
selector:pseudo-element {styles}
```

where *selector* is an element or group of elements within the document, *pseudo-element* is an abstract element based on the selector, and *styles* are the styles that you want to apply to the pseudo-element. Figure 4-20 lists some of the pseudo-elements supported by CSS.

Pseudo-elements **Figure 4-20**

Pseudo-element	Description	Example
first-letter	The first letter of the element text	`p:first-letter {font-size:14pt}`
first-line	The first line of the element text	`p:first-line {text-transform: uppercase}`
before	Content inserted directly before the element	`p:before {content:"Special!"}`
after	Content appended to the element	`p:after {content:"eof"}`

For example, to display the first letter of every paragraph in a gold fantasy font, you could apply the following style:

```
p:first-letter {font-family: fantasy; color: gold}
```

The advantage of this pseudo-element is that you don't have to mark the first letter in the HTML document; its position is inferred by the browser when it applies the style.

A pseudo-element is also useful for a design element such as a drop cap. To create a drop cap, you increase the font size of an element's first letter and float it on the left margin. Drop caps also generally look better if you decrease the line height of the first letter, enabling the surrounding content to better wrap around the letter. Finding the best combination of font size and line height is a matter of trial and error; and unfortunately what looks best in one browser might not look as good in another. After trying out several combinations for the Getting Started page, you settle on a drop cap that is 400% the size of the surrounding text, with a line height of 0.8. The following style will create this effect:

```
p:first-letter {float: left; font-size: 400%; line-height: 0.8}
```

However, Kathy only wants to apply this style to the first paragraph on each page. The first paragraph on the Getting Started page has already been given the id value firstp, so the style declaration becomes

Tip

Older browsers might not support the first-letter pseudo-element. If you still want to create a drop cap for those browsers, mark the first letter with a span element and apply your style to that element.

```
#firstp:first-letter {float: left; font-size: 400%; line-height: 0.8}
```

Because Kathy also wants the first line of that paragraph to be displayed in small caps, you will also use the first-line pseudo-element in the following style:

```
#firstp:first-line {font-variant: small-caps}
```

Add both of these styles to the scraps.css style sheet.

To create the drop cap effect:

1. Return to the **scraps.css** file in your text editor.
2. Directly above the style for the #article selector, insert the following two styles involving the first-letter and first-line pseudo-elements. See Figure 4-21:

```
#firstp:first-line {font-variant: small-caps}
#firstp:first-letter {float: left; font-size: 400%; line-height: 0.8}
```

Figure 4-21 Specifying a style for the first-line and first-letter pseudo-elements

```
#firstp:first-line   {font-variant: small-caps}
#firstp:first-letter {float: left; font-size: 400%; line-height: 0.8}

#article             {margin-left: 200px}
```

3. Close the **scraps.css** file, saving your changes, and then refresh the **start.htm** file in your Web browser. Figure 4-22 shows the final layout of the Getting Started page.

Figure 4-22 Final appearance of the Getting Started page

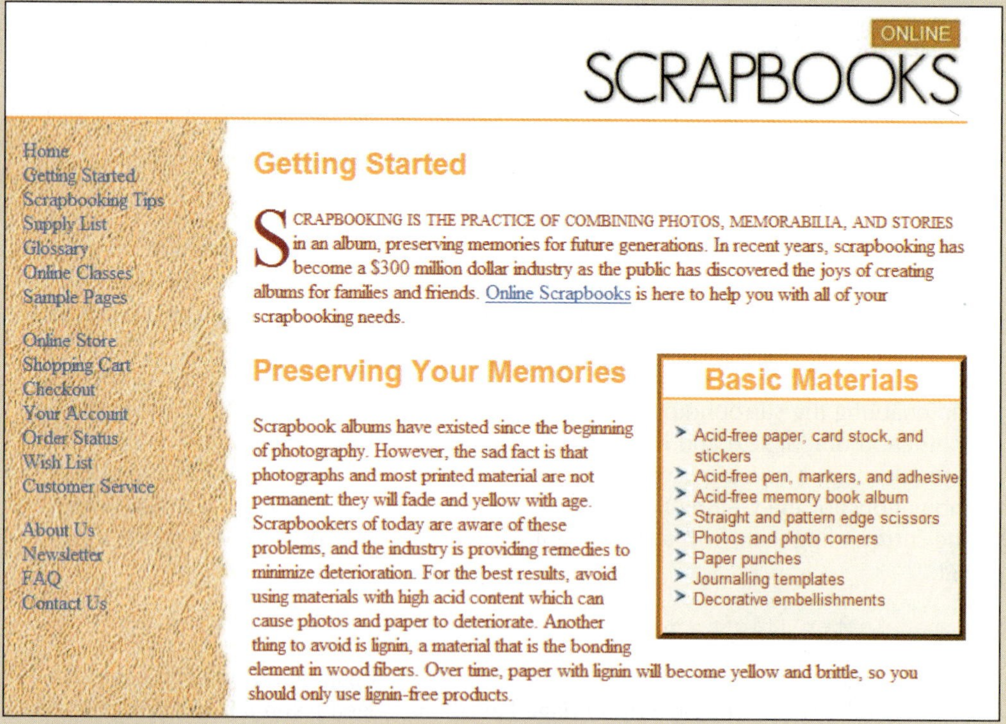
ONLINE
SCRAPBOOKS
Home
Getting Started
Scrapbooking Tips
Supply List
Glossary
Online Classes
Sample Pages
Online Store
Shopping Cart
Checkout
Your Account
Order Status
Wish List
Customer Service
About Us
Newsletter
FAQ
Contact Us
Getting Started
SCRAPBOOKING IS THE PRACTICE OF COMBINING PHOTOS, MEMORABILIA, AND STORIES in an album, preserving memories for future generations. In recent years, scrapbooking has become a $300 million dollar industry as the public has discovered the joys of creating albums for families and friends. Online Scrapbooks is here to help you with all of your scrapbooking needs.
Preserving Your Memories
Scrapbook albums have existed since the beginning of photography. However, the sad fact is that photographs and most printed material are not permanent: they will fade and yellow with age. Scrapbookers of today are aware of these problems, and the industry is providing remedies to minimize deterioration. For the best results, avoid using materials with high acid content which can cause photos and paper to deteriorate. Another thing to avoid is lignin, a material that is the bonding element in wood fibers. Over time, paper with lignin will become yellow and brittle, so you should only use lignin-free products.
Basic Materials
Acid-free paper, card stock, and stickers
Acid-free pen, markers, and adhesive
Acid-free memory book album
Straight and pattern edge scissors
Photos and photo corners
Paper punches
Journalling templates
Decorative embellishments

4. If you want to take a break before starting the next session, close any open files or programs now.

Working with Pseudo-Elements

| Reference Window

- To apply a style to the first line of an element, use the pseudo-element selector
  `selector:first-line`
  where *selector* is the name of the element or elements in the document.
- To apply a style to the first letter of an element, use the pseudo-element selector
  `selector:first-letter`
- To insert a text string before an element, use the style
  `selector:before {content: "text"}`
  where *text* is the content of the text string.
- To insert a text string after an element, use the style
  `selector:after {content: "text"}`

Generating Text with Pseudo-Elements

You can use CSS to insert text into your Web page using the before and after pseudo-elements. The before pseudo-element places text directly before the element, while the after pseudo-element placed the text directly after the element. The syntax of both pseudo-elements is

```
selector:before {content: "text"}
selector:after {content: "text"}
```

where *selector* is an element to which you want to add the *text* string. For example, the style

```
em:after {content: " !"}
```

appends an exclamation point to the end of every element marked with a <em> tag. You can use the before and after pseudo-elements in conjunction with other pseudo-elements and pseudo-classes. The code

```
a:hover:before {content: "<"}
a:hover:after {content: ">"}
```

creates a rollover effect in which the < and > characters are placed around a hypertext link when a mouse pointer hovers over the link.

The content value must be entered as a text string, and you cannot use the content property to insert HTML code. The browser displays the HTML code rather than the element the code represents. For example, if you apply the style

```
em:after {content: "<b>!</b>"}
```

the browser displays the text of opening and closing <b> tags in addition to the exclamation point. Although you cannot insert an HTML element, you can insert an HTML attribute. This is useful because attribute values are usually not displayed on the Web page, but you can automatically insert an attribute value using the attr property

```
content: attr(attribute)
```

where *attribute* is an attribute of the element. For example, the following style appends every hypertext link with the link's URL (as stored in the href attribute):

```
a:after {content attr(" [" attr(href) "] ")}
```

Note that in this example, the href attribute will be enclosed within a set of opening and closing square brackets [.]. This makes your text easy to read by using spaces or brackets to offset the generated content from its surrounding text.

Using the before and after pseudo-elements, you can create truly dynamic Web pages whose content can change based on the styles stored in different style sheets. Internet Explorer does not support the before and after pseudo-elements unless your code puts the IE browser in standards mode. You will not need to use the before and after pseudo-elements in Kathy's Web site.

Kathy is pleased with the work you've done adding special effects to the Getting Started page. She feels that the use of the first-letter and first-line pseudo-elements to create the drop cap effect added a great deal to the appearance of the page. She's also pleased with your work on the rollover effect in the list of links and the graphic image used in the Basic Materials list. In the next session, you'll expand your understanding of CSS by using the styles to directly position elements on the rendered Web page.

Review | Session 4.1 Quick Check

1. Specify the style to italicize the content of all span elements nested within paragraphs.
2. Specify the style to italicize the content of all span elements that are direct children of paragraph elements.
3. Specify the style to italicize all h2 headings that directly follow h1 headings.
4. Specify a style to display all elements that belong to the newsAlert class in boldface text.
5. Specify a style to display only span elements belonging to the newsAlert class in boldface text.
6. Specify a style in which every hypertext link is displayed with a yellow background when the mouse pointer hovers over the link.
7. Specify a style in which hovering over a hypertext link causes the Web browser to change the link's background image to the graphic file hover.jpg.
8. Specify a style that displays the first letter of every block quote in a red font.
9. Specify a style that displays the first line of every block quote in a red font.

Session 4.2

Positioning Objects with CSS

One purpose of the Online Scrapbooks Web site is to teach new scrapbookers how to create beautiful and interesting pages. Every month Kathy wants to highlight a scrapbook page that displays some noteworthy features. Figure 4-23 shows the current Samples page. (Note that because of the scraps.css style sheet, this page uses the same layout as the other pages in the Web site.) The scrapbooking sample is displayed in the main section of the document.

Initial Samples page | Figure 4-23

Kathy wants to augment the page by inserting callouts that highlight certain portions of the scrapbooking sample for the reader. She wants each callout to be placed close to the feature that it highlights. Kathy has drawn in the locations of the three callouts that she wants to add in the sketch shown in Figure 4-24.

Figure 4-24 Sketch of the Samples page

Figure 4-25 shows the text of the three callout notes.

Figure 4-25 Text of the three callout notes

Note	Text
note 1	Paste cut-out letters and words in your scrapbook to create a 3D effect. Online Scrapbooks sells professionally designed cut-out letters, words, and phrases for all occasions.
note 2	Clippings, flyers, programs, and other memorabilia are valuable sources of information that can enhance your scrapbook pages. Make sure that any material is copied to acid-free paper. Newspaper clippings are especially susceptible to deterioration.
note 3	Photographic cut-outs and textured backgrounds can add visual interest to your pages. See the online store for our wide variety of textured and embossed papers.

You'll insert each of these notes in div containers placed within the main section of the page. You'll set the id values of the three elements to note1, note2, and note3, respectively, and you'll add the class value notes to each element so that you can apply a common set of styles to all of the notes.

To insert the three notes:

1. Use your text editor to open the **samptxt.htm** from the tutorial.04\tutorial folder included with your Data Files. Enter ***your name*** and ***the date*** in the comment section of the file and save it as **samples.htm** in the same folder.
2. Directly below the h2 heading, Samples from Online Scrapbooks, insert the following div container elements, as shown in Figure 4-26:

```
<div id="note1" class="notes">
   <p>Paste cut-out letters and words in your scrapbook to create
   a 3D effect. Online Scrapbooks sells professionally  designed
   cut-out letters, words, and phrases for all occasions.</p>
</div>
<div id="note2" class="notes">
   <p>Clippings, flyers, programs, and other memorabilia are valuable
   sources of information that can enhance your scrapbook pages.
   Make sure that any material is copied to acid-free paper.
   Newspaper clippings are especially susceptible to deterioration.
   </p>
</div>
<div id="note3" class="notes">
   <p>Photographic cut-outs and textured backgrounds can add
   visual interest to your pages. See the online store for our
   wide variety of textured and embossed papers.</p>
</div>
```

Inserting text for the three notes **Figure 4-26**

```
<div id="article">
   <h2>Samples from Online Scrapbooks</h2>

   <div id="note1" class="notes">
      <p>Paste cut-out letters and words in your scrapbook to create
      a 3D effect. Online Scrapbooks sells professionally
      designed cut-out letters, words, and phrases for all occasions.</p>
   </div>
   <div id="note2" class="notes">
      <p>Clippings, flyers, programs, and other memorabilia are valuable
      sources of information that can enhance your scrapbook pages.
      Make sure that any material is copied to acid-free paper.
      Newspaper clippings are especially susceptible to deterioration.</p>
   </div>
   <div id="note3" class="notes">
      <p>Photographic cut-outs and textured backgrounds can add visual
      interest to your pages. See the online store for our wide
      variety of textured and embossed papers.</p>
   </div>

   <div id="sample_image">
      <img src="sample.jpg" alt="sample page" width="474" height="616" />
   </div>
```

Because the styles in this task will apply only to this page and no others in Kathy's Web site, you'll add an embedded style sheet to the samples.htm file to format the appearance of the three notes. Kathy wants the text to appear in a brown 8-point sans-serif font on an ivory background. She wants the note boxes to be displayed with a 3-pixel light gray inset border. The notes should be 130 pixels wide with a margin space of 5 pixels around the paragraphs.

To define a style for the three notes:

1. Scroll to the top of the samples.htm file.
2. Directly below the link element, insert the following embedded style sheet as shown in Figure 4-27:

```
<style type="text/css">
  .notes   {font-family: sans-serif; font-size: 8pt; color: brown;
            background-color: ivory;
            border: 3px inset rgb(212, 212, 212); width: 130px}
 .notes p {margin: 5px}
 </style>
```

Figure 4-27 Setting the styles for the notes text

```
   <title>Samples from Online Scrapbooks</title>
   <link href="scraps.css" rel="stylesheet" type="text/css" />
   <style type="text/css">
      .notes    {font-family: sans-serif; font-size: 8pt; color: brown;
                 background-color: ivory; border: 3px inset rgb(212, 212, 212);
                 width: 130px}
      .notes p {margin: 5px}
   </style>
</head>
```

3. Save your changes to the file.
4. Open the **samples.htm** file in your Web browser. Figure 4-28 shows the formatted appearance of the three note boxes. Note that although the boxes are placed side-by-side in this figure to make them easier to read, they should be stacked one on top of the other at the top of your Web page.

Figure 4-28 Formatted note boxes

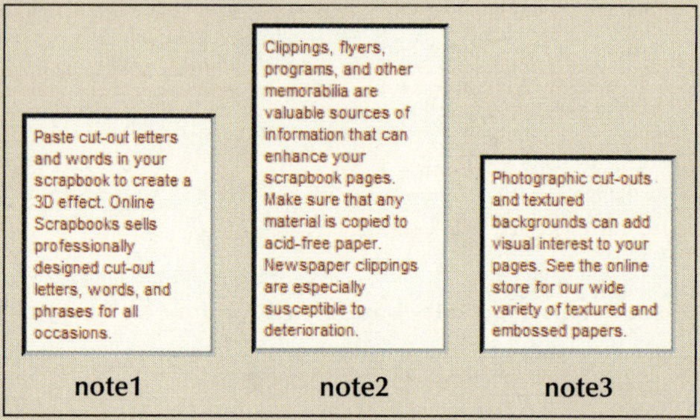

Trouble? Depending on your browser, your note boxes may look slightly different than those shown in Figure 4-28.

Now that you've entered the text and the formatting styles for the three callout notes, your next task is to position them at appropriate locations on the Samples page.

The Position Style

Positioning was one of the first enhancements to the original CSS1 specifications. Collectively, the various positioning styles were known as **CSS-Positioning**, or more commonly, **CSS-P**. CSS-P became part of the specification for CSS2, and positioning styles were some of the first CSS2 styles to be adopted by browsers.

To place an element at a specific position on the page, use the styles

```
position: type; top: value; right: value; bottom: value; left: value;
```

where *type* indicates the type of positioning applied to the element, and the top, right, bottom, and left styles indicate the coordinates of the top, right, bottom, and left edges of the element. In practice, usually only the left and top coordinates are used because the right and bottom coordinates can be inferred given the element's height and width. Coordinates can be expressed in any of the CSS measuring units.

The position style has five possible values: static, absolute, relative, fixed, and inherit. The default position is static, which enables browsers to place an element based on where it flows in the document. This is essentially the same as not using any CSS positioning at all. Any values specified for the left or top styles with a static position are ignored by the browser. You'll explore each of the other values (absolute, relative, fixed, and inherit) so that you can use them to position the notes on Kathy's Sample Pages page.

Absolute Positioning

Absolute positioning enables you to place an element at specific coordinates either on a page or within a containing element. For example, the declaration

```
position: absolute; left: 100px; top: 50px
```

places an element at the coordinates (100, 50), or 100 pixels to the right and 50 pixels down from upper-left corner of the page or the containing element. Once an element has been placed using absolute positioning, it affects the placement of other objects on the Web page. To explore how absolute positioning affects page layout, you'll use a demo containing objects that can be positioned on the Web page.

To explore absolute positioning:

1. Use your Web browser to open the **demo_positioning.htm** file from the tutorial.04\demo folder included with your Data Files.

   The demo page contains two colored boxes that you can move by changing the values in the Positioning Styles box. The boxes are initially set to their default position, which is within the flow of the other elements on the demo page. To make it easier to place the boxes at specific positions, a grid marked in pixels has been added to the page background.

2. Select **absolute** from the list box for the outer box, and then press the **Tab** key.

3. Enter **275** in the left box, and then press the **Tab** key. Enter **350** in the top box, and then press the **Tab** key again. As shown in Figure 4-29, the red outer box is placed at the page coordinates (275, 350).

Figure 4-29 Viewing absolute positioning

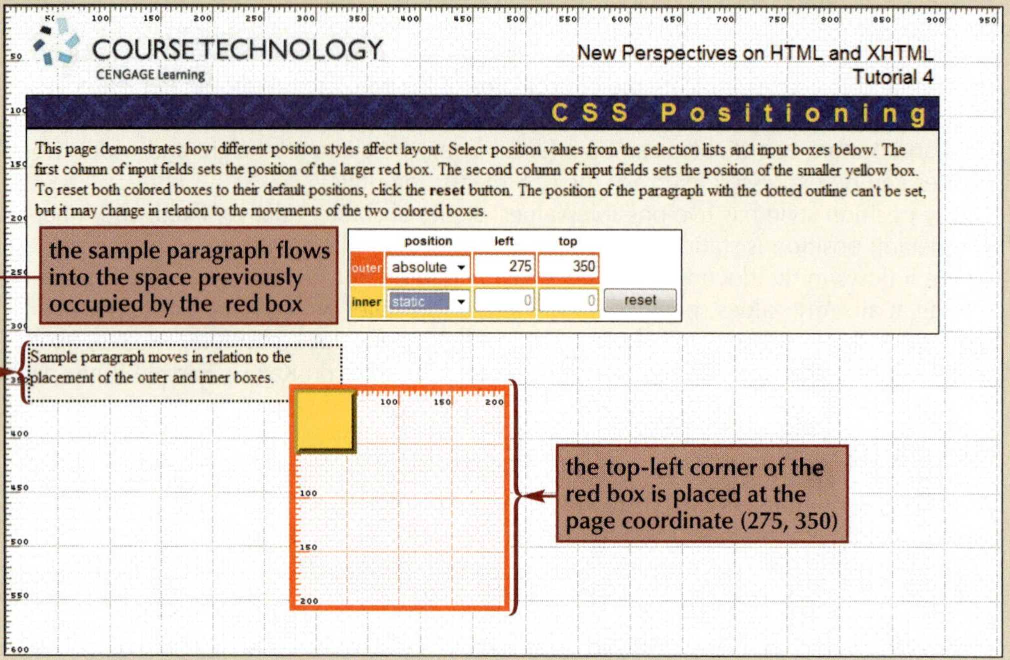

Absolute positioning takes an element out of the normal flow of a document, so that any subsequent content flows into the space previously occupied by the element. Note that on the demo page, the sample paragraph moves up into the space that was previously occupied by the red outer box.

When elements are nested within one another, the position of the element is based on the coordinates within the parent object if that object is itself placed on the page using a CSS positioning style. If the parent object is not positioned using a CSS style, then the position of the nested object is set within the next object higher up in the hierarchy of elements positioned on the page. If no other objects are positioned on the page, the top and left coordinates are based on the browser window. To see this effect, return to the demo page.

To view absolute positioning with a nested object:

1. Within the demo page, select **absolute** from the list box for the inner element.
2. Enter **90** in the left box for the inner object and **75** for the top box. As shown in Figure 4-30, the inner yellow box is placed at the (90, 75) coordinate within the outer box, not within the Web page.

Figure 4-30

Positioning a nested object

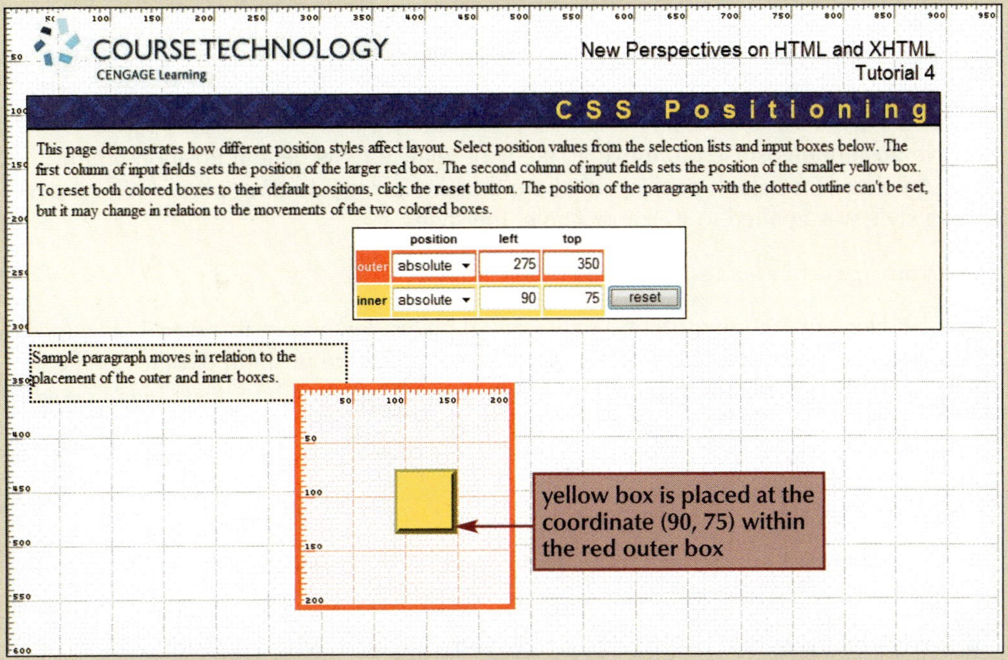

Now examine what occurs when the outer box is no longer placed on the Web page using a positioning style.

3. Select **static** from the list box for the outer element.

As shown in Figure 4-31, the red outer box is returned to its default position on the Web page. The yellow inner box is now placed at the coordinate (90, 75), but within the Web page.

Figure 4-31

Absolute positioning within a nonpositioned element

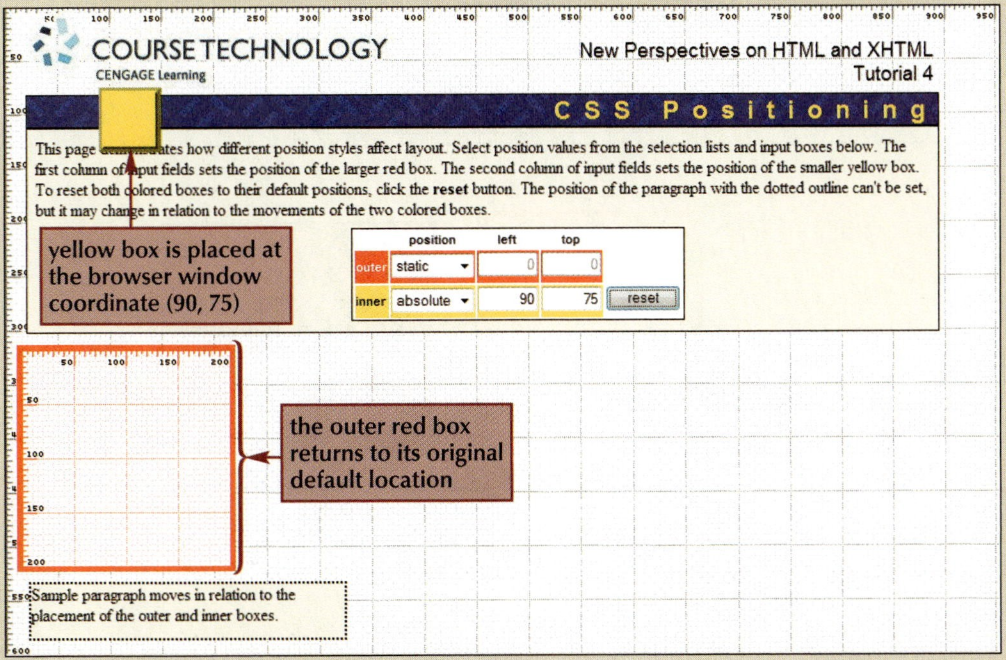

Tip

You can enter negative values for the top and left styles to move page elements up and to the left from their default locations.

4. Continue experimenting with the demo page by entering values for the top and left coordinates and observing the effect on the placement of the boxes.

Relative Positioning

Relative positioning is used to move an element relative to its default position on the page. An element's default position is where the browser would have placed it if no positioning style was applied to it. For example, the style

```
position: relative; left: 100px; top: 50px
```

places an element 100 pixels to the right and 50 pixels down from its normal placement in a browser window. Relative positioning does not affect the position of other elements on a page, which retain their original positions as if the element had never been moved. You'll use the demo page to experiment with this.

To explore relative positioning:

1. Click the **reset** button within the demo page to return both boxes to their default locations on the Web page.
2. Select **relative** from the list box for the outer element, and then enter **275** for the left value and **50** for the top value. As shown in Figure 4-32, the outer box moves 275 pixels to the right and 50 pixels down from its default location.

Figure 4-32 Relative positioning

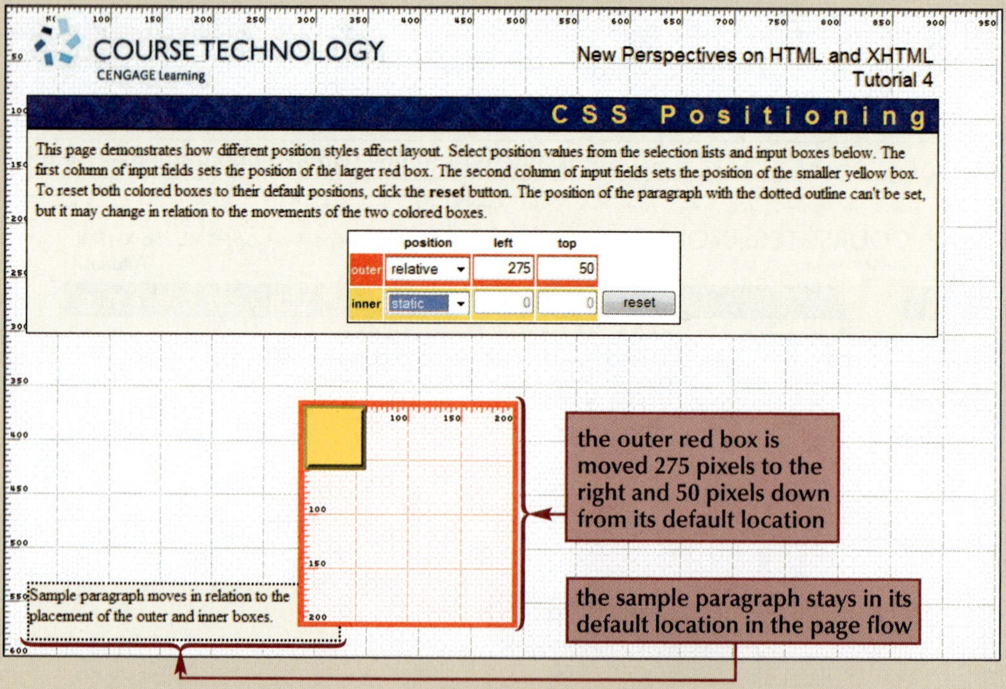

Also note that the sample paragraph does not flow into the space previously occupied by the colored boxes. The layout of the rest of the page is unaffected when relative positioning is applied.

3. Explore other combinations of absolute and relative positioning to see their effect on the layout of the demo page.

In many Web page layouts, you might want to position any object nested within a div container, but you don't need to move the container itself. In those cases, use relative positioning to place the div container with the top and left values set to 0 pixels. The position you apply to the nested object will then be based on coordinates within the div container object.

Fixed and Inherited Positioning

An element placed with absolute or relative positioning scrolls with the rest of the document. Alternately, you can fix an element at a specific spot in the document window while the rest of the page scrolls by setting the value of the position style to fixed. Note that not all browsers support the fixed position, so you should use it with some caution if it is a crucial part of your Web page layout.

You can also assign the inherit position style to an element so that it inherits the position value of its parent element. You'll explore both positioning styles on the demo page.

To explore fixed and inherited positioning:

1. Click the **reset** button within the demo page to return both boxes to their default locations on the Web page.
2. Select **fixed** from the list box for the outer element, and then enter **300** for the left and top values.

   The red box is placed at the window coordinates (300, 300). The sample paragraph moves up into the space previously occupied by the red box.

   Trouble? If you are running an older browser, you might not see any change in the position of the red box.
3. Select **inherit** from the list box for the inner element, and then enter **600** for the left value and **300** for the top value.

   The yellow box inherits the position style of its parent. In this case it uses fixed positioning and is placed to the right of the outer red box. See Figure 4-33.

Figure 4-33 **Fixed and inherited positioning**

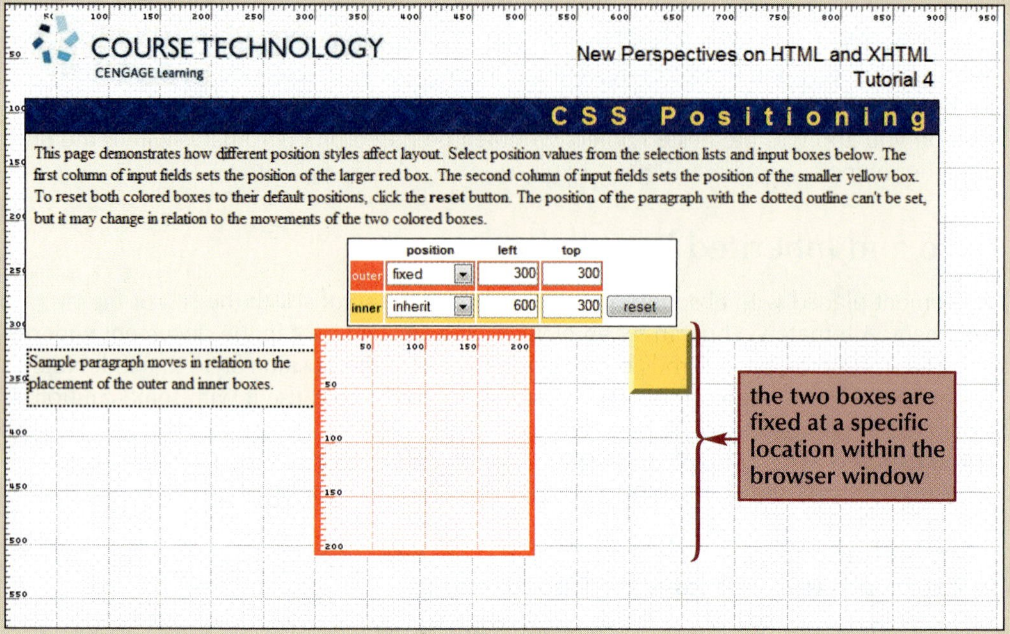

Trouble? Internet Explorer does not support the inherit position style at the time of this writing. To fix the position of the inner box, you have to choose fixed drop in the list box.

4. Resize the browser window so it's small enough to force the browser to display the vertical and horizontal scroll bars. Scroll through the document and verify that the two color boxes remain fixed at the same location within the window.
5. Continue to experiment with different positioning combinations. Close the demo page when you're finished.

Reference Window | Positioning an Object with CSS

- To position an object at a specific coordinate, use the style
  `position: type; top: value; right: value; bottom: value; left: value;`
  where *type* indicates the type of positioning applied to the object (absolute, relative, static, fixed, or inherit) and the top, right, bottom, and left styles indicate the coordinates of the object.

Now that you've seen how to work with the different positioning styles of CSS, you can apply your knowledge to position the three callout notes. After trying different values, you and Kathy settle on the following coordinates using absolute positioning:

```
note1: (600, 120)
note2: (170, 400)
note3: (570, 550)
```

You'll add styles for these positions to the embedded style sheet in the samples.htm file.

To position the three notes for the Samples page:

1. Return to the **samples.htm** file in your text editor.
2. Add the following styles to the embedded style sheet, as shown in Figure 4-34:

```
#note1 {position: absolute; left: 600px; top: 120px}
#note2 {position: absolute; left: 170px; top: 400px}
#note3 {position: absolute; left: 570px; top: 550px}
```

Figure 4-34 Setting the position of the three note boxes

```
<style type="text/css">
   .notes    {font-family: sans-serif; font-size: 8pt; color: brown;
              background-color: ivory; border: 3px inset rgb(212, 212, 212);
              width: 130px}
   .notes p {margin: 5px}
   #note1    {position: absolute; left: 600px; top: 120px}
   #note2    {position: absolute; left: 170px; top: 400px}
   #note3    {position: absolute; left: 570px; top: 550px}
</style>
```

3. Save your changes, and then reload the **samples.htm** file in your Web browser. Figure 4-35 shows the placement of the three sample notes.

Figure 4-35 Notes placed with absolute positioning

You show Kathy the revised page. She likes the position of the notes, but she points out that they are pretty big and they hide too much of the scrapbooking sample. Kathy would like you to investigate ways of making the notes less intrusive.

Working with Overflow and Clipping

Reducing the height of each note by lowering the value of its height attribute might seem like an easy solution to Kathy's first request. Unfortunately, though, this would not meet her needs because the height of each note expands to accommodate its content. If you want to force an element into a specified height and width, you have to define how the browser should handle a situation where content overflows the space allotted to the object. The syntax of the overflow style is

```
overflow: type
```

where *type* is visible (the default), hidden, scroll, or auto. A value of visible instructs browsers to increase the height of an element to fit the overflow content. The hidden value keeps an element at the specified height and width, but cuts off excess text. The scroll value keeps an element at the specified dimensions, but adds horizontal and vertical scroll bars to allow users to scroll through the overflow. Finally, the auto value keeps an element at the specified size, adding scroll bars only as they are needed. Figure 4-36 shows examples of the effect of each overflow value.

Figure 4-36 Values of the overflow style

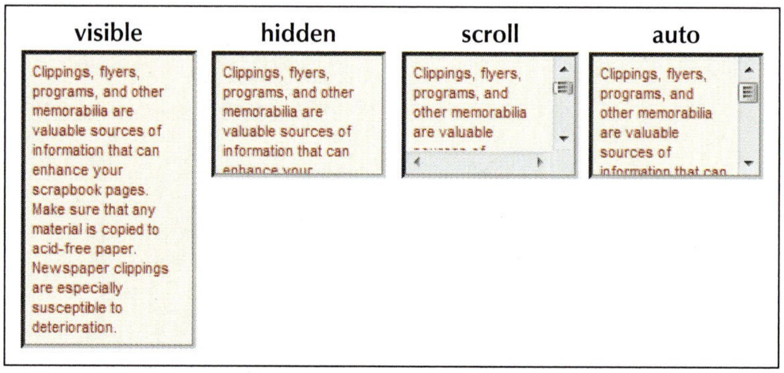

You decide to limit the height of each callout note to 90 pixels and have the browser display scroll bars as needed by setting the value of the overflow style to auto.

To define the overflow style for the callout notes:

1. Return to the **samples.htm** file in your text editor.
2. Add the following styles to the .notes selector, as shown in Figure 4-37:

```
height: 90px; overflow: auto
```

Figure 4-37 Setting the overflow style for the notes

```
<style type="text/css">
   .notes    {font-family: sans-serif; font-size: 8pt; color: brown;
              background-color: ivory; border: 3px inset rgb(212, 212, 212);
              width: 130px; height: 90px; overflow: auto}
   .notes p {margin: 5px}
   #note1    {position: absolute; left: 600px; top: 120px}
   #note2    {position: absolute; left: 170px; top: 400px}
   #note3    {position: absolute; left: 570px; top: 550px}
</style>
```

3. Save your changes, and then refresh the **samples.htm** file in your Web browser. Figure 4-38 shows the appearance of the three callout notes with heights limited to 90 pixels and scroll bars added.

Figure 4-38 Notes with scroll bars

4. Use the scroll bars to verify that the entire content of each note is still available to the user.

   Trouble? Depending on your browser, you might not see scrollbars around each note box.

5. If you want to take a break before starting the next session, you can close any open files or programs now.

Clipping an Element

Closely related to the overflow style is the clip style. The clip style allows you to define a rectangular region through which the element's content can be viewed. Anything that lies outside the boundary of the rectangle is hidden. The syntax of the clip style is

```
clip: rect(top, right, bottom, left)
```

where *top*, *right*, *bottom*, and *left* define the coordinates of the clipping rectangle. For example, a clip value of rect(10, 175, 125, 75) defines a clip region whose top and bottom edges are 10 and 125 pixels from the top of the element, and whose right and left edges are 175 and 75 pixels from the left side of the element. See Figure 4-39.

Figure 4-39 Clipping an element

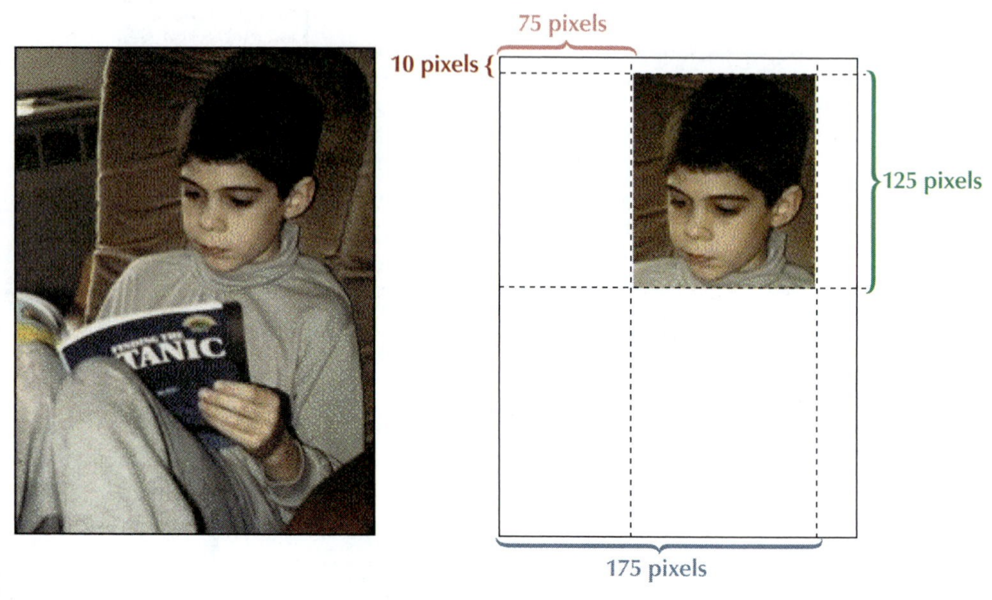

The *top*, *right*, *bottom*, and *left* values can also be set to auto, which matches the specified edge of the clipping region to the edge of the parent element. For example, a clip value of rect(10, auto, 125, 75) creates a clipping rectangle whose right edge matches the right edge of the parent element.

Reference Window | Working with Content Overflow and Clipping

- To specify how the browser should handle content that overflows an element's boundary, use the style
  `overflow: type`
  where *type* is visible (to expand the element height to match the content), hidden (to hide the excess content), scroll (to always display horizontal and vertical scroll bars), or auto (to display scroll bars if needed).
- To clip an element's content, use the style
  `clip: rect(top, right, bottom, left)`
  where *top*, *right*, *bottom*, and *left* define the boundaries of the clipping rectangle.

Limiting Width and Height

In some page layouts, you might want to limit an element's height or width. This is often desirable when you've specified the element's size using relative units that can expand or contract depending on the size of the browser window. If the browser window is very wide, the element might become too wide to be easily readable. If the browser window is too narrow, the element might be reduced to a size that is also difficult to view. Rather than allowing these problems to occur, you can specify an element's minimum or maximum height or width using the styles

```
min-width: value
min-height: value
max-width: value
max-height: value
```

where *value* is the width or height value in one of the CSS units of measure. The min and max values are usually used alongside the height and width styles to set a possible range of values for an element. For example, the style declaration

```
div {width: 80%; min-width: 200px; max-width: 700px}
```

sets the width of the div element to 80% of the Web browser window. If the browser window is 800 pixels wide, the div element will be 640 pixels wide. However, browser windows can vary in size and many users will resize their browser windows to free up desktop space. In that case, the size of the div element will vary accordingly, but it will never be allowed to get smaller than 200 pixels or larger than 700 pixels. Using the min and max styles enables the Web page designer to have some control over the page layout and avoid problems caused by either very large or very small windows.

Max-Width and Internet Explorer | InSight

As mentioned in Tutorial 3, usability studies have shown that most users are comfortable reading text that extends no more than 60 to 70 characters per line or about 30 em. Beyond this length, reading comprehension goes down rapidly and eye fatigue increases. To deal with this problem, Web page designers often use the max-width style to ensure that their Web pages are not too wide on large monitors or screens set to high resolutions.

Internet Explorer did not fully support maximum widths until IE 7. For browser versions earlier than IE7, Web page authors have had to adopt workarounds to approximate the effect of the max-width style. One popular approach, offered by Svend Tofte, is to use a CSS command introduced and supported by Internet Explorer to automatically size the width of an element based on the width of the browser window. For example, the following set of styles defines a maximum width of 800 pixels for an object:

```
max-width:800px;
width:expression(document.body.clientWidth > 800? "800px":
"auto" );
```

In this code, browsers that support maximum widths use the max-width style in the first line to set the maximum width of the object to 800 pixels. Those browsers then ignore the next line and continue on to the rest of the style sheet. Internet Explorer on the other hand, ignores the max-width style in the first line and goes directly to the second line. The second line contains a command that tests whether the browser window is wider than 800 pixels. If it is, it sets the width of the object to 800 pixels. If the browser window is not wider than 800 pixels, the object will be automatically sized by the browser to fit into whatever space is available. The result is that the object will have a maximum width under both IE and browsers that support the max-width style.

This particular workaround can be adapted for different widths and different units of measure. For more information, you can view Svend Tofte's work at *www.svendtofte.com/code/max_width_in_ie/* or do a Web search for IE workarounds to the max-width problem. As always, you should test any code to ensure that it works with a variety of browsers and operating systems.

Stacking Elements

Positioning elements can sometimes lead to objects that overlap each other. By default, elements that are formatted later in an HTML or XHTML document are stacked on top of earlier elements. In addition, elements placed using CSS positioning are stacked on top of elements that are not. To specify a different stacking order, use the style

```
z-index: value
```

where *value* is a positive or negative integer or the keyword "auto." As shown in Figure 4-40, objects are stacked based on their z-index values, with the highest z-index values placed on top. A value of auto allows the browser to determine stacking order using the default rules.

Figure 4-40 **Using the z-index style to stack elements**

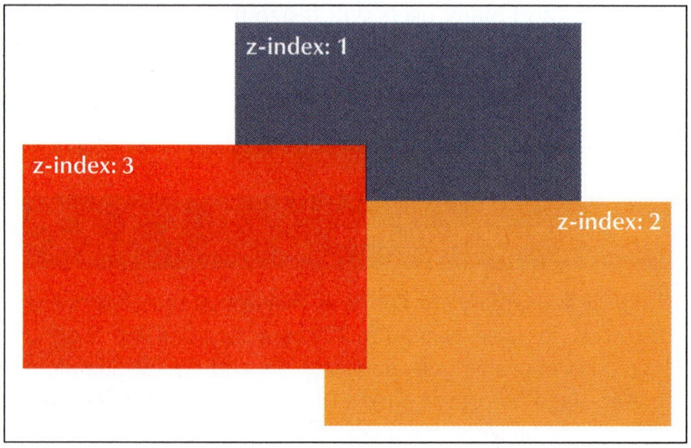

The z-index style only works for elements that are placed with absolute positioning. Also, an element's z-index value determines its position relative only to other elements that share a common parent; the style has no impact when applied to elements with different parents. Figure 4-41 shows a diagram in which the object with a high z-index value of 4 is still covered because it is nested within another object that has a low z-index value of 1.

Figure 4-41 **Nesting z-index values**

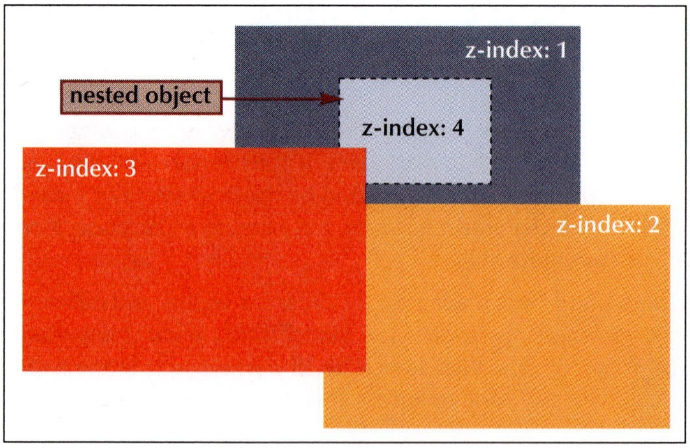

Kathy is pleased with how the notes are positioned over the scrapbooking sample, so you don't need to use the clip or z-index styles. The page looks good on computer monitors. In the next session, you'll explore styles to make your Web pages ready for print media and portable devices.

Session 4.2 Quick Check | Review

1. Specify the style to place an element with the id named logo at the coordinates (150, 75) using absolute positioning.
2. Specify a style to place the logo element 25% down from the top of the page and 10% to the right.
3. What is the style to move span elements belonging to the class highlight up 10 pixels?
4. Specify a style that moves all link elements 5 pixels down when the mouse pointer hovers over them.
5. What is the style to fix an element with the links id at the browser window coordinates (10, 50)?
6. Specify a style to set the width of all block quotes to 70% of the browser window width with a minimum width of 250 pixels and a maximum width of 650 pixels.
7. Specify a style to set the height of all block quotes to 25% of the browser window height. If the content of the block quote cannot fit within this space, include a style to add scroll bars to the block quote as needed.
8. The #title element has a z-index of 1. The #subtitle has a z-index of 5. Will the #subtitle element always be displayed on top of the #title element? Explain why or why not.

Session 4.3

Working with Different Media

Many users of the Online Scrapbooks Web site have reported to Kathy that they enjoy the monthly Samples page so much that they print the samples and store them for future reference. However, these users often find that the pages don't print well. Most users would prefer to print only the scrapbook sample, without the Online Scrapbooks header, links list, and footer. Also, they enjoy the notes that Kathy adds to the sample page, but they would like those notes to be printed on a separate page from the scrapbook sample. In Figure 4-42, Kathy has sketched the design she envisions for the printed version of the Samples page.

Figure 4-42 Kathy's proposed printed output

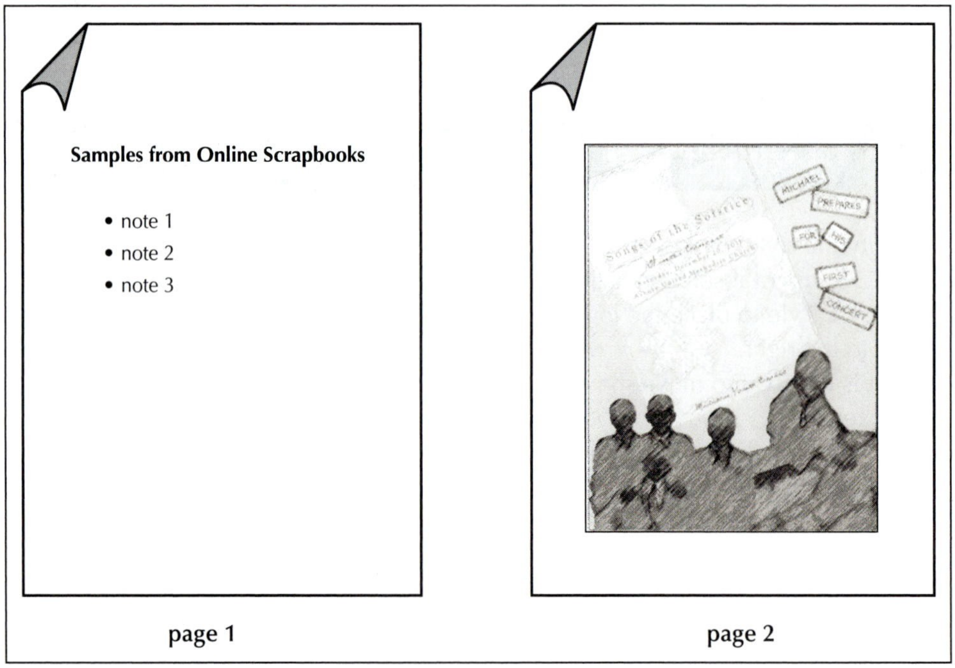

One solution to Kathy's problem would be to create two versions of the Samples page: one for computer screens and the other for printouts. However, Kathy would like to avoid having multiple versions of the same file on her Web site. She would much prefer having a separate style sheet: one that is designed for printed output. She would like you to examine how to create style sheets that are designed for specific devices such as a printer.

Media Types

By default, a style sheet is applied to all devices, and each device must determine how best to match the styles to its own requirements. For example, when you print a Web page, the Web browser and its built-in styles prepare the document for the printer. The user also has some control over that process—for example, determining the size of the page margins or the content of the printout's header or footer. However, beyond that, the user cannot control how the page is printed.

CSS2 and subsequent versions have given more control to Web page authors to specify output styles for particular devices. To do that, you use the media attribute to specify an output device in either the style element (for embedded style sheets) or in the link element (for external style sheets). The syntax of the media attribute is

```
<style type="text/css" media="type">
   ...
</style>
```

or

```
<link href="url" type="text/css" media="type" ... />
```

where *type* is the type of media used by the style sheet. Figure 4-43 lists the different values of the media attribute.

Figure 4-43 Values of the media attribute

Value	Used for
all	All output devices (the default)
aural	Speech and sound synthesizers
braille	Braille tactile feedback devices
embossed	Paged Braille printers
handheld	Small or handheld devices with small screens, monochrome graphics, and limited bandwidth
print	Printers
projection	Projectors
screen	Computer screens
tty	Fixed-width devices like teletype machines and terminals
tv	Television-type devices with low resolution, color, and limited scrollability

For example, to specify that aural browsers should render your Web page using the sounds.css style sheet, you would enter the following link element in the HTML file:

```
<link href="sounds.css" type="text/css" media="aural" />
```

In the same way, you would use the following media attribute in an embedded style sheet to indicate that its styles are intended for aural devices:

```
<style type="text/css" media="aural">
   ...
</style>
```

The media attribute can also contain a comma-separated list of media types. The following link element points to a style sheet designed for both print and screen media:

```
<link href="output.css" type="text/css" media="print, screen" />
```

Style sheets cascade through the media types in the same way they cascade through a document tree. A style sheet in which the output device is not specified is applied to all devices, unless it is superseded by a style designed for a particular device. In the following set of embedded style sheets, h1 headings are displayed in a sans-serif font for all devices; however, the text color is red for computer screens and black for printed pages:

```
<style type="text/css">
   h1 {font-family: sans-serif}
</style>
<style type="text/css" media="screen">
   h1 {color: red}
</style>
<style type="text/css" media="print">
   h1 {color: black}
</style>
```

When no value is given to the media attribute, any style defined in the embedded or external style sheet is used for all media, where applicable.

The @media Rule

It's not always convenient to maintain several different style sheets for the same document. In place of several style sheets, you can use a single style sheet broken down into different sections for each media type. This is done using the rule

```
@media type {
   styles declarations
}
```

where *type* is one of the supported media types and *style declarations* are style declarations associated with that media type. For example, the following style sheet is broken into four sections with a different collection of styles for screen, print, handheld, and television media:

```
@media screen   { body {font-size: 1em}  h1 {font-size: 2em}  }
@media print    { body {font-size: 12pt} h1 {font-size: 16pt} }
@media handheld { body {font-size: 8pt}  h1 {font-size: 12pt} }
@media tv       { body {font-size: 16pt} h1 {font-size: 24pt} }
```

In this style sheet, the font size is smallest for a handheld device (which presumably has a limited screen area), and largest for a television (which is usually viewed from a greater distance). Similar to the media attribute, the @media rule also allows you to place media types in a comma-separated list, as in the following declaration:

```
@media screen, print, handheld, tv {
   h1 {font-family: sans-serif}
}
```

Both the media attribute and the @media rule come with their own benefits and disadvantages. The @media rule enables you to consolidate all of your styles within a single style sheet; however, this consolidation can result in larger and complicated files. The alternative—placing media styles in different sheets—can make those sheets easier to maintain; however, if you change the design of your site, you might have to duplicate your changes across several style sheets.

Media Groups

The distinction among the different media types is not always immediately clear. For example, how is projection media different from screen media? The difference lies in what kind of output can be sent to the media. All output media can be described based on some common properties. CSS uses **media groups** to describe how different media devices render content. There are four media groups based on the following characteristics:

- continuous or paged
- visual, aural, or tactile
- grid (for character grid devices) or bitmap
- interactive (for devices that allow user interaction) or static (for devices that allow no interaction)

Figure 4-44 shows how all output media are categorized based on the four media groups. For example, a printout is paged (because the output comes in discrete units or pages), visual, bitmap, and static (you can't interact with it). A computer screen, on the other hand, is continuous, visual, bitmap, and can be either static or interactive.

Media groups

Figure 4-44

Media type	continuous/ paged	visual/aural/ tactile	grid/bitmap	interactive/ static
aural	continuous	aural	N/A	both
braille	continuous	tactile	grid	both
embossed	paged	tactile	grid	both
handheld	both	visual	both	both
print	paged	visual	bitmap	static
projection	paged	visual	bitmap	static
screen	continuous	visual	bitmap	both
tty	continuous	visual	grid	both
tv	both	visual, aural	bitmap	both

Media groups are important because the CSS2 specifications indicate which media *group* a particular style belongs to, rather than the specific media *device*. For example, the font-size style belongs to the visual media group because it describes the visual appearance of the document content; and as indicated in Figure 4-44, this means you can use the font-size style with handheld, print, projection, screen, tty, and tv media. However, it would have no meaning to—and will in fact be ignored by—devices whose output consists of Braille or aural communication. On the other hand, the pitch style, used to define the pitch or frequency of a speaking voice, belongs to the aural media group and is supported by aural and tv devices. By studying the media groups, you can choose the styles that apply to a given output device.

Creating Styles for Different Media

| Reference Window

- To create a style sheet for specific media, add the attribute
  `media = "type"`
  to either the link element or the style element, where *type* is one or more of the following: aural, braille, embossed, handheld, print, projection, screen, tty, tv, or all. If you don't specify a media type, the style sheet applies to all media. Multiple media types should be entered in a comma-separated list.
- To create a style for specific media from within a style sheet, add to the sheet the rule
  `@media type {style declarations}`
  where *type* is the media type and *style declarations* are the styles that are applied to the different page elements within that media.

Now that you've seen how to define the style sheet for a particular media device, you decide to create one for printers.

To create a style sheet for print media:

1. Use your text editor to open the **printtxt.css** style sheet from the tutorial.04\tutorial folder included with your Data Files. Enter ***your name*** and ***the date*** in the comment section of the file.
2. Save the file as **print.css** in the same folder.

Kathy wants you to use the print.css style sheet for any paged visual media, which includes both printed media and projected media. You'll use the scraps.css style sheet for continuous visual media, which includes computer screens, television monitors, and ttys. In the samples.htm file, add a link to the print.css style sheet and insert the media attribute to indicate which style sheets to use for which output devices.

To link Kathy's Samples page to the print.css style sheet:

1. Return to the **samples.htm** file in your text editor.
2. Directly above the link element in the document head, insert the following link element for the print.css style sheet:

```
<link href="print.css" rel="stylesheet" type="text/css"
      media="print, projection" />
```

3. Add the following media attribute to the link element for the scraps.css file to indicate that it should be used for screen, tv, and tty media:

```
media="screen, tv, tty"
```

Figure 4-45 highlights the new code in the samples.htm file.

Figure 4-45 Linking to external style sheets for different media

```
<title>Samples from Online Scrapbooks</title>
<link href="print.css" rel="stylesheet" type="text/css" media="print, projection" />
<link href="scraps.css" rel="stylesheet" type="text/css" media="screen, tv, tty" />
```

The samples.htm file also includes an embedded style sheet. Like the external style sheet, you need to create two embedded sheets: one for printers and projection devices, and the other for screens, tvs, and ttys.

To create an embedded style sheet for print media:

1. Within the samples.htm file, directly above the embedded style sheet, insert the following HTML code:

```
<style type="text/css" media="print, projection">
</style>
```

2. Add the following media attribute to the opening <style> tag for the first embedded style sheet. See Figure 4-46.

```
media="screen, tv, tty"
```

Figure 4-46 Embedded style sheets for different media

```
<style type="text/css" media="print, projection">
</style>

<style type="text/css" media="screen, tv, tty">
   .notes    {font-family: sans-serif; font-size: 8pt; color: brown;
              background-color: ivory; border: 3px inset rgb(212, 212, 212);
              width: 130px; height: 90px; overflow: auto}
   .notes p  {margin: 5px}
   #note1    {position: absolute; left: 600px; top: 120px}
   #note2    {position: absolute; left: 170px; top: 400px}
   #note3    {position: absolute; left: 570px; top: 550px}
</style>
```

3. Save your changes to the file, and then reload the **samples.htm** file in your Web browser. Confirm that the appearance of the page has not changed. (It should not change because your Web browser is treated as screen media and you haven't changed the style sheet for that media type.)

With two sets of style sheets for the different media types, you are ready to start defining the styles for printed output.

Hiding Elements

The first thing you notice when examining Kathy's sketch of the printed version of the Samples page is that many elements from the Web page—such as the list of links on the left and the address at the bottom—are missing. CSS has two styles that you can use to keep an element from being displayed in the output: the display style and the visibility style. As you've already seen in Tutorial 3, the display style supports the value "none," which causes the element to not be rendered by the output device. Alternately, you can use the visibility style, which has the syntax

```
visibility: type
```

where *type* is visible, hidden, collapse, or inherit (the default). A value of "visible" makes an element visible; the "hidden" value hides the element; a value of "collapse" is used with the tables to prevent a row or column from being displayed; and the "inherit" value causes an element to inherit the visibility style from its parent. Unlike the display style, the visibility style hides an element, but does not remove it from the flow of elements on the page. As shown in Figure 4-47, setting the display style to none not only hides an element, but also removes it from the page flow.

Comparing the visibility and display styles | **Figure 4-47**

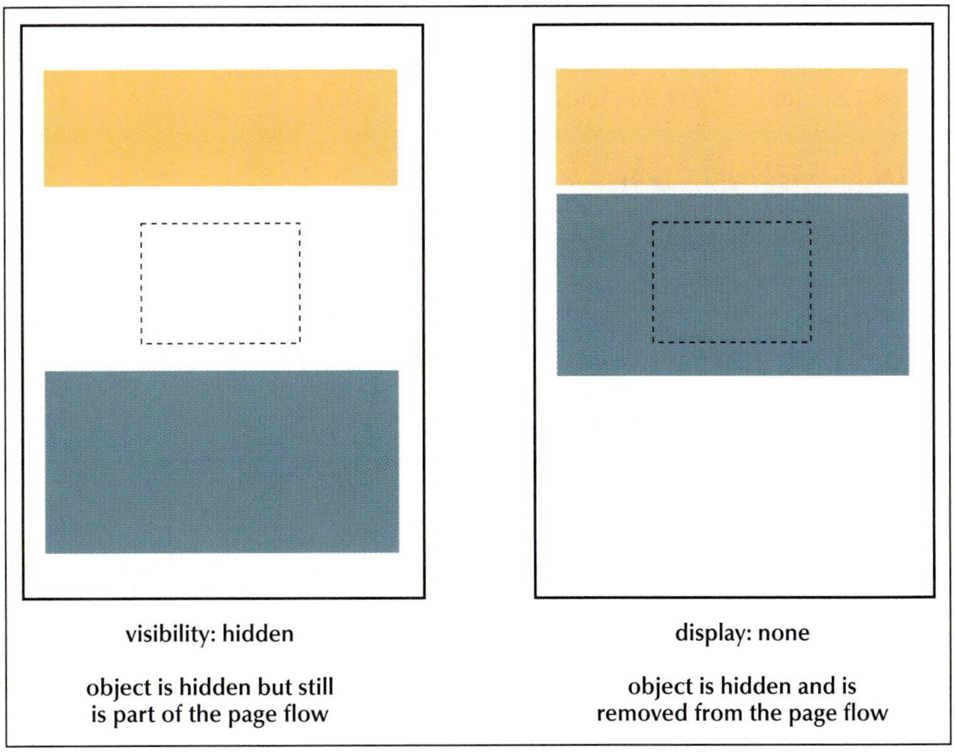
visibility: hidden
object is hidden but still is part of the page flow
display: none
object is hidden and is removed from the page flow

The display: none style is more appropriate for hiding elements in most cases. Use of the visibility: hidden style is usually reserved for scripts in which an element is alternatively hidden and made visible to create an animated effect. You'll use the display: none style to hide the #head, #links, and address selectors in the printed output.

To apply the display: none style:

1. Return to the **print.css** file in your text editor.
2. Add the following style declaration below the comment section:

```
#head, #links, address {display: none}
```

3. Kathy still wants all headings to appear in a sans-serif font in the printed version of the page. Add the following style to the sheet:

```
h1, h2, h3, h4, h5, h6 {font-family: sans-serif}
```

Figure 4-48 shows the code from the print.css style sheet.

Tip

You can also hide an element by stacking other elements on top of it using CSS positioning and the z-index style.

Figure 4-48 Using the display:none style

```
#head, #links, address {display: none}
h1, h2, h3, h4, h5, h6 {font-family: sans-serif}
```

4. Save your changes to the file.

Next, you need to modify the style for the callout notes. Kathy wants the notes to be displayed as items in a bulleted list. You can change the style of the notes to list items by applying the following display style:

```
display: list-item
```

Once the display style has been set to list-item, you can apply the same list styles you would use with elements marked with HTML's <li> tag. You decide to display each note with the bullet.jpg graphic image you used earlier in Session 1. You'll also set the text style to a 12-point sans-serif font with a margin of 20 pixels.

To set the print style of the callout notes:

1. Return to the **samples.htm** file in your text editor.
2. Add the following style to the embedded style sheet for printed output. See Figure 4-49.

```
.notes {display: list-item; list-style-image: url(bullet.jpg);
        font-family: sans-serif; font-size: 12pt;
        margin: 20px}
```

Figure 4-49 Setting the print styles for the callout notes

```
<style type="text/css" media="print, projection">
   .notes {display: list-item; list-style-image: url(bullet.jpg);
           font-family: sans-serif; font-size: 12pt; margin: 20px}
</style>
```

3. Save your changes to the file.

Now test whether the styles you've defined have been applied to the printed version of the page.

4. Reload the **samples.htm** file in your Web browser. Verify that the appearance of the page within the browser window has *not* changed.

5. Either print the Web page from within your browser or use your browser's Print Preview command to preview the printed version of the page. Figure 4-50 shows how the page appears when printed.

Figure 4-50 Preview of the Samples page

Samples from Online Scrapbooks | Page 1 of 1

notes printed as a bulleted list

Samples from Online Scrapbooks

- Paste cut-out letters and words in your scrapbook to create a 3D effect. Online Scrapbooks sells professionally designed cut-out letters, words, and phrases for all occasions.
- Clippings, flyers, programs, and other memorabilia are valuable sources of information that can enhance your scrapbook pages. Make sure that any material is copied to acid-free paper. Newspaper clippings are especially susceptible to deterioration.
- Photographic cut-outs and textured backgrounds can add visual interest to your pages. See the online store for our wide variety of textured and embossed papers.

Kathy likes the printout you created; however, she still wants the notes to appear on a separate sheet. To do this, you'll have to place a page break in the middle of the document. Although page breaks are not supported by media types such as computer screens, they are supported in printed output and for projection devices.

Using Print Styles

CSS defines printed pages by extending the box model described in Tutorial 3 to incorporate the entire page in a **page box**. As shown in Figure 4-51, the page box is composed of two areas: the **page area**, containing the content of the document, and the **margin area**, containing the space between the printed content and the edges of the page.

Figure 4-51 **The page box**

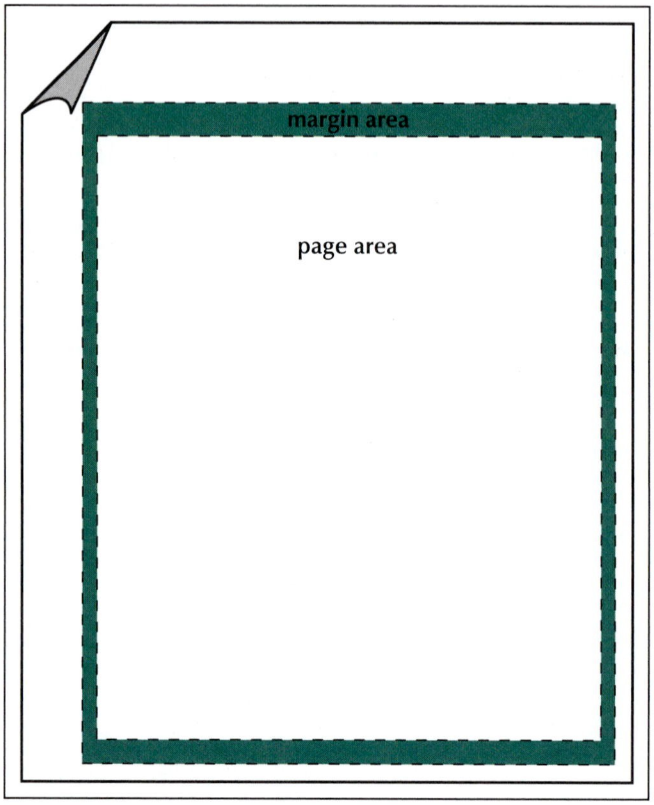

As with the box model, you can specify the size of a page box, the page margins, the internal padding, and other features. The general rule to create and define a page box is

```
@page {styles}
```

where *styles* are the styles you want applied to the page. For example, the following @page rule sets the page margin for the printed output to 5 inches:

```
@page {margin: 5in}
```

A page box does not support all of the measurement units you've used with the other elements. For example, pages do not support the em or ex measurement units. In general, you should use measurement units that are appropriate to the dimensions of your page, such as inches or centimeters.

> **Tip**
> To fit your Web document to a printed page, use absolute units such as inches and centimeters. Do not use pixels or relative units.

Page Pseudo-Classes and Named Pages

If your Web pages will require several pages when printed, you might want to define different styles for different pages. You can do this with pseudo-classes that reference specific pages. The syntax to apply a pseudo-class to a page uses the following rule

```
@page:pseudo-class {styles}
```

where *pseudo-class* is first (for the first page of the printout), left (for the pages that appear on the left in double-sided printouts), and right (for pages that appear on the right in double-sided printouts).

For example, if you are doing two-sided printing, you might want to mirror the margins of the left and right pages of the printout. The following styles result in pages in which the inner margin is set to 5 centimeters and outer margin is set to 2 centimeters:

```
@page:left {margin: 3cm 5cm 3cm 2cm}
@page:right {margin: 3cm 2cm 3cm 5cm}
```

To format specific pages other than the first, left, or right pages, you first must create a page name that contains a set of styles for the page. The syntax to create a page name is

```
@page name {styles}
```

where *name* is the label assigned to the page style. The following code creates the large_margins page name that defines a page box with 10-centimeter margins:

```
@page large_margins {margin: 10cm}
```

Once you define a page name, you can apply it to any block-level element in your document. The content of the block-level element will appear on its own page, with the browser automatically inserting page breaks before and after the element if required. To assign a page name to a block-level element, use the style

```
selector {page: name}
```

where *selector* is a CSS selector that points to a block-level element and *name* is the name of a defined page. For example, the style

```
blockquote {page: large_margins}
```

causes all block quotes to be displayed on their own separate pages using the styles defined for the large_margins page.

Setting the Page Size

Because printed media can vary in size and orientation, one of the styles supported by the page box is the size style that allows the Web author to define the default dimensions of the printed page as well as whether the pages should be printed in portrait or landscape orientation. The syntax of the size style is

```
size: width height orientation
```

where *width* and *height* are the width and height of the page, and *orientation* is the orientation of the page (portrait or landscape). If you don't specify the orientation, browsers assume a portrait orientation. To format a page as a standard-size page in landscape orientation with a 1-inch margin, you would apply the following style:

```
@page {size: 8.5in 11in landscape; margin: 1in}
```

If you remove the orientation value, as in the style

```
@page {size: 8.5in 11in; margin: 1in}
```

browsers print the output in portrait by default. Note that the page sizes and orientations chosen by the Web page author can still be overridden by the user, who may choose different settings when actually printing the page.

You can also replace the width, height, and orientation values with the keyword "auto" (to let the browser determine the page dimensions) or "inherit" (to inherit the page size from the parent element). If a page does not fit into the dimensions specified by the style, browsers will either rotate the page box 90 degrees or scale the page box to fit the sheet size.

Use the @page rule to define the print layout of the Samples page. Kathy suggests that you set the page size to 8.5 × 11 inches, in portrait orientation, with 0.5-inch margins.

To set the style of the printed page:

1. Return to the **print.css** file in your text editor.
2. As shown in Figure 4-52, add the following rule to the top of the list of style declarations:

```
@page {size: 8.5in 11in portrait; margin: 0.5in}
```

Figure 4-52 Setting the print style with the @print rule

```
@page {size: 8.5in 11in portrait; margin: 0.5in}
#head, #links, address {display: none}
h1, h2, h3, h4, h5, h6 {font-family: sans-serif}
```

3. Save your changes to the file.

Working with Page Breaks

When a document is sent to the printer, the printer decides the location of the page breaks unless that information is included as part of the print style. To specify a page break that occurs either before or after a page element, you apply the following styles:

```
page-break-before: type
page-break-after: type
```

The *type* style attribute has the following values:

- **always**, to always place a page break before or after the element
- **avoid**, to never place a page break
- **left**, to place a page break where the next page will be a left page
- **right**, to place a page break where the next page will be a right page
- **auto**, to allow the printer to determine whether or not to insert a page break
- **inherit**, to insert the page break style from the parent element

For example, if you want h1 headings to always be placed at the start of a new page, you would apply the following style in your style sheet:

```
h1 {page-break-before: always}
```

Or, if you want block quotes to always appear on their own page, you could place a page break before and after the block quote using the style:

```
blockquote {page-break-before: always; page-break-after: always}
```

Preventing a Page Break

Sometimes you want to keep the printer from inserting a page break inside of an element. This usually occurs when you have a long string of text that you don't want broken into two pages. You can prevent the printer from inserting a page break by using the style

```
page-break-inside: type
```

where *type* is auto, inherit, or avoid. To prevent a block quote from appearing on two separate pages, you could apply the following style:

```
blockquote {page-break-inside: avoid}
```

Note that the avoid type does not guarantee that there will not be a page break within the element. If the content of an element exceeds the dimensions of the sheet, the browser will be forced to insert a page break.

Working with Widows and Orphans

Even with the three page break styles, there will be situations where a printer will have to divide the contents of an element across two pages. Although this situation is largely unavoidable, designers can control the occurrence of widows and orphans in their printed output. A **widow** occurs when only a few ending lines of an element appear at the top of a page. An **orphan** is just the opposite: it occurs when only a few beginning lines of an element appear at the bottom of a page. Leaving one or two lines "stranded" on a page either as a widow or an orphan makes the material more difficult to read and is considered poor page design. The styles to control the appearance of widows and orphans in the printout are

```
widow: value
orphan: value
```

where *value* is the number of lines that must appear within the element before a page break can be inserted by the printer. The default value is 2, which means the widow or orphan must contain at least two lines of text. If you want to increase the size of widows and orphans to three lines for the paragraphs of your document, you could use the style declaration

```
p {widow: 3; orphan: 3}
```

and the printer will not insert a page break if less than three lines of a paragraph will be stranded at either the top or the bottom of a page. It's important to note that the widow and orphan values might not always be followed. Browsers attempt to use page breaks that obey the following guidelines:

- Insert all of the manual page breaks as indicated by the page-break-before, page-break-after styles, and page-break-inside styles.
- Avoid inserting page breaks where indicated in the style sheet.
- Break the pages as few times as possible.
- Make all pages that don't have a forced page break appear to have the same height.
- Avoid page breaking inside a block-level element that has a border.
- Avoid breaking inside a table.
- Avoid breaking inside of a floating element.

Only after attempting to satisfy these constraints are the Web page designer's recommendations for the widow and orphan styles applied.

You can combine all of the various page styles described above to provide the greatest control over the appearance of your printed document. The following set of styles shows how to create a style for the blockquote element that places each block quote on a separate 8.5 × 11 sheet of paper in landscape orientation:

Tip

You can repeat an element across several pages as a header or footer by placing it in the printout using fixed positioning.

```
@page quote_page {8.5in 11in landscape}
blockquote     {page: quote_page; page-break-before: always;
                                  page-break-inside: avoid;
                                  page-break-after: always}
```

Browser support for the various CSS print styles is very uneven, so you should always test your print styles on a wide variety of browsers and operating systems.

Reference Window | Working with Print Styles

- To define a page box for a printout that indicates the page size, margins, and orientation, use the declaration
  `@page {styles}`
  where *styles* are the styles that define the page.
- To set the page size and orientation, use the style
  `size: width height orientation`
  where *width* and *height* are the width and height of the page, and *orientation* is the orientation of the page (portrait or landscape).
- To insert a page break before an element, use the style
  `page-break-before: type`
  where *type* is always (to always place a page break), avoid (to never place a page break), left (to force a page break where the succeeding page will be a left page), right (to force a page break where the succeeding page will be a right page), auto (to allow the browser to determine whether or not to insert a page break), or inherit (to inherit the page break style of the parent element).
- To insert a page break after an element, use the style
  `page-break-after: type`
  where *type* has the same values as the page-break-before style.
- To apply a page break inside an element, use the style
  `page-break-inside: type`
  where *type* is auto, inherit, or avoid.

Now that you've seen how to insert page breaks into printed output, you are ready to insert a break into the printed version of the Samples page. Recall that Kathy wants the list of notes to appear on one page and the scrapbooking sample to appear on another. To do this, you can either place a page break after the third callout note or place a page break before the inline image of the scrapbooking sample. You decide to place a page break before the image. This will enable you to insert additional callout notes later without having to revise the page break structure. The sample image has been placed within a div container element with the id sample_image. To ensure that this container will start on a new page, you'll add the style below to the print.css style sheet. Kathy also wants the image centered horizontally on the page. The complete style for the #sample_image selector is:

```
#sample_image {page-break-before: always;
               text-align: center}
```

Kathy also wants the sample image itself resized to better fit the size of the page. She suggests you increase the size of the printed image to 7 inches wide by 9.1 inches tall. Because the img element for the sample image is nested within the #sample_image div container, you can set the size using the following style:

```
#sample_image img {width: 7in; height: 9.1in}
```

Add both of these styles to the print.css style sheet.

To complete the print.css style sheet:

1. As shown in Figure 4-53, add the following styles to the bottom of the **print.css** style sheet:

```
#sample_image      {page-break-before: always;
                     text-align: center}
#sample_image img {width: 7in; height: 9.1in}
```

Final print.css style sheet **Figure 4-53**

```
@page {size: 8.5in 11in portrait; margin: 0.5in}
#head, #links, address {display: none}
h1, h2, h3, h4, h5, h6 {font-family: sans-serif}

#sample_image      {page-break-before: always;
                     text-align: center}

#sample_image img {width: 7in; height: 9.1in}
```

2. Close the file, saving your changes.
3. Reload the **samples.htm** file in your Web browser.
4. Either print the Web page or use the Print Preview feature of your Web browser to view the layout and design of the printed version of the document. As shown in Figure 4-54, the printed version covers 2 pages, with the list of notes on one page and the sample image resized and centered on the second page.

Figure 4-54 Two-page printout of the samples.htm file

Samples from Online Scrapbooks Page 1 of 2

Samples from Online Scrapbooks

- Paste cut-out letters and words in your scrapbook to create a 3D effect. Online Scrapbooks sells professionally designed cut-out letters, words, and phrases for all occasions.
- Clippings, flyers, programs, and other memorabilia are valuable sources of information that can enhance your scrapbook pages. Make sure that any material is copied to acid-free paper. Newspaper clippings are especially susceptible to deterioration.
- Photographic cut-outs and textured backgrounds can add visual interest to your pages. See the online store for our wide variety of textured and embossed papers.

Samples from Online Scrapbooks Page 2 of 2

5. Close your Web browser and any other programs and files.

Styles for Handheld Devices | InSight

Although CSS allows you to create styles for handheld devices such as cell phones, PDAs, and MP3 players, effectively translating a large Web page into a smaller space is not easy. Some handheld devices support screens only up to 120 pixels wide; so you might quickly find your graphics-intensive Web page does not translate well into a portable world.

In general, if you want your Web page to be accessible to handheld devices, you should avoid using decorative images, and you should always specify alternative text for your graphic images. Also avoid floating elements. In the small, confined space of a handheld device, a floating element can behave unpredictably and ruin your page layout. Instead try to limit your page layout to a single column.

Use relative units such as the em unit and percent values to set the size of your fonts and block-level elements. If you must use pixels to specify a margin or padding size, try to keep your sizes within 5 pixels. Using larger pixel values such as 15 or 20 pixel widths can have an unpredictable effect on your page.

Finally, you have to pick and choose the features that are the most crucial to your Web page. A long list of links, while useful on a computer screen, can be distracting and difficult to navigate in a portable browser. Use the display:none style to control which elements will be sent to handheld devices.

Support for handheld browsing is still in its infancy, so don't be surprised to find a great deal of variation in the support for your HTML and CSS code among the various portable devices.

You've completed your work on the Samples page for the Online Scrapbooks Web site, and you'll be able to apply what you've learned about print styles to the other pages in the site. At the moment, most browsers support few of the page styles other than page breaking. This is sure to change in the future, however, as Web pages expand beyond the limitations of the computer screen into new media. Kathy finds this an exciting prospect, providing the opportunity to advertise the company to a whole new set of potential customers.

Session 4.3 Quick Check | Review

1. What attribute would you add to an embedded or external style sheet link to apply a style sheet to a mobile phone?
2. Which media types belong to the continuous/visual group?
3. Which media types would be most appropriate for Web browsers designed for the visually impaired?
4. What is the difference between the display:none and visibility:hidden styles?
5. Specify a style to set the page size of the printed document to 11 inches wide by 14 inches high in landscape orientation with a 1.5-inch margin.
6. Specify the style to insert a page break before every h1 heading in your document.
7. In page design, what is a widow? What is an orphan?

Review | Tutorial Summary

In this tutorial, you learned how to use Cascading Style Sheets to create interesting and flexible layouts and designs. The first session examined different types of CSS selectors, providing the Web author flexibility in creating and applying specific design styles. The first session also explored how to apply styles to unordered lists. It concluded by examining how to use CSS to create rollover effects and drop caps. The second session focused on CSS positioning styles and explored how to use CSS positioning to place elements in absolute and relative coordinates. The final session looked at applying styles to media other than computer screens, focusing on creating styles for printed output. In the session you learned how to work with page flow within printed materials by controlling the placement of page breaks before, after, and within page elements.

Key Terms

absolute positioning
attribute selector
conditional comment
contextual selector
media group
orphan
page box
pseudo-class
pseudo-element
relative positioning
rollover effect
widow

Practice | Review Assignments

Practice the skills you learned in the tutorial using the same case scenario.

Data Files needed for the Review Assignments: back.jpg, gallerytxt.htm, marker.gif, printertxt.css, sample1.jpg – sample4.jpg, scraps.jpg, and screentxt.css

Kathy stopped by to ask for your help in designing a new Web page to display scrapbooking samples sent in by different visitors to the Web site. The screen version of the Web page will show four new sample scrapbook pages each month, laid out on the page in a 2 × 2 grid. The print version of the same page will display enlarged versions of the four samples, printed on separate pages. Kathy also has some changes she wants you to make to the size navigation links. A preview of the design you'll apply to the Scrapbook Gallery page is shown in Figure 4-55.

Figure 4-55

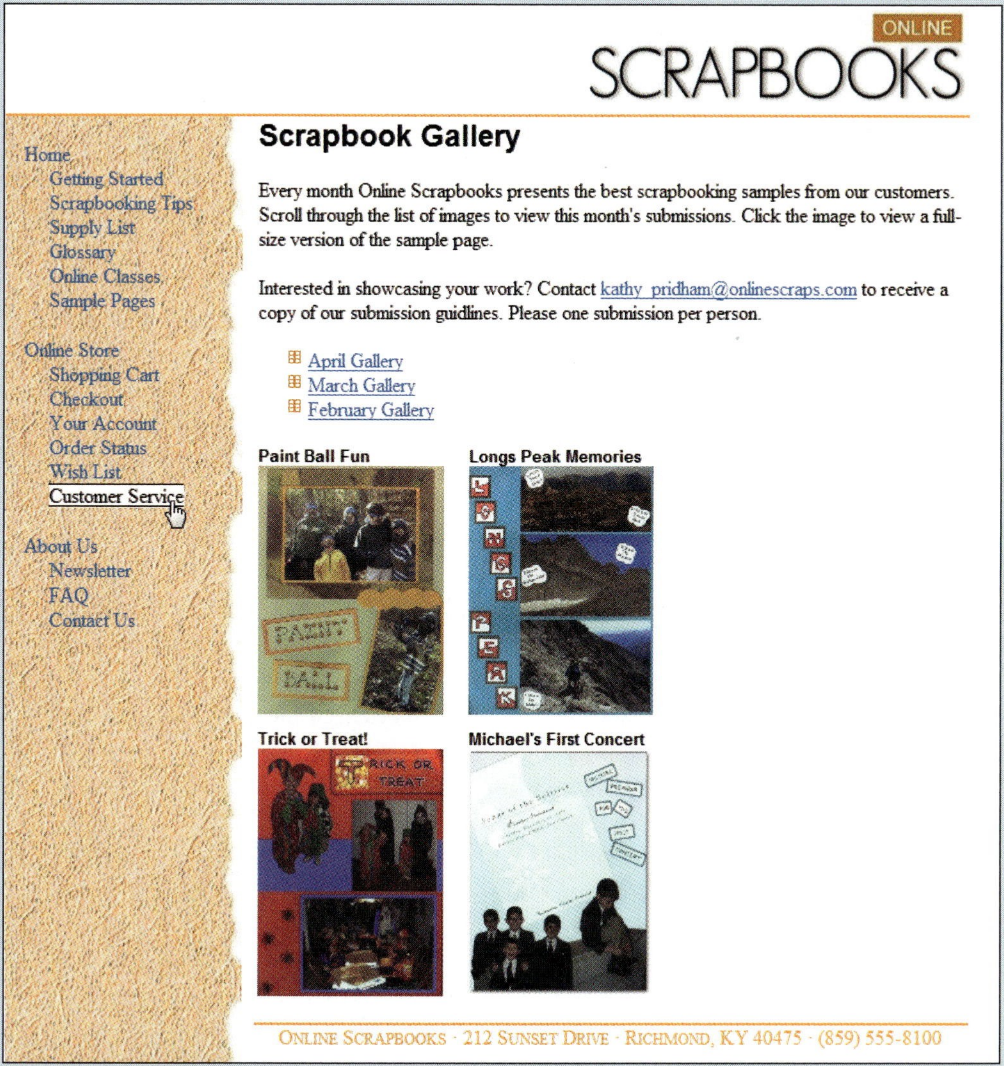

ONLINE
SCRAPBOOKS
Home
Getting Started
Scrapbooking Tips
Supply List
Glossary
Online Classes
Sample Pages
Online Store
Shopping Cart
Checkout
Your Account
Order Status
Wish List
Customer Service
About Us
Newsletter
FAQ
Contact Us
Scrapbook Gallery
Every month Online Scrapbooks presents the best scrapbooking samples from our customers. Scroll through the list of images to view this month's submissions. Click the image to view a full-size version of the sample page.
Interested in showcasing your work? Contact kathy_pridham@onlinescraps.com to receive a copy of our submission guidlines. Please one submission per person.
April Gallery
March Gallery
February Gallery
Paint Ball Fun
Longs Peak Memories
Trick or Treat!
Michael's First Concert
ONLINE SCRAPBOOKS · 212 SUNSET DRIVE · RICHMOND, KY 40475 · (859) 555-8100

Complete the following:

1. Use your text editor to open the **gallerytxt.htm**, **printertxt.css**, and **screentxt.css** files from the tutorial.04\review folder included with your Data Files. Enter ***your name*** and ***the date*** in the comment section of each file. Save the files as **gallery.htm**, **printer.css**, and **screen.css**, respectively, in the same folder. Take some time to study the content and layout of the Gallery Web page and observe how the styles in the screen.css style sheet file affects the layout and appearance of the page as it appears in your Web browser.
2. Return to the **gallery.htm** file in your text editor. Kathy wants you to format the appearance of the list of links by indenting links belonging to a particular group or class. To define the class of links, do the following:
   - Add a class attribute to the li elements in the list of links, placing the Home, Online Store, and About Us links in the newgroup class.
   - Place the other li elements in the list of links in the subgroup class.
3. The Gallery page contains four images of scrapbook page samples chosen for the May gallery. Scroll down to the four div container elements (marked with ids sample1 through sample4) and place each of the div containers in the samples class.
4. Save your changes to the **gallery.htm** file and then go to the **screen.css** style sheet file in your text editor. This style sheet will be used to design the layout of the Gallery page as it appears on computer screens.
5. Kathy wants to remove the bullet markers from the list of links. She also wants to change the layout of the links, moving them farther to the left and indenting links belonging to the subgroup class. To apply these styles, do the following:
   - For ul elements nested within the #links selector, change the marker style to none.
   - To move the list of links to the left on the Web page, set the size of the left margin to 15 pixels and the size of the left padding to 0 pixels.
   - Set the top margin of elements belonging to the newgroup class to 20 pixels.
   - Set the left margin of elements belonging to the subgroup class to 20 pixels.
6. The Gallery page also includes links to galleries from the months of February, March, and April. These links also appear in a list nested within the content div container. Kathy would like you to replace the bullet marker on this list with a graphical marker. To apply this style, set all the ul elements nested within the #content selector to use the **marker.gif** file as their bullet marker.
7. Kathy would like you to create a rollover effect for the list of links displayed on the left margin of the Web page. To create the rollover effect, add the following styles to the style sheet:
   - For links within the #links selector, remove any underlining by setting the text-decoration style to none. Do this for the link, visited, and active pseudo-classes.
   - When the mouse pointer is hovering over those links, change the font color to black and change the background color to white, and use the text-decoration style to add an underline and an overline to the link text.
8. Kathy wants the four scrapbook samples to be reduced in size and placed in a 2 x 2 grid on the Web page. To create this effect, add the following styles to the style sheet:
   - Apply absolute positioning to all elements belonging to the samples class.
   - For all img elements nested within the samples class, set the width of the image to 150 pixels, the height to 193 pixels, and the border width to 0 pixels.

- All four scrapbook samples are nested within a div container with the id samples_container. Place this div container on the Web page using relative positioning. Set the top and left coordinates of the element to 0 pixels. Set the height of samples_container to 450 pixels.
- Place the #sample1 selector at the page coordinates (0, 0). Place the #sample2 selector at the coordinates (170, 0). Place the #sample3 selector at the coordinates (0, 220). Place the #sample4 selector at the coordinates (170, 220).

9. Save your changes to the **screen.css** file. Load the **gallery.htm** file in your Web browser and verify that its layout resembles that shown in Figure 4-55. Confirm that the Web browser displays the correct rollover effect when you hover your mouse pointer over any of the links in the list on the left page margin.
10. Kathy also wants you to create a style sheet for printed versions of the Gallery page in which only the four scrapbook samples and their headings are shown, each on its own page. To create this style, return to the **printer.css** file in your text editor.
11. Add the following styles to the style sheet:
    - Set the page size to 8.5 × 11 inches, in portrait orientation, with a margin of 0.5 inches.
    - Prevent the display of the #head and #links selectors as well as the address, ul, and h2 elements and paragraphs nested within the #content selector.
    - Horizontally center all elements belonging to the samples class, and add a page break after every occurrence of this class of element.
    - Set the font size of h3 headings nested within the samples class to 18 points and the font family to sans-serif.
    - Set the size of img elements nested within the samples class to 6.5 inches wide by 8.35 inches tall. Set the border width to 0 pixels.
12. Save your changes to the **printer.css** file and return to the **gallery.htm** file.
13. Edit the link element pointing to the screen.css style sheet, adding an attribute that indicates that this style sheet should only be used for screen output.
14. Add a link pointing to the printer.css style sheet with an attribute indicating that this style sheet is used for printed output.
15. Save your changes to the **gallery.htm** file and refresh the page in your Web browser. Confirm that the appearance of the page within the browser window is unchanged. Print the Web page or use your browser's Print Preview command to confirm that the printed version of the page displays only the four scrapbook samples and their headings.
16. Submit your completed files to your instructor.

Apply | Case Problem 1

Apply your knowledge of Web site design to create a Web site for a golf course.

Data Files needed for this Case Problem: h01txt.htm – h18txt.htm, hole01.jpg – hole18.jpg, next.jpg, prev.jpg, printtxt.css, willet.jpg, and willettxt.css

Willet Creek Golf Course Willet Creek is a popular public golf course in central Idaho. You've been asked to work on the design of the course's Web site by Michael Carpenter, the head of promotion for the course. Part of the Web site contains a preview of each of the course's 18 holes, complete with yardages and shot recommendations. Each hole has been given its own Web page with a set of links to navigate from one page to another. Figure 4-56 shows a preview of the design you'll use to show one of the pages on the golf course Web site.

Figure 4-56

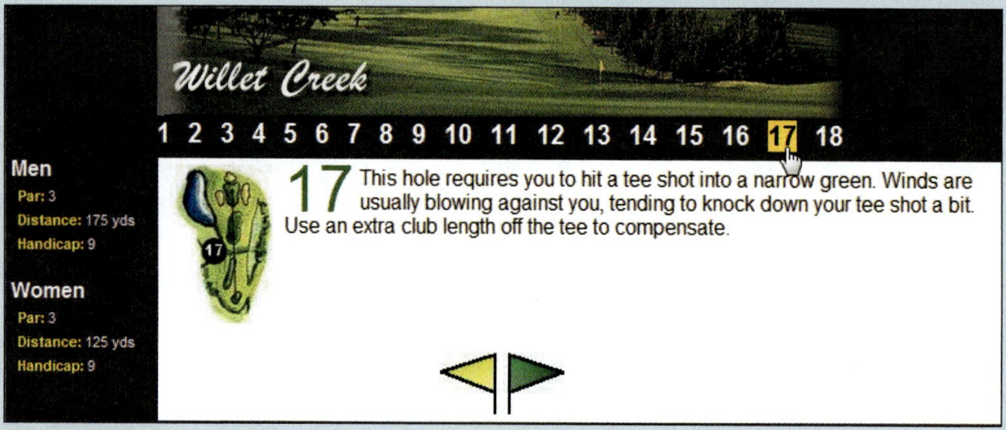

Michael also wants another style sheet designed for printed output. Figure 4-57 shows a preview of the print style used with the golf course pages.

Figure 4-57

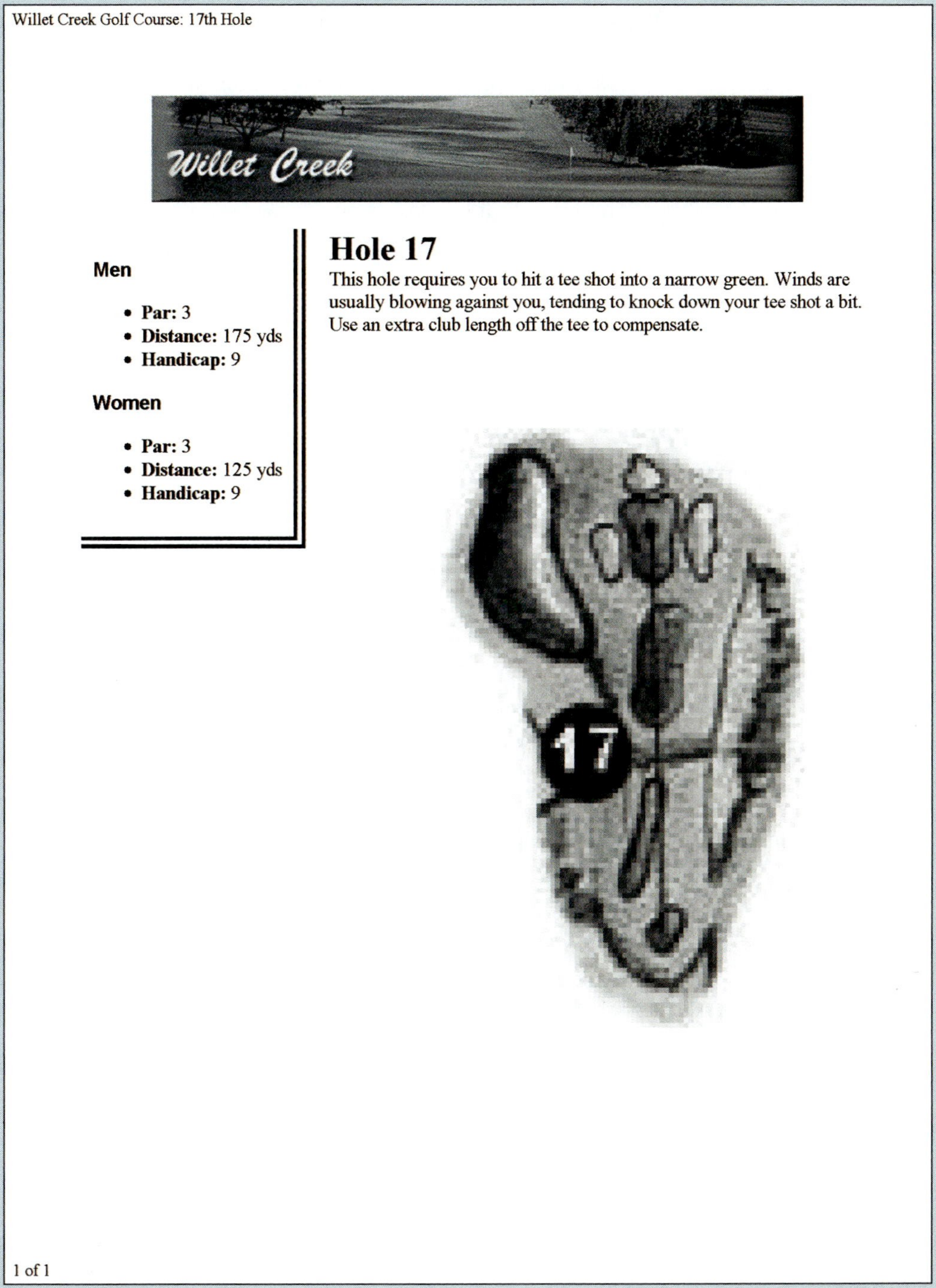
Willet Creek Golf Course: 17th Hole
Willet Creek
Men
Par: 3
Distance: 175 yds
Handicap: 9
Women
Par: 3
Distance: 125 yds
Handicap: 9
Hole 17
This hole requires you to hit a tee shot into a narrow green. Winds are usually blowing against you, tending to knock down your tee shot a bit. Use an extra club length off the tee to compensate.
17
1 of 1

Michael has already done a lot of work in setting up the page content and has even applied a few CSS styles to the page elements. He needs you to complete the task, getting the Web pages ready for the next round of golfers.

Complete the following:

1. In your text editor, open the files **h01txt.htm** through **h18txt.htm** from the tutorial.04\case1 folder included with your Data Files. Enter ***your name*** and ***the date*** in the comment section of each file and save the files as **h01.htm** through **h18.htm** in the same folder.
2. Use your text editor to open the **printtxt.css** and **willettxt.css** files, also from the tutorial.04\case1 folder included with your Data Files. Enter ***your name*** and ***the date*** in each file and save them as **print.css** and **willet.css**, respectively, in the same folder. Take some time to review the contents and layout of the Web pages, paying particular attention to the use of div container tags and id attributes to mark off different sections of the document. Also take some time to review the contents of the **willet.css** style sheet to examine what styles Michael has already created for the Web site.
3. Return to the **willet.css** file in your text editor. The list of links to each page in the Web site is contained within a div container with the id hole_list. Apply the following styles to the list and the links it contains:
   - Display each link in a bold, white font, with a font size of 1.25 em.
   - When a mouse pointer hovers over a link, change the background color to yellow and the font color to black.
   - Display each li element within the #hole_list selector as an inline element with a margin of 0 pixels, a padding space of 0 pixels above and below the element, and padding space of 5 pixels to the left and right.
4. The hole_stats div container stores statistical information about each hole, providing the par score, distance, and handicap value for men and women. Apply the following styles to this element:
   - Use absolute positioning to place the div container at the page coordinates (0, 115).
   - For h2 elements nested within the container, set the font size to 1 em and the left margin to 5 pixels. Set the size of the other margins to 0 pixels.
   - Remove the list markers from the unordered list within the container. Also, set the left margin of the list to 10 pixels, the left padding to 0 pixels, and the top margin to 0 pixels. Display the unordered list in a 0.7 em size font.
   - Display the contents of the strong element within the container in a yellow font.
5. The hole_summary div container contains a text summary of the hole and how to play it. Add a style to place the container at the coordinates (120, 115). Use absolute positioning.
6. The hole_image div container stores an image of the hole. Use absolute positioning to place this element at the coordinates (10, 5).
7. The hole_description div container contains a text description of the hole. Use absolute positioning to place this element at the coordinates (100, 5).
8. Within the hole_description container is a span element that contains the hole number. Michael would like this number to appear as a drop cap. Create this effect by floating the span element on the left margin with a line height of 0.75 with 2 pixels of padding on the right. Set the font color to green and the font size to 300%.
9. At the bottom of each page are a pair of flag images that can be clicked to move to the next hole on the course. The images are nested within a div container with the id flags. Apply the following styles to the div container and the images it contains:
   - Set the border width of img elements within the flags container to 0 pixels.

- Use absolute positioning to place the #prevFlag selector at the coordinates (220, 145).
- Use absolute positioning to place the #nextFlag selector at the coordinates (270, 145).

10. Save your changes to the **willet.css** file. Go to the **h01.htm** through **h18.htm** files in your text editor and link each file to the willet.css style sheet, specifying that the sheet is to be used with screen and tv media. Save your changes to each file, and then view the Web site in your browser. Verify that the layout resembles that shown in Figure 4-57 and that the list of links at the top of the page has a rollover effect.
11. Return to the **print.css** file in your text editor. Add the following styles to the style sheet:
    - Set the page size to 8.5 × 11 inches in portrait orientation.
    - Set the font family of the h1, h2, and h3 headings to sans-serif.
    - Horizontally align the contents of the #head selector.
    - Prevent the display of the #hole_list and #flags selectors.
    - Float the #hole_stats selector on the left margin with a 0.2-inch right margin and 0.1 inches of padding. Add a 0.1-inch double black border to the right and bottom of the element.
    - Set the font size of h2 elements nested within the #hole_stats selector to 12 points.
    - Use absolute positioning to place the #hole_image selector 3 inches from the top of the page and 3 inches from the page's left margin.
    - Set the width of img elements within the #hole_image selector to 3.54 inches wide by 5 inches tall.
    - Display the span element nested within the #hole_description selector as a block-level element. Display the text in a 20-point bold sans-serif font.
    - EXPLORE — Use the before pseudo-element to place the text "Hole" directly before the content of the span element.
12. Save your changes to the **print.css** file. Return to the **h01.htm** through **h18.htm** files in your text editor. Link each file to the print.css style sheet, indicating that this style sheet is used for print media.
13. Print **h01.htm** (or use the Print Preview feature on your Web browser) to verify that the layout of the printed Web page resembles that shown in Figure 4-57. (Note: Internet Explorer does not support the before pseudo-element, so in this browser you will not see the word "Hole" next to the hole number in the printed version of the page.)
14. Submit your completed files to your instructor.

Challenge | Case Problem 2

Test your knowledge of Web site design by completing a Civil War history page.

Data Files needed for this Case Problem: cwlogo.gif, cwpagetxt.htm, cwtxt.css, and tan.jpg

Civil War Studies Adanya Lynne is a professor of military history at Ridgeview State College in Bartlett, Tennessee. She has been working on a Web site for a course she is preparing in Civil War studies. Professor Lynne has already created some sample pages and done work on the design and layout, but she needs your help in completing the project. She would like to create a list of links in an outline format by nesting one ordered list inside of another. She's also interested in using CSS to create a drop-shadow effect on the main topic headings on her pages. To test your design, you'll create a style for a page containing the text of Lincoln's second inaugural address. A preview of the page you'll create for Professor Lynne is shown in Figure 4-58.

Figure 4-58

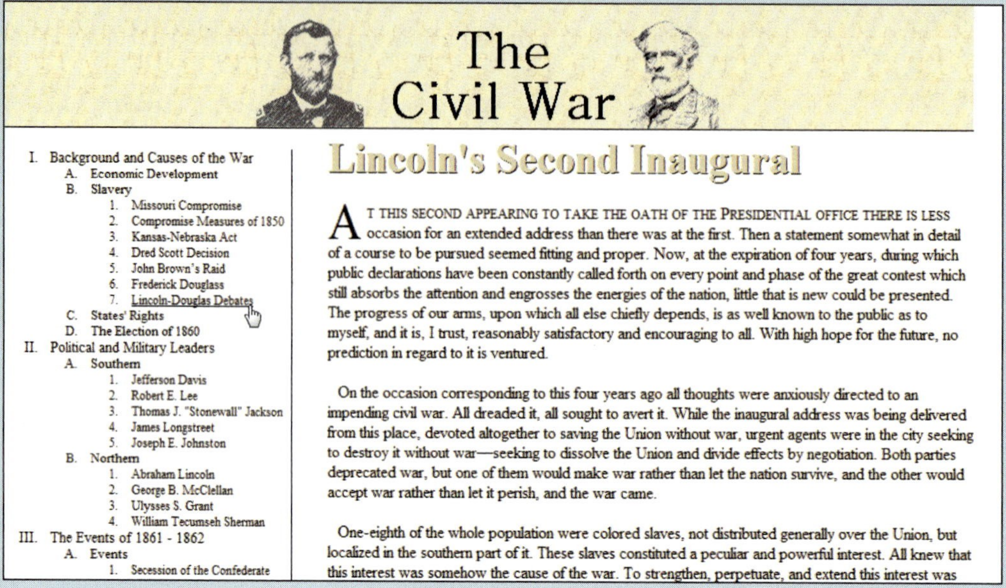

Complete the following:

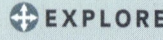

1. Use your text editor to open the **cwpagetxt.htm** and **cwtxt.css** files from the tutorial.04\case2 folder included with your Data Files. Enter ***your name*** and ***the date*** in the comment section of each file. Save the files as **cwpage.htm** and **cw.css**, respectively, in the same folder. Take some time to examine the contents and structure of the HTML file and the external style sheet.
2. Return to the **cwpage.htm** file in your text editor. Create a link to the cw.css style sheet. You do not have to specify a media attribute.
3. Scroll down the file and locate the h2 heading "Lincoln's Second Inaugural." Directly below this heading, insert another h2 heading containing exactly the same text but with the class name shadow.
4. Go to the paragraphs within the article div container. Give the first paragraph the class name first_para and give the remaining paragraphs the class name following_para.
5. Save your changes to the **cwpage.htm** file and then return to the **cw.css** file in your text editor.
6. The page_content div container contains the entire contents of the Web page. Add the following styles for the container:
   - Use relative positioning to place the container with top and left coordinates of 0 pixels.
   - Set the width of the container to 95% of the width of the document window.
   - **EXPLORE** Insert styles to set the minimum width of the container to 800 pixels and the maximum width to 1000 pixels.
7. The linkList div container contains the list of links in Adanya's Web site. Use absolute positioning to place this element at the coordinates (5, 140). Set the width to 280 pixels. Add a 1-pixel-wide solid black border to the right edge of the element.
8. Remove the underlining from the links nested within the linkList container, and change the font color to black. If a mouse pointer hovers over any of the links, have the browser underline the link text.

EXPLORE

9. The links appear in a set of nested ordered lists. Adanya wants these links to appear in an outline format. To create the outline, do the following:
   - Display the ol element using uppercase Roman numerals as the bullet marker. Set the font size to 0.9 em.
   - Display ol elements nested within another ordered list using uppercase letters as bullet markers.
   - Display ol elements nested within *two* levels of ordered lists using decimal numbers as bullet markers.
10. Use absolute positioning to place the article div container at the coordinates (320, 190).

EXPLORE

11. You can create a drop-shadow around a heading by duplicating the heading and then offsetting one heading from another. You've already duplicated the heading in the cwpage.htm file; complete the drop-shadow by applying the following styles:
    - Use absolute positioning to place the h2 element at the coordinates (320, 125). Set the font color of the heading to the RGB value (237, 227, 178) and the z-index value to 2.
    - Directly below the h2 style, insert a style to place the element belonging to the shadow class at the coordinates (321, 126), once again using absolute positioning. Set the font color to black and the z-index value to 1.
12. Adanya wants you to create drop caps and a special first line style for the paragraphs that contain the text of Lincoln's second inaugural address. Add the following styles to the style sheet:
    - Display the first line of the paragraph belonging to the first_para class in small capital letters.
    - Float the first letter of the "first_para" paragraph on the left margin of the paragraph with top and left margin values of 0 pixels and right bottom margins of 5 pixels. Set the font size to 300% and the line height to 0.75.
    - Use the text-indent style to indent the paragraphs belonging to the following_para class by 10 pixels each.
13. Save your changes to the style sheet.
14. Load the **cwpage.htm** file in your Web browser and verify that the layout matches that shown in Figure 4-58. Confirm that the Lincoln's Second Inaugural heading appears with a drop-shadow. Verify that the list of links appears in outline form and that links within the outline display a rollover effect.

EXPLORE

15. If you have a large screen monitor and access to Firefox, Opera, or another Web browser that supports minimum and maximum widths, resize your browser window and verify that the width of the page content does not exceed 1000 pixels or fall below 800 pixels even as you resize the browser window. (Note: Internet Explorer does not support minimum and maximum width styles.)
16. Submit your completed files to your instructor.

Challenge | Case Problem 3

Broaden your knowledge of CSS styles by creating an interactive map for a national park Web site.

Data Files needed for this Case Problem: image0.jpg – image9.jpg, longstxt.htm, and lpmap.jpg

Longs Peak Interactive Map Longs Peak is one of the most popular attractions of Rocky Mountain National Park (RMNP). Each year during the months of July, August, and September, thousands of people climb Longs Peak by the Keyhole Route to reach the 14,255-foot summit. Ron Bartlett, the head of the RMNP Web site team, has asked for your help in creating an interactive map of the Keyhole Route. The map will be installed at electronic kiosks in the park's visitor center. Ron envisions a map with 10 numbered waypoints along the Keyhole Route, displaying photos and text descriptions of each waypoint when a mouse pointer hovers over its corresponding numbered point. Figure 4-59 shows a preview of the online map with the first waypoint highlighted by the user.

Figure 4-59

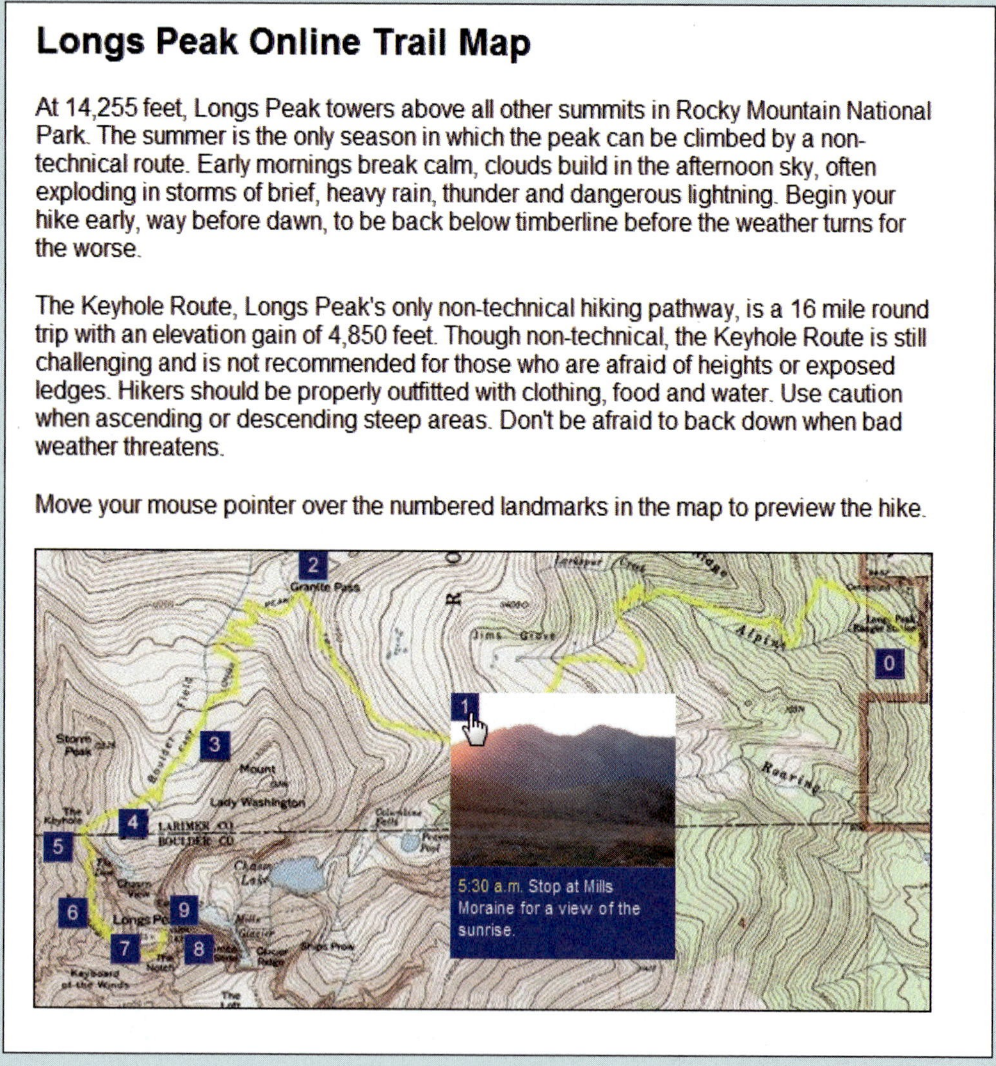
Longs Peak Online Trail Map

At 14,255 feet, Longs Peak towers above all other summits in Rocky Mountain National Park. The summer is the only season in which the peak can be climbed by a non-technical route. Early mornings break calm, clouds build in the afternoon sky, often exploding in storms of brief, heavy rain, thunder and dangerous lightning. Begin your hike early, way before dawn, to be back below timberline before the weather turns for the worse.

The Keyhole Route, Longs Peak's only non-technical hiking pathway, is a 16 mile round trip with an elevation gain of 4,850 feet. Though non-technical, the Keyhole Route is still challenging and is not recommended for those who are afraid of heights or exposed ledges. Hikers should be properly outfitted with clothing, food and water. Use caution when ascending or descending steep areas. Don't be afraid to back down when bad weather threatens.

Move your mouse pointer over the numbered landmarks in the map to preview the hike.

Ron also wants to create a print version of the waypoint descriptions. Users can print the map elsewhere on the park's Web site, so he wants the print style sheet to display just the list of waypoints in a bulleted list.

Complete the following:

1. Use your text editor to open the **longstxt.htm** file from the tutorial.04\case3 folder included with your Data Files. Enter ***your name*** and ***the date*** in the comment section at the top of the file. Save the file as **longs.htm** in the same folder. Take some time to study the contents of the file. Notice that the waypoint descriptions are nested within the online_map div container. Each waypoint description has been placed in a separate div container with the class name notes and id names ranging from point0 to point9.
2. To create a rollover effect for the nine waypoints, you need to mark the waypoint contents as hyperlinks. Within each of the nine div containers, enclose the img element and paragraph element within a single <a> tag. Point each link to the **longs.htm** file so that if a user clicks the link, it will simply refresh the current Web page.
3. Add a style to the embedded style sheet at the top of the file to remove underlining from all hypertext links.
4. Currently the online_map div container does not display the Longs Peak map. Add the following style to the embedded style sheet to display the map:
   - Set the width of the container to 600 pixels wide by 294 pixels high.
   - Add a 1-pixel-wide solid black border to the container.
   - Apply the **lpmap.jpg** graphic file as the background image.
   - Use relative positioning to place the container on the page. Set the top and left coordinates to 0 pixels.
5. In the embedded style sheet, add the following styles for all of the div containers belonging to the notes class:
   - For paragraphs nested within each note, set the font size to 8 points and the margin to 5 pixels.
   - Set the font color to yellow for each span element nested within a note.

EXPLORE

6. For each link nested within a notes class element, apply the following styles:
   - Set the width and height of the link to 20 pixels.
   - Hide any content that overflows the boundary of the link.
   - Set the background color to blue and the font color to white.
   - Set the z-index value to 1.

EXPLORE

7. When the mouse hovers over a link within a notes class element, have the browser apply the following style:
   - Change the width to 150 pixels and the height to 170 pixels.
   - Change the overflow property to visible.
   - Set the z-index value to 2.
8. Use absolute positioning to place the link nested within the #point0 selector at the coordinates (560, 60).
9. Repeat Step 8 for the nine remaining waypoints:
   - #point1 at (277, 90)
   - #point2 at (175, 0)
   - #point3 at (110, 115)
   - #point4 at (55, 165)
   - #point5 at (5, 180)

- #point6 at (15, 222)
- #point7 at (50, 245)
- #point8 at (100, 245)
- #point9 at (90, 220)

10. Go to the top of the file and add a media attribute to the embedded style sheet indicating that the sheet is designed for screen and tv media.
11. Save your changes to the file and then open **longs.htm** in your Web browser. Verify that the placement of the waypoints follows the locations shown in Figure 4-59. Confirm that when you hover your mouse over each of the nine waypoints, a description of the waypoint appears on the top of the trail map.
12. Return to the **longs.htm** file in your text editor. Create a new embedded style sheet designed for print media.
13. Scroll down to the "Longs Peak Online Trail Map" h2 heading and enclose the text "Online Trail Map" within a span element.
14. Add the following styles to the embedded print style sheet:
    - Set the font family for the page body to sans-serif.
    - Remove underlining from all hypertext links.
    - Do not display the #instructions selector, the span element nested within the h2 element, or the img element nested within elements belonging to the notes class.
    - Display the notes class of elements as list items with a disc marker. Set the margin to 20 pixels.
    - Change the display property of paragraphs nested within the notes class of elements to inline.
    - Display span elements nested within the notes class of elements in a bold font.

EXPLORE

15. Add a style that inserts the text string "Trail Itinerary" after the h2 heading.
16. Save your changes to the file.
17. Refresh the **longs.htm** file in your Web browser. By either printing the page or viewing the page within the Print Preview window, confirm that the printed page only shows a bulleted list of the waypoint descriptions. If you are running Firefox, Opera, or Safari, confirm that the heading at the top of the page reads "Longs Peak Trail Itinerary." (If you are using Internet Explorer, the title will simply read "Longs Peak.")
18. Submit your completed files to your instructor.

Create | Case Problem 4

Test your knowledge of CSS and HTML by creating a Web page design for a children's choir.

Data Files needed for this Case Problem: bizet.jpg, bizetbio.txt, bizetlist.txt, mozart.jpg, mozartbio.txt, mozartlist.txt, puccini.jpg, puccinibio.txt, puccinilist.txt, verdi.jpg, verdibio.txt, verdilist.txt, wagner.jpg, wagnerbio.txt, and wagnerlist.txt

Gresham Children's Choir Faye Dawson is an instructor for Gresham Children's Choir in Gresham, Oregon. The choir is a chance for talented youth to perform and to learn about music history. Faye is working on a Web site describing the history of opera. She's asked for your help in creating a design. Faye has provided you with information on five different composers: Bizet, Mozart, Puccini, Verdi, and Wagner. For each composer, she's given you an image file containing the composer's picture, a text file listing the composer's works, and a text file containing a biographical sketch. Use this information to design your Web site. You may supplement these files with any other material you think will enhance your site's design.

Complete the following:

1. Use your text editor to create four HTML files named **bizet.htm**, **mozart.htm**, **puccini.htm**, **verdi.htm**, and **wagner.htm**, placing them in the tutorial.04\case4 folder included with your Data Files. Enter ***your name*** and ***the date*** in a comment section of each file. Include any other comments you think will aptly document the page's purpose and history.
2. Use the provided text files and image files to create a Web page describing each composer's life and accomplishments. Include hypertext links between the five composer Web pages.
3. Create an external style sheet named **gresham.css** for your Web site. Insert a comment section in the style sheet file that includes ***your name*** and ***the date*** as well as other comments that describe the style sheet.
4. The content of the gresham.css style sheet is up to you, but it must include the following features:
   - Styles that use contextual selectors
   - A style that uses a pseudo-element and a pseudo-class
   - Styles that use positioning styles (either absolute or relative)
   - A style that creates or modifies an ordered or unordered list
   - A style to create a rollover effect
5. Create another style sheet named **printer.css** containing styles for a printed version of the pages in your Web site. Add appropriate comments to the different parts of your style sheet.
6. Test your Web site on a variety of browsers to ensure your design works under different conditions.
7. Submit your completed files to your instructor.

Review | Quick Check Answers

Session 4.1

1. `p span {font-style: italic}`
2. `p > span {font-style: italic}`
3. `h1 + h2 {font-style: italic}`
4. `.newsAlert {font-weight: bold}`
5. `span.newsAlert {font-weight: bold}`
6. `a:hover {background-color: yellow}`
7. `a:hover {background-image:url(hover.jpg)}`
8. `blockquote:first-letter {color: red}`
9. `blockquote:first-line {color: red}`

Session 4.2

1. `#logo {position: absolute; top: 75px; left: 150px}`
2. `#logo {position: relative; top: 25%; left: 10%}`
3. `span.highlight {position: relative; top: -10px}`
4. `a:hover {position: relative; top: 5px}`
5. `#links {position: fixed; top: 50px; left: 10px}`
6. `blockquote {width: 70%; min-width: 250px; max-width: 650px}`
7. `blockquote {height: 25%; overflow: auto}`
8. No. It will only be on top of other elements for which it shares a common parent.

Session 4.3

1. `media = "handheld"`
2. screen, tv, tty
3. aural, Braille, embossed
4. The display:none style hides the element and removes it from the document flow. The visibility:hidden style hides the element, but does not remove it from the document flow.
5. `@page {11in 14in landscape ; margin 1.5 in}`
6. `h1 {page-break-before: always}`
7. A widow occurs when a page break divides a block of text, leaving only one or two lines of text on the succeeding page. An orphan occurs when the page break occurs near the start of the block of text, leaving only one or two lines of text on the first page.

Ending Data Files

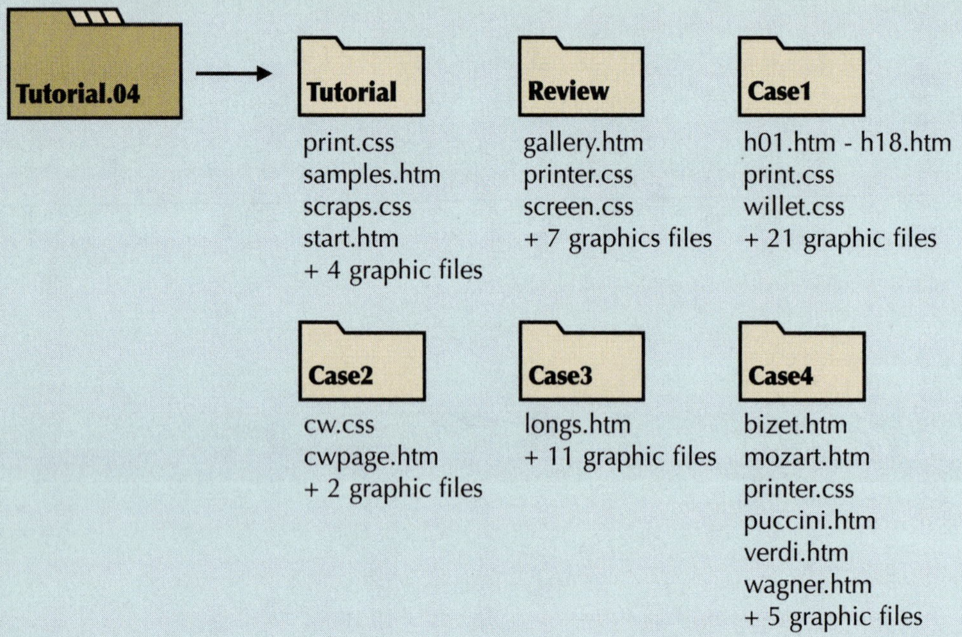

Objectives

Session 5.1
- Explore the structure of a Web table
- Create headings and cells in a table
- Create cells that span multiple rows and columns
- Create row and column groups
- Add a caption and a summary to a table

Session 5.2
- Format a table using HTML attributes
- Format a table using CSS styles
- Collapse table borders
- Display page elements in tabular form

Session 5.3
- Create a jigsaw layout
- Explore the use of tables for page layout
- Create rounded borders

Working with Web Tables

Creating a Radio Program Schedule

Case | KPAF Radio

Kyle Mitchell is the program director at KPAF, a public radio station broadcasting out of Bismarck, North Dakota. To remain viable, it's important for the station to have a presence on the Internet. With this in mind, Kyle has begun upgrading the KPAF Web site. He envisions a site in which listeners have quick and easy access to information about the station and its programs.

The Web site needs to include pages listing the KPAF morning, afternoon, and evening schedules. Kyle decides that this information is best conveyed to the listener in a table, with each column of the table displaying one day's program schedule and each row displaying the broadcast times for the various KPAF programs. Kyle has never created a Web table, so he's come to you for help in designing a Web page describing the KPAF evening schedule. Kyle wants the table you create to be easy to read and informative. He also wants you to add table styles that will enhance the appearance of the Web page.

Starting Data Files

Tutorial.05 →

Tutorial
kpaftxt.css
newshows.css
newshows.txt
roundedtxt.css
schedtxt.htm
tablestxt.css
+ 9 graphic files

Review
kpaf.css
morningtxt.htm
programstxt.css
+ 5 graphic files

Case1
jpftxt.css
stabletxt.css
sudokutxt.htm
+ 6 graphic files

Case2
caltxt.css
ccctxt.css
febtxt.htm
+10 graphic files

Case3
dhometxt.htm
dometxt.css
dtabletxt.css
+ 14 graphic files

Case4
rooms.txt
+ 9 graphic files

Session 5.1

Introducing Web Tables

You meet with Kyle in his office at KPAF to discuss the design of the new Web site. Kyle has already created a basic Web page displaying the KPAF logo and a list of links to other pages. Open this file now.

To view Kyle's data files:

1. In your text editor, open the **schedtxt.htm** and **kpaftxt.css** files, located in the tutorial.05\tutorial folder included with your Data Files. Enter ***your name*** and ***the date*** in the comment section of each file. Save the files as **schedule.htm** and **kpaf.css** in the same folder.
2. Review the **schedule.htm** file in your text editor to become familiar with its content and structure. Insert the following link element below the opening <title> tag to link the schedule.htm file to the kpaf.css style sheet:

```
<link href="kpaf.css" rel="stylesheet" type="text/css" />
```

3. Save your changes to the file and then open the **schedule.htm** file in your Web browser. Figure 5-1 shows the current appearance of the Web page.

Figure 5-1 Initial schedule page

4. Go to the **kpaf.css** style sheet in your text editor. Review the styles and compare them to the elements contained within the schedule.htm file to fully understand Kyle's design for the schedule page.
5. Close the style sheet file when you're finished reviewing it.

The first thing that Kyle needs you to add to the schedule page is KPAF's nightly schedule, which covers from 6:00 p.m. to 10:30 p.m. Kyle hands you a printout of the KPAF schedule shown in Figure 5-2. At 10:30 p.m. the station goes dark and does not broadcast again until 5:00 a.m. the following day. Kyle wants you to use HTML to recreate this table.

Figure 5-2 KPAF nightly schedule

<table>
<tr><th>Time</th><th>Monday</th><th>Tuesday</th><th>Wednesday</th><th>Thursday</th><th>Friday</th><th>Saturday</th><th>Sunday</th></tr>
<tr><td>6:00</td><td>National News</td><td>National News</td><td>National News</td><td>National News</td><td>National News</td><td>National News</td><td>National News</td></tr>
<tr><td>6:30</td><td>Local News</td><td>Local News</td><td>Local News</td><td>Local News</td><td>Local News</td><td>Local News</td><td>Local News</td></tr>
<tr><td>7:00</td><td rowspan="2">Opera Fest</td><td rowspan="2">Radio U</td><td rowspan="2">Science Week</td><td rowspan="2">The Living World</td><td>Word Play</td><td>Agri-Week</td><td rowspan="2">Folk Fest</td></tr>
<tr><td>7:30</td><td>Brain Stew</td><td>Bismarck Forum</td></tr>
<tr><td>8:00</td><td colspan="4" rowspan="4">The Classical Music Connection</td><td>Old Time Radio</td><td rowspan="4">Saturday Nite Jazz</td><td rowspan="4">The Indie Connection</td></tr>
<tr><td>8:30</td><td>The Inner Mind</td></tr>
<tr><td>9:00</td><td rowspan="2">Open Mike Nite</td></tr>
<tr><td>9:30</td></tr>
<tr><td>10:00</td><td>World News Feed</td><td>World News Feed</td><td>World News Feed</td><td>World News Feed</td><td>World News Feed</td><td>World News Feed</td><td>World News Feed</td></tr>
</table>

To create this program listing in HTML, you have to first understand the HTML table structure.

Marking Tables and Table Rows

Each table in a Web page follows a basic structure consisting of the table element and a collection of table rows nested in the table element. The general HTML code for a Web table is

```
<table>
   <tr>
   table cells
   </tr>
   <tr>
   table cells
   </tr>
...
</table>
```

where <table> marks the table element, <tr> marks each row, and *table cells* are the cells within each row. Note that the dimension of a Web table is defined by the number of rows and the number of cells within the rows. There is no HTML element to mark a table column. You'll explore how to create table cells shortly. Tables are considered block-level elements, so when rendered by a browser, they'll appear on a new line on the Web page. Like other block-level elements, you can float tables and resize them using the same styles you've already studied.

Kyle's proposed Web table has 10 rows, with the first row containing the days of the week, followed by nine rows listing the KPAF shows from 6:00 p.m. to 10:30 p.m. in half-hour intervals. For now, you'll insert tr elements for just the first three rows of the table. You'll also include a class attribute, placing the table in the schedule class of elements to distinguish it from other tables on the KPAF Web site.

To insert the table and tr elements:

1. Return to the **schedule.htm** file in your text editor.
2. Directly above the address element, insert the following code, as shown in Figure 5-3:

```
<table class="schedule">
   <tr>
   </tr>
   <tr>
   </tr>
   <tr>
   </tr>
</table>
```

Figure 5-3 Marking a table and table rows

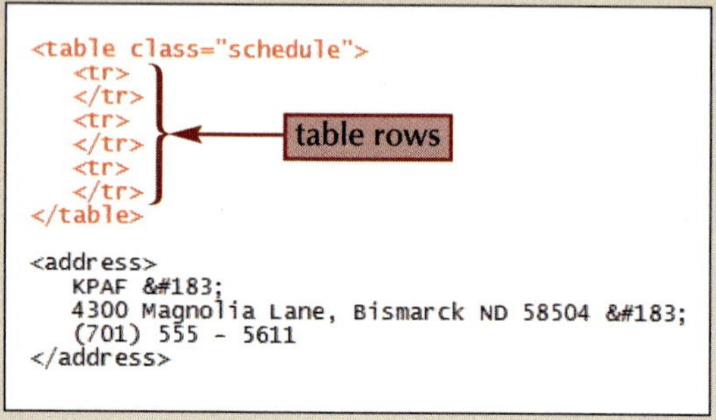


```
<table class="schedule">
   <tr>
   </tr>
   <tr>
   </tr>
   <tr>
   </tr>
</table>

<address>
   KPAF &#183;
   4300 Magnolia Lane, Bismarck ND 58504 &#183;
   (701) 555 - 5611
</address>
```

At this point you have a table with three rows but nothing within those rows. The next part of the table structure is the cells within each row.

Marking Table Headings and Table Data

There are two types of table cells: those that contain headings and those that contain data. The two tags are different so that the headings in a table are formatted differently than the rest of the cells. **Table headings**, the cells that identify the contents of a row or column, are marked using a <th> tag. You can place a <th> tag anywhere in a table, but you'll most often place one at the top of a column or at the beginning of a row. Most browsers display table headings in a bold font, centered within the table cell.

Kyle wants you to mark the cells in the first row of the radio schedule as headings because the text identifies the contents of each column. He also wants the first cells in the remaining rows displaying the time to be marked as headings. Add these cells to the first three columns of the schedule table.

To insert the table headings:

1. Return to the **schedule.htm** file in your text editor.
2. In the first table row, insert the following th elements:

```
<th>Time</th>
<th>Monday</th>
<th>Tuesday</th>
<th>Wednesday</th>
<th>Thursday</th>
<th>Friday</th>
<th>Saturday</th>
<th>Sunday</th>
```

3. Insert the heading

```
<th>6:00</th>
```

in the second table row.

4. In the third table row insert the following heading:

```
<th>6:30</th>
```

5. Figure 5-4 shows the revised code in the schedule table.

Inserting table heading cells **Figure 5-4**

table headings

```
<table class="schedule">
   <tr>
      <th>Time</th>
      <th>Monday</th>
      <th>Tuesday</th>
      <th>Wednesday</th>
      <th>Thursday</th>
      <th>Friday</th>
      <th>Saturday</th>
      <th>Sunday</th>
   </tr>
   <tr>
      <th>6:00</th>
   </tr>
   <tr>
      <th>6:30</th>
   </tr>
</table>
```

The other type of table cells is **data cells**, which are marked with the <td> tag and are used for any content that is not considered a heading. Most browsers display table data using unformatted text, left-aligned within the cell. You'll use table data cells to insert the names of the KPAF programs. KPAF airs the national and local news at 6:00 and 6:30, respectively, every night of the week. Add these broadcasts to the schedule table.

To insert table data for the next two rows of the table:

1. Return to the **schedule.htm** file in your text editor.
2. In the second table row, insert the following td elements:

```
<td>National News</td>
<td>National News</td>
<td>National News</td>
<td>National News</td>
<td>National News</td>
<td>National News</td>
<td>National News</td>
```

3. In the third table row, insert the following elements:

```
<td>Local News</td>
<td>Local News</td>
<td>Local News</td>
<td>Local News</td>
<td>Local News</td>
<td>Local News</td>
<td>Local News</td>
```

Figure 5-5 shows the newly inserted HTML code.

Figure 5-5 Inserting table data cells

```
<table class="schedule">
   <tr>
      <th>Time</th>
      <th>Monday</th>
      <th>Tuesday</th>
      <th>Wednesday</th>
      <th>Thursday</th>
      <th>Friday</th>
      <th>Saturday</th>
      <th>Sunday</th>
   </tr>
   <tr>
      <th>6:00</th>
      <td>National News</td>
      <td>National News</td>
      <td>National News</td>
      <td>National News</td>
      <td>National News</td>
      <td>National News</td>
      <td>National News</td>
   </tr>
   <tr>
      <th>6:30</th>
      <td>Local News</td>
      <td>Local News</td>
      <td>Local News</td>
      <td>Local News</td>
      <td>Local News</td>
      <td>Local News</td>
      <td>Local News</td>
   </tr>
</table>
```

table data cells

4. Save your changes to the file, and then refresh the **schedule.htm** file in your Web browser. Figure 5-6 shows the current appearance of the programming schedule. The headings are in bold and centered, and the table data is in a normal font and left-aligned.

Figure 5-6 Viewing the Web table

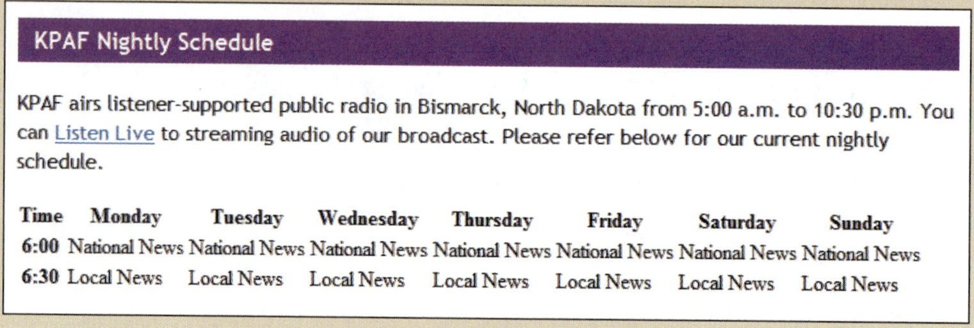
KPAF Nightly Schedule

KPAF airs listener-supported public radio in Bismarck, North Dakota from 5:00 a.m. to 10:30 p.m. You can Listen Live to streaming audio of our broadcast. Please refer below for our current nightly schedule.

Time	Monday	Tuesday	Wednesday	Thursday	Friday	Saturday	Sunday
6:00	National News	National News	National News	National News	National News	National News	National News
6:30	Local News	Local News	Local News	Local News	Local News	Local News	Local News

Trouble? If your table looks different than Figure 5-6, you might have inserted an incorrect number of table cells. Check your code and verify that you've inserted one table header and seven table data cells in each row.

Defining a Table Structure

| Reference Window

- To mark a Web table, use the element
  `<table>rows</table>`
  where *rows* are the rows of the table.
- To mark a table row, use the element
  `<tr>cells</tr>`
  where *cells* are the table cells contained within the row.
- To mark a cell containing a row or column heading, use the element
  `<th>content</th>`
  where *content* is the content of the heading.
- To mark a cell containing table data, use the element
  `<td>content</td>`
  where *content* is the content of the table data.

Tip

To place an empty table cell anywhere within a row, insert the <td> </td> tag into the row.

The table you created for Kyle has three rows and eight columns. Remember that the number of columns is determined by the maximum number of cells within each row. If one row has four cells and another row has five, the table will have five columns. The row with only four cells will have an empty space at the end, where the fifth cell should be.

Adding a Table Border

By default, there are no gridlines displayed in a Web table, making it difficult to see the table structure. You decide the table would be easier to read with gridlines marking each cell in the table. To add gridlines, insert the attribute

```
<table border="value">
   ...
</table>
```

in the table element, where *value* is the width of the table border in pixels. Figure 5-7 shows how different border values affect the appearance of a sample table.

Tables with different border sizes | **Figure 5-7**

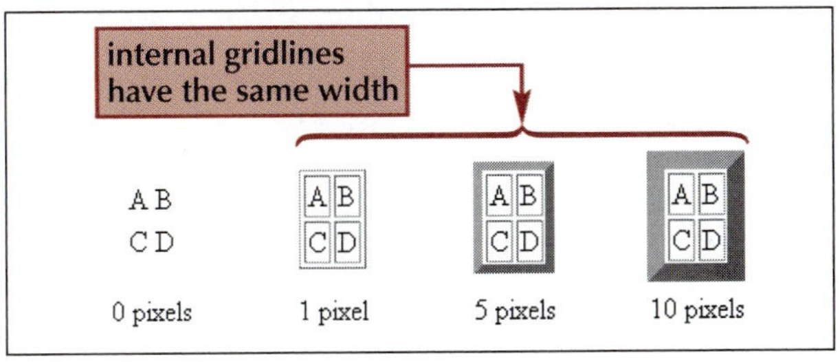

Note that the border attribute does not control the width of internal gridlines; however, to display internal gridlines you must add a border to the table. You can change the width of the internal gridlines by changing the space between the table cells, an issue you'll examine in the next session.

Reference Window | Adding a Table Border Using HTML

- To add a border to a Web table using HTML, use the border attribute

```
<table border="value"> ... </table>
```

where *value* is the size of the border in pixels.

You decide to add a 1-pixel border to the schedule table. Because of the border, your browser will also insert gridlines around each of the table cells.

To add a border to the schedule:

1. Return to the **schedule.htm** file in your text editor and add the attribute

   `border="1"`

   to the opening <table> tag, as shown in Figure 5-8.

Figure 5-8 Adding a table border

```
<table class="schedule" border="1">
   <tr>
      <th>Time</th>
      <th>Monday</th>
      <th>Tuesday</th>
      <th>Wednesday</th>
      <th>Thursday</th>
      <th>Friday</th>
      <th>Saturday</th>
      <th>Sunday</th>
   </tr>
```

table cells will be surrounded by a 1-pixel-wide border

2. Save your changes to the file, and then reload the schedule page in your Web browser. Figure 5-9 shows the revised table with the border and the internal grid-lines added.

Figure 5-9 Web table with cell borders

KPAF Nightly Schedule

KPAF airs listener-supported public radio in Bismarck, North Dakota from 5:00 a.m. to 10:30 p.m. You can Listen Live to streaming audio of our broadcast. Please refer below for our current nightly schedule.

Time	Monday	Tuesday	Wednesday	Thursday	Friday	Saturday	Sunday
6:00	National News	National News	National News	National News	National News	National News	National News
6:30	Local News	Local News	Local News	Local News	Local News	Local News	Local News

Table Border Colors | InSight

Most browsers display the table border in gray in a raised style that gives the border a 3D effect. There is no HTML attribute to change the border style, but many browsers allow you to change the color by adding the bordercolor attribute

```
<table border="value" bordercolor="color"> ... </table>
```

to the table element, where *color* is either a recognized color name or a hexadecimal color value. For example, the following HTML code adds a 10-pixel blue border to a table:

```
<table border="10" bordercolor="blue"> ... </table>
```

The exact appearance of the table border differs among browsers. Internet Explorer and Safari display the border in a solid blue color, Firefox displays the border in a raised style using two shades of blue, and Opera does not support the bordercolor attribute at all. So you should not rely on getting a consistent border color across all browsers with this attribute.

The bordercolor attribute has been deprecated by the World Wide Web Consortium (W3C) and is being gradually phased out. The recommended method is to use one of the CSS border styles discussed in Tutorial 3, but you will still see this attribute used in many Web pages.

Spanning Rows and Columns

Reviewing the schedule from Figure 5-2, you notice that several programs are longer than a half hour, and some are repeated across several days. For example, every day of the week there is national and local news at 6:00 and 6:30, respectively. Likewise, from Monday through Thursday, the hour from 7:00 to 8:00 is needed for the shows Opera Fest, Radio U, Science Week, and The Living World. And finally, the Classical Music Connection airs Monday through Thursday for two hours from 8:00 to 10:00. Rather than repeat the names of programs in all of the half-hour slots, Kyle would prefer that the table cells stretch across those hours and days.

To do this, create a **spanning cell** in which a single cell occupies more than one row or one column in the table. Spanning cells are created by inserting a rowspan or colspan attribute into a <th> or <td> tag. The syntax is

```
<th rowspan="value" colspan="value"> ... </th>
```

or

```
<td rowspan="value" colspan="value"> ... </td>
```

where *value* is the number of rows or columns that you want the table cell to cover. The spanning starts in the cell where you put the rowspan and colspan attributes and goes downward and to the right from that cell. For example, to create a data cell that spans two columns and three rows, enter the <td> tag as:

```
<td colspan="2" rowspan="3"> ... </td>
```

It's important to remember that when a cell spans multiple rows or columns, you must adjust the number of cells used elsewhere in the table. For column-spanning cells, you have to reduce the number of cells in the current row. For example, if a row contains five columns but one of the cells in the row spans three columns, you need only three cell elements in the row: two cells that occupy a single column each and one cell that spans the remaining three columns.

To see how column-spanning cells works, you'll replace the cells for the National News and Local News programs that currently occupy seven cells a piece with two cells that each span seven columns in each row.

Tip

For every extra column that a cell spans, you must delete one cell from the table row. So for a cell spanning four columns, you must delete three cells to keep from having extra cells in the row.

To create cells that span several columns:

1. Return to the **schedule.htm** file in your text editor and add the attribute

   `colspan="7"`

   to the second table cell in the second and third rows of the table.
2. Delete the remaining six table cells in both the second and the third table rows. Figure 5-10 shows the revised code for the schedule table.

Figure 5-10 Creating cells to span several columns

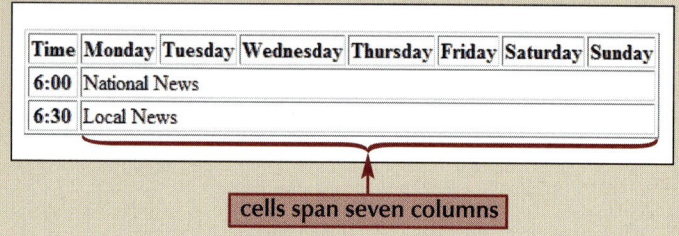

```
<table class="schedule" border="1">
   <tr>
      <th>Time</th>
      <th>Monday</th>
      <th>Tuesday</th>
      <th>Wednesday</th>
      <th>Thursday</th>
      <th>Friday</th>
      <th>Saturday</th>
      <th>Sunday</th>
   </tr>
   <tr>
      <th>6:00</th>
      <td colspan="7">National News</td>
   </tr>
   <tr>
      <th>6:30</th>
      <td colspan="7">Local News</td>
   </tr>
</table>
```

cell spans seven columns

delete the other six cells in the table row

3. Save your changes to the file, and then refresh the **schedule.htm** file in your Web browser. Figure 5-11 shows the revised appearance of the Web table.

Figure 5-11 Column-spanning cell

Time	Monday	Tuesday	Wednesday	Thursday	Friday	Saturday	Sunday
6:00	National News						
6:30	Local News						

cells span seven columns

To make the cell for the hour-long shows on Monday through Thursday, you'll need to span two rows, which lengthens the height of the cell. For row-spanning cells, you need to remove extra cells from the rows below the spanning cell. Consider the table shown in Figure 5-12, which contains three rows and four columns. The first cell spans three rows. You need four table cells in the first row, but only three in the second and third rows. This is because the spanning cell from row one occupies a position reserved for a cell that would normally appear in those rows.

Figure 5-12 Cells spanning several rows

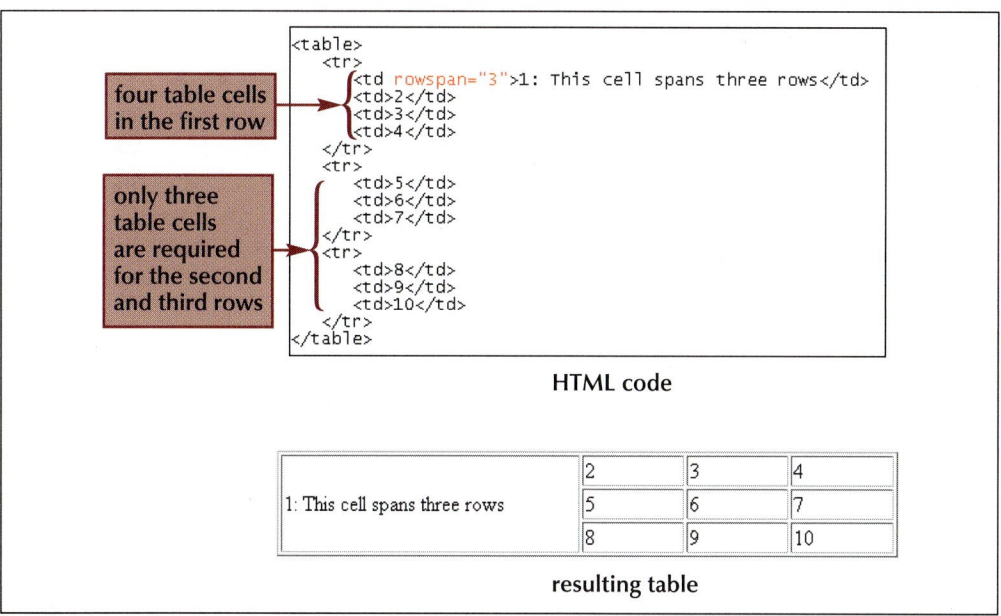

four table cells in the first row

only three table cells are required for the second and third rows

```
<table>
   <tr>
      <td rowspan="3">1: This cell spans three rows</td>
      <td>2</td>
      <td>3</td>
      <td>4</td>
   </tr>
   <tr>
      <td>5</td>
      <td>6</td>
      <td>7</td>
   </tr>
   <tr>
      <td>8</td>
      <td>9</td>
      <td>10</td>
   </tr>
</table>
```

HTML code

1: This cell spans three rows	2	3	4
	5	6	7
	8	9	10

resulting table

Creating a Spanning Cell

| Reference Window

- To create a table cell that spans several columns, add the attribute
  `colspan="value"`
  to the cell, where *value* is the number of columns covered by the cell.
- To create a table cell that spans several rows, add the attribute
  `rowspan="value"`
  to the cell, where *value* is the number of rows covered by the cell.

The 7:00 to 8:00 section of the KPAF schedule contains several programs that run for an hour. To insert these programs, you'll create row-spanning cells that span two rows in the schedule table. To keep the columns lined up, you must reduce the number of cells entered in the subsequent row.

To span several table rows:

1. Return to the **schedule.htm** file in your text editor and add the following row to the bottom of the schedule table:

```
<tr>
   <th>7:00</th>
   <td rowspan="2">Opera Fest</td>
   <td rowspan="2">Radio U</td>
   <td rowspan="2">Science Week</td>
   <td rowspan="2">The Living World</td>
   <td>Word Play</td>
   <td>Agri-Week</td>
   <td rowspan="2">Folk Fest</td>
</tr>
```

2. The next row should display table cells only for the two programs that start at 7:30. The HTML code for this table row is:

```
<tr>
   <th>7:30</th>
   <td>Brain Stew</td>
   <td>Bismarck Forum</td>
</tr>
```

Figure 5-13 shows the code for the two new table rows.

Figure 5-13 Inserting cells that span two rows

```
   <tr>
      <th>6:30</th>
      <td colspan="7">Local News</td>
   </tr>
   <tr>
      <th>7:00</th>
      <td rowspan="2">Opera Fest</td>
      <td rowspan="2">Radio U</td>
      <td rowspan="2">Science Week</td>
      <td rowspan="2">The Living World</td>
      <td>Word Play</td>
      <td>Agri-Week</td>
      <td rowspan="2">Folk Fest</td>
   </tr>
   <tr>
      <th>7:30</th>
      <td>Brain Stew</td>
      <td>Bismarck Forum</td>
   </tr>
</table>
```

3. Save your changes to the file, and then refresh the **schedule.htm** file in your Web browser. As shown in Figure 5-14, the Sunday through Thursday 7:00 p.m. programs each last an hour, spanning two table rows.

Figure 5-14 Schedule table with several one-hour programs spanning two table rows

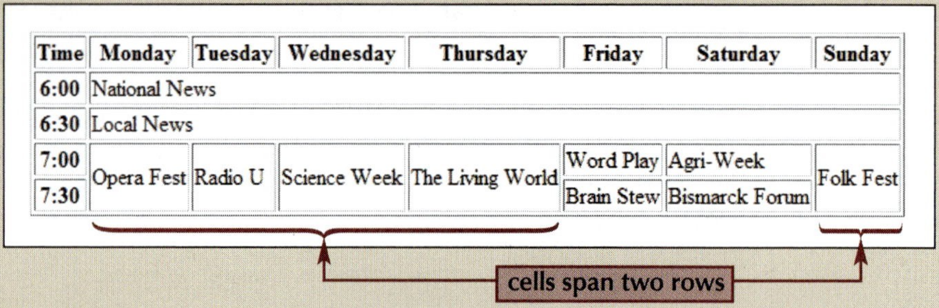

Time	Monday	Tuesday	Wednesday	Thursday	Friday	Saturday	Sunday
6:00	National News						
6:30	Local News						
7:00	Opera Fest	Radio U	Science Week	The Living World	Word Play	Agri-Week	Folk Fest
7:30					Brain Stew	Bismarck Forum	

The final part of the evening schedule includes the program Classical Musical Connection, which spans two hours on Monday through Thursday. Like the news programs, you don't want to repeat the name of the show each day; and like the four hour-long programs you just entered, you don't want to repeat the name of the show in each half-hour cell. Kyle suggests that you use both the colspan and rowspan attributes to enter a table cell that spans four rows and four columns.

Other programs in the 8:00 to 10:00 time slots, such as Saturday Nite Jazz and The Indie Connection, also span four rows, but only one column. The last program aired before KPAF signs off is the World News Feed, which is played every night from 10:00 to 10:30. You'll add these and the other late evening programs to the schedule table now.

To add the remaining KPAF evening programs:

1. Return to the **schedule.htm** file in your text editor and enter the following table row for programs airing starting at 8:00:

```
<tr>
   <th>8:00</th>
   <td rowspan="4" colspan="4">The Classical Music Connection</td>
   <td>Old Time Radio</td>
   <td rowspan="4">Saturday Nite Jazz</td>
   <td rowspan="4">The Indie Connection</td>
</tr>
```

2. The Inner Mind is the only program that starts at 8:30 during the week. Add the 8:30 starting time to the table using the following row:

```
<tr>
   <th>8:30</th>
   <td>The Inner Mind</td>
</tr>
```

3. The only program that starts at 9:00 is Open Mike Nite. Add the following row to the table to display this program in the schedule:

```
<tr>
   <th>9:00</th>
   <td rowspan="2">Open Mike Nite</td>
</tr>
```

4. There are no programs that start at 9:30, so you'll add the table row but without any programs listed. Add the following row:

```
<tr>
   <th>9:30</th>
</tr>
```

5. Complete the schedule table by adding the last table row for the World News Feed occurring every night from 10:00 to 10:30. This single program occupies a single row and spans seven columns. Add the following row:

```
<tr>
   <th>10:00</th>
   <td colspan="7">World News Feed</td>
</tr>
```

Figure 5-15 shows the code completing the structure of the schedule table.

Figure 5-15 Adding the remaining KPAF evening programs

```
<tr>
   <th>7:30</th>
   <td>Brain Stew</td>
   <td>Bismarck Forum</td>
</tr>
<tr>
   <th>8:00</th>
   <td rowspan="4" colspan="4">The Classical Music Connection</td>
   <td>Old Time Radio</td>
   <td rowspan="4">Saturday Nite Jazz</td>
   <td rowspan="4">The Indie Connection</td>
</tr>
<tr>
   <th>8:30</th>
   <td>The Inner Mind</td>
</tr>
<tr>
   <th>9:00</th>
   <td rowspan="2">Open Mike Nite</td>
</tr>
<tr>
   <th>9:30</th>
</tr>
<tr>
   <th>10:00</th>
   <td colspan="7">World News Feed</td>
</tr>
</table>
```

6. Save your changes to the file, and refresh the **schedule.htm** file in your Web browser. Figure 5-16 shows the complete evening schedule of programs offered by KPAF.

Figure 5-16 **The complete KPAF evening schedule**

<table>
<tr><th>Time</th><th>Monday</th><th>Tuesday</th><th>Wednesday</th><th>Thursday</th><th>Friday</th><th>Saturday</th><th>Sunday</th></tr>
<tr><th>6:00</th><td colspan="7">National News</td></tr>
<tr><th>6:30</th><td colspan="7">Local News</td></tr>
<tr><th>7:00</th><td rowspan="2">Opera Fest</td><td rowspan="2">Radio U</td><td rowspan="2">Science Week</td><td rowspan="2">The Living World</td><td>Word Play</td><td>Agri-Week</td><td rowspan="2">Folk Fest</td></tr>
<tr><th>7:30</th><td>Brain Stew</td><td>Bismarck Forum</td></tr>
<tr><th>8:00</th><td colspan="4" rowspan="4">The Classical Music Connection</td><td>Old Time Radio</td><td rowspan="4">Saturday Nite Jazz</td><td rowspan="4">The Indie Connection</td></tr>
<tr><th>8:30</th><td>The Inner Mind</td></tr>
<tr><th>9:00</th><td rowspan="2">Open Mike Nite</td></tr>
<tr><th>9:30</th></tr>
<tr><th>10:00</th><td colspan="7">World News Feed</td></tr>
</table>

The Web table you created matches the printout of KPAF's evening schedule. Kyle likes the clear structure of the table. He notes that many KPAF listeners tune into the station over the Internet, listening to KPAF's streaming audio feed. Since those listeners might be located in different time zones, Kyle suggests that you add a caption to the table indicating that all times in the schedule are based on the Central time zone.

Creating a Table Caption

Table captions are another part of the basic table structure and are marked using the caption element

```
<table>
   <caption>content</caption>
   ...
</table>
```

where *content* is the content contained within the caption. You can nest inline elements within a caption element. For example, the following code marks the text *Program Schedule* using the em element:

```
<table>
   <caption><em>Program Schedule</em></caption>
   ...
</table>
```

Only one caption is allowed per Web table and the <caption> tag must be listed directly after the opening <table> tag. The caption is treated as a block-level element, placed directly above the table, but you can change the placement of the caption using the following align attribute:

```
<caption align="position">content</caption>
```

In this code, *position* equals top, bottom, left, or right, to place the caption either above, below, or to the left or right sides of the table.

The interpretation of the left and right align value is not consistent among the major browsers. Netscape and Firefox follow the W3C specifications and place the captions to the left or right of the Web table. Internet Explorer and Opera still place the caption above the table, but horizontally align the caption text to the left or right. The align attribute is another example of a presentational attribute that has been deprecated in favor of style sheets, though you'll still often find it used on Web sites, both old and new.

Tip

You can also use the CSS caption-side style to align caption text.

Creating a Table Caption | Reference Window

- To create a table caption, add the caption element directly below the opening <table> tag with the syntax

```
<caption>content</caption>
```

where *content* is the content of the table caption.

Add Kyle's suggested caption to the program schedule. You do not have to specify an align value because you want the caption to be above the table.

To create a caption for the program schedule:

1. Return to the **schedule.htm** file in your text editor and insert the following caption element directly below the opening tag, as shown in Figure 5-17.

```
<caption>All times listed in central time</caption>
```

Figure 5-17 Inserting a table caption

```
<table class="schedule" border="1">
   <caption>All times listed in central time</caption>
   <tr>
      <th>Time</th>
      <th>Monday</th>
      <th>Tuesday</th>
      <th>Wednesday</th>
      <th>Thursday</th>
      <th>Friday</th>
      <th>Saturday</th>
      <th>Sunday</th>
   </tr>
```

2. Save your changes to the file and refresh the **schedule.htm** file in your Web browser. As shown in Figure 5-18, Kyle's suggested caption appears centered above the Web table.

Figure 5-18 Table caption for the KPAF programming schedule

<table>
<caption>All times listed in central time</caption>
<tr><th>Time</th><th>Monday</th><th>Tuesday</th><th>Wednesday</th><th>Thursday</th><th>Friday</th><th>Saturday</th><th>Sunday</th></tr>
<tr><th>6:00</th><td colspan="7">National News</td></tr>
<tr><th>6:30</th><td colspan="7">Local News</td></tr>
<tr><th>7:00</th><td rowspan="2">Opera Fest</td><td rowspan="2">Radio U</td><td rowspan="2">Science Week</td><td rowspan="2">The Living World</td><td>Word Play</td><td>Agri-Week</td><td rowspan="2">Folk Fest</td></tr>
<tr><th>7:30</th><td>Brain Stew</td><td>Bismarck Forum</td></tr>
<tr><th>8:00</th><td colspan="4" rowspan="4">The Classical Music Connection</td><td>Old Time Radio</td><td rowspan="4">Saturday Nite Jazz</td><td rowspan="4">The Indie Connection</td></tr>
<tr><th>8:30</th><td>The Inner Mind</td></tr>
<tr><th>9:00</th><td rowspan="2">Open Mike Nite</td></tr>
<tr><th>9:30</th></tr>
<tr><th>10:00</th><td colspan="7">World News Feed</td></tr>
</table>

Although table captions might lie outside of the borders of the Web table, they are still part of the Web table's structure. This means that they'll inherit any styles associated with the table. For example, if you create a style for the table that sets the font color to red, the caption text will also be in a red font. You'll explore how to apply styles to table captions in the next session.

Marking Row Groups

You can divide a table's rows into **row groups**, in which each group element contains different types of content and can be formatted differently. HTML supports three row groups: one to mark the header rows, another for the body rows, and a third for the footer rows. The syntax to create these three row groups is:

```
<table>
   <thead>
      table rows
   </thead>
   <tfoot>
      table rows
   </tfoot>
   <tbody>
      table rows
   </tbody>
</table>
```

where *table rows* are rows from the Web table. For example, the following code marks two rows as belonging to the table header row group:

```
<thead>
   <tr>
      <th colspan="2">KPAF Programs</th>
   </tr>
   <tr>
      <th>Time</th>
      <th>Program</th>
   </tr>
</thead>
```

Tip

The table header, table body, and table footer must all contain the same number of columns.

Order is important. The thead element must appear first, and then the tfoot element, and finally the tbody element. A table can contain only one set of thead and tfoot elements, but it can have any number of tbody elements. The reason the body group appears last and not the footer group is to allow the browser to render the footer before receiving what might be numerous groups of table body rows.

One purpose of row groups is to allow you to create different styles for groups of rows in your table. Any style that you apply to the thead, tbody, or tfoot elements is inherited by the rows those elements contain. Row groups are also used for tables that import their data from external data sources such as databases or XML documents. In those situations, a single table can span several Web pages, and it's helpful to have the rows within the thead and tfoot elements repeated on every page.

Creating Row Groups

| Reference Window

- Row groups must be entered in the following order: table header rows, table footer rows, and then table body rows.
- To create a row group consisting of header rows, add the element

```
<thead>
   rows
</thead>
```

  within the table, where *rows* are the row elements within the table header.
- To create a row group consisting of footer rows, add the following element:

```
<tfoot>
   rows
</tfoot>
```

- To create a row group consisting of rows used in the body of the table, add the following element:

```
<tbody>
   rows
</tbody>
```

  A table can have multiple table body row groups.

To indicate the structure of the schedule table, you decide to the use the thead element to mark the header row in the program schedule and the tbody element to mark the rows that include the broadcast times of each program. You do not need to specify a footer for this table.

To mark the row groups:

1. Return to the **schedule.htm** file in your text editor and enclose the first row of the table within an opening and closing set of **<thead>** tags.
2. Enclose the remaining rows of the table within an opening and closing set of **<tbody>** tags. Figure 5-19 shows the markup tags for the two new row groups.

Figure 5-19 Marking the table header and table body row groups

```
<table class="schedule" border="1">
   <caption>All times listed in central time</caption>

   <thead>
   <tr>
      <th>Time</th>
      <th>Monday</th>
      <th>Tuesday</th>
      <th>Wednesday</th>
      <th>Thursday</th>
      <th>Friday</th>
      <th>Saturday</th>
      <th>Sunday</th>
   </tr>
   </thead>

   <tbody>
   <tr>
      <th>6:00</th>
      <td colspan="7">National News</td>
   </tr>
```

```
   <tr>
      <th>9:30</th>
   </tr>
   <tr>
      <th>10:00</th>
      <td colspan="7">World News Feed</td>
   </tr>
   </tbody>

</table>
```

Marking Column Groups

As you've seen, there is no HTML tag to mark table columns—the columns are created implicitly from the number of cells within each row. However, once the columns have been determined by the browser, you can reference them through the use of **column groups**. Column groups give you the ability to assign a common format to all of the cells within a given column. Column groups are defined using the colgroup element

```
<colgroup>
   columns
</colgroup>
```

where *columns* are the individual columns with the group. The columns themselves are referenced using the following empty element:

```
<col />
```

The number of col elements must match the number of columns in the Web table. Once you create a column group, you can add id or class attributes to identify or classify individual columns. For example, the following code creates a column group consisting of three columns, each with a different class name:

```
<colgroup>
   <col class="column1" />
   <col class="column2" />
   <col class="column3" />
</colgroup>
```

The browser takes any style specified for the col element and applies it to cells within the column. So to create columns with different background colors, you could apply the inline styles

```
col.column1 {background-color: red}
col.column2 {background-color: blue}
col.column3 {background-color: yellow}
```

and the browser will display the first table column with a background color of red, the second with blue, and the third with yellow. Note that not all CSS styles can be applied to table columns. You'll explore column styles in more detail in the next session.

The col element also supports the span attribute, allowing a column reference to cover several table columns. The syntax of the span attribute is

```
<col span="value" />
```

where *value* is the number of columns referenced by the col element. The column structure

```
<colgroup>
   <col class="column1" />
   <col class="nextColumns" span="2" />
</colgroup>
```

references a group of three columns; the first column belongs to the column1 class and the next two columns belong to the nextColumns class. Note that you can also apply the span attribute to a column group itself. The following code uses two column groups to also reference three columns, the first belonging to the column1 class and the last two belonging to the nextColumns class:

```
<colgroup class="column1"></colgroup>
<colgroup class="nextColumns span="2"></colgroup>
```

Notice that in this case there are no col elements within the column group. The browser will assume the number of columns indicated by the span attribute; if no span attribute is present, the column group is assumed to have only one column.

Creating Column Groups

| Reference Window

- To create a column group, add the element
```
<colgroup>
   columns
</colgroup>
```
to the Web table, where *columns* are individual columns within the group.
- To define a column or columns within a column group, use the element
```
<col span="value" />
```
where *value* is the number of defined columns. The span attribute is not required if only one column is defined.

Now that you've seen how columns can be referenced through the use of column groups, you'll create a column group for the programming table. You'll place the first column containing the broadcast times for the different KPAF programs in one column with the class name firstCol and the remaining seven columns containing the daily program listings in a column group with the class name dayCols. These groupings will allow you to format the two sets of columns in different ways later on.

To mark the column groups:

1. Return to the **schedule.htm** file in your text editor.
2. Directly below the table caption, insert the following code, as shown in Figure 5-20:

```
<colgroup>
   <col class="firstCol" />
   <col class="dayCols" span="7" />
</colgroup>
```

Figure 5-20 Inserting a column group

```
<table class="schedule" border="1">
   <caption>All times listed in central time</caption>

   <colgroup>
      <col class="firstCol" />
      <col class="dayCols" span="7" />
   </colgroup>
```

col element spans seven columns

3. Save your changes to the file.
4. Creating row groups and column groups adds to the structure and flexibility of the table, but should not alter its appearance. To confirm that the row and column groups have not modified the table's appearance, refresh the **schedule.htm** file in your browser. Verify that the table layout is the same as that shown earlier in Figure 5-18.

Adding a Table Summary

Nonvisual browsers (such as aural browsers that are often used by visually impaired people) can't display tables, and it's cumbersome to listen to each cell being read. For these situations, it is useful to include a summary of a table's contents. While a caption and the surrounding page text usually provide clues about the table and its contents, the summary attribute allows you to include a more detailed description. The syntax of the summary attribute is

```
<table summary="description"> ... </table>
```

where *description* is a text string that describes the table's content and structure. The summary attribute fills the same role that the alt attribute fills for inline image: providing a textual (aural) alternative to what could be a long and complicated table. A user running a screen reader or other type of aural browser will first hear the summary of the table's contents, which can then aid in interpreting the subsequent reading of the table's content.

Kyle definitely wants the KPAF Web page to be accessible to users with all types of disabilities and asks that you include a summary description of the program schedule.

To add a summary to the table:

1. Return to the **schedule.htm** file in your text editor.
2. Within the opening <table> tag insert the following attribute as shown in Figure 5-21.

```
summary="This table contains the nightly KPAF program schedule aired
from Bismarck, North Dakota. Program times are laid out in
thirty-minute increments from 6:00 p.m. to 10:00 p.m., Monday through
Sunday night."
```

Inserting a table summary

Figure 5-21

```
<table class="schedule" border="1"
       summary="This table contains the nightly KPAF program schedule aired
                from Bismarck, North Dakota. Program times are laid out in
                thirty-minute increments from 6:00 p.m. to 10:00 p.m., Monday
                through Sunday night.">

   <caption>All times listed in central time</caption>
```

3. Save your changes to the file, and then reload the **schedule.htm** file in your Web browser. Verify that the summary description does *not* appear in the browser window.
4. If you plan on taking a break before starting the next session, close your open files and programs now.

Tip

In some browsers, you can view the summary description by right-clicking the table and selecting Properties from the shortcut menu.

Creating Tables with Preformatted Text | InSight

As you learned in Tutorial 1, browsers strip out white space from the HTML code when they render Web pages. You can force the browser the keep certain white space by marking your document text as **preformatted text**, in which the browser displays the spacing and line breaks exactly as you enter it. Preformatted text is created using the tag

```
<pre>content</pre>
```

where *content* is the text that will appear preformatted in the browser. One use of preformatted text is to quickly create tables, neatly laid out in rows and columns. For example, the code

```
<pre>
Time   Friday       Saturday
====   ==========   ==============
7:30   Brain Stew   Bismarck Forum
</pre>
```

is displayed by the browser exactly as typed, with the spaces as shown:

```
Time   Friday       Saturday
====   ==========   ==============
7:30   Brain Stew   Bismarck Forum
```

Preformatted text is displayed by the browser in a **monospace font** in which each letter takes up the same amount of space. One of the advantages of monospace fonts that make them useful for entering tabular data is that the relative space between characters is unchanged as the font size increases or decreases. This means that if the font size of the above table were increased or decreased, the columns would still line up.

Although you should probably use Web tables to display most of your data, you might want to consider using preformatted text for simple and quick text tables.

You've completed your work in laying out the basic structure of the KPAF program schedule. The next thing Kyle wants you to focus on is formatting the table to be attractive and professional. In the next session you'll explore how to apply design styles to make an interesting and attractive Web table.

Review | Session 5.1 Quick Check

1. There is no HTML tag that marks a column; how is the number of columns in a Web table determined?
2. How does a browser usually render text marked with the <th> tag?
3. Specify the code to add a 10-pixel-wide border to a Web table.
4. A cell contains the text "Monday" and should stretch across 2 rows and 3 columns. Specify the HTML for the cell.
5. What adjustment do you have to make when a cell spans multiple columns?
6. Captions usually appear above or below their Web tables. Explain why a caption is still part of a table's structure.
7. What are the three table row groups, and in what order should they be specified in the code?
8. Specify the code to create a column group in which the first two columns belong to the introCol class and the next three columns belong to the col1, col2, and col3 classes, respectively.
9. What is the purpose of the table summary attribute?

Session 5.2

Formatting Tables with HTML Attributes

After specifying the content and structure of the program schedule, you and Kyle are ready to format the table's appearance. There are two approaches to formatting Web tables. One is to use HTML attributes, and the other is to use CSS styles. Because you'll see both approaches used on the Internet, you'll examine both techniques, starting with the HTML attribute approach.

Setting Cell Spacing with HTML

Web tables are one of the older HTML page elements, predating the introduction of cascading style sheets. Because of this, HTML has long supported several attributes controlling a table's layout and appearance. In the last session you used one of those attributes, the border attribute, to create a table border and display internal table gridlines. The next attribute you'll consider controls the amount of space between table cells, which is known as the **cell spacing**. By default, browsers set the cell spacing to 2 pixels. To set a different cell spacing value, add the cellspacing attribute

```
<table cellspacing="value"> ... </table>
```

to the table element, where *value* is the size of the cell spacing in pixels. If you have applied a border to your table, changing the cell spacing value also impacts the size of the internal gridlines. Figure 5-22 shows how different cell spacing values affect the appearance of the table border and internal gridlines. Note that if the cell spacing is set to 0 pixels, the browser will still display an internal gridline that comes from the drop shadow that browsers apply to cell and table borders.

Cell spacing values **Figure 5-22**

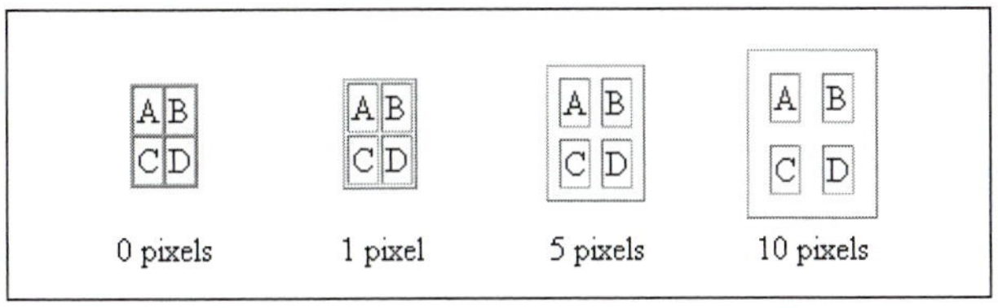

Cell spacing essentially sets the outside margins of the table cells. Unlike the CSS margin style, you can specify cell spacing values only in pixels and not other measuring units, nor can you set different cell spacing values for the different sides of the cell. Also, the effect of setting the cell spacing value is limited by the width allotted to the entire table. The browser ignores cell spacing values that would push the table beyond its defined width.

Setting Cell Padding with HTML

Related to cell spacing is **cell padding**, which is the space between the cell contents and the cell border. You set the padding using the attribute

```
<table cellpadding="value"> ... </table>
```

where *value* is the size of the cell padding. Like the cellspacing attribute, the cellpadding attribute applies to every cell in the table. Figure 5-23 shows the impact of various cell padding values on the table's appearance. Cell padding is similar to the CSS padding style, though there is no option to define padding values for different sides of the cell; and like the cellspacing attribute, cell padding values can only be expressed in pixels and not other units of measure.

Cell padding values **Figure 5-23**

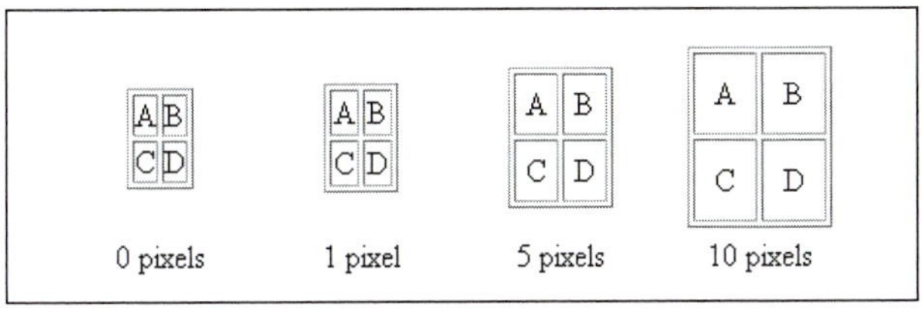

Setting Cell Padding and Cell Spacing with HTML | Reference Window

- To define the padding within table cells, add the attribute
  ```
  <table cellpadding="value"> ... </table>
  ```
  to the table element, where *value* is the size of the padding space in pixels.
- To define the space between table cells, add the attribute
  ```
  <table cellspacing="value"> ... </table>
  ```
  to the table element, where *value* is the space between table cells in pixels.

Kyle would like you to experiment with how the cellpadding and cellspacing attributes might affect the appearance of the program schedule, so you'll add these two attributes to the table element, setting the cell spacing to 3 pixels and the cell padding to 5 pixels.

To set the cell padding and cell spacing:

1. Return to the **schedule.htm** file in your text editor.
2. Within the opening <table> tag, insert the following attribute, as shown in Figure 5-24.

```
cellspacing="3" cellpadding="5"
```

Figure 5-24 Setting the cell spacing and padding values

```
<table class="schedule" border="1" cellspacing="3" cellpadding="5"
       summary="This table contains the nightly KPAF program schedule aired
                from Bismarck, North Dakota. Program times are laid out in
                thirty-minute increments from 6:00 p.m. to 10:00 p.m., Monday
                through Sunday night.">
```

3. Save your changes to the file, and then open **schedule.htm** in your Web browser. As shown in Figure 5-25, the space between and within the table cells has been increased from their default values.

Figure 5-25 Table with increased cell spacing and padding

<table>
<tr><th>Time</th><th>Monday</th><th>Tuesday</th><th>Wednesday</th><th>Thursday</th><th>Friday</th><th>Saturday</th><th>Sunday</th></tr>
<tr><th>6:00</th><td colspan="7">National News</td></tr>
<tr><th>6:30</th><td colspan="7">Local News</td></tr>
<tr><th>7:00</th><td rowspan="2">Opera Fest</td><td rowspan="2">Radio U</td><td rowspan="2">Science Week</td><td rowspan="2">The Living World</td><td>Word Play</td><td>Agri-Week</td><td rowspan="2">Folk Fest</td></tr>
<tr><th>7:30</th><td>Brain Stew</td><td>Bismarck Forum</td></tr>
<tr><th>8:00</th><td colspan="4" rowspan="4">The Classical Music Connection</td><td>Old Time Radio</td><td rowspan="4">Saturday Nite Jazz</td><td rowspan="4">The Indie Connection</td></tr>
<tr><th>8:30</th><td>The Inner Mind</td></tr>
<tr><th>9:00</th><td rowspan="2">Open Mike Nite</td></tr>
<tr><th>9:30</th></tr>
<tr><th>10:00</th><td colspan="7">World News Feed</td></tr>
</table>

Setting Table Widths and Heights in HTML

You can use HTML to set the overall width and height of the table, and of the individual cells within the table. By default, the width of tables will range from the minimum necessary to display all the cell contents without the line wrapping up to the width of the container element. To set the width of the table to a specific value, add the width attribute

```
<table width="value"> ... </table>
```

to the table element, where *value* is the width either in pixels or as a percentage of the width of the containing element. If the containing element is the page itself, you can set the table to fill the entire page width by specifying a width value of 100%. You can still never reduce a table to a width smaller than is required to display the content or larger than the width of its container. For example, if the table content requires a width of 450 pixels, then the browser will ignore any width attribute that attempts to set a smaller table size.

Many browsers also support the height attribute, which has the syntax

```
<table height="value"> ... </table>
```

where *value* is the height of the table either in pixels or as a percentage of the height of the containing element. Even though the height attribute is widely supported, it is not part of the HTML specifications nor is it supported by XHTML. Like the width attribute, the height attribute indicates only the minimum height of the table. If the table content cannot fit into the specified height, the table height increases to match the content.

You can also set the width of individual columns by applying the width attribute to either an individual column or a column group. For example, the HTML code

```
<colgroup width="100" span="7">
</colgroup>
```

sets the width of each of seven columns from the table to 100 pixels. To specify different column widths, apply the width attribute to individual col elements as in the code

```
<colgroup>
   <col width="50" />
   <col width="100" span="5" />
   <col width="50" />
</colgroup>
```

which sets the widths of the five middle columns to 100 pixels, but sets the width of the first and seventh columns to 50 pixels each. Column widths can also be expressed as a percentage of the total width of the table. A column width of 50% causes a column to occupy half of the table width. Column widths are always limited by the total width of the table and the content that each cell contains. For example, if you try to set the width of each column in a five-column table to 200 pixels but only 800 pixels of space is available, the browser will adjust the column widths down to fit the content.

> **Tip**
>
> Width and height values should always be thought of as minimum widths and heights because they will be overridden whenever the content of the table requires it.

In the code for many Web tables, you might see the width attribute applied to individual table cells. This is another way to set the width of an entire column because the remaining cells in the column will adopt that width to keep the column cells aligned. Even so, the width value for a single cell might be overridden by the browser if other cells in the column require a larger width to display their content. With the introduction of column groups, there is little need to apply the width attribute to individual table cells. Also, the W3C has deprecated the use of the width attribute with the td and th elements. As you might expect, however, you will still see it supported by many of the current browsers.

Setting Row Heights with HTML

You can use HTML to set the row heights by applying the height attribute

```
<tr height="value"> ... </tr>
```

to the tr element, where *value* is the height of the row in pixels. Internet Explorer also allows you to specify height values as a percentage of the height of the table. The height attribute is not part of the W3C specifications, but most browsers support it. As with setting the column width by setting the width of an individual cell, you can also set the row height by applying the height attribute to an individual cell within the row. This approach is also supported by most browsers even though it has been deprecated by the W3C.

Formatting Table Borders with HTML

In the last session you used the border attribute to add a border around the table and each of the table cells. You can modify the placement of the table borders using table frames and table rules. A **table frame** specifies which sides of the table (or which sides of the table cells) will have borders. To apply a frame to a table, apply the frame attribute

```
<table border="value" frame="type"> ... </table>
```

to the table element, where *value* is the width of the table border and *type* is box (the default), above, border, below, hsides, vsides, lhs, rhs, or void. Figure 5-26 describes each of these frame options.

Figure 5-26 **Values of the frame attribute**

Frame Value	Border Appearance
above	only above the table
below	only below the table
border	around all four sides of the table
box	around all four sides of the table
hsides	on the top and bottom sides of the table (the horizontal sides)
lhs	only on the left side
rhs	only on the right side
void	no border is drawn around the table
vsides	on the left and right sides of the table (the vertical sides)

Figure 5-27 shows the impact of these frame attribute values on a sample table grid.

Figure 5-27 **Frame examples**

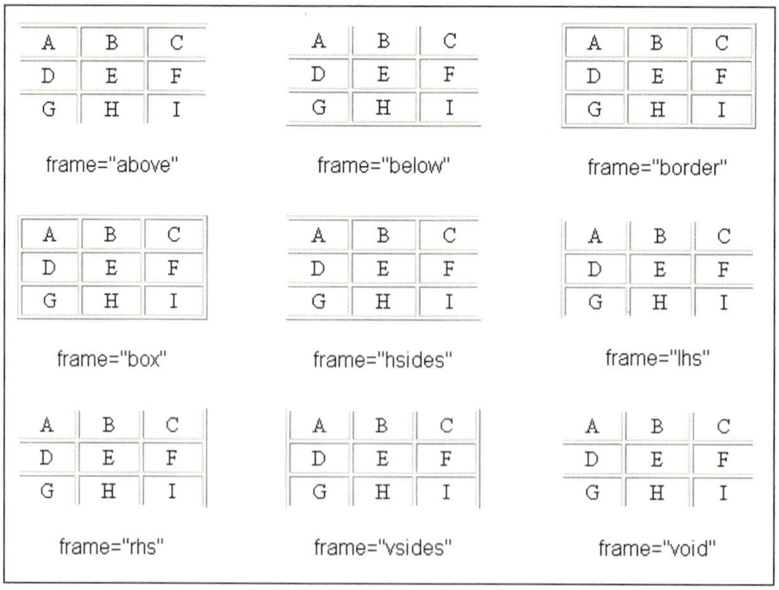

A **table rule** specifies how the internal gridlines are drawn within the table. To apply a table rule, add the rules attribute

```
<table border="value" rules="type"> ... </table>
```

to the table element, where *type* is all (the default), cols, groups, none, or rows. Figure 5-28 describes the impact of each of these rules attribute values on the placement of the internal table gridlines.

Values of the rules attribute **Figure 5-28**

Rules Value	Description of Rules
all	places gridlines around all table cells
cols	places gridlines around columns
groups	places gridlines around row groups
none	displays no gridlines
rows	places gridlines around rows

Figure 5-29 shows how these rules values would appear in a sample table.

Rules examples **Figure 5-29**

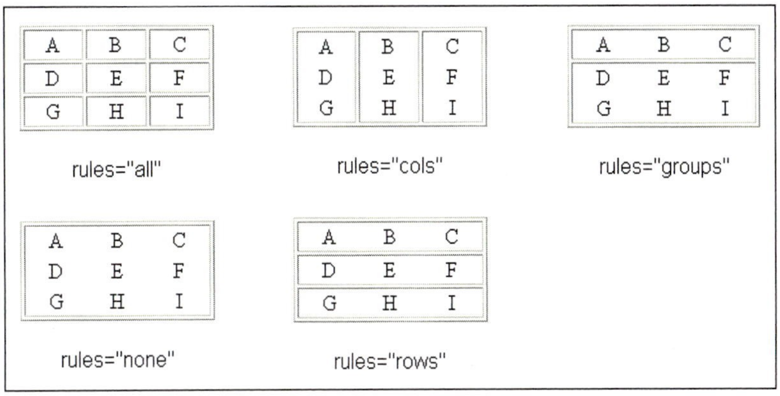

By combining frame and rules values, you can duplicate many of the same effects you could achieve using the CSS border-style property, which you'll explore shortly. Some Web page authors prefer to work with these HTML attributes because they enable them to set the appearance of the table borders from within the <table> tag rather than through an external style sheet.

Aligning Cell Contents with HTML

The final set of HTML table attributes you'll examine before looking at CSS table styles are those attributes that control how content is aligned within each table cell. By default, browsers horizontally center the contents of table header cells and left-align the contents of table data cells. You can specify a different horizontal alignment using the align attribute

```
align="position"
```

where *position* is left, center, right, justify or char. The align attribute can be applied to table rows, row groups, columns, column groups, or individual table cells. For example, the code

```
<colgroup>
   <col align="left" />
   <col span="6" align="right" />
</colgroup>
```

left-aligns the first column of the Web table and right-aligns the remaining six columns. When you apply the align attribute to the table element, it aligns the entire table with the surrounding page content but does not affect the alignment of the cells within the table. The align attribute has been deprecated for use with the table element, but not for the row, column, and cell elements within the table.

InSight | **Character Alignment**

Another alignment option included with the align attribute is the char value, which tells the browser to align the values in a cell based on the position of a particular character. The default character is a decimal point, which is represented by a period in the English language and by commas in some European languages (such as French). To line up all of the data values within a column by their decimal points, enter the following code:

```
<col align="char" />
```

You can specify a different character by adding the char attribute to the tag. You can also specify how much the alignment character is offset from the cell borders using the charoff attribute. The syntax of these attributes is

```
align="char" char="character" charoff="position"
```

where *character* is the alignment character and *position* is the position of the character within the table cell either in pixels or as a percentage of the cell's width. So the HTML code

```
<col align="char" char="," charoff="50%" />
```

aligns all of the column values by the position of the comma character. The comma character itself will be placed in the center of each cell in the column.

While useful for displaying financial or scientific data, the character alignment attributes have not received much support in the browser market, so their potential is still mostly unfulfilled.

Vertical Alignment in HTML

You can also use HTML to vertically align the contents of each table cell. The default is to place the text in the middle of the cell. To choose a different placement, apply the valign attribute

```
valign="position"
```

where *position* is top, middle, bottom, or baseline. The top, middle, and bottom options align the content with the top, middle, and bottom borders of the cell. The baseline option places the text near the bottom of the cell but aligns the bases of each letter. The valign attribute can be applied to table rows, row groups, columns, and column groups to set the vertical alignment of several cells at once.

Kyle feels that having the program names placed in the middle of each cell makes the program schedule more difficult to read. He prefers having all of the program names lined up with the top of the cells. To change the cell alignment for all of the cells in the table body, you'll apply the valign attribute to the tbody row group.

To vertically align the text in the table:

1. Return to the **schedule.htm** file in your text editor.
2. Within the opening <tbody> tag, insert the following attribute, as shown in Figure 5-30:

```
valign="top"
```

Figure 5-30 Applying the valign attribute

```
<tbody valign="top">
   <tr>
      <th>6:00</th>
      <td colspan="7">National News</td>
   </tr>
```

3. Save your changes to the file, and then reload or refresh the **schedule.htm** file in your Web browser. As shown in Figure 5-31, the text is aligned at the top of the cells.

Figure 5-31 Cell content aligned with the top of each table cell

<table>
<tr><th>Time</th><th>Monday</th><th>Tuesday</th><th>Wednesday</th><th>Thursday</th><th>Friday</th><th>Saturday</th><th>Sunday</th></tr>
<tr><th>6:00</th><td colspan="7">National News</td></tr>
<tr><th>6:30</th><td colspan="7">Local News</td></tr>
<tr><th>7:00</th><td rowspan="2">Opera Fest</td><td rowspan="2">Radio U</td><td rowspan="2">Science Week</td><td rowspan="2">The Living World</td><td>Word Play</td><td>Agri-Week</td><td rowspan="2">Folk Fest</td></tr>
<tr><th>7:30</th><td>Brain Stew</td><td>Bismarck Forum</td></tr>
<tr><th>8:00</th><td colspan="4" rowspan="4">The Classical Music Connection</td><td>Old Time Radio</td><td rowspan="4">Saturday Nite Jazz</td><td rowspan="4">The Indie Connection</td></tr>
<tr><th>8:30</th><td>The Inner Mind</td></tr>
<tr><th>9:00</th><td rowspan="2">Open Mike Nite</td></tr>
<tr><th>9:30</th></tr>
<tr><th>10:00</th><td colspan="7">World News Feed</td></tr>
</table>

Kyle likes the appearance of the program table. But he notes that this is only the evening schedule; he plans to create other Web pages for the morning and afternoon schedules. To have the tables match each other, you'll have to insert the various HTML attributes into each table's markup tags. Kyle would rather use CSS so he can easily apply the formatting he likes to all of the schedules at once. He suggests that you explore the CSS table styles before continuing your design of the evening schedule.

Formatting Tables with CSS

Starting with CSS2, Cascading Style Sheets included support for Web tables. With more browser support for these styles, CSS has gradually replaced the HTML attributes you've just reviewed (though you will still see those HTML attributes frequently used on the Web). Kyle suggests that you replace the HTML table attributes with an external style sheet that he can apply to all of the program schedule tables on the KPAF Web site.

To create the style sheet:

1. Open the **tablestxt.css** file from the tutorial.05\tutorial folder included with your Data Files. Enter ***your name*** and ***the date*** in the comment section of the file. Save the file as **tables.css** in the same folder.
2. Return to the **schedule.htm** file in your text editor and insert the following link element directly above the closing </head> tag:

```
<link href="tables.css" rel="stylesheet" type="text/css" />
```

3. Because you'll be replacing the HTML attributes with CSS styles, delete the border, cellpadding, and cellspacing attributes from the opening <table> tag.
4. Delete the valign attribute from the opening <tbody> tag.
5. Save your changes to the file.

Tip

Don't combine HTML table attributes and CSS table styles in your Web table design. Choose one or the other to avoid conflicts in the two approaches.

Now that you've linked the schedule.htm file to the tables.css style sheet and you've removed the old HTML table attributes, you are ready to begin creating the style sheet. You'll start with styles for the table border.

Table Border Styles

The first styles you'll apply to the program schedule are the border styles. Web tables use the same border styles you've already used with other page elements in previous tutorials. Unlike the HTML border attribute, you can apply one set of borders to the Web table itself and another set of borders to the individual cells within the table. You decide to add a 10-pixel purple border around the entire schedule table in the outset style. You'll also add a 1-pixel solid gray border around each cell within the table.

To add the table border styles:

1. Return to the **tables.css** file in your text editor. Add the following style to apply a border to the entire Web table:

```
table.schedule {border: 10px outset rgb(153, 0, 153)}
```

2. Add the following style to apply borders to each table cell. See Figure 5-32.

```
table.schedule th, table.schedule td
               {border: 1px solid gray}
```

Figure 5-32 **Setting the table border styles**

```
table.schedule          {border: 10px outset rgb(153,0,153)}

table.schedule th, table.schedule td
                        {border: 1px solid gray}
```

Notice that the style sheet uses contextual selectors to apply these styles only to the schedule table and not other tables that might exist on the KPAF Web site.

3. Save your changes to the style sheet and then reload the **schedule.htm** file in your Web browser. As shown in Figure 5-33, borders have now been added to the entire table and to each table cell.

Figure 5-33 Table and cell borders

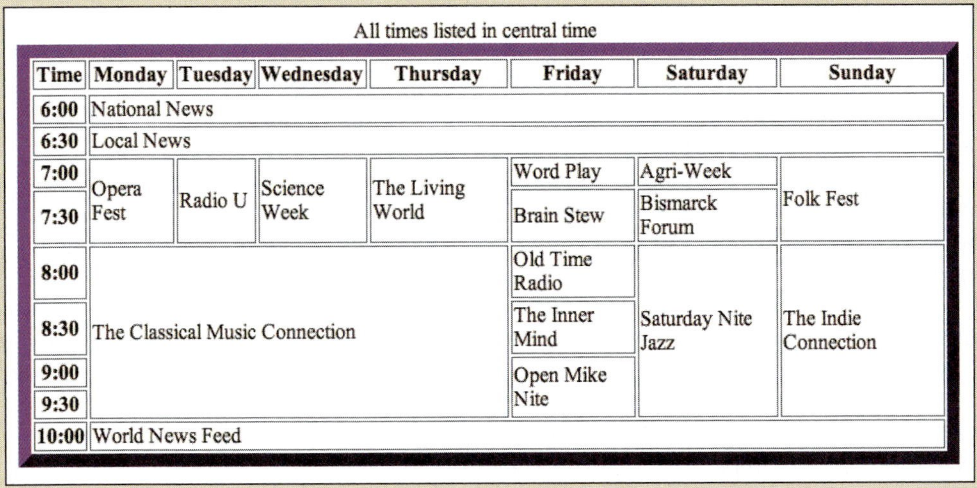

All times listed in central time

<table>
<tr><th>Time</th><th>Monday</th><th>Tuesday</th><th>Wednesday</th><th>Thursday</th><th>Friday</th><th>Saturday</th><th>Sunday</th></tr>
<tr><th>6:00</th><td colspan="7">National News</td></tr>
<tr><th>6:30</th><td colspan="7">Local News</td></tr>
<tr><th>7:00</th><td rowspan="2">Opera Fest</td><td rowspan="2">Radio U</td><td rowspan="2">Science Week</td><td rowspan="2">The Living World</td><td>Word Play</td><td>Agri-Week</td><td rowspan="2">Folk Fest</td></tr>
<tr><th>7:30</th><td>Brain Stew</td><td>Bismarck Forum</td></tr>
<tr><th>8:00</th><td colspan="4" rowspan="4">The Classical Music Connection</td><td>Old Time Radio</td><td rowspan="4">Saturday Nite Jazz</td><td rowspan="4">The Indie Connection</td></tr>
<tr><th>8:30</th><td>The Inner Mind</td></tr>
<tr><th>9:00</th><td rowspan="2">Open Mike Nite</td></tr>
<tr><th>9:30</th></tr>
<tr><th>10:00</th><td colspan="7">World News Feed</td></tr>
</table>

CSS provides for two ways of drawing the table borders. The default, shown in Figure 5-33, is to draw separate borders around the table cells and the entire table. The other approach is to collapse the borders in upon each other as shown in Figure 5-34, removing any space between the borders.

Figure 5-34 Separate and collapsed borders

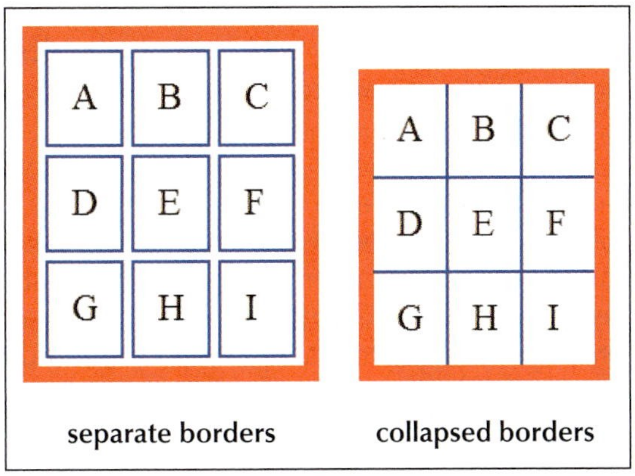

To determine whether to use the separate or collapsed border model, you apply the style

```
border-collapse: type
```

to the table element, where *type* is either separate (the default) or collapse. One of the key differences between the separate and collapse border models is that under the separate border model you can only apply borders to the table itself or to table cells. Under the collapse border model, any table object can have a border, including table rows, row groups, columns, and column groups. If the separate borders model is used, you can specify the distance between the borders by applying the style

```
border-spacing: value
```

to the table, where *value* is the space between the borders in one of the CSS units of measure. For example, the following style specifies that all borders within the table should be separated by a distance of 10 pixels:

```
table {border-collapse: separate; border-spacing: 10px}
```

The separate borders model, therefore, has the same effect as the HTML cellspacing attribute in providing additional space between table cells.

In the collapsed border model, there is no space between borders; in fact, the adjacent borders are merged together to form a single line. It's important to understand that the borders are not simply moved together, but rather they are combined into a single border. For example, if two adjacent 1-pixel-wide borders are collapsed together, the resulting border is not 2 pixels wide, but only 1 pixel wide. The situation is more complicated when the adjacent borders have different widths, styles, or colors. How would you merge a double red border and a solid blue border into a single border of only one color and style? Those kinds of differences must be reconciled before the two borders can be merged. CSS employs five rules to determine the style of the collapsed border. Listed in decreasing order of importance, the rules are:

1. If either border has a border style of hidden, the collapsed border is hidden.
2. A border style of none is overridden by any other border style.
3. If neither border is hidden, the style of the wider border takes priority over the narrower.
4. If the two borders have the same width but different styles, the border style with the highest priority is used. Double borders have the highest priority, followed by solid, dashed, dotted, ridge, outset, groove, and finally inset borders.
5. If the borders differ only in the color, the color from the table object with the highest priority is used. The highest priority color belongs to the border surrounding individual table cells, followed by the borders for table rows, row groups, columns, column groups, and finally the border around the entire table.

Any situation not covered by these rules is left to the browser to determine which border dominates when collapsing the two borders. Figure 5-35 provides an example of the first rule in action. In this example, the border around the entire table is hidden but a 1-pixel blue border is assigned to the cells within the table. When collapsed, any cell borders that are adjacent to the table border adopt the hidden border property.

Figure 5-35 **Reconciling hidden borders**

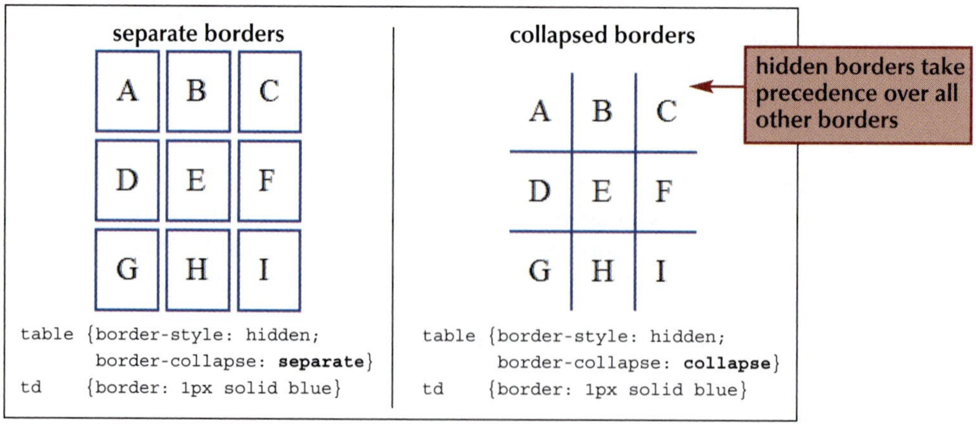

Figure 5-36 shows what happens when two borders of the same width but different styles meet. In this case, because of Rule 4, the table cell borders with the double blue lines have precedence over the solid red lines of the table border.

Figure 5-36 **Reconciling different border styles**

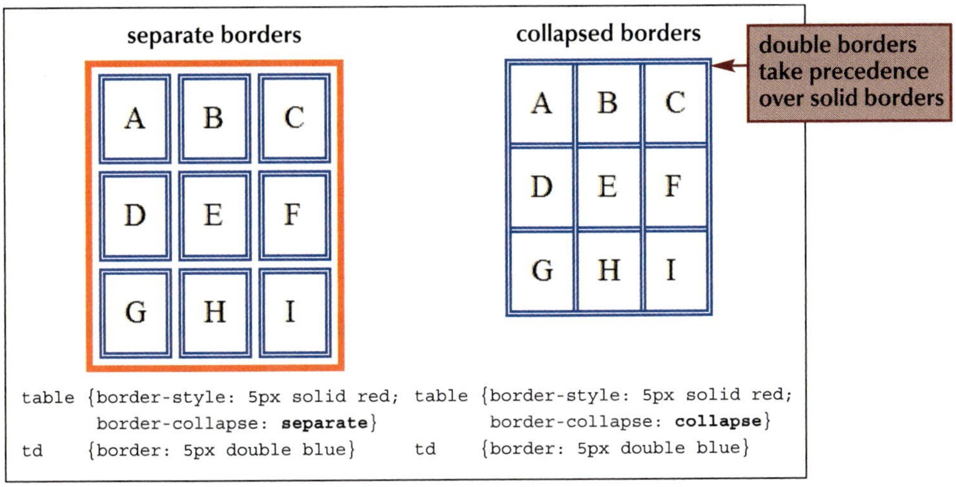
separate borders
A B C
D E F
G H I
collapsed borders
A B C
D E F
G H I
double borders take precedence over solid borders
table {border-style: 5px solid red;
border-collapse: separate}
td {border: 5px double blue}
table {border-style: 5px solid red;
border-collapse: collapse}
td {border: 5px double blue}

Although the collapse model appears more complicated at first, the rules are reasonable and allow for a wide variety of border designs.

Setting Table Borders with CSS | Reference Window

- To define the border model used by the table, apply the table style
  `border-collapse: type`
  where *type* is separate (the default) to keep all borders around cells and the table itself, separate, or collapse to merge all adjacent borders.
- To set the space between separated borders, apply the table style
  `border-spacing: value`
  where *value* is the space between the borders in any of the CSS units of measure.

For the KPAF program schedule, Kyle thinks the table would look better if there were no space between the table cells. He asks you to collapse the borders.

To collapse the cell borders:

1. Return to the **tables.css** file in your text editor. Add the following style to the table element, as shown in Figure 5-37.

   `border-collapse: collapse`

Figure 5-37 **Adding the border-collapse style**

```
table.schedule          {border: 10px outset rgb(153,0,153); border-collapse: collapse}
table.schedule th, table.schedule td
                        {border: 1px solid gray}
```

2. Save your changes to the style sheet, and then reload **schedule.htm** in your Web browser. Figure 5-38 shows the revised table design with the collapsed border layout.

Figure 5-38 **Table with collapsed borders**

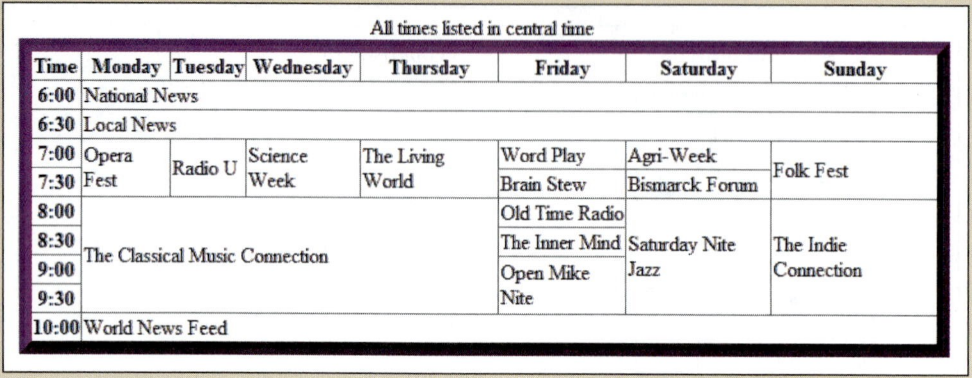

All times listed in central time

Time	Monday	Tuesday	Wednesday	Thursday	Friday	Saturday	Sunday
6:00	National News						
6:30	Local News						
7:00	Opera Fest	Radio U	Science Week	The Living World	Word Play	Agri-Week	Folk Fest
7:30					Brain Stew	Bismarck Forum	
8:00	The Classical Music Connection				Old Time Radio	Saturday Nite Jazz	The Indie Connection
8:30					The Inner Mind		
9:00					Open Mike Nite		
9:30							
10:00	World News Feed						

Notice that the browser still uses the purple outset style for the border around the entire table. This is due to Rule 3 above. Because the border around the entire table is 10 pixels wide, it takes priority over the 1-pixel-wide borders around the individual table cells under the collapsed border model.

Applying Styles to Rows and Columns

Kyle doesn't like the appearance of the table text. He suggests changing the table text to a sans-serif font that is 0.7 em units in size. He also suggests that the text in the header row appear in a white font on a purple background and that the first column of the schedule, containing the program times, appear on a light yellow background.

You can apply these styles to the row groups and column groups you created in the last session. Recall that the header row is part of the thead row group (see Figure 5-19), and the first column of the table belongs to the firstCol class of columns (see Figure 5-20). So to apply Kyle's suggested styles, you could add the following declarations to the tables.css style sheet:

```
table.schedule              {font-family: Arial, Helvetica, sans-
                            serif; font-size: 0.7em}
table.schedule thead        {color: white; background-color:
                            rgb(203,50,203)}
table.schedule col.firstCol {background-color: rgb(255,255,192)}
```

However, you notice a small problem. The first cell in the table belongs to both the header row and the first column. Will this cell have a purple background or a yellow background? Which style has precedence? Table objects, like other parts of CSS, have levels of precedence in which the more specific object has priority over the more general. Figure 5-39 shows a diagram of the different levels of precedence in the Web table structure.

Levels of precedence in Web table styles — **Figure 5-39**

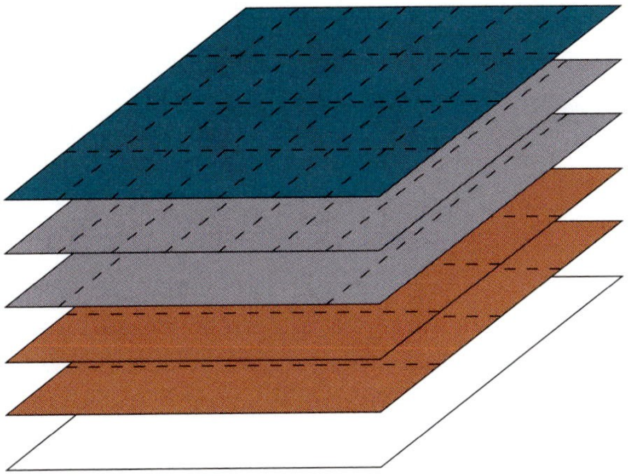

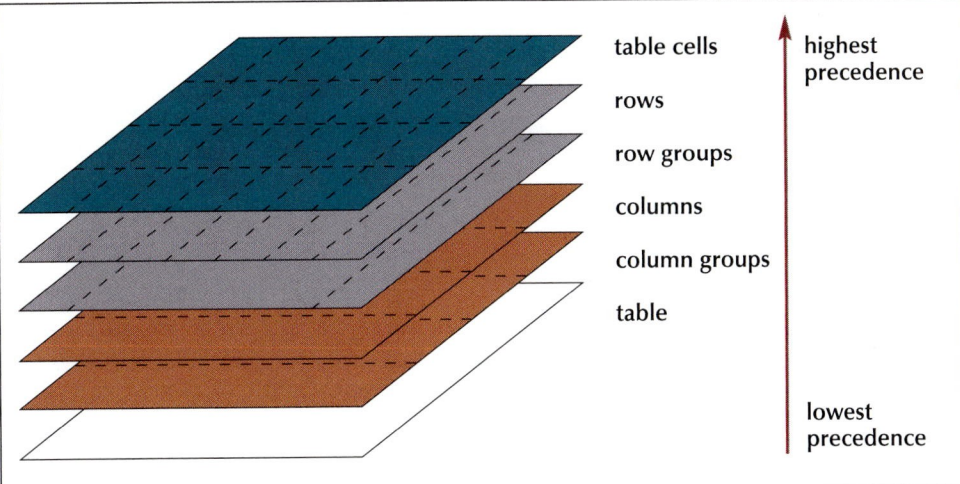

The most general styles are those applied to the entire table. Those styles are overruled by styles that are applied to column groups and then to columns. The next level up in precedence contains those styles applied to row groups and then rows. The highest level of precedence is given to those styles applied to table cells. Be aware that not all styles are supported by different layers of the table structure. In particular, columns and column groups accept only four styles: border, background, width, and visibility.

With Kyle's proposed design, the first cell should have a purple background because row groups take priority over columns or column groups. To see that this is the case, add Kyle's proposed styles to the tables.css style sheet.

To set the text and background styles in the schedule table:

1. Return to the **tables.css** file in your text editor. Add the following styles to the style declaration for the schedule table:

```
font-family: Arial, Helvetica, sans-serif; font-size: 0.7em
```

2. Go to the bottom of the style sheet and insert the following lines to create styles for the table's header row and first column as shown in Figure 5-40:

```
table.schedule thead         {color: white; background-color:
                              rgb(203,50,203)}
table.schedule col.firstCol {background-color: rgb(255,255,192)}
```

Adding font and color styles to the schedule table — **Figure 5-40**

```
table.schedule          {border: 10px outset rgb(153,0,153); border-collapse: collapse;
                         font-family: Arial, Helvetica, sans-serif; font-size: 0.7em}

table.schedule th, table.schedule td
                        {border: 1px solid gray; font-family: Arial}

table.schedule thead    {color: white; background-color: rgb(203,50,203)}

table.schedule col.firstCol
                        {background-color: rgb(255,255,192)}
```

table font styles

style applied to thead row group

style applied to first table column

3. Save your changes to the style sheet, and then reload **schedule.htm** in your Web browser. The revised table design is shown in Figure 5-41.

Figure 5-41 Applying styles to the header row and first column

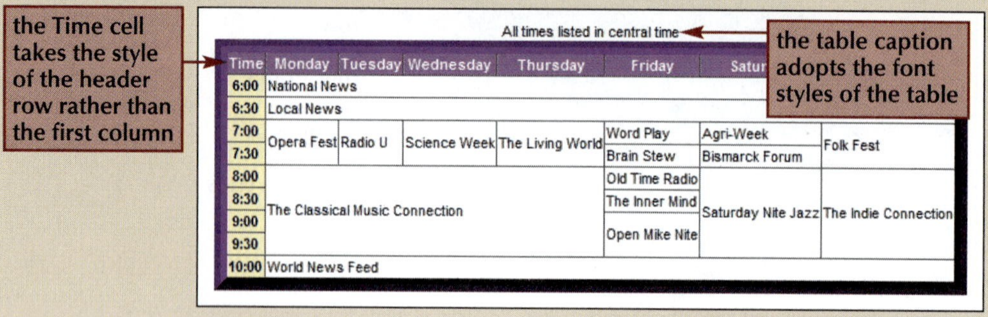

As you expected, the cell in the first column of the header row does indeed have a purple, and not a light yellow, background. Also note that all of the cells in the table and the table caption have adopted the smaller sans-serif font. This is because the font style you entered for the schedule table is inherited by all table objects unless a different font style is specified.

Using the Width and Height Styles

Reducing the font size and changing the font family has resulted in a more compact table, but Kyle thinks it could be difficult to read and wonders if you could enlarge the table. Recall that browsers will set the table width to efficiently use the page space, never making tables wider than necessary to display the content. You can use the CSS width style to specify a different table size. Widths are expressed in one of the CSS units of measure or as a percentage of the containing element. Kyle suggests that you set the width of the table to 100% so that it covers the entire width of its div container.

To set the width of the table:

1. Return to the **tables.css** file in your text editor. Add the following style to the table element, as shown in Figure 5-42.

```
width: 100%
```

Figure 5-42 Setting the width of the schedule table

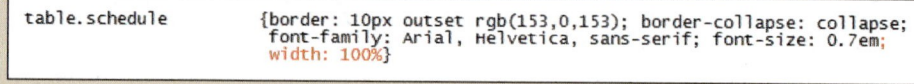

```
table.schedule          {border: 10px outset rgb(153,0,153); border-collapse: collapse;
                          font-family: Arial, Helvetica, sans-serif; font-size: 0.7em;
                          width: 100%}
```

2. Save your changes to the file, and then reload **schedule.htm** in your Web browser. Figure 5-43 shows the layout of the enlarged table.

Figure 5-43 Table width set to 100%

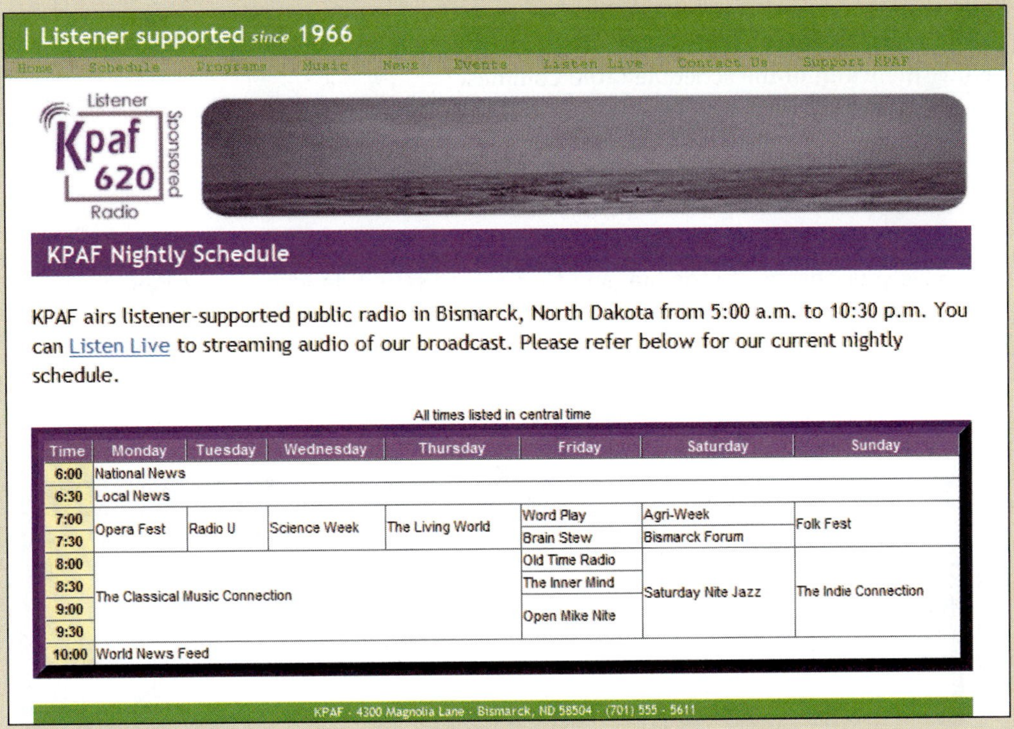

You notice that the column widths are inconsistent, with very little width given to the Time column and different widths given to different days of the week. This is because the space allotted to each column is a function of the column's content. The Web browser will attempt to fit the most content possible within each column without having the text wrap to a new line. This means that columns with more text are wider than those with less text. When the width of the entire table is increased, the added space is divided evenly among the table columns.

You can set column widths using the same width style you applied to the table itself. The column width is expressed either in a CSS unit of measure or as a percentage of the entire width of the table. You decide to set the width of the first column to 7% of the entire table width, while setting each of the seven remaining columns to 13% of the table width. Added together, 98% of the table width will be allotted to the eight table columns. The remaining table width is reserved for table and cell borders.

> **Tip**
>
> Always set the total width of the table columns to be less than 100% of the table width to allow space for table borders and padding.

You can set the column widths by applying the width style to the two column groups. The width values are applied to the individual columns within those groups. The styles are:

```
table.schedule col.firstCol {width: 7%}
table.schedule col.dayCols  {width: 13%}
```

Add these styles to the tables.css style sheet.

To set the width of the table columns:

1. Return to the **tables.css** file in your text editor. Add the following style to the firstCol selector:

   ```
   width: 7%
   ```

2. Insert the following style declaration to set the widths of the columns in the dayCols class to 13% as shown in Figure 5-44:

```
table.schedule col.dayCols {width: 13%}
```

Figure 5-44 **Setting the width of the schedule table columns**

```
table.schedule col.firstCol
                    {background-color: rgb(255,255,192); width: 7%}
table.schedule col.dayCols
                    {width: 13%}
```

3. Save your changes to the file, and then reload **schedule.htm** in your Web browser. Figure 5-45 shows the revised layout of the table.

Figure 5-45 **Revised table column widths**

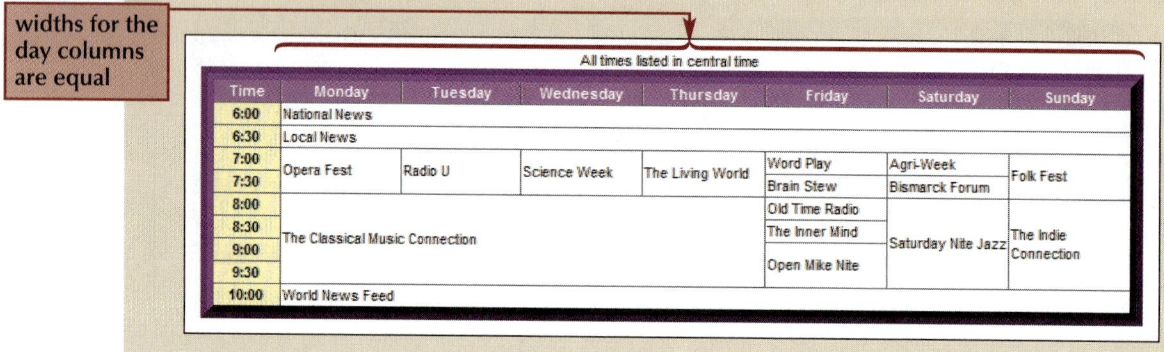
widths for the day columns are equal
All times listed in central time
Time
Monday
Tuesday
Wednesday
Thursday
Friday
Saturday
Sunday
6:00
6:30
7:00
7:30
8:00
8:30
9:00
9:30
10:00
National News
Local News
Opera Fest
Radio U
Science Week
The Living World
Word Play
Brain Stew
Agri-Week
Bismarck Forum
Folk Fest
Old Time Radio
The Inner Mind
Open Mike Nite
Saturday Nite Jazz
The Indie Connection
The Classical Music Connection
World News Feed

Kyle also wants you to increase the height of the table rows to provide more visual space for the table contents. Heights are set using the CSS height style. You can apply heights to entire table rows or individual table cells. You can also use the height style to set the height of the entire table. As with the width style, the height style should be interpreted as the minimum height for these table objects since the browser will enlarge the table, table row, or table cell if the content requires it.

You decide to set the height of the rows in the table header to 20 pixels and the height of the rows in the table body to 30 pixels. The styles to do this are:

```
table.schedule thead tr {height: 20px}
table.schedule tbody tr {height: 30px}
```

Note that you don't apply the height style to the row groups themselves because that would set the width of the entire group and not the individual rows within the group.

To set the height of the table rows:

1. Return to the **tables.css** file in your text editor and add the following styles to the bottom of the style sheet, as shown in Figure 5-46.

```
table.schedule thead tr {height: 20px}
table.schedule tbody tr {height: 30px}
```

Figure 5-46 **Setting the height of the table rows**

```
table.schedule col.dayCols
                    {width: 13%}
table.schedule thead tr {height: 20px}
table.schedule tbody tr {height: 30px}
```

▶ **2.** Save your changes to the file, and then reload **schedule.htm** in your Web browser. Verify that the heights in the table header and table body have changed.

With the increased row height, Kyle would like all of the program names in the schedule to be vertically aligned with the top of the cell borders as you did earlier with the valign HTML attribute. The equivalent CSS style is the vertical-align property introduced in Tutorial 3. Kyle also wants to increase the padding within each cell to add more space between the program names and the cell border. You'll add the following style to the style sheet:

```
table.schedule tbody td {vertical-align: top; padding: 5px}
```

To place the program names at the top of each table cell:

▶ **1.** Return to the **tables.css** file in your text editor and add the following style as shown in Figure 5-47.

```
table.schedule tbody td {vertical-align: top; padding: 5px}
```

Figure 5-47 **Aligning the data cells within the table body**

```
table.schedule thead tr {height: 20px}
table.schedule tbody tr {height: 30px}

table.schedule tbody td {vertical-align: top; padding: 5px}
```

▶ **2.** Save your changes to the file, and then reload **schedule.htm** in your Web browser. As shown in Figure 5-48, the program names are now placed at the top of each cell and the padding space between the program names and the cell borders has been increased.

Figure 5-48 **Revised table layout**

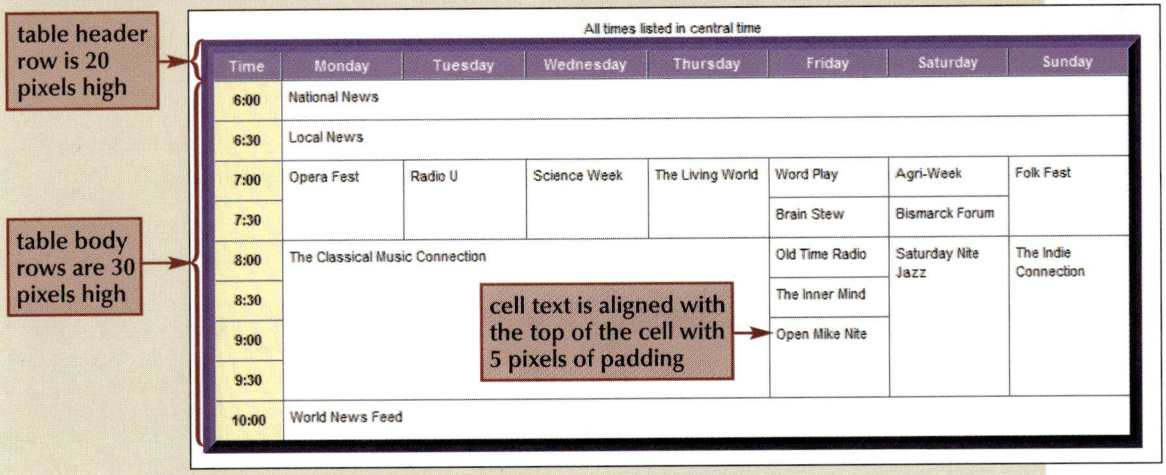

Notice that only the data cells within the tbody rows are placed at the top of the cell. The header cells are still centered vertically because they were not included in the contextual selector you specified in the style sheet.

Caption Styles

Kyle likes the new table design. His only remaining suggestion is that you align the table caption with the top-right corner of the table. Browsers usually place captions above the table, but you can specify the caption location using the caption-side style with the syntax

```
caption-side: position
```

where *position* is either top (the default) or bottom to place the caption below the Web table. To horizontally align the caption text you use the CSS text-align style. So to place the schedule caption at the top-right corner of the table, you would enter the following CSS style:

```
caption {caption-side: top; text-align: right}
```

Tip

Firefox supports caption-side values of left and right to place the caption directly to the left or right of the Web table.

Reference Window | Formatting a Table Caption with CSS

- To position a table caption, apply the style
  `caption-side: position`
  where *position* is top or bottom.

Add this style to the tables.css style sheet.

To apply a style to the table caption:

1. Return to the **tables.css** file in your text editor and add the following style, as shown in Figure 5-49:

```
table.schedule caption {caption-side: top; text-align: right}
```

Figure 5-49 Setting the caption position

```
table.schedule tbody td {vertical-align: top; padding: 5px}
table.schedule caption  {caption-side: top; text-align: right}
```

2. Close the file, saving your changes, and then reload the **schedule.htm** file in your Web browser. Figure 5-50 shows the final appearance of the Web table.

Figure 5-50 Final design of the schedule table

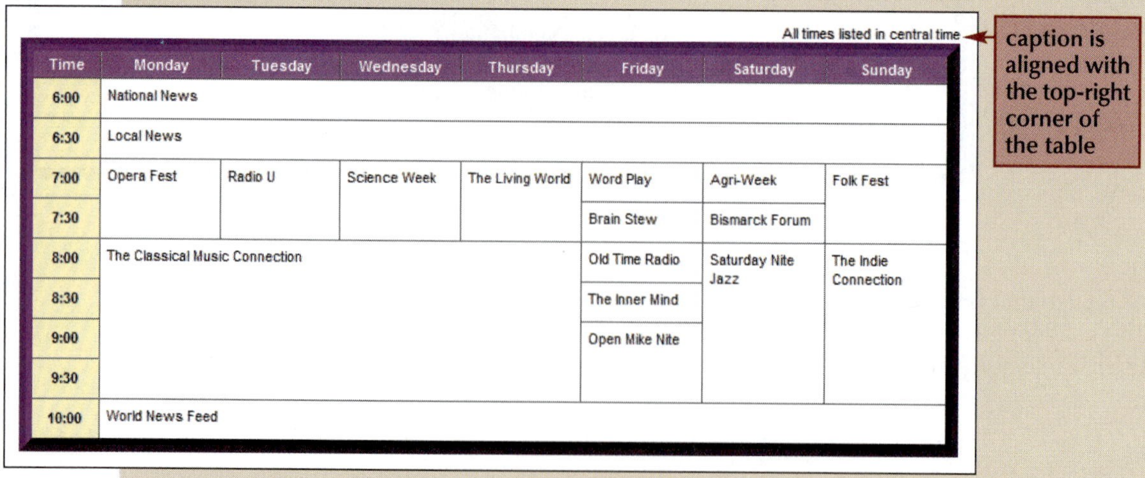
All times listed in central time

Time	Monday	Tuesday	Wednesday	Thursday	Friday	Saturday	Sunday
6:00	National News						
6:30	Local News						
7:00	Opera Fest	Radio U	Science Week	The Living World	Word Play	Agri-Week	Folk Fest
7:30					Brain Stew	Bismarck Forum	
8:00	The Classical Music Connection				Old Time Radio	Saturday Nite Jazz	The Indie Connection
8:30					The Inner Mind		
9:00					Open Mike Nite		
9:30							
10:00	World News Feed						

caption is aligned with the top-right corner of the table

3. If you want to take a break before starting the next session, close all of your files and programs now.

Applying Table Styles to Other Page Elements

As you can see, tables are useful for displaying information in an organized structure of rows and columns. Tables are so useful, in fact, that there's no reason to limit the table structure to Web tables. Using the CSS display style, you can apply the table layout to other HTML elements, such as paragraphs, block quotes, or lists. Figure 5-51 describes the various CSS table display styles and their HTML equivalents.

Table display styles **Figure 5-51**

Display Style	Equivalent HTML Element
`display: table`	table (treated as a block-level element)
`display: table-inline`	table (treated as an inline element)
`display: table-row`	tr
`display: table-row-group`	tbody
`display: table-header-group`	thead
`display: table-footer-group`	tfoot
`display: table-column`	col
`display: table-column-group`	colgroup
`display: table-cell`	td or th
`display: table-caption`	caption

For example, the following definition list contains definitions of several networking terms:

```
<dl>
   <dt>bandwidth</dt>
   <dd>A measure of data transfer speed over a network</dd>
   <dt>HTTP</dt>
   <dd>The protocol used to communicate with Web servers</dd>
</dl>
```

Rather than accepting the default browser layout for this list, it might be useful to display the text in a table. But you don't want to lose the meaning of the markup tags. After all, HTML is designed to mark content, but not indicate how that content should be rendered by the browser. To display this definition list as a table, you first enclose each set of terms and definitions within a div container tag, as follows:

```
<dl>
   <div>
      <dt>bandwidth</dt>
      <dd>A measure of data transfer speed over a network</dd>
   </div>
   <div>
      <dt>HTTP</dt>
      <dd>The protocol used to communicate with Web servers</dd>
   </div>
</dl>
```

You then apply the following style sheet to the list, which treats the entire definition list as a table, the div elements as table rows, and the definition terms and descriptions as table cells within those rows:

```
dl     {display: table; border-collapse: collapse; width: 300px}
dl div {display: table-row}
dt, dd {display: table-cell; border: 1px solid black;
        vertical-align: top; padding: 5px}
```

When viewed in a Web browser, the definition list looks exactly as if it were created using the HTML table tags as shown in Figure 5-52.

Figure 5-52 **Applying table styles to a definition list**

```
<dl>
   <div>
      <dt>bandwidth</dt>
      <dd>A measure of data transfer speed over
          a network</dd>
   </div>
   <div>
      <dt>HTTP</dt>
      <dd>The protocol used to communicate with
          Web servers</dd>
   </div>
</dl>
```

definition list code

```
dl     {display: table; border-collapse: collapse;
        width: 300px}

dl div {display: table-row}

dt, dd {display: table-cell; border: 1px solid black;
        vertical-align: top; padding: 5px}
```

table styles

bandwidth	A measure of data transfer speed over a network
HTTP	The protocol used to communicate with Web servers

definition list displayed as table

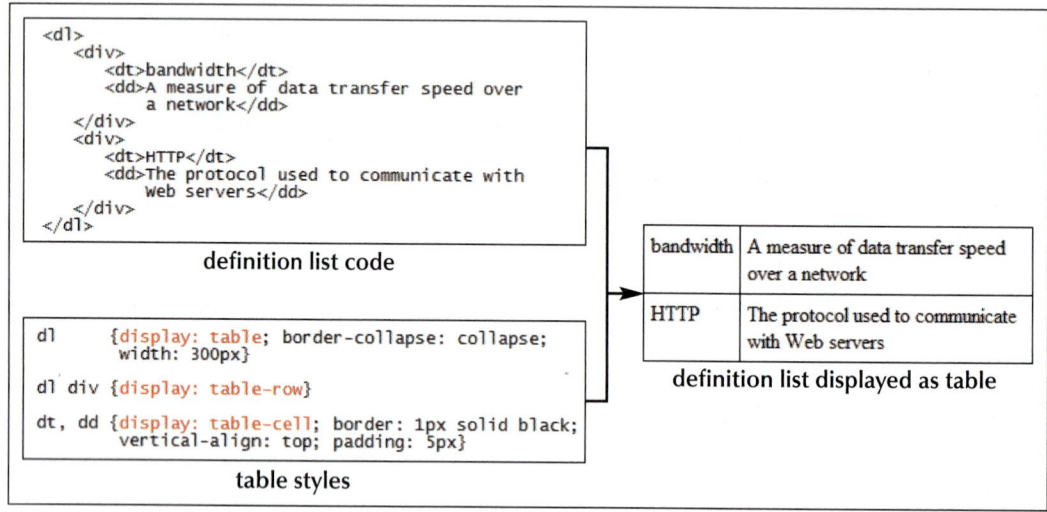

In the same way, you can display other page elements in tabular form. As long as the markup tags are nested in a way that mimics the table structure, it doesn't matter if they're table tags or not. You can display them as tables using CSS.

Kyle is pleased with the work you've done on the programming schedule page. In the next session you'll explore how to use tables for page layout and you'll study various CSS layout designs.

Review | Session 5.2 Quick Check

1. What HTML attribute do you add to the table element to set the space between cells to 10 pixels?
2. What HTML attribute would you add to the table element to display a 1-pixel border around the table but no gridlines within the table?
3. What HTML attribute would you add to the table element to add borders around the table columns?
4. What CSS style would you enter to collapse all adjacent borders in the table into single borders?
5. Two table cells have adjacent borders. One cell has a 5-pixel-wide double border and the other cell has a 6-pixel-wide solid border. If the table borders are collapsed, what type of border will the two cells share?
6. In the case of conflicting styles, which has highest precedence: the style of the row group or the style of the column group?

7. What style should you enter to align the content of all table header cells with the bottom of the cell?
8. What style would you enter to display the table caption below the table?
9. Specify the style to display ordered lists as table elements and list items as table cells.

Session 5.3

Using Tables for Page Layout

Kyle is very pleased with the work you've done on the KPAF evening schedule. He thinks the page would look even better if it included summaries of upcoming broadcasts. Figure 5-53 shows a sketch of Kyle's proposed addition. He suggests placing the program summaries in a new column to the right of the schedule table.

Figure 5-53 Kyle's proposed addition to the evening schedule page

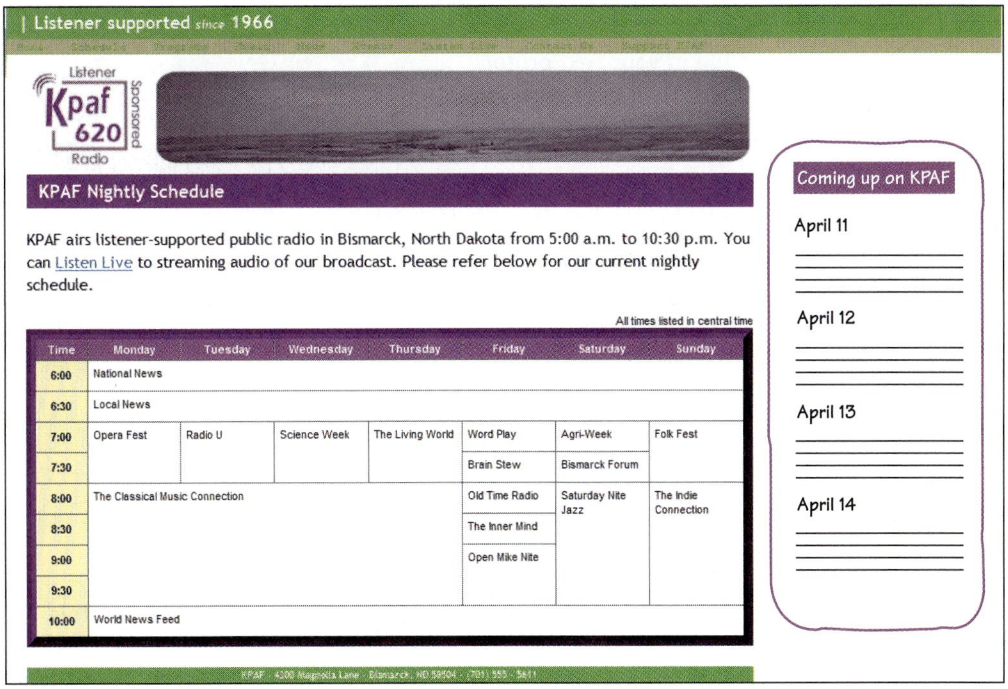

To create this new column, you'll add a new div container named right_col to the schedule.htm file.

To create the new column:

1. Return to the **schedule.htm** file in your text editor.
2. Scroll to the bottom of the file, and directly above the closing </body> tag, insert the following div container as shown in Figure 5-54.

```
<div id="right_col">
</div>
```

Figure 5-54 Inserting the right_col div element

```
      <address>
         KPAF &#183;
         4300 Magnolia Lane &#183;
         Bismarck, ND 58504 &#183;
         (701) 555 - 5611
      </address>

   </div>

   <div id="right_col">
   </div>

</body>
```

3. Save your changes to the file.

Now you'll add styles to the kpaf.css style sheet to set the width of this new column to 200 pixels. You'll use absolute positioning to place it alongside the nightly program schedule, creating a two-column layout.

To create styles for a two-column layout:

1. Open the **kpaf.css** file in your text editor.
2. Directly below the style declaration for the #page_content selector, insert the following style for the #right_col selector:

```
#right_col {width: 200px; position: absolute; top: 55px; left:
770px}
```

Figure 5-55 highlights the new style sheet code.

Figure 5-55 Adding styles to create a two-column layout

```
body            {margin: 0px}
#heading        {color: white; background-color: rgb(215, 205, 151);
                 border-bottom: 1px solid rgb(105, 177, 60)}
#page_content   {width: 730px; position: absolute; top: 55px; left: 20px}
#right_col      {width: 200px; position: absolute; top: 55px; left: 770px}
```

3. Close the style sheet file, saving your changes.

Next you'll start creating the bar that lists upcoming programs. To avoid having this look too "boxy," Kyle has proposed that the list be placed in a rectangle with rounded corners. There is no HTML element or CSS style for rounded corners, but you can simulate the effect using background images and a Web table.

Introducing the Jigsaw Layout

So far in this tutorial you've only placed text into your Web tables; however, tables can contain any page content, including inline images, headings, paragraphs, lists, and other tables. Because of this, Web designers began using tables for page layout, allowing them to have more control over the placement of different page elements. For example, a three-column layout could be simulated by enclosing the entire page within a table containing a single row with three columns. The table borders would be hidden from the user, leaving only the table content visible.

Tables support a wide variety of possible page layouts. The one that you'll explore in this session is known as a **jigsaw layout**, so called because it involves breaking up the page content into separate table cells that are then joined together like pieces in a jigsaw puzzle. Figure 5-56 shows an example of a jigsaw layout in which the page content is broken into fourteen table cells, including an image file that has been sliced into nine distinct pieces and placed on the page as a background image. When the cells are reassembled in the complete table after removing the table borders, it appears that the page content flows naturally alongside and within the graphic images or other features of the page.

Figure 5-56 A jigsaw layout

Defining the Structure of a Jigsaw Table

Figure 5-57 shows a similar jigsaw layout for Kyle's list of upcoming programs. The cell borders have been added to make the table structure clear, but they are removed in the final version of the object. The table contains three rows and three columns with eight background images. Only the middle cell contains any actual content; the remaining cells are used to display the graphic images that constitute the rounded border. When rendered by the browser without the table gridlines, it appears like a rectangle with rounded borders.

Figure 5-57 Creating a box with rounded corners

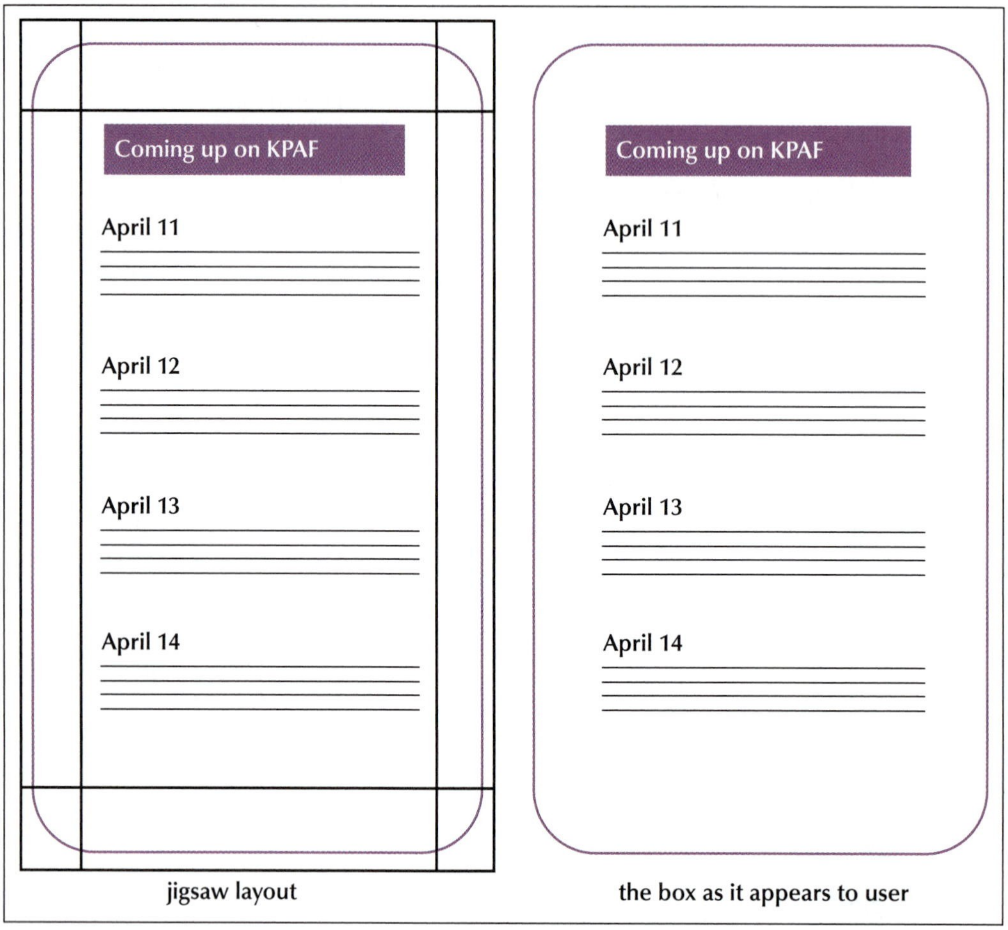

Kyle is interested in this technique and asks you to add the structure for this 3x3 table to the schedule.htm file.

To create the table:

1. Return to the **schedule.htm** file in your Web browser.
2. Within the right_col container, insert the following table. See Figure 5-58.

```
<table class="roundedBox">
   <tr>
      <td></td>
      <td></td>
      <td></td>
   </tr>
   <tr>
      <td></td>
      <td></td>
      <td></td>
   </tr>
   <tr>
      <td></td>
      <td></td>
      <td></td>
   </tr>
</table>
```

Figure 5-58 Basic table structure for the roundedBox layout

```
<div id="right_col">
   <table class="roundedBox">
      <tr>
         <td></td>
         <td></td>
         <td></td>
      </tr>
      <tr>
         <td></td>
         <td></td>
         <td></td>
      </tr>
      <tr>
         <td></td>
         <td></td>
         <td></td>
      </tr>
   </table>
</div>
```

Next you have to assign class names to the nine cells contained within the table. Remember that only the center cell will contain any content. The remaining cells will be used to display the outside borders of the rounded box. You'll assign the outside cells the class names topLeft, top, topRight, left, right, bottomLeft, bottom, and bottomRight. You'll give the inside cell the class name boxContent.

To add class values to the table cells:

1. Return to the **schedule.htm** file and add the class values **topLeft**, **top**, **topRight**, **left**, **right**, **bottomLeft**, **bottom**, and **bottomRight** to the eight outside table cells.
2. Add the class value **boxContent** to the center table cell. Figure 5-59 shows the class values in the roundedBox table.

Figure 5-59 Inserting the class attributes

```
<div id="right_col">
   <table class="roundedBox">
      <tr>
         <td class="topLeft"></td>
         <td class="top"></td>
         <td class="topRight"></td>
      </tr>
      <tr>
         <td class="left"></td>
         <td class="boxContent"></td>
         <td class="right"></td>
      </tr>
      <tr>
         <td class="bottomLeft"></td>
         <td class="bottom"></td>
         <td class="bottomRight"></td>
      </tr>
   </table>
</div>
```

3. Save your changes to the file.

Now that you've created the basic structure of the roundedBox table, you can start working on the design. Rounded boxes are useful elements of page design that Kyle will probably want to repeat throughout the KPAF Web site. So you'll insert the styles for the roundedBox table in an external style sheet named rounded.css.

To open the style sheet file and link it to the schedule file:

1. Use your text editor to open the **roundedtxt.css** file from the tutorial.05\tutorial folder included with your Data Files. Enter ***your name*** and ***the date*** in the comment section of the file. Save the file as **rounded.css**.
2. Return to the **schedule.htm** file in your text editor.
3. Directly above the closing </head> tag, insert the following link element:

```
<link href="rounded.css" rel="stylesheet" type="text/css" />
```

4. Save your changes to the file.

In a jigsaw layout, you don't want any seams to appear between the cells, so you have to collapse the table borders and set the cell padding to 0 pixels. For the KPAF Web site you also want to add space between the table and any surrounding page content, so you'll set the margin space around the table to 5 pixels.

To set the table styles:

1. Return to the **rounded.css** file in your text editor.
2. Add the following styles to the sheet, as shown in Figure 5-60:

```
table.roundedBox     {margin: 5px; border-collapse: collapse}
table.roundedBox td {padding: 0px}
```

Figure 5-60 Setting the table styles to control the spaces within the table

```
table.roundedBox     {margin: 5px; border-collapse: collapse}
table.roundedBox td {padding: 0px}
```

3. Save your changes to the file.

Next you must define the sizes of the eight cells that constitute the outer edges of the table. Because the box will vary in width and height depending on its content, the different cells need to be free to move in different directions. The left and right sides should expand in the vertical direction to accommodate the table content, while the top and bottom sides should expand horizontally. The four corner cells are fixed in size and should not expand or contract based on the table content. See Figure 5-61.

Figure 5-61 The outside table cells

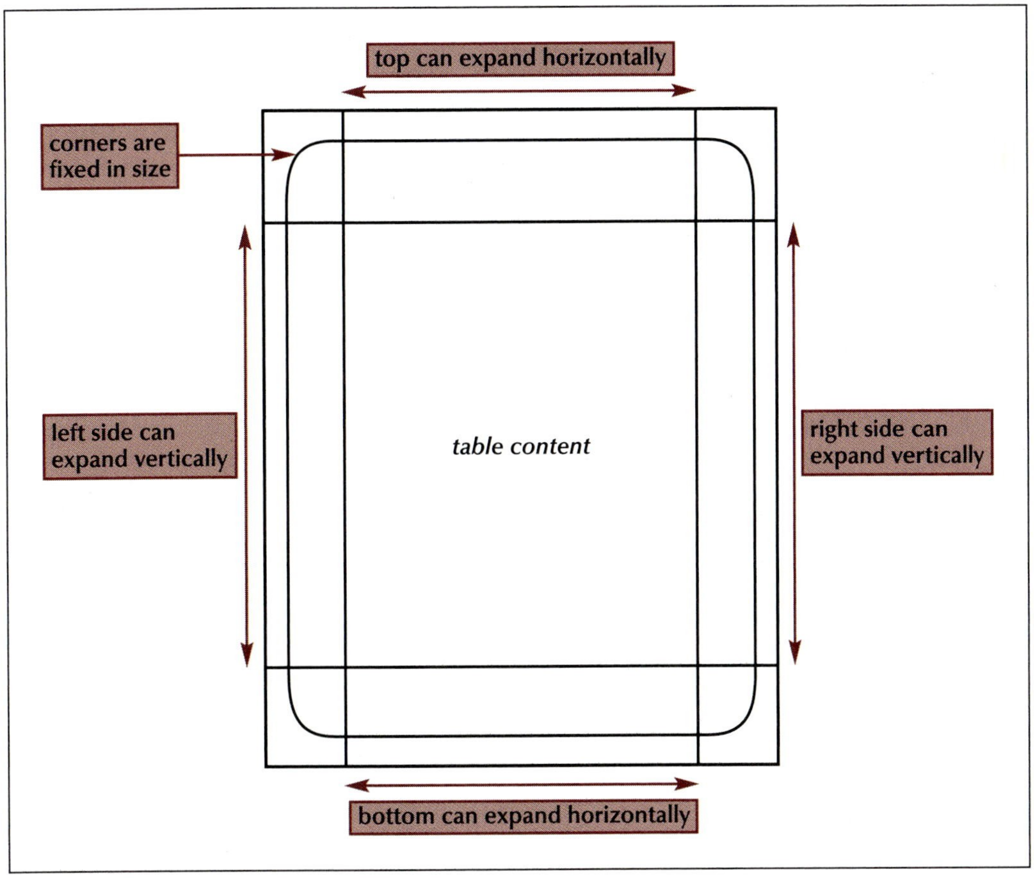

Each cell still must be large enough to display the border image files, which you'll add shortly. For example, the corner cells must be 16 pixels wide by 16 pixels high. The style for the top-left corner cell would therefore be:

```
table.roundedBox td.topLeft {width: 16px; height: 16px}
```

On the other hand, the top border is free to expand horizontally, but it must be tall enough to display the top border image. Its style would be:

```
table.roundedBox td.top {width: auto; height: 16px}
```

Remember that a width or height value of auto allows the browser to change the element to match the content. The other six border cells have similar width and height values. Add these styles to the rounded.css style sheet.

To set the dimensions of the outside cells:

1. To set the dimensions of the four corner cells, add the following styles to the bottom of the **rounded.css** style sheet:

```
table.roundedBox td.topLeft     {width: 16px; height: 16px}
table.roundedBox td.topRight    {width: 16px; height: 16px}
table.roundedBox td.bottomLeft  {width: 16px; height: 16px}
table.roundedBox td.bottomRight {width: 16px; height: 16px}
```

2. For the top and bottom cells, add the styles:

```
table.roundedBox td.top         {width: auto; height: 16px}
table.roundedBox td.bottom      {width: auto; height: 16px}
```

3. Finally, for the left and right cells, add the styles:

```
table.roundedBox td.left       {width: 16px; height: auto}
table.roundedBox td.right      {width: 16px; height: auto}
```

Figure 5-62 highlights the styles of the eight cells on the outside edge of the table.

Figure 5-62 Setting cell widths and heights

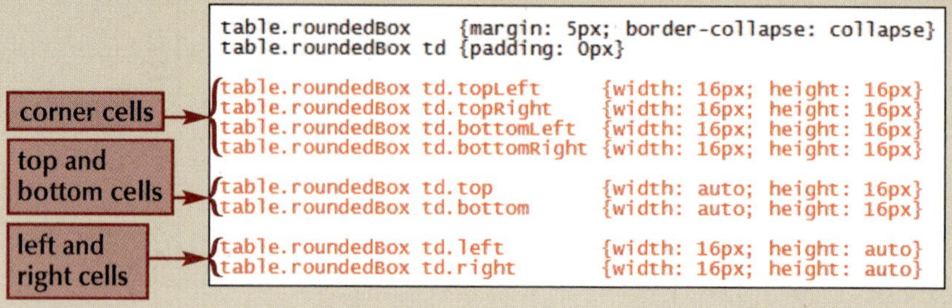

You won't set a width or height for the boxContent cell because that should expand to match whatever content you place inside.

Adding the Rounded Border

The last part of the jigsaw table is to put background images in the eight outside cells. Kyle has created eight separate files that cover the four corners and four sides of the box. The files—named topleft.png, top.png, topright.png, left.png, right.png, bottomleft.png, bottom.png, and bottomright.png—are shown in Figure 5-63.

Figure 5-63 The layout of the eight border images

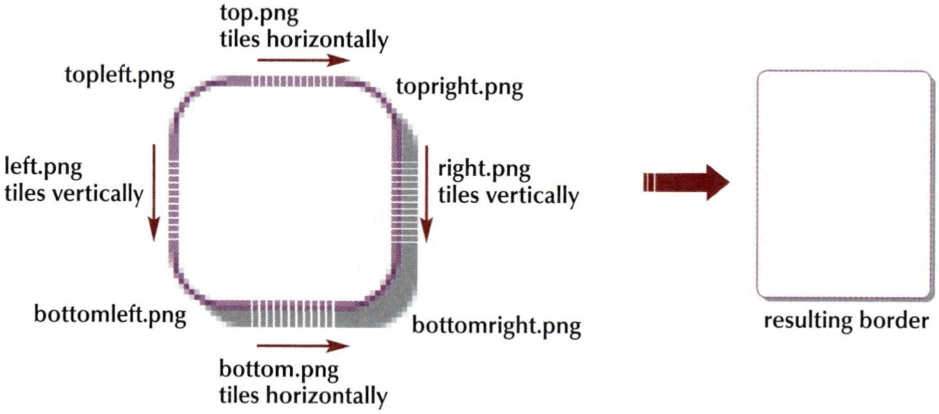

Each background image is tiled in a different way. The left and right images are tiled only in the vertical direction, filling up the entire background of the left and right cells. The top and bottom images are tiled horizontally, filling up the backgrounds of the top and bottom cells. Finally, the corner cells do no tiling, remaining fixed.

So to set the background of the top-left corner cell, you would use the following background style:

```
.topLeft {background: url(topleft.png) no-repeat top left}
```

Note that this style places the topleft.png image without tiling and fixes it in the top-left corner of the cell (if you're unclear about the background style, review the material on background styles from Tutorial 3). The style for the top border would appear as:

```
.top {background: url(top.png) repeat-x top}
```

Here the background image starts at the top of the cell and tiles in the x or horizontal direction only. The style for the left border would appear as

```
.left {background: url(left.png) repeat-y left}
```

with the tiling done only in the y or vertical direction.

Notice this style is applied to any element belonging to the topLeft, top, or left classes. This is not an accident. Later in this session, you'll reuse these background image styles, applying them to page elements other than table cells.

Add these styles to the rounded.css style sheet to insert and tile the eight background images for the roundedBox table.

Tip

If you have an object with a fixed width and height, you can create a rounded border with a single background image. If the object can vary in size, break the border graphic into separate pieces in a jigsaw layout.

To add the table background images to the style sheet:

1. Go to the bottom of the **rounded.css** style sheet and add the following styles to set the background images for the four corner cells:

```
.topLeft {background: url(topleft.png) no-repeat top left}
.topRight {background: url(topright.png) no-repeat top right}
.bottomLeft {background: url(bottomleft.png) no-repeat bottom left}
.bottomRight {background url(bottomright.png) no-repeat bottom
right}
```

2. Add the styles for the top and bottom cell backgrounds:

```
.top {background: url(top.png) repeat-x top}
.bottom {background: url(bottom.png) repeat-x bottom}
```

3. Finally add the background images for the left and right cells:

```
.left {background: url(left.png) repeat-y left}
.right {background: url(right.png) repeat-y right}
```

Figure 5-64 shows the newly inserted style code.

Setting the background images for the eight corners **Figure 5-64**

```
table.roundedBox    {margin: 5px; border-collapse: collapse}
table.roundedBox td {padding: 0px}

table.roundedBox td.topLeft     {width: 16px; height: 16px}
table.roundedBox td.topRight    {width: 16px; height: 16px}
table.roundedBox td.bottomLeft  {width: 16px; height: 16px}
table.roundedBox td.bottomRight {width: 16px; height: 16px}

table.roundedBox td.top         {width: auto; height: 16px}
table.roundedBox td.bottom      {width: auto; height: 16px}

table.roundedBox td.left        {width: 16px; height: auto}
table.roundedBox td.right       {width: 16px; height: auto}

.topLeft     {background: url(topleft.png) no-repeat top left}
.topRight    {background: url(topright.png) no-repeat top right}
.bottomLeft  {background: url(bottomleft.png) no-repeat bottom left}
.bottomRight {background: url(bottomright.png) no-repeat bottom right}

.top         {background: url(top.png) repeat-x top}
.bottom      {background: url(bottom.png) repeat-x bottom}

.left        {background: url(left.png) repeat-y left}
.right       {background: url(right.png) repeat-y right}
```

corners

top and bottom sides

left and right sides

4. Save your changes to the file.

Adding the Box Content

Now that you've created the styles that define the size and backgrounds of the eight outside cells, you can enter sample text into the roundedBox table. You'll test your styles by first inserting some simple text to verify that you have not made any errors in entering the table tags or CSS styles.

To enter sample text into the box:

1. Return to the **schedule.htm** file in your text editor.
2. Locate the center cell in the roundedBox table and insert the following text, as shown in Figure 5-65.

   `Coming Up on KPAF`

Figure 5-65 **Inserting the sample text**

```
      <address>
         KPAF &#183;
         4300 Magnolia Lane &#183;
         Bismarck, ND 58504 &#183;
         (701) 555 - 5611
      </address>
   </div>

      <div id="right_col">
         <table class="roundedBox">
            <tr>
               <td class="topLeft"></td>
               <td class="top"></td>
               <td class="topRight"></td>
            </tr>
            <tr>
               <td class="left"></td>
               <td class="boxContent">Coming Up on KPAF</td>
               <td class="right"></td>
            </tr>
            <tr>
               <td class="bottomLeft"></td>
               <td class="bottom"></td>
               <td class="bottomRight"></td>
            </tr>
         </table>
      </div>

</body>
```

3. Save your changes to the file, and then reload **schedule.htm** in your Web browser. As shown in Figure 5-66, the sample text is displayed within a rounded box that is tightly fit to the text.

Figure 5-66 **Sample text placed in a rounded box**

Trouble? If your box does not resemble the box shown in Figure 5-66, check your style sheet code against the code shown in Figure 5-64. Make sure you have separated all of the style values with semicolons, that you have entered all of the background image file names correctly, and that you have the images correctly tiled.

The advantage of the table design you've created is that it's flexible and will expand to match the content you place in the center cell.

You've tested your code against the sample text; now you can replace that text with the complete list of upcoming KPAF programs. Kyle has already written HTML code listing upcoming KPAF programs and has created a style sheet for that list. You can copy and paste that code directly into the rounded box table and then link the page to Kyle's style sheet.

To insert the descriptions of upcoming programs at KPAF:

1. In your text editor, open the **newshows.txt** file from the tutorial.05\tutorial folder included with your Data Files.
2. Copy all of the HTML code describing upcoming KPAF programs.
3. Return to the **schedule.htm** file in your text editor and scroll down to the bottom of the file.
4. Paste the copied HTML code into the center table cell, replacing the sample text you just entered (you might want to insert a line break into your text file to make the new code easier to read). Figure 5-67 shows the newly inserted code.

Figure 5-67 Inserting the text of the upcoming KPAF programs

```
<td class="boxContent">
<h1 class="newshows">Coming Up on KPAF</h1>

<ul class="newshows">
   <li>
      <h2 class="newshows">April 11 - 14</h2>
      <h3 class="newshows">The Classical Music Connection</h3>
      <p>Peter Thiesen shares his eclectic
         selections from the world of classical
         music.</p>
   </li>
   <li>
      <h2 class="newshows">April 11</h2>
      <h3 class="newshows">Opera Fest</h3>
      <p>Excerpts from <i>Turandot</i> by Giacomo Puccini.</p>
   </li>
   <li>
      <h2 class="newshows">April 12</h2>
      <h3 class="newshows">Radio U</h3>
      <p>Novelist Karen Graves reads from her latest
         work, <i>Hellion of Troy</i>.</p>
   </li>
   <li>
      <h2 class="newshows">April 13</h2>
      <h3 class="newshows">Science Week</h3>
      <p>Prof. Thomas Glass from UND discusses
         <i>String Theory and Spooky Action at a Distance</i>.</p>
   </li>
   <li>
      <h2 class="newshows">April 14</h2>
      <h3 class="newshows">The Living World</h3>
      <p>A panel discussion on
          the <i>Return of the Electric Car</i> and the latest
          in eco-news.</p>
   </li>
</ul>
</td>
```

Styles for the list of upcoming shows are contained in the newshows.css style sheet that Kyle created. You need to add a link to this style sheet to the schedule.htm file.

5. Scroll to the top of the file. Directly above the closing </head> tag, insert the following link element:

```
<link href="newshows.css" rel="stylesheet" type="text/css" />
```

6. Save your changes to the file, and then reload **schedule.htm** in your Web browser. As shown in Figure 5-68, the list of upcoming KPAF programs is presented in a box with rounded corners.

Figure 5-68 The upcoming programs sidebar

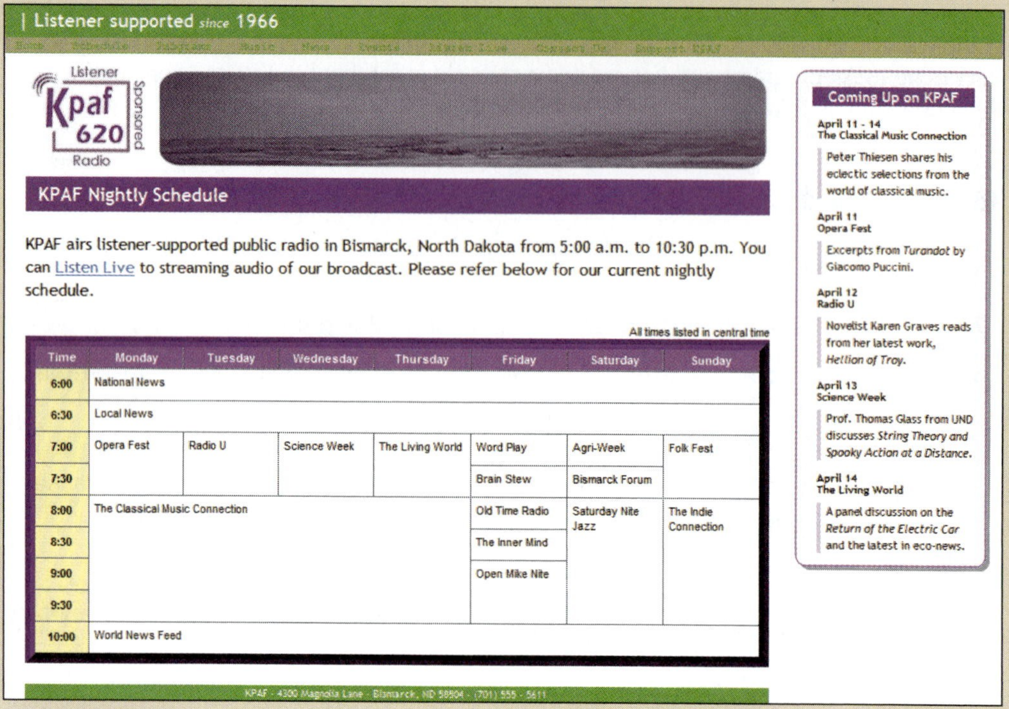

As you expected, the box expanded to fit the contents of the program list without showing any seams in the rounded border. Kyle is happy to know that this design can be easily adapted to any page content and complements you on your work.

Kyle wonders whether you should use Web tables to design other parts of his Web site. He asks you which is better for doing page layout: div containers or Web tables? You'll explore this question next.

Exploring the Controversy over Table Layouts

Using Web tables for page layout predates the introduction of CSS, and for many years the technique was one of the essential tools of the Web page designer. However, this changed with the introduction of CSS, which held the promise of simplifying the process of Web page design. But browser support for CSS was scattered and inconsistent at first, so many designers were reluctant to give up their Web table layouts. Then as more browsers began to support CSS and in particular the CSS positioning styles, Web designers began to advise against using Web tables for page layout—arguing that tables should be reserved for strictly tabular data, such as the KPAF program schedule. There are several good reasons for this:

- **Table layouts are not in the spirit of HTML**. A basic philosophy of Web page design is that the HTML code should indicate the structure of the document, but not how it should be rendered by the browser. Tables take control of layout from style sheets, putting page design back into the HTML file.

- **Table layouts are difficult to revise.** Imagine a complex table layout consisting of two columns with several levels of additional tables nested within each column. Now imagine having to revise that table structure, changing it into a three-column layout. This would not be an easy task because the page content is intertwined with the page layout. Now further imagine the difficulty of having to repeat that design change for dozens of pages across a large Web site. On the other hand, a layout created with a properly designed style sheet is much easier to maintain and revise because it is separate from the page content.
- **Tables take longer to render.** Unless the size of every element in the table is specified, the browser needs to first load the table content and then run an algorithm to determine how to size each element of the table. This can be time-consuming for a large, complex table that involves many cells and nested elements.
- **Tables can be code-heavy.** Creating a visually striking table layout often requires several table cells, rows, and columns, and some nested tables. This is particularly true if you create a jigsaw layout. Therefore, the ratio of HTML code to actual page content becomes more heavily weighted toward the HTML code, resulting in a longer file that takes longer to load and that can be difficult to interpret by people who need to edit the underlying code.
- **Tables can be inaccessible to users with disabilities.** People who use an aural or Braille browser to access a Web page formatted with a table layout can find it difficult to interpret the page content. The problem is that screen readers and speech output browsers read the HTML source code line-by-line in a linear direction, but tables sometimes convey information in several different directions. Figure 5-69 shows how a table whose content is quite clear visually becomes jumbled when presented aurally. This example shows the problems associated with a simple 3x3 table; comprehending a truly complex table layout with several levels of nested tables might be insurmountable to the visually impaired. On the other hand, an aural style sheet could be written that would more easily convey this information.

Figure 5-69 **Aural browsers and tables**

```
<table>
   <tr>
      <th>Time</th>
      <th>Thursday</th>
      <th>Friday</th>
   </tr>
   <tr>
      <th>7:00</th>
      <th>colspan="2">The Living World</th>
      <th>World Play</th>
   </tr>
   <tr>
        <th>7:30</th>
        <th>Brain Stew</th>
   </tr>
   </table>
```

HTML table code

Time	Thursday	Friday
7:00	The Living World	Word Play
7:30		Brain Stew

table displayed visually

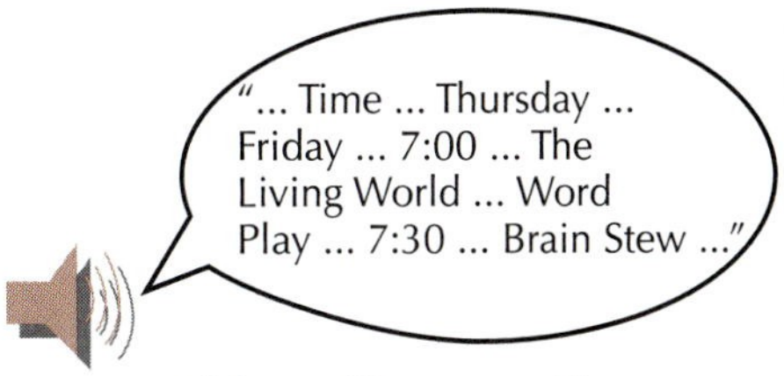

table read by an aural browser doesn't clearly convey the table contents

With the current strong browser support for CSS, there is less reason to use tables for page layout. In fact, the jigsaw layout shown earlier in Figure 5-56 could also be done using div containers positioned on the Web page with CSS. However, Web table layouts will not disappear immediately, so Web page designers must be conversant with both approaches, especially if they are called upon to support older browser versions or have the task of maintaining the code of an older Web site.

Creating a Rounded Box Using div Containers

You tell Kyle what you've learned about the controversy over Web table layouts and he agrees that the KPAF Web site should limit the use of tables to strictly tabular information. Kyle wants to add another rounded box to the schedule page, one that displays the name and description of the program currently running on KPAF. He understands your concern about using table layouts and asks whether you can create the same rounded box design using only div containers and CSS styles. As with your work on the table layout, whatever you create must be flexible enough to accommodate content of any size.

After researching the issue on the Internet, you discover there are actually hundreds of techniques that Web designers have developed over the years to create rounded borders without using tables. You decide to use one that was introduced by the Web designer Tedd Sperling (*www.sperling.com*).

Nesting div Containers

The basic idea of Tedd Sperling's approach is to nest several levels of div elements within one another. Since the div elements have no padding and no margin spaces, they will be completely superimposed upon one another—creating a stack of div elements that all occupy the same space on the Web page. Because they're stacked on top of each other, when these div elements are displayed by the browser, any background image from an element lower in the stack will be visible as long as it is not obstructed by another background image higher in the stack. Figure 5-70 shows how eight different background images from eight nested div elements would appear as a single curved border when rendered by the browser.

Figure 5-70 **Creating a rounded border using nested div elements**

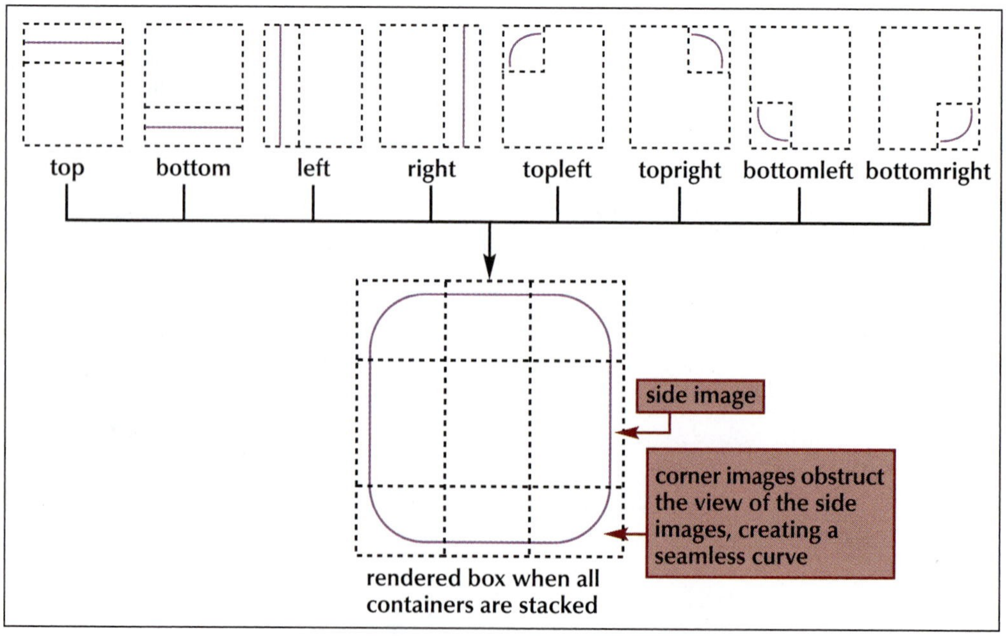

Notice that the corner images obstruct the view of the side images, so that it appears as one seamless curve around the content. To create this effect in HTML, you can nest these eight div elements

```
<div class="top"><div class="bottom">
<div class="left"><div class="right">
<div class="topLeft"><div class="topRight">
<div class="bottomLeft"><div class="bottomRight">
   <div class="boxContent">
      content
   </div>
</div></div></div></div>
</div></div></div></div>
```

where *content* is the page content you would surrounded by the rounded border. The order of the div elements is important. The corner borders must be on top of the stack because they connect the side borders, and so you list the top, bottom, left, and right sides first. The div elements for the corners (topleft, topright, bottomleft, and bottomright) are nested within them. When the browser renders these elements, it starts from the outside and moves in. The corners are therefore displayed last, appearing on top of the side borders.

Add this basic structure of nested div elements to the schedule.htm page.

To insert the div containers:

1. Return to the **schedule.htm** file in your text editor.
2. Scroll down to the bottom of the file and directly after the opening tag

```
<div id="right_col">
```

insert the following code as shown in Figure 5-71:

```
<div class="roundedBox">
   <div class="top"><div class="bottom">
   <div class="left"><div class="right">
   <div class="topLeft"><div class="topRight">
   <div class="bottomLeft"><div class="bottomRight">

      <div class="boxContent">
      </div>

   </div></div></div></div>
   </div></div></div></div>
</div>
```

Creating a set of nested div elements — **Figure 5-71**

```
<div id="right_col">

   <div class="roundedBox">
      <div class="top"><div class="bottom">
      <div class="left"><div class="right">
      <div class="topLeft"><div class="topRight">
      <div class="bottomLeft"><div class="bottomRight">

      <div class="boxContent">
      </div>

      </div></div></div></div>
      </div></div></div></div>
   </div>

   <table class="roundedBox">
      <tr>
         <td class="topLeft"></td>
         <td class="top"></td>
         <td class="topRight"></td>
      </tr>
```

3. Save your changes to the file.

You might have noticed that you repeated the same class names used earlier in Figure 5-58. That's no accident—the eight div elements fulfill the same role of creating the rounded border as the eight table cells did in the table layout. Also, because you assigned background images to any element belonging to the topLeft, topRight, and so forth classes, these div elements will have the same background images as the table cells did in the roundedBox table. The only thing you must add to this set of div elements is a style to place a 5-pixel margin around the roundedBox and 16 pixels of padding space to the boxContent element. Finally, because of how Internet Explorer treats nested div elements, you'll place the box using relative positioning to ensure that all of the nested div elements line up properly in that browser. Add these styles to the rounded.css file.

To define the style for the box and its contents:

1. Return to the **rounded.css** file and insert the following style to define the appearance of the containing box:

```
div.roundedBox {margin: 5px; position: relative}
```

2. Add the following style to set the display properties of the box's content:

```
div.boxContent {padding: 16px}
```

Figure 5-72 shows the final style definitions for the rounded box style sheet.

Figure 5-72 **Defining the styles for the box contents**

```
.topLeft     {background: url(topleft.png) no-repeat top left}
.topRight    {background: url(topright.png) no-repeat top right}
.bottomLeft  {background: url(bottomleft.png) no-repeat bottom left}
.bottomRight {background: url(bottomright.png) no-repeat bottom right}

.top         {background: url(top.png) repeat-x top}
.bottom      {background: url(bottom.png) repeat-x bottom}

.left        {background: url(left.png) repeat-y left}
.right       {background: url(right.png) repeat-y right}

div.roundedBox {margin: 5px; position: relative}
div.boxContent {padding: 16px}
```

3. Close the **rounded.css** file, saving your changes.
4. Reload the **schedule.htm** file in your Web browser. The page should now show an empty rounded box directly above the list of upcoming programs.

   Kyle asks that you add text to this box describing the program currently airing on KPAF.

5. Return to the **schedule.htm** file in your text editor and insert the following code within the boxContent div element as shown in Figure 5-73:

```
<h1 class="newshows">On the Air Now</h1>
<h2 class="newshows">Folk Fest</h2>
<p class="newshows">Featuring the best of traditional and
        contemporary folk music</p>
```

Figure 5-73 Adding text for the current program

```
<div class="roundedBox">
   <div class="top"><div class="bottom">
   <div class="left"><div class="right">
   <div class="topLeft"><div class="topRight">
   <div class="bottomLeft"><div class="bottomRight">

   <div class="boxContent">
      <h1 class="newshows">On the Air Now</h1>
      <h2 class="newshows">Folk Fest</h2>
      <p  class="newshows">Featuring the best of traditional
          and contemporary folk music</p>
   </div>

   </div></div></div></div>
   </div></div></div></div>
</div>
```

6. Save your changes to the file, and then reload **schedule.htm** in your Web browser. As shown in Figure 5-74, the name of the program currently airing on KPAF is shown in a rounded box at the top of the page.

Figure 5-74 The final KPAF nightly schedule page

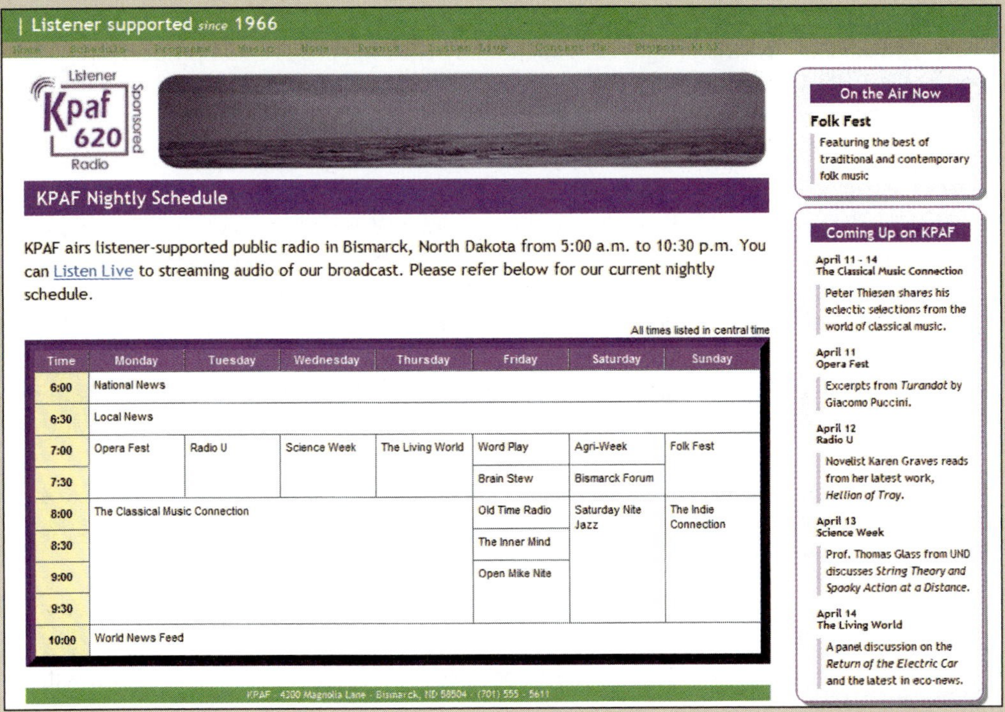

Trouble? If your rounded box does not resemble that shown in Figure 5-74, check your style code against that shown in Figure 5-72 and Figure 5-73. Common errors include misspelling class names, forgetting to separate style properties with semicolons, neglecting to close style declarations with right curly braces, and misspelling the names of style properties.

7. You can close any open files or programs now.

Kyle will talk to the KPAF programmers to write code that will automatically insert the name of the currently airing program into the rounded box you created, but for now this gives him a good idea of how the page will look to KPAF listeners.

InSight | Rounded Boxes and CSS3

The Web is a competitive environment in which designers are always looking for ways to make their pages stand out. One way is with specialized design elements like the rounded box you created in this session. Such designs can be challenging the first few times. One reason is that CSS 2.1 allows only one background image per element, so you have to "trick" browsers into displaying several images at once. How much easier the task would be if you could place multiple background images that automatically resized with the element!

This is starting to change with the introduction and adoption of CSS3 styles. In CSS3, you can define multiple backgrounds by entering them in a comma-separated list for the background-image style. The syntax is

```
background image: url(image1), url(image2), ...
```

where *image1*, *image2*, and so forth are the image files you want displayed as a background for the element. To position the images, you once again enter a comma-separated list of position values matching the background image. For example, the style

```
background-position: top left, center left
```

places the first background image in the top-left corner of the element and the second image on the center-left edge. As you increase the number of background images, you add more background-position values, one for each image.

Finally, you specify how the images are repeated by entering each repeat property in another list. The style

```
background-repeat: no-repeat, repeat-y
```

fixes the first background image in place and tiles the second image in the vertical direction.

You can see from these styles that what would require a Web table or several nested div elements can be accomplished in CSS3 with one element and a style sheet. CSS3 will also introduce styles to allow for more decorative borders, including rounded borders. To create a rounded border, you will be able to apply the style

```
border-radius: value
```

where *value* defines the curvature of the rounded corners of the border. This style has scattered browser support at the moment, though Firefox does support the following equivalent style:

```
-moz-border-radius: value
```

CSS3 is still in the development stage, so you cannot rely on it yet for designing Web sites. However, as these and other CSS3 styles are finalized and adopted by the browser market, designers will explore new possibilities for their Web sites.

You've completed your work on the design of the KPAF nightly schedule page. Kyle will discuss your final version with other people at the station and get back to you with future projects.

Review | Session 5.3 Quick Check

1. What is a jigsaw layout?
2. You are creating a table structure for a table that will be used to develop a jigsaw layout. One of the cells in the table with the id midCell needs to have a height of 20 pixels, but the width can be calculated by the browser. Specify a style to apply to the midCell table cell.
3. Why are tables especially challenging for the visually impaired?
4. You want to use the image tlcorner.jpg as the top-left background corner image for a div element with the id mainLogo. What style would you enter?

5. A div element with the id name subLogo needs to use a background image for the left side border. The div element could be any height, so the image will need to tile vertically down the element. The image comes from the file lborder.jpg. Specify a style to apply this image to the element's background.
6. You want to use an image file named bborder.jpg as the bottom border for the div element mainContent. The width of the mainContent element can vary freely, so the image file will need to tile horizontally across the element. Specify the style you would use.
7. An old Web page uses a table with one row and two columns to create a two-column layout. The Web site manager wants to move away from using table layouts. Suggest two ways of creating a two-column layout without tables.

Tutorial Summary | Review

In this tutorial you learned how to create and design Web tables, and you explored the issues surrounding using tables for page layout. The first session introduced the basic structure of the Web table. You learned how to define table rows, table cells, row groups, column groups, and captions. The session also explored how to create cells that span multiple rows and columns. The session concluded by introducing the summary attribute as a way of making table content accessible in nonvisual browsers. The second session explored how to format a table's appearance. The first half of the session looked at various HTML attributes that have long been used to format tables. The second half of the session concentrated on the CSS styles that can be applied to tables. The session ended by showing how to use CSS to make almost any page element appear as a table. The third session looked at the special topic of creating page boxes with rounded borders. The first method examined was the use of a Web table to lay out the graphical borders of the box. The second method explored how to do the same thing with nested div elements. The third session discussed the advantages and disadvantages of using tables for page layout and examined the prevalence of table-based designs on the Web today.

Key Terms

cell padding
cell spacing
column group
jigsaw layout
monospace font
preformatted text
row group
spanning cell
table data cell
table frame
table heading
table rule

Practice | Review Assignments

Practice the skills you learned in the tutorial using the same case scenario.

Data Files needed for the Review Assignments: kpaf.css, kpaf.jpg, left.jpg, morningtxt.htm, programstxt.css, right.jpg, topleft.jpg, and topright.jpg

Kyle has had a chance to work with the KPAF nightly schedule page. He wants you to make a few changes to the layout and apply the new design to a page that displays the KPAF morning schedule. Kyle has already entered much of the Web page content and style. He wants you to complete his work by creating the Web table with the morning schedule. He wants you to add some rounded and shaped corners to the table to make it stand out more on the page. Figure 5-75 shows a preview of the table you'll create for Kyle.

Figure 5-75

Complete the following:

1. Use your text editor to open the **morningtxt.htm** and **programstxt.css** files from the tutorial.05\review folder included with your Data Files. Enter ***your name*** and ***the date*** in the comment section of each file. Save the files as **morning.htm** and **programs.css**, respectively, in the same folder.
2. Go to the **morning.htm** file in your text editor. Insert a link to the **programs.css** style sheet.

3. Scroll down the file and directly below the paragraph element, insert a Web table with the class name programs.
4. Add a caption containing the text "All times central".
5. Below the caption, create a column group containing three columns. The first column element should have the class name timeColumn. The second column element should have the class name daysColumn and span six columns in the table. The last column element should have the class name lastColumn.
6. Insert the following summary for the table: "Lists the morning programs aired by KPAF from 5:00 a.m. to 12:00 p.m. (central time)".
7. Add the table header row group containing the headings shown in Figure 5-75.
8. Enter the tbody row group containing the times and names of the different KPAF programs from 5:00 a.m. to 12:00 p.m., Monday through Sunday, in half-hour intervals. Create row- and column-spanning cells to match the layout of the days and times shown in Figure 5-75.
9. Assign the cell in the top-left corner of the table the id name topLeft. Assign the cell in the top-right corner the id name topRight.
10. Close the **morning.htm** file, saving your changes.
11. Go to the **programs.css** file in your text editor. Create the following styles for the programs table:
    - Set the width of the table to 100%.
    - Display the table text according to the following list of fonts: Trebuchet MS, Arial, Verdana, and sans-serif.
    - Set the table borders to collapse.
12. Align the table caption with the bottom-right border of the table. Set the caption font size to 0.8 em.
13. Add the following styles for the table cells:
    - Set all table cells to a font size of 0.7 em.
    - Vertically align the text of all table data cells with the top of the cell.
    - Add a 1-pixel solid gray border to the left and bottom of every table data cell.
    - Add a 1-pixel solid gray border to the bottom of every table header cell.
14. Set the height of all table rows to 25 pixels.
15. Display the header row group in white font with a background color of (105, 177, 60).
16. Add the following styles for the three column types in the table:
    - Set the width of the timeColumn to 7%. Change the background color to the value (215, 205, 151). Add the background image file **left.jpg** to the column, repeated vertically and set against the left border of the column.
    - Set the width of the columns in the dayColumns group to 13%.
    - Set the width of the lastColumn column to 13%. Set the background color to white and add the background image file **right.jpg**, tiled vertically and set against the right border of the column.
17. For the table cell with the id topLeft, set the background color to the value (105, 177, 60) and add the background image file **topleft.jpg** set against the top-left corner of the cell. Do not tile the background image.
18. For the table cell with id topRight, set the background color also to the value (105, 177, 60) and add the background image file **topright.jpg**. Set the background image against the top-right border of the cell and do not tile the image.
19. Save your changes to the **programs.css** file.

20. Open the **morning.htm** file in your Web browser and verify that the table layout and design resembles that shown in Figure 5-75. (Note: If you are using Internet Explorer, you might see the caption aligned with the top-right corner of the table rather than the bottom-right.)
21. Submit your completed files to your instructor.

Apply | Case Problem 1

Apply your knowledge of Web tables and table styles to create a puzzle page.

Data Files needed for this Case Problem: gold.jpg, green.jpg, jpf.jpg, jpftxt.css, left.jpg, stabletxt.css, sudokutxt.htm, topleft.jpg, and topright.jpg

The Japanese Puzzle Factory Rebecca Peretz has a passion for riddles and puzzles. Her favorites are the Japanese logic puzzles that have become very popular in recent years. Rebecca and a few of her friends have begun work on a new Web site called The Japanese Puzzle Factory (JPF), where they plan to create and distribute Japanese-style puzzles. Eventually the JPF Web site will include interactive programs to enable users to solve the puzzles online, but for now Rebecca is interested only in the design and layout of the pages. You've been asked to help by creating a draft version of the Web page describing the Sudoku puzzle. Figure 5-76 shows a preview of the design and layout you'll create for Rebecca.

Figure 5-76

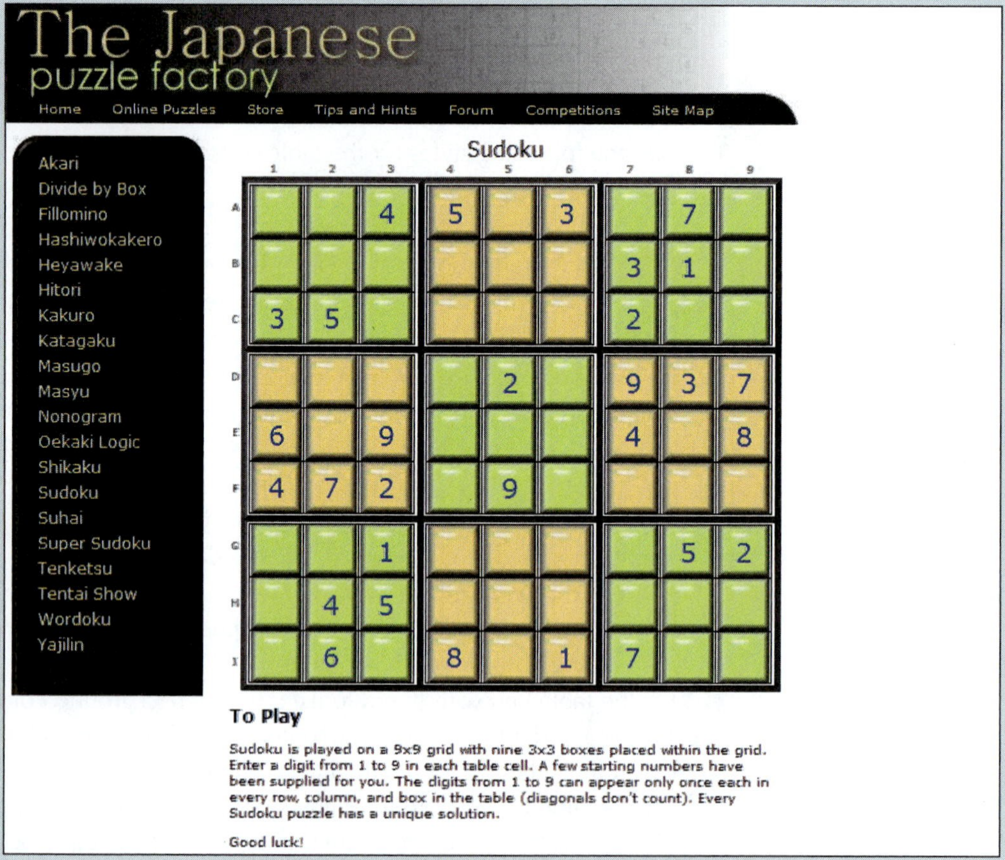

Rebecca has created some of the content and designs for this page. Your task is to complete the page by entering the code and styles for the Sudoku table as well as adding some background images to other sections of the page layout.

Complete the following:

1. Use your text editor to open the **jpftxt.css**, **stabletxt.css**, and **sudokutxt.htm** from the tutorial.05\case1 folder included with your Data Files. Enter ***your name*** and ***the date*** in the comment section of each file. Save the files as **jpf.css**, **stable.css**, and **sudoku.htm**, respectively, in the same folder.
2. Return to the **sudoku.htm** file in your text editor. Add a link to the **jpf.css** and **stable.css** style sheets.
3. Scroll down to the links div element. Rebecca wants the list of links to have rounded top corners and a shaded left corner. Mark the corner and sides by nesting the ul element within three div elements with class names of left, topLeft, and topRight.
4. Save your changes to the file, and then go to the **jpf.css** style sheet in your text editor. At the bottom of the style sheet, add the following styles:
   - For the div element belonging to the topLeft class, display the background image file **topleft.jpg** in the top-left corner of the element. Do not tile the image.
   - For the div element from the topRight class, display the background image file **topright.jpg** in the top-right corner without tiling.
   - For the div element from the left class, display the **left.jpg** background image file placed on the left border of the element and tiled in the vertical direction only.
5. Save your changes to the file, and then display the **sudoku.htm** file in your Web browser. Verify that the list of Japanese puzzles on the left margin of the page is displayed with rounded top corners and a shaded left border.
6. Return to the **sudoku.htm** file in your text editor. Scroll down to the rightColumn div element. Directly below the opening <div> tag, insert a table element that will be used to display the Sudoku puzzle. Give the table element the class name spuzzle.
7. Add a caption to the spuzzle table containing the text Sudoku.
8. Create a table head row group containing a single row. The row should display 10 heading cells. The first heading cell should be blank and the remaining nine cells should display the digits from 1 to 9.
9. Create the table body row group. The tbody should contain the following structure:
   - There are nine rows in the tbody.
   - The first cell in each row should contain a table heading cell displaying the letters A through I.
   - Starting with the first row, every third row should contain three table data cells with each cell spanning three rows and three columns. All together, these table cells will store the nine 3x3 boxes that are part of the Sudoku puzzle.
   - In the first row, put the three table data cells in the greenBox, goldBox, and greenBox classes, respectively. In the fourth row, the three data cells belong to the goldBox, greenBox, and goldBox classes. In the seventh row, the three data cells belong to the greenBox, goldBox, and greenBox classes.

EXPLORE

10. Go to each of the nine table data cells you created in the last step. Within each data cell, insert a nested table belonging to the subTable class. Within each nested table, insert three rows and three columns of data cells. Enter the digits from Figure 5-76 in the appropriate table cells. Where there is no digit, leave the table cell empty.
11. Save your changes to the file, and then go to the **stable.css** file in your text editor.
12. Collapse the borders of the spuzzle and subTable tables.

13. Add a 5-pixel outset gray border to the data cells within the spuzzle table. Set the font size of header cells within the spuzzle table to 8 pixels and the font color to gray. Set the height of header cells within the body row group of the spuzzle table to 40 pixels.
14. For data cells within the subTable table, add the following styles:
    - Set the font size to 20 pixels and the font color to blue.
    - Set the width and height to 40 pixels and center the cell text both horizontally and vertically.
    - Add a 1-pixel solid black border around the cell.
15. For table cells nested within the goldBox class of table cells, apply the background image file gold.jpg centered within the cell and not tiled (*Hint*: Use background position values of 50% for both the horizontal and vertical directions.) For cells nested within the greenBox class of table cells, set the background image to the green.jpg file, once again centered within the cell without tiling.
16. Save your changes to the file and then reload **sudoku.htm** in your Web browser. Verify that the layout and design of the Sudoku table resembles that shown in Figure 5-76.
17. Submit your completed files to your instructor.

Apply | Case Problem 2

Create a calendar table for a community civic center.

Data Files needed for this Case Problem: bottom.jpg, bottomleft.jpg, bottomright.jpg, caltxt.css, ccc.jpg, ccctxt.css, febtxt.htm, left.jpg, right.jpg, tab.jpg, top.jpg, topleft.jpg, and topright.jpg

The Chamberlain Civic Center Lewis Kern is an events manager at the Chamberlain Civic Center in Chamberlain, South Dakota. The center is in the process of updating its Web site and Lewis has asked you to work on the pages detailing events in the upcoming year. He's asked you to create a calendar page for the month of February. Lewis wants the page design to catch the reader's eye and so he suggests that you create a Web table with a background showing a spiral binding. The spiral binding graphic must be flexible to accommodate calendars of different sizes, so you'll build the borders for this image by nesting the February calendar table within eight div elements. The February calendar must list the following events:

- Every Sunday, the Carson Quartet plays at 1:00 p.m. ($8)
- February 1, 8:00 p.m.: Taiwan Acrobats ($16/$24/$36)
- February 5, 8:00 p.m.: Joey Gallway ($16/$24/$36)
- February 7-8, 7:00 p.m.: West Side Story ($24/$36/$64)
- February 10, 8:00 p.m.: Jazz Masters ($18/$24/$32)
- February 13, 8:00 p.m.: Harlem Choir ($18/$24/$32)
- February 14, 8:00 p.m.: Chamberlain Symphony ($18/$24/$32)
- February 15, 8:00 p.m.: Edwin Drood ($24/$36/$44)
- February 19, 8:00 p.m.: The Yearling ($8/$14/$18)
- February 21, 8:00 p.m.: An Ellington Tribute ($24/$32/$48)
- February 22, 8:00 p.m.: Othello ($18/$28/$42)
- February 25, 8:00 p.m.: Madtown Jugglers ($12/$16/$20)
- February 28, 8:00 p.m.: Ralph Williams ($32/$48/$64)

Lewis wants the weekend events (Friday and Saturday night) to be displayed with a light red background. A preview of the page you'll create is shown in Figure 5-77.

Figure 5-77

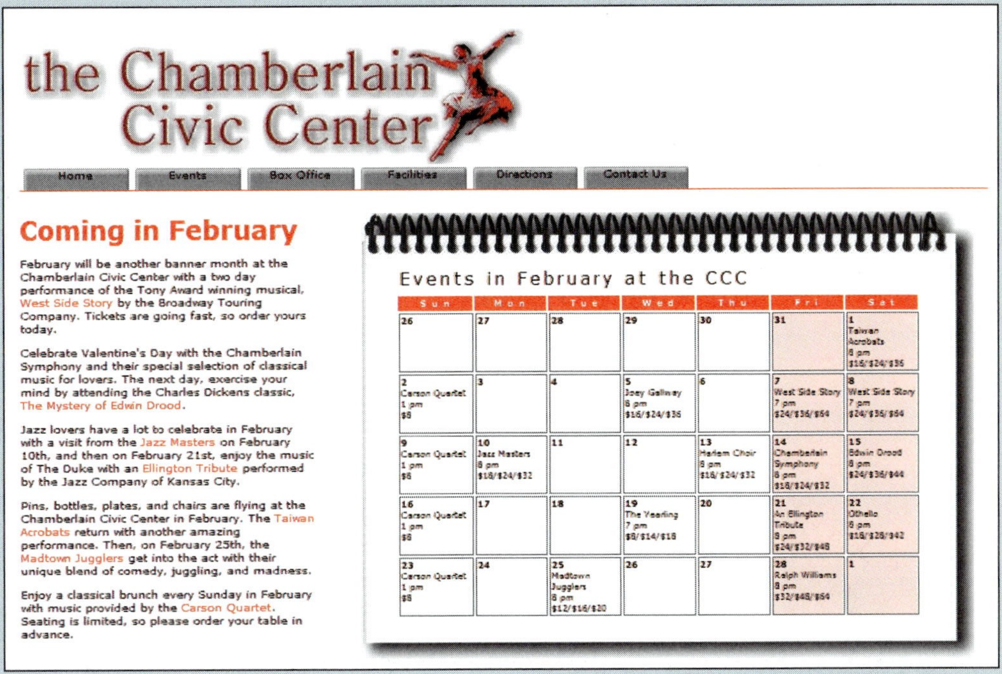

Complete the following:

1. Use your text editor to open the **caltxt.css**, **ccctxt.css**, and **febtxt.htm** from the tutorial.05\case2 folder included with your Data Files. Enter ***your name*** and ***the date*** in the comment section of each file. Save the files as **calendar.css**, **ccc.css**, and **feb.htm**, respectively, in the same folder.
2. Go to the **feb.htm** file in your text editor. Create links to the **calendar.css** and **ccc.css** style sheets.
3. Scroll down to the rightColumn div element. Within the div element, insert a table with the class name calendar. Add the caption "Events in February at the CCC" to the calendar.
4. Create a column group for the calendar consisting of two col elements. The first col element should belong to the weekdays class and span five columns. The second col element should belong to the weekends class and span two columns.
5. Create a table header row group consisting of one row of table headings displaying the three-letter abbreviations of the days of the week, starting with Sun and ending with Sat.
6. Create a table body row group containing the days in the month of February. The row group should contain five rows and seven columns of table data cells. There are no spanning cells in any of the rows or columns.
7. Each table data cell should have the following content:
   - The day of the month marked as an h3 heading (refer to Figure 5-77 for the starting and ending days in the calendar).
   - On the days in which there is a CCC event, enter the event information as a definition list with the name of the event marked as a dt element, and the time and price of the event each marked with dd elements.

8. Enclose the entire table within a set of nine nested div elements. The four outermost elements should have the ids tBorder, lBorder, rBorder, and bBorder. The next four innermost elements should have the ids tlCorner, trCorner, blCorner, and brCorner. The innermost div element should have the id boxContent.
9. Save your changes to the file, and then go to the **ccc.css** file in your text editor.
10. Apply the following background image styles to the eight div container elements:
    - For the tlCorner element, display the **topleft.jpg** image in the top-left corner of the element without tiling.
    - For the trCorner element, display the **topright.jpg** image in the top-right corner without tiling.
    - For the blCorner element, display the **bottomleft.jpg** image in the bottom-left corner without tiling.
    - For the brCorner element, display the **bottomright.jpg** image in the bottom-right corner without tiling.

EXPLORE

    - For the tBorder element, display the **top.jpg** image 39 pixels from the left edge aligned at the top border, tiling the image horizontally.
    - For the lBorder element, display the **left.jpg** image on the left border and tiled vertically.
    - For the rBorder element, display the **right.jpg** image on the right border and tiled vertically.
    - For the bBorder element, display the **bottom.jpg** image on the bottom border and tiled horizontally.
11. Set the padding space of the boxContent div element to 50 pixels.
12. Save your changes to the file, and then go to the **calendar.css** file in your text editor. Add the table styles described in the next steps to the style sheet.

EXPLORE

13. Display the borders of the table as separate borders with the space between the borders set to 5 pixels. Set the font size of the table text to 8 pixels.
14. Align the table caption with the top left of the calendar table. Set the font size of the caption to 16 pixels and the letter spacing to 3 pixels.
15. Set the width of the table columns to 14% of the width of the table. For columns belonging to the weekend class, change the background color to the value (255, 232, 232).
16. For table headings in the table header row group of the calendar table, set the background color to red, the font color to white, and the letter spacing to 5 pixels.
17. Set the height of the table row within the table header row group of the calendar table to 5%. Set the height of the table rows within the table body row group to 19% each.
18. Add a 1-pixel solid gray border to every table data cell within the calendar table. Set the vertical alignment of the cell content to the top of the cell.
19. Set the font size of h3 headings with the data table cells of the calendar table to 8 pixels and set the margin and padding spaces of the h3 headings to 0 pixels.
20. Set the margin and padding spaces of the definition list, definition descriptions, and definition terms within the tables to 0 pixels.
21. Save your changes to the file, and then open **feb.htm** in your Web browser. Verify that the layout and design of the page resemble that shown in Figure 5-77.
22. Submit your completed files to your instructor.

Challenge | Case Problem 3

Explore additional CSS table styles and image techniques by designing the home page for a manufacturer of geodesic domes.

Data Files needed for this Case Problem: blank.gif, bottom.jpg, bottomleft.jpg, bottomright.jpg, dhometxt.htm, dlogo.jpg, domepaper.css, dometxt.css, dtabletxt.css, left.jpg, leftbox.jpg, right.jpg, rightbox.jpg, tableback.jpg, top.jpg, topleft.jpg, and topright.jpg

dHome, Inc. Olivia Moore is the director of advertising for dHome, one of the nation's newest manufacturers of geodesic dome houses. She's hired you to work on the company's Web site. Olivia has provided you with all of the text you need for the Web page, and your job is to design the page's layout. You'll start by designing a draft of the company's home page. Olivia wants the page to include information about dHome's pricing structure for various dome models. The page should also contain links to other pages on the Web site. A preview of the design you'll create for Olivia is shown in Figure 5-78.

Figure 5-78

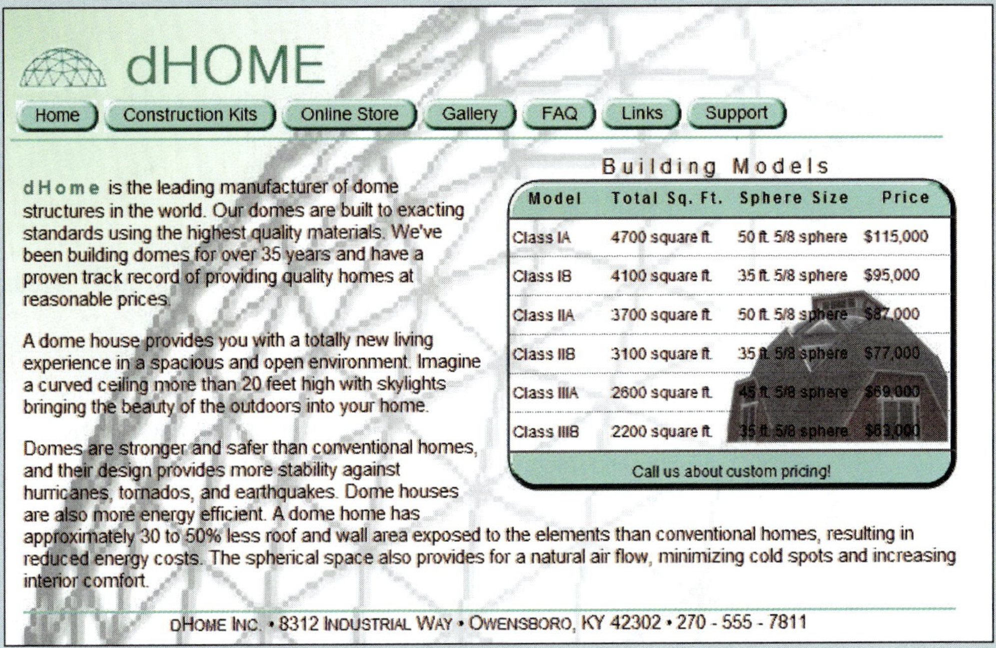

Complete the following:

1. Use your text editor to open **dhometxt.htm**, **dometxt.css**, and **dtabletxt.css** from the tutorial.05\case3 folder included with your Data Files. Enter ***your name*** and ***the date*** in the comment section of each file. Save the files as **dhome.htm**, **dome.css**, and **dtable.css**, respectively, in the same folder.
2. Go to the **dhome.htm** file in your text editor. Create links to the **dome.css** and **dtable.css** style sheets.
3. Scroll down to the pageContent div element, and above the paragraphs within that element, insert a table with the class name domeSpecs. Add the table summary, "A table describing six dome models sold by dHome, Inc." and add the caption, "Building Models".
4. Create a column group containing three col elements with class names of firstColumn, middleColumns, and lastColumn. The middleColumns element should span two columns in the table.

5. Create a table header row group containing a single table row with four table heading cells. The cells should contain the headings Model, Total Sq. Ft., Sphere Size, and Price. Mark the first cell with the id value topLeft and the last cell with the id value topRight.

EXPLORE

6. Insert a table footer row group containing a single row and three data cells. The first and third cells should be left blank. The middle cell should contain the text, "Call us about custom pricing!" and should span two columns. Mark the first cell with the id bottomleft and the last cell with the id bottomright.
7. Create the table body row group consisting of six table rows with four cells each. Insert the model, square feet, sphere size, and price values from Figure 5-78.
8. Save your changes to the **dhome.htm** file, and then go to the **dome.css** file in your text editor.
9. Many of the styles for the dHome Web page have been entered for you. Your job is to insert styles for the list of links. Make the following style changes to the unordered list within the links div element:
   - Remove the bullet marker.
   - Set the padding space to 0 pixels.
   - Set the top and left margins to 5 pixels and the right and bottom margins to 0 pixels.
10. Make the following style changes to the list elements:
    - Change the list items to inline objects, floating on the left margin.
    - Set the font size to 14 pixels and the right margin to 5 pixels.
    - Display the background image file **rightbox.jpg**, placed on the center of the right margin. Do not tile the image.
11. Make the following changes to hypertext links within list elements:
    - Display the hypertext links as block-level elements.
    - Set the font color to black and remove underlining from the links.
    - Set the top and bottom padding space to 10 pixels and the left and right padding spaces to 15 pixels.
    - Display the background image file **leftbox.jpg**, placed on the center of the left margin. Do not tile the image.
12. Change the font color of the hyperlinks within the list element to blue whenever the mouse pointer hovers over the link.
13. Save your changes to the file, and then load **dhome.htm** in your Web browser. Verify that the list of links is displayed in a single line below the dHome logo and that each link is enclosed within a rounded box of varying lengths.

EXPLORE

14. The technique used to create the rounded box behind the links is known as the *sliding door* technique. Open the **rightbox.jpg** and **leftbox.jpg** files in a graphics program and notice that the rightbox.jpg image file is extremely long compared to the text it lies behind. Why is the entire image not displayed? (Hint: Think about how the hypertext links are nested within list elements.) Look up the sliding door technique on the Web to learn more about this approach.
15. Go to **dtable.css** in your text editor. Create a style for the domeSpecs table that floats the table on the right border, sets the font size to 12 pixels, and sets the top and right margins to 0 pixels, the bottom margin to 10 pixels, and the left margin to 20 pixels. Collapse all the borders in the table.
16. Create a style for the caption, setting the font size to 16 pixels and the kerning to 5 pixels. Center the caption horizontally above the table.

17. Set the width of the first and last columns to 22% of the width of the table. Set the width of the middle columns to 28% of the table width.
18. Make the following style changes to the table row groups:
    - Add a 2-pixel-wide solid gray border to the bottom of the table head row group.
    - EXPLORE Add a 2-pixel-wide solid gray border to the top of the table footer row group and center the text of the table footer.
    - Add a 1-pixel dotted gray border to the table rows within the table body row group.
19. Make the following style changes to individual table cells and rows:
    - Set the padding of all table cells to 0 pixels above and 5 pixels on the sides.
    - Set the kerning of the table heading cells to 2 pixels.
    - Set the height of all table rows to 30 pixels.
20. EXPLORE Add the following background images to the table:
    - Apply the **left.jpg** image as a background for the first table column, placed on the left border of the column and tiled vertically.
    - Apply the **blank.gif** image as a background for the middle table columns tiled in all directions.
    - Apply the **right.jpg** image as a background for the last column, placed on the right border and tiled vertically.
    - Apply the **top.jpg** image to the table header row group, placed on the top border of the object and tiled horizontally.
    - Add the **tableback.jpg** image to the background of the entire table, placed at the 98%, 70% position with no tiling.
    - Add the **topleft.jpg**, **topright.jpg**, **bottomleft.jpg**, and **bottomright.jpg** image files to the background corners of the topLeft, topRight, bottomLeft, and bottomRight table cells. Do not tile the images.
21. Save your changes to the **dtable.css** file, and then open the **dhome.htm** file in the Firefox, Opera, or Safari browsers. Verify that the design of the table resembles that shown in Figure 5-78. (Note: Internet Explorer is unable to display the borders within the three row groups.)
22. Submit your completed files to your instructor.

Create | Case Problem 4

Create a Web page describing room reservations at a popular conference center.

Data Files needed for this Case Problem: bottom.png, bottomleft.png, bottomright.png, hcclogo.jpg, left.png, right.png, rooms.txt, top.png, topleft.png, and topright.png

Hamilton Conference Center Yancy Inwe is the facilities manager at the Hamilton Conference Center in Hamilton, Ohio. The conference center, a general-use facility for the community, hosts several organizations and clubs as well as special events and shows by local vendors. The center has recently upgraded its intranet capabilities and Yancy would like to create a Web site where employees and guests can easily track which conference rooms are available and which are being used. She would like this information displayed in a table that lays out the room use from 8:00 a.m. to 5:00 p.m. for seven rooms and halls. Eventually this process will be automated by the conference's Web server, but for now she has come to you for help in setting up a sample Web page layout and design.

Complete the following:

1. Use your text editor to create an HTML file named **conference.htm** and two style sheets named **hcc.css** and **schedule.css**. Enter ***your name*** and ***the date*** in a comment section of each file. Include any other comments you think aptly document the purpose and content of the files. Save the files in the tutorial.05\case4 folder included with your Data Files.
2. Use the text files provided to create a Web page containing the reservation information. The design of the Web page is up to you and you may supplement your Web page with any material you feel is appropriate. Place any CSS styles you design for the page in the **hcc.css** style sheet.
3. Create a table containing the room reservation information. The table structure should contain the following elements:
   - A table caption and summary
   - Table row and column groups
   - Examples of row- and/or column-spanning cells
   - Examples of both table heading and table data cells
4. Create a style for your table in the **schedule.css** style sheet. The layout and appearance of the table is up to you, but it should include the following:
   - A border style applied to one or more table objects
   - Multiple background colors
   - Use of horizontal and vertical alignment of the table cell contents
   - Different widths applied to different table columns
   - Styles applied to the table caption
5. Add a rounded-box object to your final Web page. You may use nested div elements, a Web table, or another approach to create the rounded border effect. You may use the border style graphics included in the tutorial.05\case4 folder included with your Data Files, or you may find or create your own.
6. Test your Web site on a variety of browsers to ensure your design works under different conditions.
7. Submit your completed files to your instructor.

Review | Quick Check Answers

Session 5.1

1. The number of columns is determined by the maximum number of cells within the table rows.
2. Horizontally centered and in a bold font
3. `<table border="10"> ... </table>`
4. `<td colspan="3" rowspan="2">Monday</td>`
5. You have to reduce the number of cells in the row to accommodate the spanning cell.
6. Because styles that are applied to the table element will be inherited by the caption.
7. thead, tfoot, and tbody (they should be specified in that order).
8.
```
<colgroup>
<col span="2" class="introCol" />
<col class="col1" />
<col class="col2" />
<col class="col3" />
</colgroup>
```

9. To provide more information to visually impaired users whose browsers have difficulty interpreting text in a tabular form.

Session 5.2

1. <table cellspacing="10"> ... </table>
2. <table border="1" rules="none"> ... </table>
3. rules="cols"
4. border-collapse: collapse
5. 6-pixel solid border because it is the border with the larger width
6. the row group
7. th {vertical-align: bottom}
8. caption {caption-side: bottom}
9. ul {display: table}
   ul li {display: table-cell}

Session 5.3

1. A layout in which the page content is broken down into smaller pieces which are then reassembled like pieces from a jigsaw puzzle
2. #midCell {height: 20px; width: auto}
3. Table text is read as it appears in the browser code, which can be confusing to users who cannot see the relationship between the rows and columns of the table.
4. #mainLogo {background: url(tlcorner.jpg) no-repeat 0% 0%}
5. #subLogo {background: url(lborder.jpg) repeat-y 0% 0%}
6. #mainContent {background: url(bborder.jpg) repeat-x 0% 100%}
7. You could float two div elements on the page's left page or you could place the div elements using absolute positioning.

Ending Data Files

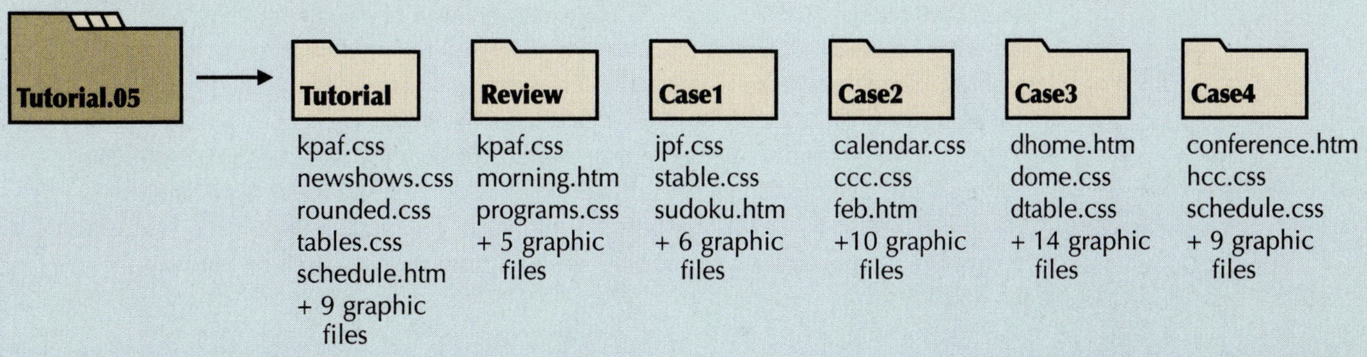

Reality Check

The Web is a valuable source of information and it is particularly valuable for those who want to learn how to write Web pages. Each Web site presents an opportunity to study how other Web page designers solved problems involving layout and design. And most Web designers are eager to share the methods, techniques, and sometimes tricks they've used to get the most out of HTML, CSS, and an occasional uncooperative browser. In this exercise, you'll use the skills and tasks you learned in Tutorials 3 through 5 to create a Web site on a hobby or personal interest of yours. First you'll research and evaluate the techniques of published Web page designers.

Please be sure *not* to include any personal information of a sensitive nature in the files you create to be submitted to your instructor for this exercise. Later on, you can update the files with such information for your personal use.

1. Web designers have come up with a variety of approaches to creating two-, three-, and four-column layouts. Search the Web for designer pages and report on the different techniques designers have used to create these classic layouts.
2. In the course of your research, you'll come across information on fixed and liquid layouts. Summarize the two approaches and compare each one's advantages and disadvantages.
3. The W3C specifications for HTML and CSS represent a "gold standard" by which all browsers are rated. Do a Web search to determine the browsers that provide the best support for the W3C specifications. Which browsers provide the poorest level of support?
4. Designers must come up with work-arounds or "hacks" to deal with the incompatibilities between browsers in implementing HTML and CSS. Search the Web and come up with three different hacks that designers use in their Web sites. Describe each hack and the problem it solves.
5. Locate a Web page whose content and layout you enjoy. Take some time to download the underlying HTML and CSS code and reconstruct exactly how the Web designer created the page. A few caveats: be respectful about your use of copyrighted material and avoid large and over-complicated Web sites. A site for a large company or organization would be difficult to interpret.
6. When you're finished studying the page's code, recreate the layout and design techniques on a page describing one of your hobbies or interests. Try to duplicate the same look and feel (as much as possible) of the site that you studied.
7. Save your completed Web site and the answers from your research and present them to your instructor.

Objectives

Session 6.1
- Explore how Web forms interact with Web servers
- Create form elements
- Create field sets and legends
- Create input boxes and form labels

Session 6.2
- Creation option buttons
- Create selection lists
- Create check boxes
- Create text area boxes
- Apply styles to Web forms

Session 6.3
- Work with form buttons
- Explore image elements and hidden fields
- Work with form actions and methods

Working with Web Forms

Creating a Donation Form

Case | The Lighthouse

Terry Ives is the director of The Lighthouse, a community center in St. Peters, Missouri. The Lighthouse provides social services, focusing on drug addiction counseling, job placement, child care, and tutoring disadvantaged youths. The Lighthouse's mission is broad and challenging, and as a nonprofit organization, money is always tight.

You've been volunteering at the center for several months, helping to upgrade the Web site's design and adding new features that will make the site more useful for clients, volunteers, and donors. Terry would like your help with one important feature: creating a page for online donations. She knows that many social service organizations receive a good percentage of their donations online; therefore, she's been working with an Internet service provider (ISP) to find out how to facilitate secure online donations. She has learned that the donations page needs a Web form that can be used to transfer payment data to the ISP's Web server for processing. Terry has asked you to create a Web form that will supply the server with the needed financial data.

Starting Data Files

Tutorial.06 →

Tutorial	Review	Case1	Case2	Case3	Case4
donatxt.htm formstxt.css main.css + 4 graphic files	main.css vformstxt.css voltxt.htm + 4 graphic files	pcg.css sformtxt.css subtxt.htm + 2 graphic files	cw.css cwquiztxt.htm qformtxt.css + 2 graphic files	orderformtxt.css pizzatxt.htm rb.css topping.txt + 4 graphic files	mclogo.jpg

Session 6.1

Introducing Web Forms

You meet with Terry to discuss the new donations page for The Lighthouse's Web site. She sketches out the appearance of a form shown in Figure 6-1 that she would like to display on the center's Web site.

Figure 6-1 **Terry's proposed donations form**

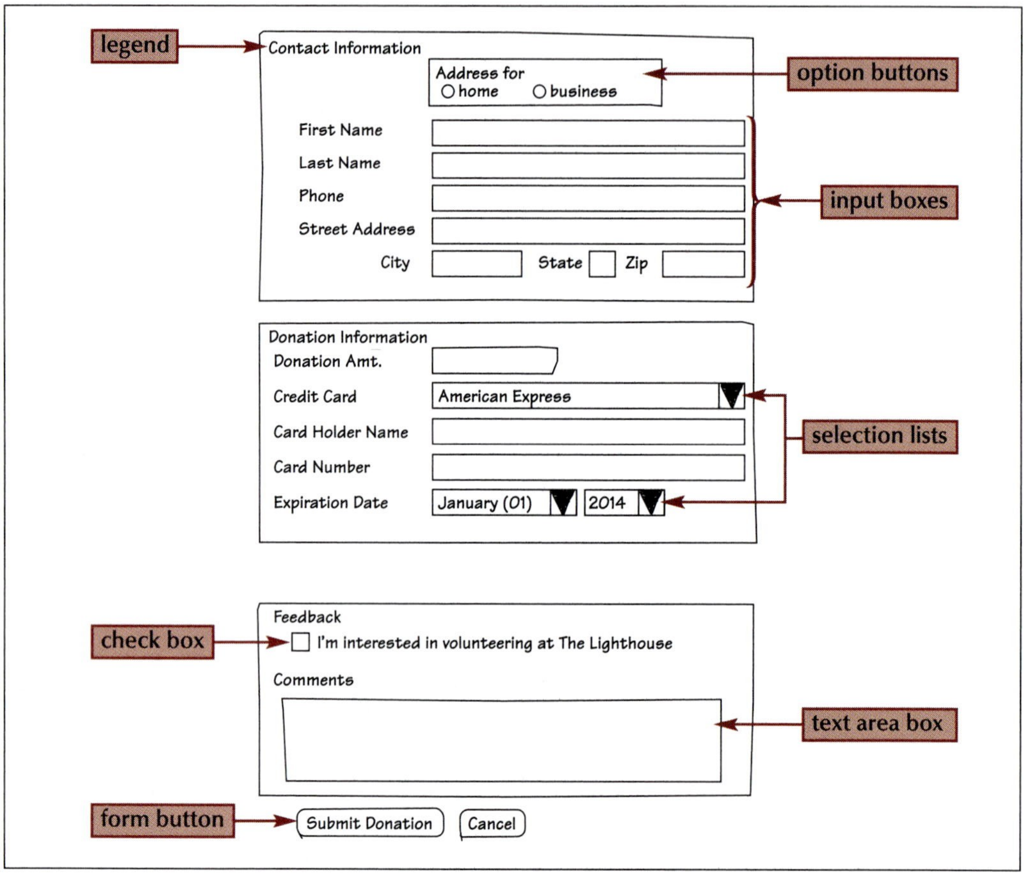

The form is divided into three topical areas. The first requests contact information from the donor, including the donor's name, phone number, and mailing address. In the second part of the form, the donor specifies the amount of the donation and provides credit card information. The final part of the form is reserved for any comments the donor has and offers a check box where donors can indicate an interest in volunteering at the center.

Parts of a Web Form

Each piece of information for a form is stored in a **field**, and the value itself is known as the **field value**. In some fields, users are free to enter anything they choose, while other fields are limited to a set of possible values. Users enter or select a field value using **control elements**, which are buttons, boxes, lists, and so on, that provide a way of associating a field value with a particular field. HTML supports the following control elements:

- **input boxes** for text and numerical entries

- **option buttons**, also called **radio buttons**, for selecting a single option from a predefined list
- **selection lists** for long lists of options, usually appearing in a **drop-down list box**
- **check boxes** for specifying yes or no
- **text areas** for extended entries that can include several lines of text

Terry's donation form includes several examples of these different control elements, each one associated with a particular field. As you'll see later, users will enter their first and last names in the firstName and lastName fields through the use of an input box control element. They'll indicate their credit card through the use of a selection list.

Forms and Server-Based Programs

Before you start work on Terry's Web form, you should understand how forms are processed on the Web. As shown in Figure 6-2, the Web form is used to collect information, but the data itself is stored and analyzed using a program running on a Web server.

The interaction between the Web form and the Web server **Figure 6-2**

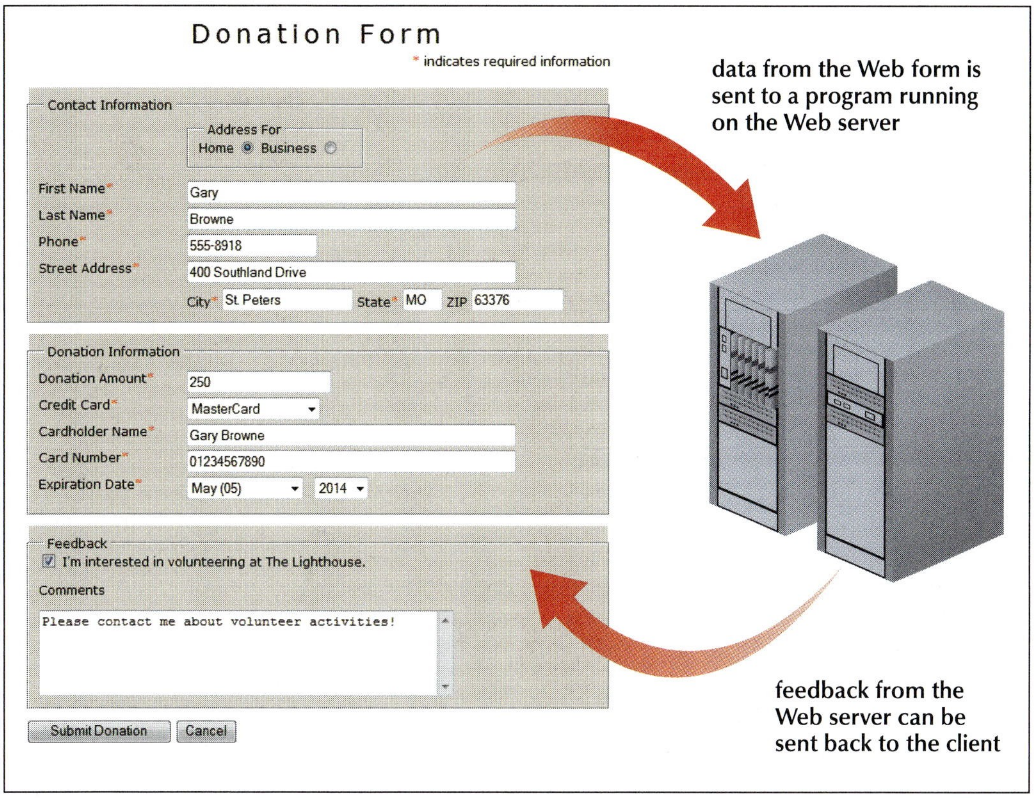

The pairing of server-based programs and Web forms early in the development of HTML represented a dramatic shift in how the Web was perceived and used. By giving users access to programs that react to user input, the Web became a more dynamic environment where companies and users could interact. Server-based programs have made many things possible, including:

- online databases containing customer information
- online catalogs for ordering and purchasing merchandise
- dynamic Web sites with content that is constantly modified and updated
- message boards for hosting online discussion forums

Because these programs run on Web servers, rather than locally, you might not have permission to create or edit them. Instead, you'll receive information about how to interact with the programs on the Web server. This usually includes a list of fields that are required by the program and a description of the type of values expected in those fields. The Web form code needs to work in conjunction with the requirements of the server-based program.

There are several reasons to restrict direct access to these programs. The primary reason is that when you run a server-based program, you are interacting directly with the server environment. Mindful of the security risks that computer hackers present and the drain on system resources caused by large numbers of programs running simultaneously, system administrators are understandably careful to maintain strict control over their servers and systems. Otherwise, people could use malicious code to inject programming into the server and possibly change the prices of items or degrade the performance of the server.

Server-based programs are written in a variety of languages. The earliest and most common of these languages are called **Common Gateway Interface (CGI) scripts**, written in a language called **Perl**. Other popular languages widely used today for writing server-based programs include:

- ASP
- ColdFusion
- C/C++
- PHP
- VBScript

Which language your Web form will interact with depends on your Web server. Check with your ISP or system administrator to find out what programs are available and what rights and privileges you have in working with them.

The ISP that hosts The Lighthouse's Web site has scripts in place to receive the data from the donation form and process it. You will not have access to these programs, so Terry just wants you to work with the Web form portion of this process. Others will test your Web form to verify that the information is being collected and processed correctly.

Creating a Web Form

Now that you're familiar with the background of server-based programs, you can begin to work on Terry's donation form. Terry has created the design of the page, leaving the right column empty for the form. Your job will be to complete the page by adding the Web form. Open Terry's document now.

To view Terry's document:

1. Start your text editor, and then open the **donatxt.htm** file located in the tutorial.06\tutorial folder included with your Data Files. Enter ***your name*** and ***the date*** in the comment section of the file. Save the file as **donations.htm** in the same folder.
2. Review the file to become familiar with its contents and structure, and then open the file in your Web browser. Figure 6-3 shows the current appearance of the page.

Figure 6-3 The initial donations page

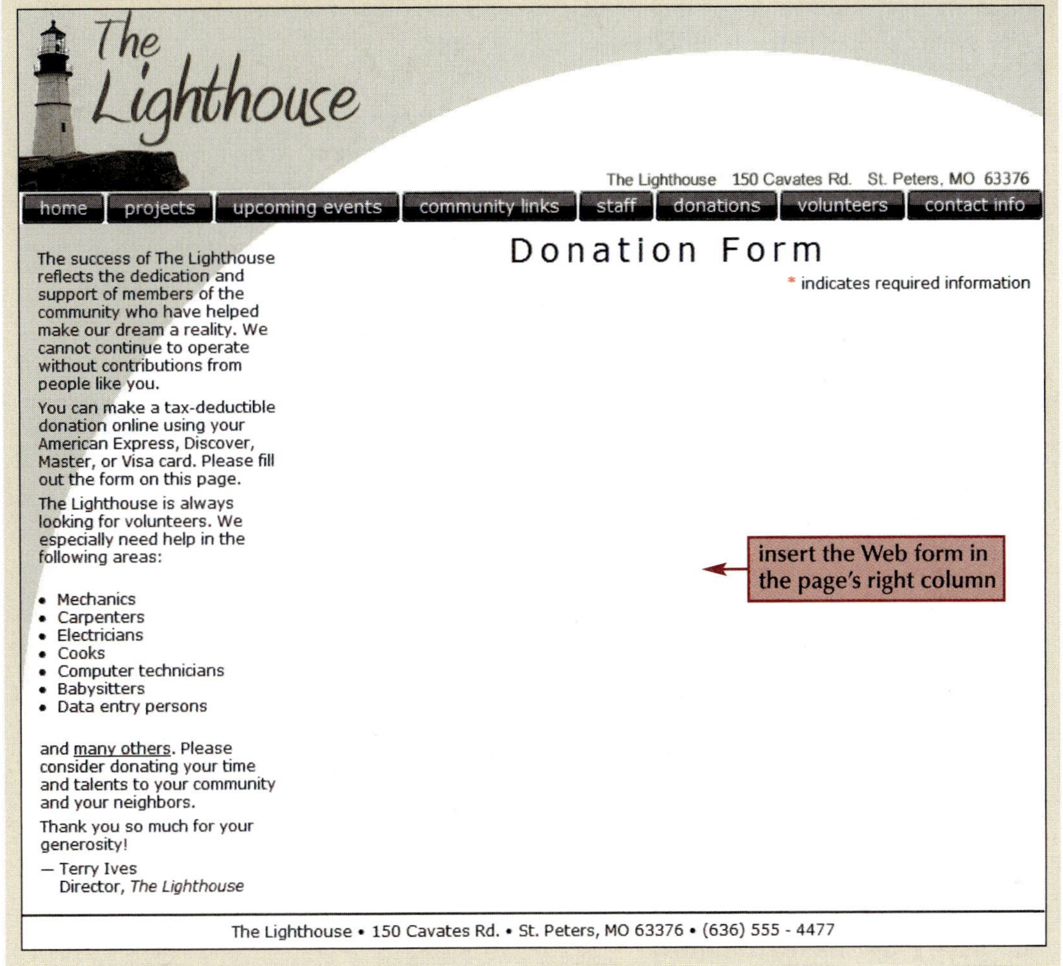
The Lighthouse
The Lighthouse 150 Cavates Rd. St. Peters, MO 63376
home
projects
upcoming events
community links
staff
donations
volunteers
contact info
Donation Form
* indicates required information
The success of The Lighthouse reflects the dedication and support of members of the community who have helped make our dream a reality. We cannot continue to operate without contributions from people like you.
You can make a tax-deductible donation online using your American Express, Discover, Master, or Visa card. Please fill out the form on this page.
The Lighthouse is always looking for volunteers. We especially need help in the following areas:
• Mechanics
• Carpenters
• Electricians
• Cooks
• Computer technicians
• Babysitters
• Data entry persons
and many others. Please consider donating your time and talents to your community and your neighbors.
Thank you so much for your generosity!
— Terry Ives
Director, The Lighthouse
insert the Web form in the page's right column
The Lighthouse • 150 Cavates Rd. • St. Peters, MO 63376 • (636) 555 - 4477

Terry suggests that you insert the Web form in the page's right column. She has already inserted a heading above where she wants the form to appear. Forms are created using the form element

```
<form attributes>
   elements
</form>
```

where *attributes* are the attributes that name the form and control how it is processed, and *elements* are the elements placed within the form. Forms typically contain many of the control elements that were discussed earlier, but can also contain page elements such as tables, paragraphs, inline images, and headings. The form element can be placed anywhere within the HTML file and a single page can contain multiple forms.

Form attributes tell the browser the location of the server-based program to be used on the form's data, how that data is to be transferred to the script, and so forth. These attributes are not needed when first designing the form, and it's actually useful to omit them at first. This prevents you from accidentally running the program on an unfinished form, causing the Web server to process incomplete information. After you've finalized the form's appearance, you can add the attributes required by the server program. You'll have a chance to do this in the last session of this tutorial.

Two attributes identify the form: the id attribute and the name attribute. Naming a form is useful for pages that contain multiple forms so you can differentiate one form from another, and it might be required for server-based programs that accept form values. The syntax of both of these attributes is

```
<form name="name" id="id"> . . . </form>
```

where *name* is the name of the form, and *id* is the id of the form. Although these two attributes might appear to do the same thing, each has its own history and role. The name attribute represents the older standard for form identification, and so is often required for older browsers and older server programs. The id attribute, on the other hand, represents the current standard under HTML and XHTML for identifying a form. For maximum compatibility with older and newer browsers and CGI scripts, you should include both attributes, setting them to the same value.

Reference Window | Inserting a Web Form

- To insert a Web form, add the elements

  ```
  <form attributes>
     elements
  </form>
  ```

  to the Web page, where *attributes* are the attributes that name the form and control how it is processed, and *elements* are the elements placed within the form.
- To identify the form, add the attributes

  ```
  id="id" name="name"
  ```

  to the opening <form> tag, where *id* is the form id and *name* is the form name. You will often set these attributes to the same value.

You are ready to add a form element named donationForm to Terry's Web page.

To insert the form element:

1. Return to the **donations.htm** file in your text editor and scroll down the file to the rightColumn div container.
2. Insert the following form element within the rightColumn div container, as shown in Figure 6-4.

   ```
   <form name="donationForm" id="donationForm">
   </form>
   ```

Figure 6-4 **Inserting a form element**

```
<div id="rightColumn">
   <h1>Donation Form</h1>
   <p><span>*</span> indicates required information</p>

   <form name="donationForm" id="donationForm">
   </form>

</div>
```

With the form element added to the donations page, you can start populating it with control elements and other form features. You'll start by adding field sets.

Creating a Field Set

A Web form like the donation form can have dozens of different fields. One way of organizing a form is to group similar fields into **field sets**. When rendered by the browser, a field set usually appears as a box surrounding the fields, separating those fields from other field sets. Field sets are created using the fieldset element, which has the syntax

```
<fieldset id="id">
   controls
</fieldset>
```

where *id* identifies the field set and *controls* are the control elements associated with fields within the field set. The *id* value is not required, but it is useful in distinguishing one field set from another. Terry wants to organize the donation form into three field sets named contact, donation, and feedback. Add these field sets to her donation form.

Tip

Field sets make it easier for users with aural browsers and screen readers to navigate your Web form.

Creating a Field Set | Reference Window

- To create a field set, add the element

```
<fieldset id="id">
   controls
</fieldset>
```

to the form, where *id* identifies the field set and *controls* are the control elements associated with fields within the field set.

To insert a field set:

1. Return to the **donations.htm** file.
2. Within the form element, insert the following three field sets, as shown in Figure 6-5:

```
<fieldset id="contact">
</fieldset>

<fieldset id="donation">
</fieldset>

<fieldset id="feedback">
</fieldset>
```

Inserting field sets **Figure 6-5**

```
<form name="donationForm" id="donationForm">
   <fieldset id="contact">
   </fieldset>

   <fieldset id="donation">
   </fieldset>

   <fieldset id="feedback">
   </fieldset>
</form>
```

3. Save your changes to the file.

Every field set can contain a legend describing its contents. The syntax of the legend element is

```
<legend>text</legend>
```

where *text* is the text of the legend. The legend element can only contain text and not other page elements. Based on Terry's sketch from Figure 6-1, you'll add the legends Contact Information, Donation Information, and Feedback to the three field sets you created.

To insert legends for the field sets:

1. Return to the **donations.htm** file.
2. Within the first field set, insert the following legend element:

```
<legend>Contact Information</legend>
```

3. In the second field set, insert the following legend element:

```
<legend>Donation Information</legend>
```

4. In the last field set, insert the following legend element:

```
<legend>Feedback</legend>
```

Figure 6-6 highlights the revised text of the HTML file.

Figure 6-6 Creating field set legends

```
<form name="donationForm" id="donationForm">
   <fieldset id="contact">
      <legend>Contact Information</legend>
   </fieldset>

   <fieldset id="donation">
      <legend>Donation Information</legend>
   </fieldset>

   <fieldset id="feedback">
      <legend>Feedback</legend>
   </fieldset>
</form>
```

5. Now you can view the three field sets in your Web browser. Save your changes to the file, and reload the **donations.htm** file in your Web browser. Figure 6-7 shows the current appearance of the form.

Figure 6-7 Appearance of the field set and legend elements

Field sets are block-level elements that expand to accommodate their content. Currently, there are no control or other page elements within the three field sets, so the field set boxes are small and narrow. By default, browsers display the legend text in the upper-left corner of the field set box. However, you can use the CSS positioning styles to move the legend position. Terry does not need you to modify the legend, so you'll leave it in its default position. Now that you've created the three field sets, you can begin to populate them with form control elements.

Creating Input Boxes

Most of the control elements in which users either type or select a data value are marked as input elements. The general syntax of this element is

```
<input type="type" name="name" id="id" />
```

where *type* specifies the type of input control, and the name and id attributes provide the field's name and id, respectively. As with the form element, you should provide both the name and the id attributes, setting them to the same value to ensure compatibility with older browsers. HTML supports 10 different input types, which are described in Figure 6-8. If no type attribute value is specified, the browser will assume a type value of text.

Appearance of control elements **Figure 6-8**

Type Value	Description	General Appearance
button	Displays a button that can be clicked to perform an action from a script	Run Program
checkbox	Displays a check box	
file	Displays a Browse button to locate and select a file	donations.htm Browse...
hidden	Creates a hidden field, not viewable on the form	
image	Displays an inline image that can be clicked to perform an action from a script	
password	Displays an input box that hides text entered by the user	•••••••••
radio	Displays an option button	
reset	Displays a button that resets the form when clicked	Cancel Donation
submit	Displays a button that submits the form when clicked	Submit Donation
text	Displays an input box that displays text entered by the user	Terry Ives

The exact appearance of each control element varies among browsers and operating systems. Figure 6-9 highlights the differences among four major browsers in how they render a control button. Because of this variation, you should not rely on the exact appearance of any particular control element when designing your Web form.

Figure 6-9 **Control elements under different browsers**

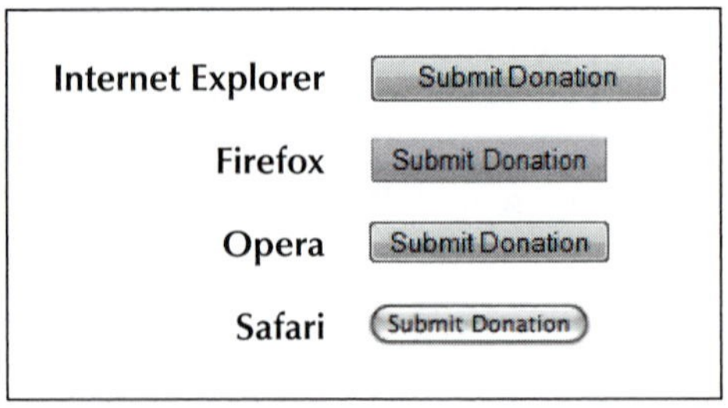

When a form is submitted to the server, the server program receives the data in **name/value pairs** in which the name or id of each field is paired with whatever field value is entered into the corresponding control element. The program then processes the data according to each name/value pair. Some server-based programs require a particular field or group of fields. For example, a CGI script whose purpose is to register users might require e-mail addresses entered into a field named e_mail. This means that before specifying a name or id value for a control, you have to learn what the server program expects that data to be named and write your HTML code accordingly. Be aware that case is usually important in specifying field names. A program might not interpret a field named e_mail in the same way as a field named E_MAIL.

The first controls you'll add to the donation form will be input boxes in which donors can enter their first and last names. The syntax to create an input box is:

```
<input type="text" name="name" id="id" />
```

You ask Terry for the ids of the first and last name fields in her donation form. She checks with the ISP hosting The Lighthouse's Web site and tells you that fields containing the donor's first and last name should be given name and id values of firstName and lastName, respectively. You can add these two input boxes to the Contact Information field set. To describe these input boxes for the user, you'll insert the text First Name and Last Name before the input boxes.

Reference Window | Inserting a Text Input Box

- To create a text input box control, use the element
  ```
  <input type="text" name="name" id="id" />
  ```
  where the name and id attributes identify the field associated with the input box.

To insert the input boxes:

1. Return to the **donations.htm** file in your text editor and scroll down to the Contact Information field set element.
2. Within the field set element, add the following text strings and input elements, as shown in Figure 6-10.

```
First Name
   <input type="text" id="firstName" name="firstName" />
Last Name
   <input type="text" id="lastName" name="lastName" />
```

Figure 6-10 Adding input box controls

```
<form name="donationForm" id="donationForm">
   <fieldset id="contact">
      <legend>Contact Information</legend>
      First Name
      <input type="text" id="firstName" name="firstName" />
      Last Name
      <input type="text" id="lastName" name="lastName" />
   </fieldset>
```

text type indicates an input text box

3. Save your changes to the file, and then reload **donations.htm** in your Web browser. Your browser should show two input boxes within the Contact Information field set box. Terry suggests that you test the input boxes.

4. Type ***your first name*** in the First Name box, press the **Tab** key, and then type ***your last name*** in the Last Name box. Figure 6-11 shows the input boxes with the sample text.

Figure 6-11 Input controls with sample data

HTML treats all form control elements as inline elements, so the input boxes that you created for Terry's form appear within the same line rather than in separate blocks. You can change this by applying the CSS display style to the input box.

Adding Field Labels

In the last set of steps, you entered descriptive text alongside the input boxes to indicate the purpose of the input box to the user. However, nothing in the HTML code explicitly associates that text with the input box. To associate text with a control element, you can use the label element

```
<label for="id">label text</label>
```

where *id* is the value of the id attribute for the field's control element, and *label text* is the text of the label. The for attribute associates the text of the label with the control element id. For example, the following code associates the label text First Name with the first-Name control element:

```
<label for="firstName">First Name</label>
<input type="text" id="firstName" />
```

Using the for attribute explicitly associates the label with the control element. You can also make this association implicitly by nesting the control element within the label as in the following code:

```
<label>
   First Name
   <input type="text" id="firstName" />
</label>
```

Notice that you do not need to include a for attribute when you nest the control element within the label element.

Which approach you take depends on how you want to lay out the form's contents. When you use the for attribute, you can place the label text anywhere within the Web page and it will still be associated with the control element. However, by nesting the control element within the label, you can treat both the control element and its label as a single object, which might make it easier to do form layout as you can move both label text and the control element around the page. Depending on the layout of your Web form, you might use both approaches.

Reference Window | Creating a Field Label

- To explicitly associate a text label with a control element, use the label element
```
<label for="id">label text</label>
```
where *id* is the id of the control element.
- To implicitly associate a text label with a control element, nest the control element within the label as follows
```
<label>
   label text
   control
</label>
```
where *control* is the control element. You do not have to include a for attribute.

For the firstName and lastName fields, you'll use the second approach, in which the control elements are nested within their label elements.

To insert the field labels:

1. Return to the **donations.htm** file in your text editor.
2. Enclose the First Name and Last Name text strings within opening and closing **<label>** tags. Indent your code to make it easier to read, as shown in Figure 6-12.

Figure 6-12 Adding field labels

```
<fieldset id="contact">
   <legend>Contact Information</legend>

   <label>
      First Name
      <input type="text" id="firstName" name="firstName" />
   </label>
   <label>
      Last Name
      <input type="text" id="lastName" name="lastName" />
   </label>

</fieldset>
```

3. Save your changes to the file, and reload the page in your Web browser.
4. Test the labels by clicking each label and verifying that the cursor appears within the corresponding control element.

Working with Form Styles and HTML Attributes

Terry stops by to see your progress on the donation form. She would prefer to have the labels placed in one column and the input boxes put in another column, rather than having both strung together in a single line. Placing labels and control elements in separate columns is a common form layout, one that has often been done with Web tables. However, you've learned that the use of Web tables for page layout is frowned upon. So, instead of a Web table, you'll lay out the form using positioning styles placed in an external style sheet. This has the advantage of making it easier to modify the form layout later on because you will not have to modify the markup code in the HTML file.

To create the form style sheet:

1. Use your text editor to open the **formstxt.css** file from the tutorial.06\tutorial folder included with your Data Files. Enter ***your name*** and ***the date*** in the comment section of the file, and then save it as **forms.css** in the same folder.
2. Return to the **donations.htm** file in your text editor and add the following link to the forms.css style sheet directly above the closing </head> tag.

```
<link href="forms.css" rel="stylesheet" type="text/css" />
```

You decide to change the display style of the label elements from inline to block so that the labels will appear on a separate line from the input boxes. Because this particular style might not apply to other labels in the donation form or on The Lighthouse's Web site, you'll add a class element named blockLabel to the label elements having this design format.

To create the blockLabel class:

1. Scroll down the **donations.htm** file and insert the class attribute

```
class="blockLabel"
```

in the First Name and Last Name labels, as shown in Figure 6-13.

Figure 6-13 Adding class names to the field labels

```
<label class="blockLabel">
   First Name
   <input type="text" id="firstName" name="firstName" />
</label>
<label class="blockLabel">
   Last Name
   <input type="text" id="lastName" name="lastName" />
</label>
```

2. Save your changes to the file.

Next, you'll create a style for the blockLabel class of labels. The style will set the display property of the label to block, and set the margins to 12 pixels above and below the label and to 0 pixels to the left and right. You'll also place the label using relative positioning, but you will not define any coordinates so that the label stays in its default position in the page flow. The complete style declaration is:

```
label.blockLabel {display: block; position: relative; margin: 12px 0px}
```

The input elements within each label will be placed using absolute positioning 150 pixels from the left margin of the label. The style declaration is:

```
label.blockLabel input {position: absolute; left: 150px}
```

Add these two styles to the forms.css style sheet.

To create styles for the blockLabel class:

1. Return to the **forms.css** file in your text editor and add the following styles to the style sheet, as shown in Figure 6-14.

```
label.blockLabel       {display: block; position: relative;
                        margin: 12px 0px}

label.blockLabel input {position: absolute; left: 150px}
```

Figure 6-14 Styles for the blockLabel labels and input elements

```
label.blockLabel       {display: block; position: relative; margin: 12px 0px}
label.blockLabel input {position: absolute; left: 150px}
```

2. Save your changes to the style sheet, and reload the donations page in your Web browser. Figure 6-15 shows the new layout of the form fields.

Figure 6-15 Revised layout of the form elements

There are some fields in the donation form that the server-based program will require for the donation to be processed. Terry wants you to mark such required fields with a red asterisk. The firstName and lastName fields are both required, so you'll mark their labels with an asterisk, adding the red style to the forms.css style sheet.

To mark the required fields:

1. Return to the **donations.htm** file in your text editor.
2. At the end of the label text for the firstName and lastName fields, insert the code

```
<span>*</span>
```

as shown in Figure 6-16.

Marking a required field | Figure 6-16

```
<label class="blockLabel">
   First Name<span>*</span>
   <input type="text" id="firstName" name="firstName" />
</label>

<label class="blockLabel">
   Last Name<span>*</span>
   <input type="text" id="lastName" name="lastName" />
</label>
```

3. Save your changes to the file and then return to the **forms.css** style sheet. Add the following style to the bottom of the sheet to display all span elements from the donation form in a red font:

   ```
   #donationForm span {color: red}
   ```

4. Save your changes to the style sheet and then reload **donations.htm** in your Web browser. Verify that the labels for the firstName and lastName variables end with a red asterisk.

Tip

Always mark the required fields in your Web form so that users know exactly which fields they must enter and which fields are optional.

Terry wants the same style applied to input boxes for each donor's phone number and street address. Both of these fields are required, so you'll also append an asterisk to the field labels.

To insert additional fields to the donation form:

1. Return to the **donations.htm** file in your text editor.
2. Directly below the label for the lastName field, insert the following fields and labels as shown in Figure 6-17.

   ```
   <label class="blockLabel">
      Phone<span>*</span>
      <input type="text" id="phone" name="phone" />
   </label>
   <label class="blockLabel">
      Street Address<span>*</span>
      <input type="text" id="street" name="street" />
   </label>
   ```

Adding the phone and street fields | Figure 6-17

```
<fieldset id="contact">
   <legend>Contact Information</legend>

   <label class="blockLabel">
      First Name<span>*</span>
      <input type="text" id="firstName" name="firstName" />
   </label>

   <label class="blockLabel">
      Last Name<span>*</span>
      <input type="text" id="lastName" name="lastName" />
   </label>

   <label class="blockLabel">
      Phone<span>*</span>
      <input type="text" id="phone" name="phone" />
   </label>

   <label class="blockLabel">
      Street Address<span>*</span>
      <input type="text" id="street" name="street" />
   </label>

</fieldset>
```

3. Save your changes to the file and then reload the donations page in your browser. Verify that the two additional input boxes have been added to the page in the same style and layout as the First Name and Last Name boxes, as shown in Figure 6-18.

Figure 6-18 **Required contact information in the donations form**

The next fields in the Contact Information field set are the city, state, and zip fields. Terry has indicated that she wants these three fields to be displayed on the same line in the form, just as they usually appear in mailing addresses. You'll add the labels for these control elements without the blockLabel class attribute so that the browser treats them as inline elements; however, you'll indent the first label for the city field by 150 pixels, lining it up with the rest of the columns in the form. You learn from Terry that the city and state fields are required by the CGI script that will process this form, so you'll add red asterisks to those two labels.

To add the city, state, and zip fields:

1. Return to the **donations.htm** file in your text editor.
2. Add the following elements to the form, as shown in Figure 6-19.

```
<label class="indentLabel">
   City<span>*</span>
   <input type="text" id="city" name="city" />
</label>
<label>
   State<span>*</span>
   <input type="text" id="state" name="state" />
</label>
<label>
   ZIP
   <input type="text" id="zip" name="zip" />
</label>
```

Figure 6-19 **Adding the city, state, and zip fields**

```
      <label class="blockLabel">
         Street Address<span>*</span>
         <input type="text" id="street" name="street" />
      </label>

      <label class="indentLabel">
         City<span>*</span>
         <input type="text" id="city" name="city" />
      </label>
      <label>
         State<span>*</span>
         <input type="text" id="state" name="state" />
      </label>
      <label>
         ZIP
         <input type="text" id="zip" name="zip" />
      </label>

   </fieldset>
```

3. Save your changes to the file and then return to the **forms.css** file in your text editor to create a style for the indentLabel class.
4. Add the following style to the bottom of the style sheet:

```
label.indentLabel {margin-left: 150px}
```

5. Save your changes to the style sheet and then reload the **donations.htm** file in your Web browser. Figure 6-20 shows the current layout of the form.

Figure 6-20 **Form layout for the city, state, and zip fields**

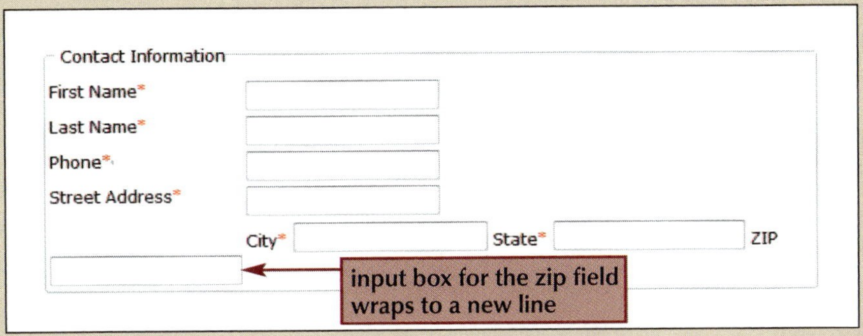

Trouble? Under some browsers such as Safari, the three input boxes will not wrap onto a new line but will instead be displayed on a single line, crossing the boundary of the field set box.

The three input boxes for the city, state, and zip fields do not fit onto a single line, causing the input box for the zip field to wrap onto a second line. By default, most browsers set the width of the input boxes to display about 20 characters of text at any one time. You can change the width of these input boxes using the CSS width style.

Setting the Width of an Input Box

Because Terry wants users to enter only a two-letter abbreviation for the state input box, you can reduce the width of that box to 3 em. The width of the zip code input box can be reduced to 7 em. Finally, she would like the width of the city and phone input boxes set at 10 em. Terry thinks the other input boxes could be wider and suggests that you set the width of the firstName, lastName, and street input boxes to 25 em. Add these styles to the forms.css style sheet.

To set the width of the input boxes:

1. Return to the **forms.css** style sheet and add the following styles to the bottom of the sheet, as shown in Figure 6-21.

```
#firstName, #lastName, #street {width: 25em}
#phone, #city                  {width: 10em}
#state                         {width: 3em}
#zip                           {width: 7em}
```

Figure 6-21 **Setting the widths of the input boxes**

```
#donationForm span      {color: red}

label.indentLabel       {margin-left: 150px}

#firstName, #lastName, #street {width: 25em}
#phone, #city                  {width: 10em}
#state                         {width: 3em}
#zip                           {width: 7em}
```

2. Save your changes to the style sheet and reload the **donations.htm** file in your Web browser. Figure 6-22 shows the layout of the form with the new widths for the input boxes.

Figure 6-22 **Input boxes with modified widths**

Applying new widths to the different input boxes has removed the line wrap from the form and made the form easier to read. The width style is one way of setting the size of an input box. For older browsers, you can also apply the size attribute to the input element as follows

```
<input type="text" size="chars" />
```

where *chars* is the number of characters displayed in the input box. For example, the tag

```
<input type="text" id="zip" name="zip" size="7" />
```

sets the width of the input box for the zip field to seven characters. This is not an exact measure because the width of individual characters varies (unless you specify a monospace font for the input box text).

Setting the Maximum Width of an Input Box

Setting the width of an input box does not limit the number of characters the box can hold. If a user tries to enter text longer than a box's width, the text scrolls to the left, hiding the extra characters. A user would not be able to see the entire text entered into the input box, but all of it would still be sent to the server for processing.

There are times when you want to limit the number of characters a user can enter in order to reduce the chance of erroneous data entry. For example, if you have a Social Security Number field, you know that only nine characters are required and that any attempt to enter more than nine characters would indicate a mistake. To set the maximum number of characters allowed for an input box, you add the attribute

```
<input type="text" maxlength="chars" />
```

to the input element, where *chars* is the maximum number of characters that can be stored in the field. For the donation form, Terry wants users to enter the two-letter state abbreviation, so she suggests that you limit the size of that input box to two characters. She also wants to limit the width of the zip code field to 10 characters, allowing users to enter a nine-digit zip code that incorporates a hyphen.

To set the maximum width of the state and zip input fields:

1. Return to the **donations.htm** file in your text editor and add the attribute

   ```
   maxlength="2"
   ```

   to the input box for the state field.

2. Add the attribute

   ```
   maxlength="10"
   ```

   to the input box for the zip field. Figure 6-23 shows the revised code.

Figure 6-23 **Setting the maximum number of characters for an input box**

```
<label>
   State<span>*</span>
   <input type="text" id="state" name="state" maxlength="2" />
</label>
<label>
   ZIP
   <input type="text" id="zip" name="zip" maxlength="10" />
</label>
```

values of the state field are limited to two characters

values of the zip field are limited to 10 characters

3. Save your changes to the file and reload **donations.htm** in your Web browser.

4. Click the input boxes for the state and zip fields, and verify that you cannot type more than two characters into the state field and more than 10 characters into the zip field.

Setting a Default Value for a Field

If you expect that most people will enter the same value into a field in your form, it might make sense to define a default value for that field. This makes data entry easier for users who want that default value, and it increases the accuracy of data entered into your Web form. To define a default value, you add the value attribute

```
<input value="value" />
```

to the input control element, where *value* is the default text or number that is displayed in the field. In the case of an input box, the default value appears in the input box when the form is initially opened.

Reference Window | Working with Input Box Attributes

- To set the size of the input box in characters, add the attribute
  `size="chars"`
  to the input element, where *chars* is the number of characters displayed in the input box.
- To set the maximum number of characters in the input box, use the attribute
  `maxlength="chars"`
  where *chars* is the maximum number of characters that can be entered into the input box.
- To set the default value of the field in the input box, use the attribute
  `value="value"`
  where *value* is the default value that will appear in the input box when the form is initially displayed.

About 80% of the online donations to The Lighthouse come from donors in St. Peters, Missouri. Terry suggests that you enter the city and state abbreviation into the form as a default value.

To set the default value for the city and state fields:

1. Return to the **donations.htm** file in your text editor and add the attribute

   ```
   value="St. Peters"
   ```

   to the input box for the city field.

2. Add the attribute

   ```
   value="MO"
   ```

   to the input box for state field, as shown in Figure 6-24.

Figure 6-24 Defining a default city and state value

```
<label class="indentLabel">
   City<span>*</span>
   <input type="text" id="city" name="city" value="St. Peters" />
</label>
<label>
   State<span>*</span>
   <input type="text" id="state" name="state" maxlength="2" value="MO" />
</label>
```

St. Peters is the default value for the city field

MO is the default value for the state field

3. Save your changes to the **donations.htm** file and then reload it in your browser. As shown in Figure 6-25, the default values of St. Peters and MO appear in the city and state fields, respectively.

Figure 6-25 Web form with default city and state values

4. If you want to take a break before starting the next session, you can close your files and programs now.

Note that if donors from places other than St. Peters, Missouri use this Web form, they can remove the default value by selecting the text and pressing the Delete key.

Navigating Forms with Access Keys | InSight

In this session, you've activated control elements either by using your mouse button or by tabbing from one control element to another. As your forms get larger with more elements, you might want to give users the ability to jump to a particular element in the form. This can be done with an access key. An **access key** is a single key on the keyboard that you type in conjunction with the Alt key for Windows users, or the Control key for Macintosh users, to jump to one of the control elements in the form. You can create an access key by adding the accesskey attribute to any of the control elements discussed in this tutorial. For example, to create an access key for the lastName field, enter the following code:

```
<input type="text" name="lastName" id="lastName" accesskey="l" />
```

If a user types Alt+l (or Command+l for Macintosh users), the input box for the lastName field is selected. Note that you must use letters that are not reserved by your browser. For example, Alt+f is used by many browsers including Internet Explorer to access the File menu. If you use an access key, you should provide some visual clues about the key's existence. The accepted method is to underline the character corresponding to the access key. For example, in the previous code, you might display the Last Name label as Last Name.

You've completed the text input boxes for the Contact Information section of the donation form. In the next session, you'll complete the layout of the form by adding new fields to the form, including option buttons, selection lists, and check boxes.

Session 6.1 Quick Check | Review

1. What is a CGI script?
2. Specify the code to create a form with the name registration.
3. Specify the code to create a field set with the id contactInfo and the legend Contact Information.
4. What are two ways of associating a field label with a control element?
5. Specify the code to create a field label with the text Phone that is associated with an input box containing the phone field.

6. What attribute would you add to the Phone input box to allow no more than 10 characters to be entered?
7. Specify the code to create an input box named subscribe with a default value of Yes.
8. What style would you enter to display all text input boxes as block-level elements?

Session 6.2

Creating Option Buttons

Donations to The Lighthouse come from both private individuals and businesses. Terry handles the receipts and thank you notes for private donations differently than those for business donations, so she would like the form to indicate whether the contact information is associated with a business or represents a home address. Terry doesn't want donors to enter this information in an input box; she would prefer that they enter the information with option buttons.

Option buttons, also called **radio buttons**, allow users to select a data value from a limited set of possible values. With option buttons, users can select only one button at a time from a group. The syntax to create a collection of option buttons is

```
<input type="radio" name="name" id="id1" value="value1" />
<input type="radio" name="name" id="id2" value="value2" />
<input type="radio" name="name" id="id3" value="value3" />
...
```

where *name* identifies the field associated with the collection of option buttons; *id1*, *id2*, *id3*, etc. identify the specific options; and *value1*, *value2*, *value3*, etc. are the field values associated with each option. Notice that all options within the group have the same *name* value. In fact, the id attribute is required only if you intend to use a field label with the option button or need some way of distinguishing one option button from another for use with a program or script.

When a group of option buttons share the same name, this puts them in a group—so that selecting one option button automatically deselects all of the others. Figure 6-26 shows an example of a Web form that uses an option button group to indicate political party affiliations.

Figure 6-26 **Creating a group of option buttons**

```
<fieldset>
   <legend>Party Affiliation</legend>

   <label for="demOption">Democrat</label>
   <input type="radio" name="party" id="demOption" value="dem" />

   <label for="gopOption">Republican</label>
   <input type="radio" name="party" id="gopOption" value="gop" />

   <label for="indOption">Independent</label>
   <input type="radio" name="party" id="indOption" value="ind" />
</fieldset>
```

HTML code

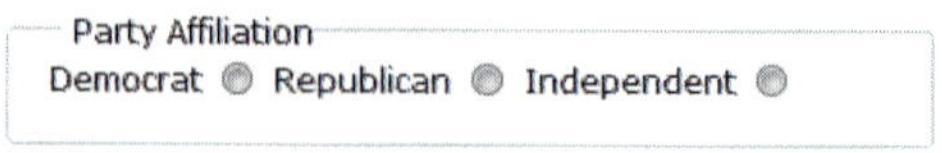

open buttons

In this sample code, all of the option buttons have the field name party but each has a different value. Because they share the same name, a user can select only one of the option buttons. The field set box provides a visual clue that all of these option buttons are part of the same field, but the field set is only there to aid in the form's appearance—it is not part of the option button syntax.

By default, an option button is unselected; but you can set an option button to be selected by adding the checked attribute to the input element:

```
<input type="radio" checked="checked" />
```

In older Web pages, you might see this code also entered as

```
<input type="radio" checked />
```

with no value provided for the checked attribute. However, this format is not supported in the official specifications for HTML and XHTML and should be avoided in new Web pages.

Tip

Use option buttons when a field has a small number of possible values, of which the user can select only one; otherwise, use a selection list.

Creating a Group of Option Buttons | Reference Window

- To create a group of option buttons associated with a single field, add the elements
```
<input type="radio" name="name" id="id1" value="value1" />
<input type="radio" name="name" id="id2" value="value2" />
<input type="radio" name="name" id="id3" value="value3" />
```
to the Web form, where *name* identifies the field associated with the collection of option buttons; *id1*, *id2*, *id3*, etc. identify the specific options; and *value1*, *value2*, *value3*, etc. are the field values associated with each option.
- To specify the default option, add the following attribute to the <input> tag:
```
checked="checked"
```

Terry wants you to insert two option buttons at the top of the Contact Information field set with the labels Home and Business. The field name you'll use for this group of option buttons is addressType. To make it clear to donors that the two option buttons are related, you'll enclose them in a field set box.

To create the option buttons for the addressType field:

1. Reopen the **donations.htm** file in your text editor.
2. Directly below the Contact Information legend, insert the following field set containing two option buttons with associated field labels:

```
<fieldset id="addressOptions">
   <legend>Address For</legend>

      <label for="homeType">Home</label>
      <input type="radio" id="homeType" name="addressType"
             value="home" />

      <label for="busType">Business</label>
      <input type="radio" id="busType" name="addressType"
             value="business" />

</fieldset>
```

Figure 6-27 shows the revised code.

Tip

Always enclose your option button groups within a field set box to provide a visual indication that the option buttons belong to the same field.

Figure 6-27 Inserting a field set containing an option button group

```
<form name="donationForm" id="donationForm">

   <fieldset id="contact">
      <legend>Contact Information</legend>

      <fieldset id="addressOptions">
         <legend>Address For</legend>

         <label for="homeType">Home</label>
         <input type="radio" id="homeType" name="addressType" value="home" />
         <label for="busType">Business</label>
         <input type="radio" id="busType" name="addressType" value="business" />

      </fieldset>

      <label class="blockLabel">
         First Name<span>*</span>
         <input type="text" id="firstName" name="firstName" />
      </label>
```

3. Save your changes to the **donations.htm** file and then reload it in your browser. Figure 6-28 shows the new field set containing the two option buttons from the addressType field.

Figure 6-28 Option buttons in the donations form

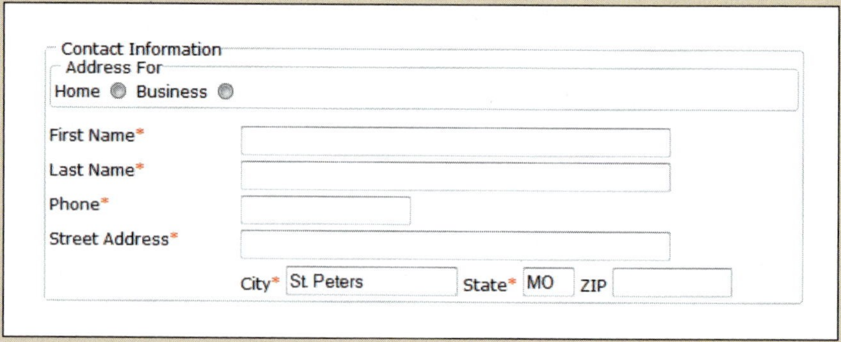

4. Test the option buttons by clicking each one, verifying that you can select only one option at a time. Also verify that you can select an option button by clicking the field label associated with the button.

You decide that the option button group would look better if it weren't as wide and if it were lined up with the other control elements in the form. You'll add this code to the style sheet.

To change the appearance of the option group:

1. Reopen the **forms.css** file in your text editor.
2. The fieldset element containing the option buttons has the id addressOptions. Add the following style to the bottom of the style sheet, as shown in Figure 6-29.

```
#addressOptions {width: 180px; margin-left: 150px}
```

Figure 6-29

Setting the format of the addressOptions field set

```
#firstName, #lastName, #street {width: 25em}
#phone, #city                  {width: 10em}
#state                         {width: 3em}
#zip                           {width: 7em}

#addressOptions          {width: 180px; margin-left: 150px}
```

3. Save your changes to the style sheet and reload the **donations.htm** file in your Web browser. Figure 6-30 shows the new appearance of the control elements in the form.

Figure 6-30

Revised format of the addressOptions field set

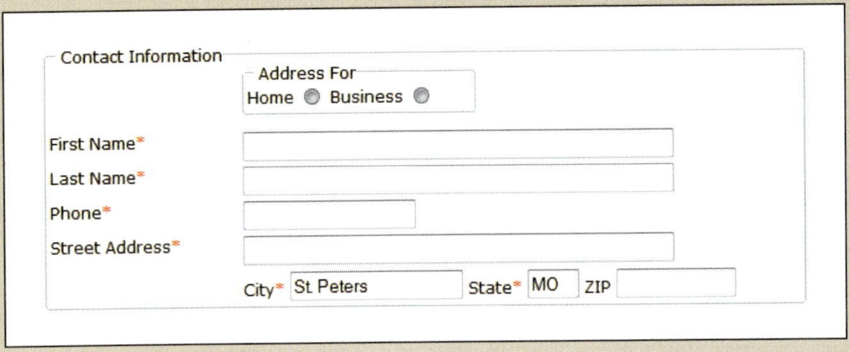

You've now entered all of the control elements for the Contact Information part of the form. Next you'll add fields that store the amount of the donation and the method of payment. You'll start by creating an input box in which donors enter the amount of their donation. You'll name this new field amount. You'll use the same blockLabel class style you used earlier in the form to format the input box and field label.

To insert an input box for the amount of the donation:

1. Return to the **donations.htm** file in your text editor.
2. Scroll down the file. Within the Donation Information field set, insert the following code, as shown in Figure 6-31.

```
<label class="blockLabel">
   Donation Amount<span>*</span>
   <input type="text" id="amount" name="amount" />
</label>
```

Figure 6-31

Adding an input box for the donation amount

```
<fieldset id="donation">
   <legend>Donation Information</legend>

   <label class="blockLabel">
      Donation Amount<span>*</span>
      <input type="text" id="amount" name="amount" />
   </label>
</fieldset>
```

3. Save your changes to the file and then reload **donations.htm** in your Web browser. Figure 6-32 shows the new donation amount input box.

Figure 6-32 Donation amount input box

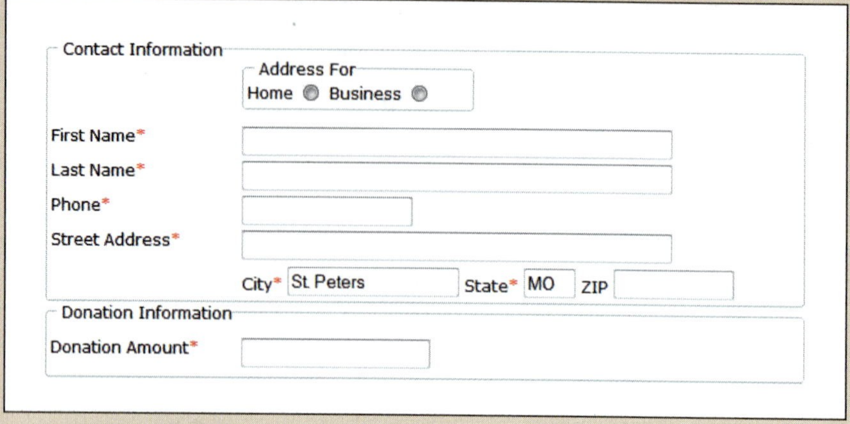

In the next field in the donation form, donors are asked to specify the credit card type. To insert this information you'll use a selection list.

Creating a Selection List

A **selection list** is a list box that presents users with a group of possible field values. A selection list fulfills the same role as a group of option buttons and is used in situations where there are too many options to be easily listed on the form with option buttons. As with option buttons, selection lists help prevent spelling mistakes and erroneous data entries that can occur with text input boxes. A selection list is created using the elements

```
<select name="name" id="id">
   <option value="value1">text1</option>
   <option value="value2">text2</option>
   ...
</select>
```

where *name* and *id* identify the field associated with the selection list; *value1*, *value2*, etc. are the possible field values; and *text1*, *text2*, etc. are the entries in the selection list. The text entries are displayed to the user, while CGI scripts retrieving data from a selection list will often work with either the field value or the text entry. Figure 6-33 shows a selection list version of the party affiliation field described earlier with option buttons.

Figure 6-33 Creating a selection list

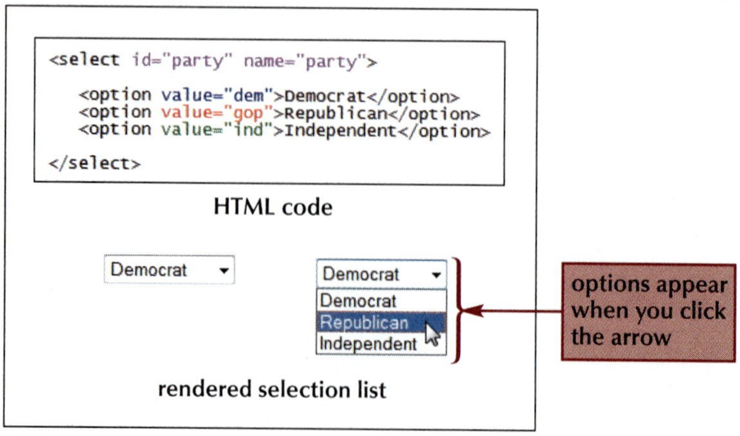

Although the first text entry is displayed in a selection list, this is not a default value for the list. To specify which of the options should be selected by default, add the following selected attribute to the option element:

```
<option selected="selected" value="value">text</option>
```

In older code, you might also see the selected attribute entered without an attribute value, appearing as

```
<option selected value="value">text</option>
```

but this is considered poor syntax and is rejected in XHTML documents.

Grouping Selection Options

In a selection list, the options are presented in the same order as they appear in the HTML code. In long selection lists it might be difficult for users to locate a particular option value. You can organize the selection list options by placing them in **option groups** using the optgroup element

```
<select>
   <optgroup label="label1">
      <option>text1</option>
      <option>text2</option>
...
   </optgroup>
   <optgroup label="label2">
      <option>text1</option>
      <option>text2</option>
...
   </optgroup>
</select>
```

where *label1*, *label2*, and so forth are the labels for the different groups of options. The text for the label appears in the selection list above each group of items but is not a selectable item from the list. Figure 6-34 shows an example of a selection list in which the options are divided into two groups.

Figure 6-34 **Organizing a selection list with option groups**

```
<label for="candidate">Candidate</label>
<select id="candidate" name="candidate">

   <optgroup label="Democrat">
      <option>Tim Harris</option>
      <option>Gary Nielsen</option>
      <option>Kate Paulenty</option>
   </optgroup>

   <optgroup label="Republican">
      <option>Barbara Alt</option>
      <option>Peter Trudea</option>
      <option>Maria Sandoval</option>
   </optgroup>

</select>
```

HTML code

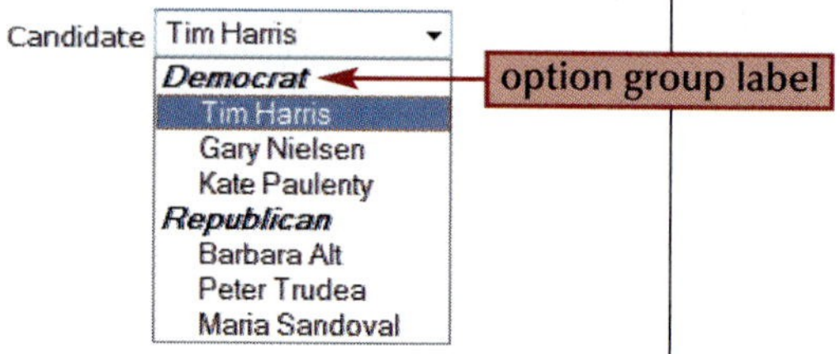

selection list option group

The appearance of the option group label is determined by the browser. You can apply a style to an entire option group including its label, but there is no CSS style to change the appearance of the option group label alone.

Setting the Selection List Size

By default, selection lists display only the currently selected option value. You can change the number of options displayed by applying the size attribute

```
<select size="value"> ... </select>
```

to the select element, where *value* is the number of items that the selection list displays in the form at a time. By specifying a value greater than 1, you change the selection list from a drop-down list box to a list box with a scroll bar that allows a user to scroll through the selection options. If you set the size attribute to be equal to the number of options in the selection list, the scroll bar either is not displayed or is dimmed, as shown in Figure 6-35.

Figure 6-35 **Setting the size of the selection list**

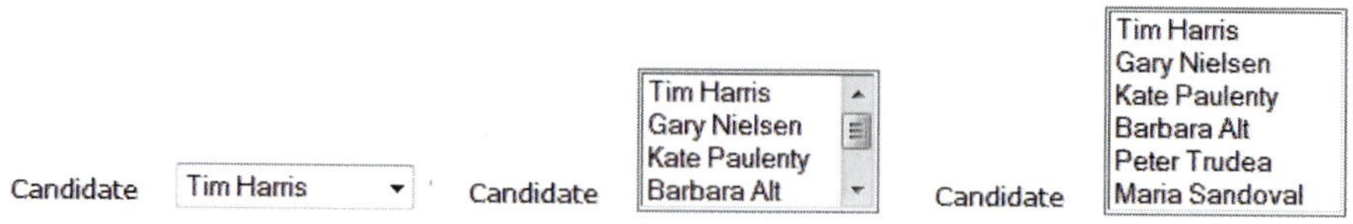

size="1" size="4" size="6"(all)

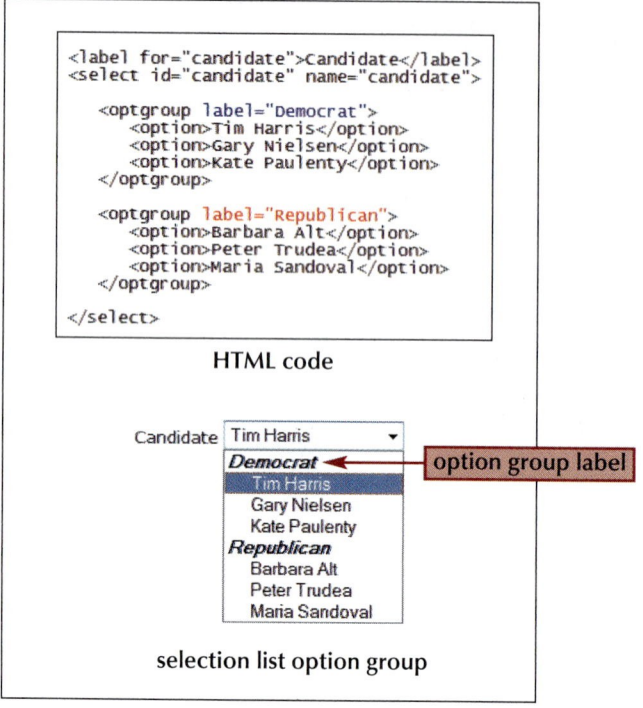

Although the size attribute defines the number of options displayed in the list box, there is no HTML attribute to set the width of the list box. The browser will make the width large enough to display the longest option text. If you want to change the width of a list box, you can use the CSS width style.

Creating a Selection List | Reference Window

- To create a selection list, add the elements

```
<select name="name" id="id">
  <option value="value1">text1</option>
  <option value="value2">text2</option>
  ...
</select>
```

  to the Web form, where *name* and *id* identify the field associated with the selection list; *value1*, *value2*, etc. are the possible field values; and *text1*, *text2*, etc. are the entries in the selection list.
- To specify the default option, add the following attribute to the <option> tag:

```
selected="selected"
```

- To set the number of options displayed at one time in the selection list, add the attribute

```
size="value"
```

  to the <select> tag, where *value* is the number of options displayed in the selection list at any one time.

Now that you've learned about selection lists, you can add one to the donation form for entering the credit card brand. The Lighthouse accepts payments from American Express, Discover, MasterCard, and Visa. The field values Terry wants you to use for these three vendors are Amex, Disc, MC, and Visa, respectively. She wants the values to be stored in a field named creditCard. The code for the selection is:

```
<select id="creditCard" name="creditCard">
   <option value="Amex">American Express</option>
   <option value="Disc">Discover</option>
   <option value="MC">MasterCard</option>
   <option value="Visa">Visa</option>
</select>
```

Terry wants the selection list displayed as a block-level element, with the field label placed alongside it.

To create a selection list for the credit card vendors:

1. Return to the **donations.htm** file in your text editor.
2. Below the donation amount input box, insert the following code, as shown in Figure 6-36.

```
<label class="blockLabel">
   Credit Card<span>*</span>
   <select id="creditCard" name="creditCard">
      <option value="Amex">American Express</option>
      <option value="Disc">Discover</option>
      <option value="MC">MasterCard</option>
      <option value="Visa">Visa</option>
   </select>
</label>
```

Figure 6-36 **Inserting a selection list**

```
<fieldset id="donation">
   <legend>Donation Information</legend>

   <label class="blockLabel">
      Donation Amount<span>*</span>
      <input type="text" id="amount" name="amount" />
   </label>

   <label class="blockLabel">
      Credit Card<span>*</span>
      <select id="creditCard" name="creditCard">
         <option value="Amex">American Express</option>
         <option value="Disc">Discover</option>
         <option value="MC">MasterCard</option>
         <option value="Visa">Visa</option>
      </select>
   </label>

</fieldset>
```

selection list options

3. Save your changes to the file, and then return to the **forms.css** style sheet in your text editor. Like the input boxes you created earlier, you want the selection list positioned 150 pixels from the left margin of the field label. Add the following style to the bottom of the style sheet, as shown in Figure 6-37:

```
#creditCard {position: absolute; left: 150px}
```

Figure 6-37 **Formatting the selection list**

```
#firstName, #lastName, #street {width: 25em}
#phone, #city                  {width: 10em}
#state                         {width: 3em}
#zip                           {width: 7em}

#addressOptions          {width: 180px; margin-left: 150px}

#creditCard              {position:absolute; left: 150px}
```

4. Save your changes to the style sheet, and then reload **donations.htm** in your Web browser. Figure 6-38 shows the selection list for the creditCard field.

Figure 6-38 **Credit card selection list in the donations form**

5. Click the selection list control for the creditCard field and verify that it displays the names of the four credit cards accepted by The Lighthouse.

The next two fields in the donation form are the cardHolder and cardNumber fields, which will be input boxes for users to enter the name on the credit card and the credit card number. You'll format these elements using the blockLabel label class, setting the width of both input boxes to 25 em.

To create input boxes for the card holder name and the credit card number:

1. Return to the **donations.htm** file in your text editor.
2. Below the selection list, insert the following control elements, as shown in Figure 6-39.

```
<label class="blockLabel">
   Cardholder Name<span>*</span>
   <input type="text" id="cardHolder" name="cardHolder" />
</label>

<label class="blockLabel">
   Card Number<span>*</span>
   <input type="text" id="cardNumber" name="cardNumber" />
</label>
```

Figure 6-39 Adding input boxes for the cardholder name and credit card number

```
<label class="blockLabel">
   Credit Card<span>*</span>
   <select id="creditCard" name="creditCard">
      <option value="Amex">American Express</option>
      <option value="Disc">Discover</option>
      <option value="MC">MasterCard</option>
      <option value="Visa">Visa</option>
   </select>
</label>

<label class="blockLabel">
   Cardholder Name<span>*</span>
   <input type="text" id="cardHolder" name="cardHolder" />
</label>

<label class="blockLabel">
   Card Number<span>*</span>
   <input type="text" id="cardNumber" name="cardNumber" />
</label>

</fieldset>
```

3. Save your changes to the file, and then return to the **forms.css** style sheet in your text editor. Add the following styles at the bottom of the file to set the width on the cardHolder and cardNumber input boxes:

   ```
   #cardHolder, #cardNumber {width: 25em}
   ```

4. Save your changes to the style sheet, and then reload **donations.htm** in your Web browser. Figure 6-40 shows the input boxes for the cardHolder and cardNumber fields.

Figure 6-40 Cardholder Name and Card Number input boxes

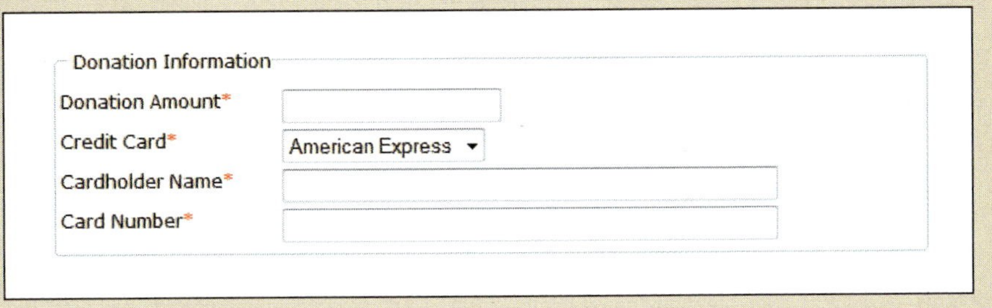

The final credit card information you need to add to the form is the expiration date. You'll add two selection lists to collect this information. One selection list will contain the month values from January (01) to December (12). The other selection list will contain the year value, ranging from 2011 to 2015.

To create selection lists for the credit card expiration date:

1. Return to the **donations.htm** file in your text editor.
2. Below the credit card number input box, insert the following code, as shown in Figure 6-41.

```
<label class="blockLabel">
   Expiration Date<span>*</span>
   <select id="expMonth" name="expMonth">
      <option value="01">January (01)</option>
      <option value="02">February (02)</option>
      <option value="03">March (03)</option>
      <option value="04">April (04)</option>
      <option value="05">May (05)</option>
      <option value="06">June (06)</option>
      <option value="07">July (07)</option>
      <option value="08">August (08)</option>
      <option value="09">September (09)</option>
      <option value="10">October (10)</option>
      <option value="11">November (11)</option>
      <option value="12">December (12)</option>
   </select>
   <select id="expYear" name="expYear">
      <option value="2011">2011</option>
      <option value="2012">2012</option>
      <option value="2013">2013</option>
      <option value="2014">2014</option>
      <option value="2015">2015</option>
   </select>
</label>
```

Figure 6-41 **Creating selection lists for the expiration month and year**

```
   <label class="blockLabel">
      Card Number<span>*</span>
      <input type="text" id="cardNumber" name="cardNumber" />
   </label>

   <label class="blockLabel">
      Expiration Date<span>*</span>
      <select id="expMonth" name="expMonth">
         <option value="01">January (01)</option>
         <option value="02">February (02)</option>
         <option value="03">March (03)</option>
         <option value="04">April (04)</option>
         <option value="05">May (05)</option>
         <option value="06">June (06)</option>
         <option value="07">July (07)</option>
         <option value="08">August (08)</option>
         <option value="09">September (09)</option>
         <option value="10">October (10)</option>
         <option value="11">November (11)</option>
         <option value="12">December (12)</option>
      </select>
      <select id="expYear" name="expYear">
         <option value="2011">2011</option>
         <option value="2012">2012</option>
         <option value="2013">2013</option>
         <option value="2014">2014</option>
         <option value="2015">2015</option>
      </select>
   </label>

</fieldset>
```

3. Save your changes to the file.

   You also have to add styles to the forms.css style sheet to line up the expMonth and expYear selection lists with the other entries in the donation form.

4. Go to the **forms.css** file in your text editor and add the following styles to the bottom of the file, as shown in Figure 6-42.

```
#expMonth {position: absolute; left: 150px}
#expYear  {position: absolute; left: 280px}
```

Figure 6-42 **Positioning the expiration month and year selection lists**

```
#creditCard           {position:absolute; left: 150px}

#cardHolder, #cardNumber {width: 25em}

#expMonth             {position: absolute; left: 150px}
#expYear              {position: absolute; left: 280px}
```

5. Save your changes to the style sheet and reload **donations.htm** in your Web browser. Figure 6-43 shows all of the control elements that collect credit card data.

Figure 6-43 **Control elements collecting credit card data**

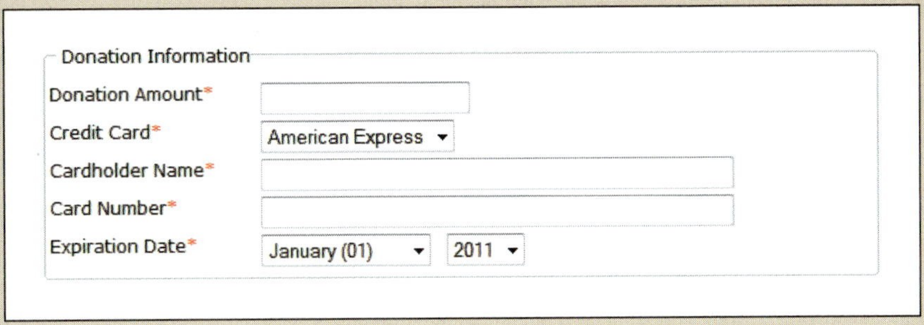

6. Test the selection lists by clicking the selection list arrows to verify that all of the year and month options are present.

Allowing for Multiple Selections

In the code you just entered for the donation form, donors were limited to a single option—a certain kind of credit card and a specific month and year for the expiration date. However, selection lists also allow for multiple selections by applying the following multiple attribute to the select element:

```
<select multiple="multiple"> . . . </select>
```

In older code, you might see the minimized version of this attribute, removing the attribute value as follows:

```
<select multiple> . . . </select>
```

However, as with the selected attribute, this is not correct HTML or XHTML syntax and so you should avoid using it.

There are two ways for users to select multiple items from a selection list. For noncontiguous selections, press and hold the Ctrl key (or the Command key on a Macintosh) while making the selections. For a contiguous selection, select the first item, press and hold the Shift key, and then select the last item in the range. This selects the two items as well as all the items between them.

If you decide to use a multiple selection list in a form, be aware that the form sends a name/value pair to the server for each option the user selects from the list. This requires the server-based program to be able to handle a single field with multiple values. Check and verify that your server-based programs are designed to handle this before using a multiple selection list. In most cases, you are better served using check boxes rather than selection lists with multiple values. You'll examine check boxes next because Terry wants donors to be able to indicate if they're interested in volunteering at The Lighthouse.

Working with Check Boxes

You use a **check box** control in situations where you are checking for the presence or absence of something, such as whether or not a donor is interested in volunteering at the center. Check boxes are created using the input element with the type attribute set to checkbox, as follows:

```
<input type="checkbox" name="name" id="id" value="value" />
```

The value attribute contains the value of the field when the check box is checked. If no value is provided, the value On is used by default. For example, the following code creates a check box for determining whether the user is a member of the Democratic party:

```
<label for="dem">Democrat?</label>
<input type="checkbox" name="dem" id="dem" value="yes" />
```

If the check box is selected, the browser will submit the name/value pair of dem/yes to the CGI script running on the Web server. A name/value pair is only sent to the server when the check box is checked by the user. By default, check boxes are not selected. To make a check box selected by default, add the following checked attribute to the input element:

```
<input type="checkbox" checked="checked" />
```

As with other form attributes, you will also see older code with this attribute used as:

```
<input type="checkbox" checked />
```

But once again, you should always provide an attribute value, even if most browsers accept this attribute without a value.

Reference Window | Creating a Check Box

- To create a check box, add the element
  `<input type="checkbox" name="name" id="id" value="value" />`
  to the Web form, where *name* and *id* identify the check box field and *value* is the value of the check box field if the check box is selected.
- To specify that the check box is selected by default, add the following attribute to the <input> tag:
  `checked="checked"`

In the next section of the donation form, Terry wants you to add a few fields for recording customer feedback and comments. Terry wants donors to be able to select a check box indicating whether they're interested in doing volunteer work at The Lighthouse in addition to providing financial support. You'll insert this field with a check box control element.

To create a check box for volunteers:

1. Return to the **donations.htm** file in your text editor and go to the Feedback field set near the bottom of the file.
2. Directly below the legend element, insert the following code, as shown in Figure 6-44.

```
<label>
   <input type="checkbox" id="volunteer" name="volunteer" />
   I'm interested in volunteering at The Lighthouse.
</label>
```

Figure 6-44 Adding a check box for the volunteer field

```
<fieldset id="feedback">
   <legend>Feedback</legend>

   <label>
      <input type="checkbox" id="volunteer" name="volunteer" />
      I'm interested in volunteering at The Lighthouse.
   </label>

</fieldset>

</form>
```

3. Save your changes to the file, and reload **donations.htm** in your Web browser. Figure 6-45 shows the new check box control added to the Feedback field set box.

Figure 6-45 The volunteer check box control

Feedback
I'm interested in volunteering at The Lighthouse.

4. Click the check box, and then click the field label to verify that you can alternately select and deselect the field with both the check box and its label.

Note that you did not specify a value for the volunteer field. When the form is eventually submitted to a CGI script, it will send the name/value pair as volunteer/on when the check box is selected in the form, which means the person would like Terry to contact him or her for volunteering. If the check box is not selected, no name/value pair will be sent, and Terry will not contact the person.

InSight | **Specifying the Tab Order**

Typically, users navigate through a Web form using the Tab key, which moves the cursor from one field to another in the order that the field tags are entered into the HTML file.

You can specify an alternate order by adding the tabindex attribute to any control element in your form. When each element is assigned a tab index number, the cursor moves through the fields from the lowest index number to the highest. For example, to assign the tab index number 1 to the firstName field from the donation form, you would enter the following tabindex attribute to the control element:

```
<input name="firstName" id="firstName" tabindex="1" />
```

This code would ensure that the cursor is in the firstName field when the form is first opened. (Fields with zero or negative tab indexes are omitted from the tab order entirely.)

Web page designers can use tab index numbers in their forms without worrying about older browsers that do not support this new standard. Such browsers simply ignore the tabindex attribute and continue to tab to the fields in the order that they appear in the HTML file.

Working with Text Area Controls

The final part of the Feedback field set includes a place where donors can offer comments about The Lighthouse. Because their comments might contain several lines of text, it would not be appropriate to enter those comments in an input box because input boxes are limited to a single line of text. Instead, you can create a control element that allows for extended text entries using the textarea element

```
<textarea name="name" id="id">
   text
</textarea>
```

where *text* is default text that is placed in the text area box. You do not have to specify default text—this would leave the text area box empty on the form.

The size of the text area box is determined by the browser. Most browsers create a text area box that is about 20 characters long and two or three lines high. To change the dimensions of the text area box, you add the row and cols attributes

```
<textarea rows="value" cols="value"> ... </textarea>
```

where the rows attribute specifies the number of lines in the text area box and the cols attribute specifies the number of characters per line. You can also set the dimensions of the textarea element using the CSS width and height styles.

Tip

The rows and cols attributes are required under strict applications of XHTML.

As you type text into a text area box, the text automatically wraps to a new line as it extends beyond the box's width. If more text is entered into the box than can be displayed, the browser automatically adds horizontal and vertical scroll bars to the box. You can control how the browser handles extra text by using the wrap attribute

```
<textarea wrap="type"> ... </textarea>
```

where *type* is one of the values described in Figure 6-46.

Values of the wrap attribute **Figure 6-46**

Value	Description
off	All the text is displayed on a single line, scrolling to the left if the text extends past the width of the box. Text goes to the next row in the box only if the Enter key is pressed. The text is sent to the CGI script in a single line.
soft	Text wraps automatically to the next line when it extends beyond the width of the input box. The text is still sent to the CGI script in a single line without any information about how the text was wrapped within the text area box.
hard	Text wraps automatically to the next line when it extends beyond the width of the input box. When the text is sent to the CGI script, the line-wrapping information is included, allowing the CGI script to work with the text exactly as it appears in the text area box.

The wrap attribute is not part of the World Wide Web Consortium (W3C) specifications for HTML or XHTML, but all browsers support it. The default wrap value is soft, which allows the text to wrap automatically to a new line—note that this information is not sent to the CGI script. If you need to include the line wraps as part of the field value, use the following attribute value:

```
wrap="hard"
```

Creating a Text Area Box

| Reference Window

- To create a text area box for multiple lines of text, use the element
```
<textarea name="name" id="id">
  text
</textarea>
```
where *name* and *id* identify the field associated with the text area box and *text* is the default text that appears in the box.
- To specify the dimensions of the box, add the attributes
```
rows="value" cols="value"
```
to the <textarea> tag, where the rows attribute specifies the number of lines in the text area box and the cols attribute specifies the number of characters per line.

You decide to use a text area box for the donor comments, setting the size of the box to 50 characters wide by five lines high.

To create the comments text area box:

1. Return to the **donations.htm** file in your text editor.
2. Below the volunteer check box, insert the following elements to create the text area box, as shown in Figure 6-47.

```
<label for="comments" class="blockLabel">Comments</label>
<textarea id="comments" name="comments"
          rows="5" cols="50">
</textarea>
```

Figure 6-47 Adding a text area box

```
<fieldset id="feedback">
   <legend>Feedback</legend>

   <label>
      <input type="checkbox" id="volunteer" name="volunteer" />
      I'm interested in volunteering at The Lighthouse.
   </label>

   <label for="comments" class="blockLabel">Comments</label>
   <textarea id="comments" name="comments" rows="5" cols="50"></textarea>

</fieldset>
```

the text area box will have five lines of 50 characters each

3. Close the file, saving your changes, and then reload **donations.htm** in your Web browser. Figure 6-48 shows the comments text area box.

Figure 6-48 Text area box in the Feedback section

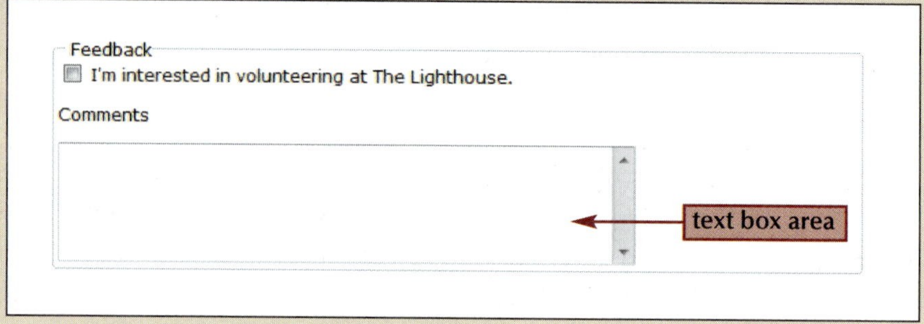

4. Type some sample text into the text area box and verify that the text wraps to a new line as you exceed the width of the box.

   Trouble? Line wraps do not occur in the middle of words. If you find your sample text is not wrapping to a new line, make sure you are entering individual words rather than a long character string.

You've added the last field to the donation form. Terry likes the layout of the form, but she thinks the field sets would look better if they had a light brown background similar to the color used in the page's background image. She also wants you to increase the space between and within each of the field set boxes.

To format the field set boxes:

1. Go to the **forms.css** style sheet file in your text editor.
2. At the top of the style sheet, add the following style, as shown in Figure 6-49.

```
fieldset {margin-bottom: 10px; padding: 10px;
          background-color: rgb(237, 233, 223)}
```

Figure 6-49 Setting the style of the fieldset elements

```
fieldset                {margin-bottom: 10px; padding: 10px; background-color: rgb(237,233,223)}
label.blockLabel        {display: block; position: relative; margin: 12px 0px}
label.blockLabel input  {position: absolute; left: 150px}
```

3. Close the file, saving your changes, and then reload **donations.htm** in your Web browser. Figure 6-50 shows the revised design of the entire donation form.

Figure 6-50 **Layout and design of the donation form**

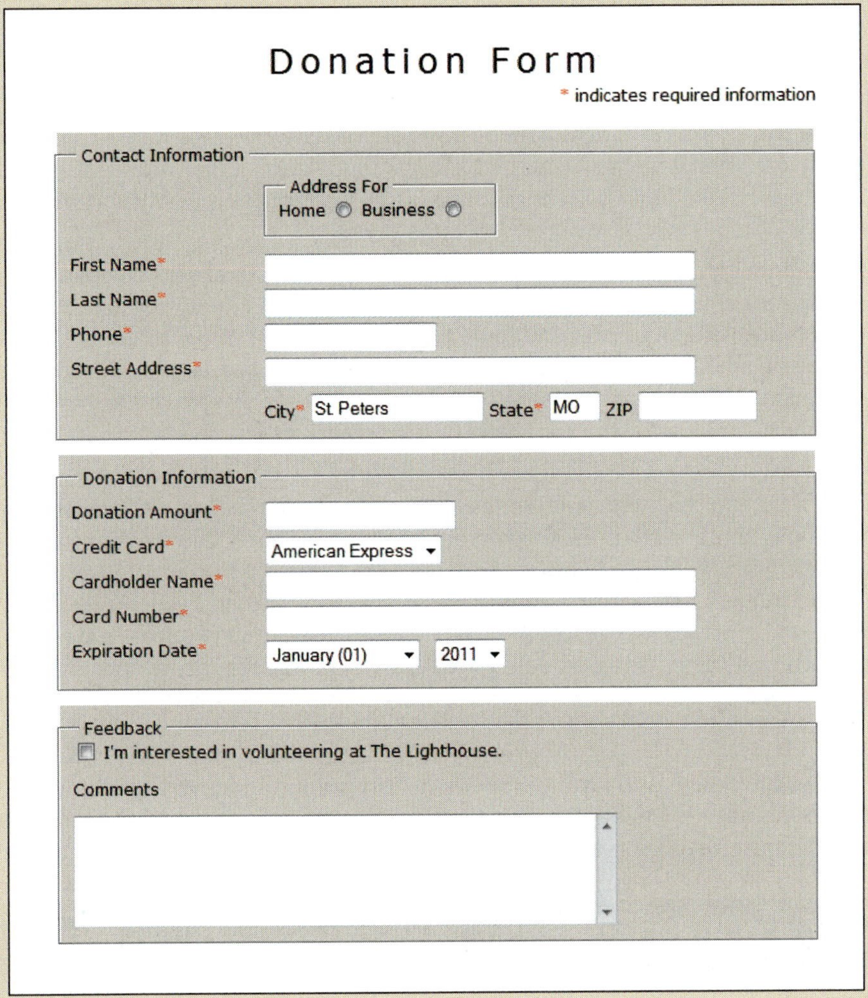

Trouble? Depending on your browser, the tan background might not extend beyond the borders of the field set.

4. Take some time to work with all of the control elements you've entered, pressing the **Tab** key to move from one element to another and entering sample data into each field.

5. If you want to take a break before starting the next session, you can close all open files and programs now.

InSight | Web Forms and CSS

When you complete a Web form, you will probably want to ensure that the various form elements appear the same across different browsers and operating systems. The most natural way of doing this would appear to be with CSS. For example, you can apply the following style to display all command buttons with blue text on a yellow background:

```
input[type=button] {color: blue; background-color: yellow}
```

The degree to which these control elements can be formatted varies from browser to browser. Safari, for example, does not apply the above style, nor does it allow any changes to be made to any input element's border or background style. Other browsers are much more lenient. However, an important question for Web designers is whether to make these kinds of style changes even if the browser allows them.

One school of thought holds that any and all parts of a Web form should be open to CSS styles to enhance creativity in the design process. A different point of view holds that control elements such as input boxes and form buttons need to be, above all, usable. The most usable control element is one that has the same design and appearance as the other control elements found elsewhere on the user's computer. When users have come to expect a certain appearance for input boxes, command buttons, check boxes, and radio buttons, they can become confused by a Web format that has a totally different style.

However, the bottom line is that because the appearance of control elements is determined by the operating system and the browser, different browsers will apply CSS styles to control elements in different ways. Research has shown that trying to achieve a uniform look for control elements is a fruitless task. The best approach is to use CSS to lightly style form controls by modifying only properties such as font color, font size, and background colors—and realize that your style changes will not be seen by all of your users. As always, any styles applied to a Web form need to be checked under a variety of browsers and operating systems.

Terry likes the design and layout of the donations form. In the next session you'll add elements to the page to enable the donation form to interact with the CGI script running on The Lighthouse's Web server.

Review | Session 6.2 Quick Check

1. Specify the code to create two option buttons for the Computer field with the values PC and Macintosh.
2. In Question 1, what attribute would you add to the code to make PC the default value for the Computer field?
3. Specify the code to create a selection list for the State field with possible values of California, Nevada, Oregon, and Washington.
4. What attribute would you add to the code in Question 3 to make Oregon the default value for the State field?
5. In Question 3, what attribute would you add to the code to display all of the possible field values in the selection list?
6. How would you modify the code in Question 3 to allow for multiple selections?
7. Specify the code to create a check box and a label for the Computer field. The text of the label should be "I use a PC" and the value of the check box should be Yes.
8. Specify the code to create a text area box for the Memo field that displays 10 lines of text, each of which displays up to 40 characters.

Session 6.3

Working with Form Buttons

Up to now, all of your control elements have involved entering field values. Another type of control element is one that performs an action. In forms, this is usually done with **form buttons**, which perform one of three actions:

- run a command
- submit the form to the CGI script running on the server
- cancel the data entry done in the form

The first type of button you'll examine is the command button.

Creating a Command Button

A **command button** runs a command on the Web page. This command can be a call to a program running on a Web server or to a program installed within the Web browser. Command buttons are created using the input element

```
<input type="button" value="text" />
```

where *text* is the text that appears on the button. By itself, a command button performs no actions on a Web page. To create an action for a command button, you have to write a script or program that runs when the button is clicked. This can be done using a programming language such as JavaScript. Because that is beyond the scope of this tutorial, we won't examine how to use command buttons on the donation page.

Creating Submit and Reset Buttons

The two other kinds of form buttons are submit and reset buttons. A **submit button** submits a form to the server for processing when clicked. Clicking the **reset button** resets a form, changing all field values to their original default values and deleting any values that the user might have entered into the form. The syntax for creating these two buttons is

```
<input type="submit" value="text" />
<input type="reset" value="text" />
```

where the *value* attribute defines the text that appears on the button.

You can also specify name and id attributes for command, submit, and reset buttons, although these attributes are not required. You would use these attributes when a form contains multiple buttons and you're running a program that needs to distinguish one button from another. You won't need to add id and name attributes to the buttons on the donation form.

Tip

Avoid overpopulating your forms with buttons; too many buttons can be confusing. If more than one button is displayed, use CSS styles to give more visual emphasis on the button that will be most often clicked by the user.

Reference Window | Creating Form Buttons

- To create a form button to run a command, use the element
  ```
  <input type="button" value="text" />
  ```
  where *text* is the text that appears on the button.
- To create a form button to submit the form and its fields and values to a CGI script, use the element
  ```
  <input type="submit" value="text" />
  ```
- To create a form button to reset the form to its default values and appearance, use
  ```
  <input type="reset" value="text" />
  ```

Terry wants the donation form to include both a submit button and a reset button. The submit button, which she wants labeled Send Donation, will send the form data to the server for processing when clicked. The reset button, which she wants labeled Cancel, will erase the user's input and reset the fields to their default values.

To add the submit and reset buttons to the donation form:

1. Return to the **donations.htm** file in your text editor.
2. Scroll to the bottom of the file. Directly below the closing </fieldset> tag for the feedback field set, insert the following input elements, as shown in Figure 6-51:
   ```
   <input type="submit" value="Submit Donation" />
   <input type="reset" value="Cancel" />
   ```

Figure 6-51 Adding submit and reset buttons

```
      </fieldset>

      <input type="submit" value="Submit Donation" />
      <input type="reset" value="Cancel" />

   </form>

</div>

<address>
   The Lighthouse &bull;
   150 Cavates Rd. &bull;
   St. Peters, MO  63376 &bull;
   (636) 555 - 4477
</address>
```

3. Save your changes to the file, and then reload **donations.htm** in your Web browser. Figure 6-52 shows the complete donations page with the Web form.

Completed donation page

Figure 6-52

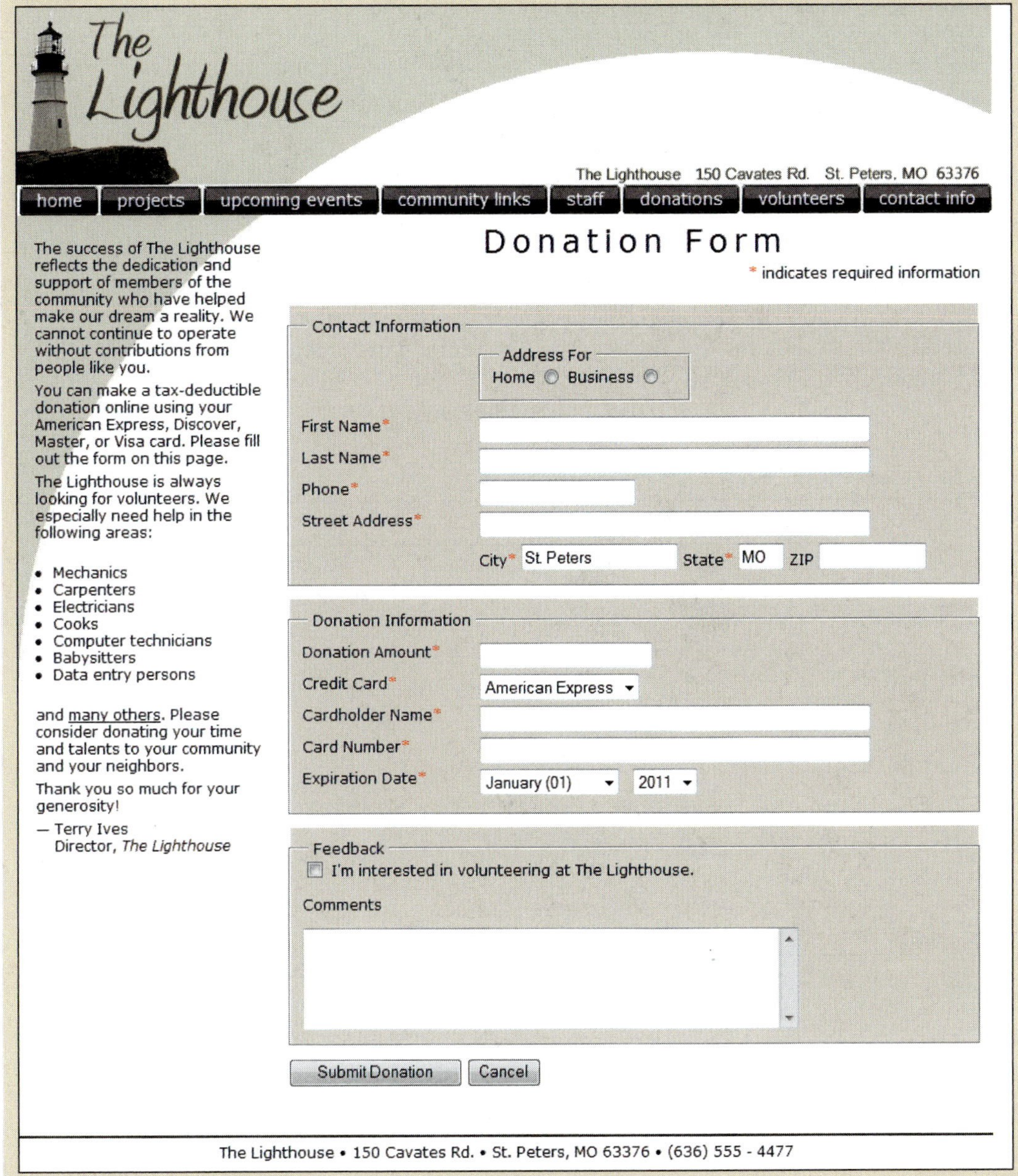
The Lighthouse
The Lighthouse 150 Cavates Rd. St. Peters, MO 63376
home
projects
upcoming events
community links
staff
donations
volunteers
contact info
The success of The Lighthouse reflects the dedication and support of members of the community who have helped make our dream a reality. We cannot continue to operate without contributions from people like you.
You can make a tax-deductible donation online using your American Express, Discover, Master, or Visa card. Please fill out the form on this page.
The Lighthouse is always looking for volunteers. We especially need help in the following areas:
Mechanics
Carpenters
Electricians
Cooks
Computer technicians
Babysitters
Data entry persons
and many others. Please consider donating your time and talents to your community and your neighbors.
Thank you so much for your generosity!
— Terry Ives
Director, The Lighthouse
Donation Form
* indicates required information
Contact Information
Address For
Home Business
First Name*
Last Name*
Phone*
Street Address*
City* St Peters
State* MO
ZIP
Donation Information
Donation Amount*
Credit Card* American Express
Cardholder Name*
Card Number*
Expiration Date* January (01) 2011
Feedback
I'm interested in volunteering at The Lighthouse.
Comments
Submit Donation
Cancel
The Lighthouse • 150 Cavates Rd. • St. Peters, MO 63376 • (636) 555 - 4477

4. Test the Cancel button by entering data into the form and then clicking the **Cancel** button. Verify that the form is reset to its initial state and default values.

Designing a Custom Button

The text of a command, submit, or reset button is determined by the value attribute. You are only allowed to specify the button label text. You can't add other elements such as an inline image to the button value. For more control over a form button's appearance you can use the button element

```
<button name="name" id="id" value="value" type="type">
   content
</button>
```

Tip

Custom buttons help personalize a Web site and make it more user friendly.

where the *name* and *value* attributes identify the button and the value sent to a server-based program, respectively; the *id* attribute specifies the button's id; the *type* attribute specifies the button type (submit, reset, or button); and *content* are page elements displayed within the button. The page content can include formatted text, inline images, and other design elements supported by HTML. Figure 6-53 shows an example of a button that contains both formatted text and an inline image.

Figure 6-53 **Creating a custom button**

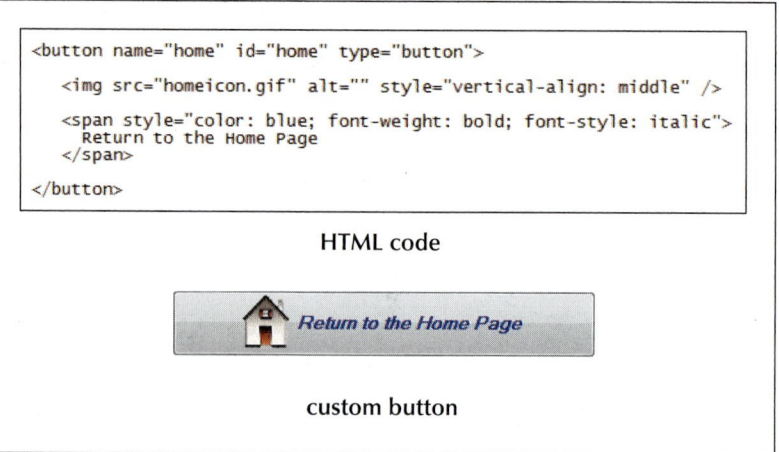

```
<button name="home" id="home" type="button">
   <img src="homeicon.gif" alt="" style="vertical-align: middle" />
   <span style="color: blue; font-weight: bold; font-style: italic">
     Return to the Home Page
   </span>
</button>
```

HTML code

custom button

Creating File Buttons

Another type of button supported by HTML is the **file button**, which is used to select files so that their contents can be submitted for processing to a program. File buttons are created by applying the attribute

```
type="file"
```

to the input element as follows:

```
<input type="file" name="name" id="id" />
```

Most browsers render file buttons as input boxes accompanied by a Browse button. As shown in Figure 6-54, when the user clicks the Browse button, a window opens from which the user can select a file. The file's location and name are then automatically inserted into the input box. When the form is submitted for processing, a script could use the value of the input box to retrieve the file as long as the Web server has access to the folder in which the file is stored.

Figure 6-54 Using a file button

```
<input type="file" id="fileName" name="fileName" />
```

HTML code

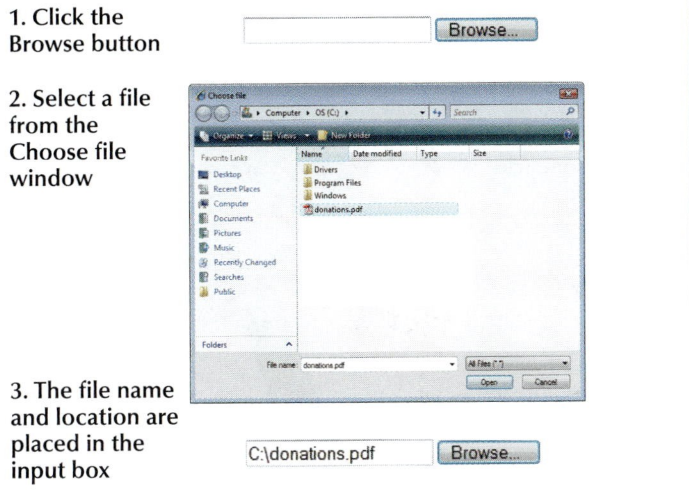
1. Click the Browse button
Browse...
2. Select a file from the Choose file window
3. The file name and location are placed in the input box
C:\donations.pdf
Browse...

You cannot change the label for the Browse button, but you can increase the size of the input box using either a CSS style or the HTML size attribute.

Creating Image Field Buttons

Another control element you can use in your Web form is an image button. Image buttons act like submit buttons, allowing a user to click an image to submit a form. The syntax for this type of control element is

```
<input type="image" src="url" name="text" id="id" />
```

where *url* is the filename and location of the inline image. The user interacts with this control element by clicking somewhere within the image.

The image field can also act as an image map by recording where within the image the user clicked. When the form is submitted to a server-based program, the coordinates of that mouse click are attached to the image's name in the format

```
name.x=coordinate&name.y=coordinate
```

where *name* is the name of the image field and *coordinate* are the coordinates of the mouse click in the *x* and *y* direction. For example, suppose your Web page contains the following inline image form element:

```
<input type="image" src="usamap.gif" name="usa" id="usa" />
```

If a user clicks the inline image at the coordinates (15, 30), the Web form sends the text string "usa.x=15&usa.y=30" to the server. Once the server-based program receives this data, it performs an action in response to that mouse click, as shown in Figure 6-55.

Figure 6-55 Using an image control field with a server-based program

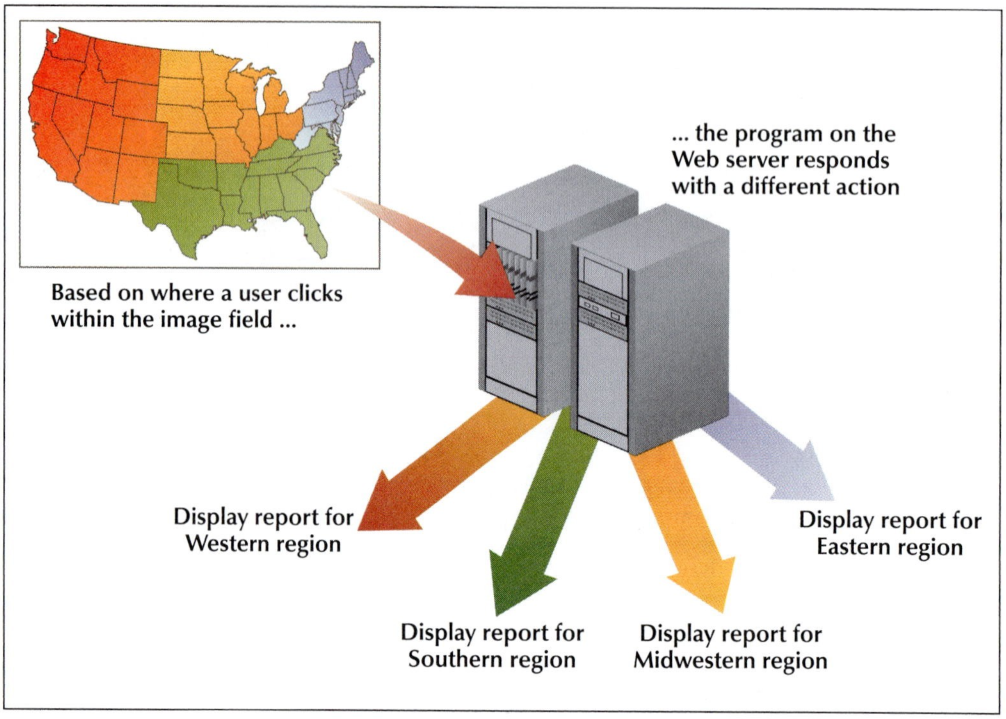

Terry doesn't need any inline image controls or file buttons in the Web form for The Lighthouse.

Working with Hidden Fields

Terry is pleased with the final appearance of the donation form. She shows the code for the form to Warren Kaughman, one of the programmers responsible for the CGI script that will process the donations. Warren notices only one thing missing from the code: the e-mail address that will receive and processes a new donation.

Unlike the other fields you've created so far, this field has a predefined value that users of the Web form should not be able to change. In fact, the e-mail address for donations should not even be displayed on the form. To accomplish this, you can use a **hidden field**, which is added to the form but not displayed on the Web page. The syntax for creating a hidden field is:

```
<input type="hidden" name="name" id="id" value="value" />
```

> **Tip**
> Even though hidden fields are not displayed by the browser, their values can still be read by examining the source code; so do not put any sensitive information in a hidden field.

You've learned from Warren that the name of the e-mail field should be eMail; the e-mail address that will receive the new donations is *donations@thelighthouse.org* (note that this is a fictional address used for the purposes of this tutorial). Now that you know both the field name and the field value, you can add the hidden field to the donation form.

Because the field is hidden, you can place it anywhere within the form element. A common practice is to place all hidden fields in one location, usually at the beginning of the form, to make it easier to read and interpret your HTML code. You should also include a comment describing the purpose of the field.

To add the hidden field to the donation form:

1. Return to the **donations.htm** file in your text editor.
2. Directly below the opening <form> tag, insert the following element, as shown in Figure 6-56.

```
<input type="hidden" name="eMail" id="eMail"
       value="donations@thelighthouse.org" />
```

Figure 6-56 **Adding a hidden field**

```
<form name="donationForm" id="donationForm">

   <input type="hidden" name="eMail" id="eMail"
          value="donations@thelighthouse.org" />

   <fieldset id="contact">
      <legend>Contact Information</legend>
```

3. Save your changes to the file.

Creating a Hidden Field

Reference Window

- To create a hidden field, add the control element
  `<input type="hidden" name="name" id="id" value="value" />`
  to the form, where *value* is the value of the hidden field, and *name* and *id* identify the hidden field.

With the e-mail field now included in the donation form, you'll return to the first tag you entered into this document, the <form> tag, and insert the attributes needed for it to interact with the CGI script running on the organization's Web server.

Working with Form Attributes

You've added all the elements needed for the form. Your final task is to specify where to send the form data and how to send it. You do this by adding the attributes

```
<form action="url" method="type" enctype="type"> ... </form>
```

to the form element, where *url* specifies the filename and location of the program that processes the form, the *method* attribute specifies how your Web browser sends data to the server, and the *enctype* attribute specifies the format of the data stored in the form's field. Next you'll examine the method and enctype attributes in more detail.

There are two possible values for the method attribute: get or post. The **get method**, the default, appends the form data to the end of the URL specified in the action attribute. The **post method**, on the other hand, sends form data in a separate data stream, allowing the Web server to receive the data through what is called **standard input**. Because it is more flexible, most Web designers prefer the post method for sending data to a server. Also, because browsers limit the size of URLs, the post method is safer—avoiding the possibility of data being truncated (this can happen using the get method if a long string is appended to a URL). The post method is also safer because the content of an extended URL can be viewed by other users and automated programs.

Don't be concerned if you don't completely understand the difference between get and post. Your Internet service provider can supply the necessary information about which of the two methods you should use when accessing the CGI scripts running on its server.

The enctype attribute determines how the form data should be encoded as it is sent to the server. Figure 6-57 describes the three most common encoding types.

Figure 6-57 **Values of the enctype attribute**

Value	Description
application/x-www-form-urlencoded	The default format. In this format, form data is transferred as a long text string in which spaces are replaced with the + character and nontext characters (such as tabs and line breaks) are replaced with their hexadecimal code values. Field names are separated from their field values with a = symbol.
multipart/form-data	Used when sending files to a server. In this format, spaces and nontext characters are preserved, and data elements are separated using delimiter lines. The action type of the form element must be set to post for this format.
text/plain	Form data is transferred as plain text with no encoding of spaces or nontext characters. This format is most often used when the action type of the form element is set to mailto.

Finally, another attribute you might use with the form element is the target attribute, used to send form data to a different browser window or frame. This is not a concern with the donation form.

Now that you've been introduced to the issues involved in sending form data to a server-based program, you are ready to make some final modifications to the donations.htm file. Warren tells you that a CGI script that processes the form is located at the URL *http://www.thelighthouse.org/cgi-bin/donation* (a fictional address) and uses the post method. You do not have to specify a value for the enctype attribute, so the browser will assume a value of application/x-www-form-urlencoded.

To add attributes to the form element:

1. Return to the **donations.htm** file and add the following attributes to the opening <form> tag, as shown in Figure 6-58.

```
action="http://www.thelighthouse.org/cgi-bin/donation"
method="post"
```

Figure 6-58 **Setting the form attributes**

```
<form name="donationForm" id="donationForm"
      action="http://www.thelighthouse.org/cgi-bin/donation"
      method="post">

  <input type="hidden" name="eMail" id="eMail"
         value="katherinehayes@thelighthouse.org" />
```

2. Close the **donations.htm** file, saving your changes.
3. You can close any other open files or programs.

Using the mailto Action

The data from the donation form must be processed using a CGI script running on the center's Web server. There is, however, a way to send form information from the Web form to an e-mail address. You can do this with the mailto action, which accesses the user's own e-mail program and uses it to mail form information to a specified e-mail address, bypassing the need to use a CGI script. The syntax of the mailto action is

```
<form action="mailto:e-mail" method="post" enctype="text/plain"> ...
</form>
```

where *e-mail* is the e-mail address of the recipient of the form. Because the mailto action does not require a server-based program, you don't have to coordinate your form with a CGI script running on the Web server.

The mailto action is not supported by earlier versions of many browsers. Another concern is that using the mailto action requires the user filling out the form to have an e-mail client program that will be able to accept the output from the Web form and use it to send an e-mail message. This might not always be the case, as different users run different types of e-mail clients or might have no e-mail client at all. Finally, messages sent via the mailto action are not encrypted for privacy and therefore are a security risk. For these reasons, you should carefully consider all of the ramifications of the mailto action before using it in one of your forms. However, if these issues are not obstacles to your project, you can use the mailto action for situations where you need to send form data to an e-mail address and a CGI script is not available.

Tips for Effective Forms | InSight

Web forms are one of the main ways of communicating with your users, so it's important for the forms to be friendly and easy to use. A well-designed form can often be the difference between a new customer and a disgruntled user who leaves your site to go elsewhere. Here are some tips to remember when designing your form:

- Mark fields that are required, but also limit the number of unrequired fields. Don't overwhelm your users with requests for information that is not really essential. Keep your forms short and to the point.
- If you need to collect a lot of information, break the form into manageable sections spread out over several pages. Allow users to easily move backward and forward through the forms without losing data.
- Provide detailed instructions about what users are expected to do. Don't assume that your form is self-explanatory.
- If you ask for personal data and financial information, provide clear assurances that the data will be secure. If possible, provide a link to a Web page describing your security practices.
- Clearly indicate what users will receive once the form is submitted, and provide feedback on the Web site and through e-mail that tells them when their data has been successfully submitted.

Finally, every Web form should undergo usability testing before it is made available to the general public. Weed out any mistakes and difficulties before your users see the form.

You've finished the donation form, and Terry has placed a copy of donation.htm in a folder on the company's Web server. From there it can be fully tested to verify that the CGI script and the form work properly together. Terry is pleased with your work on this project and will come back to you for future Web page development at The Lighthouse.

Review | Session 6.3 Quick Check

1. Specify the code to create a submit button with the text Send Form.
2. Specify the code to create a reset button with the text Cancel Form.
3. Specify the code to create an image field named Sites displaying the graphic file sites.gif.
4. Specify the code to create a hidden field named Subject with the field value Form Responses.
5. You need your form to work with a CGI script located at *http://www.j_davis.com/cgi-bin/post-query*. The Web server uses the get method. Specify the code for the form element.
6. You want to use the mailto action to send your form to the e-mail address *walker@j_davis.com*. Assume that the message is sent as plain text. Specify the code for the form element.

Review | Tutorial Summary

In this tutorial, you learned how to create and use Web forms. The first session dealt with the fundamentals of Web forms, discussing how Web forms interact with the Web server to submit information to programs running on the server. You learned how to create and format simple input boxes with form labels, and you learned how to create field sets. You also saw how to use CSS styles to format the appearance and layout of a Web form. The second session examined other types of control elements, including option buttons, selection lists, and check boxes. The session concluded by examining how to create text area boxes for extended text input. The last session showed how to create form buttons for resetting a form or submitting it to a program for processing. The session also examined some special input fields that can be used to create server-side image maps and file input boxes. The session and the tutorial concluded by examining various form attributes and discussed how data from the Web form is transferred to a CGI script running on a Web server.

Key Terms

access key
CGI script
check box
command button
Common Gateway Interface script
control element
drop-down list box
field
field set
field value
form button
get method
hidden field
input box
name/value pair
option button
option group
Perl
post method
radio button
reset button
selection list
standard input
submit button
text area box

Practice | Review Assignments

Practice the skills you learned in the tutorial using the same case scenario.

Data Files needed for the Review Assignments: back.jpg, left.jpg, lhouse.jpg, main.css, right.jpg, vformstxt.css, and voltxt.htm

Terry and the staff at The Lighthouse have been working with your form and the CGI script running on the Web server for several weeks now. They're pleased with the work you've done, so they have asked for your help in creating another Web form for the center's Web site. Terry would like a form that Lighthouse volunteers can fill out indicating their talents and interests, and ways they can help the center. A CGI script is already in place to process the information, and much of the work in designing the volunteer page has been done except for the form itself. Terry wants you to complete the page by adding the HTML and CSS code for the volunteer form. A preview of the form you'll create is shown in Figure 6-59.

Figure 6-59

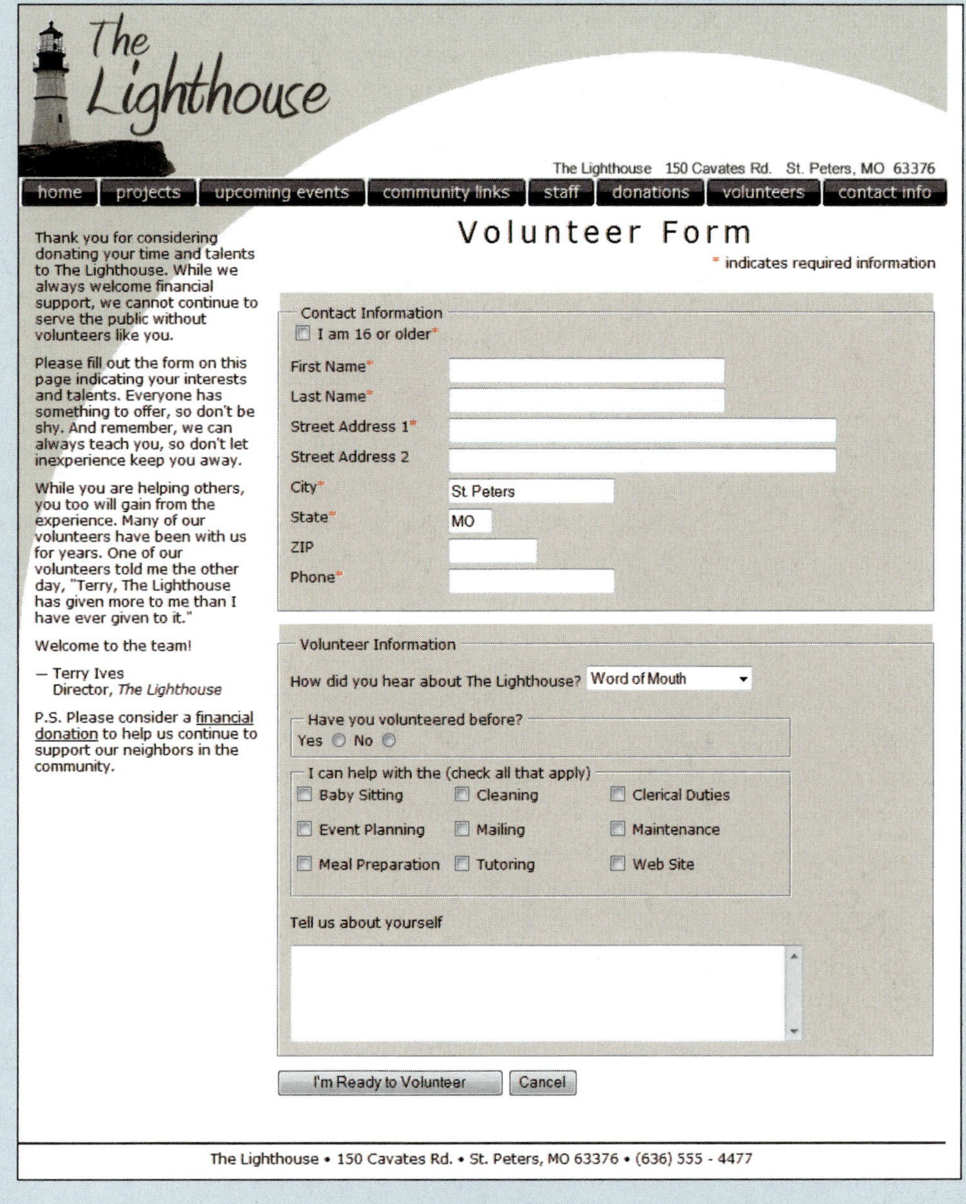

When the form is filled out, it should be sent to a CGI script at *http://www.thelighthouse.org/volunteer*. The CGI script will collect the information and e-mail it to Steve Jones, the volunteer coordinator.

Complete the following:

1. Use your text editor to open the **voltxt.htm** and **vformstxt.css** files from the tutorial.06\review folder included with your Data Files. Enter ***your name*** and ***the date*** in the comment section of each file. Save the files as **volunteer.htm** and **vforms.css**, respectively, in the same folder.
2. Go to the **volunteer.htm** file in your text editor. Scroll down to the rightColumn div container and directly below the paragraph element, insert a form element with the name and id volunteerForm. Have the form perform the action of submitting the form data to the CGI script at *http://www.thelighthouse.org/cgi-bin/volunteer* using the post method.
3. Directly below the opening <form> tag, insert a hidden field named eMail with the value *stevejones@thelighthouse.org*.
4. Create a field set with the legend Contact Information. Give the fieldset element the id contactFields.
5. Below the field set legend, insert a label element with the text "I am 16 or older*". Enclose the asterisk symbol in a span element. Directly before the label text, but still nested within the label element, insert a check box with the field name ageOK.
6. Below the label element you just entered, insert the contact information for the volunteer. There are eight contact fields: fName, lName, street1, street2, city, state, zip, and phone. For each field, do the following:
   - Create an input box nested within a label element. The labels for the eight fields are First Name*, Last Name*, Street Address 1*, Street Address 2, City*, State*, ZIP, and Phone*.
   - Enclose the asterisks within a span element.
   - Place each label element within the blockLabel class.
7. Set the maximum number of characters in the state and zip fields to two and 10 characters, respectively.
8. Set the default value of the city and state fields to St. Peters and MO, respectively.
9. Below the contactFields field set, insert another field set with the legend Volunteer Information. Give the field set the id volunteerInfo.
10. Directly below the Volunteer Information legend, insert a selection list for the infoSource field. Add the following code for the selection list:
    - Enclose the selection list within a label element with the class blockLabel.
    - Directly before the selection list within the label element, insert the text "How did you hear about The Lighthouse?"
    - Add the following five options to the selection list: Word of Mouth, TV or Radio Ad, The Internet, The Phonebook, and College/High School. Give the five options the values talk, ads, internet, phonebook, and schools, respectively.

11. After the selection list label, insert a field set with the id experience and the legend "Have you volunteered before?" Within the field set, create two option buttons with the following code:
    - Before each option button, insert a label with the text strings "Yes" and "No". Use the for attribute to assign the labels to the prevYes and prevNo fields, respectively.
    - After each label, insert an option button belonging to the prevExp field. The ids of the option buttons should be prevYes and prevNo, respectively, and the values of the buttons should be yes and no.
12. After the experience field set, insert another field set with the id interestFields and the legend "I can help with the (check all that apply)".
13. Within the interestFields field set, insert nine check boxes. Format the check boxes as follows:
    - Enclose each check box within a label element. Give the label elements ids of interest1 through interest9.
    - Give the check box controls the field names of babysitting, cleaning, clerical, events, mailing, maintenance, food, tutoring, and web.
    - After each check box within the label element, insert the text strings "Baby Sitting", "Cleaning", "Clerical Duties", "Event Planning", "Mailing", "Maintenance", "Meal Preparation", "Tutoring", and "Web Site".
14. Below the interestFields field set, insert a label associated with the comments field. Place the label in the blockLabel class and give it the text "Tell us about yourself".
15. After the label, insert a text area box for the comments field. The text area box should have five lines of 55 characters each.
16. After the text area box, insert submit and reset buttons. The text of the submit button should be "I'm Ready to Volunteer" and the text of the reset button should be "Cancel".
17. Go to the top of the file and link the file to the **vforms.css** style sheet.
18. Close the **volunteer.htm** file, saving your changes.
19. Go to the **vforms.css** file in your text editor and add the following styles to the style sheet:
    - Set the background color of all fieldset elements to the value (237, 233, 223) with 10 pixels of padding and a bottom margin of 10 pixels.
    - Display all span elements within field sets in a red font.
    - Display all labels belonging to the blockLabel class as block-level elements, with relative positioning. Set the width of the labels to 450 pixels. Set the top and bottom margins to 12 pixels and the left and right margins to 0 pixels.
    - Place all input elements nested within blockLabel labels with absolute positioning 140 pixels to the left of the label's left margin.
    - Set the width of the fName and lName input boxes to 250 pixels. Set the width of the street1 and street2 input boxes to 350 pixels. Set the width of the phone and city input boxes to 150 pixels. Set the width of the state input box to 40 pixels and the width of the zip input box to 80 pixels.
    - Set the width of the experience field to 450 pixels with 5 pixels of padding.
20. Terry wants the nine check boxes that constitute different volunteer opportunities to be displayed in a grid of three rows and three columns. To create this layout:
    - Place the interestFields field set with relative positioning. Set the size of the field set box to 450 pixels wide by 120 pixels high. Set the padding to 5 pixels.
    - Place the interest1 through interest9 label elements with absolute positioning.

- Set the top coordinate of the interest1 through interest3 labels to 20 pixels, interest4 through interest6 to 50 pixels and interest7 through interest9 to 80 pixels.
- Set the left coordinate of the interest1, interest4, and interest7 labels to 0 pixels; interest2, interest5, and interest8 to 140 pixels; and interest3, interest6, and interest9 to 280 pixels.

21. Save your edits to **vforms.css**, and then open **volunteer.htm** in your Web browser. Verify that the layout and design of the form resembles that shown in Figure 6-59.
22. Submit your completed files to your instructor.

Apply | Case Problem 1

Apply your knowledge of Web forms to create a subscription form for a newspaper.

Data Files needed for this Case Problem: parch.jpg, pcg.css, pcglogo.jpg, sformtxt.css, and subtxt.htm

The Park City Gazette Kevin Webber, the editor of the Park City Gazette of Estes Park, Colorado, has asked for your help in developing a subscription page for the newspaper's Web site. The page includes a form where customers can enter the length of the subscription they want to purchase, their mailing address, and their credit card information. Kevin has already created much of the layout and text of the Web page. Your job is to add the fields and control elements for the subscription form. A preview of the Web page you'll create for Kevin is shown in Figure 6-60.

Figure 6-60

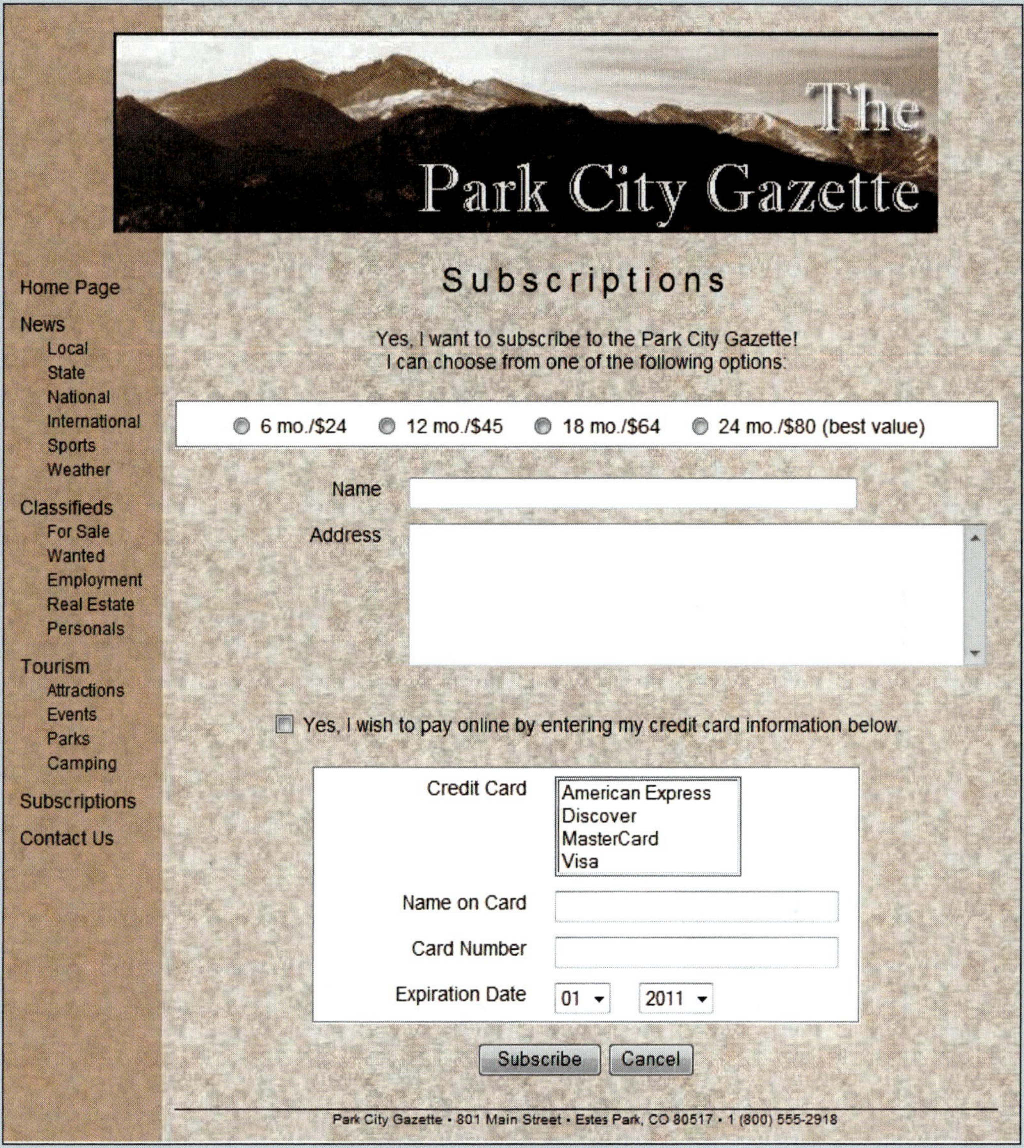

The form contains several labels and control elements placed side-by-side in two columns. To create this two-column layout, you'll float the labels and control elements on the left margin. You'll identify the labels that are floated by putting them into the floatLabel class. The floated control elements will belong to the floatCtrl class.

Complete the following:

1. Use your text editor to open the **sformtxt.css** and **subtxt.htm** files from the tutorial.06\case1 folder included with your Data Files. Enter ***your name*** and ***the date*** in the comment section of each file. Save the files as **sform.css** and **subscription.htm**, respectively, in the same folder.
2. Go to the **subscription.htm** file in your text editor and insert a link to the **sform.css** style sheet.
3. Scroll down the file and insert a form element with the id subForm, directly below the paragraph in the rightColumn div container.

4. At the top of the form, Kevin wants an option list showing the four different payment plans. Insert a field set with the id subPlans. Within the field set do the following:
   - Insert four option buttons belonging to the subplan field.
   - Give the option buttons the ids plan1 through plan4 and the values 1 through 4.
   - After each option button, insert a label element associated with the preceding option button. The text of the four labels is "6 mo./$24", "12 mo./$45", "18 mo./$64", and "24 mo./$80 (best value)".
5. After the subPlans field set, insert a label containing the text "Name". Associate the label with the cName field and put it in the class floatLabel.
6. After the label, insert an input box for the cName field. Place the input box in the floatCtrl field and set the size of the input box to 50 characters.
7. Insert another label containing the text "Address" associated with the address field and belonging to the floatLabel class. After the label, insert a text area box for the address field. Set the size of the box to six rows by 50 columns and place the text area box in the floatCtrl field.
8. Insert a label with the id agreeLabel associated with the agree field. Place the label in the floatLabel class. Within the label element, insert a check box for the agree field. After the check box, but within the label element, insert the text "Yes, I wish to pay online by entering my credit card information below."
9. Insert a field set with the id payment. At the top of the field set, insert a label belonging to the floatLabel class, containing the text "Credit Card" and associated with the cardType field.

EXPLORE

10. Insert a selection list for the cardType field. Do the following for the selection list:
    - Place the selection list in the floatCtrl class.
    - Set the selection list to display four items.
    - Add the following options to the selection list: American Express, Discover, MasterCard, and Visa.
    - Set the values of the four options to: Amex, Disc, MC, and Visa.
11. Below the selection list, insert two labels. The first label should contain the text "Name on Card" and should be associated with the cardName field. The second label should contain the text "Card Number" and should be associated with the cardNumber field. Put both labels in the floatLabel class.
12. Directly after each label, insert an input box. The first input box should be for the cardName field; the second input box is for the cardNumber field. For both input boxes, set the width to 30 characters and place the input box into the floatCtrl class.
13. Insert a label belonging to the floatLabel class and containing the text "Expiration Date". After the label, insert two selection lists for the expMonth and expYear field. Do the following for the selection lists:
    - Place both selection lists in the floatCtrl class.
    - Add 12 options to the expMonth selection list containing the text "01" through "12". The values of the options should range from 1 to 12.
    - Add five options to the expYear selection list containing the text "2011" through "2015". Set the values of each option to match the option text.
14. Insert a field set with the id buttons. Within the field set, insert a submit and reset button. Give the submit button the value Subscribe. Give the reset button the value Cancel.
15. Use the CGI script at *http://www.theparkcitygazette.com/subscribe* with the post method.
16. Save your changes to the file.

17. Go to the **sform.css** file in your text editor and add the following styles to the style sheet:
    - Set the background color of the subPlans field set to white. Set the padding to 5 pixels and the bottom margin to 20 pixels. Center the contents of the field set.
    - For label elements within the subPlans fieldset element, set the right margin to 15 pixels.
    - Display objects belonging to the floatLabel class as block-level elements, floated on the left margin but only when the left margin is clear. (*Hint*: Use the clear style.) Set the width to 150 pixels and the bottom margin to 10 pixels. Right-align the label text.
    - Display objects belonging to the floatCtrl class as block-level elements, floated on the left margin. Set the left margin to 20 pixels and the bottom margin to 10 pixels.
    - Set the width of the agreeLabel label to 600 pixels with top/bottom margins of 20 pixels and left/right margins of 0 pixels. Center the label text.
    - Display the payment field set only when the left margin is clear. Set the background color to white. Set the width of the field set to 400 pixels with a left margin of 100 pixels and 5 pixels of padding.
    - Center the contents of the buttons field set with top/bottom margins of 10 pixels and left/right margins of 0 pixels. Set the border style to none.
18. Save your changes to the **sform.css** file and open **subscription.htm** in your Web browser. Verify that the layout and content of the Web form resemble that shown in Figure 6-60.
19. Submit your completed files to your instructor.

Apply | Case Problem 2

Apply your knowledge of Web forms to create a form for an online quiz.

Data Files needed for this Case Problem: cw.css, cwlogo.gif, cwquiztxt.htm, qformtxt.css, and tan.jpg

Civil War Studies Adanya Lynne, a professor of military history at Ridgeview State College in Bartlett, Tennessee, has been preparing a series of online quizzes for her students. She has created the basic Web page design and layout, but has come to you for help in designing the quiz form. She envisions a series of multiple choice questions displayed in a collection of option buttons. Students will be able to click answers on the form and then submit their answers to a CGI script running on the Web server for their scores. Figure 6-61 shows a preview of the page you'll create for Professor Lynne.

Figure 6-61

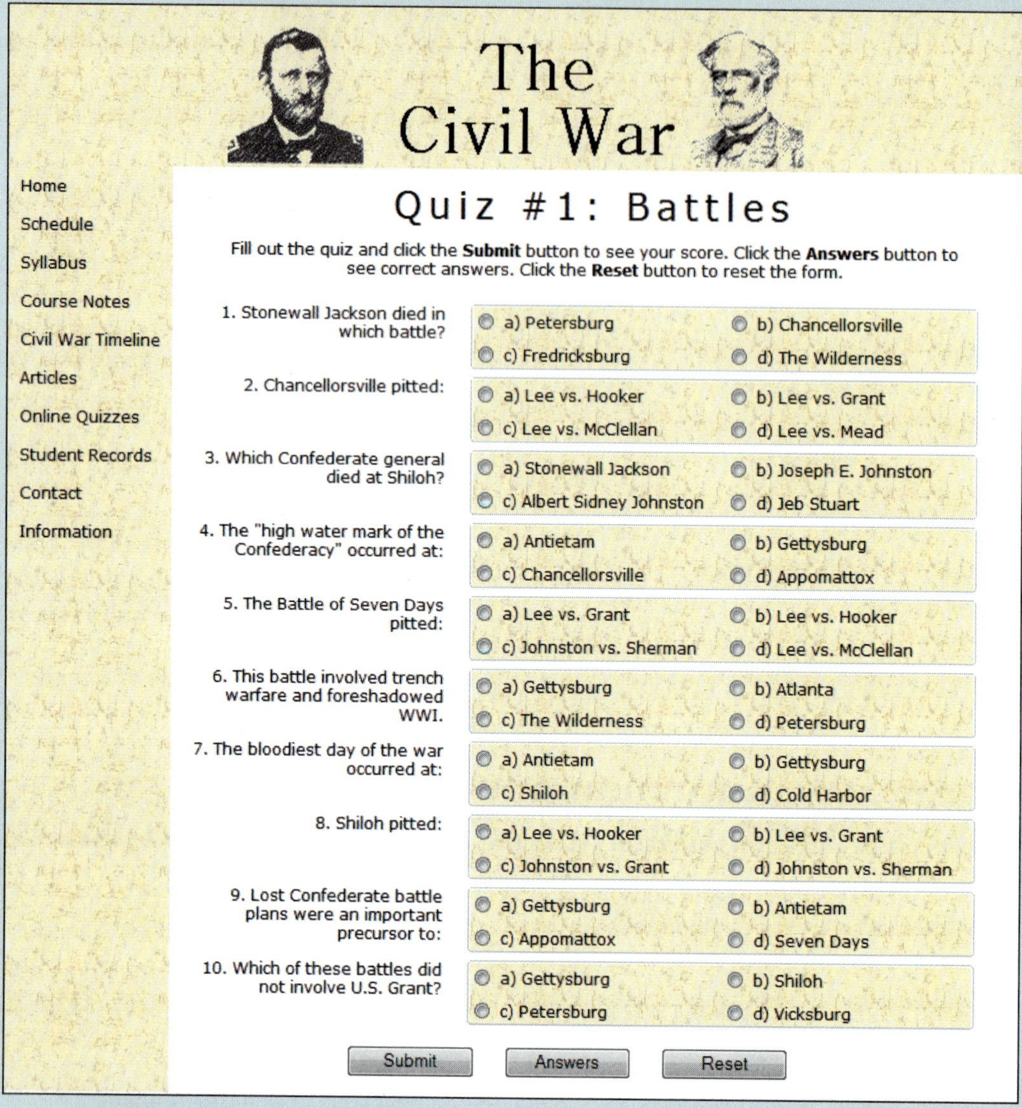

Complete the following:

1. Use your text editor to open the **cwquiztxt.htm** and **qformtxt.css** files from the tutorial.06\case2 folder included with your Data Files. Enter ***your name*** and ***the date*** in the comment section of each file. Save the files as **cwquiz.htm** and **qform.css**, respectively.
2. Go to the **cwquiz.htm** file in your text editor and insert a link to the **qform.css** style sheet.
3. Scroll down the file to the rightColumn div element. Professor Lynne has inserted the 10 questions for the online quiz. Enclose the questions in a form element with the id quizForm. Call the CGI script at *http://www.ridgeviewcollmil.edu/quiz* using the post method.
4. Go to the first question and enclose the text of the question in a div element with the class name question.
5. Enclose the set of answers for the first question within a field set.

6. Place a label element around each possible answer for the first question. Put the first answer in the class answerA, the second answer in the class answerB, the third answer in the class answerC, and the fourth answer in the class answerD.
7. Within each of the four labels for the answers to the first question, insert an option button directly before the text of the answer. Assign the ids ans1a, ans1b, ans1c, and ans1d to the four option buttons. Assign the field name question1 to each of the four option buttons. Finally, set the values for the four option buttons to a, b, c, and d.
8. Associate each of the four labels with a different id. Associate the first label with the ans1a field, the second with ans1b, the third with ans1c, and the fourth with ans1d.
9. Repeat Steps 4 through 8 for the remaining nine questions in the quiz, with the following changes:
   - Change the ids for the four option buttons to the question number. For example, the ids for the second question are: ans2a, ans2b, ans2c, and ans2d.
   - Change the field name of the four option buttons to the number of the question. For example, the field name for the second question is question2, for the third question is question3, and so forth.
10. After the last question, insert a div element with the id buttons. Within the element, insert a submit button with the value Submit, a command button with the value Answers, and a reset button with the value Reset.
11. Save your changes to the file.
12. Go to the **qform.css** file in your text editor and add the following styles to the style sheet:
    - Float all elements of the question class on the left margin. Set their widths to 200 pixels and right-align the text. Set the clear style to left so that the element is only displayed when the left margin is clear.
    - Display all field sets as block-level elements floated on the left margin. Set the size of the field sets to 400 pixels wide by 50 pixels high. Add a 20-pixel left margin and a 5-pixel bottom margin. Set the position property to relative. Finally, display the **tan.jpg** file as the background image for the field sets.
    - Use absolute positioning to place all elements of the answerA class at the coordinates (0, 0), place answerB class elements at the coordinates (200, 0), place answerC class elements at (0, 25), and place answerD class elements at (200, 25).
    - Center the contents of the div element with the buttons id. Set the width to 600 pixels and the top/bottom padding to 10 pixels. Set the left/right padding to 0 pixels.
    - For input elements within the buttons div element, set the width to 100 pixels, set the top/bottom margin to 0 pixels, and set the left/right margin to 10 pixels.
13. Save your changes to the file and open **cwquiz.htm** in your Web browser. Verify that the layout and design resemble that shown in Figure 6-61.
14. Submit your completed files to your instructor.

Challenge | Case Problem 3

Explore different form controls needed to create an online order form for a pizzeria.

Data Files needed for this Case Problem: buttonball.jpg, leftball.jpg, orderformtxt.css, pizzatxt.htm, rb.css, redball.jpg, rightball.jpg, and topping.txt

Red Ball Pizza Alice Nichols is the owner of Red Ball Pizza, a new pizzeria in Ormond Beach, Florida. You've been working with Alice on creating a Web site for the restaurant. Alice wants to give customers the ability to submit orders online. She has contacted programmers at the restaurant's ISP to process the orders, but she needs a Web form to collect those orders. She's asked you to design a form that would allow customers to select items from the Red Ball Pizza menu. A preview of the Web page you'll create is shown in Figure 6-62.

Figure 6-62

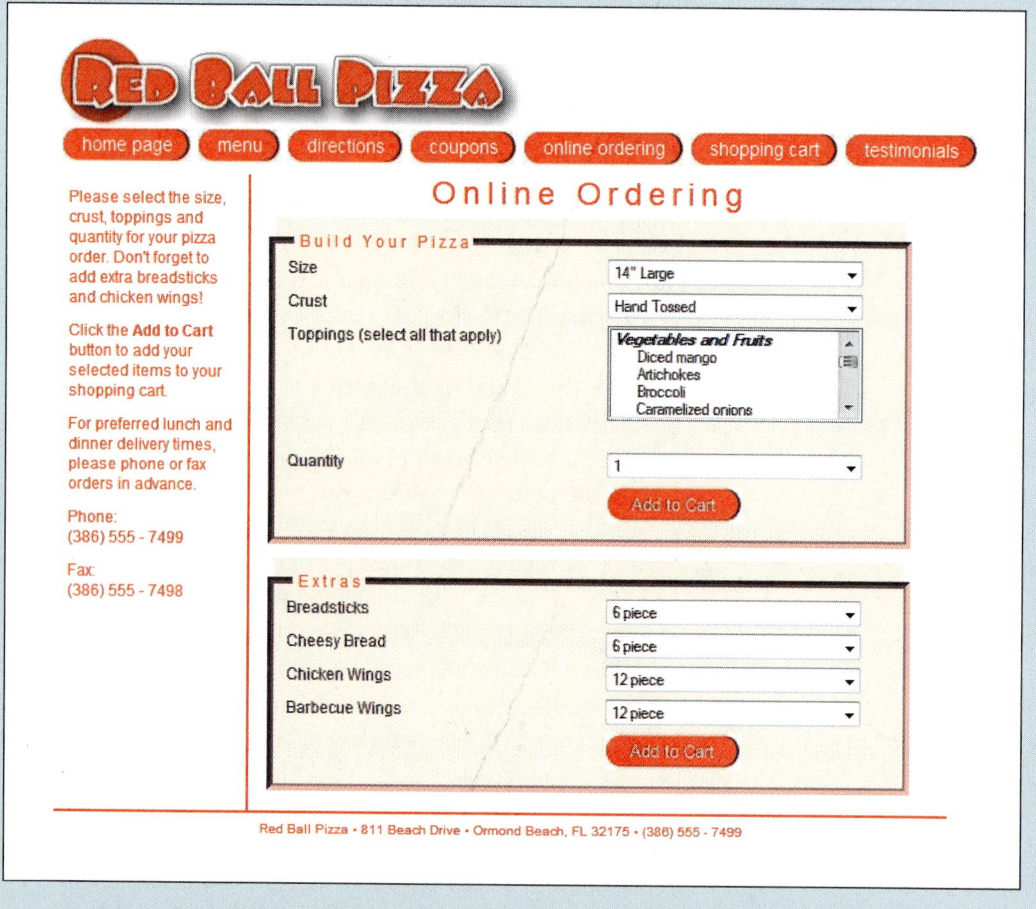

Complete the following:

1. Use your text editor to open the **orderformtxt.css** and **pizzatxt.htm** files from the tutorial.06\case3 folder included with your Data Files. Enter ***your name*** and ***the date*** in the comment section of each file. Save the files as **orderform.css** and **pizza.htm**, respectively.
2. Go to the **pizza.htm** file in your text editor and create a link to the **orderform.css** style sheet.
3. Scroll down the file to the rightCol div element and insert a form element directly below the h1 heading.

4. Create a field set with the id pizzaType and the legend Build your Pizza.

EXPLORE

5. Insert a label element with the text Size. Within the label element, insert a selection list for the size field. Add the following options: 12" Regular, 14" Large, 16" Extra Large, and 20" Family Size. Set the option values to 12, 14, 16, and 20. Make 14" Large the default selection.
6. Insert a label element with the text "Crust". Within the label element, insert a selection list for the crust field. Add the following options: Thin, Thick, Hand Tossed, and Deep Dish. Make the option values thin, thick, hand, and dish. Make Hand Tossed the default selection.

EXPLORE

7. Insert a label element containing the text "Toppings (select all that apply)". Within the label element, insert the toppings field. Set the size of the selection list to five entries and allow users to make multiple selections.

EXPLORE

8. Within the topping selection list, insert the list of toppings from the **topping.txt** file. Break the options into option groups with labels Vegetables and Fruits, Meats, and Cheeses. You do not have to specify option values.
9. Insert a label element with the text Quantity. Give the label the id qLabel. Within the label element, insert a selection list for the qty field. Insert the numbers 1 through 10 for both the option text and option values.

EXPLORE

10. After the selection list, insert an image control element displaying the image **buttonball.jpg**.
11. Insert a field set with the id extras and the legend Extras.
12. Within the field set, insert a label element containing the text "Breadsticks". Inside the label, insert a selection list for the bread field containing the options 6 piece, 12 piece, and 18 piece. The option values are 6, 12, and 18.
13. Repeat Step 12 for the cheesy bread menu item. The label text is "Cheesy Bread" and the field name is cbread.
14. Insert a label element containing the text "Chicken Wings". Inside the label, insert a selection list for the wings field containing the options 6 piece, 12 piece, 18 piece, and 24 piece with the values 6, 12, 18, and 24. Make 12 the default selection.
15. Repeat Step 14 for the Barbecue Wings menu item. The label text is "Barbecue Wings" and the field name is bwings.
16. After the selection list, insert an image control element displaying the image **buttonball.jpg**.
17. Save your changes to the **pizza.htm** file.
18. Go to the **orderform.css** file in your text editor and add the following styles to the style sheet:
    - Set the margin and padding space of the form element to 0 pixels.
    - Set the bottom margin of the fieldset element to 10 pixels. Set the other margin sizes to 0 pixels. Change the background color to ivory. Add a 5-pixel inset border with the color value (255, 192, 192).
    - Display field set legends in a red font with the kerning set to 3 pixels.
    - Display label elements as blocks with relative positioning. Set the width to 400 pixels, set the top margin to 5 pixels, the bottom margin to 10 pixels, and the left/right margins to 0 pixels.
    - Display select elements using absolute positioning with the top coordinate set to 0 pixels and the left coordinate set to 250 pixels. Set the font size to 12 pixels.
    - For the label with the id qLabel, set the top margin to 80 pixels.
    - Display input elements with a left margin of 250 pixels.

19. Save your changes to the file and then open **pizza.htm** in your Web browser. Verify that the design and layout resemble that shown in Figure 6-62.
20. Submit your completed files to your instructor.

Create | Case Problem 4

Test your knowledge of Web forms by creating an order form for an online computer store.

Data Files needed for this Case Problem: mclogo.jpg

Millennium Computers You are employed at Millennium Computers, a discount mail-order company specializing in computers and computer components. You've been asked by your supervisor, Sandy Walton, to create an order form Web page so that customers can purchase products online. Your order form is for computer purchases only. There are several options for customers to consider when purchasing computers from Millennium. Customers can choose from the following:

- Processor Speed: 2.4 GHz, 3.2 GHz, 4 GHz
- Memory: 1 GB, 2 GB, 4 GB, 8 GB
- Monitor Size: 15″, 17″, 19″, 21″
- Hard Drive: 240 GB, 500 GB, 750 GB, 1 TB
- DVD burner: yes/no
- LAN card: yes/no
- Media card reader: yes/no

Complete the following:

1. Use your text editor to create an HTML file named **pc.htm** and two style sheets named **mill.css** and **oform.css**. Enter ***your name*** and ***the date*** in a comment section of each file. Include any other comments you think will aptly document the purpose and content of the files. Save the files in the tutorial.06\case4 folder included with your Data Files.
2. Design a Web page for the Millennium Computers Web page. Insert any styles you create in the mill.css style sheet. You are free to use the **mclogo.jpg** file and whatever text or images you wish to complete the look and content of the Web page.
3. Within the **pc.htm** file, insert a Web form containing the following elements:
   - Input boxes for the customer's first name, last name, street address, city, state, zip code, and phone number. The field names are fName, lName, street, city, state, zip, and phone.
   - Selection lists for the processor speed, memory, monitor size, and hard drive size. The field names are pSpeed, mem, monitor, and hd. The option values should match the option text.
   - Option buttons for the DVD burner, LAN card, and media card reader options. The field names are dvd, LAN, and mCard.
   - A check box for the warranty field that asks whether customers want the 24-month extended warranty.
   - A text area box requesting additional information or comments on the order.
   - Three form buttons: a submit button with the text "Send Order", a reset button with the text "Cancel Order", and a command button with the text "Contact Me".
   - Name the form cOrder and submit the form using the post method to the CGI script located at *http://www.mill_computers.com/orders/process.cgi*.
4. Create a style for your form in the **oform.css** style sheet. The layout and appearance of the form is up to you.

5. Test your Web site on a variety of browsers to ensure your design works under different conditions.
6. Submit your completed files to your instructor.

Review | Quick Check Answers

Session 6.1

1. A CGI script is a program running on a Web server that receives data from a form and uses it to perform a series of tasks.
2. `<form id="registration" name="registration"> ... </form>`
3.
```
<fieldset id="contactInfo">
   <legend>Contact Information</legend>
   </fieldset>
```
4. Either with the for attribute (explicitly) or by nesting the control element within the label (implicitly)
5. `<label for="phone">Phone</label>`
6. `maxlength="10"`
7. `<input type="text" id="subscribe" name="subscribe" value="Yes" />`
8. `input[type="text"]{display: block}`

Session 6.2

1.
```
<input type="radio" name="Computer" value="PC" />
<input type="radio" name="Computer" value="Macintosh" />
```
2.
```
<input type="radio" name="Computer" value="PC
" checked="checked" />
```
3.
```
<select id="State" name="State">
   <option>California</option>
   <option>Nevada</option>
   <option>Oregon</option>
   <option>Washington</option>
</select>
```
4. `<option selected="selected">Oregon</option>`
5. `<select id="State" name="State" size="4">`
6. `<select id="State" name="State" multiple="multiple">`
7.
```
<label for="Computer">I use a PC</label>
<input type="checkbox" name="Computer" id="Computer" value="Yes" />
```
8.
```
<textarea rows="10" cols="40" id="Memo" name="Memo">
</textarea>
```

Session 6.3

1. `<input type="submit" value="Send Form" />`
2. `<input type="reset" text="Cancel Form" />`
3. `<input type="image" id="Sites" name="Sites" src="sites.gif" />`
4. `<input type="hidden" id="Subject" name="Subject"`
   `value="Form Responses" />`
5. `<form action="http:www.j_davis.com/cgi-bin/post-query"`
   `method="get"> ...</form>`
6. `<form action="mailto:walker@j_davis.com" method="text/plain" />`

Ending Data Files

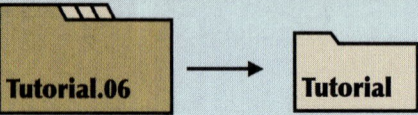

Tutorial.06 →

Tutorial
donations.htm
forms.css
main.css
+ 4 graphic files

Review
main.css
vforms.css
volunteer.htm
+ 4 graphic files

Case1
pcg.css
sform.css
subscription.htm
+ 2 graphic files

Case2
cw.css
cwquiz.htm
qform.css
+ 2 graphic files

Case3
orderform.css
pizza.htm
rb.css
+ 4 graphic files

Case4
mill.css
oform.css
pc.htm
+ 1 graphic file

Objectives

Session 7.1
- Explore various multimedia applications on the Web
- Learn about sound file formats and properties
- Embed a sound clip
- Work with object parameters
- Work with ActiveX objects
- Insert IE conditional comments

Session 7.2
- Learn about video file formats and properties
- Embed a video clip
- Work with the embed element
- Nest embedded objects

Session 7.3
- Explore the history of Java
- Embed a Java applet
- Work with applet parameters

Working with Multimedia

Enhancing a Web Site with Sound, Video, and Applets

Case | Jumbo Popcorn

Maxine Michaels is a movie buff and has a special fondness for classic movies and musicals. To pursue her interests, she's started a Web site called Jumbo Popcorn containing articles, reviews, and news about movies and cinematic history.

Maxine wants to enhance her Web site by adding sound and video so that users can not only read about movies, but also enjoy audio and video clips of famous movie moments. Maxine is aware that there are several technical issues involved with putting multimedia clips on her Web site. She's asked you to help complete a sample page describing the 1951 classic movie, *Royal Wedding*, starring Fred Astaire and Jane Powell. Note: To complete this tutorial, you should have Adobe Flash and Apple QuickTime on your computer. If you are running Windows, you should also have Windows Media Player.

Starting Data Files

Tutorial.07 →

Tutorial
CreditRoll.class
jp.css
jumbotxt.htm
overture.mp3
rwdance.mov
rwdance.swf
rwdance.wmv
+ 2 text files
+ 15 graphic files

Review
CreditRoll.class
astairetxt.htm
fabio.css
fasong.mp3
hatrack.mov
hatrack.swf
hatrack.wmv
+ 1 text file
+ 16 graphic files

Case1
devotion.mp3
fireice.mp3
poetry.css
PopBtn.class
PopMenu.class
rftxt.htm
+ 6 graphic files

Case2
roadtxt.txt
rw.css
rwlogo.jpg
trailridge.swf

Case3
Cmplx.class
Controls.class
fractaltxt.htm
FracPanel.class
fstyles.css
Mandel.class
mandel.swf
+ 2 graphic files

Case4
beethoven.mp3
CreditRoll.class
+ 2 text files
+ 2 graphic files

Session 7.1

Introducing Multimedia

You and Maxine sit down to discuss her new cinema Web site. She's completed much of the work on the *Royal Wedding* Web page and wants to show you her progress. Open her page now.

To view Maxine's document:

1. In your text editor, open the **jumbotxt.htm** file located in the tutorial.07\tutorial folder included with your Data Files. Enter ***your name*** and ***the date*** in the comment section of the file. Save the file as **jumbo.htm** in the same folder.
2. Take some time to review the contents of the file. Maxine has already created a style sheet for the document stored in the **jp.css** file. You will not have to make any changes to the style sheet file.
3. Open **jumbo.htm** in your Web browser. Figure 7-1 shows the current layout of the page.

Figure 7-1 The initial Royal Wedding Web page

Royal Wedding is one of a handful of Metro-Goldwyn-Mayer productions from the early 1950s whose original copyrights were never renewed. This means that versions of the movie are now in the public domain and that Maxine can add sound and video clips from the film to this Web page without worrying about the copyright. One of her audio clips contains the first few seconds from the film's overture. She would like to add that clip to the Listen Up box in the upper-right corner of the Web page. She also has a brief excerpt from a Fred Astaire dance number that she wants to add to the In Focus box in the lower-right corner of the page.

Multimedia and Bandwidth

When creating Web pages that include multimedia elements such as sound and video, one of the most important factors that you need to consider is the issue of bandwidth. **Bandwidth** is a measure of the amount of data that can be sent through a communication pipeline each second. Bandwidth values range from slow connections—such as landlines, which can transfer data at a maximum rate of 56 kilobits per second—to high-speed direct network connections capable of transferring data at several gigabytes per second. In the early days of the Web, efforts to include multimedia elements in Web sites were hampered by low-bandwidth connections, as most users connected to the Internet over slow landlines. Under those conditions, a Web site containing more than one or two multimedia clips would be inaccessible to most users.

This situation led to two developments. One was to make high-speed Internet access more available to the general public through the use of cable modems and DSL. The second development was reducing the size of large multimedia clips through file compression technology that doesn't sacrifice sound or video quality. Paired together, the two developments have made multimedia much more accessible to most Internet users. One of the most popular sites on the Web is YouTube, which is almost solely dedicated to the creation and dissemination of user-created video.

External and Embedded Media

As shown in Figure 7-2, multimedia is made available on the Web in two different ways: as external and embedded media. With **external media**, the media file is accessed through a link that the user clicks to download the media file to his or her computer. An advantage of using an external file is that users don't have to retrieve a multimedia clip; they do so only if they want to. This is useful in situations where a user has a low-bandwidth connection and wants to choose whether to spend time downloading a large multimedia file.

Figure 7-2 **Comparing external and embedded media**

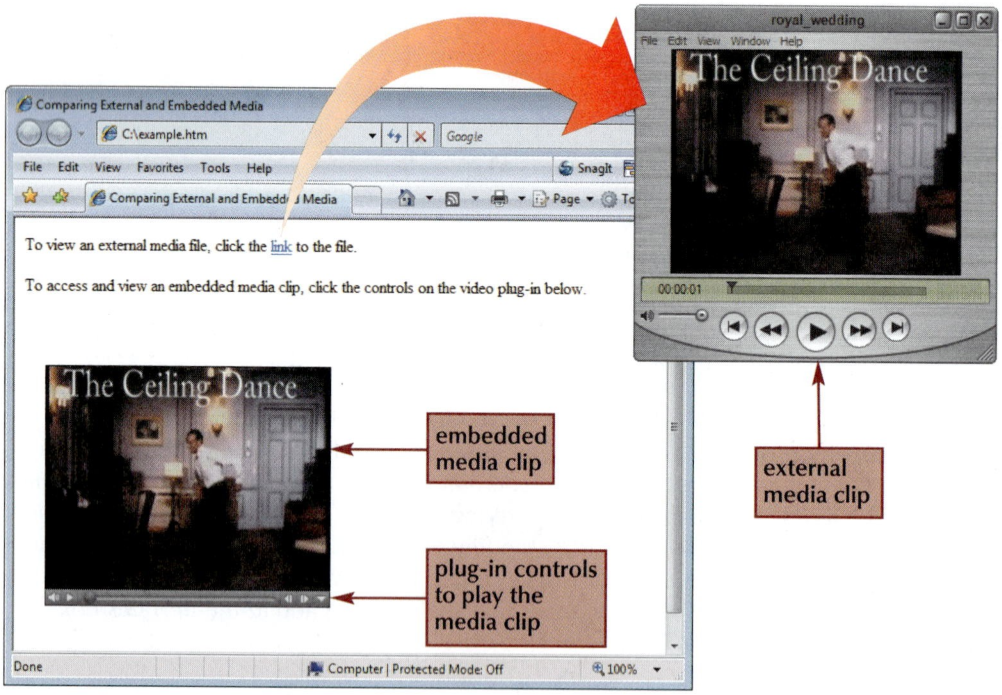

You add external media to a Web page through a hypertext link. For example, to create a link to a sound file named royal.mp3, you could add the following hypertext link to your Web page:

```
<a href="royal.mp3">Music from Royal Wedding</a>
```

When this link is clicked, the royal.mp3 sound file will be downloaded to the user's computer, where it can be played by a media player program such as Apple's QuickTime Player. The sound file will also be stored in one of the user's folders, where it can be played again and again.

Embedded media, on the other hand, is displayed within the Web page in a fashion similar to an inline image. The controls to play the media clip are also displayed as part of the Web page. Users who wish to play the clip do not leave the Web page to do so; instead, they click the player controls. Because embedded media appears within the page, you can supplement it with other material such as text that describes the clip's content and purpose. In essence, embedded media becomes part of the content of the page just as inline images become part of the page content.

To play embedded media, users' browsers often will have access to a **plug-in** or **add-on**—an extra component added to a program (such as a Web browser) to provide a feature or capability not included in the program. In Figure 7-2, a video plug-in has been added to the Web browser to provide the capability of displaying and playing a video clip within the Web page. Most browsers have a collection of plug-ins preinstalled for your use; you can also download and install additional plug-ins from the browser's manufacturer as the need arises.

Maxine has decided that she would like to use embedded media on her Web site to provide users with even more information about classic movies and the actors who appear in them. Your first task will be to embed an audio clip on the *Royal Wedding* Web page. Before doing that, you should learn about the various audio formats available and explore the differences in their sound quality and file size.

Tip

You can view a list of plug-ins installed on Firefox and Opera by entering *about:plugins* in the browser address bar. For Internet Explorer, click Manage Add-ons from the Tools menu and then select Enable or Disable Add-ons to view the list.

Exploring Digital Audio

If you want to add sound to your Web site, it's helpful to understand some of the issues involved in converting sound into a format that can be played on your users' computers and over their Internet connections. Sound is composed of combinations of sound waves; and every sound wave can be described on the basis of two components: amplitude and frequency. Figure 7-3 shows a basic sound wave. The **amplitude** is the height of the sound wave and it relates to the sound's volume—the higher the amplitude, the louder the sound. The **frequency** is the speed at which the sound wave moves and it relates to the sound's pitch—the higher the frequency, the higher the pitch.

Figure 7-3 A simple sound wave

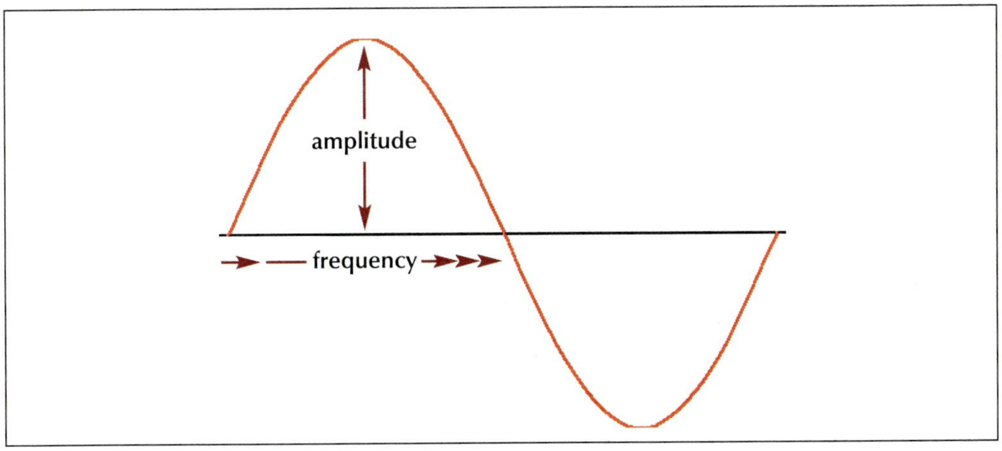

When you hear sound, your ears hear a continuously varying signal created by the vibrations that sound makes on your eardrum; to store that sound in a computer file, it must be converted into discrete pieces or bits of information. A digital recording of that sound takes measurements of the amplitude at different moments in time; each measurement is called a **sample**. The number of samples taken per second is called the **sampling rate**, a value that is measured in kilohertz (kHz). As shown in Figure 7-4, a higher sampling rate means that more samples are taken per second, resulting in a digital recording that more closely matches the original sound. There is a trade-off, however, as increasing the sampling rate also increases the size of a sound file. This might not be a problem with a CD recording, but it can be an issue when transferring sound over an Internet connection—where it's important to keep file sizes compact.

Figure 7-4 **Different sampling rates**

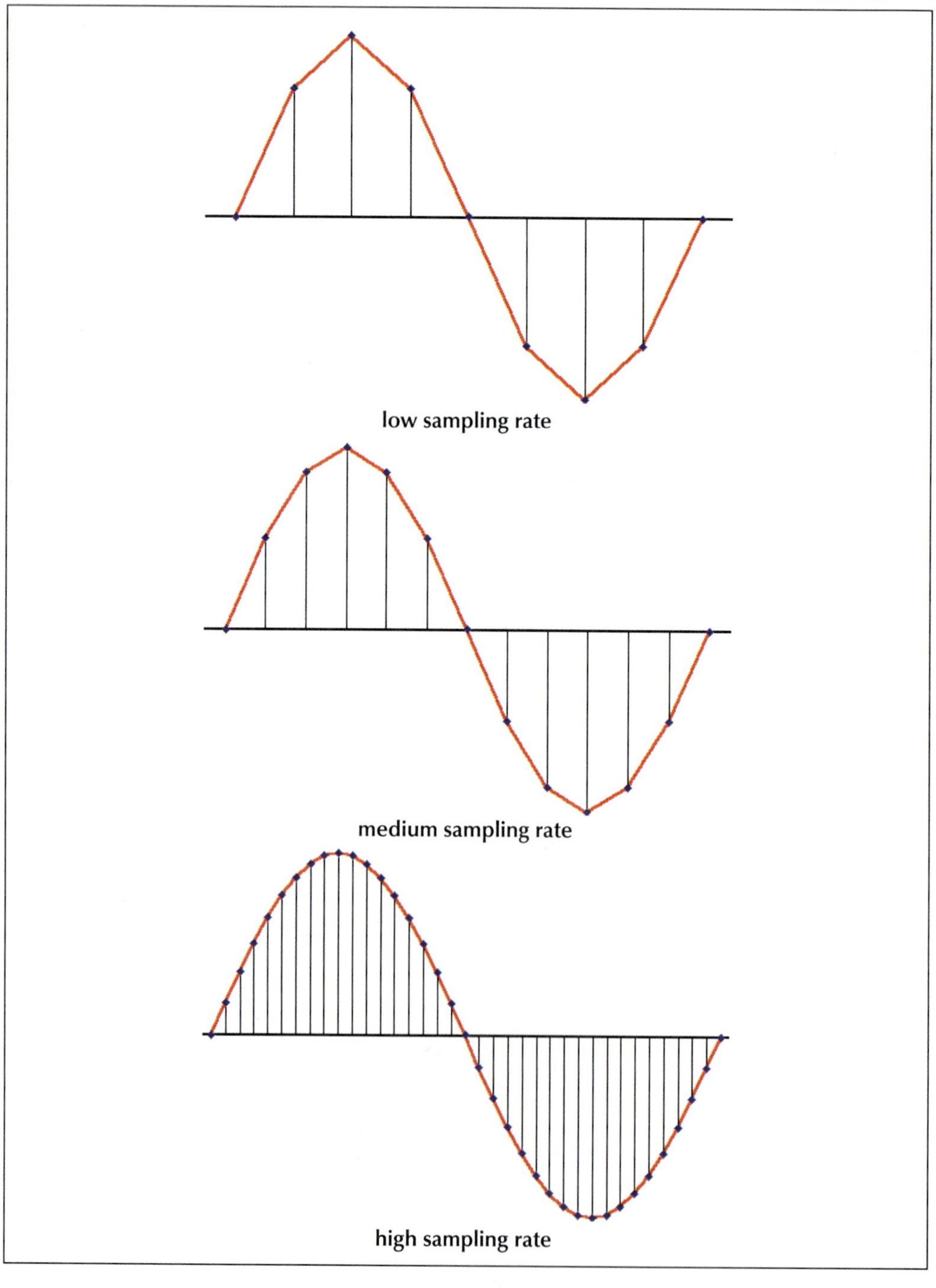

The second factor in converting sound to digital form is the sample resolution. **Sample resolution** or **bit depth** indicates the precision in measuring the sound within each sample. Three commonly used sample resolution values are 8 bit, 16 bit, and 32 bit. As shown in Figure 7-5, increasing the sample resolution creates a digital sound file that represents the analog signal more accurately, but this results in a larger file. For most applications, saving sound files at the 16-bit resolution provides a good balance between sound quality and file size.

Different sampling resolutions **Figure 7-5**

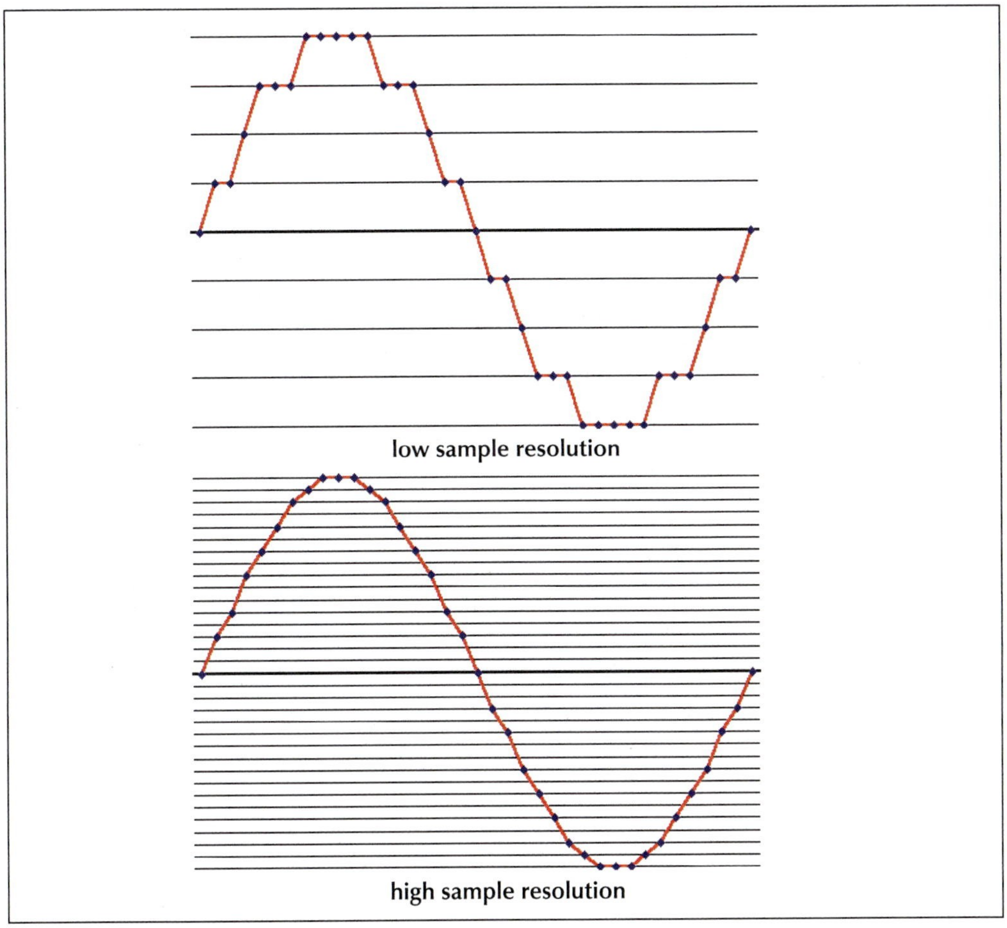

Another factor affecting audio quality is the number of sound channels. Typically, the choice is between stereo (two channels) or monaural (a single channel). Stereo provides a richer sound than mono, but with the trade-off of approximately doubling the size of the sound file.

The size of an audio clip is therefore related to the sampling rate, the sample resolution, and the number of channels. The total size can be expressed in terms of the **bitrate**, which is the number of bits of data required for each second of sound. For music stored on compact discs, the bitrate is determined by multiplying the sampling rate by the sample resolution by the number of channels. A typical CD track has a bitrate value of 1411 Kbps, which is too high for practical use on the Web. Therefore, sound files used on the Web must employ **file compression**, a process that reduces the size of the audio file but sometimes at the expense of sound quality. The most common file compression format is the MP3 format used throughout the Web as well as on portable music players and cell phones. MP3s can achieve near-CD quality sound at bitrates of 192 to 320 Kbps. The standard bitrate for MP3s is 192 Kbps, which results in some minor sound degradation but also requires only 13% of the size required for CD-quality sound. If the sound clip involves spoken words and not music, even greater sound compression can be used without affecting the overall quality of the recording. Therefore, MP3 is one of the sound formats ideally suited for use on the Internet. Figure 7-6 lists some of the other common sound file formats that Maxine might consider for her Web site.

Figure 7-6 **Common sound file formats on the Web**

Format	Description
AIFF/AIFC	Audio Interchange File Format. AIFF was developed by Apple for use on the Macintosh operating system. AIFF sound files can be either 8 bit or 16 bit, can be mono or stereo, and can be recorded at several different sampling rates.
AU	Also called mlaw (mu-law) format. One of the oldest sound formats, it is primarily used on UNIX workstations. AU sound files have 8-bit sample resolutions, use a sampling rate of 8 kHz, and are recorded in mono.
MIDI	Musical Instrument Digital Interface. MIDI files cannot be used for general sound recording, like other sound formats, but are limited to synthesizers and music files. The MIDI format represents sound by recording each note's pitch, length, and volume. MIDI files tend to be much smaller in size than other sound formats.
MP3	The most popular format for downloading and storing music, MP3 compresses sound files to roughly one-tenth the size of uncompressed files while maintaining good audio quality.
RealAudio	A popular sound format on the Web, RealAudio files are designed for real-time playing over low- to high-bandwidth connections. RealAudio files tend to be much smaller than AU or WAV files, but the sound quality is usually not as good.
SND	The SND format is used primarily on the Macintosh operating system for creating system sounds. This format is not widely supported on the Web.
WAV	WAV is the standard audio format for Windows PCs and is commonly used for storing uncompressed CD-quality sound files. In its uncompressed format, a WAV file will require about 10 megabytes per minute of sound; however, compression algorithms are available to reduce the file size.
WMA	Windows Media Audio is a proprietary audio format developed by Microsoft to compete with MP3s, offering near or better levels of compression than MP3s.

Maxine has created a 30-second MP3 sound clip from the overture of *Royal Wedding* and stored it in a sound file named overture.mp3. The file is a monaural recording with sample rate of 44 kHz and a bitrate of 96 Kbps, which she feels is adequate for use on her Web site. You'll next explore how to embed this clip into her Web page.

The MIDI Format | InSight

Another popular sound format for the Web is the MIDI format. **MIDI (Musical Instrument Digital Interface)**, a standard sound format for synthesizers and sound cards, uses mathematical functions to describe the pitch, length, and volume of each note in a musical piece. Because MIDI is a widely supported standard, sounds created on one synthesizer can be played and manipulated on another synthesizer. Sound-editing software can also be used to manipulate the MIDI files, creating new sounds and sound effects. An additional advantage of MIDI files is that they are much smaller compared with most sound formats. A MIDI composition lasting several minutes is less than 20 kilobytes in size, while a similar file in WAV format would be several megabytes in size, and MP3s for similar musical pieces might be several hundred kilobytes in size. However, the major drawback of the MIDI format is that it is limited to instrumental music—it cannot be used for general sounds, such as speech.

Working with Embedded Objects

Most browsers support two elements for embedding objects such as sound clips within a Web page: the embed element and the object element. The embed element is the older approach, initially introduced by the Netscape browser to support multimedia plug-ins; it is supported by most browsers. However, because it is not part of the World Wide Web Consortium (W3C) specifications, it will be rejected by strict applications of XHTML. To be in strict compliance with the W3C specifications, you should use the object element, which is supported by all major browsers. You'll explore both the object element and the embed element in this tutorial, starting with the object element. The syntax of the object element is

```
<object attributes>
   parameters
</object>
```

where *attributes* are the attributes that define the object and *parameters* are values that determine how the embedded object is rendered and played within the browser. The object element can be used with almost any type of content, from sound and video clips to graphic images, PDF files, and even the content of other Web pages. The W3C's original vision was to have the object element used for all nontextual content. For example, the object element could be used in place of the img element for the display of inline images, though this is rarely done. The primary use of the object element is for sound and video clips.

Object Data Sources and MIME Types

To specify the source of the content displayed within the object, you add the data attribute

```
<object data="url"> ... </object>
```

to the opening <object> tag, where *url* is the filename and location of the object file. For example, the following code specifies the overture.mp3 file as the object's data source:

```
<object data="overture.mp3"> ... </object>
```

Because the object element can be used with a wide variety of data types, you indicate the type of object by adding the type attribute

```
type="MIME type"
```

to the <object> tag, where *MIME type* describes the type of data contained in the object. **MIME types** or **Multipurpose Internet Mail Extension types** identify the type of data contained in the file and provide information about how that data should be interpreted. One common MIME type you've used since Tutorial 3 is text/css, which identifies a text file as containing CSS style declarations. The MIME type for mp3 files is audio/mpeg, though audio/x-mpeg is also supported by most browsers. Figure 7-7 lists the MIME types for other sound file formats.

Figure 7-7 **Sound file MIME types**

Format	File Extension	MIME Type
AIFC	aifc	audio/x-aiff
AIFF	aif	audio/x-aiff
AIFF	aiff	audio/x-aiff
AU	au	audio/basic
MIDI	mid	audio/mid
MIDI	rmi	audio/mid
MP3	mp3	audio/mpeg
MP3	mp3	audio/x-mpeg
RealAudio	ra	audio/x-pn-realaudio
RealAudio	ram	audio/x-pn-realaudio
SND	snd	audio/basic
WAV	wav	audio/wav
WAV	wav	audio/x-wav

InSight | MIME Types

The MIME type designation was first introduced as a way of attaching nontextual content to e-mail messages. With the growth of the World Wide Web, the use of MIME types expanded to include the flow of information across the Web. Each MIME type contains a header that indicates the type of data content. The header has the general form

```
type/subtype
```

where *type* is the general data type and *subtype* is a special classification of data within that type. The possible values for *type* are: application, audio, image, message, model, multipart, text, and video. Within these types there can be dozens or hundreds of subtypes. The subtype value can often be determined by examining the file extension of the object. For example, a JPEG image is identified as image/jpeg. Note that different file extensions can be associated with the same MIME type. JPEG image files can end in .jpe, .jfif, .jpg, or .jpeg, but all are designated as image/jpeg.

MIME types also include information that tells the computer how to handle and interpret the object data. Most operating systems give the administrator the ability to associate MIME types with specific programs. You can view and change these associations in the Windows or Macintosh Control Panel. For example, you can direct your computer to associate image/jpeg content with a particular graphics program, which tells the operating system to use that graphics program to always open files containing image/jpeg content. Note that any changes you make in the Control Panel might impact how your browser handles and displays multimedia content.

Maxine is ready for you to add an object element for the overture.mp3 file to the jumbo.htm file.

To insert the object element:

1. Return to the **jumbo.htm** file in your text editor and scroll down to the section in the middle of the document containing a short bio of Burton Lane, the composer of the music for *Royal Wedding*.
2. Directly after the h2 heading, insert the following HTML code, as shown in Figure 7-8:

```
<p style="text-align: center">

   <object data="overture.mp3" type="audio/mpeg">
   </object>

</p>
```

Figure 7-8 Inserting the object element

```
<div class="boxContent">
   <h2>Listen Up</h2>

   <p style="text-align: center">

      <object data="overture.mp3" type="audio/mpeg">
      </object>

   </p>

   <p>The music for <i>Royal Wedding</i> was composed by Burton Lane,
      who is best known for his work in <i>Finian's Rainbow </i>(1947)
      and his Grammy Award-winning <i>On a Clear Day You Can See
      Forever </i>(1965). Lane's greatest musical accomplishment may
      very well be his discovery of an 11-year-old singing phenom named
      Frances Gumm, whom the world now knows better as Judy Garland.</p>
</div>
```

MIME type of an MP3 sound file

MP3 sound file

Tip

For large media clips, you can have your browser display a text message as it loads the media file by adding the attribute `standby="text"` where *text* is the text to be displayed temporarily in place of the media clip.

The code you've just entered tells the browser the source and type of object, but it doesn't give any indication of how the sound clip should be rendered and played. Some of that will be determined by the plug-in used by the browser, but you can also add explicit instructions to control how the plug-in will operate and interact with the sound file.

Setting the Object Width and Height

An embedded sound clip is displayed with controls that allow the user to start, pause, rewind, and control the volume of the playback. So part of inserting the sound clip also includes defining how many of these controls appear on the Web page. This is done by setting the size of the sound clip using the attribute

```
width="value" height="value"
```

where the width and height attributes set the size of the control in pixels. The width and height attributes are required for XHTML code.

For sound clips, you should set the height to at least 25 pixels to allow enough space to display the control buttons. The width determines how many control buttons are displayed. In some cases, you might only need to display the play button; while in other cases, you'll want to display all of the buttons available with the plug-in. Figure 7-9 shows the minimum widths needed to display controls for two popular sound plug-ins: QuickTime and Windows Media Player.

Figure 7-9 Plug-in controls under different width values

Plug-in	Width	Description	Image
QuickTime Player	17px	Displays only the play button	
	33px	Adds the popup menu button	
	49px	Adds a volume control	
	74px	Adds a progress bar	
	106px	Adds fast-forward and reverse buttons	
	150px	Extends the length of the progress bar	
Windows Media Player	42px	Displays only the play button	
	66px	Adds the stop button	
	164px	Adds fast-forward and reverse buttons	
	279px	Adds a volume control	

You decide to set the height of the sound control for Maxine's Web page to 25 pixels and the width to 280 pixels to ensure all of the sound control buttons appear on the Web page.

To set the width and height of the sound control:

1. Return to the **jumbo.htm** file in your text editor and add the following attributes to the <object> tag, as shown in Figure 7-10:

```
width="280" height="25"
```

Figure 7-10 Setting the object width and height

```
<p style="text-align: center">
   <object data="overture.mp3" type="audio/mpeg"
    width="280" height="25">
   </object>
</p>
```

2. Save your changes to the file.

The width and height attributes define the space allotted to the controls for the sound clip. But to define how users will interact with those controls, you must specify the control parameters.

Working with Parameters

Every plug-in has a collection of **parameters** that define the appearance and behavior of the embedded object. These parameters are defined by adding the parameter elements

```
<object attributes>
   <param name="name1" value="value1" />
   <param name="name2" value="value2" />
   <param name="name3" value="value3" />
...
</object>
```

within the <object> tag, where *name1*, *name2*, *name3*, and so forth are the parameter names and *value1*, *value2*, *value3*, etc. are the values of each parameter. The parameter names and values are based on the type of object being embedded and on the plug-in used to display the object. One parameter common to most plug-ins for embedded sound is the src parameter, which defines the source of the sound file. So to set the source of your object to the overture.mp3 file, you would enter the following src parameter:

```
<object attributes>
   <param name="src" value="overture.mp3" />
</object>
```

Although the src parameter is similar to the data attribute you've already studied, it's required for some browsers such as Internet Explorer, so you should include it in addition to the data attribute. Figure 7-11 list some other parameters supported by QuickTime and Windows Media Player.

Figure 7-11 Parameters for QuickTime and Windows Media Player

Plug-in	Parameter	Description	Value(s)
QuickTime Player	autoplay	Starts playing the clip automatically when the page loads	true | false
	bgcolor	Sets the background color for the space allotted to the object	*#rrggbb | color name*
	controller	Specifies whether or not to show the object controls	true | false
	endtime	Specifies the time in the clip at which playback ends	*hh:mm:ss*
	href	Specifies a page to load when the user clicks on the object	*url*
	loop	Plays the clip in a continuous loop, forward, backward, or both (*palindrome*)	true | false | *palindrome*
	src	The source of the clip	*url*
	starttime	Specifies the time in the clip at which playback begins	*hh:mm:ss*
	volume	Sets the initial audio volume	0 - 255
Windows Media Player	autostart	Starts playing the clip automatically when the page loads	true | false
	filename	The source of the clip	*url*
	mute	Specifies whether or not the clip should be initially muted	true | false
	selectionstart	Specifies the time in the clip at which playback begins	*seconds*
	selectionstop	Specifies the time in the clip at which playback ends	*seconds*
	playcount	Specifies the number of times the clip will play	*integer*
	showcontrols	Specifies whether or not to show the object controls	true | false
	volume	Sets the initial audio volume	-10,000 - 0

For example, if you want your sound clip to play automatically when the page is opened, you would enter the following parameter if the browser uses the QuickTime plug-in:

```
<param name="autoplay" value="true" />
```

For Windows Media Player, the parameter to start the clip automatically is:

```
<param name="autostart" value="true" />
```

If a plug-in encounters a parameter it doesn't recognize, it will ignore it. So if you don't know which plug-in the browser will use to play your multimedia clip, you should include both parameter values in your HTML code. Figure 7-11 shows only a small list of the parameters associated with the two popular media players. You can get more information on other parameters and their values from each player's home page on the Web. Remember that users can always set the default options for their plug-ins. So if you are not sure, for example, that the sound controls will be displayed by the plug-in, you can always turn on that feature using either the controller parameter (for QuickTime) or the showcontrols parameter (for Windows Media Player).

Inserting an Object Element | Reference Window

- To insert an object, use the general syntax
```
<object data="url" type="MIME type"
 width="value" height="value">
    parameters
</object>
```
  where *url* is the URL of the filename and location of the object file, *MIME type* specifies the data type of the object, *value* specifies the width and height sizes in pixels, and *parameters* are parameters associated with the embedded object.
- To insert a parameter, use the tag
```
<param name="name" value="value" />
```
  where *name* is the name of the parameter and *value* is the parameter's value.

Maxine suggests that you add a few parameter elements to the code for the overture.mp3 sound clip. She wants to ensure that the browser always displays the sound clip controls and she doesn't want the clip to start automatically. Because you don't know which plug-in the browser will run, you'll add the following parameter elements to the file:

```
<param name="src" value="overture.mp3" />
<param name="autoplay" value="false" />
<param name="autostart" value="false" />
<param name="controller" value="true" />
<param name="showcontrols" value="true" />
```

Add this code to the jumbo.htm file.

To enter parameter values for the embedded sound clip:

1. Return to the **jumbo.htm** file in your text editor, and within the object tag, insert the following parameter elements as shown in Figure 7-12:
```
<param name="src" value="overture.mp3" />
<param name="autoplay" value="false" />
<param name="autostart" value="false" />
<param name="controller" value="true" />
<param name="showcontrols" value="true" />
```

Adding object parameters **Figure 7-12**

```
<object data="overture.mp3" type="audio/mpeg"
 width="280" height="25">
   <param name="src" value="overture.mp3" />
   <param name="autoplay" value="false" />
   <param name="autostart" value="false" />
   <param name="controller" value="true" />
   <param name="showcontrols" value="true" />
</object>
```

2. Save your changes to the file and then reload **jumbo.htm** in your Web browser. Depending on your browser, you might see controls for the QuickTime Player or for the Windows Media Player, as shown in Figure 7-13.

Figure 7-13 Plug-ins for the overture.mp3 plug-in

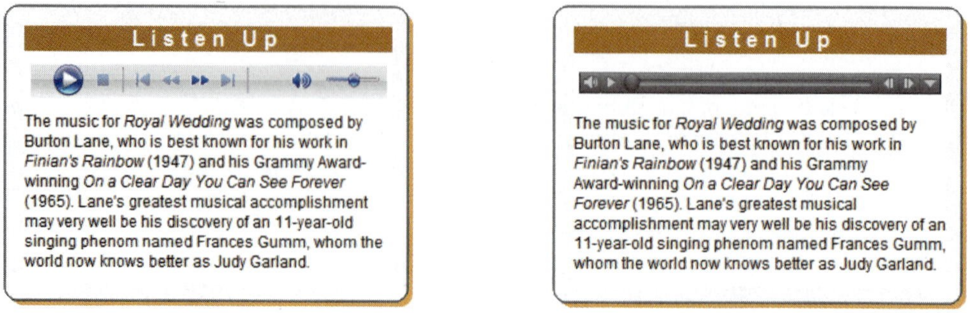

sound clip with Windows Media Player | sound clip with QuickTime Player

Trouble? If you don't see any sound controls on the Web page, your browser might not have the necessary plug-ins installed. If this is the case, you might be prompted by the browser to either activate or download and install the necessary plug-ins. You can also install plug-ins by going to the Web site for your browser; it should have links to all of the popular multimedia plug-ins. Talk to your instructor or technical resource person for permission before installing any programs on a lab computer.

3. Click the embedded sound clip and then click the **Play** button on the sound controls to start playing the sound clip.

You show the Web page to Maxine. She appreciates the work you've done but wonders why some users will see the QuickTime plug-in and others will see Windows Media Player. You explain that the choice of plug-in is determined by the settings on users' browsers. Maxine would prefer that QuickTime Player be used because it is a standard that is available for both Windows and Macintosh. She asks whether you can specify a particular plug-in to be used with a media clip.

Working with ActiveX Components

Different browsers support embedded media in different ways. For example, Internet Explorer supports a technology called ActiveX to play embedded media. **ActiveX** is a technology developed by Microsoft involving reusable software components that can be run from within a variety of Windows programs. For example, a programmer could create an ActiveX component to display a drop-down list box to be run within Internet Explorer, and that same component could be run from within Microsoft Word or Microsoft Excel. Another ActiveX component could be created to play video clips or sound files. The media player shown in Figure 7-13 is one example of an ActiveX control for playing such files.

There are literally thousands of ActiveX components available to the programmer and end user. The problem is that ActiveX is a technology designed only for Windows, and thus you cannot rely solely upon it if you're developing a program or Web site that will be used under a variety of operating systems.

The classid Attribute

Each ActiveX control is identified by a unique string of characters called the **class id**. The class id value is determined by the manufacturer of the ActiveX control. Figure 7-14 lists the class id values for several ActiveX controls that Maxine can use in creating her Web site.

Figure 7-14 **Class ids for ActiveX controls**

ActiveX Control	Class ID
Flash Shockwave Player	D27CDB6E-AE6D-11cf-96B8-444553540000
QuickTime Player	02BF25D5-8C17-4B23-BC80-D3488ABDDC6B
RealAudio Player	CFCDAA03-8BE4-11cf-B84B-0020AFBBCCFA
Windows Media Player	6BF52A52-394A-11d3-B153-00C04F79FAA6
Java applet	8AD9C840-044E-11D1-B3E9-00805F499D93

To insert a specific ActiveX control into your Web page, you would add the classid attribute

```
classid="clsid:id"
```

to the <object> tag, where *id* is the class id of the ActiveX control. For example, to insert the ActiveX control for the QuickTime Player, you would add the following classid attribute to the <object> tag:

```
classid="clsid:02BF25D5-8C17-4B23-BC80-D3488ABDDC6B"
```

Class id values are not case sensitive, so you can use upper- or lower-case letters in your HTML code; but you do have to enter the entire class id string with no omissions or errors. Given the length of the class id text string, this makes writing code for ActiveX objects a bit cumbersome. You can find the class id values for each ActiveX control by viewing the manufacturer's documentation.

Tip

You can avoid typing mistakes by saving all of your class id values in a text file that you can use for copying and pasting.

The codebase Attribute

When browsers encounter plug-ins or ActiveX controls they don't recognize, they usually leave a blank space where the embedded object would normally appear. One way of dealing with this problem is to provide the browser with information about where a working version of the plug-in or control can be downloaded. This is done by adding the codebase attribute

```
codebase="url"
```

to the <object> tag, where *url* is the filename and location of the program. In some cases, these programs are stored in installation files called **cab** or **cabinet files**, which automatically install the necessary software on the user's computer. You can usually find the location of installation programs in the manufacturer's documentation. For the ActiveX QuickTime Player, the URL for the cabinet file is *http://www.apple.com/qtactivex/qtplugin.cab*. So to embed an object using the ActiveX version of the QuickTime Player, you would enter the following code in your Web page:

```
<object classid="clsid:02BF25D5-8C17-4B23-BC80-D3488ABDDC6B"
        codebase="http://www.apple.com/qtactivex/qtplugin.cab">

   parameters

</object>
```

When Internet Explorer encounters this object, it will first attempt to insert the ActiveX QuickTime control into the Web page. If it can't find an ActiveX control on the computer with that class id value, it will then access the cab file at the URL specified in the codebase attribute and prompt the user to install the ActiveX control from that location. This frees the user from having to search for the program file.

Reference Window | Inserting an ActiveX Control

- To insert an ActiveX control for Internet Explorer, use the object element

```
<object data="url" type="MIME type"
 width="value" height="value"
 classid="clsid:id" codebase="url">
   parameters
</object>
```

where *id* is the class id of the ActiveX control, and the codebase attribute specifies the location where the ActiveX control can be downloaded and installed.

Maxine wants you to add both the classid and codebase attributes for the QuickTime Player to the <object> tag for the overture.mp3 sound clip. This will cause the browser to either play the clip using the ActiveX control for the QuickTime Player or to prompt the user to download the control from Apple's Web site.

To insert the classid and codebase attributes:

1. Return to the **jumbo.htm** file in your text editor.
2. Within the opening <object> tag for the overture.mp3 sound clip, insert the following attributes, as shown in Figure 7-15:

```
classid="clsid:02BF25D5-8C17-4B23-BC80-D3488ABDDC6B"
codebase="http://www.apple.com/qtactivex/qtplugin.cab"
```

Figure 7-15 Adding the classid and codebase attributes

```
<object data="overture.mp3" type="audio/mpeg"
 classid="clsid:02BF25D5-8C17-4B23-BC80-D3488ABDDC6B"
 codebase="http://www.apple.com/qtactivex/qtplugin.cab"
 width="280" height="25">
   <param name="src" value="overture.mp3" />
   <param name="autoplay" value="false" />
   <param name="autostart" value="false" />
   <param name="controller" value="true" />
   <param name="showcontrols" value="true" />
</object>
```

Trouble? The file **activexlist.txt** located in the tutorial.07/tutorial folder contains a list of class ids and codebases for various ActiveX components. You can use the copy and paste feature of your text editor to copy the code values from that file into the jumbo.htm file, rather than typing them.

3. Save your changes to the file and then reload **jumbo.htm** in the Internet Explorer Web browser. Verify that the browser either displays the QuickTime Player controls to play this audio clip or prompts you to activate or download the QuickTime ActiveX component for the QuickTime Player.
4. Open **jumbo.htm** in a non-Internet Explorer browser such as Firefox or Opera. Note that the QuickTime Player controls are now missing from the Web page. What happened?

With the classid and codebase attributes, you were able to embed the ActiveX QuickTime control for the Internet Explorer browser, but at the expense of removing it from other browsers. The problem is that ActiveX controls are designed for the Internet Explorer browser; other browsers do not support them. When those browsers encounter the classid attribute in the code you just entered, they're unable to process the <object> tag and so they ignore the embedded object altogether.

One way to resolve this problem is with Internet Explorer conditional comments.

Internet Explorer Conditional Comments

By now you've realized that Internet Explorer implements HTML and CSS differently than other browsers. Sometimes the easiest way to reconcile the two approaches is to run one set of code for Internet Explorer and another set of code for the other browsers. In Tutorial 4, you were briefly introduced to Internet Explorer's conditional comment, which allows you to run different code for different versions of Internet Explorer as well as for different browsers. The general syntax of an Internet Explorer conditional comment is

```
<!--[if condition IE version]><!-->
   HTML code
<!--<![endif]-->
```

where *condition* is a condition that is either true or false, *version* is the version number of an IE browser, and *HTML code* is code that will be run if the condition is true. If you want to run code only for Internet Explorer (regardless of the version), you would enter the following code:

```
<!--[if IE]><!-->
   HTML code
<!--<![endif]-->
```

If a non-IE browser encounters this code structure, it will interpret the whole structure as one long HTML comment and will not attempt to parse any of the HTML code within the comment tags. So you can insert the entire opening <object> tag within the following structure and it will be run only within Internet Explorer:

```
<!--[if IE]><!-->
   <object data="overture.mp3" type="audio/mpeg"
    classid="02BF25D5-8C17-4B23-BC80-D3488ABDDC6B"
    codebase=http://www.apple.com/qtactivex/qtplugin.cab
    width="280" height="25">
<!--<![endif]-->
```

You can also mark code that will only be run if the browser is *not* Internet Explorer. The general syntax uses conditional comments in the form

```
<!--[if !IE]><!-->
   HTML code
<!--<![endif]-->
```

where *HTML code* is code that will only be parsed if the browser is *not* Internet Explorer. Here, !IE is a conditional statement that means "not Internet Explorer." So to create an opening <object> tag for non-IE browsers that doesn't have the classid and codebase attributes, you would enter the following code:

```
<!--[if !IE]><!-->
   <object data="overture.mp3" type="audio/mpeg"
    width="280" height="25">
<!--<![endif]-->
```

Reference Window | Inserting IE Conditional Comments

- To insert an Internet Explorer conditional comment, use the general syntax
```
<!--[if condition IE version]><!-->
   HTML code
<!--<![endif]-->
```
where *condition* is a condition that is either true or false, *version* is the version number of an IE browser, and *HTML code* is code that will be run if the condition is true.
- To insert a conditional comment that runs code only for Internet Explorer, enter the following:
```
<!--[if IE]><!-->
   HTML code
<!--<![endif]-->
```
- To insert a conditional comment that runs code only for non-IE browsers, enter:
```
<!--[if !IE]><!-->
   HTML code
<!--<![endif]-->
```

Figure 7-16 shows how you can insert a sound clip tailored to both IE and non-IE browsers using both sets of conditional comments. Internet Explorer will insert the sound clip using the ActiveX QuickTime control, while non-IE browsers will insert the sound clip using a plug-in chosen by the browser.

Figure 7-16 **Writing code for IE and non-IE browsers**

Internet Explorer will run the code for the ActiveX QuickTime component

```
<!--[if IE]><!-->
   <object data="overture.mp3" type="audio/mpeg"
    classid="clsid:02BF25D5-8C17-4B23-BC80-D3488ABDDC6B"
    codebase="http://www.apple.com/qtactivex/qtplugin.cab"
    width="280" height="25">
<!--<![endif]-->

<!--[if !IE]><!-->
   <object data="overture.mp3" type="audio/mpeg"
    width="280" height="25">
<!--<![endif]-->

      <param name="src" value="overture.mp3" />
      <param name="autoplay" value="false" />
      <param name="autostart" value="false" />
      <param name="controller" value="true" />
      <param name="showcontrols" value="true" />
   </object>
```

Non-IE browsers will run the standard code for the embedded MP3 sound clip

```
<!--[if IE]><!-->
   <object data="overture.mp3" type="audio/mpeg"
    classid="clsid:02BF25D5-8C17-4B23-BC80-D3488ABDDC6B"
    codebase="http://www.apple.com/qtactivex/qtplugin.cab"
    width="280" height="25">
<!--<![endif]-->

<!--[if !IE]><!-->
   <object data="overture.mp3" type="audio/mpeg"
    width="280" height="25">
<!--<![endif]-->

      <param name="src" value="overture.mp3" />
      <param name="autoplay" value="false" />
      <param name="autostart" value="false" />
      <param name="controller" value="true" />
      <param name="showcontrols" value="true" />
   </object>
```

Add this structure to the jumbo.htm file.

To insert a set of conditional comments:

1. Return to the **jumbo.htm** file in your text editor.
2. Directly above the opening <object> tag for the overture.mp3 sound clip, insert:

```
<!--[if IE]><!-->
```

3. Directly below the opening <object> tag, insert:

```
<!--<![endif]-->

<!--[if !IE]><!-->
   <object data="overture.mp3" type="audio/mpeg"
    width="280" height="25">
<!--<![endif]-->
```

Figure 7-17 shows the revised code for the overture.mp3 embedded sound clip.

Figure 7-17 Conditional comments for the overture.mp3 sound file

```
<!--[if IE]><!-->
   <object data="overture.mp3" type="audio/mpeg"
    classid="clsid:02BF25D5-8C17-4B23-BC80-D3488ABDDC6B"
    codebase="http://www.apple.com/qtactivex/qtplugin.cab"
    width="280" height="25">
<!--<![endif]-->

<!--[if !IE]><!-->
   <object data="overture.mp3" type="audio/mpeg"
    width="280" height="25">
<!--<![endif]-->

      <param name="src" value="overture.mp3" />
      <param name="autoplay" value="false" />
      <param name="autostart" value="false" />
      <param name="controller" value="true" />
      <param name="showcontrols" value="true" />
   </object>
```

4. Save your changes to the file and then verify that the embedded sound clip appears in both Internet Explorer and in non-Internet Explorer browsers such as Firefox and Opera.
5. If you want to take a break before starting the next session, you can close your files and programs now.

You tell Maxine that you've found a workaround for the class id issue and now both Internet Explorer and non-Internet Explorer browsers should be able to display the overture.mp3 file using QuickTime Player (if it is installed). Conditional comments are only one way of writing code that reconciles the differences between how browsers handle embedded objects. You'll explore another technique later in this tutorial that involves nesting one object within another.

Creating Background Sound

The clip you've entered into Maxine's Web page will play only when clicked by the user. You might want to enhance a Web page by adding background music that starts when the page is loaded by the browser and whose controls are hidden on the Web page. The parameters for Windows Media Player to create a hidden clip that starts automatically are

```
<param name="autostart" value="true" />
<param name="showcontrols" value="false" />
```

while for QuickTime Player the parameter values are

```
<param name="autoplay" value="true" />
<param name="hidden" value="true" />
```

If you want the background music to play continuously as long as the page is open, you would add the parameter

```
<param name="playcount" value="0" />
```

for Windows Media Player, and you would use

```
<param name="loop" value="true" />
```

for QuickTime Player. In both cases, once the background music reaches the end of the file, this code will make it loop back to the beginning.

Another way of creating background sound for Internet Explorer is to use the bgsound element

```
<bgsound src="url" balance="value" loop="value" volume="value" />
```

where *url* is the filename and location of the background sound clip, the balance attribute defines how the sound should be balanced between the left and right speakers, the loop attribute defines how many times the sound clip is played, and the volume attribute indicates the volume, ranging from 0 (muted) to 10,000 (the loudest). To have the sound clip play continuously, set the loop value to infinite. The bgsound element is supported only by Internet Explorer and is not part of the specifications for HTML or XHTML.

Tip

Most background music is created from MIDI files because that format allows for longer music clips with a much smaller file size.

If you choose to create background music for your Web site, make sure you pick a sound clip that will not irritate your users. Background music can be annoying, especially if the music clip is set to loop indefinitely with no way of shutting it off!

Maxine is pleased with your work on the overture.mp3 sound clip. In the next session you'll use the same techniques to embed a video clip on her Web page.

Review | Session 7.1 Quick Check

1. Describe two ways of making multimedia content available on your Web site.
2. Define the following terms: bandwidth, sampling rate, sample resolution, and bitrate.
3. Specify the code to create an embedded object containing the sound file royal.wav.
4. What are two possible MIME types that you could use to specify the data type of the royal.wav sound file?
5. Assuming that the royal.wav file will be played using Windows Media Player, what attribute would you add to the <object> tag to display only the play and stop buttons?
6. What parameter would you enter to start playing the royal.wav file when the page is loaded? (Assume that Windows Media Player is used to play the sound clip.)
7. What classid value would you add to the <object> tag to tell the browser to use the Windows Media Player ActiveX control to play the royal.wav file?
8. Specify the code you would enter to run all of the commands from Questions 3 through 7 only for the Internet Explorer browser.

Session 7.2

Exploring Digital Video

Maxine's next task for you is to embed a video clip on her Web page of Fred Astaire dancing in *Royal Wedding*. Displaying video is one of the most popular uses of the Web. With high-speed connections more available to the public, video has transitioned from simply a source of entertainment to an essential source of content and information. For example, sites such as *www.cnn.com* routinely include important information in embedded video clips to supplement their news articles.

Digital video can be recorded using digital camcorders, digital cameras, and cell phones, and with video capture boards installed on computers to record images from television, DVDs, and VCRs. You can also create video clips using computer animation software. When creating a video clip for distribution on the Web, you must determine what size and type of video will work best when played back over the viewer's Internet connection. You also must consider what video format will be most accessible to your users. The goal is to create video that will be easily playable by the most people, with a smooth playback that is easy to watch. Before embedding Maxine's video clip, you'll first examine some of the issues involved in creating digital video files.

Data Rates and Video Quality

A video file is composed of a series of single images or **frames** that are played in rapid succession to create the illusion of motion. Most frames are sized to have width-to-height ratios or **aspect ratios** of 4:3. The two most common frame sizes for the Web are 160 × 120 pixels and 320 × 240 pixels. With high-bandwidth connections becoming increasingly available, frame sizes as high as 640 × 480 pixels are becoming more common.

When a video is played, the frames are rapidly shown in sequence, giving the illusion of motion. The number of frames shown in a given amount of time is called the **frame rate**, commonly expressed in frames per second (fps). Higher frame rates usually, but not always, result in a smoother animation. For comparison, DVDs typically render video at 24 fps, while frame rates of 10 to 15 fps, commonly used on the Web, can still result in videos of good quality.

However, the frame rate is not the only factor that determines the quality of a video. Another more important factor is the **data rate**, which is the amount of data that has to be processed by the video player each second to play the video clip. The size of the frame, the frame rate, and the bit rate of any audio attached to the video also are factored into the calculation of the data rate. When settling on a data rate for video embedded on a Web site, you should take into account the bandwidth of the connection to your Web site. The bandwidth must be large enough to accommodate the amount of information processed each second to smoothly play the video. If the user attempts to play a video with too high of a data rate, the playback will be choppy and uneven as the connection tries in vain to keep up with the pace of the clip. A common mistake is to assume that a high-quality video clip with a fast frame rate will result in the best video for the user. This is not necessarily the case. For slower connections, a lower-quality clip with a slower frame rate might actually look and perform better.

A general rule of thumb is that for a local area network, you should be able to get good quality playback at a data rate of 400 to 600 kilobytes per second (Kbps). For DSL and ISDN, keep the data rate at 350 Kbps or less. If your viewers are connecting at low bandwidth such as through a dial-up line, the data rate should be kept below 100 Kbps. If you are running a video installed on your own computer or on a very fast network connection, you can work with data rates of a megabyte per second or more.

Tip

Use video editing software to create several versions of your video clips, varying the frame rate, frame size, and bit rate to determine which combinations result in the best playback for your target bandwidth.

You can reduce the data rate by reducing the frame size, using monaural rather than stereo sound, and reducing the frame rate. The content of your video clip also has an impact on the data rate. A so-called "talking head" video in which there is a narrator in front of a largely static background can be saved with a low frame rate at little cost in video quality; on the other hand, a clip with a lot of motion (such as the dance sequence that Maxine wants to use for her site) would become choppy and uneven when played at a low frame rate.

Finally, video size can be greatly reduced through the use of file compression. When a compressed video is replayed, each frame is decompressed as it is rendered. The technology that compresses and decompresses a media clip is called a **codec** (short for *co*mpression/*dec*ompression). Many different codecs are available, each with its own advantages and disadvantages. Some codecs create smaller video files but at the expense of choppier playback. Video editing software allows you to choose the codec for your video clip, but you might need to experiment to determine which codec provides the best file compression without sacrificing video quality. Recent developments in video editing have introduced codecs that greatly reduce video size, resulting in high-quality video at data rates that are reasonable even under lower bandwidths.

Video File Formats

As with the sound formats you examined in the last session, there are a variety of video formats in use on the Web. Figure 7-18 lists some of the video file formats that Maxine will consider for her Web site.

Video formats **Figure 7-18**

Format	Filename Extension	MIME Type	Description
AVI	.avi	video/x-msvideo	Audio/Video Interleaved. AVI is a common video file format developed by Microsoft for use with Windows. It is not always possible to play AVI files on non-Windows computers unless special software has been installed on the computer.
Flash Video	.flv	video/x-flv	FLV is a proprietary file format developed by Adobe to deliver video over the Internet using the popular Adobe Flash Player. It is the preferred file format for online video sites such as YouTube and Google Video.
MPEG	.mpg, .mpeg, .mp3	video/mpeg	Moving Pictures Group. The MPEG format allows for high compression of the video file, resulting in a smaller file size. MPEG files have good support across various browsers and operating systems but tend to be much larger than flash videos.
QuickTime	.mov	video/quicktime	QuickTime is a video format developed by Apple Computer for Windows and Apple computers. Like MPEG, QuickTime employs a compression algorithm that can result in smaller file sizes. QuickTime files require QuickTime Player, available for either Windows or the Macintosh.
RealVideo	.rm, .rv	application/ vnd.rn-realmedia	RealVideo is a video format developed by RealNetworks for transmitting live video over the Internet at both low and high bandwidths. It uses a variety of data compression techniques and requires the installation of the RealPlayer media player.
Shockwave Flash	.swf	application/ x-shockwave-flash	SWF is a proprietary file format developed by Adobe to deliver multimedia and vector graphics on the Web. An SWF file can contain animations, video, audio, interactive scripts, and control buttons. SWF files can be played using Adobe Flash Player either as a browser plug-in or a stand-alone player.
Windows Media	.wmv	video/x-ms-wmv	Developed by Microsoft, WMV is a popular video format for creating streaming video on the Web. The WMV format offers good compression and video quality, but is primarily designed for Windows users.

The format you should use for your Web page depends a great deal on your target audience. You want a video format that users will be able to play without having to install additional software, and it should be a format that will result in good video quality with reasonable data rates. Currently, the most popular video format by far is Flash video, which is used throughout the Web, including such popular sites as YouTube, MySpace, and Google Video.

Media Players

> **Tip**
>
> Only use codecs that are commonly available to your audience. Most users will not want to watch a video clip if they have to go through the process of installing another codec.

There are four standard media players for use with video on the Web: Windows Media Player, QuickTime, Flash, and RealPlayer. In the last session, you examined Windows Media Player and QuickTime Player for use with audio clips. You can apply similar techniques to play video clips with those players. Figure 7-19 details the video formats that each player typically supports. Note that these media players support other formats than those listed here, and in some cases the user can install additional codecs to enable the player to support even more formats.

Figure 7-19 **Video formats, media players and plug-ins**

Video Format	Adobe Flash Player	Windows Media Player	QuickTime Player	RealPlayer
.asf		yes		
.avi		yes		
.mov	yes		yes	
.mp4	yes		yes	yes
.mpg		yes	yes	yes
.rm				yes
.swf	yes			
.wmv		yes		

No matter which video format Maxine chooses for her Web site, her viewers will need to have access to a media player to view the files. Windows Media Player comes preinstalled on Windows computers, QuickTime comes preinstalled on the Macintosh, Flash comes preinstalled on both operating systems, and RealPlayer comes preinstalled on neither. Recent market surveys have indicated that almost 99% of Internet viewers have access to Adobe Flash Player, 83% can run Microsoft Windows Media Player, 68.4% have access to QuickTime Player, and 52.6% have RealPlayer (source: *www.adobe.com/products/player_census/flashplayer*). Based on these findings, you strongly recommend to Maxine that she develop video for her site to take advantage of the popularity of Adobe Flash Player.

Working with Flash

> **Tip**
>
> Because online services compress your video for you, submit the highest-quality video you can to their site. Don't provide a compressed version of your video because the site will only compress it even more, further degrading video quality.

Now that Maxine has decided on Flash for her video clips, she can either use a free online service such as YouTube (*www.youtube.com*) to host her video or she can host the video on her own Web site. One problem with an online service is that she has no control over the final video quality. Online services tend to apply heavy compression to their video files and limit the choices for both frame rate and frame size. For example, the dimension of a YouTube video is set to 320 × 240 pixels with a data rate of 314 Kbps and frame rates of 25 fps. If these settings do not work well for your video clip, you do not have the option of changing them within YouTube.

Maxine decides that she will create and edit the video clip herself so that she has control over the final appearance of the video and its quality. There are several software packages available for creating a Flash video. The most expensive and extensive is Adobe Flash Professional, which is used by professional video developers. Users who don't want to spend several hundreds of dollars can find decent editing programs for much less. Look for editing software that allows you to convert other video file formats into Flash and gives you control over video quality.

There are two main file formats involved in creating a Flash video. The first is the **flv** or **Flash Video** format that contains the video clip that will be displayed by Adobe Flash Player. An flv file is usually created by converting video from another format such as avi or mpeg. To play Flash video, the video must be stored within a Shockwave Flash file. A **Shockwave Flash** or **swf** file contains the video, audio, animations, interactive scripts, program controls, and other features that provide real-time interactive animation for the viewer. One advantage of an swf file is that programmers can create their own players, containing video controls tailored to the specific needs of their Web site. It's not uncommon to observe Web sites containing players reflecting the Web site's content or design. For example, video played with YouTube's player will display the YouTube logo at the bottom-right corner of each frame. This is different from QuickTime Player and Windows Media Player, whose controls are designed by Apple and Microsoft, respectively, and therefore have a common look and feel on any Web site.

Working with Flash editing software, Maxine has created an swf file containing the video clip of Fred Astaire dancing on the ceiling from *Royal Wedding*. She wants you to insert this file as an embedded object on her Web page.

Embedding a Flash Player

To embed a Flash Player, you use many of the same techniques you used in the last session to embed the overture.mp3 sound clip. Most browsers embed a Flash Player using the object element

```
<object type="application/x-shockwave-flash"
        data="file.swf" width="value" height="value">
   <param name="movie" value="file.swf" />
   parameters
</object>
```

where *file.swf* is the swf file containing the Flash animation. On the other hand, Internet Explorer inserts the Flash Player as an ActiveX control. The object code for Internet Explorer is

```
<object type="application/x-shockwave-flash"
        data="file.swf" width="value" height="value"
        classid="clsid:D27CDB6E-AE6D-11cf-96B8-444553540000"
        codebase="http://download.macromedia.com/pub/shockwave/cabs/
                  flash/swflash.cab#version=9,0,115,0">
   <param name="movie" value="file.swf" />
   parameters
</object>
```

You can support both approaches by applying the same conditional comments you used in the last session for the QuickTime plug-in.

Reference Window | Embedding Shockwave Flash

- To embed a Shockwave Flash file as an ActiveX control, enter

```
<object type="application/x-shockwave-flash"
        data="file.swf" width="value" height="value"
        classid="clsid:D27CDB6E-AE6D-11cf-96B8-444553540000"
        codebase="http://download.macromedia.com/pub/shockwave/cabs/
                  flash/swflash.cab#version=9,0,115,0">

   <param name="movie" value="file.swf" />
   parameters

</object>
```

  where *file.swf* is the Shockwave Flash file and *parameters* are parameters associated with the Flash Player.
- To embed a Shockwave Flash file for non-IE browsers, use the following:

```
<object type="application/x-shockwave-flash"
        data="file.swf" width="value" height="value">

   <param name="movie" value="file.swf" />
   parameters
</object>
```

Maxine has stored her video clip in a Flash Player with the filename rwdance.swf. The clip has a frame size of 280 × 210 pixels and a frame rate of 25 fps. Because she'll be testing this on her local computer only, she set the data rate at 500 Kbps. Later, when she places this clip on her Web server, she might reduce the frame and data rates to something more appropriate for the lower bandwidth.

Add this clip to her Web page now.

To embed the Flash Player:

1. Return to the **jumbo.htm** file in your text editor.
2. Scroll down the file to the In Focus paragraph. Directly after the paragraph, insert the following code to define the properties of the object element for Internet Explorer users:

```
<p style="text-align: center">

<!--[if IE]><!-->
   <object data="rwdance.swf" type="application/x-shockwave-flash"
    classid="clsid:D27CDB6E-AE6D-11cf-96B8-444553540000"
    codebase=http://download.macromedia.com/pub/shockwave/
cabs/flash/swflash.cab#version=9,0,115,0"
    width="280" height="239">
<!--<![endif]-->
```

   Trouble? You can copy and paste the class id and codebase values from the **activexlist.txt** file located in the tutorial.07\tutorial folder included with your Data Files. Despite its length, enter the class id value without inserting blank spaces or pressing the Enter key.

3. Next, insert the following code to define the properties of the object element under non-IE browsers.

```
<!--[if !IE]><!-->
   <object data="rwdance.swf" type="application/x-shockwave-flash"
    width="280" height="239">
<!--<![endif]-->
```

4. Finally, complete the code for the Flash video by adding the param element and the closing </object> and </p> tags. Figure 7-20 shows the complete code for the embedded object.

```
      <param name="movie" value="rwdance.swf" />
   </object>

</p>
```

Embedding a Shockwave Flash file | **Figure 7-20**

```
<div class="boxContent">
   <h2>In Focus</h2>

   <p>The high point of <i>Royal Wedding</i> is the "Ceiling Dance" in
      which Fred Astaire appears to literally dance on the ceiling and walls
      of his hotel room. The effect was accomplished by putting the whole set
      inside of a 20-foot diameter rotating cage. As the cage turned, Astaire
      would seamlessly dance across the four sides of the box, creating the
      illusion of weightlessness. The same technique would later be used
      to simulate a zero gravity environment in <i>2001: A Space
      Odyssey</i>.</p>

   <p style="text-align: center">

   <!--[if IE]><!-->
      <object data="rwdance.swf" type="application/x-shockwave-flash"
       classid="clsid:D27CDB6E-AE6D-11cf-96B8-444553540000"
       codebase="http://download.macromedia.com/pub/shockwave/cabs/flash/swflash.cab#version=9,0,115,0"
       width="280" height="239">
   <!--<![endif]-->

   <!--[if !IE]><!-->
      <object data="rwdance.swf" type="application/x-shockwave-flash"
       width="280" height="239">
   <!--<![endif]-->

         <param name="movie" value="rwdance.swf" />
      </object>

   </p>

</div>
```

5. Save your changes to the file.

6. Refresh or reload the **jumbo.htm** file in your Web browser.

7. Below the In Focus paragraph, your browser should display an embedded video clip, as shown in Figure 7-21. Click the **play** button to begin playing the clip.

The embedded video clip from *Royal Wedding* | **Figure 7-21**

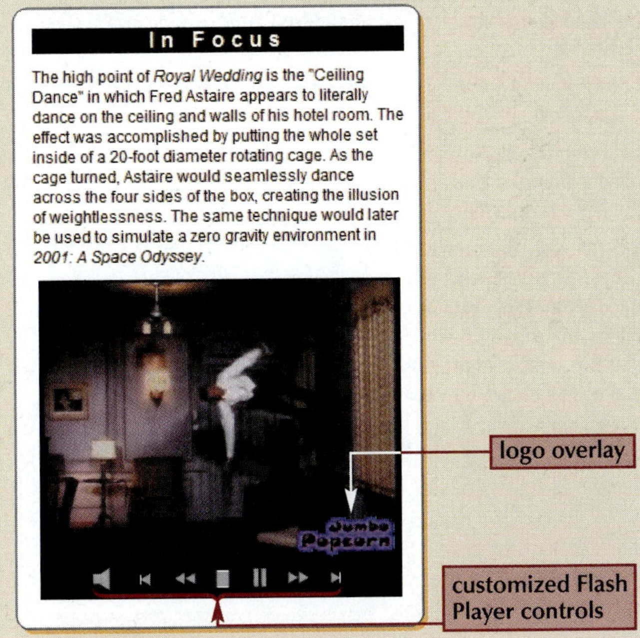

Trouble? If the clip doesn't play or it doesn't appear on the Web page, check your code against that shown in Figure 7-20 and in Steps 2 through 4. It is also possible that you do not have Flash Player installed on your computer. Contact your instructor or technical resource person if you need to install Flash.

Note that the codebase attribute specified above is for version 9 of Flash Player. If a more recent version of the player is available, Internet Explorer checks this Web site using the url from this codebase and prompts the user to install the most recent version. Also note that the URL references the Macromedia.com Web site. Macromedia, the original creator of Flash, was acquired by Adobe Systems in 2005. Adobe choose to keep the Macromedia Web site URL's active to accommodate current HTML code.

The Flash Player that Maxine created for her Web site has a few interesting features. She customized the video control buttons, and she placed the Jumbo Popcorn logo in the lower-right corner of the player. This demonstrates a few of the features of Flash that have made it so popular for designers who want to customize the multimedia on their Web sites.

Tip

You can also use Shockwave Flash Player to embed audio clips on your Web site, customizing the player and appearance of the clip using Flash editing software.

Flash Parameters

The movie you just embedded had a single parameter that identified the swf file. Flash supports other parameters to give more control over the appearance and behavior of the Flash file. Figure 7-22 lists some of the other Flash attributes and parameters.

Figure 7-22 **Flash Player parameters and values**

Parameter	Description	Value(s)
bgcolor	Sets the background color of the Flash player	*#rrggbb* | *color name*
flashvar	Contains text values that are passed to the Flash player as variables to control the behavior and content of the movie	*text*
id	Identifies the embedded Flash movie so that it can be referenced	*text*
loop	Plays the movie in a continuous loop	true | false
menu	Displays the full Flash pop-up when the user right-clicks the movie	true | false
name	Names the embedded Flash movie so that it can be referenced	*text*
play	Starts playing the movie automatically when the page loads	true | false
quality	Sets the playback quality of the movie; low values favor playback speed over quality; high values favor display quality over playback speed	low | autolow | autohigh | medium | high | best
scale	Defines how the movie clip is scaled within the defined space; a value of showall makes the entire clip visible in the specified area without distortion; a value of noborder scales the movie to fill the specified area, without distortion but possibly with some cropping; a value of exactfit makes the entire movie visible in the specified area without trying to preserve the original aspect ratio	showall | noborder | exactfit
wmode	Sets the appearance of the Flash player against the page background; a value of window causes the movie to play within its own window on the page; a value of opaque hides everything on the page behind the clip; a value of transparent allows the page background to show through transparent colors in the movie	window | opaque | transparent

For example, if you want to set the playback quality of the Flash movie to high, you would add the following parameter to the object element:

```
<param name="quality" value="high" />
```

Note that Flash movies with high display quality may suffer from ragged playback, so you must test your video clips to ensure that the speed of the clip is still sufficient for the viewer.

Maxine suggests that you set the playback quality of the rwdance.swf clip to high. She also asks you to change the menu settings so that viewers will only see the brief version of the pop-up menu rather than the full version. Using a brief Flash pop-up menu is a standard approach on the Web so that viewers cannot change the playback settings chosen by the clip's author.

To add parameters to the Flash Player:

1. Return to the **jumbo.htm** file in your text editor.
2. Add the following parameters to the object element for the rwdance.swf file, as shown in Figure 7-23:

```
<param name="quality" value="high" />
<param name="menu" value="false" />
```

Figure 7-23 **Adding the quality and menu parameters**

```
<!--[if !IE]><!-->
   <object data="rwdance.swf" type="application/x-shockwave-flash"
    width="280" height="239">
<!--<![endif]-->

      <param name="movie" value="rwdance.swf" />
      <param name="quality" value="high" />
      <param name="menu" value="false" />
   </object>
```

3. Save your changes to the file and then reload **jumbo.htm** in your Web browser.
4. Click the **play** button to verify that the clip still plays properly within your browser.
5. Right-click the embedded video and verify that the pop-up menu has only two entries: Settings and About Adobe Flash Player.

You show Maxine the embedded video. She agrees that it adds a lot to the Web page and that the player is easy to use. Although she will continue to use Flash for this site, it's possible that she'll want to use a different video format in the future. She asks you to research how to create embedded video clips with QuickTime Player and Windows Media Player.

Exploring QuickTime Video

QuickTime movies are displayed in the same player you used in the last session for the overture.mp3 file, and therefore much of the code you used for that audio clip can be applied to a QuickTime movie. Once again you need two sets of opening <object> tags: one for Internet Explorer, in which the QuickTime Player is inserted as an ActiveX control, and the other for non-IE browsers, in which the video clip is inserted as a plug-in. You can use the same classid and codebase attribute values for the movie player. The MIME type for QuickTime videos is video/quicktime.

Maxine has created a QuickTime version of the dance clip, saved as rwdance.mov, that she wants you to embed on a sample Web page. Because the code structure will be pretty close to what you used to embed the Flash Player, you can use the jumbo.htm file as a starting point.

To embed the QuickTime movie:

1. Return to the **jumbo.htm** file in your text editor and save the file as **jumbo_mov.htm** in the tutorial.07\tutorial folder. Scroll down to the section of the file containing the Flash movie.
2. Change the data attribute in both <object> tags from

   ```
   data="rwdance.swf"
   ```

   to

   ```
   data="rwdance.mov"
   ```

3. Change the type attribute in both <object> tags from

   ```
   type="application/x-shockwave-flash"
   ```

   to

   ```
   type="video/quicktime"
   ```

4. Change the value of the classid attribute to:

   ```
   classid="clsid:02BF25D5-8C17-4B23-BC80-D3488ABDDC6B"
   ```

   Trouble? You can copy and paste the classid value from the code you entered earlier for the embedded overture.mp3 sound clip.
5. Change the value of the codebase attribute to:

   ```
   codebase="http://www.apple.com/qtactivex/qtplugin.cab"
   ```

6. Delete the three parameters from the embedded object and replace them with the following QuickTime parameters:

   ```
   <param name="src" value="rwdance.mov" />
   <param name="autoplay" value="false" />
   <param name="controller" value="true" />
   ```

   These are the same parameters you used in the last session for the overture.mp3 sound clip. Figure 7-24 highlights the revised code for the embedded QuickTime movie.

Figure 7-24 Embedding a QuickTime movie

```
<p style="text-align: center">

<!--[if IE]><!-->
   <object data="rwdance.mov" type="video/quicktime"
    classid="clsid:02BF25D5-8C17-4B23-BC80-D3488ABDDC6B"
    codebase="http://www.apple.com/qtactivex/qtplugin.cab"
    width="280" height="239">
<!--<![endif]-->

<!--[if !IE]><!-->
   <object data="rwdance.mov" type="video/quicktime"
    width="280" height="239">
<!--<![endif]-->

      <param name="src" value="rwdance.mov" />
      <param name="autoplay" value="false" />
      <param name="controller" value="true" />
   </object>

</p>
```

7. Save your changes to the **jumbo_mov.htm** file and then open it in your browser. Your browser should show controls for the QuickTime Movie Player, as shown in Figure 7-25. Click the **play** button to start the movie.

Figure 7-25 **The QuickTime video player**

All of the parameters discussed earlier in Figure 7-11 for sound also apply to video. The player also supports other parameters specifically related to video. Figure 7-26 lists some of the other QuickTime parameters you can use with embedded video.

Figure 7-26 **Parameters of the QuickTime Player**

Parameter	Description	Value(s)
autohref	Automatically loads the Web page specified in *url*	*url*
goto	Plays a movie from the numbered list specified in the qtnext parameter	*integer*
href	Loads *url* when the viewer clicks the movie	*url*
kioskmode	Does not include the Save option in the movie controller bar	true
movieid	Identifies the movie so that it can be referenced	*text*
moviename	Names the movie so that it can be referenced	*text*
playeveryframe	Does not drop any frames from the video playback	true | false
qtnext	Specifies a numbered list of movies to play in the player	n=<*url*>T<target> | GOTO*n*
qtsrc	Loads a file or stream different from the one specified in the src parameter	*url*
qtsrcchokedspeed	Limits the outgoing bandwidth from the server to a specified data rate	*date rate*
saveembedtags	Preserves the current parameter values when loading a new movie	true
scale	Defines how the movie should be rescaled to fit the defined space; use tofit to change the movie's dimension to fit the space, aspect to fit the movie to the space while retaining the aspect ratio, and *n* to scale the movie by a factor of *n*	tofit | aspect | *n*
showlogo	Shows the QuickTime logo until the movie is ready to play	true | false
target	Places the movie within the QuickTime player or within a named frame, or replaces the current movie with the new movie	quicktimeplayer | *frame* | myself

For example, you can use the QuickTime parameters to format the size of the video clip. The width and height attributes define the space reserved for the QuickTime Player, but within that space you can resize the video clip using the parameter

```
<param name="scale" value="scale" />
```

where *scale* is tofit, aspect, or a numeric value. A value of tofit fits the video clip and the video controls exactly to the available space (even if that distorts the image). The aspect value fits the width of the video clip and player to space while retaining its aspect ratio. If a numeric value is specified, it indicates the factor by which the video is rescaled while retaining its aspect ratio. For example, to reduce the video to 70% of its size, you would enter the following parameter:

```
<param name="scale" value="0.7" />
```

If you reduce the size of the player relative to the space available for it, you can apply a background color using the bgcolor parameter. Background colors are entered using either the color name or a hexadecimal color value (for discussion of hexadecimal color values, see Tutorial 3). Maxine suggests you experiment with these parameters by reducing the size of the player and presenting it on a light brown background.

To format the video's appearance:

1. Return to the **jumbo_mov.htm** file in your text editor.
2. Add the following parameters to the QuickTime object as shown in Figure 7-27:

```
<param name="scale" value="0.7" />
<param name="bgcolor" value="#F0BC4C" />
```

Figure 7-27
Setting the movie scale and background color

```
<!--[if !IE]><!-->
   <object data="rwdance.mov" type="video/quicktime"
    width="280" height="239">
<!--<![endif]-->

        <param name="src" value="rwdance.mov" />
        <param name="autoplay" value="false" />
        <param name="controller" value="true" />
        <param name="scale" value="0.7" />
        <param name="bgcolor" value="#F0BC4C" />
   </object>
```

3. Close the file, saving your changes, and then reload **jumbo_mov.htm** in your Web browser. As shown in Figure 7-28, the video is rescaled to 70% of its original size and displayed on a light brown background.

Figure 7-28
Rescaling the QuickTime Player

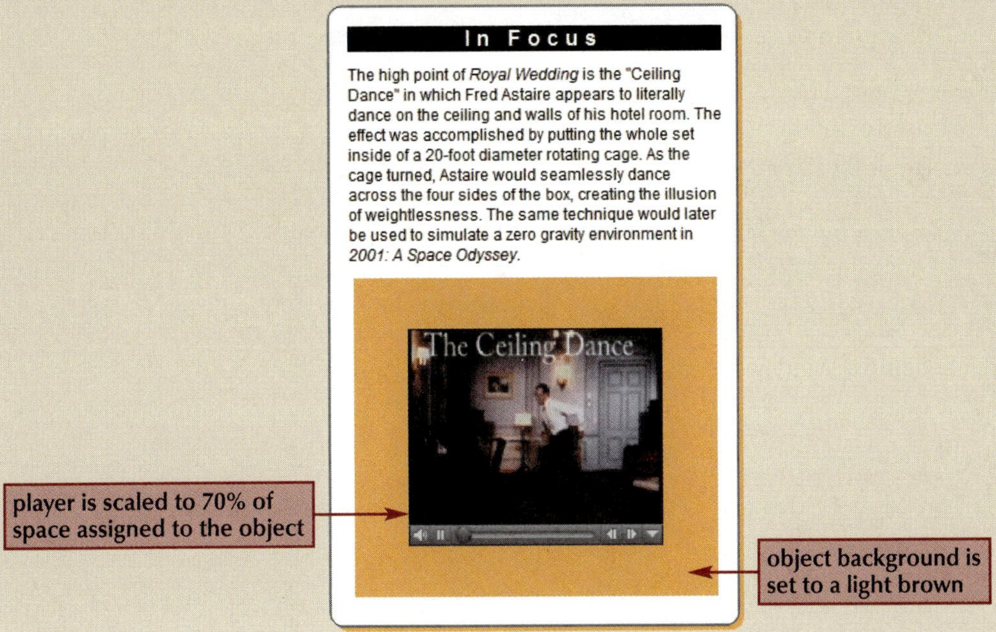

Rescaling the video does not change the file size or the data rate. It only changes how the browser renders the clip on the page. If you need to resize the clip to reduce its file size or data rate, you must use video editing software.

Exploring Windows Media Player

Maxine has also created a version of the video clip for Windows Media Player that she wants you to test. You can embed this clip as an ActiveX object for IE browsers and as a plug-in for non-IE browsers. Once again, you'll use the same structure for the Windows Media Player as you did for the Flash Player you created earlier.

To embed the Windows Media Player:

1. Reopen the **jumbo.htm** file in your text editor and save the file as **jumbo_wmv.htm** to the tutorial.07\tutorial folder. Scroll down to the code for the embedded Flash Player.
2. Change the data attribute in both <object> tags from

   ```
   data="rwdance.swf"
   ```

   to

   ```
   data="rwdance.wmv"
   ```

3. Change the type attribute in both <object> tags from

   ```
   type="application/x-shockwave-flash"
   ```

   to

   ```
   type="video/x-ms-wmv"
   ```

4. Change the value of the classid attribute to:

   ```
   classid="clsid:6BF52A52-394A-11d3-B153-00C04F79FAA6"
   ```

   Trouble? You can copy and paste the classid value from the **activexlist.txt** file located in the tutorial.07\tutorial folder.

5. Change the value of the codebase attribute to:

   ```
   codebase="http://activex.microsoft.com/activex/controls/
             mplayer/en/nsmp2inf.cab#Version=6,4,5,715"
   ```

6. Change the value of the height attribute in both <object> tags to

   ```
   height="245"
   ```

7. Delete the three parameters from the embedded object and replace them with the following Windows Media Player parameters:

   ```
   <param name="url" value="rwdance.wmv" />
   <param name="autostart" value="false" />
   <param name="showcontrols" value="true" />
   ```

   Figure 7-29 highlights the revised code for the embedded Windows Media Player.

Tip

To display the movie controls, add about 30 pixels to the height of a video played by Windows Media Player. For QuickTime Player, increase the height by about 20 pixels.

Figure 7-29 Embedding a Windows Media video

```
<p style="text-align: center">

<!--[if IE]><!-->
   <object data="rwdance.wmv" type="video/x-ms-wmv"
    classid="clsid:6BF52A52-394A-11d3-B153-00C04F79FAA6"
    codebase="http://activex.microsoft.com/activex/controls/mplayer/en/nsmp2inf.cab#Version=6,4,5,715"
    width="280" height="245" >
<!--<![endif]-->

<!--[if !IE]><!-->
   <object data="rwdance.wmv" type="video/x-ms-wmv"
    width="280" height="245" >
<!--<![endif]-->

      <param name="url" value="rwdance.wmv" />
      <param name="autostart" value="false" />
      <param name="showcontrols" value="true" />
   </object>

</p>
```

8. Close the file, saving your changes to the **jumbo_wmv.htm** file and then open it in your browser. Your browser should show controls for the Windows Media Player, as shown in Figure 7-30. Click the **play** button to start the movie.

The Windows Media Player **Figure 7-30**

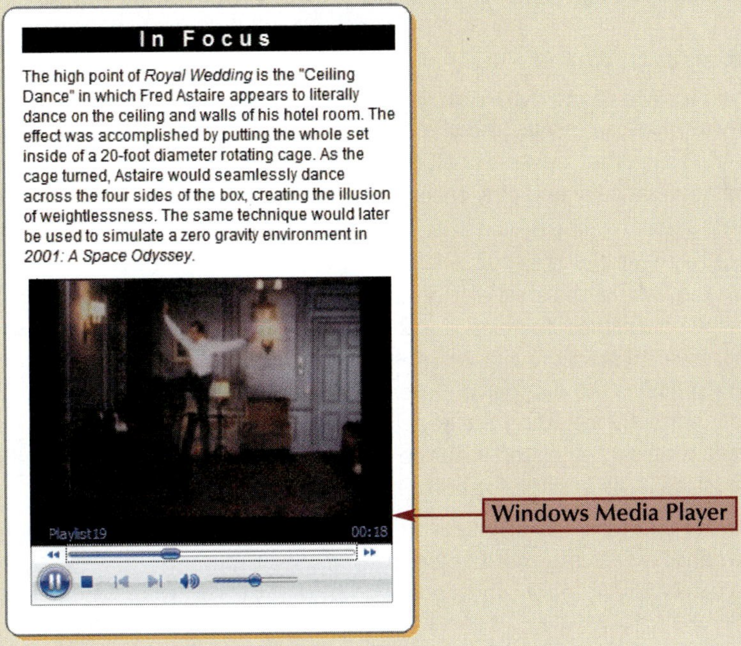

Like the other players, the Windows Media Player includes support for several parameters specifically related to playing videos. Figure 7-31 lists some of the parameters you might consider using in addition to those shown earlier in Figure 7-11.

Video-related parameters of the Windows Media Player **Figure 7-31**

Parameter	Description	Value(s)
fullscreen	Specifies whether the video content is played back in full-screen mode	true | false
rate	Specifies the playback rate, where a value of 0.5 indicates a playback at half-speed and a value of 2 plays the video back at twice normal speed	*value*
stretchtofit	Specifies whether the video automatically sizes to fit the video window	true | false
url	Specifies the name of the media file to play	*url*
windowlessvideo	Specifies whether the Windows Media player renders the video in windowless mode, in which the video is rendered directly on the page where you can apply special effects or overlay the video with text	true | false

Maxine does not need you to make any other changes to the code for Windows Media Player.

InSight | **Using a Dynamic Resource with Inline Images**

Internet Explorer users can combine inline images and video clips by adding the dynsrc attribute

```
<img src="url" dynsrc="url" />
```

to the <img> tag, where the dynsrc attribute specifies the url of a video version of the inline image. Browsers that can display the video version will automatically load and play the clip for the viewer, while other browsers will display only the inline image. By default, the video clip will start automatically and play once; however, you can control this behavior by adding the attributes

```
start="type" loop="value" controls
```

to the <img> tag, where the start attribute tells the browser when to start the video clip and has two possible values: fileopen to start playing the clip when the browser opens the file, and mouseover to start the clip when the user hovers the mouse over the video. The loop attribute specifies the number of times to play the clip and can be either an integer or the keyword infinite. By including the keyword controls within the <img> tag, you can display any player controls associated with the video clip. Be aware that the space allotted to the image must be large enough for both the clip and the player controls.

For example, the following tag displays the rwdance.jpg inline for non-IE browsers and the video clip rwdance.avi for Internet Explorer:

```
<img src="rwdance.jpg" dynsrc="rwdance.avi" start="mouseover"
loop="1" />
```

The movie will not start until the user hovers the mouse pointer over the video; then the clip will play once and stop. No player controls will be displayed with the image.

Because the dynsrc attribute is supported only by Internet Explorer, you should use it only in situations where you are sure that the IE browsers will be used by viewers, such as for Web pages on a company's intranet.

Introducing the embed Element

The <object> tag represents the W3C standard for inserting multimedia content. Although it is supported by current browsers, it might not be supported by older browser versions. To make your pages backward compatible, you can use the embed element along with the object tag to insert multimedia content. The syntax of the embed element is

```
<embed src="url" attributes></embed>
```

where *url* is the source of the multimedia content and *attributes* are the attributes that define that content and how it is rendered by the browser. Figure 7-32 lists some of the attributes associated with the embed element. Note that many of the attributes match the attributes and parameters associated with the object element. The only required attribute is the src attribute; the other attributes listed in Figure 7-32 are optional.

Attributes of the embed element — Figure 7-32

Attribute	Description	Value(s)
align	Specifies the horizontal alignment of the embedded element	absbottom | absmiddle | baseline | bottom | left | middle | right | texttop | top
alt	Specifies alternate text to be displayed in place of the embedded element	*text*
classid	Provides the classid for an ActiveX object or Java applet inserted as an embedded element	*text*
code	The location of class file used with embedded Java applets	*url*
codebase	The location of a Java applet class file if it differs from the location of the Web page	*url*
height	The height of the embedded element in pixels	*value*
id	Provides the id of the embedded element	*text*
name	Provides the name of the embedded element	*text*
pluginspage	Provides the location of a document containing instructions for installing the plug-in if it is not already installed	*url*
pluginurl	Provides the location of an installation file for installing the plug-in specified by the embedded element	*url*
src	The source of the media file used by the embedded element	*url*
type	The MIME type of the embedded element	*mime-type*
width	The width of the embedded element in pixels	*value*

For example, to insert a Flash Player using the <embed> tag, you would enter the following HTML code:

```
<embed src="file.swf" type="application/x-shockwave-flash"
       pluginspage="http://www.macromedia.com/go/getflashplayer"
       width="value" height="value">
</embed>
```

Note that the pluginspage attribute provides a url for browsers that do not have the Shockwave Flash plug-in. Users running such a browser would be prompted with an option to install the player so they wouldn't have to search for the player on their own.

The <embed> tag to insert the QuickTime Player is:

```
<embed src="file.mov" type="video/quicktime"
       pluginspage="http://www.apple.com/quicktime/download"
       width="value" height="value">
</embed>
```

Finally, the <embed> tag to insert the Windows Media Player has the following form:

```
<embed src="file.wmv" type="video/x-ms-wmv"
       pluginspage="http://www.microsoft.com/Windows/MediaPlayer"
       width="value" height="value">
</embed>
```

The embed element does not support the <param> tag, so any features specific to a particular player are added as attributes to the <embed> tag. So the parameter element

```
<param name="name" value="value" />
```

for an object would be entered using the following attribute in the <embed> tag:

```
<embed name="value" ...> </embed>
```

For example, the following code applies the autostart, bgcolor, controller, and scale values as attributes rather than parameters in embedding the rwdance.mov QuickTime video:

```
<embed src="rwdance.mov" type="video/quicktime"
       pluginspage="http://www.apple.com/quicktime/download"
       width="280" height="239"
       autoplay="false" controller="true" scale="0.7"
       bgcolor="#F0BC4C">
</embed>
```

Compare this code to the code you entered earlier, shown in Figure 7-27. Notice that all of the <param> tags in that code have been replaced by attributes within the <embed> tag.

Reference Window | Using the embed Element

- To insert an object using the embed element, enter
  `<embed src="url" attributes></embed>`
  where *url* is the url of the embedded file and *attributes* are attributes associated with the embedded object.

Nesting Embedded Objects

When you add embedded content to your Web pages, you need to provide support for as many browser configurations as possible. Users might access your page using an older browser that supports only the <embed> tag and not the <object> tag. Other users might be running browsers without the capability of displaying embedded content, or they might have turned off those features for their browsers to speed up their Web browsing. To accommodate all of those situations, your code needs to match the capabilities of the variety of browsers and browser settings. You've already studied one way of accommodating different browser capabilities through the use of conditional comments; another important approach is to nest media objects within one another.

As shown in Figure 7-33, the idea behind nesting media clips is to first attempt to display the clip using the <object> tag; if that fails, the browser attempts to display the media clip using the <embed> tag. Finally, if the browser is unable to embed the media clip using either the <object> or the <embed> tag, it will still be able to display a hypertext link to the media clip.

Figure 7-33 Nesting embedded objects

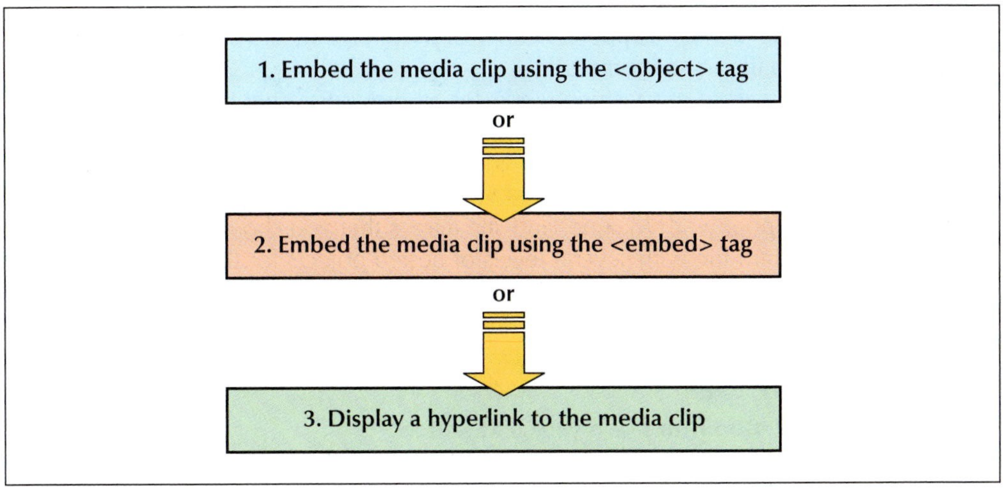

The general syntax of this approach is therefore:

```
<object data="url" attributes>
   <embed src="url" attributes>
      <a href="url">Link to media clip</a>
   </embed>
</object>
```

Browsers that can display the media clip using the <object> tag will ignore any elements nested within the<object> tag other than <param> tags. If a browser cannot work with the <object> tag, it will ignore it and attempt to display the contents of the <embed> tag. Finally, if the browser cannot display the contents of the <embed> tag, it will ignore it as well and display the hypertext link.

Figure 7-34 shows how to use this approach to insert a QuickTime movie clip first as an ActiveX control, then as an embedded object using the <embed> tag, and finally as a hypertext link.

Figure 7-34 HTML code to nest a QuickTime movie

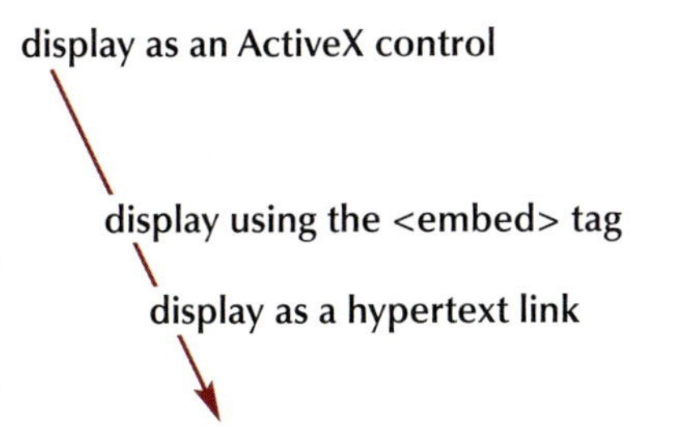


```
<object data="video.mov" type="video/quicktime"
 classid="clsid:02BF25D5-8C17-4B23-BC80-D3488ABDDC6B"
 codebase="http://www.apple.com/qtactivex/qtplugin.cab"
 width="320" height="260">

   <param name="src" value="video.mov" />
   <param name="autoplay" value="false" />

      <embed src="video.mov" type="video/quicktime"
       pluginspage="http://www.apple.com/quicktime/download"
       width="320" height="260" autoplay="false">

         Click to <a href="video.mov">download</a> the movie clip.

      </embed>

</object>
```

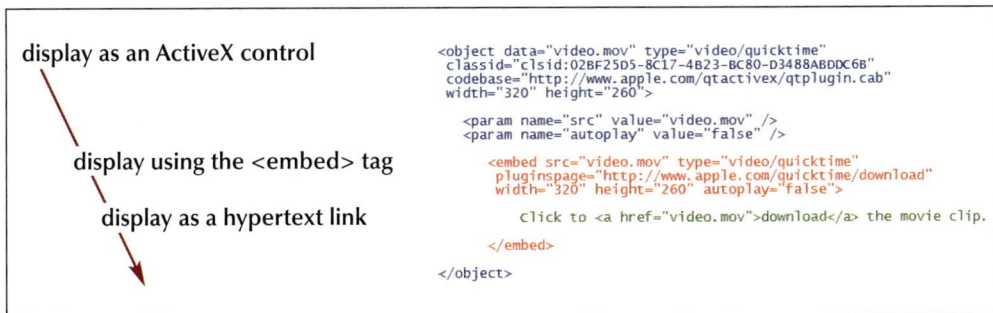

You can also nest <object> tags within one another. The following general code shows three levels of nested objects:

```
<object data="video.mov" type="video/quicktime">
   <object data="video.wmv" type="video/x-ms-wmv">
      Click to <a href="video.avi">download</a> the movie clip.
   </object>
</object>
```

The uppermost level uses the <object> tag to insert a QuickTime movie clip. If that video format is not supported by the browser, the browser will then attempt to display the clip in .wmv format. If the browser supports neither of those objects, it will display a hypertext link to the video file in .avi format.

Nesting <object> tags in this fashion works for all browsers other than Internet Explorer prior to version 7. Earlier versions of Internet Explorer will treat the nested <object> tags as separate objects and will display both of them within the Web page. You can override this behavior by hiding one of the embedded objects using CSS.

You discuss this option with Maxine, and she agrees that you should augment the code for the jumbo.htm file with several levels of nested objects for the sound and video clips from *Royal Wedding*.

To nest the media clips:

1. Return to the **jumbo.htm** file in your text editor.
2. Scroll to the object element for the overture.mp3 audio clip.
3. Directly above the closing </object> tag, insert the following embed element, as shown in Figure 7-35:

```
<embed src="overture.mp3" type="audio/mpeg"
 width="280" height="25"
 autoplay="false" autostart="false"
 controller="true" showcontrols="true">

   Click to <a href="overture.mp3">download</a> the movie overture.

</embed>
```

Figure 7-35 **Object nesting for the overture.mp3 file**

```
<!--[if IE]><!-->
   <object data="overture.mp3" type="audio/mpeg"
    classid="clsid:02BF25D5-8C17-4B23-BC80-D3488ABDDC6B"
    codebase="http://www.apple.com/qtactivex/qtplugin.cab"
    width="280" height="25">
<!--<![endif]-->

<!--[if !IE]><!-->
   <object data="overture.mp3" type="audio/mpeg"
    width="280" height="25">
<!--<![endif]-->

      <param name="src" value="overture.mp3" />
      <param name="autoplay" value="false" />
      <param name="autostart" value="false" />
      <param name="controller" value="true" />
      <param name="showcontrols" value="true" />

      <embed src="overture.mp3" type="audio/mpeg"
       width="280" height="25"
       autoplay="false" autostart="false"
       controller="true" showcontrols="true">

         Click to <a href="overture.mp3">download</a> the movie overture.

      </embed>

   </object>
```

the <embed> tag will be used by browsers that do not support the <object> tag

browsers that do not support embedded MP3 files will still display a hypertext link to the file

Note that the attributes of the embed element duplicate the parameters and parameter values used for the object element.

4. Scroll down to the object element for the rwdance.swf file. Above the closing </object> tag, insert the following code as shown in Figure 7-36:

```
<embed src="rwdance.swf" type="application/x-shockwave-flash"
 width="280" height="239"
 movie="rwdance.swf" quality="high" menu="false">

   To view the movie clip, install Adobe Flash.

</embed>
```

Figure 7-36 **Object nesting for the rwdance.swf file**

```
<!--[if IE]><!-->
   <object data="rwdance.swf" type="application/x-shockwave-flash"
    classid="clsid:D27CDB6E-AE6D-11cf-96B8-444553540000"
    codebase="http://download.macromedia.com/pub/shockwave/cabs/flash/swflash.cab#version=9,0,115,0"
    width="280" height="239">
<!--<![endif]-->

<!--[if !IE]><!-->
   <object data="rwdance.swf" type="application/x-shockwave-flash"
    width="280" height="239">
<!--<![endif]-->

      <param name="movie" value="rwdance.swf" />
      <param name="quality" value="high" />
      <param name="menu" value="false" />

      <embed src="rwdance.swf" type="application/x-shockwave-flash"
       width="280" height="239"
       movie="rwdance.swf" quality="high" menu="false">

         To view the movie clip, install Adobe Flash.

      </embed>

   </object>
```

browsers that do not support Flash will display a message suggesting that Flash be installed

5. Save your changes and then reload the **jumbo.htm** file in your Web browser. Verify that both embedded media clips still play correctly within your browser.

As long as you have support for MP3 files and Flash, you should not see any change within your Web page. The nested objects and hypertext links only appear to users who do not have the plug-ins or add-ons installed for these objects. You can test object nesting within your browser by temporarily disabling the multimedia plug-ins. Each browser has a different method for disabling plug-ins. For example, the Opera browser allows users to turn off plug-ins from the Preferences window. Firefox requires the user to remove or rename the plug-in files from the Mozilla Firefox\plugins folder. Under Internet Explorer, you can disable plug-ins and add-ons by selecting Manage Add-ons from the Tools menu and clicking Enable or Disable Add-ons to open the Manage Add-Ons dialog box. From that dialog box, you can select and disable each plug-in associated with Internet Explorer. Figure 7-37 shows the appearance of the Web page in Internet Explorer with both QuickTime and Flash disabled.

Figure 7-37 The Web page with disabled plug-ins

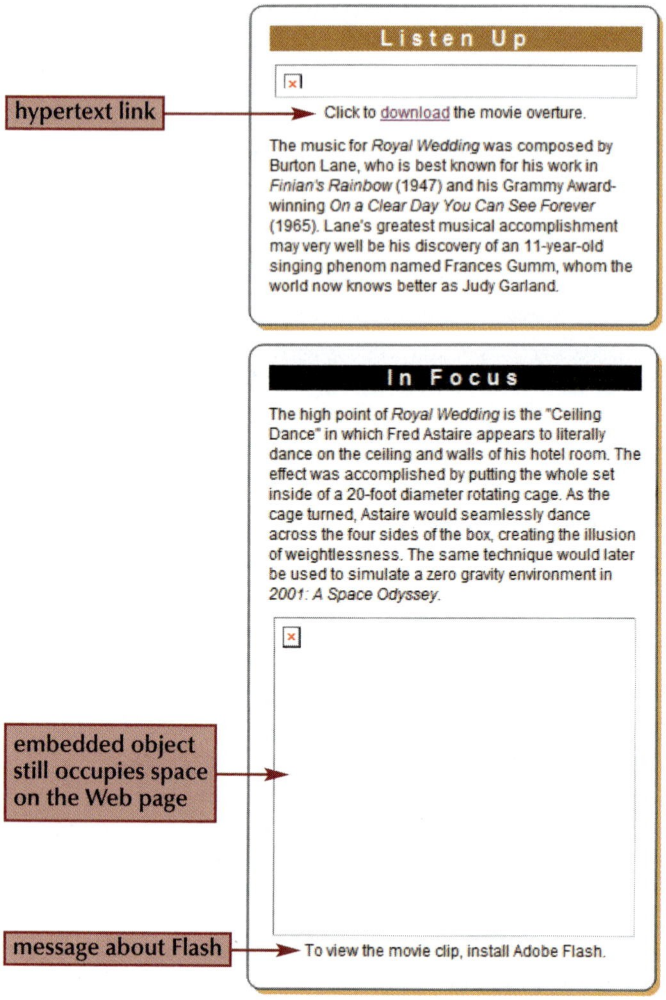

Notice that the embedded objects still occupy space within the Web page even if they're unable to be displayed by the browser.

Embedded Video and YouTube | InSight

One of the largest and most popular online sites for sharing videos is YouTube. Exact numbers are difficult to come by, but the site is estimated to house tens of millions of videos viewed by millions of users each day. YouTube applies a common format to all of its videos, limiting them to a frame size of 320 × 240 pixels with a data rate of 314 Kbps. Although the site accepts videos in wmv, avi, mov, mpeg, and mp4 formats, the files are converted to flv format before being added to the YouTube library. Audio is stored in mp3 format at a bit rate of 65 Kbps.

A video stored on the YouTube server can be viewed either by going to the YouTube Web site or by embedding the YouTube movie player on one's own Web site. The HTML code to embed a YouTube video on your Web site is

```
<object width="425" height="355">
   <param name="movie" value="http://www.youtube.com/v/id"/>
   <param name="wmode" value="transparent" />
   <embed src="http://www.youtube.com/v/id"
          type="application/x-shockwave-flash" wmode="transparent"
          width="425" height="355">
   </embed>
</object>
```

where the url *www.youtube.com/v/id* points to a video file stored on the YouTube server. The id string *youtube_id* is a special id that YouTube assigns to each video in its library. For example, the source for a clip from *Royal Wedding* is (as of this writing) at *www.youtube.com/v/ac6o8PXthzQ&hl=en*.

Maxine is pleased with the work you've done embedding video in several different formats on sample pages for her Web site. In the next session, you'll explore how to work with applets by adding a scrolling marquee to Maxine's sample Web page.

Session 7.2 Quick Check | Review

1. What are four factors that contribute to the calculation of a video's data rate?
2. Why does saving Web video at a high frame rate and data rate not always result in a high-quality video?
3. What is a codec?
4. What is the difference between a Flash flv file and a Flash swf file?
5. What is the MIME type of a Flash animation?
6. What parameter do you add to an embedded Flash animation to set the playback quality to high?
7. What parameter do you add to an embedded QuickTime video to fit the video clip to the object space while retaining its aspect ratio?
8. Specify the code you would enter to insert an embed element containing the QuickTime movie file astaire.mov. Assume the dimensions of the clip are 320 × 160 pixels.

Session 7.3

Introducing Java

Maxine has included a cast list for *Royal Wedding* on her Web site. Currently, the list displays only a few of the actors and actresses from the movie. Maxine would like to expand the list to include more of the cast as well as the director, producers, and writers; however, doing so would result in a list so long that it would ruin her page layout. Instead of a long list, Maxine envisions a scrolling cast list mimicking the credits that appear at the end of a movie. Maxine has seen scrolling text on other Web sites and wonders if you could add a similar feature to her Web page. You can do so with a programming language called Java.

As with many computing innovations, Java came from some unexpected sources. In the early 1990s, programmers at Sun Microsystems envisioned a day when common appliances and devices, such as refrigerators, toasters, and garage door openers, would be networked and controllable using a single operating system. Such an operating system would need to be portable because it would obviously need to be able to work with a wide variety of devices. The programmers began development on such an operating system and based it on a language called **Oak**. The project did not succeed at that point (perhaps the world was not ready for toasters and refrigerators to communicate), but the initial work on Oak was so promising that Sun Microsystems saw its potential for use on the Internet. Oak was modified in 1995 and renamed **Java**.

Each Java program works with a **Java Virtual Machine** (**JVM**), a software program that runs the Java code and returns the results to the user's computer. Java Virtual Machines can be created for different operating systems, so a Java program can be run from any operating system, including UNIX, Windows, DOS, and the Macintosh. Just as Web pages were designed at the beginning to be platform-independent, so was Java, and it became a natural fit for use on the Web. Netscape incorporated a Java Virtual Machine into Netscape Navigator version 2.0. Microsoft wasted little time in including its own JVM with Internet Explorer version 3.0. Because of the popularity of Java, JVMs are usually installed as part of the operating system or along with the user's Web browser. Java is still used throughout the Web today, though many of the uses of Java are now being supplied by Flash, which is easier to program.

A Java program is not a stand-alone application, but instead runs in conjunction with a hosting program such as a Web browser. The program is therefore a "mini" application or **applet**. When the user connects to a Web page containing a Java applet, the applet is downloaded along with the Web page from a Web server, but the applet itself runs within the user's Web browser. This frees up the Web server for other tasks, as shown in Figure 7-38.

Applets and Java Virtual Machines

Figure 7-38

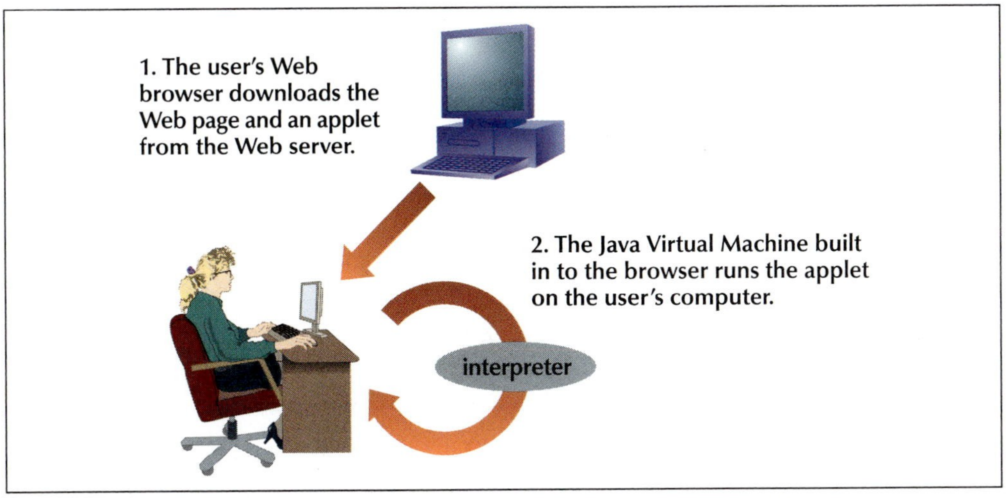

1. The user's Web browser downloads the Web page and an applet from the Web server.
2. The Java Virtual Machine built in to the browser runs the applet on the user's computer.
interpreter

Applets are embedded within Web pages just like the sound and video clips you embedded in the first two sessions of this tutorial. The applet runs within an **applet window**, which can be resized and positioned anywhere within the page.

Several libraries of Java applets are available on the Web. Some applets are free to download and use for non-commercial purposes. In other cases, programmers charge a fee for use of their applets. You can find Java applets for a variety of tasks, including stock market tickers, games, animations, and utilities for your browser or Web page.

A Java program is stored in an executable file called a **class file**, which has the file extension .class. Some Java applets might require several .class files to run properly. Each class file is run within a Java Virtual Machine. This is different from other programs on your computer, such as your Web browser, which are run by your computer's operating system.

Working with Java Applets

Java applets are embedded using the same <object> tag you used for sound and video clips. The general syntax of an embedded Java applet is

```
<object classid="id" type="application/x-java-applet"
        width="value" height="value">
   parameters
</object>
```

where *id* is the class id of the Java applet, the width and height attributes define the dimensions of the applet window, and *parameters* are the parameters associated with the applet. Internet Explorer and non-IE browsers differ in the class id values they use for Java. To embed a Java applet under Internet Explorer, you would use the code

```
<object classid="clsd:clsid:8AD9C840-044E-11D1-B3E9-00805F499D93"
        type="application/x-java-applet"
        width="value" height="value">
   <param name="code" value="file" />
   parameters
</object>
```

where *file* is the name of the file containing the Java applet. For non-IE browsers, Java is installed as a plug-in and the object code is

```
<object classid="java:file" type="application/x-java-applet"
        width="value" height="value">
   parameters
</object>
```

where once again *file* is the name of the file containing the Java applet. Note that for non-IE browsers, you do not need the code parameter. To reconcile the two approaches, you can use IE conditional comments as you did for the embedded sound and video clips in the first two sessions.

Reference Window | Embedding a Java Applet

- To embed a Java applet as an ActiveX object for Internet Explorer, enter

```
<object classid="clsd:clsid:8AD9C840-044E-11D1-B3E9-00805F499D93"
        type="application/x-java-applet"
        width="value" height="value">
   <param name="code" value="file" />
   parameters
</object>
```

  where the width and height attributes define the dimensions of the applet window, *file* is the filename of the class file, and *parameters* are the parameters associated with the applet.
- To embed a Java applet for non-IE browsers, use

```
<object classid="java:file" type="application/x-java-applet"
        width="value" height="value">
   parameters
</object>
```

Embedding a Java Applet

Maxine has located a Java applet to display text in a scrolling marquee. The name of the class file is CreditRoll.class. Embed this applet in her Web page both as an ActiveX object for Internet Explorer and a plug-in for non-IE browsers.

To embed the Java applet:

1. Return to the **jumbo.htm** file in your text editor and scroll up to the paragraph listing the cast members.
2. Directly above the cast list within the paragraph, insert the following code for IE browsers:

```
<!--[if IE]><!-->
   <object classid="clsid:8AD9C840-044E-11D1-B3E9-00805F499D93"
    type="application/x-java-applet"
    width="260" height="130">
      <param name="code" value="CreditRoll.class" />

<!--<![endif]-->
```

   Trouble? You can copy and paste the ActiveX classid from the **activexlist.txt** file located in the tutorial.07\tutorial folder included with your Data Files.

3. Add the following code to insert the <object> tag for non-IE browsers:

```
<!--[if !IE]><!-->
   <object classid="java:CreditRoll.class"
           type="application/x-java-applet"
           width="260" height="130">
<!--<![endif]>
```

4. After the cast list, insert the following closing tag:

```
</object>
```

Figure 7-39 highlights the newly inserted code.

Figure 7-39 **Insert an object element for a Java applet**

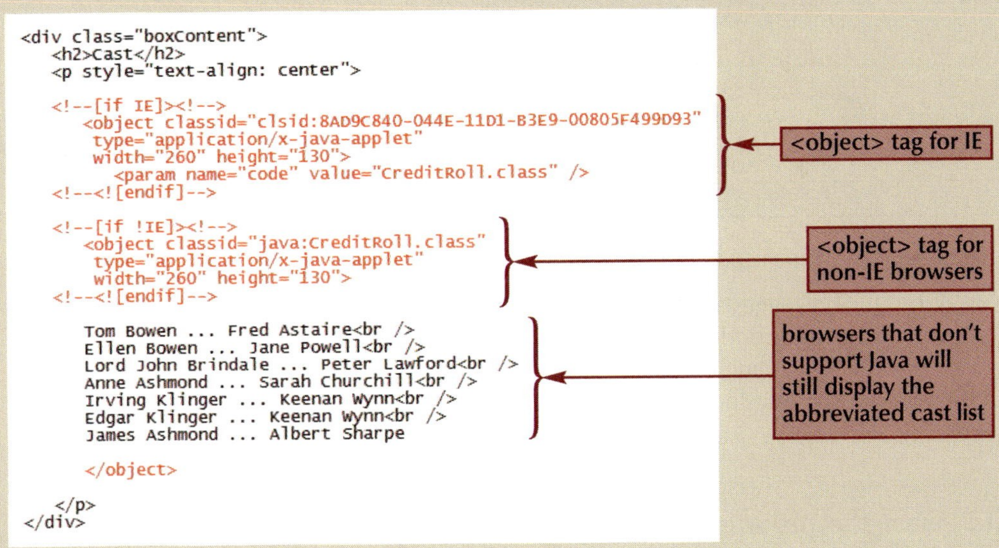
<div class="boxContent">
<h2>Cast</h2>
<p style="text-align: center">
<!--[if IE]><!-->
<object classid="clsid:8AD9C840-044E-11D1-B3E9-00805F499D93"
type="application/x-java-applet"
width="260" height="130">
<param name="code" value="CreditRoll.class" />
<!--<![endif]-->
<!--[if !IE]><!-->
<object classid="java:CreditRoll.class"
type="application/x-java-applet"
width="260" height="130">
<!--<![endif]-->
Tom Bowen ... Fred Astaire
Ellen Bowen ... Jane Powell
Lord John Brindale ... Peter Lawford
Anne Ashmond ... Sarah Churchill
Irving Klinger ... Keenan Wynn
Edgar Klinger ... Keenan Wynn
James Ashmond ... Albert Sharpe
</object>
</p>
</div>
<object> tag for IE
<object> tag for non-IE browsers
browsers that don't support Java will still display the abbreviated cast list

5. Save your changes to the file.

Notice that you kept the cast list that Maxine previously entered in this document nested within the <object> tag. If this page is opened by a browser that does not support Java, it will ignore the <object> tags but will still display the abbreviated cast list.

Inserting Java Parameters

The CreditRoll applet contains several parameters that define the text being scrolled, the speed of the scrolling, and the font and background styles. Figure 7-40 describes the parameters used by the CreditRoll applet.

Figure 7-40 **Parameters of the CreditRoll.class**

Parameter	Description
bgcolor	The background color of the applet window, expressed as a hexadecimal color value
fadezone	The text in the applet window fades in and out as it scrolls; this parameter sets the size of the area in which the text fades (in pixels)
textcolor	The color value of the text in the applet window
font	The font used for the scrolling text in the applet window
text*x*	Each line of text in the applet window requires a separate text*x* parameter, where *x* is the line number; for example, the parameter text1 sets the text for the first line in the applet window, text2 sets the text for the second line in the applet window, and so forth
url	Specifies the Web page that is opened if the applet window is clicked
repeat	Specifies whether the text in the applet window is repeated; setting this parameter's value to yes causes the text to scroll continuously
speed	The speed at which the text scrolls, expressed in milliseconds between each movement
vspace	The space between each line of text, in pixels
fontsize	The point size of the text in the applet window

Maxine would like the credit roll to appear in a 14-point white font on a brown background. She suggests setting the speed of the scrolling to 100, which is 100 milliseconds or 1/10 of a second between each movement of the text. She wants 3 pixels of space between each line of text and a fadezone value of 20 pixels. The scrolling should run continuously. Add these parameters and values to the object code for the CreditRoll applet.

To insert the parameters for the CreditRoll applet:

1. Return to the **jumbo.htm** file in your text editor.
2. Add the following parameters directly above the text for the cast list to set the font style of the scrolling text:

```
<param name="fontsize" value="14" />
<param name="bgcolor" value="CE9314" />
<param name="textcolor" value="FFFFFF" />
```

3. Add the following parameters to set the scrolling speed, the space between the lines of text, and the size of the fadezone:

```
<param name="speed" value="100" />
<param name="vspace" value="3" />
<param name="fadezone" value="20" />
```

4. Finally, set the CreditRoll applet to repeatedly scroll the text without stopping by adding the following parameter, as shown in Figure 7-41:

```
<param name="repeat" value="yes" />
```

Figure 7-41 Adding parameters for font style and scrolling speed

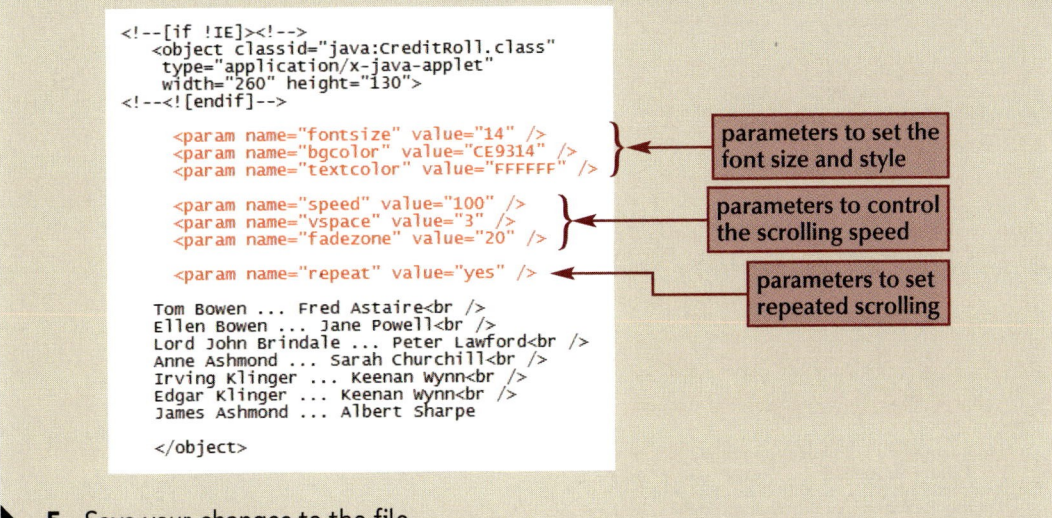

```
<!--[if !IE]><!-->
   <object classid="java:CreditRoll.class"
    type="application/x-java-applet"
    width="260" height="130">
<!--<![endif]-->

      <param name="fontsize" value="14" />
      <param name="bgcolor" value="CE9314" />
      <param name="textcolor" value="FFFFFF" />

      <param name="speed" value="100" />
      <param name="vspace" value="3" />
      <param name="fadezone" value="20" />

      <param name="repeat" value="yes" />

   Tom Bowen ... Fred Astaire<br />
   Ellen Bowen ... Jane Powell<br />
   Lord John Brindale ... Peter Lawford<br />
   Anne Ashmond ... Sarah Churchill<br />
   Irving Klinger ... Keenan Wynn<br />
   Edgar Klinger ... Keenan Wynn<br />
   James Ashmond ... Albert Sharpe

   </object>
```

parameters to set the font size and style

parameters to control the scrolling speed

parameters to set repeated scrolling

5. Save your changes to the file.

Next you must specify the text of the rolling marquee. The credit roll text is entered into parameters named text*x*, where *x* is the number of the line in the credit roll. Because of the length of the cast list, parameters named text1 through text19 have already been created for you and stored in a separate file in the tutorial.07\tutorial folder.

The credit roll applet also supports a parameter named url that adds a link to the credit roll, opening a Web page when a user clicks the applet window. Maxine suggests that you link the credit roll to a Web page from the Internet Movie Database describing *Royal Wedding*. The url of the Web page is *www.imdb.com/title/tt0043983/*.

Add parameters for the credit roll text and the url to the embedded applet.

To add the scrolling text and url:

1. Copy the parameter text from the **creditlist.txt** (in the tutorial.07\tutorial folder included with your Data Files).
2. Return to the **jumbo.htm** file in your text editor and paste the parameter text directly below the <param> tag for the repeat parameter.
3. Add the following parameter to set the url associated with the CreditRoll applet:

```
<param name="url" value="http://www.imdb.com/title/tt0043983" />
```

Figure 7-42 shows the revised code of the file.

Figure 7-42 Specifying the marquee text

```
<param name="repeat" value="yes" />

<param name="text1" value="Royal Wedding" />
<param name="text2" value="Produced by: Arthur Freed" />
<param name="text3" value="Directed by: Stanley Donen" />
<param name="text4" value="Written by: Alan Jay Lerner" />
<param name="text5" value="Orignal Music by: Burton Lane" />
<param name="text6" value="---- o ----" />
<param name="text7" value="" />
<param name="text8" value="Fred Astaire ... Tom Bowen" />
<param name="text9" value="Jane Powell ... Ellen Bowen" />
<param name="text10" value="Peter Lawford ... Lord John Brindale" />
<param name="text11" value="Sarah Churchill ... Anne Ashmond" />
<param name="text12" value="Keenan Wynn ... Irving Klinger" />
<param name="text13" value="Keenan Wynn ... Edgar Klinger" />
<param name="text14" value="Albert Sharpe ... James Ashmond" />
<param name="text15" value="Eddie ... Wilson Benge" />
<param name="text16" value="Charles Gordon ... Francis Bethencourt" />
<param name="text17" value="Dick ... William Cabanne" />
<param name="text18" value="Harry ... Jimmy Fairfax" />
<param name="text19" value="Billy ... John Hedloe" />

<param name="url" value="http://www.imdb.com/title/tt0043983" />

Tom Bowen ... Fred Astaire<br />
Ellen Bowen ... Jane Powell<br />
Lord John Brindale ... Peter Lawford<br />
Anne Ashmond ... Sarah Churchill<br />
Irving Klinger ... Keenan Wynn<br />
Edgar Klinger ... Keenan Wynn<br />
James Ashmond ... Albert Sharpe

</object>
```

marquee text

url of the scrolling marquee

4. Save your changes to the file and then reload **jumbo.htm** in your Web browser. Verify that the Cast box contains a scrolling marquee of the cast from *Royal Wedding*. Figure 7-43 shows the completed Web page with all of the embedded objects.

Completed Web page **Figure 7-43**

5. Click the scrolling marquee box and verify that your Web browser opens a Web page from the Internet Movie Database describing the film.

You show Maxine the scrolling marquee, which she likes very much. She asks how the page will appear for users who don't have Java. You tell her that the page will show the abbreviated cast list used earlier. That text is still present in the Web page, though it won't be displayed if the CreditRoll applet can be run.

Maxine also wants you to include information for users about how to install Java if they don't have it. For Internet Explorer, you can do this by adding the following codebase attribute to the <object> tag:

```
codebase="http://java.sun.com/update/1.6.0/jinstall-6-windows-i586.cab"
```

If Internet Explorer doesn't have Java installed or has a later version installed, this code prompts users to decide whether or not to upgrade their Java support. For other browsers, you can insert a link to a Java download page at *http://www.java.com/en/download*, which users can click to manually install or update their version of Java.

Maxine would like you to add code for both approaches to the jumbo.htm file.

To provide installation support for Java:

1. Return to the **jumbo.htm** file in your text editor.
2. Add the following codebase attribute to the <object> tag for Internet Explorer users, as shown in Figure 7-44:

```
codebase="http://java.sun.com/update/1.6.0/jinstall-6-windows-
i586.cab"
```

Figure 7-44 Specifying the codebase for Internet Explorer

```
<!--[if IE]><!-->
   <object classid="clsid:8AD9C840-044E-11D1-B3E9-00805F499D93"
    codebase="http://java.sun.com/update/1.6.0./jinstall-6-windows-i586.cab"
    type="application/x-java-applet"
    width="260" height="130">
      <param name="code" value="CreditRoll.class" />
<!--<![endif]-->
```

3. Scroll down the file and add the following code after the last cast entry, as shown in Figure 7-45:

```
<br /><br />
To view a scrolling marquee, get the latest
<a href="http://java.sun.com/products/plugin/downloads">
   Java Plug-in.
</a>
```

Figure 7-45 Text displayed when Java is not installed

```
Tom Bowen ... Fred Astaire<br />
Ellen Bowen ... Jane Powell<br />
Lord John Brindale ... Peter Lawford<br />
Anne Ashmond ... Sarah Churchill<br />
Irving Klinger ... Keenan Wynn<br />
Edgar Klinger ... Keenan Wynn<br />
James Ashmond ... Albert Sharpe

<br /><br />
To view a scrolling marquee, get the latest
<a href="http://java.sun.com/products/plugin/downloads">
   Java Plug-in.
</a>

</object>
```

4. Close the file, saving your changes.

You can temporarily disable Java in your Web browser to test whether or not the message from Figure 7-45 will be displayed to the user. The commands to disable Java will usually be found in the Options or Preferences window of your browser. For example, to disable Java in the Firefox browser, select Options from the Tools menu to open the Options dialog box, and then click the Content tab. Deselect the Enable Java check box to disable Java. The Enable Java check box for Opera is located under the Advanced tab in the Preferences dialog box. For Safari, it's located under the Security tab of the Preferences dialog box. Finally, for Internet Explorer, you can disable Java by opening the Manage Add-ons dialog box and disabling the Java plug-in. Figure 7-46 shows the appearance of the movie credit box when Java is disabled.

Figure 7-46 Text for Java-less browsers

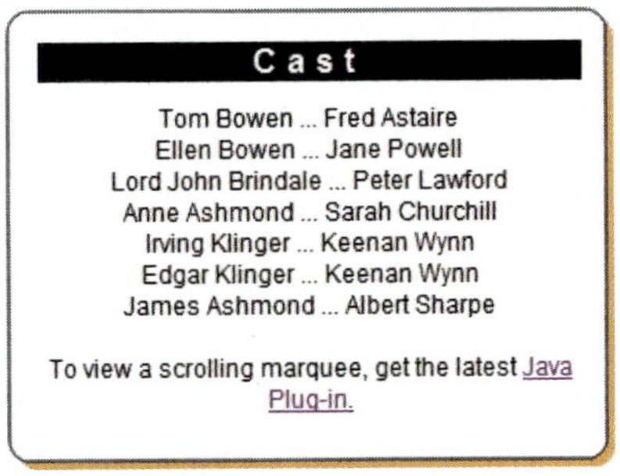

Creating a Scrolling Marquee with Internet Explorer | InSight

As an alternative to using a Java applet to create a box with scrolling text, if you know that users accessing your Web page will be using Internet Explorer, you can take advantage of Internet Explorer's marquee element to create a theater-style marquee. The general syntax of the marquee element is

```
<marquee attributes>content</marquee>
```

where *attributes* are the attributes that control the behavior of the marquee and *content* is the text content that appears in the marquee box. To control the scrolling of the text within the marquee, use the attributes

```
behavior="type" direction="type" loop="value"
```

where behavior is either scroll (to scroll the text across the box), slide (to slide the text across the box and stop), or alternate (to bounce the text back and forth across the box); the direction attribute defines the direction of the scrolling (left, right, down, or up); and the loop attribute determines how often the marquee plays (either an integer or infinite).

To control the speed of the text within a marquee, use the attributes

```
scrollamount="value" scrolldelay="value"
```

where the scrollamount attribute determines the amount of space, in pixels, that the text moves each time it advances across the page, and the scrolldelay attribute is the amount of time, in milliseconds, between text advances.

Browsers that do not support the marquee element display the entire marquee text without any scrolling; so if you use this element, be sure to leave room for your text to appear in non-IE browsers.

Exploring the Applet Element

Older browsers might not support the <object> tag for inserting Java applets. If you expect some users to be running older browsers, you can still allow them to view your applet by using the applet element

```
<applet code="file" width="value" height="value" alt="text">
   parameters
</applet>
```

where *file* is the name of the Java class file, the width and height attributes set the dimension of the applet window, the alt attribute defines alternate text to be displayed by the browser if it doesn't support Java, and *parameters* are the parameters associated with the applet. For example, to embed the CreditRoll.class applet using the <applet> tag, you could enter the code

```
<applet code="CreditRoll.class" width="260" height="130">
   parameters
</applet>
```

with *parameters* being the same <param> tags you used with the object element. Like the <embed> tag discussed in the last session, the <applet> tag is not part of the W3C specifications for HTML and XHTML and is gradually being phased out, though you might still encounter it in the code for older Web pages.

Embedding Other Objects

In this tutorial you've used the object element to embed sound clips, video clips, and Java applets. However, you can use the object element for many other purposes. Any type of content can be embedded using <object> tags. In fact, the original vision of the object element was to act as a general container for any content not directly entered into the HTML code of the Web page. Maxine suggests that you explore a few examples.

Inserting Inline Images

You can use the <object> tag to insert all of your inline images. One advantage of entering images as embedded objects is that you can apply markup tags for the alternate text. For example, the inline image

```
<img src="jplogo.jpg" alt="Jumbo Popcorn" width="300" height="200" />
```

can be replaced with the embedded object

```
<object data="jplogo.jpg" type="image/jpeg"
 width="300" height="200">
   <h1>Jumbo Popcorn</h1>
</object>
```

Tip

You can turn an embedded image into an image map by adding the usemap attribute to the <object> tag.

Another advantage of treating images as embedded objects is that you can provide the user with different formats of the same graphic image. For example, the following code allows the browser to first display the Jumbo Popcorn logo in png format:

```
<object data="jplogo.png" type="image/png">
   <object data="jplogo.jpg" type="image/jpg">
      <h1>Jumbo Popcorn</h1>
   </object>
</object>
```

If that format is not supported, the browser displays the logo as a jpeg. Finally, if the browser does not support either format or is a nongraphical browser, it displays the text Jumbo Popcorn marked as an h1 heading.

You can also nest videos and inline images. For example, you can embed a video clip and nest an image object within the video clip, allowing the browser to choose which type of object to display.

Embedding an HTML file

Web pages themselves can be embedded as objects. To embed a Web page you use the <object> tags

```
<object data="url" type="text/html"
        width="value" height="value">
</object>
```

where *url* is the URL of the HTML file to be embedded. When you embed a Web page, that file is displayed within the dimensions specified by the width and height attributes. The browser will automatically add horizontal and vertical scroll bars to allow users to scroll around the document. Figure 7-47 shows an example that Maxine might want to use on the Jumbo Popcorn Web site in which previews of two Web pages are shown embedded within her Web site.

Embedding Web pages as objects **Figure 7-47**

Embedding one Web page within another can also be accomplished using frames, a topic that will be discussed in the next tutorial.

You've completed your work on Maxine's sample page describing the *Royal Wedding* movie. She likes the media clips and Java applet you've inserted in the Web page and looks forward to adding more features.

Review | Session 7.3 Quick Check

1. What is a Java Virtual Machine?
2. What are class files?
3. Specify the code you would enter to display the stockmarket.class applet in an applet window that is 500 pixels wide × 400 pixels high. Assume that the code is written for Internet Explorer.
4. What code would you enter for the previous question for non-IE browsers?
5. What Internet Explorer element could you use to create a scrolling marquee?
6. Specify the code to embed the image file logo.jpg as an object. If the browser does not support embedded objects, have it display the text "Millennium Computers" as an h2 heading.
7. Specify the code to display the HTML file glossary.htm as an embedded Web page in a window that is 400 pixels wide × 200 pixels high.

Review | Tutorial Summary

In this tutorial, you learned how to work with multimedia on your Web pages. The tutorial explored the use of the object element to embed various types of multimedia. The first session focused on sound, starting with a discussion of the issues surrounding working with digital sound. The session then explored how to embed sound files of different types either as plug-ins or ActiveX objects. The second session explored the use of video, focusing on three video formats: Flash, QuickTime, and Windows Media video. The session also examined some of the issues involved with working with video servers such as YouTube. The final session looked at embedded Java applets within a Web page. The tutorial ended by examining how to embed other objects, such as images and other Web pages, into a Web page.

Key Terms

ActiveX
add-on
amplitude
applet
applet window
aspect ratio
bandwidth
bit depth
bitrate
cab files
cabinet files
class file
class id
data rate
embedded media
external media
file compression
Flash video
flv
frame (video file)
frame rate
frequency
Java
Java Virtual Machine
MIDI
MIME type
MP3
Multipurpose Internet Mail Extension type
Oak
parameter
plug-in
sample resolution
sampling rate
Shockwave Flash
swf

Practice | Review Assignments

Practice the skills you learned in the tutorial using the same case scenario.

Data Files needed for the Review Assignments: astairetxt.htm, bottom.png, bottomleft.png, bottomright.png, button.jpg, CreditRoll.class, fa1.gif - fa5.gif, fabio.css, fasong.mp3, filmlist.txt, hatrack.mov, hatrack.swf, hatrack.wmv, jplogo.jpg, left.png, popcorn.jpg, right.png, top.png, topleft.png, and topright.png

Maxine has been working on the Jumbo Popcorn Web site for several weeks now. She has come back to you for help with completing another page. This page will feature the life of Fred Astaire. She has created a sound clip and a video clip that she wants you to embed on the Web page. She's also interested in creating another scrolling marquee, this one listing some of the many movies that Fred Astaire starred in during his life. A preview of the page you'll create is shown in Figure 7-48.

Figure 7-48

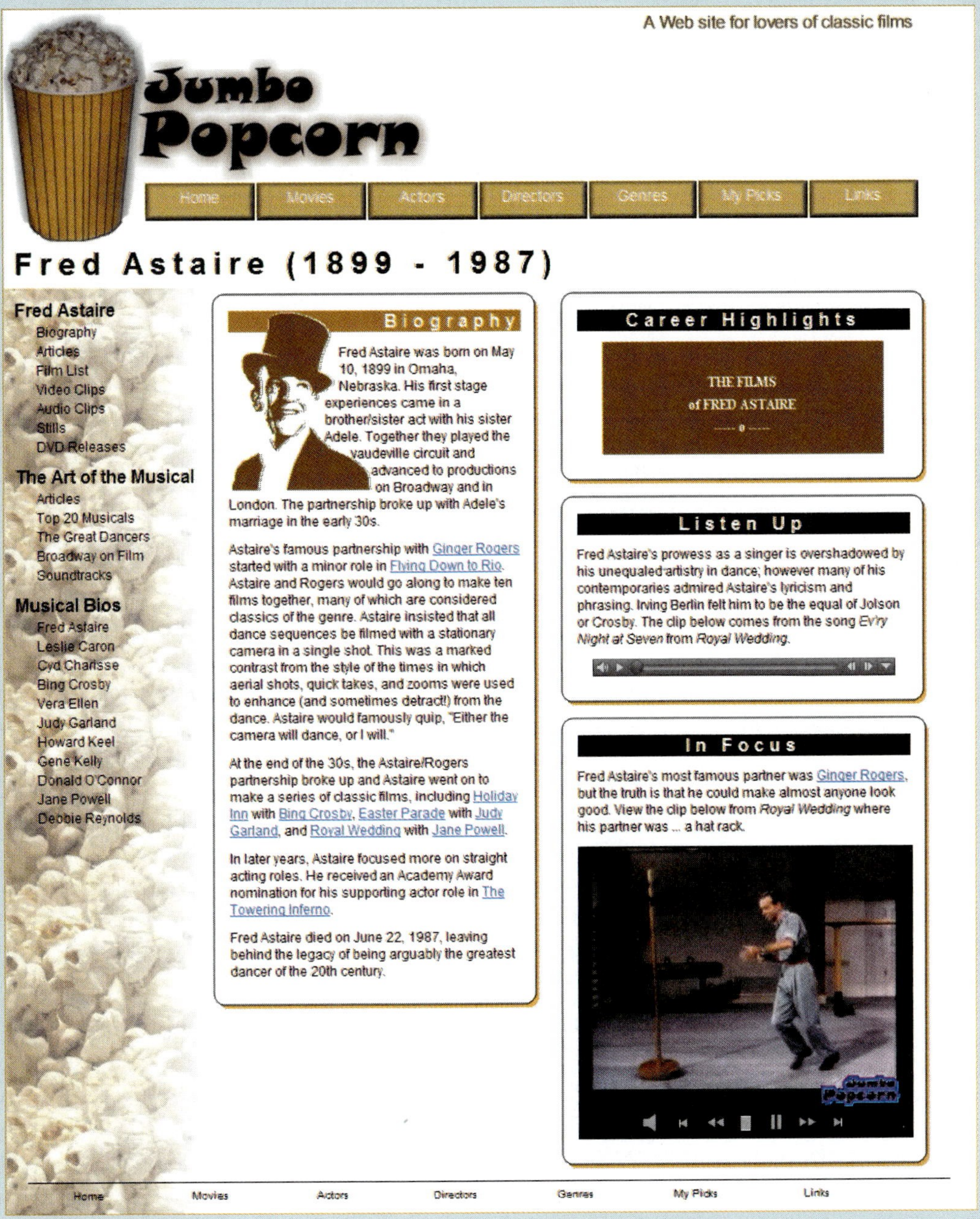

Complete the following:

1. Use your text editor to open the **astairetxt.htm** file from the tutorial.07\review folder included with your Data Files. Enter ***your name*** and ***the date*** in the comment section of the file. Save the files as **astaire.htm** in the same folder.
2. Scroll down the file and locate the paragraph below the Career Highlights heading. Within this paragraph, Maxine would like to insert a rolling marquee displaying a list of classic Fred Astaire movies. Insert an embedded object to display the CreditRoll applet both as an ActiveX object (for Internet Explorer) and as a plug-in (for non-IE browsers). Set the dimensions of the applet window to 260 pixels wide × 100 pixels high.
3. Add the following parameters to the CreditRoll applet:
   - Display the marquee text in a 12-point font with a background hexadecimal color value of 996600 and a text color of FFFFFF.
   - Set the scrolling speed to 150, the vspace value to 3 pixels, and the fadezone value to 10 pixels. Have the marquee repeat the scrolling without stopping.
   - When users click the marquee, have the browser display the IMDB Fred Astaire biography located at *www.imdb.com/name/nm0000001*.
   - Copy and paste the parameters from the **filmlist.txt** file (located in the tutorial.07\review folder included with your Data Files) to insert the marquee text.
4. For browsers that do not support Java, display the brief list of Astaire movies found in the original data file, followed by a hypertext link to the page *www.java.com/en/download*.
5. Scroll down the file and locate the second paragraph below the Listen Up heading. Within this heading, insert an embedded object to play the **fasong.mp3** sound clip within the QuickTime Media Player. The clip should be inserted as an ActiveX control for Internet Explorer and as a plug-in for non-IE browsers. Set the dimensions of the player to 280 pixels wide × 16 pixels high.
6. Add QuickTime parameters to the sound clip to set the source to the fasong.mp3 file, to display the QuickTime sound controls, and to not autoplay the sound file.
7. For older browsers that do not support the <object> tag, nest the embed element within the <object> tag to play the fasong.mp3 sound clip.
8. For browsers that do not support embedded sound files, have the Web page display a hypertext link to the fasong.mp3 file.
9. Scroll down to the second paragraph below the In Focus heading. Insert an embedded Flash Player both as an ActiveX control and as a plug-in to play the **hatrack.swf** file. Set the dimensions of the movie clip to 310 pixels wide × 260 pixels high.
10. Set the parameters of the movie clip to play the movie at high quality and to turn off the Flash Player menu.
11. For older browsers that may not support the object element, nest the embed element within the <object> tag to play the hatrack.swf file. For browsers that do not support Java at all, have the browser display a message telling users that they must have Adobe Flash Player installed to play the movie clip.
12. Save your changes to the file and then open **astaire.htm** in your Web browser. Verify that you can play the embedded sound file and movie file, and that the CreditRoll applet starts automatically within the page.
13. Return to the **astaire.htm** file in your text editor. Save the file as **astaire_mov.htm** in the same folder. Change the embedded movie from Flash Player to QuickTime Player, playing the **hatrack.mov** file. Set the autoplay parameter to false and the controller parameter to true. For users who do not have QuickTime installed, have the browser display text suggesting that they install QuickTime Player.

14. Save your changes to the file and then open **astaire_mov.htm** in your Web browser. Verify that you can play the embedded movie clip with QuickTime Player.
15. Return to the **astaire_mov.htm** file in your text editor and save it as **astaire_wmv.htm** in the same folder. Change the embedded movie from QuickTime Player to Windows Media Player, playing the **hatrack.wmv** file. Change the parameter values and the text message accordingly to match the parameters required by Windows Media Player.
16. Save your changes and open **astaire_wmv.htm** in your Web browser. Verify that you can play the embedded movie clip using Windows Media Player.
17. Submit your completed files to your instructor.

Apply | Case Problem 1

Apply your knowledge of multimedia to create a poetry page with audio samples from an American poet.

Data Files needed for this Case Problem: button0.gif - button3.gif, devotion.mp3, fireice.mp3, poetry.css, PopBtn.class, PopMenu.class, rflogo.gif, rftxt.htm, and tan.jpg

American Poetry 121 Professor Debra Li of the English Department at Carston University in Columbia, Mississippi has asked you to help her create a Web page devoted to the works of the poet Robert Frost for her American Poetry 121 class. With your help, she has created a Web page that contains a short biography of the poet and the complete text of two of his works. Professor Li would like to add sound clips of the two poems to the page so that her students can listen to Frost's poetry as well as read it.

She also wants you to create links to other Frost pages on the Web. She's located a Java applet that creates a set of graphical buttons that act as hypertext links. Professor Li thinks this applet would also make her page more interesting. The Java applet uses the PopMenu.class file with the parameters shown in Figure 7-49.

Figure 7-49

Parameter	Defines
`labelpos="type"`	The default label position for all of the buttons on the menu, where *type* is either right or below.
`labelposn="type"`	The label position for the *n*th button, starting with labelpos0, labelpos1, etc.
`textn="text"`	The text for the *n*th button, starting with text0, text1, etc.
`srcn="url"`	The URL of the image file to be displayed in the *n*th button, starting with src0, src1, etc.
`hrefn="url"`	The URL to be opened when the *n*th button is clicked, starting with href0, href1, etc.
`frame="target"`	The target of the links when the applet is used with frames; the default is _top.

A preview of the completed page is shown in Figure 7-50.

Figure 7-50

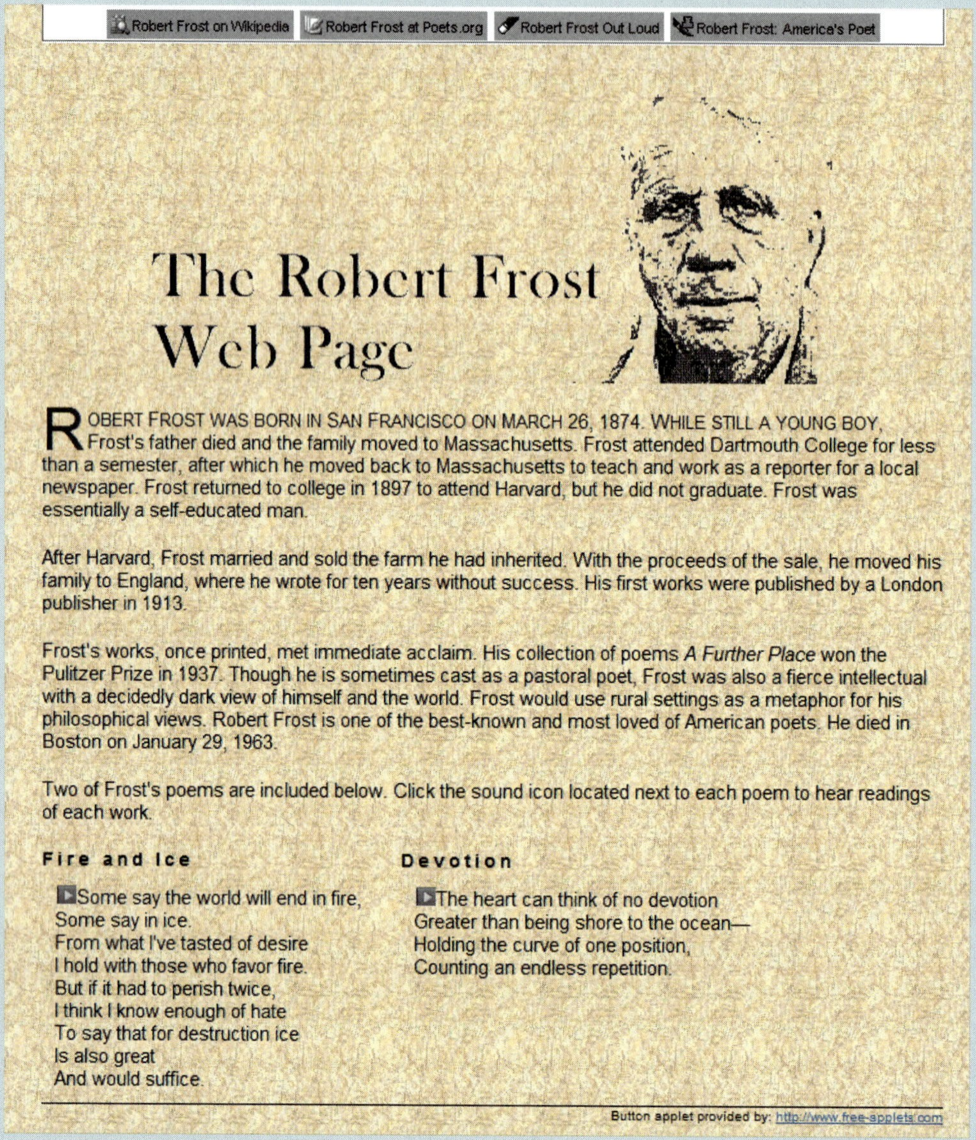

Complete the following:

1. Use your text editor to open the **rftxt.htm** file from the tutorial.07\case1 folder included with your Data Files. Enter ***your name*** and ***the date*** in the comment section of the file. Save the file as **rf.htm** in the same folder. Scroll to the links div container. Within the container, Debra has already inserted linked text to four Robert Frost sites on the Web.
2. Insert the **PopMenu.class** Java applet as both an ActiveX object and a plug-in. Set the width of the applet to 700 pixels wide × 30 pixels high.
3. Set the labelpos parameter of the applet to right.
4. Insert parameters src0 through src3, text0 through text3, and href0 through href3 to store the source of the button image, the button text, and the button hypertext link for the four linked buttons. Use the values button0.gif through button3.gif for the button images and the hypertext links to the four Robert Frost sites for the values of the text and href parameters.

5. If the user's browser does not support Java, have it display the hypertext links to the four Robert Frost sites.
6. Scroll down the file to the paragraph for the Fire and Ice poem. Directly above the first line of the poem, insert an embedded QuickTime Player to play the **fireice.mp3** file. Have your code support the QuickTime Player both as an ActiveX object and as a plug-in. Set the height of player to 16 pixels and set the width to only display the QuickTime play button.
7. Add the src, autoplay, and controller parameters to set the source of the QuickTime audio file, to turn off autoplay, and to display the player's sound controls.
8. If the user's browser does not support the QuickTime Player, use the following code instead:

```
<p>Click to <a href="fireice.mp3">download</a> the sound clip</p>
```

9. Repeat Steps 6 through 8 for the Devotion poem, using the sound file **devotion.mp3**.
10. Save your changes to the file and then view it in your Web browser. Verify that the four linked buttons at the top of the page connect the user to the four Robert Frost sites. Also verify that by clicking the player buttons, you can hear a reading of each of the Robert Frost poems.
11. Turn off support for Java and QuickTime within your browser. Verify that your browser displays the hypertext links you specified as alternatives to the embedded media.
12. Submit your completed files to your instructor.

Apply | Case Problem 2

Apply your knowledge of embedded video to create a travel guide page with a video tour.

Data Files needed for this Case Problem: roadtxt.htm, rw.css, rwlogo.jpg, and trailridge.swf

Roadways Karen Upton loves to travel and spends more than half of the year behind the wheel exploring the byways and roadways for her online travel guide, *Roadways*. Karen's Web site is a place where others who share her passion for travel can gather to share stories, advice, and their love for travel. Karen would like to upgrade her site by adding video tours of some of her favorite roadways. She's come to you for help in adding this feature to her site. Karen presents you with a sample page; she has already created the video and descriptive text for Trail Ridge Road, the highest paved continuous highway in the United States. A preview of the page you'll create for Karen is shown in Figure 7-51.

Figure 7-51

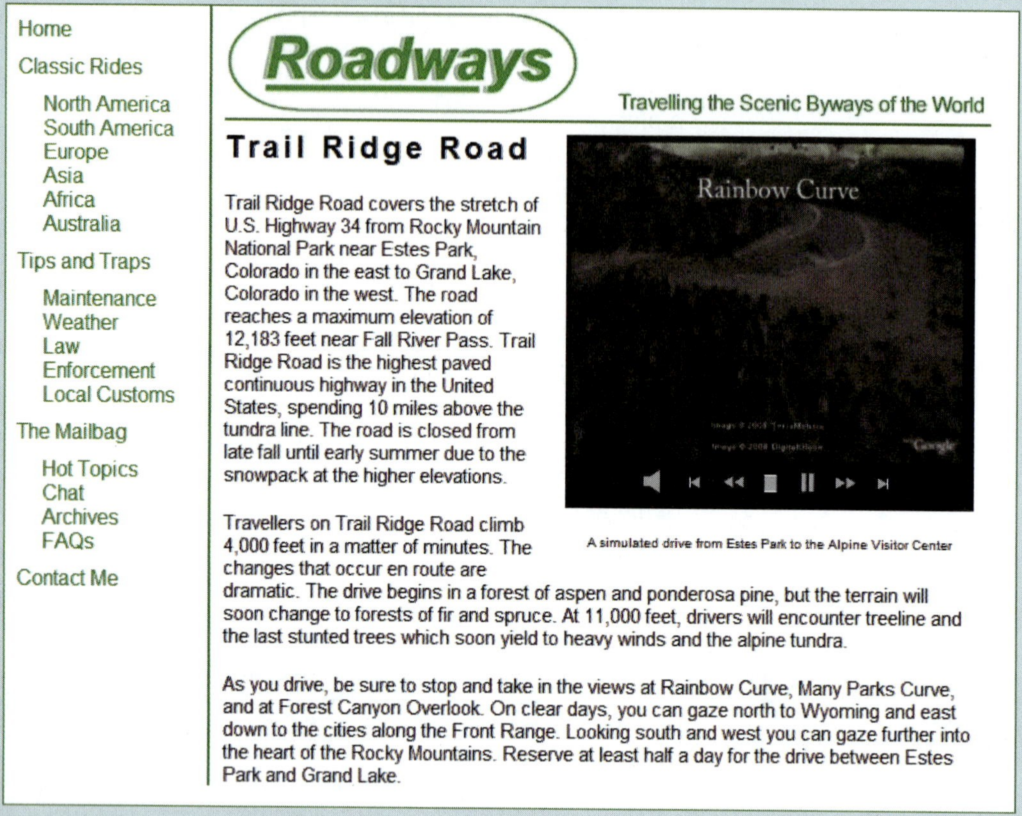
Home
Classic Rides
North America
South America
Europe
Asia
Africa
Australia
Tips and Traps
Maintenance
Weather
Law Enforcement
Local Customs
The Mailbag
Hot Topics
Chat
Archives
FAQs
Contact Me
Roadways
Travelling the Scenic Byways of the World
Trail Ridge Road
Rainbow Curve
A simulated drive from Estes Park to the Alpine Visitor Center
Trail Ridge Road covers the stretch of U.S. Highway 34 from Rocky Mountain National Park near Estes Park, Colorado in the east to Grand Lake, Colorado in the west. The road reaches a maximum elevation of 12,183 feet near Fall River Pass. Trail Ridge Road is the highest paved continuous highway in the United States, spending 10 miles above the tundra line. The road is closed from late fall until early summer due to the snowpack at the higher elevations.
Travellers on Trail Ridge Road climb 4,000 feet in a matter of minutes. The changes that occur en route are dramatic. The drive begins in a forest of aspen and ponderosa pine, but the terrain will soon change to forests of fir and spruce. At 11,000 feet, drivers will encounter treeline and the last stunted trees which soon yield to heavy winds and the alpine tundra.
As you drive, be sure to stop and take in the views at Rainbow Curve, Many Parks Curve, and at Forest Canyon Overlook. On clear days, you can gaze north to Wyoming and east down to the cities along the Front Range. Looking south and west you can gaze further into the heart of the Rocky Mountains. Reserve at least half a day for the drive between Estes Park and Grand Lake.

Complete the following:

1. Use your text editor to open the **roadtxt.htm** file from the tutorial.07\case2 folder included with your Data Files. Enter ***your name*** and ***the date*** in the comment section of the file. Save the file as **roadways.htm** in the same folder.
2. Scroll down to the div element with the id movie. Within the div container, insert an embedded object for the **trailridge.swf** file. The file should be inserted as an ActiveX control for Internet Explorer users and as a plug-in for users of non-IE browsers.
3. Set the dimensions of the video clip to 320 pixels × 280 pixels.
4. Set the value of the movie parameter to trailridge.swf, the quality parameter to high, and the menu parameter to false.
5. For users of older browsers, nest within your video object an embed element to play the trailridge.swf video clip. Set the attributes of the embed element similar to those that you used for the object element.
6. If users do not have Adobe Flash Player installed, display the message "To play this clip you need Adobe Flash Player."
7. Save your changes to file and then view the page in your Web browser. Verify that you can play the embedded video clip.
8. Submit your completed files to your instructor.

Challenge | Case Problem 3

Explore how to use a Java applet to create a Web page describing the mathematics of fractals.

Data Files needed for this Case Problem: Cmplx.class, Controls.class, fback.jpg, flogo.jpg, FracPanel.class, factaltxt.htm, fstyles.css, Mandel.class, and mandel.swf

Franklin High School Fractals are geometric objects that closely model the seemingly chaotic world of nature. Doug Hefstadt, a mathematics teacher at Franklin High School in Lake Forest, Illinois, has just begun a unit on fractals for his senior math class. He's used the topic of fractals to construct a Web page to be placed on the school network, and he needs your help to complete the Web page. He has a video clip of a fractal that he wants placed on the Web page, along with a Java applet that allows students to interactively explore the Mandelbrot Set, a type of fractal object. He wants your assistance in putting these two objects on his Web page. A preview of the page you'll create is shown in Figure 7-52.

Figure 7-52

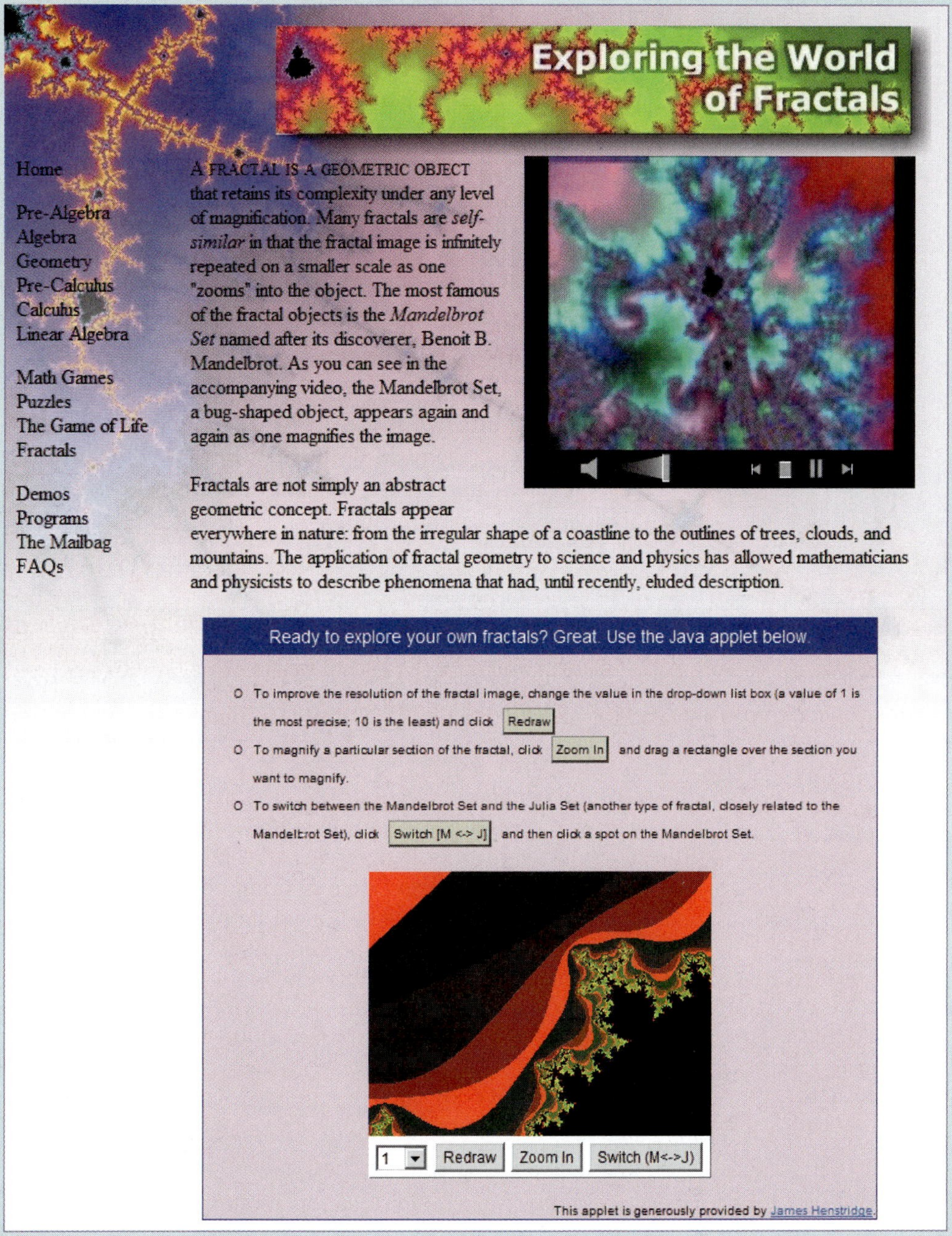

Complete the following:

1. Use your text editor to open the **fractaltxt.htm** file from the tutorial.07\case3 folder included with your Data Files. Enter ***your name*** and ***the date*** in the comment section of the file. Save the file as **fractal.htm** in the same folder.
2. Scroll down to the div element with the id movie. Within this div element, insert the **mandel.swf** Flash file both as an ActiveX object and as a plug-in, set the width of the player window to 320 pixels and the height to 260 pixels.

EXPLORE

3. The fractal movie might take several seconds to load into the Web page. Doug would like the object window to display a message indicating this fact. For both <object> tags, insert the standby attribute to display the text message "Loading movie. Please wait."
4. Set the value of the movie parameter to mandel.swf, the value of the quality parameter to high, and the value of the menu parameter to false.
5. For older browsers, nest an embed element within your <object> tags to insert the **mandel.swf** file. Include all necessary attributes for the embed element.
6. Within the embed element, insert the text string "To play this clip, you need Adobe Flash Player" to have a message for users who do not have Adobe Flash Player installed.
7. Scroll down to the demo div element. Within this element, insert a Java applet for the **Mandel.class** file, both as an ActiveX object and as a plug-in. Set the width of the applet window to 280 pixels and the height to 240 pixels.

EXPLORE

8. Within the <object> tag, insert the Mandel.class file using the applet object. Set the width of the applet to 280 pixels and the height to 240 pixels.
9. If the browser does not support Java, have it display the text "Your browser does not support Java applets" in place of the Mandel.class applet.
10. Save your changes to the file.
11. Open the Web page in your browser and verify that the video plays correctly.

EXPLORE

12. Test the fractal applet to verify that you can use it to zoom into the Mandelbrot Set at different levels of magnification.
13. Submit your completed files to your instructor.

Create | Case Problem 4

Test your knowledge of embedded media by creating a multimedia Web page for a youth orchestra.

Data Files needed for this Case Problem: beethoven.mp3, byso.jpg, bysoinfo.txt, bysologo.jpg, CreditRoll.class, and schedule.txt

Boise Youth Symphony Orchestra The Boise Youth Symphony Orchestra is one of the premier young people's orchestras in the United States. Denise Young, the BYSO artistic director, has asked you to help create a Web site that contains information about the orchestra. Denise has a short excerpt from the first movement of Beethoven's *Symphony No. 8 in F Major, Op. 93* that the orchestra played in their most recent spring concert. She would like you to embed the clip in the Web page. She also has a schedule of upcoming events and concerts that she would like displayed in a scrolling marquee.

The design of the Web site is up to you, but you can use the following files in creating the Web page:

- **beethoven.mp3**, an MP3 containing an excerpt from the first movement of Beethoven's *Symphony No. 8 in F Major, Op. 93*
- **byso.jpg**, a photo of the orchestra
- **bysoinfo.txt**, general information about the orchestra

- **bysolog.jpg, the BYSO logo**
- **CreditRoll.class**, the scrolling marquee applet
- **schedule.txt**, the orchestra's schedule of upcoming events

Complete the following:

1. Use your text editor to create an HTML file named **byso.htm** and a style sheet named **bstyles.css**. Enter ***your name*** and ***the date*** in a comment section of each file. Include any other comments you think will aptly document the purpose and content of the files. Save the files in the tutorial.07\case4 folder included with your Data Files.
2. Go to the **byso.htm** file in your text editor and design the Web page using the files you've been given and any other supplements you have. Place all of your styles in the **bstyles.css** style sheet.
3. The page should contain the **beethoven.mp3** sound file embedded with the QuickTime Player. Make sure your code works with both as an ActiveX control and a browser plug-in for non-IE browsers.
4. Include code to support browsers that use the embed element rather than the object element to display your media clip.
5. If the users do not have support for embedded media, have your Web page display a link to the **beethoven.mp3** file.
6. Use the schedule information from the **schedule.txt** file to create a scrolling marquee of upcoming BYSO events. The exact parameter values are left up to you. The scrolling marquee should be readable by both IE and non-IE browsers. Set the URL of the CreditRoll applet to *www.cityofboise.org*.

EXPLORE

7. Within the code for the scrolling marquee, include code for older browsers that might only support the applet element.
8. If the user's browser does not support Java at all, have the Web page display a message indicating this fact and suggesting that Java be installed to view the marquee. Include a hypertext link to a Web site where Java can be downloaded and installed.
9. Save your changes to the file and view the page in your Web browser. Verify that you can play both media clips and view the scrolling marquee.

EXPLORE

10. If you are working on your own computer or have permission to turn off support within your browser for embedded media and Java, turn off that support temporarily and verify that the page degrades well, showing the hypertext links and the message about installing Java.
11. Submit your completed files to your instructor.

Review | Quick Check Answers

Session 7.1

1. Either as external media in which the user downloads the multimedia file from a hypertext link or as embedded media that is displayed within the Web page.
2. Bandwidth is a measure of the amount of data that can be sent through the communication pipeline each second. Sampling rate is the number of samples taken per second from a sound source. Sample resolution indicates the precision in measuring the sound within each sample. Bitrate is a measure of the amount of data required for each second of sound.
3. `<object data="royal.wav" type="audio/wav"></object>`
4. audiop/wav and audio/x-wav
5. `<param name="showcontrols" value="true" />`
6. `<param name="autostart" value="true" />`
7. `classid ="clsid: 6BF52A52-394A-11d3-B153-00C04F79FAA6"`
8.
```
<!--[if IE]><!-->
    <object data="royal.wav" type="audio/wav"
     classid ="clsid: 6BF52A52-394A-11d3-B153-00C04F79FAA6">
       <param name="showcontrols" value="true" />
       <param name="autostart" value="true" />
    </object>
<!--<![endif]-->
```

Session 7.2

1. The frame size, the frame rate, the bitrate of the audio, the amount of compression.
2. If the bandwidth is not sufficient to keep up with the data rate required by the video, the quality of the video will be greatly degraded.
3. An algorithm that compresses and decompresses a video clip to reduce the overall file size.
4. The Flash flv file is the actual video file. The swf file is a container that contains the video file, other animations, scripts, and special controls to play the video.
5. application/x-shockwave-flash
6. `<param name="quality" value="high" />`
7. `<param name="scale" value="aspect" />`
8.
```
<embed src="astaire.mov" type="video/quicktime" width="320"
height="160"></embed>
```

Session 7.3

1. A Java Virtual Machine is a program in which a Java applet is run, thus making Java applets portable across a variety of operating systems.
2. Class files are the executable Java applet files that are run by a Java Virtual Machine.
3.
```
<object classid="clsid: 8AD9C840-044E-11D1-B3E9-00805F499D93"
 type="application/x-java-applet" width="500" height="400">
  <param name="code" value="stockmarket.class" />
</object>
```
4.
```
<object type="application/x-java-applet"
 classid="java:stockmarket.class"
 width="500" height="400">
</object>
```
5. the <marquee> tag
6.
```
<object data="logo.jpg" type="image/jpeg">
  <h2>Millennium Computers</h2>
</object>
```
7.
```
<object data="glossary.htm" type="text/html" width="400"
height="200">
</object>
```

Ending Data Files

Tutorial.07 →

Tutorial
- CreditRoll.class
- jp.css
- jumbo.htm
- jumbo_mov.htm
- jumbo_wmv.htm
- overture.mp3
- rwdance.mov
- rwdance.swf
- rwdance.wmv
- + 15 graphic files

Review
- astaire.htm
- astaire_mov.htm
- astaire_wmv.htm
- CreditRoll.class
- fabio.css
- fasong.mp3
- hatrack.mov
- hatrack.swf
- hatrack.wmv
- + 16 graphic file

Case1
- devotion.mp3
- fireice.mp3
- poetry.css
- PopBtn.class
- PopMenu.class
- rf.htm
- + 6 graphic files

Case2
- roadways.txt
- rw.css
- rwlogo.jpg
- trailridge.swf

Case3
- Cmplx.class
- Controls.class
- FracPanel.class
- fractal.htm
- fstyles.css
- Mandel.class
- mandel.swf
- + 2 graphic files

Case4
- bstyles.css
- beethoven.mp3
- byso.htm
- CreditRoll.class
- + 2 graphic files

Objectives

Session 8.1
- Explore the uses of frames in a Web site
- Create a frameset consisting of rows and columns of frames
- Display a document within a frame
- Format the appearance of a frame

Session 8.2
- Create links targeted at frames
- Direct a link to a target outside of a frame layout
- Format the color and size of frame borders
- Create an inline frame

Designing a Web Site with Frames

Using Frames to Organize a Web Site

Case | Cliff Hangers

One of the most popular climbing schools and touring agencies in Colorado is Cliff Hangers. Located in Boulder, Cliff Hangers specializes in teaching beginning through advanced climbing techniques. The school also sponsors several climbing tours, leading individuals on some of the most exciting climbs in North America.

Debbie Chen is the owner of the school and is always looking for ways to market her programs and improve the visibility of the school.

She knows that some Web sites use frames to display several Web pages in a single browser window and has asked you to help develop a frame-based Web site for Cliff Hangers.

Starting Data Files

Tutorial.08 →

Tutorial
clifftxt.htm
linkstxt.htm
philosphtxt.htm
tourstxt.htm
+ 17 HTML files
+ 3 style sheets
+ 29 graphic files

Review
lefttxt.htm
lessonstxt.htm
links1txt.htm
links2txt.htm
links3txt.htm
middletxt.htm
newlayouttxt.htm
righttxt.htm
+ 16 HTML files
+ 4 style sheets
+ 25 graphic files

Case1
maptxt.htm
nhpolytxt.htm
notestxt.htm
+ 13 HTML files
poli.css
+ 2 graphic files

Case2
browyer.css
listingtxt.htm
+ 17 graphic files

Case3
messtxt.htm
mxxtxt.htm
+ 9 HTML files
+ 2 style sheets
+ 22 graphic files

Case4
tempa1stxt.htm - tempa5s1txt.htm
tempest.jpg

Session 8.1

Introducing Frames

Web authors often dedicate individual Web pages to a particular topic or group of topics. One page might contain a list of links, another page might display contact information for the company or organization, and another page might describe the business philosophy. As more pages are added to the site, the designer often needs a way to display information from several pages at the same time—such as a list of links remaining on the page at the same time as the contact information is displayed.

One common solution is to duplicate that information (such as the list of links) across the Web site, but this strategy presents problems. It requires a great deal of time and effort to repeat (or copy and paste) the same information over and over again. Also, each time a change is required, the edit must be repeated on each page where the information appears—a process that could easily result in errors.

Such considerations contributed to the creation of frames. A **frame** is a section of a browser window capable of displaying the contents of an entire Web page. Figure 8-1 shows an example of a browser window containing two frames. The frame on the left displays the contents of a Web page containing a list of links for the University of Michigan Documents Center. The frame on the right displays the site's home page.

Figure 8-1 A framed Web site

This Web site illustrates a common use of frames: displaying a table of contents in one frame, while showing individual pages from the site in another frame. Figure 8-2 illustrates how a list of links can remain on the screen while the user navigates through the contents of the site. Using this layout, a designer can easily change the list of links without having to change every page on the site because the links are stored on only one page.

Figure 8-2 Activating a link within a frame

Drawbacks of Frame-Based Layouts | InSight

As convenient as they look at first, frame-based Web sites do have drawbacks. One drawback is that the browser must load multiple HTML files, increasing the amount of time a user must wait to work with the site. With high-speed connections this is less of a concern than it once was, but it is still something to consider.

Another problem with frames is that they make it difficult for users to bookmark the Web site contents. Browsers will allow the user to bookmark the entire frame or individual pages, but there is no way to create a bookmark that displays a page as it appears within the frame.

Also, some frame-based sites don't work well with Internet search engines such as Yahoo! and Google. The problem is that most search engines base their results on the contents and keywords found within the Web page. However, because frames do not have any content (they only display the content from other pages), the home page from a frame-based site might not score high on the results from a search engine.

For these reasons, many Web designers suggest that if you want to use frames, you should also provide a nonframed version of your Web site, giving users links to both versions so they can choose which version they wish to use.

Planning Your Frames

Before you start creating your frames, you must plan their appearance and determine how you want to use them. There are several issues to consider:

- What information will be displayed in each frame?
- How do you want the frames placed on the Web page? What is the size of each frame?
- Which frames will be static—that is, always showing the same content?
- Which frames will change in response to links being clicked?
- What Web pages will users first see when they access the site?
- Should users be permitted to resize the frames to suit their needs?

As you progress with your design for the Cliff Hangers Web site, you'll consider each of these questions. Debbie has already created the Web pages for the site; your job is to create the frame layout and insert the correct files into the various frames. Figure 8-3 describes the different Web pages you'll work with in this project.

Figure 8-3 **Web pages on the Cliff Hangers Web site**

Topic	Filename	Content
Biographies	staff.htm	Links to biographical pages of Cliff Hangers staff
Home page	home.htm	The Cliff Hangers home page
Lessons	lessons.htm	Climbing lessons offered by Cliff Hangers
Logo	head.htm	A page containing the company logo
Philosophy	philosph.htm	Business philosophy of Cliff Hangers
Table of contents	links.htm	Links to Cliff Hangers Web pages
Tours	diamond.htm	Description of the Diamond climbing tour
Tours	eldorado.htm	Description of the Eldorado Canyon climbing tour
Tours	grepon.htm	Description of the Petit Grepon climbing tour
Tours	kieners.htm	Description of the Kiener's Route climbing tour
Tours	lumpy.htm	Description of the Lumpy Ridge climbing tour
Tours	nface.htm	Description of the North Face climbing tour

Debbie has organized the pages by topic, such as tour descriptions, climbing lessons, and company philosophy. Two of the files, links.htm and staff.htm, do not focus on a particular topic, but contain links to other Cliff Hangers Web pages.

Debbie has carefully considered how this material should be organized on the Web site and what information the user should see first. She has sketched a layout that illustrates how she would like the frames to be organized, as shown in Figure 8-4.

Debbie's proposed frame layout **Figure 8-4**

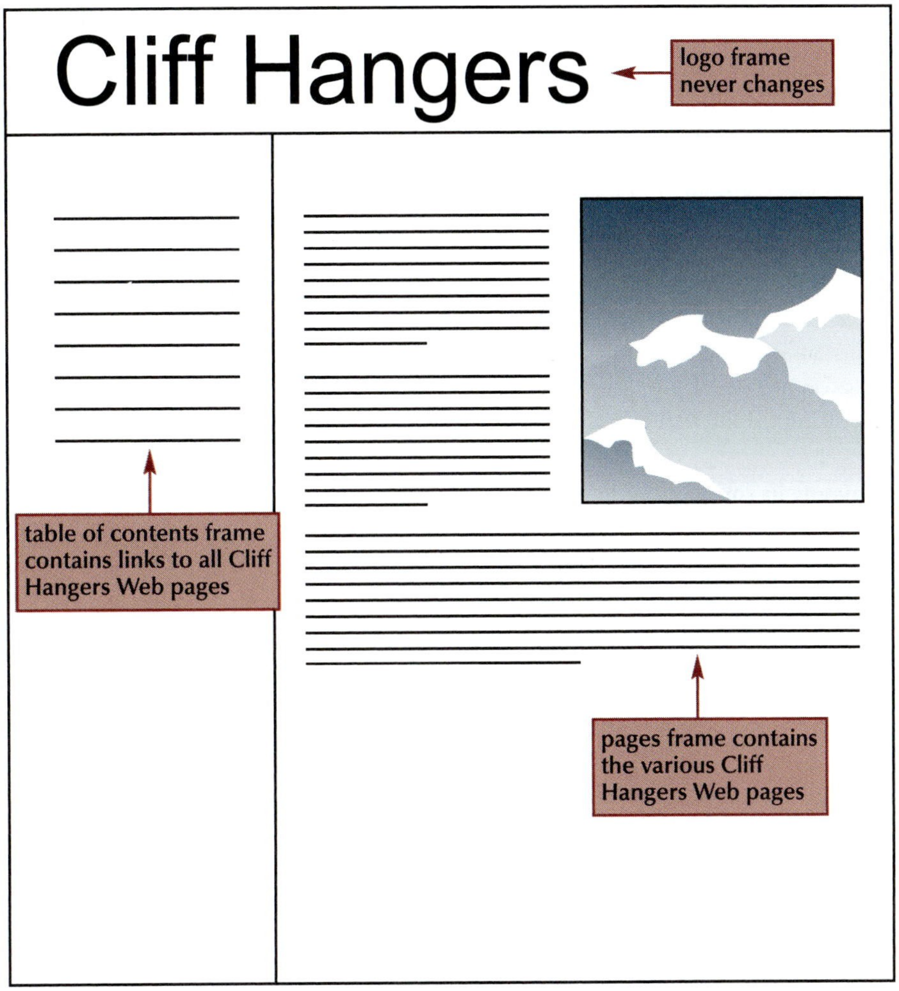

As you can see in Figure 8-4, Debbie would like you to create three frames. She would like the school's logo (which will contain the phone and address information) to appear in the top frame, and she wants that frame to always display that information. She wants the frame on the left to display a list of the Web pages on the Cliff Hangers Web site. Finally, Debbie wants the frame on the lower right to display the contents of the page corresponding to the link that a user clicks from the left frame.

Your first task is to enter the HTML code for the frame layout that Debbie has described.

Creating a Frameset

Frames are organized into a **frameset**, which is HTML code that defines the layout and content of the frames within the browser window. The syntax for creating a frameset is

```
<html>
   <head>
      <title>title</title>
   </head>
   <frameset>
      frames
   </frameset>
</html>
```

where *frames* are the individual frames within the frameset. You'll learn how to create these frames shortly. An HTML file can contain several framesets nested within one another.

Note that the frameset element replaces the body element in this HTML document. Because this HTML file displays the contents of other Web pages, it is not technically a Web page and thus does not include a page body. Later in the tutorial, you'll explore situations in which you would include a body element to support browsers that do not display frames. For now, you'll concentrate on defining the appearance and content of the frames.

Specifying Frame Size and Orientation

Framesets lay out frames in either rows or columns, but not both. Figure 8-5 shows two framesets: one in which the frames are laid out in three columns, and another in which they are placed in three rows.

Figure 8-5 **Frame layouts in rows and columns**

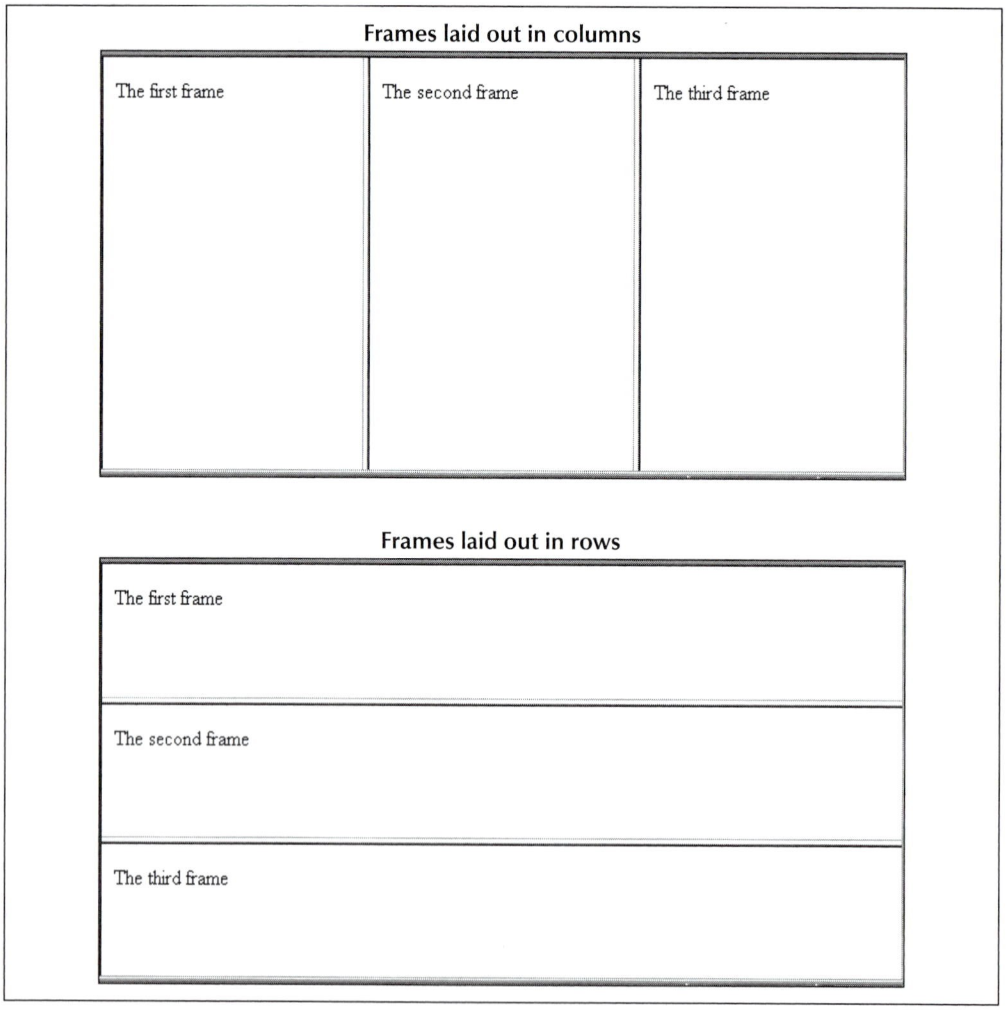

To lay out the frames in rows, you add the rows attribute

```
<frameset rows="row1,row2,row3,..."> ... </frameset>
```

to the <frameset> tag, where *row1, row2, row3,* etc. is the height of each row in the frameset. To lay out the frames in columns, you use the cols attribute

```
<frameset cols="col1,col2,col3,..."> ... </frameset>
```

where *col1, col2, col3,* etc. are the widths of each column. There is no limit to the number of rows or columns you can specify for a frameset; however, you can lay out a frameset only in rows or in columns, but not both. If your site requires frames in both rows and columns, you must nest one frameset within another.

Row and column sizes can be specified in three ways: in pixels, as a percentage of the total size of the frameset, or by an asterisk (*), which instructs the browser to allocate any unclaimed space in the frameset to the given row or column. For example, the attribute

```
rows="160, *"
```

creates two frames set up as rows. The first row has a height of 160 pixels, and the height of the second row is equal to whatever space remains in the browser window area. You can combine all three units of measure to make your framed site look good on different-sized monitors. The attribute

```
cols="160, 25%, *"
```

creates a layout consisting of three columns, with the first column at 160 pixels wide, the second column at 25% of the width of the frameset, and the third column covering whatever space is left, as shown in Figure 8-6.

Sizing frames **Figure 8-6**

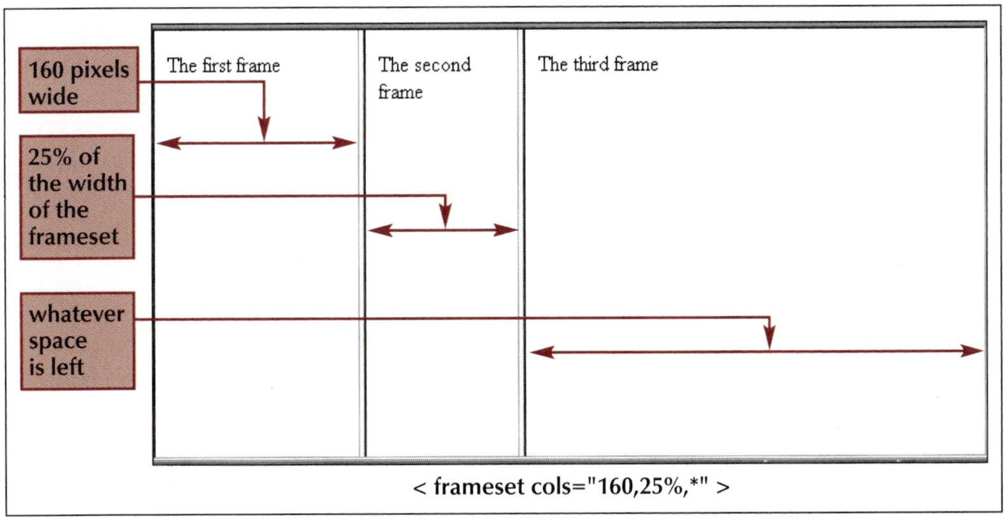

Tip

Set the size of at least one of the rows or columns to * to ensure that the frames fill up the entire browser window.

You can also use multiple asterisks. In that case, the browser divides the remaining display space equally among the frames designated with asterisks. For example, the attribute

```
rows="*, *, *"
```

creates three rows, each with a height that is one-third of the total height of the frameset.

Reference Window | Creating a Frameset

- To create a frameset, enter the frameset element

```
<frameset>
   frames
</frameset>
```

  where *frames* are the individual frames within the frameset.
- The frames of a frameset must be laid out in rows or columns. To lay out the frames in rows, add the attribute

```
rows="row1, row2, row3, ..."
```

  to the opening <frameset> tag, where *row1*, *row2*, *row3*, etc. are the heights of the rows in pixels or percentages. To allow a row to fill the browser window space not specified for other rows, use the value *.
- To lay out the frames in columns, add the attribute

```
cols="col1, col2, col3, ..."
```

  to the opening <frameset> tag, where *col1*, *col2*, *col3*, etc. are the widths of the columns in pixels or percentages.

The first frameset you'll create for the Cliff Hangers Web site has two rows. The top row will display the company logo. You'll set the height of the row to 85 pixels. The rest of the Web site will be displayed in the second row, and you'll set that row's height to occupy the rest of the browser window.

To create a frameset:

1. Use your text editor to open the **clifftxt.htm**, **linkstxt.htm**, **philosphtxt.htm**, and **tourstxt.htm** files from the tutorial.08\tutorial folder included with your Data Files. Enter ***your name*** and ***the date*** in the comment section of each file and save them as **cliff.htm**, **links.htm**, **philosph.htm**, and **tours.htm**, respectively, in the same folder.
2. Return to the **cliff.htm** file in your text editor.
3. Insert the following frameset directly after the closing </head> tag, as shown in Figure 8-7:

   <frameset rows="85,*">

   </frameset>

Figure 8-7 Inserting a frameset

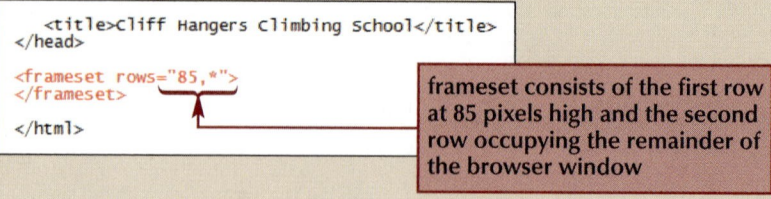

```
   <title>Cliff Hangers Climbing School</title>
</head>

<frameset rows="85,*">
</frameset>

</html>
```

frameset consists of the first row at 85 pixels high and the second row occupying the remainder of the browser window

The initial frameset is now defined. Next you must specify the content of the frameset.

Creating a Frame

The first row of the frameset will contain a frame displaying the company logo. To create a frame, you use the frame element

```
<frame src="url" />
```

where *url* is the URL of the document displayed within the frame.

Debbie saved the page containing the company logo and address as head.htm. You'll place this document in the first frame of the frameset, as shown in Figure 8-8.

> **Tip**
>
> The frame source does not need to be an HTML file. You can insert graphics files within frames as well. However, frames must always be nested within a frameset.

Figure 8-8 Placing the head.htm file

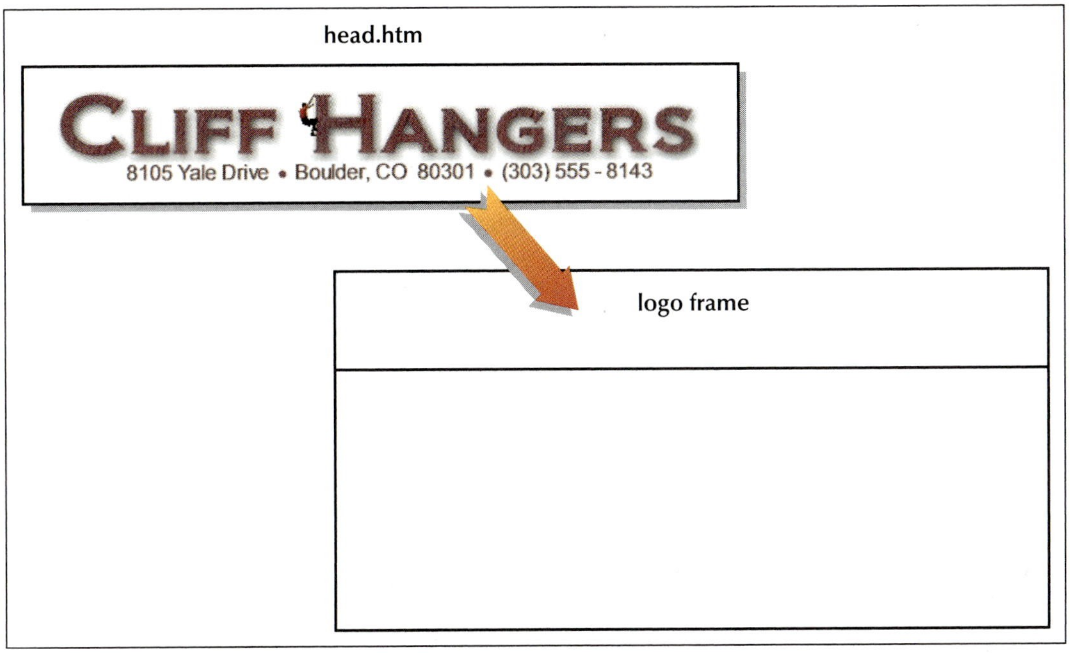

Create a Frame | Reference Window

- To create a frame, use the element
  ```
  <frame src="url" />
  ```
  where *url* is the URL of the document displayed in the frame.

To set the source of the first frame:

1. After the opening <frameset> tag, insert the following frame element, as shown in Figure 8-9.

   ```
   <!-- Company Logo -->
   <frame src="head.htm" />
   ```

> **Tip**
>
> Add comments to your <frame /> tags so that it's clear what content will be displayed within each frame.

Figure 8-9 **Inserting the frame element**

```
<frameset rows="85,*">
   <!-- Company Logo -->
   <frame src="head.htm" />
</frameset>

</html>
```

file displayed within the frame

2. Save your changes to the file.

You have successfully specified the source for the first row of the frameset. In the second row you'll insert another frameset.

Nesting Framesets

As noted earlier, a frameset places frames in either rows or columns, but not both. Therefore, to create a layout containing frames in both rows and columns, you must nest one frameset within another. Debbie wants the second row of the current frame layout to contain two columns: the first column will display a table of contents, and the second column will display the Web pages for the various lessons and tours that Cliff Hangers offers. You'll specify a width of 140 pixels for the first column, and whatever remains in the display area will be allotted to the second column.

To nest a frameset:

1. Directly below the <frame /> tag you just entered, insert the following lines of code, as shown in Figure 8-10:

```
<!-- Nested Frameset -->
<frameset cols="140,*">
</frameset>
```

Figure 8-10 **Nesting a frameset**

```
<frameset rows="85,*">
   <!-- Company Logo -->
   <frame src="head.htm" />

   <!-- Nested Frameset -->
   <frameset cols="140,*">
   </frameset>

</frameset>
```

2. Save your changes to the file.

Next, you'll specify the sources for the two frames in the nested frameset. The frame in the first column should display the links.htm file, which is Debbie's table of contents. The Cliff Hangers home page, home.htm, should be displayed in the second frame. Figure 8-11 shows the contents of these two pages and their locations in the frameset.

Figure 8-11

Placing the links.htm and home.htm files in the frame layout

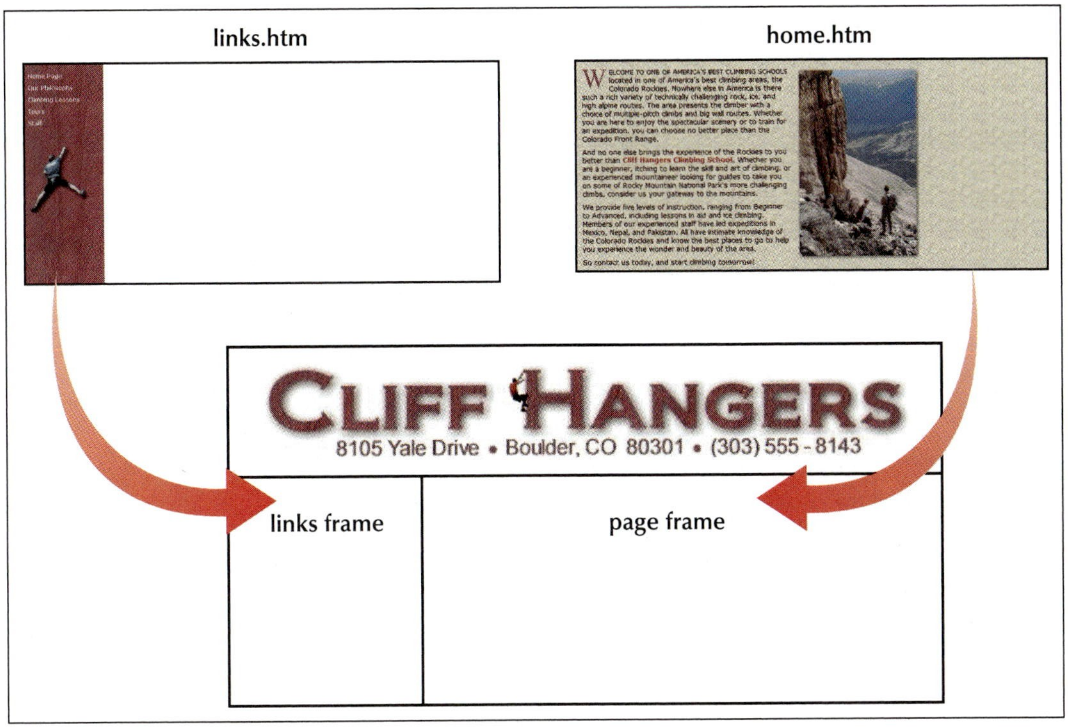

To insert the two frames of the nested frameset:

1. Directly below the opening <frameset> tag of the nested frameset, insert the following code, as shown in Figure 8-12.

```
<!-- List of Links -->
<frame src="links.htm" />

<!-- Cliff Hangers Web Pages -->
<frame src="home.htm" />
```

Figure 8-12

Inserting the frame columns

```
<frameset rows="85,*">
   <!-- Company Logo -->
   <frame src="head.htm" />

   <!-- Nested Frameset -->
   <frameset cols="140,*">
      <!-- List of Links -->
      <frame src="links.htm" />

      <!-- Cliff Hangers Web Pages -->
      <frame src="home.htm" />
   </frameset>

</frameset>
```

2. Save your changes to the file.
3. Open the **cliff.htm** file in your Web browser. As shown in Figure 8-13, the browser lays out the contents of the three Web pages within frames in the browser window.

Figure 8-13 Initial frame layout of the Cliff Hangers Web site

CLIFF HANGERS
8105 Yale Drive • Boulder, CO 80301 • (303) 555 - 8143
contents of the head.htm file
vertical scroll bar for page content outside of the frame
Home Page
Our Philosophy
Climbing Lessons
Tours
Staff
WELCOME TO ONE OF AMERICA'S BEST CLIMBING SCHOOLS located in one of America's best climbing areas, the Colorado Rockies. Nowhere else in America is there such a rich variety of technically challenging rock, ice, and high alpine routes. The area presents the climber with a choice of multiple-pitch climbs and big wall routes. Whether you are here to enjoy the spectacular scenery or to train for an expedition, you can choose no better place than the Colorado Front Range.
And no one else brings the experience of the Rockies to you better than Cliff Hangers Climbing School. Whether you are a beginner, itching to learn the skill and art of climbing, or an experienced mountaineer looking for guides to take you on some of Rocky Mountain National Park's more challenging climbs, consider us your gateway to the mountains.
We provide five levels of instruction, ranging from Beginner to Advanced, including lessons in aid and ice climbing. Members of our experienced staff have led expeditions in Mexico, Nepal, and Pakistan. All have intimate knowledge of the Colorado Rockies and know the best places to go to help you experience the wonder and beauty of the area.
So contact us today, and start climbing tomorrow!
links.htm
home.htm

Although the browser window displays the three Web pages from the Cliff Hangers Web site, the design of the frame layout could use some refinement. Part of the logo has been cut off in the head frame. Whenever page content does not entirely fit within the frame borders, the browser displays horizontal and vertical scroll bars to allow the user to scroll through the rest of the page content within the frame. Scroll bars do not appear in the two other frames because all of the page content from the links.htm and home.htm files fits within their frames. Debbie doesn't want the scroll bars to appear, so you need to format the frame so that it displays all of the company logo.

Formatting a Frame

You can control three attributes of a frame: the appearance of scroll bars, the size of the margin between the source document and the frame border, and whether or not users are allowed to change the frame size. The first attribute you'll work with is the scrolling attribute.

Hiding and Displaying Scroll Bars

By default, a scroll bar is displayed when the content of the source page does not fit within a frame. You can override this setting using the scrolling attribute. The syntax for this attribute is

```
scrolling="type"
```

where *type* can be either yes (to always display a scroll bar) or no (to never display a scroll bar). If you don't specify a setting for the scrolling attribute, the browser displays a scroll bar when the page content doesn't fit in the frame.

Debbie thinks that a scroll bar is inappropriate for the logo frame, and she wants to ensure that a scroll bar is never displayed for that frame. Therefore, you need to add the

```
scrolling="no"
```

attribute to the frame element. However, Debbie does want scroll bars for the other two frames, as needed, so the default value for those frames is sufficient.

To remove the scroll bars from the logo frame:

1. Return to the **cliff.htm** file in your text editor.
2. Within the frame element for the logo frame, insert the following attribute, as shown in Figure 8-14:

   scrolling="no"

Figure 8-14 **Removing the scroll bars from the logo frame**

hide the frame scroll bars

```
<frameset rows="85,*">
   <!-- Company Logo -->
   <frame src="head.htm" scrolling="no" />

   <!-- Nested Frameset -->
   <frameset cols="140,*">
      <!-- List of Links -->
      <frame src="links.htm" />

      <!-- Cliff Hangers Web Pages -->
      <frame src="home.htm" />
   </frameset>

</frameset>
```

3. Save your changes to the file and then reload **cliff.htm** in your Web browser. Verify that the scroll bars have been removed from the logo frame.

   Although the scroll bar for the logo frame has been removed, depending on your screen size, the logo contained in the head.htm file might still be cut off.

> **Tip**
>
> To view changes in the frame layout or for frame properties in some older browsers, you might have to reload rather than simply refresh the Web site.

When working with frames, keep in mind that you should remove scroll bars from a frame only when you are convinced that the entire Web page will be visible in the frame. To do this, you should view your Web page using several different monitor settings. Few things are more irritating to Web site visitors than to discover that some content is missing from a frame with no scroll bars available to reveal the missing content. To ensure that the head.htm file will fit in the logo frame, you need to modify the frame margins.

Setting Frame Margins

When your browser displays a Web page in a frame, it places a margin between the Web page and the frame borders. If the margin is too large, part of the Web page might not fit within the frame. This is what occurred with the logo frame. Generally, you want the margin to be big enough to keep the source's text or images from running into the frame's borders. However, you do not want the margin to take up too much space, either.

You've already noted that the margin height for the logo frame is too large, and this has shifted some of the text beyond the border of the frame. To fix this problem, you need to specify a smaller margin for the frame so that the logo can move up and allow all of the text to be displayed in the frame.

The attribute for specifying margin sizes for a frame is

```
marginheight="value" marginwidth="value"
```

where the marginheight value specifies the amount of space, in pixels, above and below the frame source, and the marginwidth value specifies the amount of space to the left and right of the frame source. You do not have to specify both the margin height and width. However, if you specify only one, the browser assumes that you want to use the same value for both. Setting margin values is a process of trial and error as you determine what combination of margin sizes looks best.

To correct the problem with the logo frame, you'll decrease its margin size to 0 pixels. This setting will allow the entire logo to be displayed within the frame. You don't need to change the margins of the other frames.

To set the size of the internal frame margins:

1. Return to the **cliff.htm** file in your text editor.
2. Within the frame element for the logo frame, insert the following attribute, as shown in Figure 8-15:

   marginheight="0"

Figure 8-15 Set the frame margin height

```
<frameset rows="85,*">
   <!-- Company Logo -->
   <frame src="head.htm" scrolling="no" marginheight="0" />

   <!-- Nested Frameset -->
   <frameset cols="140,*">
      <!-- List of Links -->
      <frame src="links.htm" />

      <!-- Cliff Hangers Web Pages -->
      <frame src="home.htm" />
   </frameset>

</frameset>
```

the margin above and below the head.htm file will be 0 pixels

3. Save your changes to the file and then reload **cliff.htm** in your Web browser. As shown in Figure 8-16, the entire logo should now be visible within the frame with no scroll bars showing.

Figure 8-16 Revised frame layout

CLIFF HANGERS
8105 Yale Drive • Boulder, CO 80301 • (303) 555 - 8143
the entire Cliff Hangers logo appears within the frame
Home Page
Our Philosophy
Climbing Lessons
Tours
Staff
WELCOME TO ONE OF AMERICA'S BEST CLIMBING SCHOOLS located in one of America's best climbing areas, the Colorado Rockies. Nowhere else in America is there such a rich variety of technically challenging rock, ice, and high alpine routes. The area presents the climber with a choice of multiple-pitch climbs and big wall routes. Whether you are here to enjoy the spectacular scenery or to train for an expedition, you can choose no better place than the Colorado Front Range.
And no one else brings the experience of the Rockies to you better than Cliff Hangers Climbing School. Whether you are a beginner, itching to learn the skill and art of climbing, or an experienced mountaineer looking for guides to take you on some of Rocky Mountain National Park's more challenging climbs, consider us your gateway to the mountains.
We provide five levels of instruction, ranging from Beginner to Advanced, including lessons in aid and ice climbing. Members of our experienced staff have led expeditions in Mexico, Nepal, and Pakistan. All have intimate knowledge of the Colorado Rockies and know the best places to go to help you experience the wonder and beauty of the area.
So contact us today, and start climbing tomorrow!

Formatting a Frame

| Reference Window

- To control whether a frame contains a scroll bar, add the attribute
  `scrolling="type"`
  to the frame element, where *type* is either yes (scroll bar) or no (no scroll bar). If you do not specify the scrolling attribute, a scroll bar appears only when the content of the frame source cannot fit within the boundaries of the frame.
- To control the amount of space between the frame source and the frame boundary, add the attribute
  `marginwidth="value" marginheight="value"`
  to the frame element, where the width and height values are expressed in pixels. The margin width is the space to the left and right of the frame source. The margin height is the space above and below the frame source. If you do not specify a margin height or width, the browser assigns dimensions based on the content of the frame source.
- To keep users from resizing frames, add the following attribute to the frame element:
  `noresize="noresize"`

Debbie is satisfied with the changes you've made to the Web page. Your next task is to prevent users from resizing the frames.

Controlling Frame Resizing

By default, users can resize frame borders in the browser by simply clicking and dragging a frame border with their mouse. However, some Web designers prefer to freeze, or lock, frames so that users cannot resize them. This ensures that the Web site appears as the designer intended. Debbie would like you to do this for the Cliff Hangers Web site. The attribute for controlling frame resizing is

```
noresize="noresize"
```

Many browsers also allow you to insert this attribute as simply

```
noresize
```

without an attribute value. However, this form is not supported by XHTML because XHTML requires all attributes to have attribute values. You'll follow this principle in the code we create for Debbie's Web site.

To prevent users from resizing the frames on the Cliff Hangers site:

1. Return to the **cliff.htm** file in your text editor.
2. Within each of the three <frame /> tags in the file, add the attribute

   noresize="noresize"
3. Save your changes to the file and then reload **cliff.htm** in your Web browser.
4. Verify that the frames are now locked in and cannot be resized by the user.
5. If you want to take a break before starting the next session, you can close any open files and programs now.

Debbie is pleased with the progress you've made on the Cliff Hangers site. In the next session you'll modify the properties of the links in the table of contents frame so that all links open with the page frame.

Review | Session 8.1 Quick Check

1. What are frames, and why are they useful in displaying and designing a Web site?
2. Why is the <body> tag unnecessary for pages that contain frames?
3. What HTML code do you use to create three rows of frames with the height of the first row set to 200 pixels, the height of the second row set to 50% of the display area, and the height of the third row set to occupy the remaining space?
4. What HTML code do you use to specify home.htm as a source for a frame?
5. What HTML code do you use to remove the scroll bars from the frame for home.htm?
6. What HTML code do you use to set the size of the margin above and below the contents of the home.htm frame to 3 pixels?
7. What is the size of the margins to the right and left of the frame in Question 6?
8. What code would you use to prevent users from moving the frame borders in home.htm?

Session 8.2

Working with Frames and Links

Now that you've created frames for the Cliff Hangers Web site, you're ready to work on formatting the links for the Web page. The links page contains five links, which point to the pages as shown in Figure 8-17:

- The Home Page link points to home.htm.
- The Our Philosophy link points to philosph.htm.
- The Climbing Lessons link points to lessons.htm.
- The Tours link points to tours.htm.
- The Staff link points to a frameset stored in the staff.htm file.

Figure 8-17 **Links within the table of contents frame**

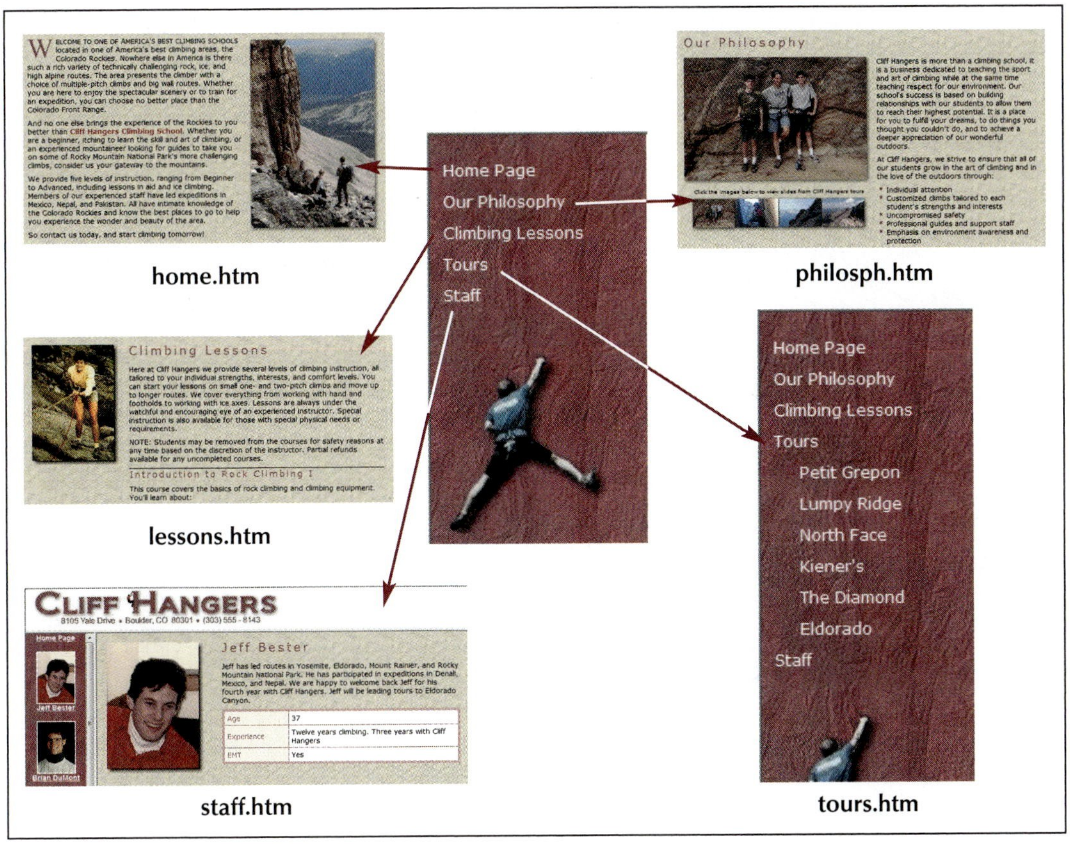

By default, clicking a link within a frame opens the linked file inside the same frame. However, this is not the way Debbie wants each of the links to work. She wants the links to work as follows:

- The Home, Our Philosophy, and Climbing Lessons pages should appear in the lower-right frame.
- The Tours page should appear in the table of contents frame.
- The frameset from the staff.htm file should occupy the entire browser window.

To specify the location in which to open a hypertext link, you must first assign each frame a name. This is done by adding the attribute

```
name="name"
```

to the frame element, where *name* is the name assigned to the frame. Case is important in assigning names. The frame name "information" differs from the frame name "INFORMATION." Also, frame names cannot contain spaces. For the Cliff Hangers frameset, you'll name the three frames logo, links, and pages.

Reference Window | Directing a Link to a Frame

- First, assign a name to a frame by adding the name attribute
  `name="name"`
  to the <frame> tag, where *name* is the name of the frame.
- To point the target of a link to a named frame, add the following attribute to the hypertext link:
  `target="name"`
- To point all links in a document to the same target, add the following element to the head section of the document:
  `<base target="name" />`

You need to name the frames in the Cliff Hanger site so that you can specify where Debbie's various pages will open when users click the links in the left frame.

To assign frame names:

1. Return to the **cliff.htm** file in your text editor.
2. Within the first <frame /> tag, insert the following attribute:
   name="logo"
3. Within the second <frame /> tag, insert the following attribute:
   name="links"
4. Within the last <frame /> tag, insert the following attribute:
   name="pages"
   Figure 8-18 highlights the revised code in the file.

Figure 8-18 Setting the frame names

```
<frameset rows="85,*">
   <!-- Company Logo -->
   <frame src="head.htm" scrolling="no" marginheight="0" noresize="noresize" name="logo"

   <!-- Nested Frameset -->
   <frameset cols="140,*">
      <!-- List of Links -->
      <frame src="links.htm" noresize="noresize" name="links" />

      <!-- Cliff Hangers Web Pages -->
      <frame src="home.htm" noresize="noresize" name="pages" />
   </frameset>

</frameset>
```

5. Save your changes to the file.

Now that you've named the frames, the next task is to specify the pages frame as the target for the Home Page, Our Philosophy, and Climbing Lessons links—so that clicking each of these links opens the corresponding file in the pages frame. In Tutorial 2, you learned how the target attribute can be used to open a hypertext link in a new browser window. You can also use the target attribute to open a linked target in a frame. To point the link to a specific frame, add the attribute

```
target="name"
```

to the <a> tag for the hypertext link, where *name* is the name you've assigned to a frame on your Web page. For the links to home.htm, philosph.htm, and lesson.htm, the *name* value is pages because all of these links should open within the pages frame of the Cliff Hangers frameset. Add these target names to the hypertext links within the links.htm file.

To specify the target for the hypertext links:

1. Open the **links.htm** file from the tutorial.08\tutorial folder with your text editor.
2. Within the <a> tags for the Home Page, Our Philosophy, and Climbing Lessons links, enter the following attribute, as shown in Figure 8-19:

   target="pages"

Figure 8-19 Assigning a target to a link

```
<ul>
   <li><a href="home.htm" target="pages">Home Page</a></li>
   <li><a href="philosph.htm" target="pages">Our Philosophy</a></li>
   <li><a href="lessons.htm" target="pages">Climbing Lessons</a></li>
   <li><a href="tours.htm">Tours</a></li>
   <li><a href="staff.htm">Staff</a></li>
</ul>
```

3. Save your changes to the file.
4. Reload the **cliff.htm** file in your Web browser.
5. Click the **Our Philosophy** link in the links frame. Verify that the Our Philosophy page opens in the pages frame, as shown in Figure 8-20.

Figure 8-20 Viewing the philosophy page

Home Page
Our Philosophy
Climbing Lessons
Tours
Staff
Our Philosophy
Cliff Hangers is more than a climbing school, it is a business dedicated to teaching the sport and art of climbing while at the same time teaching respect for our environment. Our school's success is based on building relationships with our students to allow them to reach their highest potential. It is a place for you to fulfill your dreams, to do things you thought you couldn't do, and to achieve a deeper appreciation of our wonderful outdoors.
At Cliff Hangers, we strive to ensure that all of our students grow in the art of climbing and in the love of the outdoors through:
Individual attention
Customized climbs tailored to each student's strengths and interests
Uncompromised safety
Professional guides and support staff
Emphasis on environment awareness and protection
Here, you are more than students, you are partners in the climbing experience.
Click the images below to view slides from Cliff Hangers tours

6. Click the links for the **Home Page** and the **Climbing Lessons** links and verify that both pages are also displayed within the pages frame.

   Trouble? If you click one of the other links in the frame, the browser will open the file in the links frame. Reload or refresh the **cliff.htm** file to restore the frameset to its original appearance.

Using Reserved Target Names

The remaining two tags in the list of links point to a list of the tours offered by Cliff Hangers, stored in the tours.htm file, and to a staff information page, stored in the staff.htm file. The tours.htm file does not contain information about individual tours; instead, it is an expanded table of contents of pages on the Cliff Hangers Web site. The purpose of the tours.htm page is to replace the links.htm page when a user clicks the Tours link. The links frame will then display the table of contents shown in Figure 8-21. A user can click on an individual tour name to open a page about that tour.

Figure 8-21 **Links to the tour pages**

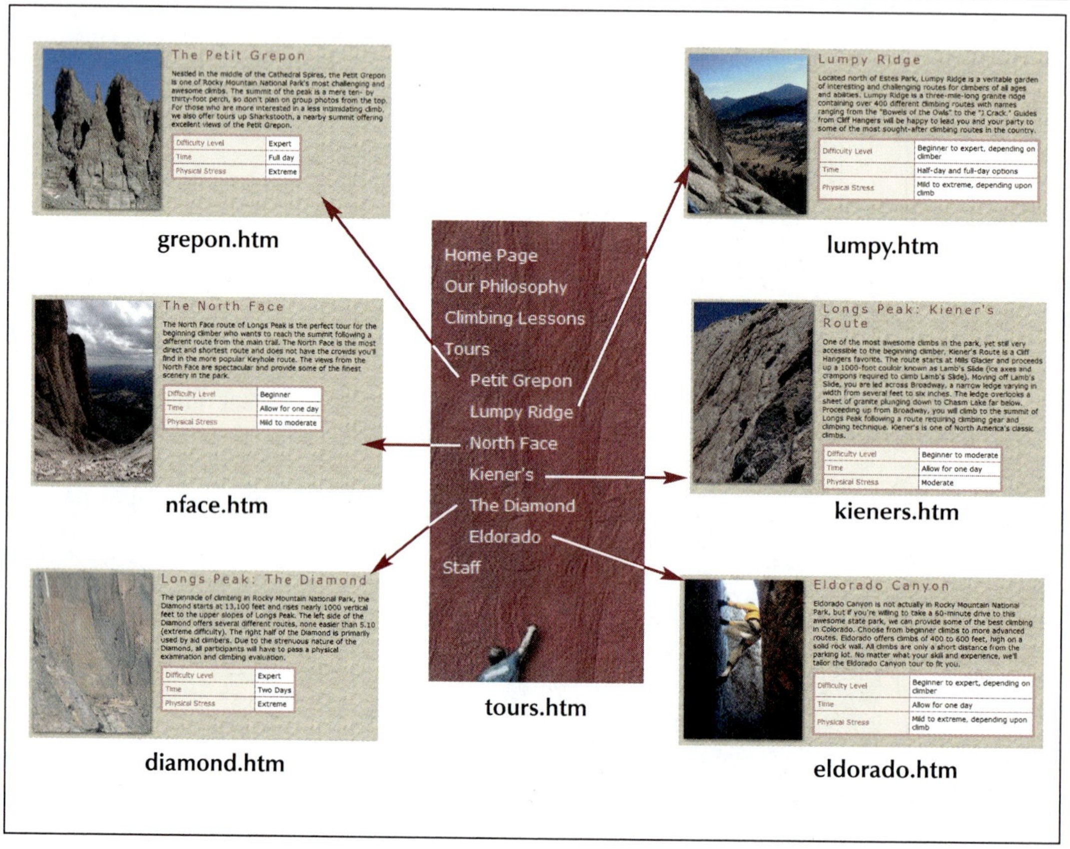

To have tours.htm appear in the links frame when a user clicks the Tours link, you can specify links (the name of the frame) as the target. However, you can also do this using reserved target names. A **reserved target name** is a special name that can be used in place of a frame name as a target. This is useful when the name of the frame is unavailable, when you want the page to appear in a new window, or when you want the page to replace the current browser window. Figure 8-22 describes the reserved target names.

Figure 8-22 Reserved target names

Reserved Target Name	Function in a Frameset
_blank	Loads the target document into a new browser window
_self	Loads the target document into the frame containing the link
_parent	Loads the target document into the parent of the frame containing the link
_top	Loads the document into the full display area, replacing the current frameset

All reserved target names begin with the underscore character (_) to distinguish them from other target names. Note that reserved target names are case-sensitive, so you must enter them in lowercase letters. Debbie wants the contents of the tours.htm file to be displayed in the links frame. You can specify this behavior by adding the target

```
_self
```

to the hypertext link for the tours.htm file.

To add the _self reserved target name to the Tours link:

1. Return to **links.htm** in your text editor.
2. Within the hypertext link for the tours.htm file, insert the following attribute, as shown in Figure 8-23:

   target="_self"

Figure 8-23 Using the _self target

```
<ul>
   <li><a href="home.htm" target="pages">Home Page</a></li>
   <li><a href="philosph.htm" target="pages">Our Philosophy</a></li>
   <li><a href="lessons.htm" target="pages">Climbing Lessons</a></li>
   <li><a href="tours.htm" target="_self">Tours</a></li>
   <li><a href="staff.htm">Staff</a></li>
</ul>
```

3. Save your changes to the file.
4. Reload **cliff.htm** in your Web browser and verify that when you click the Tours link, the tours.htm file opens in the links frame.

Next you'll work with the links in the tours.htm file. Debbie wants each tour page that is linked to the tours.htm page to appear in the pages frame when a user clicks its respective link. When a Web site contains many links that should all open in the same frame, instead of inserting the same target attributes for each link, you can instead specify the target by inserting the base element

```
<base target="name" />
```

in the head section of the document. This way, hypertext links will by default open in the target specified by *name*. You decide to use the base element in the tours.htm file, setting the default target for all hypertext links to the pages frame. The tours.htm file also contains a link that takes the user back to the links.htm file when the user clicks the Tours link again. So, when a user clicks the Tours link the first time, the browser loads the tours.htm file (the expanded table of contents); and when a user clicks the Tours link again, the browser returns to the links.htm file. You'll specify _self as the target for this particular link.

To modify the targets for the tours.htm file:

1. Use your text editor to open the **tours.htm** file from the tutorial.08\tutorial folder included with your Data Files.
2. Insert the following tag directly above the </head> closing tag:

   <base target="pages" />

3. Add the attribute

   target="_self"

   to the hypertext link in the links.htm file. Figure 8-24 highlights the revised code in the tours.htm file.

Figure 8-24 Adding targets to the tours page

```
   <base target="pages" />
</head>

<body style="background: url(wall3.jpg) repeat-y">

   <ul>
      <li><a href="home.htm">Home Page</a></li>
      <li><a href="philosph.htm">Our Philosophy</a></li>
      <li><a href="lessons.htm">Climbing Lessons</a></li>
      <li><a href="links.htm" target="_self">Tours</a></li>
      <ul>
         <li><a href="grepon.htm">Petit Grepon</a></li>
         <li><a href="lumpy.htm">Lumpy Ridge</a></li>
         <li><a href="nface.htm">North Face</a></li>
         <li><a href="kieners.htm">Kiener's</a></li>
         <li><a href="diamond.htm">The Diamond</a></li>
         <li><a href="eldorado.htm">Eldorado</a></li>
      </ul>
      <li><a href="staff.htm">Staff</a></li>
   </ul>
```

by default, all links will open in the page frame

4. Save your changes to the file and then reload **cliff.htm** in your Web browser.
5. Verify that the Tours link works as you intended. When you click the link, the table of contents list should alternately collapse and expand.
6. Click some of the links to the individual tour pages to verify that they appear correctly in the pages frame, as shown in Figure 8-25.

Figure 8-25 Viewing the Lumpy Ridge tour page

As you can see, clicking the Tours link gives the effect that the list is expanding and contracting; but in reality, one table of contents file is simply being replaced by another.

The final link you must create points to a Web page of staff biographies. Debbie asked another employee to produce the contents of this Web page, and the results are shown in Figure 8-26.

The Cliff Hangers staff page — **Figure 8-26**

As you can see, this Web page also uses frames. If you specify the pages frame as the target for the staff.htm page, the result is a series of nested framesets, as shown in Figure 8-27.

Nesting one frameset within another — **Figure 8-27**

This is not what Debbie wants. She wants the Staff Web page to load into the full display area, replacing the frame layout with its own layout. To target a link to the full display area, you use the _top reserved target name. The _top target is often used when one frameset is accessed from another frameset.

You should also use the _top target when you are linking to pages outside of your Web site. For example, if Debbie wanted to add a link to the Colorado Tourism Board Web site, she wouldn't want that Web site to appear within a frame on the Cliff Hangers Web site. Having the Tourism Board Web site appear within the Cliff Hangers frameset could easily confuse users, making it appear as if the Colorado Tourism Board is a component of the Cliff Hangers Climbing School.

Tip

In a frame layout, always have Web pages that lie outside of your Web site open in a new Window or tab to avoid making external pages appear to be part of your frameset.

To apply the _top target to the staff link:

1. Return to the **links.htm** file in your text editor.
2. Enter the attribute

   target="_top"

   to the <a> tag for the Staff link, as shown in Figure 8-28.

Figure 8-28 Setting the target of the Staff link

```
<ul>
   <li><a href="home.htm" target="pages">Home Page</a></li>
   <li><a href="philosph.htm" target="pages">Our Philosophy</a></li>
   <li><a href="lessons.htm" target="pages">Climbing Lessons</a></li>
   <li><a href="tours.htm" target="_self">Tours</a></li>
   <li><a href="staff.htm" target="_top">Staff</a></li>
</ul>
```

the staff.htm page will occupy the complete browser window

3. Save your changes to the file.
4. Return to the **tours.htm** file in your text editor, and repeat Step 2 to ensure that the Staff link on that page also opens in the full browser window. Save your changes to the file.
5. Reload **cliff.htm** in your Web browser. Verify that clicking the **Staff** link displays the full frameset for the Staff pages within the browser window.
6. Click the **Home Page** link at the top of the links frame to return to the cliff.htm file in your browser.

Debbie has viewed all the links on the Cliff Hangers Web site and is quite satisfied with the results. However, she wonders what would happen if a user accesses her site with a browser that does not display frames. Although most browsers do display frames, she also must consider the needs of people who access the Cliff Hangers Web site with screen readers and other nonvisual browsers. If possible, she wants to accommodate browsers that don't support frames.

Using the noframes Element

You can use the noframes element to make your Web site viewable with browsers that do not support frames (known as frame-blind browsers). The noframes element marks a section of your HTML file as code that browsers incapable of displaying frames can use. The noframes element is nested within the frameset element and uses the syntax

```
<html>
<head>
   <title>title</title>
</head>
<frameset>
   frames
   <noframes>
      <body>
         page content
      </body>
   </noframes>
</frameset>
</html>
```

where *page content* is the content that you want the browser to display in place of the frames. There can be only one noframes element in the document. When a browser that supports frames processes this code, it ignores everything within the noframes element and concentrates solely on the code to create the frames. When a browser that doesn't support frames processes this HTML code, it ignores the frameset and frame elements and renders whatever appears within the <body> tags. This way, both types of browsers are supported within a single HTML file.

Cliff Hangers has been using the nonframed Web site displayed in Figure 8-29 for several years.

Figure 8-29 **Frameless version of the Cliff Hangers home page**

CLIFF HANGERS
8105 Yale Drive • Boulder, CO 80301 • (303) 555 - 8143
Home Page
Our Philosophy
Climbing Lessons
Tours
Petit Grepon
Lumpy Ridge
North Face
Kiener's
The Diamond
Eldorado
Staff
WELCOME TO ONE OF AMERICA'S best climbing schools located in one of America's best climbing areas, the Colorado Rockies. Nowhere else in America is there such a rich variety of technically challenging rock, ice, and high alpine routes. The area presents the climber with a choice of multiple-pitch climbs and big wall routes. Whether you are here to enjoy the spectacular scenery or to train for an expedition, you can choose no better place than the Colorado Front Range.
And no one else brings the experience of the Rockies to you better than Cliff Hangers Climbing School. Whether you are a beginner, itching to learn the skill and art of climbing, or an experienced mountaineer looking for guides to take you on some of Rocky Mountain National Park's more challenging climbs, consider us your gateway to the mountains.
We provide five levels of instruction, ranging from Beginner to Advanced, including lessons in aid and ice climbing. Members of our experienced staff have led expeditions in Mexico, Nepal, and Pakistan. All have intimate knowledge of the Colorado Rockies and know the best places to go to help you experience the wonder and beauty of the area.
So contact us today, and start climbing tomorrow!

Reference Window | Supporting Frame-Blind Browsers

- To provide content for browsers that do not support frames, add the code

```
<noframes>
<body>
 page content
</body>
</noframes>
```

to the document, where *page content* is the content that will appear on the Web page.

To display this page for frame-blind browsers, while still making your framed version available as the default, you decide to copy the HTML code from the nonframed Web page and place it within a pair of <noframes> tags in the cliff.htm file.

To insert the noframes code:

1. Return to the **cliff.htm** file in your text editor.

   First you must create a link to the noframes.css style sheet, which contains the style declarations for the elements in the noframes version of the Web page.

2. Directly above the closing </head> tag, insert the following link to the noframes.css style sheet:

   ```
   <link href="noframes.css" rel="stylesheet" type="text/css" />
   ```

3. Scroll down the file and directly after the closing </frameset> tag near the middle of the file, insert the following:

   ```
   <!-- Noframes version of this page -->
   <noframes>


   </noframes>
   ```

4. Save your changes to the file.

   Now copy the body content from the noframes.htm file into the cliff.htm file.

5. Open the **noframes.htm** file in the tutorial.08\tutorial.folder included with your Data Files.

6. Copy the HTML code for the page content, including both the opening and the closing <body> tags in the selection.

7. Return to the **cliff.htm** file in your text editor and paste the copied code within the noframes element you inserted in Step 3. Figure 8-30 shows the revised code in the cliff.htm file.

Figure 8-30

Inserting the noframes version of the Cliff Hangers home page

```
   <title>Cliff Hangers Climbing School</title>
   <link href="noframes.css" rel="stylesheet" type="text/css" />
</head>

<frameset rows="85,*">
   <!-- Company Logo -->
   <frame src="head.htm" scrolling="no" marginheight="0" noresize="noresize" name="logo" />

   <!-- Nested Frameset -->
   <frameset cols="140,*">
      <!-- List of Links -->
      <frame src="links.htm" noresize="noresize" name="links" />

      <!-- Cliff Hangers Web Pages -->
      <frame src="home.htm" noresize="noresize" name="pages" />
   </frameset>

   <!-- Noframes version of this page -->
   <noframes>
      <body>
         <div id="head"><img src="chlogo.jpg" alt="Cliff Hangers" /></div>

         <div id="pageContent">
            <div id="leftCol">
```

```
               <p>We provide five levels of instruction, ranging from Beginner to Advanced,
                  including lessons in aid and ice climbing. Members of our experienced staff
                  have led expeditions in Mexico, Nepal, and Pakistan. All have intimate
                  knowledge of the Colorado Rockies and know the best places to go
                  to help you experience the wonder and beauty of the area.</p>
               <p>So contact us today, and start climbing tomorrow!</p>
            </div>

         </div>
      </body>

   </noframes>

</frameset>
```

8. Save your changes to the file and then reload **cliff.htm** in your Web browser. Browsers that support frames should not look any different because the noframes version will be rendered only by frame-blind browsers.

Tip

You can also support frame-blind browsers by creating two versions of your Web site: one using frames and the other without frames. Provide your users with an opening splash screen to let them pick which version to load.

Of the major browsers, only Opera allows the user to disable frames to test the noframes element. To disable frames in Opera, click Preferences from the Tools menu to open the Preferences dialog box, click Content from the Advanced tab, and then click the Style options button. Deselect the Enable frames check box to turn off support for frames.

InSight | **Making Frames Work with Search Engines**

By their nature, frames are not friendly to search engines because they don't have any page content for the search engines to index. However, there are a few things you can do to make your frames more accessible. One is to add <meta /> tags to the head section of the document with keywords that the search engines can use in creating their search indices. However, <meta /> tags are only a partial solution because not all search engines use them.

For a more complete solution, always include page content within a <noframes> element. The page content should be extensive enough to describe your site's purpose and contents, providing enough information for search engines to create a proper index for your site. Search engines also take into account that most Web sites cover multiple pages. Therefore, part of the indexing process undertaken by a search engine is to navigate through all of the links within a Web site, creating a list of important keywords as it goes. This means that you should also include any navigation links within the <noframes> section of your file so that the search engines will be able to see those links and act upon them.

By using <meta /> tags and enclosing important page content within the <noframes> tag, you can make your site much more accessible to search engines, removing one of the drawbacks often associated with frames.

Working with Frame Borders

Some browsers support additional attributes that you can use to change border size and appearance. For example, you can remove borders from your frames to free up more space for text and images, or you can change the color of the frame borders so that they match or complement the color scheme for your Web site.

Setting the Frame Border Color

To change the color of a frame's border, many browsers support the bordercolor attribute. The syntax for this attribute is

```
bordercolor="color"
```

where *color* is either a color name or a hexadecimal color value. The attribute can be applied either to an entire set of frames, by applying it to the frameset element, or to individual frame elements within the frameset. The bordercolor attribute is not part of the official specifications for HTML and XHTML, so you should not rely on it for your frame design.

Debbie wonders how the Cliff Hangers Web site would look with brown frame borders. You'll use the bordercolor attribute to experiment with this.

To set the frame border color:

1. Return to the **cliff.htm** file.
2. In the opening <frameset> tag, enter the following attribute:

   bordercolor="brown"

3. Save your changes to the file and then reload **cliff.htm** in your Web browser. If your Web browser supports the bordercolor attribute for frames and framesets, your Web site should look like Figure 8-31.

Figure 8-31 Setting the frame border color to brown

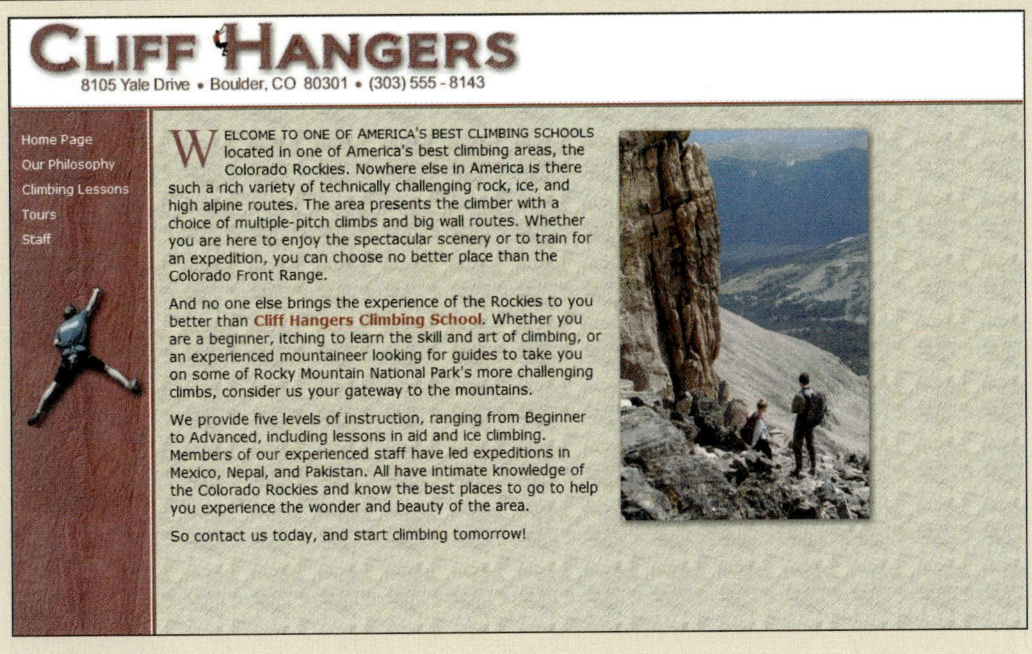

Setting the Frame Border Width

You can also remove the frame borders entirely by applying the frameborder attribute

```
<frame frameborder="value" />
```

to the frame element, where a frameborder value of 0 removes the frame border and a value of 1 displays the border. Different browsers respond in different ways to this attribute, and some browsers do not support the attribute at all. Other browsers require you to apply the border attribute

```
<frameset border="value"> ... </frame>
```

to the frameset element to remove frame borders, where *value* is the size of the border in pixels. Note that the border attribute is applied to the frameset element, while the frameborder attribute is applied only to the frame element. Like bordercolor, the border attribute is not part of the specifications for HTML and is not supported by XHTML.

Hiding a Frame Border | Reference Window

- To specify whether a frame border is displayed, add the attribute
  `frameborder="value"`
  to the <frame> tag, where *value* is 0 to hide the border and 1 to display it.

Debbie decides that although the brown borders look fine, the page might look cleaner without any borders at all. To ensure compatibility with the greatest number of browsers, you'll use both the frameborder and the border attributes in your HTML code.

To remove the frame borders:

1. Return to the **cliff.htm** file in your Web browser.
2. Delete the bordercolor attribute that you added to the opening <frameset> tag in the previous set of steps. You don't need this attribute because you're going to remove the frame borders entirely.
3. Insert the attribute

   border="0"

   within the opening <frameset> tag.
4. Insert the attribute

   frameborder="0"

   within each of the three <frame> tags. Figure 8-32 highlights the revised code.

Figure 8-32 **Removing frame borders**

```
<frameset rows="85,*" border="0">
   <!-- Company Logo -->
   <frame src="head.htm" scrolling="no" marginheight="0" noresize="noresize" name="logo" frameborder="0" />

   <!-- Nested Frameset -->
   <frameset cols="140,*">
      <!-- List of Links -->
      <frame src="links.htm" noresize="noresize" name="links" frameborder="0" />

      <!-- Cliff Hangers Web Pages -->
      <frame src="home.htm" noresize="noresize" name="pages" frameborder="0" />
   </frameset>
```

5. You've finished your edits on this file. Close the **cliff.htm** file, saving your changes.
6. Reload **cliff.htm** in your Web browser. As shown in Figure 8-33, the borders are removed from the frames in the frame layout.

Figure 8-33 **Final frame layout**

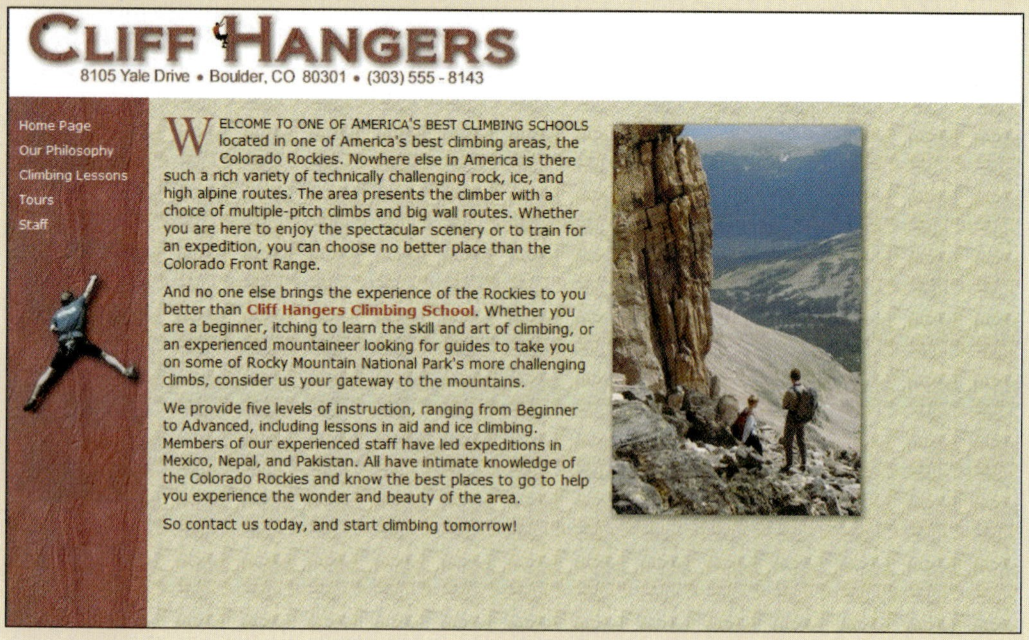

CLIFF HANGERS
8105 Yale Drive • Boulder, CO 80301 • (303) 555 - 8143
Home Page
Our Philosophy
Climbing Lessons
Tours
Staff
WELCOME TO ONE OF AMERICA'S BEST CLIMBING SCHOOLS located in one of America's best climbing areas, the Colorado Rockies. Nowhere else in America is there such a rich variety of technically challenging rock, ice, and high alpine routes. The area presents the climber with a choice of multiple-pitch climbs and big wall routes. Whether you are here to enjoy the spectacular scenery or to train for an expedition, you can choose no better place than the Colorado Front Range.
And no one else brings the experience of the Rockies to you better than Cliff Hangers Climbing School. Whether you are a beginner, itching to learn the skill and art of climbing, or an experienced mountaineer looking for guides to take you on some of Rocky Mountain National Park's more challenging climbs, consider us your gateway to the mountains.
We provide five levels of instruction, ranging from Beginner to Advanced, including lessons in aid and ice climbing. Members of our experienced staff have led expeditions in Mexico, Nepal, and Pakistan. All have intimate knowledge of the Colorado Rockies and know the best places to go to help you experience the wonder and beauty of the area.
So contact us today, and start climbing tomorrow!

By removing the borders, you've created more space for the text and images on each Web page. You've also created the impression of a seamless Web page, which some Web designers prefer in order to give the illusion of a single Web page rather than three separate ones. However, other Web designers believe that hiding frame borders can confuse users as they navigate the Web site.

Creating Inline Frames

Another type of frame used on Web sites is an **inline frame** in which the frame appears not within a frameset but within the body of a Web page. Much like an inline image displays the contents of graphics file or an embedded object displays a video clip, an inline frame displays the contents of a Web page. Inline frames are created using the iframe element

```
<iframe src="url" width="value" height="value">
   alternate content
</iframe>
```

where *url* is the URL of the document you want displayed in the inline frame and *alternate content* is content displayed by browsers that don't support inline frames. The width and height attributes are required, and they set the size of the inline frame in pixels. For example, the following code displays the contents of the jobs.htm file within an inline frame that is 500 pixels wide × 200 pixels high; browsers that don't support inline frames will display a paragraph containing a link to the jobs.htm file:

```
<iframe src="jobs.htm" width="500" height="200">
   <p>
      View the online <a href="jobs.htm">jobs listings</a>.
   </p>
</iframe>
```

If the contents of the jobs.htm file cannot fit within the specified dimensions, the Web browser will automatically add the necessary horizontal and vertical scroll bars to enable the user to scroll through the contents of the file.

Inline frames support many of the same features as inline images. You can resize them, float them on the page margins, and specify the size of the margin around the frame. You can also use many of the attributes associated with frame elements. Figure 8-34 summarizes some of the attributes associated with inline frames. Note that some of the listed attributes have been deprecated by the World Wide Web Consortium (W3C). You can replace many of these attributes using CSS style sheets.

Tip

You can also use the <object> tag discussed in Tutorial 7 to display the contents of one Web page within another.

Figure 8-34 **Attributes of inline frames**

Attribute	Description
align="*position*"	Aligns the inline frame with the surrounding content (deprecated)
border="*value*"	Sets the size of the border around the frame in pixels (deprecated)
frameborder="1 | 0"	Specifies whether to display the inline frame border (1 = display; 0 = no frame border)
height="*value*"	Sets the height of the frame in pixels
hspace="*value*"	Sets the horizontal margin around the frame in pixels (deprecated)
marginheight="*value*"	Sets the vertical margin within the frame in pixels
marginwidth="*value*"	Sets the horizontal margin within the frame in pixels
name="*text*"	Specifies the name of the frame
scrolling="yes | no"	Specifies whether or not to display scroll bars around the frame
src="*url*"	Sets the source of the document within the inline frame
style="*styles*"	Provides inline styles to be applied to the frame
vspace="*value*"	Sets the vertical margin around the frame in pixels (deprecated)
width="*value*"	Sets the width of the frame in pixels

Debbie would like to use inline frames on the Cliff Hangers Philosophy page to create a slide show for users to view high-resolution images from Cliff Hangers tours and classes. As shown in Figure 8-35, Debbie wants to give users the option to click on thumbnail versions of the photo images that would then load the larger images onto the Web page.

Figure 8-35 **Creating a slide show with inline frames**

Our Philosophy
Click the images below to view slides from Cliff Hangers tours
Our Philosophy
Click the images below to view slides from Cliff Hangers tours
clicking the thumbnail image loads a new image into the inline frame

Like frames within framesets, inline frames support the name attribute. This attribute provides a way of targeting the inline frame for hypertext links. For example, if you set the name of an inline frame to docs, the hypertext link

```
View the online <a href="jobs.htm" target="docs">job listings</a>
```

will open the jobs.htm file within the docs inline frame.

Creating an Inline Frame

| Reference Window

- To create an inline frame within a Web page, add the code

```
<iframe src="url" width="value" height="value">
    alternate content
</iframe>
```

where *url* is the URL of the document you want displayed in the inline frame and *alternate content* is content displayed by browsers that don't support inline frames. The width and height attributes define the size of the inline frame in pixels.

- To create a link to an inline frame, first add the name attribute

```
<iframe src="url" width="value" height="value" name="name">
    alternate content
</iframe>
```

to the <iframe>, where *name* is the name of the inline frame. Then, add the name of the frame to the hypertext link as follows:

```
<a href="url" target="name"> text </a>
```

The linked document will then appear within the *name* inline frame.

To create the inline frame:

1. Open the **philosph.htm** file in your text editor.
2. Scroll down to the leftCol div container and locate the inline image for the philosph1.jpg file.
3. Directly after the opening <div id="leftCol"> tag, insert the following opening <iframe> tag:

<iframe src="philosph1.jpg" name="slide" width="380" height="260"
scrolling="no" marginwidth="0" marginheight="0"
frameborder="0">

4. Directly below the inline image for the philosph1.jpg file, insert the closing **</iframe>** tag, as shown in Figure 8-36.

Creating an inline frame | Figure 8-36

```
<div id="leftCol">
   <iframe src="philosph1.jpg" name="slide" width="380" height="260"
           scrolling="no" marginwidth="0" marginheight="0" frameborder="0">

      <img src="philosph1.jpg" alt="" width="380" height="260" />

   </iframe>

   <p>Click the images below to view slides from Cliff Hangers tours<br />
      <img src="slides.jpg" alt="" width="380" height="73" />
   </p>
```

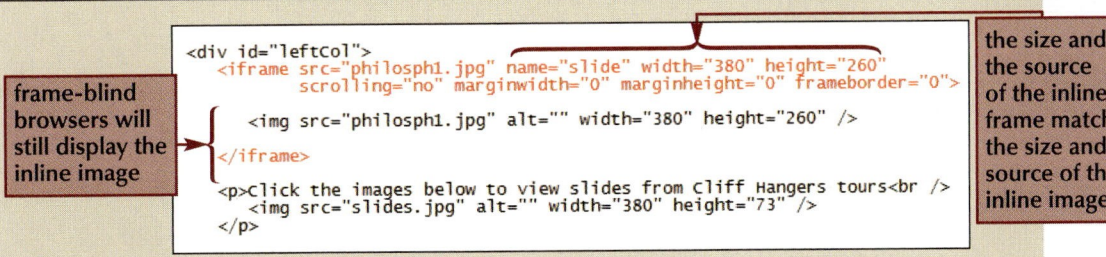

frame-blind browsers will still display the inline image

the size and the source of the inline frame match the size and source of the inline image

5. Save your changes to the file and then reload the **cliff.htm** file in your Web browser. Click the **Our Philosophy** link from the links frame and verify that the Our Philosophy page still displays the philosph1.jpg image.

Tip

To replace an inline image with an inline frame, match the size of the frame to the size of the image and remove any internal margins and frame borders.

Because you sized the inline frame to match the size of the inline image and removed the frame border and internal margins, you should not see any difference between the appearance of the inline frame and the appearance of the inline image. Note that you've given the inline image the name slide. Like the other frames in this tutorial, you must assign the inline frame name so that it can be a target for hypertext links in other documents.

Next you'll create an image map for the image containing the thumbnail versions of the high-resolution images. Recall from Tutorial 2 that image maps are created using the map and area elements. For the thumbnail images, each image map hot spot can be defined using a rectangular shape. Figure 8-37 shows the coordinates of the four rectangular hot spots.

Figure 8-37 **Rectangular hot spots in the thumbnail images**

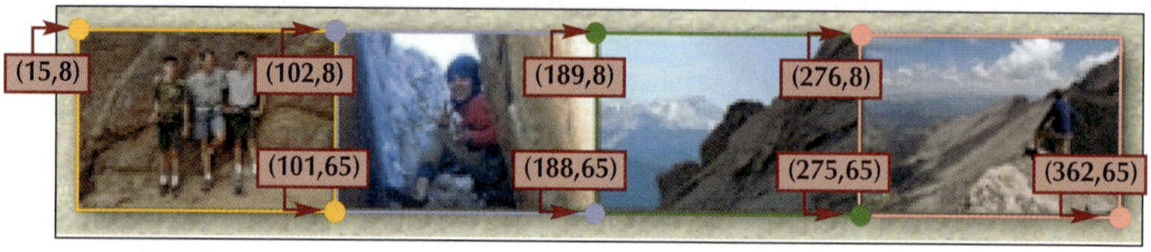

The area elements corresponding to these four hot spots are:

```
<area shape="rect" coords="15,8,101,65" href="philosph1.jpg" />
<area shape="rect" coords="102,8,188,65" href="philosph2.jpg" />
<area shape="rect" coords="189,8,275,65" href="philosph3.jpg" />
<area shape="rect" coords="276,8,362,65" href="philosph4.jpg" />
```

To have each hot spot open the high-resolution jpeg image within the inline frame, you also must add the attribute

```
target="slide"
```

to the <area> tag because you named the inline frame with the slide target name. Debbie wants you to add the image map to the philosph.htm file using the hot spots listed above.

To create an image map for the thumbnail images:

1. Within the **philosph.htm** file, scroll down to the slides.jpg inline image and insert the following attributes:

   usemap="#thumbmap" style="border-width: 0px"

2. Directly below the inline image, insert the following thumbmap image map:

```
<map name="thumbmap" id="thumbmap">
   <area shape="rect" coords="15,8,101,65" href="philosph1.jpg"
         target="slide" />
   <area shape="rect" coords="102,8,188,65" href="philosph2.jpg"
         target="slide" />
   <area shape="rect" coords="189,8,275,65" href="philosph3.jpg"
         target="slide" />
   <area shape="rect" coords="276,8,362,65" href="philosph4.jpg"
         target="slide" />
</map>
```

Figure 8-38 highlights the revised code for the file.

Figure 8-38 Adding the image map for the inline frame

```
<div id="leftcol">
  <iframe src="philosph1.jpg" name="slide" width="380" height="260"
          scrolling="no" marginwidth="0" marginheight="0" frameborder="0">

     <img src="philosph1.jpg" alt="" width="380" height="260" />

  </iframe>

  <p>Click the images below to view slides from Cliff Hangers tours<br />
     <img src="slides.jpg" alt="" width="380" height="73"
        usemap="#thumbmap" style="border-width: 0px" />

     <map name="thumbmap" id="thumbmap">
        <area shape="rect" coords="15,8,101,65" href="philosph1.jpg" target="slide" />
        <area shape="rect" coords="102,8,188,65" href="philosph2.jpg" target="slide" />
        <area shape="rect" coords="189,8,275,65" href="philosph3.jpg" target="slide" />
        <area shape="rect" coords="276,8,362,65" href="philosph4.jpg" target="slide" />
     </map>
  </p>
```

3. Close the **philosph.htm** file, saving your changes.
4. Reload the **cliff.htm** file in your Web browser and click the **Our Philosophy** link.
5. Click each of the four thumbnail images and verify that the Web page displays the corresponding image in the inline frame above the row of thumbnails.
6. You can close any open files or programs now.

Keeping Pages Within Their Frames | InSight

In a frame-based layout, ideally you want all of your Web pages to be accessed only within the context of the frameset. However, with Web search engines such as Google and Yahoo!, this might not always be the case. For example, a user might enter your Web site not from the home page containing the frameset but from another page, thereby bypassing the frame layout you created for all the pages in your Web site. Accessing the Web page outside of its frame context can make it difficult for the user to navigate through the rest of your Web site, especially if you've placed all of your hypertext links on another page.

One way to avoid this problem is to force browsers to always access your Web site through the frameset. You can do this by running a short JavaScript program. JavaScript is a programming language developed for use with HTML and Web browsers. Use the code

```
<script type="text/javascript">
  if (top.location == self.location) top.location = "frame.htm";
</script>
```

in the head section of any document within the site, where *frame.htm* is the file containing the frameset. When the browser attempts to open the page outside of the frameset, this code will force the browser to open the frame.htm file instead. This code can also be used with documents that should only appear within an inline frame. In that case, frame.htm is the Web page containing the inline frame and the code prevents documents from appearing outside of the inline frame.

You've completed your work for Debbie and the Cliff Hangers Climbing School. Using frames, you've created an interesting presentation that is both attractive and easy to navigate. Debbie is pleased and will get back to you if she needs any additional work done.

Review | Session 8.2 Quick Check

1. When you click a link inside a frame, in what frame does the target Web page appear by default?
2. What attribute would you use to assign the name Address to a frame?
3. What attribute would you add to a link to direct it to a frame named News?
4. What attribute would you use to point a link to the document sales.htm, with the result that the sales.htm file is displayed in the entire browser window?
5. What tag would you use to direct all links in a document to the News target?
6. Describe what you would do to make your Web page readable both by browsers that support frames and by those that do not.
7. How would you set the frame border width to 5 pixels?
8. Specify the code to create an inline frame that is 300 pixels wide × 200 pixels high and contains the Web page glossary.htm.

Review | Tutorial Summary

In this tutorial, you learned how to create and use frames. In the first session, you learned how to create a frameset and arrange the frames in rows or columns within a set. You also learned how to specify which document appears within each frame. The first session concluded with a discussion of some of the frame attributes used to control the frame's appearance. The second session explored how to direct a link's target to a specific frame. In addition, you learned some of the other attributes that can be used to format a frame's appearance. The session also showed how to support browsers that don't recognize frames. The tutorial concluded by demonstrating how to create inline frames.

Key Terms

frame (Web design)
frameset
inline frame
reserved target name

Practice | Review Assignments

Practice the skills you learned in the tutorial using the same case scenario.

Data Files needed for the Review Assignments: lefttxt.htm, lessonstxt.htm, links1txt.htm, links2txt.htm, links3txt.htm, middletxt.htm, newlayouttxt.htm, righttxt.htm, 16 HTML files, 4 external style sheets, and 25 graphic files

Debbie has asked you to revise the layout for the Cliff Hangers Web site. She would like the links to appear in separate frames so that users can always click a link for a specific page or collection of pages no matter where they are on the Web site. Figure 8-39 shows a preview of the new frame layout you'll create for her Web site.

Figure 8-39

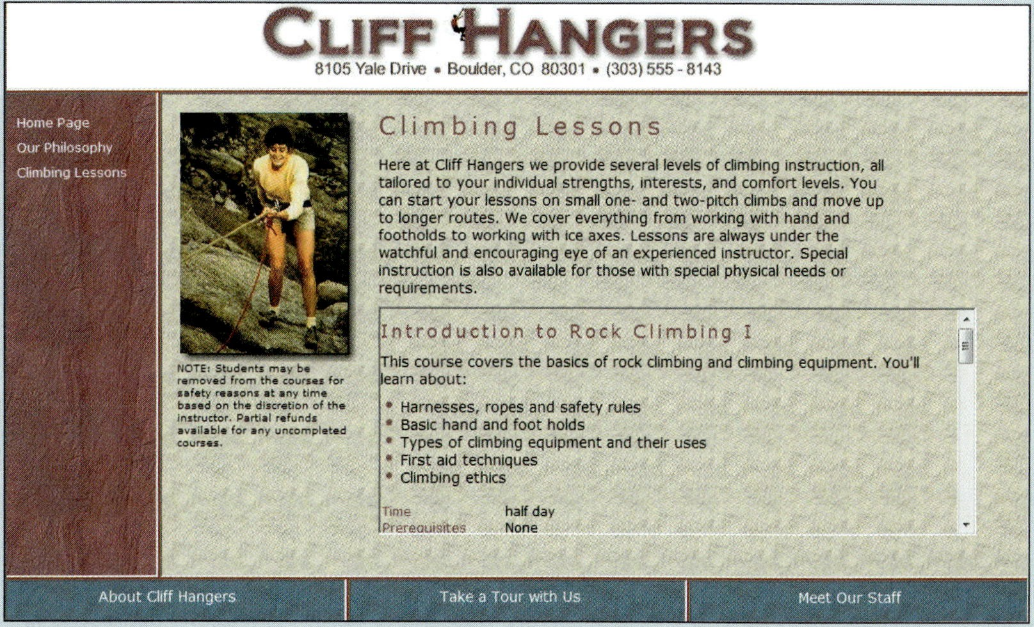

This is a large Web site containing 53 files; however, you'll only have to create the following files in order to complete the frame layout for the site:

- left.htm — a file containing a link to a list of Web pages describing Cliff Hangers
- lessons.htm — a file describing the lessons offered by Cliff Hangers
- links1.htm — a file containing the list of Web pages describing Cliff Hangers
- links2.htm — a file containing the list of tours offered by Cliff Hangers
- links3.htm — a file containing the list of Cliff Hangers staff members
- middle.htm — a file containing a link to the list of tours offered by Cliff Hangers
- newlayout.htm — a frame layout for the Cliff Hangers Web site
- right.htm — a file containing a link to the list of Cliff Hangers staff members

Complete the following:

1. Use your text editor to open the **lefttxt.htm**, **lessonstxt.htm**, **links1txt.htm**, **links2txt.htm**, **links3txt.htm**, **middletxt.htm**, **newlayouttxt.htm**, and **righttxt.htm** from the tutorial.08\review folder included with your Data Files. Enter ***your name*** and ***the date*** in the comment section of each file and save them as **left.htm**, **lessons.htm**, **links1.htm**, **links2.htm**, **links3.htm**, **middle.htm**, **newlayout.htm**, and **right.htm**, respectively, in the same folder.

2. Go to the **newlayout.htm** file in your text editor. This file will contain the frame layout for the Cliff Hangers Web site. Create a frameset consisting of three rows. Set the height of the first row to 85 pixels, set the height of the third row to 40 pixels, and let the second row occupy the remaining space between the first and third rows. Set the border color of the frameset to brown.
3. Within the frameset, insert a frame and nest two more framesets. Name the frame top and display the head.htm file within it. Set the margin height of the frame to 0 pixels. Set the first frameset to display two columns, with the first column 150 pixels wide and the second column occupying the remaining space. Set the second frameset to display three columns of equal width.
4. Within the first nested frameset, insert two frames named links and docs. Set the margin width of both frames to 0 pixels. Display the links1.htm file in the first frame and the home.htm file in the second frame.
5. Within the second nested frameset, insert three frames containing the files left.htm, middle.htm, and right.htm. Name the frames left, middle, and right. Set the margin width of all frames to 0 pixels.
6. Within the head section of the file, insert a link to the **noframes.css** style sheet.
7. For browsers incapable of displaying frames, have the file display page contents copied from the **noframes.htm** file. Remember to include the opening and closing <body> tags.
8. Close the file, saving your changes to the file.
9. Go to the **links1.htm** file in your text editor. Set the default target for all links in the file to the docs frame. Close the file, saving your changes.
10. Repeat Step 9 for the **links2.htm** and **links3.htm** files.
11. Go to the **left.htm** file in your text editor. Set the target of the hypertext link in the file to the links frame. Close the file, saving your changes.
12. Repeat Step 11 for the **middle.htm** and **right.htm** files.
13. Go to the **lessons.htm** file in your text editor. Deb wants to insert an inline frame within this file, displaying a list of lessons offered by Cliff Hangers. At the bottom of the page, insert an inline frame in which to display the **lessonlist.htm** file. Set the width of the inline frame to 600 pixels wide × 220 pixels high.
14. For browsers that do not support inline frames, have the browsers display a hypertext link pointing to the **lessonslist.htm** file.
15. Close the **lessons.htm** file, saving your changes.
16. Open the **newlayout.htm** file in your Web browser. Verify that you can view all of the Web pages from the Cliff Hangers site within the appropriate frames.
17. Go to the **Climbing Lessons** page on the Web site and verify that the list of climbing lessons appears within an inline frame with a vertical scroll bar.
18. Submit your completed files to your instructor.

Apply | Case Problem 1

Apply your knowledge of frames to create a politics Web site.

Data Files needed for this Case Problem: belknap.htm, carroll.htm, cheshire.htm, coos.htm, elections.htm, grafton.htm, hillsborough.htm, maptxt.htm, merrimack.htm, nhmap.jpg, nhplogo.jpg, nhpolytxt.htm, notestxt.htm, poli.css, rockingham.htm, statewide.htm, strafford.htm, sullivan.htm, and title.htm

NH PoliWeb Kevin Unger runs a Web site in New Hampshire called NH PoliWeb, which provides articles and news on New Hampshire politics. On part of his Web site, Kevin wants to post recent election results for statewide offices broken down by county. He's decided to use a frame layout with an image map of the New Hampshire counties in one frame and the election results in another. He's asked for your help in creating the frame design. Figure 8-40 shows a preview of the Web site you'll create for Kevin.

Figure 8-40

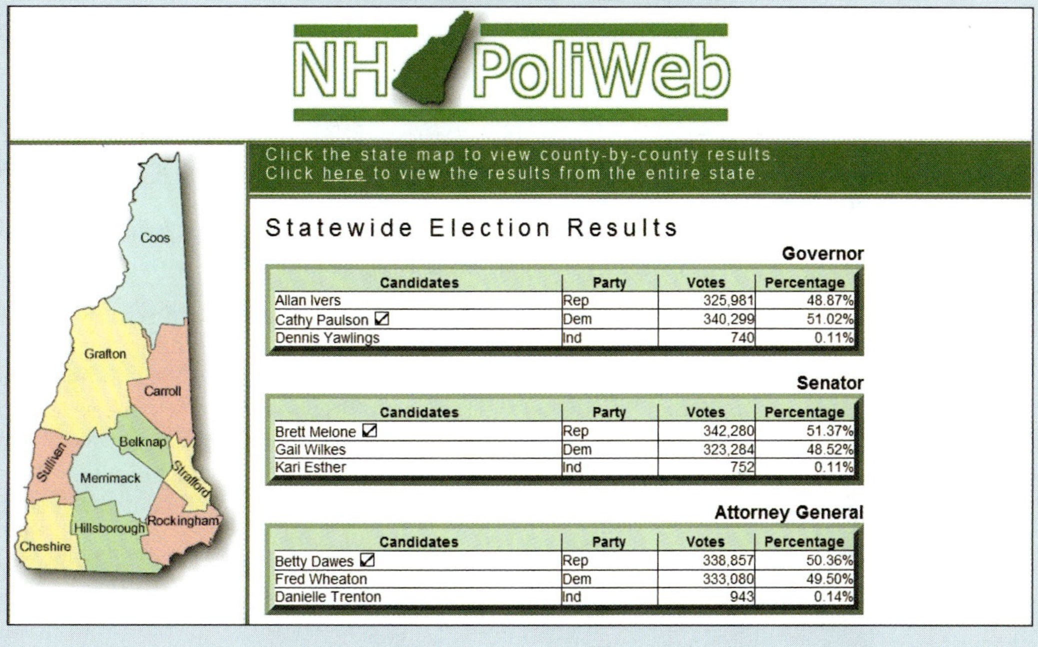

Complete the following:

1. Use your text editor to open **maptxt.htm**, **nhpolytxt.htm**, and **notestxt.htm** from the tutorial.08\case1 folder included with your Data Files. Enter ***your name*** and ***the date*** in the comment section of each file. Save the files as **map.htm**, **nhpoly.htm**, and **notes.htm**, respectively, in the same folder.
2. Go to the **nhpoly.htm** file in your text editor. Create a frameset that consists of two rows, with the top row set at 130 pixels and the bottom row occupying the remaining space in the browser window. Set the frame border color to green.
3. Display the title.htm file in the first frame of the frameset. Set the margin width of the frame to 0 pixels and name the frame top.
4. Nest a second frameset within the first frameset consisting of two columns, with the left column set at 235 pixels wide and the right column occupying the remaining space in the browser window.
5. Display the map.htm file in the first frame of the nested frameset. Name the frame links and set the margin width to 0 pixels.

6. Nest a third frameset within the main frameset, consisting of two rows. Set the width of the first row to 50 pixels and the second row to whatever space is left in the browser window.
7. Display the notes.htm file in the first frame. Name the frame notes and set the margin width to 0 pixels. Name the second frame documents and display the statewide.htm file in it. Set the margin width to 0.
8. For browsers that don't support frames, display the page content copied from the elections.htm file.
9. Save your changes to the **nhpoly.htm** file.
10. Return to the **map.htm** file in your text editor. Set the default target of all hypertext links in the file to the documents frame. Save your changes to the file.
11. Return to the **notes.htm** file in your text editor. Set the target of the hypertext link in the file to the documents frame. Save your changes to the file.
12. Open **nhpoly.htm** in your Web browser. Verify that the frame layout resembles that shown in Figure 8-40. Also verify that all the links open in the documents frame.
13. Submit your completed files to your instructor.

Apply | Case Problem 2

Apply your knowledge of frames to create inline frames for photos on a realty Web site.

Data Files needed for this Case Problem: back.jpg, brlogo.jpg, browyer.css, img01.jpg - img13.jpg, l20481.jpg, listingtxt.htm, and pback.jpg

Browyer Realty Linda Browyer is the owner of Browyer Realty, a real estate company in Owatonna, Minnesota. She's asked you to help her design a Web page for her current listings. Linda envisions a Web page that displays basic information about a listing, including the owner's description. She would like to have several photos of the listing on the page; but rather than cluttering up the layout with several images, she would like users to be able to view different images by clicking a link on the page. Linda wants the images to open within the listing page, not on a separate Web page. Figure 8-41 shows a preview of the page you'll create for Linda.

Figure 8-41

Complete the following:

1. Use your text editor to open **listingtxt.htm** from the tutorial.08\case2 folder included with your Data Files. Enter ***your name*** and ***the date*** in the comment section of the file and save it as **listing.htm**.
2. Locate the inline image for the img01.jpg file (it's floated off the left side of the second paragraph). Use this image as the alternate content for an inline frame, enclosing the image within an inline frame with the following attributes:
   - The source of the frame is the img01.jpg file.
   - The name of the frame is slide.
   - The frame is 300 pixels wide and 225 pixels high.
   - The frame's internal margin width and height are 0 pixels.
   - Do not display scroll bars around the frame.
3. Insert a comment above the floating frame indicating its purpose on the Web page.
4. Change each of the 13 entries in the list of photos to a link. Direct the first entry to img01.jpg, the second entry to img02.jpg, and so forth.
5. Direct the 13 links you created in the previous step to the inline frame (named slide in Step 2).
6. Save your changes to the file.
7. Using your Web browser, open **listing.htm**. Verify that each link displays a different photo on the Web page and that the rest of the page remains unchanged.
8. Submit your completed files to your instructor.

Challenge | Case Problem 3

Explore how to nest inline frames to create an interactive slide show for an astronomy Web site.

Data Files needed for this Case Problem: messtxt.htm, mxxtxt.htm, 9 HTML files, 2 external style sheets, and 22 graphic files

SkyWeb Astronomy Dr. Andrew Weiss of Central Ohio University maintains an astronomy page called SkyWeb for his students. On his Web site, he discusses many aspects of astronomy and observing. One of the pages he wants your help with involves the Messier catalog, which is a list of deep sky objects of particular interest to astronomers and amateur observers.

Dr. Weiss wants his page to contain a slide show of various Messier objects, displaying both a photo of the object and a text box describing the object's history and features. He wants his users to be able to click a forward or backward button to move through the slide show, and he wants the rest of the Web page to remain unchanged as users view the presentation. Figure 8-42 shows a preview of the page that Dr. Weiss wants to create.

Figure 8-42

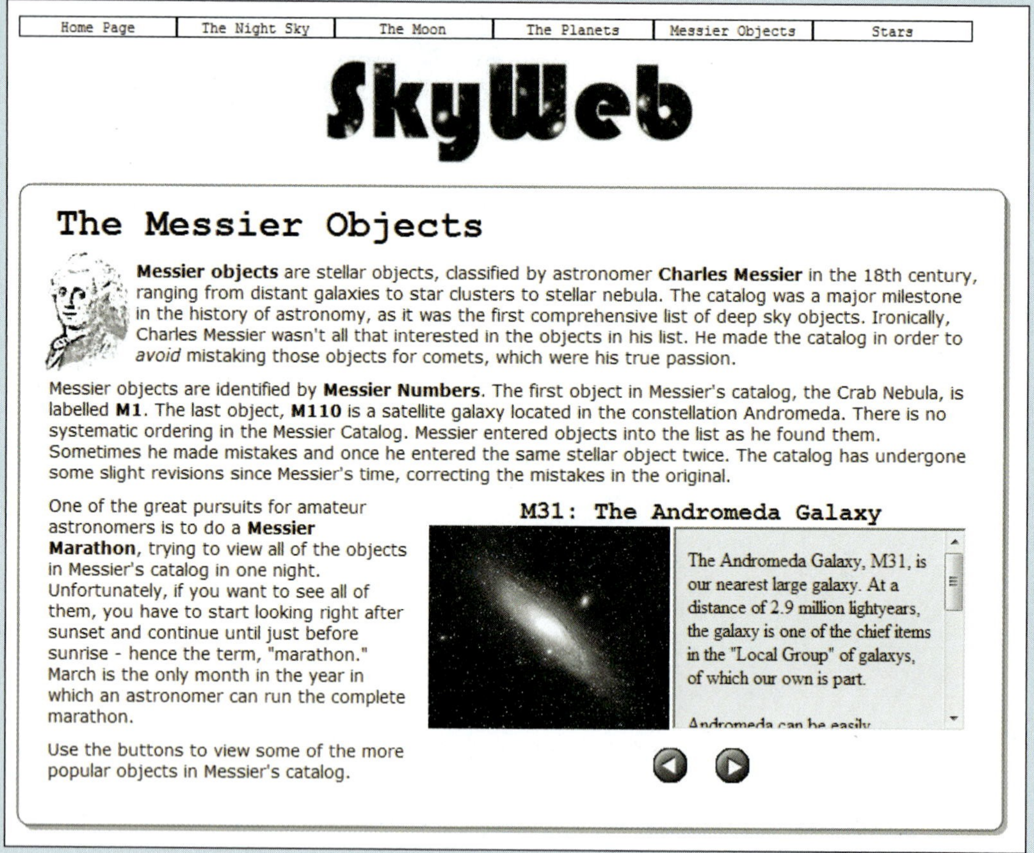

To create a presentation like this, you can nest one inline frame inside of another. Dr. Weiss has created the text you need for the Web site. Your job is to create the frames needed to complete the Web page.

Complete the following:

1. Using your text editor, open **mxxtxt.htm** from the tutorial.08\case3 folder included with your Data Files. This file will act as a model for pages that display descriptions and images of the Messier objects. You'll start by using this file to create the page for Messier object M01. Enter ***your name*** and ***the date*** in the comment section of this file and save the file as **m01.htm** in the same folder.
2. Replace the text of the page title and the h1 heading with M01: The Crab Nebula.
3. Replace the inline image mxx.jpg with the image file **m01.jpg**.
4. Replace the inline image mxxdesc.jpg with an inline frame with the same id name and dimensions. Set the source of the inline frame to the **m01desc.htm** file.
5. Copy the page content (excluding the opening and closing <body> tags) from the **m01desc.htm** file and paste that content within the inline frame to provide alternate text for browsers that don't support inline frames.
6. Point the hypertext link for the Previous button to the file **m57.htm**. (You'll create this file shortly.)
7. Point the hypertext link for the Next button to the file **m13.htm**. (This is another file you'll create shortly.)
8. Close the file, saving your changes.
9. **EXPLORE** Using your work on the m01.htm file as a guide, use your text editor with the **mxxtxt.htm** file to create similar Web pages for the other eight Messier objects. Save the files as **m13.htm**, **m16.htm**, **m20.htm**, **m27.htm**, **m31.htm**, **m42.htm**, **m51.htm**, and **m57.htm**. Be sure to enter ***your name*** and ***the date*** in the comment section of each file. The titles for these pages are:
   - M13: Hercules Globular Cluster
   - M16: The Eagle Nebula
   - M20: The Trifid Nebula
   - M27: The Dumbbell Nebula
   - M31: The Andromeda Galaxy
   - M42: The Orion Nebula
   - M51: The Whirlpool Galaxy
   - M57: The Ring Nebula

   The inline frame for each page should point to the file containing descriptive text on the Messier object. For example, the floating frame for the m13.htm file should display the m13desc.htm file, and so forth.

   The Previous and Next buttons on each page should point to the previous and next Messier object files. For example, the buttons in m27.htm should point to m20.htm and m31.htm. The Next button for m57.htm should point to m01.htm. Save your changes to all the files, and then close them.
10. Use your text editor to open the **messtxt.htm** file. Enter ***your name*** and ***the date*** in the comment section of the file. Save the file as **messier.htm**.
11. Scroll down to the div container with the slide show id. Within the id, insert an inline frame with the following properties:
    - Set the source of the frame to the **m01.htm** file.
    - Set the frame dimensions to 460 pixels wide × 240 pixels high.
    - Set the internal margins to 0 pixels.
    - Set the width of the frame border to 0 pixels.
    - For browsers that don't display inline frames, display a text message indicating that they need inline frames to view the slide show and include a hypertext link to the **m01.htm** file.

EXPLORE 12. Save your changes to the file, and then open **messier.htm** in your Web browser. Click the Previous and Next buttons and verify that you can navigate through the list of Messier objects without disturbing the rest of the Web page. Verify that you can use the scroll bars around the description box to view descriptions of each object.

EXPLORE 13. Return to the **m01.htm** file in your text editor. Add code to the head section of the document to force the file to always appear within the inline frame of the messier.htm file.

14. Repeat Step 13 for **m13.htm**, **m16.htm**, **m20.htm**, **m27.htm**, **m31.htm**, **m42.htm**, **m51.htm**, and **m57.htm**.

EXPLORE 15. Attempt to the open the **m01.htm** file in your Web browser. Verify that when you attempt to load the file, the browser automatically opens the **messier.htm** file (with the m01.htm file showing) instead, preventing users from seeing the m01.htm file outside the contents of the rest of the Web site.

16. Submit your completed files to your instructor.

Create | Case Problem 4

Test your knowledge of frames by creating a frame layout for a Shakespeare play.

Data Files needed for this Case Problem: tempa1s1txt.htm, tempa1s2txt.htm, tempa2s1txt.htm, tempa2s2txt.htm, tempa3s1txt.htm, tempa3s2txt.htm, tempa3s3txt.htm, tempa4s1txt.htm, tempa5s1txt.htm, and tempest.jpg

Mansfield Classic Theatre Steve Karls, the director of Mansfield Classic Theatre in Mansfield, Ohio, has come back to you for help on his Web site listing the great plays of classic theatre. He has decided to place the entire text of Shakespeare's *The Tempest* on his Web site. He would like to use a frame layout, with the dialog from the scenes displayed in one frame and a list of links to each scene in the play displayed in another frame. He wants a third frame that displays the logo for the company's production of *The Tempest* and a fourth frame that contains links to sites on the Web containing commentary on William Shakespeare and *The Tempest*. He has already created the HTML files for nine scenes from the play and has created a graphics file containing the logo. He needs your help in creating the frame layout.

Complete the following:

1. Open the **tempa1s1txt.htm** through **tempa5s1txt.htm** files from the tutorial.08\case4 folder in your text editor. Within each file, insert a comment section containing ***your name*** and ***the date***. Save the files as **tempa1s1.htm** through **tempa5s1.htm**, respectively, in the same folder.
2. You are free to design the pages with any styles or content you think will enhance the site. Save any styles in an external style sheet named **ws.css** in the tutorial.08\case4 folder.
3. Use your text editor to create an HTML file named **tempest.htm** that will contain the frame layout for the Web site. Save the file in the tutorial.08\case4 folder included with your Data Files. Enter ***your name*** and ***the date*** in a comment section of the file. Include any other comments you think will aptly document the purpose and content of the file.
4. Use your text editor to create an HTML file named **scenelist.htm** that will contain a list of links to the nine scenes from the five acts of *The Tempest*. Save the file in the tutorial.08\case4 folder. Enter ***your name*** and ***the date*** in a comment section of the file.

5. Use your text editor to create an HTML file named **weblinks.htm** that will contain a list of links to five sites you locate on the Web containing commentary or articles on *The Tempest* or Shakespeare. Save the file in the tutorial.08\case4 folder. Enter ***your name*** and ***the date*** in a comment section of the file.
6. In the **tempest.htm** file, create a frameset layout containing the following four frames:
   - A frame displaying the dialog from a scene in the play
   - A frame displaying the **scenelist.htm** file
   - A frame displaying the logo for the production of *The Tempest* (use the file tempest.jpg)
   - A frame containing the **weblinks.htm** file
7. The layout of the frameset is up to you, but it should be designed so that links to each scene from the play open in the frame displaying the scene dialogue, and links to external Web sites open in the entire browser window, replacing the frameset.
8. For sites that do not support frames, have them display a Web page with the name of the play in an h1 heading and the text "Read an online version of Shakespeare's *The Tempest* from the Mansfield Classic Theatre."

EXPLORE

9. Add JavaScript code to the head section of each page on the Web site so that if a user attempts to open the file in a browser, the browser will load the entire frameset from tempest.htm.
10. Open **tempest.htm** in your Web browser and verify that all of the pages are readable within the frame layout and all of the hypertext links open in the correct frame or browser window.

EXPLORE

11. Open the individual files in your Web browser and verify that the frameset contained within the **tempest.htm** file opens instead.
12. Submit your completed files to your instructor.

Review | Quick Check Answers

Session 8.1

1. A frame is a section of a browser window capable of displaying the contents of an entire Web page. Frames do not require the same information (such as a list of links) to be repeated on multiple pages of a Web site. They also enable a Web designer to update content in one place in order to affect an entire Web site.
2. Because there is no page body in a frame document. The frame document displays the content of other pages.
3. `<frameset rows="200,50%,*"> ... </frameset>`
4. `<frame src="home.htm" />`
5. `<frame src="home.htm" scrolling="no" />`
6. `<frame src="home.htm" marginheight="3" />`
7. 3 pixels
8. `<frame src="home.htm" noresize="noresize" />`

Session 8.2

1. The frame containing the link
2. `name="Address"`
3. `target="News"`
4. `target="_top"`

5. Place the tag <base target="News" /> in the head element of the document.
6. Create a section starting with the <noframes> tag. After the <noframes> tag, enter a <body> tag to identify the text and images you want frame-blind browsers to display. Complete this section with a </body> tag followed by a </noframes> tag.
7. <frameset border="5">
8. <iframe src="glossary.htm" width="300" height="200"></iframe>

Ending Data Files

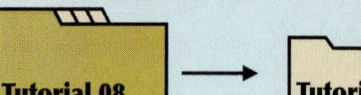

Tutorial.08 →

Tutorial
cliff.htm
links.htm
philosph.htm
tours.htm
+ 17 HTML files
+ 3 style sheets
+ 29 graphic files

Review
left.htm
lessons.htm
links1.htm
links2.htm
links3.htm
middle.htm
newlayout.htm
right.htm
+ 16 HTML files
+ 4 style sheets
+ 25 graphic files

Case1
map.htm
nhpoly.htm
notes.htm
poli.css
+ 13 HTML files
+ 2 graphic files

Case2
browyer.css
listing.htm
+ 17 graphic files

Case3
messier.htm
+ 9 HTML files
+ 2 style sheets
+ 21 graphic files

Case4
scenelist.htm
tempa1s1.htm - tempa5s1.htm
tempest.htm
tempest.jpg
weblinks.htm
ws.css

Objectives

Session 9.1

- Describe the history and theory of XHTML
- Understand the rules for creating valid XHTML documents
- Apply a DTD to an XHTML document
- Understand how to apply the XHTML namespace

Session 9.2

- Test an XHTML document under the transitional DTD
- Test an XHTML document under the strict DTD
- Explore the use of character and parsed character data

Working with XHTML

Creating a Well-Formed, Valid Document

Case | Wizard Works Fireworks

Wizard Works is one of the largest sellers of brand-name and customized fireworks in the central states. Its Web site produces the bulk of the company's sales. Tom Blaska, the head of advertising for Wizard Works, helps develop the content and design of the company's Web site. Because the Web site has been around for many years, some of the code dates back to the earliest versions of HTML. Tom would like the Web site code to be updated to reflect current standards and practices. Specifically, he wants you to look into rewriting the Web site code in XHTML rather than HTML. He also would like you to find ways to verify that the code used by Wizard Works meets XHTML standards.

Starting Data Files

Tutorial.09 →

Tutorial	Review	Case1	Case2	Case3	Case4
dtd_list.txt workstxt.htm wwtxt.css + 4 graphic files	dtd_list.txt founttxt.htm + 2 graphic files	breaktxt.htm dinnrtxt.htm dtd_list.txt lunchtxt.htm + 4 graphic files	dtd_list.txt gargtxt.htm + 5 graphic files	casttxt.htm dtd_list.txt + 6 graphic files hebdtxt.htm hightxt.htm laketxt.htm scottxt.htm + 4 HTML files	address.txt astro.txt chem.txt dtd_list.txt + 1 graphic file elect.txt eng.txt physics.txt

Session 9.1

Introducing XHTML

You meet with Tom to discuss upgrading the Wizard Works site to conform to the current standards for XHTML. He has brought files for the site's home page to the meeting and he suggests that you upgrade the home page file to XHTML standards before continuing to the rest of the Web site.

To open the Wizard Works home page:

1. Use your text editor to open the **workstxt.htm** and **wwtxt.css** files from the tutorial.09\tutorial folder included with your Data Files. Enter ***your name*** and ***the date*** in the comment section of each file and save them as **works.htm** and **ww.css**, respectively, in the same folder.
2. Open **works.htm** in your Web browser. Figure 9-1 shows the current layout and design of the page.

Figure 9-1 Wizard Works home page

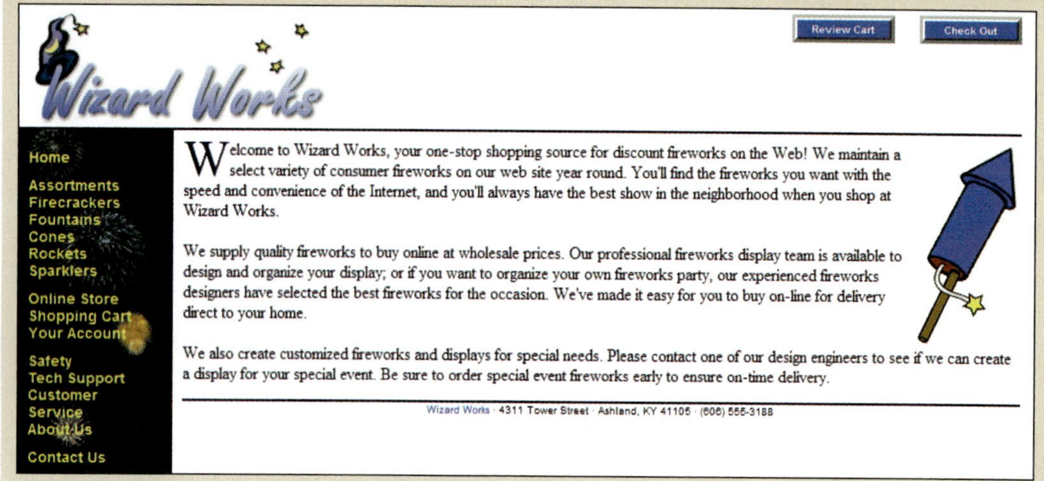

Before you can create your first XHTML document, you should review some of the history of the language. The beginnings of XHTML go back to SGML.

SGML

Standard Generalized Markup Language or **SGML** is a language introduced in 1980 that describes the structure and content of documents or any type of information that is readable by machines. SGML is **device-independent** and **system-independent**, meaning that documents written in SGML can be used, in theory, on almost any type of device under almost any type of operating system. SGML has been and remains the chosen vehicle for creating structured documents in businesses and government organizations of all sizes. Think of the daunting task involved in documenting all of the parts used in a jet airplane while at the same time organizing those documents so that engineers, mechanics, and developers can use them to quickly retrieve and edit information they need. SGML provides tools to manage documentation projects of this magnitude.

However, because of its power, scope, and flexibility, SGML is a difficult language to learn and apply. The official specification for SGML is over 150 pages long and covers some scenarios and cases that are rarely encountered by even the most experienced programmer. This means that the use of SGML is limited to organizations that can afford the cost and overhead of maintaining complex SGML environments. For example, SGML is not intended for the World Wide Web, where Web page authors need a language that is easy to use.

HTML as an SGML Application

SGML is more often used in creating **SGML applications**, which are markup languages that are based on the SGML architecture and that can be applied to specific, not general, types of information. One such SGML application is HTML. Because HTML is an SGML application, it shares several of the properties of SGML, such as device-independence, which is why the same Web page can be rendered by PCs, cell phones, printers, and screen readers.

One problem with HTML that you may have noticed is that various Web browsers developed their own unique flavors of HTML to provide customers with new and useful features not available with other browsers. For example, the Netscape browser saw a need for frames, so it introduced a version of HTML that included the frameset and frame elements, both of which were not part of standard HTML at that time. Likewise, Microsoft saw a need for internal frames and introduced the iframe element into Internet Explorer—another innovation that represented a departure from standard HTML. Although these extensions were later adopted into the official HTML specifications by the World Wide Web Consortium (W3C), many other extensions were not adopted—for example, Internet Explorer's marquee element used to create blocks of scrolling text. The result can sometimes be a confusing mixture of competing HTML standards—one kind of HTML for each browser and, even worse, for each browser version. Although the innovations offered by Netscape, Microsoft, and others certainly increased the scope and power of HTML, they did so at the expense of clarity. Web designers could no longer create Web sites without taking a lot of time and effort to ensure their sites worked across various browsers and browser versions.

A second problem with HTML is that it can be applied inconsistently. For example, the following code does not follow HTML specifications because the h1 element has not been closed with an ending </h1> tag:

```
<body>
   <h1>Web Page Title
</body>
```

Although this code does not follow the correct syntax, most browsers render it correctly. Likewise, the following code would likely be interpreted correctly even though the colspan attribute value is not enclosed in quotation marks:

```
<td colspan=2>Heading</td>
```

Although a browser that is very forgiving of mistakes in syntax might seem beneficial to the Web page designer, it also can cause confusion as different Web pages employ HTML code in markedly different ways. This behavior also affects the browser design. By making allowances for inconsistently applied HTML code, the source code for the browser must be larger and more complex to deal with all contingencies. This can become an issue for browsers that run on handheld devices, which are more limited in the space they allot for software. So it is actually better for everyone if Web page code adheres to certain standards for content and structure. The path to a cleaner version of HTML involved rewriting HTML in terms of XML.

XML and XHTML

Extensible Markup Language or **XML** can be thought of as "SGML light"—a language like SGML used to create markup languages but without SGML's complexity and size. XML has been used to create several markup languages, including MathML for mathematical content, CML for documenting chemical structures, and MusicML for describing musical scores. Individual users can also create their own markup languages tailored for specific needs. For example, a business might design an XML document that contains elements for recording inventory and pricing data. This code

```
<work>
   <work-number>K. 331</work-number>
   <work-title>Piano Sonata in A Major</work-title>
</work>
<identification>
   <creator type="composer">Wolfgang Amadeus Mozart</creator>
   <rights>Copyright 2003 Recordare LLC</rights>
</identification>
```

is an excerpt from a MusicML document describing Mozart's *Piano Sonata in A Major*. Aside from the different tag names, the appearance of this code is very similar to what you've seen with HTML, which is to be expected because both are markup languages. This leads to **XHTML**, which is a reformulation of HTML written in XML. As with HTML and XML, the W3C maintains the specifications and standards for XHTML. The W3C has released or is in the process of developing different versions of XHTML. Figure 9-2 summarizes these versions.

Figure 9-2 **Versions of XHTML**

Version	Date Released	Description
XHTML 1.0	2001	This version is a reformulation of HTML 4.01 in XML and combines the strength of HTML 4.0 with the power of XML. XHTML brings the rigor of XML to Web pages and provides standards for more robust Web content on a wide range of browser platforms.
XHTML 1.1	2002	A minor update to XHTML 1.0 that allows for modularity and simplifies writing extensions to the language.
XHTML 2.0	not yet released	The latest version, designed to remove most of the presentational features left in HTML. XHTML 2.0 is not backward-compatible with XHTML 1.1.
XHTML 5.0	not yet released	A version of HTML 5.0 written under the specifications of XML; unlike XHTML 2.0, XHTML 5.0 will be backward-compatible with XHTML 1.1.

The most widely supported version of XHTML is XHTML 1.0, with the specifications most closely matching the specifications for HTML 4.0 (the latest W3C version of HTML at the time of this writing). XHTML 1.1 is a restructuring of XHTML 1.0 in which different elements are placed within modules. This allows browsers to support only the portions of the XHTML language that are relevant to their needs. Figure 9-3 describes some of the different modules in XHTML 1.1.

Figure 9-3 XHTML 1.1 modules

Module	Use	Supported Elements and Attributes
Structure	Used to define the basic structure of the document	body, head, html, title
Metainformation	Used to add meta-information to the document	meta
Text	Used for text content	abbr, acronym, address, blockquote, br, cite, code, dfn, div, em, h1, h2, h3, h4, h5, h6, kbd, p, pre, q, samp, span, strong, var
Presentation	Used for presentational elements	b, big, hr, i, small, sub, sup, tt
List	Used for list content	dl, dt, dd, ol, ul, li
Object	Used for embedded objects	object, param
Image	Used for inline images	img
Client-side Image Map	Used for client-side image maps	area, map
Hypertext	Used for links	a
Frames	Used for frames	frameset, frame, noframes
Iframe	Used for inline frames	iframe
Forms	Used for Web forms	button, fieldset, form, input, label, legend, select, optgroup, option, textarea
Table	Used for Web tables	caption, col, colgroup, table, tbody, td, tfoot, th, thead, tr
Scripting	Used for adding scripts to the document	noscript, script
Style Sheet	Used for accessing style sheets	style
Style Attribute	Used for adding the style attribute to individual elements	attribute: style attribute (deprecated)
Legacy	Used for deprecated elements and attributes	basefont, center, dir, font, isindex, menu, s, strike, uattributes: align, alink, background, bgcolor, color, face, link, size, text, type, vlink

For example, an aural browser that works only with text might support only modules that deal with text content, and not modules that deal with images or embedded objects. This enables browser developers to reduce the sizes of their applications to fit the requirements of specific devices. Browser developers can also use XHTML Basic, a version of XHTML 1.1 that limits the modules to those useful with handheld devices.

XHTML 2.0 is still in draft form and so it is not supported in the Web community. When completed, this version is expected to represent a great departure from previous versions of XHTML and HTML. In fact, documents written in XHTML 2.0 will not be backward-compatible with earlier XHTML versions—a point that concerns many developers. The development of XHTML 2.0 will likely require the development of new XHTML modules or revisions to existing XHTML modules. For this reason, a great deal of development effort is also going into HTML 5.0 (and its XML version, XHTML 5.0), which will provide more support for multimedia elements as well as features for entering and retrieving data.

In the end, any future version of XHTML must have wide-ranging browser support before it can be easily adopted for general use. Browser support does not occur automatically, nor is acceptance of any revisions to XHTML uniform across all browsers. So even after the specifications for new versions of XHTML are finalized, it will be many years before XHTML 1.0 can be entirely replaced.

Creating an XHTML Document

Because XHTML documents are also considered XML documents, the first line of an XHTML file contains a prolog indicating that the document adheres to the syntax rules of XML. The form of the XML prolog is

```
<?xml version="value" encoding="type" ?>
```

where the version attribute indicates the XML version of the document and the encoding attribute specifies character encoding. XHTML documents are written in XML 1.0. The encoding depends on the character set being used; but unless you are including special international characters, you can set the encoding value to UTF-8 (for a discussion of encoding and character sets, see Tutorial 2). So for most XHTML documents, you can include the following prolog:

```
<?xml version="1.0" encoding="UTF-8" ?>
```

Reference Window | Adding an XML Prolog

- To declare that a document is written in XML, enter
  `<?xml version="value" encoding="type" ?>`
  as the first line of the file, where the version attribute indicates the XML version of the document and the encoding attribute specifies the character encoding.
- For XHTML documents, use the prolog
  `<?xml version="1.0" encoding="UTF-8" ?>`
  where *row1*, *row2*, *row3*, etc. are the heights of the rows in pixels or percentages.

Tip

You can also indicate the encoding used in your XHTML file by adding a meta element to the head section with the content attribute set to the MIME type and character set employed in the document.

The first thing you need to do for Tom's Wizard Works file is to add an XML prolog.

To insert an XML prolog:

1. Return to the **works.htm** file in your text editor.
2. At the top of the file, insert the following XML prolog, as shown in Figure 9-4:

   <?xml version="1.0" encoding="UTF-8" ?>

Figure 9-4 Inserting the XML prolog

```
<?xml version="1.0" encoding="UTF-8" ?>
<html>
<head>
```

3. Save your changes to the file.

Note that the prolog is not strictly required for XHTML documents and can be omitted. You should also be aware that older browsers might not be able to interpret XHTML documents that start with a prolog, though this has become less of a problem in recent years.

Creating Well-Formed Documents

To make XML documents follow specific rules for content and structure, they are evaluated with an XML parser. An **XML parser** is a program that checks the document for errors in syntax and content, and reports any errors it finds. An XML document that employs the correct syntax is known as a **well-formed** document, as shown in Figure 9-5.

Figure 9-5 Testing for well-formedness

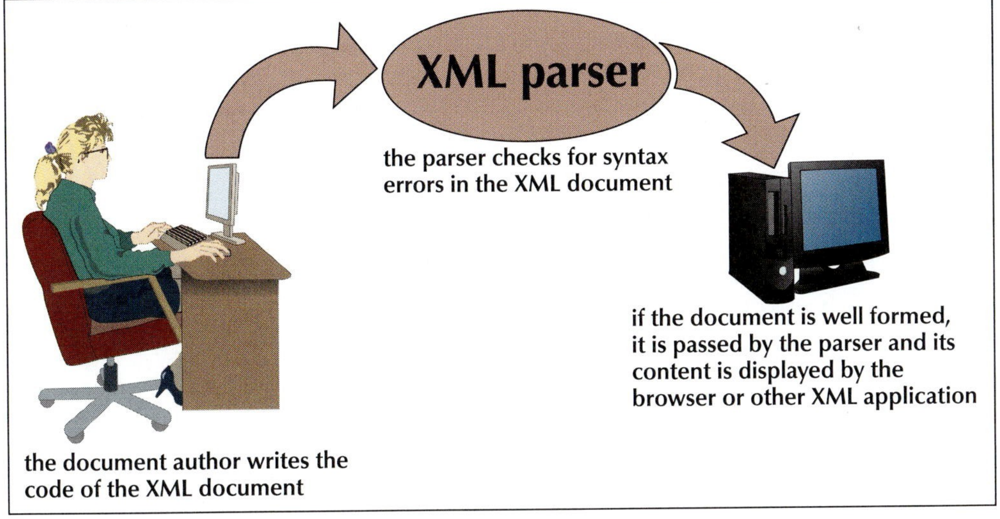
XML parser
the parser checks for syntax errors in the XML document
if the document is well formed, it is passed by the parser and its content is displayed by the browser or other XML application
the document author writes the code of the XML document

With HTML, browsers usually accept documents that violate HTML syntax as long as the violation is not too severe. However, an XML parser will reject any XML document that is not well formed. For example, the sample code described earlier

```
<body>
   <h1>Web Page Title
</body>
```

is not an example of well-formed code because it violates the basic rule that every two-sided tag must have both an opening and closing tag. When you write XHTML code, it's important to be familiar with all of the rules of proper syntax. Figure 9-6 lists seven syntax requirements that all XML documents (and therefore all XHTML documents) must follow.

Figure 9-6 Rules for well-formed XML

Rule	Incorrect	Correct
Element names must be lowercase	`<P>This is a paragraph.</P>`	`<p>This is a paragraph.</p>`
Elements must be properly nested	`<p>This text is <b>bold.</p></b>`	`<p>This text is <b>bold.</b></p>`
All elements must be closed	`<p>This is the first paragraph.` `<p>This is the second paragraph.`	`<p>This is the first paragraph.</p>` `<p>This is the second paragraph.</p>`
Empty elements must be terminated	`This is a line break `	`This is a line break `
Attribute names must be lowercase	`<td ALIGN="right">`	`<td align="right">`
Attribute values must be quoted	`<table width=620>`	`<table width="620">`
Attributes must have values	`<option selected>`	`<option selected="selected">`

In addition to the rules specified in Figure 9-6, all XML documents must also include a single root element that contains all other elements. For XHTML, that root element is the html element. You should already be familiar with most of these rules because you've been working with well-formed HTML from the first tutorial. However, if you examine older Web pages you may find document code that violates that basic syntax, but which most browsers nonetheless support.

In some older HTML documents, you might find cases of **attribute minimization**, a situation in which some attributes lack attribute values. XHTML does not allow attribute minimization. Figure 9-7 lists the minimized attributes that are in some HTML documents, along with their XHTML-compliant versions.

Figure 9-7 **Attribute minimization in HTML and XHTML**

HTML	XHTML
compact	compact="compact"
checked	checked="checked"
declare	declare="declare"
readonly	readonly="readonly"
disabled	disabled="disabled"
selected	selected="selected"
defer	defer="defer"
ismap	ismap="ismap"
nohref	nohref="nohref"
noshade	noshade="noshade"
nowrap	nowrap="nowrap"
multiple	multiple="multiple"
noresize	noresize="noresize"

For example, in earlier versions of HTML, the following code was used to indicate that a radio button should be selected by default:

```
<input type="radio" checked>
```

In XHTML, this code would be rewritten as

```
<input type="radio" checked="checked" />
```

Failure to make this change would cause the XHTML document to be rejected as not well formed.

Tip

A minimized attribute can be updated to XHTML by using the name of the attribute as the attribute's value.

Creating Valid XHTML Documents

In addition to being well formed, XML documents can also be checked to see if they are valid. A **valid** document is a well-formed document that also contains only approved elements, attributes, and other features of the language. If the code

```
<body>
   <mainhead>Web Page Title</mainhead>
</body>
```

were entered into an XHTML file, the code would be considered well formed because it complies with the syntax rules of XML—but it would not constitute valid XHTML code because XHTML does not support the <mainhead> tag. To specify what the correct content and structure is for a document, the developers of an XML-based language can create a collection of rules called the **document type definition** or **DTD**. As shown in Figure 9-8, an XML parser tests the content of the document against the rules in the DTD. If it does not conform to those rules, the parser will reject the document as not valid.

Figure 9-8 Testing for validity

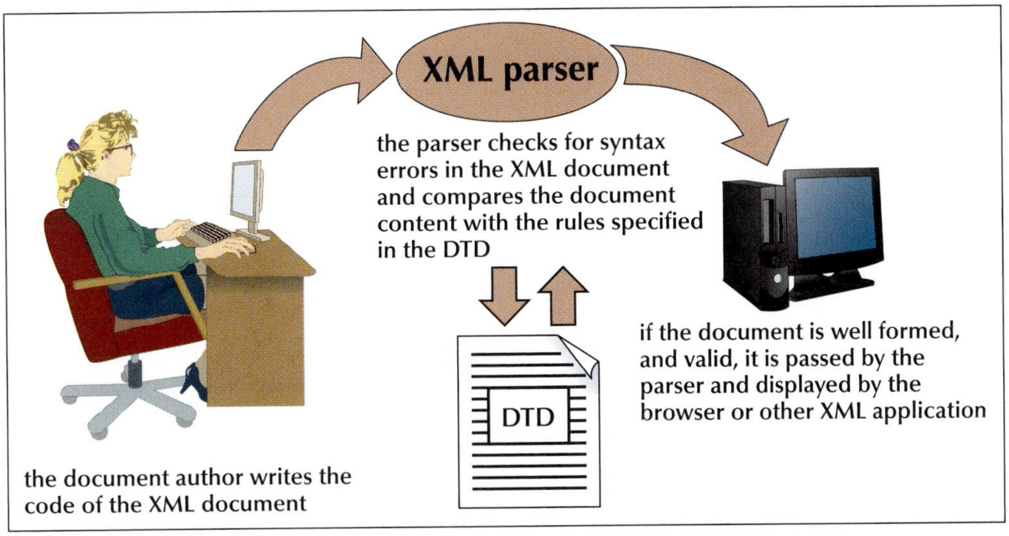
XML parser
the parser checks for syntax errors in the XML document and compares the document content with the rules specified in the DTD
DTD
if the document is well formed, and valid, it is passed by the parser and displayed by the browser or other XML application
the document author writes the code of the XML document

For example, an XML document for a business might contain elements that store the name of each product in inventory. The DTD for that document could require that each product name element be accompanied by an id attribute value, and that no products share the same name or id. An XML parser would reject any XML document for that business that didn't satisfy those rules, even if the document was well formed. In this way, XML differs from HTML which does not include a mechanism to force Web page authors to adhere to rules for syntax and content.

Transitional, Frameset, and Strict DTDs

There are several different DTDs associated with HTML and XHTML documents. Some of the DTDs represent older versions of HTML. For example, if you want to create a document that is validated only against the standards of HTML 2.0, there is a DTD available for that. However, for most purposes you'll focus on the three DTDs used with XHTML 1.0:

- **transitional:** The transitional DTD supports many of the presentational features of HTML, including the deprecated elements and attributes. It is best used for older documents that contain deprecated features.
- **frameset:** The frameset DTD is used for documents containing frames and also supports deprecated elements and attributes.
- **strict:** The strict DTD does not allow any presentational features or deprecated HTML elements and attributes, and does not support frames or inline frames. It is best used for documents that must strictly conform to the latest standards.

If you need to support older browsers, you should use the transitional DTD, which recognizes deprecated elements and attributes such as the font element and the bgcolor attribute. If you need to support older browsers in a framed Web site, you should use the frameset DTD. If you only need to support more current browsers and want to weed out any use of deprecated features, and you have no need to support frames, then you should use the strict DTD.

In addition to browser-specific elements (such as Internet Explorer's marquee element), the following elements are not allowed under the strict DTD:

- applet
- basefont
- center
- dir
- font
- frame
- frameset
- iframe
- isindex
- menu
- noframes
- s
- strike
- u

Note that these elements are allowed in the transitional DTD. The frameset DTD supports these elements as well as the frame, frameset, and noframes elements. Therefore, the code

```
<font color="red">Wizard Works</font>
```

which uses the deprecated font element to format text, would be considered valid code under the transitional and frameset DTDs but not under the strict DTD.

In addition to prohibiting the use of certain elements, the strict DTD also enforces a particular structure on the document. For example, you cannot place a block-level element within an inline element. Figure 9-9 lists the prohibited child elements under the strict DTD.

Figure 9-9 **Child elements prohibited under the strict DTD**

Element	Prohibited Children
inline element	block-level elements
body	a, abbr, acronym, b, bdo, big, br, button, cite, code, dfn, em, i, img, input, kbd, label, map, object, q, samp, select, small, span, strong, sub, sup, textarea, tt, var
button	button, form, fieldset, iframe, input, isindex, label, select, textarea
blockquote	a, abbr, acronym, b, bdo, big, br, button, cite, code, dfn, em, i, img, input, kbd, label, map, object, q, samp, select, small, span, strong, sub, sup, textarea, tt, var
form	a, abbr, acronym, b, bdo, big, br, cite, code, dfn, em, form, i, img, kbd, map, object, q, samp, small, span, strong, sub, sup, tt, var
label	label
pre	big, img, object, small, sub, sup
all other page elements	big, small

For example, the following code would be disallowed under the strict DTD because it places an inline image as a child of the body element:

```
<body>
   <img src="logo.jpg" alt="Wizard Works" />
</body>
```

However, you could make this code compliant with the strict DTD by placing the inline image within a paragraph:

```
<body>
   <p><img src="logo.jpg" alt="Wizard Works" /></p>
</body>
```

The goal of this rule is to enforce the inline nature of the img element. Because an inline image is displayed inline within a block element such as a paragraph, it should not be found outside of that context. For the same reason, form elements like the input or select elements should be found only within a form, not outside of one.

Finally, all three DTDs require that the following elements be present in every valid XHTML document:

- html
- head
- title
- body

Although the html, head, and body elements are generally expected under HTML, XHTML requires that every valid document include the title element as well. Any XHTML document that omits the title element is rejected.

The Valid Use of Attributes

DTDs also include different rules for attributes and their use. Under the strict DTD, deprecated attributes are not allowed. A list of these prohibited attributes with their corresponding elements is displayed in Figure 9-10.

Figure 9-10 Prohibited attributes under the strict DTD

Element	Prohibited Attributes
a	target
area	target
base	target
body	alink, bgcolor, link, text, vlink,
br	clear
caption	align
div	align
dl	compact
form	name, target
h*n*	align
hr	align, noshade, size, width
img	align, border, hspace, name, vspace
input	align
li	type, value
link	target
map	name
object	align, border, hspace, vspace
ol	compact, start
p	align
pre	width
script	language
table	align, bgcolor
td	bgcolor, height, nowrap, width
th	bgcolor, height, nowrap, width
tr	bgcolor
ul	type, compact

Many of the attributes listed in Figure 9-10 are so-called presentational attributes because they define how the browser should render the associated element on the Web page. All of the attributes listed in Figure 9-10 are supported in the transitional and frameset DTDs. Therefore, the code

```
<img src="logo.jpg" alt="Wizard Works" align="left" />
```

which uses the align attribute to float an inline image on the left margin of the page, would not be valid under the strict DTD because the align attribute is prohibited; however, it would be allowed under the frameset and transitional DTDs. To make this code valid under all three DTDs, you could replace the align attribute with an inline style that employs the float style:

```
<img src="logo.jpg" alt="Wizard Works" style="float: left" />
```

You may also find that you must make changes to older HTML code in the use of the name attribute. The strict DTD requires the use of the id attribute in place of the name attribute, so the tags

```
<a name="top">
<form name="order">
```

```
<img name="logo" />
<map name="parkmap">
```

would be written in strict XHTML as

```
<a id="top">
<form id="order">
<img id="logo" />
<map id="parkmap">
```

Finally, unlike the transitional and frameset DTDs, the strict DTD does not support the target attribute. This means that you cannot open links in secondary browser windows if you want your code to be strictly compliant with XHTML. This decision was not greeted with enthusiasm by many developers, so the target attribute was reintroduced in XHTML 1.1 as part of the Target module. If your users' browsers support XHTML 1.1 and the Target module, you can use the target attribute in all of your links.

Whereas some attributes are prohibited, others are required. A list of the required attributes and the elements they're associated with is shown in Figure 9-11.

Tip

The transitional and frameset DTDs also require the use of the id attribute, but do not reject documents that contain both the name and id attributes. For those DTDs, it's best to include both attributes if you want to make your code backward-compatible.

Required XHTML attributes — **Figure 9-11**

Element	Required Attributes
applet	height, width
area	alt
base	href
basefont	size
bdo	dir
form	action
img	alt, src
map	id
meta	content
optgroup	label
param	name
script	type
style	type
textarea	cols, rows

For example, an inline image is valid only if it contains both the src and alt attributes, and a form element is valid only if it contains an action attribute.

Although the list of rules for well-formed and valid documents may seem long and onerous, they simply reflect good coding practice. You would not, for example, want to create a Web page without a page title, or an inline image without alternate text. In addition to being required for valid well-formed code, there are many advantages to using DTDs. Perhaps their most significant advantage is the help they provide in troubleshooting documents. If you create or edit your XHTML code by hand, you can easily make mistakes in syntax, content, or structure. Using a DTD enables you to test your document and correct any mistakes.

Inserting the DOCTYPE Declaration

To specify which DTD is used by the XHTML document, you add a DOCTYPE declaration directly after the XML prolog. The syntax of the DOCTYPE declaration for a general XML document is

```
<!DOCTYPE root type "id" "url">
```

where *root* is the name of the root element of the document, *type* identifies the type of DTD (either PUBLIC or SYSTEM), *id* is an id associated with the DTD, and *url* is the location of an external file containing the DTD rules. For XHTML documents, you set the value *root* to html and the *type* value to PUBLIC. Web browsers do not need to store the location of the external file containing the rules of any of the three DTDs. Therefore, the DOCTYPE declaration for XHTML documents has the simpler form

```
<!DOCTYPE html PUBLIC "id">
```

where *id* is the id for the DTD. Figure 9-12 lists the complete DOCTYPE declarations for different versions of HTML and XHTML. Note that you can validate a document not only against different versions of XHTML 1.0, but even down to the W3C's specifications for HTML 2.0, which can be beneficial if you need to develop code for older browser versions. You can access the most recent versions of these DTDs on the W3C Web site.

Figure 9-12 **DOCTYPE declarations for different versions of HTML and XHTML**

DTD	DOCTYPE
HTML 2.0	<!DOCTYPE html PUBLIC "-//IETF//DTD HTML 2.0//EN">
HTML 3.2	<!DOCTYPE html PUBLIC "-//W3C//DTD HTML 3.2 Final//EN">
HTML 4.01 strict	<!DOCTYPE html PUBLIC "-//W3C//DTD HTML 4.01//EN" "http://www.w3.org/TR/html4/strict.dtd">
HTML 4.01 transitional	<!DOCTYPE html PUBLIC "-//W3C//DTD HTML 4.01 Transitional//EN" "http://www.w3.org/TR/html4/loose.dtd">
HTML 4.01 frameset	<!DOCTYPE html PUBLIC "-//W3C//DTD HTML 4.01 Frameset//EN" "http://www.w3.org/TR/html4/frameset.dtd">
XHTML 1.0 strict	<!DOCTYPE html PUBLIC "-//W3C//DTD XHTML 1.0 Strict//EN" "http://www.w3.org/TR/xhtml1/DTD/xhtml1-strict.dtd">
XHTML 1.0 transitional	<!DOCTYPE html PUBLIC "-//W3C//DTD XHTML 1.0 Transitional//EN" "http://www.w3.org/TR/xhtml1/DTD/xhtml1-transitional.dtd">
XHTML 1.0 frameset	<!DOCTYPE html PUBLIC "-//W3C//DTD XHTML 1.0 Frameset//EN" "http://www.w3.org/TR/xhtml1/DTD/xhtml1-frameset.dtd">
XHTML 1.1	<!DOCTYPE html PUBLIC "-//W3C//DTD XHTML 1.1//EN" "http://www.w3.org/TR/xhtml11/DTD/xhtml11.dtd">

Setting the Document DTD

| Reference Window

- To apply the XHTML 1.0 strict DTD, add the following line after the XML declaration:
```
<!DOCTYPE html PUBLIC "-//W3C//DTD XHTML 1.0 Strict//EN"
 "http://www.w3.org/TR/xhtml1/DTD/xhtml1-strict.dtd">
```
- To apply the XHTML 1.0 transitional DTD, use the following:
```
<!DOCTYPE html PUBLIC "-//W3C//DTD XHTML 1.0 Transitional//EN"
 "http://www.w3.org/TR/xhtml1/DTD/xhtml1-transitional.dtd">
```
- To apply the XHTML 1.0 frameset DTD, use the following:
```
<!DOCTYPE html PUBLIC "-//W3C//DTD XHTML 1.0 Frameset//EN"
 "http://www.w3.org/TR/xhtml1/DTD/xhtml1-frameset.dtd">
```

Tom suggests that you associate the Wizard Works Web site with the transitional DTD for XHTML 1.0. To do that, you'll add the DOCTYPE declaration for XHTML 1.0 transitional. Because the code for the DOCTYPE declaration can be long and complicated, a text file with the declarations from Figure 9-12 has been created for you to copy from.

To insert a DOCTYPE declaration:

1. In your text editor, open the **dtd_list.txt** file from the tutorial.09\tutorial folder included with your Data Files.
2. Copy the DOCTYPE declaration for the XHTML 1.0 transitional DTD—the third DTD from the bottom of the file.
3. Close the file and return to the **works.htm** file in your text editor.
4. Directly after the XML prolog, paste the copied DOCTYPE declaration. Figure 9-13 highlights the revised code in the file.

Figure 9-13 **Inserting the DOCTYPE declaration**

```
<?xml version="1.0" encoding="UTF-8" ?>

<!DOCTYPE html PUBLIC "-//W3C//DTD XHTML 1.0 Transitional//EN"
  "http://www.w3.org/TR/xhtml1/DTD/xhtml1-transitional.dtd">

<html>
<head>
```

5. Save your changes to the file.

Setting the XHTML Namespace

Another modification you can make to the works.htm file is to add a namespace declaration to the html element. Understanding the concept of a namespace requires looking more into how XML operates. As was noted earlier, XHTML is only one of hundreds of languages built on the foundation of XML. For example, another XML-based language, MathML, is used for documents containing mathematical content, symbols, equations, and operations. For a math professor interested in creating a Web site, MathML provides many elements and attributes not available with HTML or XHTML. It would be useful for the professor to have a document language that combined features from both XHTML and MathML.

Recall from the history of HTML that browser developers dealt with the issue of needing new features in their documents by adding extensions to the HTML language. XML (and through it, XHTML) deals with this problem by allowing elements and attributes from several different XML-based languages to be combined within a single document. Ideally, therefore, our math professor could combine elements of XHTML and MathML in his document without having to invent a new language or modify the specifications of an old one.

The problem is that you need a way of identifying which element goes with which language. This is done by using namespaces. A **namespace** is a unique identifier for the elements and attributes originating from one particular language, such as XHTML or MathML. There are two types of namespaces: default and local. For now you'll only focus on the default namespace. A **default namespace** is the namespace that is assumed to be applied to the root element and any element within it—which includes, by default, any element within the document. To declare a default namespace, you add the xmlns (XML namespace) attribute

```
<root xmlns="namespace">
```

to the markup tag for the document's root element, where *root* is the name of the root element and *namespace* is the namespace id. Every XML-based language has a namespace id. For example, if you wish to declare that the elements in your document belong to the XHTML namespace by default, you would add the following attribute to the opening <html> tag:

```
<html xmlns="http://www.w3.org/1999/xhtml">
```

The namespace id for XHTML looks like a url, but it's not treated as one by the XML parser. The id can actually be any string of characters as long as it uniquely identifies the document namespace. For XHTML, it was decided to use http://www.w3.org/1999/xhtml as the unique identifier.

Reference Window | Setting the XHTML Namespace

- To set XHTML as the default namespace for a document, add the xmlns attribute to the html element with the following value:

```
<html xmlns="http://www.w3.org/1999/xhtml">
```

If you don't intend to combine different XML-based languages within the same document, it's still a good idea to add a namespace to an XHTML file. In practical terms, an XHTML document is still interpretable by most browsers without a namespace. However, the W3C requires that the XHTML namespace be added to the html element to avoid any possible confusion in the future when mixed documents become more prevalent. Tom would like you to add the default namespace to his works.htm file.

To add the XHTML namespace:

1. Locate the opening <html> tag in the **works.htm** file.
2. Within the tag, insert the following attribute, as shown in Figure 9-14:

```
xmlns="http://www.w3.org/1999/xhtml"
```

Figure 9-14 Declaring the XHTML namespace

```
<?xml version="1.0" encoding="UTF-8" ?>

<!DOCTYPE html PUBLIC "-//W3C//DTD XHTML 1.0 Transitional//EN"
  "http://www.w3.org/TR/xhtml1/DTD/xhtml1-transitional.dtd">

<html xmlns="http://www.w3.org/1999/xhtml">
<head>
```

3. Close the file, saving your changes.
4. If you want to take a break before starting the next session, you can close any open files or programs now.

Namespaces in Compound Documents | InSight

One of the features of XML is the ability to combine several languages into a single document. For the elements of the different languages to coexist, you assign one language as the default namespace for the document so that all elements are assumed to belong to that language. Elements that do not belong to the default namespace belong instead to a **local namespace**. The existence of a local namespace is indicated by adding a prefix to the markup tag as follows

```
<prefix:element> ...</prefix:element>
```

where *prefix* is the prefix for the local namespace and *element* is the name of element within that local namespace. For example, the following code contains elements from both XHTML and MathML (the markup language for mathematical documents):

```
<p>
  <ml:mi>x</ml:mi>
  <ml:mo>+</ml:mo>
  <ml:mn>1</ml:mn>
</p>
```

The namespace prefix for MathML is ml, and the MathML element names are mi, mo, and mn. To create a local namespace, you add the attribute

```
xmlns:prefix="namespace"
```

to the html root element, where *prefix* is the prefix you'll use to mark elements in this local namespace and *namespace* is the namespace id. Every XML-based language has a unique namespace id. For example, to declare a local namespace for MathML, you would add the following code to the html element:

```
<html xmlns:ml="http://www.w3.org/1998/math/MathML">
```

Most browsers do not include built-in support to render elements from non-XHTML languages, but you can often add support for different XML-based languages by installing browser add-ins. You can also create style sheets to display non-XHTML elements on your Web page. See your browser's documentation for more information.

With the addition of the XHTML namespace, you have converted the Tom's HTML document into XHTML format. In the next session, you'll test this document to determine whether it passes the W3C tests for well-formedness and validity.

Review | **Session 9.1 Quick Check**

1. What is a well-formed document? What is a valid document?
2. Why is the following code not well formed?:

```
<img src="logo.jpg" alt="Wizard Works">
```

   How would you correct it?

3. Why is the following code not well formed?:

```
<input type="radio" disabled />
```

   How would you correct it?

4. Why is the following code not valid under strict XHTML?:

```
<blockquote>
   For more information go to the <a href="faq.htm"FAQ page</a>
</blockquote>
```

   Suggest a correction for the problem.

5. Why is the following code not valid under strict XHTML?:

```
<img src="logo.jpg" alt="Wizard Works" align="right" />
```

   How would you fix it?

6. Why is the following code not valid under transitional XHTML?:

```
<map name="parkmap"> ... </map>
```

   Suggest a change to the code that would correct the problem and make the code backward-compatible with older browsers.

7. What declaration would you add to an XHTML document to associate it with the XHTML strict DTD?
8. What line do you add to the start of your file to declare it as an XML document?

Session 9.2

Testing under XHTML Transitional

In the last session you converted Tom's Web page document from HTML format into XHTML format. By adding the DOCTYPE declaration and XML namespace, you can test the document for well-formedness and validity. To test the document, you must submit the file to an XML parser. There are several parsers available on the Web. You'll use the one hosted on the W3C Web site.

To access the W3C validator page:

1. Use your browser to open the Web page at **http://validator.w3.org**.
2. Click the **Validate by File Upload** tab on the Web page.

   Trouble? Depending on the current format of the validator page, it might not exactly match the figures and screen shots in this session. Use whatever buttons or forms exist on the Web page.

3. Click the **Browse** button and locate the **works.htm** file from the tutorial.09\tutorial folder included with your Data Files.
4. Select the file and click the **Open** button. The filename and path will be displayed in the File input box, as shown in Figure 9-15.

Figure 9-15 **Selecting a file for validation**

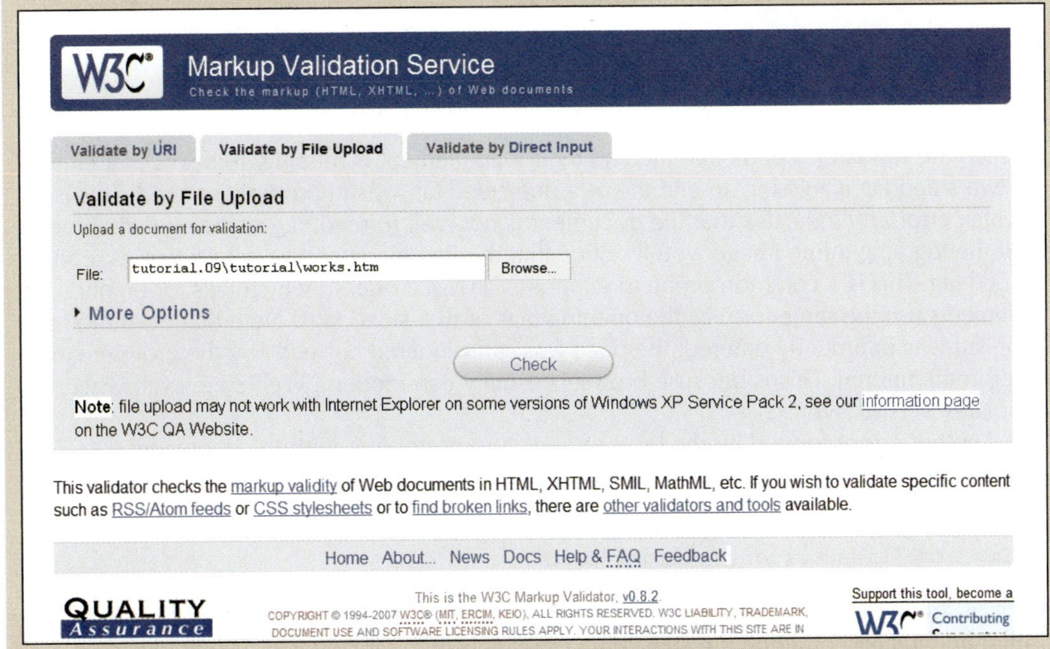
Markup Validation Service
Check the markup (HTML, XHTML, ...) of Web documents
Validate by URI
Validate by File Upload
Validate by Direct Input
Validate by File Upload
Upload a document for validation:
File: tutorial.09\tutorial\works.htm
Browse...
More Options
Check
Note: file upload may not work with Internet Explorer on some versions of Windows XP Service Pack 2, see our information page on the W3C QA Website.
This validator checks the markup validity of Web documents in HTML, XHTML, SMIL, MathML, etc. If you wish to validate specific content such as RSS/Atom feeds or CSS stylesheets or to find broken links, there are other validators and tools available.
Home About... News Docs Help & FAQ Feedback
QUALITY Assurance
This is the W3C Markup Validator, v0.8.2.
Support this tool, become a
Contributing

5. Click the **Check** button. The validator reports several errors in the file, as shown in Figure 9-16.

Figure 9-16 **Results of the first validation test**

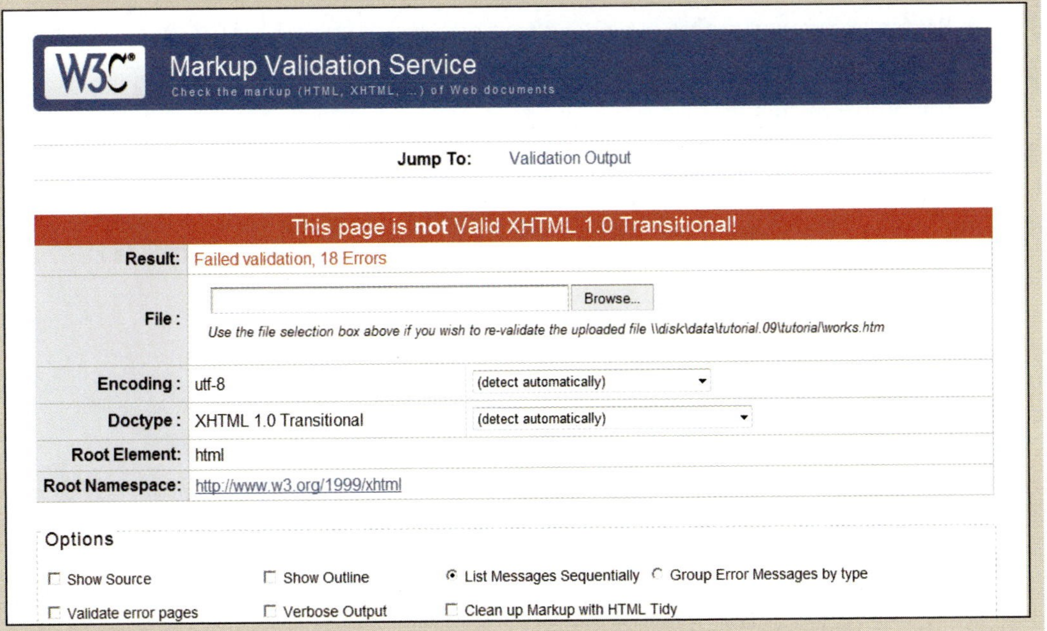
Markup Validation Service
Check the markup (HTML, XHTML, ...) of Web documents
Jump To: Validation Output
This page is not Valid XHTML 1.0 Transitional!
Result: Failed validation, 18 Errors
File: Browse...
Use the file selection box above if you wish to re-validate the uploaded file \\disk\data\tutorial.09\tutorial\works.htm
Encoding: utf-8 (detect automatically)
Doctype: XHTML 1.0 Transitional (detect automatically)
Root Element: html
Root Namespace: http://www.w3.org/1999/xhtml
Options
Show Source
Show Outline
List Messages Sequentially
Group Error Messages by type
Validate error pages
Verbose Output
Clean up Markup with HTML Tidy

Tip

You can test a different DTD on the validator page without editing the file by selecting the DTD from the Doctype list box.

6. Scroll down the Web page to read the validator's summary of the errors.

A total of 18 errors were reported by the validator. This doesn't mean that there are 18 separate mistakes in the file. In some cases, the same mistake results in several errors being noted in the report, and fixing one mistake can result in several of the errors reported by the validator being resolved. In a large error list, it's unlikely that you can fix everything at once. It's best to fix the most obvious mistakes first to reduce the size of the list, leaving the more subtle errors to be fixed last. Tom wants you to examine the error list in more detail. The first error reported was:

```
Line 28, column 55: end tag for "img" omitted, but OMITTAG NO
was specified
<img src="logo.jpg" alt="Wizard Works" align="left">
```

When the validator reports that the end tag for an element is missing, it means that either a two-sided tag is missing an end tag or a one-sided tag was improperly entered. This is a syntax error and indicates that the document is not well formed. If you examine the code for the logo.jpg inline image, you'll notice that the img element was not written as a one-sided tag. This is a common problem with older HTML code, in which tags for empty elements use the same form as the opening tags of two-sided tags. Note that even though the tag was improperly entered, the page was still rendered correctly by the browser earlier in the tutorial. This is because browsers usually can render a Web page even when it violates XHTML syntax.

Another error reported by the browser indicates a problem with the document's validity:

```
Line 52, column 40: required attribute "alt" not specified
<img src="firework.gif" align="right">
```

This is an inline image without the alt attribute. Because the alt attribute is required for all inline images, omitting it results in an error. This inline image was also not inserted using a one-sided tag, resulting in a syntax error as well. You'll fix these errors and resubmit the file for testing.

To fix and resubmit the file:

1. Return to the **works.htm** file in your text editor.
2. Locate the img element for the logo.jpg file and change it to a one-sided tag using the proper syntax.
3. Locate the img element for the firework.gif image, add the attribute

   ```
   alt=""
   ```

   and change the tag to a one-sided tag. Figure 9-17 shows the revised code in the file.

Figure 9-17 Modifying the img elements in the document

```
<body bgcolor="white">
<div id="head">
   <img src="logo.jpg" alt="Wizard Works" align="left" />
   <a href="#" target="new">Review Cart</a>
   <a href="#" target="new">Check Out</a>
</div>

<div id="linklist">
   <a href="#">Home</a>
   <a href="#" class="newgroup">Assortments</a>
   <a href="#">Firecrackers</a>
   <a href="#">Fountains</a>
   <a href="#">Cones</a>
   <a href="#">Rockets</a>
   <a href="#">Sparklers</a>
   <a href="#" class="newgroup">Online Store</a>
   <a href="#">Shopping Cart</a>
   <a href="#">Your Account</a>
   <a href="#" class="newgroup">Safety</a>
   <a href="#">Tech Support</a>
   <a href="#">Customer Service</a>
   <a href="#">About Us</a>
   <a href="#" class="newgroup">Contact Us</a>
</div>

<div id="main">
   <img src="firework.gif" align="right" alt="" />
   <p class="firstp">
      Welcome to Wizard Works, your one-stop shopping source for discount
      fireworks on the Web! We maintain a select variety of consumer fireworks
      on our Web site year round. You'll find the fireworks you want with the
      speed and convenience of the Internet, and you'll always have the best
      show in the neighborhood when you shop at Wizard Works.
```

correct the syntax error for the one-sided <img /> tag

add the required alt attribute for the img element and fix the syntax error

4. Save your changes to the file.
5. Return to your Web browser and refresh or reload the Web page to resubmit the validation check on the **works.htm** file. You might be queried as to whether or not you wish to resend the previous information. If so, click the **Retry** or **OK** button.

   Trouble? If clicking the Refresh or Reload button does not resubmit the page for testing, you can click the Browse button on the form to reselect the works.htm file from the tutorial.09\tutorial folder, and then click the Revalidate button.

   Figure 9-18 shows the new validation report.

Tip

To test the code from international documents, select a different encoding value from the Encoding list box on the validator page.

Figure 9-18 Results of the second validation test

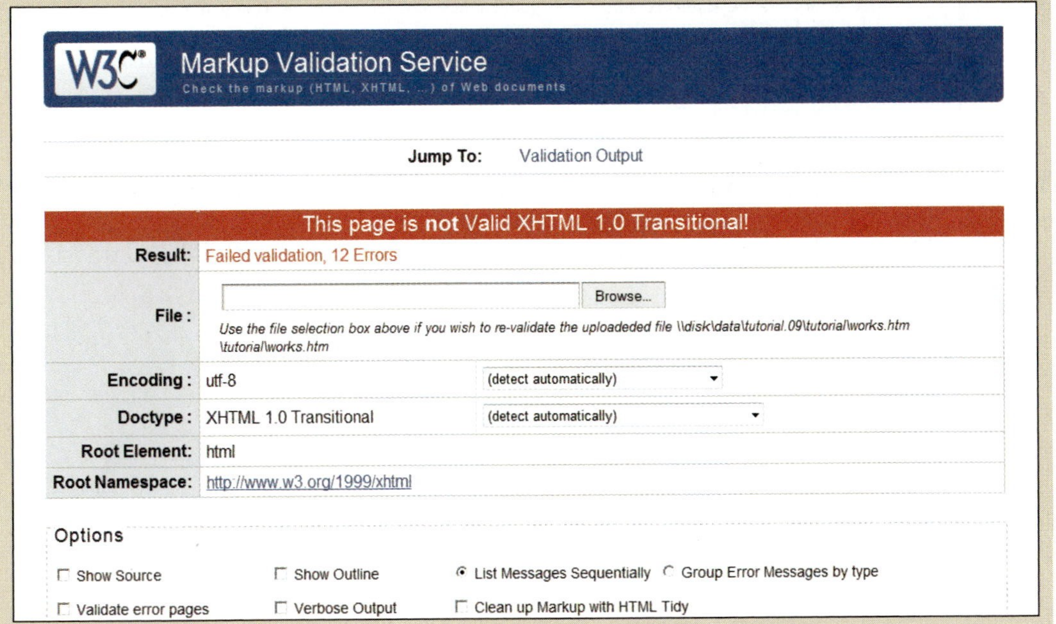

By fixing these errors, you reduced the size of the error list from 18 to 12. You can trim that down even more. The first error in the latest list states

```
Line 59, column 5: document type does not allow element "p" here;
 missing one of "object", "applet", "map", "iframe", "button", "ins",
"del" start-tag
<p>
```

which can indicate that an element has been improperly nested within the p element—but read on. Another error states

```
Line 78, column 5: tag for "p" omitted, but OMITTAG NO was
specified
</div>
```

which indicates that the paragraph element was not properly closed with the closing </p> tag. In this case, the same mistake has caused both errors. By not closing the paragraph element, it appears that other elements have been improperly placed inside of it. By adding the closing tag, both errors should be corrected.

To fix the errors in the Web page paragraphs:

1. Return to the **works.htm** file in your text editor.
2. Locate the three paragraph elements in the main section and add closing </p> tags to each paragraph, as shown in Figure 9-19.

Figure 9-19 Closing the paragraph elements

```
<div id="main">
   <img src="firework.gif" align="right" alt="" />
   <p class="firstp">
      Welcome to Wizard Works, your one-stop shopping source for discount
      fireworks on the Web! We maintain a select variety of consumer fireworks
      on our web site year round. You'll find the fireworks you want with the
      speed and convenience of the Internet, and you'll always have the best
      show in the neighborhood when you shop at Wizard Works.</p>
   <p>
      We supply quality fireworks to buy online at wholesale prices. Our
      professional fireworks display team is available to design and organize
      your display; or if you want to organize your own fireworks party, our
      experienced fireworks designers have selected the best fireworks for the
      occasion. We've made it easy for you to buy on-line for delivery direct
      to your home.</p>
   <p>
      We also create customized fireworks and displays for special needs. Please
      contact one of our design engineers to see if we can create a display for
      your special event. Be sure to order special event fireworks early to ensure
      on-time delivery.</p>
```

3. Save your changes and return to the W3C validator page. Click the **Refresh** or **Reload** button in your browser to redo the validation check. As shown in Figure 9-20, the page should now pass the validation check under the XHTML 1.0 transitional DTD.

Figure 9-20

Successful validation under XHTML transitional

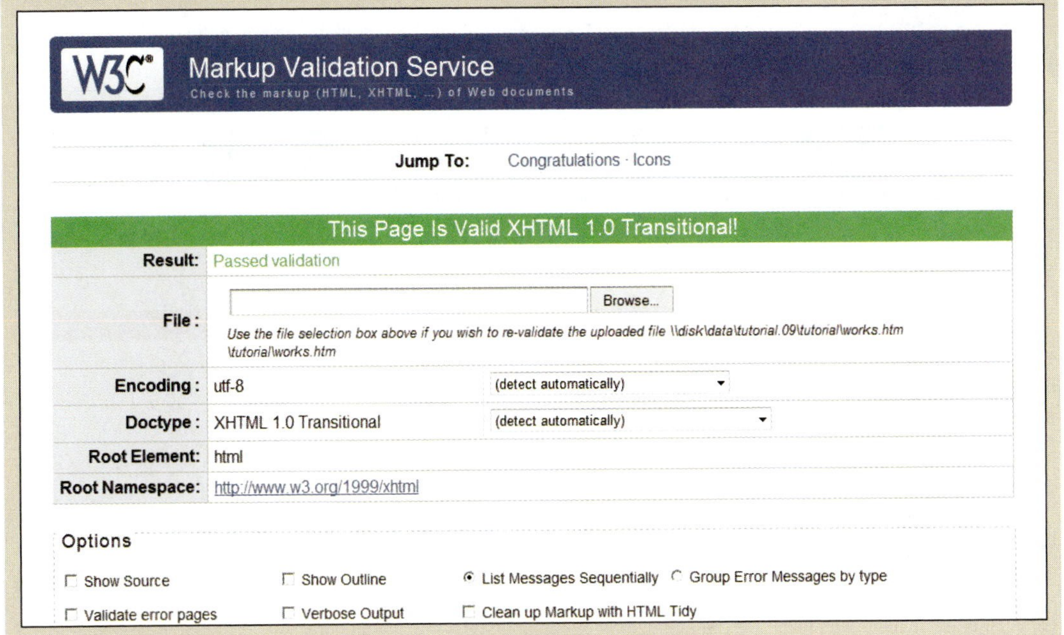

Testing under XHTML Strict

Now that the Web page has passed the validation check for XHTML 1.0 transitional, Tom wants the page tested under XHTML 1.0 strict. To perform this test, you first must change the DOCTYPE declaration to use the strict XHTML 1.0 DTD.

To change the DOCTYPE declaration:

1. Reopen the **dtd_list.txt** file from the tutorial.09\tutorial folder in your text editor. Copy the DOCTYPE declaration for XHTML 1.0 strict and then close the file.
2. Return to the **works.htm** file in your text editor.
3. Paste the copied DOCTYPE declaration into the file, replacing the previous declaration for XHTML 1.0 transitional. Figure 9-21 highlights the revised code in the file.

Figure 9-21

Pasting the XHTML 1.0 strict DOCTYPE declaration

```
<?xml version="1.0" encoding="UTF-8" ?>
<!DOCTYPE html PUBLIC "-//W3C//DTD XHTML 1.0 Strict//EN"
  "http://www.w3.org/TR/xhtml1/DTD/xhtml1-strict.dtd">
<html xmlns="http://www.w3.org/1999/xhtml">
<head>
```

With the new DOCTYPE declaration pasted into the works.htm file, you can retest the document using the same validator page on the W3C Web site.

To test the file under the strict DTD:

1. Save your changes to the **works.htm** file.

2. Return to the W3C validator page. Click the **Refresh** or **Reload** button in your browser to redo the validation check. As shown in Figure 9-22, the page fails the test under XHTML 1.0 strict.

Figure 9-22 **Results of the XHTML strict validation test**

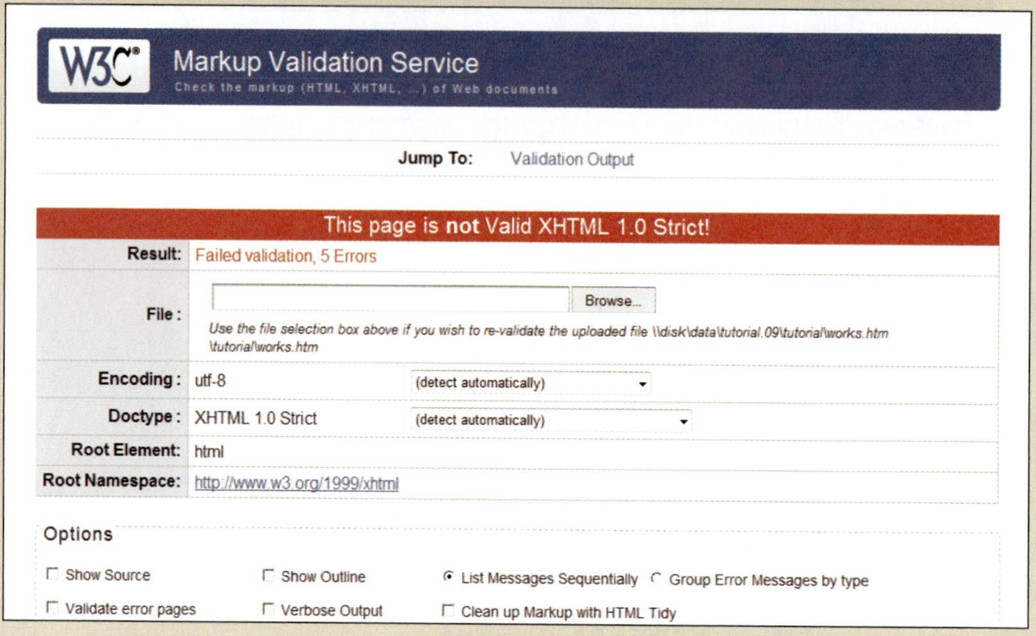

Tip

You can view extended comments on your page errors by checking the Verbose Output check box on the validator page.

Five errors are reported by the W3C validator page. The first two are:

```
Line 26, column 14: there is no attribute "bgcolor"
<body bgcolor="white">
Line 28, column 48: there is no attribute "align"
<img src="logo.jpg" alt="Wizard Works" align="left" />
```

Both errors reference presentational attributes that are not supported under the XHTML 1.0 strict DTD. The first attribute, bgcolor, is used to set the background color of the Web page. The align attribute referenced in the second error message is used to float the inline image on the left page margin. You can fix both errors by removing the attributes and replacing them with the background-color and float styles added to the ww.css style sheet.

To replace the attributes with styles:

1. Return to the **works.htm** file in your Web browser.
2. Delete the attribute

   bgcolor="white"

   from the opening <body> tag.
3. Go down two lines in the file and delete the attribute

   align="left"

   from the <img /> tag for the logo.jpg file.
4. Scroll down the file and delete the attribute

   align="right"

   from the <img /> tag for the firework.gif graphic.

5. Save your changes to the file and then open the **ww.css** file in your text editor.
6. Add the style

   `background-color: white`

   to the list of style properties for the body element.
7. Directly below the styles for the #head a:hover selector, insert the following style declaration for images nested within the #head selector:

   `#head img {float: left}`
8. Directly below the styles for the #main selector, insert the following style declaration:

   `#main img {float: right}`

   Figure 9-23 highlights the revised code in the style sheet file.

Modifying the ww.css style sheet **Figure 9-23**

```
body                  {background-image: url(back.jpg); background-repeat: repeat-y;
                       font-size: 16px; margin-right: 20px; background-color: white}

#head                 {position: absolute; top: 0px; left: 0px; width: 100%; font-size: 16px;
                       font-family: sans-serif; background-color: white; text-align: right;
                       border-bottom: 2px solid black; padding-top: 5px}
#head a               {color: white; background-color: blue; font-size: 10px; font-weight: bold;
                       text-decoration: none; text-align: center; border: 5px outset white;
                       width: 100px; padding: 2px; margin-left: 20px}
#head a:hover         {color: black; background-color: yellow; border: 5px inset white}
#head img             {float: left}

#linklist             {position: absolute; top: 125px; left: 0px; font-size: 14px;
                       font-weight: bold; font-family: sans-serif; width: 140px; padding: 10px}
#linklist a           {color: rgb(247,233,64); text-decoration: none; display: block}
#linklist a:hover     {color: white; text-decoration: underline}
#linklist .newgroup   {margin-top: 10px}

#main                 {position: absolute; top: 125px; left: 160px}
#main img             {float: right}

.firstp:first-letter {font-size: 300%; line-height: 0.8; float: left}

address               {border-top: 2px solid black; font-style: normal; font-size: 10px;
                       font-family: sans-serif; text-align: center; margin-top: 15px}
```

9. Save your changes to the file, and then return to the **W3C validator page** in your Web browser. Refresh or reload the **works.htm** page and verify that the number of errors in the page has dropped to three.

The next error reported by the validator is:

```
Line 29, column 22: there is no attribute "target"
<a href="#" target="_new">Review Cart</a>
```

The target attribute is not supported in XHTML strict, so it will have to be removed from the Web page. This means that if Tom wants to work with XHTML strict, he will not be able to direct his hypertext links to new browser windows or tabs.

To remove the target attribute:

1. Return to the **works.htm** file in your Web browser.
2. Delete the attribute

   `target="_new"`

   from the hypertext links for the Review Cart and Check Out links located at the top of the Web page body.

3. Save your changes to the file and then reload or refresh the **W3C validator page** in your Web browser. The number of errors in the Web page has dropped to two.

InSight | **The target Attribute and Strict XHTML**

The decision not to support the target attribute under strict XHTML was a controversial one. Many Web page designers prefer to have some links open in new browser windows or tabs, rather than in the window or tab that displays their site, to allow users to stay at their site while also browsing on other sites.

One problem is that the ability to open a new window or tab is strictly browser-dependent. For example, cell phones and PDAs don't support opening new windows, and those devices are becoming increasingly important tools for viewing the Web. Another argument is that the action of opening a link in a new window should be left to the user's preference; it should not be forced on users by the Web site designer. Most browsers provide users the ability to choose where to open links, and that is where the decision should reside. Finally, there is the opinion that opening new browser windows for the user is actually confusing to new users who can get lost as the number of open windows increases with each site they visit.

However, despite these reasons, many Web designers still want to direct links to new browser windows. One way to allow a link to be opened in a new window but still retain valid code under XHTML strict is to use JavaScript to open the link. The following code shows a JavaScript command that can be added to any hypertext link to force the link to open in a new window:

```
<a href="url" onclick="window.open(this.href); return false;"
              onkeypress="window.open(this.href); return false;">
   linked text
</a>
```

Note that for this approach to work, the user's browser must have JavaScript enabled. This is the default state for most browsers. However, if JavaScript is not enabled, the JavaScript code will be ignored and the link will open in the current browser window or tab.

The last two errors in the works.htm file involve using the <font> tag and the color attribute. The reported errors are as follows:

Line 73, column 18: **there is no attribute "color"**

```
<font color="blue">Wizard Works</font> &#183;
```

Line 73, column 24: **element "font" undefined**

```
<font color="blue">Wizard Works</font> &#183;
```

To fix this problem, you'll remove the unsupported font element and color attribute, replacing them with the following supported code:

```
<span style="color: blue">Wizard Works</span> &#183;
```

Make this change to the works.htm file.

To replace the font and color attributes:

1. Return to the **works.htm** file in your text editor.
2. Scroll to the bottom of the file and replace

```
<font color="blue">Wizard Works</font>
```

with the following, as shown in Figure 9-24:

```
<span style="color: blue">Wizard Works</span>
```

Figure 9-24 **Replacing the font element and color attribute**

```
    <address>
       <span style="color: blue">Wizard Works</span> &#183;
       4311 Tower Street &#183;
       Ashland, KY  41105 &#183;
       (606) 555-3188
    </address>
</div>
```

3. Save your changes to the file and then reload or refresh the **W3C validator page** in your Web browser. As shown in Figure 9-25, the validator should now report that the code for the works.htm file passes validation under XHTML strict.

Figure 9-25 **Successful validation under XHTML strict**

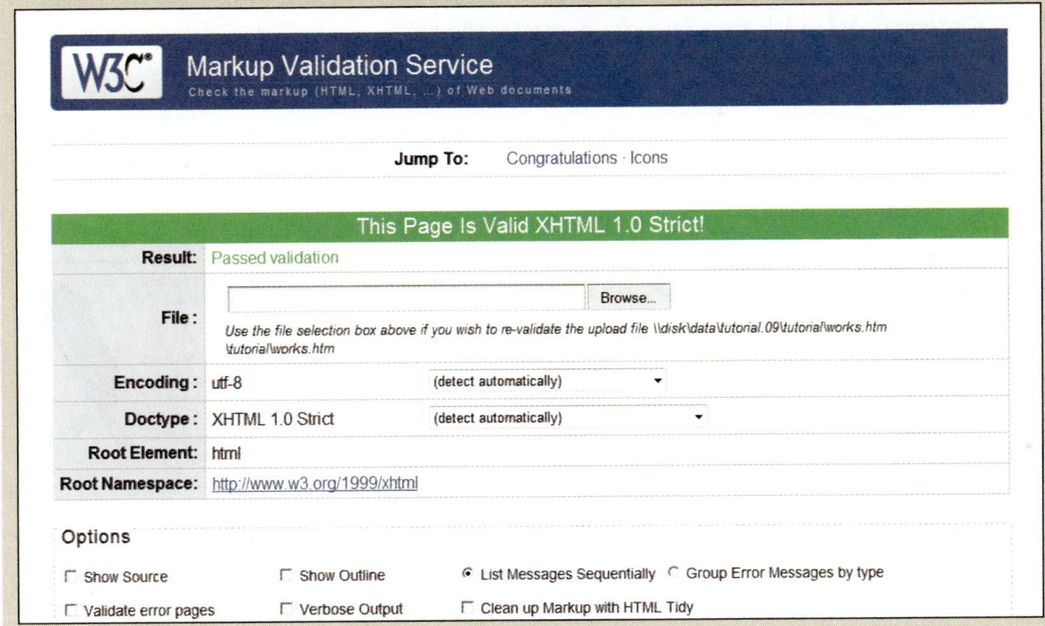

Once you have a document that passes the validation test, you might want to make a note of this on your Web page. The W3C provides code that you can paste into your document to advertise this fact. Tom suggests that you add this code to the Wizard Works Web page.

To insert the W3C validation notice:

1. Scroll to the bottom of the **W3C validator page** and select the code sample directly to the right of the second validation icon image (the blue image).
2. Click **Edit** from your browser menu and then click **Copy**.
3. Return to the **works.htm** file in your text editor and paste the following code directly below the closing </address> tag, as shown in Figure 9-26:

```
<p>
   <a href="http://validator.w3.org/check?uri=referer">
      <img src="http://www.w3.org/Icons/valid-xhtml10-blue"
           alt="Valid XHTML 1.0 Strict" height="31" width="88" />
   </a>
</p>
```

You can indent the code to make it easier to read.

Figure 9-26 Inserting the code for the W3C validation icon

```
<address>
   <span style="color: blue">Wizard Works</span> &#183;
   4311 Tower Street &#183;
   Ashland, KY  41105 &#183;
   (606) 555-3188
</address>

<p>
   <a href="http://validator.w3.org/check?uri=referer">
      <img src="http://www.w3.org/Icons/valid-xhtml10-blue"
           alt="Valid XHTML 1.0 Strict" height="31" width="88" />
   </a>
</p>

</div>
```

4. Save your changes to the **works.htm** file and then close it.
5. Reopen **works.htm** in your Web browser. As shown in Figure 9-27, the validation icon appears in the bottom-right corner of the page.

Figure 9-27 Final Wizard Works page

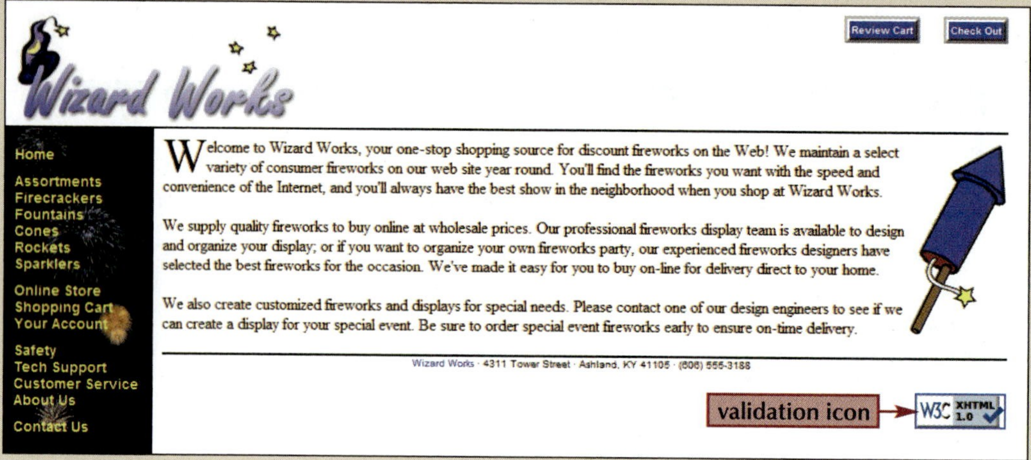

You show the completed Web page to Tom. He's pleased with your work in updating the file to meet the specifications for XHTML. He is sure that these changes will help the Web site in the future as the company tries to stay current with the latest developments in XHTML.

Using Style Sheets and XHTML

Although XHTML and HTML files are simple text documents, not all text is the same. Browsers and parsers distinguish between two types of text: parsed character data and unparsed character data. **Parsed character data** or **PCDATA** is text that is processed (parsed) by a browser or parser. The following code is an example of PCDATA:

```
<title>Wizard Works</title>
```

When a browser encounters this string of characters, it processes it and uses that information to change the text of the browser's title bar. In PCDATA, you cannot enter character symbols such as <, >, and & directly into a document as text because they are used to process information. The < and > symbols are used to mark the beginning and end of element tags.

The & symbol is used to indicate a special character. If you want to display a < symbol in your document, for example, you must use the special character symbol <.

Unparsed character data or **CDATA** is text that is not processed by the browser or parser. In CDATA, you can use any character you like without worrying about it being misinterpreted—browsers and parsers essentially ignore it. The DTDs for XML and XHTML specify whether an element contains CDATA or PCDATA. Most elements contain PCDATA. This prevents document authors from putting symbols such as < into the element content.

However, this also has an impact on embedded style sheets. The content of an embedded style sheet is treated as PCDATA, meaning that a parser attempts to process the information contained in the style sheet's characters. This can cause problems if the style sheet contains a character that could be processed by the parser. For example, the following embedded style sheet contains the > character, which a parser would interpret as the end of an element tag:

```
<style type="text/css">
   p > img {float: left}
</style>
```

A parser encountering this code would probably invalidate the document (assuming that the code didn't crash the page entirely). This problem also occurs with JavaScript (a topic you'll cover in the next tutorial), in which the <, >, and & symbols are frequently used.

One way of dealing with this problem is to use a special construct called a **CDATA section**, which marks a block of text as CDATA so that parsers ignore any text within it. The syntax of the CDATA section is

```
<![CDATA[
   text
]]>
```

where *text* is the content that you want treated as CDATA. To apply this to your style sheet, you could place the CDATA section within the style element as follows:

```
<style type="text/css">
<![CDATA[
   p > img {float: left}
]]>
</style>
```

The problem with this solution is that many browsers do not understand or recognize CDATA sections, and this can cause problems in displaying your page. In the end, the best solution is often to replace all embedded style sheets in XHTML documents with external style sheets. This has the added advantage of completely removing style from content because all the styles are placed in separate files. Note that this is not an issue if the embedded style sheet doesn't contain any characters that can't be processed by the XML parser.

Review | Session 9.2 Quick Check

1. An XHTML transitional validation test reports the following error:

```
Line 51, column 3:
 tag for "br" omitted, but OMITTAG NO was specified
<br>
```

   Suggest a possible cause of the error and how you would correct it.

2. A validation test under XHTML 1.0 strict reports the following error:

```
Line 59, column 12: there is no attribute "align"
<p align="left">
```

   Suggest a possible cause of the error and how you would correct it.

3. A validation test under XHTML 1.0 strict reports the following error:

```
Line 22, column 14: there is no attribute "name"
<form name="orders">
```

   Suggest a possible cause of the error and how you would correct it.

4. Suggest how to write code for a hypertext link to open in a new browser window and still be valid under the XHTML strict DTD.
5. What is the difference between PCDATA and CDATA?
6. Why would you want to place an embedded style sheet within a CDATA section?

Review | Tutorial Summary

In this tutorial, you learned how to create and work with XHTML documents. The first session reviewed the history of XHTML and its development from XML. You learned about well-formed and valid documents as well as the different DTDs associated with XHTML. The session then discussed how certain coding practices in HTML documents would lead to syntax errors in XHTML. The session examined the XML prolog and DOCTYPE declarations, as well as issues around specifying the XHTML namespace. The session concluding by discussing how XHTML can be used with other XML languages to create combined documents. In the second session you learned how to use an online validator to test a document for well-formedness and validity. The tutorial concluded with a discussion of the syntax issues surrounding embedded styles sheets.

Key Terms

attribute minimization
CDATA
CDATA section
character encoding
character set
default namespace
document type definition
DTD
frameset DTD
local namespace
namespace
parsed character data
parser
PCDATA
strict DTD
transitional DTD
UCS
Unicode
Universal Character Set
unparsed character data
valid
well formed
XML parser

Practice | Review Assignments

Practice the skills you learned in the tutorial using the same case scenario.

Data Files needed for the Review Assignments: back.jpg, dtd_list.txt, founttxt.htm, and logo.jpg

Tom has another file that he wants you to update to XHTML. This page contains an order form for some of the fountains sold by Wizard Works. The file has some older HTML elements and syntax in it, so he wants you to confirm that the file is well formed and valid after you've updated it for XHTML. Figure 9-28 shows a preview of the completed Web page.

Figure 9-28

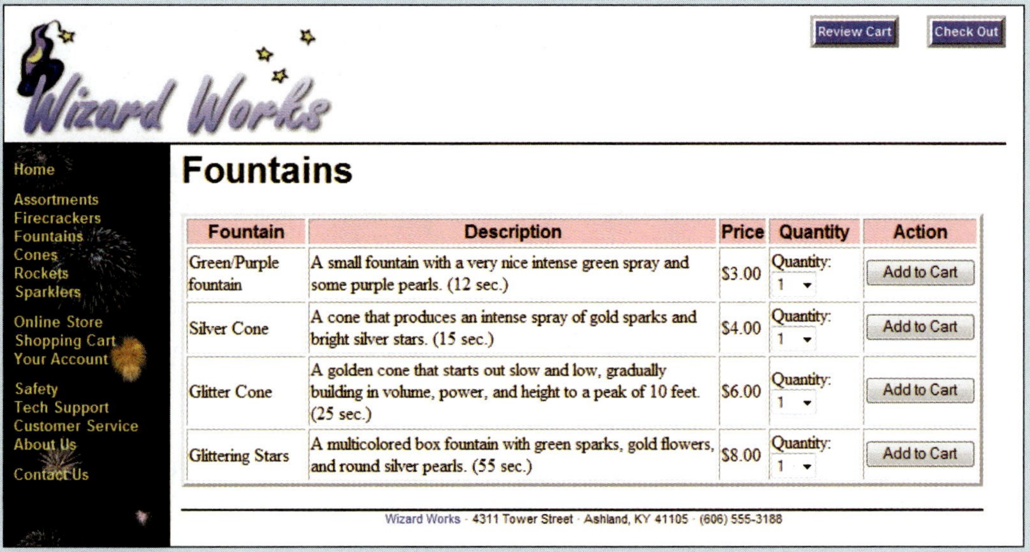

Complete the following:

1. Use your text editor to open **founttxt.htm** from the tutorial.09\review folder included with your Data Files. Enter ***your name*** and ***the date*** in the comment section of the file and save the file as **fountain.htm** in the same folder.
2. Insert an XML prolog at the top of the file, setting the version number to 1.0 and the character encoding to UTF-8.
3. Below the XML prolog, insert a DOCTYPE declaration indicating that this document conforms to the XHTML 1.0 strict DTD (you can copy the code for this declaration from the **dtd_list.txt** file in the tutorial.09\review folder).
4. Set the default namespace for the document to the XHTML namespace.
5. Use a validator to test whether the document is well formed and valid under the XHTML 1.0 strict DTD. If any deprecated presentational attributes are found, replace them with the equivalent inline style. Note that when this form is run, its action should use the CGI script at *http://wizardworksstore.com/cgi/cart*.
6. After the document passes XHTML 1.0 strict, save your changes and view the page in your Web browser to ensure that it still looks like Figure 9-28.
7. Submit your completed files to your instructor.

Apply | Case Problem 1

Use the skills you learned in this tutorial to convert an online menu to XHTML format.

Data Files needed for this Case Problem: breakfst.jpg, breaktxt.htm, dinner.jpg, dinnrtxt.htm, dtd_list.txt, lunch.jpg, lunchtxt.htm, and tan.jpg

Kelsey's Diner You've been asked to update the Web pages for Kelsey's Diner, a popular restaurant in Worcester, Massachusetts. Cindy Towser, the manager of the diner, would like the pages that display her breakfast, lunch, and dinner menus updated so that they comply with XHTML standards. A preview of one of the menu pages is shown in Figure 9-29.

Figure 9-29

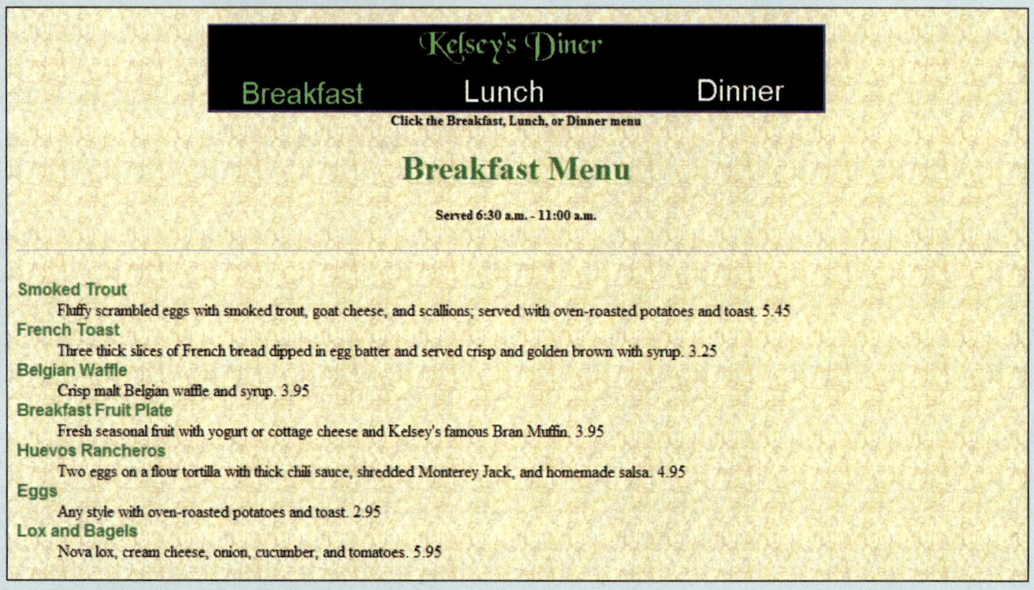

Complete the following:

1. Use your text editor to open **breaktxt.htm**, **lunchtxt.htm**, and **dinnrtxt.htm** from the tutorial.09\case1 folder included with your Data Files. Enter ***your name*** and ***the date*** in the comment section of each file and save the files as **breakfst.htm**, **lunch.htm**, and **dinner.htm**, respectively, in the same folder.
2. Go to the **breakfst.htm** file in your text editor and insert an XML prolog at the top of the file. Use the default values for the version and encoding attributes.

3. After the XML prolog, insert a DOCTYPE declaration for the XHTML 1.0 strict DTD (you may copy the entry from the **dtd_list.txt** file in the tutorial.09\case1 folder for the code of this declaration).
4. Set the default namespace of the document to the XHTML namespace.
5. Test the file on the validator and make a note of the errors reported. Here are some possible ways to fix the errors:
   - Convert any deprecated presentational attributes to an embedded style.
   - Correct syntax errors for one-sided tags.
   - Replace any prohibited attributes (such as the name attribute) with an equivalent valid attribute.
   - Replace the formatting done with the b and font elements with a span element and an embedded style.
6. Save your changes to **breakfst.htm** and continue to test the file until it passes the XHTML 1.0 strict validation test.
7. Repeat Steps 2 through 6 for the **lunch.htm** and **dinner.htm** files.
8. Test the completed Web site on your browser and verify that you can move among the pages by clicking the image map links in the logo at the top of the page.
9. Submit your completed files to your instructor.

Apply | Case Problem 2

Use the skills you've learned in this tutorial to update an old product page.

Data Files needed for this Case Problem: cassini.jpg, dtd_list.txt, gargtxt.htm, gbar.jpg, glogo.jpg, maa.jpg, and oneil.jpg

Middle Age Arts Nicole Swanson is the head of the Web site team at Middle Age Arts, a company that creates and sells replicas of historical European works of art for home and garden use. She has recently started a project to update the old HTML code in the site's many pages. She's asked you to update the page describing the company's collection of decorative gargoyles. She wants the page to comply with XHTML 1.0 strict standards. Figure 9-30 shows a preview of the completed Web page.

Figure 9-30

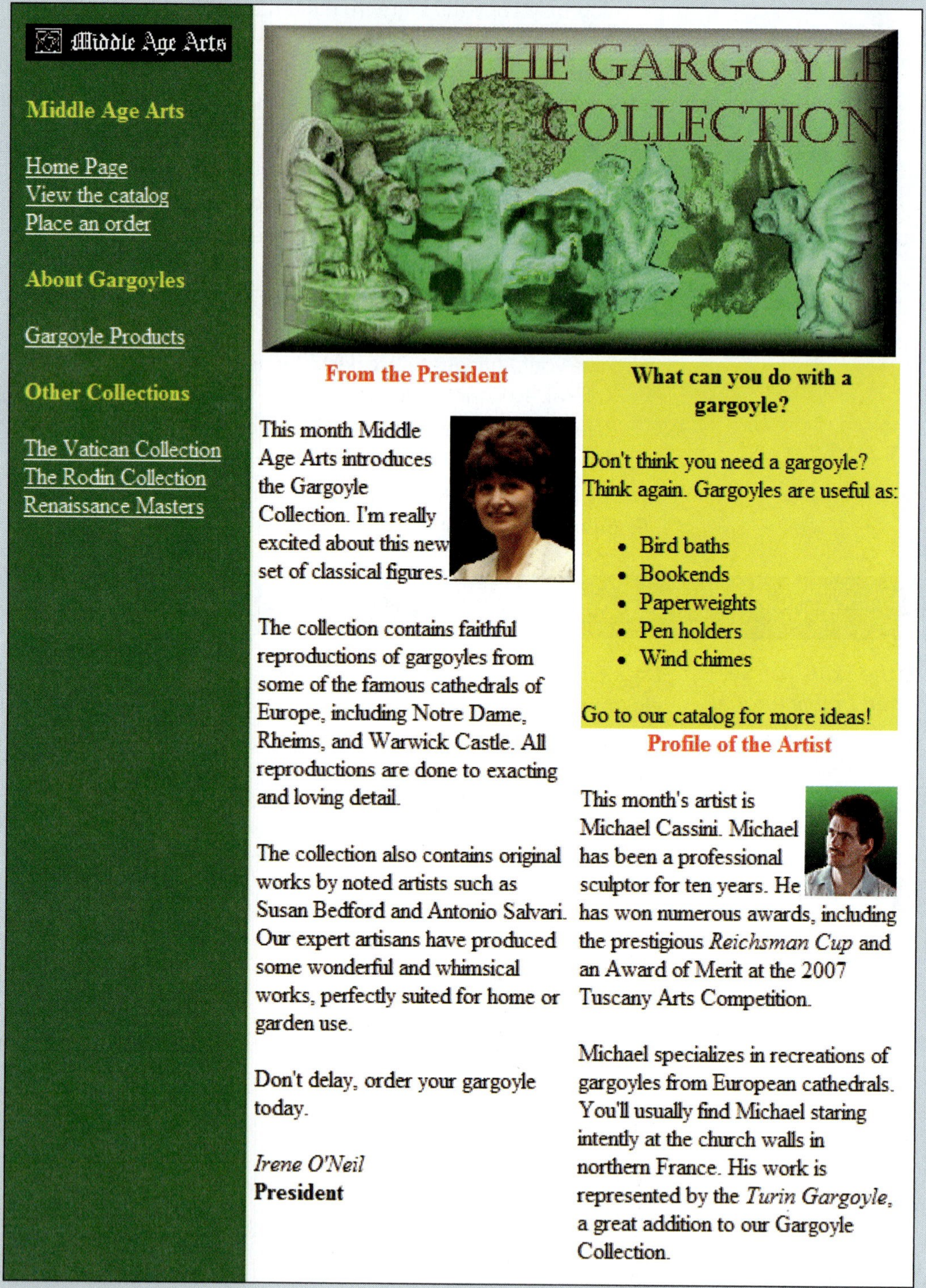
Middle Age Arts
Middle Age Arts
Home Page
View the catalog
Place an order
About Gargoyles
Gargoyle Products
Other Collections
The Vatican Collection
The Rodin Collection
Renaissance Masters
THE GARGOYLE COLLECTION
From the President
This month Middle Age Arts introduces the Gargoyle Collection. I'm really excited about this new set of classical figures.
The collection contains faithful reproductions of gargoyles from some of the famous cathedrals of Europe, including Notre Dame, Rheims, and Warwick Castle. All reproductions are done to exacting and loving detail.
The collection also contains original works by noted artists such as Susan Bedford and Antonio Salvari. Our expert artisans have produced some wonderful and whimsical works, perfectly suited for home or garden use.
Don't delay, order your gargoyle today.
Irene O'Neil
President
What can you do with a gargoyle?
Don't think you need a gargoyle? Think again. Gargoyles are useful as:
Bird baths
Bookends
Paperweights
Pen holders
Wind chimes
Go to our catalog for more ideas!
Profile of the Artist
This month's artist is Michael Cassini. Michael has been a professional sculptor for ten years. He has won numerous awards, including the prestigious Reichsman Cup and an Award of Merit at the 2007 Tuscany Arts Competition.
Michael specializes in recreations of gargoyles from European cathedrals. You'll usually find Michael staring intently at the church walls in northern France. His work is represented by the Turin Gargoyle, a great addition to our Gargoyle Collection.

Complete the following:

1. Use your text editor to open **gargtxt.htm** from the tutorial.09\case2 folder included with your Data Files. Enter ***your name*** and ***the date*** in the comment section and save the file as **gargoyle.htm** in the same file.
2. Insert an XML prolog at the top of the file. Use the standard attribute defaults for an XHTML file.

3. After the XML prolog, insert a DOCTYPE declaration for the XHTML 1.0 strict DTD.
4. Set the default namespace of the document to the XHTML namespace.
5. Test the file on the validator. Fix the errors as follows:
   - Convert the attributes for the body element into styles in an embedded style sheet. (*Hint*: The link, alink, and vlink attributes are used to set the colors of hyperlinks, active links, and visited links in the Web page.)
   - Use proper syntax for any empty elements.
   - Set the color and text alignment of an h4 element using an inline style.
   - Ensure that all two-sided tags are properly closed.
   - Use the float style to align all inline images.
   - Use an inline style to set a table cell's width and background color.
   - Remove all deprecated elements and attributes.
6. Save your final version of the file once it passes the validation test for XHTML 1.0 strict, and then test it in your browser to ensure that it looks like Figure 9-30.
7. Submit your completed files to your instructor.

Challenge | Case Problem 3

Explore how to create a valid XHTML document using the frameset DTD.

Data Files needed for this Case Problem: cast.htm, castles.jpg, casttxt.htm, dtd_list.txt, hebd.htm, hebdtxt.htm, hebrides.jpg, high.htm, highland.jpg, hightxt.htm, lake.htm, lake.jpg, laketxt.htm, scottxt.htm, tourlist.gif, and tslogo.gif

Travel Scotland! Travel Scotland! is an online Web site that books tours of Scotland and the British Isles. You've recently been hired by Travel Scotland! to update the company's Web site. Fiona Findlay, the head of advertising for the company, has given you a set of pages in a framed Web site that describe four of the company's tours. She would like you to update the code so that it complies with XHTML standards for the transitional and frameset DTDs. A preview of the completed Web site is shown in Figure 9-31.

Figure 9-31

Complete the following:

1. Use your text editor to open the files **casttxt.htm**, **hebdtxt.htm**, **hightxt.htm**, **laketxt.htm**, and **scottxt.htm** from the tutorial.09\case3 folder included with your Data Files. Enter ***your name*** and ***the date*** in the comment section of each file and then save the files as **casttour.htm**, **hebdtour.htm**, **hightour.htm**, **laketour.htm**, and **scotland.htm,** respectively, in the same folder.
2. Go to the **scotland.htm** file in your text editor and insert an XML prolog at the top of the file.
3. Below the XML prolog, insert a DOCTYPE declaration that indicates that this file conforms to the standards for XHTML 1.0 transitional.
4. Set the default namespace to the XHTML namespace.
5. EXPLORE: Enclose the styles from the embedded style sheet within a CDATA section.
6. Save your changes and submit the page for validation. Correct any errors reported by the validator. (*Hint*: If alternate text is required for the image map hot spots, use the text displayed in the **tourlist.gif** graphic.)
7. Go to the **casttour.htm** file in your text editor and insert an XML prolog at the top of the file.
8. EXPLORE: Specify that the document uses the XHTML 1.0 frameset DTD and the XHTML namespace.
9. EXPLORE: Save your changes and submit the page for validation. Correct any errors in syntax or validity under the frameset DTD.
10. EXPLORE: Repeat Steps 7 through 9 for the **hebdtour.htm**, **hightour.htm**, and **laketour.htm** files.
11. Test the Web site in your browser to verify that the inline frames and the framed pages work correctly.
12. Submit your completed files to your instructor.

Create | Case Problem 4

Test your knowledge of XHTML by creating a well-formed valid document for an educational site.

Data Files needed for this Case Problem: address.txt, astro.txt, chem.txt, dtd_list.txt, elect.txt, eng.txt, mwslogo.gif, and physics.txt

Maxwell Scientific Maxwell Scientific is an online Web site that sells science kits and educational products. Chris Todd, the head of the Web site development team, is leading an effort to update the company's Web site. He has given you some text files and graphic images. You may supplement this material with any additional files and resources at your disposal. Your job will be to develop this material into a Web site that is compliant with XHTML 1.0 strict standards. To ensure that the completed Web page is both well formed and valid, he wants you to test it on a validator before submitting it to him.

Complete the following:

1. Use your text editor to create the following HTML files in the tutorial.09\case4 folder: **astro.htm**, **chem.htm**, **elect.htm**, **eng.htm**, and **physics.htm**. Include ***your name*** and ***the date*** in a comment section for each file, along with a description of the purpose of the page.
2. Use the content from the **address.txt**, **astro.txt**, **chem.txt**, **elect.txt, eng.txt**, and **physics.txt** to create the content of each Web page. The design of the Web site and each individual page is up to you. Store any styles you create in an external style sheet named **mw.css** in the tutorial.09\case4 folder.

3. Each page should be designed as an XHTML 1.0 strict document. Include all necessary declarations and namespaces.
4. Test all of your pages against a validator to ensure that each page fulfills the requirements of the XHTML 1.0 strict DTD.
5. Submit your completed files to your instructor.

Review | Quick Check Answers

Session 9.1

1. An XML document that employs the correct syntax is known as well formed. A well-formed XML document that also contains the correct content is known as a valid document.

2. It employs the wrong syntax for the img element, it should be:

```
<img src="logo.jpg" alt="Wizard Works" />
```

3. The disabled attribute has no value. The correct form is:

```
<input type="radio" disabled="disabled" />
```

4. The blockquote element cannot contain the a element as a child element. You can correct this problem by nesting the <a> within a paragraph or other block-level element.

5. The align attribute is not a support attribute in the strict DTD. You can correct this as follows:

```
<img src="logo.jpg" alt="Wizard Works" style="float: right" />
```

6. The map element requires the id attribute to be valid. The following is a valid form:

```
<map name="parkmap" id="parkmap">
```

7. `<!DOCTYPE html PUBLIC "-//W3C//DTD XHTML 1.0 Strict//EN"` "http://www.w3.org/TR/xhtml1/DTD/xhtml1-strict.dtd">

8. `<?xml version="1.0" encoding="UTF-8" standalone="no" ?>`

Session 9.2

1. The br element should be created with an empty tag as

```
<br />
```

2. The align attribute is not supported under XHTML 1.0 strict because it is a presentational attribute used to align text or page content. You can achieve the same result by applying the style text-align: left to the paragraph element.

3. The error occurs because under the strict DTD there is no support for the name attribute within the <form> tag. Replace the name attribute with the id attribute as follows:

```
<form id="orders">
```

4. Use the following JavaScript commands within the <a> tag for the hypertext link:

```
onclick="window.open(this.href); return false;"onkeypress="window.
open(this.href); return false;">
```

5. CDATA or character data is text that is not processed by the browser or XML parser. PCDATA or parsed character data is processed by the browser or the XML parser and so will be interpreted in terms of the rules of syntax for XML.
6. To force the browser or XML parser to treat the style sheet commands as character data and not as text to be processed, thereby avoiding the situation where style sheet code will be interpreted as XHTML code.

Ending Data Files

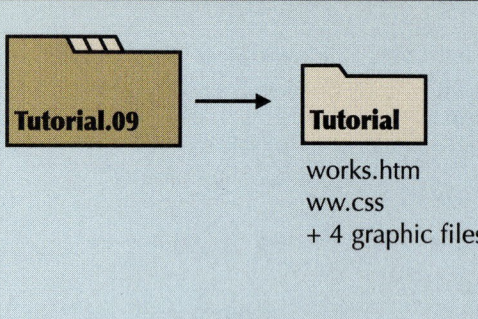

Tutorial.09 →

Tutorial
works.htm
ww.css
+ 4 graphic files

Review
fountain.htm
+ 2 graphic files

Case1
breakfst.htm
dinner.htm
lunch.htm
+ 4 graphic files

Case2
gargoyle.htm
+ 5 graphic files

Case3
casttour.htm
hebdtour.htm
hightour.htm
laketour.htm
scotland.htm
+ 4 HTML files
+ 6 graphic files

Case4
astro.htm
chem.htm
elect.htm
eng.htm
mw.css
physics.htm
+ 1 graphic file

Tutorial 10

Objectives

Session 10.1
- Learn the history of JavaScript
- Create a script element
- Understand basic JavaScript syntax
- Write text to a Web page with JavaScript

Session 10.2
- Learn about JavaScript data types
- Declare and work with variables
- Create and call a JavaScript function

Session 10.3
- Access an external JavaScript file
- Add comments to JavaScript code
- Learn about basic debugging techniques and tools

Programming with JavaScript

Hiding E-Mail Addresses on a Library Web Site

Case | Monroe Public Library

Kate Howard is the head of technical services at Monroe Public Library in Monroe, Ohio. One of her jobs is to maintain the library's Web site. In previous years, the library has made its staff directory, including e-mail links to library employees, available online. Kate thinks that this is an important part of making the library more accessible to everyone. However, Kate has become concerned about the security issues involved with making the staff's e-mail addresses so accessible. Kate is aware that e-mail addresses can be scanned from an HTML file and used to send junk mail to the recipients.

She would like to have some way of scrambling the e-mail addresses within the HTML code while still making them viewable when the page is rendered by a Web browser. Kate has approached you for help in writing a program to accomplish this.

Starting Data Files

Tutorial.10 →

Tutorial
mpl.jpg
mplstyles.css
mpltxt.htm
spam.js

Review
mpl2txt.htm
mplstyles.css
random.js
+ 11 graphic files

Case1
datetime.js
skymaptxt.htm
skyweb.css
+ 26 graphic files

Case2
ads.js
fronttxt.htm
random.js
styles.css
+ 7 graphic files

Case3
back.jpg
functions.js
sunday.htm - saturday.htm
todaytxt.htm
+ 2 style sheets

Case4
functions.js
logo.jpg

Session 10.1

Introducing JavaScript

You meet with Kate to discuss her goals regarding the e-mail addresses on the library's staff directory page. She shows you the content and page layout she has created.

To open the staff directory page:

1. Use your text editor to open **mpltxt.htm** from the tutorial.10\tutorial folder included with your Data Files. Enter ***your name*** and ***the date*** in the comment section at the top of the file and save the file as **mpl.htm** in the same folder.
2. Take some time to scroll through the document to become familiar with its contents and structure.
3. Open **mpl.htm** in your Web browser. Figure 10-1 shows the initial appearance of the Web page.

   Note that the staff directory table contains a column in which Kate wants to insert links to each employee's e-mail address; right now the column is empty.

Figure 10-1 Monroe Public Library Staff page

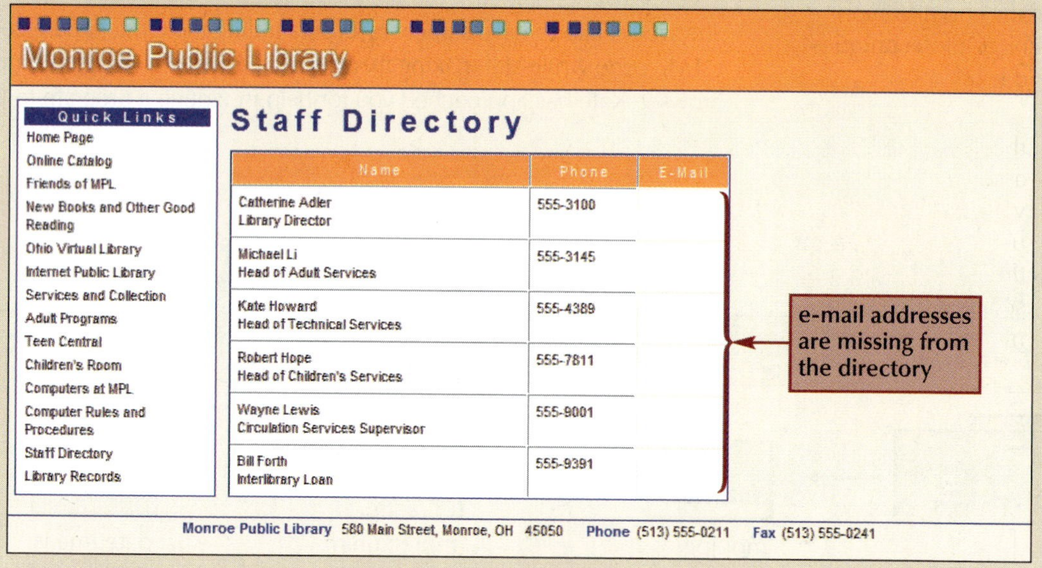

Although the staff directory page has proven invaluable in making library employees more responsive to the needs of the public, Kate is concerned about the security risks of putting e-mail addresses in that directory. Kate is most concerned about spam. **Spam** is essentially junk e-mail—messages that advertise products and services not requested by the recipient. A **spammer** is a person who sends these unsolicited e-mails, sometimes in bulk e-mailings involving tens of thousands of recipients. Aside from the annoyance of receiving unsolicited e-mail, spam costs companies thousands—and sometimes millions—of dollars each year by consuming valuable resources on mail servers and other devices forced to process the messages. Spam also reduces productivity by forcing employees to wade through numerous spam messages every day to find messages that are truly relevant.

One way that spammers collect e-mail addresses is through the use of e-mail harvesters. An **e-mail harvester** is a program that scans documents, usually Web pages, looking for e-mail addresses. Any e-mail address the harvester finds within the document code is added to a database, which can then be used for sending spam. So by putting the staff's e-mail addresses in the HTML code for the staff directory, Kate is also making them available to e-mail harvesters. See Figure 10-2.

Figure 10-2 Harvesting e-mail addresses

```
<tr>
   <td>Catherine Adler<br />Library Director</td>
   <td>555-3100</td>
   <td><a href="mailto:cadler@mpl.gov">cadler@mpl.gov</a>
   </td>
</tr>
<tr>
   <td>Michael Li<br />Head of Adult Services</td>
   <td>555-3145</td>
   <td><a href="mailto:mikeli@mpl.gov">mikeli@mpl.gov</a>
   </td>
</tr>
<tr>
   <td>Kate Howard<br />Head of Technical Services</td>
   <td>555-4389</td>
   <td><a href="mailto:khoward@mpl.gov">khoward@mpl.gov</a>
   </td>
</tr>
```

e-mail addresses in the staff directory

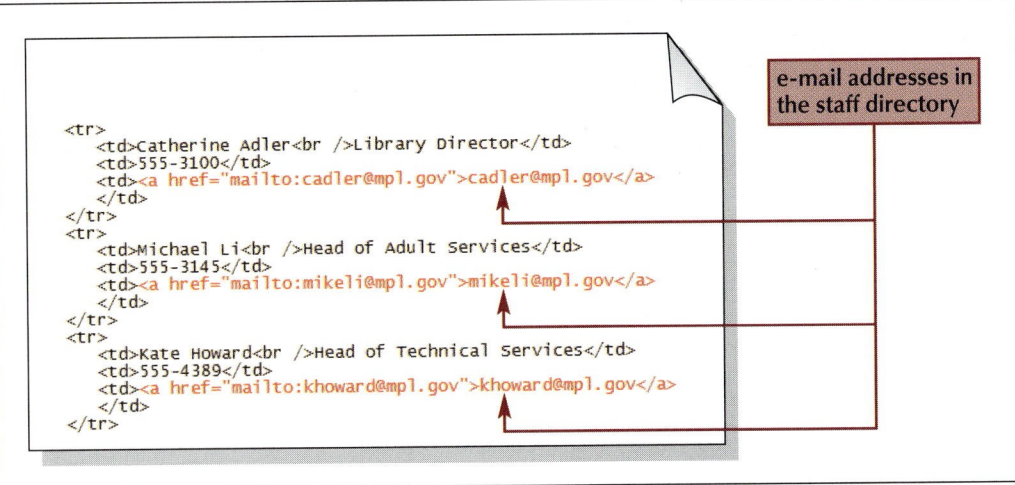

Kate would like you to scramble the e-mail addresses so that they don't appear within the Web page code; but when a browser loads and renders the page for a user, the e-mail addresses are unscrambled. See Figure 10-3. This mechanism will thwart most e-mail harvesters examining the document's HTML code while making the addresses available to users viewing the page on the Web. Note that some e-mail harvesters can still view both the underlying code and the page as they are rendered by a browser, so the proposed scrambling method is not 100% effective. However, because this technique will thwart many e-mail harvesters, Kate accepts it as a compromise solution.

Figure 10-3 Scrambling e-mail addresses

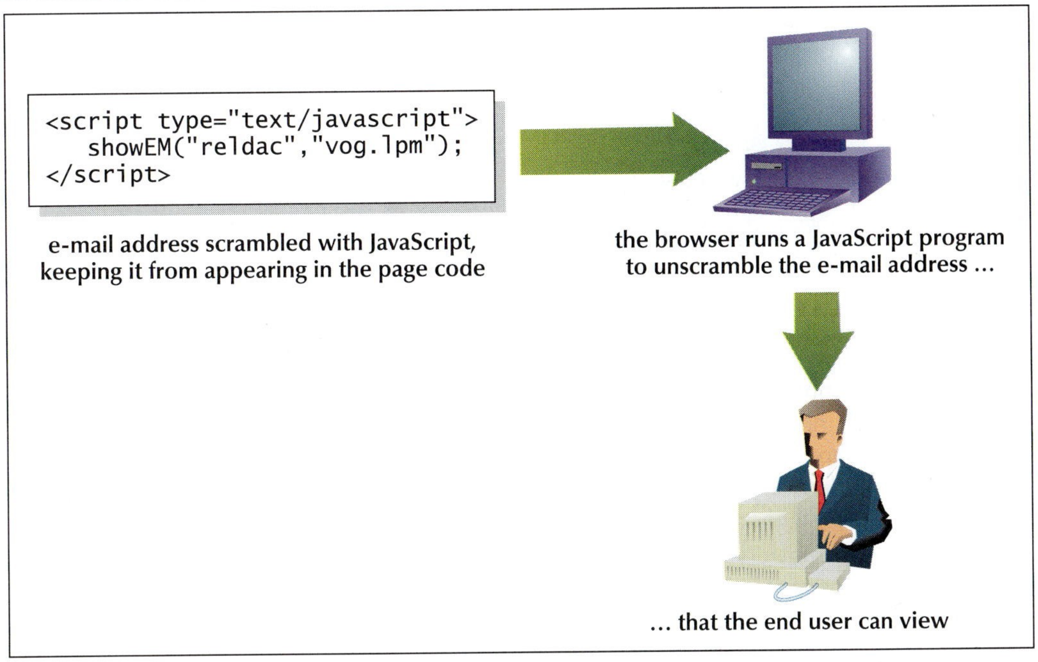

Neither HTML nor XHTML has features that allow you to scramble and unscramble the e-mail addresses from Kate's staff directory. This is not a standard function of Web browsers either. Therefore, you'll have to write a program to do this. Kate doesn't want library patrons to have to download any special applications; she wants the scrambling and unscrambling to appear behind the scenes of the library Web page. After some discussion, you decide that JavaScript is well suited to this task. You'll start on this project by first finding out just what JavaScript is and how to use it.

Server-Side and Client-Side Programming

Programming on the Web comes in two types: server-side programming and client-side programming. In **server-side programming**, a program is placed on the server that hosts a Web site. The program is then used to modify the contents and structure of Web pages. In some cases, users can interact with the program, requesting that specific information be displayed on a page, but the interaction is done remotely from the user to the server. See Figure 10-4.

Figure 10-4 **Server-side programming**

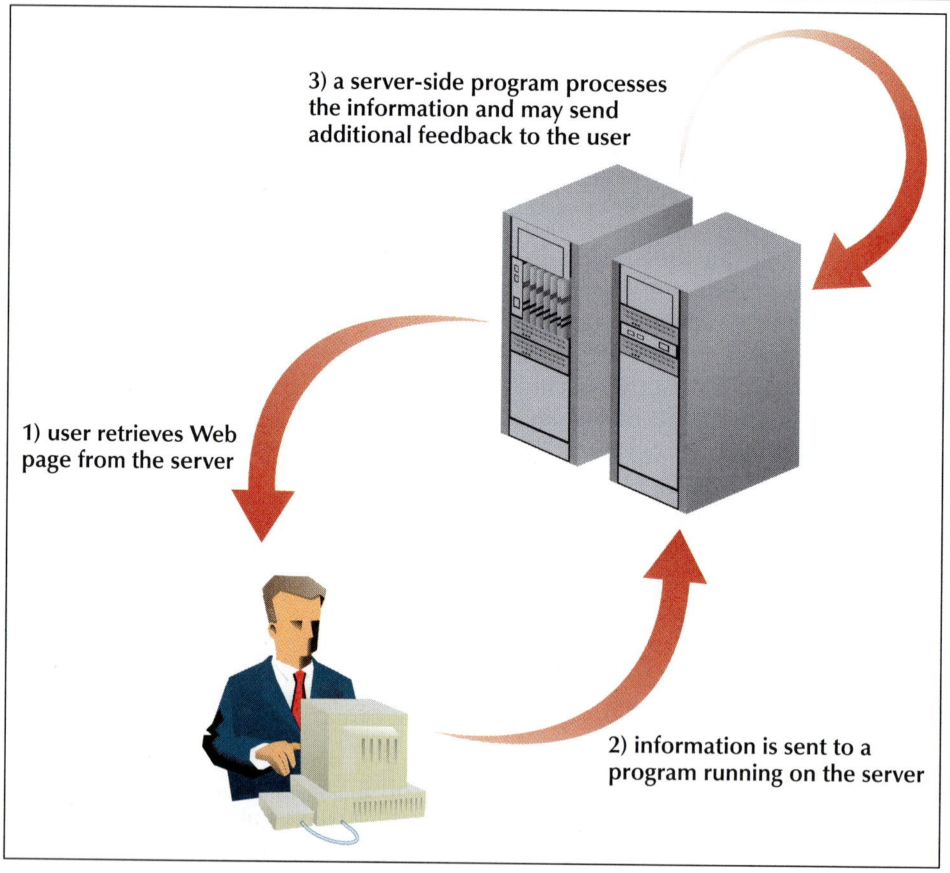
3) a server-side program processes the information and may send additional feedback to the user
1) user retrieves Web page from the server
2) information is sent to a program running on the server

There are advantages and disadvantages to this approach. A program running on a server can be connected to a database containing information not usually accessible to end users, enabling them to perform tasks not available on the client side. This enables Web pages to support such features as online banking, credit card transactions, and discussion groups. However, server-side programs use Web server resources, and in some cases a server's system administrator might place limitations on access to server-side programs to prevent users from continually accessing the server and potentially overloading the system. If the system is overloaded, an end user might have to sit through long delays as the server-side program handles multiple requests for information and action.

Client-side programming solves many of these problems by running programs on each user's computer rather than remotely off the server. See Figure 10-5.

Client-side programming **Figure 10-5**

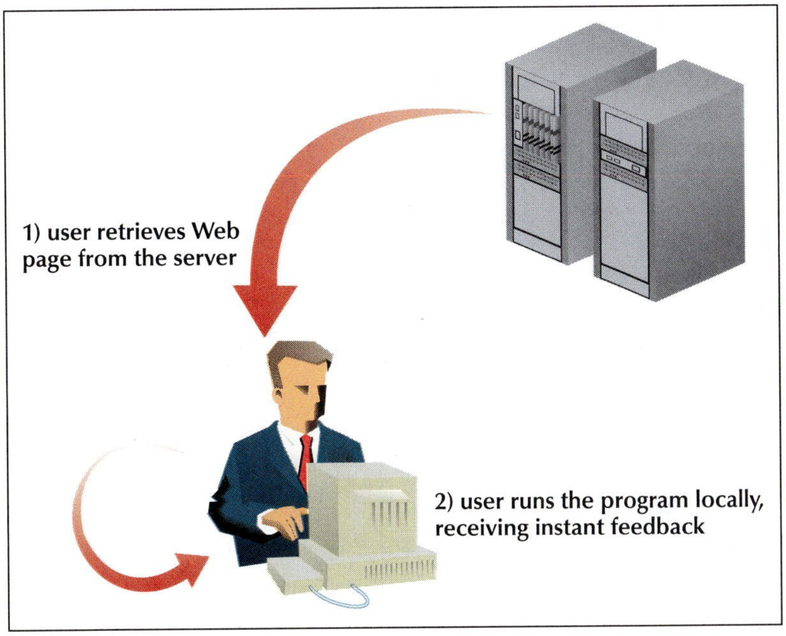
1) user retrieves Web page from the server
2) user runs the program locally, receiving instant feedback

Computing is thereby distributed so that the server is not overloaded with program-related requests. Client-side programs also tend to be more responsive because users do not have to wait for data to be sent over the Internet to a Web server. However, client-side programs can never completely replace server-side programming. For example, jobs such as running a search or processing a purchase order must be run from a central server because only the server contains the database needed to complete these types of operations.

In many cases, a combination of server-side and client-side programming is used. For example, Web forms typically use client-side programs to validate a user's entries (such as ensuring that all address information has been completely entered) and use server-side programs to submit the validated form for further processing (such as sending a purchase order to a central database). See Figure 10-6.

Figure 10-6 Combining client-side and server-side programming

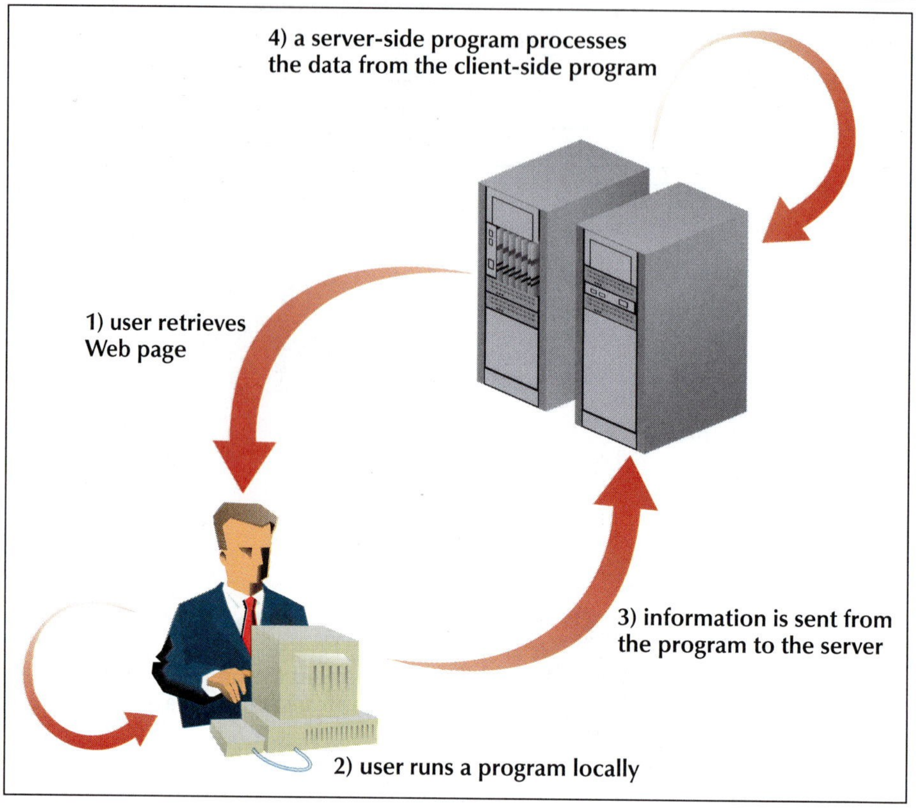

In this tutorial you'll work only with client-side programming. However, it's important to be aware that in many cases, a complete Web program includes both client-side and server-side elements.

The Development of JavaScript

Several programming languages can be run on the client side. One client-side programming language that you worked with in Tutorial 7 is Java. When Java was introduced, its advantages were quickly apparent and it was soon in wide use in many different browsers. However, creating a Java applet required access to the Java Development Kit (JDK), so nonprogrammers found it difficult to write their own Java applets.

To simplify this process, a team of developers from Netscape and Sun Microsystems created a subset of Java called **JavaScript**, which was different from Java in several important ways. Java is a **compiled language**, meaning that the program code must be submitted to a compiler that manipulates it, translating the code into a more basic language that machines can understand. For Java, this compiled code is the Java applet. Therefore, to create and run a program written in a compiled language, you need both the compiler and an application or operating system that can run the compiled code.

On the other hand, JavaScript is an **interpreted language**, meaning that the program code is executed directly without compiling. You need only two things to use JavaScript: 1) a text editor to write the JavaScript commands, and 2) a Web browser to run the commands and display the results. This means that JavaScript code can be inserted directly into an HTML or XHTML file, or placed in a separate text file that is linked to the Web page. JavaScript is not as powerful a computing language as Java, but it is simpler to use and meets the needs of most users who want to create programmable Web pages. Figure 10-7 highlights some of the key differences between Java and JavaScript.

Figure 10-7 Comparing Java and JavaScript

Java	JavaScript
A compiled language	An interpreted language
Requires the JDK (Java Development Kit) to create the applet	Requires a text editor
Requires a Java virtual machine or interpreter to run the applet	Requires a browser that can interpret JavaScript code
Applet files are distinct from the HTML and XHTML code	JavaScript programs are integrated with HTML and XHTML code
Source code is hidden from the user	Source code is accessible to the user
Powerful, requiring programming knowledge and experience	Simpler, requiring less programming knowledge and experience
Secure; programs cannot write content to the hard disk	Secure; programs cannot write content to the hard disk; however, there are more security holes than in Java
Programs run on the client side	Programs run on the client side

Through the years, JavaScript has undergone several revisions. Internet Explorer actually supports a slightly different version of JavaScript called **JScript**. Although JScript is almost identical to JavaScript, some JavaScript commands are not supported in JScript, and vice versa. In addition, although it is tempting to use commands available in the latest JavaScript or JScript versions, these commands might prevent your programs from running on older browsers. For these reasons, you should always test your JavaScript programs on a variety of Web browsers.

Because of the proliferation of competing versions and revisions of scripting languages, the responsibility for developing a scripting standard has been transferred to an international body called the **European Computer Manufacturers Association** (**ECMA**). The standard developed by the ECMA is called **ECMAScript**—though browsers still refer to it as JavaScript. Other client-side programming languages are also available to Web page designers, such as the Internet Explorer scripting language **VBScript**. However, because of the nearly universal support for JavaScript, you'll use this language for your work on the library Web site.

Working with the Script Element

JavaScript programs can be placed directly in an HTML file or they can be saved in an external text file. Placing JavaScript code in a Web page file means that users only need to retrieve one file from the server. In addition, because the code and the page it affects are both within the same file, it can be easier to locate and fix programming errors. However, if you place the code in a separate file, the programs you write can be shared by the different pages on your Web site. In this tutorial, you'll work with JavaScript code entered into an HTML file as well as code stored in an external file. You'll first examine how to insert JavaScript code directly into an HTML file.

Creating a Script Element

Scripts are entered into an HTML or XHTML file using the script element. The syntax of the script element is

```
<script type="mime-type">
   script commands
</script>
```

where *mime-type* defines the language in which the script is written and *script commands* are commands written in the scripting language. The type attribute is required for XHTML documents and should be used for HTML documents as well. The MIME type for JavaScript programs is text/javascript; meaning that for JavaScript programs, you would use the following form:

```
<script type="text/javascript">
   JavaScript commands
</script>
```

You might see other ways of entering script elements into Web page code. In earlier versions of HTML, the language attribute was used in place of the type attribute to indicate the script language. For older browsers, you indicate that the scripting language is JavaScript using the following form:

```
<script language="JavaScript">
   JavaScript commands
</script>
```

The language attribute has been deprecated and is not supported by strict applications of XHTML, so you should use the type attribute in its place if you want to conform with current standards.

Note that the script element can be used with programming languages other than JavaScript. Other client-side scripting languages are identified by using a different value for the type attribute. For example, if you use VBScript from Microsoft, the MIME type is text/vbscript. You won't use VBScript in this tutorial.

Reference Window | Creating a Script Element

- To place a JavaScript script element into the Web page, insert the two-sided tag
  ```
  <script type="mime-type">
     script commands
  </script>
  ```
  where *mime-type* defines the language in which the script is written and *script commands* are commands written in the scripting language.
- For JavaScript programs, set the *mime-type* to text/javascript.

Placing the Script Element

When a browser encounters a script element within a file, it treats any lines within the element as commands to be run. Script elements are processed in the order in which they appear within an HTML file; there is no limit to the number of script elements that you can use within a Web page. Scripts can be placed in either the head section or the body section of a document. When placed in the body section, a browser interprets and runs them as it loads the different elements of the Web page. Although a single page can contain many script elements, the browser still can work with them as a single unit. So JavaScript commands that are created in one script element can be referenced by commands in other script elements.

Writing a JavaScript Statement

Now that you've reviewed some of the basics involved in entering JavaScript into your HTML files, you'll examine how to enter JavaScript code. Every JavaScript program consists of a series of statements. Each **statement**—also known as a **command**—is a single line that indicates an action for the browser to take. A statement should end in a semicolon, employing the syntax

```
JavaScript statement;
```

where *JavaScript statement* is the code that the browser runs. The semicolon is the official way of notifying the browser that it has reached the end of the statement. Most browsers are very forgiving and still interpret most statements correctly even if you neglect to include the ending semicolon. However, it is good programming practice to include the semicolons and some browsers require them.

JavaScript and XML Parsers | InSight

Using JavaScript code within an XHTML file can lead to problems because XHTML parsers attempt to process the symbols in JavaScript code. Because character symbols such as angle brackets (<>) and the ampersand (&) are often used in JavaScript programs, this can lead to a page being rejected by an XHTML parser. To avoid this problem, you can place your JavaScript code within a CDATA section as follows:

```
<script type="text/javascript">
<![CDATA[
   JavaScript code
]]>
</script>
```

where *JavaScript code* is the code contained in the JavaScript program. The CDATA section marks the text of the JavaScript code as data that should not be processed by XHTML parsers. Unfortunately, the CDATA section is not well supported by current browsers.

A third alternative is not to embed your scripts within XHTML files at all, but instead to place them in external files. This practice has the added advantage of separating program code from page content. If you need to create valid XHTML documents, this is probably the best solution.

Writing Output to a Web Document

The first JavaScript program you add to Kate's document is a program that writes the text of an e-mail address into the Web page. Although you could enter the e-mail address directly, you use this opportunity to experiment with JavaScript. You also build on this simple statement as you progress through the rest of the tutorial. You insert the e-mail address for Catherine Adler as the first entry in the staff directory. Her e-mail address is cadler@mpl.gov. To write this text to the Web document, you insert the following statement:

```
<script type="text/javascript">
   document.write("cadler@mpl.gov");
</script>
```

This document.write() statement tells the browser to send the text string cadler@mpl.gov to the Web page document. To see how your browser applies this command, enter the script element and command into Kate's mpl.htm file.

To write text to the Web page using JavaScript:

1. Return to the **mpl.htm** in your text editor.
2. Locate the table cell after the entry for Catherine Adler and insert the following code, as shown in Figure 10-8:

```
<script type="text/javascript">
   document.write("cadler@mpl.gov");
</script>
```

Figure 10-8 Inserting a script element

```
<tr>
   <td>Catherine Adler<br />Library Director</td>
   <td>555-3100</td>
   <td>
      <script type="text/javascript">
         document.write("cadler@mpl.gov");
      </script>
   </td>
</tr>
```

script to write content to the Web document

3. Save your changes to the file and then reload **mpl.htm** in your Web browser. As shown in Figure 10-9, the text of Catherine's e-mail address should appear in the staff directory.

Figure 10-9 Text generated by JavaScript

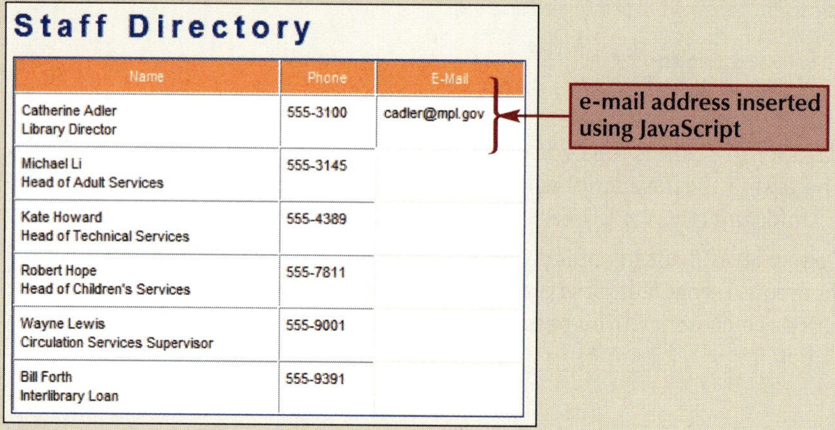
Staff Directory
Name
Phone
E-Mail
Catherine Adler
Library Director
555-3100
cadler@mpl.gov
Michael Li
Head of Adult Services
555-3145
Kate Howard
Head of Technical Services
555-4389
Robert Hope
Head of Children's Services
555-7811
Wayne Lewis
Circulation Services Supervisor
555-9001
Bill Forth
Interlibrary Loan
555-9391
e-mail address inserted using JavaScript

Trouble? Internet Explorer might display a yellow alert bar at the top of the browser window with a warning that it has restricted access to active content for security reasons. This is done to enable users to prevent their browsers from running unwanted scripts. To run the script, click the information bar and choose Allow Blocked Content from the pop-up menu, and then click Yes in the dialog box that follows.

Note that the placement of the script element tells the browser where to place the new text. Because the script element is placed between the opening and closing <td> tags, the text generated by the script is placed there as well. In more advanced JavaScript programs, you can direct your output to specific locations in the Web page document—but that's beyond the scope of this tutorial.

The document.write() Method

The document.write() method, which you just used to display the e-mail text, is one of the basic ways in JavaScript to send output to the Web document. Why is it called a method? In JavaScript, many commands involve working with objects in the Web page and browser. An **object** is any item—from the browser window itself to a document displayed in the browser to an element displayed within the document. Even the mouse pointer, the window scrollbars, or the browser application itself can be treated as an object. A **method** is a process by which JavaScript manipulates or acts upon the properties of an object. In this case, you've used the write() method to write new text into the document object. The document.write() method has the general syntax

```
document.write("text");
```

where *text* is a string of characters that you want written to the Web document. The text string can also include HTML tags. For example, the following statement writes the text Monroe Public Library marked as an h1 heading into a document:

```
document.write("<h1>Monroe Public Library</h1>");
```

When a browser encounters this statement, it places the text and the markup tags into the document and renders that text as if it had been entered directly into the HTML file.

Kate wants the e-mail addresses in the staff directory to appear as hypertext links. This requires placing the e-mail addresses within <a> tags and adding the href attribute value indicating the destination of each link. For example, the code to create a link for Catherine Adler's e-mail address is:

```
<a href="mailto:cadler@mpl.gov">cadler@mpl.gov</a>
```

Tip

Another method to write text to the Web page is the document.writeln() method, which is identical to the document.write() method except that it adds a line break to the end of the text.

Writing this text string requires you to include quotation marks around the href attribute value. Because text strings created with the document.write() method must be enclosed in quotes as well, you have to place one set of quotes within another. This is done by using both single and double quotation marks. If you want to write a double quotation mark as part of the code sent to the document, you enclose the quotation marks within single quotation marks. To write single quotation marks, you enclose them within a set of double quotation marks. The type of quotation mark must always be different. If you try to enclose double quotes within another set of double quotes, the browser won't know when the quoted text string begins and ends. The following JavaScript code encloses the href attribute value in single quotes and uses double quotes to mark the entire text to be written to the Web page document:

```
document.write("<a href='mailto:cadler@mpl.gov'>");
document.write("cadler@mpl.gov");
document.write("</a>");
```

Note that this example places the entire code into three separate document.write() commands. Although you could use one long text string, it might be more difficult to read and to type without making a mistake. A browser treats these consecutive commands as one long string of text to be written into the document.

Reference Window | Writing to the Web Page

- To write text to the Web page with JavaScript, use the method
  `document.write("text")`
  where *text* is the HTML code to be written to the Web page.

You're ready to add the code for the link to Catherine Adler's e-mail address.

To write the e-mail link for Catherine Adler:

1. Return to the **mpl.htm** file in your text editor.
2. Directly after the opening <script> element, insert the following command:

   ```
   document.write("<a href='mailto:cadler@mpl.gov'>");
   ```

3. Directly before the closing </script> tag, insert the following command:

   ```
   document.write("</a>");
   ```

   Figure 10-10 shows the revised code in the file.

Figure 10-10 Inserting several document.write() commands

```
<tr>
   <td>Catherine Adler<br />Library Director</td>
   <td>555-3100</td>
   <td>
      <script type="text/javascript">
         document.write("<a href='mailto:cadler@mpl.gov'>");
         document.write("cadler@mpl.gov");
         document.write("</a>");
      </script>
   </td>
</tr>
```

4. Save your changes and then reopen **mpl.htm** in your Web browser.
5. Hover your mouse pointer over the e-mail address to verify that it is a link. As shown in Figure 10-11, the link to the e-mail address should appear in the browser's status bar.

Figure 10-11 Viewing an e-mail link

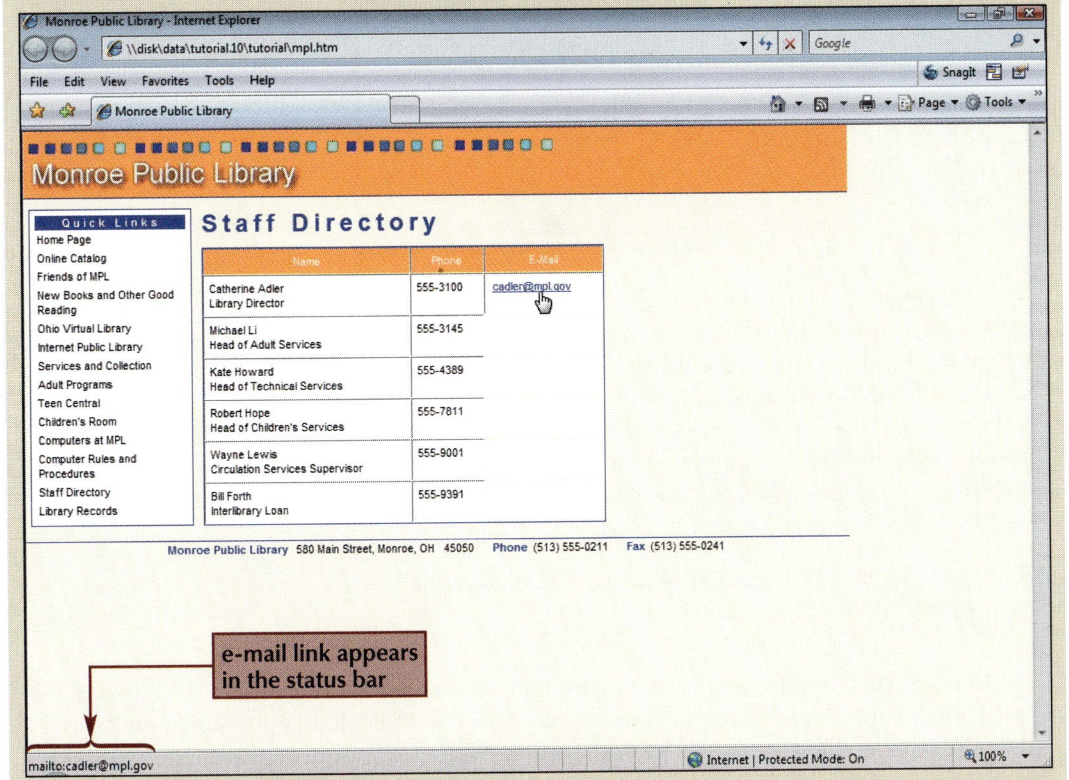

Trouble? If the link does not appear, verify that you included the opening and closing quotation marks in the JavaScript commands you just entered.

6. If you want to take a break before starting the next session, you can close any open files or programs now.

Understanding JavaScript Syntax

Besides the use of semicolons, there are some other syntax rules you should keep in mind when writing JavaScript statements. JavaScript is case sensitive so you must pay attention to whether or not letters are capitalized. For example, the following statements are not equivalent as far as JavaScript is concerned:

```
document.write("</a>");
Document.write("</a>");
```

The first command writes the HTML tag </a> to a Web page document. The second command is not recognized by a browser as a legitimate command and results in an error message. Figure 10-12 shows the error message generated by the Internet Explorer browser. The browser does not recognize the word Document (as opposed to document) and so cannot process the command. You'll examine how to handle this type of error later in this tutorial.

Figure 10-12 **An Internet Explorer error message resulting from improper case**

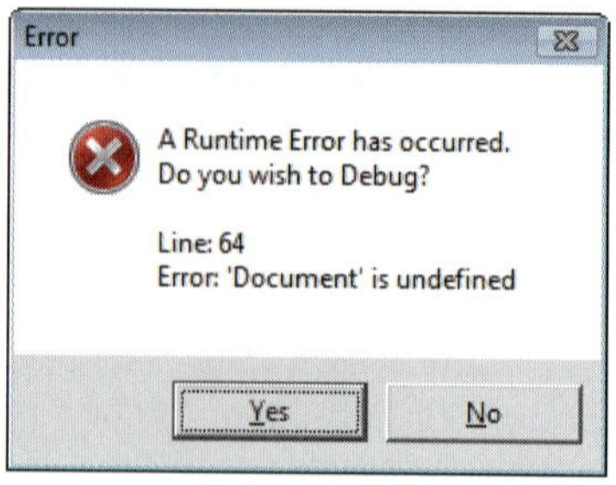

Like HTML, JavaScript ignores most occurrences of extra white space so you can indent your code to make it easier to read. You can see examples of this in Figure 10-10, where the newly entered statements are indented several spaces to make the commands stand out from the opening and closing <script> tags.

However, unlike HTML, you must be careful about line breaks occurring within a statement. A line break cannot be placed within the name of a JavaScript command or within a quoted text string without causing an error in the code. For example, the following line break is not allowed:

```
document.write("<a href='mailto:cadler@mpl.gov'>
cadler@mpl.gov
</a>");
```

It is good practice not to break a statement into several lines if you can avoid it. If you must break a long statement into several lines, you can indicate that the statement continues on the next line using a backslash, as follows:

```
document.write("<a href='mailto:cadler@mpl.gov'> \
cadler@mpl.gov \
</a>");
```

If the line break occurs within a quoted text string, you can also break the string into several distinct text strings placed over several lines by adding a plus symbol (+) at the end of each line, as follows:

```
document.write("<a href='mailto:cadler@mpl.gov'>" +
"cadler@mpl.gov" +
"</a>");
```

> **Tip**
> You can write a long text string to a Web page by breaking the text string into several document.write() statements.

The + symbol used in this command combines several text strings into a single text string. However, breaking a single statement into several lines is usually not recommended because of the possibility of introducing errors into the code. It should be done only with very long and complicated statements.

Supporting Non-JavaScript Browsers | InSight

For browsers that don't support scripts or that have their support for client-side scripts disabled, you can specify alternative content using the noscript element. The syntax of the noscript element is

```
<noscript>
   alternative content
</noscript>
```

where *alternative content* is the content a browser should display in place of accessing and running the script. For example, the following code displays a text message indicating that the page requires the use of JavaScript:

```
<script type="text/javascript">
   JavaScript statements
</script>
<noscript>
   <p>This page requires JavaScript. Please turn on JavaScript
      if your browser supports it and reload the page.</p>
</noscript>
```

Browsers that support client-side scripts and have that support enabled ignore the content of the noscript element.

You've completed the first phase of creating a script to scramble e-mail addresses in Kate's staff directory. At this point you've worked on learning how to create and run JavaScript code to write text to a Web document. In the next session you'll add the ability to create and work with variables and functions.

Session 10.1 Quick Check | Review

1. What is a client-side program? What is a server-side program?
2. What tag do you enter in your HTML code to create a script element for the JavaScript programming language?
3. What JavaScript command writes the text Public Library as an h2 heading to a Web document?
4. What JavaScript command would you enter to write the following tag to a Web document?

   ```
   <h2 id="sub">Public Library</h2>
   ```

5. How do you enter a single JavaScript statement on two lines?
6. Why would the following command produce an error message?

   ```
   document.Write("Monroe Public Library");
   ```

7. What code should you enter in an HTML file to display the following paragraph for browsers that don't support JavaScript?

   ```
   <p><i>JavaScript required</i></p>
   ```

Session 10.2

Working with Variables

In the previous session you learned how to write page content to a Web page using the document.write() method. Because you used this method to specify a text string explicitly, the code did little more than what you could have accomplished by entering the e-mail link directly into an HTML tag. However, the document.write() method is much more powerful and versatile when used in conjunction with variables. A **variable** is a named item in a program that stores information. Most JavaScript programs use variables to represent values and text strings. Variables are useful because they can store information created in one part of a program and use that information elsewhere. Variable values can also change as the program runs, enabling the program to display different values under varying conditions.

Declaring a Variable

It's common practice to introduce variables in your code by declaring them. **Declaring** a variable tells the JavaScript interpreter to reserve memory space for the variable. The statement to declare a variable is

```
var variable;
```

where *variable* is the name assigned to the variable. For example, the following statement creates a variable named emLink:

```
var emLink;
```

You can declare multiple variables by entering the variable names in a comma-separated list. The following statement declares three variables named emLink, userName, and emServer:

```
var emLink, userName, emServer;
```

JavaScript imposes some limits on variable names:

- The first character must be either a letter or an underscore character (_).
- The remaining characters can be letters, numbers, or underscore characters.
- Variable names cannot contain spaces.
- You cannot use words that JavaScript has reserved for other purposes. For example, you cannot name a variable document.write.

Tip

To avoid programming errors, use a consistent pattern for case in variable names.

Like other aspects of the JavaScript language, variable names are case sensitive. The variable names emLink and emlink represent two different variables. One common programming mistake is to forget this important fact and to use uppercase and lowercase letters interchangeably in variable names.

Assigning a Value to a Variable

Once a variable has been created or declared, you can assign it a value. The statement to assign a value to a variable is

```
variable = value;
```

where *variable* is the variable name and *value* is the value assigned to the variable. For example, the following statement stores the text string cadler in a variable named userName:

```
userName = "cadler";
```

You can combine the variable declaration and the assignment of a value in a single statement. The following statements declare the userName and emServer variables, and set their initial values:

```
var userName = "cadler", emServer = "mpl.gov";
```

Note that declaring a variable with the var keyword is not required in JavaScript. The first time you use a variable, JavaScript creates the variable in computer memory. The following statement both creates the director variable (if it has not already been declared in a previous statement) and assigns it an initial value:

```
director = "Catherine Adler";
```

Although it's not required, it's considered good programming style to include the var command whenever you create a variable. Doing so helps you keep track of the variables a program uses and also makes it easier for others to read and interpret your code.

Tip

To make your code easier to interpret, place all of your variable declarations at the beginning of your program, along with comments describing the purpose of each variable.

Declaring a JavaScript Variable | Reference Window

- To declare a JavaScript variable, run the statement
  `var variable`
  where *variable* is the name assigned to the variable.
- To declare a JavaScript variable and set its initial value, use
  `var variable = value;`
  where *value* is the initial value of the variable.

Using what you've learned about variables, you're ready to add two variables to the script element you created in the last session. The first variable, userName, will store the text string cadler, which is Catherine Adler's username on the library's mail server. The second variable, emServer, will store the text string mpl.gov, which is the domain name of the mail server. Later you'll revise this code to place different values in these variables, but you start with these two fixed values. By breaking up Catherine Adler's e-mail address into two parts, you'll make it easier to hide the e-mail address from e-mail harvesters.

To create two JavaScript variables:

1. Return to the **mpl.htm** file in your text editor.
2. Locate the script element you created in the last session. Directly below the opening <script> tag, insert the following code, as shown in Figure 10-13:

```
var userName = "cadler";
var emServer = "mpl.gov";
```

Figure 10-13 **Declaring JavaScript variables**

```
<tr>
   <td>Catherine Adler<br />Library Director</td>
   <td>555-3100</td>
   <td>
      <script type="text/javascript">
         var userName = "cadler";
         var emServer = "mpl.gov";

         document.write("<a href='mailto:cadler@mpl.gov'>");
         document.write("cadler@mpl.gov");
         document.write("</a>");
      </script>
   </td>
</tr>
```

3. Save your changes to the file.

Working with Data Types

So far, the examples you've explored have used variables that store text strings. However, JavaScript variables can store different types of information. The type of information stored in a variable is referred to as its **data type**. JavaScript supports the following data types:

- numeric value
- text string
- Boolean value
- null value

A **numeric value** is any number, such as 13, 22.5, or -3.14159. Numbers can also be expressed in scientific notation, such as 5.1E2 for the value 5.1×10^2 (or 510). Numeric values are specified without any quotation marks. So if you wished to store the value 2007 in the year variable, you would use the statement

```
year = 2007;
```

rather than

```
year = "2007";
```

A **text string** is any group of characters, such as "Hello" or "Happy Holidays!" or "421 Sunrise Lane." Text strings must be enclosed within either double or single quotation marks, but not both. The string value 'Hello' is acceptable, but the string value "Hello' is not.

A **Boolean value** indicates the truth or falsity of a statement. There are only two Boolean values: true and false. For example, the following statement sets the value of the useSafari variable to true and the value of the useIE variable to false:

```
useSafari = true;
useIE = false;
```

Tip

If a Boolean variable's value is left undefined, it is interpreted by JavaScript as having a value of false.

Boolean values are most often used in programs that must act differently based on different conditions. The useSafari variable cited above might be used in a program that tests whether a user is running the Safari browser. If the value is set to true, the program might be written to run differently for the user than if the value were set to false.

Finally, a **null value** indicates that no value has yet been assigned to the variable. This can also be done explicitly using the keyword null in assigning a value to the variable, as in the statement

```
emLink = null;
```

or implicitly by simply declaring the variable without assigning it a value, as follows:

```
var emLink;
```

In either case, the emLink variable will have a null value until it is assigned a value using one of the other data types.

In JavaScript, a variable's data type is always determined by the context in which it is used. This means that a variable can switch from one data type to another within a single program. In the following two statements, the variable Month starts out as a numeric variable with an initial value of 5, but then becomes a text string variable containing the text March:

```
Month = 5;
Month = "March";
```

When variables are not strictly tied to specific data types like this, programmers refer to the language as a **weakly typed language**; JavaScript is one such language. Other programming languages are **strongly typed languages**, forcing the programming to explicitly identify a variable's data type. In those languages, the above code would result in an error because a given variable cannot store more than one type of data.

A weakly typed language such as JavaScript relieves the programmer from the task of assigning a data type to a variable. However, this can lead to unpredictable results if you aren't careful. For example, in JavaScript the + symbol can be used with either numeric values or text strings. When used with numeric values, it returns the sum of the values—so that the code

```
var total = 5 + 4;
```

stores the value 9 in the total variable. When used with text strings, the + symbol combines the text strings—so that the code

```
var emLink = "cadler" + "@" + "mpl.gov";
```

stores the text string cadler@mpl.gov in the emLink variable. However, when used with both text strings and numeric values, the + symbol treats the numeric value as a text string so that the code

```
x = 5;
y = "4";
z = x+y;
```

stores the text string 54 in the z variable because the y variable stores "4" as a text string, not a number. This result is not readily apparent from the code without a prior understanding of how JavaScript handles text and numeric values. This is one of the limitations of a weakly typed language in which data types are inferred by the rules of the language and not by the programmer.

To see how the + symbol works with text string variables, you'll add a third variable to your script. The emLink variable will be used to store the complete e-mail address for Catherine Adler by combining the userName variable with the emServer variable.

To create the emLink variable:

1. Return to the **mpl.htm** file in your text editor.
2. Directly below the command to create the emServer variable, insert the following command, as shown in Figure 10-14:

```
var emLink = userName + "@" + emServer;
```

Figure 10-14 **Creating the emLink variable**

```
<script type="text/javascript">
   var userName = "cadler";
   var emServer = "mpl.gov";
   var emLink = userName + "@" + emServer;

   document.write("<a href='mailto:cadler@mpl.gov'>");
   document.write("cadler@mpl.gov");
   document.write("</a>");
</script>
```

the value stored in the emLink variable is cadler@mpl.gov

3. Save your changes to the file.

After you've created a variable, you can use it in JavaScript statements in place of the value it contains. The following code writes the text string Monroe Public Library to a Web page:

```
var libName = "Monroe Public Library";
document.write(libName);
```

You can also use the + symbol to combine a variable with a text string and then write the combined text string to the document. The following statements send the text string

```
<p>Welcome to the Monroe Library</p>
```

to the Web document:

```
var libName = "Monroe Library";
document.write("<p>Welcome to the "+libName+"</p>");
```

You can use the document.write() command with the variables you've already created to write the hypertext link for Catherine Adler's e-mail address. The code is as follows:

```
document.write("<a href='mailto:" + emLink + "'>");
document.write(emLink);
document.write("</a>");
```

If the text string cadler@mpl.gov is stored in the emLink variable, these commands will write the following code to the Web page:

```
<a href='mailto:cadler@mpl.gov'>
caldler@mpl.gov
</a>
```

Notice that the document.write() command nests single quotes within double quotes so that the HTML code written to the Web page includes the value of the href attribute within a set of single quotation marks. You'll add this JavaScript code to the Web page, replacing the previous document.write() commands.

To replace the document.write() commands in the script:

1. Return to the **mpl.htm** file in your text editor.
2. Replace the three document.write() commands in the script with the following code, as shown in Figure 10-15:

```
document.write("<a href='mailto:" + emLink + "'>");
document.write(emLink);
document.write("</a>");
```

Figure 10-15

Writing the value of the emLink variable to the Web page

```
<script type="text/javascript">
   var userName = "cadler";
   var emServer = "mpl.gov";
   var emLink = userName + "@" + emServer;

   document.write("<a href='mailto:" + emLink + "'>");
   document.write(emLink);
   document.write("</a>");
</script>
```

3. Save your changes to the file and then reload **mpl.htm** in your Web browser. The hypertext link for Catherine Adler's e-mail address should remain unchanged from what was shown earlier in Figure 10-11.

Creating a JavaScript Function

So far, in writing code for the staff directory page, you've focused on the e-mail address of only one person. However, five other individuals are listed in the staff directory. If you wanted to use JavaScript to write the e-mail links for the rest of the directory, you could repeat the code you used for Catherine Adler's entry five more times. However, JavaScript provides a simpler way of doing this.

When you want to reuse the same JavaScript commands throughout your Web page, you store the commands in a function. A **function** is a collection of commands that performs an action or returns a value. Every function includes a **function name**, which identifies it, and a set of commands that are run when the function is called. Some functions also require **parameters**, which are variables associated with the function. The general syntax of a JavaScript function is

```
function function_name(parameters){
   JavaScript commands
}
```

where *function_name* is the name of the function, *parameters* is a comma-separated list of variables used in the function, and *JavaScript commands* are the statements run by the function. Function names, like variable names, are case sensitive. For example, weekDay and WEEKDAY are treated as different function names. A function name must begin with a letter or underscore (_) and cannot contain any spaces. The following is an example of a function named showMsg() that writes a paragraph to a Web document:

```
function showMsg() {
   document.write("<p>Welcome to the Monroe Library</p>");
}
```

There are no parameters to this function. If you had stored the name of the library in a function parameter named libName, the showMsg() function would look as follows:

```
function showMsg(libName) {
   document.write("<p>Welcome to the" + libName +"</p>");
}
```

If the libName parameter had the value Monroe Public Library, then the HTML code

```
<p>Welcome to the Monroe Public Library</p>
```

would be sent to the Web document.

Rather than rewrite the code for generating the e-mail link for each person in the staff directory, you'll put the commands in a function named showEM(). The code for the showEM() function is as follows:

```
function showEM(userName,emServer) {
   var emLink = userName+"@" + emServer;
   document.write("<a href='mailto:" + emLink + "'>");
   document.write(emLink);
   document.write("</a>");
}
```

Tip

Organize your functions by placing them all within the document head rather than scattered throughout the Web page.

Compare the code for this function to the script you created in Figure 10-15. Note that userName and emServer variables from that earlier code are used here as parameters of the showEM() function.

Add the showEM() function to the document head of the mpl.htm file.

To insert the showEM() function:

1. Return to the **mpl.htm** file in your text editor.
2. Directly above the closing </head> tag, insert the following script element and function, as shown in Figure 10-16:

```
<script type="text/javascript">
   function showEM(userName,emServer) {
      var emLink = userName + "@"+emServer;
      document.write("<a href='mailto:" + emLink + "'>");
      document.write(emLink);
      document.write("</a>");
   }
</script>
```

Figure 10-16 **Inserting the showEM() function**

```
<title>Monroe Public Library</title>
<link href="mplstyles.css" rel="stylesheet" type="text/css" />

<script type="text/javascript">
   function showEM(userName, emServer) {
      var emLink = userName + "@" + emServer;
      document.write("<a href='mailto:" + emLink + "'>");
      document.write(emLink);
      document.write("</a>");
   }
</script>
</head>
```

Calling a Function

When a browser encounters a function, it bypasses it without executing any of the code it contains. The function is executed only when called by another JavaScript command. If the function has any parameters, the initial values of the parameters are set when the function is called. The expression to call a function and run the commands it contains has the following form:

```
function_name(parameter values)
```

where *function_name* is the name of the function and *parameter values* is a comma-separated list of values that match the parameters of the function. For example, to call the showMsg() function described earlier using the text string Monroe Public Library as the value of the libName parameter, you would run the command

```
showMsg("Monroe Public Library");
```

The HTML code

```
<p>Welcome to the Monroe Public Library</p>
```

would be written to the document.

Parameter values can also themselves be variables. The following commands store the library name in a text string variable named libText and call the showMsg() function using that variable as the parameter value:

```
var libText="Cutler Public Library";

showMsg(libText);
```

The result is that the following HTML code is written to the Web document:

```
<p>Welcome to the Cutler Public Library</p>
```

Functions can be called repeatedly with different parameter values to achieve different results. For example, the following code calls the showMsg() function twice with different parameter values to display two welcome paragraphs for the Monroe and Cutler Public Libraries:

```
var libText = "Monroe Public Library";
showMsg(libText);
var libText2 = "Cutler Public Library";
showMsg(libText2);
```

You can use a function call to run the showEM() function you just entered. To write a hypertext link for Catherine Adler's e-mail address, the function call is as follows:

```
showEM("cadler","mpl.gov");
```

As a result, the userName parameter has an initial value of cadler and the emServer parameter has the initial value of mpl.gov. You're ready to replace the commands you entered earlier to write the hypertext link for Catherine Adler's e-mail address with this function call.

To call the showEM() function:

1. Return to the **mpl.htm** file in your text editor, and scroll down the file to the script element containing the JavaScript code for Catherine Adler's e-mail address.

2. Replace all of the commands within the script element with the following command, as shown in Figure 10-17:

```
showEM("cadler","mpl.gov");
```

Figure 10-17 Calling the showEM() function

```
<tr>
   <td>Catherine Adler<br />Library Director</td>
   <td>555-3100</td>
   <td>

      <script type="text/javascript">
         showEM("cadler","mpl.gov");
      </script>

   </td>
</tr>
```

3. Save your changes to the file and then reload **mpl.htm** in your Web browser. The link to Catherine Adler's e-mail address should once again appear in the staff table, unchanged from Figure 10-11.

Using the function call gives the same result as the code you used earlier. However, the great advantage is that you can reuse the showEM() function for other e-mail addresses in the staff directory by simply changing the parameter values. You don't have to reenter all four of the program lines. For longer programs this is a substantial improvement.

Reference Window | Creating and Calling a JavaScript Function

- To create a JavaScript function that performs an action, insert the structure
  ```
  function function_name(parameters){
     JavaScript commands
  }
  ```
  where *function_name* is the name of the function, *parameters* is a comma-separated list of variable names used in the function, and *JavaScript commands* are the statements run by the function.
- To create a JavaScript function that returns a value, use
  ```
  function function_name(parameters){
     JavaScript commands
     return value;
  }
  ```
  where *value* is the value returned by the function.
- To call a JavaScript function, run the command
  ```
  function_name(values)
  ```
  where *function_name* is the name of the JavaScript function and *values* is a comma-separated list of values for each of the parameters of the function.

Kate asks you to call the showEM() function for the other e-mail addresses in the staff table.

To add the remaining e-mail addresses:

1. Return to the **mpl.htm** file in your text editor.
2. Locate the entry for Michael Li. His e-mail address is mikeli@mpl.gov. Add the following script element to the empty table cell that directly follows the Michael Li entry:

```
<script type="text/javascript">
   showEM("mikeli","mpl.gov");
</script>
```

3. Kate Howard's e-mail address is khoward@mpl.gov. Insert the following script element in the empty table cell for her entry in the staff directory:

```
<script type="text/javascript">
   showEM("khoward","mpl.gov");
</script>
```

Trouble? You can use the copy and paste feature of your text editor because the additions you'll make to the file in these steps are so similar. If you're not sure where to place these script elements, refer to Figure 10-18.

4. Robert Hope's e-mail address is rhope@mpl.gov. Enter the following script element for his entry:

```
<script type="text/javascript">
   showEM("rhope","mpl.gov");
</script>
```

5. Wayne Lewis's e-mail address is wlewis@mpl.gov. Enter the following script element in the empty table cell for his entry:

```
<script type="text/javascript">
   showEM("wlewis","mpl.gov");
</script>
```

6. Bill Forth's e-mail address is bforth@mpl.gov. Enter the following code in the empty table cell for his entry:

```
<script type="text/javascript">
   showEM("bforth","mpl.gov");
</script>
```

Figure 10-18 shows the revised code in the mpl.htm file.

Figure 10-18 **Inserting the remaining e-mail addresses**

```
<tr>
   <td>Michael Li<br />Head of Adult Services</td>
   <td>555-3145</td>
   <td>
      <script type="text/javascript">
         showEM("mikeli","mpl.gov");
      </script>
   </td>
</tr>
<tr>
   <td>Kate Howard<br />Head of Technical Services</td>
   <td>555-4389</td>
   <td>
      <script type="text/javascript">
         showEM("khoward","mpl.gov");
      </script>
   </td>
</tr>
<tr>
   <td>Robert Hope<br />Head of Children's Services</td>
   <td>555-7811</td>
   <td>
      <script type="text/javascript">
         showEM("rhope","mpl.gov");
      </script>
   </td>
</tr>
<tr>
   <td>Wayne Lewis<br />Circulation Services Supervisor</td>
   <td>555-9001</td>
   <td>
      <script type="text/javascript">
         showEM("wlewis","mpl.gov");
      </script>
   </td>
</tr>
<tr>
   <td>Bill Forth<br />Interlibrary Loan</td>
   <td>555-9391</td>
   <td>
      <script type="text/javascript">
         showEM("bforth","mpl.gov");
      </script>
   </td>
</tr>
```

7. Save your changes to the file and reload **mpl.htm** in your Web browser. Figure 10-19 shows the complete list of e-mail addresses in the staff directory. Verify that each e-mail address is a hypertext link by hovering your mouse pointer over the address text and observe the destination of the link in the browser's status bar.

Figure 10-19 **The complete list of e-mail address links in the staff directory**

Name	Phone	E-Mail
Catherine Adler Library Director	555-3100	cadler@mpl.gov
Michael Li Head of Adult Services	555-3145	mikeli@mpl.gov
Kate Howard Head of Technical Services	555-4389	khoward@mpl.gov
Robert Hope Head of Children's Services	555-7811	rhope@mpl.gov
Wayne Lewis Circulation Services Supervisor	555-9001	wlewis@mpl.gov
Bill Forth Interlibrary Loan	555-9391	bforth@mpl.gov

8. If you want to take a break before starting the next session, you can close any open files and programs now.

Creating a Function to Return a Value

You created the showEM() function to perform the action of writing a text string to your Web document. The other use of functions is to return a calculated value. For a function to return a value, it must include a return statement. The syntax of a function that returns a value is

```
function function_name(parameters){
   JavaScript commands
   return value;
}
```

where *value* is the calculated value that is returned by the function. For example, the following CalcArea() function calculates the area of a rectangular region by multiplying the region's length and width:

```
function CalcArea(length, width) {
   var area = length*width;
   return area;
}
```

In this function, the value of the area variable is returned by the function. You can then call the function to retrieve this value. The following code uses the function to calculate the area of a rectangle whose dimensions are 8 × 6 units:

```
var x = 8;
var y = 6;
var z = CalcArea(x,y);
```

The first two commands assign the values 8 and 6 to the x and y variables, respectively. The values of both of these variables are then sent to the CalcArea() function as the values of the length and width parameters. The CalcArea() function uses these values to calculate the area, which it then returns, assigning that value to the z variable. As a result of these commands, a value of 48 is assigned to the z variable.

Functions that return a value can be placed within larger expressions. For example, the following code calls the CalcArea() function within an expression that multiplies the area value by 2:

```
var z = CalcArea(x,y)*2;
```

When this command is run, the value of the CalcArea() function is returned, multiplied by 2, and then stored in the z variable. Using the above parameter values, the value of the z variable is 96.

Functions and Variable Scope | InSight

As you've seen, the commands within a function are run only when called. This has an impact on how variables within the function are treated. Every variable you create has a property known as **scope**, which indicates where you can reference a variable within the Web page. A variable's scope can be either local or global. A variable created within a JavaScript function has **local scope** and can be referenced only within that function. Variables with local scope are sometimes referred to as **local variables**. In the function you created in this session, the emLink variable has local scope and can be referenced only within the showEM() function. Parameters such as the userName and emServer parameters from the showEM() function also have local scope and are not recognized outside of the function in which they're used. When the showEM() function stops running, those variables and their values are not held in the computer memory and their values can no longer be accessed.

Variables not declared within functions have **global scope** and can be referenced from within all script elements on the Web page. Variables with global scope are often referred to as **global variables**.

You've successfully added the showEM() function to the staff directory page. In the next session you'll continue to add features to that function, including the ability to scramble and unscramble e-mail addresses to further hide them from e-mail harvesters.

Session 10.2 Quick Check | Review

1. Specify the JavaScript command to declare a variable named weekday with an initial value of Friday.
2. Describe two uses of the + symbol.
3. What are the four data types supported by JavaScript?
4. Specify the JavaScript command to write the code

   ```
   <img src='file' alt='' />
   ```

   to the Web page, where *file* is the value stored in the fileName variable.
5. What are the two purposes of a JavaScript function?
6. Write a JavaScript function named CalcVol() to calculate the volume of a rectangular solid. The function should have three parameters named x, y, and z, and return the value of a variable named Vol that is equal to x*y*z.
7. Write the JavaScript statement to call the CalcVol() function with values of x = 3, y = 10, and z = 4, storing the result of the function in a variable named TotalVol.
8. What is variable scope?

Session 10.3

Accessing an External JavaScript File

You show your work on the staff directory to Kate. She's happy that you were able to use JavaScript to generate the e-mail addresses, but she's still concerned that the text of each employee's username and mail server are present in the document as parameter values of the showEM() function. She would like to have those values hidden from any e-mail harvesters that might be scanning the document code. You discuss the issue with a programmer friend who sends you a file containing the following function:

```
function stringReverse(textString) {
   if (!textString) return '';
   var revString='';
   for (i = textString.length-1; i>=0; i--)
      revString+=textString.charAt(i);
   return revString;
}
```

Interpreting the code contained within this function is beyond the scope of this tutorial, but for now it is sufficient to know in general what the function does. The function has a single parameter named textString, which stores a string of characters. The function then creates a variable name revString that stores the characters from textString in reverse order, and that reversed text string is returned by the function. For example, if you called the function in the statements

```
userName = stringReverse("reldac");
emServer = stringReverse("vog.lpm");
```

the userName variable would have the value cadler, and the emServer variable would have the value mpl.gov (the text strings reldac and vog.lpm in reverse order). You show this function to Kate and she agrees that this will be sufficient to hide the actual username and server name from most e-mail address harvesters.

The stringReverse() function has already been entered for you and stored in a file named spam.js. To access JavaScript code and functions placed in external files, you employ the same script element you've been using to insert JavaScript commands directly into the staff directory document. The code to access an external script file is

```
<script src="url" type="mime-type"></script>
```

where *url* is the URL of the external document and *mime-type* is the language of the code in the external script file. For example, to access the code in the spam.js file, you would add the following script element to your Web document:

```
<script type="text/javascript" src="spam.js"></script>
```

> **Tip**
>
> Place all script elements that reference external files in the document head so that those programs are immediately loaded by the Web browser and can be referenced by any code within the Web page.

It's a common practice for JavaScript programmers to create libraries of functions located in external files that are easily accessible to pages on the entire Web site. Any new functions added to the external file are then instantly accessible to each Web page without having to edit the contents of those pages. External files containing JavaScript commands and functions always have the file extension .js to distinguish them from files containing script commands from other languages.

When a browser encounters a script element that points to an external file, it loads the contents of the external file into the Web document just as if the programmer had entered the code from the external file directly into the Web file. See Figure 10-20.

Using an external script file **Figure 10-20**

```
function stringReverse(textString) {
   if (!textString) return '';
   var revString='';
   for (i = textString.length-1; i>=0; i--)
      revString+=textString.charAt(i)
   return revString;
}
```

```
<title>Monroe Public Library</title>
<link href="mplstyles.css" rel="stylesheet" type="text/css" />
<script src="spam.js" type="text/javascript"></script>
<script type="text/javascript">
   function showEM(userName, emServer) {
      var emLink = userName + "@" + emServer;
      document.write("<a href='mailto:" + emLink + "'>");
      document.write(emLink);
      document.write("</a>");
   }
</script>
</head>
```

Accessing an External JavaScript File | Reference Window

- To access the code stored in an external file, add the script element
  `<script src="url" type="mime-type"></script>`
  to the Web page, where *url* is the URL of the external document and *mime-type* is the language of the code in the external script file.
- For JavaScript files, set the *mime-type* to text/javascript.
- JavaScript files usually have the file extension .js.

You insert a script element into the staff directory page to access the code from the spam.js file.

To access the code in the spam.js file:

1. Return to the **mpl.htm** file in your text editor.
2. Directly above the opening <script> tag in the head section of the file, insert the following script element, as shown in Figure 10-21:

```
<script src="spam.js" type="text/javascript"></script>
```

Inserting a link to an external script file **Figure 10-21**

```
   <title>Monroe Public Library</title>
   <link href="mplstyles.css" rel="stylesheet" type="text/css" />

   <script src="spam.js" type="text/javascript"></script>

   <script type="text/javascript">
      function showEM(userName, emServer) {
         var emLink = userName + "@" + emServer;
         document.write("<a href='mailto:" + emLink + "'>");
         document.write(emLink);
         document.write("</a>");
      }
   </script>
</head>
```

Next you'll want to confirm that the stringReverse() function from the spam.js file is working correctly. To test the function, call it to reverse the text string values of the userName and emServer parameters in the showEM() function.

To test the stringReverse() function:

1. Scroll down to the showEM() function.
2. Insert the following two lines of code at the top of the function, as shown in Figure 10-22:

```
userName = stringReverse(userName);
emServer = stringReverse(emServer);
```

Figure 10-22 Calling the stringReverse() function

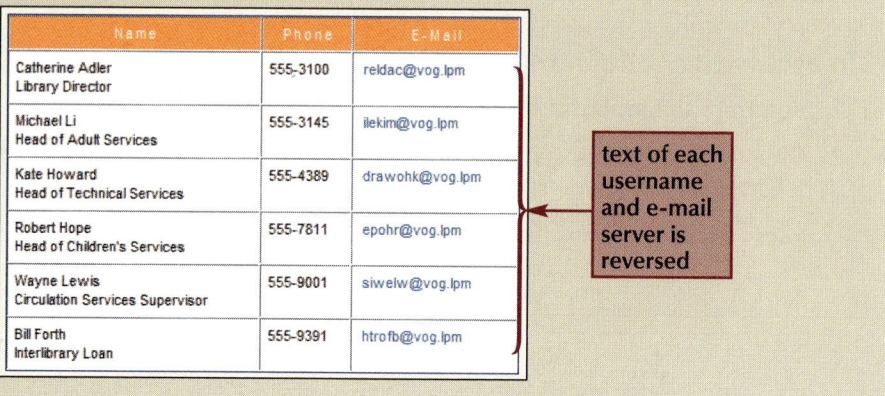

```
<script type="text/javascript">
   function showEM(userName, emServer) {

      userName = stringReverse(userName);
      emServer = stringReverse(emServer);

      var emLink = userName + "@" + emServer;
      document.write("<a href='mailto:" + emLink + "'>");
      document.write(emLink);
      document.write("</a>");
   }
</script>
```

reverse the order of the characters in the userName and emServer parameters

3. Save your changes to the file, and then reload **mpl.htm** in your Web browser. As shown in Figure 10-23, the text of the username and mail server portions of each employee's e-mail address appears reversed on the Web page.

Figure 10-23 Staff directory with e-mail addresses reversed

Name	Phone	E-Mail
Catherine Adler Library Director	555-3100	reldac@vog.lpm
Michael Li Head of Adult Services	555-3145	ilekim@vog.lpm
Kate Howard Head of Technical Services	555-4389	drawohk@vog.lpm
Robert Hope Head of Children's Services	555-7811	epohr@vog.lpm
Wayne Lewis Circulation Services Supervisor	555-9001	siwelw@vog.lpm
Bill Forth Interlibrary Loan	555-9391	htrofb@vog.lpm

text of each username and e-mail server is reversed

The stringReverse() function appears to be working correctly. Of course, you don't want the e-mail addresses to be reversed in the rendered document; you want those addresses to appear correctly. Instead, you want the code within the document reversed to thwart e-mail harvesters. This means that you need to enter the username and e-mail server names in reverse order.

To change the userName and emServer parameter values:

1. Return to the **mpl.htm** file in your text editor.
2. Scroll down the file to the script element for Catherine Adler's e-mail address and change the value of the userName parameter from cadler to **reldac**. Change the value of the emServer parameter from mpl.gov to **vog.lpm**.
3. Change the parameter values for Michael Li's e-mail address to **ilekim** and **vog.lpm**.
4. Change the parameter values for Katherine Howard's e-mail address to **drawohk** and **vog.lpm**.

5. Change the parameter values for Robert Hope's e-mail address to **epohr** and **vog.lpm**.
6. Change the parameter values for Wayne Lewis's e-mail address to **siwelw** and **vog.lpm**.
7. Finally, change the parameter values for Bill Forth's e-mail address to **htrofb** and **vog.lpm**. Figure 10-24 highlights the revised code in the file.

Figure 10-24 Entering the reversed userName and emServer parameter values

```
<tr>
   <td>Catherine Adler<br />Library Director</td>
   <td>555-3100</td>
   <td>
      <script type="text/javascript">
         showEM("reldac","vog.lpm");
      </script>
   </td>
</tr>

<tr>
   <td>Michael Li<br />Head of Adult Services</td>
   <td>555-3145</td>
   <td>
      <script type="text/javascript">
         showEM("ilekim","vog.lpm");
      </script>
   </td>
</tr>
<tr>
   <td>Kate Howard<br />Head of Technical Services</td>
   <td>555-4389</td>
   <td>
      <script type="text/javascript">
         showEM("drawohk","vog.lpm");
      </script>
   </td>
</tr>
<tr>
   <td>Robert Hope<br />Head of Children's Services</td>
   <td>555-7811</td>
   <td>
      <script type="text/javascript">
         showEM("epohr","vog.lpm");
      </script>
   </td>
</tr>
<tr>
   <td>Wayne Lewis<br />Circulation Services Supervisor</td>
   <td>555-9001</td>
   <td>
      <script type="text/javascript">
         showEM("siwelw","vog.lpm");
      </script>
   </td>
</tr>
<tr>
   <td>Bill Forth<br />Interlibrary Loan</td>
   <td>555-9391</td>
   <td>
      <script type="text/javascript">
         showEM("htrofb","vog.lpm");
      </script>
   </td>
</tr>
```

8. Save your changes to the file and reload **mpl.htm** in your Web browser. As shown in Figure 10-25, the text characters of the e-mail addresses for staff members now appear in the correct order.

Figure 10-25 Final staff directory page

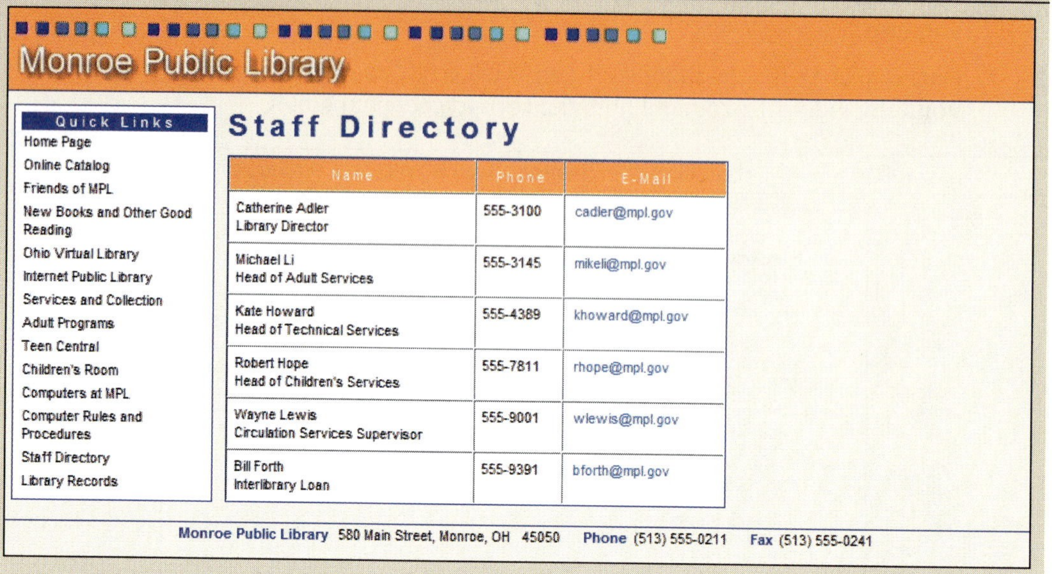

You review your progress with Kate. As she scans through the code in the HTML file, she's pleased to note that none of the e-mail addresses for the six staff members appears in any readable form. By breaking the e-mail addresses into two parts (the userName and the emServer parts) and entering the text in reverse order, you have effectively hidden the actual addresses from harvesting programs.

Commenting JavaScript Code

Kate is pleased to see how JavaScript can unscramble the e-mail addresses and present them to users in a readable form. However, she is concerned that in the future, she might forget how this program is designed to work. She would like you to add some comments to the code you created.

Inserting Single-Line and Multiline Comments

Commenting your code is an important programming practice. It helps other people who examine your code to understand what your programs are designed to do and how they work. It can even help you in the future when you return to edit the programs you've written and need to recall the programming choices you made. In JavaScript, comments can be added to script elements on either single or multiple lines. The syntax of a single-line comment is

```
// comment text
```

where *comment text* is the JavaScript comment. Single-line comments can be placed within the same line as a JavaScript command, making it easier to interpret each command in your code. The following is an example of a JavaScript statement that includes a single-line comment:

```
document.write(emLink); // write e-mail address to the Web page
```

For more extended comments, you place the comment text on several lines using the following structure:

```
/*
   comment text spanning
   several lines
*/
```

The following is an example of a multiline comment applied to a JavaScript program:

```
/*
   The showEM() function displays a link to the user's e-mail address.
   The text of the user and e-mail server names are entered in
   reverse order to thwart e-mail harvesters.
*/
```

Inserting JavaScript Comments

| Reference Window

- To insert a single-line comment into a JavaScript program, use
  ```
  // comment text
  ```
  where *comment text* is the JavaScript comment. Single-line comments can be placed on the same line as a JavaScript command.
- To insert several lines of comments, use the following:
  ```
  /*
    comment text spanning
    several lines
  */
  ```

Kate would like you to add comments to the showEM() function you created.

To add comments to your JavaScript code:

1. Return to the **mpl.htm** file in your text editor.
2. Add the following multiline comment directly below the opening function statement for the showEM() function:
   ```
   /*
      The showEM() function displays a link to the user's
      e-mail address.
      The text of the user and e-mail server names are entered in
      reverse order to thwart e-mail harvesters.
   */
   ```
3. Add the following single-line comment to the end of the line that reverses the value of the userName parameter:
   ```
   // reverse the text of the userName parameter
   ```
4. Add the following comment to the end of the line that reverses the value of the emServer parameter:
   ```
   // reverse the text of the emServer parameter
   ```
5. Finally, add the following comment to the end of the line creating the emLink variable:
   ```
   // combine the text of userName and emServer
   ```
   Figure 10-26 displays these comments in the mpl.htm file.

Figure 10-26 **Adding comments to the showEM() function**

```
<script type="text/javascript">
   function showEM(userName, emServer) {
      /*
         The showEM() function displays a link to the user's e-mail address.
         The text of the user and e-mail server names are entered in
         reverse order to thwart e-mail harvesters.
      */

      userName = stringReverse(userName); // reverse the text of the userName parameter
      emServer = stringReverse(emServer); // reverse the text of the emServer parameter

      var emLink = userName + "@" + emServer; // combine the text of userName and emServer
      document.write("<a href='mailto:" + emLink + "'>");
      document.write(emLink);
      document.write("</a>");
   }
</script>
```

6. Close the **mpl.htm** file, saving your changes.
7. Reopen **mpl.htm** in your Web browser and verify that you have not introduced any errors by adding comments to the showEM() function.
8. You can close any open files or programs now.

You show the commented version of the showEM() function to Kate. She agrees that it will help her better remember the purpose of the function and how the function works.

Using Comments to Hide JavaScript Code

Comments have another purpose besides documenting the code used in a JavaScript application. Older browsers that do not support JavaScript can present a problem for Web designers. If such browsers encounter JavaScript commands, they might display the program code as part of the Web page body. To avoid this problem, you can hide a script from these browsers using both HTML and JavaScript comment lines. The following is the syntax for doing this:

```
<script type="text/javascript">
   <!--Hide from nonJavaScript browsers
        JavaScript commands
   // Stop hiding from older browsers -->
</script>
```

When a Web browser that doesn't support scripts encounters this code, it ignores the <script> tag, as it does any tag it doesn't recognize. The next line it sees is the start of the HTML comment tag, which doesn't close until the arrow symbol (-->) in the second-to-last line. This means that the browser ignores the entire JavaScript program. It similarly ignores the final </script> tag.

On the other hand, a browser that does support JavaScript recognizes the <script> tag and ignores any HTML tags found between the <script> and </script> tags. Therefore, in this example, it bypasses the comment tag in the second line and processes the JavaScript program as written. The JavaScript comment, which starts with the double slash symbol (//) in the second-to-last line, is included to help other users understand and interpret your code.

Hiding JavaScript code from older browsers is not as important as it once was, so you will not add this feature to the JavaScript code for the staff directory page.

Debugging Your JavaScript Programs

As you work with JavaScript, you will inevitably encounter scripts that fail to work because of an error in the code. To fix a problem with a program, you need to debug it. **Debugging** is the process of searching code to locate a source of trouble. To debug a program, you must first determine the type of error present in your code.

There are three types of errors: load-time errors, run-time errors, and logical errors. A **load-time error** occurs when a script is first loaded by the browser. As the page loads, the browser reads through the code looking for mistakes in syntax. For example, suppose you had neglected to include the closing parenthesis, as in the following command from the showEM() function:

```
document.write("</a>";
```

In this case, you would be making a mistake in the syntax of the document.write() method. When a load-time error is uncovered, the JavaScript interpreter halts loading the script. Depending on the browser, an error message might also appear. Figure 10-27 shows the message generated by the above error in Internet Explorer. An error message can include the line number and character number of the error. This does not mean that the error occurred at this location in the document—the source of the trouble could be much earlier in the script. The message simply indicates the location at which the JavaScript interpreter was forced to cancel loading the script.

Reporting a load-time error **Figure 10-27**

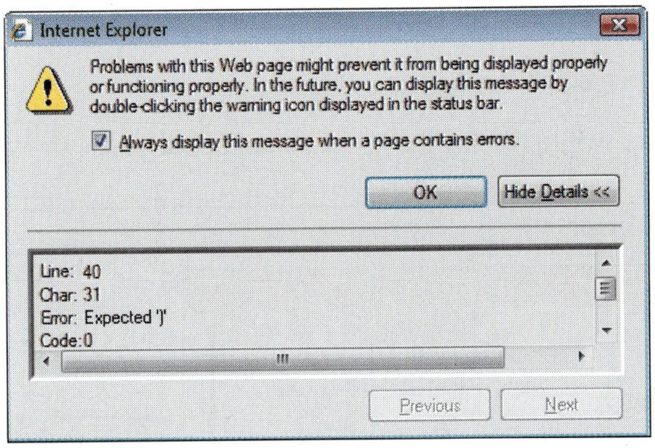

A **run-time error** occurs after a script has been successfully loaded and is being executed. In a run-time error, the mistake occurs when the browser cannot complete a line of code. One common source of a run-time error is mislabeling a variable name. For example, the line of code

```
document.write(emlink);
```

in the showEM() function would result in the run-time error shown in Figure 10-28.

Figure 10-28 **Reporting a run-time error**

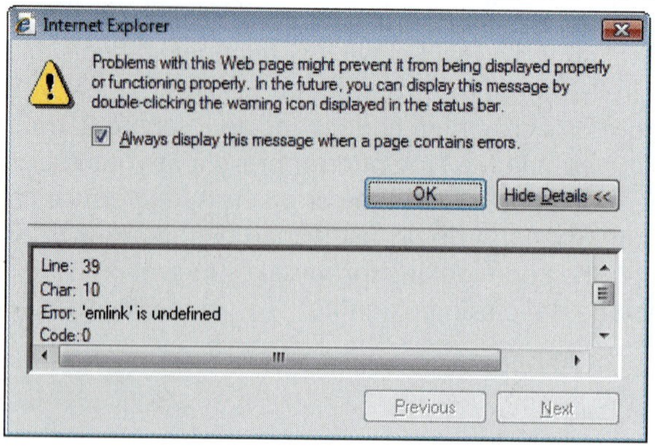

The mistake in this line of code is that there is no variable named emlink in the showEM() function—the variable name should be emLink (recall that variable names are case sensitive). When a browser attempts to write the contents of the emlink variable to the Web document, it discovers that no such variable exists and reports the run-time error. When a JavaScript interpreter catches a run-time error, it halts execution of the script and displays an error message indicating the location where it was forced to quit.

Logical errors are free from syntax and structural mistakes, but result in incorrect results. A logical error is often the hardest to fix and sometimes requires you to meticulously trace every step of your code to detect the mistake. Suppose you had incorrectly entered the line of code to create the emLink variable, placing the server name before the username, as follows:

```
var emLink = emServer + "@" + userName;
```

In this case, a browser would display the list of e-mail addresses as shown in Figure 10-29.

Figure 10-29 **Displaying a logical error**

Name	Phone	E-Mail
Catherine Adler Library Director	555-3100	mpl.gov@cadler
Michael Li Head of Adult Services	555-3145	mpl.gov@mikeli
Kate Howard Head of Technical Services	555-4389	mpl.gov@khoward
Robert Hope Head of Children's Services	555-7811	mpl.gov@rhope
Wayne Lewis Circulation Services Supervisor	555-9001	mpl.gov@wlewis
Bill Forth Interlibrary Loan	555-9391	mpl.gov@bforth

usernames and e-mail server names are displayed in the wrong order

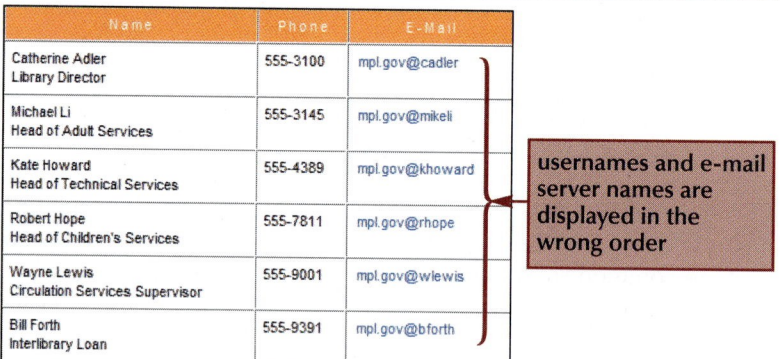

Although the browser did not report any mistakes, this is obviously not the way Kate wants e-mail addresses displayed!

Common Mistakes in JavaScript Programs | InSight

When you begin writing JavaScript programs, you will invariably encounter mistakes in your code. Some common sources of programming error include:

- Misspelling a variable name: For example, if you named a variable ListPrice, then misspellings or incorrect capitalization—such as listprice, ListPrices, or list_price—will result in the program failing to run correctly.
- Mismatched parentheses or braces: The following code results in an error because the function lacks the closing brace:
```
function Area(width, height) {
  var size = width*height;
```
- Mismatched quotes: If you neglect the closing quotes around a text string, JavaScript treats the text string as an object or variable, resulting in an error. The following code results in an error because the closing double quote is missing from the firstName variable:
```
var firstName = "Sean';
var lastName = "Lee";
document.write(firstName+" " + lastName);
```
- Missing quotes: When you combine several text strings using the + symbol, you might neglect to quote all text strings. For example, the following code generates an error because of the missing quotes around the <br /> tag:
```
document.write("MidWest Student Union" + <br />);
```

As you become more experienced in writing JavaScript code, you'll be able to quickly spot these types of errors, making it easier for you to debug your programs.

Debugging Tools and Techniques

There are several techniques you can employ to avoid making programming mistakes and to quickly locate the mistakes you do make. One is to write **modular code**, which is code that entails breaking up a program's different tasks into smaller, more manageable chunks. A common strategy when creating modular code is to use functions that perform a few simple tasks. The different functions can then be combined and used in a variety of ways.

If you do encounter a logical error in which the incorrect results are displayed by the browser, you can monitor the changing values of your variables using an alert dialog box. An **alert dialog box** is a dialog box generated by JavaScript that displays a text message with an OK button. Clicking the OK button closes the dialog box, allowing the browser to resume running the JavaScript code. The command to create an alert dialog box is

```
alert(text);
```

where *text* is the text string that you want displayed in the dialog box. You can also use a variable name in place of a text string. For example, the command

```
alert(emLink);
```

displays the current value of the emLink variable. Figure 10-30 shows the appearance of this dialog box for the first entry in the library staff directory. Alert dialog boxes are useful in determining what is happening to your variable values while a program is running.

Figure 10-30 Displaying a variable value in an alert dialog box

Browsers also offer various tools for debugging JavaScript programs. Microsoft offers the **Microsoft Script Debugger**, a debugger available for use with its Internet Explorer browser running under Windows XP. The Microsoft Script Debugger is available for free from the Microsoft Web site and is also included with the Microsoft Office XP suite. When the Microsoft Script Debugger is installed on your system, it displays a prompt when it encounters a load-time or run-time error in one of your scripts. See Figure 10-31.

Figure 10-31 Runtime Error dialog box

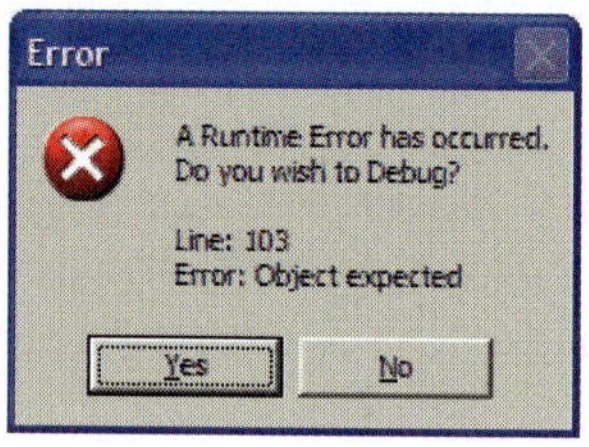

> **Tip**
>
> To enable script debugging on Internet Explorer, you might have to turn on script debugging from the Advanced tab on the Internet Explorer Options dialog box.

Clicking the Yes button opens the Microsoft Script Debugger window, highlighting the source of the error. As shown in Figure 10-32, the source of this particular error is that the showEM() function was referenced as showem(). Because function names are case sensitive, the browser was unable to locate the function and reported an error. You can learn more about the script debugger using the online help provided with the Microsoft Script Debugger or at the Microsoft Web site.

Microsoft Script Debugger window **Figure 10-32**

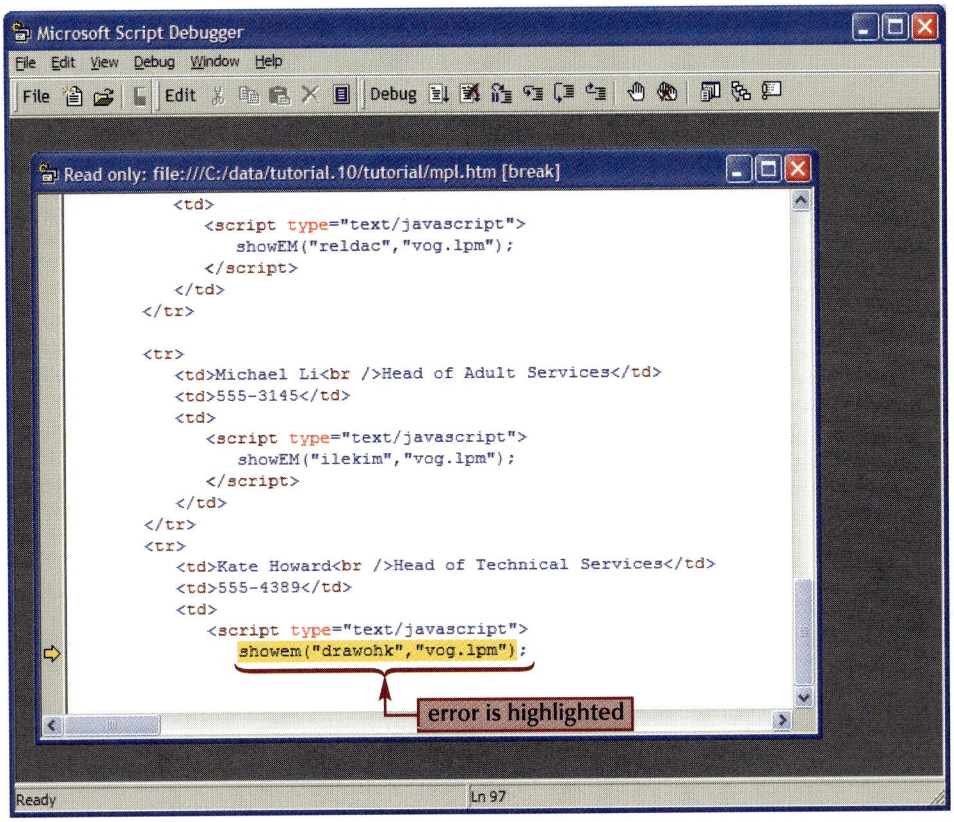

Firefox also provides the **Firefox Error Console** that displays all of the errors generated within the current document. To view the list of errors, type javascript: in the address bar as shown in Figure 10-33.

Figure 10-33 Accessing the Firefox Error Console

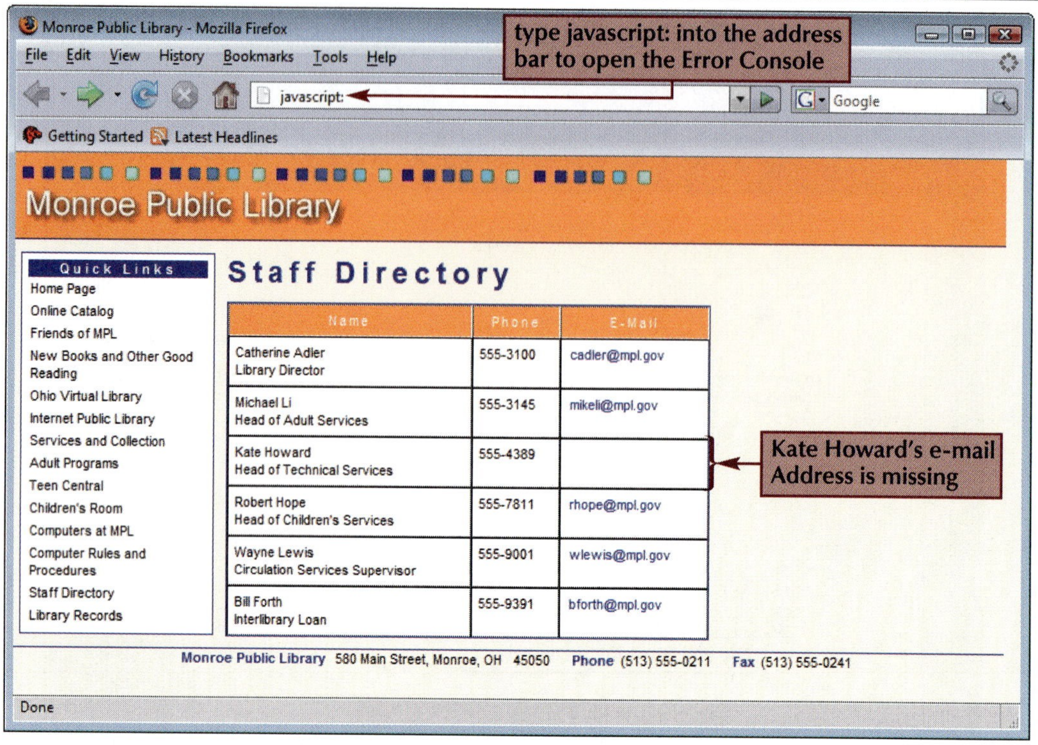

The Error Console appears as another Firefox browser window, as shown in Figure 10-34. Within the Error Console is an Evaluate box in which you can insert JavaScript commands to evaluate your code and variable values at the point at which the error occurred.

Figure 10-34 The Firefox Error Console

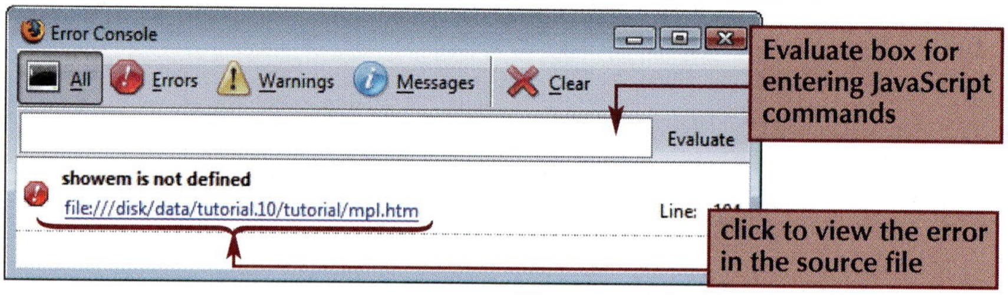

The Error Console also includes a hypertext link to another Firefox window that displays the code for the source file. The point at which the error was first detected (not necessarily the source of the error) is highlighted in this window, as shown in Figure 10-35.

Figure 10-35 Highlighting the source of the error

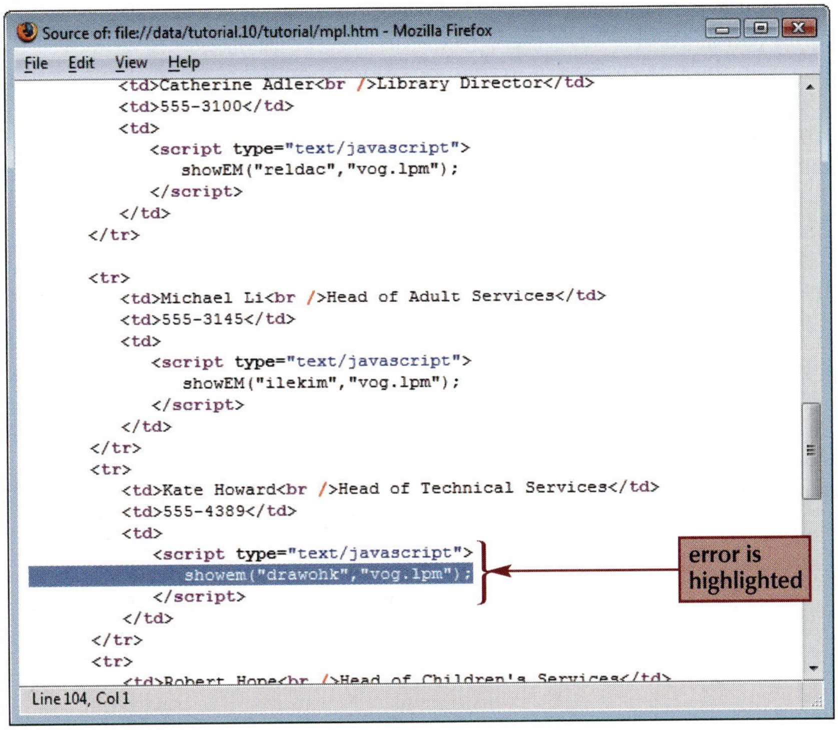

Tip

Firefox's Error Console will also display syntax errors from your CSS style sheet or other warnings generated by mistakes in the HTML code.

You can learn more about Firefox's Error Console by using the online help in the console window. Because errors inevitably creep into any programming task you undertake, it's important to be familiar with the various debugging tools available to you.

You've completed your work on the staff directory for the Monroe Public Library. Kate will call you again as other issues with the library's Web site arise.

Session 10.3 Quick Check | Review

1. Specify the code to access the JavaScript file library.js.
2. Specify the code to enter the single-line JavaScript comment Library of JavaScript functions.
3. Specify the code to enter following multiline JavaScript comment:

   `The library.js file contains a collection of`
   `JavaScript functions for use with the file index.htm`

4. What is debugging?
5. What code would you enter to display the value of the userName variable in an alert dialog box?
6. What are the three types of errors generated by mistakes in a JavaScript program?
7. Your code has a misspelled variable name. What type of error will result from the mistake?

Review | Tutorial Summary

In this tutorial you learned how to create and run Web page programs written in the JavaScript language. In the first session, you learned about the history of JavaScript and how it compares to Java. You then studied how to create a script element and how to use JavaScript to write text to a Web document. In the second session, you learned how to create and use variables as well as how to write and call a JavaScript function. The third session examined how to access code in external JavaScript files. The session then demonstrated how to document your code with comments. The tutorial concluded with a discussion of common scripting errors and an overview of some tools and techniques you can use to ensure that your code is error free.

Key Terms

alert dialog box
Boolean value
client-side programming
command
compiled language
data type
debugging
declaring
ECMA
ECMAScript
e-mail harvester
European Computer Manufacturers Association
Firefox Error Console
function
function name
global scope
global variable
human input validation
interpreted language
JavaScript
JScript
load-time error
local scope
local variable
logical error
method
Microsoft Script Debugger
modular code
null value
numeric value
object
parameter
run-time error
scope
server-side programming
spam
spammer
statement
strongly typed language
text string
variable
VBScript
weakly typed language

Practice | **Review Assignments**

Practice the skills you learned in the tutorial using the same case scenario.

Data Files needed for the Review Assignments: 0.jpg through 9.jpg, mpl2txt.htm, mpl.jpg, mplstyles.css, and random.js

Kate has a new assignment for you. One of the pages on the Monroe Public Library Web site is the library records page, which contains sensitive information about library patrons and the books they have checked out. Kate has created a Web form in which a staff member enters a username and password before getting access to the library records. However, Kate has heard that some hackers create programs that search for Web forms that open confidential pages. One technique of these hackers is to have automated programs that submit thousands of username/password combinations, hoping to break into the system. Kate knows that some sites use human input validation to thwart these programs.

Human input validation is a technique that requires the entry of some piece of information that humans can easily enter, but automated programs cannot. One approach is to display a series of images containing numbers or letters and request that the user enter the numbers or letters being displayed. Because most automated programs can't "see" images, they cannot answer this question; most humans, on the other hand, can enter the requested information without trouble. Kate suggests you write a program that shows five images, each displaying a random number between 0 and 9. In addition to entering a username and password, users will be required to enter the numbers they see on the screen. Figure 10-36 shows a preview of the completed Web page.

Figure 10-36

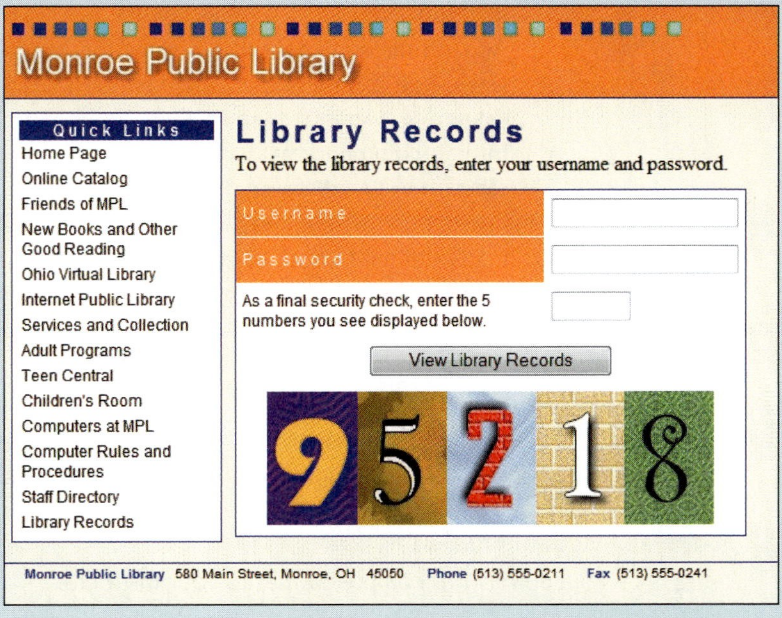

Your job is to write a script to display the random images. The images have been stored in files named 0.jpg through 9.jpg. To help you, Kate has located a file that contains a JavaScript function to return a random integer from 0 to *size*, where *size* is the largest integer to be returned. The name of the function is randomInteger, so to call the function, you use the command

```
randomInteger(size)
```

For example, to return a random integer from 0 to 5, you would run the command

```
randomInteger(5)
```

The randomInteger() function has been saved for you in the random.js file.

Complete the following:

1. Use your text editor to open **mpl2txt.htm** from the tutorial.10\review folder included with your Data Files. Enter ***your name*** and ***the date*** in the comment section of the file and save the file as **mpl2.htm** in the same folder.
2. In the head section, just above the closing </head> tag, insert a script element that accesses the code in the random.js file.
3. Add a second script element for the code that you'll add to the mpl2.htm file.
4. Within the second script element, create a function named showImg(). The purpose of this function is to write an inline image tag into the current document. The function has no parameters. Add the following statements to the function:
   a. Add the following multiline comment to the start of the function, just below the opening showImg() function statement:
      ```
      The showImg() function displays a random image from the
      0.jpg through 9.jpg files.
       The random image is designed to thwart hackers attempting to enter
      the library records database by requiring visual confirmation.
      ```
   b. Declare a variable named imgNumber equal to the value returned by the randomInteger() function. Use 9 as the value of the size parameter in the randomInteger() function.
   c. Append the statement that creates the imgNumber variable with the following single-line comment:
      ```
      Return a random number from 0 to 9.
      ```
   d. Insert a command that writes the text
      ```
      <img src='imgNumber.jpg' alt='' />
      ```
   to the document, where *imgNumber* is the value of the imgNumber variable.
5. Scroll down to the bottom of the file and locate the last table cell in the document. Within this empty table cell, insert a script element.
6. Within the script element, call the showImg() function five times. You do not need to specify a parameter value.
7. Save your changes to the file.
8. Open **mpl2.htm** in your Web browser. Verify that each time you refresh the Web page, a different sequence of five image numbers appears at the bottom of the Web form. Debug your code as necessary using any of the tools or techniques described in this tutorial.
9. Submit your completed files to your instructor.

Apply | Case Problem 1

Use the skills you learned in this tutorial to create an online star map.

Data Files needed for this Case Problem: datetime.js, mask.gif, sky0.jpg through sky23.jpg, skymaptxt.htm, skyweb.css, and skyweb.jpg

SkyWeb Astronomy Dr. Andrew Weiss of Central Ohio University maintains an astronomy page called SkyWeb for his students. On his Web site he discusses many aspects of astronomy and stargazing. One of the tools of the amateur stargazer is a planisphere, which is a handheld device composed of two flat disks: one disk shows a map of the constellations, and the other disk contains a window corresponding to the part of the sky that is visible at a given time and date. When a user rotates the second disk to the current date and time, the constellations that appear in the window correspond to the constellations currently visible in the nighttime sky.

Dr. Weiss has asked for your help in constructing an online planisphere for his Web site. He has created 24 different sky charts, named sky0.jpg through sky23.jpg, that represent 24 different rotations of the nighttime sky. He has also created an image containing a transparent window through which a user can view a selected sky chart. A preview of the completed Web page is shown in Figure 10-37.

Figure 10-37

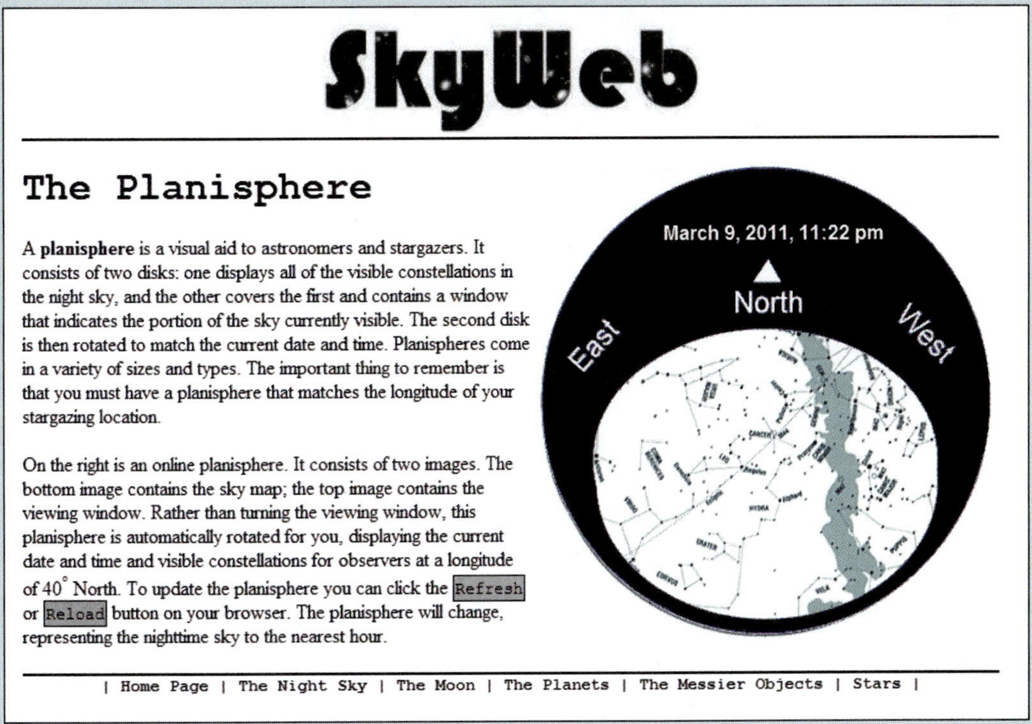

Dr. Weiss has designed the page layout. He needs your help in creating JavaScript code to display the current date and time, and to display the correct sky chart for that date and time. To do this, you've been provided with two functions:

- The showDateTime() function, which returns the current date and time in the text string

    Month Day, *Year*, *hour*:*time* am/pm

where *Month* is the name of the current month, *Day* is the current day, *Year* is the current year, *hour* is the current hour, *minute* is the current minute, and am/pm changes based on the current time.

- The getMap() function, which returns a number from 0 to 23. The number matches the number of the sky map image to show based on the current date and time.

Both functions have been placed in an external JavaScript file named datetime.js.

Complete the following:

1. Use your text editor to open the **skymaptxt.htm** file from the tutorial.10\case1 folder included with your Data Files. Enter ***your name*** and ***the date*** in the comment section of the file. Save the file as **skymap.htm** in the same folder.
2. Directly below the link element in the head section, insert a script element accessing the datetime.js file.
3. Below the script element, insert another script element that contains the following statements:
   a. Insert a multiline comment containing the following text:
   ```
   timeStr is a text string containing the current date and time
   mapNum is the number of the map to display in the planisphere
   ```
   b. Declare a variable named timeStr equal to the value returned from the showDateTime() function.
   c. Declare a variable named mapNum equal to the value returned from the getMap() function.
4. Scroll down the file to the div element with id value maps and replace the line
   ```
   <img id="sky" src="sky0.jpg" alt="" />
   ```
   with a script element that writes the following HTML code:
   ```
   <img id='sky' src='mapNum.jpg' alt='' />
   ```
   where *mapNum* is the value of the mapNum variable.
5. Scroll down a few lines and replace the date/time value January 1, 2011, 12:00 a.m. with a script element that writes the value of the timeStr variable to the Web page.
6. Save your changes to the file and then open **skymap.htm** in your Web browser. Verify that the planisphere displays the current date and time.
7. EXPLORE — If you're able to modify the date/time settings on your computer, change the date and time and then reload or refresh the page to verify that the date/time value changes and that the map also changes. Debug your code as necessary.
8. Submit your completed files to your instructor.

Apply | Case Problem 2

Use JavaScript to display random banner ads.

Data Files needed for this Case Problem: ad1.jpg through ad5.jpg, ads.js, fp.jpg, fronttxt.htm, logo.jpg, random.js, and styles.css

Ridgewood Herald Tribune Maria Ramirez manages advertising accounts for the *Ridgewood Herald Tribune* in Ridgewood, New Jersey. Recently, the paper has put more of its content online. To offset the cost of the Web site, Maria is selling ad space on the company's home page. She is looking at creating banner ads to be displayed on the paper's masthead, with each ad linked to the advertiser's Web site. Because ad space on the paper's home page is the most valuable, Maria has decided to sell space to five companies, with the selection of the banner ad determined randomly each time a user opens the page.

Maria has asked for your help in writing the JavaScript code to display banner ads randomly. She has provided a collection of functions that will be useful to you:

- The randInt() function, which returns random integers from 1 to *n*. To call the randInt() function, use the following expression:
  `randInt(n)`
- The adDescription() function, which returns the description of the *n*th ad from a list of ad descriptions. To call the function, use the following expression:
  `adDescription(n)`
- The adLink() function, which returns the URL of the *n*th ad of the collection. To call the function, use the following expression:
  `adLink(n)`

The random.js file contains the randInt() function. The ads.js file contains the adDescription() and adLink() functions. Figure 10-38 shows a preview of the completed Web page with one of the random banner ads displayed at the top of the page.

Figure 10-38

Complete the following:

1. Use your text editor to open the **fronttxt.htm** file from the tutorial.10\case2 folder included with your Data Files. Enter ***your name*** and ***the date*** in the comment section of the file. Save the file as **front.htm** in the same folder.
2. After the link element in the head section, insert a script element accessing the functions in the random.js file.
3. Insert another script element accessing the functions in the ads.js file.

4. Scroll down the file to the div element with the id ads. Replace the content of the div element with a script element containing the following statements:
   a. Declare a variable named rNumber equal to the value returned from the randInt() function using 5 as the parameter value. Append the following comment to the statement:
      `generate a random integer from 1 to 5`
   b. Declare a variable named rAd equal to the text string returned from the adDescription() function using rNumber as the parameter value. Append the following comment to the statement:
      `description of the random ad`
   c. Declare a variable named rLink equal to the URL returned from the adLink() function using rNumber as the parameter value. Append the following comment:
      `URL of the random ad`
   d. Insert a command to write the text
      ```
      <a href="url">
         <img src="adn.jpg" alt="description"/>
      </a>
      ```
      to the Web document, where *url* is the value of the rLink variable, *n* is the value of the rNumber variable, and *description* is the value of the rAd variable.
5. Save your changes to the file.
6. Open **front.htm** in your Web browser. Refresh the Web page multiple times, verifying that different banner ads appear each time the page is refreshed. Debug your code as necessary.
7. Submit your completed files to your instructor.

Challenge | Case Problem 3

Explore how to write a script to display the daily calendar of events at a student union.

Data Files needed for this Case Problem: back.jpg, friday.htm, functions.js, monday.htm, mw.css, saturday.htm, schedule.css, sunday.htm, thursday.htm, todaytxt.htm, tuesday.htm, and wednesday.htm

Midwest Student Union Sean Lee manages the Web site for the student union at MidWest University in Salina, Kansas. The student union provides daily activities for the students on campus. As Web site manager, part of Sean's job is to keep the Web site up to date on the latest activities sponsored by the union. At the beginning of each week, she revises a set of seven Web pages detailing the events for each day in the upcoming week.

Sean would like the Web site to display the current day's schedule in an inline frame within the Web page named Today at the Union. To do this, her Web page must be able to determine the day of the week and then load the appropriate file into the frame. She would also like the Today at the Union page to display the current day and date. Figure 10-39 shows a preview of the page she wants you to create.

Figure 10-39

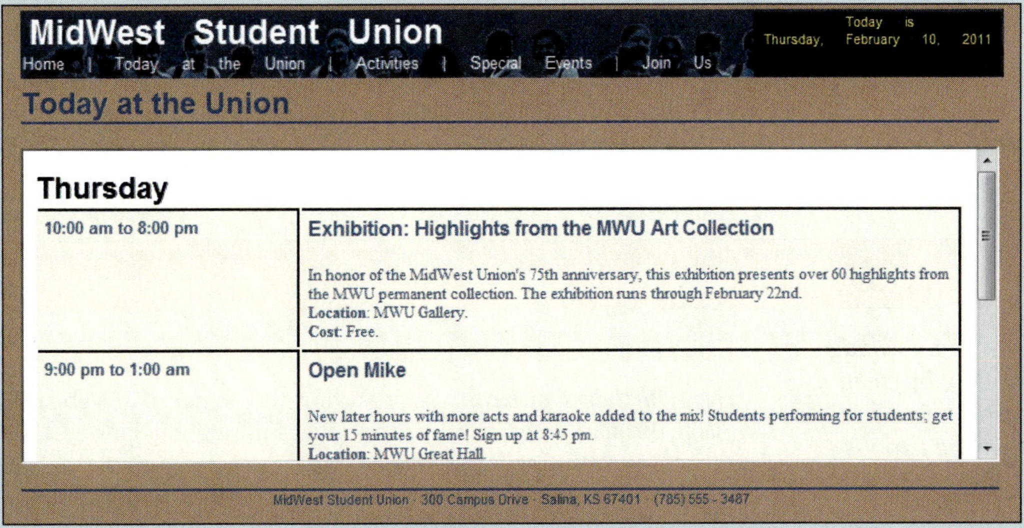

Sean has created the layout of the page, and she needs you to write the scripts to insert the current date and the calendar of events for the current day. To assist you, she has located two functions:

- The showDate() function, which returns a text string containing the current date in the format *Weekday*, *Month Day*, *Year*. The function has no parameter values.
- The weekDay() function, which returns a text string containing the name of the current weekday, from Sunday through Saturday. This function also has no parameter values.

The two functions are stored in an external JavaScript file named functions.js. The daily schedules have been stored in files named sunday.htm through saturday.htm.

Complete the following:

1. Use your text editor to open the **todaytxt.htm** file from the tutorial.10\case3 folder included with your Data Files. Enter ***your name*** and ***the date*** in the comment section of the file and save it as **today.htm**.
2. In the head section just above the closing </head> tag, insert a script element accessing the functions.js file.
3. Scroll down the file and locate the div element with the id dateBox. Within this element insert a script element. The script should run the following two commands:
   a. Write the following HTML code to the Web page:
   ```
   Today is <br />
   ```
   EXPLORE
   b. Write the text string returned by the showDate() function to the Web document.
4. Scroll down the file and locate the h2 heading Today at the Union. Within the empty paragraph that follows this heading, insert another script element. Within the script element, do the following:
   a. Insert the following multiline comment:
   ```
   Display the daily schedule in an inline frame.
   Daily schedules are stored in the files
   sunday.htm through saturday.htm.
   ```
   EXPLORE
   b. Insert a command to write the HTML code
   ```
   <iframe src='weekday.htm'></iframe>
   ```
   to the Web page, where *weekday* is the text string returned by the weekDay() function.

5. Save your changes to the document.
6. Open **today.htm** in your Web browser. Verify that it shows the current date and that the daily schedule matches the current weekday.

EXPLORE

7. If you have the ability to change your computer's date and time, change the date to different days of the week and refresh the Web page. Verify that the date and the daily schedule change to match the new date you selected. Debug your code as necessary.
8. Submit your completed files to your instructor.

Create | Case Problem 4

Test your knowledge of JavaScript by creating a splash screen displaying famous birthdays.

Data Files needed for this Case Problem: functions.js and logo.jpg

HappyBirthdayNews.com Linda Chi is the owner of a Web site called HappyBirthdayNews.com that specializes in birthday gifts and memorabilia. To make her site more interesting for users, Linda wants to create a splash screen that displays the current date and a famous birthday occurring on that date. She has asked for your help in writing the JavaScript code to generate the welcome message. She has designed the page's style and content, and has also located the following JavaScript functions:

- The showDate() function, which returns the current date in the text string *Weekday, Month Day, Year*, where *Weekday* is the day of the week, *Month* is the name of the month, *Day* is the day of the month, and *Year* is the four-digit year value. The showDate() function has no parameters.
- The dayNumber() function, which returns the day number of the current date, ranging from 1 (the first day of the year) to 366 (the last day of the year). The dayNumber() function has no parameters.
- The showBirthDay() function, which returns a text string describing a famous birthday on the given date. The function has a single parameter—*day*—which is equal to the day number of the famous birthday you want to view.

The three functions have already been saved for you in a file named functions.js. Figure 10-40 shows one possible solution to this problem.

Figure 10-40

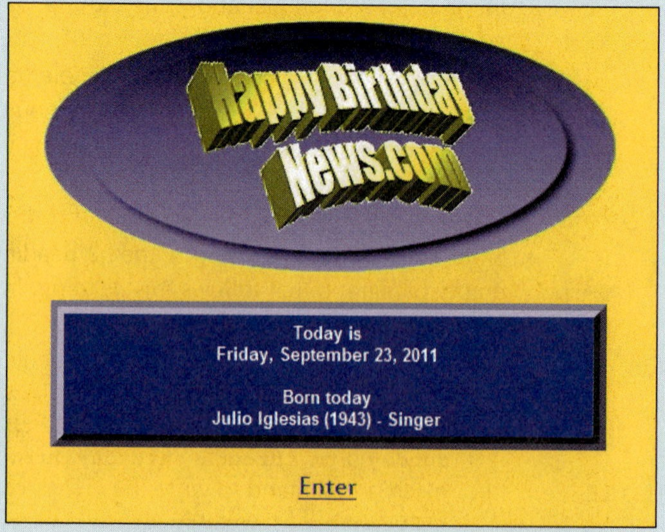

Complete the following:

1. Use your text editor to create the file **birthday.htm** and save it in the tutorial.10\case4 folder included with your Data Files. Create a comment section containing ***your name*** and ***the date*** as well as a brief description of the Web page.
2. Create a splash screen introducing the HappyBirthday.com Web site. The content and design of the site are up to you. You can use the **logo.jpg** graphic file as the logo for the Web site and supplement it with any other content or graphics you find.
3. Use your knowledge of JavaScript to add the following features to the Web page:
   - A page element that displays the current date
   - A page element that displays the name of a famous person born on that date
   - Any comments that document each of the variables you use in writing your JavaScript code and any functions you create
4. Save your changes to the file and then open it in your Web browser. Verify that the page displays the current date and a famous person's birthday for that date.

EXPLORE

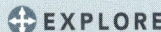

5. If you're able to change the date on your computer's clock, change the date and refresh the Web page. Verify that the page displays the new date and a new famous birthday. Debug your code as necessary.
6. Submit your completed files to your instructor.

Review | Quick Check Answers

Session 10.1

1. A client-side program is a program that is run on a user's computer, usually with a Web browser. A server-side program runs off of a Web server.

2.
```
<script type="text/javascript"> ... </script>
```
3.
```
document.write("<h2>Public Library</h2>");
```
4.
```
document.write('<h2 id="sub">Public Library</h2>');
```
5. Place the backslash (\) symbol at the end of the line to indicate that the statement continues on the next line.

6. JavaScript is case sensitive, so this statement should read:
```
document.write("Monroe Public Library");
```
7.
```
<noscript>
   <p><i>JavaScript required</i></p>
</noscript>
```

Session 10.2

1.
```
var weekday = "Friday";
```
2. To calculate the sum of numeric values or to combine text strings into a single text string
3. numeric, text, Boolean, and null
4.
```
document.write("<img src='" + fileName + "' alt='' />");
```
5. To perform an action or to return a value
6.
```
function CalcVol(x, y, z) {
   Vol = x*y*z;
   return Vol;
}
```

7. `TotalVol = CalcVol(3, 10, 4);`
8. Scope indicates where you can reference a variable within the Web page.

Session 10.3

1.
```
<script src="library.js" type="text/javascript"></script>
```
2. `// Library of JavaScript functions.`
3.
```
/*
   The library.js file contains a collection of
   JavaScript functions for use with the file index.htm
*/
```
4. Debugging is the process of searching code to locate a source of trouble.
5. `alert(userName);`
6. load-time error, run-time error, and logical error
7. a run-time error

Ending Data Files

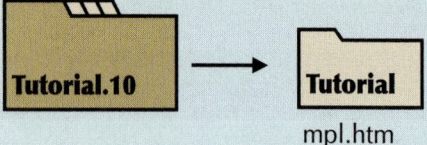

Tutorial.10 →

Tutorial
mpl.htm
mpl.jpg
mplstyles.css
spam.js

Review
mpl2.htm
mplstyles.css
random.js
+ 11 graphic files

Case1
datetime.js
skymap.htm
skyweb.css
+ 26 graphic files

Case2
ads.js
front.htm
random.js
style.css
+ 7 graphic files

Case3
back.jpg
functions.js
sunday.htm - saturday.htm
today.htm
+ 2 style sheets

Case4
birthday.htm
functions.js
logo.jpg
styles.css

Reality Check

The Web is constantly changing, offering users new and innovative ways of presenting information and exchanging data. Some of the greatest innovations do not always come from large and well-financed companies, but from entrepreneurs who see ways of bringing something new to the Internet community. In this exercise you will explore the dynamic world of the Web.

Please be sure *not* to include any personal information of a sensitive nature in the files you create to be submitted to your instructor for this exercise. Later on, you can update the files with such information for your personal use.

1. Research the history and development of some of the most important sites on the Web and prepare a report exploring what new features those sites brought to the Web. For example, how did sites such as Google, MySpace, and YouTube change our perception of the Internet? What features did these sites offer that had not previously been part of the Web?
2. Explore the impact that new technology has had on Web page development and the development of XHTML. Focus on the impact of MP3 players, cell phones, and high-speed wireless connections.
3. The most dominant browser on the market is Internet Explorer, but it does not always follow the specifications set forth by the World Wide Web Consortium (W3C). One of the challenges for a Web site designer is the different standards used by Internet Explorer compared to Web browsers that do follow the W3C recommendations. Investigate many of the key differences between Internet Explorer and the W3C specifications for CSS and HTML. Also examine how Web designers resolve these differences.
4. When a Web site changes its content, it's useful to be able to notify users of that fact. One way of informing users of new and interesting material is by creating a feed of the site using RSS. Explore the concepts behind RSS, including the use of RSS in creating audio and video feeds for podcasts.
5. All information on the Web is stored on Web servers. Users interact with the Web using Web browsers run on their PCs and Macintoshes. One approach to make communication between the server and the browser more seamless is called AJAX. Do a Web search on AJAX technology and examine how AJAX has affected the way users interact with Web servers.
6. How is the Web changing? Examine some of the latest trends in the development of the Web. Research the goals of the languages currently in development by the W3C. How will these new languages change the way people design Web sites in the future?
7. Assume that you're a designer who wishes to create a Web site that reports on issues involved with Web page design and changes to the Web. Create a Web site that summarizes what you've learned about the changing nature of the Web. The design and content of the Web site is up to you, but the site should include the following features:
   - At least three pages, one each describing a different aspect of the changing nature of the Web
   - A convenient list of links to enable users to quickly access topics of interest on your Web site
   - Links to all external sites containing the information you've gathered

- At least one external style sheet used by all of the pages on your Web site
- At least one Web table listing some of the information you've gathered for your report
- A Web form in which users can sign up for a newsletter about the changing nature of the Web and HTML
- At least one example of an inline frame that displays the contents of an external Web site
- An audio or video clip introducing your site's contents to the viewer (if you have the ability to create or locate a clip)

8. All of your code should be compliant with the XHTML 1.0 strict DTD. Test your code to ensure its validity.
9. Submit your completed files to your instructor.

Objectives

- Create an image with irregular line wrap
- Insert and format a Web table
- Insert and format an inline frame
- Embed an MP3 sound clip
- Insert and format a Web form

Creating a Music School Web Site

Case | Young Notes

Brenda is the owner of Young Notes, a private music school that has recently opened in Brownwood, Texas. She has asked for your help in setting up the school's Web site. Eventually the Web site will be extensive, covering all of the services offered by the school, but for now Brenda wants you to create a site with five Web pages. The first page will contain the site's home page, describing the Young Notes school. The second page will contain a description of the lessons offered by the school and will include a Web table with a fee schedule. The third page will contain a list of a few members of the Young Notes staff. Brenda wants the staff biographies to appear within an inline frame on the Web page. The fourth page will contain a list of upcoming Young Notes concerts and recitals. Brenda wants you to include a sound clip from last year's Honors Award Concert. The last page will display a Web form that students and their parents can submit to get more information about Young Notes.

Brenda has created much of the site's content and many of the site's styles. She needs you to add a graphic image of a Young Notes student, a table with information on lessons, an inline frame for the staff biographies, a sound clip from last year's concert, and a form for prospective families to fill out to get more information about the school. She also needs you to insert styles into her style sheets for these new elements and to link the Web pages together. Once you're finished, she will use your work as a starting point for planning the final version of the site.

Starting Data Files

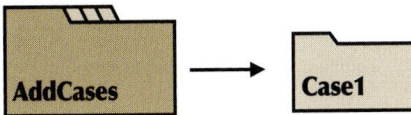

AddCases → Case1

applicationtxt.htm
eventstxt.htm
fstylestxt.css
lessonstxt.htm
stafftxt.htm
tstylestxt.css
youngtxt.htm
ystylestxt.css
+ 4 HTML files
+ 1 style sheet
+ 11 graphic files
+ 1 MP3 file

Complete the following:

1. Use your text editor to open the **applicationtxt.htm**, **eventstxt.htm**, **fstylestxt.css**, **lessonstxt.htm**, **stafftxt.htm**, **tstylestxt.css**, **youngtxt.htm**, and **ystylestxt.css** files from the addcases/case1 folder included with your Data Files. Enter ***your name*** and ***the date*** in the comment section of each file. Save the files as **application.htm**, **events.htm**, **fstyles.css**, **lessons.htm**, **staff.htm**, **tstyles.css**, **young.htm**, and **ystyles.css**, respectively, in the same folder.
2. Go to the **young.htm** file in your text editor. This file contains the Young Notes home page. Brenda wants you to add a graphic of a student to the page with an irregular line wrap around the image. Figure AC1-1 shows a preview of the completed page.

Figure AC1-1

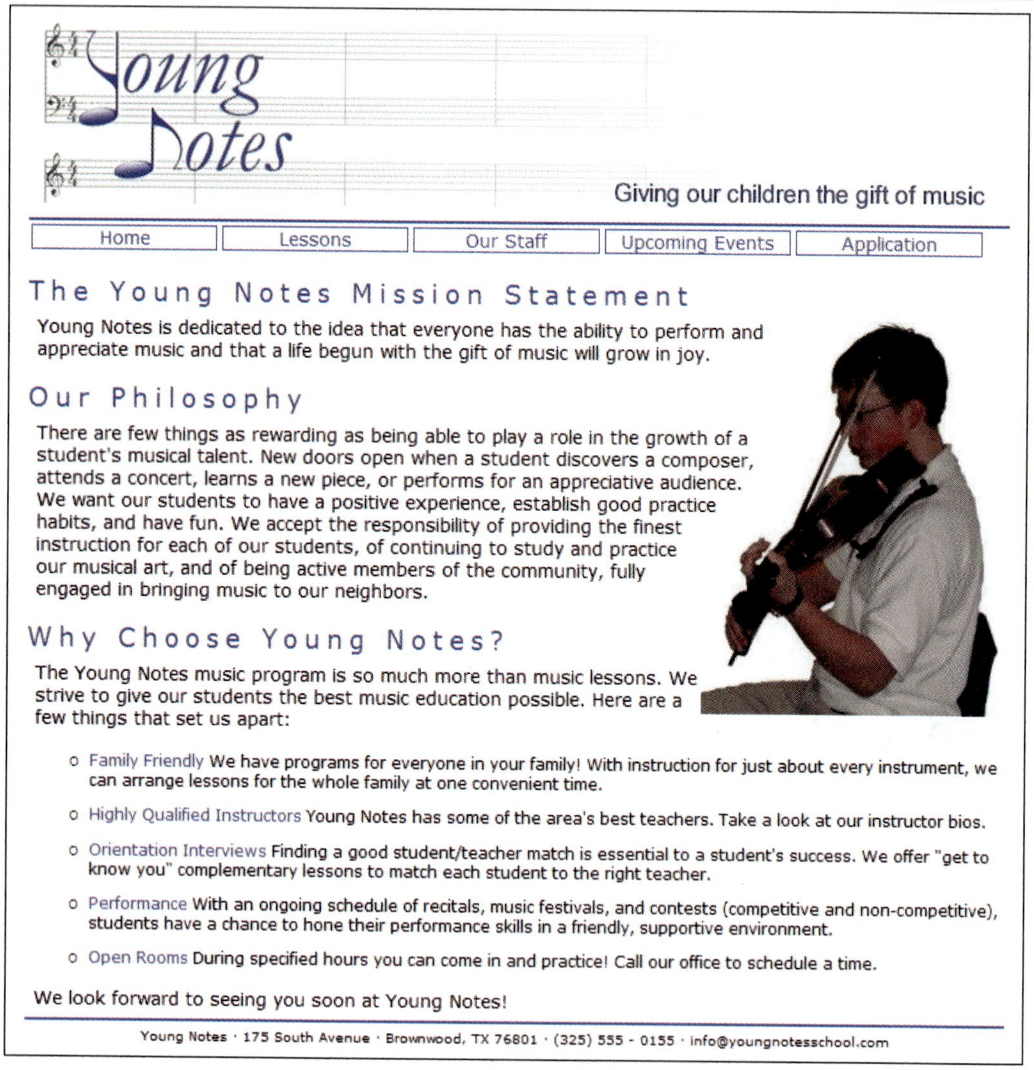

3. To insert the graphic, add five inline image elements at the top of the first paragraph after the initial h2 heading. Set the source of the inline images to **student1.jpg** through **student5.jpg**. Specify an empty text string for the alt attribute.
4. Link the **young.htm** file to the **ystyles.css** style sheet and then close the file, saving your changes.

5. Go to the **ystyles.css** style sheet in your text editor. At the bottom of the file, insert a style to float all img elements nested with the #main selector on the right margin, but only when the right margin is clear of other floating elements. Set the margin around the image elements to 0 pixels, except for the left margin, which should be set to 10 pixels.
6. Save the **ystyles.css** file, and then open the **young.htm** file in your Web browser. Verify that the page resembles that shown in Figure AC1-1 and that the text of the home page wraps around the graphic files that comprise the student image.
7. Go to the **lessons.htm** file in your text editor. This file contains a short summary of the music lessons offered by Young Notes. Figure AC1-2 shows a preview of the completed Web page.

Figure AC1-2

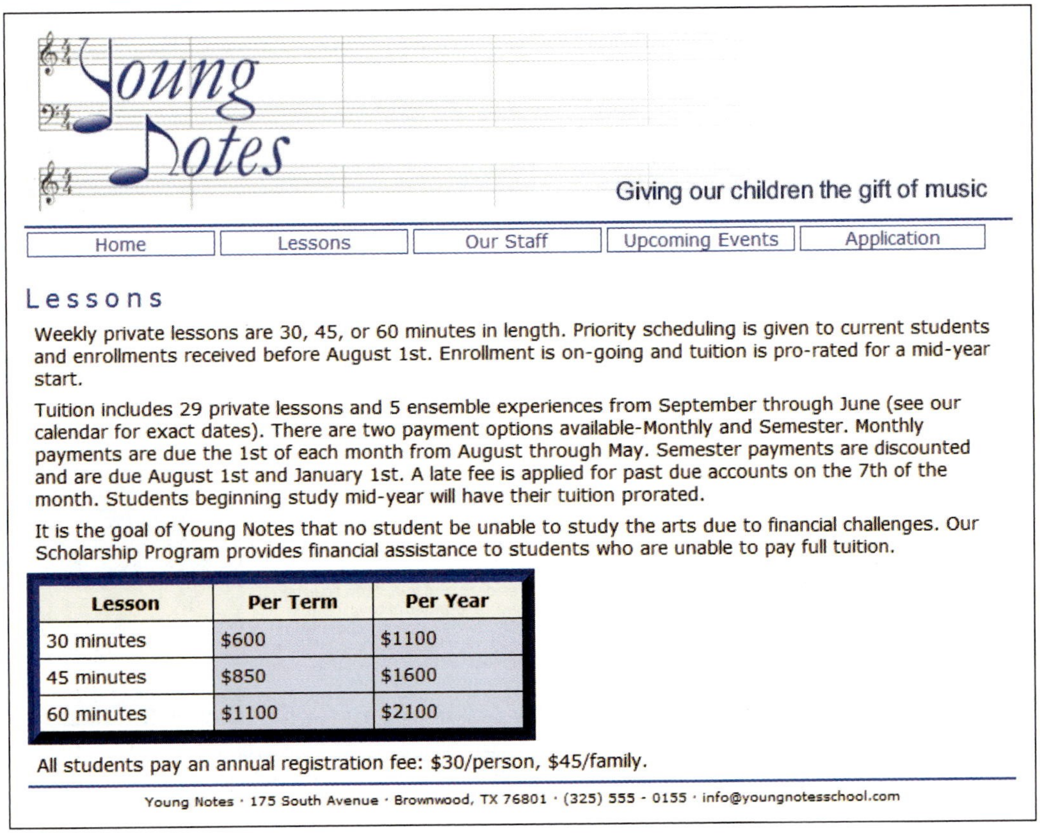
Young Notes

Giving our children the gift of music

Home | Lessons | Our Staff | Upcoming Events | Application

Lessons

Weekly private lessons are 30, 45, or 60 minutes in length. Priority scheduling is given to current students and enrollments received before August 1st. Enrollment is on-going and tuition is pro-rated for a mid-year start.

Tuition includes 29 private lessons and 5 ensemble experiences from September through June (see our calendar for exact dates). There are two payment options available-Monthly and Semester. Monthly payments are due the 1st of each month from August through May. Semester payments are discounted and are due August 1st and January 1st. A late fee is applied for past due accounts on the 7th of the month. Students beginning study mid-year will have their tuition prorated.

It is the goal of Young Notes that no student be unable to study the arts due to financial challenges. Our Scholarship Program provides financial assistance to students who are unable to pay full tuition.

Lesson	Per Term	Per Year
30 minutes	$600	$1100
45 minutes	$850	$1600
60 minutes	$1100	$2100

All students pay an annual registration fee: $30/person, $45/family.

Young Notes · 175 South Avenue · Brownwood, TX 76801 · (325) 555 - 0155 · info@youngnotesschool.com

8. At the bottom of the file directly above the last paragraph, insert a Web table containing the following elements.
   a. A table heading row group consisting of one row with three heading cells containing the text Lesson, Per Term, and Per Year.
   b. A table body row group containing three rows of table data cells with the values shown in Figure AC1-2.
   c. A column group containing one column element belonging to the firstCol class and another column element belonging to the feeColumns class. The feeColumns element should span two columns in the Web table.
9. Link the **lessons.htm** file to the **tstyles.css** style sheet and then close the file, saving your changes.

10. Go to the **tstyles.css** file in your text editor. Add the following styles to the style sheet.
    a. Set the font size of the table element to 14 pixels. Add a 10-pixel offset border with the color value (68, 76, 169) around the table. Set the table borders to collapse in case of conflicts with other borders. Set the width of the table to 400 pixels.
    b. Set the background color of the table heading row group to ivory.
    c. Vertically align the text of all table header and table data cells with the top of the cell. Add 5 pixels of padding to those cells. Surround those cells with a 1-pixel-wide solid black border.
    d. Change the background color of table columns belonging to the feeColumns class to the value (232, 232, 255).
11. Close the file, saving your changes, and then in your browser, view the Lessons page. Verify that the layout and format of the Web table resemble that shown in figure AC1-2.
12. Go to the **staff.htm** file in your text editor. This file contains the code for the Young Notes staff page. The biographies of four staff members will appear within an inline frame. The code for the four bio pages has already been done for you. Figure AC1-3 shows a preview of the completed staff page.

Figure AC1-3

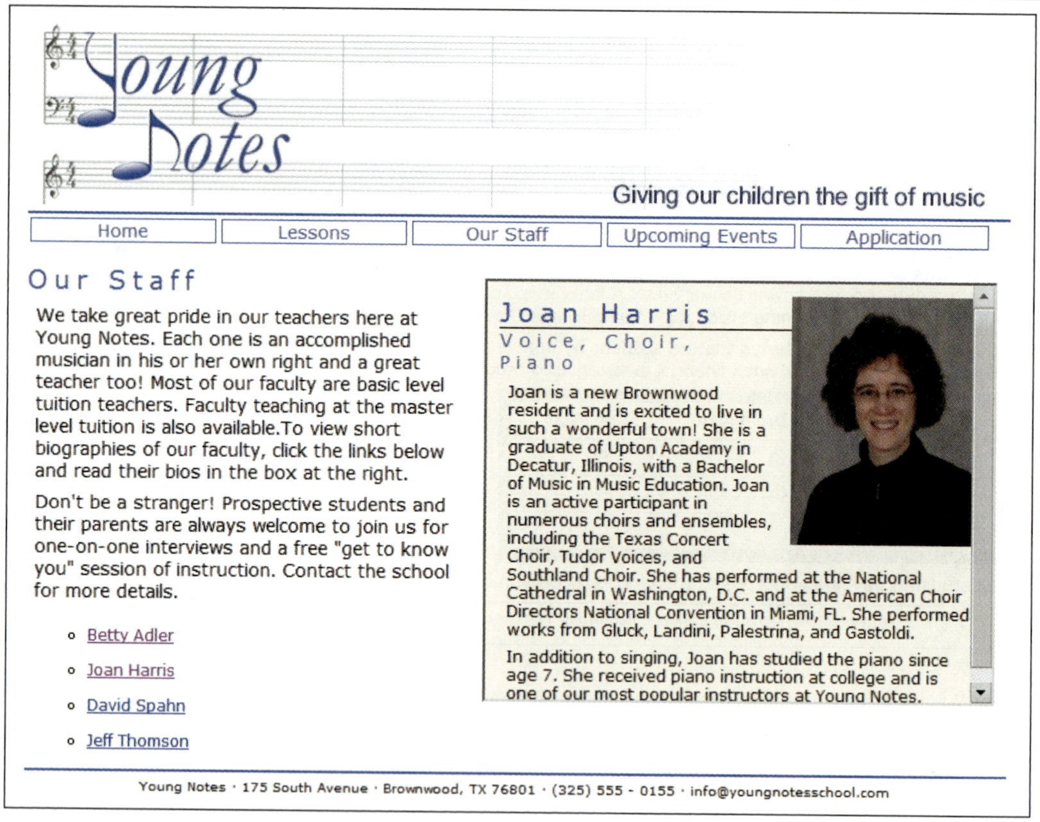

13. Directly above the Our Staff h2 heading, insert an inline frame. Add the following attributes to the frame:
    a. Set the source of the frame to the **badler.htm** file.
    b. Give the frame the name and id bio.
    c. Set the width and height of the frame to 400 pixels by 320 pixels.
    d. Set the margin height and width to 10 pixels.

14. Scroll down to the unordered list of hypertext links for the four staff members listed in this page. Set the target of the four links to open in the bio inline frame you created.
15. Close the **staff.htm** file, saving your changes, and then return to the **ystyles.css** file in your text editor.
16. Add a style to float inline images within the #main selector on the right margin. Set the margin around the inline frame to 10 pixels.
17. Close the **ystyles.css** file, saving your changes. Go to the Our Staff page in your Web browser and verify that each of the four staff bios appears within the inline frame you created.
18. Go to the **events.htm** file in your text editor. This file lists the upcoming events sponsored by Young Notes. Brenda wants you to add an embedded sound clip from a concert performed last year. Figure AC1-4 shows a preview of the page with the embedded sound clip.

Figure AC1-4

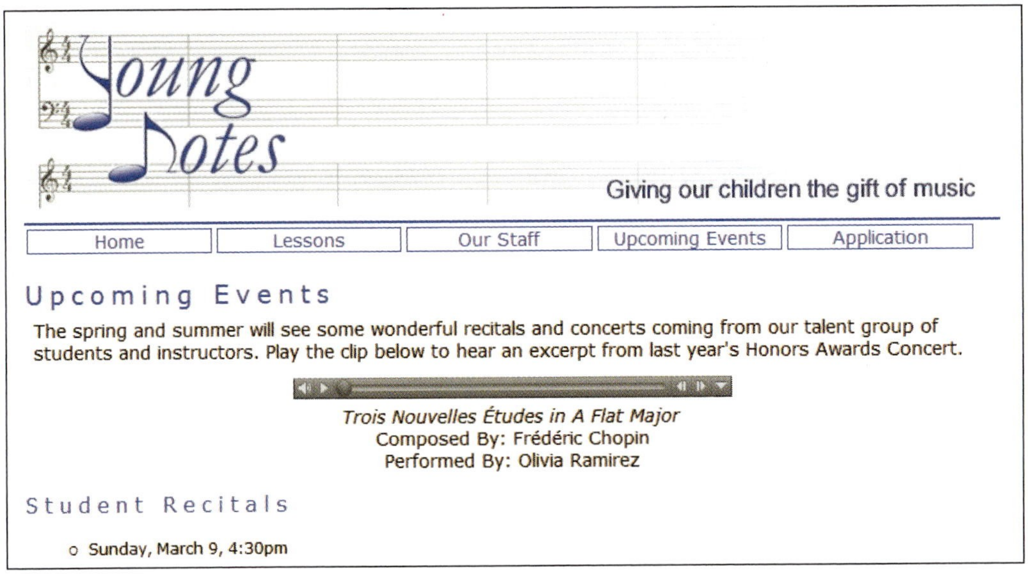

19. In the empty second paragraph directly above the <br /> tag, insert the embedded sound clip using the QuickTime player. Embed the clip as follows:
    a. Use the IE conditional comments to create different HTML code for IE and non-IE browsers.
    b. Embed the chopin.mp3 file with dimensions of the clip being 350 pixels wide by 26 pixels high.
    c. Set the mime-type of the audio file to audio/mpeg.
    d. For IE browsers, embed the clip as an ActiveX object. Include the appropriate class id and codebase values.
    e. Display the QuickTime controls for the player, and do not have the clip start automatically.
    f. For older browsers that do not support the <object> tag, display the clip using the <embed> tag. Set the attribute values of the <embed> tag to match what you set with the <object> tag.
    g. If the browser does not support embedded sound clips, display a hypertext link to the chopin.mp3 file.

20. Close the **events.htm** file, saving your changes. Go to the Upcoming Events page in your Web browser and verify that the embedded sound clip appears under the paragraph text.
21. If you can turn off support for embedded sound clips within your browser, turn off the support and verify that the page displays a link to the chopin.mp3 file.
22. Go to the **application.htm** file in your text editor. In this file you'll insert a Web form that students and adults can fill out and submit to find out more information about Young Notes. Figure AC1-5 shows a preview of the Web page you'll create.

Figure AC1-5

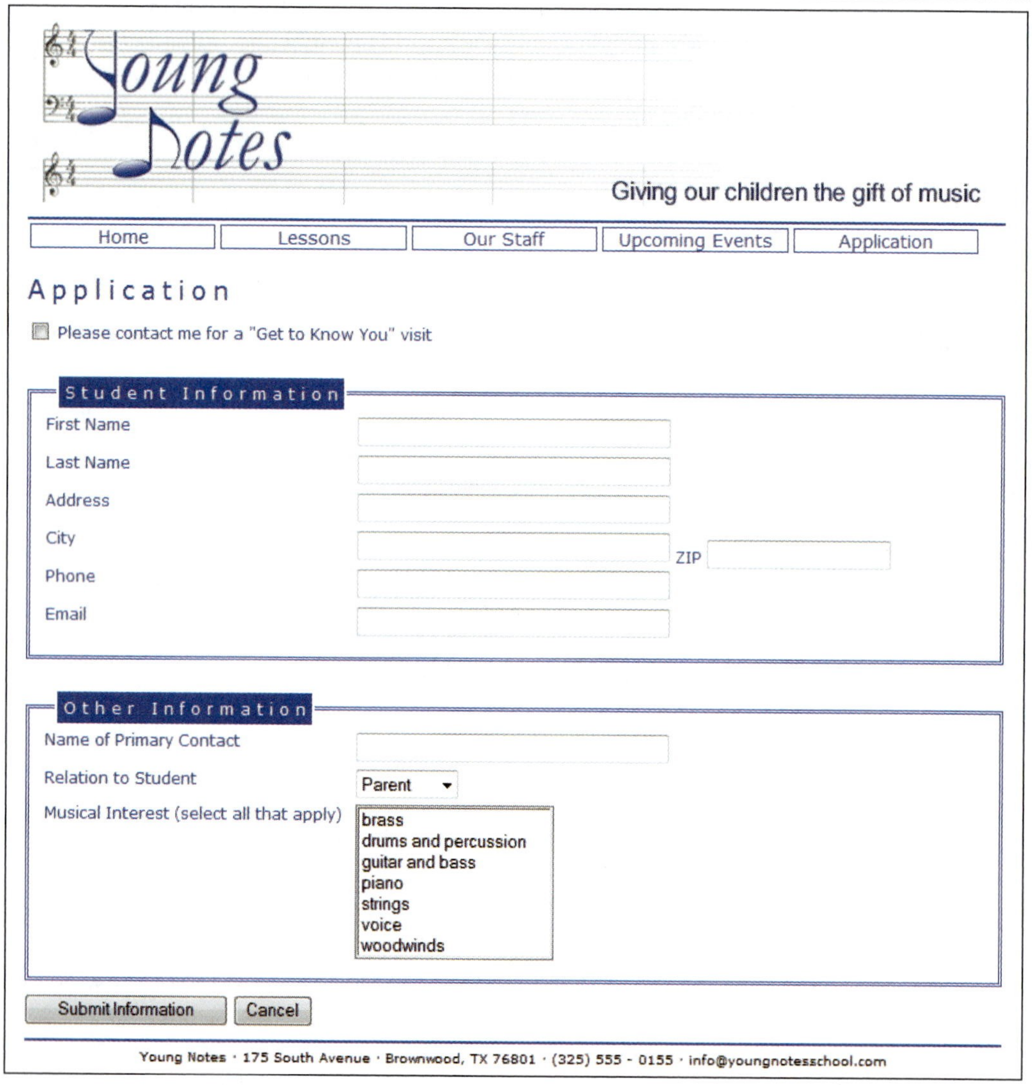

23. Directly below the Application h2 heading, insert a form element. Set the name and id the form to interestForm. Have the form access the CGI script located at *www.youngnotesschool.orgcgi-bin/interest* using the post method.
24. Within the form insert a hidden field named email. Set the value of the hidden field to the e-mail address, info@youngnotesschool.org.
25. Insert a check box field named call. Next to the check box insert a label containing the text, Please contact me for a "Get to Know You" visit.

26. Create a fieldset with the id contactFields and the legend Student Information. Within the fieldset insert the following:
    a. An input box for the fName field. Directly before the input box insert a label for the fName field containing the text, First Name.
    b. Insert a label with the text Last Name, associated with the lName field. Add an input box for the lName field directly after the label.
    c. Insert a label with the text Address, associated with the address field. Add an input box for the text field directly after the label.
    d. Insert a label with the text City, associated with the city field. Add an input box for the city field directly after the label.
    e. Insert a label for the text ZIP, associated with the zip field. Add an input box for the zip field directly after the label.
    f. Insert a label for the phone field containing the text Phone, associated with the phone field. Add an input box for the phone field directly after the label.
    g. Insert a label for the email field containing the text Email, associated with the email field. Add an input box for the email field directly after the label.
    h. Place all of the labels and input box within the contactFields fieldset, within the blockEntry class, except the label and input box for the zip field.
    i. Insert line breaks by placing the <br /> tag after the input boxes for the fName, lName, zip, and phone fields.
27. Below the contactFields field set, insert another field set with the id otherFields. Add the legend containing the text Other Information.
28. Add the following elements to the otherFields field set:
    a. Insert a label containing the text Name of Primary Contact, and associated with the pcontact field. After the label insert an input box for the pcontact field.
    b. Insert a label for the ctype field containing the text Relation to Student. After the label insert a selection list for the ctype field and containing the options Parent and Guardian. The values of the two options are also Parent and Guardian.
    c. Insert a label for the interest field containing the text Musical Interest (select all that apply). After the label insert a selection list containing the text shown in Figure AC1-5. The option values associated with text are: brass, drums, guitar, piano, strings, voice, and woodwinds. Set the size of the selection list to seven entries and allow users to select multiple options from the list.
    d. Place all of the labels, input boxes, and selection lists from the fieldset in the blockEntry class.
    e. Insert line breaks after the pcontact input box and the ctype selection list using the <br /> element.
29. After the otherFields field set, insert a submit button and a cancel button containing the text Submit Information, and Cancel, respectively.
30. Link the **application.htm** file to the **fstyles.css** style sheet. Close the **application.htm** file, saving your changes.
31. Go to the **fstyles.css** file in your text editor. Add the following styles to the style sheet:
    a. Set the font size of the form element to 12 pixels and the font color to the value (68, 76, 169). Set the top and bottom margins of the form to 10 pixels.
    b. Add a 3-pixel double border in the color value (68, 76, 169) to all field sets in the form. Set the top and bottom margin of field sets to 10 pixels. Set the left and right margins of the field sets to 0 pixels. Set the padding of the field sets to 5 pixels.
    c. Display field set legends in a white font on a background color value of (68, 76, 169). Set the letter spacing, padding, and margin of the field set legends to 5 pixels.

d. Place all labels belonging to the blockEntry class in the form using absolute positioning. Set the value of the large style property to 30 pixels.
e. Set the width of all input boxes belonging to the blockEntry class to 250 pixels. Set the left margin of those input boxes to 250 pixels as well. Set the bottom margin to 5 pixels.
f. Set the left margin of all selection lists in the blockEntry class to 250 pixels. Set the bottom margin of those selection lists to 5 pixels.

32. Save your changes to the file, and then go to the Application page in the Young Notes Web site. Verify that the layout and content of the application form resemble that shown in Figure AC1-5.
33. Submit your completed files to your instructor.

Ending Data Files

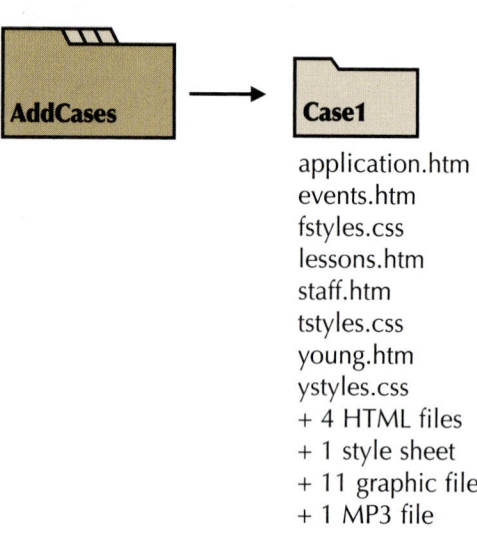

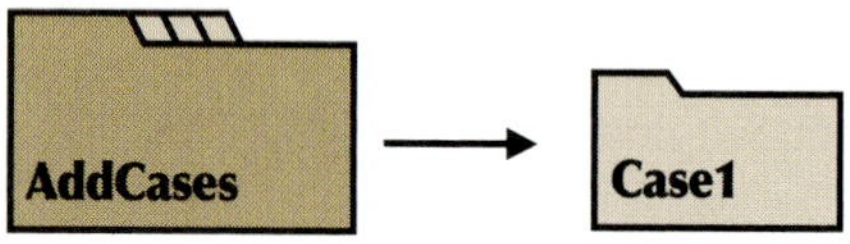

application.htm
events.htm
fstyles.css
lessons.htm
staff.htm
tstyles.css
young.htm
ystyles.css
+ 4 HTML files
+ 1 style sheet
+ 11 graphic files
+ 1 MP3 file

Additional Case 2

Objectives

- Convert an HTML document to XHTML
- Add rounded corners to a box
- Create a drop-cap
- Generate content with JavaScript
- Create a style sheet for printed output
- Generate content with CSS

Creating a Culinary Web Site

Case | Cornucopia Online

Gary Kendrick is the owner and manager of a shop selling gourmet products. Gary's company began under the name *Cornucopia* and is based in his hometown of Bristol, Connecticut. The store originally was a small shop in which Gary raised and sold turkeys—still a main feature of the company. As the company grew in popularity, Gary branched out into other fields and products, eventually moving its operations to the Web under the name *Cornucopia Online*.

The company has been in operation for several years and Gary is looking at revising the Web site's design and layout. He has hired you as part of his Web site development team. Some of the work on the new design has already been completed; he would like you to complete the design of the site's home page and work on the Recipe of the Week page.

Because of the store's origins in selling turkeys and other poultry, Gary is aware that Thanksgiving and the holidays are a busy time for Cornucopia Online. So, besides the HTML code you'll write, Gary also wants you to add a JavaScript program to the site's home page that will display a countdown message informing customers of the number of days remaining until Thanksgiving.

Starting Data Files

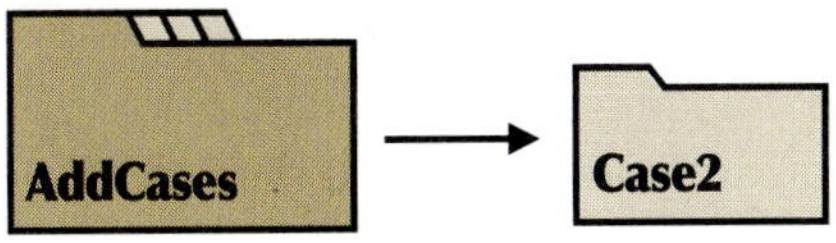

cornstylestxt.css
corntxt.htm
countdowntxt.js
printstylestxt.css
recipetxt.htm
tday.js
+ 5 graphic files

Complete the following:

1. Use your text editor to open the **cornstylestxt.css**, **corntxt.htm**, **countdowntxt.js**, **printstylestxt.css** and **recipetxt.htm** files from the addcases/case2 folder included with your Data Files. Enter ***your name*** and ***the date*** in the comment section of each file. Save the files as **cornstyles.css**, **corn.htm**, **countdown.js**, **printstyles.css**, and **recipe.htm**, respectively, in the same folder.
2. Go to the **corn.htm** file in your text editor. This file will be used for the Cornucopia Online home page. A preview of the final version of the page is shown in Figure AC2-1.

Figure AC2-1

3. Link the page to the **cornstyles.css** style sheet.
4. Change the file from an HTML file into an XHTML file by adding an xml prolog, a DOCTYPE declaration for the XHTML strict DTD, and an xml namespace attribute to the opening <html> tag.
5. Gary wants to have a decorative border around the contents of the main div element. To create this decorative border, enclose the contents of the main div element (but not the main div element itself) within a set of four container div elements with id names, bottom, left, corner, and boxContent.

6. Gary also wants to create a drop-cap effect for the first paragraph of text on the home page. Locate the article div element and set the id of the first paragraph within that container to the value firstPara.
7. Save your changes, and then open the **cornstyles.css** file in your text editor.
8. At the bottom of the file, insert a style declaration for the first line of the firstPara div element to display the text of the first line in small capital letters.
9. Insert a style declaration that applies the following styles to the first letter of the firstPara div element:
   a. Float the text on the left margin.
   b. Set the font size to 350% of the normal font size.
   c. Set the line height to 0.8 and the margin to 5 pixels to the right and below the letter, but 0 pixels to the left and above.
   d. Display the first letter in a serif font with the text color value (173, 89, 28).
10. For the #corner selector, display the **corner.jpg** graphic image in the bottom left corner of the element, without repeating. Display the **bottom.jpg** image at the bottom of the div element with the id bottom. Repeat the image only horizontally. Display the **left.jpg** image on the left edge of the div element with the id left. Tile the image only vertically.
11. Set the width of the element with the id boxContent to 740 pixels. Set the padding size to 40 pixels at the bottom and left edge of the element and 0 pixels at the top and right edges.
12. Save your changes, and then open **corn.htm** in your Web browser. Verify that the drop-cap, first line, and decorative borders match Figure AC2-1.
13. Gary has located some JavaScript programs to display the current date and to calculate the number of days until Thanksgiving from the current date. The program to display the current date is named showDate(). The program to calculate the days until Thanksgiving is called daysToThanksgiving(). He's stored both of these programs in the **tday.js** file. Return to the **corn.htm** file in your text editor and insert an external script element pointing to the **tday.js** external JavaScript file.
14. Gary wants you to store the code that writes the days until Thanksgiving in another external script file. Open the **countdown.js** file in your text editor and insert a function named countdown(). The function has no parameters, but should include commands to write the following HTML code to the Web document:
```
Today is: <br />
date
<br /><br /> There are:
days
days until Thanksgiving
```
    where *date* is the text returned by the showDate() function and *days* is the text returned by the daysToThanksgiving() function. Neither function requires a parameter value.
15. Close **countdown.js**, saving your changes, and then return to the **corn.htm** file in your text editor. Insert an external script element pointing to the **countdown.js** file.
16. Scroll down to the div element with the id head. Within this div container, insert another div element with the id countdown. Within that div element, insert a script element that calls the countdown() function.
17. Close the **corn.htm** file, saving your changes, and then return to the **cornstyles.css** file in your text editor. At the bottom of the file, insert a style declaration that applies the following format to the countdown div element:
   a. Set the width of the element to 150 pixels and the top/bottom margins to 10 pixels. Set the left/right margins to 0 pixels.

b. Set the padding to 5 pixels.
c. Set the font size to 10 pixels.
d. Float the div element on the right margin.
e. Add a 2-pixel solid border with the color value (173, 89, 28).

18. Close **cornstyles.css**, saving your changes, and then reload **corn.htm** in your Web browser. Verify that in the upper-right corner there is a box with a message as in Figure AC2-1, indicating the date and the number of days until Thanksgiving.
19. Open **recipe.htm** in your text editor. The page displays the Recipe of the Week, shown in Figure AC2-2.

Figure AC2-2

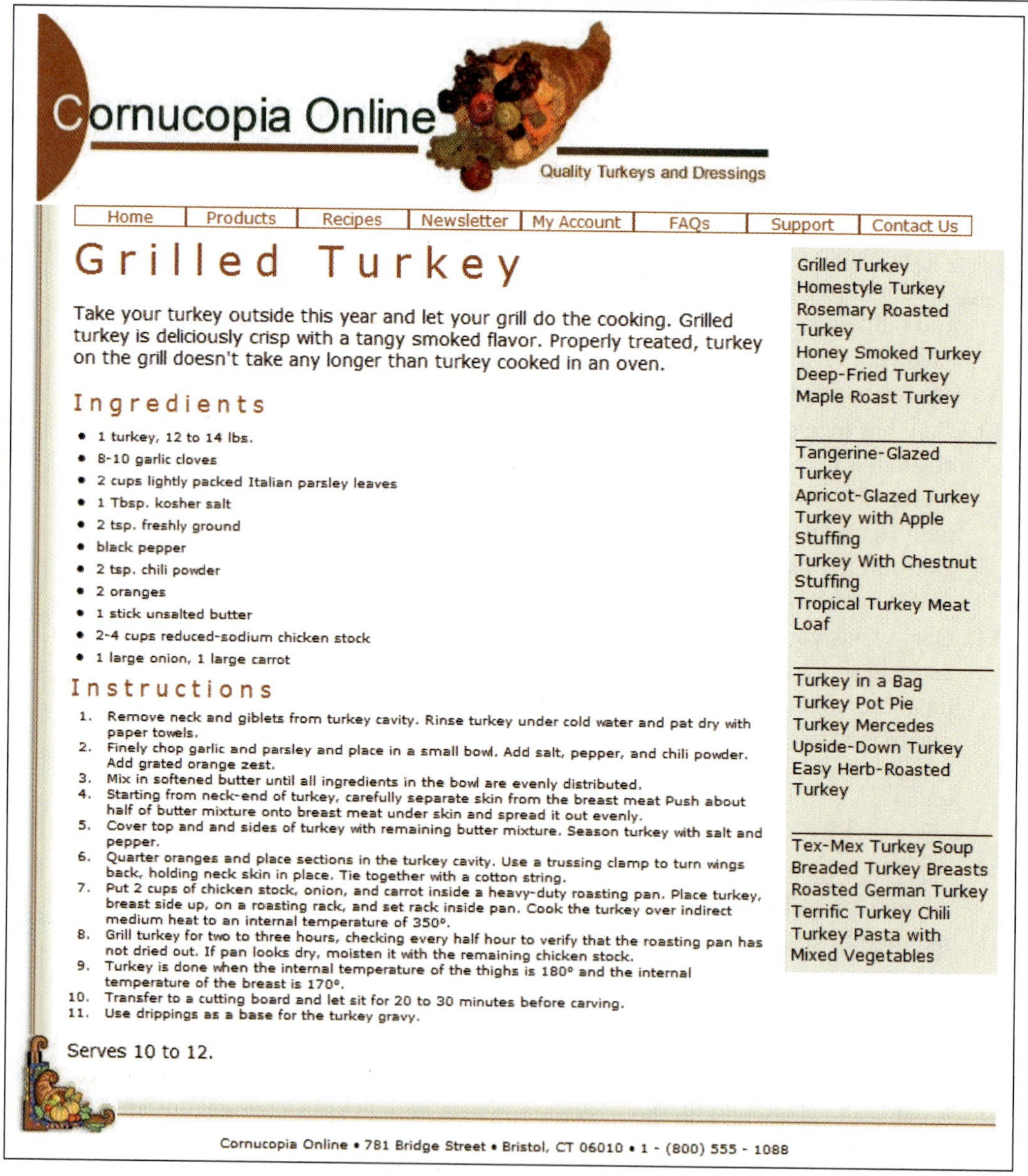

20. Change the format of the file from HTML to XHTML using the XHTML script DTD.
21. Insert a link to the **cornstyles.css** style sheet.

22. As you did for the **corn.htm** file, enclose the contents of the main div element with four container div elements with ids, bottom, left, corner, and boxContent.
23. Save your changes to the file, and then open **recipe.htm** in your Web browser. Verify that the layout and design resemble that shown in Figure AC2-2.
24. Gary wants the printed version of this page to display just the recipe for grilled turkey. Figure AC2-3 shows a preview of the printed output. To create a style sheet for printed output, go to the **printstyles.css** file in your text editor.

Figure AC2-3

Cornucopia Online Recipe Page

Recipe of the Week: Grilled Turkey

Take your turkey outside this year and let your grill do the cooking. Grilled turkey is deliciously crisp with a tangy smoked flavor. Properly treated, turkey on the grill doesn't take any longer than turkey cooked in an oven.

Ingredients

- 1 turkey, 12 to 14 lbs.
- 8-10 garlic cloves
- 2 cups lightly packed Italian parsley leaves
- 1 Tbsp. kosher salt
- 2 tsp. freshly ground
- black pepper
- 2 tsp. chili powder
- 2 oranges
- 1 stick unsalted butter
- 2-4 cups reduced-sodium chicken stock
- 1 large onion, 1 large carrot

Instructions

1. Remove neck and giblets from turkey cavity. Rinse turkey under cold water and pat dry with paper towels.
2. Finely chop garlic and parsley and place in a small bowl. Add salt, pepper, and chili powder. Add grated orange zest.
3. Mix in softened butter until all ingredients in the bowl are evenly distributed.
4. Starting from neck-end of turkey, carefully separate skin from the breast meat Push about half of butter mixture onto breast meat under skin and spread it out evenly.
5. Cover top and and sides of turkey with remaining butter mixture. Season turkey with salt and pepper.
6. Quarter oranges and place sections in the turkey cavity. Use a trussing clamp to turn wings back, holding neck skin in place. Tie together with a cotton string.
7. Put 2 cups of chicken stock, onion, and carrot inside a heavy-duty roasting pan. Place turkey, breast side up, on a roasting rack, and set rack inside pan. Cook the turkey over indirect medium heat to an internal temperature of 350°.
8. Grill turkey for two to three hours, checking every half hour to verify that the roasting pan has not dried out. If pan looks dry, moisten it with the remaining chicken stock.
9. Turkey is done when the internal temperature of the thighs is 180° and the internal temperature of the breast is 170°.
10. Transfer to a cutting board and let sit for 20 to 30 minutes before carving.
11. Use drippings as a base for the turkey gravy.

Serves 10 to 12.

1 of 1

25. Insert an @page rule that defines the size of the printed output as an 8½ × 11″ sheet of paper, with ½″ margins, in portrait orientation.
26. Add a style to prevent the display of the elements with the head, links, and links2 ids. Also hide the address element.
27. Add a style to display h1 and h2 headings in a sans-serif font.
28. For h1 headings, insert a style that automatically inserts the text Recipe of the Week: directly before the h1 heading text.
29. Close the **printstyles.css** file, saving your changes.
30. Return to the **recipe.htm** file in your text editor. Insert a link to the **printstyles.css** file, indicating that this style sheet should only be used for print media.
31. Indicate that the **cornstyles.css** style sheet should be used only for screen media.
32. Close the **recipe.htm** file, saving your changes. Reload the file in your Web browser and either print the page or use the print preview feature of your Web browser to confirm that the print layout resembles that shown in Figure AC2-3. (Note: Internet Explorer does not support the CSS style to insert content, so the printed heading under IE will read just Grilled Turkey.)
33. Using an XHTML validator, test whether the **corn.htm** and **recipe.htm** files pass validation under the strict XHTML DTD. Correct errors until the files pass validation.
34. Submit your completed files to your instructor.

Ending Data Files

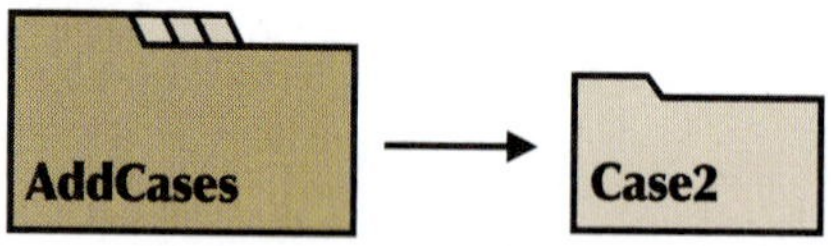

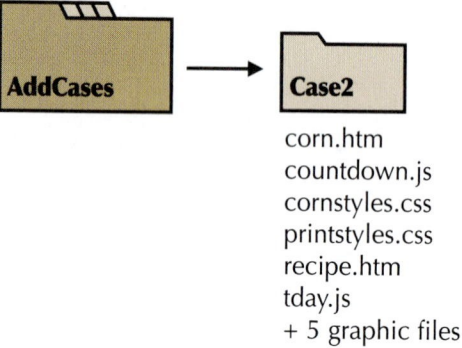

corn.htm
countdown.js
cornstyles.css
printstyles.css
recipe.htm
tday.js
+ 5 graphic files

Additional Case 3

Objectives

- Design a complete Web site from scratch
- Create an online survey form
- Generate content using a JavaScript function
- Create a style sheet for a complete Web site
- Test a Web site against the XHTML strict DTD

Creating an Online Newsletter

Case | Twin Life Magazine

Twin Life is a magazine created for parents of twins, triplets, and other multiple-birth children. Recently the company has decided to go online and publish parts of its monthly magazine on the World Wide Web. Elise Howard, the magazine's editor, has asked you to create a Web site for the contents of *Twin Life*.

Elise envisions a total of five Web pages for the site: a front page, a news page, a monthly features page, a page of special articles, and a customer survey page. She gave you a disk containing text files of the articles and image files she wants you to include. You are free to supplement these files with any other appropriate material.

Starting Data Files

AddCases → **Case3**

calendar.txt
chicago.txt
CreditRoll.class
dates.js
deliver.txt
editor.txt
mbirths.txt
rates.txt
recipe.txt
roles.txt
staff.txt
survey.txt
talk.txt
twintips.txt
+ 8 graphic files

Complete the following:

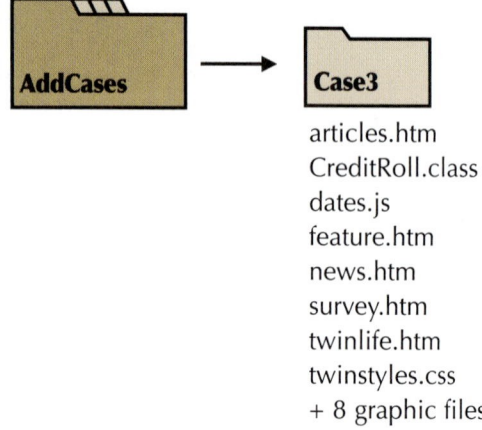

1. Use your text editor to create the following html files: **articles.htm**, **feature.htm**, **news.htm**, **survey.htm**, **twinlife.htm**, and **twinstyles.css** in the addcases/case3 folder included with your Data Files. Enter ***your name, the date,*** and ***a description*** in the comment section of each file.
2. The **twinlife.htm** file should contain the home page for the newsletter. The **articles.htm** should contain a page of articles about twins and child care. The **feature.htm** should contain an advice column and a recipe of the month. The **news.htm** file should contain a page of news stories. Finally, the **survey.htm** should contain a Web form requesting information from newsletter subscribers. Use the text files for the content of these pages, though you are free to supplement these pages with additional material.
3. The design of the Web site is up to you, but it should incorporate the following:
   - Each page should be written to the standards of the XHTML strict DTD.
   - The page should have at least one Web form, a Web table, and an inline frame.
   - All formatting should be done in the **twinstyles.css** style sheet.
   - Each page should contain links to all of the other pages in the Web site so that users can easily navigate from one page to another.
4. The list of upcoming events (found in the **calendar.txt** file) should be displayed in a scrolling window, using the CreditRoll.class Java applet. You need to determine the values of each parameter in the applet, aside from the TEXTx parameters.
5. The home page should display the current date. Use the showDate() function from the dates.js JavaScript file to generate the text of the current date.
6. The magazine's logo (**twinlogo.gif**) should include an image map linking to the five Web pages in the Web site. You will have to determine the coordinates for each hotspot using either your image editing software or an image map editor.
7. A Submit button and a Reset button should be included with the online survey form. The form should be submitted to a CGI script at: *http://www.twinlifemag.com/cgi/survey*.
8. Test all of the files in your Web site against a validator to verify that they pass validation under the XHTML strict DTD.
9. Submit the completed files to your instructor.

Ending Data Files

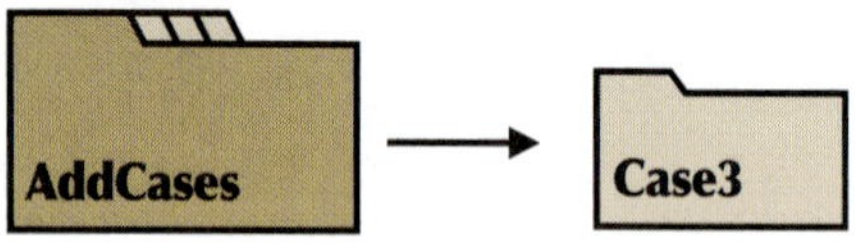

articles.htm
CreditRoll.class
dates.js
feature.htm
news.htm
survey.htm
twinlife.htm
twinstyles.css
+ 8 graphic files

Objectives

Session 11.1
- Work with event handlers
- Insert a value into a Web form field
- Create and work with date objects
- Extract information from date objects

Session 11.2
- Work with arithmetic, unary, conditional, and logical operators
- Understand the properties and methods of the Math object
- Understand how JavaScript works with numeric values
- Run time-delayed and timed-interval commands

Working with Operators and Expressions

Creating a New Year's Day Countdown Clock

Case | Tulsa's New Year's Bash

Every year on December 31st, Tulsa, Oklahoma, rings in the New Year with a daylong celebration. The New Year's Bash includes races, jugglers, tasting booths, live bands, and dances, and is capped by fireworks at midnight. The bash has become so big that partygoers come from miles away to join in the fun, and planning for the celebration starts early.

Hector Sadler manages promotion for the New Year's Bash. One of his responsibilities is to maintain a Web site that advertises the event and builds up anticipation for it. Hector wants to include a countdown clock on the site's home page that displays the current date and the number of days, hours, minutes, and seconds remaining before the fireworks go off. You will write the JavaScript code to create this clock for Hector.

Starting Data Files

Tutorial.11 →

Tutorial
clocktxt.htm
functxt.js
newyear.css
+ 3 graphic files

Review
datestxt.js
eventstxt.htm
tulsa.css
+ 1 graphic file

Case1
functions.js
oaetxt.htm
quiz.css
+ 6 graphic files

Case2
hometxt.htm
randtxt.js
styles.css
tips.js
+ 2 graphic files

Case3
je.css
worldtxt.htm
zonestxt.js
+ 2 graphic files

Case4
mall.txt
malltxt.htm
timetxt.js
+ 4 graphic files

Session 11.1

Introducing onevent Processing

The New Year's Bash is still six months away, but it's not too soon to sit down with Hector to discuss creating the countdown clock for the Web site. Hector envisions a clock that updates itself every second to add a dynamic effect to the site's home page. Hector already created a Web page that displays a static value for the date, time, and amount of time left until the New Year. You'll look at this file now.

To view the clock Web page:

1. Use your text editor to open **clocktxt.htm** from the tutorial.11/tutorial folder included with your Data Files, enter ***your name*** and ***the date*** in the comment section of the file, and then save the file as **clock.htm** in the same folder.
2. Scroll through the file and familiarize yourself with its contents.
3. Open **clock.htm** in your Web browser. Figure 11-1 shows the initial version of the Web page.

Figure 11-1 **The initial clock page**

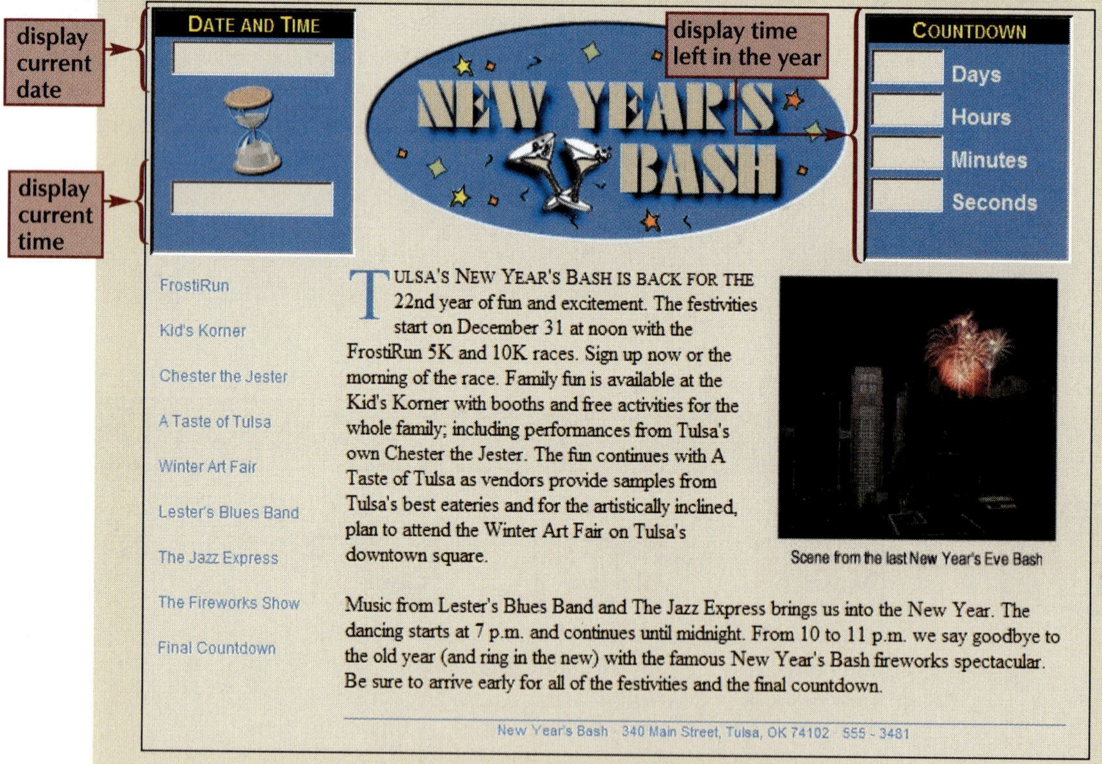

At the top of the Web page are Web form fields in which the current date, time, and countdown clock will appear. The form's name is clockform. Figure 11-2 shows the names of the fields within the form along with sample values for each field.

Form field names | Figure 11-2

Hector wants these values to be constantly updated to reflect the current date and time. To do this, you'll write a JavaScript function that calculates the current date and time as well as the time remaining until New Year's Day, and then updates those values once every second. You'll start creating this function by exploring how to insert values into a Web form. The general command to insert a value into a field is

```
document.form.field.value = field_value;
```

where *form* is the name of the Web form, *field* is the name of the field, and *field_value* is the value you want to place into the field. For example, for Hector's Web page, the current date is stored in the dateNow field of the clockform Web form. To set this value to the text string 2/24/2011, you would use the following JavaScript command:

```
document.clockform.dateNow.value = "2/24/2011";
```

Similarly, to display the text 2:35:05 p.m. in the timeNow field, you would use the following JavaScript command:

```
document.clockform.timeNow.value = "2:35:05 p.m.";
```

You'll use this information as you work on Hector's Web page. You'll begin by placing sample date and time values into the clockform Web form using a JavaScript function named NYClock(). For now, you'll insert the text string "99" in the fields for days, hours, minutes, and seconds left in the year. This text string will act as a placeholder until you learn how to calculate the actual values, but including this text allows you to confirm that your code is correctly writing text to the Web form fields.

To create the NYClock() function:

1. Return to the **clock.htm** file in your text editor.
2. Above the closing </head> tag, insert the following embedded script, as shown in Figure 11-3:

```
<script type = "text/javascript">
   function NYClock() {
   // display the current date and time
      document.clockform.dateNow.value = "2/24/2011";
      document.clockform.timeNow.value = "2:35:05 p.m.";

   // calculate the time left until the New Year's Bash
      document.clockform.daysLeft.value = "99";
      document.clockform.hrLeft.value = "99";
      document.clockform.minLeft.value = "99";
      document.clockform.secLeft.value = "99";
   }
</script>
```

Figure 11-3 **Inserted NYClock function**

```
<title>Tulsa's New Year's Bash</title>
<link href="newyear.css" rel="stylesheet" type="text/css" />

<script type="text/javascript">

   function NYClock() {
   // display the current date and time
      document.clockform.dateNow.value = "2/24/2011";
      document.clockform.timeNow.value = "2:35:05 p.m.";

   // calculate the time left until the New Year's Bash
      document.clockform.daysLeft.value = "99";
      document.clockform.hrLeft.value = "99";
      document.clockform.minLeft.value = "99";
      document.clockform.secLeft.value = "99";
   }

   </script>
</head>
```

writes sample dates and times to the dateNow and timeNow fields

writes placeholder values to the daysLeft, hrLeft minLeft and secLeft fields

The single-line comments make it easier to interpret the commands in the function. Be sure to enter the code exactly as shown in Figure 11-3, including matching the use of upper- and lowercase letters. Recall that JavaScript is a case-sensitive language and programs will not run correctly if the case is incorrect.

3. Save your changes to the file.

Because these values will be updated constantly while the page is displayed by a user's browser, the NYClock() function needs to run when the page is initially loaded, and then repeatedly thereafter. This is in contrast to the code you wrote in the previous tutorial, which ran only once when the page was loaded by the browser. That code ran either when it was encountered within a script element or was called as part of a function. Because you'll need to control when and how often the NYClock() function is run, you must learn how to work with events.

Understanding Events and Event Handlers

An **event** is an action that occurs within a Web browser or Web document. Most objects have specific events associated with them. For example, one event associated with a Web form button is the action of being clicked by a user. Another event occurs when a user hovers the pointer over the button without clicking it. A Web document also has associated events such as the action of being loaded or unloaded by a browser. Each event can be associated with one or more JavaScript programs that run in response to the event's occurrence.

To associate a program with an event, you add an event handler to the object in which the event occurs. An **event handler** is a statement that tells browsers what code to run in response to the specified event. One way of inserting an event handler is to add it as an attribute of the element in the Web document. The syntax to insert an event handler as an attribute is:

```
<element onevent = "script" ...> ...
```

In this event handler, *element* is the name of the element, *event* is the name of an event, and *script* is a command or collection of commands to be run in response to the event. If you intend to run several commands in response to an event, it's easiest to place them within a function and run the function using a single command. One commonly used event handler, onclick, runs a program in response to a user clicking an element with the mouse button. The event handler in the following code runs the calcTotal() function when a user clicks the input button:

```
<input type = "button" value = "Total Cost" onclick = "calcTotal()" />
```

Figure 11-4 lists other event handlers you can use with the elements in a Web page. You can also view an extended list of event handlers in the appendices.

JavaScript event handlers **Figure 11-4**

Category	Event Handler	Description
Window and document event handlers	onload	The browser has completed loading the document.
	onunload	The browser has completed unloading the document.
	onerror	An error has occurred in the JavaScript program.
	onmove	The user has moved the browser window.
	onresize	The user has resized the browser window.
	onscroll	The user has moved the scroll bar within the browser window.
Form event handlers	onfocus	The user has entered an input field.
	onblur	The user has exited an input field.
	onchange	The content of an input field has changed.
	onselect	The user has selected text within an input or text area field.
	onsubmit	The user has submitted the Web form.
	onreset	The user has reset the Web form.
Mouse and keyboard event handlers	onkeydown	The user has pressed a key.
	onkeypress	The user has pressed and released a key.
	onclick	The user has clicked the mouse button.
	ondblclick	The user has double-clicked the mouse button.
	onmousedown	The user has pressed the mouse button.
	onmouseup	The user has released the mouse button.
	onmousemove	The user has moved the pointer over the element.
	onmouseout	The user has moved the pointer off of the element.

For the clock Web page, you want to run the NYClock() function when the page is loaded. Loading is one of the events associated with the Web page, and can be handled by adding the following event handler attribute to the <body> tag:

```
<body onload = "NYClock()">
```

You'll add this event handler to the clock.htm file.

To insert the onload event handler to the clock Web page:

1. In the <body> tag of the clock.htm file, click after the word body, press the **Spacebar**, and then type the following attribute, as shown in Figure 11-5:

   ```
   onload="NYClock()"
   ```

onload event handler attribute inserted in the <body> tag **Figure 11-5**

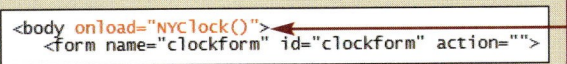

```
<body onload="NYClock()">
  <form name="clockform" id="clockform" action="">
```

event handler to run the NYClock() function when the page is loaded

2. Save your changes to the file.

3. Reload **clock.htm** in your Web browser. The page opens, displaying the field values you specified in the previous set of steps. See Figure 11-6.

Figure 11-6 **Field values inserted into the clockform Web form**

Trouble? If you receive an error message when loading the page, check the code in the NYClock() function and the onload event handler. Some common programming errors that might have occurred within the NYClock() function include mismatching uppercase and lowercase letters, misspelling variable names, forgetting to close up double quotes, and forgetting to enclose command blocks and functions within curly braces.

InSight | Running JavaScript Commands as Hypertext Links

Another way to run a JavaScript command in response to an event is to treat it as a hypertext link. This method is similar to running the command in response to a click event within an element. The syntax for running a JavaScript command as a hypertext link is

```
<a href = "javascript:script">content</a>
```

where *script* is the command (or commands) you want to run when a user clicks the link. For example, the following code runs the calcTotal() function when a user clicks the link:

```
<a href = "javascript:calcTotal()">
   Calculate total cost
</a>
```

This technique was often used for older browsers that did not support event handlers, or for elements that did not support the onclick event handler. This issue was more prevalent when event handlers were a new feature of HTML and JavaScript. Now, running JavaScript commands through hypertext links is considered a bad practice because it misuses the href attribute, which should be reserved for linked documents and not commands. However, you might see this code still being run in older Web sites.

Reference Window | Running a Script in Response to an Event

- To insert an event handler as an element attribute, use the syntax

```
<element onevent = "script"> ...
```

where *element* is the Web page element, *event* is the name of an event associated with the element, and *script* is a command to be run in response to the event.

Working with Date Objects

Now that you've created the initial form of the NYClock() function, you need some way of generating the date and time information rather than typing the values directly into the JavaScript code. To work with dates, JavaScript supports a **date object**, which contains information about a specified date and time. Date objects are created using the following command:

```
variable = new Date("month day, year hours:minutes:seconds");
```

In this command, *variable* is the name of the variable that contains the date object, and *month*, *day*, *year*, *hours*, *minutes*, and *seconds* indicate the date and time to be stored in the object. Time values are entered using 24-hour time; for example, a time of 2:35 p.m. would be entered as 14:35. The following command stores a date object in a variable named thisDate that corresponds to a date of February 24, 2011 and a time of 2:35:05 p.m.:

```
thisDate = new Date("February 24, 2011 14:35:05");
```

If you omit the hours, minutes, and seconds values, JavaScript assumes that the time is 0 hours, 0 minutes, and 0 seconds—in other words, midnight of the specified day. If you omit both the date and time information, JavaScript returns the current date and time, which it gets from the system clock on the user's computer. The following command creates a variable named thisDate that contains the current date and time:

```
thisDate = new Date();
```

You can also create a date object using the following command:

```
variable = new Date(year, month, day, hours, minutes, seconds);
```

In this command, *year*, *month*, *day*, *hours*, *minutes*, and *seconds* are the values of the date and time, and the *month* value is an integer from 0 to 11, where 0 = January, 1 = February, and so forth. Time values are again expressed in 24-hour time. The following command creates a date object for February 24, 2011, at 2:35:05 p.m.:

```
thisDate = new Date(2011, 1, 24, 14, 35, 5);
```

Creating a Date and Time Variable | Reference Window

- To store a date and time in a variable, use the JavaScript command
  `variable = new Date("month day, year hours:minutes:seconds")`
  where *variable* is the name of the variable that contains the date object, and *month*, *day*, *year*, *hours*, *minutes*, and *seconds* indicate the date and time to be stored in the object. Time values are entered in 24-hour time.
- To store a date and time using numeric values, use the JavaScript command
  `variable = new Date(year, month, day, hours, minutes, seconds)`
  where *year*, *month*, *day*, *hours*, *minutes*, and *seconds* are the values of the date and time, and the *month* value is an integer from 0 to 11, where 0 = January, 1 = February, and so forth. Time values are entered in 24-hour time.
- To create a date object containing the current date and time, use the following JavaScript command:
  `variable = new Date()`

Now that you've seen how to store date and time information in a variable, you'll create a variable named today that stores a date object. You'll use February 24, 2011 as the initial date and 2:35:05 p.m. as the initial time. Later in this tutorial, you'll set the value of the today variable to the current date and time. For now, using a preset date and time lets you check that any calculations based on this date are correct. You'll add the today variable to the NYClock() function you just created.

To create the today variable:

1. Return to the **clock.htm** file in your text editor.
2. Insert the following lines at the beginning of the NYClock() function, as shown in Figure 11-7:

```
// the today variable contains the current date and time
   var today = new Date("February 24, 2011 14:35:05");
```

Figure 11-7 Date object added to the NYClock() function

variable storing the date object

```
function NYClock() {
// the today variable contains the current date and time
   var today = new Date("February 24, 2011 14:35:05");

// display the current date and time
   document.clockform.dateNow.value = "2/24/2011";
   document.clockform.timeNow.value = "2:35:05 p.m.";

// calculate the time left until the New Year's Bash
   document.clockform.daysLeft.value = "99";
   document.clockform.hrLeft.value = "99";
   document.clockform.minLeft.value = "99";
   document.clockform.secLeft.value = "99";
}
```

3. Save your changes to the file.

Retrieving the Date, Month, and Hour Values

A date object stores a numeric value that is equal to the number of milliseconds (1/1000 of a second) between the specified date and time and January 1, 1970. For example, a date object with the date and time of February 24, 2011 at 2:35:05 p.m. has a hidden value equal to 1,298,579,705,000 milliseconds. Fortunately, you don't have to work with this value. Instead, JavaScript provides **date methods**, which are methods you can use to retrieve information from a date object or to change a date object's value.

To extract the day of the month from a given date object, JavaScript provides the getDate() method. The syntax to apply the getDate() method is

```
DateObject.getDate()
```

where *DateObject* is a date object (or a variable that contains a date object). For example, the following code extracts the day value from the thisDate variable and stores the result in the thisDay variable:

```
thisDate = new Date("February 24, 2011 14:35:05");
thisDay = thisDate.getDate();
```

After running these commands, the value of the thisDay variable is 24.

A similar method exists for extracting the value of the current month. This method is named getMonth(). Because JavaScript starts counting the months with 0 for January, you must add 1 to the month number returned by the getMonth() method to translate the value to the common system of numbering months from 1 to 12. The following JavaScript code extracts the current month number, increases it by 1, and stores it in a variable named thisMonth:

```
thisDate = new Date("February 24, 2011 14:35:05");
thisMonth = thisDate.getMonth()+1;
```

In this code, the value of the thisMonth variable is 2.

Finally, the getFullYear() method extracts the four-digit year value from the date object. The following code stores the value of the current year in a variable named thisYear:

```
thisDate = new Date("February 24, 2011 14:35:05");
thisYear = thisDate.getFullYear();
```

In this case, the value of the thisYear variable is 2011.

Comparing the getFullYear() and getYear() Methods | InSight

The two methods to extract the year information from a date object are getFullYear() and getYear(). As you've seen, the getFullYear() method extracts the year value as a four-digit number. However, JavaScript originally used the getYear() method, which returns a two-digit year value. For example, with the getYear() method, a date object from the year 1996 returns the value 96. This approach of returning only the two-digit year value was an example of the so-called Y2K Bug in which programs that relied on two-digit year values would begin to show mistakes with the start of the new century in the year 2000.

The getYear() method is still supported by JavaScript, but it returns a four-digit year value for dates past the year 2000. For example, a date object from the year 2009 that uses the getYear() method returns 2009 and not 09. To avoid confusion between two- and four-digit year values, you should always use the getFullYear() method.

Retrieving the Hour, Minute, and Second Values

In addition to methods for extracting date, month, and hour values from a date object, JavaScript supports similar methods for extracting the hours, minutes, and seconds values from a date object. These methods are:

```
DateObject.getSeconds()
DateObject.getMinutes()
DateObject.getHours()
```

In these methods, *DateObject* is a date object or a variable containing a date object. Hours are expressed in 24-hour time. So, the code

```
thisDate = new Date("February 24, 2011 14:35:05");
thisHour = thisDate.getHours();
```

stores the value 14 in the thisHour variable. Figure 11-8 summarizes the methods for retrieving date and time values from date objects.

Figure 11-8 Methods to extract date and time values from date objects

Method	Retrieves	Value (when the thisDate variable stores the date object for "June 15, 2011 14:35:28")
thisDate.getSeconds()	Retrieves the seconds value	28
thisDate.getMinutes()	Retrieves the minutes value	35
thisDate.getHours()	Retrieves the hours value (in 24-hour time)	14
thisDate.getDate()	Retrieves the day of the month value	15
thisDate.getDay()	Retrieves the day of the week value (0 = Sunday, 1 = Monday, 2 = Tuesday, 3 = Wednesday, 4 = Thursday, 5 = Friday, 6 = Saturday)	3
thisDate.getMonth()	Retrieves the month value (0 = January, 1 = February, 2 = March, etc.)	5
thisDate.getFullYear()	Retrieves the four-digit year value	2011
thisDate.getTime()	Retrieves the time value, as expressed in milliseconds, since January 1, 1970	1,308,166,505,000

Reference Window | Retrieving Date and Time Values

- To retrieve the year value from a date object named DateObject, use the method
  `DateObject.getFullYear()`
  where *DateObject* is a variable containing a date object.
- To retrieve the month value, use the method
  `DateObject.getMonth()`
  where a month value of 0 equals the first month of the year (January), a month value of 1 equals the second month of the year (February), and so forth.
- To retrieve the day of the month value, use the following method:
  `DateObject.getDate()`
- To retrieve the day of the week value, use the method
  `DateObject.getDay()`
  where a value of 0 equals the first weekday (Sunday), a value of 1 equals the second weekday (Monday), and so forth.
- To retrieve the hours value, use the following method:
  `DateObject.getHours()`
- To retrieve the minutes value, use the following method:
  `DateObject.getMinutes()`
- To retrieve the seconds value, use the following method:
  `DateObject.getSeconds()`

Setting Date and Time Values

In addition to retrieving date and time values, you can also use JavaScript to set these values. This is most often used in programs where you have to change the value of a date object from one particular date or time to another. For example, the following code uses the setFullYear() method to change the date stored in the thisDate variable from February 24, 2011 to February 24, 2012:

```
thisDate = new Date("February 24, 2011");
thisDate.setFullYear(2012);
```

Figure 11-9 summarizes the other methods supported by JavaScript for setting date and time values.

Methods to set date and time values for date objects **Figure 11-9**

Method	Description
DateObject.setSeconds(*value*)	Sets the seconds value of *DateObject* to *value*
DateObject.setMinutes(*value*)	Sets the minutes value of *DateObject* to *value*
DateObject.setHours(*value*)	Sets the hours value of *DateObject* to *value*
DateObject.setDate(*value*)	Sets the day of the month value of *DateObject* to *value*
DateObject.setMonth(*value*)	Sets the month number of *DateObject* to *value* (0 = January, 1 = February, etc.)
DateObject.setFullYear(*value*)	Sets the four-digit year value of *DateObject* to *value*
DateObject.setTime(*value*)	Sets the time of *DateObject* in milliseconds since January 1, 1970

You'll create a function that uses the setFullYear() method in the next session.

Tip

JavaScript does not support daylight savings time (also known as summer time); the computer's operating system makes adjustments for daylight savings time.

Creating a Date and Time Function

You'll use the methods associated with date objects that you just learned to create functions that extract the date and time values from a date object, and then return those values in formatted text strings. The first function you'll create is named showDate() and has the following code:

```
function showDate(dateObj) {
   thisDate = dateObj.getDate();
   thisMonth = dateObj.getMonth()+1;
   thisYear = dateObj.getFullYear();
   return thisMonth + "/" + thisDate + "/" + thisYear;
}
```

The showDate() function has a single parameter named dateObj, which stores the date object to be evaluated. The function extracts the day of the month, the month number, and the four-digit year value, and returns a text string combining all of the values in the format

```
month/day/year
```

where *month* is the value of the thisMonth variable, *day* is the value of the thisDate variable, and *year* is the value of the thisYear variable. You'll call this function by placing the generated text string into the dateNow field of the Web form on the clock Web page.

The following code for the showTime() function is similar:

```
function showTime(dateObj) {
   thisSecond = dateObj.getSeconds();
   thisMinute = dateObj.getMinutes();
   thisHour = dateObj.getHours();
   return thisHour + ":" + thisMinute + ":" + thisSecond;
}
```

The showTime() function extracts the hours, minutes, and seconds values from the date object, returning the text string

```
hour:minute:second
```

where *hour* is the value of the thisHour variable, *minute* is the value of the thisMinute variable, and *second* is the value of the thisSecond variable.

You'll add both the showDate() and showTime() functions to an external JavaScript file so that you can access them from any page of Hector's Web site.

To create the showDate() and showTime() functions:

1. Use your text editor to open the **functxt.js** file from the tutorial.11/tutorial folder included with your Data Files, enter ***your name*** and ***the date*** in the comment section at the top of the file, and then save the file as **functions.js** in the same folder.
2. Below the comment section, insert the following two functions, as shown in Figure 11-10:

```
function showDate(dateObj) {
   thisDate = dateObj.getDate();
   thisMonth = dateObj.getMonth()+1;
   thisYear = dateObj.getFullYear();
   return thisMonth + "/" + thisDate + "/" + thisYear;
}

function showTime(dateObj) {
   thisSecond=dateObj.getSeconds();
   thisMinute=dateObj.getMinutes();
   thisHour=dateObj.getHours();
   return thisHour + ":" + thisMinute + ":" + thisSecond;
}
```

Figure 11-10 showDate() and showTime() functions

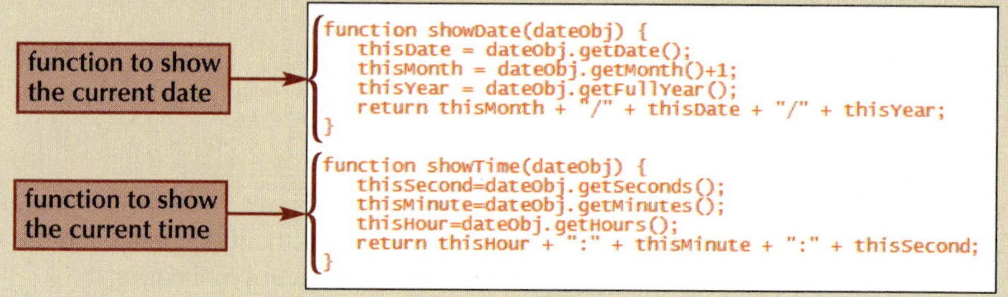
function to show the current date
function to show the current time
function showDate(dateObj) {
thisDate = dateObj.getDate();
thisMonth = dateObj.getMonth()+1;
thisYear = dateObj.getFullYear();
return thisMonth + "/" + thisDate + "/" + thisYear;
}
function showTime(dateObj) {
thisSecond=dateObj.getSeconds();
thisMinute=dateObj.getMinutes();
thisHour=dateObj.getHours();
return thisHour + ":" + thisMinute + ":" + thisSecond;
}

3. Save your changes to the file.

You can call these two functions to display the date and time text strings in the showDate and showTime fields of the Web form. To call the functions, you first must create a link to the functions.js file.

To call the showDate() and showTime() functions:

1. Return to the **clock.htm** file in your text editor.
2. Directly above the opening <script> tag, insert the following external script element:

```
<script type="text/javascript" src="functions.js"></script>
```

3. In the embedded script element, replace the date value in the dateNow field with:

```
showDate(today)
```

4. In the embedded script element, replace the time value in the timeNow field with:

```
showTime(today)
```

Figure 11-11 shows the revised code for the clock.htm file.

Figure 11-11 Code to call the showDate() and showTime() functions

```
<script type="text/javascript" src="functions.js"></script>
<script type="text/javascript">

   function NYClock() {
   // the today variable contains the current date and time
      var today = new Date("February 24, 2011 14:35:05");

   // display the current date and time
      document.clockform.dateNow.value = showDate(today);
      document.clockform.timeNow.value = showTime(today);

   // calculate the time left until the New Year's Bash
      document.clockform.daysLeft.value = "99";
      document.clockform.hrLeft.value = "99";
      document.clockform.minLeft.value = "99";
      document.clockform.secLeft.value = "99";
   }
```

link to the external functions.js file

displays the text from the showDate() and showTime() functions in the Web form

5. Save your changes to the file.
6. Reopen or refresh **clock.htm** in your Web browser. Figure 11-12 shows the current values in the page's Web form. The date value has not changed but the time value is displayed in 24-hour format.

Figure 11-12 Revised countdown clock values

Hector reviews the current output and sees two things that he wants changed. The time values should be displayed in 12-hour time rather than 24-hour time. Also, a minute or second value less than 10 should have a zero placed before its value as a placeholder. In other words, instead of displaying

14:35:5

Hector wants the time to read

2:35:05 p.m.

In the next session, you'll add these features to the countdown clock and create functions to calculate the number of days, hours, minutes, and seconds remaining in the year.

Session 11.1 Quick Check | Review

1. What is an event handler?
2. What attribute would you add to a button element to run the showImage() function when the button is clicked?
3. What HTML code creates a link that runs the showImage() function when the link is clicked?

4. What JavaScript command creates a variable named examDate storing the following date and time: May 8, 2011 at 6:55:28 p.m.?
5. What command extracts the month value from the examDate variable? What value would be returned by this method?
6. What command extracts the four-digit year value from the examDate variable?
7. What command changes the day of the month value in the examDate variable from 8 to 9 (while leaving all of the other date and time values unchanged)?
8. What command creates a variable named currentTime that stores the current date and time?

Session 11.2

Working with Operators and Operands

In the previous session, you worked with date objects to display specified dates and times on a Web page. In this session, you'll learn how to perform calculations with dates and JavaScript variables. To perform a calculation, you need to insert a JavaScript statement that contains an operator. An **operator** is a symbol used to act upon an item or a variable within a JavaScript expression. The variables or expressions that operators act upon are called **operands**. An operator is a very basic concept. In fact, you've been using operators throughout this and the previous tutorial. For example, you've been using the + operator to combine text strings and add numeric values. The following statement from the showDate() function uses the + operator to increase the value of dateObj.getMonth() by 1:

```
thisMonth = dateObj.getMonth()+1;
```

You have also used the + operator to combine text strings, as in the following statement from the showDate() function, which displays dates in the format *month/date/year*:

```
thisMonth + "/" + thisDate + "/" + thisYear;
```

Using Arithmetic and Unary Operators

The + operator belongs to a group of operators called **arithmetic operators** that perform simple mathematical calculations. Figure 11-13 lists some of the arithmetic operators and gives examples of how they work.

Figure 11-13 Arithmetic operators

Operator	Description	Example
+	Combines or adds two items	Men = 20; Women = 25; Total = Men + Women;
–	Subtracts one item from another	Income = 1000; Expense = 750; Profit = Income – Expense;
*	Multiplies two items	Width = 50; Length = 20; Area = Width * Length;
/	Divides one item by another	Persons = 50; Cost = 200; CostPerPerson = Cost / Persons;
%	Calculates the remainder after dividing one value by another	TotalEggs = 64; CartonSize = 12; EggsLeft = TotalEggs % CartonSize;

The arithmetic operators shown in Figure 11-13 are also known as **binary operators** because they work with two operands in an expression. JavaScript also supports **unary operators**, which work on only one operand. Unary operators can make code more compact and efficient. One of the unary operators is the **increment operator**, which increases the value of the operand by 1. The increment operator is indicated by the ++ symbol. For example, the following two expressions increase the value of *x* by 1. The first uses the binary operator indicated by the + symbol, and the second uses the increment operator indicated by the ++ symbol.

```
x = x + 1;
x++;
```

A similar operator is the **decrement operator**, indicated by the -- symbol, which decreases the operand's value by 1. Thus the following two expressions have the equivalent impact of reducing the value of *x* by 1:

```
x = x - 1;
x--;
```

Both the increment and decrement operators can be placed either before or after the operand. The placement impacts the value ultimately assigned by JavaScript. If the operator is placed before the operand, the increment or decrement happens *before* the operand is evaluated. If the operator is placed after the operand, the operand is evaluated *after* it is incremented or decremented. For example, if the variable *x* has an initial value of 5, then the statement

```
y = x++;
```

assigns a value of 5 to *y* and 6 to *x*. This is because the statement combines two actions. It first assigns *y* the value of *x* using

```
y = x;
```

setting the value of *y* to 5. The expression then increments the value of *x* using

```
x = x + 1;
```

increasing the *x* value to 6. The end result is that *y* is equal to 5 and *x* is equal to 6. If you switch the order so that the increment operator appears *before* the expression as follows

```
y = ++x;
```

then JavaScript modifies the values of *x* and *y* in the following order

```
x = x + 1;
y = x;
```

incrementing *x* by 1 and *then* assigning that value to *y*. The end result is that both *x* and *y* have a final value of 6.

Tip

To avoid misinterpreting the actions of an increment or decrement operator, read the action of the operator from left to right, updating the value of the operand as you go.

Another unary operator is the **negation operator**, which changes the sign of (or negates) an item's value. Figure 11-14 summarizes the three unary operators.

Figure 11-14 **Unary operators**

Operator	Description	Example	Equivalent To
++	Increases the item's value by 1	x++	x = x + 1
--	Decreases the item's value by 1	x--	x = x – 1
-	Changes the sign of the item's value	-x	x = 0 – x

Using Assignment Operators

JavaScript statements also use operators when assigning values to items. These types of operators are called **assignment operators**. The most common assignment operator is the equal sign (=), which assigns the value of one expression to another. You can also combine the act of assigning a value and changing a value within a single operator. For example, the following two expressions both add the value of the *x* variable to the value of the *y* variable and then store the new value back in the *x* variable, creating the same result:

```
x = x + y;
x += y;
```

An assignment operator can also be used with numbers to increase a variable by a specific amount. Both of the following expressions increase the value of the *x* variable by 2:

```
x = x + 2;
x += 2;
```

Tip

Always type += for the addition assignment operator; do not insert a space between the two symbols or JavaScript will report a syntax error.

A common use of the += operator is to concatenate text strings to create a single, long text string. This is useful in situations where a text string that covers several lines might be difficult to store in a variable using a single statement. However, you can use the += operator to do this, as follows:

```
quote = "To be or not to be: ";
quote += "That is the question. ";
quote += "Whether 'tis nobler in the mind to suffer ";
quote += "the slings and arrows of outrageous fortune, ";
quote += "Or to take arms against a sea of troubles";
quote += "And by opposing end them.";
...
```

Continuing in this fashion, the quote variable eventually contains the complete text of Hamlet's soliloquy by using a series of short, simple expressions rather than one long and cumbersome expression. This technique is often used to store long text strings within a variable. Other assignment operators are described in Figure 11-15.

Assignment operators **Figure 11-15**

Operator	Description	Example	Equivalent To
=	Assigns the value of the expression on the right to the expression on the left	x = y	
+=	Adds two expressions	x += y	x = x + y
-=	Subtracts the expression on the right from the expression on the left	x -= y	x = x – y
*=	Multiplies two expressions	x *= y	x = x * y
%=	Calculates the remainder from dividing the expression on the left by the expression on the right	x %= y	x = x % y

After you master the syntax, you can use assignment operators to create efficient and compact expressions. New JavaScript programmers might prefer to use the longer form for such expressions. However, experienced JavaScript programmers make substantial use of assignment operators to reduce program size.

Calculating the Days Left in the Year

You'll use operators and date objects to create a function that calculates the number of days remaining in the year. This function, which you'll name calcDays(), has a single parameter named currentDate that contains a date object for the current date and time. The function needs to do the following:

```
function calcDays(currentDate) {
   create a date object for January 1 of the next year
   calculate the difference between currentDate and January 1
}
```

Because you want the calcDays() function to be available to other pages of the Web site, you'll add this function structure to the functions.js file.

To create the calcDays() function:

1. If you took a break after the previous session, make sure the clock.htm and functions.js files are open in a text editor and the clock.htm file is open in your Web browser.
2. Return to the **functions.js** file in your text editor.
3. At the bottom of the file, insert the following function, as shown in Figure 11-16:

```
function calcDays(currentDate) {

   // create a date object for January 1 of the next year
   // calculate the difference between currentDate and January 1
}
```

Figure 11-16 **calcDays() function**

```
function calcDays(currentDate) {
   // create a date object for January 1 of the next year
   // calculate the difference between currentDate and January 1
}
```

4. Save your changes to the file.

Next, you will enter the commands for the calcDays() function. The first line creates the January 1 date object. You need to specify a year value, so you'll use 2011 as a placeholder, as shown in the following command:

```
newYear = new Date("January 1, 2011");
```

Using 2011 as the year is only a temporary step. You really want to display the value of the current year plus 1. You can determine this value by extracting the year value from the currentDate parameter and adding 1 to it using the following command:

```
nextYear = currentDate.getFullYear()+1;
```

You'll use the setFullYear() method to set the year value of the newYear date object, as follows:

```
newYear.setFullYear(nextYear);
```

The following command calculates the time difference between New Year's Day and the current day by subtracting one date object from the other:

```
days = newYear - currentDate;
```

However, JavaScript measures time in terms of milliseconds, not days. So, this difference shows the number of milliseconds between the current date and time and the next New Year's Day. To express this value in days, you need to divide the difference by the number of milliseconds in one day. The revised expression is

```
days = (newYear - currentDate)/(1000*60*60*24);
```

because 1000 milliseconds are in one second, 60 seconds are in one minute, 60 minutes are in one hour, and 24 hours are in one day. Putting all of these commands together, the complete calcDays() function is:

```
function calcDays(currentDate) {
   // create a date object for January 1 of the next year
      newYear = new Date("January 1, 2011");
      nextYear = currentDate.getFullYear()+1;
      newYear.setFullYear(nextYear);

   // calculate the difference between currentDate and January 1
      days = (newYear - currentDate)/(1000*60*60*24);

      return days;
}
```

You'll add these commands and comments to the calcDays() function.

To revise the calcDays() function in the functions.js file:

1. Below the first comment line in the calcDays() function, add the following lines:

```
newYear = new Date("January 1, 2011");
nextYear = currentDate.getFullYear()+1;
newYear.setFullYear(nextYear);
```

2. Below the next comment line, add the following line:

```
days = (newYear - currentDate)/(1000*60*60*24);
```

3. Complete the function by adding the following command to return the value of the days variable:

```
return days;
```

Figure 11-17 shows the revised code in the calcDays() function.

Figure 11-17 **Commands added to the calcDays() function**

```
function calcDays(currentDate) {
   // create a date object for January 1 of the next year
      newYear = new Date("January 1, 2011");
      nextYear = currentDate.getFullYear()+1;
      newYear.setFullYear(nextYear);

   // calculate the difference between currentDate and January 1
      days = (newYear - currentDate)/(1000*60*60*24);

      return days;
}
```

divides by the number of milliseconds in a day

4. Save your changes to the file, and then close the file.

You can use the calcDays() function to calculate the number of days remaining in the year, displaying that value in the daysLeft field of the Web form on the New Year's Bash Web page. You'll add this function to the clock.htm file, replacing the placeholder value of 99 that you specified earlier for the number of days remaining in the year.

To add the calcDays() function to the clock.htm file:

1. Return to the **clock.htm** file in your text editor.
2. Directly above the line that sets the value of the daysLeft field, insert the following line:

```
var days = calcDays(today);
```

3. Change the line that sets the value of the daysLeft field to the following:

```
document.clockform.daysLeft.value = days;
```

Figure 11-18 highlights the revised code in the clock.htm file.

Figure 11-18 **Code to call the calcDays function**

```
function NYClock() {
// the today variable contains the current date and time
   var today = new Date("February 24, 2011 14:35:05");

// display the current date and time
   document.clockform.dateNow.value = showDate(today);
   document.clockform.timeNow.value = showTime(today);

// calculate the time left until the New Year's Bash
   var days = calcDays(today);
   document.clockform.daysLeft.value = days;
   document.clockform.hrLeft.value = "99";
   document.clockform.minLeft.value = "99";
   document.clockform.secLeft.value = "99";
}
```

calls the calcDays() function to calculate the days remaining in the year

replaces the placeholder value "99" with the days variable

4. Save your changes to the file.
5. Reload or refresh **clock.htm** in your Web browser. The daysLeft field at the top of the page displays the calculated number of days until the New Year's Bash. See Figure 11-19.

Figure 11-19 **Days left until New Year's Day displayed**

Trouble? If no value appears in the Days field, you might have made an error when entering the code. In your text editor, check the code in the calcDays() function against the code shown in Figure 11-17, making corrections as needed. Save the file and then repeat Step 5.

The value displayed in the daysLeft field is 310.3923, indicating that slightly more than 310 days are left until the start of the New Year's Bash. The fractional part of the value represents how much of the last day is remaining until midnight on New Year's Eve. Because Hector is interested only in the exact number of days, hours, minutes, and seconds until the party begins, you have to modify this value by extracting the days amount and then converting the fractional part to hours, minutes, and seconds. You can do this by using some of the built-in JavaScript functions for mathematical calculations.

Working with the Math Object and Math Methods

One way of performing this type of calculation is to use JavaScript's Math object. The **Math object** is an object that can be used for performing mathematical tasks and storing mathematical values.

Using Math Methods

The Math object supports several different **Math methods**, which store functions used for performing advanced calculations and mathematical operations such as generating random numbers, extracting square roots, and calculating trigonometric values. The syntax for applying a Math method is

```
Math.method(expression)
```

where *method* is the method you'll apply to an expression. For example, to calculate the square root of a number, you can use the sqrt method, which has the following syntax:

```
Math.sqrt(expression)
```

When applied to the *x* variable, the following commands result in the value 4 being stored in the *y* variable:

```
x = 16;
y = Math.sqrt(x);
```

Figure 11-20 lists the JavaScript Math methods and describes how to apply them.

Tip

Case is important in applying the Math object; you must use "Math" instead of "math" for the name of the Math object.

Figure 11-20 Math methods

Math Method	Returns
Math.abs(*x*)	the absolute value of *x*
Math.acos(*x*)	the arc cosine of *x* in radians
Math.asin(*x*)	the arc sine of *x* in radians
Math.atan(*x*)	the arc tangent of *x* in radians
Math.atan2(*x*, *y*)	the angle between the x-axis and the point (*x*, *y*)
Math.ceil(*x*)	*x* rounded up to the next highest integer
Math.cos(*x*)	the cosine of *x*
Math.exp(*x*)	e^x
Math.floor(*x*)	*x* rounded down to the next lowest integer
Math.log(*x*)	the natural logarithm of *x*
Math.max(*x*, *y*)	the larger of *x* and *y*
Math.min(*x*, *y*)	the smaller of *x* and *y*
Math.pow(*x*, *y*)	x^y
Math.random()	a random number between 0 and 1
Math.round(*x*)	*x* rounded to the nearest integer
Math.sin(*x*)	the sine of *x*
Math.sqrt(*x*)	the square root of *x*
Math.tan(*x*)	the tangent of *x*

InSight | Generating Random Numbers

One of the most useful applications of JavaScript is to create dynamic pages that can change in a random fashion. A commercial Web site might need to display banner ads in a random order so that customers see a different ad each time they access the page. To create these kinds of effects, you need a script that generates a random value. JavaScript accomplishes this using the Math.random() method, which returns a random value between 0 and 1. You can enlarge the range of possible random values by multiplying the random number by the desired size of the range. To apply the range to a different interval, you add the lower boundary to the random number. So, to generate a random number from 20 to 30, you can apply the following expression:

```
20 + 10*Math.random();
```

In many cases, you will want to limit the random number to integer values. To force the random number to be an integer, you apply either the Math.ceil() method to round the value to the next highest integer or the Math.floor() method to round the value to the next lowest integer. You should not use the Math.round() method. Although the Math.round() method would round the random value to the nearest integer within the defined range, the range's lower and upper value would appear less often than the other integers. As a result, each integer would not have an equal chance of being selected. To generate a random integer from 20 to 30, you would apply the Math.floor method as follows:

```
Math.floor(20 + 11*Math.random());
```

This expression multiplies the random value by 11, not 10, because there are 11 integers in the range from 20 to 30. You can combine all of these operations in a customized function that returns a random integer for a specified range and lower boundary. The code for the function is:

```
function randInt(lower, size) {
    return Math.floor(lower + size*Math.random());
}
```

With the randInt() function, you can generate a random integer from 1 to 10 using the following expression:

```
var randInteger = randInt(1, 10);
```

To create a random integer from a different range of values, simply change the values for the lower and size parameters in the randInt() function.

Using Math Constants

Many functions require the use of mathematical constants, such as π and e. Rather than entering the numeric values of these constants directly into code, you can reference one of the built-in constants stored in the JavaScript Math object. The syntax to access one of these mathematical constants is

```
Math.CONSTANT
```

where *CONSTANT* is the name of one of the mathematical constants supported by the Math object, shown in Figure 11-21.

Figure 11-21 Math constants

Math Constant	Description
Math.E	The natural logarithm base, e (approximately 2.7183)
Math.LN10	The natural logarithm of 10 (approximately 2.3026)
Math.LN2	The natural logarithm of 2 (approximately 0.6931)
Math.LOG10E	The base 10 logarithm of e (approximately 0.4343)
Math.LOG2E	The base 2 logarithm of e (approximately 1.4427)
Math.PI	The value π (approximately 3.1416)
Math.SQRT1_2	The value of 1 divided by the square root of 2 (approximately 0.7071)
Math.SQRT2	The value of the square root of 2 (approximately 1.4142)

For example, the formula to calculate the volume of a sphere is $4 \pi r^3/3$ where *r* is the radius of the sphere. To reference the value of π in a calculation of the sphere's volume, you would apply the Math.PI constant. To cube the value of *r*, you would use the method Math.pow(*r*, 3). Putting these together, a function to return the volume of a sphere given the radius is:

```
function sphereVolume(radius) {
   volume = 4*Math.PI*Math.pow(radius, 3)/3;
   return volume;
}
```

To calculate the volume of a sphere that is two units in radius, you could enter the expression

```
x = sphereVolume(2);
```

and JavaScript would assign a value of 33.5103 to the *x* variable.

You don't need to use any Math constants for the New Year's Bash Web site. However, the countdown clock does need to display only the integer portion of the days left in the year. You can calculate this value using the Math.floor() method, which rounds a value down to the next lowest integer. For the days left value of 310.39 currently in the countdown clock, this method returns the integer value 310. You'll apply this method to the value displayed in the daysLeft field.

To apply the Math.floor() method:

1. Return to the **clock.htm** file in your text editor.
2. Change the statement that sets the value of the daysLeft field to the following two lines, as shown in Figure 11-22:

```
// display days rounded to the next lowest integer
document.clockform.daysLeft.value = Math.floor(days);
```

Figure 11-22 Code to apply the Math.floor() method

```
    // display days rounded to the next lowest integer
    document.clockform.daysLeft.value = Math.floor(days);
    document.clockform.hrLeft.value = "99";
    document.clockform.minLeft.value = "99";
    document.clockform.secLeft.value = "99";
}
```

3. Save your changes to the file, and then reopen or refresh **clock.htm** in your Web browser. The daysLeft field displays the daysLeft value as an integer. See Figure 11-23.

Figure 11-23 daysLeft value displayed as an integer

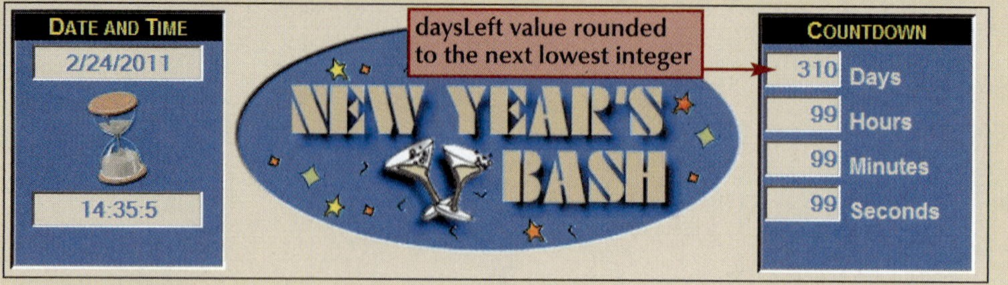

Calculating the Hours, Minutes, and Seconds Left in the Year

Next you want to calculate the hours, minutes, and seconds left in the year. The Math.floor() function determined that the number of whole days left in the year is 310. The difference between this number and 310.3923... is 0.3923..., which represents the fractional part of the current day remaining. You need to convert this value to hours. You can do this by multiplying 0.3923... by 24 (the number of hours in a single day). The JavaScript command to calculate the number of hours remaining in the current day is:

```
var hours = (days - Math.floor(days))*24;
```

Based on this calculation, the value of the hours variable is 9.4152 hours or almost 9 and a half hours. The fractional part of this value represents the minutes and seconds left within the current hour. As with the days variable in the previous set of steps, you need to round this value down to the next lowest integer using the Math.floor function, as shown in the following expression:

```
Math.floor(hours)
```

The value of the hours variable will then be equal to 9. You'll add these two expressions to the JavaScript code in the clock.htm file.

To calculate the hours left in the day:

1. Return to the **clock.htm** file in your text editor.
2. Below the statement that sets the value of the daysLeft field value, insert the following two lines:

```
// calculate the hours left in the current day
   var hours = (days - Math.floor(days))*24;
```

3. Change the statement that sets the value of the hoursLeft field to the following, as shown in Figure 11-24:

```
// display hours rounded to the next lowest integer
document.clockform.hrLeft.value = Math.floor(hours);
```

Figure 11-24 Hours variable added to the code

```
function NYClock() {
// the today variable contains the current date and time
   var today = new Date("February 24, 2011 14:35:05");

// display the current date and time
   document.clockform.dateNow.value = showDate(today);
   document.clockform.timeNow.value = showTime(today);

// calculate the time left until the New Year's Bash
   var days = calcDays(today);

   // display days rounded to the next lowest integer
   document.clockform.daysLeft.value = Math.floor(days);

   // calculate the hours left in the current day
   var hours = (days - Math.floor(days))*24;

   // display hours rounded to the next lowest integer
   document.clockform.hrLeft.value = Math.floor(hours);
   document.clockform.minLeft.value = "99";
   document.clockform.secLeft.value = "99";
}
```

calculates the hours left in the current day

4. Save your changes to the file, and then reopen or refresh **clock.htm** in your Web browser. The hoursLeft field displays the hours left in the current day. See Figure 11-25.

Figure 11-25 Hours left in the day

The technique to calculate the minutes left in the current hour is similar to the one you used to calculate the hours left in the current day. You multiply the difference between the hours value and whole hours value by 60 (the number of minutes in an hour) to express the fractional part in terms of minutes, as shown in the following command:

```
var minutes = (hours - Math.floor(hours))*60;
```

Finally, to calculate the seconds left in the current minute, you multiply the fractional part of the minutes variable by 60 (the number of seconds in a minute), as follows:

```
var seconds = (minutes - Math.floor(minutes))*60;
```

As with the days and hours variables, you want to display only the integer part of the minutes and seconds variables by using the Math.floor() method. You'll add these commands to the NYClock() function.

To calculate the minutes and seconds left:

1. Return to the **clock.htm** file in your text editor.
2. Below the statement that sets the value of the hrLeft field value, insert the following lines:

```
// calculate the minutes left in the current hour
var minutes = (hours - Math.floor(hours))*60;
```

3. Change the statement that sets the value of the minLeft field to:

```
// display minutes rounded to the next lowest integer
document.clockform.minLeft.value = Math.floor(minutes);
```

4. Below the statement that sets the value of the minLeft field value, insert the following lines:

```
// calculate the seconds left in the current minute
var seconds = (minutes - Math.floor(minutes))*60;
```

5. Change the statement that sets the value of the secondsLeft field to:

```
// display seconds rounded to the next lowest integer
document.clockform.secLeft.value = Math.floor(seconds);
```

Figure 11-26 highlights the changes to the code.

Figure 11-26 Minutes and seconds variables added to the code

```
function NYClock() {
// the today variable contains the current date and time
   var today = new Date("February 24, 2011 14:35:05");

// display the current date and time
   document.clockform.dateNow.value = showDate(today);
   document.clockform.timeNow.value = showTime(today);

// calculate the time left until the New Year's Bash
   var days = calcDays(today);

   // display days rounded to the next lowest integer
   document.clockform.daysLeft.value = Math.floor(days);

   // calculate the hours left in the current day
   var hours = (days - Math.floor(days))*24;

   // display hours rounded to the next lowest integer
   document.clockform.hrLeft.value = Math.floor(hours);

   // calculate the minutes left in the current hour
   var minutes = (hours - Math.floor(hours))*60;

   // display minutes rounded to the next lowest integer
   document.clockform.minLeft.value = Math.floor(minutes);

   // calculate the seconds left in the current minute
   var seconds = (minutes - Math.floor(minutes))*60;

   // display seconds rounded to the next lowest integer
   document.clockform.secLeft.value = Math.floor(seconds);
}
```

calculates the minutes left in the current hour

calculates the seconds left in the current minute

6. Save your changes to the file.

7. Reopen or refresh **clock.htm** in your Web browser. The Web form displays the time left in whole number values of days, hours, minutes, and seconds. See Figure 11-27.

Figure 11-27 Time left in terms of days, hours, minutes, and seconds

In some cases, the countdown value may show an extra (or missing) hour, minute, or second. Why is that? Several factors are involved. One is the presence of daylight savings time, which moves the clock forward (or backward) one hour. If your time interval crosses this event, the hour value will appear off as an hour is added to or subtracted from the time interval. Another factor is that the day is not evenly divided into seconds (that's why JavaScript measures time in milliseconds). A fraction of a second is always left over each day. As the days accumulate, these fractions of a second add up. Most time devices, such as atomic clocks, account for this accumulation by adding a "leap second" on certain days of the year. The effect of adding these leap seconds is included in any time calculations you make with JavaScript. As you can see, more is going on in calculating the time difference between one date and another than may appear at first glance.

Controlling How JavaScript Works with Numeric Values

As you perform mathematical calculations using JavaScript, you'll encounter situations in which you need to work with the properties of numeric values themselves. JavaScript provides several methods that allow you to examine the properties of numbers and specify how they're displayed on a Web page.

Handling Illegal Operations

Some mathematical operations can return results that are not numeric values. For example, you cannot divide a number by a text string. If you attempt to perform the operation

```
var x = 5/"A";
document.write(x);
```

in a script, the Web page would display the value NaN, which stands for Not a Number. This is JavaScript's way to indicate that you are attempting an operation that should involve a numeric value, but doesn't. You can check for the presence of this particular error using the function isNaN(). The syntax of the function is

```
isNaN(value)
```

where *value* is the value or variable you want to test for being numeric. The isNaN() function returns a Boolean value: true if the value is not numeric (i.e., NaN) and false if otherwise. The use of the isNaN() function is one way to locate illegal operations in code in which nonnumeric values are treated as numeric.

Another illegal operation is attempting to divide a number by 0, such as in the following code:

```
var x = 5/0;
document.write(x);
```

This code results in the value Infinity being written to the Web page. The Infinity value indicates that you've attempted a numeric calculation whose result is greater than the largest numeric value supported by JavaScript. An Infinity value also exists for operations whose result is less than the smallest numeric value. JavaScript is limited to numeric values that fall between approximately 1.8×10^{-308} and 1.8×10^{308}. Any operation that exceeds those bounds, such as dividing a number by 0, causes JavaScript to assign a value of Infinity to the result. You can check for this outcome using the function

```
isFinite(value)
```

where *value* is the value you want to test for being finite. Like the isNaN() function, the isFinite() function returns a Boolean value: true if *value* is a finite number falling within JavaScript's acceptable range and false if the numeric value falls outside that range or if *value* is not a number at all.

Tip

A program that reports a run-time or logical error may have a mismatched data value; use the isFinite() and isNaN() functions to determine the state of your data values.

Specifying the Number Format

When JavaScript displays a numeric value, it displays all of the calculated digits in that value. This can result in long numeric strings of digits. For example, the code

```
var x = 1/4;
var y = 1/3;
document.write("x = " + x);
document.write("y = " + y);
```

causes the following two text strings to be written to the Web page:

```
x = 0.25
y = 0.3333333333333333
```

In most cases, you don't need to display a calculated value to 16 digits. With currency values, you usually want to display results only to two decimal places. To control the number of digits displayed by the browser, you can apply the method

```
value.toFixed(n)
```

where *value* is the value or variable and *n* is the number of decimal places that should be displayed in the output. The following examples show the toFixed() method applied to different numeric values:

```
testValue = 2.835;
testValue.toFixed(0)   // returns "3"
testValue.toFixed(1)   // returns "2.8"
testValue.toFixed(2)   // returns "2.84"
```

Note that the toFixed() method limits the number of decimals displayed by a value and converts the value into a text string. Also, the toFixed() method rounds the last digit in an expression rather than truncating it.

Tip

Older browsers do not support the toFixed() method. You must create custom functions to round a number to a certain number of digits for those browsers.

Converting Between Numbers and Text Strings

Sometimes you might need to convert a number to a text string and vice versa. One way to convert a number to a text string is by using the + operator to add a text string to a number. For example, the following code uses the + operator to concatenate a numeric value with an empty text string. The result is to create a text string containing the characters 123.

```
testNumber = 123;              // numeric value
testString = testNumber + "";  // text string
```

To convert a text string to a number, you can apply an arithmetic operator (other than the + operator) to the text string. The following code takes the text string "123" and multiplies it by 1. The end result is that JavaScript converts the text string "123" to the numeric value 123.

```
testString = "123";          // text string
testNumber = testString*1;   // numeric value
```

Another way of converting a text string to a numeric value is to use the parseInt() function, which extracts the leading integer value from a text string. The syntax of the parseInt() function is

```
parseInt(text)
```

where *text* is the text string or variable from which you need to extract the leading integer value. The parseInt() function determines whether the first nonblank character in the text string is a number. If it is, the function then parses the text string from left to right until the end of the number or a decimal point is encountered. Any characters in the string after that are discarded. The parseInt() function returns only the first integer in the string; it does not return decimal points or numbers to the right of a decimal. If a text string does not begin with a number, the parseInt() function returns the value NaN, indicating that there is no accessible number in the text string. The following are some sample values returned by the parseInt() function:

```
parseInt("120 lbs")                  // returns 120
parseInt("206.58 lbs")               // returns 206
parseInt("weight equals 55 lbs")     // returns NaN
```

You can also use the parseFloat() function to extract numeric values other than integers from text strings. The parseFloat() function has the syntax

```
parseFloat(text)
```

where *text* is a text string or variable containing a text string. The parseFloat() function works like the parseInt() function except that it retrieves both integers and numbers with decimals. The following are sample values returned by the parseFloat() function:

```
parseFloat("120 lbs")                  // returns 120
parseFloat("206.58 lbs")               // returns 206.58
parseFloat("weight equals 55 lbs")     // returns NaN
```

Because the countdown clock is not performing any calculations on values within the Web form, you don't need to use the parseInt() or parseFloat() functions in your code. However, you will use these functions in the Case Problems at the end of the tutorial. Figure 11-28 summarizes the different JavaScript methods and functions used to work with numeric values.

Numeric functions and methods **Figure 11-28**

Function or Method	Description
isFinite(*value*)	Returns a Boolean value indicating whether *value* is finite and a legal number
isNaN(*value*)	Returns a Boolean value, which has the value true if *value* is not a number
parseFloat(*string*)	Extracts the first numeric value from a text string
parseInt(*string*)	Extracts the first integer value from a text string
value.toExponential(*n*)	Returns a text string displaying *value* in exponential notation with *n* digits to the right of the decimal point
value.toFixed(*n*)	Returns a text string displaying *value* to *n* decimal places
value.toPrecision(*n*)	Returns a text string displaying *value* to *n* significant digits either to the left or to the right of the decimal point

Reference Window | Using Numeric Methods and Functions

- To display a numeric value to a set number of digits, use the function
  `value.toFixed(n)`
  where *value* is the numeric value and *n* is the number of digits to the right of the decimal place to be displayed. The toFixed() method converts the numeric value to a text string.
- To extract an integer from the beginning of a text string, use
  `parseInt(string)`
  where *string* is a text string that starts with an integer value.
- To extract a numeric value from the beginning of a text string, use
  `parseFloat(string)`
  where *string* is a text string that starts with a numeric value.
- To test whether a value represents a number, use
  `isNaN(value)`
  where *value* can be either a text string, a numeric value, or another data type. The isNaN() function returns the Boolean value true if *value* is not a number, and false if it is.

InSight | Rounding Values

Online ordering is one of the most common uses of the Web and requires calculations of monetary values. For example, suppose you needed to calculate a 2% sales tax on a customer's purchase of an item that costs $25.49. One way of doing this is to use the following code, which multiplies the price by the tax rate and stores the value in the tax variable:

```
var price = 25.49;
var taxrate = 0.02;
var tax = price*taxrate;
```

The tax value from this calculation is 0.5098, which is not an acceptable currency value. You could use the toFixed() function discussed earlier to display the result to only two decimal places. However, recall that the toFixed() function doesn't change a variable's value, only how it is displayed. Instead, you need to round the actual value of the tax variable to the hundredths digit. There are no Math methods for rounding values to specific numbers of decimal places. To round a currency value to two digits, you must first multiply the value by 100, apply the Math.round() method to round the value to the nearest integer, and then divide that result by 100. For the tax rate example, 0.5098 multiplied by 100 is 50.98; that value rounded to the nearest integer is 51; dividing that number by 100 results in a currency value of $0.51. In JavaScript, this sequence of operations can be placed in a single expression as follows:

```
Math.round(100*tax)/100;
```

In general, if *n* is the number of decimal places you want to round the value to, you multiply and divide the value by 10*n*. You could use this fact to create a custom function to round values to a specified number of decimal places. The following code uses the pow() method of the Math object to create a general rounding function that rounds values to *n* decimal places:

```
function roundValue(value, n) {
    return Math.round(Math.pow(10,n)*value)/Math.pow(10,n);
 }
```

The roundValue() function multiplies the value variable by a power of 10, rounds it to the nearest integer, and then divides it by the same power of 10. The end result is the value variable rounded to the number of digits specified by the n parameter. The roundValue() function also allows for a negative value for the n parameter. This has the effect of rounding a value to the nearest ten, hundred, thousand, and so forth. For example, the expression

```
roundValue(238414, -3)
```

rounds the value to the nearest thousand, returning a value of 238,000.

Working with Conditional, Comparison, and Logical Operators

Hector wants the countdown clock to display the current time using 12-hour format rather than 24-hour format. In 24-hour format, the hour values range from 0 hours (representing 12:00 a.m.) up to 23 hours (representing 11:00 p.m.). A time of 14:35 in 24-hour format is equivalent to 2:35 p.m. in 12-hour format. To convert 24-hour time to 12-hour time, the code needs to apply the following rules:

- If the hour value is less than 12, display the time as a.m.; otherwise, display the time as p.m.
- If the hour value is greater than 12, subtract 12 from the value.
- If the hour value is equal to 0, change it to 12.

Using a Conditional Operator

The code needs to run different operations based on the hours value. You can specify these options through the use of a conditional operator. A **conditional operator** is a ternary operator that tests whether a certain condition is true or not. If the condition is true, one value is returned; if the condition is not true, a different value is returned. The syntax of a conditional operator is

```
(condition) ? trueValue : falseValue
```

where *condition* is an expression that is either true or false, *trueValue* is the value returned if the condition is true, and *falseValue* is the value returned if the condition is false. You can use a conditional operator to assign a value to a variable using the statement

```
variable = (condition) ? trueValue : falseValue
```

where *variable* is the variable to which the resulting value is assigned.

Using Comparison Operators

To create expressions that have true or false values, you use comparison operators. A **comparison operator** is an operator that compares the value of one expression to another. One commonly used comparison operator is the less than operator (**<**), which is used to determine whether one value is less than another. The following expression demonstrates the use of the less than (<) comparison operator:

```
x < 100
```

If *x* is less than 100, then this expression is true; but if *x* is greater than or equal to 100, the expression is false. Figure 11-29 lists the comparison operators supported by JavaScript.

Figure 11-29 **Comparison operators**

Operator	Description	Example
==	Returns true if the values are equal	x == y
!=	Returns true if the values are not equal	x != y
>	Returns true if the value on the left is greater than the value on the right	x > y
<	Returns true if the value on the left is less than the value on the right	x < y
>=	Returns true if the value on the left is greater than or equal to the value on the right	x >= y
<=	Returns true if the value on the left is less than or equal to the value on the right	x <= y

Tip

The symbols in the == comparison operator must be entered without a space between the two = symbols.

When you want to test whether two values are equal, you use a double equal sign (==) rather than a single equal sign. The single equal sign (=) is an assignment operator and is reserved for that purpose. To test whether *x* is equal to 100, use the following expression:

```
x == 100
```

If *x* is equal to 100, then this expression returns the Boolean value true; otherwise, it returns the Boolean value false.

Using Logical Operators

JavaScript also supports **logical operators** that allow you to connect several expressions. Figure 11-30 lists the logical operators supported by JavaScript. The logical operator && returns a value of true only if both of the expressions are true. For example, the statement

```
(x < 100) && (y == 100)
```

is true only if *x* is less than 100 and *y* is equal to 100.

Figure 11-30 **Logical operators**

<table>
<tr><th>Operator</th><th>Description</th><th>Example
(when x = 20 and y = 25)</th><th>Value</th></tr>
<tr><td>&&</td><td>Returns true when both expressions are true</td><td>(x == 20) && (y == 25)</td><td>TRUE</td></tr>
<tr><td>||</td><td>Returns true when at least one expression is true</td><td>(x == 20) || (y < 10)</td><td>TRUE</td></tr>
<tr><td>!</td><td>Returns true if the expression is false and false if the expression is true</td><td>!(x == 20)</td><td>FALSE</td></tr>
</table>

You'll use conditional, comparison, and logical operators to write code for the three rules described above to convert 24-hour time to 12-hour time. First, you need a variable named ampm that indicates whether the time is a.m. or p.m. Recall that the value of the current hour is stored in the thisHour variable. If the value of the thisHour variable is less than 12, the value of the ampm variable is a.m.; otherwise, its value is p.m. The conditional operator for this rule is:

```
ampm = (thisHour < 12) ? " a.m." : " p.m.";
```

The second rule should check whether the thisHour value is greater than 12. If so, the rule should subtract 12 from the thisHour value; otherwise, it should leave the value unchanged. You do this using the following command:

```
thisHour = (thisHour > 12) ? thisHour - 12 : thisHour;
```

The third rule should check whether thisHour is equal to 0. If so, the rule should change the value of thisHour to 12; otherwise, it should leave the value unchanged. The code for this rule is:

```
thisHour = (thisHour == 0) ? 12 : thisHour;
```

You'll add these commands to the showTime() function in the functions.js file.

To modify the showTime() function:

1. Return to the **functions.js** file in your text editor.
2. Within the showTime() function, below the statement that creates the thisHour variable, insert the following commands:

```
// change thisHour from 24-hour time to 12-hour time by:
// 1) if thisHour < 12 then set ampm to " a.m." otherwise set
it to " p.m."
var ampm = (thisHour < 12) ? " a.m." : " p.m.";

// 2) subtract 12 from the thisHour variable
thisHour = (thisHour > 12) ? thisHour - 12 : thisHour;

// 3) if thisHour equals 0, change it to 12
thisHour = (thisHour == 0) ? 12 : thisHour;
```

3. Change the return statement as follows to modify the text string returned by the function so that it displays the ampm value at the end of the text string:

```
return thisHour + ":" + thisMinute + ":" + thisSecond + ampm;
```

Figure 11-31 shows the revised code in the showTime() function.

Figure 11-31 Code to change the thisHour variable to 12-hour format

```
function showTime(dateObj) {
   thisSecond=dateObj.getSeconds();
   thisMinute=dateObj.getMinutes();
   thisHour=dateObj.getHours();

   // change thisHour from 24-hour time to 12-hour time by:
   // 1) if thisHour < 12 then set ampm to " a.m." otherwise set it to " p.m."
   var ampm = (thisHour < 12) ? " a.m." : " p.m.";

   // 2) subtract 12 from the thisHour variable
   thisHour = (thisHour > 12) ? thisHour - 12 : thisHour;

   // 3) if thisHour equals 0, change it to 12
   thisHour = (thisHour == 0) ? 12 : thisHour;

   return thisHour + ":" + thisMinute + ":" + thisSecond + ampm;
}
```

4. Save your changes to the file.
5. Reload or refresh **clock.htm** in your Web browser. The revised clock displays time in 12-hour format. See Figure 11-32.

Figure 11-32 **Time displayed in 12-hour format**

The time value should display minutes and seconds values with a leading zero if they are less than 10. In other words, Hector wants the clock to display 2:35:05 p.m., not 2:35:5 p.m. You can make this change by adding another conditional operator to the showTime() function. With this final modification, the statement to change the displayed value of the thisMinute variable becomes:

```
thisMinute = thisMinute < 10 ? "0"+thisMinute : thisMinute;
```

You enclose the value 0 in quotes, which causes JavaScript to treat the 0 as a text string rather than a numeric value. Also, if the value of the thisMinute variable is not less than 10, you leave it unchanged. The code to change the display of the thisSecond variable is similar:

```
thisSecond = thisSecond < 10 ? "0"+thisSecond : thisSecond;
```

You'll add these two commands to the showTime() function and then reload the Web page.

To change the minutes and seconds format:

1. Return to the **functions.js** file in your text editor.
2. Add the following commands, as shown in Figure 11-33:

```
// add leading zeros to minutes and seconds less than 10
thisMinute = thisMinute < 10 ? "0"+thisMinute : thisMinute;
thisSecond = thisSecond < 10 ? "0"+thisSecond : thisSecond;
```

Figure 11-33 **Code to change the format of the minutes and seconds values**

```
function showTime(dateObj) {
   thisSecond=dateObj.getSeconds();
   thisMinute=dateObj.getMinutes();
   thisHour=dateObj.getHours();

   // change thisHour from 24-hour time to 12-hour time by:
   // 1) if thisHour < 12 then set ampm to " a.m." otherwise set it to " p.m."
   var ampm = (thisHour < 12) ? " a.m." : " p.m.";

   // 2) subtract 12 from the thisHour variable
   thisHour = (thisHour > 12) ? thisHour - 12 : thisHour;

   // 3) if thisHour equals 0, change it to 12
   thisHour = (thisHour == 0) ? 12 : thisHour;

   // add leading zeros to minutes and seconds less than 10
   thisMinute = thisMinute < 10 ? "0"+thisMinute : thisMinute;
   thisSecond = thisSecond < 10 ? "0"+thisSecond : thisSecond;

   return thisHour + ":" + thisMinute + ":" + thisSecond + ampm;
}
```

3. Save your changes, and then close the file.

4. Reload or refresh **clock.htm** in your Web browser. The revised clock displays the formatted minutes and seconds values. See Figure 11-34.

Figure 11-34 Minutes and seconds values in the revised format

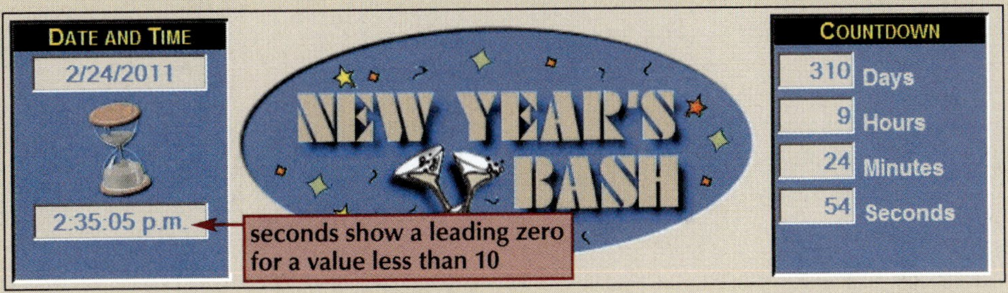

You've completed work on the showTime() and showDate() functions. Because your purpose is to display the current date and time (and the time remaining in the year), you'll replace the test date of February 24, 2011 with the current date and time. Recall that a date object stores the current date and time when you do not specify a date/time value.

To display the current date and time:

1. Return to the **clock.htm** file in your text editor.
2. Change the command to create the today variable to the following, as shown in Figure 11-35:

```
var today = new Date();
```

Figure 11-35 Current date and time in the NYClock() function

```
function NYClock() {
// the today variable contains the current date and time
   var today = new Date();

// display the current date and time
   document.clockform.dateNow.value = showDate(today);
   document.clockform.timeNow.value = showTime(today);
```

inserts the current date and time

3. Save your changes, and then reload or reopen **clock.htm** in your Web browser. The Web page displays the current date and time as well as the time remaining in the year.
4. Refresh the Web page, and then verify that the browser updates the date/time information as well as the amount of time remaining in the year.

Running Timed Commands

You've completed the functions required for the countdown clock, but the clock is largely static, changing only when the page is loaded by the browser. Hector wants the clock to be updated constantly so that it always shows the current time and the time remaining until the New Year's Bash. To do this, you need to run the function at certain times. JavaScript provides two methods for doing this: time-delayed commands and timed-interval commands.

Working with Time-Delayed Commands

A **time-delayed command** is a JavaScript command that is run after a specified amount of time has passed. The syntax to run a time-delayed command is

```
setTimeout("command", delay);
```

where *command* is a JavaScript command and *delay* is the delay time in milliseconds before the browser runs the command. The command must be placed within either double or single quotation marks. For example, the following command sets a 5-millisecond delay before the browser runs the showClock() function:

```
setTimeout("showClock()", 5);
```

In some JavaScript programs, you may want to cancel a time-delayed command. This can occur in programs where other actions by the user remove the need to run a time-delayed command. To cancel the command, you run the command

```
clearTimeout();
```

and JavaScript will cancel the time-delayed command before it is run by the browser.

There is no limit to the number of time-delayed commands a browser can process. To distinguish one time-delayed command from another, you can assign a unique identification to each command. This ID becomes important when you want to cancel a specific command out of several time-delayed commands being processed by the browser. You store the ID value of each time-delayed command as a variable as follows

```
timeID = setTimeout("command",delay);
```

where *timeID* is a variable that stores the ID of the command. After you've assigned an ID to a time-delayed command, you can cancel it using the clearTimeout method

```
clearTimeout(timeID);
```

where once again *timeID* is the variable that stores the ID of the command.

Running Commands at Specified Intervals

The other way to time JavaScript commands is by using a **timed-interval command**, which instructs the browser to run the same command repeatedly at specified intervals. The method to run such a command is

```
setInterval("command",interval);
```

where *command* is the JavaScript command that is to be run repeatedly, and *interval* is the interval in milliseconds before the command is run again. To instruct the browser to stop running the command, you use the following method:

```
clearInterval();
```

As with time-delayed commands, you may have several timed-interval commands running simultaneously. To distinguish one timed-interval command from another, you store the time ID in a variable using the setInterval() method as follows

```
timeID = setInterval("command",interval);
```

where *timeID* is a variable that stores the ID of the timed-interval command. To halt the repeating command, you use the clearInterval() method with the *timeID* variable as follows:

```
clearInterval(timeID);
```

An important point to remember about the setTimeout() and setInterval() methods is that after a browser processes a request to run a command at a later time, the browser doesn't stop. Instead, the browser proceeds to any other commands running in the script and processes those commands without delay. For example, you might try to run three functions at 50-millisecond intervals using the following structure:

```
setTimeout("function1()",50);
setTimeout("function2()",50);
setTimeout("function3()",50);
```

However, a browser would execute this code by running all three functions almost simultaneously 50 milliseconds later. To run the functions with a separation of about 50 milliseconds between one function and the next, you would need to use three different delay times, as follows:

```
setTimeout("function1()",50);
setTimeout("function2()",100);
setTimeout("function3()",150);
```

In this case, a user's browser would run the first function after 50 milliseconds, the second function 50 milliseconds after that, and the third function after another 50 milliseconds has passed.

You have only one function to run for Hector's Web page: the NYClock() function. Because the function should run once every second, you will use the following command, which runs the NYClock() function continuously at intervals of 1000 milliseconds or one second:

```
setInterval("NYClock()", 1000)
```

You will replace the event handler in the <body> tag with this setInterval method. The revised event handler is:

```
onload = "setInterval('NYClock()', 1000)"
```

This event handler causes a browser displaying the page to run the NYClock() function one second after loading the page and then rerun that program every second thereafter. Because the event handler is enclosed in double quotation marks, you must use single quotation marks to enclose the name of the function to avoid confusion about which set of quotation marks refers to the onload attribute and which refers to the function being run.

To run the NYClock() function every second:

1. Return to the **clock.htm** file in your text editor.
2. Change the attribute of the onload event handler in the <body> tag to the following, as shown in Figure 11-36:

   ```
   onload="setInterval('NYClock()',1000)"
   ```

Figure 11-36 Command to run the function at timed intervals

runs the NYClock() function every second after the page loads

```
<body onload="setInterval('NYClock()', 1000)">
   <form name="clockform" id="clockform" action="">

   <div id="clock">
      <h4>Time</h4>
      <p>
         <input size="12" id="dateNow" name="dateNow" /><br />
         <img src="clock.jpg" alt="" /><br />
         <input size="12" id="timeNow" name="timeNow" />
      </p>
   </div>
```

3. Close the file, saving your changes.
4. Reload or reopen **clock.htm** in your Web browser. The countdown clock appears one second after the page loads, and both the countdown clock and the current time update continually as the NYClock() function is run again and again.

Reference Window | Running Timed Commands

- To run a command after a delay, use the method
  `timeID = setTimeout("command", delay)`
  where *command* is the command to be run, *delay* is the delay time in milliseconds, and *timeID* is a variable that stores the ID associated with the time-delayed command.
- To repeat a command at set intervals, use the method
  `timeID = setInterval("command", interval)`
  where *interval* is the time, in milliseconds, between repeating the command.
- To cancel a specific time-delayed command, use the method
  `clearTimeout(timeID)`
  where *timeID* is the ID of the time-delayed command.
- To clear all time-delayed commands, use the following method:
  `clearTimeout()`
- To cancel a repeated command, use the method
  `clearInterval(timeID)`
  where *timeID* is the ID of the repeated command.
- To clear all repeated commands, use the following method:
  `clearInterval()`

You've completed the countdown clock for the New Year's Bash. Hector will continue to work on the event's Web site and get back to you with any new projects or concerns.

Review | Session 11.2 Quick Check

1. How do you use a unary operator to increase the value of the thisMonth variable by 1?
2. How do you use an assignment operator to increase the value of the thisMonth variable by 1?
3. What command rounds the value of the thisMonth variable to the nearest integer?
4. What conditional operator changes the value of the thisMonth variable to 12 if it equals 11 but otherwise leaves the value unchanged?

5. What function tests whether the value of the thisMonth variable is a number?
6. What command displays the value of the thisDay variable with no decimal places?
7. What statement runs the function calcMonth() after a 0.5-second delay?
8. What statement runs the function calcMonth() every 0.5 seconds?

Tutorial Summary | Review

In this tutorial, you learned how to work with date objects, math functions, and timed commands to create a countdown clock. In the first session, you created event handlers that allow you to run functions in response to particular events occurring within a Web page and Web browser. You also set the values of fields within a Web form. The rest of the first session introduced the date object and discussed how to work with the properties and methods of dates in order to display a specified date in a Web form. In the second session, you worked with JavaScript operators to calculate the amount of time left in the year from a specified date. You used a Math object to convert this value into days, hours, minutes, and seconds. The second session then discussed how to work with numeric values in JavaScript. The session also covered how to use comparison operators to apply different possible values to a single variable. The session concluded with a discussion of timed commands, which run a function at a specified time interval.

Key Terms

arithmetic operator
assignment operator
binary operator
comparison operator
conditional operator
date method
date object
decrement operator
event
event handler
increment operator
logical operator
Math method
Math object
negation operator
operand
operator
time-delayed command
timed-interval command
unary operator

Practice | Review Assignments

Practice the skills you learned in the tutorial using the same case scenario.

Data Files needed for the Review Assignments: datestxt.js, eventstxt.htm, logo.jpg, tulsa.css

Hector has been promoted to general manager of promotion for all of Tulsa's special events. He wants you to create something similar to the New Year's Bash countdown clock for all of the events sponsored by the city. Hector envisions a Web page displaying a list of special events that includes each event's name, the date that it will occur, and the time remaining until the event (in days, hours, minutes, and seconds). Hector wants the following events listed on the Web page:

- Heritage Day on January 14 at 10:00 a.m.
- Spring Day Rally on May 21 at 12:00 p.m.
- July 4th Fireworks on July 4 at 9:00 p.m.
- Summer Bash on September 1 at 12:00 p.m.
- Holiday Party on December 1 at 11:30 a.m.
- New Year's Bash on December 31 at 3:30 p.m.

Like the countdown clock, the contents of the Web site should be constantly updated by a user's browser. Hector has already created the Web page's design and layout, but wants you to write the JavaScript program to run the clocks. Figure 11-37 shows a preview of the completed Web page.

Figure 11-37

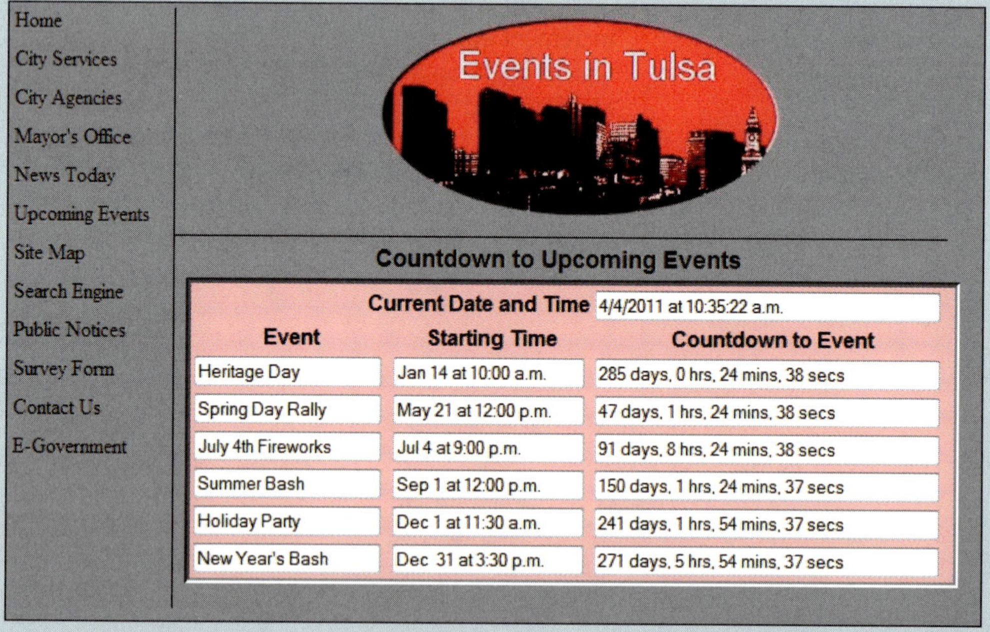

Complete the following:

1. Use your text editor to open the **eventstxt.htm** file from the tutorial.11/review folder, enter ***your name*** and ***the date*** in the head section, and then save the file as **events.htm** in the same folder. Use your text editor to open the **datestxt.js** file from the tutorial.11/review folder, enter ***your name*** and ***the date*** in the comment section, and then save the file as **dates.js** in the same folder.

2. Go to the **dates.js** file in your text editor. The file contains a single function named showDateTime() that displays the date and time of a date object in a formatted text string. Below this function, insert a function named **changeYear()** that will change a date's year value if the date has already been passed in the current calendar year. To create the changeYear parameter, do the following:
   a. Specify two parameters for the changeYear function: today and holiday. The **today** parameter is used to store a date object representing the current date. The **holiday** parameter is used to store a date object representing one of the events in Hector's list.
   b. In the first line of the function, use the getFullYear() date method to extract the four-digit year value from the today variable and store the value in a variable named **year**.
   c. In the second line, use the setFullYear() date method to set the full year value of the holiday date object to the value of the year variable. This changes the date of the holiday event to the current year.
   d. In the third line, use a conditional operator involving the year variable. The operator's test condition is whether the value of the holiday date object is less than the today date object. If it is, the event has already passed in the current year and the value of the year variable should increase by 1. If it is not, the event has not yet occurred and the year value should remain unchanged.
   e. In the fourth line of the function, set the full year value of the holiday date object to the value of the year variable.
3. Below the changeYear() function, create a function named **countdown()** that will return a text string displaying the number of days, hours, minutes, and seconds between a starting date and a stopping date. Create the function as follows:
   a. Specify two parameters for the function: start and stop. The **start** parameter will contain a date object for the starting date. The **stop** parameter will contain a date object for the stopping date.
   b. In the first line of the function, calculate the time difference between stop and start, storing the difference in a variable named **time**.
   c. Convert the time difference into days, hours, minutes, and seconds, and return the following text string

      ***days* days, *hours* hrs, *minutes* mins, *seconds* secs**

      where *days*, *hours*, *minutes*, and *seconds* are variables that store the integer values of the days, hours, minutes, and seconds. (*Hint:* Use the commands in the NYClock() function from the tutorial as a guide for converting the time difference into days, hours, minutes, and seconds.)
4. Close the file, saving your changes.
5. Go to the **events.htm** file in your text editor. Above the closing </head> tag, insert an external script element to access the code in the dates.js file; and then, below that element, insert a second script element for code to be embedded in the events.htm file.
6. Within the embedded script element, create a function named **showCountdown()**. The showCountdown() function has no parameters. Within the function, do the following:
   a. Create a variable named **today** containing a date object. Use the current date and time shown in Figure 11-37. Create six additional date objects in variables named **Date1** through **Date6**. Assign the dates and times from the six events in Hector's list to the Date1 through Date6 variables. Use a year value of **2011** for these six dates (you'll set the current year value in a later step).

b. Using the today variable as the parameter value, call the showDateTime() function and store the value returned by the function in the thisDay field of the eventform Web form.

c. Using today as the first parameter value and Date1 as the second parameter value, call the changeYear() function. Calling this function sets the correct year value for the first event in Hector's list. Repeat this step for the Date2 through Date6 variables.

d. Call the countdown() function using the today variable as the first parameter value and the Date1 variable as the second. Display the result returned by this function in the count1 field of the eventform Web form. Running this command displays the time remaining until the first event in Hector's list. Repeat this step for the other five events.

7. Add an event handler to the <body> tag that runs the showCountdown() function when the page is loaded by the browser.
8. Save your changes to the file.
9. Open **events.htm** in your Web browser. Verify that it shows the same date, time, and countdown values shown in Figure 11-37.
10. Return to the **events.htm** file in your text editor. Modify the initial value of the today variable so that it always uses the current date and time.
11. Modify the event handler in the <body> tag so that it runs the showCountdown() function every tenth of a second after the page is loaded.
12. Close the file, saving your changes.
13. Reload or refresh **events.htm** in your Web browser and verify that it shows a countdown clock with the current date and time.
14. Submit your completed files to your instructor.

Apply | Case Problem 1

Use JavaScript to create and run an exam timer.

Data Files needed for this Case Problem: oaetxt.htm, figa.jpg, figb.jpg, figc.jpg, figd.jpg, figures.jpg, functions.js, oae.jpg, quiz.css

Online Aptitude Exams Grunwald Testing, Inc. creates and administers a series of aptitude tests for schools, government agencies, and private firms. The company has been exploring the feasibility of putting some of its tests online. John Paulson is directing the effort and has asked you to help design a sample test page. The company's tests are graded on two measures: the number of correct answers by the respondents and the time required to complete the exam. John wants you to work on creating an online timer that starts the moment users begin work on an exam and stops once users have submitted their answers. The exam questions will be hidden from users until the clock starts. After users submit their answers, the exam questions will close and an alert box will appear showing the number of correct answers and the time, in seconds, taken to complete the exam. John has already collected some of the functions you'll need for this page in a separate file named functions.js. The file contains two functions:

- The showQuiz() function displays the quiz questions on the Web page.
- The gradeQuiz() function returns the number of correct answers in a submitted quiz, highlights the correct answers on the page, and disables the quiz, preventing users from changing their answers.

You will write the code to start and stop the quiz timer as well as to call the functions to show and grade a completed quiz. Figure 11-38 shows a preview of the exam page in action.

Figure 11-38

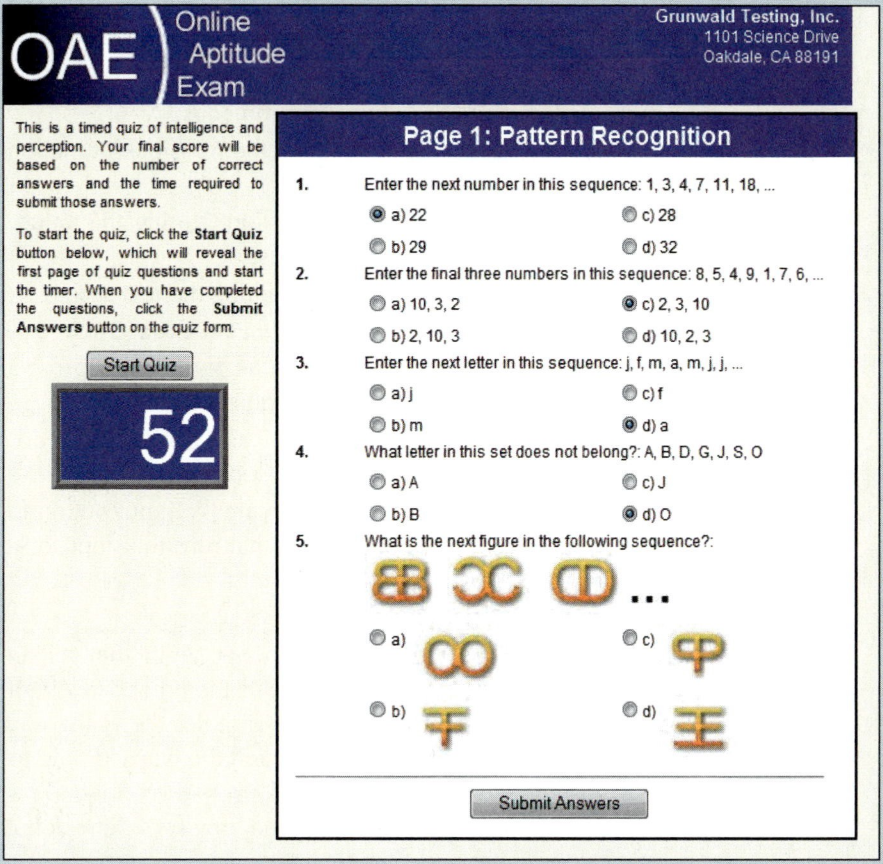

Complete the following:

1. Use your text editor to open the **oaetxt.htm** file from the tutorial.11/case1 folder, enter ***your name*** and ***the date*** in the head section, and then save the file as **oae.htm** in the same folder.
2. Above the closing </head> tag, insert an external script element that points to the functions.js file in the tutorial.11/case1 folder.
3. Below this script element, insert another script element. Within the script element, declare two variables. The first variable is named **seconds** and will store the current elapsed time that the user has worked on the exam. The second variable is named **clockId** and will reference the commands used to repeatedly update the clock value. Set the initial value of the seconds variable to 0. Do not set an initial value for the clockId variable.
4. Create a function named **runClock()** that will update the time value in the Web page's clock. There are no parameters. Add the following commands to the function:
   a. Use a unary operator to increase the value of the seconds variable by 1.
   b. Change the value of the quizclock field in the quiz form to the value of the seconds variable.
5. Create a function named **startClock()** that will start the Web page clock and then repeatedly update the elapsed time displayed in the clock. There are no parameters to this function. Add the following commands:
   a. Call the showQuiz() function to display the questions in the online exam.

   b. Call the runClock() function every second, storing the ID of this timed-interval command in the clockId variable.
6. Create a function named **stopClock()** that will stop the timer, display the user's score, and disable the exam to prevent further entry. There are no parameters to this function. Add the following commands:
   a. Halt the repeated calls to the runClock() function. (*Hint:* Use the clearInterval() method.)
   b. Call the gradeQuiz() function, storing the value returned by the function in a variable named **correctAns**.
   c. Display an alert box containing the text string

      `You have correctAns correct of 5 in timer seconds.`

      where *correctAns* is the value of the correctAns variable and *timer* is the value of the quizclock field in the quiz form.
7. Locate the input button for the Start Quiz button. Add an event handler attribute that runs the startClock() function when the button is clicked.
8. Go to the end of the file and locate the input button for the Submit Answers button. Add an event handler attribute that runs the stopClock() function when the button is clicked.
9. Save your changes to the file.
10. Open **oae.htm** in your Web browser. Verify that clicking the Start Quiz button displays the quiz questions and starts the timer. Then verify that clicking the Submit Answers button stops the timer, disables the exam, and displays an alert box with the number of correct answers and the elapsed time to complete the exam. (*Hint:* To restore the timer and the Web form to their original state, you will have to reload the page in the browser. Clicking the browser's Refresh button will not remove the Web form values or zero the timer.)
11. Submit your completed files to your instructor.

Apply | Case Problem 2

Use JavaScript to display a random text box.

Data Files needed for this Case Problem: hometxt.htm, logo.jpg, randtxt.js, styles.css, tips.js, work.jpg

The Home Center Tom Vogel manages The Home Center, a Web site for do-it-yourself enthusiasts. The site contains articles, forums, and products for home repair and maintenance. Tom thinks it would be helpful for users to see a short home repair tip on the site's home page. He wants a different tip to appear each time a user loads the page, and has created a collection of 10 tips to display randomly on the page. Tom has already obtained two functions to display the tip title and text:

- The tipTitle() function returns the title of the nth tip title. The value of *n* is entered as a parameter of the function.
- The tipText() function returns the text of the nth tip of the tip collection. The value of *n* is entered as a parameter of the function.

The tipTitle() and tipText() functions have been stored in the tips.js file. You will create a function that randomly selects a tip from this collection and then writes the title and text of that tip to an appropriate spot on the Web page. A preview of the completed Web page is shown in Figure 11-39.

Figure 11-39

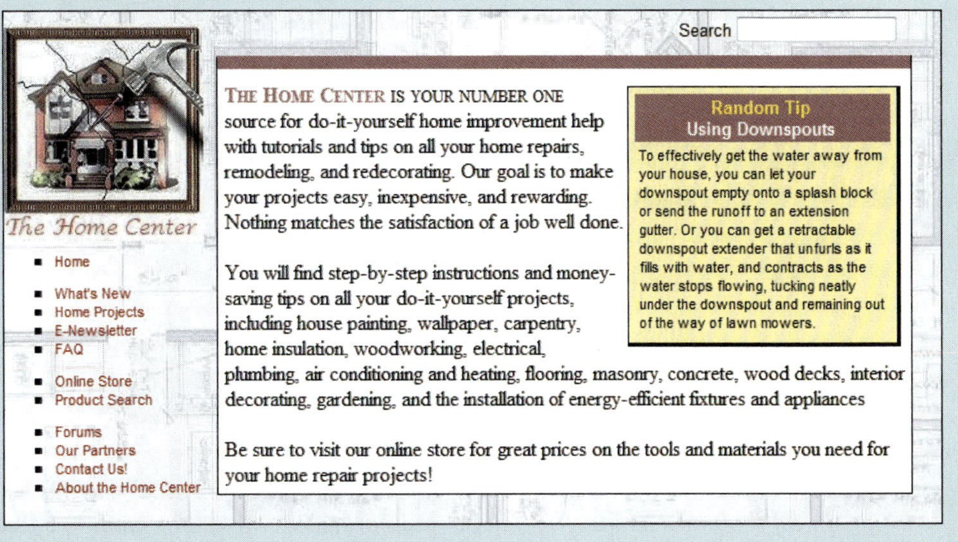

Complete the following:

1. Use your text editor to open the **hometxt.htm** file from the tutorial.11/case2 folder, enter ***your name*** and ***the date*** in the head section, and then save the file as **home.htm** in the same folder. Use your text editor to open the **randtxt.js** file, enter ***your name*** and ***the date*** in the comment section, and then save the file as **random.js** in the same folder.

EXPLORE

2. Within the random.js file, create a function named **randInt()** that will generate a random integer within a given range. The function has two parameters: lower and upper, where lower is the lowest integer in the range and upper is the highest integer in the range. Add the following commands to the function:
   a. Declare a variable named **size** that is equal to the number of integers in the given range. (*Hint:* The size of the range is one more than the difference between the highest and lowest integer.)
   b. Use the Math.floor() and Math.random() methods as well as the lower parameter and size variable to generate a random integer. (*Hint:* See the section on generating a random integer in this tutorial for guidance.)
3. Close the file, saving your changes.
4. Go to the **home.htm** file in your text editor. Above the closing </head> tag, insert two external script elements: one that links to the tips.js file and another that links to the random.js file you just created.
5. Scroll down the document to the div element with an ID value of "tip" and replace the contents of this element with an embedded script element. Within the script element do the following:
   a. Declare a variable named **tipNum** that is equal to a random integer between 1 and 10 returned by the randInt() function you created in the random.js file.
   b. Use a series of document.write() statements to write the HTML code

```
<h1>Random Tip<br />title</h1>
<p>tip</p>
```

   to the Web page, where *title* is the title of the random title as generated by the tipTitle() function and *tip* is the text of the random tip as generated by the tipText() function.

6. Save your changes to the file.
7. Open **home.htm** in your Web browser and verify that a random tip appears in the floating tip box each time you reload or refresh the Web page.
8. Submit your completed files to your instructor.

Challenge | Case Problem 3

Explore how to use JavaScript to create a world clock.

Data Files needed for this Case Problem: worldtxt.htm, zonestxt.js, je.css, logo.jpg, map.jpg

Jackson Electronics Jackson Electronics is a global company that manufactures and sells quality electronic equipment and components. The company has six corporate offices at different locations around the globe, and employees must keep in constant communication with the different offices. David Lin maintains the corporate Web site and asks you for help with a problem. He wants to augment the Web page that displays the location of the corporate offices to display the local time at each location. This will give employees important information when they want to call or fax data from one office to another. To create this world clock, David needs to know how JavaScript's date object works with different time zones.

The Earth is divided into 24 time zones. Each time zone is referenced in comparison to the time kept in Greenwich, England, which is known as standard time or Greenwich mean time (GMT). You can determine how Greenwich mean time differs from your local time using the getTimezoneOffset() method. For example, if the today variable contains a date object and is run on a computer in New York, the expression

```
today.getTimezoneOffset()
```

returns the value 300 because Greenwich mean time is 300 minutes or five hours ahead of New York time. With this information, you can determine Greenwich time by adding the offset value to your computer's local time. Because JavaScript measures time in milliseconds, you must multiply the offset by the number of milliseconds in one minute. The following code calculates the number of hours using this function:

```
today.getTimezoneOffset()*60*1000
```

You can determine the time anywhere in the world if you know Greenwich time and the other location's offset from GMT. David has compiled the following list of the six corporate offices and the time difference in minutes between each of those cities and GMT:

- Office 1: Houston (–360)
- Office 2: London (0)
- Office 3: New York (–300)
- Office 4: Seattle (–480)
- Office 5: Sydney (660)
- Office 6: Tokyo (540)

The number in parentheses indicates the number of minutes the city is offset from GMT. A negative value indicates that the city is behind GMT, and a positive value indicates that it is ahead of GMT. Tokyo, for example, is 540 minutes or nine hours ahead of Greenwich.

David already designed the contents of the world map Web page, but he needs your help in programming the times for the six offices. Figure 11-40 shows a preview of the completed Web page.

Figure 11-40

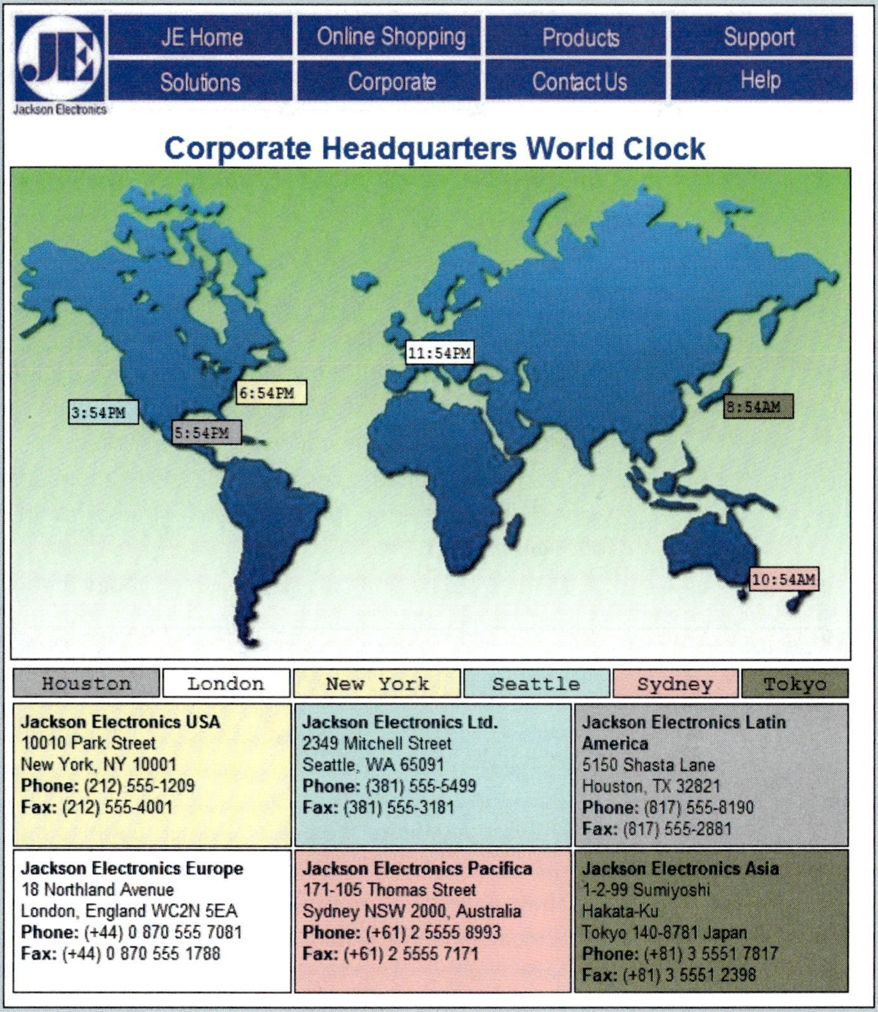

Complete the following:

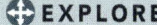

1. Use your text editor to open the **worldtxt.htm** file from the tutorial.11/case3 folder, enter ***your name*** and ***the date*** in the head section, and then save the file as **world.htm** in the same folder. Use your text editor to open the **zonestxt.js** file from the tutorial.11/case3 folder, enter ***your name*** and ***the date*** in the comment section, and then save the file as **zones.js** in the same folder.
2. Within the **zones.js** file, create a function named **addTime()** that will create a new date object by adding a specified number of milliseconds to an initial time value. The function has two parameters: **oldTime** and **milliSeconds**. The oldTime parameter stores a date object representing an initial time value. The milliSeconds parameter stores the amount of time, in milliseconds, that should be added to the oldTime parameter. Add the following commands to the function:
   a. Create a date object named **newTime**, but do not specify a value for its date or time.

   EXPLORE

   b. Using the getTime() method, extract the number of milliseconds contained in the oldTime parameter and add this to the milliSeconds parameter. Store the sum in a variable named **newValue**.

EXPLORE

c. Using the setTime() method, set the time value of the newTime date object to the value of the newValue variable.
d. Return the value of the newTime date object.

3. Below the addTime() function, create a function named **showTime()** that will return a text string showing the time in 12-hour format. The function has a single parameter named **time**, which contains the date and time that you want displayed. Using the show Time() function from the tutorial as a guide, have this function return the text string

   `hour:minute AM/PM`

   where *hour* is the hour value in 12-hour format, *minute* is the minute value, and AM/PM is either AM or PM, depending on the time of day.
4. Save your changes to the zones.js file.
5. Go to the **world.htm** file in your text editor. Above the closing </head> tag, insert an external script element to access the functions you created in the zones.js file and then insert a second embedded script element.
6. Within the embedded script element, create a function named **worldClock()** that will calculate the time in different time zones. Within this function, do the following:
   a. Create a date object variable named **today** that is equal to the current date and time.

EXPLORE

   b. Apply the getTimezoneOffset() method to the today variable to calculate the offset of your computer's clock from GMT in minutes. Change this value to milliseconds by multiplying the value by 60 and then by 1000. Store the result in a variable named **offSet**.
   c. Call the addTime() function using today as the first parameter value and offSet as the second. Store the value returned by this function in a variable named **GMT**. The GMT variable represents the current date and time in Greenwich.

EXPLORE

   d. Calculate the current date and time at Jackson Electronics' first office (Houston). To calculate this value, call the addTime() function with GMT as the first parameter and the second parameter equal to the number of milliseconds that Houston is offset from GMT. (*Hint:* Because Houston is 360 minutes behind Greenwich, the offset from GMT is equal to (–360)*60*1000.) Store the date object returned by the addTime() function in a variable named **time1**. Repeat this step to create variables named **time2** through **time6** for the other five office locations using the offset values listed above.
   e. The current times for the six office locations are to be displayed in input fields named **place1** through **place6** in the zones Web form. To display the value of the place1 field, call the showTime() function using the time1 variable as the parameter value. Repeat this step for the five remaining input fields.
7. Add an event handler attribute to the <body> tag to run the worldClock() function when the page is loaded by the browser and every second thereafter.
8. Close the file, saving your changes.
9. Open **world.htm** in your Web browser. Verify that the page shows the current time for the six office locations and that these times are correctly offset from Greenwich.
10. Submit your completed files to your instructor.

Note: This is a simplified example of a very complex problem. Different countries apply time zones in different ways. For example, China spans several time zones but applies a uniform time throughout the country. Some countries also shift their time(s) twice a year during daylight savings time (also known as summer time) whereas others do not apply daylight savings time at all. For example, the reported times in the Case Problem will be off by one hour during daylight savings time for the Seattle, Houston, and New York clocks. To create a truly accurate world clock, you would have to take into account all the various idiosyncrasies of global timekeeping.

Create | Case Problem 4

Test your knowledge of JavaScript by creating a countdown clock for the opening of a shopping mall.

Data Files needed for this Case Problem: malltxt.htm, mall.txt, timetxt.js, logo.jpg, mall1.jpg, mall2.jpg, mall3.jpg

The Cutler Mall Alice Samuels is the director of promotion for the Cutler Shopping Mall, a large new mall opening on March 23 at 9:00 a.m. in Cutler, Iowa. She asked you to design the Web page announcing the mall's opening. She's provided the text of the page as well as several graphic images; however, she also wants you to program a countdown clock that displays the days, hours, and minutes until the mall opens. The final design of the site is up to you, and you may supplement the provided material with your own.

Complete the following:

1. Use your text editor to open the **malltxt.htm** file from the tutorial.11/case4 folder, enter ***your name*** and ***the date*** in the head section, and then save the file as **mall.htm** in the same folder.
2. Insert a Web form named **mallclock** that has the following fields:
   - A **dayNow** field that displays the current date in the format month/day/year
   - A **timeNow** field that displays the time in 12-hour format
   - A **days** field that displays the number of days until the mall opens
   - An **hours** field that displays the number of hours left in the current day
   - A **minutes** field that displays the number of minutes left in the current hour; round this value to the nearest minute
3. Add the remaining content to the Web page. Refer to the **mall.txt** text file in the tutorial.11/case4 folder for the content that Alice wants you to include. Insert any styles for the Web page in an external file named **mall.css**. Link the mall.htm file to this style sheet.
4. Use your text editor to open the **timetxt.js** file from the tutorial.11/case4 folder, enter ***your name*** and ***the date*** in the comment section, and then save the file as **time.js** in the same folder.
5. In the file, add the following functions (refer to the functions and codes from the tutorial case for help in writing these functions):
   - A **daysDiff()** function that calculates the number of days, rounded down to the next lowest integer, between a starting date and a stopping date
   - An **hoursDiff()** function that calculates the number of hours left in the current day rounded down to the next lowest integer
   - A **minutesDiff()** function that calculates the number of minutes left in the current hour rounded down to the next lowest integer
   - A **showDate()** function that displays the value of a date object in the format *month/day/year*

- A **showTime()** function that displays the value of a date object in the format *hour:minute* a.m./p.m.

6. Insert an external script element to access the functions in the time.js script file from the mall.htm file.
7. Add an embedded script to the mall.htm file to use the functions from the time.js file to create a function named **countDownClock()** that displays the current date and time in the document as well as the days, hours, and minutes remaining until the mall opening. Assume an opening date of March 23 and an opening time of 9:00 a.m. For the year, use a starting year value of the current year; but if the current date falls after March 23 of the current year, change the year value for the opening date to the next year. (*Hint:* Apply conditional operators along with the getFullYear() and setFullYear() functions to set the year value of the opening date.)
8. Have the countDownClock() function run when the page initially opens and then every 60 seconds thereafter.
9. Submit your completed files to your instructor.

Review | Quick Check Answers

Session 11.1

1. An event handler is an attribute added to an element that instructs Web browsers to run a script command or commands when an event (such as a mouse click) occurs within the element.
2. `onclick = "showImage()"`
3. `<a href = "javascript:showImage()"> ... </a>`
4. `var examDate = new Date("May 8, 2011 18:55:28");`
5. `examDate.getMonth() // The value returned would be 4.`
6. `examDate.getFullYear()`
7. `examDate.setDate(9);`
8. `currentTime = new Date();`

Session 11.2

1. `thisMonth++`
2. `thisMonth += 1;`
3. `Math.round(thisMonth)`
4. `thisMonth = (thisMonth == 11) ? 12 : thisMonth;`
5. `IsNan(thisMonth)`
6. `thisDay.toFixed(0);`
7. `setTimeout("calcMonth", 500);`
8. `setInterval("calcMonth", 500);`

Ending Data Files

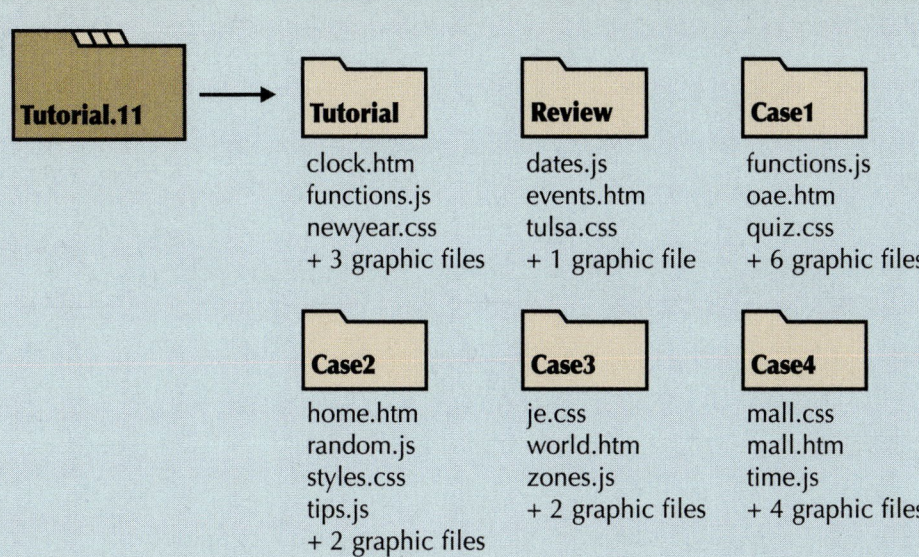

Tutorial.11 →

Tutorial
- clock.htm
- functions.js
- newyear.css
- + 3 graphic files

Review
- dates.js
- events.htm
- tulsa.css
- + 1 graphic file

Case1
- functions.js
- oae.htm
- quiz.css
- + 6 graphic files

Case2
- home.htm
- random.js
- styles.css
- tips.js
- + 2 graphic files

Case3
- je.css
- world.htm
- zones.js
- + 2 graphic files

Case4
- mall.css
- mall.htm
- time.js
- + 4 graphic files

Tutorial 12

Objectives

Session 12.1
- Create an array
- Populate and reference values from an array
- Work with array methods

Session 12.2
- Work with For loops
- Work with While loops
- Loop through the contents of an array
- Work with If, If... Else, and multiple conditional statements

Session 12.3
- Use arrays, loops, and conditional statements to create a table
- Work with break, continue, and label commands

Working with Arrays, Loops, and Conditional Statements

Creating a Monthly Calendar

Case | The Chamberlain Civic Center

With first-class concerts, performances from Broadway touring companies, and shows from famous comics, singers, and other entertainers, the Chamberlain Civic Center (CCC) is a popular attraction in South Dakota. Maria Valdez is the new publicity director for the center. Part of her job is to oversee the development of the center's Web site. After reviewing the Web site, Maria wants you to make a few changes.

In addition to links connecting visitors to the site's main features, the CCC home page provides a brief description of the events for the current month. Maria thinks it would be helpful to place a monthly calendar at the top of the home page so that visitors could quickly see the day each event will be held. Maria does not want staff members to construct the calendar manually each month. Instead, she wants a program added to the site that displays the monthly calendar for the current date. She asks you to help write a program that automatically generates the calendar.

Starting Data Files

Tutorial.12 →

Tutorial
ccctxt.htm
caltxt.js
+ 2 CSS files
+ 3 graphic files

Review
caltxt.htm
yeartxt.js
+ 2 CSS files
+ 3 graphic files

Case1
clisttxt.htm
list.js
lhouse.css
logo.jpg

Case2
electtxt.htm
votes.js
results.css
+2 graphics files

Case3
aucttxt.htm
styles.css
logo.jpg

Case4
lunartxt.htm
lunartxt.js
moonfunc.js
atro.css
caltxt.css
+ 17 graphics files

Session 12.1

Introducing the Monthly Calendar

Maria has drawn her idea for creating the monthly calendar on a printout of the Chamberlain Civic Center's home page. The printout shows the events from the previous month, March 2011. The main text of the page contains a description of May events at the CCC. Maria wants the monthly calendar for May to appear in the upper-right corner of the page so that users can relate the events to the dates on the calendar. Figure 12-1 shows how Maria envisions the calendar on the Web page.

Figure 12-1 **Monthly calendar to add to home page**

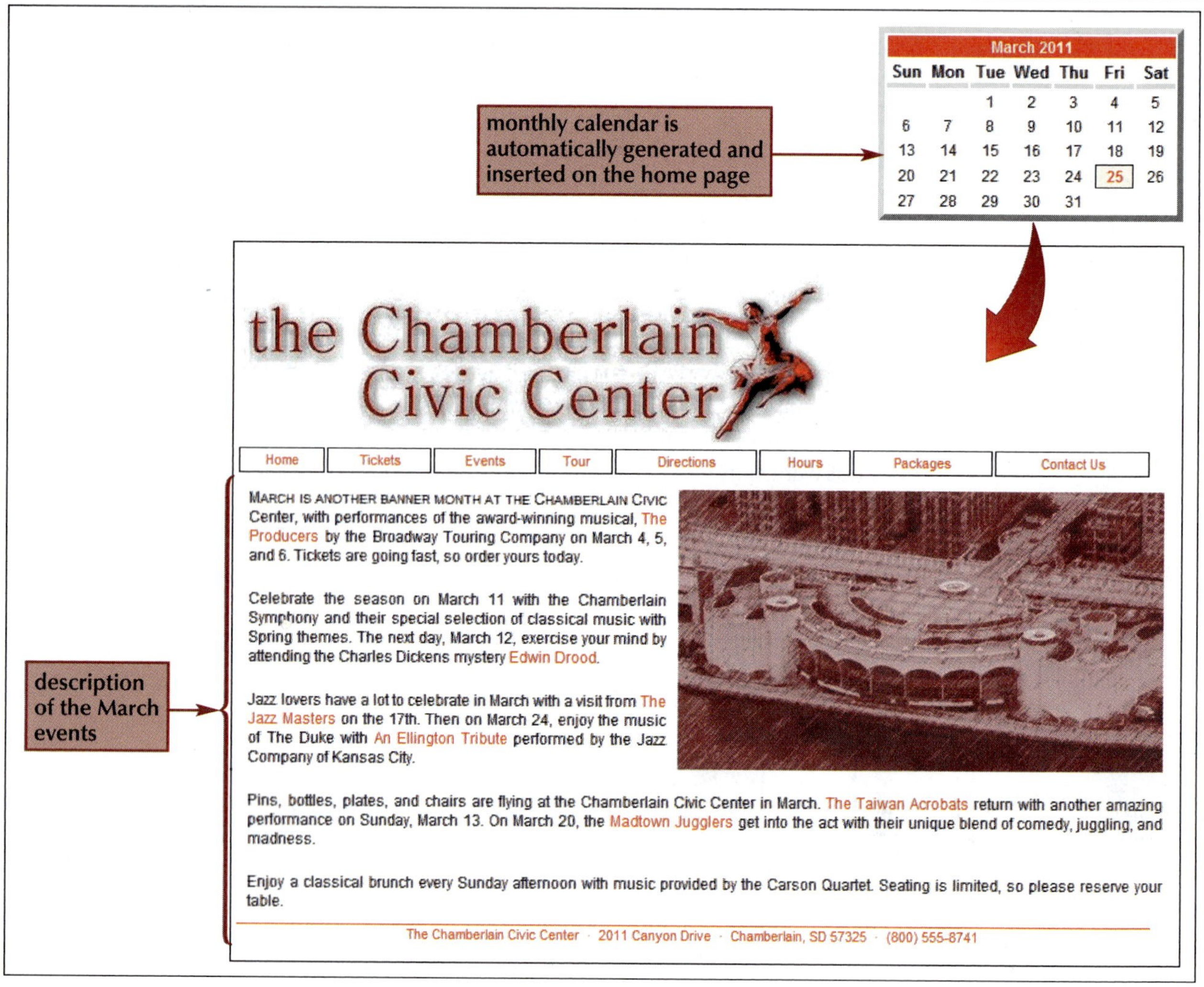

March 2011
Sun Mon Tue Wed Thu Fri Sat
1 2 3 4 5
6 7 8 9 10 11 12
13 14 15 16 17 18 19
20 21 22 23 24 25 26
27 28 29 30 31
monthly calendar is automatically generated and inserted on the home page
the Chamberlain Civic Center
Home Tickets Events Tour Directions Hours Packages Contact Us
March is another banner month at the Chamberlain Civic Center, with performances of the award-winning musical, The Producers by the Broadway Touring Company on March 4, 5, and 6. Tickets are going fast, so order yours today.
Celebrate the season on March 11 with the Chamberlain Symphony and their special selection of classical music with Spring themes. The next day, March 12, exercise your mind by attending the Charles Dickens mystery Edwin Drood.
Jazz lovers have a lot to celebrate in March with a visit from The Jazz Masters on the 17th. Then on March 24, enjoy the music of The Duke with An Ellington Tribute performed by the Jazz Company of Kansas City.
Pins, bottles, plates, and chairs are flying at the Chamberlain Civic Center in March. The Taiwan Acrobats return with another amazing performance on Sunday, March 13. On March 20, the Madtown Jugglers get into the act with their unique blend of comedy, juggling, and madness.
Enjoy a classical brunch every Sunday afternoon with music provided by the Carson Quartet. Seating is limited, so please reserve your table.
The Chamberlain Civic Center · 2011 Canyon Drive · Chamberlain, SD 57325 · (800) 555-8741
description of the March events

Maria wants the program you write to be easily usable on other Web pages. She envisions placing the entire JavaScript code for the calendar in an external file named calendar.js and running it from a single function. She also wants the styles for the calendar to be placed in a single external file named calendar.css. Figure 12-2 shows how these files create the monthly calendar. Accessing and displaying the monthly calendar table should then require only a minimal amount of recoding within any page at the CCC site.

Files to create and format the monthly calendar **Figure 12-2**

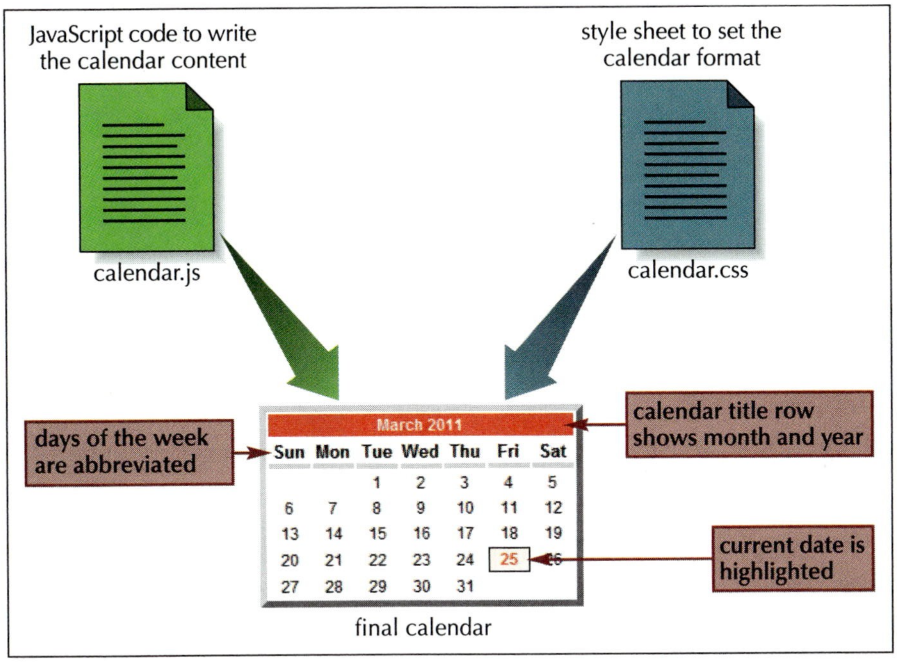

Maria has already created the styles required for the calendar table, but has left the coding to you. You'll add links to both the calendar.js and calendar.css files on the Chamberlain Civic Center's home page.

To access the CCC files:

1. Use your text editor to open the **ccctxt.htm** and **caltxt.js** files from the tutorial.12/tutorial folder, enter ***your name*** and ***the date*** in the comment section at the top of each file, and then save the files as **ccc.htm** and **calendar.js**, respectively.
2. Return to the **ccc.htm** file in your text editor, and then add the following code above the closing </head> tag to create links to both the calendar.css style sheet and the calendar.js JavaScript file, as shown in Figure 12-3:

```
<link href="calendar.css" rel="stylesheet" type="text/css" />
<script src="calendar.js" type="text/javascript"></script>
```

Code to link the JavaScript and style sheet files **Figure 12-3**

```
<title>The Chamberlain Civic Center</title>
<link href="ccc.css" rel="stylesheet" type="text/css" />

<link href="calendar.css" rel="stylesheet" type="text/css" />
<script src="calendar.js" type="text/javascript"></script>
```

3. Save your changes to the file.

Reviewing the Calendar Style Sheet

Before you start writing the code to create the monthly calendar, you will look at the styles in the calendar.css style sheet. Maria has assigned class names and IDs to different parts of the table. The five classes and IDs you'll use when creating the monthly calendar are:

- The entire calendar is set in a table with the ID **calendar_table**.
- The cell containing the calendar title has the ID **calendar_head**.
- The seven cells containing the days of the week abbreviations all belong to the class **calendar_weekdays**.
- The cells containing the dates of the month all belong to the class **calendar_dates**.
- The cell containing the current date has the ID **calendar_today**.

For each of these parts, calendar.css has a style declaration. Figure 12-4 shows the style sheet contained in the calendar.css file.

Figure 12-4 **Contents of the calendar.css style sheet**

```
#calendar_table    {float: right; background-color: white; font-size: 9pt;
                    font-family: Arial, Helvetica, sans-serif;
                    border-style: outset; border-width: 5px; margin: 0px 0px 5px 5px}

#calendar_head     {background-color: rgb(223,29,29); color: ivory; letter-spacing: 2px}

.calendar_weekdays {width: 30px; font-size: 10pt; border-bottom-style: solid}

.calendar_dates    {text-align: center; background-color: white}

#calendar_today    {font-weight: bold; color: rgb(223,29,29); background-color: ivory;
                    border: 1px solid black}
```

As you create the code that writes this table, you need to make sure that you add the ID and class attributes to the appropriate table and cell tags. Placing this information in a separate style sheet lets you modify the table's appearance without having to rewrite the code that generates the table.

Adding the calendar() Function

Because Maria wants the calendar application to be available to any page of the CCC site, you'll place all of the commands in a single function named calendar(). The first commands you will add to the function use the document.write() method to write the HTML code for a table element with the ID calendar_table. The initial code for the calendar() function is:

```
function calendar() {
   document.write("<table id='calendar_table'>");
   document.write("</table>");
}
```

You'll call this function by adding the command in a script element within the ccc.htm file. You'll add this code to the calendar.js and ccc.htm files now.

To begin work on the calendar() function:

1. Return to the **calendar.js** file in your text editor, and then, at the bottom of the file, add the following code, as shown in Figure 12-5:

```
function calendar() {
   document.write("<table id='calendar_table'>");
   document.write("</table>");
}
```

Figure 12-5 Code for the calendar() function

```
function calendar() {
   document.write("<table id='calendar_table'>");
   document.write("</table>");
}
```

2. Save your changes to the file.
3. Return to the **ccc.htm** file in your text editor, and then locate the div element with the ID head. The calendar should be placed as a table element within this section of the page.
4. Insert the following code to run the calendar() function to create the table, as shown in Figure 12-6:

```
<script type="text/javascript">
   calendar();
</script>
```

Figure 12-6 Code to call the calendar() function

```
<body>
   <div id="head">
      <script type="text/javascript">
         calendar();
      </script>
      <img src="ccc.jpg" alt="Chamberlain Civic Center" />
   </div>
```

5. Close the file, saving your changes.
6. Open **ccc.htm** in your Web browser, and then verify that the browser does not report any coding errors. The calendar table does not appear on the Web page because you haven't yet created any content for the table.

   Trouble? If you are running Internet Explorer, you may need to allow the browser to run the script on the page.

At this point, you've completed all of the coding needed in the ccc.htm file. All of the remaining work to build the calendar() function is done in the calendar.js file. The three main tasks to complete the calendar table are:

- Creating the table header row
- Creating the table row containing the names of the days of the week
- Creating the rows containing the days of the month

In this first session, you'll learn how to create the header row for the calendar table. In the second and third sessions, you'll complete the rest of the table.

Working with Arrays

Maria wants the header row of the calendar table to display the text *Month*, *Year* where *Month* is the name of the month and *Year* is the four-digit year value. Recall that date objects support methods that allow you to extract the date's month number. For example, a date object storing the date March 18, 2011 has a month value of 2 (because month values start with 0 for the month of January). Maria wants the month name rather than the month number to appear in the table, but no existing date method returns the name of the month. Instead, you will have to write code to associate each month number with a month name. One way of doing this is through an array.

An **array** is a collection of data values organized under a single name. Each individual data value has a number or **index** that distinguishes it from other values in the array. The general form of an array value is

```
array[i]
```

where *array* is the name of the array and *i* is the index of a specific value in the array. The first item in any array has an index value of 0, the second item has an index value of 1, and so on. For example, the expression

```
monthName[4]
```

references the fifth (not the fourth) item in the monthName array.

Creating and Populating an Array

To create an array, you run the command

```
var array = new Array(length);
```

where *array* is the name of the array and *length* is the number of items in the array. The *length* parameter is optional. If you omit the *length* parameter, the array expands to match the number of items defined for it. When the length of an array is defined, JavaScript allots only the amount of memory needed to generate the array, so the code runs more efficiently. To create an array named monthName for the 12 month names, you can enter the command

```
var monthName = new Array(12);
```

or you can omit the array length and enter the command

```
var monthName = new Array();
```

Tip

Arrays without a defined length can take up more memory on your computer system.

After you create an array, you can populate it with values using the same commands you use for any variable. The only difference is that you must specify both the array name and the index number of the array item. The command to set the value of a specific item in an array is

```
array[i] = value;
```

where *array* is the name of the array, *i* is the index of the array item, and *value* is the value assigned to the item. For example, to insert the month names into the monthName array, you could run the following commands:

```
monthName[0] = "January";
monthName[1] = "February";
monthName[2] = "March";
. . .
monthName[10] = "November";
monthName[11] = "December";
```

A more compact way of creating and populating an array is to specify the array values when the array is initially declared. The syntax for this statement is

```
var array = new Array(values);
```

where *values* is a comma-separated list of values. The following command creates and populates the monthName array in a single statement:

```
var monthName = new Array("January", "February", "March", "April", "May",
"June", "July", "August", "September", "October", "November", "December");
```

A final way to create an array is with an **array literal**, in which the array values are entered into a bracketed list. The expression to create an array literal is

```
var array = [values];
```

where *values* is a comma-separated list of item values. The following command creates an array literal of month names:

```
var monthName = ["January", "February", "March", "April", "May", "June",
"July", "August", "September", "October", "November", "December"];
```

Array values do not need to all be the same data type. You can mix numeric values, text strings, and other data types within a single array, as in the following statement:

```
var x = new Array("JavaScript", 3.14, true, null);
```

Tip

Be careful when using array literals to populate an array. Some early browser versions do not support this method.

Now that you've seen how to create and populate an array, you will create an array of month names to use in creating the calendar application. You will insert the array in a function named writeCalTitle() that you will use to write the header row of the calendar table. The function has a single parameter named calendarDay that will store a date object containing the date to be highlighted in the calendar. The initial code for the writeCalTitle() function is:

```
function writeCalTitle(calendarDay) {
   var monthName = new Array("January", February", "March", "April",
  "May", "June", "July", "August", "September", "October", "November",
  "December");
}
```

You'll add this function to the calendar.js file.

To create the writeCalTitle() function:

1. Return to the **calendar.js** file in your text editor.
2. At the bottom of the file, insert the following code, as shown in Figure 12-7, being sure that each array item value is enclosed within a set of double quotation marks and that the line does not wrap within a quoted text string:

```
function writeCalTitle(calendarDay) {
   var monthName = new Array("January", "February", "March",
  "April", "May", "June", "July", "August", "September",
  "October", "November", "December");
}
```

Figure 12-7 Code for the monthName array

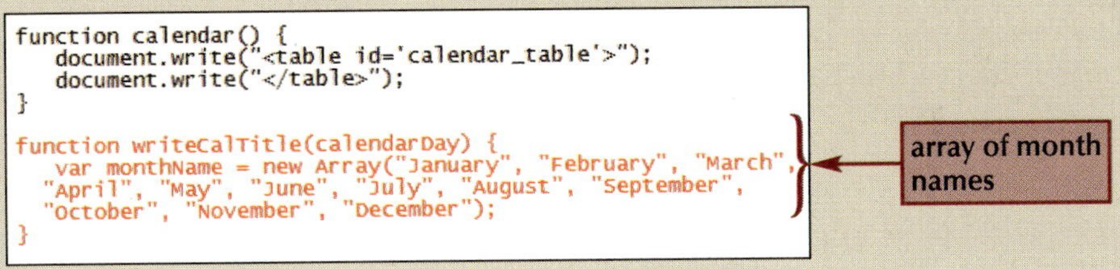

```
function calendar() {
   document.write("<table id='calendar_table'>");
   document.write("</table>");
}

function writeCalTitle(calendarDay) {
   var monthName = new Array("January", "February", "March",
  "April", "May", "June", "July", "August", "September",
  "October", "November", "December");
}
```

The function needs to extract the month value and year value from the calendarDay parameter using the getMonth() and getFullYear() date methods introduced in the previous tutorial. You'll store the values in variables named thisMonth and thisYear as follows:

```
var thisMonth=calendarDay.getMonth();
var thisYear=calendarDay.getFullYear();
```

Finally, the function will write the HTML code for the first table row of the monthly calendar. The monthly calendar will have seven columns, so the row containing the calendar title has to span seven columns. Recall that the heading row will also have the ID calendar_head. The HTML code for the heading row has the form

```
<tr>
   <th id='calendar_head' colspan='7'>
      Month Year
   </th>
</tr>
```

where *Month* is the month name and *Year* is the four-digit year value. The year value is simply the value of the thisYear variable. The thisMonth variable tells you the month value and ranges from 0 (for January) to 11 (for December). The month values match the index numbers from the monthName array. For example, the first item in the monthName array is January, which has an index value of 0. To retrieve the name of the month, you can use the following expression:

```
monthName[thisMonth]
```

So, the code to write the first row of the calendar table is:

```
document.write("<tr>");
document.write("<th id='calendar_head' colspan='7'>");
document.write(monthName[thisMonth]+" "+thisYear);
document.write("</th>");
document.write("</tr>");
```

You will complete the writeCalTitle() function by adding the commands to create the thisMonth and thisYear variables and to write the HTML code for the first table row.

To complete the writeCalTitle() function in the calendar.js file:

1. Insert the following commands into the writeCalTitle() function, as shown in Figure 12-8:

```
var thisMonth=calendarDay.getMonth();
var thisYear=calendarDay.getFullYear();

document.write("<tr>");
document.write("<th id='calendar_head' colspan='7'>");
document.write(monthName[thisMonth]+" "+thisYear);
document.write("</th>");
document.write("</tr>");
```

Figure 12-8
Completed writeCalTitle() function

```
function writeCalTitle(calendarDay) {
   var monthName = new Array("January", "February", "March",
  "April", "May", "June", "July", "August", "September",
  "October", "November", "December");

   var thisMonth=calendarDay.getMonth();
   var thisYear=calendarDay.getFullYear();

   document.write("<tr>");
   document.write("<th id='calendar_head' colspan='7'>");
   document.write(monthName[thisMonth]+" "+thisYear);
   document.write("</th>");
   document.write("</tr>");
}
```

code to write the header row of the calendar table

2. Save your changes to the file.

Creating and Populating Arrays

| Reference Window

- To create an array, run the command
  `var array = new Array(length);`
  where *array* is the name of the array and *length* is the number of items in the array. The optional *length* parameter limits the array to a specific size to save space.
- To set a value of an item within an array, use the command
  `array[i] = value;`
  where *i* is the index of the array item and *value* is the value assigned to the item.
- To create and populate an array, use the command
  `var array = new Array(values);`
  where *values* is a comma-separated list of values.
- To create an array literal, use the following command:
  `var array = [values];`

Next, you must specify a date for the calendar to display. For now, you will add a date object named calDate to the calendar() function that stores the date March 18, 2011. You will then call the writeCalTitle() function using this date as the value for the calendarDay parameter.

To revise the calendar() function:

1. Insert the following statement at the beginning of the calendar() function to create the calDate variable:

```
var calDate = new Date("March 18, 2011");
```

2. Insert the following command to call the writeCalTitle() function, as shown in Figure 12-9:

```
writeCalTitle(calDate);
```

Figure 12-9 Code to call the writeCalTitle() function

```
function calendar() {
   var calDate = new Date("March 18, 2011");

   document.write("<table id='calendar_table'>");
   writeCalTitle(calDate);
   document.write("</table>");
}

function writeCalTitle(calendarDay) {
   var monthName = new Array("January", "February", "March",
  "April", "May", "June", "July", "August", "September",
  "October", "November", "December");

   var thisMonth=calendarDay.getMonth();
   var thisYear=calendarDay.getFullYear();

   document.write("<tr>");
   document.write("<th id='calendar_head' colspan='7'>");
   document.write(monthName[thisMonth]+" "+thisYear);
   document.write("</th>");
   document.write("</tr>");
}
```

test date for the calendar table

3. Save your changes to the file.

4. Reopen or refresh **ccc.htm** in your Web browser. The calendar table appears in the upper-right corner of the page, displaying only the title March 2011. See Figure 12-10.

Figure 12-10 Calendar title displayed

Trouble? If the table does not appear on the Web page, your JavaScript code may contain a mistake. Check your code against the code shown in the figures. Common sources of error include forgetting to close all quoted text strings, failing to match the use of upper- and lowercase letters in function names and variable names, and misspelling function names and variable names.

Working with Array Length

To increase the size of an array, you can simply add more items to it. Unlike in other programming languages, JavaScript arrays do not need to stay at a fixed size, even if you defined a value for the *length* parameter when the array was declared. In addition, you do not have to define a value for every item in an array. The following commands create an array of 100 items even though only the first and last items actually have defined values. The other array items have null values and are not stored in memory:

```
var x = new Array();
x[0] = "start";
x[99] = "stop";
```

Arrays such as the x array with several missing or null items are called **sparse arrays**. To determine the size of an array, you can use the length property, which has the syntax

```
array.length
```

where *array* is the name of the array and *length* is one more than the highest index in the array. The value of the length property is always equal to one more than the highest index number in the array (because index numbers start with the value 0 rather than 1). For the sparse array defined above, the length is 100, even though only two items in the array have defined values.

Changing the value of the length property changes the size of an array. Increasing the array length adds more items to an array, but the items have null values until they are defined. Decreasing the array length truncates an array, removing any defined items whose indexes are not included in the new length. For example, running the command

```
monthName.length = 3;
```

on the monthName array reduces the monthName array to the following three items: January, February, and March.

Specifying Array Length

| Reference Window

- To determine the size of an array, use the property
  array.length
  where *array* is the name of the array and *length* is one more than the highest index in the array.
- To add more items to an array, run the command
  array[*i*] = *value*;
  where *i* is an index value higher than the highest index currently in the array.
- To remove items from an array, run the command
  array.length = *value*;
  where *value* is an integer that is smaller than the highest index currently in the array.

Reversing an Array

Arrays are associated with a collection of methods that allow you to change their contents, order, and size. You can also use these methods to combine different arrays into a single array and to convert arrays into text strings. Though you will not need to use these methods with the calendar() function, you'll examine them for future projects. Each method is applied using the syntax

```
array.method()
```

where *array* is the name of an array and *method* is the name of the method. Some array methods have parameter values that control how they are applied to an array. You will examine a few of these array methods.

By default, array items are placed in an array either in the order in which they are defined, or explicitly by index number. JavaScript supports two methods for changing the order of these items: reverse() and sort(). The reverse() method, as the name suggests, reverses the order of items in the array, making the last items first and vice-versa. In the following set of commands, the reverse() method is used to change the order of the values in the weekDay array:

```
var weekDay = new Array("Sun", "Mon", "Tue", "Wed", "Thu", "Fri", "Sat");
weekDay.reverse();
```

After running the reverse() method, the weekDay array contains the items in the following order: Sat, Fri, Thu, Wed, Tue, Mon, and finally, Sun. So, the expression weekDay[5] returns the text string Sun.

Sorting an Array

The sort() method arranges array items in alphabetical order. This can cause problems if you apply the sort() method to data values that are not usually treated in alphabetical order. For example, applying the command

```
weekDay.sort();
```

to the weekDay array causes the array to store the weekday abbreviations in the order Fri, Mon, Sat, Sun, Thu, Tue, Wed. Also, if you apply the sort() method to numeric values, the method treats the values as text strings and sorts them in order by their first digits, rather than by their true numerical values. This sorting, which is analogous to arranging words in alphabetical order, can lead to unexpected results. For example, the following commands create and sort an array named x:

```
var x = new Array(3, 45, 1234, 24);
x.sort();
```

The sorted x array will store items in the order 1234, 24, 3, 45, because this is the order of those numbers when sorted by their first digits. To correctly sort nontextual data, you must create a **compare function** that compares the values of two adjacent items in the array at a time. The general form of the compare function is

```
function fname(a, b) {
   compare the values of a and b
   return a negative, positive, or 0 value based on the comparison
}
```

where *fname* is the name of the compare function and *a* and *b* are two parameters used by the function. The a and b parameter values are compared to determine which is greater. The function then returns a negative, positive, or 0 value based on that comparison. For example, the following compare function compares the numeric difference between the *a* and *b* parameters:

```
function numSort(a, b) {
   return a-b;
}
```

The value returned by the function is used to sort the item in the array, comparing items from the array taken two at a time. If the returned value is 0, the order of the two items remains unchanged. If the value is positive, the first of the two items is assigned a higher index than the second. If the value is negative, the second of the two items is assigned a higher index than the first. To apply a compare function to the sort() method, you use the expression

```
array.sort(function)
```

where *function* is the name of the compare function. To use the numSort() compare function in sorting the x array in numeric order, you run the following command:

```
x.sort(numSort)
```

Because of how the numSort() function works, the values of the resulting x array are now sorted in ascending numeric order rather than alphabetic, yielding the array entries: 3, 24, 45, and 1234. To sort the array in decreasing numeric order, you need a different compare function. The following function can be used to sort numeric values in decreasing numeric order:

```
function numSortDesc(a, b) {
   return b-a;
}
```

In this function, the comparison process returns the value (b–a) rather than (a–b).

Tip

You can also sort an array in descending order by sorting it and then applying the reverse() method to the sorted array.

Shuffling an Array | InSight

In some code, you may want to rearrange an array in random order. For example, you may be writing a JavaScript code to simulate a randomly shuffled deck of cards. You can shuffle an array using the same sort() method you use to place the array in a defined order. The trick is to create a compare function that randomly returns a positive, negative, or 0 value. The following compare function is a simple approach to this problem:

```
function randOrder(){
  return 0.5 - Math.random();
}
```

To randomly sort an array, you apply this function to the sort() method. For example, if you create the array

```
var poker = new Array(52);
poker[0] = "2H";
poker[1] = "3H";
...
```

containing poker cards, you can shuffle the array contents using the following command:

```
poker.sort(randOrder)
```

After running this command, the contents of the poker array will be placed in random order. This is a useful technique if you are writing an online poker program using JavaScript.

Extracting and Inserting Array Items

In some scripts, you want to extract a section of an array, known as a **subarray**. For example, you might want to extract only the names of the summer months—June, July, and August—from the monthName array. To create a subarray, you can use the slice() method, which extracts a part of an array. The original contents of the array are unaffected, but the extracted items can be stored in another array. The syntax of the slice() method is

```
array.slice(start, stop)
```

where *start* is the index of the array item at which the slicing starts and *stop* is the index before which the slicing ends. The *stop* value is optional. If no *stop* value is provided, the array is sliced to the end of the array. For example, if you want to slice the monthName array, extracting only the summer months, you use the following command:

```
summerMonths = monthName.slice(5, 8);
```

The summerMonths array will contain the values June, July, and August. Remember that arrays start with the index value 0, so the sixth month of the year (June) has an index value of 5 and the ninth month of the year (September) has an index value of 8. Related to the slice() method is the splice() method, which is a general purpose method for extracting and inserting array items. The syntax of the splice() method is

```
array.splice(start, size)
```

where *start* is the index of the array item at which to start extracting items from the array and *size* is the number of items to extract. If no *size* value is specified, items are removed up through the end of the array. For example, if you want to extract the summer months from the monthName array using the splice() method, you run the following command:

```
summerMonths = monthName.splice(5, 3);
```

One of the important differences between the slice() and splice() methods is that the splice() method extracts the selected items and also removes them from the original array. Applying the splice() method to the monthName array above creates a subarray of the summer months and removes those three months from the monthName array. This is not true of the slice() method, which leaves the contents of the monthName array unaffected.

You can also use the splice() method to insert new items into an array. To insert new array items, you use the expression

```
array.splice(start, size, values)
```

where *values* is a comma-separated list of new values to replace the old values in the array. If you want to replace the first three month names with their first letters, for example, you apply the following splice() method to the monthName array:

```
monthName(0, 3, "J", "F", "M");
```

The values in the monthName array would now be J, F, M, April, May, and so on.

In some cases, you want to work only with items at the beginning or end of an array. The most efficient methods to insert or remove those items are the push(), pop(), unshift(), and shift() methods. The push() method appends new items to the end of an array and has the syntax

```
array.push(values)
```

where *values* is a comma-separated list of values to be appended to the end of the array. To remove the last item from an array, use the pop() method, which has the following syntax:

```
array.pop()
```

The push() and pop() methods are often used with programs that employ the "last-in-first-out" principle, in which the last item added to an array is the first item that is removed. The following set of commands demonstrates how to use the push() and pop() methods to expand and contract an array of values. The most recent additions to the array are popped out first because recent additions are added to the end of an array by default.

```
var x = new Array("a", "b", "c");
x.push("d", "e"); // x now contains ["a", "b", "c", "d", "e"]
x.pop();          // x now contains ["a", "b", "c", "d"]
x.pop();          // x now contains ["a", "b", "c"]
```

The unshift() method is similar to the push() method except that it inserts new items at the start of the array. Likewise, the shift() method is akin to the pop() method except that it removes the first array item, not the last.

Using Array Methods

| Reference Window

- To reverse the order of items in an array, use the method
  `array.reverse()`
  where *array* is the name of the array.
- To sort an array in alphabetical order, use the following method:
  `array.sort();`
- To sort an array in any order, use
  `array.sort(function)`
  where *function* is the name of a compare function that returns a positive, negative, or 0 value.
- To extract items from an array without affecting the array contents, use
  `array.slice(start, stop)`
  where *start* is the index of the array item at which the slicing starts and *stop* is the index before which the slicing ends. If no *stop* value is provided, the array is sliced to the end of the array.
- To add or remove items in an array, use
  `array.splice(start, size)`
  where *start* is the index of the array item at which the splicing starts and *size* is the number of items to splice from or into the array. If no *splice* value is specified, the array is spliced to its end.
- To add new items to the end of an array, use
  `array.push(values)`
  where *values* is a comma-separated list of values.
- To remove the last item from an array, use the following method:
  `array.pop()`

Figure 12-11 summarizes several of the other methods that can be applied to arrays. Arrays are a powerful and useful feature of the JavaScript language. The methods associated with arrays can be used to simplify and expand the capabilities of Web page scripts. Be aware, however, that older browsers might not support all of these array methods. Use these array methods with caution when you want to support a wide range of browser versions.

Figure 12-11 Array methods

Array Method	Description
array.concat(*array1*, *array2*, ...)	Joins *array* to two or more arrays, creating a single array containing the items from all the arrays.
array.join(*separator*)	Joins all items in *array* into a single text string. The array items are separated using the text in the separator parameter. If no separator is specified, a comma is used.
array.pop()	Removes the last item from *array*.
array.push(*values*)	Appends *array* with new items, where *values* is a comma-separated list of item values.
array.reverse()	Reverses the order of items in *array*.
array.shift()	Removes the first item from *array*.
array.slice(*start*, *stop*)	Extracts the *array* items starting with the start index up to the *stop* index, returning a new subarray.
array.splice(*start*, *size*, *values*)	Extracts *size* items from *array* starting with the item with the index *start*. To insert new items into the array, specify the array item in a comma-separated *values* list.
array.sort(*function*)	Sorts *array* where *function* is the name of a function that returns a positive, negative, or 0. If no *function* is specified, *array* is sorted in alphabetical order.
array.toString()	Converts the contents of *array* to a text string with the array values in a comma-separated list.
array.unshift(*values*)	Inserts new items at the start of *array*, where *values* is a comma-separated list of new values.

You set up the first parts of the online calendar in this session. In the next session, you'll complete the monthly calendar by working with loops and conditional statements.

Review | Session 12.1 Quick Check

1. What is an array?
2. What command creates an array named dayNames?
3. What command both creates and populates the dayNames array with the abbreviations of the seven days of the week (starting with Sun and going through Sat)?
4. What expression returns the third value from the array dayNames?
5. What command creates the dayNames array as an array literal?
6. What command sorts the dayNames array in alphabetical order?
7. What command extracts the middle five values from the dayNames array?
8. What command converts the contents of the dayNames array to a text string with each value separated by a comma?

Session 12.2

Working with Program Loops

Now that you're familiar with the properties and methods of arrays, you'll continue working on the calendar() function. So far, you've created only the header row, which displays the calendar's month and year. The next row of the table will contain the three-letter abbreviations of the seven days of the week, starting with Sun and continuing through

Sat. Each abbreviation needs to be placed within an element with the class name calendar_weekdays. Using a document.write() command for each line of HTML, you could generate this table row with the following code:

```
document.write("<tr>");
document.write("<th class='calendar_weekdays'>Sun</th>");
document.write("<th class='calendar_weekdays'>Mon</th>");
document.write("<th class='calendar_weekdays'>Tue</th>");
document.write("<th class='calendar_weekdays'>Wed</th>");
document.write("<th class='calendar_weekdays'>Thu</th>");
document.write("<th class='calendar_weekdays'>Fri</th>");
document.write("<th class='calendar_weekdays'>Sat</th>");
document.write("</tr>");
```

This code contains a lot of repetitive text. Imagine if you had to repeat essentially the same string of code dozens, hundreds, or even thousands of times. The code would become unmanageably long. Programmers deal with this kind of situation by creating program loops. A **program loop** is a set of commands that is executed repeatedly until a stopping condition has been met. Two commonly used program loops in JavaScript are the For and While loops.

Exploring the For Loop

In a For loop, a variable known as a **counter variable** is used to track the number of times a set of commands is run. Each time through the loop, the value of the counter variable is increased or decreased by a set amount. When the counter variable reaches or exceeds a specified value, the For loop stops. The general structure of a For loop is

```
for (start; continue; update) {
   commands
}
```

where *start* is an expression that sets the initial value of a counter variable, *continue* is a Boolean expression that must be true for the loop to continue, *update* is an expression that indicates how the value of the counter variable should change each time through the loop, and *commands* is the JavaScript commands that are run each time through the loop.

Suppose you want to set a counter variable to range in value from 0 to 3 in increments of 1. You could use the following expression to set the initial value of the variable:

```
var i = 0;
```

The name of the counter variable here is i, which is a common variable name often applied in program loops. The next expression in the For loop structure defines the stopping condition for the program loop. The following expression sets the loop to continue as long as the value of the counter variable is less than 4:

```
i < 4;
```

Finally, the following update expression uses the increment operator to indicate that the value of the counter variable increases by 1 each time through the program loop:

```
i++;
```

Putting all of these expressions together, you get the following For loop:

```
for (var i = 0; i < 4; i++) {
   commands
}
```

The collection of commands that is run each time through a loop is collectively known as a **command block**, a feature you've already worked with in functions. Command blocks are easily distinguished by their opening and closing curly braces { }. If a For loop contains only a single command, you don't need the command block and can leave out the curly braces.

The following is an example of a For loop that writes the value of the counter variable to a table cell on the Web page.

```
for (var i = 0; i < 4; i++) {
   document.write("<td>" + i + "</td>");
}
```

As shown in Figure 12-12, each time through the loop, the value displayed in the table cell is changed by 1.

Figure 12-12 For loop being run

```
<table border="2">
   <tr>
      <script type="text/javascript">
         for (var i=0; i < 4; i++) {
            document.write("<td>" + i + "</td>");
         }
      </script>
   </tr>
</table>
```

For loop

Parts of the For Loop	Expressions	Counter Values	Code Written to the Page
start	var i=0	0	<td>0</td>
continue	i < 4	1	<td>1</td>
		2	<td>2</td>
update	i++	3	<td>3</td>

Values during the For loop

0	1	2	3

resulting table

For loops can be nested inside one another. Figure 12-13 shows the code used to create a table with three rows and four columns. This example uses two counter variables, named rowNum and colNum. The rowNum variable loops through the values 1, 2, and 3. In addition, for each value of the rowNum variable, the colNum variable loops through the values 1, 2, 3, and 4. Each time the value of the colNum variable changes, a new cell is added to the table. Each time the value of the rowNum variable changes, a new row is added to the table.

Nested For loops **Figure 12-13**

```
<table border="2">
   <script type="text/javascript">
      for (var rowNum=1; rowNum < 4; rowNum++) {
         document.write("<tr>");
         for (var colNum=1; colNum < 5; colNum++) {
            document.write("<td>"+rowNum+" , "+colNum+"</td>");
         }
         document.write("</tr>");
      }
   </script>
</table>
```

nested For loops

rowNum Values	colNum Values	Code Written to the Page
1		<tr>
1	1	<td>1,1</td>
1	2	<td>1,2</td>
1	3	<td>1,3</td>
1	4	<td>1,4</td>
1		</tr>
2		<tr>
2	1	<td>2,1</td>
2	2	<td>2,2</td>
2	3	<td>2,3</td>
2	4	<td>2,4</td>
2		</tr>
...		
3	4	<td>3,4</td>
3		</tr>

resulting table

1,1	1,2	1,3	1,4
2,1	2,2	2,3	2,4
3,1	3,2	3,3	3,4

The update expression is not limited to increasing the counter by 1. You can use the other operators introduced in the previous tutorial to create a wide variety of increment patterns. Figure 12-14 shows a few of the many different ways of updating the value of the For loop's counter variable.

Counter values in the For loop **Figure 12-14**

For Loop	Counter Values
for (var i =1 ; i <= 5; i++)	i = 1, 2, 3, 4, 5
for (var i = 5; i > 0; i--)	i = 5, 4, 3, 2, 1
for (var i = 0; i <= 360; i+=60)	i = 0, 60, 120, 180, 240, 300, 360
for (var i =1 ; i <= 64; i*=2)	i = 1, 2, 4, 8, 16, 32, 64

Using For Loops and Arrays

For loops are often used to cycle through the different values contained within an array. The general structure of accessing each value from an array is

```
for (var i = 0; i < array.length; i++) {
   commands involving array[i]
}
```

where *array* is the array containing the values to be looped through and *i* is the counter variable used in the loop. The counter variable in this case represents the index number of an item from the array. The length property is used to determine the size of the array. The last item in the array has an index value of one less than the array's length (because array indices start with zero), so you only continue the loop when the array index is less than the length value.

With this information, you can create a function that employs arrays and a For loop to create a row displaying the names of the seven days of the week. First, you need to use the following code to create an array named dayName containing the three-letter abbreviations of each day:

```
var dayName = new Array("Sun", "Mon", "Tue", "Wed", "Thu", "Fri", "Sat");
```

Then, you'll loop through the values of the dayName array, displaying each value in a header cell with the class name calendar_weekdays, as follows:

```
document.write("<tr>");
for (var i = 0;i<dayName.length;i++) {
   document.write("<th class='calendar_weekdays'>"+dayName[i]+"</th>");
}
document.write("</tr>");
```

You'll add these commands to a new function named writeDayNames(), and then apply the function to your monthly calendar.

To create the writeDayNames() function in the calendar.js file:

1. If you took a break after the previous session, make sure the calendar.js file is open in your text editor and the ccc.htm file is open in your Web browser.
2. At the bottom of the **calendar.js** file, insert the following function:

```
function writeDayNames() {
   var dayName = new Array("Sun", "Mon", "Tue", "Wed", "Thu",
                           "Fri", "Sat");
   document.write("<tr>");
   for (var i = 0;i<dayName.length;i++) {
      document.write("<th class='calendar_weekdays'> "+dayName[i]+
         "</"</th>");
   }
   document.write("</tr>");
}
```

3. Scroll up to the calendar() function, and then insert **writeDayNames()** below the command that calls the writeCalTitle() function, as shown in Figure 12-15.

Figure 12-15 Code for the writeDayNames() function

```
function calendar() {
   var calDate = new Date("March 18, 2011");

   document.write("<table id='calendar_table'>");
   writeCalTitle(calDate);
   writeDayNames();
   document.write("</table>");
}
```

```
function writeDayNames() {
   var dayName = new Array("Sun", "Mon", "Tue", "Wed", "Thu",
                           "Fri", "Sat");
   document.write("<tr>");
   for (var i=0;i < dayName.length;i++) {
      document.write("<th class='calendar_weekdays'> "+dayName[i]+"</th>");
   }
   document.write("</tr>");
}
```

function to write the days of the week

4. Save your changes to the file.
5. Reopen or refresh **ccc.htm** in your Web browser. The monthly calendar displays a second row containing the abbreviations of the seven days of the week. See Figure 12-16.

Figure 12-16 Calendar with day names

Exploring the While Loop

The For loop is only one way of creating a program loop in JavaScript. Before continuing with the calendar() function, you'll investigate a few others. Similar to the For loop is the While loop, in which a command block is run as long as a specific condition is met. Unlike the For loop, the condition in a While loop does not depend on the value of a counter variable. The general syntax of the While loop is

```
while (continue) {
   commands
}
```

where *continue* is any Boolean expression. The Boolean expression is tested before attempting to run the command block. If the expression returns a value of true, the command block is run; otherwise, the command block is skipped and the program loop ends. Every While loop includes a condition under which the loop stops. Without this stop condition, While loops would run without end, causing users' browsers to crash.

The following code shows how to create the table shown in Figure 12-12 as a While loop. In this loop, the command block is run as long as the value of the i variable remains less than 4. Each time through the command block, the loop writes the value of the i variable into a table cell and then increases the value of the i variable by 1.

```
var i = 0;
while (i < 4) {
   document.write("<td>"+i+"</td>");
   i++;
}
```

Like For loops, While loops can be nested within one another. The following code demonstrates how to create the 3 × 4 table shown in Figure 12-13 using nested While loops. Again, the initial values of the counter variables are set before the While loops are run and are updated within the command blocks.

```
var rowNum = 1;
while (rowNum < 4) {
   document.write("<tr>");
   var colNum = 1;
   while (colNum < 5) {
      document.write("<td>"+rowNum+","+colNum+"</td>");
      colNum++;
   }
   document.write("</tr>");
   rowNum++;
}
```

Tip

Use a For loop when your loop contains a counter variable. Use a While loop for a more general stopping condition.

Because For loops and While loops share many of the same characteristics, which one you choose for a given application is often a matter of personal preference. In general, For loops are used whenever you have a counter variable and While loops are used for conditions that don't easily lend themselves to using counters.

Exploring the Do/While Loop

In the For and While loops, the test to determine whether to continue the loop is made before the command block is run. JavaScript also supports a program loop called Do/While that tests the condition to continue the loop right after the latest command block is run. The structure of the Do/While loop is as follows:

```
do {
   commands
   }
while (continue);
```

For example, the following code is used to create the table shown in Figure 12-12 as a Do/While loop:

```
var i = 0;
do {
   document.write("<td>"+i+"</td>");
   i++;
   }
while (i < 4);
```

The Do/While loop is usually used when the program loop should run at least once before testing for the stopping condition.

Creating Program Loops | Reference Window

- To create a For loop, use the syntax
```
for (start; continue; update) {
   commands
}
```
where *start* is an expression that sets the initial value of a counter variable, *continue* is a Boolean expression that must be true for the loop to continue, *update* is an expression that indicates how the value of the counter variable should change each time through the loop, and *commands* are the JavaScript commands that are run each time through the loop.
- To create a While loop, use the following syntax:
```
while (continue) {
   commands
}
```
- To create a Do/While loop, use the following syntax:
```
do {
   commands
   }
while (continue);
```
- To loop through the contents of an array, enter the For loop
```
for (var i = 0; i < array.length; i++) {
   commands involving array[i]
}
```
where *i* is a counter variable representing the indices of the array items and *array* is the array to be looped through.

Evaluating Arrays with Customized Functions | InSight

Program loops and conditional statements are very helpful in creating customized functions to extract information from arrays. Let's look at some examples. The following function returns the maximum value from an array:

```
function maxValue(arr) {
   var maxVal = arr[0];
   for (var i = 0; i < arr.length; i++) {
      if (arr[i] > maxVal) maxVal=arr[i];
   }
   return maxVal;
}
```

The maxValue() function loops through all the entries in the arr array, testing whether each item's value is greater than the maxVal variable. The function then returns the value of maxVal, which represents the maximum value found among all of the values in the array. The statement

```
var maximumValue = maxValue(dataArray);
```

returns the maximum value from the dataArray array, storing the answer in the maximumValue variable. To find the minimum value, revise the function with an If condition that tests whether values of arr[i] are less than the current minimum.

To return a random value from an array, the following function uses the Math.random() method along with the Math.floor() method and the length property to generate a random integer between 0 and the value of the array length:

```
function randValue(arr) {
   return arr[Math.floor(Math.random()*arr.length)];
}
```

The following statment shows how to call the function, returning a randomly chosen entry from the dataArray array:

```
var randomValue = randValue(dataArray);
```

Working with Conditional Statements

Your next task in the calendar application is to enter the table rows for the days of the month. Each table cell within those rows will contain a number for the corresponding day of the month. After reaching the last day of the month, you'll stop writing table cells and rows. This process requires some kind of program loop. The number of times this loop runs depends on the number of days in the current month. Because months have differing numbers of days, you need to create the following array containing the length of each month to use in conjunction with the loop:

```
var dayCount = new Array(31,28,31,30,31,30,31,31,30,31,30,31);
```

You'll create this array within a function named daysInMonth(). Like the writeCalTitle() function you created earlier, the daysInMonth() function has a single parameter, calendarDay, representing a date object. The function creates two variables, thisYear and thisMonth, containing the four-digit year value and month value. The thisMonth variable is used to supply the index from which the number of days in the month is returned by the function.

To start creating the daysInMonth() function:

1. Return to the **calendar.js** file in your text editor.
2. At the bottom of the file, insert the following code, as shown in Figure 12-17:

```
function daysInMonth(calendarDay) {
   var thisYear = calendarDay.getFullYear();
   var thisMonth = calendarDay.getMonth();
   var dayCount = new Array(31,28,31,30,31,30,31,31,30,31,30,31);
   return dayCount[thisMonth]; // return the number of days in the
   month
}
```

Figure 12-17 Initial daysInMonth() function

```
function writeDayNames() {
   var dayName = new Array("Sun", "Mon", "Tue", "Wed", "Thu",
                           "Fri", "Sat");
   document.write("<tr>");
   for (var i=0;i < dayName.length;i++) {
      document.write("<th class='calendar_weekdays'> "+dayName[i]+"</th>");
   }
   document.write("</tr>");
}

function daysInMonth(calendarDay) {
   var thisYear = calendarDay.getFullYear();
   var thisMonth = calendarDay.getMonth();
   var dayCount = new Array(31,28,31,30,31,30,31,31,30,31,30,31);
   return dayCount[thisMonth]; // return the number of days in the month
}
```

function to return the number of days in a given month

The dayCount array you've created has one problem: February sometimes has 29 days, not 28 days. Figure 12-18 shows the general process to determine whether a particular year is a leap year. Any year that is not divisible by 4 is not a leap year. So, a year such as 2015 is not a leap year because it is not divisible by 4. Beyond that, the situation is a little more complex. In most cases, a year that is divisible by 4 is a leap year. The only exceptions are years that occur at the turn of the century that are divisible by 100. These years are not leap years unless they are also divisible by 400. Thus, years such as 1800, 1900, and 2100 are not leap years even though they are divisible by 4. Years such as 2000 and 2400 are leap years because they are divisible by 400.

Process to calculate leap years — Figure 12-18

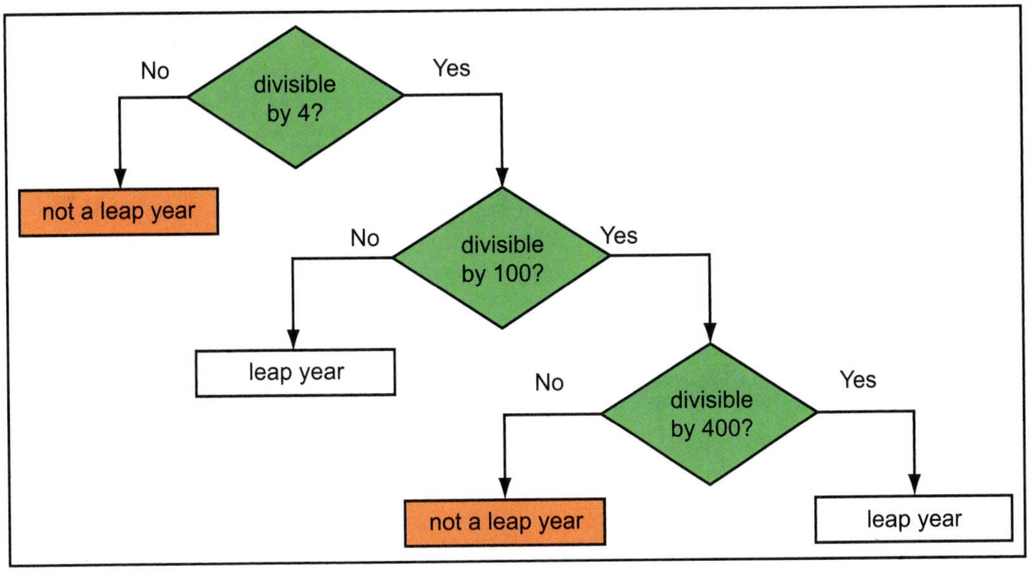

For the daysInMonth() function to determine whether February has 28 or 29 days, it must examine the year value and then set the value for the number of days in February to either 28 or 29 based on the year value. You can do this through a conditional statement. A **conditional statement** is a statement that runs a command or command block only when certain circumstances are met.

Exploring the If Statement

The most common conditional statement is the If statement. The syntax of the If statement is

```
if (condition) {
   commands
}
```

where *condition* is a Boolean expression that is either true or false, and *commands* is the command block that is run if *condition* is true. If only one command is run, you can eliminate the command block and enter the If statement as follows:

```
if (condition) command;
```

The *condition* expression uses the same comparison and logical operators you've used in the conditional operator from the previous tutorial. Unlike a comparison operator that changes the value of a variable based on a condition, a conditional statement determines whether to run a particular command or command block. For example, the following If statement sets the value of the dayCount array for February to 29 if the year value is 2012 (a leap year):

```
if (thisYear == 2012) {
   dayCount[1] = 29;
}
```

For the calendar application, you need to create a conditional expression that indicates whether the current year is a leap year. Start by looking at methods of determining whether the year is divisible by 4. One way is to use the % operator, which is also known as the modulus operator. The **modulus operator** returns the integer remainder after dividing one integer by another. For example, the expression

```
2015 % 4
```

> **Tip**
>
> A common programming error is to use = instead of == to test whether two items are equal. The = symbol assigns values; it does not compare objects.

returns the value 3 because 3 is the remainder after dividing 2015 by 4. To test whether a year value is divisible by 4, you use the conditional expression

```
thisYear % 4 == 0
```

where the thisYear variable contains the four-digit year value. The following is the complete If statement to change the value of the dayCount array for the month of February:

```
if (thisYear % 4 == 0) {
   dayCount[1] = 29;
}
```

Nesting If Statements

The above If statement works as a simple approximation, but it is not completely accurate because it doesn't take into account century years. You need to include a second test to account for the different leap year rule applicable during century years. The general structure of this nested If statement is:

```
if (thisYear % 4 == 0) {
   if statement for century years
}
```

The nested If statement needs to test for two conditions: (1) the year is not divisible by 100, and (2) the year is divisible by 400. The expressions for the two conditions are:

```
thisYear % 100 != 0
thisYear % 400 == 0
```

If either of those two conditions is true for a year evenly divisible by 4, then the year is a leap year. Note that you use the != operator to test for an inequality in the first expression. You then combine these two expressions into a single expression using the or operator (||). The combined expression is:

```
(thisYear % 100 != 0) || (thisYear % 400 == 0)
```

Finally, you place this conditional expression in a nested If statement. Following is the complete code:

```
if (thisYear % 4 == 0) {
   if ((thisYear % 100 !=0) || (thisYear % 400 == 0)) {
      dayCount[1] = 29;
   }
}
```

Under this set of nested If statements, the number of days in February is 29 only if the thisYear variable is divisible by 4 *and* only if it also is divisible by 400 or *not* divisible by 100. Take some time to compare this set of nested If statements with the chart shown in Figure 12-18 to confirm that it satisfies all possible conditions for leap years. Putting this nested If statement into the daysInMonth() function returns the number of days for any month in any given year.

By adding this nested If statement to the daysInMonth() function, you arrive at the final version of the function:

```
function daysInMonth(calendarDay) {
   var thisYear = calendarDay.getFullYear();
   var thisMonth = calendarDay.getMonth();
   var dayCount = new Array(31,28,31,30,31,30,31,31,30,31,30,31);
   if (thisYear % 4 == 0) {
      if ((thisYear % 100 !=0) || (thisYear % 400 == 0)) {
         dayCount[1] = 29; // this is a leap year
      }
   }
   return dayCount[thisMonth]; // return the number of days in the
                                  month
}
```

You'll complete the daysInMonth() function in the calendar.js file.

To create the final daysInMonth() function:

1. In the **calendar.js** file, before the final return statement in the daysInMonth() function, insert the following nested If structure, as shown in Figure 12-19:

```
if (thisYear % 4 == 0) {
   if ((thisYear % 100 != 0) || (thisYear % 400 == 0)) {
      dayCount[1] = 29; // this is a leap year
   }
}
```

Figure 12-19 Complete daysInMonth() function

```
function daysInMonth(calendarDay) {
   var thisYear = calendarDay.getFullYear();
   var thisMonth = calendarDay.getMonth();
   var dayCount = new Array(31,28,31,30,31,30,31,31,30,31,30,31);

   if (thisYear % 4 == 0) {
      if ((thisYear % 100 != 0) || (thisYear % 400 == 0)) {
         dayCount[1] = 29; // this is a leap year
      }
   }

   return dayCount[thisMonth]; // return the number of days in the month
}
```

nested If statement to test for the presence of a leap year

2. Save your changes to the file.

Exploring the If...Else Statement

The If statement runs a command or a command block only if the conditional expression returns the value true; it does nothing if a value of false is returned. On some occasions, you may want to choose between two alternate sets of commands. In those cases, you use an If...Else structure, in which one set of commands is run if the conditional expression is true and a different set of commands is run if the expression is false. The general structure of an If...Else statement is:

```
if (condition) {
   commands if condition is true
} else {
   commands if otherwise
}
```

If only a single expression is run in response to the If statement, you can use the following abbreviated form:

```
if (condition) command if condition is true
else command if otherwise;
```

The following example shows an If...Else statement that runs one of two possible document.write() commands:

```
if (day == "Friday") document.write("Thank goodness it's Friday")
else document.write("Today is " + day);
```

In this statement, the text "Thank goodness it's Friday" is written to the document if the value of the day variable is Friday. Otherwise, the text string "Today is *day*" is written to the document, where *day* is the value of the day variable.

Like the If statement, If...Else statements can be nested. With a nested If...Else statement, you place the inner statements within command blocks. The following nested If... Else statement chooses between three possible text strings to write to a document:

```
if (day == "Friday") document.write("Thank goodness it's Friday")
else {
   if (day == "Monday") document.write("Blue Monday")
   else document.write("Today is " + day);
}
```

Tip

To make it easier to interpret nested If statements, always indent your code, lining up all of the commands for one set of nested statements.

Some programmers advocate always using curly braces even if the command block contains only a single command. This practice visually separates one Else clause from another. Also, when reading through nested statements, it can be helpful to remember that an Else clause usually pairs with the nearest preceding If statement.

Using Multiple Else...If Statements

For more complex scripts, you may need to choose from several alternatives. In these cases, you can specify multiple Else clauses, each with its own If statement. This is not a new type of conditional structure, but rather a way of taking advantage of the syntax rules inherent in the If...Else statement. The general structure for choosing from several alternatives is

```
if (condition 1) {
   first command block
}  else if (condition 2) {
   second command block
}  else if (condition 3) {
   third command block
}  else {
   default command block
}
```

where *condition 1*, *condition 2*, *condition 3*, and so on are the different conditions to be tested. This construction should always include a final Else clause that is run by default if none of the previous conditional expressions return the value true. When a browser runs this series of statements, it stops examining the remaining Else clauses when it encounters the first true Else clause (because there no longer is an Else condition to investigate). The following example is a structure that employs multiple Else...If conditions:

```
if (day == "Friday") {
   document.write("Thank goodness it's Friday");
} else if (day == "Monday") {
   document.write("Blue Monday");
} else if (day == "Saturday") {
   document.write("Sleep in today");
} else {
   document.write("Today is "+day);
}
```

Tip

To simplify code, keep your nesting of multiple If statements to three or less (if possible). For more conditions, use the case/switch structure.

Working with Conditional Statements | Reference Window

- To test a single condition, use the construction
```
if (condition) {
   commands
}
```
where *condition* is a Boolean expression and *commands* is a command block run if the conditional expression is true.
- To test between two conditions, use the following construction:
```
if (condition) {
   commands if condition is true
} else {
   commands if otherwise
}
```
- To test multiple conditions, use the construction
```
if (condition 1) {
   first command block
} else if (condition 2) {
   second command block
} else if (condition 3) {
   third command block
} else {
   default command block
}
```
where *condition 1*, *condition 2*, *condition 3*, and so on are the different conditions to be tested. If no conditional expressions return the value true, the default command block is run.

Exploring the Switch Statement

When you need to choose from several possible conditions, a series of Else...If statements might be too cumbersome to work with. A simpler structure is the Switch statement (also known as the Case statement), in which different commands are run based upon various possible values of a variable. The syntax of a Switch statement is

```
switch (expression) {
   case label1: commands1
   break;
   case label2: commands2
   break;
   case label3: commands3
   break;
...
   default: default commands
}
```

where *expression* is an expression that returns a value other than a Boolean value; *label1*, *label2*, *label3*, and so on are possible values of that expression; *commands1*, *commands2*, *commands3*, and so on are the commands to run for each matching label; and *default commands* are the commands to be run if no label matches the value returned by *expression*. The previous Else...If statement could be rewritten as the following Switch statement:

```
switch (day) {
   case "Friday": document.write("Thank goodness it's Friday"); break;
   case "Monday": document.write("Blue Monday"); break;
   case "Saturday": document.write("Sleep in today"); break;
   default: document.write("Today is "+day);
}
```

Tip

Use the Switch statement for conditional statements that involve variables with several possible values.

As the browser moves through the different case values, it executes any command or command block in which the label matches the expression's value. The break statement is optional and is used to halt the execution of the Switch statement once a match has been found. For programs in which you want to allow for multiple matching cases, you can omit the break statements and JavaScript will continue moving through the Switch statements, running all matching commands.

Reference Window | Creating a Switch Statement

- To create a Switch statement to test for different values of an expression, use the structure

```
switch (expression) {
   case label1: commands1
   break;
   case label2: commands2
   break;
   case label3: commands3
   break;

...

   default: default commands
}
```

where *expression* is an expression that returns a value other than a Boolean value; *label1*, *label2*, *label3*, and so on are possible values of that expression; *commands1*, *commands2*, *commands3*, and so on are the commands to run for each matching label; and *default commands* are the commands to be run if no label matches the value returned by *expression*.

At this point, you are familiar with all of the tools you will need for completing the calendar() function. In the next session, you'll enter the code to create a monthly calendar for any date you choose.

Review | Session 12.2 Quick Check

1. What is a program loop? Name three types of program loops supported by JavaScript.
2. What expressions would you place in a For statement to use a counter variable named i that starts with the value 0 and continues up to 100 in increments of 10?

3. What For statement creates a table row consisting of five table cells? Assume the table cells display the text "Column *i*" where *i* is the value of the counter variable and the value of the counter variable ranges from 1 to 5 in increments of 1.
4. What is a conditional statement? What is the most commonly used conditional statement?
5. What code writes the text "Internet Explorer Browser" to the document if the Boolean variable WebBrowser equals true?
6. The WebBrowser variable has been changed to a text string variable that can equal either "IE" or "Mozilla". Write an If...Else statement to display the text "Internet Explorer Browser" if WebBrowser equals "IE" and "Mozilla Browser" otherwise.
7. The WebBrowser variable can now equal "IE", "Opera", "Safari", or "Firefox". Write a series of Else...If statements that write the name of the browser to the document. If WebBrowser equals none of the four text strings listed above, write the text "Generic Browser" to the document.
8. Answer Question 7 using a Switch statement. Use a break statement to break off from processing the Switch statement once a match has been found.

Session 12.3

Creating the calendar() Function

You are ready to complete the calendar application. You've already written the code that writes the calendar title and the row of abbreviated day names. In this session, you'll complete the calendar by adding in table rows and cells displaying the days of the month. Figure 12-20 shows a preview of the calendar you'll create for a date of March 25, 2011.

Monthly calendar **Figure 12-20**

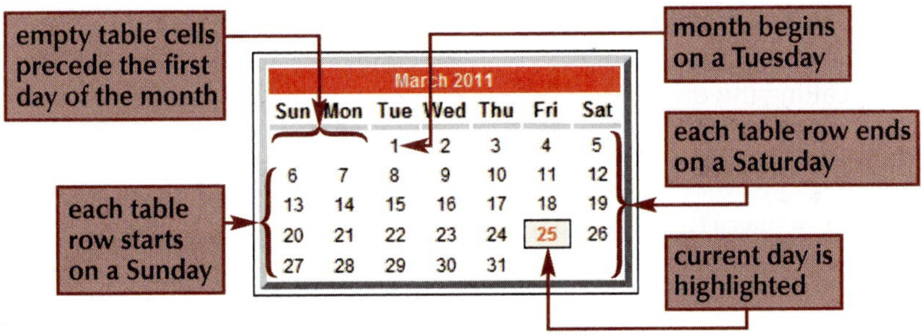

To complete this table, the program code must do the following:

- Calculate the day of the week in which the month starts.
- Write blank table cells for the last days of the previous month at the start of a table row.
- Loop through all of the days of the current month, writing each date in a different table cell, starting a new table row on each Sunday.

You'll place all of these commands in a function named writeCalDays(). The function will have a single parameter named calendarDay containing a date object for the current date. You'll add this function to the calendar.js file.

To insert the writeCalDays() function:

1. If you took a break after the previous session, make sure the calendar.js file is open in your text editor and the ccc.htm file is open in your Web browser.
2. At the bottom of the **calendar.js** file, insert the following function, as shown in Figure 12-21:

```
function writeCalDays(calendarDay) {
   // determine the starting day of the week
   // write blank cells preceding the starting day
   // write cells for each day of the month
}
```

Figure 12-21 **Code to begin the writeCalDays() function**

```
function daysInMonth(calendarDay) {
   var thisYear = calendarDay.getFullYear();
   var thisMonth = calendarDay.getMonth();
   var dayCount = new Array(31,28,31,30,31,30,31,31,30,31,30,31);

   if (thisYear % 4 == 0) {
      if ((thisYear % 100 != 0) || (thisYear % 400 == 0)) {
         dayCount[1] = 29; // this is a leap year
      }
   }

   return dayCount[thisMonth]; // return the number of days in the month
}

function writeCalDays(calendarDay) {
   // determine the starting day of the week
   // write blank cells preceding the starting day
   // write cells for each day of the month
}
```

initial writeCalDays() function

3. Save your changes to the file.

Setting the First Day of the Month

To loop through all of the days of the month, you'll need to keep track of the day currently being written to the calendar table. You'll store this information in a variable named dayCount. The initial value of the dayCount variable will be set to 1 and will increase up to the total number of days in the month. You can determine the total days in the month by calling the daysInMonth() function you created in the previous session. The first two lines of the writeCalDays() function are:

```
var dayCount = 1;
var totalDays = daysInMonth(calendarDay);
```

Next, you reset the value of the calendarDay variable so that it is equal to the first day of the month. This is done using the setDate() method. The command is:

```
calendarDay.setDate(1);
```

Finally, the code must determine on which day of the week this date falls. The getDay() method returns this information, with values ranging from 0 (Sunday) to 6 (Saturday). You'll store this value in a variable named weekDay. The following command declares the weekDay variable:

```
var weekDay = calendarDay.getDay();
```

You'll add these commands to the writeCalDays() function.

To declare the initial variables in the writeCalDays() function:

1. Below the first comment line in the writeCalDays() function, insert the following commands, as shown in Figure 12-22:

```
var dayCount = 1;
var totalDays = daysInMonth(calendarDay);
calendarDay.setDate(1);                    // set the date to the first
 day of the month
var weekDay = calendarDay.getDay();  // the day of week of the
 first day
```

Figure 12-22

Code to set the first day of the month

```
function writeCalDays(calendarDay) {
   // determine the starting day of the week
   var dayCount = 1;
   var totalDays = daysInMonth(calendarDay);
   calendarDay.setDate(1);              // set the date to the first day of the month
   var weekDay = calendarDay.getDay();  // the day of week of the first day

   // write blank cells preceding the starting day
   // write cells for each day of the month
}
```

2. Save your changes to the file.

Placing the First Day of the Month

Prior to the first day of the month, the calendar table should show only empty table cells. The value of the weekDay variable indicates how many empty table cells you need to create. For example, if the value of the weekDay variable is 4 (Thursday), you know that there are four blank table cells—corresponding to Sunday, Monday, Tuesday, and Wednesday—that need to be written at the start of the first table row. The following loop creates the blank table cells:

```
document.write("<tr>");
for (var i = 0; i < weekDay; i++) {
   document.write("<td></td>");
}
```

If weekDay equals 0—indicating that the month starts on a Sunday—then no blank table cells will be written because the value of the counter variable i is never less than the value of the weekDay variable. You'll insert these commands into the writeCalDays() function.

To write the initial blank cells of the first table row:

1. Below the second comment line, insert the following For loop, as shown in Figure 12-23:

```
document.write("<tr>");
for (var i = 0; i < weekDay; i++) {
   document.write("<td></td>");
}
```

Figure 12-23

Code to write the preceding blank table cells

```
function writeCalDays(calendarDay) {
   // determine the starting day of the week
   var dayCount = 1;
   var totalDays = daysInMonth(calendarDay);
   calendarDay.setDate(1);              // set the date to the first day of the month
   var weekDay = calendarDay.getDay();  // the day of week of the first day

   // write blank cells preceding the starting day
   document.write("<tr>");
   for (var i=0; i < weekDay; i++) {
      document.write("<td></td>");
   }

   // write cells for each day of the month
}
```

loop to write empty table cells to the calendar table

2. Save your changes to the file.

3. Reopen or refresh **ccc.htm** in your Web browser and verify that no run-time errors have been introduced by incorrectly typing any of the code. The appearance of the page remains unchanged from Figure 12-16.

Writing the Calendar Days

Now that the code determines into which table cell the initial date is placed, the rest of the function will be devoted to inserting the remaining dates. This is done using a While loop. Each time through the loop, the function should write the table cells containing the calendar dates, and, if necessary, add new rows to the table. At the end of the command block, the dayCount variable should be increased, moving to the next day in the month. The general structure of the While loop is:

```
while (dayCount <= totalDays) {
   write the table rows and cells
   move to the next day
}
```

You'll add this While loop to the writeCalDays() function.

To insert the While loop to the writeCalDays() function:

1. Below the last comment line in the writeCalDays() function, insert the following While loop, as shown in Figure 12-24:

```
while (dayCount <= totalDays) {
   // write the table rows and cells
   // move to the next day
}
```

Figure 12-24 While loop for adding the calendar days

```
function writeCalDays(calendarDay) {
   // determine the starting day of the week
   var dayCount = 1;
   var totalDays = daysInMonth(calendarDay);
   calendarDay.setDate(1);                // set the date to the first day of the month
   var weekDay = calendarDay.getDay();    // the day of week of the first day

   // write blank cells preceding the starting day
   document.write("<tr>");
   for (var i=0; i < weekDay; i++) {
      document.write("<td></td>");
   }

   // write cells for each day of the month
   while (dayCount <= totalDays) {
      // write the table rows and cells
      // move to the next day
   }
}
```

loop to write the cells containing day numbers

2. Save your changes to the file.

Each new table row in the calendar table starts with a Sunday. The first command in the While loop's command block needs to determine whether the value of the weekDay variable corresponds to a Sunday. If so, the function will write the opening <tr> tag for the table row. The If statement appears as follows:

```
if (weekDay == 0) document.write("<tr>");
```

This expression uses the same weekDay variable you used previously to determine the day on which the month started. As you proceed through the While loop, the value of this variable is constantly updated to reflect the current calendar date being written. The next step is to write a table cell containing the date. Because every date belongs to the class calendar_dates (refer to Figure 12-4), the code is:

```
document.write("<td class='calendar_dates'>"+dayCount+"</td>");
```

Finally, because every table row ends with a Saturday, you also must test whether the day being written falls on a Saturday. If this is the case, you need to write a </tr> to end the table row. The command to do this is:

```
if (weekDay == 6) document.write("</tr>");
```

In the final part of the command block for the While loop, you update the values of the dayCount, calendarDay, and weekDay variables so that the next time through the loop they point to the next day in the calendar. The commands are similar to what you used to set the initial values of these variables before the While loop, except that you increase the dayCount variable by 1 using the ++ increment operator as follows:

```
dayCount++;
calendarDay.setDate(dayCount);
weekDay = calendarDay.getDay();
```

The complete code for the While loop is:

```
while (dayCount <= totalDays) {
   // write the table rows and cells
   if (weekDay == 0) document.write("<tr>");
   document.write("<td class='calendar_dates'>"+dayCount+"</td>");
   if (weekDay == 6) document.write("</tr>");
```

```
      // move to the next day
      dayCount++;
      calendarDay.setDate(dayCount);
      weekDay = calendarDay.getDay();
   }
```

After the While loop is finished running, you'll write a closing </tr> tag to ensure that the table row is closed off if the last day of the month does not fall on a Saturday. You do not need to write blank table cells at the end of the month like you did at the beginning because browsers will simply ignore any missing table cells at the end of a table row.

To add commands to the While loop:

1. Below the first comment line within the While loop, insert the following commands:

```
if (weekDay == 0) document.write("<tr>");
document.write("<td class='calendar_dates'>"+dayCount+"</td>");
if (weekDay == 6) document.write("</tr>");
```

2. Below the second comment line within the While loop, insert the following commands:

```
dayCount++;
calendarDay.setDate(dayCount);
weekDay = calendarDay.getDay();
```

3. Below the While loop, insert the following command:

```
document.write("</tr>");
```

Figure 12-25 shows the revised code for the writeCalDays() function.

Figure 12-25 **Commands added to the While loop**

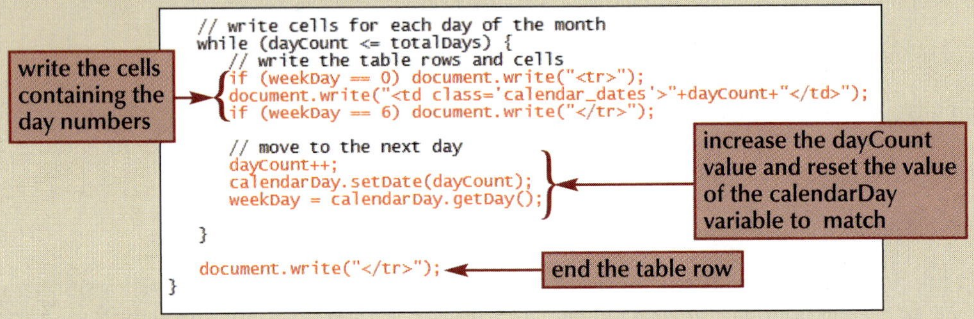
// write cells for each day of the month
while (dayCount <= totalDays) {
// write the table rows and cells
if (weekDay == 0) document.write("<tr>");
document.write("<td class='calendar_dates'>"+dayCount+"</td>");
if (weekDay == 6) document.write("</tr>");
// move to the next day
dayCount++;
calendarDay.setDate(dayCount);
weekDay = calendarDay.getDay();
}
document.write("</tr>");
}
write the cells containing the day numbers
increase the dayCount value and reset the value of the calendarDay variable to match
end the table row

4. Save your changes to the file.

Next, you have to run the writeCalDays() function from the calendar() function. You can then test the monthly calendar to verify that it correctly lays out the dates in the calendar.

To test the calendar() function:

1. Scroll up to the calendar() function, and then insert the following command, as shown in Figure 12-26:

```
writeCalDays(calDate);
```

Figure 12-26 **Code to call the writeCalDays() function**

```
function calendar() {
   var calDate = new Date("March 18, 2011");

   document.write("<table id='calendar_table'>");
   writeCalTitle(calDate);
   writeDayNames();
   writeCalDays(calDate);
   document.write("</table>");
}
```

2. Save your changes to the file.
3. Reload **ccc.htm** in your Web browser. The monthly calendar shows all of the dates laid out in different table cells and rows. See Figure 12-27.

Figure 12-27 **Monthly calendar table**

Highlighting the Current Date

Maria likes the calendar's appearance but mentions that the calendar should also highlight the current date. To indicate the current date, the corresponding table cell should have the ID calendar_today. As shown in Figure 12-4, a different style is applied to the table cell with this ID. As you loop through each day in the calendar, you need to insert an If statement that tests whether the day being written to the table represents the current date. If it does, you write the HTML code

```
<td class='calendar_dates' id='calendar_today'>day</td>
```

where *day* is the day number; otherwise, the script should write

```
<td class='calendar_dates' >day</td>
```

omitting the ID attribute. To do this test, you'll create a new variable named currentDate, setting it equal to the date value returned by applying the getDate() date object method to the calendarDay parameter. You need to create this variable before the While loop because the While loop alters the value of the calendarDay parameter as it moves through the calendar rows and cells.

To highlight the current date in the calendar:

1. Return to the **calendar.js** file in your text editor, and then scroll down to the writeCalDays() function.
2. Insert the following line of code as the first command in the function:

```
var currentDay = calendarDay.getDate();
```

3. In the While loop, replace the command that writes the table cell for each day with the following If structure:

```
if (dayCount == currentDay) {
   // highlight the current day
   document.write("<td class='calendar_dates' id='calendar_
      today'>"+dayCount+"</td>");
} else {
   // display the day as usual
   document.write("<td class='calendar_dates'>"+dayCount+"</td>");
}
```

Figure 12-28 shows the final version of the writeCalDays() function.

Figure 12-28 Code to highlight the current day

```
function writeCalDays(calendarDay) {
   var currentDay = calendarDay.getDate();

   // determine the starting day of the week
   var dayCount = 1;
   var totalDays = daysInMonth(calendarDay);
   calendarDay.setDate(1);              // set the date to the first day of the month
   var weekDay = calendarDay.getDay();  // the day of week of the first day

   // write blank cells preceding the starting day
   document.write("<tr>");
   for (var i=0; i < weekDay; i++) {
      document.write("<td></td>");
   }

   // write cells for each day of the month
   while (dayCount <= totalDays) {
      // write the table rows and cells
      if (weekDay == 0) document.write("<tr>");

      if (dayCount == currentDay) {
         // highlight the current day
         document.write("<td class='calendar_dates' id='calendar_today'>"+dayCount+"</td>");
      } else {
         // display the day as usual
         document.write("<td class='calendar_dates'>"+dayCount+"</td>");
      }

      if (weekDay == 6) document.write("</tr>");

      // move to the next day
      dayCount++;
      calendarDay.setDate(dayCount);
      weekDay = calendarDay.getDay();

   }

   document.write("</tr>");
}
```

write the cell for the current day using the calendar_today ID

4. Save your changes to the file.
5. Reload **ccc.htm** in your Web browser. March 18 is highlighted in the calendar because this is the date specified in the calendar() function. See Figure 12-29.

Figure 12-29 Completed home page for the CCC

the Chamberlain Civic Center
March 2011
Sun Mon Tue Wed Thu Fri Sat
1 2 3 4 5
6 7 8 9 10 11 12
13 14 15 16 17 18 19
20 21 22 23 24 25 26
27 28 29 30 31
Home
Tickets
Events
Tour
Directions
Hours
Packages
Contact Us
March is another banner month at the Chamberlain Civic Center, with performances of the award-winning musical, The Producers by the Broadway Touring Company on March 4, 5, and 6. Tickets are going fast, so order yours today.
Celebrate the season on March 11 with the Chamberlain Symphony and their special selection of classical music with Spring themes. The next day, March 12, exercise your mind by attending the Charles Dickens mystery Edwin Drood.
Jazz lovers have a lot to celebrate in March with a visit from The Jazz Masters on the 17th. Then on March 24, enjoy the music of The Duke with An Ellington Tribute performed by the Jazz Company of Kansas City.
Pins, bottles, plates, and chairs are flying at the Chamberlain Civic Center in March. The Taiwan Acrobats return with another amazing performance on Sunday, March 13. On March 20, the Madtown Jugglers get into the act with their unique blend of comedy, juggling, and madness.
Enjoy a classical brunch every Sunday afternoon with music provided by the Carson Quartet. Seating is limited, so please reserve your table.
The Chamberlain Civic Center · 2011 Canyon Drive · Chamberlain, SD 57325 · (800) 555-8741
highlighted date specified in the calendar() function

Setting the Calendar Date

Maria is pleased with the calendar application, but wants it to display dates other than March 18, 2011. You can display specific dates by changing the value of the calDate variable in the calendar() function. Another option is to include the date value as a parameter value in the calendar() function, allowing the calendar() function to be easily used for any date. Maria asks you to make this change.

It would be ideal if the calendar() function worked like the JavaScript Date() method, creating a monthly calendar for a specified date with the command

```
calendar("March 18, 2011")
```

but producing the calendar for the current month if no date is specified, for example

```
calendar()
```

To test for the presence or absence of a parameter value, you insert an If condition that tests whether the parameter value is null. If the parameter value is null, the value of the calDate variable is set to the current date; otherwise, the calDate variable is set to the date specified in the calendarDay parameter. The revised calendar() function would appear as follows:

```
function calendar(calendarDay) {
   if (calendarDay == null) calDate = new Date()
   else calDate = new Date(calendarDay);
...
```

You'll edit the calendar() function to add this feature and then retest the calendar() function using both the current date and a date that you specify.

To complete and test the calendar() function:

1. Return to the **calendar.js** file in your text editor.
2. Go to the calendar() function and add the parameter **calendarDay** to the function line.
3. Replace the first line of the calendar() function with the following If statement:

```
if (calendarDay == null) calDate=new Date()
else calDate = new Date(calendarDay);
```

Figure 12-30 highlights the revised code of the calendar() function.

Figure 12-30 Final calendar() function

```
function calendar(calendarDay) {
   if (calendarDay == null) calDate=new Date()
   else calDate = new Date(calendarDay);

   document.write("<table id='calendar_table'>");
   writeCalTitle(calDate);
   writeDayNames();
   writeCalDays(calDate);
   document.write("</table>");
}
```

add the calendarDay parameter to the function

if no calendarDay is specified, use the current date

otherwise, use the date from the calendarDay parameter

4. Save your changes to the file.
5. Close the **calendar.js** file, and then refresh **ccc.htm** in your Web browser. Verify that the monthly calendar for the current date appears at the top of the Web page.
6. Open the **ccc.htm** file in your text editor, and then change the statement that runs the monthly calendar to the following, as shown in Figure 12-31:

```
calendar("March 25, 2011");
```

Figure 12-31 Code to display the monthly calendar for March 25, 2011

```
<body>
   <div id="head">
      <script type="text/javascript">
         calendar("March 25, 2011");
      </script>
      <img src="ccc.jpg" alt="Chamberlain Civic Center" />
   </div>
```

7. Close the **ccc.htm** file, saving your changes.
8. Reopen **ccc.htm** in your Web browser, and then verify that the monthly calendar for March 25, 2011 appears on the Web page.
9. Close your Web browser.

Maria is pleased with the final version of the calendar() function. Because of how the function and style sheets were designed, she can use this utility in many of the other pages on the CCC Web site with only a minimal amount of recoding in the Web documents.

Managing Program Loops and Conditional Statements

Although you are finished with the calendar() function, you should still become familiar with some features of program loops and conditional statements for future work with these JavaScript structures. You'll examine three features in more detail: the break, continue, and label commands.

Exploring the break Command

You briefly saw how to use the break command in creating a Switch statement, but the break command can be used anywhere within program code. The purpose of the break command is to terminate any program loop or conditional statement. When a browser runs a break command, it passes control to the statement immediately following it. The break statement is most often used to exit a program loop without waiting for the loop to end when the stopping condition is met. The syntax of the break command is:

```
break;
```

In some cases, you may need to create a loop that examines an array for the presence or absence of a particular value such as a customer ID number or name. The code for the loop might look as follows:

```
for (var i = 0; i< names.length; i++) {
   if (names[i] == "Valdez") {
      document.write("Valdez is in the list");
   }
}
```

Although this loop indicates whether the names array contains the text string Valdez, what would happen if the array had tens of thousands of entries? It would be time consuming to keep examining the array if Valdez was encountered within the first few array items. This is where the break command can be helpful to avoid wasting processing time. The following For loop breaks off when it encounters the Valdez text string, keeping the browser from needlessly examining the rest of the array:

```
for (var i = 0; i< names.length; i++) {
   if (names[i] == "Valdez") {
      document.write("Valdez is in the list");
      break;  // stop processing the For loop
   }
}
```

Exploring the continue Command

The continue command is similar to the break command except that instead of stopping the program loop altogether, the continue command stops processing the commands in the current iteration of the loop and jumps to the next iteration. For example, you could create a For loop to add the values from an array. The code for this For loop would be:

```
var total = 0;
for (var i = 0; i < data.length; i++) {
   total += data[i];
}
```

Each time through the loop, the value of the current entry in the data array is added to the total variable. When the For loop is finished, the total variable is equal to the sum of the values in the data array. However, what would happen if this were a sparse array containing several empty entries? In that case, when a browser encountered a missing or null value, that value would be added to the total variable; this would result in the value of the total variable also being equal to missing or null. One way to fix this problem would be to use the continue statement, jumping out of the loop if a missing or null value were encountered. The revised code would look as follows:

```
var total = 0;
for (var i = 0; i < data.length; i++) {
   if (data[i] == null) continue;  // continue with the next iteration
   total += data[i];
}
```

In this code, the value of the total variable is not updated if a null value is encountered but rather the loop jumps to the next step in the iteration.

Exploring Statement Labels

Labels are used to identify statements in JavaScript code so that you can reference those statements elsewhere in a program. The syntax of the label is

```
label: statement
```

where *label* is the text of the label and *statement* is the statement identified by the label. You've already seen labels with the Switch statement, but they can also be used with other program loops and conditional statements to provide more control over how statements are processed. Labels are often used with break and continue commands to direct a program to the statement that it should go to if it needs to break off or continue a program loop. The syntax to reference a label in such cases is simply:

```
break label;
```

or

```
continue label;
```

For example, the following nested For loop contains two labels: one for the outer loop and the other for the inner loop. The program breaks to the outer loop when the variable i is equal to the variable j:

```
//outer_loop:
for(i=1; i<4; i++) {
   document.write("<br />"+"outer "+i+": ");
   //inner_loop:
   for(j=1; j<4; j++) {
      document.write("inner "+j+" ");
      if(j==x)    //break outer_loop;
   }
}
```

As the code is run, it writes the following text to the document:

```
<br />outer 1: inner 1
<br />outer 2: inner 1
<br />outer 2: inner 2
<br />outer 3: inner 1
<br />outer 3: inner 2
<br />outer 3: inner 3
```

Some programmers discourage the use of break, continue, and label statements because they create confusing code as a script jumps in and out of loops. Most of the tasks you perform with these statements can also be performed by carefully setting up the conditions for program loops. For example, to create the same output from the above code without labels or the break command, you could define the counter variable used in the inner loop so that it is always less than or equal to the counter value of the outer loop. The following code demonstrates how this might be done:

```
for(i=1; i<4; i++) {
   document.write("<br />"+"outer "+i+": ");
   for(j=1; j<=i; j++) {
      document.write("inner "+j+" ");
   }
}
```

Tip

Avoid using break and continue statements to cut off loops unless necessary. Instead, set break conditions in the conditional expression of the loop.

Using Multidimensional Arrays | InSight

A matrix is a multidimensional array in which each item is referenced by two or more index values. The following is an example of a two-dimensional matrix consisting of three rows and four columns.

```
| 4  15   8  2 |
| 1   3  18  6 |
| 3   7  10  4 |
```

In this matrix, each value is referenced by a row index number and column index number. The value 18, for example, is located in the second row and third column and has the index numbers (2, 3).

Although matrices are commonly used in various programming languages, JavaScript does not support them. You can mimic the behavior of matrices in JavaScript by nesting one array within another. For example, the following code creates the array mArray as an array literal with another set of arrays nested within it. The values of the mArray variable match the values of the matrix shown above.

```
var mArray = [ [4, 15, 8, 2], [1, 3, 18, 6], [3, 7, 10, 4] ]
```

Values within the mArray variable can be accessed with the expression

```
mArray[x][y]
```

where *x* represents the index of the mArray variable and *y* represents an index of the nested array. For example, the expression

```
mArray[1][2]
```

returns the value 18. Proceeding in this fashion, you can treat a nested array like a matrix, allowing you to duplicate some of the features associated with matrices.

Review | Session 12.3 Quick Check

1. What command extracts the day of the week value from a date object variable named thisDate?
2. What day of the week value is returned for a date occurring on a Friday?
3. What command changes the thisDate variable to the fifth day of the month?
4. A function named showDate() has an optional parameter named thisDate. What expression tests whether the showDate() function was called with a value set for the thisDate parameter?
5. What command breaks out of a program loop?
6. What command forces the script to go to the next iteration of the current program loop?

Review | Tutorial Summary

In this tutorial, you learned how work to with arrays, program loops, and conditional statements to create an application that produces a monthly calendar for any given date. In the first session, you created and populated arrays, and you learned some JavaScript methods to sort and modify arrays. The second session dealt with program loops and conditional statements. You learned how to repeat sections of code multiple times in either For or While loops. Using the If statement, you saw how to run commands only when certain conditions are met. In the third session, you applied what you learned about program loops and conditional statements to complete the calendar application. The third session concluded with a discussion of the break, continue, and label commands.

Key Terms

array
array literal
command block
compare function
conditional statement
counter variable
index
modulus operator
program loop
sparse array
subarray

Practice | Review Assignments

Practice the skills you learned in the tutorial using the same case scenario.

Data files needed for this Review Assignment: caltxt.htm, yeartxt.js, back.jpg, ccc.jpg, photo.jpg, styles.css, yearly.css

Maria finds the calendar() function you created an incredibly useful feature for the CCC Web site. However, she wants you to create a new calendar application that displays monthly calendars for the entire year on a single page. The calendar would still highlight the current date (or a date specified by the user) within the table. Figure 12-32 shows a preview of the yearly calendar that you'll create for Maria.

Figure 12-32

To combine all of the monthly calendars into one calendar, you'll use JavaScript to write a larger 3 x 4 table in which each table cell contains a monthly calendar. Maria has already created the Web page layout and a style sheet for both the Web page and the yearly calendar. You'll create the functions that generate the Web table containing the yearly calendar.

Complete the following:

1. Using your text editor, open **caltxt.htm** and **yeartxt.js** from the tutorial.12/review folder, enter ***your name*** and ***the date*** in the head section of each file, and then save the files as **calendar.htm** and **yearly.js**, respectively.
2. Go to the **yearly.js** file in your text editor. Many of the functions to create the individual monthly calendars have already been created. Insert a function named **writeMonthCell()** directly below the heading section. The purpose of this function is to place a monthly calendar within a table cell. The function has two parameters: **calendarDay** and **currentTime**. The calendarDay parameter contains a date object for the first day of the month to be displayed in the monthly calendar. The currentTime parameter contains the time value of the date that should be highlighted in the yearly table. Add the following commands to the writeMonthCell() function:
   a. Write the following HTML code to the document:
   ```
   <td class='yearly_months'>
   ```
   b. Call the writeMonth() function using calendarDay and currentTime as the parameter values. The purpose of the writeMonth() function is to write a monthly calendar into the table cell.
   c. Write a closing </td> tag to the document.
3. Above the writeMonthCell() function, insert a function named **yearly()**. The purpose of this function is to write the entire yearly calendar containing all of the separate monthly calendars as cells within the larger table. The function has a single parameter named **calDate**. Add the following commands to the function:
   a. If calDate equals null, set the calendarDay variable equal to a date object pointing to the current date and time; otherwise, calendarDay equals a date object using the text string specified in the calDate parameter.
   b. Create a variable named **currentTime** equal to the time value of the calendarDay variable. (*Hint:* Use the getTime() date object method to extract the time value from calendarDay.)
   c. Create a variable named **thisYear** equal to the four-digit year value from the calendarDay variable.
   d. Write the HTML code
   ```
   <table id='yearly_table'><tr>
      <th id='yearly_title' colspan='4'>
         this year
      </th>
   </tr>
   ```
   to the document, where *this year* is the value of the thisYear variable. This code represents the heading of the calendar table.
   e. Create a variable named **monthNum**, setting its initial value equal to –1. The purpose of the monthNum variable is to keep track of the month value of the current month being written in the calendar.
   f. Create a For loop that writes the rows of the yearly table. Create a counter variable named **i** that goes from 1 to 3 in increments of 1. The first command within the For loop should write the opening <tr> tag to the document.

g. Within the For loop you just created, add a nested For loop that writes the individual cells of the yearly table. The counter variable j of the nested For loop should go from 1 to 4 in increments of 1. In this nested For loop, add the following commands: (1) increase the value of monthNum by one; (2) use the setDate() date object method to change the day value of calendarDay to 1 (the first day of the month); (3) use the setMonth() date object method to change the month value of calendarDay to monthNum; and (4) call the writeMonthCell() function using calendarDay and currentTime as the parameter values.

h. After the nested For loop, but still within the outer loop, write a closing </tr> tag to the document.

i. After the nested loops, write a closing </table> tag to the document.

4. Locate the writeDayNames() function in the document. Within this function, change the values of the dayName array from three-letter abbreviations of the day names to the one-letter abbreviations **S**, **M**, **T**, **W**, **R**, **F**, and **S**.
5. Close the **yearly.js** file, saving your changes.
6. Go to the **calendar.htm** file in your text editor. In the head section of the document, add links to both the yearly.css style sheet and the yearly.js external script file.
7. Scroll down the document and locate the div element with the ID main. After the h1 heading in this element, insert an embedded script element. Within the script, run the command yearly() using the date **June 7, 2011** as the parameter value.
8. Save your changes to the file.
9. Open **calendar.htm** in your Web browser. Verify that the yearly calendar shown in Figure 12-32 is displayed on the Web page.
10. Return to the **calendar.htm** file in your text editor. Change the yearly() function so that no parameter value is specified (so that the function uses the current date). Save your changes and reload calendar.htm in your Web browser. Verify that the calendar for the current year is displayed and that the current date is the only one highlighted in the calendar.
11. Close any open files, and then submit your completed Web site to your instructor.

Apply | Case Problem 1

Use arrays, loops, and conditional statements to create a list of contributors.

Data Files needed for this Case Problem: clisttxt.htm, lhouse.css, list.js, logo.jpg

The Lighthouse The Lighthouse is a charitable organization located in central Kentucky that matches donors with needy groups. The fundraising coordinator for The Lighthouse is Aaron Kitchen. On a Web page available only to Lighthouse staff, Aaron wants to display a list of information on recent donations, including the name and address of the donor, the amount donated, and the date of the donation. A list of donations from the last month has been downloaded from an external database and stored in a collection of arrays named firstName, lastName, street, city, state, zip, amount, and date. Aaron needs your help in displaying the data from those arrays in a Web table. He also wants a summary table that displays the total number of contributors and the total contribution amount. Figure 12-33 shows a preview of the Web page you'll create.

Figure 12-33

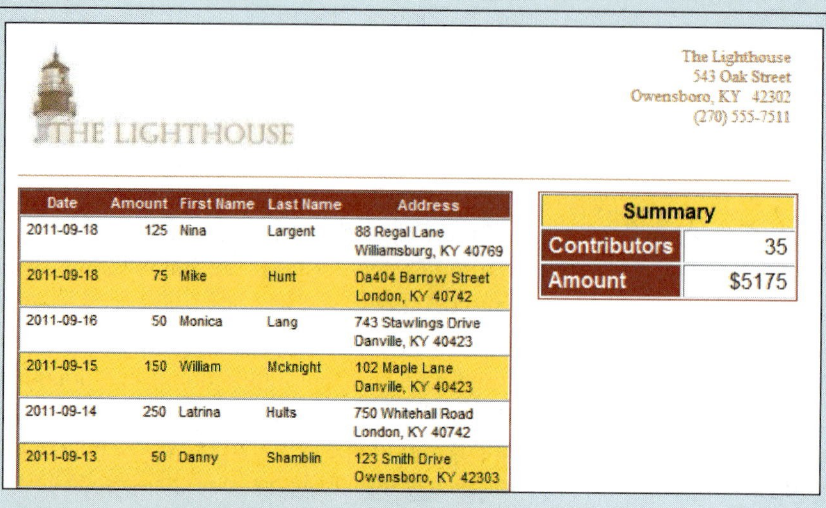

Complete the following:

1. Using your text editor, open **clisttxt.htm** from the tutorial.12/case1 folder, enter ***your name*** and ***the date*** in the head section, and then save the file as **clist.htm**.
2. The firstName, lastName, street, city, state, zip, amount, and date arrays have been created and populated for you in the list.js file. In the head section of the document, insert a script element that points to this file.
3. Below the script element you just created, insert another script element that contains the function **amountTotal()**. The purpose of the amountTotal() function is to return the sum of all of the values in the amount array. There are no parameters for this function. Add the following commands to the function:
   a. Declare a variable named **total**, setting its initial value to 0.
   b. Create a For loop that loops through all of the values in the amount array. At each iteration of the loop, add the current value of the array item to the value of the total variable.
   c. After the For loop is completed, return the value of the total variable.
4. Scroll down the document and locate the div element with the ID data_list. Within the div element, add a script element that contains the following commands:
   a. Write the following code to the document to create the header row for the table of contributions:
   ```
   <table border='1' rules='rows' cellspacing='0'>
      <tr>
         <th>Date</th><th>Amount</th><th>First Name</th>
         <th>Last Name</th><th>Address</th>
      </tr>
   ```
   b. Create a For loop in which the counter variable starts at 0 and, while the counter is less than the length of the amount array, increase the counter in increments of 1.
   c. Display every other row in the data list with a yellow background. To do this, within the For loop, insert an If condition that tests whether the counter variable is divisible evenly by 2 (*Hint:* Use the % modulus operator). If the counter variable is divisible by 2, write the following HTML tag:
   ```
   <tr>
   ```
   Otherwise, write the following tag:
   ```
   <tr class='yellowrow'>
   ```

d. Next, within the For loop, write the HTML code
```
<td>date</td><td class='amt'>amount</td>
<td>firstName</td><td>lastName</td>
```
to the document, where *date*, *amount*, *firstName*, and *lastName* are the values of the date, amount, firstName, and lastName arrays for the index indicated by the current value of the For loop's counter variable.

e. Finally, within the For loop, write the HTML code
```
<td>street<br />
   city, state zip</td>
</tr>
```
to the document, where *street*, *city*, *state*, and *zip* are the values of the street, city, state, and zip arrays for the current index value.

5. Go to the div element with the ID totals. Insert a script element that writes the HTML code
```
<table border='1' cellspacing='1'>
   <tr>
      <th id='sumTitle' colspan='2'>
         Summary
      </th>
   </tr>
   <tr>
      <th>Contributors</th>
      <td>contributions</td>
   </tr>
   <tr>
      <th>Amount</th>
      <td>$total</td>
   </tr>
</table>
```
to the document, where *contributions* is the length of the amount array and *total* is the value returned by the amountTotal() function you created earlier.

6. Close the file, saving your changes.
7. Open **clist.htm** in your Web browser. Verify that a list of 35 contributions totaling $5175 is displayed in the table and that alternate rows of the contributor list have a yellow background.
8. Submit your completed Web site to your instructor.

Apply | Case Problem 2

Use arrays, loops, and conditional statements to create a horizontal bar chart.

Data Files needed for this Case Problem: electtxt.htm, votes.js, back.jpg, logo.jpg, results.css

VoterWeb VoterWeb is an online source for election news and results from national, state, and local races. Faye Summerall is one of the managers of the Web site development team. Faye wants to add horizontal bar charts to the Web pages displaying election results. The length of each bar should correspond to the percentage of votes that the corresponding candidate receives in a given race. She has asked you to develop a JavaScript program that automatically writes the bar chart. Figure 12-34 shows a preview of the Web page for a series of Congressional races.

Figure 12-34

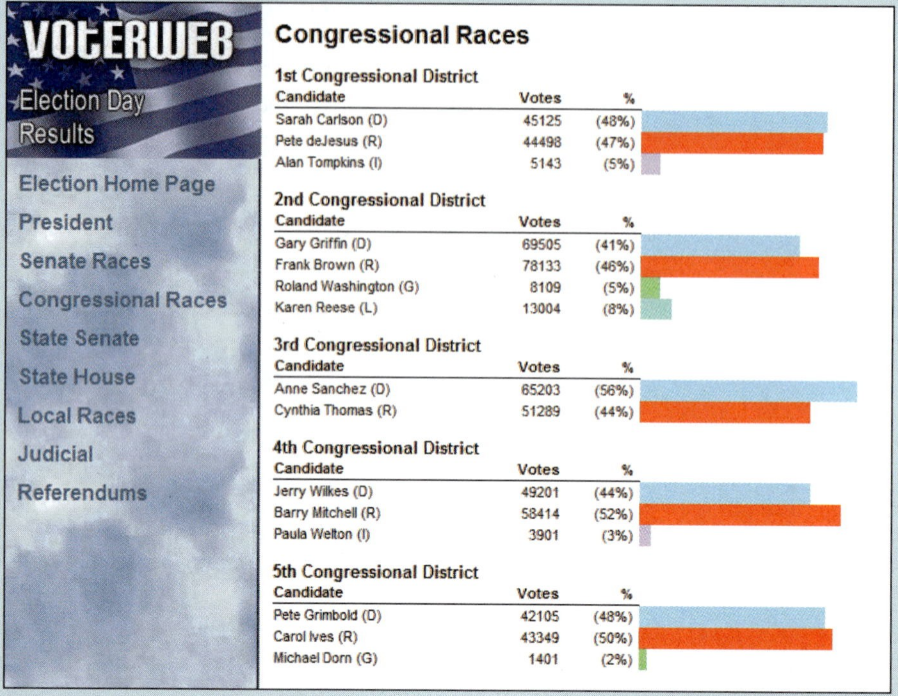

The horizontal bar charts will be created within table rows. The length of each bar will be determined by the number of blank table cells it contains. For example, to display a horizontal bar representing 45% of the vote, you'll write 45 blank table cells. The color of each bar is determined by the background color of its table cells. To apply the background color, you'll add class attributes to the blank table cells. A style in the results.css style sheet determines the background color for each class of table cells.

The data for each election has been stored in arrays in an external file named votes.js. The file includes data from five elections for different Congressional seats. The names of the races have been stored in an array named race. The name1 array contains the candidate names for the first race, the name2 array contains the candidate names for the second race, and so on through the name5 array. The party affiliations for each candidate in the first race have been stored in the party1 array, for the second race in the party2 array, and so forth. The votes1 through votes5 arrays store the votes for each candidate in each of the five races.

Complete the following:

1. Using your text editor, open **electtxt.htm** from the tutorial.12/case2 folder, enter ***your name*** and ***the date*** in the head section, and then save the file as **election.htm**.
2. Open the **votes.js** file from the tutorial.12/case2 folder in your text editor, study the contents to become familiar with the different arrays and their contents, and then close the file. Return to the **election.htm** file in your text editor, and then add a script element to the head section of the file that points to the votes.js file.

3. Insert another script element in the head section. In this script element, insert a function named **totalVotes()**. The purpose of this function is to calculate the sum of all the values within an array. The function has a single parameter, votes, representing one of the five vote arrays (vote1 through vote5). Add the following commands to the function:
   a. Declare a variable named **total**, setting its initial value to 0.
   b. Create a For loop that loops through each of the items in the votes array, adding that item's value to the total variable.
   c. After the For loop is completed, return the value of the total variable.
4. Insert another function named **calcPercent()**. The purpose of this function is to calculate a percentage, rounded to the nearest integer. The function has two parameters: **item** and **sum**. Have the function return the value of the item variable divided by sum, multiplied by 100, and then rounded to the nearest integer. (*Hint*: Use the Math.round() method to round the calculated percentage.)
5. Insert a function named **createBar()**. The purpose of this function is to write the blank table cells that make up each horizontal bar in the election results. The function has two parameters: **partyType** and **percent**. The partyType parameter stores the party affiliation of the candidate (D, R, I, G, or L). The percent parameter stores the percentage the candidate received in the election, rounded to the nearest integer. Add the following commands to the function:

EXPLORE

   a. Create a Switch statement that tests the value of the partyType parameter. If partyType equals D, store the following text string in a variable named **barText**:
      `<td class='dem'> </td>`
      If partyType equals R, barText should equal:
      `<td class='rep'> </td>`
      If partyType equals I, barText should equal:
      `<td class='ind'> </td>`
      If partyType equals G, barText should equal:
      `<td class='green'> </td>`
      Finally, if partyType equals L, barText should equal:
      `<td class='lib'> </td>`
      Make sure you add break commands after each case statement so that the browser does not attempt to test additional cases after it has found a match.
   b. Create a For loop in which the counter variable goes from 1 up through the value of the percent parameter in increments of 1. At each iteration, write the value of the barText variable to the Web document.
6. Insert a function named **showResults()**. The purpose of this function is to show the results of a particular race. The function has four parameters: **race**, **name**, **party**, and **votes**. The race parameter contains the name of the race. The name parameter contains the array of candidate names. The party parameter contains the array of party affiliations. Finally, the votes parameter contains the array of votes for each candidate in the race. Add the following commands to the function:
   a. Declare a variable named **totalV** equal to the value returned by the totalVotes() function using votes as the parameter value.

b. Write the HTML code

```
<h2>race</h2>
<table cellspacing='0'>
   <tr>
      <th>Candidate</th>
      <th class='num'>Votes</th>
      <th class='num'>%</th>
   </tr>
```

to the document, where *race* is the value of the race parameter.

c. Create a For loop in which the counter variable starts at 0 and, while the counter is less than the length of the name array, increase the counter in increments of 1. At each iteration of the For loop, run the commands outlined in the following five steps.

d. Write the HTML code

```
<tr>
   <td>name (party)</td>
   <td class='num'>votes</td>
```

where *name*, *party*, and *votes* are the entries in the name, party, and votes arrays for the index indicated by the counter variable.

e. Create a variable named **percent** equal to the value returned by the calcPercent() function. Use the current value from the votes array for the value of the item parameter, and totalV for the value of the sum parameter.

f. Write the HTML code

```
<td class='num'>(percent%)</td>
```

where *percent* is the value of the percent variable.

g. Call the **createBar()** function using the current value of the party array and percent as the parameter values.

h. Write a closing </tr> tag to the document.

i. After the For loop has completed, write a closing </table> tag to the document.

7. Scroll down the document. After the Congressional Races h1 heading, insert a script element containing the following commands:
   a. Call the showResults() function using race[0], name1, party1, and votes1 as the parameter values.
   b. Repeat the previous command for the remaining four races, using race[1] through race[4] as the parameter value for the race parameter, party2 through party5 for the party parameter, name2 through name5 for the name parameter, and votes2 through votes5 for the votes parameter.
8. Save your changes to the file, and then open **election.htm** in your Web browser. Verify that the correct percentages for each candidate appear and that a horizontal bar chart representing that percent value is displayed next to each candidate.
9. Submit your completed Web site to your instructor.

Challenge | Case Problem 3

Explore how to use JavaScript to create an auction log.

Data Files needed for this Case Problem: aucttxt.htm, logo.jpg, styles.css

Schmitt AuctionHaus David Schmitt owns Schmitt AuctionHaus, an auction center located in rural Indiana that specializes in estate and farm sales and auctions. David has been looking at ways to improve the bidding process for silent auctions in which applicants enter their name and bid for various items. David wants to create a Web page containing bidding information on various items at the auction center. The bidding could be displayed on a kiosk or terminal in the auction center, giving customers a quick look at the current status of different items for sale. David asked you to help design a Web form to track bids for a sales item. The form should include the name of the item, the current highest bid, a list of the bidding history for the item, and a form in which new bids can be entered. Because mistakes are sometimes made in entering a bid, David wants the ability to remove the last bid from the list. Figure 12-35 shows a preview of a sample page you'll create for David.

Figure 12-35

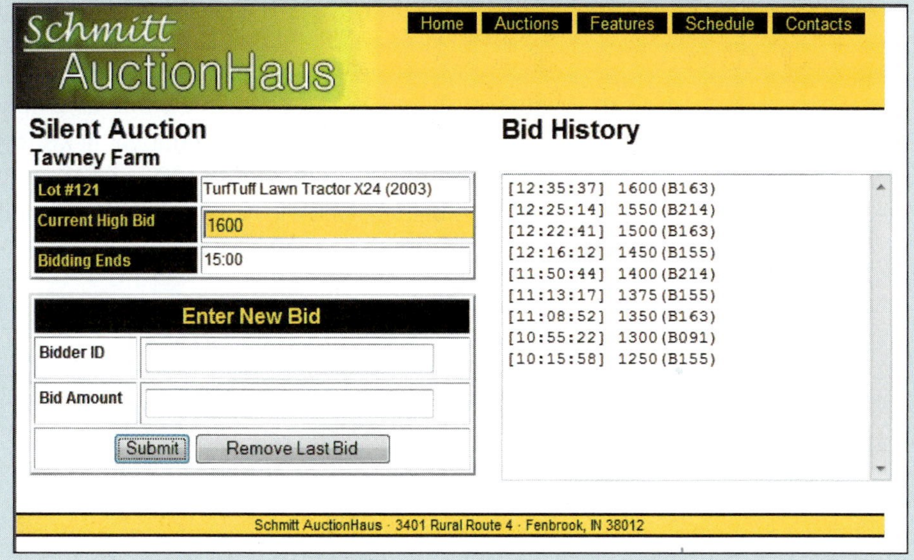

The layout and styles used on the page have already been created. You'll program the script that enters new bids and updates the box displaying the bid history and the highest current bid. You need to collect three pieces of information from each bid: the bid amount, the bidder ID, and the time when the bid was placed. You'll record this information in three arrays named bids, bidders, and bidTime, respectively.

Complete the following:

1. Using your text editor, open **aucttxt.htm** from the tutorial.12/case3 folder, enter ***your name*** and ***the date*** in the head section, and then save the file as **auction.htm**.
2. In the head section of the file, insert an embedded script element. Within the script element, create three new arrays named **bids**, **bidders**, and **bidTime**. Do not populate these arrays with any values.

3. Insert a function named **writeBid()**. The purpose of this function is to write the bidding history and the highest current bid to the Web page. There are no parameters for this function. Add the following commands to the function:
   a. Declare a variable named **historyText**, setting its initial value to an empty text string. This variable will be used to record the bidding history.

   EXPLORE

   b. Insert a For loop in which the counter variable goes from 0 through the length of the bids array in increments of 1. Each time through the loop, append the text string
   ***bidTime bids (bidders)* \n**
   to the historyText variable, where *bidTime*, *bids*, and *bidders* are the current items in the bidTime, bids, and bidders array based on the value of the counter variable. Note that \n is an escape character indicating a new line and causes the next entry to the historyText variable to be placed on a new line.

   EXPLORE

   c. After the For loop finishes, write the value of the historyText variable to the text area box with the name **bidList**. (*Hint:* To write text into a form field, run the command
   `document.form.field.value = text;`
   where *form* is the name of the form, *field* is the name of the form field, and *text* is the text string to be written to the field. In this example, the name of the form is bidForm and the name of the field is bidList.)
   d. Write the value of the first item in the bids array to the highBid field.
   e. Set the values of the bidId and bidAmount fields to empty text strings.
4. Create a function named **addBid()**. The purpose of this function is to add a bid to the start of the bids, bidders, and bidTime arrays. Add the following commands:

   EXPLORE

   a. Using the unshift() array method, insert the current value of the bidId field to the start of the bidders array.
   b. Use the unshift() array method to insert the current value of the bidAmount field at the start of the bids array.
   c. Declare a variable named **now** containing a date object for the current date and time.
   d. Extract the hours, minutes, and seconds values from the now variable, storing these values in variables named **hours**, **minutes**, and **seconds**.
   e. Use a conditional operator to insert leading zeroes in the minutes and seconds values if they are less than 10.
   f. Create a variable named **timeText** equal to the text
   [*hours*:*minutes*:*seconds*]
   where *hours*, *minutes*, and *seconds* are the values of the hours, minutes, and seconds variables.
   g. Using the unshift() array method, insert the value of the timeText variable at the start of the bidTime array.
   h. Call the writeBid() function. Remember that there are no parameters for this function.
5. Create a function named **removeBid()**. The purpose of this function is to remove the first entry from the bidders, bids, and bidTime arrays. Add the following commands:

   EXPLORE

   a. Using the shift() array method, remove the first entry from the bidders array.
   b. Repeat the previous step to remove the first entry from the bidders and bidTime arrays.
   c. Call the writeBid() function.

6. Scroll down the document to the Submit input button. Add an event handler attribute to run the addBid() function when the button is clicked.
7. Add an event handler attribute to the Remove Last Bid button to run the removeBid() function when the button is clicked.
8. Save your changes to the file.
9. Open **auction.htm** in your Web browser. Enter new bids in the Bidder ID and Bid Amount input fields. Click the Submit button to update the bidding history and Current High Bid field. Verify that the newest bid entries are placed at the top of the bidding history. Click the Remove Last Bid button and verify that the latest bid is removed from the list.
10. Submit your completed Web site to your instructor.

Create | Case Problem 4

Use your knowledge of arrays, loops, and conditional statements to create a lunar calendar.

Data Files needed for this Case Problem: caltxt.css, lunartxt.htm, lunartxt.js, astro.css, moonfunc.js, phase0.jpg through phase15.jpg, skyweb.jpg

SkyWeb Dr. Andrew Weiss of the SkyWeb astronomy Web site is working on a Web page describing the phases and properties of the Moon. Dr. Weiss wants the page to contain a table describing the current conditions of the Moon, including the Moon phase, age (days since the last new moon), distance from the Earth, and position in the nighttime sky. He also wants the page to contain a lunar calendar for the current month. A lunar calendar is a calendar that displays the phases of the Moon on each day of the month. A preview of the page that Dr. Weiss wants you to create is shown in Figure 12-36.

Figure 12-36

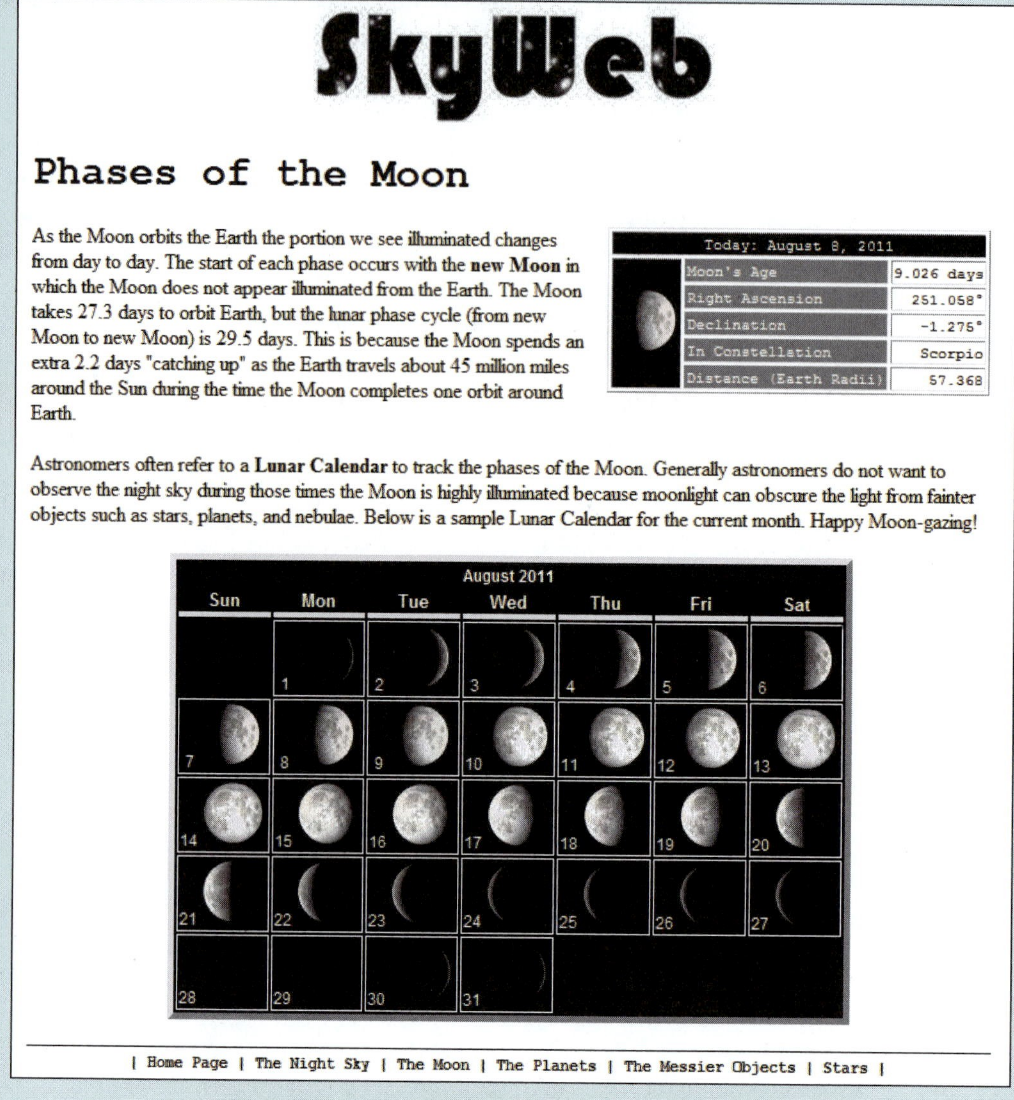

Dr. Weiss has designed the basic layout for the page. He wants you to write scripts to generate the lunar calendar as well as to insert data on the current lunar conditions in a summary table located at the top of the page. To help you in creating this page, Dr. Weiss has supplied a file named moonfunc.js containing the functions described in Figure 12-37.

Figure 12-37

Function	Description
calcMPhase(cDay)	Returns the phase number (from 0 to 15) of the Moon for the date stored in cDay
calcMAge(cDay)	Returns the age of the Moon for the date stored in cDay
calcMDist(cDay)	Returns the distance in Earth radii between the Earth and the Moon on the date stored in cDay
calcMDec(cDay)	Returns the declination (latitude on the nighttime sky) of the Moon on the date stored in cDay
calcMRA(cDay)	Returns the right ascension (longitude on the nighttime sky) of the Moon on the date stored in cDay
calcMZodiac(cDay)	Returns the name of the constellation or sign of the zodiac in which the Moon resides on the date stored in cDay

Each function has a date object parameter named cDay that you can use to return information on the Moon's status for that day. Dr. Weiss has also supplied a collection of 16 images named phase0.jpg through phase15.jpg. Each file contains an image of the Moon from a particular phase in its cycle. The file phase0.jpg contains an image of the new Moon, phase8.jpg contains an image of a full moon, and so on. Dr. Weiss points out that you can use the calcMPhase() function he's supplied to determine which of the 16 images to display for any given day.

The layout and appearance of the lunar calendar are up to you. You can also supplement the contents of this Web page with any other material you think is appropriate for the subject.

Complete the following:

1. Using your text editor, open the **caltxt.css**, **lunartxt.htm**, and **lunartxt.js** files from the tutorial.12/case4 folder. Enter ***your name*** and ***the date*** in each file. Save the files as **calendar.css**, **lunar.htm**, and **lunarcal.js**, respectively. The calendar.css file will be used to store the style sheet for the lunar calendar you'll create. The lunar.htm file contains the Web page that Dr. Weiss wants to display on the SkyWeb Web site. The lunarcal.js file will contain the functions required to create the lunar calendar.
2. Go to the **lunar.htm** file in your text editor. In the head section, add links to the **calendar.css** style sheet, the **moonfunc.js** JavaScript file, and the **lunarcal.js** JavaScript file.
3. Insert a script element in the head section containing the following:
   a. A variable named **calendarDay** containing a date object with the date set to **August 8, 2011**.
   b. A function named **writeDate()**. The purpose of this function is to display a date in the format Month Day, Year, where Month is the name of the month, Day is the day of the month, and Year is the four-digit year value. The function has a single parameter, **calendarDay**, which contains the date object to be formatted.
4. Scroll down to the summary table in the body of the document. Add the following to the table:
   a. In the table's title cell, display the text "Today: *today*", where *today* is the date from the calendarDay variable formatted using the writeDay() function.
   b. In the lunarimg cell, display the lunar image for the date in calendarDay. (*Hint:* Use the calcMPhase() function to return the phase number of the image.)

   c. In the cell next to the Moon's Age label, display the text "*age* days", where *age* is the age of the Moon on calendarDay.
   d. In the cell next to the Right Ascension label, display the text "*ra*°", where *ra* is the right ascension of the Moon on calendarDay.
   e. In the cell next to the Declination label, display the text "*dec*", where *dec* is the declination of the Moon on calendarDay.
   f. In the cell next to the In Constellation label, display the text "*zodiac*", where *zodiac* is the constellation that the Moon resides in on calendarDay.
   g. In the cell next to the Distance label, display the text "*distance*", where *distance* is the distance from the Earth to the Moon in Earth radii on calendarDay.
5. Scroll down to the lunar_cal div element. Within this element, insert a script that calls the function lunar_calendar() for the date in calendarDay.
6. Save your changes to the lunar.htm file.
7. Go to the **lunarcal.js** file in your text editor. Create a function named **lunar_calendar()** that displays a lunar calendar. The function should have a single parameter named **calendarDay** that contains the date you want to use for the calendar. You can use the calendar() function created in the tutorial as a model for your function and any supporting functions required to complete the calendar. The calendar does not have to highlight the current date.
8. Go to the **calendar.css** file in your text editor and create the styles required for your lunar calendar. You can use the calendar.css file from the tutorial as a model, or you can create a layout you choose.
9. After completing your work in the lunarcal.js and calendar.css files, open **lunar.htm** in your Web browser. Verify that the lunar calendar and the Moon data follow the information shown in Figure 12-37.
10. Submit your completed Web site to your instructor.

Review | Quick Check Answers

Session 12.1

1. An array is a collection of data values organized under a single name with each value referenced by an index number.
2. `var dayNames = new Array();`
3. `var dayNames = new Array("Sun", "Mon", "Tue", "Wed", "Thu", "Fri", "Sat");`
4. `dayNames[2]`
5. `var dayNames = ["Sun", "Mon", "Tue", "Wed", "Thu", "Fri", "Sat"];`
6. `dayNames.sort();`
7. `dayNames.slice(1,6);`
8. `dayNames.toString();`

Session 12.2

1. A program loop is a set of commands that is executed repeatedly until a stopping condition has been met. Three program loops supported by JavaScript are the For, While, and Do/While loops.
2. `for (var i = 0; i<=100; i+=10)`

3.
```
document.write("<tr>");
    for (var i=1; i<=5; i++) {
       document.write("<td>Column "+i+"</td>");
    }
document.write("</tr>");
```

4. A conditional statement is a statement that runs a command block only when certain conditions are met. The most commonly used conditional statement is the If statement.

5.
```
if (WebBrowser) document.write("Internet Explorer Browser");
```
or
```
if (WebBrowser == true) document.write("Internet Explorer Browser");
```

6.
```
if (WebBrowser == "IE") document.write("Internet Explorer Browser")
else document.write("Mozilla Browser");
```

7.
```
if (WebBrowser == "IE") document.write("Internet Explorer Browser")
else if (WebBrowser == "Opera") document.write("Opera Browser")
else if (WebBrowser == "Safari") document.write("Safari Browser")
else if (WebBrowser == "Firefox") document.write("Firefox Browser")
else document.write("Generic Browser");
```

8.
```
switch (WebBrowser) {
   case "IE": document.write("Internet Explorer Browser"); break;
   case "Opera": document.write("Opera Browser"); break;
   case "Safari": document.write("Safari Browser"); break;
   case "Firefox": document.write("Firefox Browser"); break;
   default: document.write("Generic Browser");
}
```

Session 12.3

1. `thisDate.getDay();`
2. 5
3. `thisDate.setDate(5);`
4. `if (thisDate != null) ...`
5. `break;`
6. `continue;`

Ending Data Files

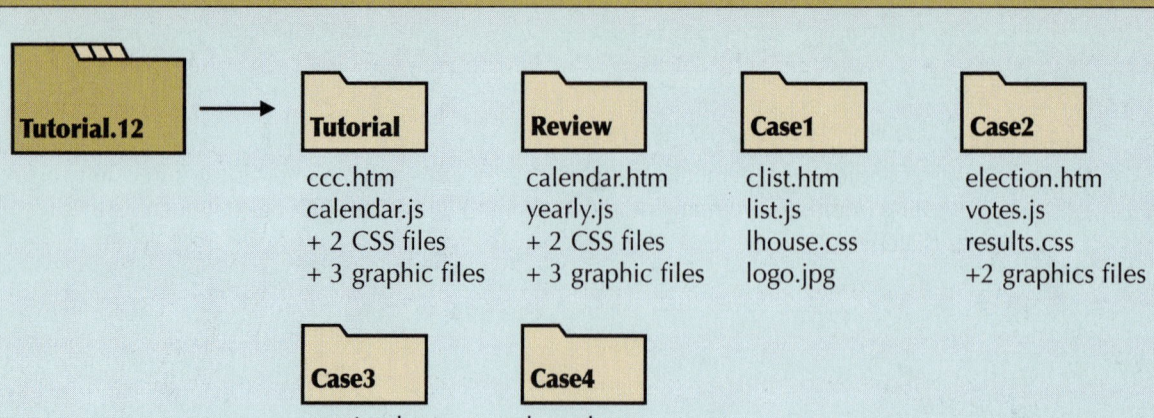

Tutorial.12 →

Tutorial
ccc.htm
calendar.js
+ 2 CSS files
+ 3 graphic files

Review
calendar.htm
yearly.js
+ 2 CSS files
+ 3 graphic files

Case1
clist.htm
list.js
lhouse.css
logo.jpg

Case2
election.htm
votes.js
results.css
+2 graphics files

Case3
auction.htm
styles.css
logo.jpg

Case4
lunar.htm
lunarcal.js
moonfunc.js
astro.css
calendar.css
+ 17 graphics files

Objectives

Session 13.1
- Learn about objects and the document object model
- Reference documents objects by ID, name, and tag name
- Work with object collections
- Work with object properties and CSS styles

Session 13.2
- Study the syntax of object methods
- Apply an event handler to an object
- Work with mouse events
- Employ object detection to avoid programming errors

Session 13.3
- Create an animation with timed functions
- Explore how to create sliding and tabbed menus
- Retrieve values from a style sheet
- Create custom objects

Working with Objects and Styles

Creating a Pull-Down Menu

Case | The 221B Blog

Kyle Harris is a fan of mystery stories. His favorites are the Sherlock Holmes stories by Sir Arthur Conan Doyle. Kyle decided to create a Web site for other fans of the fictional detective called The 221B Blog, named after the street number of Holmes' Baker Street address.

On his Web site, Kyle has added a discussion forum, links to other mystery Web sites, and a place for members to post artwork, essays, and fan fiction. Kyle has also created links to the online text versions of all of the 56 short stories and four novels in the Sherlock Holmes canon. Kyle is concerned that so many links on the site's home page will be difficult for users to manage. He's seen sites in which lists of links are stored in pop-up or pull-down menus, remaining out of sight until needed by the user. Kyle wants to add a similar feature to his Web site and has asked you to help him write the code.

Starting Data Files

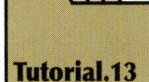

Tutorial.13 →

Tutorial
holmestxt.htm
menustxt.js
shblogtxt.css
+ 2 graphic files

Review
sherlocktxt.htm
slidestxt.js
mblog.css
+ 3 graphic files

Case1
printertxt.htm
jemenustxt.js
je.css
+ 4 graphic files

Case2
hanjietxt.htm
puzzletxt.js
jpf.css
+ 2 graphic files

Case3
bysotxt.htm
marqueetxt.js
bstyles.css
+ 2 graphic files

Case4
dinnerplate.txt
+ 2 graphic files

Session 13.1

Introducing Pull-Down Menus

Kyle asks you to help him update the home page of his 221B Blog Web site. The home page will have links to online versions of every story in the Sherlock Holmes canon. The links have been placed in separate div elements organized into five collections: *The Adventures of Sherlock Holmes, The Memoirs of Sherlock Holmes, The Return of Sherlock Holmes, The Case Book of Sherlock Holmes,* and *His Last Bow*. You'll open the home page to see the content of these collections and study how Kyle has organized and designed the home page.

To view the 221B Blog home page:

1. Use your text editor to open the **holmestxt.htm** and the **shblogtxt.css** files from the tutorial.13/tutorial folder, enter ***your name*** and ***the date*** in the comment section of each file, and then save the files as **holmes.htm** and **shblog.css**, respectively.
2. Explore the content of both files in your text editor, making note of the structure, IDs, and class names used for the different sections of the holmes.htm file.
3. Open **holmes.htm** in your Web browser. Figure 13-1 shows the initial appearance of the Web page.

Figure 13-1 **The initial 221B Blog page**

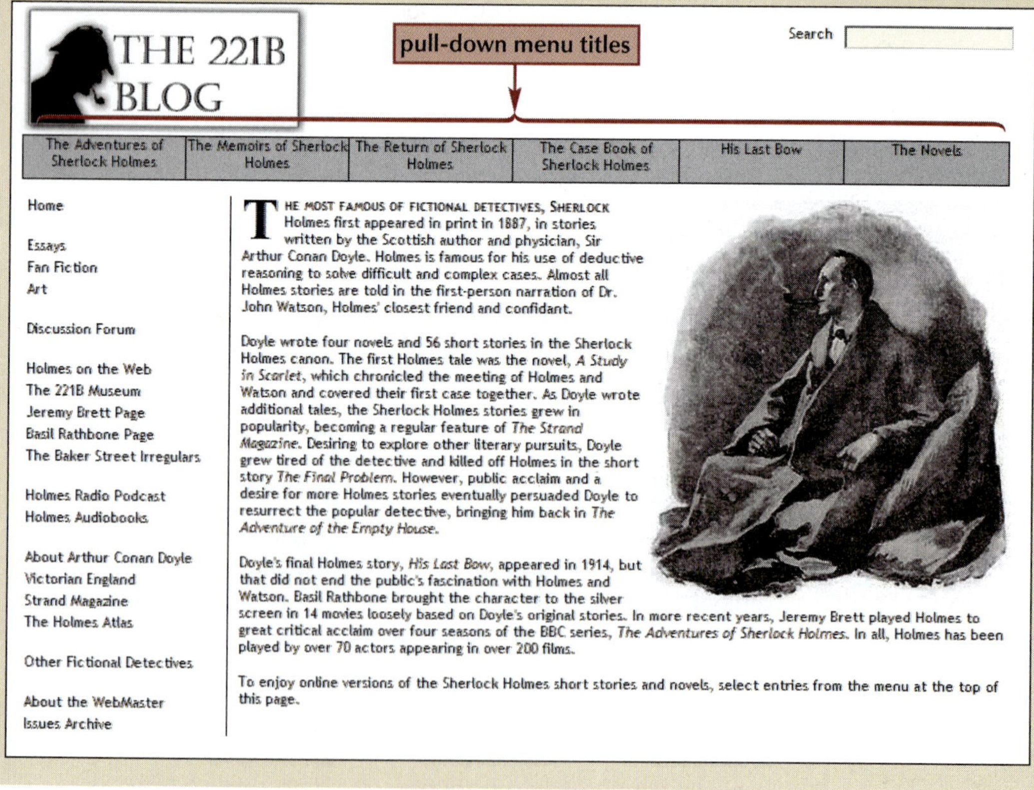

Kyle has placed the five collection titles in their own div element and given them IDs of menu1 through menu6. Each collection title has the class name menu. Kyle has also created div elements containing a list of stories and novels for each collection. The lists have been placed in separate div elements with the class name menuList and IDs ranging from menu1List to menu6List. Currently those lists are hidden, but you can reveal them by modifying the display property of the menuList class in the shblog style sheet.

To display the lists of stories and novels:

1. Return to the **shblog.css** file in your text editor.
2. Scroll down the style sheet and change the display property of the menuList class from none to **block**. See Figure 13-2.

Figure 13-2

Display property for the menuList class modified

displays the menuList elements as blocks

```
.menuList           {position: absolute; top: 146px; width: 140px; z-index: 2;
                     background-color: ivory; border: 1px solid black; display: block}

.menuList li        {margin: 5px}
.menuList a         {display: block; width: 132px}
.menuList a:hover   {background-color: rgb(151, 151, 151); color: white}
```

Tip

You can also hide or display page elements by setting the value of the visibility style to hidden or visible.

3. Save your changes to the style sheet, and then refresh **holmes.htm** in your Web browser. The six pull-down menus are displayed in the browser window. See Figure 13-3.

Figure 13-3

Menu lists displayed on the 221B Blog home page

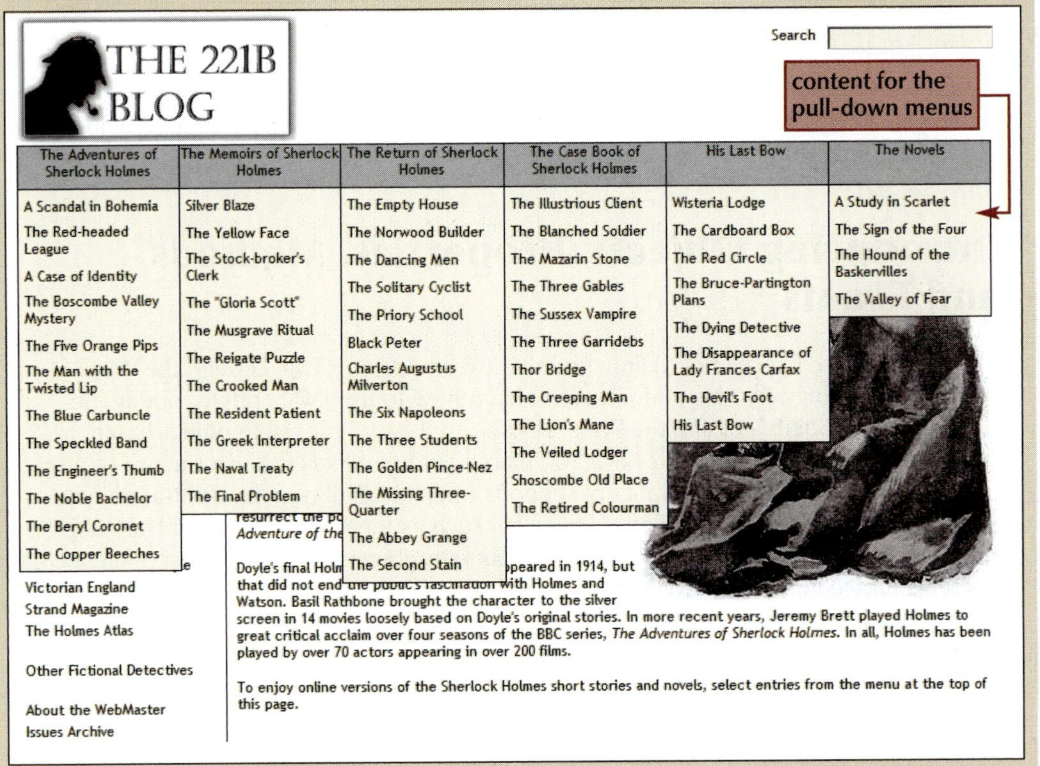

4. Return to the **shblog.css** file in your text editor, change the display property of the menuList class from block back to **none**, and then save and close the file.

Each entry in the six lists will act as a hypertext link to a new page that contains the complete text of the selected story or novel. Kyle wants these titles and lists to act as pull-down menus. In a **pull-down menu**, a menu title is always visible to the user, identifying the entries in the menu. When a user clicks the title or in some cases moves the pointer over the title, the rest of the menu is displayed, often accompanied by the effect of a menu being "pulled down" from the title. See Figure 13-4. To display a different pull-down menu, users click or move the pointer over another menu title. To hide a pull-down menu, users click the menu title again or they can click or move the pointer to a spot on the main browser page.

Figure 13-4 Pull-down menu being created

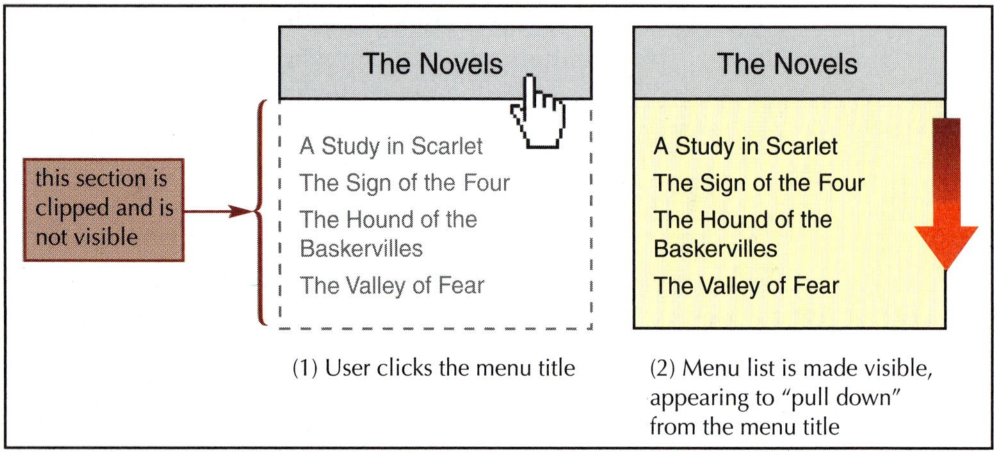

To save space on the home page and to avoid obscuring the contents of the rest of the page, Kyle wants you to write a program that duplicates the pull-down menu effect for the six menu lists. You'll use JavaScript to control the action of hiding and displaying each menu list.

Introducing Objects, Properties, Methods, and Events

So far, you've used JavaScript mainly to write text strings of HTML code to the Web document. Starting with this tutorial, you'll learn how to use JavaScript to modify the contents of the document and the Web browser itself. JavaScript is an **object-based language**, which means that it is based on manipulating objects through the use of properties, methods, and events. JavaScript supports three kinds of objects. **Built-in objects** are objects intrinsic to the JavaScript language, such as the Math, array, and Date objects you've used in the previous few tutorials. **Document objects** are objects that reference elements and features of the Web document or Web browser. You'll study these kinds of objects in this tutorial. **Customized objects** are objects created by the user. You won't use customized objects with Kyle's Web page, but you'll examine how to create them later in the tutorial.

Every object has **properties** that describe its appearance, purpose, or behavior. Every object also has **methods**, which are actions that the object performs. Finally, objects can be associated with **events**, which are actions undertaken by the user or the browser that impact the object in some way.

JavaScript objects share some characteristics with common, everyday objects. An oven, for example, has certain properties, such as model name, age, size, and temperature. An oven also has associated methods, such as heating and cooking. Some of those methods change the properties of the oven, such as the oven's internal temperature or its state of cleanliness. Finally, an event that impacts an oven is when the user turns the oven on or off.

Similarly, JavaScript objects have their own set of objects, properties, methods, and events. The Web browser itself is an object, and the page you're viewing within the browser is also an object. If the page contains a form, the form is an object as are any elements within the form. A paragraph is also an object, and the text within that paragraph can be considered its own object. Each object has properties. The browser object has a property that indicates its type, such as Firefox or Internet Explorer, and another property that indicates its version number. A form object has a name or id property that distinguishes it from other forms. An object that has been placed on a page has properties for its page coordinates. Most objects also have methods. Documents can be opened or closed. The page background color can be set. The font of a paragraph can be changed in color or resized. And, of course, the user or the browser interacts with these objects by initiating events with a keyboard or mouse.

You've already been working with objects, properties, methods, and events throughout the last three tutorials. You've seen the effect of adding an onload attribute to the <body> tag to run a function in response to the event of loading the document. You've also used the onclick attribute to run code in response to the click of the mouse. The command you've used most often, the document.write() command, uses the write() method to write HTML text to the document object. In this tutorial, you'll learn about other objects and their properties, methods, and events. You'll start by examining the JavaScript objects that describe the contents of the Web browser and Web document.

Exploring the Document Object Model

All of the objects within documents and browsers need to be organized in a systematic way. This organized structure of objects is called the **document object model (DOM)**. The goal is to make every object related to the document or to the Web browser accessible to a scripting language such as JavaScript. Several document object models have been used with JavaScript. To better understand how JavaScript relates to the document object model, let's review the history of how these models developed.

Development of a Common DOM

The first document object model for the Web was introduced in Netscape Navigator 2.0. This is often referred to as the **basic model**, or in some cases, the **DOM Level 0**. The basic model did not include all objects, but it did support some common objects such as the browser window, the Web document, and the browser itself. Under the basic model, a programmer could reference these objects in the scripting language; but in most cases, the programmer could not modify their properties once the page was loaded by the browser. Only form elements could be modified after the page was loaded; the rest of the page was static and could not be changed. Internet Explorer 3.0 was the first version of Internet Explorer to support the basic model.

Netscape versions 3 and 4 further expanded the scope of the document object model by adding image rollovers and the ability to initiate programs in response to mouse and keyboard actions by the user. Internet Explorer 4.0 introduced the **IE4 DOM**, the chief feature being that all Web page elements were now part of the document object model. CSS attributes also became part of the IE4 DOM, allowing users to manipulate CSS styles with JavaScript commands. Unfortunately, the approach adopted by Internet Explorer was incompatible with the Netscape 4 approach.

The browser wars had reached a stage at which two fundamentally incompatible document object models were in use, and programmers who wanted to create dynamic Web pages had to work hard to reconcile the differences between the two models. At this point, the World Wide Web Consortium (W3C) stepped in—much like it did with HTML—to develop specifications for a common document object model.

The first specification, **DOM Level 1**, released in October 1998, provided support for all elements contained within HTML and XML documents. An update to this specification was released in September 2000 and fixed some errors from the earlier release.

The second specification, **DOM Level 2**, was released in November 2000. This specification enhanced the document object model by providing an event model that specified how events are captured as they progress through the objects in a Web browser. DOM Level 2 also extended the style sheet model to work with CSS style sheets and provided a range model to allow programmers to manipulate sections of text within a document. The DOM Level 2 specifications were placed within six different modules, allowing browser developers to support those sections of the DOM that were important to them.

The most recent specification is **DOM Level 3**, which was released in April 2004. DOM Level 3 provides a framework for working with document loading and saving, as well as for working with XML, namespaces, DTDs, and document validation. This tutorial refers to all of the DOM levels released and supported by the W3C as the **W3C DOM** unless highlighting specific aspects unique to a particular level.

Figure 13-5 summarizes the different document object models that have been introduced and supported by the browser market throughout the years.

Figure 13-5 **Document object models**

DOM	Description
DOM Level 0 (Basic Model)	The basic DOM that supported few page and browser objects and allowed dynamic content only for form elements
DOM Level 0 + Images	The basic DOM with added support for image rollovers
Netscape 4 (layers)	The basic DOM with support for the Netscape 4 layer element and the ability to capture events within the browser
Internet Explorer 4	An expanded DOM allowing dynamic content for most page elements
Internet Explorer 5	The IE 4 DOM with additional refinements and enhancements
W3C DOM Level 1	The first DOM specification by the W3C, which supported all page and browser elements and handled all events occurring within the browser
W3C DOM Level 2	The second DOM specification, allowing for the capture of events, manipulation of CSS styles, working with element text, and document subsets
W3C DOM Level 3	The third DOM specification, providing a framework for working with document loading and saving, as well as working with DTDs and document validation

Be aware that if you're writing code that will be read by older browsers, you may be limited to supporting earlier DOM versions. At the time of this writing, current browsers support almost all of the specifications for DOM Level 1, most if not all of DOM Level 2, and partially DOM Level 3. Internet Explorer also supports the specifications for the IE4 DOM, but has some gaps in its support for DOM Levels 2 and 3. Most browsers, other than Opera, do not support the IE4 DOM at all. The scope of the tasks in these tutorials is mostly limited to the treatment of objects through DOM Level 2, unless otherwise noted. Features specific to the IE4 DOM are examined as circumstances warrant.

The Document Tree

Each document object model organizes objects into a hierarchy known as a **document tree**. Figure 13-6 shows part of this hierarchy for DOM Level 2. The topmost object in the hierarchy is the window object, which represents the browser window. Within the browser window are objects for the Web page document, each frame, the history of Web pages visited, and even the browser itself. Those objects can themselves contain yet another level of objects. For example, the document object contains objects for Web forms, images, applets, inline frames, and links. As document object models encompass more objects, the tree structure itself became more elaborate, including more of the objects within the window, browser, and document. The object hierarchy for the W3C Level 1 and Level 2 DOMs includes a structure for individual tags, tag attributes, and text strings within an HTML file.

Document tree **Figure 13-6**

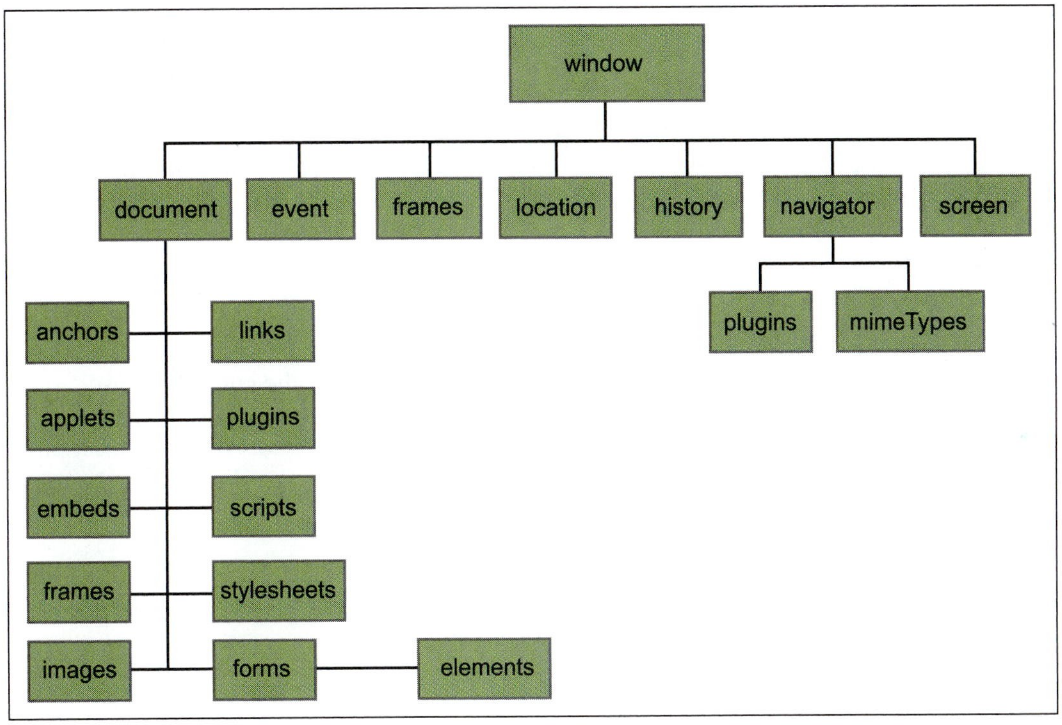

Referencing Objects

After the document object model defines how the objects within the browser and document are organized, it can be used by any scripting language, such as JavaScript. Once you understand how to work with a document object model, you can apply these lessons to several other programming languages. These tutorials explore how JavaScript interacts with the DOM, so you'll start by examining how to reference a particular element or groups of elements within a document object model using JavaScript.

Object Names

Each object is identified by an **object name**. Figure 13-7 lists the object names for some of the objects at the top of the object hierarchy. You've been using one of these objects, the document object, throughout the last three tutorials.

Figure 13-7 Object names

Object Name	Description
window	The browser window
document	The Web document displayed in the window
document.body	The body of the Web document displayed in the browser window
event	Events or actions occurring within the browser window
history	The list of previously visited Web sites within the browser window
location	The URL of the document currently displayed in the browser window
navigator	The browser itself
screen	The screen displaying the document

As indicated by the document tree in Figure 13-6, many objects are nested within other objects. To indicate the location of an object within the hierarchy, you separate each level using a dot. This is often referred to as **dot syntax**. The general form is

```
object1.object2.object3. ...
```

where *object1* is at the top of the hierarchy, *object2* is a child of *object1*, *object3* is a child of *object2*, and so on. To reference the document object displayed within the browser window, you could use the following nested form:

```
window.document
```

However, in most cases, you do not have to indicate an object's location within the entire hierarchy of the document tree. For example, when you simply use the document object name, JavaScript assumes that the object is located within the current browser window. If you have multiple browser windows open, you may need to explicitly indicate the window containing the document object you want to access. For now, all scripts apply to the currently active window.

Working with Object Collections

When more than one of the same type of object exists, these objects are organized into arrays called **object collections**. For example, the object reference

```
document.images
```

references all of the inline image objects in the current document (and implicitly within the current browser window). Figure 13-8 lists some other examples of object collections found with the document, navigator, and window objects.

Figure 13-8 Object collections

Object Collection	Description
document.anchors	All anchors
document.applets	All applets
document.embeds	All embed elements
document.forms	All Web forms
document.*form*.elements	All elements within a specific *form*
document.images	All inline images
document.links	All links
document.plugins	All plug-ins in the document
document.styleSheets	All style sheet elements
navigator.plugins	All plug-ins supported by the browser
navigator.mimeTypes	All mime-types supported by the browser
window.frames	All frames within the browser window

To reference a specific object within a collection, you can use either

```
collection[idref]
```

or

```
collection.idref
```

where *collection* is a reference to the object collection and *idref* is either an index number representing the position of the object in the array or the value of the name or ID assigned to the element. As with other arrays, the first object in the collection has an index number of 0. For example, if the first inline image within the document has the tag

```
<img src = "logo.jpg" id = "logoImg" />
```

you can reference the image using any of the following expressions:

```
document.images[0]
document.images["logoImg"]
document.images.logoImg
```

To avoid long object references in your code, you can store the reference in a variable. The statement

```
var firstImg = document.images[0]
```

stores the object reference to the first inline image in the variable firstImg.

Because object collections are essentially arrays, they support the length property; so you can always determine the number of items in an object collection using the following expression:

```
collection.length
```

The number of inline images within the document is returned by the following expression:

```
document.images.length
```

Finally, as with arrays, you can use a for loop to go through all of the items within the collection. The general form is

```
for (var i = 0; i< collection.length; i++) {
   commands
}
```

where *collection* is again a reference to an object collection and *commands* are commands that can be applied to each item within the collection.

Referencing Objects by Name and ID

Not all elements are associated with an object collection. For example, no object collection specifically references div elements. However, you can create object collections based on the names of element tags using the expression

```
object.getElementsByTagName(tag)
```

where *object* is an object in the document and *tag* is the name of an HTML tag nested within that object. To create an array of all div elements within the current document, you would use the following expression:

```
document.getElementsByTagName("div")
```

The getElementsByTagName() method can also be used to create an array of all elements in a document by using the * wildcard character in place of the tag name. For example, the following code creates an array of all HTML tags in the current document in the allElems variable:

```
allElems = document.getElementsByTagName("*");
```

You can also create object collections based on the ID attribute of the element. The object reference is

```
document.getElementById(id)
```

where *id* is the value of the ID attribute. So, to reference the element

```
<div id = "mainHeading">
   ...
</div>
```

from the document, you would use the following object reference:

```
document.getElementById("mainHeading")
```

The getElementById () method is associated only with the document object, unlike the getElementsByTagName() method, which can be applied to any element within the document. Also, because ID values are meant to be unique, the getElementById() method returns only a single object, not an object collection.

Tip

Case is important with the getElementById method. A common error is to enter the code as getElementByID, incorrectly capitalizing the final letter, resulting in an error.

Finally, you can create references to objects by the value of their name attribute with the expression

```
document.getElementsByName(name)
```

where *name* is the value of the name attribute. Because more than one element can share the same name (such as radio buttons within a Web form), this method returns an object collection rather than a single object. The getElementsByName() method, like the getElementById() method, is applied only to the document object.

Object References in the Internet Explorer DOM | InSight

Before the development of a common document object model, each browser put forth its own DOM—and with it, its own collection of object names and object syntax. Starting with version 4.0, Internet Explorer introduced the IE document object model. Because of the dominance of the Internet Explorer browser, programmers had to write code that would accommodate both the IE DOM as well as the DOM supported by the W3C. Versions of Internet Explorer after IE 4.0 provided more support for the W3C DOM, so you can use much of the W3C document object model; but you may occasionally need to support the IE DOM, especially if your Web site needs to work with earlier versions of the Internet Explorer browser.

One chief area of difference between the IE DOM and the W3C DOM lies in how document elements are referenced. The IE DOM supports the object reference

```
document.all
```

which references an object collection consisting of all elements within the document. To reference an element within this collection by its ID, you can use any of the following expressions:

```
document.all[id]
document.all.id
```

Note that the document.all object collection is not supported in the W3C DOM and would cause the program to fail if it were used in a browser that did not support the IE DOM. The IE DOM also allowed object references consisting only of the object's ID value. So to reference the element with the mainHeading, ID any of the following object references would be supported under the IE DOM:

```
document.all["mainHeading"]
document.all.mainHeading
mainHeading
```

The IE DOM also allows references to objects by their tag name using the tags object collection

```
document.all.tags(tag)
```

where *tag* is the tag name. Thus to create an array of all paragraph elements under the IE DOM, you could enter the following expression:

```
document.all.tags("p")
```

As with the getElementsByTagName() method, you can create an array of all elements in the document by using the wildcard character * in place of the tag name. Again, the tags collection is not part of the W3C DOM and would cause the program to fail when used with non-IE browsers.

Reference Window | Referencing Objects

- To reference an object as part of the collection in a document, use either
  `collection[idref]`
  or
  `collection.idref`
  where *idref* is either an index number representing the position of the object in the collection or the value of the ID or name attribute assigned to that element.
- To reference a document object based on its ID, use
  `document.getElementById(id)`
  where *id* is the value of the element's ID attribute.
- To reference an array of elements based on the tag name, use
  `object.getElementsByTagName(tag)`
  where *object* is an object reference and *tag* is the name of the element tag.
- To reference an array of elements based on the value of the name attribute, use
  `document.getElementsByName(name)`
  where *name* is the value of the name attribute.

Working with Object Properties

Most objects are associated with one or more properties. The syntax of an object property is

```
object.property
```

where *object* is the object name and *property* is the name of a property associated with the object. To set the value of an object property, you enter the statement

```
object.property = expression
```

where *expression* is a JavaScript expression that returns a value.

Object Properties and HTML Attributes

Many of the properties associated with document objects correspond to the HTML attributes associated with document elements. For example, the img element

```
<img id = "logoImg" src = "logo.jpg" />
```

from an HTML file has the following equivalent JavaScript expression:

```
document.images["logoImg"].src = "logo.jpg";
```

The object properties that mirror HTML attributes follow certain conventions. The first is that all properties must begin with a lowercase letter. If the HTML attribute consists of multiple words, then the initial word is lowercase, but the first letter of subsequent words is an uppercase letter, also known as **camel case**. For example, the maxlength attribute from an input element in an HTML document

```
<input type = "text" id = "fName" maxlength = "15" />
```

can be expressed in camel case as follows:

```
document.getElementById("fName").maxLength = 15;
```

If the name of the HTML attribute is a reserved JavaScript name or keyword, the attribute is prefaced with the text string html. The for attribute in the label element

```
<label id = "fLabel" for = "fName">
```

is mirrored by the following JavaScript expression:

```
document.getElementById("fLabel").htmlFor = "fName";
```

One exception to this convention is the class attribute. Because the class name is reserved by JavaScript for other purposes, references to the HTML class attribute use the className property. In Kyle's document, the HTML code

```
<div id = "menu1" class = "menu">
```

which is used to mark the first menu title, has the following equivalent JavaScript expression:

```
document.getElementById("menu1").className = "menu";
```

Once you are comfortable with these conventions, you can easily transfer your knowledge of HTML elements and attributes to their equivalent JavaScript expressions involving object names and properties. Also, because the document object model mirrors the HTML code, you can modify the attribute values of most HTML elements through your JavaScript program.

The only properties you cannot change are the **read-only properties**, which have fixed values. One such property is the appVersion property of the navigator object, which identifies the Web browser version currently in use. However, keep in mind that you cannot upgrade your browser by simply running a JavaScript command to change the value of the appVersion property.

> **Tip**
>
> The className property and the class attribute are not limited to single values. Both the property and the attribute can store a space-separated list of class names used for assigning more than one class to the same object or element.

Object Properties and CSS Styles

CSS styles can also be set in the document object model through the use of the style property. The general syntax of the style property is

```
object.style.attribute
```

where *object* is a document object, and *attribute* is a CSS style attribute applicable to that object. For example, the following command mirrors the effect of applying the CSS font-size style by setting the font size of the first h1 heading in the document to 24 pixels:

```
document.getElementsByTagName("h1")[0].style.fontSize = "24px";
```

Because JavaScript does not support hyphenated letters for property names, the CSS style attribute is formatted in camel case with each hyphenated word entered with an initial capital letter.

You can use the style property to retrieve an element's style values, but only if the style is set as an inline style. For example, if the HTML file contains the tag

```
<div id = "main" style = "width: 200px">
```

you can retrieve the style value and store it in a variable using the following command:

```
widthValue = document.getElementById("main").style.width;
```

The widthValue variable will contain the text string 200px. If you need to extract the numeric value, you would use the parseInt() method described in an earlier tutorial as follows:

```
widthValue = parseInt(document.getElementById("main").style.width);
```

As with HTML attributes, one advantage of the style object is that you can apply your knowledge of CSS styles quickly and easily to your JavaScript code, allowing you to modify the appearance of your document objects through your program.

InSight | Using Classes Versus the Style Object

JavaScript allows styles to be changed in two ways. One approach is to modify the object's appearance by using the style object. For example, to change the font color of an element with the ID heading1 to red, you can run the following command:

```
document.getElementById("heading1").style.color = "red";
```

Another approach is to keep all style changes in a style sheet under different class names. A part of the CSS style sheet to change the font color to red might look like

```
.redText {color: red}
```

allowing the programmer to change the font color by changing the class name as follows:

```
document.getElementById("heading1").className = "redText";
```

There are several good reasons to use classes for this task rather than the style object. First, it is easier to maintain consistent styles for a Web site because all styles are confined to a style sheet rather than spread across style sheets and JavaScript programs. Second, it is usually easier to later modify a style in the style sheet rather than in what might be a long and complex JavaScript program. Finally, test speeds done by Peter-Paul Koch of quirksmode.org have shown that browsers are more responsive and apply style changes more quickly by changing the element class rather than by modifying the style properties directly.

Still, situations exist in which it would be inconvenient to create different classes for every minor change in an object's appearance. Most programmers use a combination of different classes and the style object in their JavaScript programs.

Reference Window | Working with Object Properties

- To set the value of an object property, use
  `object.property = expression`
  where *object* is the object reference, *property* is the object property, and *expression* is the value you want to assign to the property.
- To apply a CSS style to a document object, use
  `object.style.attribute = expression`
  where *attribute* is a CSS style attribute written in camel case and *expression* is a text string containing the value of the CSS style.

Creating an Array of Menus

You have enough information to begin writing the program that generates pull-down menus for Kyle's Web page. The first step is to create an array of all of the elements in Kyle's Web page containing menu titles. All of the menu title elements belong to the menu class. Because JavaScript does not have a built-in object collection to select objects based on their class name, you'll have to write your own. One approach is to loop through the collection of elements in the document, checking each element to determine whether it belongs to the menu class. If it does, it can be added to an array of objects sharing that class name. The code for this loop appears as follows:

```
var menus = new Array();
var allElems = document.getElementsByTagName("*");

for (var i = 0; i < allElems.length; i++) {
   if (allElems[i].className == "menu") menus.push(allElems[i]);
}
```

The code creates two variables. The menus variable starts as an empty array. The allElems variable stores the object collection containing all elements in the Web document. The for loop then loops through each object in the allElems collection and uses the push() method to push each object belonging to the menu class into the menus array. The end result is that the menus array is populated only with document objects that belong to the menu class.

You'll place this code in a new function named init() that you'll add to an external JavaScript file.

To create the init() function:

1. Use your text editor to open the **menustxt.js** file from the tutorial.13/tutorial folder, enter ***your name*** and ***the date*** in the comment section, and then save the file as **menus.js**.
2. Directly below the comment section, insert the following text, as shown in Figure 13-9:

```
function init() {
   var menus = new Array();
   var allElems = document.getElementsByTagName("*");

   for (var i = 0; i < allElems.length; i++) {
      if (allElems[i].className == "menu") menus.push(allElems[i]);
   }
}
```

Figure 13-9 **Code for the init() function**

```
function init() {
   var menus = new Array();
   var allElems = document.getElementsByTagName("*");

   for (var i=0; i < allElems.length; i++) {
      if (allElems[i].className == "menu") menus.push(allElems[i]);
   }
}
```

3. Save your changes to the file.

In this session, you have learned about the document object model, objects, and properties. In the next session, you'll continue to develop a program to create a system of pull-down menus for Kyle's Web site.

Review | Session 13.1 Quick Check

1. What is the document object model?
2. What is the object name for the user's Web browser?
3. What expression references the second hypertext link in the document?
4. An element from the Web document has the ID value footer. Provide an expression referencing this object.
5. What expression references the second paragraph element from the Web document?
6. What JavaScript command sets the action attribute of the first form in a document to the following text string: http://www.avalon.com/mailer.cgi?
7. What JavaScript command changes the second div element in the document to the blueBackground class?
8. What JavaScript command applies a 2 pixel solid black border to the document element with the ID main?
9. Specify the program code to loop through all of the hypertext links in a document, changing their text decoration style to none.

Session 13.2

Exploring Object Methods

After exploring the syntax of JavaScript objects and properties, you continue your work on the pull-down menu program for Kyle's Web site. The next step in exploring JavaScript's document object model is to learn how to work with object methods. You've been using object methods throughout the last three tutorials, but it's time to formalize that understanding. The syntax for applying a method to an object is

```
object.method(parameters)
```

where *object* is the name of the object, *method* is the method to be applied, and *parameters* is a comma-separated list of parameter values used with the method. In the previous tutorials, you applied the write method to the document object to write text into the page. In that case, there was only one parameter value, consisting of the text string to be written into the document. Figure 13-10 provides other examples of applying methods to objects. Note that not every method requires a parameter.

Examples of object methods — Figure 13-10

Expression	Action
location.reload()	Reload the current page in the browser
document.forms[0].reset()	Reset the first form in the Web page
document.forms[0].submit()	Submit the first form in the Web page
document.write("Sherlock Holmes Novels")	Write "Sherlock Holmes Novels" to the Web page
history.back()	Go back to the previous page in the browser's history list
thisDay.getFullYear()	Return the four-digit year value from the thisDay date object
Math.rand()	Return a random value using the Math object
navigator.javaEnabled()	Return a Boolean value indicating whether Java is enabled in the browser
window.close()	Close the browser window
window.print()	Print the contents of the browser window
window.scroll(*x*, *y*)	Scroll the browser window to the (*x*, *y*) coordinate

Working with Object Methods | Reference Window

- To apply a method to an object, use

  `object.method(parameters)`

  where *object* is the object reference, *method* is the method to be applied, and *parameters* is a comma-separated list of parameter values used by the method.

Working with Event Handlers

Finally, you'll examine how to use JavaScript to apply an event to an object. All objects can be affected by events initiated by the user or browser. In previous tutorials, you used event handlers with the HTML attribute

```
<element onevent = "script" ...>
```

where *element* is the name of an HTML element, *event* is a user- or browser-initiated event, and *script* is a JavaScript command or function to be run in response to the event. The on*event* attribute can also be treated as a property of a JavaScript object so that you can assign the same event handler using the statement

```
object.onevent = function;
```

where *object* is an object in the document or browser and *function* is a JavaScript function run in response to the event. For example, the HTML tag

```
<div id = "heading1" onclick = "showlogo()">
```

is mirrored by the following JavaScript command:

```
document.getElementById("heading1").onclick = showlogo;
```

JavaScript assigns only the name of the function to the on*event* property. It doesn't call the function itself. So the following statement would be rejected as a violation of JavaScript syntax:

```
document.getElementById("heading1").onclick = showlogo();
```

Using an event handler as an object property provides programmers with greater flexibility in designing scripts. The function assigned to an event can be changed at one or more points in a program or modified in response to other events initiated by the user or browser. Also, a Web page could contain dozens or hundreds of elements requiring event handlers. Rather than assigning event handlers as attributes to each element tag, a program could loop through this collection of elements, assigning the event handlers automatically.

The other important advantage of treating an event handler as an object property is that it removes scripting from the HTML code, placing it within the external script file. An important goal in Web site design is to separate document content (HTML) from document design (CSS) from document programming (JavaScript). The HTML file should contain little or no style attributes and little or no scripting. Placing event handlers in HTML tags violates this principle; so whenever possible, event handlers should be placed within an external JavaScript file.

One main disadvantage of treating an event handler as object property is the difficulty of passing parameter values to the function assigned to the event. In addition, you can assign only one function at a time to a particular object and event. You can work around this limitation by having the function assigned to the event call two or more other functions when it is run.

Tip

Event handlers can be assigned to document objects only *after* the object has been loaded by the browser.

In the previous session, you began to write the init() function, which generates the collection of menuList elements found in Kyle's document. You'll run this function immediately after the page loads. If you were using event handlers as attributes, you could add the onload attribute to the <body> tag as follows:

```
<body onload = "init()">
```

In JavaScript, to run the init() function when the page is finished loading into the browser window, you run the following statement:

```
window.onload = init;
```

You'll add this command to the menus.js file, and then link the JavaScript file to Kyle's Web page.

To add the onload event handler:

1. If you took a break after the previous session, make sure the menus.js file is open in a text editor and the holmes.htm file is open in your Web browser.
2. Return to the **menus.js** file in your text editor, and then directly above the init() function, insert the following command, as shown in Figure 13-11:

```
window.onload = init;
```

Figure 13-11 Code for the event handler object

```
window.onload = init;        runs the init() function after the page
                             is loaded into the browser window

function init() {
   var menus = new Array();
   var allElems = document.getElementsByTagName("*");

   for (var i = 0; i < allElems.length; i++) {
      if (allElems[i].className == "menu") menus.push(allElems[i]);
   }
}
```

3. Save your changes to the file, and then return to the **holmes.htm** file in your text editor.
4. Link to the menus.js file by adding the following tag to the head section of the document:

```
<script type = "text/javascript" src = "menus.js"></script>
```

5. Close the file, saving your changes. With the onload event handler added to the JavaScript file, you do not need to modify the holmes.htm file anymore. All modifications and additions to your program can be done from within the menus.js file.
6. Reopen or refresh **holmes.htm** in your Web browser. The Web page loads without any errors being reported by your browser.

   Trouble? If your browser reports an error, you may have made a mistake in entering the init() function in the previous session. Open the menus.js file in a text editor, compare your code to the code shown in Figure 13-11, making sure that your code matches both uppercase and lowercase letters and that all text strings are closed with quotation marks. Repeat Steps 5 and 6.

Programming a Pull-Down Menu

You can begin to write the code to create pull-down menus for Kyle. The pull-down menus are opened by clicking any of the six menu titles on Kyle's Web page. You've already created the menus array containing the menu title objects. You use JavaScript to add onclick event handlers to each of the titles to run the changeMenu() function when the title is clicked. The code to create the onclick event handlers is:

```
for (var i = 0; i < menus.length; i++) {
   menus[i].onclick = changeMenu;
}
```

This code loops through all of the items in the menus array. For each item, it adds the onclick event handler, associating the changeMenu() function (which you'll create shortly) with the action of clicking the menu title. Nothing in the code you just entered specifies how many menus are present in the document. This code works for any number of pull-down menus. Kyle could later insert additional pull-down menus to his page or apply this code to other Web pages as long as the menu titles all belong to the menu class.

You'll add the above code to the init() function now.

To add event handlers to the menus:

1. Return to the **menus.js** file in your text editor, and then, at the end of the init() function, add the following code:

```
for (var i = 0; i < menus.length; i++) {
   menus[i].onclick = changeMenu;
}
```

2. Below the init() function, insert the following code for the changeMenu() function:

```
function changeMenu() {
   // this function changes the pull-down menu displayed in the document

}
```

Figure 13-12 highlights the newly inserted code.

Figure 13-12 Event handlers added to the menu titles

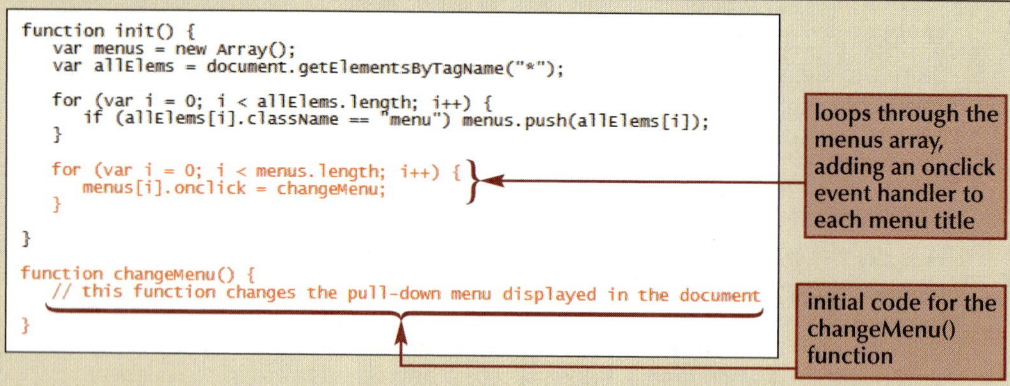

function init() {
var menus = new Array();
var allElems = document.getElementsByTagName("*");
for (var i = 0; i < allElems.length; i++) {
if (allElems[i].className == "menu") menus.push(allElems[i]);
}
for (var i = 0; i < menus.length; i++) {
menus[i].onclick = changeMenu;
}
}
function changeMenu() {
// this function changes the pull-down menu displayed in the document
}
loops through the menus array, adding an onclick event handler to each menu title
initial code for the changeMenu() function

3. Save your changes to the file.

The purpose of the changeMenu function is to change the pull-down menu from one menu list to another. To do that, you need to keep track of what, if any, pull-down menus are currently displayed in the document. You'll store this information in a variable named activeMenu that contains the object reference of the current pull-down menu. If no pull-down menu is being displayed, the value of the activeMenu variable is set to null.

You'll add this variable to the menus.js file, setting its initial value to null.

To create the activeMenu variable:

1. Return to the **menus.js** file in your text editor.
2. Directly above the init() function, insert the following declaration for the active-Menu variable, as shown in Figure 13-13:

```
var activeMenu = null;
```

Figure 13-13 activeMenu variable inserted

```
var activeMenu = null;

function init() {
   var menus = new Array();
   var allElems = document.getElementsByTagName("*");

   for (var i = 0; i < allElems.length; i++) {
      if (allElems[i].className == "menu") menus.push(allElems[i]);
   }

   for (var i = 0; i < menus.length; i++) {
      menus[i].onclick = changeMenu;
   }

}
```

the activeMenu variable stores the object reference of the pull-down menu

3. Save your changes to the file.

The activeMenu variable is defined outside of the context of the init() function to give it global scope, allowing you to reference it in any of the functions within the menus.js file. The initial value of the activeMenu is set to null because, when the page opens, no pull-down menu is visible in the document.

Using the `this` Keyword

As users click different menu titles, the value of the activeMenu variable will be changed and updated in the changeMenu() function. Kyle assigned the menu titles ID values of menu1 through menu6, and he assigned the corresponding pull-down menu lists ID values of menu1List through menu6List. If you know the ID of the menu title the user clicked, you can derive the ID of the corresponding menu list by simply adding the text string List. Because any of the six menu titles in Kyle's document can activate the changeMenu() function, how do you know which one the user clicked? To determine that, you use JavaScript's keyword `this`. The **`this` keyword** references the currently active object in the Web browser. When the changeMenu() function is run, the currently active object is the menu title that was just clicked by the user. From the `this` keyword, you can determine the ID of that menu title using the expression

```
this.id
```

which for Kyle's Web page is equal to one of the text strings from menu1 through menu6. Therefore, the ID of the corresponding pull-down menu is:

```
this.id + "List"
```

Using this information, you'll add the following code to the changeMenu() function:

```
closeOldMenu();

menuID = this.id + "List";
activeMenu = document.getElementById(menuID);
activeMenu.style.display = "block";
```

The first line of this code calls a function named closeOldMenu() to close the currently displayed menu. The next two lines set the object reference of the activeMenu variable to point to the new pull-down menu. Finally, the last line displays the new pull-down menu by changing its CSS display style to block.

You'll add these lines of code to the changeMenu() function.

To edit the changeMenu() function:

1. Within the changeMenu() function, insert the following lines of code, as shown in Figure 13-14:

```
closeOldMenu();

menuID = this.id + "List";
activeMenu = document.getElementById(menuID);
activeMenu.style.display = "block";
```

Figure 13-14 Code for the changeMenu() function

```
function changeMenu() {
   // this function changes the pull-down menu displayed in the document

   closeOldMenu();

   menuID = this.id + "List";
   activeMenu = document.getElementById(menuID);
   activeMenu.style.display = "block";
}
```

this keyword references the object that called the changeMenu() function

2. Save your changes to the file.

Next, you'll create the closeOldMenu() function whose purpose is to close the pull-down menu that is no longer active. The function first must test whether there is an active menu to close (to avoid generating an error message if no menu is active). It does this using the following if condition:

```
function closeOldMenu() {
   if (activeMenu) {
      commands
   }
}
```

If the activeMenu variable is null (meaning that no menu is currently open), then the if condition returns a value of false; otherwise, it will return a value of true and run the command block. The commands in the command block are as follows:

```
function closeOldMenu() {
   if (activeMenu) {
      activeMenu.style.display = "none";
      activeMenu = null;
   }
}
```

Thus, if JavaScript has determined that there is an open pull-down menu, it sets the display style of the menu to none, rehiding it from the user, and then resets the activeMenu variable to null.

You'll add this function to the menus.js file, and then test your code in your browser.

Tip

You can avoid some programming errors when working with document objects by enclosing commands within if statements that verify those objects exist and are supported by your browser.

To insert the closeOldMenu() function and test your page:

1. At the bottom of the **menus.js** file, insert the following function, as shown in Figure 13-15:

```
function closeOldMenu() {
   if (activeMenu) {
      activeMenu.style.display = "none";
      activeMenu = null;
   }
}
```

Figure 13-15 Code for the closeOldMenu() function

```
function changeMenu() {
   // this function changes the pull-down menu displayed in the document

   closeOldMenu();

   menuID = this.id + "List";
   activeMenu = document.getElementById(menuID);
   activeMenu.style.display = "block";

}

function closeOldMenu() {
   if (activeMenu) {
      activeMenu.style.display = "none";
      activeMenu = null;
   }
}
```

closes the currently-opened pull-down menu

2. Save your changes to the file.
3. Refresh or reopen the **holmes.htm** file in your Web browser.
4. Click each of the six menu titles at the top of the page and verify that clicking a menu title opens the corresponding pull-down menu while closing any previously opened pull-down menu. See Figure 13-16.

Figure 13-16 Pull-down menu being tested

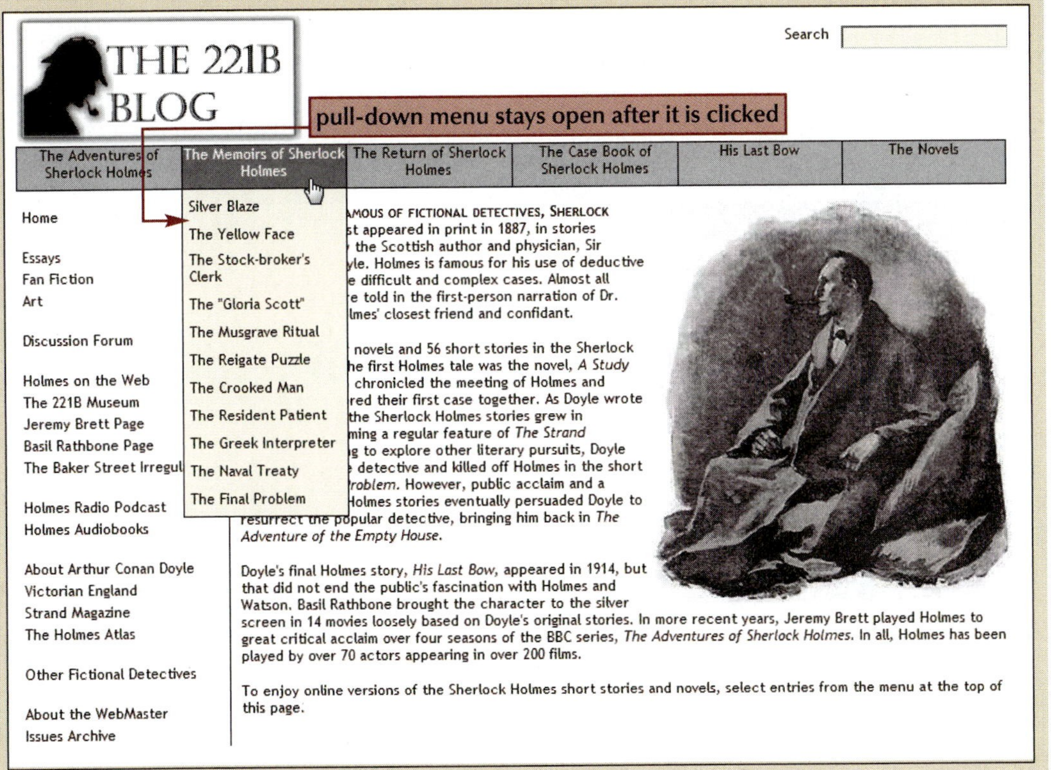

5. Click within the page content. The pull-down menu remains open.

You need to revise the code to make the pull-down menus disappear if the user clicks elsewhere within the body of the Web page. You can do this by adding the onclick event handler to the page's logo, list of links, and main text to run the closeOldMenu() function.

To add the onclick event handlers:

1. Return to the **menus.js** file in your text editor.
2. At the bottom of the init() function, insert the following statements, as shown in Figure 13-17:

```
document.getElementById("logo").onclick = closeOldMenu;
document.getElementById("linkList").onclick = closeOldMenu;
document.getElementById("main").onclick = closeOldMenu;
```

Figure 13-17 **Code for the onclick event handlers**

```
function init() {
   var menus = new Array();
   var allElems = document.getElementsByTagName("*");

   for (var i = 0; i < allElems.length; i++) {
      if (allElems[i].className == "menu") menus.push(allElems[i]);
   }

   for (var i = 0; i < menus.length; i++) {
      menus[i].onclick = changeMenu;
   }

   document.getElementById("logo").onclick = closeOldMenu;
   document.getElementById("linkList").onclick = closeOldMenu;
   document.getElementById("main").onclick = closeOldMenu;
}
```

runs the closeOldMenu() function when the user clicks within the page logo, the list of links, or the main text

3. Save your changes to the file, and then refresh the **holmes.htm** file in your Web browser.
4. Verify that you can close all of the pull-down menus by clicking anywhere within the page logo, main text, or list of links. If you click a blank area of the document window outside of the page content, the pull-down menu does not close.

Object Detection with JavaScript | InSight

In the closeOldMenu() function, you enclosed the commands within an if statement that verified the existence of the activeMenu object. This is because you had to confirm the existence of the activeMenu object before you could apply the display style property to it. This process of confirming support for an object is known as **object detection** and has the general form

```
if (object) {
   commands
}
```

where *object* is a JavaScript reference to an object and *commands* are commands that apply if that object exists and is supported by the browser. If the condition of the if statement fails, then the browser skips all of the statements in *commands*, avoiding an error that could cause the program to fail.

For example, the following statement verifies that the browser supports the document.images collection before attempting to use that object in a for loop:

```
if (document.images) {
   for (var i = 0; i < document.images.length; i++) {
      document.images[i].style.border = "1px solid black";
   }
}
```

Object detection can also be used with methods. To detect support for a method, include the method name without the brackets. The code

```
if (window.focus) {
   commands
}
```

confirms that the browser supports the window.focus() method before attempting to run commands involving it.

Object detection is often used when reconciling inconsistencies between different object models. The IE4 DOM employs the document.all object to reference all objects found within the Web page document, but this object is not supported in the W3C DOM. To write commands specifically for the IE4 DOM, you could enclose them within the following if statement:

```
if (document.all) {
   IE4-specific commands
}
```

You can also employ object detection for the W3C DOM. The if condition

```
if (document.getElementById && document.createElement) {
   W3C DOM commands
}
```

can be used to confirm that the browser supports the features of the W3C DOM.

Object detection is an important tool for the JavaScript programmer and should be used whenever there is a question about the support for an object or method.

Adding Handlers for Mouse Events

Kyle has one more suggestion for the pull-down menu system. As the users move the pointer from one menu title to another, he wants the displayed pull-down menu to change with it, as shown in Figure 13-18.

Figure 13-18 Pull-down menu changes by moving the pointer

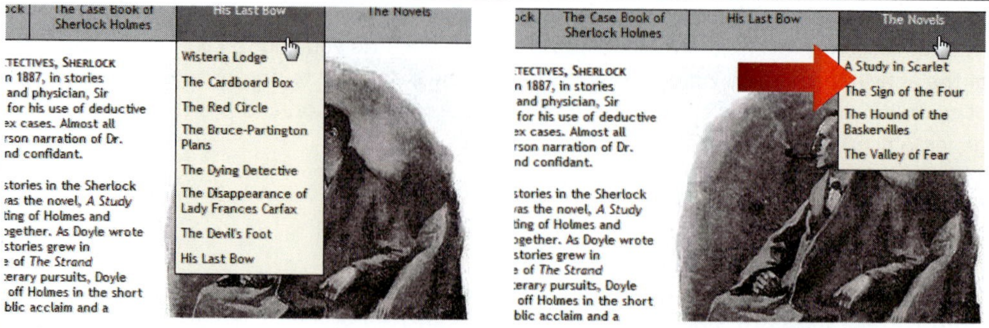

moving the pointer from one menu title to another changes the pull-down menu

To create this effect, you have to add an event handler that responds to the motions of the pointer. One such event handler is onmouseover, which is activated whenever the pointer initially moves over an object. You'll add an onmouseover event handler to the menu titles that activates the function moveMenu() in response.

Tip

To run a function in response to the pointer moving off of an object, use the onmouseout event handler.

To add the onmouseover event handler:

1. Return to the **menus.js** file in your text editor.
2. Within the second for loop in the init() function, add the following line of code:

```
menus[i].onmouseover = moveMenu;
```

3. Directly below the init() function, insert the following code:

```
function moveMenu() {
   // this function moves the pull-down menu from one title to another

}
```

Figure 13-19 highlights the newly added code in the file.

Figure 13-19 Code for the onmouseover event handler

```
function init() {
   var menus = new Array();
   var allElems = document.getElementsByTagName("*");

   for (var i = 0; i < allElems.length; i++) {
      if (allElems[i].className == "menu") menus.push(allElems[i]);
   }

   for (var i = 0; i < menus.length; i++) {
      menus[i].onclick = changeMenu;
      menus[i].onmouseover = moveMenu;
   }

   document.getElementById("logo").onclick = closeOldMenu;
   document.getElementById("linkList").onclick = closeOldMenu;
   document.getElementById("main").onclick = closeOldMenu;

}
function moveMenu() {
   // this function moves the pull-down menu from one title to another

}
```

runs the moveMenu() when the pointer initially moves over a menu title

4. Save your changes to the file.

The code for the moveMenu() function is similar to the code you entered for the changeMenu() function except that it must be enclosed within an if statement to verify that a pull-down menu is already opened. Kyle wants the moveMenu() function to be run only when the user is moving the pointer from one pull-down menu to another, not just whenever the pointer moves over a menu title. The code for the moveMenu() function is therefore:

```
if (activeMenu) {
   closeOldMenu();

   menuID = this.id + "List";
   activeMenu = document.getElementById(menuID);
   activeMenu.style.display = "block";
}
```

You'll add this code to the moveMenu() function.

To edit the moveMenu() function:

1. Within the moveMenu() function insert the following code, as shown in Figure 13-20:

```
if (activeMenu) {
   closeOldMenu();

   menuID = this.id + "List";
   activeMenu = document.getElementById(menuID);
   activeMenu.style.display = "block";
}
```

Figure 13-20 Code for the moveMenu() function

```
function moveMenu() {
   // this function moves the pull-down menu from one title to another

   if (activeMenu) {
      closeOldMenu();

      menuID = this.id + "List";
      activeMenu = document.getElementById(menuID);
      activeMenu.style.display = "block";
   }
}
```

2. Save your changes to the file.
3. Reopen or refresh the **holmes.htm** file in your Web browser.
4. Click the menu titles for the pull-down menus and verify that as you move the pointer over the other menu titles, the browser automatically opens the corresponding menu.
5. Click outside the pull-down menus to close them.

Kyle likes the changes to the pull-down menus you created. He is pleased that you were able to create a menu system that effectively manages all of the links to the Sherlock Holmes stories and novels.

Review | Session 13.2 Quick Check

1. What is the syntax for applying an object method?
2. What object and method reload the current Web page in the browser?
3. What command runs the showMenu() function whenever the user clicks the element with the ID value pullMenu?
4. What JavaScript code runs the showLinks() function whenever a user clicks a hypertext in the Web document?
5. What is the syntax error in the following code?:

```
document.getElementById("slide").onclick = loadImage();
```

6. What is object detection?
7. What code runs the command showMenu(), but only if the user's browser supports the IE4 DOM?
8. What JavaScript command runs the showMenu() function when the user initially moves the pointer over the element with the ID value pullMenu?

Session 13.3

Animating a Pull-Down Menu

Kyle has been reviewing the Web site and the site's home page. The pull-down menu code you wrote works well. Kyle has one more request: He wants you to add the illusion of the menu being pulled down or unrolled from the menu title so that the menu would appear in stages rather than all at once, as shown in Figure 13-21. Kyle thinks this would add some visual appeal to the site's home page.

Figure 13-21 **Animated pull-down menu**

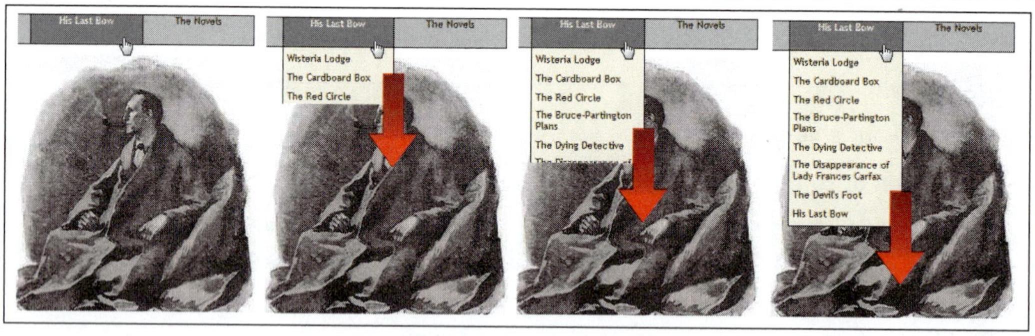

You can create this effect in several ways. One way is to use the CSS clip style. Recall that the clip style makes only part of an object visible by "clipping" a rectangular section out of the object. The syntax of the clip style is

```
clip: rect(top, right, bottom, left)
```

where *top*, *right*, *bottom*, and *left* define the coordinates of the top, right, bottom, and left corners of the clipping rectangle. For example, the following style creates a clipping rectangle that is located in the upper-left corner of the object and is 150 pixels wide and 200 pixels high:

```
clip: rect(0px, 150px, 200px, 0px)
```

For Kyle's pull-down menus, you want to start with a clipping rectangle that is located in the upper-left corner of the object with a width at least as great as the width of the menu and a height of 0 pixels. You would then gradually increase the height of the rectangle, leaving the other dimensions unchanged.

The initial size of the clipping rectangle can be set by adding the following command to the changeMenu() and moveMenu() functions:

```
activeMenu.style.clip = "rect(0px, 150px, 0px, 0px)";
```

The value of the *right* parameter is set to 150 pixels to ensure that the entire width of the menu is displayed. The rest of the parameters are set to 0 pixels to hide the menu from the user. You'll add this command to both functions.

To apply the clip style:

1. If you took a break after the previous session, make sure the menus.js file is open in a text editor and the holmes.htm file is open in a Web browser.
2. Return to the **menus.js** file in your text editor.
3. Within the changeMenu() and moveMenu() functions, insert the following command, as shown in Figure 13-22:

```
activeMenu.style.clip = "rect(0px, 150px, 0px, 0px)";
```

Figure 13-22 Clip style applied

```
function moveMenu() {
   // this function moves the pull-down menu from one title to another

   if (activeMenu) {
      closeOldMenu();

      menuID = this.id + "List";
      activeMenu = document.getElementById(menuID);
      activeMenu.style.clip = "rect(0px, 150px, 0px, 0px)";
      activeMenu.style.display = "block";
   }
}

function changeMenu() {
   // this function changes the pull-down menu displayed in the document

   closeOldMenu();

   menuID = this.id + "List";
   activeMenu = document.getElementById(menuID);
   activeMenu.style.clip = "rect(0px, 150px, 0px, 0px)";
   activeMenu.style.display = "block";
}
```

4. Save your changes to the file.

When a user opens a pull-down menu, JavaScript should repeatedly apply the clip style to the menu, increasing the value of the *bottom* parameter until it exceeds a certain value after which point the entire object is displayed. You can repeatedly modify the clip style by placing the command to do so within a function and then running that function at timed intervals using the setInterval() method described in Tutorial 11. The general form of the function, which we'll call rollDown(), is:

```
function rollDown() {
   increase the clip height value
   if the height is less than the maximum value
      clip the menu
   else
```

```
        stop running the function
}
```

To run this function, you need to add two more global variables to the menus.js file. One is the clipHgt variable, which keeps track of the current value of the height of the clipping rectangle. The other is the timeID variable, which stores the ID of the timed interval function so that it can be halted once the entire menu is displayed. You'll add both of these variables to the file.

To add the clipHgt and timeID variables:

1. Scroll to the top of the **menus.js** file.
2. Directly above the init() function, insert the following two variable declarations, as shown in Figure 13-23:

```
var clipHgt = 0;
var timeID;
```

Figure 13-23 Code for the clipHgt and timeID variables

```
var activeMenu = null;
var clipHgt = 0;
var timeID;
```

The initial value of the clipHgt is set to 0 because the pull-down menus will start out clipped to a rectangle with a height of 0 pixels.

The code for the rollDown() function is:

```
function rollDown() {
   clipHgt = clipHgt + 10;
   if (clipHgt < 400) {
      activeMenu.style.clip = "rect(0px, 150px," + clipHgt + "px, 0px)";
   } else {
      clearInterval(timeID);
      clipHgt = 0;
   }
}
```

Every time the function is run, the value of the clipHgt variable is increased by 10. As long as the clipping height is less than 400, the activeMenu object is clipped up to the height of the clipHgt value. Once the clipHgt value exceeds 400, the clearInterval() method is called, halting the timed execution of the function, and the clipHgt variable value is reset to 0. A maximum value of 400 was chosen for the clipHgt variable because all of the menu lists on Kyle's Web page are less than 400 pixels in height.

You'll add the rollDown() function to the file.

Tip

Clipping an object beyond the object's borders has no impact on how the object is displayed by the browser.

To add the rollDown() function:

1. At the bottom of the **menus.js** file, insert the following function, as shown in Figure 13-24:

```
function rollDown() {
   clipHgt = clipHgt + 10;
   if (clipHgt < 400) {
      activeMenu.style.clip = "rect(0px, 150px," + clipHgt + "px,
       0px)";
   } else {
```

```
            clearInterval(timeID);
            clipHgt = 0;
        }
    }
```

Figure 13-24 Code for the rollDown() function

```
function closeOldMenu() {
   if (activeMenu) {
      activeMenu.style.display = "none";
      activeMenu = null;
   }
}

function rollDown() {
   clipHgt = clipHgt + 10;
   if (clipHgt < 400) {
      activeMenu.style.clip = "rect(0px, 150px," + clipHgt + "px, 0px)";
   } else {
      clearInterval(timeID);
      clipHgt = 0;
   }
}
```

increases the clipping height by 10 pixels

if the height is less than 400 pixels, clips the menu

otherwise stops running the rollDown() function and resets the clipHgt value to 0

2. Save your changes to the file.

To complete the illusion of a menu unrolling as the height of the clipping rectangle increases, you'll call the rollDown() function every millisecond using the setInterval() method. To keep track of the function, you'll store the ID of the timed function in the timeID variable you declared earlier.

You'll add the setInterval() method to both the moveMenu() and changeMenu() functions.

To call the rollDown() function:

1. Within the moveMenu() and changeMenu() functions, insert the following command directly after the statement that sets the display style of the activeMenu object to display, as shown in Figure 13-25:

```
timeID = setInterval("rollDown()", 1);
```

Figure 13-25 Code to call the rollDown() function

```
function moveMenu() {
   // this function moves the pull-down menu from one title to another

   if (activeMenu) {
      closeOldMenu();

      menuID = this.id + "List";
      activeMenu = document.getElementById(menuID);
      activeMenu.style.clip = "rect(0px, 150px, 0px, 0px)";
      activeMenu.style.display = "block";
      timeID = setInterval("rollDown()", 1);
   }
}

function changeMenu() {
   // this function changes the pull-down menu displayed in the document

   closeOldMenu();

   menuID = this.id + "List";
   activeMenu = document.getElementById(menuID);
   activeMenu.style.clip = "rect(0px, 150px, 0px, 0px)";
   activeMenu.style.display = "block";
   timeID = setInterval("rollDown()", 1);
}
```

runs the rollDown() function once every millisecond until it is cleared

Finally, you need to turn off the rollDown() function whenever your program closes a pull-down menu. This prevents a situation where the rollDown() function is running for a menu that has already been closed. To turn off the function, you'll add a clearInterval() method to the closeOldMenu() function.

2. Scroll down to the closeOldMenu() function, and then insert the following command, as shown in Figure 13-26:

```
clearInterval(timeID);
```

Figure 13-26 **Code to clear the rollDown() function timer**

```
function closeOldMenu() {
   if (activeMenu) {
      clearInterval(timeID);
      activeMenu.style.display = "none";
      activeMenu = null;
   }
}
```

clears the timer, halting the operation of the rollDown() function

3. Close the **menus.js** file, saving your changes.
4. Reopen or refresh **holmes.htm** in your Web browser.
5. Click the menu titles on the Web page and verify that each pull-down menu is opened with the illusion of being rolled out or pulled down on the Web page.

Kyle is pleased with the pull-down menu effect you created. The rolling down effect is exactly what he wanted.

Creating Other Types of Menus

Pull-down menus are only one type of menu you can create with JavaScript. Menu styles fall into four general classes: pull-downs, pop-ups, sliding, and tabbed.

Creating Pop-Up Menus

Pop-up menus are closely associated with pull-down menus. In a **pop-up menu**, a user clicks an object on the page and the menu appears, sometimes elsewhere on the page. Unlike pull-down menus, pop-up menus are not usually associated with a menu bar or a list of menu titles. To close a pop-up menu, a user clicks either the menu itself or another item on the page.

One common way to create a pop-up menu for the Web is to place the menu contents within a set of <div> container tags, hidden on the page using the visibility style attribute. When a user clicks an object on the page, a JavaScript program is run that unhides the menu. To rehide the menu, a second JavaScript program is run that changes the menu's visibility property back to hidden.

Creating Sliding Menus

In a **sliding menu**, a menu is partially hidden either off the Web page or behind another object. When the user clicks the visible part of the menu, the menu "slides" into a fully visible position, as shown in Figure 13-27.

Figure 13-27 **Sliding menu**

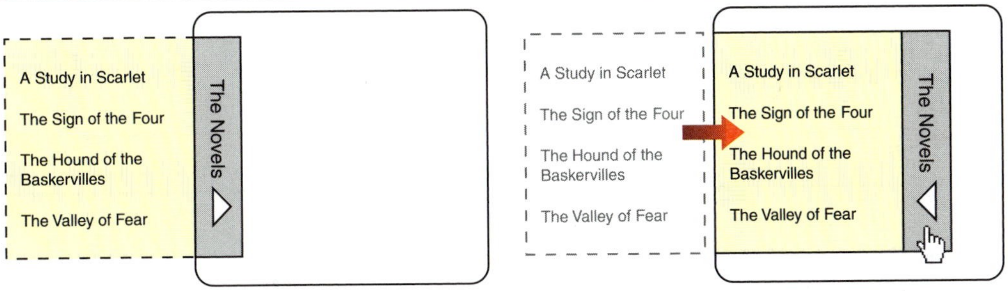

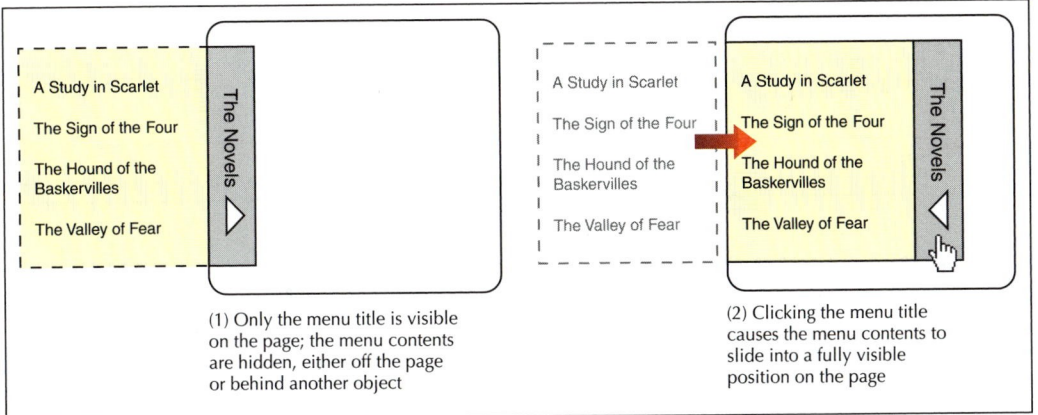

(1) Only the menu title is visible on the page; the menu contents are hidden, either off the page or behind another object

(2) Clicking the menu title causes the menu contents to slide into a fully visible position on the page

To create a sliding menu, use the positioning styles of the object to place it in a location where it is partially obscured. To place the object off the page, use absolute positioning and set the top and left styles to negative values. For example, the style declaration

```
position: absolute; top: -50px; left: -10px;
```

sets the object 50 pixels above and 10 pixels to the left of the visible browser window. To place a sliding menu behind another object, use the z-index style to set it below the other image on the page.

Once the sliding menu has been partially obscured, you can move the image across the page by modifying the values of the top or left style. For example, to set the top position to 20 pixels, you can apply the command

```
object.style.top = "20px";
```

where *object* is the document reference to an object. To create the illusion of moving an object across the page, you can employ the same technique of calling a function at timed intervals that you used with the rolling down effect on Kyle's Web page. The following code demonstrates how you can move an object horizontally across the page at the rate of 5 pixels every millisecond.

```
timeID = setInterval("moveItemRight()", 1);

function moveItemRight() {
   currentPos = parseInt(object.style.left);
   if ((currentPos + 5) <= 250) {
      object.style.left = leftPos + 5 + "px";
   } else {
      clearInterval(timeID);
   }
}
```

In this code, the object continues to move right until its left coordinate exceeds 250 pixels, at which time the moveItemRight() function will no longer be called by the browser. To keep track of the current position of the object, you use the parseInt() method to extract the numeric value from the object's left property. For example, if the value of the left property is 150px, the value of the currentPos variable will be 150.

Tip

To change an object's left or top position, the initial position style should be set either as an inline style or within the JavaScript program.

Creating Tabbed Menus

In a **tabbed menu**, several menus are stacked on the page with one part of each menu visible to the user. When you click the visible part of a menu, the selected menu moves to the top of the stack, making its contents visible to the user, as shown in Figure 13-28.

Figure 13-28 **Tabbed menu**

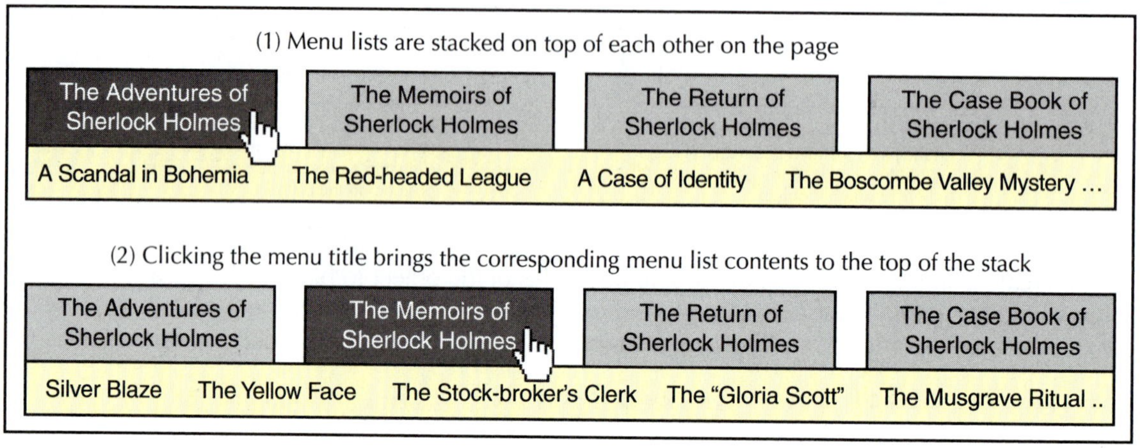

To create a tabbed menu system, you need to ensure that part of each menu is always visible, no matter where it is located in the stack. To move items to the top of the stack, you can simply change the value of the z-index style for the selected menu, setting the value to one higher than the z-index value of the menu currently on top of the stack. For example, if menu3List is on top of the stack and you want to move menu5List to the top, you could run this set of commands

```
menu3List = document.getElementById("menu3List");
menu5List = document.getElementById("menu5List");
maxZ = menu3List.style.zIndex;
menu5List.style.zIndex = maxZ+1;
```

and the menu5List object would be displayed on top of the menu3List object. An important point to remember is that when referencing a style such as the z-index style, the initial style value must be set either within the JavaScript program or as an inline style.

Retrieving Style Sheet Values | InSight

The style property can be used to set styles and to retrieve inline style values, but it cannot retrieve style values set in an external style sheet. This is because the style that the browser ultimately applies to an object is a computed value determined by resolving competing style declarations within the style sheet, the HTML code, and the browser itself. To access a computed style, the W3C DOM supports the getComputedStyle method

```
document.defaultView.getComputedStyle(object, pseudo)
```

where *object* is the reference to an object in the document and *pseudo* is a CSS pseudo-element within the object. If no pseudo-element exists, you can set the value of the *pseudo* parameter to null. For example, the following code retrieves the computed styles for the menu object:

```
menu = document.getElementById("menu");
mStyles = document.defaultView.getComputedStyle(menu, null);
```

To retrieve a specific style value for an object, you apply the getPropertyValue method

```
getPropertyValue(style)
```

where *style* is the name of a CSS style property. Therefore, to retrieve the value of the width property for the menu object, you apply the following command:

```
menuWidth = mStyles.getPropertyValue("width")
```

The IE DOM doesn't support these methods. Instead, to retrieve the computed style, you apply the following currentStyle method:

```
object.currentStyle[style]
```

Thus, to retrieve the width property for the menu object under the IE DOM, you use:

```
menuWidth = menu.currentStyle["width"]
```

If you're creating a Web site under both document object models, you can resolve the syntax differences between the two DOMs by applying object detection. The general code has the form

```
if (window.getComputedStyle) {
   W3C DOM
} else if (object.currentStyle) {
   IE DOM
}
```

where *object* is the object containing the CSS styles you want to retrieve and *W3C DOM* and *IE DOM* are the commands applicable under the W3C and IE document object models.

Exploring Custom Objects

In this tutorial, you worked with JavaScript's built-in objects and document objects to create Kyle's pull-down menu system. A third kind of object is custom objects created by the user. Although you don't need to use custom objects for Kyle's Web site, creating a custom object to handle particular tasks or calculations can greatly expand your code's flexibility and power.

The new Operator

You've seen how objects can be referenced and stored in variables using the new operator. The general syntax of the new operator is

```
var obj = new object();
```

where *object* is the general name of the object and *obj* is a variable that contains a specific example of the object. Specific objects are referred to as **instances** of the object, while the general object itself is the **object class**. You've already worked with this kind of statement with JavaScript's built-in objects such as the statement

```
var thisDate = new Date();
```

which creates an instance of a date object from the Date class of objects, or the following command that creates an instance of a JavaScript array object from the Array object class:

```
var timeValues = new Array();
```

The new operator is also used to create customized objects. For example, to create a class of objects for rectangles, you could enter the following statement:

```
var rectangle1 = new rect();
```

JavaScript will treat rect as a new object class and rectangle1 as a particular instance of that rect class. Neither the rect object class nor the specific instance of that object stored in the rectangle1 variable have any properties or methods associated with them. You'll examine how to define properties for these objects.

Defining Customized Properties

Properties are defined for instances of objects by simply adding the property name to the object variable. For example, the following two statements add the width and height properties to the rectangle1 object instance, setting their values to 5 and 6, respectively:

```
rectangle1.width = 5;
rectangle1.height = 6;
```

Once you define these property values, you can reference them the same way you would any of the built-in JavaScript object properties. For example, to calculate the area of rectangle1, you could run the following command:

```
var area1 = rectangle1.width*rectangle1.height;
```

To change the value of rectangle1's width, you would just run another command referencing the width property, and so on.

Note that the width and height properties were defined only for the rectangle1 instance, not for the rect class of objects. If you created a second instance called rectangle2, it would not have either the width or the height properties until you explicitly defined them in an expression.

Running Object Constructors

For an object class to have built-in object properties, you have to run an object constructor. An **object constructor** is a function that defines the properties of a whole class of objects. The syntax of an object constructor is

```
var obj = new object();

function object() {
   properties
}
```

where *object* is the name of the new object class and *properties* are commands that set the names of properties associated with the object class. The name of the new object class is the same as the function that defines it. To define properties within this function, you use the JavaScript keyword this as the object name. So, to create width and height properties for the rect class, you could run the following code:

```
function rect() {
   this.width;
   this.height;
}
```

Note that you didn't define a value for the width and height properties, but that can be done after a specific instance of the rect object is created. So, to create an instance of the rect class, you would run the commands:

```
var rectangle2 = new rect();
rectangle2.width = 4;
rectangle2.height = 8;
```

You can also add parameters to the constructor function to allow users to define initial values for the properties of the object. For the rect object, this could appear as the following:

```
function rect(w, h) {
   this.width = w;
   this.height = h;
}
```

Now, to define the initial dimensions of the rectangle, you could run the single command

```
var rectangle2 = new rect(4, 8);
```

and values for the rectangle2.width and rectangle2.height properties would be automatically inserted by the object constructor.

Creating Customized Methods

As you've seen in this tutorial, methods are actions associated with objects. Another way to say this is that methods are functions associated with objects. However, in JavaScript, functions are themselves considered objects (remember that almost everything is an object to JavaScript). So, to create a method for an object, you can associate a function with the object. The general syntax for associating a function with an object is

```
object.method = function;
```

where *object* is a customized object, *method* is the name of the method, and *function* is the name of a function on which the method is based. After a method has been associated with an object, you can run it in the usual way. For example, if you create a function named calcArea() that calculates the area of an object given its width and height, the function is:

```
function calcArea() {
   return this.width*this.height;
}
```

This function again uses the `this` keyword to refer to the current object being processed. Next, you'll associate this method with the rectangle1 object to create a method named area as follows:

```
rectangle1.area = calcArea;
```

Defining the area method doesn't run it; to run the method, you apply it as follows

```
var area1 = rectangle1.area();
```

and JavaScript automatically applies the calcArea() function in running the area method. If rectangle1's width property is equal to 5 and the height property is equal to 6, the area1 variable will store the value 30. Again, this method is defined only for the rectangle1 instance, not for the class of rect objects. To make the area method a part of the rect class, you must add it to the constructor function. The complete code for the rect constructor function would look like the following:

```
function rect(w, h) {
   this.width = w;
   this.height = h;
   this.area = calcArea;
}
```

Now you can use the area method with any instance of the rect class of objects. The following code creates a 7 × 4 rectangle object and calculates the area using the customized area method:

```
var rectangle3 = new rect(7, 4);
var area3 = rectangle3.area();
```

As you can see, by defining customized objects, properties, and methods, the code is greatly simplified. You can also add to the constructor function's method to calculate the rectangle's perimeter or increase the rectangle's width or height by set amounts. Although the rectangle object is a simple application of this technique, the general approach can be used for a wide range of complicated objects and features.

At this point, you've completed your work on Kyle's Web page. Through the use of JavaScript objects, properties, and methods, you've placed a large list of links on the page. Kyle is pleased with the final project.

Review | Session 13.3 Quick Check

1. What command applies a clipping rectangle to the mainDIV element located in the top-left corner of the object, having a width of 100 pixels and a height of 50 pixels?
2. What command repeats the function slideMenu() every second?
3. What command increases the value of the top coordinate of the Menu1 object by 5 pixels?
4. What command increases the z-index of the Menu1 object by 1?
5. The width value of the menu1 object has been set to 100 pixels in an external style sheet. What value is returned by the following expression?:

   ```
   document.getElementById("menu1").style.width
   ```

6. You want to retrieve the value of the font-size attribute for the Menu1 object based on the value set in the Web page's external style sheet. Specify the commands to do this under the W3C DOM and the IE DOM.
7. Indicate the commands to construct an object class named circle. Provide the class of circle objects with a property named radius and a method named circum() that returns the circle's circumference (equal to $2\pi r$ where r is the radius). Assume that the circle's radius can be set as a parameter named r of the constructor function.
8. Using the object constructor you defined in the previous question, specify the code to create an instance of the circle object named circle1 with the circle's radius set to 5. Store the circumference in a variable named circum1.

Tutorial Summary | Review

This tutorial introduced the concept of the JavaScript object. The first session covered the fundamentals of objects, including the relation of Web elements and features to the document object model. You examined how to access object collections from the DOM and how to reference Web page elements based on tag name, ID value, and name value. You then learned how to create an array of Web page elements all sharing the same class value. The second session focused on how to use knowledge of objects, properties, and events to create an interactive pull-down menu system for a Web page. You explored the use of event handlers as object properties and saw how to employ the onclick and onmouseover event handlers in a JavaScript program. The third session refined the pull-down menu system created in the second session by adding animation using the setInterval() method and the CSS clip style. In this session, you explored how to write code for sliding menus and tabbed menus. The session concluded with a quick overview of techniques to create and employ custom objects.

Key Terms

basic model
built-in object
camel case
customized object
document object
document object model (DOM)
document tree
DOM Level 0
DOM Level 1
DOM Level 2
DOM Level 3
dot syntax
event
IE4 DOM
instance
method
object class
object collection
object constructor
object detection
object name
object-based language
pop-up menu
property
pull-down menu
read-only property
sliding menu
tabbed menu
`this` keyword
W3C DOM

Practice | Review Assignments

Practice the skills you learned in the tutorial using the same case scenario.

Data files needed for this Review Assignment: sherlocktxt.htm, slidestxt.js, arrow.gif, logo.jpg, mblog.css, sh.jpg

Kyle has made some modifications to the page layout of his Web site. Rather than having two sets of links—one at the top and one at the bottom—he has placed all of the links in the left page margin. There are still a lot of links on the page. Kyle wants you to design a sliding menu system in which hidden menus slide horizontally across the page to be revealed to the user. A preview of the completed page is shown in Figure 13-29.

Figure 13-29

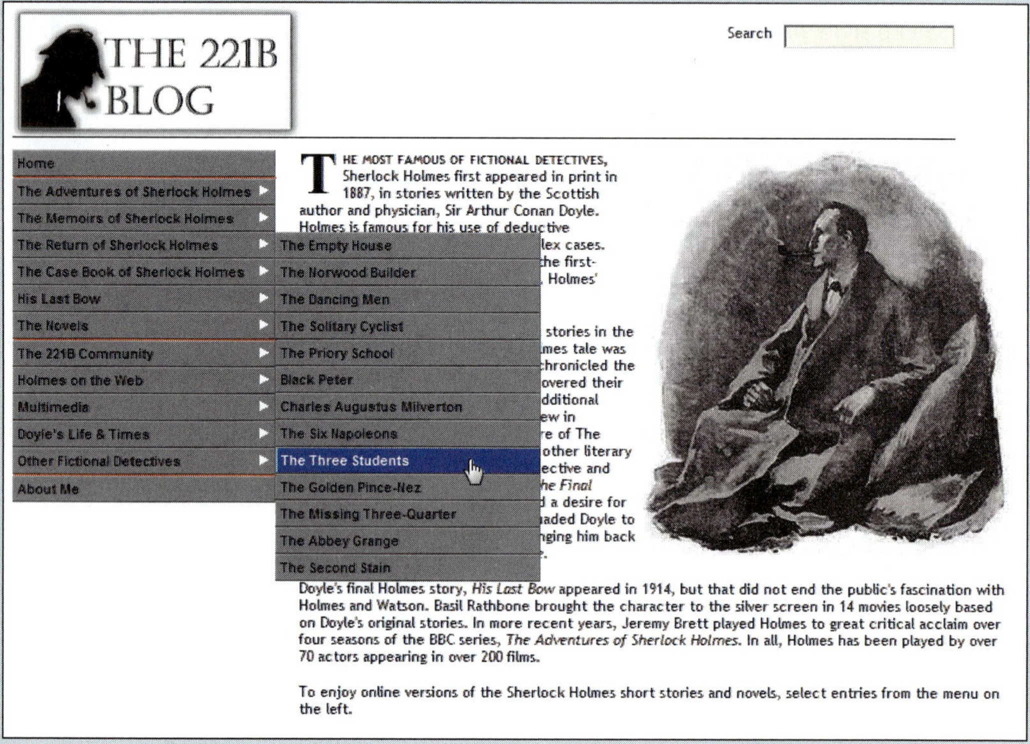

The structure of the links on this revised page has also changed. Rather than having menu titles and menu lists placed in separate div containers, Kyle opted to create a series of nested ordered lists containing the links. You'll have to take this new structure into account when you write your program.

Kyle also wants to change how the menus are activated. Menus should be displayed when the user clicks the menu title from the list of links. Menus should close whenever: (a) the user clicks another menu title, (b) the user clicks the main part of the page or the page head, and (c) the user clicks the same menu title twice. He does not want menu titles to be activated by the motions of the pointer.

Complete the following:

1. Using your text editor, open **sherlocktxt.htm** and **slidestxt.js** from the tutorial.13/review folder, enter ***your name*** and ***the date*** in the head section of each file, and then save the files as **sherlock.htm** and **slides.js**, respectively.

2. Study the code of the **sherlock.htm** file in your text editor to understand the structure of the list of links on the page. Then, link the file to the **slides.js** JavaScript file and close it.
3. Return to the **slides.js** file in your text editor. Below the comments, insert a command to run the function makeMenus() when the browser has completed loading the page.
4. Add the following three global variables to the file:
   - **currentSlide** used to reference the sliding menu currently displayed in the document. Set its initial value to null.
   - **timeID** used to reference timed interval commands. Set its initial value to null.
   - **leftPos** used to store the left coordinate of the active sliding menu. Set its initial value to 0.
5. Add the **makeMenus()** function. The purpose of this function is to create a reference to all sliding menus in the document and to apply event handlers to objects in the document. Add the following commands to the function:
   a. Create an instance of the array object named **slideMenus**.
   b. Use the getElementsByTagName() method to store all of the elements in the document in an array named **allElems**.
   c. Loop through the elements in the allElems array, pushing all of the elements belonging to the slideMenu class into the slideMenus array.
   d. Loop through all of the items in the slideMenus array and apply the onclick event handler to those objects to run the showSlide() function. Also, for each object in the slideMenus array, reference the first ul element within that object and set the value of the ul elements left style property to 0px. This command moves all sliding menus (enclosed in unordered lists) to the far left of the page.
   e. Add onclick event handlers to the elements with ID values of head and main, running the closeSlide() function.
6. Add the **showSlide()** function to the file. The purpose of this function is to display a sliding menu on the Web page. In the first line of the function, create a variable named **slideList** that stores an object reference to the first ul element nested within the current object (as referenced by the `this` keyword).
7. Add an if statement to the showSlide() function. The purpose of the if statement is to test whether a sliding menu is currently displayed on the page. If the currentSlide object is not equal to null and the ID of the currentSlide is equal to the ID of the slideList variable, then run the closeSlide() function; otherwise, do the following:
   a. Run the closeSlide() function.
   b. Set the currentSlide variable equal to the slideList variable.
   c. Set the display style of the currentSlide variable to block.
   d. Run the moveSlide() function repeated at intervals of 1 millisecond. Store the ID of the timed function in timeID.
8. Add the **closeSlide()** function. The purpose of this function is to close any active sliding menu. Use object detection to confirm that the currentSlide variable is not equal to null and then run the following commands:
   a. Clear the timed function referenced by the timeID variable.
   b. Set the left style of the currentSlide object to 0px and set the display style to none.
   c. Set the value of currentSlide to null.

9. Add the **moveSlide()** function. The purpose of this function is to move a sliding menu horizontally across the page until the left coordinate of the menu exceeds 220 pixels. Add the following commands to the function:
    a. Increase the value of the leftPos variable by 5.
    b. If the value of the left position of the currentSlide object is less than or equal to 220, then set the left style of that object to the coordinates *leftPos*px where *leftPos* is the value of the leftPos variable.
    c. Otherwise, clear the timed function referenced by the timeID variable and reset the value of the leftPos variable to 0.
10. Close the file, saving your changes.
11. Open **sherlock.htm** in your Web browser. Click the links from the list containing a white triangle and verify that clicking those titles results in a submenu containing additional links sliding across the page. Also, verify that you can close a menu by clicking another title, clicking the same title twice, or clicking elsewhere in the main body of the Web page.
12. Submit the completed project to your instructor.

Apply | Case Problem 1

Use JavaScript to create a tabbed menu system.

Data Files needed for this Case Problem: printertxt.htm, jemenustxt.js, back.jpg, back2.jpg, je.css, logo.jpg, printer.jpg

Jackson Electronics Tara Dawson is in charge of Web site development for the product portion of the Jackson Electronics (JE) Web site. Recently the company began an overhaul of the site's design. One goal of the overhaul is to improve navigation of the site by placing links to different pages within a system of online menus. Tara asked you to work on the design of the home page describing JE's printer products.

Tara wants you to program a tabbed menu at the top of the page that will direct customers to the main sections of the JE Web site. This menu appears on every page in the site. Another list of links will direct users to pages directly related to the different JE printer products. Figure 13-30 shows a preview of the page's Electronics menu after the user clicked the Electronics tab on the menu.

Figure 13-30

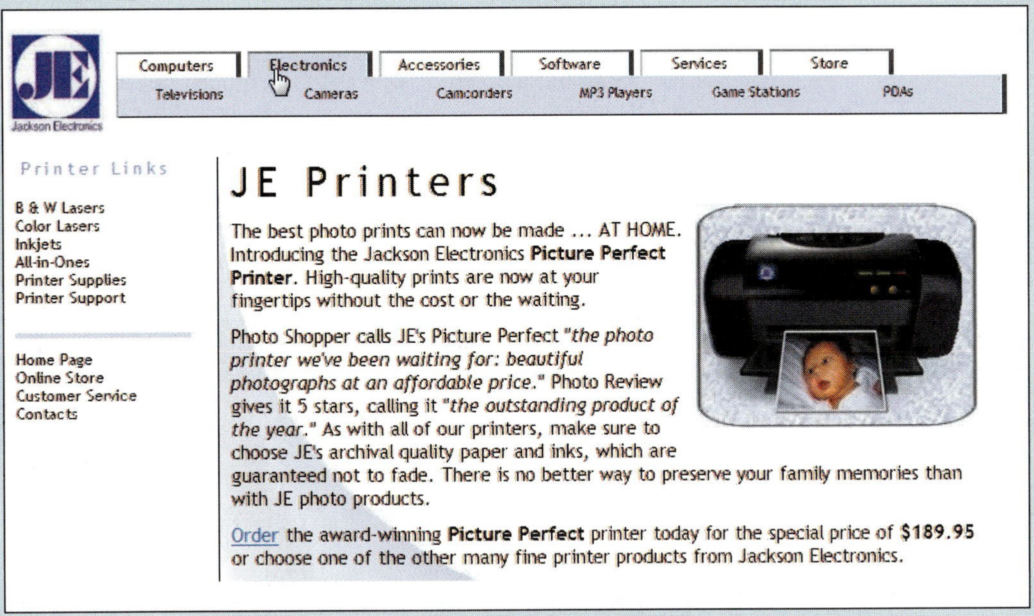

Complete the following:

1. Using your text editor, open the **printertxt.htm** and **jemenustxt.js** files from the tutorial.13/case1 folder, enter ***your name*** and ***the date*** in the comment section of each file, and then save the files as **printer.htm** and **jemenus.js**, respectively.
2. Examine the HTML code in the printer.htm file so that you are familiar with the structure of the list of links that make up the tabbed menu. When you're finished, link the file to the **jemenus.js** JavaScript file, and then close the printer.htm file.
3. Return to the **jemenus.js** file in your text editor. At the top of the file, create two global variables. The first, **currentTab**, will reference the current menu tab being displayed on the page. Set its initial value to null. The second variable, **maxZ**, will store the z-index of the currently displayed tab. Set its initial value to 1.
4. Add an event handler to run the setTabs() function after the page loads.
5. Create the **setTabs()** function. The purpose of this function is to create an array of all menu tabs in the document and to initialize the value of the currentTab object. Within the function, do the following:
    a. Declare an empty array named **menuTabs**.
    b. Use the getElementsByTagName() method to store all of the elements in the document in an array named **allElems**.
    c. Loop through the elements in the allElems array, pushing all of the elements belonging to the tab class into the menuTabs array.
    d. Set the currentTab object equal to the first item in the menuTabs array.
    e. For every item in the menuTabs array, add an onclick event handler that runs the showTab function.
6. Create the **showTab()** function. The purpose of this function is to show the currently selected tab and hide the old tab menu. Add the following commands to the function:
    a. Set the background color of the currentTab object to white.
    b. Increase the value of the maxZ variable by 1.

c. Declare a variable named tabList that references the first ul element nested within the this object.
d. Set the z-index value of the tabList object to the value of the maxZ variable.
e. Point the currentTab object to the tabList object.
f. Set the background color of the currentTab object to the color value (221, 221, 255).

7. Save your changes to the file.
8. Open the **printer.htm** file in your browser and verify that as you click different menu tabs at the top of the page, the browser displays a different submenu within the tab.
9. Submit the completed project to your instructor.

Apply | Case Problem 2

Use JavaScript to make an online puzzle interactive.

Data Files needed for this Case Problem: hanjietxt.htm, puzzletxt.js, blackbar.gif, jpf.css, jpf.jpg.

The Japanese Puzzle Factory Rebecca Peretz has been working on The Japanese Puzzle Factory Web site for several months. Created for people like her who share a love for Japanese logic puzzles, Rebecca is interested in using JavaScript to create online interactive puzzles.

Rebecca has asked you to help her create an online version of a hanjie puzzle. In a hanjie puzzle, users are presented with a blank grid in which they must click certain cells to reveal a hidden image. Each cell in the grid can be either dark or left blank. The clues to which cells darken are given by the headings of each table row or column, which lists the blocks of cells within the row or column that are to be darkened. For example, a column heading of 3 8 1 indicates that within the column there is a block of three dark cells, followed by a block of eight dark cells, and then a single dark cell. The space between the darkened blocks of cells can vary and is determined by the user, who studies the clues found in other row and column headings.

Rebecca has created a Web page containing a hanjie puzzle. The grid has been placed in a 20 × 25 table with row and column headings indicating the blocks of cells within each row or column to be darkened. The initial grid is blank. Rebecca wants users to be able to darken a table cell by clicking it. She also wants users to be able to check their progress by clicking a form button on the Web page. Users should also be able to reveal the puzzle's solution by clicking a form button. A preview of the Web page is shown in Figure 13-31.

Figure 13-31

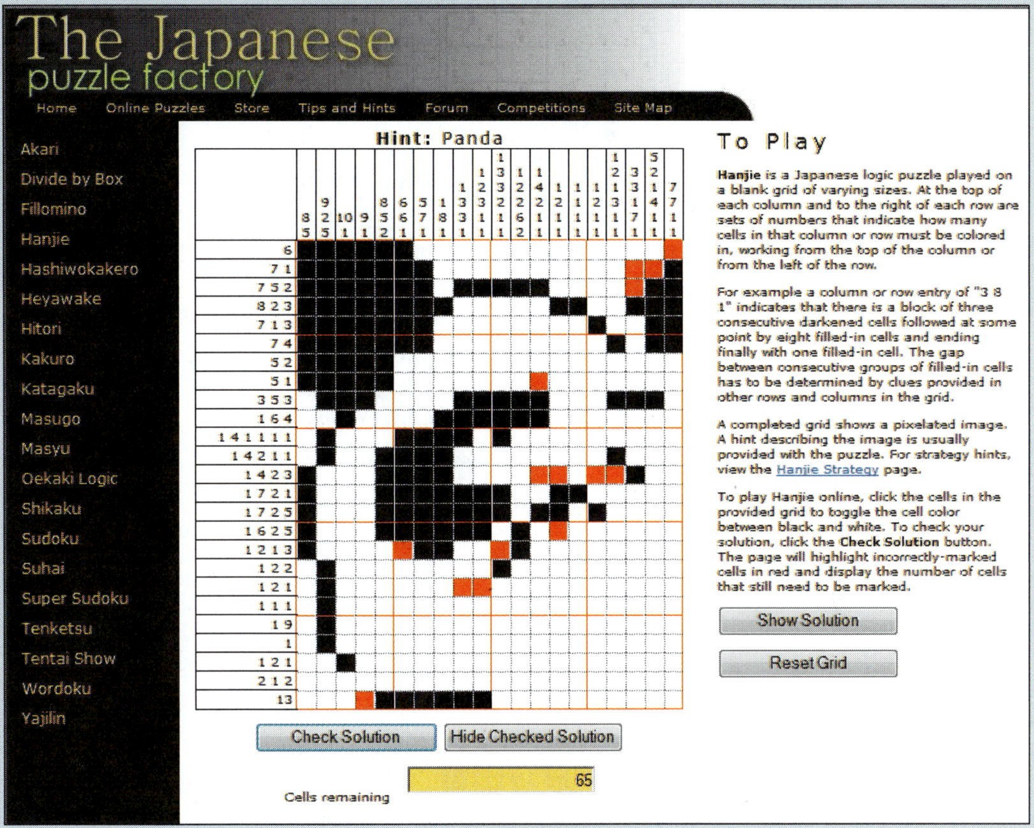

Rebecca has already written the HTML code for the puzzle page and has completed the CSS style sheet formatting the page's appearance and layout. She needs you to write the JavaScript code to make the puzzle interactive.

Complete the following:

1. Using your text editor, open the **hanjietxt.htm** and **puzzletxt.js** files in the tutorial.13/case2 folder, enter ***your name*** and ***the date*** in the comment section of each file, and then save the files as **hanjie.htm** and **puzzle.js**, respectively.
2. Go to the **hanjie.htm** file in your text editor, study the contents and structure of the file, add a link to the **puzzle.js** external script file, and then close the file, saving your changes.
3. Return to the **puzzle.js** file in your text editor, and then add an event handler to the file, running the function setPuzzle() when the page is loaded.
4. Declare a global variable named **allCells**. The purpose of this variable will be to store the object collection of all of the cells in the hanjie puzzle grid.
5. Create the **setPuzzle()** function. The purpose of this function is to set the value of the allCells variable and to add event handlers to all of the cells within the puzzle. Add the following commands to this function:
   a. The cells in the hanjie puzzle have been stored in a table element with the ID name puzzleCells. Create a variable named **puzzleTable** that points to this object.
   b. Set the value of the allCells variable to point to all of the td elements within puzzleTable.

   c. Loop through the allCells object collection and for each item in the collection, set the background color to white and add an event handler that runs the changeColor() function when the cell is clicked.
   d. Within the Web page there are four input buttons with ID names of solution, hide, check, and uncheck. For the solution button, add an onclick event handler that runs the showSolution() function. For the hide button, add an onclick event handler to run the hideSolution() function. For the check button, add an onclick event handler to run the checkSolution() function. Finally, for the uncheck button, add an onclick event handler to run the uncheckSolution() function.
6. Create the **changeColor()** function. The purpose of this function is to toggle the background color of the active cell between black and white. Add a command to the function containing a conditional operator that tests whether the background style of the active object is equal to black. If it is, change the background color to white; otherwise, change the background color to black.
7. Create the **showSolution()** function. The purpose of this function is to reveal the hidden solution to the hanjie puzzle. The cells from the puzzle that should be filled in all belong to the dark class. To create the showSolution() function, add the following commands:
   a. Create a loop that loops through all of the objects within the allCells object collection.
   b. For each item within the allCells object collection, test whether the class name of the object is equal to dark. If so, change the background color to black; otherwise, change the background color to white.
   c. After the loop has completed, set the value of the checkCount field to 0.
8. Create the **hideSolution()** function. The purpose of this function is to reset the hanjie puzzle, hiding the solution and any guesses made by the user. Add the following commands to the function:
   a. Loop through all of the objects within the allCells object collection. For each item in the collection, set the background color to white.
   b. After the loop has completed, set the value of the checkCount field to an empty text string.
9. Create the **checkSolution()** function. The purpose of this function is to check whether the user's solution matches the actual solution of the hanjie puzzle. The function should display all incorrectly clicked cells in red. It should also count and display the number of cells that should be clicked but aren't. Add the following commands to the function:
   a. Declare a variable named **checkCount** and set its initial value to 0. The checkCount variable will keep track of the number of unclicked cells in the hanjie puzzle solution.
   b. Create a loop that loops through all of the objects in the allCells object collection.
   c. Within the loop, insert an if statement that tests whether the background color of the current item is black and the class name is not equal to dark; if so, change the background color to red. Otherwise, test whether the class name is equal to dark and the background color is white; if so, increase the value of the checkCount variable by 1.
   d. After the loop is finished, display the value of the checkCount variable in the checkCount field.

10. Create the **uncheckSolution()** function. The purpose of this function is to hide the results of checking the user's solution. Add the following commands to the function:
    a. Loop through all of the objects in the allCells object collection.
    b. For every object in the collection, test whether the background color is equal to red; if so, change the background color to black.
    c. After the loop is completed, display an empty text string in the checkCount field.
11. Close the **puzzle.js** file, saving your changes.
12. Open the **hanjie.htm** file in your Web browser. Click different cells within the puzzle, verifying that you can toggle the background color of each cell between white and black. Click the Show Solution button and verify that it reveals the hidden solution to the hanjie puzzle. Click the Reset Grid button and verify that it hides the puzzle's solution. Click some cells on the puzzle, attempting to solve or partially solve the puzzle, and then click the Check Solution button. Verify that cells that should not be selected are highlighted with a red background color, and that the number of unclicked cells appears in the Cells remaining input box. Click the Hide Checked Solution button and verify that the puzzle returns to your original solution.
13. Submit the completed Web site to your instructor.

Challenge | Case Problem 3

Explore how to use JavaScript to create a scrolling marquee.

Data Files needed for this Case Problem: bysotxt.htm, marqueetxt.js, bstyles.css, byso.jpg, bysologo.jpg

Boise Youth Symphony Orchestra Denise Young is the artistic director of the Boise Youth Symphony Orchestra from Boise, Idaho. She's asked for your help in writing JavaScript programs to augment the content of the group's Web site. One element that Denise wants to add to the site's home page is a list of upcoming concerts and events. Such lists can be long and cumbersome, and Denise has heard that she should keep the site's home page content to not much more than one full screen in height. She wants to place the list of upcoming events in a vertically scrolling marquee. A preview of the page with the scrolling marquee created using JavaScript is shown in Figure 13-32.

Figure 13-32

The marquee has been placed in a div container element. Descriptions of each event within the marquee have also been placed within their own separate div containers and positioned within the marquee using absolute positioning. To create the scrolling marquee, you'll use JavaScript to alter the top position of each event, rerunning the function at timed intervals to create the illusion of text moving vertically within the marquee box. All of the CSS styles and HTML tags have already been written for you. You need to write the JavaScript program to create the marquee effect.

Complete the following:

1. Using your text editor, open the **bysotxt.htm** and **marqueetxt.js** files from the tutorial.13/case3 folder, enter ***your name*** and ***the date*** in the comment section of each file, and then save the files as **byso.htm** and **marquee.js**, respectively.
2. Examine the HTML code in the byso.htm file. Pay close attention to how the different events within the marquee box are structured. Also compare the structure of the document with the styles contained in the bstyles.css style sheet file. When you understand how the marquee content is structured and laid out, link the file to the marquee.js JavaScript file.
3. Return to the **marquee.js** file in your text editor. Within the file, create three global variables named **timeID**, **marqueeTxt**, and **marqueeOff**. The timeID variable will store the ID of the time interval function used to scroll the marquee text. The marqueeTxt variable will store the array of text items in the marquee. The marqueeOff variable will store a Boolean value indicating if the marquee is not running. Set its initial value to true.

4. Have the browser run the defineMarquee() function when the page loads.
5. Create the **defineMarquee()** function. The purpose of this function is to set up the marquee object and define the event handlers that run the marquee. Add the following to the function:
   a. Populate the contents of the marqueeTxt array with all of the elements from the document that belong to the marqueeTxt class.

   EXPLORE

   b. For every item in the marqueeTxt array, store the value of the top style from the CSS style sheet in a variable named **topValue**. (*Hint:* To extract the values from the style sheet, use object detection to determine the calculated CSS style value. Refer to the InSight in Session 13.3 for more information.) After you have calculated a value for the topValue variable, store that value in the top style property for the current item in the marqueeTxt array.

   EXPLORE

   c. The Web page has two form buttons with ID values of startMarquee and stopMarquee. Add event handlers to these buttons to run the startMarquee() and stopMarquee() functions, respectively.
6. Create the **startMarquee()** function. The purpose of this function is to start the marquee scrolling. Add the following commands to the function:
   a. Insert an if condition that tests whether the value of the marqueeOff variable is true.
   b. If marqueeOff is true, then run the moveText() function at intervals of 50 milliseconds. Store the ID of the time interval in the timeID variable. Set the value of the marqueeOff variable to false.
7. Create the **stopMarquee()** function. The purpose of this function is to pause the marquee. Add the following commands to the function:
   a. Clear the time interval function indicated by the timeID variable.
   b. Reset the marqueeOff variable to true.

EXPLORE

8. Create the **moveText()** function. The purpose of this function is to move the text within the marquee in a vertical direction. Add the following commands to the function:
   a. Create a for loop that loops through each item in the marqueeTxt array.
   b. For each item, store the value of the top style in the variable topPos. Be sure to use the parseInt() method to extract the numeric value from the text string.
   c. If the value of topPos is less than –110, set the value of the top style for the marquee item to 700px; otherwise, decrease the value of the top style by 1. The value of –110 was chosen to allow the text to scroll up and off of the marquee box and out of sight from the user. The 700-pixel value was chosen to move the marquee text back down and below the marquee box, allowing it to scroll back into view from the bottom of the box.
9. Save your changes to the file.

EXPLORE

10. Open the **byso.htm** file in your Web browser. Click the Start Marquee button and verify that the text scrolls vertically up through the marquee box, reappearing again at the bottom of the box. Click the Pause Marquee button and verify that the scrolling action is paused until the Start Marquee button is pressed again.
11. Submit the completed project to your instructor.

Create | Case Problem 4

Test your knowledge of objects, properties, and methods by designing a menu system for a cooking Web site.

Data Files needed for this Case Problem: dinnerplate.txt, dplogo.jpg, torte.jpg

DinnerPlate Tara Anderson runs a Web site called *dinnerplate.com* in which people who share her love for cooking can post their favorite recipes, share tips, and learn about the art and science of cooking. Tara wants to put several links on the site's home page, linking her users to specific recipes for breakfast, lunch, and dinner, as well as recipes organized by food groups and dietary concerns. Worried that so many links will overwhelm the page layout, Tara would like to place these links in a simple-to-use menu system, written in JavaScript. Knowing that you have worked with JavaScript in the past, Tara has asked for your help in redesigning her home page with a JavaScript menu application.

Complete the following:

1. Use your text editor to create three files named **dinner.css**, **dinnerplate.htm**, and **menus.js**. Enter ***your name***, ***the date***, and a brief description of the files in the comment section of each document. Save the files in the tutorial.13/case4 folder.
2. The content for the dinnerplate.htm file is located in the **dinnerplate.txt** file. Use this content to design the site's home page. The design and layout of the page are up to you. You can also supplement the Web page with any additional content or features you decide are appropriate. The links on the page can all point to # to avoid having to create an extended folder of Web pages.
3. Place any formatting styles in the **dinner.css** file. Link the home page to both the dinner.css file and the menus.js file.
4. Add JavaScript commands to the **menu.js** file to create a menu system for the list of links in the dinnerplate.htm file. You can choose any type of menu system that you believe will work with the content of the page. Document your code to make it easy for other users to understand and interpret your program.
5. Test your code against the list of links in the **dinnerplate.htm** file, verifying that you can open and close the menus in a simple and intuitive way.
6. Submit the completed Web site to your instructor.

Review | Quick Check Answers

Session 13.1

1. The document object model is the organized structure of objects found within a Web document and within the Web browser.
2. `navigator`
3. `document.links[1]`
4. `document.getElementById("footer")`
5. `document.getElementsByTagName("p")[1]`
6. `document.forms[0].action = "http://www.avalon.mailer.cgi";`
7. `document.getElementsByTagName("div")[1].className = "blueBackground";`
8. `document.getElementById("main").style.border = "2px solid black";`
9.
```
for (var i = 0; i < document.links.length; i++) {
    document.links[i].style.textDecoration = "none";
}
```

Session 13.2

1. `object.method()`

   where *object* is the name of the object and *method* is a method that applies to the object.

2. `location.reload()`
3. `document.getElementById("pullMenu").onclick = showMenu;`
4. ```
   for (var i = 0; i < document.links.length; i++) {
      document.links[i].onclick = showLinks;
   }
   ```
5. You do not include the parentheses when assigning a function to an event handler. The correct form of the expression is:

   `document.getElementById("slide").onclick = loadImage;`
6. Object detection is the confirmation that an object exists or is supported by the browser before attempting to use it in an expression.
7. `if (document.all) showMenu();`
8. `document.getElementById("pullMenu").onmouseover = showMenu;`

Session 13.3

1. ```
   document.getElementById("mainDIV").style.clip = "rect(0px, 100px,
   50px, 0px)";
   ```
2. `setInterval("slideMenu()", 1000);`
3. ```
   document.getElementById("Menu1").style.top =
   parseInt(document.getElementById("Menu1").style.top) + 5 + "px";
   ```
4. `document.getElementById("Menu1").style.zIndex += 1;`
5. No value is returned. The problem is that you cannot use the style property to read CSS style values from a style sheet. You can only read style values set in other JavaScript commands or with the style attribute in an inline style.
6. For the IE DOM, use:

   `document.getElementById("Menu1").currentStyle("font-size")`

   For the W3C DOM, use:

   ```
   document.defaultView.getComputedStyle(document.
   getElementById("Menu1"), null).getPropertyValue("font-size")
   ```
7. ```
   function circle(r) {
      this.radius = r;
      this.circum = calcCircum;
   }

   function calcCircum() {
      return 2*Math.Pi*this.radius;
   }
   ```
8. ```
   var circle1 = new circle(5);
   var circum1 = circle1.circum;
   ```
   ```

Ending Data Files

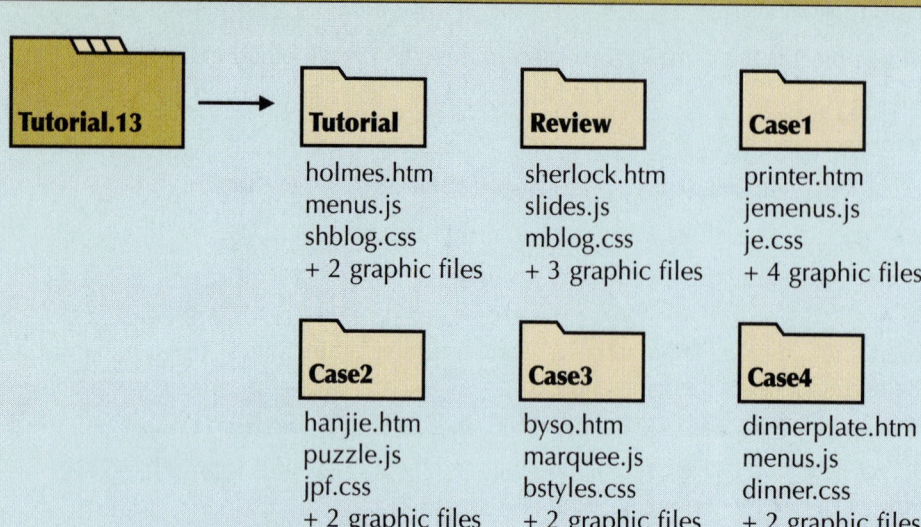

Tutorial.13 →

Tutorial
holmes.htm
menus.js
shblog.css
+ 2 graphic files

Review
sherlock.htm
slides.js
mblog.css
+ 3 graphic files

Case1
printer.htm
jemenus.js
je.css
+ 4 graphic files

Case2
hanjie.htm
puzzle.js
jpf.css
+ 2 graphic files

Case3
byso.htm
marquee.js
bstyles.css
+ 2 graphic files

Case4
dinnerplate.htm
menus.js
dinner.css
+ 2 graphic files

Objectives

Session 14.1
- Understand how to reference form element objects
- Extract data from Web form fields
- Create a calculated field

Session 14.2
- Understand the principles of form validation
- Perform a client-side validation
- Work with string objects

Session 14.3
- Work with regular expressions
- Apply regular expressions to zip code fields
- Validate credit card numbers

Working with Forms and Regular Expressions

Validating a Web Form with JavaScript

Case | GPS-ware

GPS-ware is a company that specializes in mapping and global positioning software and hardware. The company is in the planning stages of making its products available online. Carol Campbell is heading the development effort and asks you to help develop a Web form for domestic sales.

A GPS-ware employee has already created three Web forms for the Web site. The forms include fields in which users enter the details of their purchases, delivery information, and credit card data. Carol wants the forms to automatically calculate the cost of a user's order and validate any data the user has entered. All of this should be done before the form is submitted to the Web server for processing.

Starting Data Files

Tutorial.14 →

Tutorial
done.htm
form1txt.htm
form2txt.htm
form3txt.htm
contacttxt.js
ordertxt.js
paytxt.js
gpsware.css
+ 2 graphic files

Review
done.htm
ordertxt.htm
formtxt.js
gps.css
+ 2 graphic files

Case1
mpltxt.htm
linkstxt.js
mplstyles.css
mpl.jpg

Case2
done.htm
exptxt.htm
reporttxt.js
exp.css
+ 3 graphic files

Case3
conftxt.htm
sumtxt.htm
formstxt.js
conf.css
summary.css
+ 4 graphic files

Case4
info.txt
functions.js
+ 2 graphic files

Demo
demo_form1.htm
demo_form2.htm
demo_regcodes.htm
demo_regexp.htm
+ 3 graphic files

Session 14.1

Working with Forms and Fields

GPS-ware has three forms related to online ordering that you'll be working with. Figure 14-1 shows the structure of these forms. Customers enter order information in the first form, delivery information in the second form, and method of payment in the third form.

Figure 14-1 **GPS-ware online ordering forms**

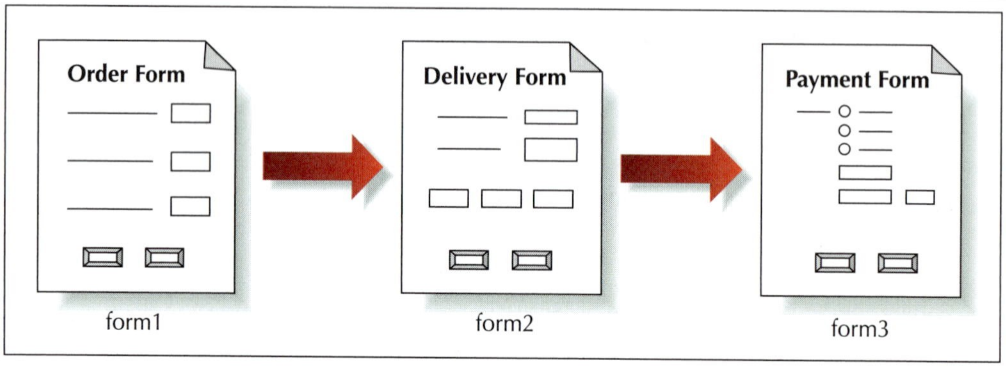

You'll open the files used on the GPS-ware Web site.

To open the order forms:

1. Use your text editor to open the **form1txt.htm**, **form2txt.htm**, **form3txt.htm**, **ordertxt.js**, **contacttxt.js**, and **paytxt.js** files from the tutorial.14/tutorial folder, enter ***your name*** and ***the date*** in the comment section of each file, and then save the files as **form1.htm**, **form2.htm**, **form3.htm**, **order.js**, **contact.js**, and **payment.js**, respectively.
2. Close all the files except form1.htm and order.js, return to the **form1.htm** file in your text editor, and then review the HTML code used in the file.
3. In the head section of the document, insert the following code to create a link to the order.js JavaScript file:

```
<script type = "text/javascript" src = "order.js"></script>
```

4. Close the file, saving your changes.
5. Open **form1.htm** in your Web browser. Figure 14-2 shows the current content and layout of the page, including the names assigned to the different form elements.

GPS-ware order form and element names

Figure 14-2

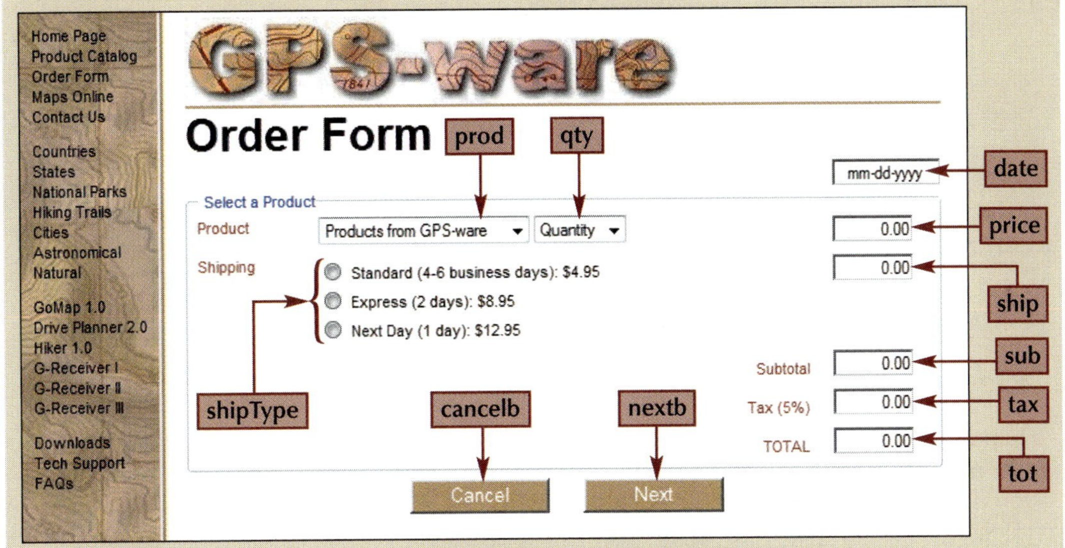

The date field and any fields that display the cost of the product, tax, or shipping are set to read-only. You cannot enter data in the fields; the values can only be set using JavaScript.

Customers use the order form to select a GPS-ware product to purchase, indicating the product name, quantity, and shipping method. Customers can choose from three shipping options: standard, which costs $4.95 and arrives in four to six business days; express, which costs $8.95 and arrives in two days; and overnight, which costs $12.95. The company also charges a 5% tax on online orders. Carol wants this form to calculate the cost of the purchased items, add the shipping cost, determine the tax, and then calculate the total order cost. All of these calculations should be done automatically by the browser. At the top of the form is a date field, which will display the current date. Carol wants the Web browser to enter this information automatically as well.

To set up the form, you'll create a function named startForm() that runs automatically after the page is loaded. You'll place this function and other JavaScript functions used with the form1.htm file in the order.js file.

To insert the startForm() function:

1. Return to the **order.js** file in your text editor.
2. Directly below the comment section, add the following statement to run the startForm() function when the page is loaded:

```
window.onload = startForm;
```

3. Below the todayTxt() function, insert the following code for the startForm() function, as shown in Figure 14-3:

```
function startForm() {
}
```

Figure 14-3 Code for the startForm() function

```
window.onload = startForm;

function todayTxt() {
   var Today = new Date();
   return Today.getMonth() + 1 + "-" + Today.getDate() + "-" + Today.getFullYear();
}

function startForm() {
}
```

4. Save your changes to the file.

Referencing a Web Form

To program the behavior and contents of a Web form, you must work with the properties and methods of the form object and the elements it contains. As shown in Figure 14-4, Web forms and their elements are part of the hierarchy of objects within a Web document.

Figure 14-4 Forms hierarchy

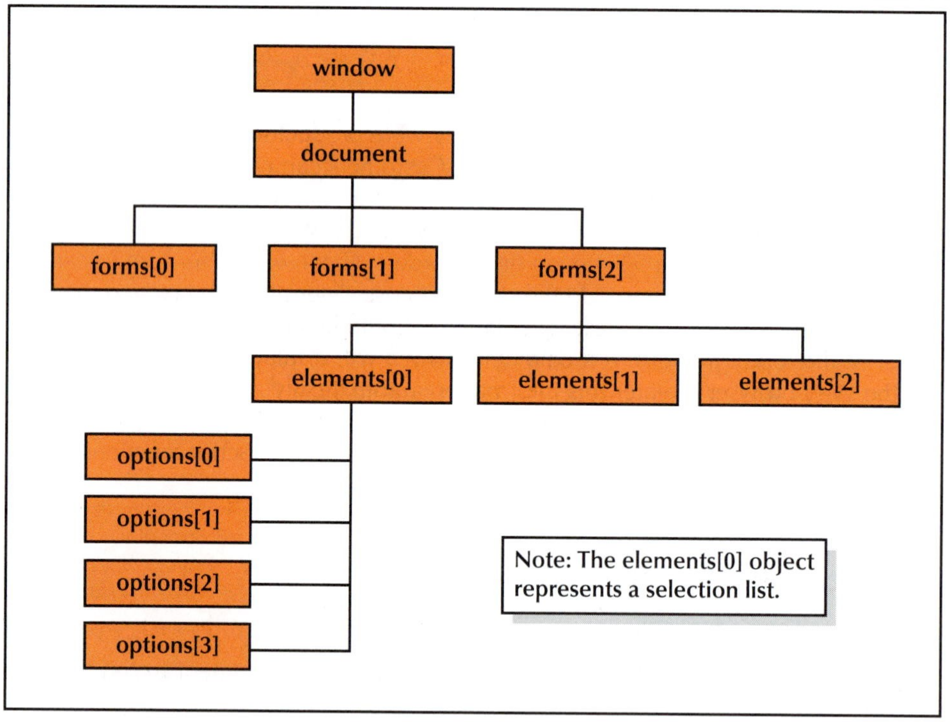

Because a Web page can contain multiple Web forms, JavaScript supports an object collection for forms. You can access a form within the current document using the object reference

```
document.forms[idref]
```

where *idref* is the ID or index number of the form. JavaScript also allows you to reference a form by its name attribute, using the object reference

```
document.webform
```

where *webform* is the value of the name attribute assigned to the form. In addition, you can always use the document.getElementById() method to reference a form based on the value of its ID attribute.

Carol assigned the ID form1 to the form, and this form is the first (and only) form on the Web page. Based on this information, you can access the form using either of the following object references:

```
document.forms[0]
```

or

```
document.forms["form1"]
```

Tip

Because XHTML under the strict DTD does not support the name attribute of the form element, you must use the ID attribute to identify form elements.

Referencing a Form Element

The elements within a form, including all input fields, buttons, and labels, are organized into an elements collection. You can reference a form element by its position in the elements collection as follows

```
formObject.elements[idref]
```

where *formObject* is the reference to the form, and *idref* is the index number of the element within the form or the value of the name or ID attribute for the element. You can also reference the element using the syntax

```
formObject.idref
```

where *idref* is either the name or the ID of the element. For example, the first element in Carol's order form is the date input box. To reference this object, you use any of the following expressions:

```
document.forms[0].elements[0]
document.forms[0].elements["date"]
document.forms[0].date
```

If the element is a selection list, it contains its own object collection consisting of the options within the list. Likewise, option buttons belonging to the same group have a unique syntax. You'll examine how to work with both selection lists and option buttons later in this session.

Figure 14-5 lists the object references for the fields and buttons in Carol's order form. The object references are drawn from the element names, which were displayed earlier in Figure 14-2.

Figure 14-5 Objects in the order form

Object	Reference
order form	document.forms[0]
date field	document.forms[0].date
product selection list	document.forms[0].prod
quantity selection list	document.forms[0].qty
price of the product field	document.forms[0].price
group of shipping options	document.forms[0].shipType
shipping cost field	document.forms[0].ship
subtotal field	document.forms[0].sub
tax field	document.forms[0].tax
total field	document.forms[0].tot
cancel button	document.forms[0].cancelb
next button	document.forms[0].nextb

Reference Window | **Referencing Form Objects**

- To access a Web form, use the object reference
  `document.forms[idref]`
  where *idref* is the ID or index number of the form. You can also use
  `document.fname`
  where *fname* is the name of the form.
- To reference an element within a form, use the object reference
  `formObject.elements[idref]`
  where *formObject* is the object reference to the form and *idref* is the ID or index number of the form element. You can also use
  `formObject.ename`
  where *ename* is the name of the form element.

Working with Input Fields

The first task on Carol's list is to display the current date in the Web form. To change the value of the date field, you need to work with the properties and methods of input fields.

Setting the Field Value

You use the value property to set the value contained in a field such as an input box. The general syntax of the value property is

```
formObject.element.value = fieldvalue;
```

where *formObject* is a reference to the Web form, *element* is the object reference to an element within the form, and *fieldvalue* is the value you want placed in the field. For example, to have the date field display the text string 6-23-2011, you would run the following command:

```
document.forms[0].date.value = "6-23-2011";
```

The value property is one of many properties and methods associated with input fields. Figure 14-6 shows some of the others.

Properties and methods of the input field — Figure 14-6

Property	Description
defaultvalue	The default value that is initially displayed in the field
form	References the form containing the field
maxlength	The maximum number of characters allowed in the field
name	The name of the field
size	The width of the input field in characters
type	The type of input field (button, check box, file, hidden, image, password, radio, reset, submit, text)
value	The current value of the field

Method	Description
blur()	Remove the focus from the field
focus()	Give focus to the field
select()	Select the field

Working with Fields | Reference Window

- To set the value of a form field, use the object property
  `field.value = fieldValue`
  where *field* is the reference to the form field and *fieldValue* is the value you want to assign to the field.
- To move the focus to a form field, use the following method:
  `field.focus()`

Carol created a function named todayTxt() that returns a text string with the current date in the format *mm-dd-yyyy*. She's already stored this function in the order.js file. Using this function, you can display the current date in the date field with the following command:

```
document.forms[0].date.value = todayTxt();
```

You'll add this command to the startForm() function.

To display the current date in the form:

1. Within the startForm() function in the order.js file, insert the following command:

   `document.forms[0].date.value = todayTxt();`

2. Save your changes to the file.

Navigating Between Fields

Carol wants the product selection list to be selected automatically when the form opens, so it is ready for data entry. When a form element is selected either by clicking it or moving into it using keyboard buttons or arrows, it receives the **focus** of the browser. To program this action, you use the focus() method, which has the following general syntax:

```
formObject.element.focus();
```

Running this command makes the *element* the selected object in the Web form. JavaScript can also deselect a form object by using the blur() method, which has the following general syntax:

```
formObject.element.blur();
```

Tip

Applying the blur() method to an object deselects that object on the Web page without selecting anything else. You can also blur a field by applying the focus to another object on the page.

Using the focus() and blur() methods, you can alternately select and deselect elements in the Web form, controlling the user's navigation through the form. The product selection list has the field name prod. So to force this field to be selected automatically when the page opens, you run the following command:

```
document.forms[0].prod.focus();
```

You'll add this command to the startForm() function.

To select the product selection list:

1. In the **order.js** file, add the following command to the end of the startForm() function, as shown in Figure 14-7:

   ```
   document.forms[0].prod.focus();
   ```

Figure 14-7 Focus set to the prod field

```
function startForm() {
    document.forms[0].date.value = todayTxt();
    document.forms[0].prod.focus();
}
```

2. Save your changes to the file, and then reload **form1.htm** in your Web browser. The current date appears in the date field and the product selection list is selected. See Figure 14-8.

Figure 14-8 Current date and focus added to the form

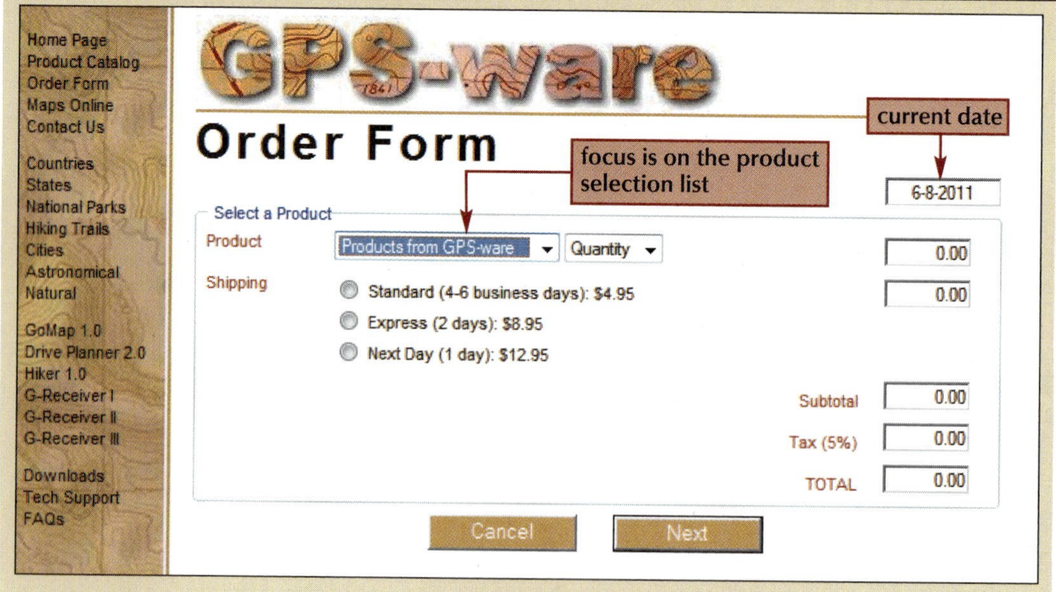

Working with Selection Lists

In the rest of the form, you need to create functions to calculate the cost of a customer's order. This involves: (1) determining the price of the order (equal to the price of the product multiplied by the quantity ordered), (2) determining the shipping cost, (3) calculating the sales tax, and (4) adding all of these costs to determine the grand total. You'll start by creating a function to calculate the price of the order.

The product prices and quantities are both placed within selection lists. However, unlike an input box, no value property exists for an entire selection list, only for each option within the list. For example, the product selection list contains the following options and values:

Tip

Guard against data entry errors in Web forms by using selection lists and radio buttons whenever possible.

```
<select name = "prod" id = "prod">
   <option value = "0">Products from GPS-ware</option>
   <option value = "19.95">GoMap 1.0 ($19.95)</option>
   <option value = "29.95">Drive Planner 2.0 ($29.95)</option>
   <option value = "29.95">Hiker 1.0 ($29.95)</option>
   <option value = "149.50">G-Receiver I ($149.50)</option>
   <option value = "199.50">G-Receiver II ($199.50)</option>
   <option value = "249.50">G-Receiver III ($249.50)</option>
</select>
```

JavaScript organizes all of the options into an options collection contained within the selection list object. The syntax to reference a particular option in the collection is

```
selection.options[idref]
```

where *selection* is the reference to the selection list object and *idref* is the index number or ID of the option. Each option in the selection list supports text and value properties specifying the text and value associated with the option. Figure 14-9 shows the text and value properties for the different options in the product selection list.

Figure 14-9 Properties in the product selection list

object	object.text	object.value
document.forms[0].prod.options[0]	Products from GPS-ware	0
document.forms[0].prod.options[1]	GoMap 1.0 ($19.95)	19.95
document.forms[0].prod.options[2]	Drive Planner 2.0 ($29.95)	29.95
document.forms[0].prod.options[3]	Hiker 1.0 ($29.95)	29.95
document.forms[0].prod.options[4]	G-Receiver I ($149.50)	149.50
document.forms[0].prod.options[5]	G-Receiver II ($199.50)	199.50
document.forms[0].prod.options[6]	G-Receiver III ($249.50)	249.50

Figure 14-10 summarizes the properties of both selection list objects and selection list option objects.

Figure 14-10 **Properties of selection list and selection list options**

selection list	Property	Description
	length	The number of options in the list
	name	The name of the selection list
	options	The collection of options in the list
	selectedIndex	The index number of the currently selected option in the list
selection list option	**Property**	**Description**
	defaultSelected	A Boolean value indicating whether the option is selected by default
	index	The index value of the option
	selected	A Boolean value indicating whether the option is currently selected
	text	The text associated with the option
	value	The value associated with the option

Because there is no value property for the entire selection list, you use the value or text of the selected option in any calculations you need to perform. To determine the currently selected option in a list, you use the selectedIndex property of the selection list object. The following code demonstrates how you would determine the price associated with a product selected by a customer:

```
product = document.forms[0].prod;
pIndex = product.selectedIndex;
productPrice = product.options[pIndex].value;
```

In this code, the product variable stores the object reference to the product selected in the form1 Web form. The pIndex variable stores the index of the currently selected option (whatever that may be). Finally, the productPrice variable stores the value of that selected option, which is the product's price. The code to determine the quantity ordered is similar:

```
quantity = document.form1.qty;
qIndex = quantity.selectedIndex;
quantityOrdered = quantity.options[qIndex].value;
```

To calculate the total price for a given product, you multiply the price of the product by the quantity ordered. The following calcPrice() function performs the necessary calculation to determine the price, and then displays the value in the price field of the Web form:

```
function calcPrice() {
   product = document.forms[0].prod;
   pIndex = product.selectedIndex;
   productPrice = product.options[pIndex].value;

   quantity = document.forms[0].qty;
   qIndex = quantity.selectedIndex;
   quantityOrdered = quantity.options[qIndex].value;

   document.forms[0].price.value = productPrice*quantityOrdered;
}
```

You'll add this function to the order.js file.

To add the calcPrice() function:

1. Return to the **order.js** file in your text editor.
2. At the bottom of the file, insert the following calcPrice() function, as shown in Figure 14-11:

```
function calcPrice() {
   product = document.forms[0].prod;
   pIndex = product.selectedIndex;
   productPrice = product.options[pIndex].value;

   quantity = document.forms[0].qty;
   qIndex = quantity.selectedIndex;
   quantityOrdered = quantity.options[qIndex].value;

   document.forms[0].price.value = productPrice*quantityOrdered;
}
```

Figure 14-11 Code for the calcPrice() function

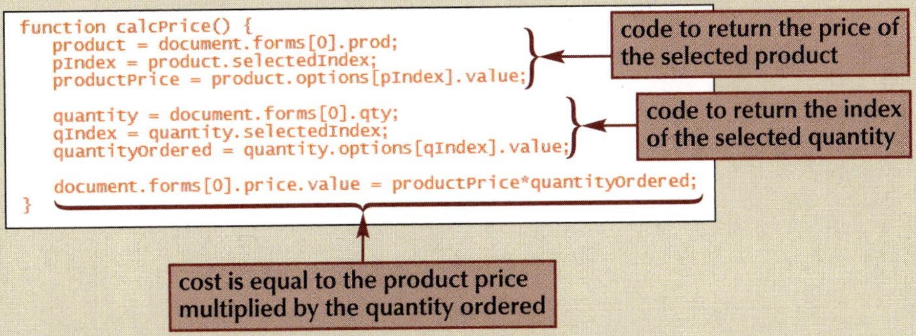
function calcPrice() {
product = document.forms[0].prod;
pIndex = product.selectedIndex;
productPrice = product.options[pIndex].value;
quantity = document.forms[0].qty;
qIndex = quantity.selectedIndex;
quantityOrdered = quantity.options[qIndex].value;
document.forms[0].price.value = productPrice*quantityOrdered;
}
code to return the price of the selected product
code to return the index of the selected quantity
cost is equal to the product price multiplied by the quantity ordered

3. Save your changes to the file.

You want to run the calcPrice() function whenever a user selects a new option from either the product or the quantity selection lists. One way of doing this is to use the onchange event handler, which runs a command whenever the selected option in the list changes. You can add the onchange event handler to the product and quantity selection lists to associate the calcPrice() function with the action of changing the prod or qty selection, as follows:

```
document.forms[0].prod.onchange = calcPrice;
document.forms[0].qty.onchange = calcPrice;
```

You'll add these two commands to the startForm() function, and then test them by reloading the form1 Web page.

To apply the onchange event handler:

1. Scroll the order.js file up to the startForm() function.
2. Within the startForm() function, add the following commands, as shown in Figure 14-12:

```
document.forms[0].prod.onchange = calcPrice;
document.forms[0].qty.onchange = calcPrice;
```

Figure 14-12 Code to insert the onchange event handler

```
function startForm() {
   document.forms[0].date.value = todayTxt();
   document.forms[0].prod.focus();

   document.forms[0].prod.onchange = calcPrice;
   document.forms[0].qty.onchange = calcPrice;
}
```

runs the calcPrice() function when the selected product or the selected quantity changes

3. Save your changes to the file, and then reload **form1.htm** in your Web browser.
4. Select **Hiker 1.0 ($29.95)** from the selection list in the product list box, and then select **2** from the quantity list box. As you select these options (changing the selected options in the list), the value in the price field is updated. See Figure 14-13.

Figure 14-13 Order price calculated based on the selected product and quantity

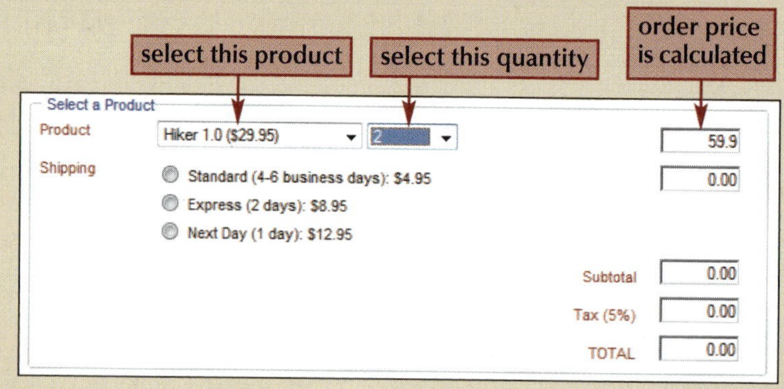

5. Select other product and quantity options, verifying that the price field automatically changes in response. For some product/quantity combinations, the value in the price field is not displayed with a two-digit cents value. You'll learn to format the calculated output to always show the price in dollars and cents later in this session.

Reference Window | Working with Selection Lists

- To determine which option in a selection list has been selected, use the object property
  `selection.selectedIndex`
  where *selection* is the selection list object.
- To extract the text of an option in a selection list, use the object reference
  `selection.options[idref].text`
  where *idref* is the index number or ID of the option.
- To extract the value of an option in a selection list, use the following object reference:
  `selection.options[idref].value`

Creating Selection Lists with Multiple Values | InSight

Some selection lists are set up to collect multiple selections. In those cases, the selectedIndex property returns only the index number of the first selected item. If you want to determine the indices of all the selected items, you must create a for loop that runs through all of the options in the list, checking each to determine whether the selected property is true (indicating that the option was selected by the user). If the option is selected, it can then be added to an array of the selected options using the push() method. The general structure of the for loop is

```
var selectedOpt = new Array();
for (var i = 0; i < selection.options.length; i++) {
   if (selection.options[i].selected) {
      selectedOpt.push(selection.options[i]);
   }
}
```

where *selection* is a selection list object within a Web form. After this code is run, the selectedOpt array will contain all of the options within the selection list that have been chosen by the user. To work with the selected options, you can create a for loop that loops through all of the items in the selectedOpt array to extract the text and value properties from each.

Working with Option Buttons and Check Boxes

Your next task is to display the cost of the shipping option that a user selects. Carol has placed the shipping options within a group of option buttons using the following HTML tags:

```
<input type = "radio" name = "shipType" id = "ship1" value = "4.95" />
<input type = "radio" name = "shipType" id = "ship2" value = "8.95" />
<input type = "radio" name = "shipType" id = "ship3" value = "12.95" />
```

Carol wants you to write a program that will enter the shipping value into the Web form whenever the user clicks one of these three option buttons.

Using Option Buttons

Because each option button in a group shares a common name value, JavaScript places the individual buttons within that group into an array. Individual option buttons have the reference

```
options[idref]
```

where *options* is the name assigned to the group of option buttons and *idref* is either the index number or the ID of the individual option button within that group. In Carol's form, either of the following object references could be used for the first shipType option button:

```
document.forms[0].shipType[0]
document.forms[0].shipType["ship1"]
```

Tip

You can also reference an option button by using the getElementById() method.

Figure 14-14 describes some of the properties associated with option buttons.

Figure 14-14 **Properties of option buttons**

Property	Description
checked	A Boolean value indicating whether the option button is currently selected
defaultChecked	A Boolean value indicating whether the option button is selected by default
name	The name of the option button
value	The value associated with the option button

You can use a for loop to move through all of the option buttons within the group. You'll use this for loop to assign an onclick event handler to each button, running the calcShipping() function (which you'll create shortly) when the button is clicked. The JavaScript code for the for loop is:

```
for (var i = 0; i < document.forms[0].shipType.length; i++) {
   document.forms[0].shipType[i].onclick = calcShipping;
}
```

You'll add this code to the startForm() function.

To add onclick event handlers to the shipType option buttons:

1. Return to the **order.js** file in your text editor.
2. Within the startForm() function, insert the following code, as shown in Figure 14-15:

```
for (var i = 0; i < document.forms[0].shipType.length; i++) {
   document.forms[0].shipType[i].onclick = calcShipping;
}
```

Figure 14-15 **onclick event handlers added to the shipType field**

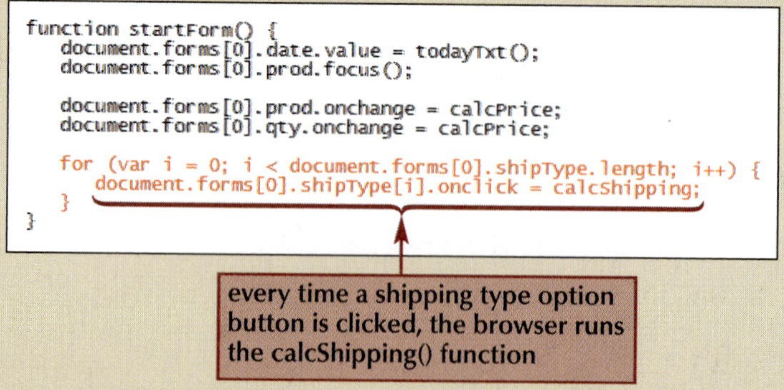

function startForm() {
document.forms[0].date.value = todayTxt();
document.forms[0].prod.focus();
document.forms[0].prod.onchange = calcPrice;
document.forms[0].qty.onchange = calcPrice;
for (var i = 0; i < document.forms[0].shipType.length; i++) {
document.forms[0].shipType[i].onclick = calcShipping;
}
}
every time a shipping type option button is clicked, the browser runs the calcShipping() function

3. Save your changes to the file.

The calcShipping() function takes the value of the clicked option button and places it in the ship field of the Web form. The code for the function is:

```
function calcShipping() {
   document.forms[0].ship.value = this.value;
}
```

The function uses the this keyword to reference the option button that was clicked, running the calcShipping() function. You'll add this function to the order.js file and test it in your Web browser.

To add and test the calcShipping() function:

1. Scroll to the bottom of the file, and then insert the following function, as shown in Figure 14-16:

```
function calcShipping() {
   document.forms[0].ship.value = this.value;
}
```

Figure 14-16 Code for the calcShipping() function

```
   document.forms[0].price.value = productPrice*quantityOrdered;
}
function calcShipping() {
   document.forms[0].ship.value = this.value;
}
```

the this keyword references the currently selected object

2. Save your changes to the file, and then reload **form1.htm** in your Web browser.
3. Click the **Standard** option button, and then verify that 4.95 appears in the ship field input box. See Figure 14-17.

Figure 14-17 Shipping cost based on the selected shipping option button

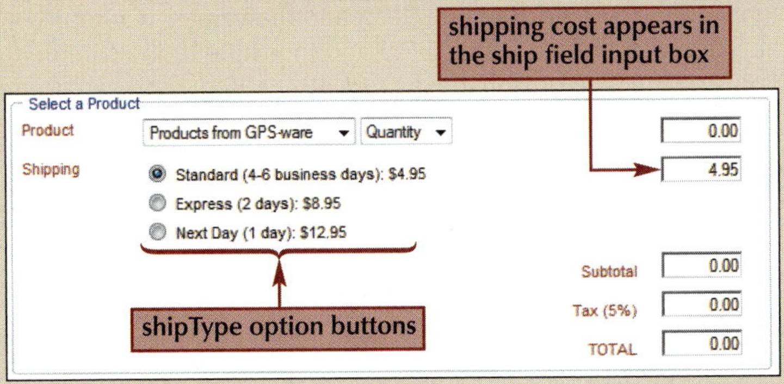

4. Click the other shipping option buttons and verify that the corresponding shipping cost appears in the ship field's input box.

Reference Window | **Working with Option Button Groups**

- To reference a specific option button within a group, use the object reference
  `options[idref]`
  where *options* is the reference to the option button group and *idref* is the ID or index number of the option button.
- To determine whether an option button is currently checked, use the object property
  `options[idref].checked`
  which returns the Boolean value true if the button is checked.
- To determine which button in the option button group is checked, create a for loop that examines each option button's checked property, returning the index of the checked button.

Working with Check Boxes

Carol's order form contains no check boxes, which work the same way as option buttons. Like an option button, a check box supports the checked property, indicating whether the box is checked. In addition, the value associated with a check box is stored in the value property of the check box object. However, this value is applied only when the check box is checked; if a check box is not checked, its field has no value assigned to it. As with option buttons, you can run a function in response to the click event by applying the onclick event handler to the check box. However, unlike option buttons, each entry field has only one check box.

Creating Calculated Fields

To complete Carol's Web form, you need to calculate the form's remaining values: the subtotal (the product price plus the shipping cost), the sales tax, and the total cost of the order (the subtotal plus the sales tax). JavaScript treats the contents of input fields as text strings. This means you cannot simply add the input field values together because JavaScript would append the text strings rather than add the values they represent. For example, if the value in the price field is 39.9 and the value in the ship field is 9.95, adding the two field values returns the text string 39.99.95. If you want to treat the contents of input fields as numeric values, you must first convert them from text strings to numbers.

One way of converting a text string to a numeric value is to use the parseFloat() method. Recall that the parseFloat() method extracts the leading numeric value from a text string, returning a number instead of a text string in the process. The following set of commands uses the parseFloat() method to add the numeric values stored in the price and ship fields, storing the result in the sub field:

```
priceVal = parseFloat(document.forms[0].price.value);
shipVal = parseFloat(document.forms[0].ship.value);
document.forms[0].sub.value = priceVal + shipVal;
```

You'll use these commands in a function named calcTotal(), which calculates the values of the subtotal, tax, and total fields.

To create the calcTotal() function:

1. Return to the **order.js** file in your text editor.
2. Scroll to the bottom of the file, and then insert the following function, as shown in Figure 14-18:

```
function calcTotal() {
   priceVal = parseFloat(document.forms[0].price.value);
   shipVal = parseFloat(document.forms[0].ship.value);
   document.forms[0].sub.value = priceVal + shipVal;
}
```

Figure 14-18 Code for the calcTotal() function

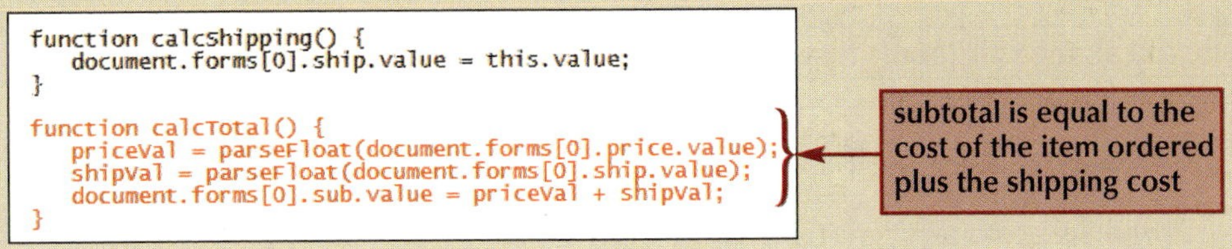

```
function calcShipping() {
   document.forms[0].ship.value = this.value;
}

function calcTotal() {
   priceVal = parseFloat(document.forms[0].price.value);
   shipVal = parseFloat(document.forms[0].ship.value);
   document.forms[0].sub.value = priceVal + shipVal;
}
```

subtotal is equal to the cost of the item ordered plus the shipping cost

You need to calculate the sales tax on the purchase, which is 5% of the subtotal, and the total cost of the sale, which is the cost of the sales tax plus the purchase cost. These two values are stored in the tax and tot fields, respectively. The code to calculate and store these values is:

```
taxVal = 0.05*(priceVal + shipVal);
document.forms[0].tax.value = taxVal;
document.forms[0].tot.value = priceVal + shipVal + taxVal;
```

You'll add these statements to the calcTotal() function.

To complete the calcTotal() function:

1. Insert the following commands in the calcTotal() function, as shown in Figure 14-19:

```
taxVal = 0.05*(priceVal + shipVal);
document.forms[0].tax.value = taxVal;

document.forms[0].tot.value = priceVal + shipVal + taxVal;
```

Figure 14-19 Code to calculate 5% sales tax and the total price

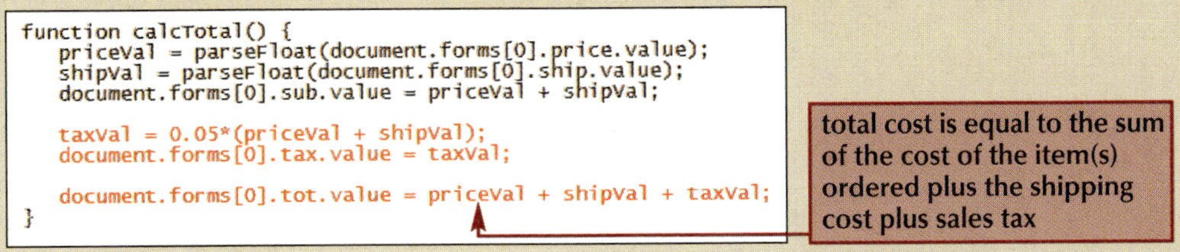

```
function calcTotal() {
   priceVal = parseFloat(document.forms[0].price.value);
   shipVal = parseFloat(document.forms[0].ship.value);
   document.forms[0].sub.value = priceVal + shipVal;

   taxVal = 0.05*(priceVal + shipVal);
   document.forms[0].tax.value = taxVal;

   document.forms[0].tot.value = priceVal + shipVal + taxVal;
}
```

total cost is equal to the sum of the cost of the item(s) ordered plus the shipping cost plus sales tax

2. Save your changes to the file.

You want to run the calcTotal() function whenever a customer makes a selection on the form. This occurs when a product or quantity is picked from a selection list or when a shipping option is selected. Because you have already created event handlers for each of those actions to run the calcPrice() and calcShipping() functions, you can simply add a command to the end of those functions to run calcTotal().

To run the calcTotal() function:

1. Scroll up the file and insert the following command into both the calcPrice() and calcShipping() functions, as shown in Figure 14-20:

```
calcTotal();
```

Figure 14-20 Code to call the calcTotal() function

```
function calcPrice() {
   product = document.forms[0].prod;
   pIndex = product.selectedIndex;
   productPrice = product.options[pIndex].value;

   quantity = document.forms[0].qty;
   qIndex = quantity.selectedIndex;
   quantityOrdered = quantity.options[qIndex].value;

   document.forms[0].price.value = productPrice*quantityOrdered;

   calcTotal();
}

function calcShipping() {
   document.forms[0].ship.value = this.value;

   calcTotal();
}
```

calls the calcTotal() function to update the total value displayed on the Web form

2. Save your changes to the file, and then reload **form1.htm** in your Web browser.
3. Select **Drive Planner 2.0 ($29.95)** from the product selection list, select **2** from the quantity selection list, and then click the **Standard (4–6 business days): $4.95** option button. As you select each option, the subtotal, tax, and total values automatically update in the Web form. See Figure 14-21.

Figure 14-21 Subtotal, tax, and total values updated based on the selected options

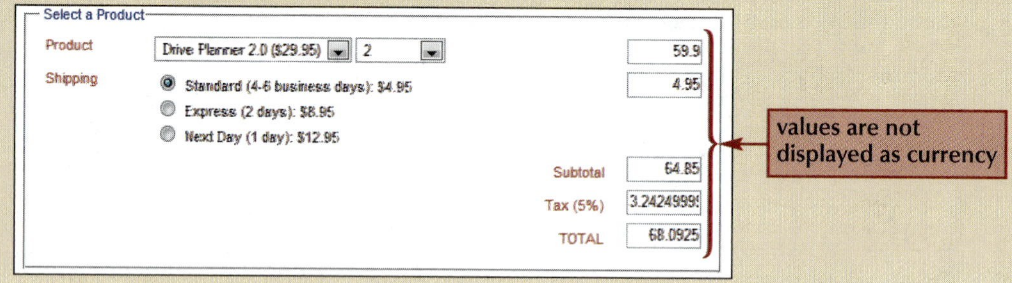

Using the options you selected, the form automatically calculates the subtotal value to be $64.85, the tax value to be approximately $3.24, and the total cost of the order to be about $68.09. Because of how numeric values are stored and calculated, the sales tax and the total price are displayed beyond two-decimal-point accuracy. All the monetary values need to be displayed only to two decimal places because they represent dollars and cents. To do this, you can apply the toFixed() method to the numeric values, which converts a number to a text string, displaying the value to a specified number of digits. Recall that the syntax of the toFixed() method is

```
value.toFixed(n)
```

where *value* is the numeric value and *n* is the number of digits displayed by the browser. You'll apply this method to the values calculated by JavaScript.

To apply the toFixed() method:

1. Return to the **order.js** file in your text editor.
2. In the calcPrice() function, change the statement that sets the value of the price field to:

```
document.forms[0].price.value = (productPrice*quantityOrdered).
toFixed(2);
```

3. In the calcTotal() function, change the statements that set the values of the sub, tax, and tot field to the following:

```
document.forms[0].sub.value = (priceVal + shipVal).toFixed(2);
document.forms[0].tax.value = taxVal.toFixed(2);
document.forms[0].tot.value = (priceVal + shipVal + taxVal).
toFixed(2);
```

You do not have to make any changes to the calcShipping() function because the three shipping values stored in the selection list are already in currency format. Figure 14-22 shows the revised code.

Figure 14-22 toFixed() method applied to currency values

```
function calcPrice() {
   product = document.forms[0].prod;
   pIndex = product.selectedIndex;
   productPrice = product.options[pIndex].value;

   quantity = document.forms[0].qty;
   qIndex = quantity.selectedIndex;
   quantityOrdered = quantity.options[qIndex].value;

   document.forms[0].price.value = (productPrice*quantityOrdered).toFixed(2);

   calcTotal();
}

function calcShipping() {
   document.forms[0].ship.value = this.value;

   calcTotal();
}

function calcTotal() {
   priceVal = parseFloat(document.forms[0].price.value);
   shipVal = parseFloat(document.forms[0].ship.value);
   document.forms[0].sub.value = (priceVal + shipVal).toFixed(2);

   taxVal = 0.05*(priceVal + shipVal);
   document.forms[0].tax.value = taxVal.toFixed(2);

   document.forms[0].tot.value = (priceVal + shipVal + taxVal).toFixed(2);
}
```

displays the value to two decimal places

4. Save your changes to the file, and then reload **form1.htm** in your Web browser.
5. Select **G-Receiver I ($149.50)** from the product selection list, select **3** from the quantity selection list, and then click the **Next Day (1 day): $12.95** shipping option button. Figure 14-23 shows the resulting values in the order form.

Figure 14-23 Currency values formatted to two decimal places

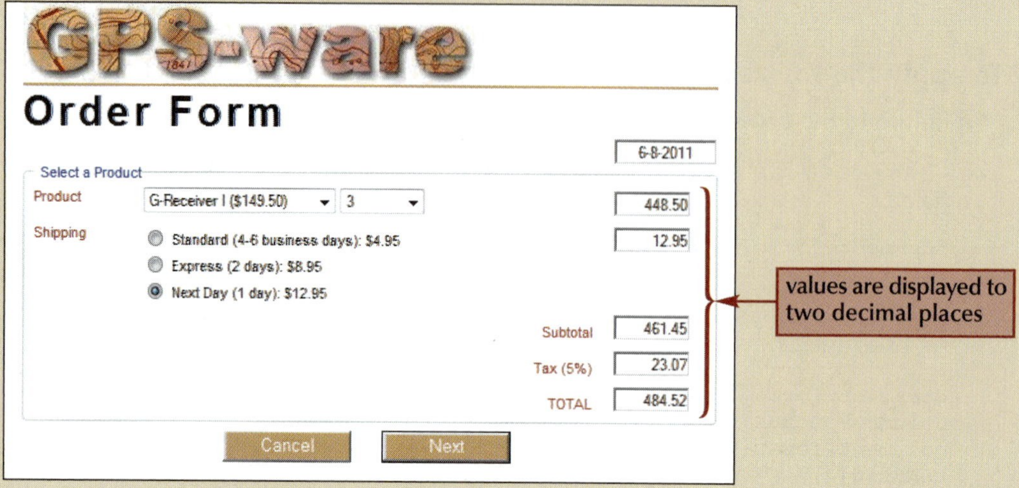

6. Continue to experiment with different order options to verify that the form correctly calculates the total price of each order.

You've created all the calculated fields needed for the order form of Carol's Web site. In the next session, you'll explore ways to ensure that Web forms are correctly filled out and to notify users of errors when they're not.

Review | Session 14.1 Quick Check

1. Specify the object reference to the second Web form in a document.
2. Specify the object reference to the lastname input field found in the register Web form.
3. What command changes the value of the lastname field to Carol Campbell? What command moves the cursor to the lastname field?
4. Specify the object reference to the fourth option in the statename selection list. Assume that the name of the Web form is register.
5. What expression returns the index number of the selected option from the statename selection list?
6. What expression indicates whether the contactme check box field in the register Web form is selected?
7. What expression converts the value 3.14159 to a text string displaying the value rounded to two decimal places?

Session 14.2

Working with Form Validation

Carol appreciates the order form's ability to automatically calculate the different costs associated with an order, but she is concerned that the form contains nothing to prevent customers from filling it out incorrectly. For example, users could submit an order without specifying a shipping option. Carol wants the form to contain some checks on whether a customer has correctly filled it out.

Carol is requesting one type of **form validation**, a process by which the server or a user's browser checks a form for data entry errors. On the Web, validation can occur on the client side or the server side. As shown in Figure 14-24, **server-side validation** sends a form to the Web server for checking. If an error is found, the user is notified and asked to resubmit the form. In **client-side validation**, the Web browser checks the form, which is not submitted to the server until it passes inspection.

Figure 14-24 Server-side and client-side validation

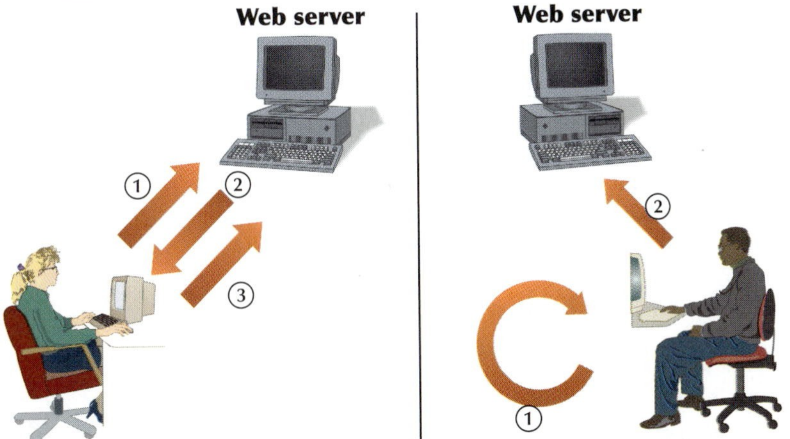

Server-side validation

1) The user submits the form to the Web server.

2) The Web server validates the user's responses and, if necessary, returns the form to the user for correction.

3) After correcting any errors, the user resubmits the form to the Web server for another validation.

Client-side validation

1) The user submits the form, and validation is performed on the user's computer.

2) After correcting any errors, the user submits the form to the Web server.

In practice, server-side and client-side validation are used together. Client-side validation provides immediate feedback to users and lessens the load on servers by distributing some of the validation tasks to users' computers. The server then has the task of performing a final check on submitted data before processing it. Carol is aware that GPS-ware's Web server might handle hundreds of orders per hour on a good business day, and anything that can be done to reduce the load on the server helps. Carol wants you to ensure that, before the form can be submitted to the server, a customer has:

1. selected a GPS-ware product
2. selected a quantity of the product to order
3. selected a shipping option

If these conditions are not met, Carol wants the user's browser to alert the customer of the problem and refuse to submit the form to the server.

Submitting a Form

When a user completes a form and then clicks the submit button, the form initiates a submit event. By default, the browser initiates the action indicated in the form's action and method attributes. The code for the <form> tag in the form1.htm file is

```
<form id = "form1" method = "post" action = "form2.htm">
```

so that when the form is successfully completed by the user, the browser will use the post method to submit the form and retrieve the form2.htm file. Clicking the Next button submits the form for processing.

To control this submission process, JavaScript provides the onsubmit event handler that can be added to the form element. The syntax of the onsubmit event handler is

```
formObj.onsubmit = function;
```

where *function* is a function that returns the Boolean value true or false. If the function returns a value of false, the submit event is cancelled, whereas a value of true allows the submit event to continue unabated. For the order form, you'll create a function named checkForm1() that will verify that all of the form data has been correctly entered. You'll create an onsubmit event handler to run this function now.

To apply an onsubmit event handler:

1. Return to the **order.js** file in your text editor.
2. Go to the startForm() function, and then at the end of the function insert the following statement, as shown in Figure 14-25:

```
document.forms[0].onsubmit = checkForm1;
```

Figure 14-25 Code for the onsubmit event handler

```
function startForm() {
   document.forms[0].date.value = todayTxt();
   document.forms[0].prod.focus();

   document.forms[0].prod.onchange = calcPrice;
   document.forms[0].qty.onchange = calcPrice;

   for (var i = 0; i < document.forms[0].shipType.length; i++) {
      document.forms[0].shipType[i].onclick = calcShipping;
   }

   document.forms[0].onsubmit = checkForm1;
}
```

browser runs the checkForm1() function when the form is submitted

Next, you will create the checkForm1() function. The initial form of the function is:

```
function checkForm1() {
   if (document.forms[0].prod.selectedIndex == 0) {
       return false;}
   else if (document.forms[0].qty.selectedIndex == 0) {
       return false;}
   else if (document.forms[0].ship.value == "0.00") {
       return false;}
   else return true;
}
```

The checkForm1() function tests three if conditions. It first tests whether a product has been selected by examining the selectedIndex property. A value of 0 indicates the user has not selected a product. It then tests whether a quantity has been selected by once again examining the value of the selectedIndex property. Finally, it tests whether the value of the ship field is equal to 0.00, which indicates that the user has not selected a shipping option. If any of those three conditions is satisfied, the function returns the value of false, which cancels the form submission. On the other hand, if none of the conditions is satisfied, indicating that the user has selected a product, a quantity, and a shipping option, the function returns a value of true and the form is submitted by the browser.

You'll add the checkForm1() function to the order.js file.

To insert the checkForm1() function:

1. At the bottom of the file, insert the following code, as shown in Figure 14-26:

```
function checkForm1() {
   if (document.forms[0].prod.selectedIndex == 0) {
       return false;}
   else if (document.forms[0].qty.selectedIndex == 0) {
       return false;}
   else if (document.forms[0].ship.value == "0.00") {
       return false;}
   else return true;
}
```

Figure 14-26 Code for the checkForm1() function

```
   document.forms[0].tot.value = (priceVal + shipVal + taxVal).toFixed(2);
}

function checkForm1() {
   if (document.forms[0].prod.selectedIndex == 0) {
      return false;}
   else if (document.forms[0].qty.selectedIndex == 0) {
      return false;}
   else if (document.forms[0].ship.value == "0.00") {
      return false;}
   else return true;
}
```

verifies that the user has selected a product, a quantity, and a shipping option

2. Save your changes to the file.

Alerting the User

It is not enough to simply reject forms that have been improperly filled out. You also need to notify users of their error so they can correct the mistake. One way of notifying the user is through an alert box. An **alert box** is a dialog box that displays an informative message to the user along with an OK button that closes the box when clicked. Alert boxes are created using the method

```
alert(message);
```

where *message* is the text that appears in the dialog box. For example, to create an alert box that displays the message "You must select a GPS-ware product", you would run the following command:

```
alert("You must select a GPS-ware product");
```

You'll add similar alert messages to each of the three conditions under which the form would be rejected by the browser.

To insert the alert boxes:

1. Directly before the first return false; line in the checkForm1() function, insert the following command:

```
alert("You must select a GPS-ware product");
```

2. Directly before the second return false; line, insert the following command:

```
alert("You must select a quantity to order");
```

3. Directly before the last return false; line, insert the following command:

```
alert("You must select a shipping option");
```

Figure 14-27 highlights the inserted code for the three alert boxes.

Figure 14-27 Code to add alert boxes

```
function checkForm1() {
   if (document.forms[0].prod.selectedIndex == 0) {
      alert("You must select a GPS-ware product");
      return false;}
   else if (document.forms[0].qty.selectedIndex == 0) {
      alert("You must select a quantity to order");
      return false;}
   else if (document.forms[0].ship.value == "0.00") {
      alert("You must select a shipping option");
      return false;}
   else return true;
}
```

displays an alert box

4. Save your changes to the file, and then reload **form1.htm** in your Web browser.

5. Click the **Next** button without selecting any products, quantities, or shipping options on the form. The browser displays an alert box indicating that you have not selected a product to order, which is the first mistake found in the form. See Figure 14-28.

Figure 14-28 Web form being validated

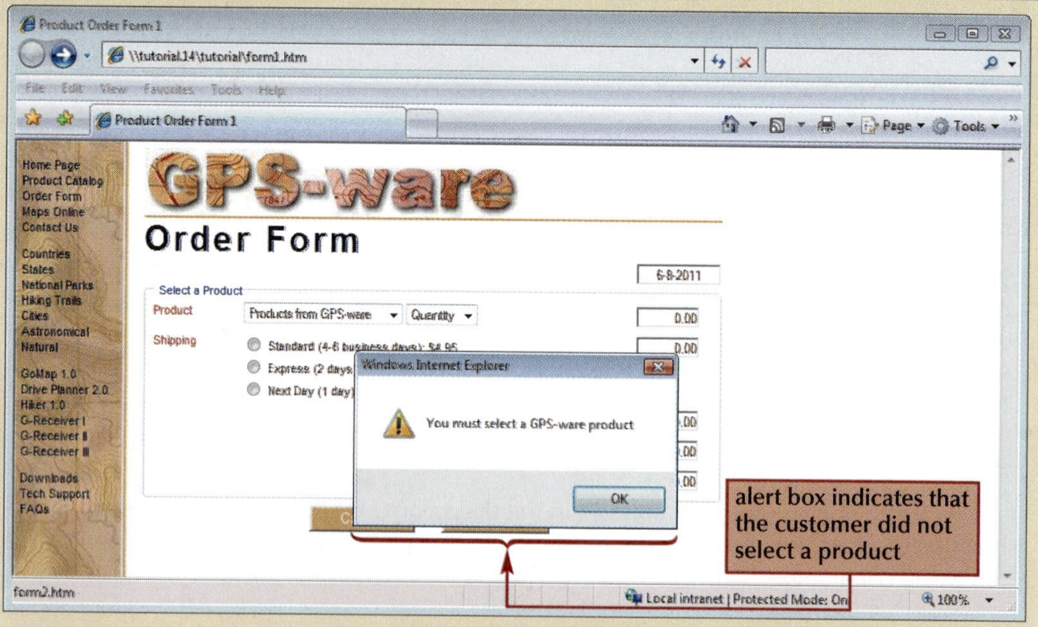

6. Click the **OK** button to close the alert box.
7. Continue to test the form by omitting one of three required pieces of information, submit the form, and then verifying that the browser fails to accept the form.
8. Correctly complete the order form, and then click the **Next** button. Verify that the browser accepted the completed form and displayed the second of Carol's three Web forms.

Due to the way that the code for the checkForm1() function is written, only the first error that JavaScript discovers will be reported to the user. Even if you omit all three items in the order, only the lack of a chosen product will be reported.

Resetting a Form

The other event associated with Web forms is the reset event, which occurs when a user clicks a form reset button. Clicking the reset button has the effect of resetting all form fields to their default values. You can control how the reset event is handled by adding an onreset event handler to the form element in the same way that you use the onsubmit event handler to manage form submission.

In Carol's order form, the Cancel button plays the role of the reset button. However, Carol wants to modify what happens when the form is reset. Recall that the first action this form takes is to insert the current date into the date field. Carol wants the reset button to both reset the fields to their default values and rerun the startForm() function, which inserts the current date into the date field. You can perform both of these actions by having the browser reload the document when the reset event is initiated. When the page is reloaded, the startForm() function runs automatically and the fields return to their default values. To reload the current page, you run the following command:

```
location.reload();
```

You'll add this command to a function named resetForm1(), and then attach that function to the onreset event handler for the Web form.

Tip

You can use JavaScript to highlight missing or erroneous data values by modifying the display style of the input fields in the Web form. For example, modify the border style to highlight incorrect or missing data values with a red border.

To apply the onreset event handler:

1. Return to the **order.js** file in your text editor.
2. Add the following command to the bottom of the startForm() function:

```
document.forms[0].onreset = resetForm1;
```

3. Directly below the startForm() function, insert the following function, as shown in Figure 14-29:

```
function resetForm1() {
   location.reload();
}
```

Figure 14-29 Code to insert the onreset event handler

```
function startForm() {
   document.forms[0].date.value = todayTxt();
   document.forms[0].prod.focus();

   document.forms[0].prod.onchange = calcPrice;
   document.forms[0].qty.onchange = calcPrice;

   for (var i = 0; i < document.forms[0].shipType.length; i++) {
      document.forms[0].shipType[i].onclick = calcShipping;
   }

   document.forms[0].onsubmit = checkForm1;
   document.forms[0].onreset = resetForm1;
}

function resetForm1() {
   location.reload();
}
```

runs the resetForm1() function when the form is reset

4. Close the file, saving your changes.
5. Reload **form1.htm** in your Web browser.
6. Select a product to order, a quantity, and a shipping option, and then click the **Cancel** button at the bottom of the form. Verify that the page reloads, setting the fields to their default values and displaying the current date in the date field. The product selection list is the selected field in the form.

Reference Window | Validating a Web Form

- To validate a Web form when it is submitted, add the event handler
  `formObj.onsubmit = function;`
  to the form element, where *function* is a function that returns a Boolean value. A value of false cancels the submission of the form, whereas a value of true allows the form to be submitted.
- To control the resetting of a form, add the event handler
  `formObj.onreset = function;`
  where *function* is a function that is run when the reset event is initiated.

Working with Text Strings

You've completed your work on the first Web form. The second form collects contact information from the user for delivering the purchased item. As with the form1.htm file, all JavaScript code for this file will be stored in the external JavaScript file contact.js. You'll create a link to this file now.

To view the form2.htm file:

1. Open the **form2.htm** file in your text editor.
2. In the head section of the document, create a link to the contact.js script file.
3. Review the contents and code of the file, and then close the file, saving your changes.
4. Open **form2.htm** in your Web browser. Figure 14-30 shows the initial layout of the file.

Figure 14-30

Delivery form and element names

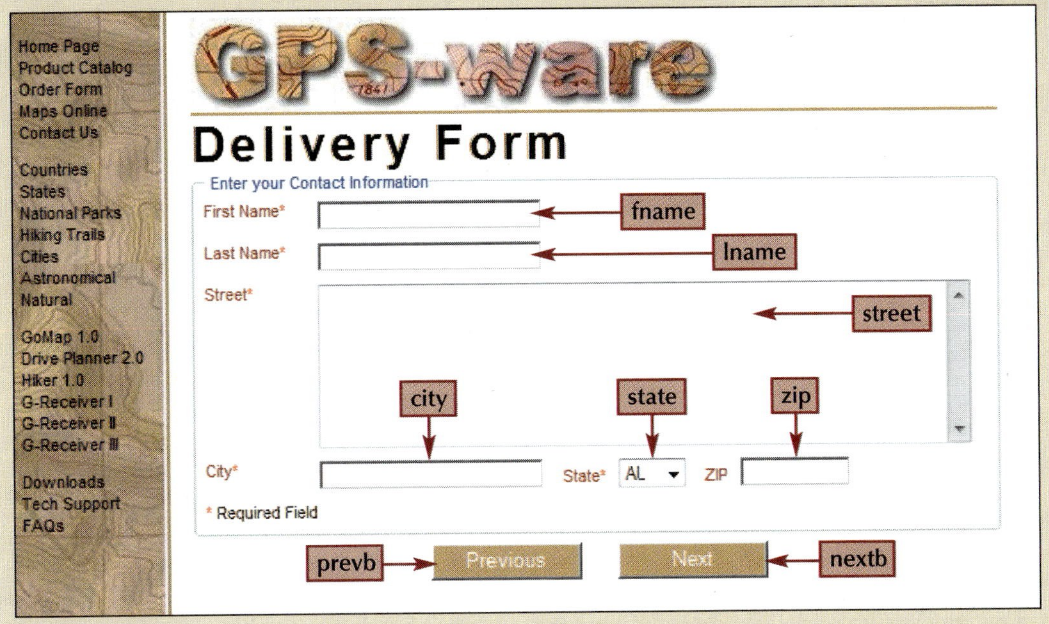

Figure 14-31 lists the object references for each element in the form.

Figure 14-31

Objects in the delivery form

Object	Reference
first name field	document.forms[0].fname
last name field	document.forms[0].lname
street text area box	document.forms[0].street
city field	document.forms[0].city
state selection list	document.forms[0].state
ZIP code field	document.forms[0].zip
previous button	document.forms[0].prevb
next button	document.forms[0].nextb

Although this form requires no calculations, Carol wants you to implement the following validation checks before the form is accepted by the browser:

1. A customer must specify a first name, last name, street address, and city.
2. If a zip code is entered, it should consist of five digits with no nonnumeric characters.

Because you need to apply these validation checks to text strings, you'll take a deeper look at the properties and methods of text strings.

Using the String Object

JavaScript can store a text value in an object called a **String object**. The most common way to create a String object is to use the object constructor

```
stringVariable = new String(text);
```

where *stringVariable* is a variable that stores the text string, and *text* is the text of the string. This approach has the advantage of explicitly identifying a variable as containing a text string, rather than having JavaScript implicitly create a String object based on the content of a variable.

Calculating the Length of a Text String

One of the properties associated with String objects is the length property, which returns the number of characters in the text string, including all white spaces and nonprintable characters. For example, the following code uses the length property to calculate the number of characters in the stringVar variable:

```
stringVar = "GPS-ware Products";
lengthValue = stringVar.length;
```

After running this code, the lengthValue variable will have the value 17.

The length property is commonly used for functions that process text strings one character at a time and need a way of knowing when to stop. You can also use the length property to validate the entries in Web forms. Carol wants to require customers to enter a first and last name, a street address, and a city. Because these are required values, the length of the text entered in each of these fields must be greater than 0. You'll use the length property to verify this condition for each of these fields in your first set of validation checks for the delivery form, storing those tests in a function named checkForm2(). As with the earlier checkForm1() function, you'll have the browser display an appropriate alert dialog box the first time it encounters an invalid field. The following is the initial code for the checkForm2() function:

```
function checkForm2() {
   if (document.forms[0].fname.value.length == 0)
      {alert("You must enter a first name");
       return false;}
   else if (document.forms[0].lname.value.length == 0)
      {alert("You must enter a last name");
       return false;}
   else if (document.forms[0].street.value.length == 0)
      {alert("You must enter a street address");
       return false;}
   else if (document.forms[0].city.value.length == 0)
      {alert("You must enter a city name");
       return false;}
   else return true;
}
```

The checkForm2() function only verifies that an entry has been made in these fields; it does not test whether those entries make any sense. You'll add the checkForm2() function to the contact.js file.

To insert the checkForm2() function:

1. Open the **contact.js** file in your text editor.
2. Below the comment section, insert the following code, as shown in Figure 14-32:

```
function checkForm2() {
   if (document.forms[0].fname.value.length == 0)
      {alert("You must enter a first name");
       return false;}
   else if (document.forms[0].lname.value.length == 0)
      {alert("You must enter a last name");
       return false;}
```

```
        else if (document.forms[0].street.value.length == 0)
           {alert("You must enter a street address");
            return false;}
        else if (document.forms[0].city.value.length == 0)
           {alert("You must enter a city name");
            return false;}
        else return true;
    }
```

Figure 14-32 Code for the checkForm2() function

```
function checkForm2() {
   if (document.forms[0].fname.value.length == 0)
      {alert("You must enter a first name");
       return false;}
   else if (document.forms[0].lname.value.length == 0)
      {alert("You must enter a last name");
       return false;}
   else if (document.forms[0].street.value.length == 0)
      {alert("You must enter a street address");
       return false;}
   else if (document.forms[0].city.value.length == 0)
      {alert("You must enter a city name");
       return false;}
   else return true;
}
```

verifies that the user entered something in the fname, lname, street, and city fields

3. Because this is a long piece of code, take some time to ensure that you have entered the code correctly. Make sure that you enclosed all command blocks within curly braces {} and that you used the == symbol rather than a single = symbol in the conditional statements.

You want the checkForm2() function to run when the user submits the delivery form. To do that, you once again add an onsubmit event handler to the form element when the page is initially loaded by the browser.

To insert the onsubmit event handler:

1. Directly above the checkForm2() function, insert the following code, as shown in Figure 14-33:

```
window.onload = startForm;

function startForm() {
   document.forms[0].onsubmit = checkForm2;
}
```

Figure 14-33 Code to call the checkForm2() function

```
window.onload = startForm;

function startForm() {
   document.forms[0].onsubmit = checkForm2;
}

function checkForm2() {
   if (document.forms[0].fname.value.length == 0)
      {alert("You must enter a first name");
       return false;}
```

runs the checkForm2() function when the user submits the form

2. Save your changes to the file, and then reload **form2.htm** in your Web browser.

   As with the previous form, the Next button submits the form for processing. In this case, submitting the form causes the browser to load the form3.htm file.

3. Click the **Next** button without entering any contact information in the first name, last name, street, or city fields. Verify that the browser displays an alert box, indicating that you have not specified a first name.

4. Click the **OK** button to close the alert box, and then continue to test the form by omitting different required fields and clicking the **Next** button. Verify that you must enter all the required information before the browser will accept the completed form.

Tip

A common form design is to place asterisks next to each required field as a visual clue to the user indicating which fields are required.

Working with String Object Methods

Carol's second validation check involves examining the digits in the zip field. At the moment Carol is only considering five-digit postal codes, so this field should be five characters long and consist only of numeric characters. (You will look at how to validate extended postal codes that include a dash and additional digits in the next session.)

To validate the zip code, you'll create a function named checkZip(). The checkZip() function will return a Boolean value of true if the text string matches the pattern for zip codes and false if otherwise. The initial version of this function will check only the length of the text string. Because the zip field is not a required field in Carol's form, you'll allow valid text strings to contain either zero or five digits; any other length will be invalid. The initial code for the checkZip() function is:

```
function checkZip(zip) {
   if (zip.length != 0 && zip.length != 5) return false
   else return true;
}
```

You'll add this function to the contact.js file.

To insert the checkZip() function:

1. Return to the **contact.js** file in your text editor.

2. At the bottom of the file, insert the following function, as shown in Figure 14-34:

```
function checkZip(zip) {
   if (zip.length != 0 && zip.length != 5) return false
   else return true;
}
```

Figure 14-34 **Initial checkZip() function**

```
   else if (document.forms[0].city.value.length == 0)
      {alert("You must enter a city name");
       return false;}
   else return true;
}

function checkZip(zip) {
   if (zip.length != 0 && zip.length != 5) return false
   else return true;
}
```

verifies that the length of the zip code is either 0 or 5

3. Save your changes to the file.

The checkZip() function can confirm that the zip code contains five characters, but it does not check whether each of those characters are digits. To do that, you'll use some of the JavaScript methods associated with string objects.

JavaScript supports methods that allow you to examine the individual characters within a text string. A character is identified by its placement in the text string. Like arrays and object collections, the first character has an index value of 0, the second has an index value of 1, and so on. If you want to reference a character with a particular index, use the charAt() method

```
string.charAt(i)
```

where *string* is the string object and *i* is the index of the character. For example, the expression

```
"GPS-ware".charAt(2)
```

returns the third character from the text string, which in this case is an uppercase S. The charAt() method extracts only a single character. To extract longer text strings, known as **substrings**, use the slice() method

```
string.slice(start, end)
```

where *start* is the starting index and *end* is the index at which the slicing stops. If you do not specify an *end* value, the substring is extracted to the end of the text string. For example, the statement

```
"GPS-ware Products For Sale".slice(9,17)
```

returns the substring Products, because it starts at index number 9 and ends right before index number 17. You can also extract substrings based on their length using the method

```
string.substr(start, length)
```

where *length* is the number of characters in the substring. If you do not specify a *length* value, JavaScript extracts the substring to the end of the string. To extract the word Products from the previous text string, you can also use:

```
"GPS-ware Products For Sale".substr(9,8)
```

Both the slice() and substr() methods are limited in that they create only a single substring. In some cases, you may need to break a text string into several substrings. For example, you may need to break a long sentence into individual words. Another common use would be to break a field in which customers enter both their first and last names into two strings. Rather than run the substr() or slice() methods several times on the same text string, you can create an array of substrings in a single expression using the method

```
strArray = string.split(str)
```

where *strArray* is the array that will store the substrings and *str* is a text string that marks the break between one substring and another, which is known as a **delimiter**. The command

```
words = "GPS-ware Products For Sale".split(" ")
```

splits the text string at each occurrence of a blank space, storing the substrings in the words array. The substrings stored in the words array are:

```
words[0] = "GPS-ware"
words[1] = "Products"
words[2] = "For"
words[3] = "Sale"
```

The characters specified in the delimiter are not placed in the substrings. This is one technique you can use to remove character strings from a large text string.

Other string object methods are used to search for the occurrence of particular substrings within larger text strings. The most often used method is the indexOf() method, which has the following syntax:

```
string.indexOf(str, start)
```

The indexOf() method returns the index value of the first occurrence of the substring *str* within *string*. The *start* parameter is optional and indicates from which character to start the search. The default value of the *start* parameter is 0, indicating that the search should start with the first character. For example, the expression

```
"GPS-ware Products For Sale".indexOf("P")
```

returns the value 1 because the first occurrence of an uppercase P in the text occurs as the second character in the text string. To locate the next occurrence of P, you can set the *start* value to 2 so that the search starts with the third character in the string. The expression

```
"GPS-ware Products For Sale".indexOf("P",3)
```

returns the value 9. If no occurrence of the substring exists, the indexOf() method returns the value –1. For this reason, the indexOf() method is often used to test whether a text string contains a particular substring.

Tip

You can use the indexOf() method to test for the presence or absence of a character. If the method returns the value –1, the character does not appear in the text string.

Reference Window | Working with String Objects

- To determine the number of characters in a text string, use the object property
  `string.length`
  where *string* is a text string object.
- To extract a character from a text string, use the method
  `string.charAt(i)`
  where *i* is the index of the character. The first character in the text string has an index number of 0.
- To extract a substring from a text string, use the method
  `string.slice(start, end)`
  where *start* is the starting index and *end* is the index at which the substring stops. If you do not specify an *end* value, the substring is extracted to the end of the string.
- To split a string into several substrings, use the command
  `strArray = string.split(str)`
  where *strArray* is the array that will store the substrings and *str* is a text string that marks the break between one substring and another.
- To search a string, use the method
  `string.indexOf(str, start)`
  where *str* is the substring to search for within the larger string and *start* is the index of the character from which to start the search. If you do not specify a *start* value, the search starts with the first character in the string.

Figure 14-35 summarizes the different string object methods used to extract information from text strings.

Methods to extract strings **Figure 14-35**

Method	Description	Example (text= "GPS-ware Products")
`string.charAt(i)`	Returns the *i*th character from *string*	`text.charAt(4);` // returns "w"
`string.charCodeAt(i)`	Returns the *i*th character's Unicode value from the *string*	`text.charCodeAt(4);` // returns 119
`string.concat(str2, str3, ...)`	Appends *string* with the text strings *str2*, *str3*, etc.	`text.concat(" Sale");` // returns "GPS-ware Products Sale"
`String.fromCharCode(n1, n2, ...)`	Returns a text string consisting of characters whose Unicode values are *n1*, *n2*, etc.	`String.fromCharCode(71,80,83);` // returns "GPS"
`string.indexOf(str, start)`	Searches *string*, beginning at the *start* index number, returning the index number of the first occurrence of *str*; if no *start* value is specified, the search begins with the first character	`text.indexOf("P",5);` // returns 9
`string.lastIndexOf(str,start)`	Searches *string*, beginning at the *start* index number, returning the index number of the last occurrence of *str*; if no *start* value is specified, the search begins with the first character	`text.lastIndexOf("P");` // returns 9
`string.slice(start, end)`	Extracts a substring from *string*, between the *start* and *end* index values; if no *end* value is specified, the substring extends to the end of the string	`text.slice(4,8);` // returns "ware"
`string. split(str)`	Splits *string* into an array of string characters at each occurrence of *str*	`word=text.split(" ");` // word[0] = "GPS-ware" // word[1] = "Products"
`string.substr(start, length)`	Returns a substring from *string* starting at the *start* index value and continuing for *length* characters; if no *length* value is specified, the substring continues to the end of *string*	`text.substr(9,4);` // returns "Prod"
`string.substring(start, end)`	Extracts a substring from *string*, between the *start* and *end* index values; if no *end* value is specified, the substring extends to the end of the string (identical to the slice() method)	`text.substring(4,8);` // returns "ware"

To further explore the string extraction methods, you'll use the charAt() and indexOf() methods to create a function that determines whether a text string is composed of only numeric characters. The code for the isNonNumeric() function is:

```
function isNonNumeric(tString) {
   validchars = "0123456789";
   for (var i = 0; i < tString.length; i++) {
      char = tString.charAt(i);
      if (validchars.indexOf(char) == -1) return true;
   }
   return false;
}
```

This function first stores the digits from 0 to 9 in a text string stored in the validchars variable. The code then loops through each of the characters in the tString variable, extracting the character at each index using the charAt() method. Each character is then tested using the indexOf() method to determine whether it matches one of the characters in the validchars text string. If it cannot be found in that text string, the indexOf() method returns the value –1, and you know that the text string contains at least one nonnumeric character. The function will then halt, returning the value true. If the loop concludes without locating at least one nonnumeric character, the function returns the value false.

You'll add this command to the contact.js file.

To insert the isNonNumeric() function:

1. Below the checkZip() function, insert the following code, as shown in Figure 14-36:

```
function isNonNumeric(tString) {
   validchars = "0123456789";

   for (var i = 0; i < tString.length; i++) {
      char = tString.charAt(i);
      if (validchars.indexOf(char) == -1) return true;
   }

   return false;
}
```

Figure 14-36 Code for the isNonNumeric() function

```
function checkZip(zip) {
   if (zip.length != 0 && zip.length != 5) return false
   else return true;
}

function isNonNumeric(tString) {
   validchars = "0123456789";

   for (var i = 0; i < tString.length; i++) {
      char = tString.charAt(i);
      if (validchars.indexOf(char) == -1) return true;
   }

   return false;
}
```

function returns the value true if tString contains a non-numeric character

2. Save your changes to the file.

Next, you'll call this function from the checkZip() function to determine whether the zip code value entered by the customer consists of only numeric characters. If the isNonNumeric() function returns the value of true, it indicates that nonnumeric characters appear in the zip code entered by the user, and the zip code should be rejected as false.

To modify the checkZip() function:

1. Add and revise the following code from the checkZip() function, as shown in Figure 14-37:

```
else if (isNonNumeric(zip)) return false
else return true;
```

Code to check the zip code validity — Figure 14-37

```
function checkZip(zip) {
   if (zip.length != 0 && zip.length != 5) return false
   else if (isNonNumeric(zip)) return false
   else return true;
}
```

verifies that the zip field contains only numeric characters

2. Add the following code to the function to call the checkZip() function from within the checkForm2() function to confirm that the user has entered a valid zip code before the form is submitted, as shown in Figure 14-38:

```
else if (checkZip(document.forms[0].zip.value) == false)
   {alert("Invalid zip code");
    return false;}
```

Code to call the checkZip() function — Figure 14-38

```
function checkForm2() {
   if (document.forms[0].fname.value.length == 0)
      {alert("You must enter a first name");
       return false;}
   else if (document.forms[0].lname.value.length == 0)
      {alert("You must enter a last name");
       return false;}
   else if (document.forms[0].street.value.length == 0)
      {alert("You must enter a street address");
       return false;}
   else if (document.forms[0].city.value.length == 0)
      {alert("You must enter a city name");
       return false;}
   else if (checkZip(document.forms[0].zip.value) == false)
      {alert("Invalid zip code");
       return false;}
   else return true;
}
```

verifies that a valid zip code has been entered

3. Save your changes to the file, and then reload **form2.htm** in your browser.
4. Enter text into the first name, last name, street, and city fields, and then click the **Next** button to submit the delivery form. Your browser displays the contents of Carol's third Web form.
5. Return to the **form2.htm** page, enter the value **abcde** into the zip field, and then click the **Next** button. Your browser displays an alert box and fails to accept the form.
6. Repeat Step 5, entering the values **123**, **1234a**, and **12345** into the zip field. Your browser displays an alert box and fails to accept the form for the zip code values 123 and 1234a, but accepts the form for the zip code value 12345.

InSight | Extracting a Text String from an Array

Arrays often contain text values. One of the string methods supported by JavaScript allows you to extract these text strings, placing them within a single String object. The syntax of the toString() method is

```
array.toString()
```

where *array* is the array containing a collection of text values. The values from the array are returned in a comma-separated text string list. For example, if the array contains the abbreviated days of the week

```
wDay = new Array('Sun','Mon','Tue','Wed','Thu','Fri','Sat');
```

then running the command

```
wDayStr = wDay.toString();
```

stores the following text string in the wDayStr variable:

```
"Sun,Mon,Tue,Wed,Thu,Fri,Sat"
```

The toString() method can also be used with objects other than arrays. When used with other objects, the toString() method returns a text string representing the object. For example, when applied to a Date object, the toString() method returns the date value as a text string. When used with a numeric value, the toString() method returns the value as a text string.

Formatting Text Strings

Another set of JavaScript methods allows you to format a text string's appearance. For example, to display a text string in all uppercase letters, you would use the method

```
string.toUpperCase()
```

where *string* is the string object. To change the text GPS-ware to all uppercase letters, you would use the following JavaScript expression:

```
"GPS-ware".toUpperCase()
```

Figure 14-39 lists other formatting methods for string objects along with their equivalent HTML tags. Running these methods does not add the HTML tags to the object, but rather achieves the same effects that you would get if you applied those formatting tags to the text string.

You may notice that many of the HTML tags shown in Figure 14-39 have been deprecated in favor of style sheets. In the same way, the string formatting methods are not often used in preference to formatting text strings using the style object. The most common formatting methods are the toUpperCase() and toLowerCase() methods. At this point, you don't need to do any text formatting for Carol's Web forms.

Figure 14-39 Methods to format strings

Method	Description	HTML Equivalent
string.anchor(*text*)	Creates an anchor with the anchor name *text*	`<a name="text">string</a>`
string.big()	Changes the size of the *string* font to big	`<big>string</big>`
string.blink()	Changes *string* to blinking text	`<blink>string</blink>`
string.bold()	Changes the font weight of *string* to bold	`<bold>string</bold>`
string.fixed()	Changes the font of *string* to a fixed width font	`<tt>string</tt>`
string.fontcolor(color)	Changes the color of *string* to the hexadecimal *color* value	`<font color="color">string</font>`
string.fontsize(*value*)	Changes the font size of *string* to *value*	`<font size="value">string</font>`
string.italics()	Changes *string* to italics	`<i>string</i>`
string.link(*url*)	Changes *string* to a link pointing to *url*	`<a href="url">string</a>`
string.small()	Changes the size of the *string* font to small	`<small>string</small>`
string.strike()	Adds strikethrough characters to *string*	`<strike>string</strike>`
string.sub()	Changes *string* to a subscript	`<sub>string</sub>`
string.sup()	Changes *string* to a superscript	`<sup>string</sup>`
string.toLowerCase()	Changes *string* to lowercase letters	
string.toUpperCase()	Changes *string* to uppercase letters	

In the next session, you'll continue to explore how to validate text entries through the use of regular expressions and how to validate financial data.

Session 14.2 Quick Check | Review

1. What is server-side validation? What is client-side validation?
2. A function named testForm()validates a Web form. What event handler should you add to the form element to run the validation before the form is submitted?
3. What expression returns the number of characters in the username string object?
4. What expression returns the first character from the username string? What expression returns the last character from the string?

5. What expression returns the first five characters from the username string?
6. E-mail addresses are usually written in the format *username@domain*. Write code that breaks an e-mail variable into two text strings: one containing *username* and the other containing *domain*.
7. Government e-mail addresses will often end with .gov. What expression tests whether the e-mail string object contains the .gov substring?
8. What expression changes the username string object to uppercase letters?

Session 14.3

Introducing Regular Expressions

Carol likes the form validation functions you created for the delivery form, but she is concerned about the function that validates the zip code. Domestic zip codes come in two forms: five digits (*nnnnn*) and five digits followed by a hyphen and four more digits (*nnnnn-nnnn*). In recent years, the second version has become more common and Carol wants the validation functions to support either format. Although you could revise the checkZip() function to accommodate the extended zip code format, a more flexible approach is to use a regular expression.

A **regular expression** is a text string that defines a character pattern. One use of regular expressions is **pattern matching**, in which a text string is tested to see whether it matches the pattern defined by a regular expression. In the zip code example, you might create a regular expression for the pattern of five digits followed by a hyphen and another four digits, and then verify that a customer's zip code matches that pattern. Pattern matching is just one use of regular expressions. They can also be used to extract substrings, insert new text, or replace old text. The greatest advantage of regular expressions is that the code is compact and powerful, so that what might take several lines of code using other methods can be done in a single line with a regular expression. However, with this power comes complexity: The syntax of regular expressions can be intimidating to new programmers, taking time and practice to master.

Creating a Regular Expression

You create a regular expression in JavaScript using the command

```
re = /pattern/;
```

where *pattern* is the text string of the regular expression and *re* is the object that stores the regular expression. This syntax for creating regular expressions is sometimes referred to as a **regular expression literal**. A regular expression is treated by a JavaScript interpreter as an object with a collection of properties and methods that can be applied to it. You'll explore some of those properties and methods later in this session. For now, you'll work on understanding the language of regular expressions. To help you understand regular expressions, you'll use a demo page in which you can enter a regular expression and apply pattern matching against a sample text string. Before continuing with Carol's order forms, you'll explore how to write and interpret regular expression patterns.

To view the regular expressions demo:

1. In your Web browser, open the **demo_regexp.htm** file from the tutorial.14/demo folder. The demo page contains a text box in the upper-left corner into which you enter sample text. Below the text box, you can enter a predefined regular expression or type your own. To match the regular expression against the sample text, you click the Pattern Test button.
2. Type the following text into the text box in the upper-left corner of the page, as shown in Figure 14-40:

```
GPS-ware Products Are Prepared With Care
```

Figure 14-40 Regular expression sdemo page

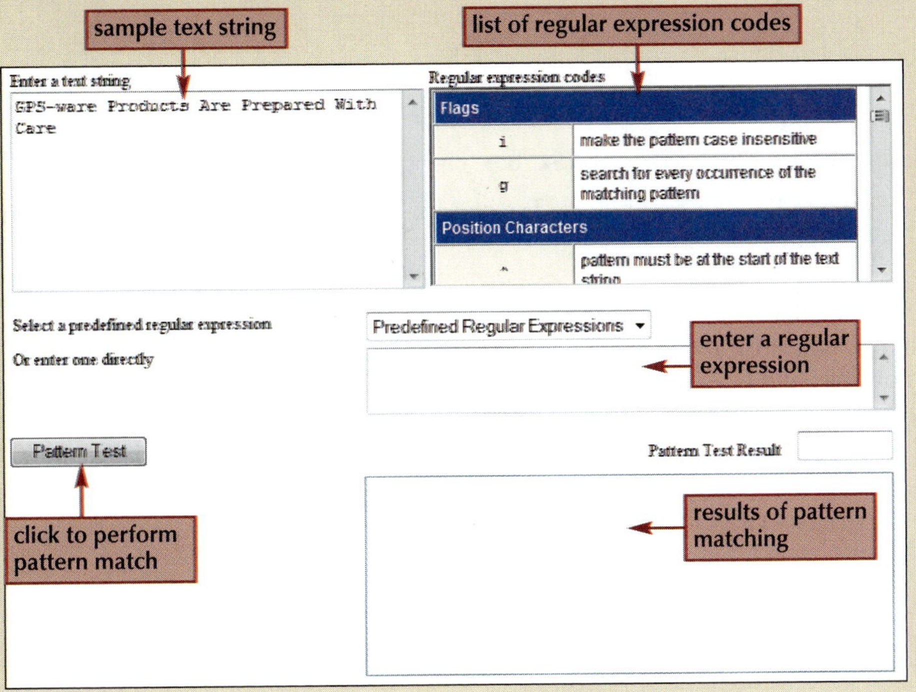

Matching a Substring

The most basic regular expression consists of a substring that you want to locate in the text string. The regular expression to match the first occurrence of a substring is

/*chars*/

where *chars* is the text of the substring. Regular expressions are case sensitive, so *chars* must match the uppercase and lowercase letters of the substring you are searching for. To see how this applies to the text string you have already entered on the demo page, you'll create regular expressions to locate the occurrences of the substrings "are" and "Are".

To match a simple substring:

1. Click the **Or enter one directly** text box for the regular expression (located directly below the drop-down list box), and then type **/are/**.

2. Click the **Pattern Test** button. The first occurrence of the "are" substring is highlighted and the Pattern Test Result field displays the word "match," indicating that a matching pattern has been found in the text string. See Figure 14-41.

Figure 14-41 Matched substring

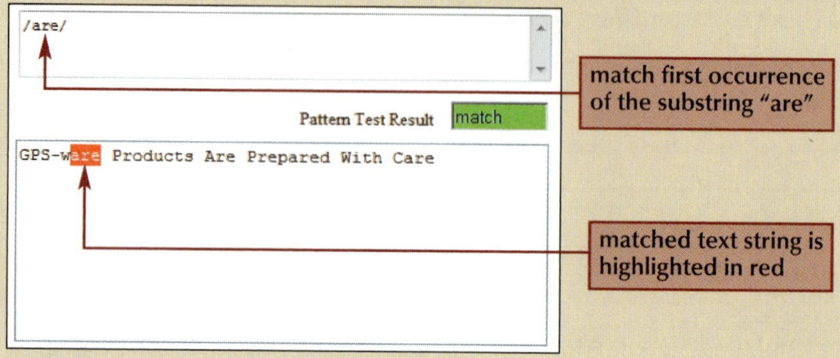
/are/
Pattern Test Result
match
GPS-ware Products Are Prepared With Care
match first occurrence of the substring "are"
matched text string is highlighted in red

3. In the Or enter one directly text box, change the regular expression to **/Are/**.
4. Click the **Pattern Test** button. The pattern now matches the word "Are" occurring later in the text string.

Be aware that spaces are considered characters in a regular expression pattern. Although JavaScript allows some flexibility in the use of white space, regular expressions do not. The patterns / GPS / and /GPS/ are considered two completely different regular expressions because the substring "GPS" is surrounded by blank spaces in one pattern but not the other.

Tip

Do not insert spaces to make a regular expression more readable; adding spaces to a regular expression changes its results.

Setting Regular Expression Flags

By default, pattern matching stops after the first match is discovered; also, the matching is case sensitive. You can override both of these default behaviors by adding single character flags to the end of the regular expression. For example, to make a regular expression insensitive to case (that is, capitalization doesn't affect the results), append the regular expression pattern with the character i as follows:

```
/pattern/i
```

To allow a global search for all matches in a text string, append the regular expression with the character g as follows:

```
/pattern/g
```

Finally, to apply both at the same time, simply append both the i and g flags to the regular expression, as follows:

```
/pattern/ig
```

You'll apply these flags in the regular expression demo.

To apply global and case-insensitive flags:

1. In the Or enter one directly text box, change the regular expression to **/are/ig**.
2. Click the **Pattern Test** button. All examples of the text string "are" are highlighted regardless of case. See Figure 14-42.

Figure 14-42 Substring being matched using the g and i flags

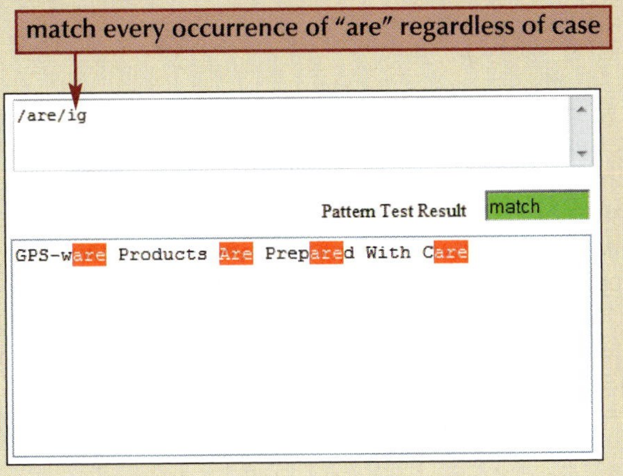
match every occurrence of "are" regardless of case
/are/ig
Pattern Test Result
match
GPS-ware Products Are Prepared With Care

Defining Character Positions

So far, you have used regular expressions to match simple text strings, which is not much more than you could have accomplished using the string object methods from the previous session. The true power (and complexity) of regular expressions comes with the introduction of special characters that allow you to match text based on the type, content, and placement of the characters in a text string. The first such characters you will consider are positioning characters. The four positioning characters are described in Figure 14-43.

Figure 14-43 Positioning characters

Character	Description	Example
^	Indicates the beginning of the text string	/^GPS/ matches "GPS-ware" but not "Products from GPS-ware"
$	Indicates the end of the text string	/ware$/ matches "GPS-ware" but not "GPS-ware Products"
\b	Indicates the presence of a word boundary	/\bart/ matches "art" and "artists" but not "dart"
\B	Indicates the absence of a word boundary	/art\B/ matches "dart" but not "artist"

Regular expressions recognize the beginning and end of a text string, indicated by the ^ and $ characters, respectively. The following pattern uses the ^ character to mark the start of the text string:

```
/^GPS/
```

In this pattern, any text string starting with the characters "GPS" would be matched. The expression would not match the GPS substring occurring elsewhere in the text string. In the same way, the end of the text string is indicated by the $ character. The following expression matches any text string that ends with the characters "-ware":

```
/-ware$/
```

The ^ and $ characters are often used together to define a pattern for a complete text string. For example, the pattern

```
/^GPS-ware$/
```

matches only a string containing the text "GPS-ware" and nothing else.

The other positioning characters are used to locate words within a text string. The term *word* has a special meaning in regular expressions. **Words** are composed of word characters. A **word character** is any letter, number, or underscore. Symbols such as *, &, and – are not considered word characters, nor are spaces, periods, and tabs. The string "R2D2" is considered a single word, but "R2D2&C3PO" is considered two words, with the & symbol acting as a boundary between the words. In a regular expression, the presence of a word boundary is indicated with the \b symbol. The pattern

```
/\bart/
```

matches any word that starts with the characters "art", but does not match "art" found in other locations within a text string. For example, this pattern would match the word "artist", but not the word "dart". The \b symbol can also indicate a word boundary at the end of a word. The regular expression

```
/art\b/
```

matches any word that ends in "art"—such as "dart" or "heart"—but not "artist". By using the \b symbol at both the beginning and the end of a pattern, you can define a complete word. The pattern

```
/\bart\b/
```

matches only the word "art" and nothing else. In some cases, you want to match substrings only within words. In these situations, you use the \B symbol, which indicates the absence of a word boundary. The regular expression

```
/\Bart\B/
```

matches the substring "art" only when it occurs inside of a word such as in "hearts" or "darts".

Tip

Regular expression symbols have opposite meanings when expressed in uppercase letters: \B means the opposite of \b and \w means the opposite of \W.

To view the effect of word boundaries on regular expressions:

1. In the Or enter one directly text box on the demo page, change the regular expression to **/\bare\b/gi**.
2. Click the **Pattern Test** button. Only the word "Are" is highlighted because it is the only occurrence in the text string where "are" appears as a complete word. See Figure 14-44.

Figure 14-44 Whole word being matched

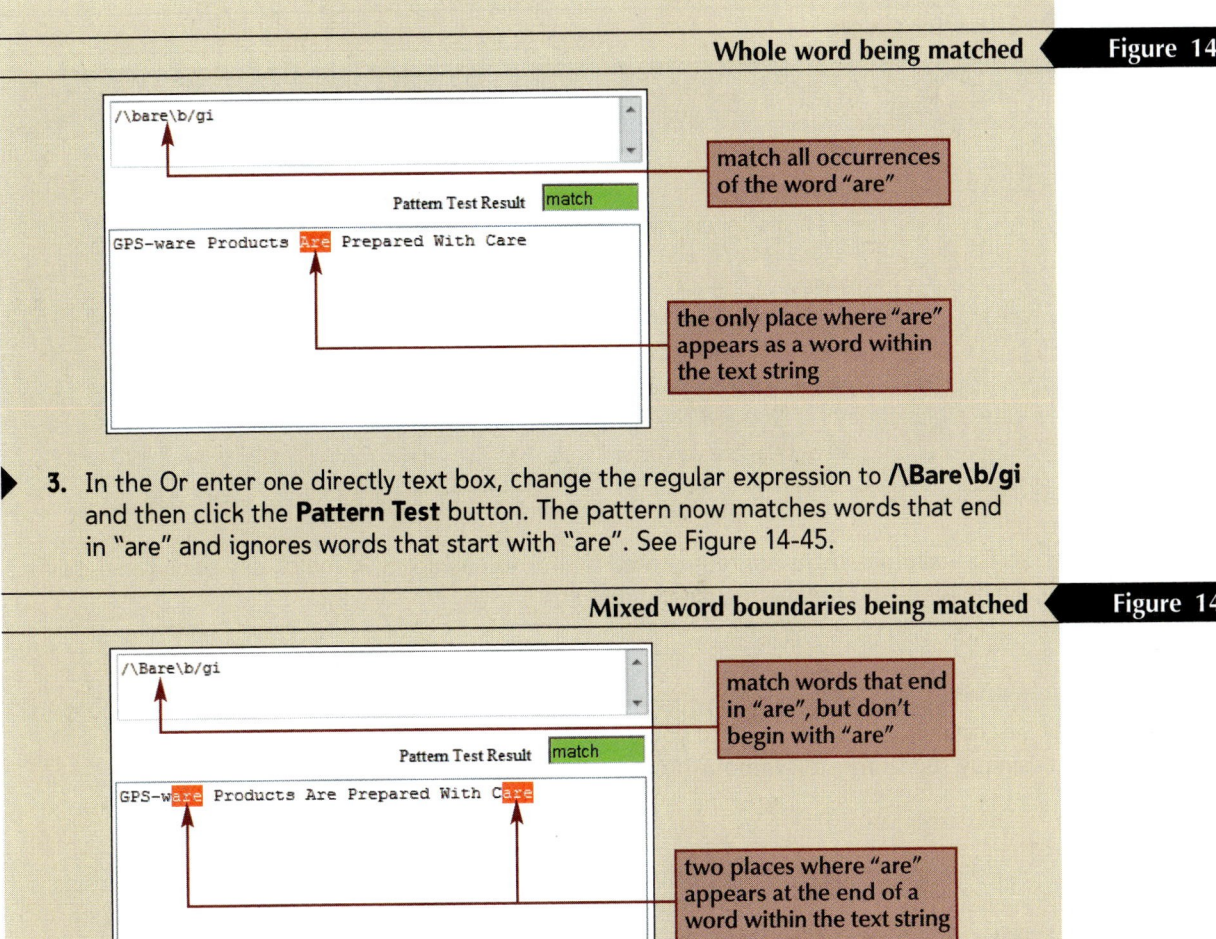

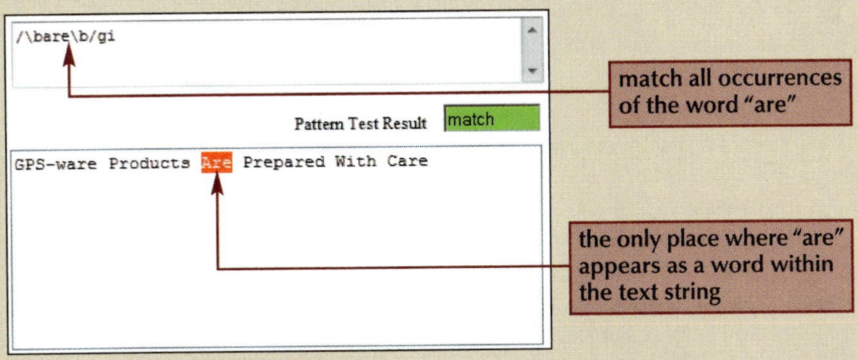
/\bare\b/gi
Pattern Test Result
match
GPS-ware Products Are Prepared With Care
match all occurrences of the word "are"
the only place where "are" appears as a word within the text string

3. In the Or enter one directly text box, change the regular expression to **/\Bare\b/gi** and then click the **Pattern Test** button. The pattern now matches words that end in "are" and ignores words that start with "are". See Figure 14-45.

Figure 14-45 Mixed word boundaries being matched

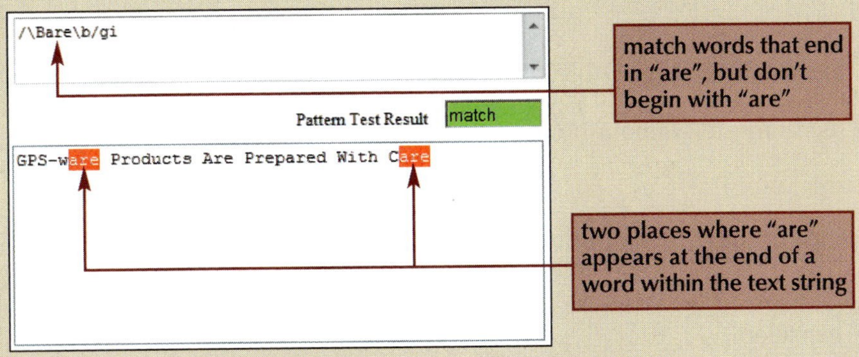
/\Bare\b/gi
Pattern Test Result
match
GPS-ware Products Are Prepared With Care
match words that end in "are", but don't begin with "are"
two places where "are" appears at the end of a word within the text string

4. In the Or enter one directly text box, change the regular expression to **/\Bare\B/gi** and then click the **Pattern Test** button to locate all instances of the substring "are" that occur within a word. The pattern now matches only the substring "are" found within the word "Prepared".

Defining Character Types and Character Classes

Another class of regular expression characters indicates character type. The three general types of characters are: word characters, digits (numbers 0 to 9), and white space characters (blank spaces, tabs, and new lines). Figure 14-46 describes the regular expression symbols for these character types.

Figure 14-46 **Character classes**

Character	Description	Example
\d	A digit (from 0 to 9)	/\dth/ matches "5th" but not "ath"
\D	A non-digit	/\Ds/ matches "as" but not "5s"
\w	A word character (an upper- or lowercase letter, a digit, or an underscore)	/\w\w/ matches "to" or "A1" but not "$x" or " *"
\W	A non-word character	/\W/ matches "$" or "&" but not "a", "B", or "3"
\s	A white space character (a blank space, tab, new line, carriage return, or form feed)	/\s\d\s/ matches " 5 " but not "5"
\S	A non-white space character	/\S\d\S/ matches "345" or "a5b" but not "5"
.	Any character	/./ matches anything

For example, digits are represented by the \d character. To match any occurrence of a single digit, you use the regular expression

```
/\d/
```

which would find matches in such text strings as 105, 6, or U2, because these all contain an instance of a single digit. If you want to match several consecutive digits, you can simply repeat the \d symbol. The regular expression

```
/\d\d\d/
```

matches the occurrence of any three consecutive digits. It would find matches in strings such as 105, 1250, or EX500. If you want to limit matches only to words consisting of three-digit numbers, you can use the \b character to mark the boundaries around the digits. The pattern

```
/\b\d\d\d\b/
```

would match strings such as 105 or 229, but not 1250 or EX500.

This barely scratches the surface of regular expressions, but you have enough information to create a regular expression for a five-digit zip code. Its pattern is:

```
/^\d\d\d\d\d$/
```

This regular expression matches only a text string that contains five digits and no other characters (recall that the ^ and $ symbols mark the beginning and end of the entire text string). You'll test this pattern now on the demo page.

To test the zip code pattern:

1. In the Enter a text string box, change the text to **12345**.
2. In the Or enter one directly text box, change the regular expression to **/^\d\d\d\d\d$/** and then click the **Pattern Test** button. The demo page highlights all of the digits in the test string indicating a complete match.
3. Continue experimenting with the pattern, trying sample text strings of **1**, **123**, and **1234a**. Verify that the demo reports a valid match only if you enter a five-digit value with no other characters or numbers.

With just one regular expression, you have achieved what took several lines of code to do in the previous session. This gives you some idea of the power of regular expressions in detecting character patterns.

No character type matches only letters. However, you can specify a collection of characters known as a **character class** to limit the regular expression to a select group of characters. The syntax to define a character class is

```
[chars]
```

where *chars* are characters in the class. To create a negative character class that matches any character not in the class, preface the list of characters with the caret symbol (^) as follows:

```
[^chars]
```

The negative character set uses the same ^ symbol that you used to mark the beginning of a text string. Although the symbol is the same, the meaning is very different in this context.

To explore working with a character class, you'll use the demo page to create character classes that match vowels and consonants.

Tip

For more general character matching, use the \w symbol, which matches any word character, or the \s symbol, which matches any white space character.

To create a character class:

1. In the Enter a text string box, change the sample text to **GPS Products For Sale**.
2. In the Or enter one directly text box, change the regular expression to **/[aeiou]/gi** and then click the **Pattern Test** button. Every vowel in the sample text string is highlighted.
3. In the Or enter one directly text box, change the regular expression to **/[^aeiou]/gi** to create a pattern that doesn't match vowels, and then click the **Pattern Test** button. The demo selects all characters in the text string other than a, e, i, o, and u.

   The regular expression still selects white space characters such as blank spaces. To remove the blank spaces from the text string, you change the regular expression by adding the \s symbol to the list of characters that are not selected.
4. In the Or enter one directly text box, change the regular expression to **\[^aeiou\s]/gi** and then click the **Pattern Test** button. Including the \s symbol in the regular expression selects only the consonants in the text string. See Figure 14-47.

Figure 14-47 All consonant characters being matched

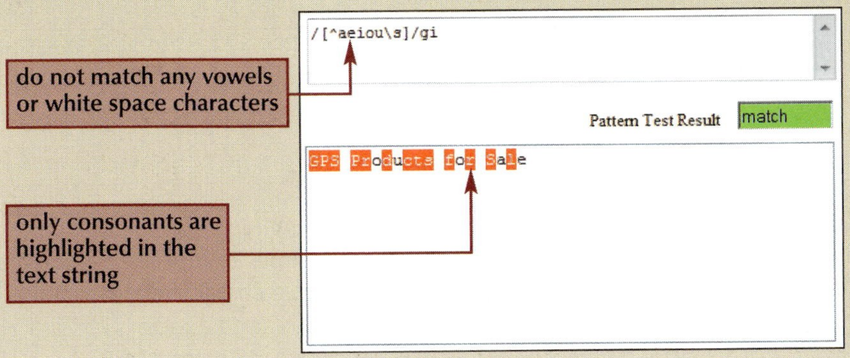
/[^aeiou\s]/gi
do not match any vowels or white space characters
Pattern Test Result
match
GPS Products For Sale
only consonants are highlighted in the text string

For a larger character class, you can define a range of characters by separating the starting and ending characters in the range with a hypen because characters are arranged in sequential and alphabetical order, to create a character class for all lowercase letters, you would use:

```
[a-z]
```

For uppercase letters, you would use:

```
[A-Z]
```

For both uppercase and lowercase letters, you would use:

```
[a-zA-Z]
```

You can continue to add ranges of characters to a character class. The following character class matches only uppercase and lowercase letters and digits:

```
[0-9a-zA-Z]
```

Figure 14-48 summarizes the syntax for creating regular expression character classes.

Figure 14-48 **Character classes**

Character	Description	Example
[*chars*]	Match any character in the list of characters, *chars*	/[tap]/ matches "tap" and "pat
[^*chars*]	Do not match any character in *chars*	/[^tap]/ matches neither "tap" nor "pat"
[*char1*-*charN*]	Match characters in the range *char1* through *charN*	/[a-c]/ matches the lowercase letters a through c
[^*char1*-*charN*]	Do not match characters in the range *char1* through *charN*	/[^a-c]/ does not match the lowercase letters a through c
[*a-z*]	Match lowercase letters	/[a-z][a-z]/ matches any two consecutive lowercase letters
[*A-Z*]	Match uppercase letters	/[A-Z][A-Z]/ matches any two consecutive uppercase letters
[*a-zA-Z*]	Match letters	/[a-zA-Z][a-zA-Z]/ matches any two consecutive letters
[*0-9*]	Match digits	/[1][0-9]/ matches the numbers "10" through "19"
[*0-9a-zA-Z*]	Match digits and letters	/[0-9a-zA-Z][0-9a-zA-Z]/ matches any two consecutive letters or numbers

Specifying Repeating Characters

So far, the regular expression symbols have applied to single characters. Regular expressions also include symbols that indicate the number of times to repeat a particular character. To specify the exact number of times to repeat a character, you append the character with the symbols

```
{n}
```

where *n* is the number of times to repeat the character. For example, to specify that a text string should contain only five digits, such as a zip code, you could use either

```
/^\d\d\d\d\d$/
```

or the more compact form

```
/^\d{5}$/
```

If you don't know how many times to repeat a character, you can use the symbol * for 0 or more repetitions, + for 1 or more repetitions, or ? for 0 repetitions or 1 repetition. Figure 14-49 describes these and other repetition characters supported by regular expressions.

Figure 14-49 **Repetition characters**

Repetition Character(s)	Description	Example
*	Repeat 0 or more times	/\s*/ matches 0 or more consecutive white space characters
?	Repeat 0 or 1 time	/colou?r/ matches "color" or "colour"
+	Repeat 1 or more times	/\s+/ matches 1 or more consecutive white space characters
{*n*}	Repeat exactly *n* times	/\d{9}/ matches a nine-digit number
{*n*, }	Repeat at least *n* times	/\d{9,}/ matches a number with at least nine digits
{*n*,*m*}	Repeat at least *n* times but no more than *m* times	/\d{5,9}/ matches a number with 5 to 9 digits

You'll practice using some of the repetitive symbols to create regular expressions on the demo page.

To apply a repetition pattern:

1. In the Enter a text string box, change the sample text to **To be or not to be. That is the question.**
2. In the Or enter one directly text box, change the regular expression to **/\bt[a-zA-Z]*\b/gi** to create a regular expression to match all words that begin with the letter t followed by any number of uppercase or lowercase letters, and then click the **Pattern Test** button. Words of varying length beginning with the letter t are selected. See Figure 14-50.

Figure 14-50 **Repetitive characters being used**

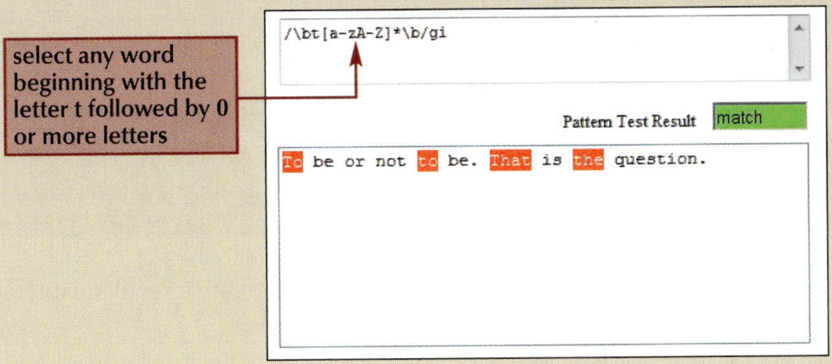
select any word beginning with the letter t followed by 0 or more letters
/\bt[a-zA-Z]*\b/gi
Pattern Test Result
match
To be or not to be. That is the question.

3. In the Or enter one directly text box, change the regular expression to **/\bt[a-zA-Z]{2}\b/gi** to revise the regular expression pattern to limit the number of letters after the initial letter t to two, and then click the **Pattern Test** button. The word "the" is highlighted, which is the only three-letter word beginning with the letter t.

Using Escape Sequences

Many commonly used characters are reserved by the regular expression language. The forward slash character / is reserved to mark the beginning and end of a regular expression literal. The ?, +, and * characters are used to specify the number of times a character can be repeated. What if you need to use one of these characters in a regular expression? For example, how would you create a regular expression matching the date pattern *mm/dd/yyyy* when the / character is already used to mark the boundaries of the regular expression?

In these cases, you use an escape sequence. An **escape sequence** is a special command inside the regular expression that tells the JavaScript interpreter not to interpret what follows as a character. In the regular expression language, escape sequences are marked by the backslash character \. You have been using escape sequences for several pages now—for example, you used the characters \d to represent a numeric digit, while d simply represents the letter d. The \ character can also be applied to reserved characters to indicate their use in a regular expression. For example, the escape sequence \$ represents the $ character while the escape sequence \\ represents a single \ character. Figure 14-51 provides a list of escape sequences for other special characters.

Figure 14-51 **Escape sequences**

<table>
<tr><th>Escape Sequence</th><th>Represents</th><th>Example</th></tr>
<tr><td>\/</td><td>The / character</td><td>/\d\/\d/ matches "5/9" "3/1" but not "59" or "31"</td></tr>
<tr><td>\\</td><td>The \ character</td><td>/\d\\\d/ matches "5\9" or "3\1" but not "59" or "31"</td></tr>
<tr><td>\.</td><td>The . character</td><td>/\d\.\d\d/ matches "3.20" or "5.95" but not "320" or "595"</td></tr>
<tr><td>*</td><td>The * character</td><td>/\[a-z]{4}*/ matches "help*" or "pass*"</td></tr>
<tr><td>\+</td><td>The + character</td><td>/\d\+\d/ matches "5+9" or "3+1" but not "59" or "39"</td></tr>
<tr><td>\?</td><td>The ? character</td><td>/[a-z]{4}\?/ matches "help?" or "info?"</td></tr>
<tr><td>\|</td><td>The | character</td><td>/a\|b/ matches "a|b"</td></tr>
<tr><td>\(\)</td><td>The (and) characters</td><td>/\(\d{3}\)/ matches "(800)" or "(555)"</td></tr>
<tr><td>\{ \}</td><td>The { and } characters</td><td>/\{[a-z]{4}\}/ matches "{pass}" or "{info}"</td></tr>
<tr><td>\^</td><td>The ^ character</td><td>/\d+\^\d/ matches "321^2" or "4^3"</td></tr>
<tr><td>\$</td><td>The $ character</td><td>/\$\d{2}\.\d{2}/ matches "$59.95" or "$19.50"</td></tr>
<tr><td>\n</td><td>A new line</td><td>/\n/ matches the occurrence of a new line in the text string</td></tr>
<tr><td>\r</td><td>A carriage return</td><td>/\r/ matches the occurrence of a carriage return in the text string</td></tr>
<tr><td>\t</td><td>A tab</td><td>/\t/ matches the occurrence of a tab in the text string</td></tr>
</table>

You'll enter an escape sequence on the demo page to create a regular expression for the date pattern.

To use an escape sequence:

1. In the Enter a text string box, change the sample text to the date **5/21/2012**.
2. In the Or enter one directly text box, change the regular expression to **/^\d{1,2}\/\d{1,2}\/\d{4}$/** to match date values.
3. Click the **Pattern Test** button. As shown in Figure 14-52, the test date you entered matches the regular expression pattern, which consists of one or two digits followed by a forward slash and then another one or two digits followed by a forward slash and then ending with four digits.

Figure 14-52 Escape sequence being used

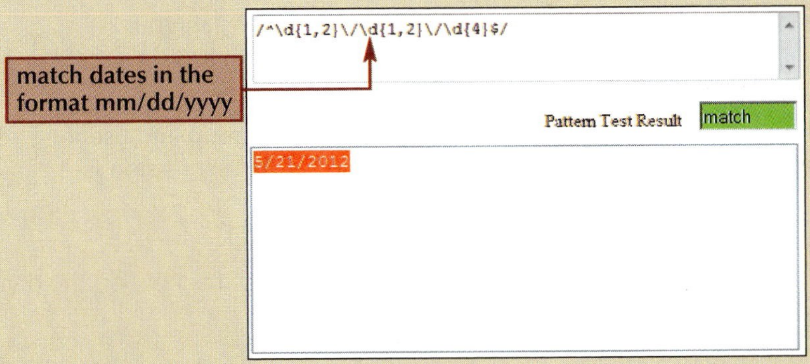

4. Test the regular expression against other text strings and verify that it matches any date in the format *mm/dd/yyyy*. The regular expression you used for the date format also matches some invalid date patterns such as 23/99/0007 or 0/0/0000 because the regular expression does not check that the month values range from 1 to 12 or that the day values range from 1 to 31.

Tip

Explore the date expressions available from the selection list on the demo page to learn more about writing expressions involving dates.

Specifying Alternate Patterns and Grouping

In some regular expressions, you may want to define two possible patterns for the same text string. You can do this by joining different patterns using the | character. The general form is

```
pattern1|pattern2
```

where *pattern1* and *pattern2* are two distinct patterns. For example, the expression

```
/^\d{5}$|^$/
```

matches a text string that either contains only five digits or is empty. You'll explore how to use the alternate character on the demo page by creating a regular expression that matches the titles Mr., Mrs., or Miss.

To specify alternate regular expression patterns:

1. In the Enter a text string box, change the sample text to **Mr.**
2. In the Or enter one of your own text box, change the regular expression pattern to **/Mr\.|Mrs\.|Miss/** and then click the **Pattern Test** button. The pattern test result shows a match.
3. Repeat Steps 1 and 2 to change the sample text to **Mrs.** and then to **Miss** and verify that both regular expressions match the sample text.

Another useful technique in regular expressions is to group character symbols. Once you create a group, the symbols within that group can be treated as a single unit. The syntax to create a group is

```
(pattern)
```

where *pattern* is a regular expression pattern. Groups are often used with the alternation character to create regular expressions that match different variations of the same text. For example, a phone number might be entered with or without an area code. The pattern for the phone number without an area code, matching such numbers as 555-1234, is:

```
/^\d{3}-\d{4}$/
```

If an area code is included in the format 800-555-1234, the pattern is:

```
/^\d{3}-\d{3}-\d{4}$/
```

To allow the area code to be added, you place it within a group and use the ? repetition character applied to the entire area code group. The regular expression is

```
/^(\d{3}-)?\d{3}-\d{4}$/
```

which matches either 555-1234 or 800-555-1234. You'll try this now on the demo page.

To group a pattern:

1. In the Enter a text string box, change the sample text to **555-1234**.
2. In the Or enter one directly text box, change the regular expression pattern to **/^(\d{3}-)?\d{3}-\d{4}$/** and then click the **Pattern Test** button. The pattern test result shows a match. See Figure 14-53.

Figure 14-53 Group of optional characters being created

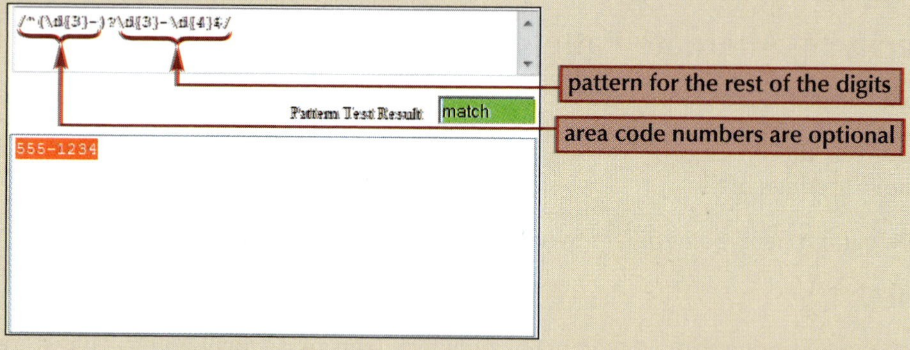

3. In the Enter a text string box, change the phone number to **800-555-1234** and then click the **Pattern Test** button to verify that this form of the phone number also matches the regular expression.
4. Continue to explore other test strings and regular expression patterns, and then close the demo page when you are finished.

Using the Regular Expression Object Constructor | InSight

The regular expression literal that you explored with the demo is only one way of creating a regular expression. Another approach is to create a regular expression object using the object constructor, which has the format

```
re = new RegExp(pattern, flags)
```

where *re* is a regular expression object, *pattern* is a text string of the regular expression pattern, and *flags* is a text string of the regular expression flags. The following two commands are equivalent as far as JavaScript is concerned:

```
var re = /GPS-ware/ig;
var re = new RegExp("GPS-ware","ig");
```

JavaScript treats the regular expression pattern used with the object constructor as a text string. Even though they are not regular expressions, such text strings can also contain escape sequences, which can be used to insert non-textual characters such as tabs or returns. To avoid conflict between escape sequences designed for text strings and escape sequences designed for regular expressions, you must insert an additional escape character \ for each regular expression escape sequence. The regular expression literal

```
/\b\w*\b\s\d{3}/
```

appears in the object constructor as

```
new RegExp("\\b\\w*\\b\\s\\d{3}")
```

In most cases, you will use the regular expression literal form in code. The new RegExp() operator is most often used when a script needs to retrieve the regular expression text string from another source, such as a data entry field.

Creating a Regular Expression | Reference Window

- The syntax to create a regular expression literal is
  ```
  re = /pattern/flags
  ```
  where *re* is the regular expression object, *pattern* is the regular expression pattern, and *flags* are the flags assigned to the regular expression.
- The syntax to create a regular expression with the object constructor is
  ```
  re = new RegExp(pattern, flags)
  ```
  where *pattern* is the text string of the regular expression and *flags* is the text string of the regular expression flags.

Working with the Regular Expression Object

Now that you have reviewed the syntax involved in writing a regular expression, you can use regular expressions in JavaScript programs. As noted earlier, a regular expression is treated as an object with its own collection of properties and methods. Before applying regular expressions to Carol's Web forms, you'll look at some of the methods associated with regular expressions.

Exploring Regular Expression Methods

One method associated with regular expressions is the test() method, which is used to determine whether a text string contains a substring that matches the pattern defined by a regular expression. The syntax of the test() method is

```
re.test(string)
```

where *re* is a regular expression object and *string* is the text string you want to test. The test() method returns the Boolean value true if a match is located within the text string and false otherwise. For example, the following code uses the test() method to compare the text string stored in the zipstring variable with the regular expression object stored in the regx variable:

```
zipstring = document.forms[0].zip.value;
regx = /^\d{5}$/;
testvalue = regx.test(zipstring);
```

If zipstring matches the pattern, the testvalue variable will have a value of true; otherwise, it will have a value of false. If you need to know where within the text string the match occurs, use the following search() method:

```
re.search(string)
```

The search() method returns the index of the first matching substring from *string*. If no match is found, it returns the value –1, just like the indexOf() method discussed in the previous session. All searches occur from the start of the text string. Unlike the indexOf() method, you cannot begin the search() method at a location other than the start of the text string.

You can also use regular expression methods that extract substrings from a text string. The match() method creates an array of substrings from a text string that match the pattern defined in a regular expression. The syntax of the match() method is

```
results = re.match(string)
```

where *results* is an array containing each matched substring. For example, the following set of commands extracts the individual words from the text string, placing each word in the words array:

```
regx = /\b\w+\b/g;
words = "GPS-ware Products For Sale".match(regx);
```

The global flag must be set to locate all matches in the text string. Without the g flag, only the first match is returned.

Similar to the match() method is the split() method, which breaks a text string into substrings at each location where a pattern match is found, placing the substrings into an array. You saw how to use the split() method in the previous session when it was applied to string objects. It can likewise be used with regular expressions. The following code shows how to split a text string at each word boundary followed by one or more white space characters:

```
regx = /\b\s*/g;
words = "GPS-ware Products For Sale".split(regx);
```

In this example, each element in the words array contains a word from the sample text string.

Besides pattern matching and extracting substrings, regular expressions can also be used to replace text. The syntax of the replace method is

```
string.replace(re,newsubstr)
```

where *string* is a text string containing text to be replaced, *re* is a regular expression defining the pattern of a substring, and *newsubstr* is the replacement substring. The following code shows how to apply the replace() method to change a text string:

```
oldtext = "<h1>GPS-ware Products</h1>";
regx = /h1/g;
newtext = oldtext.replace(regx,"h2");
```

In this code, the regular expression matches all of the occurrences of the h1 substring in the sample text string. When the replace() method is applied to the oldtext variable, it replaces all occurrences of h1 with h2. The result is the newtext variable that contains the text string <h2>GPS-ware Products</h2>. If you neglect to include the g flag, only the first occurrence of the substring is replaced.

Figure 14-54 summarizes the methods associated with the regular expression object.

Tip

The replace() method is helpful in programs that revise and edit the code of HTML and XHTML documents.

Methods of the regular expression object | **Figure 14-54**

Method	Description
re.compile(*pattern*,*flags*)	Compiles or recompiles a regular expression *re*, where *pattern* is the text string of the new regular expression pattern and *flags* are flags applied to the *pattern*
re.exec(*string*)	Executes a search on *string* using the regular expression *re*; pattern results are returned in an array and reflected in the properties of the global RegExp object
re.match(*string*)	Performs a pattern match in *string* using the *re* regular expression; matched substrings are stored in an array
string.replace(*re*, *newsubstr*)	Replaces the substring defined by the regular expression *re* in the text string *string* with *newsubstr*
string.search(*re*)	Searches *string* for a substring matching the regular expression *re*; returns the index of the match, or −1 if no match is found
string.split(*re*)	Splits *string* at each point indicated by the regular expression *re*; the substrings are stored in an array
re.test(*string*)	Performs a *pattern* match on the text string *string* using the regular expression *re*, returning the Boolean value true if a match is found and false otherwise

Working with Regular Expressions | Reference Window

- To test whether a text string matches a regular expression, use the method
  ```
  re.test(string)
  ```
  where *re* is the regular expression object and *string* is the text string to be tested. The test() method returns the Boolean value true when a match is found and false when no match is found.
- To search a text string, use:
  ```
  re.search(string)
  ```
  The search() method returns the index of the first matching substring from the text string. If no match is found, it returns the value −1.
- To create an array of the matching substrings from a text string, use
  ```
  results = re.match(string)
  ```
  where *results* is an array containing each matched substring.
- To split a string into substrings, use
  ```
  results = string.split(re)
  ```
  where *results* is an array containing the substrings, *string* is the original text string, and *re* is a regular expression that indicates the splitting points in the text string.
- To replace a substring with a new substring, use
  ```
  string.replace(re, newsubstr)
  ```
  where *string* is the text string containing the text to be replaced, *re* is a regular expression defining the substring to be replaced, and *newsubstr* is the replacement substring.

Validating a Zip Code Using Regular Expressions

You'll use your knowledge of regular expressions to create a new function to validate customers' entries in the zip field. In the first line of the function, you'll create a regular expression that matches either a five-digit or a nine-digit zip code or an empty text string (when the zip code is not required for delivery). The regular expression is:

```
/^\d{5}(-\d{4})?$|^$/
```

This regular expression matches zip codes in the form *nnnnn* or *nnnnn-nnnn*; it also uses the alternation character | to allow for empty text strings. Study this regular expression until you understand how it works. You'll use this regular expression in the following function:

```
function checkZipRE(zip) {
   regx = /^\d{5}(-\d{4})?$|^$/;
   return regx.test(zip);
}
```

The second line of the function uses the test() method to determine whether a customer's zip code matches that pattern, returning the test result. Compared to the checkZip() function you created in the previous session, this more compact function tests for greater variations in zip code patterns than the original function. This demonstrates the power of regular expressions.

You'll add this function to the validation tests for Carol's delivery form.

To create the checkZipRE() function:

1. Return to the **contact.js** file in your text editor.
2. Directly below the checkForm2() function, insert the following code:

```
function checkZipRE(zip) {
   regx = /^\d{5}(-\d{4})?$|^$/;
   return regx.test(zip);
}
```

3. Change the checkForm2() function so that it calls the **checkZipRE()** function to validate the zip code field. Figure 14-55 highlights the revised code.

Figure 14-55 Code for the checkZipRE() function

code to call the checkZipRE() function

```
   else if (document.forms[0].city.value.length == 0)
      {alert("You must enter a city name");
       return false;}
   else if (checkZipRE(document.forms[0].zip.value) == false)
      {alert("Invalid zip code");
       return false;}
   else return true;
}

function checkZipRE(zip) {
   regx = /^\d{5}(-\d{4})?$|^$/;
   return regx.test(zip);
}
```

regular expression for a U.S. zip code

4. Close the file, saving your changes, and then reload **form2.htm** in your Web browser.
5. Enter sample text into the first name, last name, street, and city fields.

6. In the zip field, enter sample zip code values in both the *nnnnn* and *nnnnn-nnnn* formats. Verify that the Web form is successfully submitted and the next form, form3.htm, is loaded when the zip code field is entered in the proper format or left blank.

You've completed the validation checks for the delivery form.

Validating Financial Data

The final of Carol's three forms is the form3.htm file, a payment form into which customers enter the credit card information that indicates how they will pay for their order. Figure 14-56 shows the contents of the payment form along with the field names.

Figure 14-56 Payment form and field names

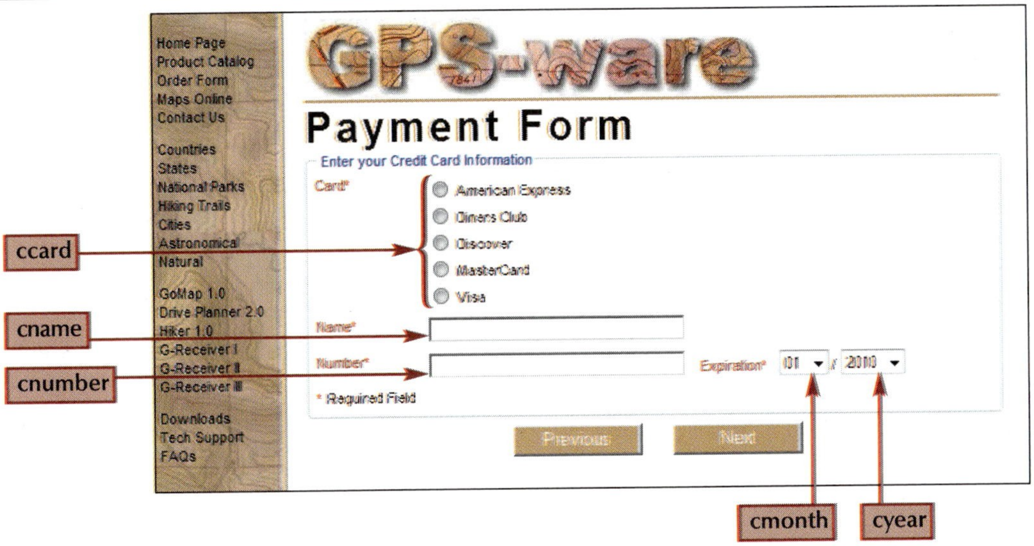

The customer's credit card data will eventually be validated on the Web server against a financial database. However, you can do some validation checks on the client side to weed out problems before they get to the server. Carol already inserted some validation checks in the payment.js file, which has already been attached to the form3.htm file. The validation checks are stored in the following two functions:

```
function checkForm3() {
   if (selectedCard() == -1)
      {alert("You must select a credit card");
       return false;}
   else if (document.forms[0].cname.value.length == 0)
      {alert("You must enter the name on your credit card");
       return false;}
   else if (document.forms[0].cnumber.value.length == 0)
      {alert("You must enter the number on your credit card");
       return false;}
   else return true;
}
```

and

```
function selectedCard() {
   card = -1;
   for (var i = 0; i < document.forms[0].ccard.length; i++) {
      if (document.forms[0].ccard[i].checked) card = i;
   }
   return card;
}
```

The checkForm3() function verifies that: (1) the customer has selected a credit card, (2) the customer has entered the name on the card, and (3) the customer has entered the number on the card. Although you have no way of knowing whether the name and number are real or accurate credit card accounts, the checkForm3() function verifies that the customer has entered something into those fields. The checkForm3() function tests whether one of the five credit cards on the payment form has been selected by calling the selectedCard() function. The selectedCard() function goes through all of the option buttons from the ccard field and returns the index number (0 to 4) of the checked option button. If no option button is checked (meaning that the customer has not selected a credit card from the list), then it returns a value of –1 and the form is not validated.

Removing Blank Spaces from Credit Card Numbers

Beyond verifying that a customer has entered something for each field, Carol wants the form to test whether the customer has entered a legitimate credit card number. Credit card numbers often appear on credit cards broken up by spaces to make it easier for cardholders to read them. Before you examine the actual card numbers, you want to remove any blank spaces that a customer entered into the credit card number field. You can do this by creating a regular expression that searches for any occurrence of white space in the credit card number field, and then by applying the replace() method to replace each occurrence of white space with an empty text string. The regular expression to match all occurrences of white space in a text string is:

```
wsregx = /\s/g
```

When applied to a text string containing spaces such as

```
123 45 6789
```

the spaces are removed, resulting in the text string

```
123456789
```

You add the g flag so that the regular expression searches the entire text string, instead of stopping at the first occurrence of white space. To replace those white spaces with empty text strings, you apply the following replace() method, storing the revised text string in the cnum variable:

```
var cnum = document.forms[0].cnumber.value.replace(wsregx,"");
```

You'll add both of these commands to a function named checkNumber() that you'll build upon to validate customers' credit card numbers.

To insert the checkNumber() function:

1. Open the **payment.js** file in your text editor.
2. Directly below the selectedCard() function, insert the following function, as shown in Figure 14-57:

```
function checkNumber() {
   wsregx = /\s/g;
   var cnum = document.forms[0].cnumber.value.replace(wsregx,"");
}
```

Code to remove white space from credit card numbers — **Figure 14-57**

```
function selectedCard() {
   var card = -1;
   for (var i = 0; i < document.forms[0].ccard.length; i++) {
      if (document.forms[0].ccard[i].checked) card = i;
   }
   return card;
}

function checkNumber() {
   wsregx = /\s/g;
   var cnum = document.forms[0].cnumber.value.replace(wsregx,"");
}
```

regular expression that matches all white space in the text string

replaces each white space character with an empty text string

Validating Credit Card Number Patterns

Each type of credit card has a certain pattern to its numbers that uniquely identifies it. GPS-ware accepts five different credit cards: American Express, Diners Club, Discover, MasterCard, and Visa. Figure 14-58 lists the number pattern for each type of card, along with a regular expression that matches the described pattern.

Credit card number patterns — **Figure 14-58**

Credit Card	Number Pattern	Regular Expression
American Express	Starts with 34 or 37 followed by 13 other digits	`/^3[47]\d{13}$/`
Diners Club	Starts with 300, 301, 302, 303, 304, or 305 followed by 11 digits, or starts with 36 or 38 followed by 12 digits	`/^30[0-5]\d{11}$\|^3[68]\d{12}$/`
Discover	Starts with 6011 followed by 12 other digits	`/^6011\d{12}$/`
MasterCard	Starts with 51, 52, 53, 54, or 55 followed by 14 other digits	`/^5[1-5]\d{14}$/`
Visa	Starts with a 4 followed by 12 or 15 other digits	`/^4(\d{12}|\d{15})$/`

To validate the credit card number entered by a customer, you can use the test() method with the regular expressions shown in Figure 14-58. Recall that the selected-Card() function returns the index number of the selected option button in Carol's Web form. In this case, the index numbers for the different credit card options are: 0 = American Express, 1 = Diners Club, 2 = Discover, 3 = MasterCard, and 4 = Visa. The following code uses a switch statement to define the regular expression pattern for each credit card, storing the regular expression in the cregx variable:

```
switch (selectedCard()) {
   case 0: cregx = /^3[47]\d{13}$/; break;
   case 1: cregx = /^30[0-5]\d{11}$|^3[68]\d{12}$/; break;
   case 2: cregx = /^6011\d{12}$/; break;
   case 3: cregx = /^5[1-5]\d{14}$/; break;
   case 4: cregx = /^4(\d{12}|\d{15})$/; break;
}
return cregx.test(cnum);
```

The function ends by testing the selected regular expression pattern against the credit card number stored in the cnum variable. A value of true indicates that the credit card number matches the corresponding pattern, whereas a value of false indicates that the number does not match the pattern and is invalid.

You'll add these commands to the checkNumber() function.

To create tests based on credit card number patterns:

1. Insert the following commands in the checkNumber() function, as shown in Figure 14-59:

```
switch (selectedCard()) {
   case 0: cregx = /^3[47]\d{13}$/; break;
   case 1: cregx = /^30[0-5]\d{11}$|^3[68]\d{12}$/; break;
   case 2: cregx = /^6011\d{12}$/; break;
   case 3: cregx = /^5[1-5]\d{14}$/; break;
   case 4: cregx = /^4(\d{12}|\d{15})$/; break;
}
return cregx.test(cnum);
```

Figure 14-59 Code to check credit card number patterns

```
function checkNumber() {
   wsregx = /\s/g;
   var cnum = document.forms[0].cnumber.value.replace(wsregx,"");

   switch (selectedCard()) {
      case 0: cregx = /^3[47]\d{13}$/; break;
      case 1: cregx = /^30[0-5]\d{11}$|^3[68]\d{12}$/; break;
      case 2: cregx = /^6011\d{12}$/; break;
      case 3: cregx = /^5[1-5]\d{14}$/; break;
      case 4: cregx = /^4(\d{12}|\d{15})$/; break;
   }

   return cregx.test(cnum);
}
```

credit card patterns for five credit companies

2. Save your changes to the file.

Next, you'll call this function from the checkForm3() function to add it to the list of validation checks already present in the payment form.

To check for valid credit card number patterns:

1. Add the following commands to the checkForm3() function, as shown in Figure 14-60:

```
else if (checkNumber() == false)
   {alert("Your card number is not valid");
    return false;}
```

Figure 14-60

Final checkForm3() function

```
function checkForm3() {
   if (selectedCard() == -1)
      {alert("You must select a credit card");
       return false;}
   else if (document.forms[0].cname.value.length == 0)
      {alert("You must enter the name on your credit card");
       return false;}
   else if (document.forms[0].cnumber.value.length == 0)
      {alert("You must enter the number on your credit card");
       return false;}
   else if (checkNumber() == false)
      {alert("Your card number is not valid");
      return false;}
   else return true;
}
```

checks that the card number is valid

2. Save your changes to the file, and then reload **form3.htm** in your Web browser.

   You'll test the form for valid credit card numbers.

3. Enter sample text in the name field so that the form is not invalidated for lack of a cardholder name.

4. Click each of the credit card option buttons and enter the corresponding sample credit card numbers shown in Figure 14-61. Verify that the form accepts the valid numbers and rejects the invalid ones.

Figure 14-61

Valid and invalid credit card number patterns

Credit Card	Valid	Invalid
American Express	34 12345 67890 127	35 12345 67890 127
Diners Club	303 12345 67890 1	310 12345 67890 1
Discover	6011 12345 67890 19	6012 12345 67890 19
MasterCard	51 12345 67890 1235	59 12345 67890 1235
Visa	4 12345 67890 12349	8 12345 67890 12349

5. Continue testing other combinations of credit card numbers to verify that only numbers that match the card patterns described in Figure 14-58 are accepted by the browser.

Testing with the Luhn Formula

One last test that you can do on the client side weeds out mistakes a customer might make when entering the credit card number. All credit card numbers must satisfy the **Luhn Formula**, or **Mod10 algorithm**, which is a formula developed by a group of mathematicians in the 1960s to provide a quick validation check on an account number by adding up the digits in the number. Almost all institutions that employ unique account or identification numbers, including credit card companies, use numbers that satisfy the Luhn Formula. The following steps, also shown in Figure 14-62, determine whether a particular number satisfies the Luhn Formula:

1. Starting from the second to the last digit in the account number, separate every other digit into two groups, moving to the left.
2. Double the value of each digit in the first group (the group containing the first digit you selected).
3. Calculate the sum of the digits in each group.

4. Add the values of the two sums together.
5. If the total sum is evenly divisible by 10, then the number satisfies the Luhn Formula.

Figure 14-62 **Luhn Formula**

Luhn Formula

1) Divide the number into alternate groups starting from the second to last digit and moving left

2) Double the digits in the first group (containing the digit you started with)

3) Sum the digits in both groups

4) Add the digit sums

5) Divide the total digit sum by 10; if evenly divisible, the number is valid

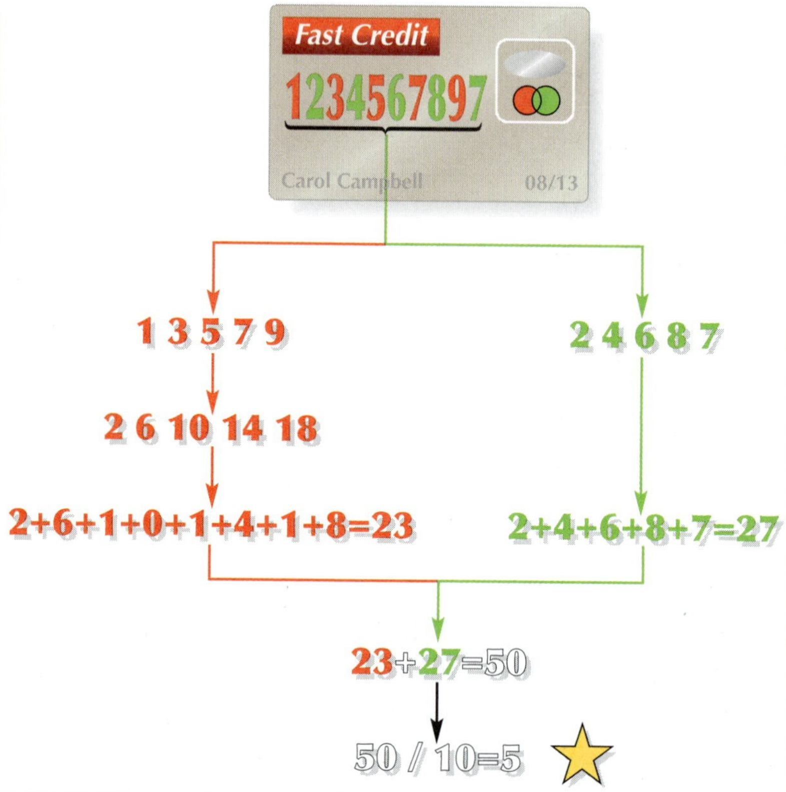

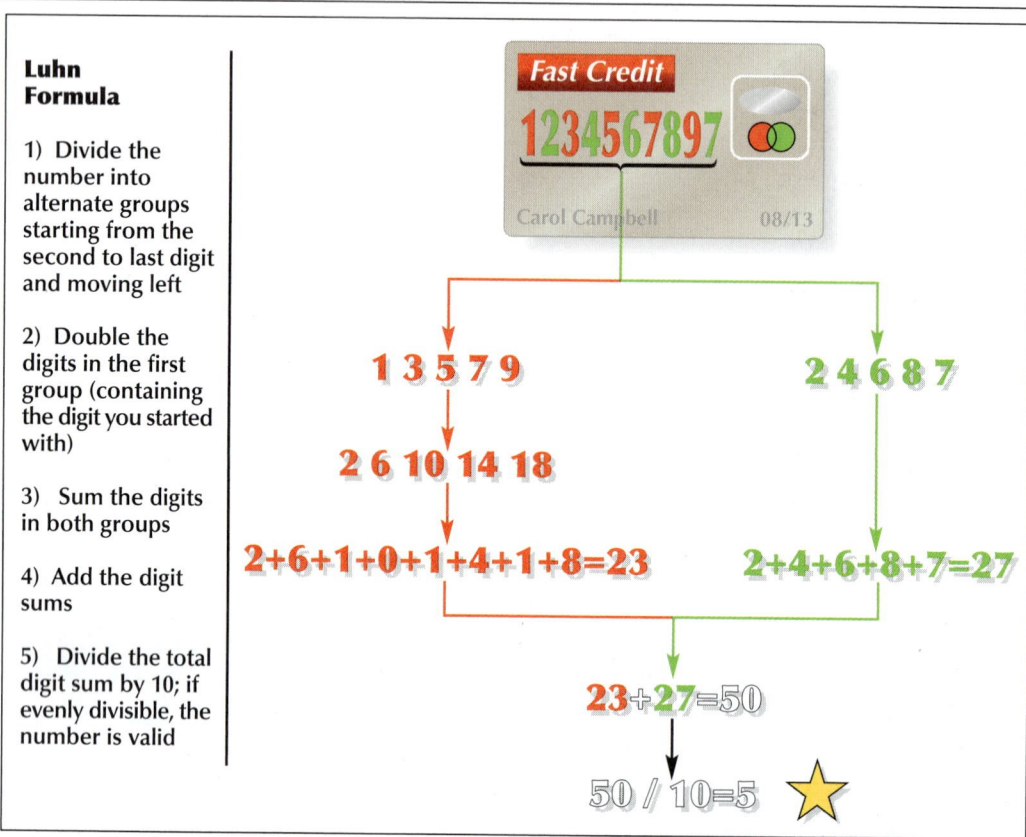

A function to calculate the Luhn Formula has already been created and is stored in the payment.js file. The code for the luhn() function is:

```
function luhn(num) {
   var luhnTotal = 0;
   for (var i = num.length-1; i >= 0; i--) {
      luhnTotal += parseInt(num.charAt(i));
      i--;
      num2 = new String(num.charAt(i)*2);
      for (j = 0; j < num2.length; j++) {
         luhnTotal += parseInt(num2.charAt(j));
      }
   }
   return (luhnTotal % 10 == 0);
}
```

The luhn() function has a single parameter, num, which contains the text string of the account number to be validated. It assumes that all white space characters have already been removed from the text string. The function loops through each digit in the text string, adding up the digit sums. Each time it encounters a digit that should be doubled, it stores the doubled digit in a string object named num2, which is then summed before continuing through the larger number string. A running total of the digit sum is stored in the luhnTotal variable. After the last digit has been added, the function uses the % operator to test whether dividing luhnTotal by 10 results in a remainder of 0. If it does, a Boolean value of true is returned by the function; otherwise, it returns a Boolean value of false. Study the code in this function. Although this function may seem daunting at first, it is composed entirely of string object methods and properties that you learned earlier in this tutorial.

You can call the luhn() function from the checkNumber() function you just created. The checkNumber() function will then have two tests: first it will check whether the selected card number matches the number pattern of the credit card company, and then it will check whether the card number fulfills the criterion of the Luhn Formula. You'll add the test for the Luhn Formula to your code.

To add a test for the Luhn Formula:

1. Return to the **payment.js** file in your text editor.
2. In the checkNumber() function, change the return statement to the following, as shown in Figure 14-63:

```
return (cregx.test(cnum) && luhn(cnum));
```

Figure 14-63 **Final checkNumber() function**

```
function checkNumber() {
   wsregx = /\s/g;
   var cnum = document.forms[0].cnumber.value.replace(wsregx,"");

   switch (selectedCard()) {
      case 0: cregx = /^3[47]\d{13}$/; break;
      case 1: cregx = /^30[0-5]\d{11}$|^3[68]\d{12}$/; break;
      case 2: cregx = /^6011\d{12}$/; break;
      case 3: cregx = /^5[1-5]\d{14}$/; break;
      case 4: cregx = /^4(\d{12}|\d{15})$/; break;
   }

   return (cregx.test(cnum) && luhn(cnum));
}
```

return value is true only if the card number matches the regular expression pattern and passes the Luhn Formula

The checkNumber() function uses the && logical operator so that a value of true is returned only if the credit card number matches the correct pattern and satisfies the Luhn Formula.

3. Close the file, saving your changes.
4. Reload **form3.htm** in your Web browser.
5. Click **American Express** from the list of credit cards, and then enter a sample cardholder name in the name field.
6. In the Number field, enter **34 12345 67890 123** and then click the **Next** button. Your browser alerts you that the number is not valid.
7. In the Number field, change the credit card number to **34 12345 67890 127** and then click the **Next** button. The number is accepted and a Web page opens, indicating that the order has been submitted successfully.

At this point, the customer's order could be sent to the Web server for further processing and validation checks. Obviously, the server would have to consult financial databases to verify that the credit card information represented a real account; but adding these validation checks on the client side allows the customer's program to filter out errors that the company's server would otherwise have to deal with.

Passing Data Between Forms

To simplify form validation for the GPS-ware Web site, Carol divided the data that she wanted collected into three separate forms. When customer input is spread out over several forms, you usually need some way of passing collected data along as customers move from one form to another. One way of doing this is with cookies, which are beyond the scope of this tutorial. Another approach is to append form data to a URL.

Appending Form Data

To append form data to a URL, you set the form's action to a URL and set the method of the form to "get". For example, the <form> tag

```
<form action = "report.htm" method = "get">
```

tells the browser to open the report.htm file using the get method when the current Web form is submitted for processing. When the report.htm file is opened by the browser, data from the calling form will be appended to its URL as follows

```
http://server/path/report.htm?field1=value1&field2=value2& ...
```

where *server* and *path* are the server and path names for the Web page; *field1*, *field2*, and so on are the names of the fields in the calling Web form; and *value1*, *value2*, and so on are the values stored in each of those fields. For example, if your Web form contains fields named firstname and lastname with values of Carol and Campbell, respectively, then the following form data is appended to report.htm's URL when it's opened in the browser:

```
http://server/path/report.htm?firstname=Carol&lastname=Campbell
```

The field/value pairs are appended to the form element after the ? character. To retrieve the form data, you must extract the substring that appears after the ? symbol, ignoring any text that appears before the ? symbol.

Extracting a Substring from a URL

You can reference the URL of the current Web page using the location object, which stores the complete text of the URL. The location object supports several properties to extract only parts of that URL. To extract only the text of the URL occurring from the ? character onward, use the following object property:

```
location.search
```

For example, the value of the location.search property for the URL noted above would consist of the following substring:

```
?firstname=Carol&lastname=Campbell
```

To remove the initial ? symbol, apply the slice() method discussed in the previous session. The expression

```
location.search.slice(1)
```

results in the following text string:

```
firstname=Carol&lastname=Campbell
```

After you have the field names and values in this substring, you can extract the form information using what you learned about string methods and regular expressions. This involves formatting the substring contents and splitting the substring into separate pieces.

Extracting Form Data from a Substring

Before you can extract form data from a substring, you must format the substring. URLs cannot contain blank spaces, so any blanks in the form data are replaced with the + symbol. For example, if a Web form contains a single field named username with a field value of Carol Campbell, the form data would be stored in the following text string:

```
username=Carol+Campbell
```

To replace every occurrence of a + symbol with a blank space, you can apply the regular expression along with the replace() method

```
plusregx = /\+/g;
formdata.replace(plusregx, " ");
```

where *formdata* is a text string containing the form data appended to a URL. You must use the escape symbol \ to reference the + character in the regular expression.

The other part of formatting the substring is to remove all escape characters from the form data. Characters such as / and : will not appear in the form data because they are reserved for use in describing the URL path. Instead of those characters, the URL will display the escape character codes: %2F for the / character and %3A for the : character. Other special characters have similar escape codes. You can remove these codes, replacing them with the actual characters using the unescape() method

```
unescape(string)
```

where *string* is the text containing escape character codes. To remove any escape codes from the form data, you would apply the following command:

```
formdata = unescape(formdata)
```

Tip

You can reverse the effect of the unescape() method by applying the escape() method to the text string.

Once you've reformatted the form data string, you can split the field/value pairs. Recall that the general syntax of the field/value pairs is

```
field1=value1&field2=value2& ...
```

with each field/value pair separated by an & symbol and the fields separated from their values by an = symbol. To split the fields and values into separate substrings, you can apply the split() method to the regular expression

```
splitregx = /[&=]/g;
formArray = formdata.split(splitregx);
```

where *formArray* is an array in which each item is either a field name or a field value. The regular expression uses a group to match all occurrences of either the & symbol or the = symbol. After running these commands, the contents of *formArray* will be:

```
formArray[0] = field1
formArray[1] = value1
formArray[2] = field2
formArray[3] = value2
...
```

At this point, you can reference each field name and field value by its location in the *formArray* and incorporate those values in your JavaScript program. Putting this all together, a function that extracts form data from a URL could appear as follows:

```
function retrieveData() {
   formString = location.search.slice(1);
   formData = formString.replace(/\+/g, " ");
   formData = unescape(formData);
   formArray = formData.split(/[&=]/g);
}
```

To see how transferring data from one form to another works in practice, you'll look at a demo page.

To view the form demo:

1. Open **demo_form1.htm** from the tutorial.14/demo folder in your Web browser.
2. Enter ***your name***, ***your age***, and ***your city*** in the appropriate fields in the form. See Figure 14-64.

Figure 14-64 **Form data being entered**

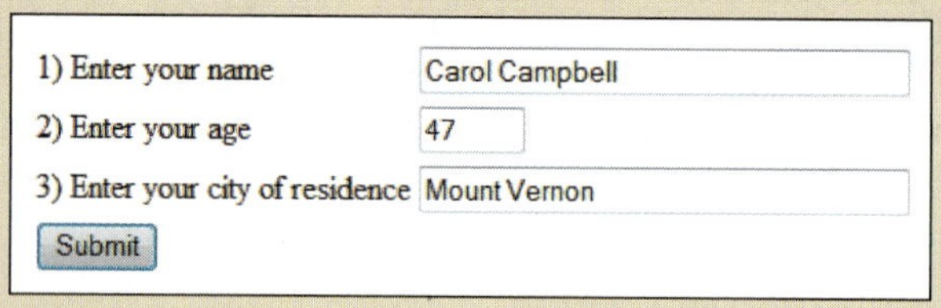

3. Click the **Submit** button. The values you entered in the first form are retrieved from the URL and displayed in the form on the second Web page. See Figure 14-65.

Figure 14-65 **Form data retrieved from the URL**

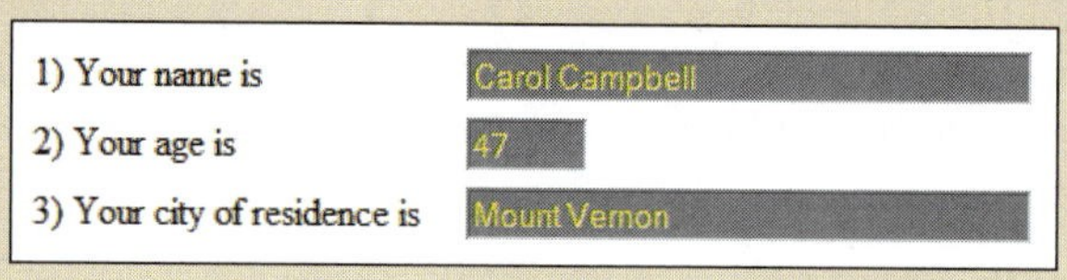

4. Close your Web browser and any open files.

At this point, you won't add the ability to pass form data to Carol's Web form, though she may want you to add this feature in the future. You've completed your work on Carol's order forms.

Review | Session 14.3 Quick Check

1. What regular expressions match every occurrence of the substring "GPS" in a text string, regardless of case?
2. What regular expression matches the first occurrence of the word "products"?
3. A Social Security number consists of nine digits. Write a regular expression to match this pattern.
4. Social Security numbers can be entered either as *ddddddddd* or *ddd-dd-dddd*. Write a regular expression to match either pattern.

5. Write a regular expression that matches any of the substrings "street", "avenue", or "lane". Make the match case insensitive and match every occurrence of the substring in the text string.
6. What JavaScript command tests whether the text string "username" matches the pattern specified in the regular expression object reuser?
7. What JavaScript command splits the text string "date" at every occurrence of the / character?
8. What is the Luhn Formula?
9. What object property extracts any form data appended to the URL of the current Web document?

Tutorial Summary | Review

This tutorial explored how JavaScript can be used to validate Web forms. In the first session, you learned how to reference different elements in a Web form, including input boxes, selection lists, and option button groups. You saw how to extract values from form fields and use them to create calculated fields. You also learned about some of the difficulties in displaying numeric values in a Web form, and techniques to create nicely formatted output. The second session introduced the concept of form validation: comparing the benefits and costs of client-side and server-side validation. You learned how to validate a form before allowing it to be processed, and you learned about the properties and methods associated with string objects. The third session introduced the language of regular expressions. You learned how to create a regular expression to match a wide variety of patterns, and you learned about the properties and methods associated with regular expression objects. In the third session, you employed regular expressions to validate both zip code and credit card data. You also learned about the Luhn Formula and how it could be used to validate credit card numbers before they are submitted to a Web server. The third session concluded with a discussion of passing data from one Web page to another, with special emphasis on passing field names and values from one Web form to another.

Key Terms

alert box
character class
client-side validation
delimiter
escape sequence
focus
form validation
Luhn Formula
Mod10 algorithm
pattern matching
regular expression
regular expression literal
server-side validation
string object
substring
word
word character

Practice | Review Assignments

Practice the skills you learned in the tutorial using the same case scenario.

Data Files needed for the Review Assignments: ordertxt.htm, formtxt.js, border.jpg, done.htm, gps.css, gpsware.jpg

Carol has a few changes she wants you to make to the first order form. Rather than displaying the GPS-ware products in a selection list, Carol wants the product names to appear as separate fields. This allows customers to purchase more than one product without having to open a second form. Also, instead of displaying the quantity to order in a selection list, Carol wants the quantity value placed in an input field, so that customers can specify any quantity in their order. Finally, Carol wants your script to confirm that a shipping option has been selected before the order is submitted to the Web server. Figure 14-66 shows a preview of the new order form.

Figure 14-66

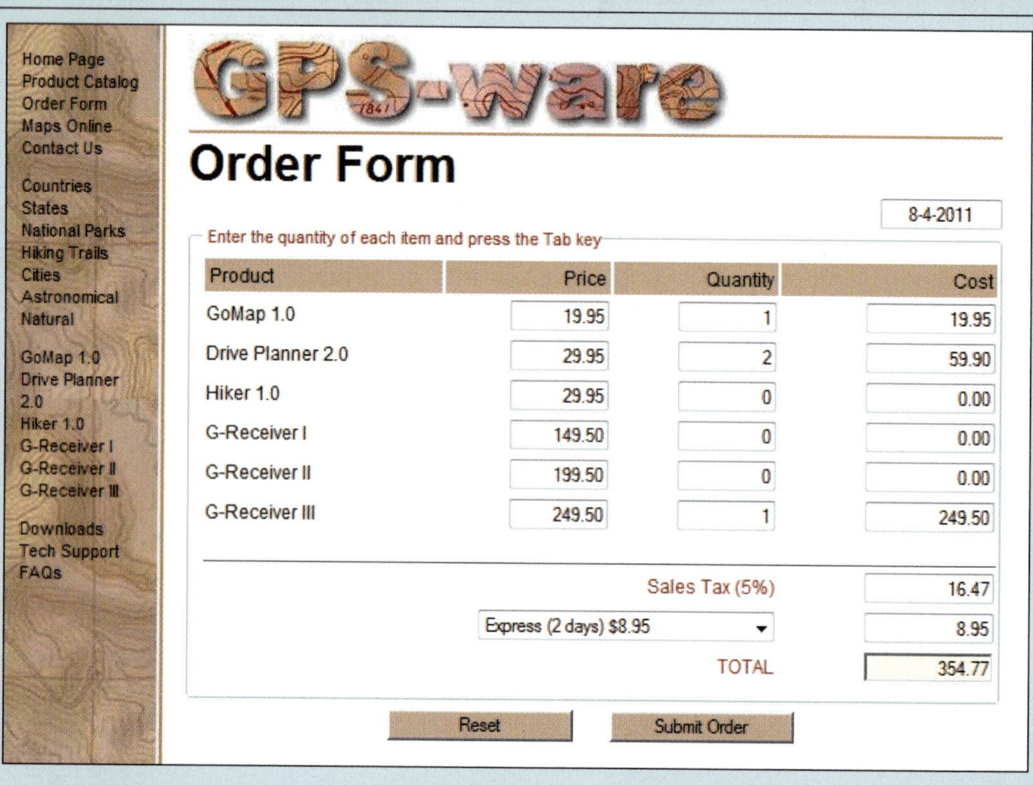

Carol wants the new form to include the following features:

- When a customer opens the form, the current date should appear in the date field.
- When a customer enters a new quantity in the Quantity column, the cost should update automatically.
- Customers should be prevented from entering anything other than digits in the Quantity column. If a value other than a digit is entered, the customer should be notified of the error and the quantity value that was entered incorrectly should be reset to 0.
- When a customer selects a shipping option, the total cost should be automatically updated to reflect the shipping price.
- The form cannot be submitted unless a shipping option has been selected.

Complete the following:

1. Use your text editor to open the **ordertxt.htm** and **formtxt.js** files from the tutorial. 14/review folder, enter ***your name*** and ***the date*** in the comment section of each file, and then save the files as **order.htm** and **form.js**, respectively.
2. Go to the **order.htm** file in your text editor, and review the contents of the file, noting the IDs and names used for the elements in the document. Insert a link to the **form.js** file in the head section of the file and close the document.
3. Go to the **form.js** file in your text editor. Below the comment section, insert an event handler to run the initForm() function when the page loads.
4. Create a function named **initForm()**. The purpose of this function is to initialize the contents of the Web page and form. Add the following commands to the function:
   a. Set the value of the date field to the value returned by the todayTxt() function.
   b. Set the focus of the Web browser on the qty1 field.
   c. Add onblur event handlers for the qty1 through qty6 fields, running the calcCost() function whenever these fields lose the focus of the Web browser.
   d. Add an onchange event handler to the shipping field, running the calcShipping() function when the value of the field changes.
5. Create a function named **productCosts()**. The purpose of this function is to return the sum of the total costs of the six GPS-ware products in the order form. The costs of items are stored in input fields named cost1 through cost6. Have the function do the following:
   a. Create a variable named **pc1** that is equal to the value of the cost1 field. Use the parseFloat() function to convert the field's value from a text string to a number.
   b. Use the same process to create variables **pc2** through **pc6**, which are equal to the numeric values of the cost2 through cost6 fields.
   c. Return the sum of the pc1 through pc6 variables.
6. Create a function named **shipExpense()**. The purpose of the shipExpense() function is to return the cost of the selected shipping option. The shipping options are stored within a selection list named shipping. Have the function do the following:
   a. Create a variable named **sindex** equal to the selected index from the shipping selection list.
   b. Return the numeric value of the option from the shipping selection list whose index is equal to the sindex variable. Be sure to use the parseFloat() function to convert the option value from a text string to a number.
7. Create a function named **calcTotal()**. The purpose of the calcTotal() function is to display the cost of the sales tax and also the total cost of the order. Add the following commands to the function:
   a. Create a variable named **ordercost** that is equal to the value returned by the productCosts() function. Create a variable named **ordertax** that is equal to 5% of the ordercost variable. Create a variable named **ordership** that is equal to the value returned by the shipExpense() function. Finally, create a variable named **ordertotal** that is equal to the sum of the ordercost, ordertax, and ordership variables.
   b. Store the value of the ordertax variable in the tax field. Display to two decimal places.
   c. Store the value of the ordertotal variable in the total field. Also display the value to two decimal places.

8. Create a function named **calcShipping()**. The purpose of the function is to display the cost of the selected shipping option and to update the total order costs. Add the following commands to the function:
   a. Store the value returned by the shipExpense() function in the shipcost field.
   b. Run the calcTotal() function.
9. Create a function named **calcCost()**. The purpose of the calcCost() function is to display the cost of the quantity of items ordered by a customer and to update the total cost of the order. This function will also test whether a customer has correctly entered an integer in one of the quantity fields. The price of each item is stored in the price*item* field, where *item* is the item number. The cost of each item is stored in the cost*item* field. And the quantity ordered by each item is stored in the qty*item* field. For the order.htm file, the value of *item* ranges from 1 to 6. To complete the calcCost() function, add the following commands:
   a. Create a variable named **iNum** that is equal to the ID of the currently selected object, using the slice() method to slice off the first three characters from the ID. (*Hint:* Use the this keyword to reference the currently selected object.)
   b. Create a variable named **price** that references the price*item* field, where *item* is the value of the iNum variable (*Hint*: Use the document.forms[0].elements collection along with the field's name to reference the price*item* field.)
   c. Create a variable named **qty** that references the qty*item* field.
   d. Create a variable named **cost** that references the cost*item* field.
   e. Create a regular expression object named **reqty** for a text string containing one or more digits and no other characters.
   f. Still within the calcCost() function, test whether the value of the qty object matches the pattern defined by the reqty regular expression. If the pattern matches, then: (1) Set the value of the cost object equal to the value of the price object multiplied by the value of the qty object. Display the value of the cost object to two decimal places; (2) Run the calcTotal() function. If the pattern does not match (meaning that the customer has not entered a quantity value in integers), then: (i) Display the alert message **Please enter a digit greater than or equal to 0**, (ii) Set the value of the qty object to 0, and (iii) Set the focus back to the qty object using the focus() method.
10. Create a function named **validateForm()**. The purpose of this function is to ensure that the form has been filled out correctly before it is submitted. Add the following commands to the function:
    a. Test whether the selected index in the shipping field is equal to 0. If it is (meaning that no shipping method has been chosen by the customer), then: (1) Display the alert message **You must select a shipping option**, and (2) Return the value false.
    b. Otherwise, return the value true.
11. Create a function named **resetForm()**. This function will run until the form is reset. Add a command to the function to reload the current document.
12. Close the **form.js** file, saving your changes. Open **order.htm** in your Web browser and verify that it correctly updates the total cost of the order as you change the values in the quantity column. Also verify that the form will not accept any quantity values other than integers. Check that the cost of shipping changes to reflect the shipping method selected by the customer, and that the form cannot be submitted unless a shipping method has been selected. Verify that clicking the Reset button reloads the Web page.
13. Submit your completed files to your instructor.

Apply | Case Problem 1

Use JavaScript to create a select and go navigation list.

Data Files needed for this Case Problem: mpltxt.htm, linkstxt.js, mpl.jpg, mplstyles.css

The Monroe Public Library At the Monroe Public Library, Denise Kruschev works on the library's Web site. One of her responsibilities is to add content to the site that will be of interest to the library's patrons. Denise's latest assignment is to create a Web page containing links to hundreds of government Web sites. She knows that a long list of links will fill the page, making the page difficult to use. Instead, Denise wants to use "select and go navigation," in which the links are placed within a selection list. When a user selects a link from the list, the linked page should open automatically. Denise already set up the selection lists, but she asks you to help write the JavaScript program. Figure 14-67 shows a preview of the Web page.

Figure 14-67

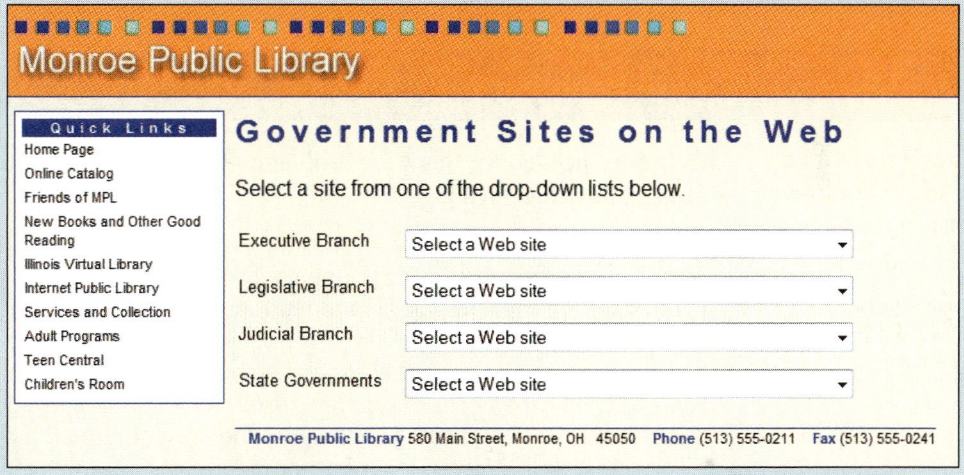

Complete the following:

1. Use your text editor to open the **mpltxt.htm** and **linkstxt.js** files from the tutorial.14/case1 folder, enter ***your name*** and ***the date*** in the comment section of each file, and then save the files as **mpl.htm** and **links.js**, respectively.
2. Go to the **mpl.htm** file in your text editor and create a link to the **links.js** file.
3. Scroll through the mpl.htm file, studying the code. Each option in the selection list contains a value referencing the URL of a government Web site. Close the file, saving your changes.
4. Go to the **links.js** file in your text editor and insert an event handler to run the init() function when the page is loaded.
5. Create the **init()** function. Within this function do the following:
   a. Create a variable named **allSelect** that references all of the selection elements in the document.
   b. For each item within the allSelect object collection, add an onchange event handler that runs the loadLink() function when the selection list changes.

6. Create the **loadLink()** function. The purpose of this function is to cause the browser to load a URL from a selection list. Add the following commands to the function:
   a. Create a variable named **sIndex** that points to the index of the selected option in the current selection list. (*Hint:* Use the this keyword to reference the current selection list.)

EXPLORE

   b. Web pages can be loaded using the command
      `location.href = url;`
      where *url* is the URL of the Web page. Enter this command into the function using the value of the selected option from the selection list as the value of *url*. (*Hint:* Use the sIndex variable to point to the selected option from the current selection list.)
7. Save your changes to the file.
8. Open **mpl.htm** in your Web browser. Verify that by clicking the links from the selection lists on the page you can bring up the corresponding government Web sites.
9. Submit your completed files to your instructor.

Apply | Case Problem 2

Use JavaScript to create an online travel expense report.

Data Files needed for this Case Problem: exptxt.htm, reporttxt.js, back.jpg, done.htm, exp.css, links.jpg, logo.jpg

DeLong Enterprises Kay Ramirez is the payroll manager for DeLong Enterprises, a manufacturer of computer components. The company has been busy putting corporate information on the company's intranet. Kay is heading a project to put all of the payroll-related forms and reports online. She asks you to help write a program for the online travel expense form. The travel expense report form requires employees to itemize their various travel expenses for corporate trips. Kay wants scripts added to the form to ensure that all of the required data is entered in the correct format. If a required data field is left blank or if data is entered in an improper format, Kay wants the program to highlight the field in yellow and refuse submission of the form to the corporate Web server. Kay wants the form to support the following features:

- The employee must enter a last name, a first name, a Social Security number, an address for the reimbursement check, and a summary of the trip.
- The employee must enter the account ID number in the format ACT*nnnnnn*, the department ID number in the format DEPT*nnn*, and the project ID number in the format PROJ*nnnnn*.
- For each day in which the employee has recorded an expense, the travel date must be entered.
- When the employee enters a travel, lodging, or meal expense, the subtotal of expenses for that day and the total cost of the trip should update automatically.
- Travel expenses must be entered as digits (either with or without the two-digit decimal place) and displayed to two digits.

A preview of the completed form is displayed in Figure 14-68.

Figure 14-68

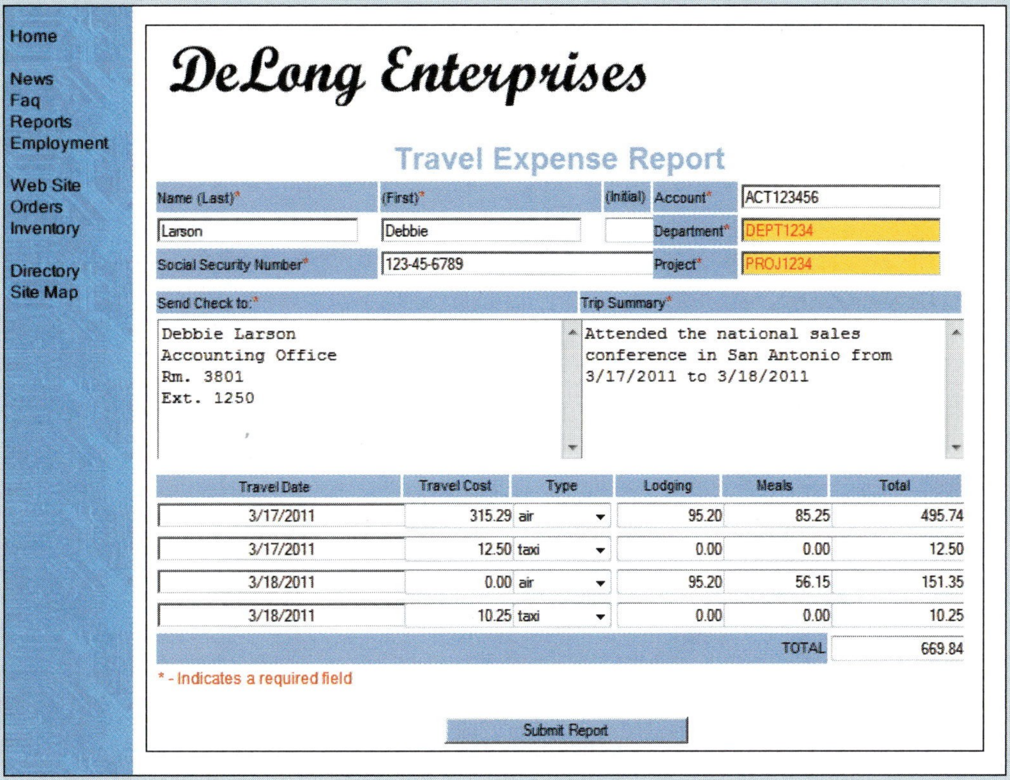

Complete the following:

1. Use your text editor to open the **exptxt.htm** and **reporttxt.js** files from the tutorial.14/case2 folder, enter ***your name*** and ***the date*** in the comment section of each file, and then save the files as **exp.htm** and **report.js**, respectively.
2. Go to the **exp.htm** file in your text editor, insert a link to the **report.js** script file in the head section of the document, review the content and elements used in the document, and then close the file, saving your changes.
3. Return to the **report.js** file in your text editor, and then add an event handler to the file, running the initPage() function when the page is loaded by the browser.
4. Insert the **initPage()** function. The purpose of this function is to set up the initial conditions for the exp.htm page. Add the following commands to the function:
   a. Declare an array variable named **dataFields**. This array will point to the input elements in the expense report for daily expenses of travel, lodging, and meals.
   b. The input elements for the daily travel, lodging, and meal expenses all belong to the expenseEntry class. Use a For loop to populate the content of the dataFields array with the object collection of all elements belonging to the expenseEntry class.
   c. For each item in the dataFields array, add an onblur event handler that runs the update() function whenever the focus leaves the dataFields element.
   d. Add an event handler to the Web form that runs the validateForm() function when the form is submitted to the browser.

5. Create a function named **testLength()**. The purpose of the testLength() function is to test whether the user has entered any text in a required field. If no text has been entered, the function should highlight the field and return the value false. If any text has been entered, the function should remove any highlighting and return the value true. The function has a single parameter named **field** that represents the field object to be tested. To complete the function, insert the following commands:
   a. Insert a conditional expression that tests whether the length of the field value is equal to 0.
   b. If the length is equal to 0, then: (i) Change the background color of the field object to yellow and (ii) Return the Boolean value false; otherwise: (i) Change the background color of the field object to white and (ii) Return the Boolean value true.
6. Create a function named **testPattern()**. The purpose of this function is to compare the value of a field against a regular expression pattern. If the field's value does not match the regular expression, the function should highlight the field on the form and return the Boolean value false. If the field's value does match the regular expression, the function should remove any highlighting and return the Boolean value true. The function has two parameters: the **field** parameter, representing the field object to be tested; and **regx**, a regular expression containing the pattern used for the testing. To complete the testPattern() function, insert the following commands:
   a. Insert a conditional expression that employs the test() method to test whether the value of the field object matches the regular expression contained in the regx parameter.
   b. If the test() method returns the value false, then: (i) Change the background color of the field object to yellow, (ii) Change the color of the field object to red, and (iii) Return the Boolean value false; otherwise: (i) Change the background color of the field object to white, (ii) Change the color of the field object to black, and (iii) Return the Boolean value true.
7. Create a function named **validateForm()**. The purpose of this function is to validate the form before it can be submitted to the server by calling the testPattern() and testLength() functions you just created. The function has no parameters. Add the following commands to the function:
   a. Create a variable named **isValid**. The purpose of this variable is to record whether the form is valid or not. Set the initial value of the isValid variable to true.
   b. Call the testLength() function with the lname field object as the parameter. (*Hint*: Use the object reference document.forms[0].lname.) If the value returned by the testLength() function is false, set the value of the isValid variable to false. Repeat this step for the fname, address, and summary fields.
   c. Call the testPattern() function with a reference to the account field as the field parameter value. For the regx parameter, insert a regular expression literal that matches a text string containing only the text "ACT" followed by six digits. If the value returned by the testPattern() function is false, set the value of the isValid variable to false.
   d. Call the testPattern() function with the department field for the field parameter. The regx parameter should contain a regular expression literal for a text string containing only the characters "DEPT" followed by three digits. If the value of the testPattern() function is false, set the value of the isValid variable to false.
   e. Repeat the previous step for the project field, using a regular expression that matches a text string containing only the characters "PROJ" followed by five digits.

   f. Call the testPattern() function for the ssn field (containing the Social Security number of the employee). The regular expression should match either a nine-digit number or a text string in the form *nnn-nn-nnnn*. If the testPattern() function returns the value false, set the value of the isValid variable to false.
   g. Insert a conditional statement that tests whether the value of the isValid variable is false. If it is false, then display the following alert message: **Please fill out all required fields in the proper format.**
   h. Return the value of the isValid variable.
8. Add a function named **calcRow()**. The purpose of this function is to return the subtotal of the expenses within a single row in the travel expense table. The function has a single parameter named **row**, which represents the number of the table row (from 1 to 4) upon which the calculations will be performed. Add the following commands to the function:
   a. Create a variable named **travel** that is equal to the numeric value of the travel*row* field, where *row* is the value of the row parameter. (*Hint*: Use the object reference document.forms[0].elements["travel"+*row*].value.) Be sure to use the parseFloat() function to convert the field value to a number. In the same fashion, create a variable named **lodge** that is equal to the numeric value of the lodge*row* field and a variable named **meal** that is equal to the numeric value of the meal*row* field.
   b. Return the sum of the travel, lodge, and row variables.
9. Create a function named **calcTotal()**. The purpose of this function is to return the total of all expenses in the travel expense table by calling the calcRow() function for each of the four rows in the table. The function has no parameters. Add the following commands to the function:
   a. Create a variable named **totalExp** and set its initial value to 0.
   b. Insert a For loop with a counter that runs from 1 to 4.
   c. Within the For loop, increase the value of the totalExp variable by the value returned by the calcRow() function using the value of the counter as the value of the row parameter.
   d. Return the value of the totalExp variable.
10. Create a function named **update()**. The purpose of this function is to update the expense values displayed throughout the table and to verify that the employee has entered a valid expense amount. The function will be called whenever the employee exits from one of the 12 expense fields in the table (initiating the blur event). Add the following commands to the function:
   a. Create a variable named **numRegExp** that contains the regular expression literal /^\d*(\.\d{0,2})?$/. This pattern matches any text string that only contains a number with or without two decimal place accuracy.
   b. Insert a conditional statement that tests whether the value property of the currently selected object matches the numRegExp pattern. (*Hint:* Use the this keyword to reference the currently selected object.)
   c. If the condition is met (meaning that the employee has entered a valid expense amount), then run the following commands: (i) Use the toFixed() method to display the value of the current object to two decimal places, (ii) Insert a For loop with a counter that runs from 1 to 4. Within the For loop, set the value of the sub*i* field to the value returned by the calcRow() function, where *i* is the value of the For loop counter. Format the value to appear to two decimal places. (iii) Set the value of the total field equal to the value returned by the calcTotal() function. Display the total field value to two decimal places.

d. If the condition is not met (meaning that the user has entered an invalid number), then: (i) Display the alert message **Invalid currency value**, (ii) Change the value property of the current object to **0.00**, and (iii) Return the focus to the current object.

11. Save your changes to the file. Open **exp.htm** in your Web browser. Test the operation of the travel expense table, verifying that it automatically updates the travel expenses as you add new values to the table.
12. Test the form validation commands by attempting to submit the form under the following conditions: (i) Without all of the required fields filled out and (ii) With invalid entries for the account, department, project, and Social Security number fields. The form should highlight the errors and alert you of the mistakes.
13. Submit your completed files to your instructor.

Challenge | Case Problem 3

Explore how to pass data between Web forms.

Data Files needed for this Case Problem: conftxt.htm, sumtxt.htm, back.jpg, conf.css, edge.jpg, formstxt.js, links.jpg, logo.jpg, summary.css

The CGIP Conference Rajiv Rammohan is a Web site consultant for the annual conference of Computer Graphics and Image Processing. This year, the conference is putting all of its registration forms and documents online. Rajiv is working on the form in which participants will enter their registration information. Rajiv wants the form to have the following features.

- The participant must enter a first name, a last name, an address, an e-mail address, and a phone number.
- Phone numbers must follow the pattern *nnn-nnn-nnnn*.
- The participant can indicate whether he or she is a member of the ACGIP to receive a discount on the registration fee.
- The form should calculate the total registration fee. The fee is equal to $145 plus $30 for every person attending the conference banquet. ACGIP members receive a $25 discount on the registration fee.

When a form is submitted, Rajiv wants the browser to display a page summarizing all of the participant's registration information and selections. Figure 14-69 shows a preview of both the registration form and the summary page.

Figure 14-69

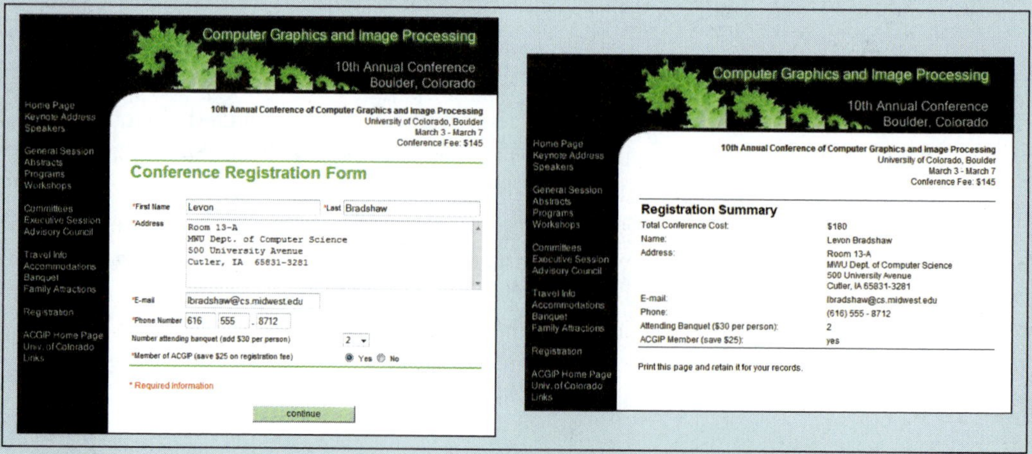

Complete the following:

1. Use your text editor to open the **conftxt.htm, sumtxt.htm**, and **formstxt.js** files from the tutorial.14/case3 folder, enter ***your name*** and ***the date*** in the comment section of each file, and then save the files as **conf.htm, summary.htm**, and **forms.js**, respectively.
2. Go to the **conf.htm** file in your text editor, and examine the contents of the file and the Web form. Note that the form has a hidden field named total. In this field, you'll store the total cost of the registration.
3. Link the file to the **forms.js** script file, and then close conf.htm, saving your changes.
4. Go to the **forms.js** file in your text editor, and then add an event handler to run the init() function when the page is loaded. Below this statement, add the init() function, which consists of a single command to assign the submitForm() function to the onsubmit event handler for the first Web form in the document. You'll create the submitForm() function shortly.
5. Create a function named **calcCost()**. The purpose of this function is to calculate the total registration fee. Add the following commands to the function:
   a. Create a variable named **cost** and set its initial value to 145, the default cost of the conference.
   b. Retrieve the value of the selected index property from the guests selection list. This value indicates the number of guests invited to the banquet. Multiply the selected index value by 30 and add this to the cost variable.
   c. If the first member radio button is checked, subtract 25 from the value of the cost variable.
   d. Set the value of the hidden total field on the Web form equal to the value of the cost variable.
6. Create a function named **testLength()**. The purpose of the function is to test whether the user has entered any text in a required field. The function has a single parameter named **field** that represents the field object to be tested. To complete the function:
   a. Insert a conditional expression that tests whether the length of the field value is equal to 0.
   b. If the length is equal to 0, then: (i) Change the background color of the field object to yellow and (ii) Return the Boolean value false. Otherwise: (i) Change the background color of the field object to white and (ii) Return the Boolean value true.
7. Create a function named **testPattern()**. The purpose of this function is to compare the value of a field against a regular expression pattern. The function has two parameters: the field parameter, representing the field object to be tested; and reg, a regular expression literal containing the pattern used for the testing. To complete the testPattern() function:
   a. Insert a conditional statement that employs the test() method to test whether the value of the field object matches the regular expression contained in the reg parameter.
   b. If the test() method returns the value false, then: (i) Change the background color of the field object to yellow, (ii) Change the color of the field object to red, and (iii) Return the Boolean value false. Otherwise: (i) Change the background color of the field object to white, (ii) Change the color of the field object to black, and (iii) Return the Boolean value true.

8. Create a function named **submitForm()**. The purpose of this function is to validate the form and calculate the total registration fee. Add the following commands to the function:
   a. Create a variable named **valid**. Set the initial value of the variable to true.
   b. Call the testLength() function using the fname field as the parameter. If the function returns the value false, change the value of the valid variable to false. Repeat this step for the lname, address, and email fields.
   c. The phone number is divided into three fields named phone1, phone2, and phone3, representing the area code, exchange, and local number. The phone1 and phone2 fields should both contain only three digits. The phone3 field should contain only four digits. Call the testPattern() function for each field along with the appropriate regular expression literal to test whether the entries in these fields match the specified patterns. If the value returned by the testPattern() function is false for any of the fields, set the value of the valid variable to false.
   d. Insert a conditional statement that tests whether neither of the member radio buttons is checked. If neither has been checked, then: (i) Change the background color of each member radio button to yellow, and (ii) Set the value of the valid variable to false. (*Hint*: To test whether neither radio button has been checked, use the condition: ((*form*.member[0].checked || *form*.member[1].checked) == false) where *form* is the object reference to the registration form.)
   e. If the valid variable is false, then display the alert message **Enter all required information in the appropriate format**; otherwise, run the calcCost() function.
   f. Return the value of the valid variable.
9. Save your changes to the forms.js file, and then open the **conf.htm** file in your Web browser. Verify that the form cannot be submitted unless all of the required fields are filled out, the phone number is entered in the appropriate format, and the user has indicated whether he or she is a member of the ACGIP. A valid form should open the summary.htm file with a list of field names and values appended to the URL.

   Note that browsers differ in how they change the background color of option buttons. If you are running Internet Explorer, the background color of the option buttons changes to yellow. If you are running Firefox, the background color of the option buttons does not turn yellow. If you are running Opera, the internal color of the option buttons changes.

EXPLORE

10. Go to the **summary.htm** file in your text editor. Add an embedded script element to the head section of the document. Add the following commands to the script element:
    a. Create a variable named **searchString** that is equal to everything but the first character of the location.search object.
    b. Use the replace() method to replace every occurrence of the + character in the searchString variable with a blank space. Store the revised text string in a variable named **formString**.
    c. Apply the unescape() method to the formString variable to remove any escape characters from the string. Store the revised text string in a variable named **dataString**.
    d. Use the split() method to split the dataString at every occurrence of a & or = character. Store the substrings in an array named **data**.

EXPLORE

11. Scroll down the file to see that embedded script elements have already been entered for you on the Web page. You need to write the field values from the data array you created in the last step into the appropriate places on the Web page. Field values are stored in data[1], data[3], data[5], and so on, where the index is an odd number.

    The total cost of the conference is stored in data[1]. In the first script element, use the document.write() method to write the value of data[1] preceded by a $ character. The participant's first name and last name are stored in data[3] and data[5], respectively. In the second script element, write the values data[3] and data[5], separated by a blank space.

EXPLORE

12. The next row in the table displays the participant's address. This value is stored in data[7]. However, the value came from a textarea field that could contain multiple lines of text. Each line return must be converted into <br /> tags to preserve the appearance of the address text. To write the participant's address, do the following:
    a. Create a regular expression literal named **reg** that matches the occurrence of every new line character. (*Hint*: Use the \n escape sequence to represent the new line character.)
    b. Use the replace() method with the reg regular expression object to replace every occurrence of the new line character in the data[7] text string with the substring <br />. Store the revised text string in a variable named **address**.
    c. Write the address variable to the document.
13. Write the remaining field values to the remaining table cells. Use data[9] for the e-mail address; data[11], data[13], and data[15] for the phone number; data[17] for the number of banquet guests; and data[19] for ACGIP membership.
14. Save your changes to the file.
15. Reopen **conf.htm** in your Web browser. Fill out the form correctly, including a multi-line address in the address field. Submit the form. Verify that the field values and total cost of the conference are written to the table cells on the summary page. Also verify that the summary page retains the line breaks in the address field.
16. Submit your completed files to your instructor.

Create | Case Problem 4

Create an order form for a commercial Web site.

Data Files needed for this Case Problem: back.jpg, functions.js, info.txt, logo.jpg,

Wizard Works Wizard Works is a leading seller of custom and brand name fireworks in the United States. Roger Blaine supervises the company's Web site development team. He asks you to work on the order form for the company's line of custom fountains. Roger wants the following elements to appear on the form:

- Data entry fields from which the customer can select an item to order and the quantity of the item
- Data entry fields from which the customer can select a shipping option (standard for $4.95, express for $8.95, or next day for $12.95)
- Data entry fields for the customer's first name, last name, address, and phone number
- Data entry fields for the customer's credit card type (Wizard Works accepts American Express, Diners Club, Discover, MasterCard, and Visa), name of the cardholder, credit card number, and expiration date

The final design of the order form is up to you. Roger has provided several files to aid you in creating the order form. You can supplement this material with material of your own.

Complete the following:

1. Use your text editor to create the following files: **works.htm**, **done.htm**, **ww.css**, and **valid.js**. Enter a comment section in each file describing the purpose of the file and containing ***your name*** and ***the date***.
2. Using the material found in the **info.txt** file in the tutorial.14/case4 folder, create the content for the works.htm file. Place the design styles in the ww.css file. Place the JavaScript code to work with the order in the valid.js file. Note that another JavaScript file, functions.js, is also available for your use in creating your Web page.
3. Add links to the works.htm file connecting that document to the ww.css file, the valid.js file, and the functions.js file.
4. Design the form so that it opens the done.htm file using the post method when the form is successfully submitted to the browser. Edit the done.htm file, so that it displays a message that the order form has been correctly filled out.
5. Go to the valid.js file and create functions to do the following:
   a. Automatically calculate the total cost of the order, including the shipping cost. The cost of the order should be formatted to two decimal places.
   b. Confirm that the customer has ordered an item, selected a quantity, specified a shipping option, and entered a first name, last name, address, phone number, cardholder name, and card number.
   c. Confirm that the phone number uses one of the following patterns: *(ddd) ddd-dddd, ddd-ddd-dddd, or ddd ddd dddd.*
   d. Confirm that the customer has selected a credit card type, entered a credit card name, and entered a credit card number that both matches the number pattern for the selected card and fulfills the Luhn Formula.
   e. Use regular expressions to test whether the credit card numbers match the card patterns specified by the card company. See the info.txt file for information on the appropriate number patterns for each card.
   f. If the form is valid, have the browser submit the form; otherwise, indicate to the customer that the form is invalid.
6. Test your Web form, verifying that it performs all calculations and validation tasks correctly. You can use the list of credit card numbers shown in Figure 14-61 to test your validation rules for both the pattern of the numbers and the numbers' adherence to the Luhn Formula.
7. Submit your completed files to your instructor.

Review | Quick Check Answers

Session 14.1

1. `document.forms[1]`
2. `document.forms["register"].elements["lastname"]`

   or

   `document.register.lastname`
3. `document.register.lastname.value = "Carol Campbell";`
4. `document.register.lastname.focus();`

5. `document.register.statename.option[3]`
6. `document.register.statename.selectedIndex`
7. `document.register.contactme.checked`
8. `3.14159.toFixed(2)`

Session 14.2

1. Server-side validation is validation that occurs on the Web server. Client-side validation is the validation of a data entry form that occurs on the user's Web browser.
2. `formObj.onsubmit = testForm;`
3. `username.length`
4. `username.charAt(0)`

   `username.charAt(username.length-1)`
5. `username.slice(0,5)`
6. `words = email.split("@")`

   words[0] contains the *username*; words[1] contains the *domain*
7. `email.indexOf("gov")`
8. `username.toUpperCase()`

Session 14.3

1. `/GPS/gi`
2. `/\bproducts\b/`
3. `/^\d{9}$/`
4. `/^\d{9}$|^\d{3}-\d{2}-\d{4}$/`

   or

   `/^\d{3}-?\d{2}-?\d{4}$/`

   Other solutions are also possible.
5. `/(street|avenue|lane)/ig`
6. `reuser.test(username)`
7. `date.split(/\//g)`
8. The Luhn Formula is a formula developed by a group of mathematicians in the 1960s to provide a quick validation check for a number string. It calculates the sum of digits in an account number to verify that the number is valid.
9. `location.search`

Ending Data Files

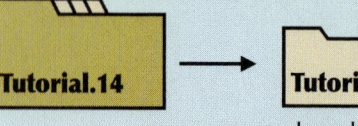

Tutorial.14 →

Tutorial
- done.htm
- form1.htm
- form2.htm
- form3.htm
- contact.js
- order.js
- payment.js
- gpsware.css
- + 2 graphic files

Review
- done.htm
- order.htm
- form.js
- gps.css
- + 2 graphic files

Case1
- mpl.htm
- links.js
- mplstyles.css
- mpl.jpg

Case2
- done.htm
- exp.htm
- report.js
- exp.css
- + 3 graphic files

Case3
- conf.htm
- summary.htm
- forms.js
- conf.css
- summary.css
- + 4 graphic files

Case4
- done.htm
- works.htm
- functions.js
- valid.js
- ww.css
- + 2 graphic files

Objectives

Session 15.1
- Compare the IE and W3C event models
- Study how events propagate under both event models
- Write a cross-browser function to capture and remove event handlers

Session 15.2
- Study the properties of the event object
- Reference the event object under both event models
- Retrieve information about the mouse pointer

Session 15.3
- Work with the cursor style
- Capture keyboard events
- Halt the propagation of events under both event models
- Prevent the default action associated with an event

Working with the Event Model

Creating a Drag-and-Drop Jigsaw Puzzle

Case | Kiddergarden

Peter Burnham is the owner of Kiddergarden, a family-friendly Web site containing games, puzzles, stories, and other activities for young children and their parents. Pete recently asked you to help develop content for the site. One of the first projects he wants you to create is an online jigsaw puzzle.

To create the jigsaw puzzle with JavaScript, you need to write code that allows the user to drag and drop objects from one location on the Web page to another. Creating this effect requires you to work with the properties and features of the JavaScript event model, as the layout of the page responds to the actions of the user's mouse.

Starting Data Files

Tutorial.15 →

Tutorial
jigsawtxt.htm
jpuzzletxt.js
kgfunctxt.js
kg.css
+ 29 graphic files

Review
blockstxt.htm
libtxt.js
slidetxt.js
sbblocks.css
+ 29 graphic files

Case1
booktxt.htm
comtxt.js
bw.css
+ 2 graphic files

Case2
badgertxt.htm
flibtxt.js
slidetxt.js
styles.css
+ 15 graphic files

Case3
crosstxt.htm
makepuzzle.js
runtxt.js
pcg.css
puzzle.css
+ 4 graphic files

Case4
library.js
pm.txt
+ 18 graphic files

Session 15.1

Setting up the Jigsaw Puzzle

Pete has started working on the online jigsaw puzzle. He has already designed the Web page on which you will insert the puzzle. He also has already created some of the scripts to set up the puzzle. Before starting, you'll review his work.

To view Pete's files:

1. Use your text editor to open the **jigsawtxt.htm**, **jpuzzletxt.js**, and **kgfunctxt.js** files from the tutorial.15/tutorial folder, enter ***your name*** and ***the date*** in the comment section of each file, and then save the files as **jigsaw.htm**, **jpuzzle.js**, and **kgfunctions.js**, respectively.
2. Return to the **jigsaw.htm** file in your text editor.
3. Study the contents of the file, paying attention to the document's structure.
4. Open **jigsaw.htm** in your Web browser. Figure 15-1 shows the initial layout and contents of the file.

Figure 15-1 Initial jigsaw.htm page

The puzzle is divided into two sections. The left section contains the puzzle grid. Each square in the puzzle grid is represented by a div element positioned absolutely on the page. There are 25 grid pieces with IDs of grid0 through grid24. Each grid piece belongs to the grid class. The styles to place the grid pieces are defined in the kg.css style sheet.

The right section includes 25 div elements that will contain the individual puzzle pieces. The 25 pieces have IDs ranging from piece0 through piece24, each belonging to the pieces class. Like the grid squares, the puzzle pieces have been placed on the Web page using absolute positioning. At this point, no images are displayed on the puzzle pieces. Pete already split the puzzle image into 25 equally sized JPEG files named piece0.jpg through piece24.jpg. To display these images on the puzzle pieces, you'll set the background-image style of each piece to point to a different JPEG file.

Pete has written a function in the jpuzzle.js file to initialize the properties of the grid and puzzle pieces. The current code in the file includes the following:

```
var grids = new Array();
var pieces = new Array();

window.onload = init;

function init() {
   var allElem = document.getElementsByTagName("*");

   for (var i = 0; i < allElem.length; i++) {
      if (allElem[i].className == "grid") grids.push(allElem[i]);
      if (allElem[i].className == "pieces") pieces.push(allElem[i]);
   }

}
```

The code populates the grids and pieces array with elements that have class names of grid and pieces, respectively. To add background images to the 25 elements in the pieces array, you can add the following loop to the init() function:

```
for (var i = 0; i < pieces.length; i++) {
   pieces[i].style.backgroundImage = "url(piece" + i + ".jpg)";
}
```

You'll insert this code in the jpuzzle.js file, and then link this script file to the jigsaw.htm page.

To apply background images to the puzzle pieces:

1. Return to the **jpuzzle.js** file in your text editor.
2. Within the init() function, insert the following for loop, as shown in Figure 15-2:

```
for (var i = 0; i < pieces.length; i++) {
   pieces[i].style.backgroundImage = "url(piece" + i + ".jpg)";
}
```

Figure 15-2 Code to add background images to the puzzle pieces

```
function init() {

   var allElem = document.getElementsByTagName("*");

   for (var i = 0; i < allElem.length; i++) {
      if (allElem[i].className == "grid") grids.push(allElem[i]);
      if (allElem[i].className == "pieces") pieces.push(allElem[i]);
   }

   for (var i = 0; i < pieces.length; i++) {
      pieces[i].style.backgroundImage = "url(piece" + i + ".jpg)";
   }
}
```

sets the background image for each puzzle piece

3. Save your changes to the file.
4. Return to the **jigsaw.htm** file in your text editor.
5. Within the head section of the file, insert a script element to link the Web page to the jpuzzle.js script file.
6. Save your changes to the file, and then reload **jigsaw.htm** in your Web browser. The 25 puzzle pieces display a different background image, presenting the complete puzzle to the user. See Figure 15-3.

Figure 15-3 Jigsaw puzzle image

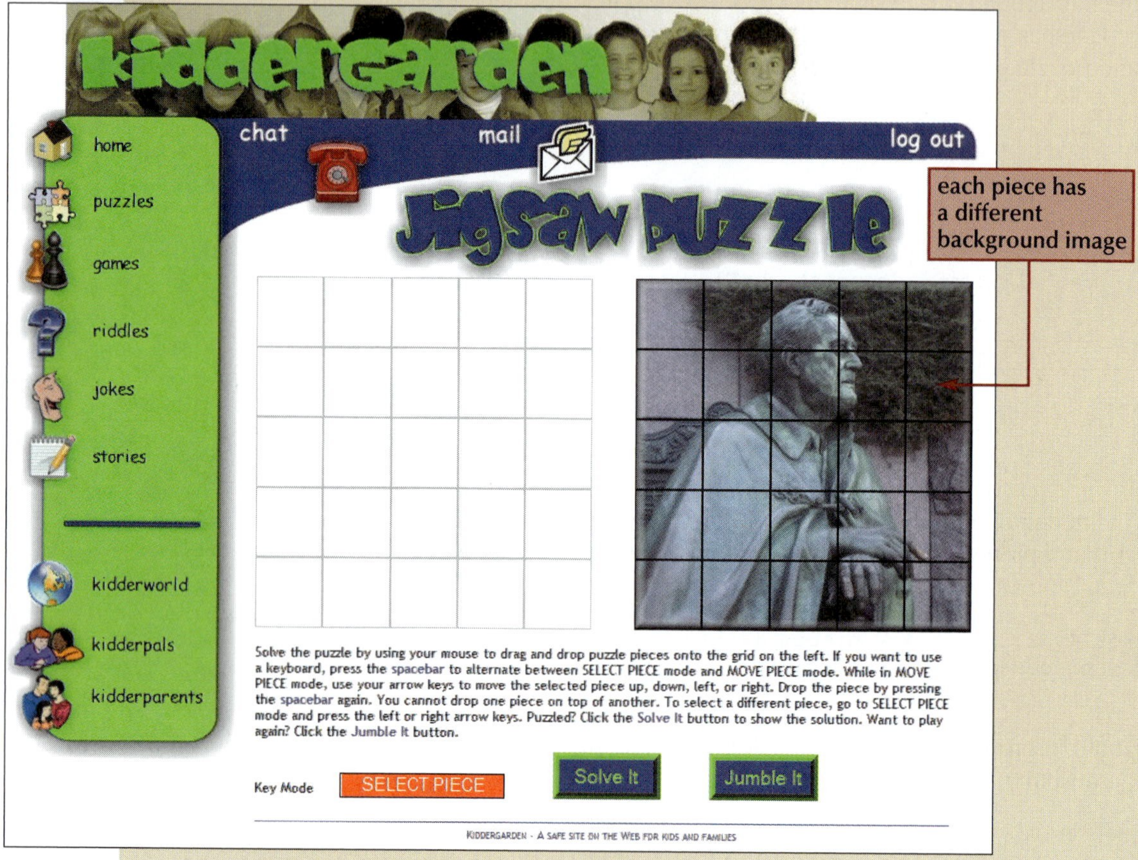

Pete wants the background images to appear in random order. To do this, you'll create an array of integers from 0 up to the number of puzzle pieces, sorted in random order. Pete has already written code to randomize the contents of an array. The code

```
function randomArray(size) {
   var ra = new Array(size);
   for (var i = 0; i < ra.length; i++) ra[i] = i;
   ra.sort(randOrder);
   return ra;
}

function randOrder() {
   return 0.5 - Math.random();
 }
```

contains a function named randomArray() that returns an array of integers ranging from 0 up to the value of the size parameter in random order. Pete saved this function and other functions in the kgfunctions.js file. The kgfunctions.js file will act as a library of functions that Pete can use in a variety of programs. You'll link the jigsaw.htm file to this script file and use the randomArray() function to randomize the order of the puzzle piece images.

To randomize the order of the puzzle piece images:

1. Return to the **jpuzzle.js** file in your text editor, and then scroll down to the init() function.
2. Directly before the second for loop that sets up the background images, add the following line to create an array of random integers ranging from 0 up to the length of the pieces array:

   ```
   var randomIntegers = randomArray(pieces.length);
   ```

3. In the command to set the background image, change `i` to the following:

   ```
   randomIntegers[i]
   ```

   Figure 15-4 highlights the newly inserted and revised code in the file.

Figure 15-4 Code to create random background images

```
for (var i = 0; i < allElem.length; i++) {
   if (allElem[i].className == "grid") grids.push(allElem[i]);
   if (allElem[i].className == "pieces") pieces.push(allElem[i]);
}

var randomIntegers = randomArray(pieces.length);
for (var i = 0; i < pieces.length; i++) {
   pieces[i].style.backgroundImage = "url(piece" + randomIntegers[i] + ".jpg)";
}
```

creates an array of random integers from 0 up to pieces.length

random integer

4. Save your changes to the file.
5. Return to the **jigsaw.htm** file in your text editor, and then insert a script element in the head section of the file, linking the file to the kgfunctions.js file.
6. Close the file, saving your changes, and then reload **jigsaw.htm** in your Web browser. The puzzle piece images are randomized. See Figure 15-5.

Figure 15-5 Puzzle pieces in jumbled order

Trouble? If the pieces on your Web page do not match the placement shown in Figure 15-5, this is because the pieces are displayed in random order.

Finally, the code to manage the jigsaw puzzle requires you to work with the position and dimensions of the grid and puzzle pieces. Pete placed this information in the kg.css file. This information is not available to the JavaScript code unless you retrieve it. The kgfunctions.js file contains the following function to retrieve the value of any style applied to a specified object:

```
function getStyle(object, styleName) {
   if (window.getComputedStyle) {
      return document.defaultView.getComputedStyle(object,
null).getPropertyValue(styleName);
   } else if (object.currentStyle) {
      return object.currentStyle[styleName]
   }
}
```

In this function, the object parameter refers to an object in the current document and the styleName parameter is the name of a CSS style. Recall that the W3C DOM and the IE DOM use different approaches to retrieve calculated styles from the browser. The W3C DOM uses the getComputedStyle and getPropertyValue methods, whereas the IE DOM uses the currentStyle method. This function uses object detection to apply whichever method is supported by the user's browser.

Tip

Make the JavaScript code as generic as possible so it can be applied to a variety of Web pages and layouts. Confine code that explicitly defines an object's size or Web page position to the page's style sheet. The number of objects within a collection should be determined solely by the code for the HTML file.

To retrieve the value of the width property for the first puzzle piece in Pete's document, you could apply the following expression:

```
getStyle(pieces[0],"width");
```

You'll add code to the init() function in the jpuzzle.js that loops through each puzzle piece and grid object, and applies the getStyle() function to retrieve and set the top, left, width, and height style values for each item.

To retrieve and set the size and location of the grid and puzzle pieces:

1. Return to the **jpuzzle.js** file in your text editor.
2. Add the following code to the second for loop within the init() function to retrieve and set the top, left, width, and height style values for each puzzle piece:

```
pieces[i].style.top = getStyle(pieces[i],"top");
pieces[i].style.left = getStyle(pieces[i],"left");
pieces[i].style.width = getStyle(pieces[i],"width");
pieces[i].style.height = getStyle(pieces[i],"height");
```

3. Insert the following for loop at the bottom of the init() function to retrieve and set the top, left, width, and height style values for each grid object:

```
for (var i = 0; i < grids.length; i++) {
   grids[i].style.top = getStyle(grids[i],"top");
   grids[i].style.left = getStyle(grids[i],"left");
   grids[i].style.width = getStyle(grids[i],"width");
   grids[i].style.height = getStyle(grids[i],"height");
}
```

Figure 15-6 shows the inserted code.

Figure 15-6 Code to retrieve and set the size and location styles

```
  var randomIntegers = randomArray(pieces.length);
  for (var i = 0; i < pieces.length; i++) {
     pieces[i].style.backgroundImage = "url(piece" + randomIntegers[i] + ".jpg)";
     pieces[i].style.top = getStyle(pieces[i],"top");
     pieces[i].style.left = getStyle(pieces[i],"left");
     pieces[i].style.width = getStyle(pieces[i],"width");
     pieces[i].style.height = getStyle(pieces[i],"height");
  }

  for (var i = 0; i < grids.length; i++) {
     grids[i].style.top = getStyle(grids[i],"top");
     grids[i].style.left = getStyle(grids[i],"left");
     grids[i].style.width = getStyle(grids[i],"width");
     grids[i].style.height = getStyle(grids[i],"height");
  }
}
```

retrieves and sets the postion and size of each puzzle piece

retrieves and sets the position and size of each grid object

the getStyle() function retrieves the style values from the style sheet

4. Save your changes to the file.

At this point, you've retrieved and set all of the properties for the puzzle pieces and grid on Pete's jigsaw puzzle page. Your next task is to start writing code so the user can interact with those objects.

Introducing the Event Model

Pete sketched his idea for the operation of the jigsaw puzzle, as shown in Figure 15-7. He wants users to be able to drag each puzzle piece from its initial location in the right section of the page onto one of the 25 grid pieces in the left section. Clicking a piece selects it, the motions of the mouse pointer move the piece, and then releasing the mouse button drops the piece in its new location on the page.

Figure 15-7 **Puzzle piece being dragged onto the grid**

To give users this ability, the code must be able to change the position of the selected puzzle piece based on the motions of the pointer. This requires the code to work with the actions and events associated with the user's mouse.

So far, you have worked with user-initiated events in two ways. One way is by adding an on*event* attribute to the HTML code of the document. The code

```
<div id = "piece0" class = "pieces" onclick = "movePiece()">
</div>
```

binds a function named movePiece() to the action of clicking the piece0 object. One problem with this approach is that it places JavaScript code directly in the HTML file, whereas ideally page content and the code that modifies it should be separated as much as possible.

The second way is by applying an event handler as a value of the onclick property, as in the following JavaScript statement:

```
pieces[0].onclick = movePiece;
```

This way of applying an event handler is also known as **traditional binding** because it binds the movePiece() function to the click action. In most cases, traditional binding works well, but it is limited to binding only one function with a specific event. For example, the statements

```
pieces[0].onclick = movePiece;
pieces[0].onclick = dropPiece;
```

contradict each other under traditional binding. The last event handler specified in the code supersedes any earlier event handlers. In this case, the browser will run only the dropPiece() function in response to the click event on pieces[0]. If you're working on a small contained Web site, this problem may be manageable. The problem becomes unmanageable, however, if you are working on a large sprawling Web site that involves hundreds or thousands of files. When you apply an event handler using traditional binding, you might not even be aware that you're overwriting another event handler elsewhere in the site.

One way of dealing with this problem is to place the two functions within a third function that is then attached to the event. The following code shows an example of this approach:

```
pieces[0].onclick = runProgram;

function runProgram() {
   movePiece();
   dropPiece();
}
```

This approach works as long as the code does not need to use the `this` keyword. Recall that the `this` keyword returns the object that called the event handler. In most programs involving event handlers, you want to know this information. In the previous code samples, pieces[0] was the object that invoked the event handler, so you could always reference it using the `this` keyword. In this case, the movePiece() and dropPiece() functions are not directly called by the pieces[0] object, but rather by the runProgram() function. This makes a big difference in how the `this` keyword is interpreted because now it doesn't refer to pieces[0] at all, but instead refers to the object in which the runProgram() function resides, which for JavaScript is the window object. So with this code, there is no immediate way of associating the movePiece() and dropPiece() functions with the object that initiated them, which would be a problem if your program requires that information.

InSight | Using Anonymous Functions and Event Handlers

Another type of function supported by JavaScript is an anonymous function. As the name implies, an **anonymous function** is a function without a name. The general syntax of an anonymous function is

```
function (parameters) {
    function code
}
```

where *parameters* are the parameters of the function and *function code* are the commands executed by the function. The advantage of anonymous functions is that you can insert them anywhere you would place an expression. For example, if you want to display a couple of alert boxes when the Web page is loaded, you could put the command to display the alert boxes in the following statement:

```
window.onload = function () {
    alert("Page Loaded");
    alert("Proceed with data entry");
}
```

You will often find anonymous functions used with event handlers in situations where the function code needs to be run only once and nowhere else in the code. Rather than cluttering the code with additional functions, you can keep all of the function commands directly inline with the event handler.

The W3C and IE Event Models

Because of the limitations associated with traditional binding of events and objects, a third approach to working with user-initiated events is to use an **event model**, which is a model that describes how events interact with objects. There are two event models. One used by the World Wide Web Consortium (W3C) and the other used by the Internet Explorer browser. Because these event models are incompatible in many areas, your JavaScript code needs to reconcile the differences between the two models. The **IE event model** is supported by Internet Explorer and Opera. The **W3C event model** is supported by Firefox, Netscape, Safari, Opera, and other major browsers.

One key difference involves how events are initiated and propagated throughout the document.

Event Bubbling and Event Capturing

Consider the object hierarchy shown in Figure 15-8 that involves several nested objects. If the user clicks the innermost span object, which element receives the click event? Under the IE event model, each object receives the event though at different points in time.

Event bubbling in the IE event model **Figure 15-8**

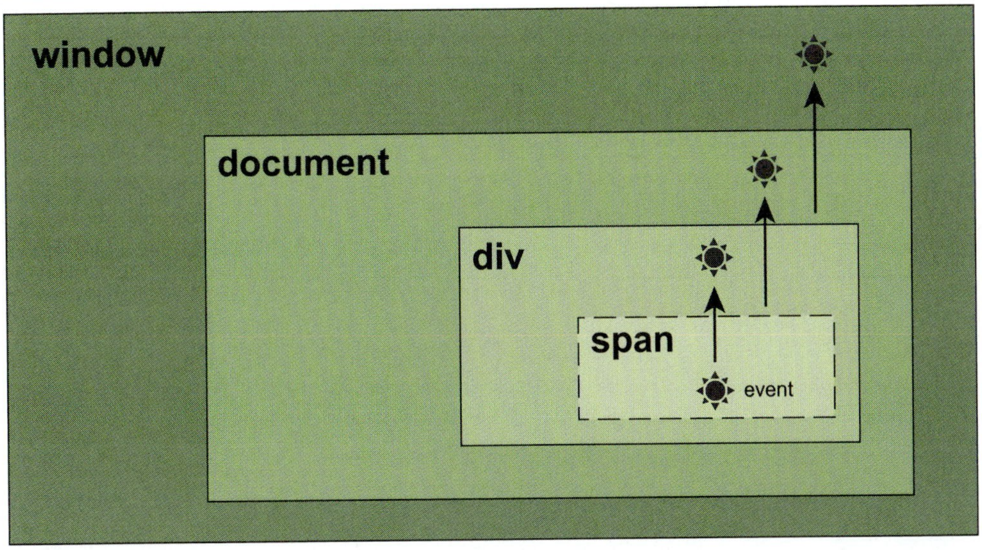

Internet Explorer does this by applying **event bubbling**, in which an event is initiated at the bottom of the object tree and rises to the top of the hierarchy. As shown in Figure 15-8, the event is first recognized by the span object, then the div object, then the Web page document, and finally the browser window itself.

Another way of propagating events through the document is by event capturing, as shown in Figure 15-9. In **event capturing**, events are initiated at the top of the object hierarchy and drop down the object tree to the lowest object. In Figure 15-9, the window object is the first object in which the event is noticed, followed by the document object, then the div element, and finally the span element. Event capturing is not supported in the IE event model but was introduced in an early version of the Netscape browser.

Event capturing **Figure 15-9**

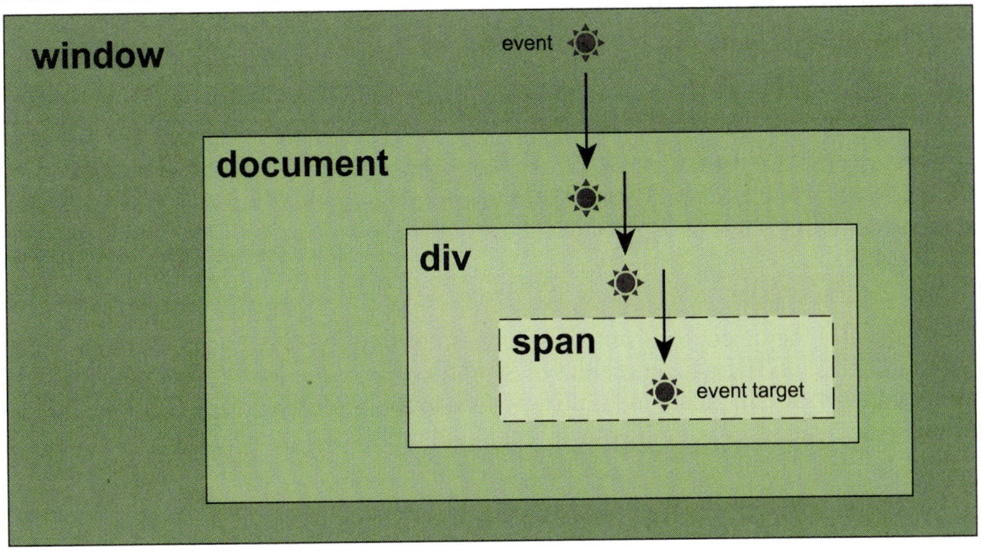

The W3C event model supports both event bubbling and event capturing, as shown in Figure 15-10. Under the W3C event model, an event starts at the top of the object hierarchy and moves down the object tree until it reaches the target of the event. At that point, the event bubbles back up the object hierarchy.

Figure 15-10 **Event propagation in the W3C event model**

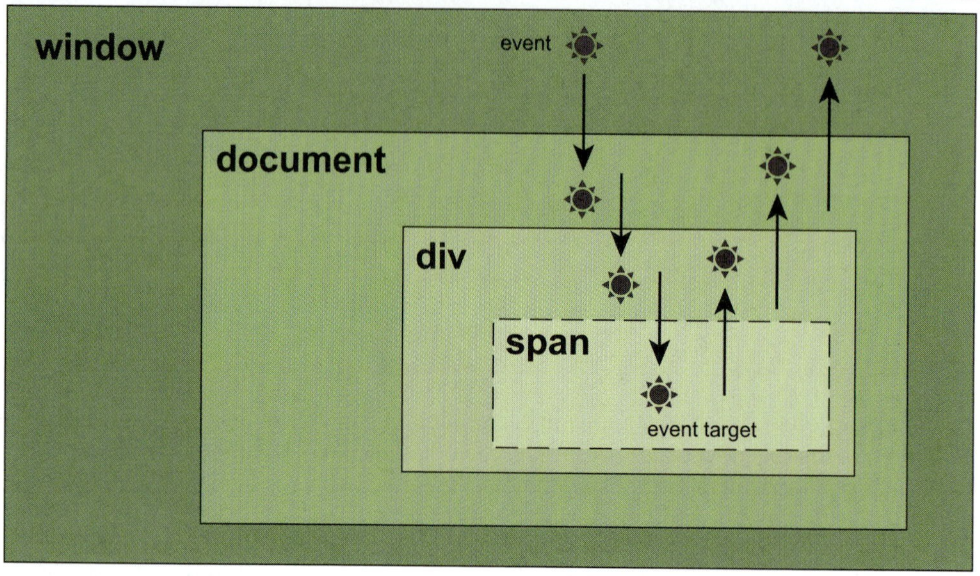

Under the W3C event model, the progress that an event makes through the DOM is split into three phases:

- A **capture phase** as the event moves down the object hierarchy
- A **target phase** in which the event reaches the object from which the event originated
- A **bubbling phase** in which the event moves back up the object hierarchy

The W3C event model is particularly powerful because it allows you to run a function that responds to an event at any phase in this process.

Tip

The order in which an event ascends and descends through the objects in the DOM is based on the object hierarchy, not the placement of the objects on the Web page.

Attaching and Listening for Events

As an event propagates through the object hierarchy (either by bubbling or capturing or both), you can use JavaScript to assign a function to the event as it passes. The IE event model accomplishes this using the attachEvent method

```
object.attachEvent(onevent, function)
```

where *object* is the object receiving the event, on*event* is the text string describing the event, and *function* is the function that runs in response to the event. Unlike traditional event binding, you can attach multiple functions to the same event. For example, the following code attaches both the movePiece() and dropPiece() functions to the action of clicking the pieces[0] object:

```
pieces[0].attachEvent("onclick", movePiece);
pieces[0].attachEvent("onclick", dropPiece);
```

When the pieces[0] object is clicked, both functions will be run in response. So there is no problem with one event handler overwriting another.

The W3C event model does not support the attachEvent method. Instead, it uses the addEventListener method

```
object.addEventListener(event, function, capture)
```

where *object* is the object receiving the event, *event* is a text string naming the event, *function* is a function that runs in response to the event, and *capture* is a Boolean value that tells the browser when to listen for the occurrence of the event. A *capture* value of true tells the browser to listen for the event during the capture phase, whereas a *capture* value of false tells the browser to listen during the bubbling phase. To run both the movePiece() and dropPiece() functions under the W3C event model, you could apply the following code:

```
pieces[0].addEventListener("click", movePiece, false);
pieces[0].addEventListener("click", dropPiece, false);
```

In this case, both functions would run in response to a mouse click event occurring within the pieces[0] object. Note that the *capture* value is set to false for both event handlers so that the functions are triggered during the bubbling phase.

For the jigsaw puzzle page, you'll reconcile the syntax difference between the IE and W3C event models using the following addEvent() function:

```
function addEvent(object, evName, fnName, cap) {
   if (object.attachEvent)
       object.attachEvent("on" + evName, fnName);
   else if (object.addEventListener)
       object.addEventListener(evName, fnName, cap);
}
```

The function has four parameters: object representing the object receiving the event, evName containing the name of the event, fnName specifying the function associated with the event, and cap specifying whether the event is in the capture phase or the bubbling phase. Note that the function uses object detection to determine which event model is supported by the user's browser. You can apply this function to the click events for the pieces[0] object as follows

```
addEvent(pieces[0], "click", movePiece, false);
addEvent(pieces[0], "click", dropPiece, false);
```

and the browser will correctly bind the two functions to the click event under either event model.

You'll add this function to the kgfunctions.js file.

> **Tip**
>
> The attachEvent method identifies events with the name on*event*; the addEventListener method uses the event name *event* without the "on" prefix. Label events for the IE event model as onclick or onload, and use click or load for the W3C event model. Event names should be in lowercase letters.

To insert the addEvent() function:

1. Go to the **kgfunctions.js** file in your text editor.
2. Scroll to the bottom of the file, and then insert the following code, as shown in Figure 15-11:

```
function addEvent(object, evName, fnName, cap) {
   if (object.attachEvent)
       object.attachEvent("on" + evName, fnName);
   else if (object.addEventListener)
       object.addEventListener(evName, fnName, cap);
}
```

Figure 15-11 **Code to add event handlers with the addEvent() function**

```
function randOrder(){
   return 0.5 - Math.random();
}

function addEvent(object, evName, fnName, cap) {
   if (object.attachEvent)
       object.attachEvent("on" + evName, fnName);
   else if (object.addEventListener)
       object.addEventListener(evName, fnName, cap);
}
```

attaches a function to the event under the IE event model

adds an event to the function under the W3C event model

Removing Events

Both event models allow you to remove event handlers from objects. The IE event model uses the detachEvent method

```
object.detachEvent(onevent, function)
```

where again *object* is the object in which the event occurs, *event* is the name of the event, and *function* is the function previously attached to the object. To detach the movePiece() function from the mouse click event on pieces[0], you run the following command:

```
pieces[0].detachEvent("onclick", movePiece);
```

The W3C event model employs the removeEventListener method

```
object.removeEventListener(event, function, capture)
```

where *object, event, function,* and *capture* have the same meanings as they did for the addEventListener method. Likewise, the command

```
pieces[0].removeEventListener("click", movePiece, false);
```

removes the click event handler from the pieces[0] object, but only during the bubbling phase of the event model. An event handler that was added for the capture phase would not be affected by this command.

To create a function to remove event handlers from an object that works for both event models, you use object detection, as shown in the following code:

```
function removeEvent(object, evName, fnName, cap) {
   if (object.detachEvent)
       object.detachEvent("on" + evName, fnName);
   else if (object.removeEventListener)
       object.removeEventListener(evName, fnName, cap);
}
```

You will add this function to the kgfunctions.js file.

To insert the removeEvent() function:

1. Scroll to the bottom of the **kgfunctions.js** file, and then insert the following code below the addEvent() function, as shown in Figure 15-12:

```
function removeEvent(object, evName, fnName, cap) {
   if (object.detachEvent)
       object.detachEvent("on" + evName, fnName);
   else if (object.removeEventListener)
       object.removeEventListener(evName, fnName, cap);
}
```

Figure 15-12 Code to remove event handlers with the removeEvent() function

```
function addEvent(object, evName, fnName, cap) {
   if (object.attachEvent)
      object.attachEvent("on" + evName, fnName);
   else if (object.addEventListener)
      object.addEventListener(evName, fnName, cap);
}

function removeEvent(object, evName, fnName, cap) {
   if (object.detachEvent)
      object.detachEvent("on" + evName, fnName);
   else if (object.removeEventListener)
      object.removeEventListener(evName, fnName, cap);
}
```

removes a function from the event under the IE event model

removes a function from an event under the W3C event model

2. Save your changes to the file.

You will verify that the cross-browser functions work by creating a simple function to display an alert dialog box whenever the user presses the mouse button within one of those puzzle pieces.

To test the addEvent() function:

1. Return to the **jpuzzle.js** file in your text editor.
2. Add the following line to the second for loop that sets the properties of the items in the pieces array:

```
addEvent(pieces[i], "mousedown", mouseGrab, false);
```

3. Directly below the init() function, insert the following function:

```
function mouseGrab() {
   alert("Puzzle piece clicked");
}
```

Figure 15-13 highlights the code added to the file.

Figure 15-13 Code to respond to the mousedown event with the mouseGrab() function

```
    var randomIntegers = randomArray(pieces.length);
    for (var i = 0; i < pieces.length; i++) {
       pieces[i].style.backgroundImage = "url(piece" + randomIntegers[i] + ".jpg)";
       pieces[i].style.top = getStyle(pieces[i],"top");
       pieces[i].style.left = getStyle(pieces[i],"left");
       pieces[i].style.width = getStyle(pieces[i],"width");
       pieces[i].style.height = getStyle(pieces[i],"height");

       addEvent(pieces[i], "mousedown", mouseGrab, false);
    }

    for (var i = 0; i < grids.length; i++) {
       grids[i].style.top = getStyle(grids[i],"top");
       grids[i].style.left = getStyle(grids[i],"left");
       grids[i].style.width = getStyle(grids[i],"width");
       grids[i].style.height = getStyle(grids[i],"height");
    }

}

function mouseGrab() {
   alert("Puzzle piece clicked");
}
```

runs the mouseGrab() function in response to pressing the mouse button down within the puzzle piece

mouseGrab() function

4. Save your changes to the file, and then reload **jigsaw.htm** in your Web browser.
5. Click the puzzle pieces on the page and verify that each time you press the mouse button on a piece, an alert dialog box appears.

Reference Window | Working with Document Events

IE Event Model

- To attach a function to an object, run
  `object.attachEvent(onevent, function);`
  where *object* is the object receiving the event, on*event* is the text string of the event handler, and *function* is the function that runs in response to the event. Multiple functions can be attached to the same event in the same object.
- To detach a function, run the following:
  `object.detachEvent(onevent, function);`

W3C Event Model

- To run a function when an event reaches an object, use
  `object.addEventListener(event, function, capture);`
  where *object* is the object receiving the event, *event* is the text string describing the event, *function* is the function to run in response to the event, and *capture* equals true if the event is moving down the document tree and false if the event is bubbling up the tree.
- To stop listening for an event, run the following:
  `object.removeEventListener(event, function, capture);`

Tracking Event Handlers | InSight

Complex applications may have several event handlers associated with each object. For some applications, you may need to know whether a function has already been attached to an event. With traditional event binding, you can determine this by examining the event handler property. For example, if you create the following event handler for the pieces[0] array object

```
pieces[0].onclick = movePiece;
```

you can display the contents of the movePiece() function in an alert box using the following command:

```
alert(pieces[0].onclick)
```

If the expression returns a null or undefined value, you know that no function has been registered with the event. If a function has been registered with the event, the alert box will display the function's code.

The situation is different with the attachEvent or addEvent methods. With those methods, you cannot retrieve a list of functions registered with that event. This issue is dealt with in Level 3 of the W3C DOM, which introduces the eventListenerList attribute, which creates a list of event handlers registered to an object. There is not a great deal of browser support for the eventListenerList attribute at the time of this writing, so you should not rely upon it.

In this session, you set up the jigsaw puzzle and added cross-browser functions to handle events in the IE and W3C event models. In the next session, you'll work with mouse events to give users the ability to drag and drop puzzle pieces.

Session 15.1 Quick Check | Review

1. Specify code that uses an anonymous function to display an alert box with the message Click Detected whenever the user clicks the mouse in the Web page document.
2. How do events propagate through the document tree under the IE event model?
3. Under the IE event model, what command attaches the function calcTotal() to the Total object in response to the click event?
4. What command detaches the function in the previous question?
5. Describe how events propagate under the W3C event model.
6. Under the W3C event model, what command runs the calcTotal() function when the Total object is clicked during the bubbling phase?
7. What command removes the function in the previous question?

Session 15.2

Introducing the Event Object

In the previous session, you examined how events propagate and are handled within the IE and W3C event models. However, this is only part of what is involved with an event model. You also need to get information about an event itself. If a user has clicked a mouse button in a document, you may need to know where the pointer was located in the browser window when this happened. If the user has pressed a key on the keyboard, you may want to know which key was pressed. Information about the event is stored in an **event object**. The two event models provide different ways of working with event objects. First, let's look at the event object under the IE event model.

Working with IE Event Object

In the IE event model, the event object has the object reference

```
window.event
```

or, more simply:

```
event
```

Under the IE event model, the event object is a global object—one that is never declared by you, but is accessible in any function you write. This system works because only one event is being processed at any given time in your code. So under the IE event model, there is no need to reference multiple event objects.

The event object supports a wide variety of properties. A partial list is described in Figure 15-14.

Figure 15-14 Common properties of the IE event object

Property	Description
event.button	Returns the number indicating which mouse button the user pressed (1 = left, 2 = right, 4 = middle)
event.cancelBubble	Set this property to true to cancel event bubbling; set it to false to continue event bubbling
event.fromElement	For mouseover and mouseout events, returns the object from which the pointer is moving
event.returnValue	Set this property to false to cancel the default action of the event; set it to true to retain the default action
event.srcElement	Returns the object in which the event was generated
event.toElement	For mouseover and mouseout events, returns the object to which the pointer is moving
event.type	Returns a text string indicating the type of event

Different events can call the same function. For example, your code may call the movePiece() function in response to both a mouse click and the act of pressing down a keyboard key. If you want to know which of these two events initiated the function, you can use the type property, as in the following expression:

```
event.type
```

This expression returns the value click if the function is run in response to the mouse click event, and returns the value keydown if the event that initiated the function is the user pressing a keyboard key down.

Working with the W3C Event Object

The W3C event model uses a different event object than the IE event object. In the W3C event model, the event object is inserted as the parameter of whatever function responds to the event. You can give the event object any parameter name, but the standard practice is to name the parameter e. For example, to run the movePiece() function when a user presses the mouse button anywhere within the document, you could insert the JavaScript commands

```
document.addEventListener("mousedown", movePiece, false);

function mouseGrab(e) {
   commands
}
```

and the browser will run the mouseGrab() function in response to the mousedown event. Information about the event is stored in the e parameter of the mouseGrab() function. Because functions are called by specific events, no confusion exists over which event the e parameter is referring to. Figure 15-15 lists some of the common properties associated with the W3C event object.

Common properties of the W3C event object **Figure 15-15**

Property	Description
evt.bubbles	Returns a Boolean value indicating whether *evt* can bubble
evt.button	Returns the number of the mouse button pressed by the user (0 = left, 1 = middle, 2 = right)
evt.cancelable	Returns a Boolean value indicating whether *evt* can have its default action canceled
evt.currentTarget	Returns the object that is currently handling the event
evt.eventPhase	Returns the phase in the propagation of *evt* (1 = capture, 2 = target, 3 = bubbling)
evt.relatedTarget	For mouseover events, returns the object that the mouse left when it moved over the target of the event; for mouseout events, returns the object that the mouse entered when leaving the target
evt.target	Returns the object that initiated the event
evt.timeStamp	Returns the date and time that the event was initiated
evt.type	Returns a text string indicating the event type

Like the IE event model, the W3C event model supports the type property to return the type of event that called the function. Again, the expression

```
evt.type
```

returns the type of event, where *evt* is the parameter of the event handler function.

Reconciling the Two Event Objects

You can reconcile the two event objects using the || (or) logical operator. The basic code is

```
function function(e) {
   var evt = e || window.event;
   commands
}
```

where *function* is the name of the function called by the event handler. The evt variable stores either the W3C event object as indicated by the e parameter or the window.event object. Thus under either event model, evt will point to the event object. To see this effect in action, revise the mouseGrab() function you created in the previous session to display the type of event initiated by the user.

To revise the mouseGrab() function:

1. If you took a break after the previous session, make sure the jpuzzle.js and kgfunctions.js files are open in a text editor, and the jigsaw.htm file is open in your Web browser.
2. Return to the **jpuzzle.js** file in your text editor.
3. Add the **e** parameter to the mouseGrab() function.
4. Insert the following command in the function:

   ```
   var evt = e || window.event;
   ```

5. Change the command to display the alert box to:

   ```
   alert("Event: " + evt.type);
   ```

   Figure 15-16 highlights the new code in the file.

Figure 15-16 Code to reconcile the two event objects

```
function mouseGrab(e) {
   var evt = e || window.event;

   alert("Event: " + evt.type);
}
```

uses either the e parameter or the window.event object, depending on which is supported by the user's browser

6. Save your changes to the file, and then reload **jigsaw.htm** in your Web browser.
7. Click the puzzle pieces on the page and verify that each time you press the mouse button, an alert dialog box like the one shown in Figure 15-17 appears.

Figure 15-17 Alert dialog box

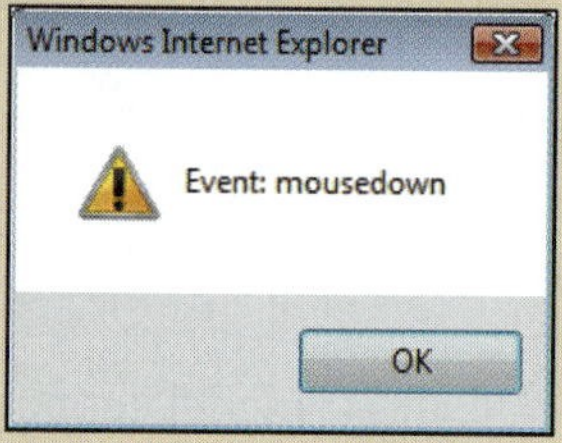

Tip

To ensure that you are fully reconciling the differences between the event models, always test your code with Internet Explorer and a browser that supports the W3C event model, such as Firefox, Opera, or Safari.

Locating the Source of an Event

It is often important to know in what object a particular event was initiated. For the jigsaw puzzle, it will be particularly important to know which of the 25 puzzle pieces were clicked by the user. The IE and W3C event models use different properties to determine the source of an event. Recall that in the IE event model, events bubble up from the first object affected at the bottom of the object tree. That object is the source of the event and is returned by the IE event model's srcElement property.

The W3C event model references the source of an event using the target property, which points to the target of the event as it moves up and down the object tree. You can work with both properties using the || (or) expression, as in the following code:

```
var eventSource = e.target || event.srcElement
```

Here, the browser will use the object reference from the event model it supports. You'll use this expression in the moveGrab() function to store the reference of the puzzle piece clicked by the user in a variable named mousePiece. Because you'll be referencing this piece in other functions, you'll set up the mousePiece variable as a global variable.

To locate the source of the mousedown event:

1. Return to the **jpuzzle.js** file in your text editor, and then directly below the statement to declare the pieces array, insert the following line:

   ```
   var mousePiece = null;
   ```

2. Scroll down the file, and then directly below the statement to declare the evt variable, add the following line to the mouseGrab() function:

   ```
   mousePiece = evt.target || evt.srcElement;
   ```

   You use evt as the object reference because the code already reconciled the difference between the two event models in how they reference the event object.

3. Change the command to display the alert box to the following:

   ```
   alert("Event: " + evt.type + " on " + mousePiece.id);
   ```

   The value of the id property is taken from the id attribute in the jigsaw.htm file. Pieces have id attribute values ranging from piece0 to piece24. Figure 15-18 highlights the changed code.

Figure 15-18 Code to create the mousePiece variable

```
var grids = new Array();
var pieces = new Array();
var mousePiece = null;

function mouseGrab(e) {
   var evt = e || window.event;
   mousePiece = evt.target || evt.srcElement;

   alert("Event: " + evt.type + " on " + mousePiece.id);
}
```

4. Save your changes to the file, and then reload **jigsaw.htm** in your Web browser.

5. Click the puzzle pieces on the page and verify that the browser displays an alert box similar to the one shown in Figure 15-19.

Figure 15-19 Alert dialog box displaying the event and its source

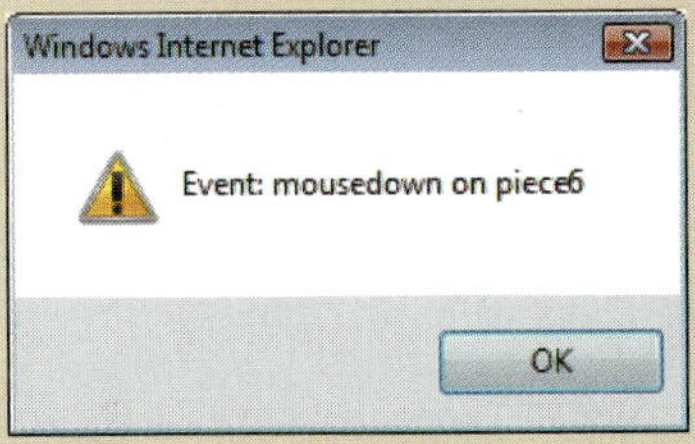

InSight | Event Propagation and the `this` Keyword

Events propagate through the object hierarchy under both event models. In the IE event model, the event bubbles up from the bottom of the object tree. In the W3C event model, events move down and then up the object tree. As you have seen, you can use the IE event model's srcElement property to indicate the source of the event bubbling, or the W3C event model's target property to indicate the target of the event. But how do you track the course of the event as it propagates through the object tree?

Under the W3C event model, the `this` keyword will return the object currently handling the event. You can also use the currentTarget property of the event object to return this information. If you need to know whether the object is reacting to the event during the capture phase or the bubbling phase, you can use the eventPhase property. Thus, under the W3C event model, you can always determine which object is currently handling the event and when it's being handled in the event propagation.

Unfortunately, the IE event model is not so accommodating. Because the window.event object in the IE event model is a global object, it does not contain information about individual objects that may be handling the event as it bubbles through the object hierarchy. The `this` keyword points not to the object handling the event, but rather to the window object. This is a huge limitation of the IE event model. This is not a problem if you use traditional binding in which the `this` keyword will point to the object handling the event, but you have to deal with the limitations of traditional binding, such as the inability to assign more than one function to a particular event.

JavaScript programmers have tackled this problem and have written several customized functions to overcome the limitations of the IE event model and inconsistencies between the two event models. You can find many of these functions on the Web.

Reference Window | Working with the Event Object

IE Event Model

- To reference the event object, use the following property:
  `window.event`
  or
  `event`
- To return the object that initiated the event bubbling, use the following property:
  `event.srcElement`

W3C Event Model

- To reference the event object, use
  `evt`
  where *evt* is the parameter of the function assigned to the event.
- To return the object that initiated an event, use the following property:
  `evt.target`
- To return the object that is currently handling an event, use the property
  `evt.currentTarget`
  or use the keyword
  `this`

Working with Mouse Events

You are ready to write a script to enable users to drag and drop the jigsaw puzzle pieces. You've already created the mouseGrab() function that will run whenever the user presses down the mouse button within one of the puzzle pieces. The function already identifies the piece that was selected by the user; but to create the drag-and-drop effect, you also need to know where on the page the pointer and the piece are located.

Determining the Mouse Position

The location of the puzzle piece is given by the top and left style properties that you retrieved and set in the previous session. The location of the pointer can be determined from the properties of the event object. Not surprisingly, the two event models support different properties to determine an event's location. Figure 15-20 summarizes these properties and their support in the two event models. For actual browser support, you must test these properties against your specific browser.

Figure 15-20 **Location properties of the event object**

Property	Returns	Event Model
evt.clientX *evt*.clientY	Returns the x and y coordinates of the event, *evt*, within the browser window	IE, W3C
evt.screenX *evt*.screenY	Returns the x and y coordinates of the event within the computer screen	IE, W3C
evt.offsetX *evt*.offsetY	Returns the x and y distances of the event from the object in which the event was initiated	IE
evt.x *evt*.y	Returns the x and y coordinates of the event relative to the element that initiated the event	IE
evt.pageX *evt*.pageY	Returns the x and y coordinates of the event within the document	W3C
evt.layerX *evt*.layerY	Returns the x and y coordinates of an event relative to its absolutely positioned parent element	W3C

The only properties supported by both event models are the screenX, screenY and the clientX, clientY properties. The screenX, screenY properties provide the coordinates of the event within the entire computer screen. The clientX, clientY properties provide the location of the event within the browser window.

Only the W3C event model provides the pageX, pageY properties to retrieve the location of the event within the document. Although the IE event model doesn't support the pageX, pageY properties, you can duplicate those values with the following code:

```
pageX = event.clientX +
        document.documentElement.scrollLeft +
        document.body.scrollLeft;
pageY = event.clientY +
        document.documentElement.scrollTop +
        document.body.scrollTop;
```

In this code, the location of the event within the browser window is added to however much of the remaining page is scrolled off to the left or top of the document window. The resulting pageX and pageY values are the x and y coordinates of the event within the entire document.

Tip

All location properties of the event object are measured in pixels.

For the puzzle page, you only need to know the location of the pointer relative to the browser window, not the Web page. You'll use the clientX and clientY properties to record the position of the pointer when the user presses the mouse button on the puzzle piece, storing the coordinates in the mouseX and mouseY variables.

To locate the coordinates of the mousedown event:

1. Return to the **jpuzzle.js** file in your text editor.
2. Directly below the statement that sets the value of the mousePiece variable in the mouseGrab() function, insert the following lines:

```
var mouseX = evt.clientX; // x-coordinate of pointer
var mouseY = evt.clientY; // y-coordinate of pointer
```

3. Delete the line displaying the alert dialog box because you no longer need it in your program. Figure 15-21 shows the revised code of the mouseGrab() function.

Figure 15-21 Code to retrieve the location of the pointer

```
function mouseGrab(e) {
   var evt = e || window.event;
   mousePiece = evt.target || evt.srcElement;

   var mouseX = evt.clientX; // x-coordinate of pointer
   var mouseY = evt.clientY; // y-coordinate of pointer
}
```

position of the pointer at the moment the mouse button is pressed down

The next item to add to the mouseGrab() function is code to calculate the distance between the pointer and the selected puzzle piece. You'll need this information to keep the piece a constant distance from the pointer as it moves across the page. The current coordinates of the puzzle piece are stored in the top and left style properties. Because both these styles and the mouse position are measured in pixels, you can calculate the distance between them using the following statements:

```
diffX = parseInt(mousePiece.style.left) - mouseX;
diffY = parseInt(mousePiece.style.top) - mouseY;
```

Figure 15-22 shows the representation of the diffX and diffY variables based on the layout of the jigsaw puzzle page. Because the left and top style values include the px substring (as in "280px"), you need to use the parseInt method to extract the numeric value of the coordinate.

Figure 15-22 Distance from the pointer to the puzzle piece

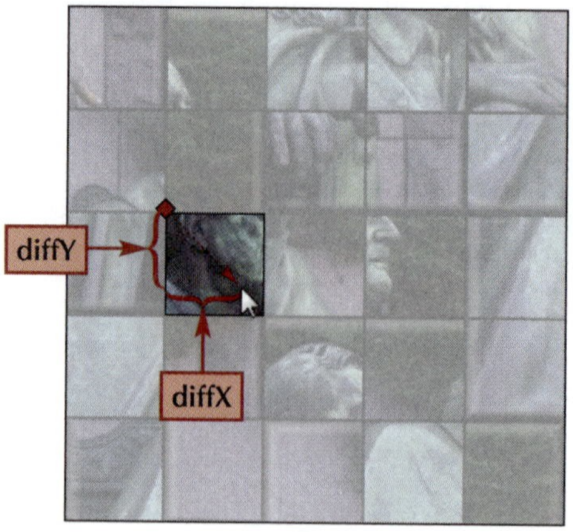

Because diffX and diffY will be used in other functions in this application, you'll declare them as global variables.

To create the diffX and diffY variables:

1. Scroll to the top of the **jpuzzle.js** file, and directly below the declaration of the mousePiece variable, insert the following lines:

```
var diffX = null;
var diffY = null;
```

2. Scroll down and within the mouseGrab() function, insert the following, as shown in Figure 15-23:

```
/* Calculate the distance from the pointer to the piece */
diffX = parseInt(mousePiece.style.left) - mouseX;
diffY = parseInt(mousePiece.style.top) - mouseY;
```

Figure 15-23 Code to calculate the value of the diffX and diffY variables

```
var grids = new Array();
var pieces = new Array();
var mousePiece = null;
var diffX = null;
var diffY = null;
```

```
function mouseGrab(e) {
   var evt = e || window.event;
   mousePiece = evt.target || evt.srcElement;

   var mouseX = evt.clientX; // x-coordinate of pointer
   var mouseY = evt.clientY; // y-coordinate of pointer

   /* Calculate the distance from the pointer to the piece */
   diffX = parseInt(mousePiece.style.left) - mouseX;
   diffY = parseInt(mousePiece.style.top) - mouseY;
}
```

3. Save your changes to the file.

The final task in the mouseGrab() function is to assign event handlers that will run whenever the pointer is moved or the mouse button is released. You'll assign a function named mouseMove() to the action of moving the pointer, and a function named mouseDrop() to the action of releasing the mouse button. The code to assign these two functions is:

```
addEvent(document, "mousemove", mouseMove, false);
addEvent(document, "mouseup", mouseDrop, false);
```

You'll add these two commands to the mouseGrab() function.

To create event handlers for the mousemove and mouseup events:

1. Within the mouseGrab() function, add the following event handlers, as shown in Figure 15-24:

```
/* Add event handlers for mousemove and mouseup events */
addEvent(document, "mousemove", mouseMove, false);
addEvent(document, "mouseup", mouseDrop, false);
```

Figure 15-24 Code to add event handlers for the mousemove and mouseup events

```
function mouseGrab(e) {
   var evt = e || window.event;
   mousePiece = evt.target || evt.srcElement;

   var mouseX = evt.clientX; // x-coordinate of pointer
   var mouseY = evt.clientY; // y-coordinate of pointer

   /* Calculate the distance from the pointer to the piece */
   diffX = parseInt(mousePiece.style.left) - mouseX;
   diffY = parseInt(mousePiece.style.top) - mouseY;

   /* Add event handlers for mousemove and mouseup events */
   addEvent(document, "mousemove", mouseMove, false);
   addEvent(document, "mouseup", mouseDrop, false);
}
```

2. Save your changes to the file. The mouseGrab() function is complete.

Reference Window | Locating an Event

- To locate the x and y coordinates of an event within the computer screen, use the properties
  `evt.screenX`
  `evt.screenY`
  where *evt* is the event object in either the IE or W3C event model.
- To locate the x and y coordinates of an event within the browser window, use the following properties:
  `evt.clientX`
  `evt.clientY`
- To locate the x and y coordinates of an event within the Web page, use the properties
  `evt.pageX`
  `evt.pageY`
  where *evt* is the W3C event object. For the IE event model, use the following expression for the x-coordinate:
  ```
  event.clientX + document.documentElement.scrollLeft
  + document.body.scrollLeft
  ```
  For the y coordinate, use the following expression:
  ```
  event.clientY + document.documentElement.scrollTop
  + document.body.scrollTop;
  ```

Creating a Function for Mouse Movement

Your next task is to create the mouseMove() function, which will allow users to move puzzle pieces from one location to another. To move mousePiece across the Web page, the mouseMove() function needs to perform the following tasks:

- Determine the current location of the pointer.
- Maintain mousePiece at a constant distance from the pointer.

Keeping the piece a constant distance from the pointer as it moves across the page, as shown in Figure 15-25, will create the illusion that the pointer is dragging the puzzle piece.

Puzzle piece maintains a constant distance from the pointer — **Figure 15-25**

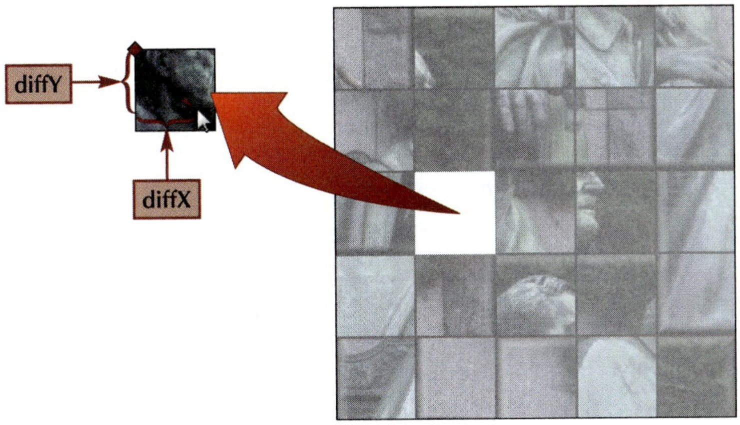

The distance between the puzzle piece and the pointer has already been stored in the diffX and diffY variables calculated in the mouseGrab() function. To set the new location of mousePiece, you add the values of diffX and diffY to the current location of the pointer, using the commands

```
mousePiece.style.left = mouseX + diffX + "px";
mousePiece.style.top = mouseY + diffY + "px";
```

where mouseX and mouseY are the current coordinates of the pointer. You have to add the px unit to the left and top styles to indicate to the browser that these coordinates are measured in pixels.

You'll add these commands to a mouseMove() function that you'll create now.

To create the mouseMove() function:

1. Directly below the mouseGrab() function, insert the following function, as shown in Figure 15-26:

```
function mouseMove(e) {
   var evt = e || window.event;
   var mouseX = evt.clientX;
   var mouseY = evt.clientY;

   mousePiece.style.left = mouseX + diffX + "px";
   mousePiece.style.top = mouseY + diffY + "px";
}
```

Code to move the puzzle piece with the mouseMove() function — **Figure 15-26**

```
   /* Add event handlers for mousemove and mouseup events */
   addEvent(document, "mousemove", mouseMove, false);
   addEvent(document, "mouseup", mouseDrop, false);
}

function mouseMove(e) {
   var evt = e || window.event;
   var mouseX = evt.clientX;
   var mouseY = evt.clientY;

   mousePiece.style.left = mouseX + diffX + "px";
   mousePiece.style.top = mouseY + diffY + "px";
}
```

new location of the puzzle piece

2. Save your changes to the file.

Dropping the Puzzle Piece

The next function to create for the jigsaw puzzle is the mouseDrop() function. This function runs whenever the user releases the mouse button, initiating the mouseup event. In response, the mouseDrop() function will cause the browser to stop running the mouseMove() function. With the mouseMove() function no longer being called, the puzzle piece will stop following the pointer across the page, making it appear that the piece was dropped on the page. To halt the mouseMove() function, you'll use the removeEvent() function you created in the previous session. The code for the mouseDrop() function is:

```
function mouseDrop(e) {
   removeEvent(document, "mousemove", mouseMove, false);
   removeEvent(document, "mouseup", mouseDrop, false);
}
```

This code first removes the event handler for the mousemove event, halting the mouseMove() function. It then removes the event handler for the mouseup event (you want the mouseDrop() function to be run only when you're in the process of moving a puzzle piece). You'll add this function to the jpuzzle.js file.

To create and test the mouseDrop() function:

1. Directly below the mouseMove() function, insert the following function, as shown in Figure 15-27:

```
function mouseDrop(e) {
   removeEvent(document, "mousemove", mouseMove, false);
   removeEvent(document, "mouseup", mouseDrop, false);
}
```

Figure 15-27 Code to drop the puzzle piece with the mouseDrop() function

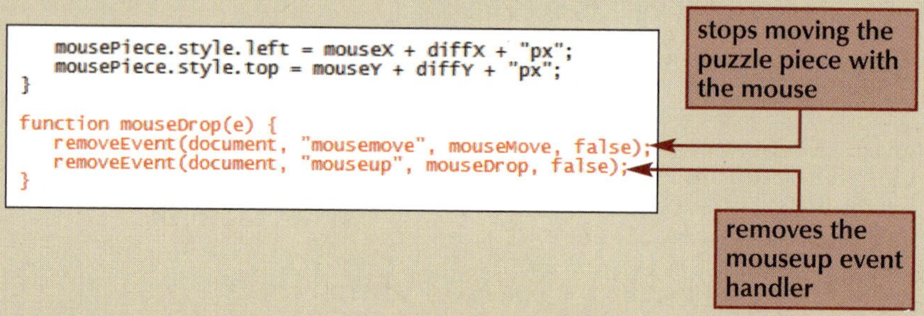
mousePiece.style.left = mouseX + diffX + "px";
mousePiece.style.top = mouseY + diffY + "px";
}
function mouseDrop(e) {
removeEvent(document, "mousemove", mouseMove, false);
removeEvent(document, "mouseup", mouseDrop, false);
}
stops moving the puzzle piece with the mouse
removes the mouseup event handler

2. Save your changes to the file, and then reload **jigsaw.htm** in your Web browser.
3. Move the pointer over any of the 24 puzzle pieces in the right section, and then press and hold down the mouse button.
4. Move the pointer to the grid in the left section and verify that the puzzle piece moves across the page, following the pointer. See Figure 15-28.

Puzzle piece being dragged **Figure 15-28**

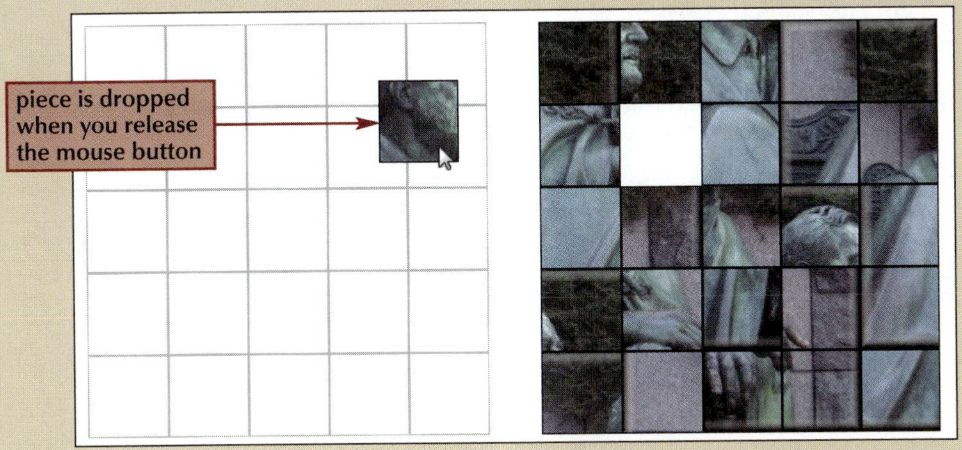
piece is dropped
when you release
the mouse button

5. Release the mouse button, and verify that the puzzle piece drops and remains at the new page location.

Refining the Jigsaw Puzzle

Pete reviews the jigsaw.htm page. While working with the puzzle, he notices that in some instances, the piece being moved disappears behind other objects on the page, as shown in Figure 15-29. He wants you to make sure the dragged puzzle piece always appears on top.

Hidden puzzle piece **Figure 15-29**

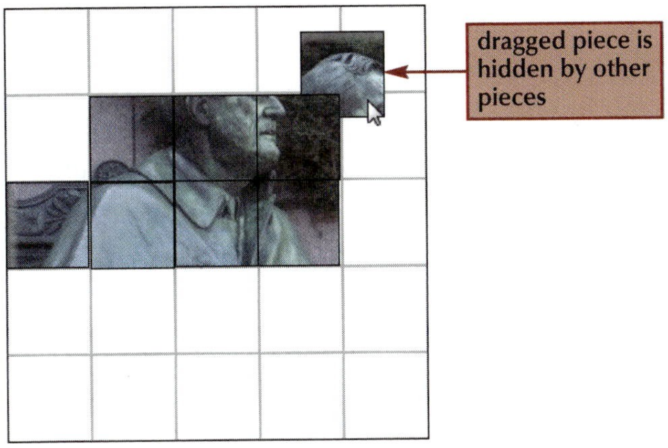
dragged piece is
hidden by other
pieces

Keeping Dragged Items on Top

To keep the dragged puzzle piece on top, you'll create a variable named maxZ that stores the maximum value of the z-index style for objects on the page. Each time you grab a piece, the value of maxZ is increased by 1 and then applied to the z-index style of the newly selected piece. As the piece is dragged across the page, it will have the highest z-index of any object on the page and will always appear on top of other objects.

You'll declare maxZ as a global variable, setting its initial value to 1.

To create and apply the maxZ variable:

1. Return to the **jpuzzle.js** file in your text editor, and then directly below the declaration of the diffY variable, insert the following line:

```
var maxZ = 1;
```

2. Scroll down to the mouseGrab() function, and then insert the following two lines, as shown in Figure 15-30:

```
maxZ++;
mousePiece.style.zIndex = maxZ; // place the piece above
other objects
```

Figure 15-30 Code to declare the maxZ variable

```
var diffX = null;
var diffY = null;
var maxZ = 1;

function mouseGrab(e) {
   var evt = e || window.event;
   mousePiece = evt.target || evt.srcElement;

   maxZ++;
   mousePiece.style.zIndex = maxZ; // place the piece above other objects

   var mouseX = evt.clientX; // x-coordinate of pointer
   var mouseY = evt.clientY; // y-coordinate of pointer
```

3. Save your changes to the file.

4. Reload **jigsaw.htm** in your Web browser, and verify that the currently selected puzzle piece always remains on top of the other objects on the page.

Preventing Hidden Pieces

A second problem Pete foresees occurs when one puzzle piece is dropped on top of another piece, hiding it from the user. Pete wants you to add a feature that prevents the user from dropping one piece upon another. To do this, you'll use the withinIt() function that Pete already created and stored in the kgfunctions.js file. The withinIt() function shown below compares the position of two objects:

```
function withinIt(object1, object2) {
   var within = false;
   var x1 = parseInt(object1.style.left);
   var y1 = parseInt(object1.style.top);

   var left = parseInt(object2.style.left);
   var top = parseInt(object2.style.top);
   var width = parseInt(object2.style.width);
   var height = parseInt(object2.style.height);

   var bottom = top + height;
   var right = left + width;

   if ((x1 > left && x1 < right) && (y1 > top && y1 < bottom)) within = true;
   return within;
}
```

If the upper-left corner of the first object falls within the boundaries of the second, the function returns the value true; otherwise, it returns the value false.

You'll use this function to confirm that the piece you're dropping will not cover another puzzle piece. The following dropValid() function does this by looping through all of the items in the pieces array, comparing the position of the specified object to the position of each piece:

```
function dropValid(object) {

   for (var i = 0; i < pieces.length; i++) {
      if (withinIt(object, pieces[i])) return false;
   }

   return true;
}
```

If the object falls within the boundary of any piece in the array, the dropValid() function returns the value false. If the for loop concludes without finding a match, the function returns the value true. Only a true value will indicate that the object will not cover any puzzle piece.

You'll add the dropValid() function to the jpuzzle.js file, and then call it from within the mouseDrop() function to check that the dragged piece can be dropped without hiding another puzzle piece.

To insert and call the dropValid() function:

1. Return to the **jpuzzle.js** file in your text editor, and then directly below the init() function, insert the following function:

```
function dropValid(object) {

   for (var i = 0; i < pieces.length; i++) {
      if (withinIt(object, pieces[i])) return false;
   }

   return true;
}
```

2. Scroll down to the mouseDrop() function, and after the opening function line, insert the following statement:

```
if (dropValid(mousePiece)) {
```

3. Indent the next two lines of code, and then insert } (a closing curly brace) to complete the if statement. Figure 15-31 shows the revised code.

Figure 15-31 Code to ensure that the piece can be dropped with the dropValid() function

```
   for (var i = 0; i < grids.length; i++) {
      grids[i].style.top = getStyle(grids[i],"top");
      grids[i].style.left = getStyle(grids[i],"left");
      grids[i].style.width = getStyle(grids[i],"width");
      grids[i].style.height = getStyle(grids[i],"height");
   }
}

function dropValid(object) {

   for (var i = 0; i < pieces.length; i++) {
      if (withinIt(object, pieces[i])) return false;
   }

   return true;
}
```

verifies that the upper-left corner of the object does not fall within any puzzle piece

```
function mouseDrop(e) {
   if (dropValid(mousePiece)) {
      removeEvent(document, "mousemove", mouseMove, false);
      removeEvent(document, "mouseup", mouseDrop, false);
   }
}
```

validates the position of the piece before dropping it

4. Save your changes to the file, and then reload **jigsaw.htm** in your Web browser.
5. Verify that you can drop puzzle pieces everywhere on the Web page except where the upper-left corner of the piece covers another puzzle piece.

Snapping a Piece to the Puzzle Grid

Pete wants the jigsaw pieces to snap into position on the grid to make it easier for users to view the completed puzzle and to line up all individual pieces. To apply this effect, you'll use the withinIt() function again to determine whether a puzzle piece has been dropped on top of any of the 25 grid pieces in the left section of the Web page. If this has happened, you'll line up the piece with the grid square.

The following function accomplishes this task by looping through all of the items in the grids array, comparing the position of each grid square to the position of the specified object:

```
function alignPiece(object) {
   for (var i = 0; i < grids.length; i++) {
      if (withinIt(object, grids[i])) {
            object.style.left = grids[i].style.left;
            object.style.top = grids[i].style.top;
            break;
      }
   }
}
```

If the withinIt() function returns a value of true, the top and left style values of the object are set to the top and left style values of the grid square, snapping it into place.

You'll add the alignPiece() function to the jpuzzle.js file, and then apply it to any puzzle piece dropped on the Web page by calling the function from within the mouse-Drop() function.

To insert and call the alignPiece() function:

1. Return to the **jpuzzle.js** file in your text editor, and then directly below the dropValid() function, insert the following function:

```
function alignPiece(object) {
   for (var i = 0; i < grids.length; i++) {
      if (withinIt(object, grids[i])) {
            object.style.left = grids[i].style.left;
            object.style.top = grids[i].style.top;
            break;
      }
   }
}
```

2. Scroll down to the mouseDrop() function and directly before the first removeEvent statement, insert the following:

```
alignPiece(mousePiece);
```

Figure 15-32 shows the inserted code.

Figure 15-32 Code to snap a piece to the grid with the alignPiece() function

```
function dropValid(object) {

   for (var i = 0; i < pieces.length; i++) {
      if (withinIt(object, pieces[i])) return false;
   }

   return true;
}

function alignPiece(object) {
   for (var i = 0; i < grids.length; i++) {
      if (withinIt(object, grids[i])) {
            object.style.left = grids[i].style.left;
            object.style.top = grids[i].style.top;
            break;
      }
   }
}
```

checks whether the upper-left corner of the object falls within any grid square

```
function mouseDrop(e) {
   if (dropValid(mousePiece)) {
      alignPiece(mousePiece);
      removeEvent(document, "mousemove", mouseMove, false);
      removeEvent(document, "mouseup", mouseDrop, false);
   }
}
```

snaps the dropped piece to the grid

3. Save your changes to the file, and then reload **jigsaw.htm** in your Web browser.
4. Verify that when you drop a puzzle piece onto the grid, the upper-left corner of the piece automatically aligns to the grid square.

InSight | Tracking Mouse Movements

Because many JavaScript applications involve the pointer moving into and out of objects, both the IE and the W3C event models include special event properties to help track the movements of the mouse. You will usually be concerned with two events: onmouseover occurring when the mouse initially moves over an object, and onmouseout occurring when the mouse initially moves out from an object.

You may need to know what object the mouse is coming from or going to during these events. Under the W3C event model, this information is stored in the relatedTarget property

```
evt.relatedTarget
```

where *evt* is the parameter of the event handler function. The relatedTarget property will reference the object the mouse is either going from (during the onmouseover event) or going to (during the onmouseout event). The IE event model uses two properties to convey this information. The following property determines what object the pointer is coming from during the onmouseover event:

```
event.fromElement
```

The following property determines what object the mouse is going to during the onmouse-out event:

```
event.toElement
```

One source of confusion with the onmouseover and onmouseout events is that they will run whenever the pointer moves in or out of the object, or in or out of any of the nested elements of the object. A Web page that involves several levels of nested elements may cause the event handlers to run at incorrect moments. Because of this problem, the IE event model also supports the onmouseenter and onmouseleave events. These events run only for the specified object and not for any elements nested within that element. The W3C event model has no equivalent property.

Pete is pleased with the refinements you made to the jigsaw puzzle so far. In the next session, you'll continue to work with the properties of the jigsaw puzzle and you'll explore how to work with keyboard events.

Review | Session 15.2 Quick Check

1. What is the reference for the event object in Internet Explorer? What is the reference in the W3C event model?
2. What property determines the type of event associated with the event object?
3. What properties determine the screen coordinates of an event?
4. What properties determine the window coordinates of an event?
5. What technique ensures that a dragged item will always be on top as it moves across a Web page?
6. What does the `this` keyword reference under the IE event model? What does it reference under the W3C event model?
7. Under both the IE and W3C event models, what event property determines what object the mouse is coming from during the mouseover event?
8. Under both the IE and W3C event models, what event property determines what object the mouse is going to during the mouseout event?

Session 15.3

Formatting a Drag-and-Drop Action

Pete wants the Web page to provide users with more visual feedback. For example, when a user hovers the pointer over one of the puzzle pieces, he wants the pointer to change to to indicate that the object is clickable. When an object is being moved across the page, Pete wants the pointer to change to .

Setting the Cursor Style

To set the style of the pointer as it hovers over an object, you can apply the cursor style

```
object.style.cursor = cursorType;
```

where *object* is an object on the Web page and *cursorType* identifies the style of cursor applied to the pointer. Figure 15-33 lists the different *cursorType* values and the appearance of the cursor under the Windows operating system (the pointer will appear differently under different operating systems and setups).

Mouse cursor styles **Figure 15-33**

Cursor	Style	Cursor	Style
	crosshair		n-resize
	default		ne-resize
	help		e-resize
	move		se-resize
	pointer		s-resize
	text		sw-resize
	wait		w-resize
	url(*url*) where *url* is the URL of a file containing the cursor image		nw-resize

You can also set a cursor style directly in the CSS style sheet using the following style declaration:

```
cursor: cursorType
```

In addition to the types listed in Figure15-33, the cursor style supports an auto *cursorType* value, which allows the user's browser to determine the appearance of the pointer. Many browsers also support an extended list of cursor styles not shown in Figure 15-33. Check your browser documentation for more information.

Reference Window | Setting Cursor Styles

- To change the appearance of a pointer, use the cursor style
  `object.style.cursor = cursorType;`
  where *object* is an object on the Web page and *cursorType* is the type of cursor to be displayed when the pointer hovers over the object.
- To change the pointer using CSS, add the following style to the style declaration for the element:
  `cursor: cursorType`

Pete wants to set the cursor style for each of the puzzle pieces as . When the user is dragging the piece, he wants the cursor to change to . After the customer drops the puzzle piece, the cursor style should return to . To make this change, you'll add commands to the init(), mouseGrab(), and mouseDrop() functions that set the cursor style when the page loads, during the mousedown event, and after the piece has been dropped during the mouseup event.

To set the cursor style:

1. If you took a break after the previous session, make sure the jpuzzle.js and kgfunctions.js files are open in a text editor, and the jigsaw.htm file is open in your Web browser.
2. Return to the **jpuzzle.js** file in your text editor, scroll down to the init() function, and then within the for loop that retrieves and sets the style properties for the puzzle pieces, add the following command:

```
pieces[i].style.cursor = "pointer";
```

3. Scroll down to the mouseGrab() function and below the statement that sets the z-index style, add the following command:

```
mousePiece.style.cursor = "move";
```

4. Scroll down to the mouseDrop() function and at the end of the command block for the if statement, insert the following command:

```
mousePiece.style.cursor = "pointer";
```

Figure 15-34 highlights the revised code in the file.

Tip

You apply your own custom cursors using the style cursor: url(*url*), where url is the location of the cursor image file.

Figure 15-34 Code to set the cursor style of the puzzle pieces

```
function init() {

   var allElem = document.getElementsByTagName("*");

   for (var i = 0; i < allElem.length; i++) {
      if (allElem[i].className == "grid") grids.push(allElem[i]);
      if (allElem[i].className == "pieces") pieces.push(allElem[i]);
   }

   var randomIntegers = randomArray(pieces.length);
   for (var i = 0; i < pieces.length; i++) {
      pieces[i].style.backgroundImage = "url(piece" + randomIntegers[i] + ".jpg)";
      pieces[i].style.top = getStyle(pieces[i],"top");
      pieces[i].style.left = getStyle(pieces[i],"left");
      pieces[i].style.width = getStyle(pieces[i],"width");
      pieces[i].style.height = getStyle(pieces[i],"height");
      pieces[i].style.cursor = "pointer";


function mouseGrab(e) {
   var evt = e || window.event;
   mousePiece = evt.target || evt.srcElement;

   maxZ++;
   mousePiece.style.zIndex = maxZ; // place the piece above other objects
   mousePiece.style.cursor = "move";


function mouseDrop(e) {
   if (dropValid(mousePiece)) {
      alignPiece(mousePiece);
      removeEvent(document, "mousemove", mouseMove, false);
      removeEvent(document, "mouseup", mouseDrop, false);
      mousePiece.style.cursor = "pointer";
   }
}
```

5. Save your changes to the file, and then reopen **jigsaw.htm** in your Web browser.
6. Verify that as you drag and drop the puzzle pieces, the mouse cursor changes between  and .

   Trouble? If you don't see a change in the pointer's appearance, you might be using the Safari or Opera browsers. At the time of this writing, the Safari and Opera browsers do not support the move cursor style.

Highlighting the Grid Square

Pete also wants the jigsaw puzzle page to highlight the grid square that the selected piece is being dragged over. This will help users to see which grid square the piece will be dropped into if the mouse button is released. Although it might seem that you could highlight the grid square because the pointer is hovering over it, this is not the case. The pointer is hovering over the puzzle piece, and the actions of the mouse then bubble up from the puzzle piece to the document object and then to the browser window. Even though the grid square and puzzle piece appear in close proximity on the page, they are actually separated in terms of the object hierarchy.

Instead, you can employ the same concepts you used in the previous session to determine which grid square the piece is hovering over. The following code shows how to highlight squares in the puzzle grid:

```
var hoverGrid = null;
function highlightGrid(object) {
   if (hoverGrid) hoverGrid.style.backgroundColor = "";

   for (var i = 0; i < grids.length; i++) {
      if (withinIt(object, grids[i])) {
         hoverGrid = grids[i];
         hoverGrid.style.backgroundColor = "rgb(192, 255, 192)";
         break;
      }
   }
}
```

The first line declares a global variable named hoverGrid. The hoverGrid variable will reference which of the 25 grid squares the puzzle piece is currently hovering over. The highlightGrid() function is then employed to highlight that grid square. To ensure that only one grid square is highlighted at a time, the function starts by removing the background color of the current hoverGrid square, if it exists. The function then loops through all of the grid squares, testing whether the object lies within the boundaries of any of the squares. If it finds a match, it sets hoverGrid to point to the selected square, changes the background color of that square to a light green, and discontinues the for loop. The effect is that only one grid square will be displayed with a light green background at a time, and only when the object is hovering over it.

To see this function in action, you'll add it to the jpuzzle.js file.

To add the highlightGrid() function:

1. Return to the **jpuzzle.js** file in your text editor, and then below the declaration for the maxZ variable, insert the following line:

```
var hoverGrid = null;
```

2. Below the alignPiece() function, insert the following function:

```
function highlightGrid(object) {
   if (hoverGrid) hoverGrid.style.backgroundColor = "";

   for (var i = 0; i < grids.length; i++) {
      if (withinIt(object, grids[i])) {
         hoverGrid = grids[i];
         hoverGrid.style.backgroundColor = "rgb(192, 255, 192)";
         break;
      }
   }
}
```

Figure 15-35 highlights the added code.

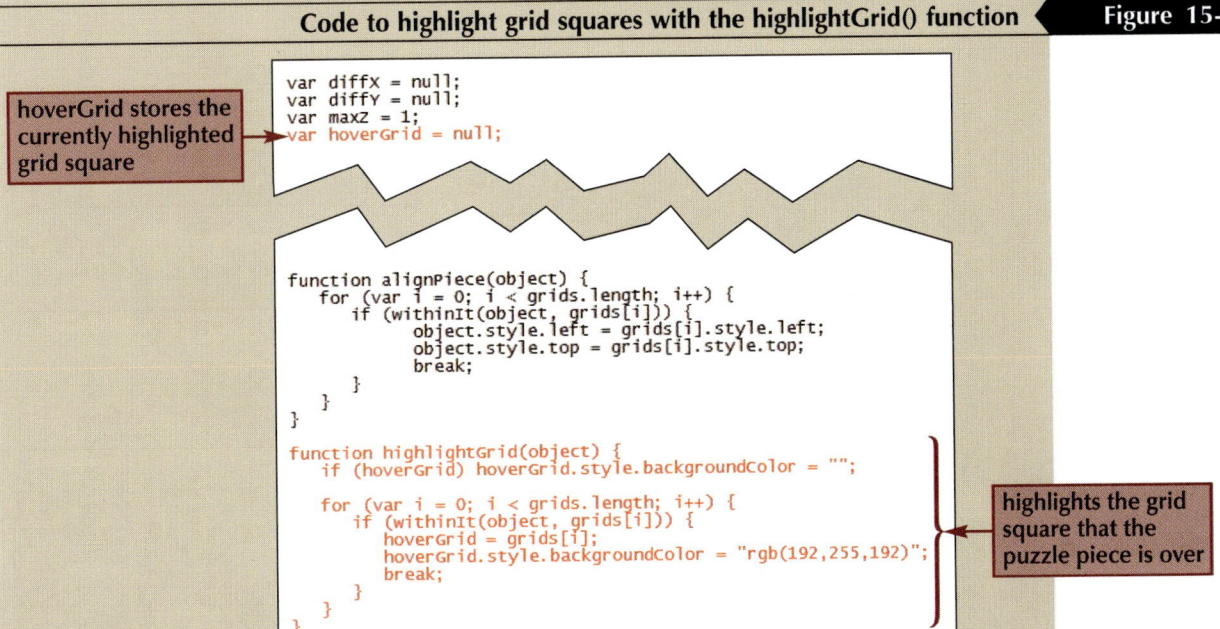

Figure 15-35 Code to highlight grid squares with the highlightGrid() function

hoverGrid stores the currently highlighted grid square

```
var diffX = null;
var diffY = null;
var maxZ = 1;
var hoverGrid = null;
```

```
function alignPiece(object) {
   for (var i = 0; i < grids.length; i++) {
      if (withinIt(object, grids[i])) {
            object.style.left = grids[i].style.left;
            object.style.top = grids[i].style.top;
            break;
      }
   }
}

function highlightGrid(object) {
   if (hoverGrid) hoverGrid.style.backgroundColor = "";

   for (var i = 0; i < grids.length; i++) {
      if (withinIt(object, grids[i])) {
         hoverGrid = grids[i];
         hoverGrid.style.backgroundColor = "rgb(192,255,192)";
         break;
      }
   }
}
```

highlights the grid square that the puzzle piece is over

You want the highlightGrid() function to run as the user drags a puzzle piece across the Web page.

3. Scroll down to the mouseMove() function and at the end of the function, insert the following statement, as shown in Figure 15-36:

```
highlightGrid(mousePiece);
```

Figure 15-36 Code to apply the highlightGrid() function while moving a puzzle piece

```
function mouseMove(e) {
   var evt = e || window.event;
   var mouseX = evt.clientX;
   var mouseY = evt.clientY;

   mousePiece.style.left = mouseX + diffX + "px";
   mousePiece.style.top = mouseY + diffY + "px";
   highlightGrid(mousePiece);
}
```

highlights the grid square under the moving piece

4. Save your changes to the file, and then reload **jigsaw.htm** in your Web browser.

5. Drag a puzzle piece over the puzzle grid and verify that the background color of the grid squares changes to light green, as shown in Figure 15-37.

Figure 15-37 Highlighted grid square

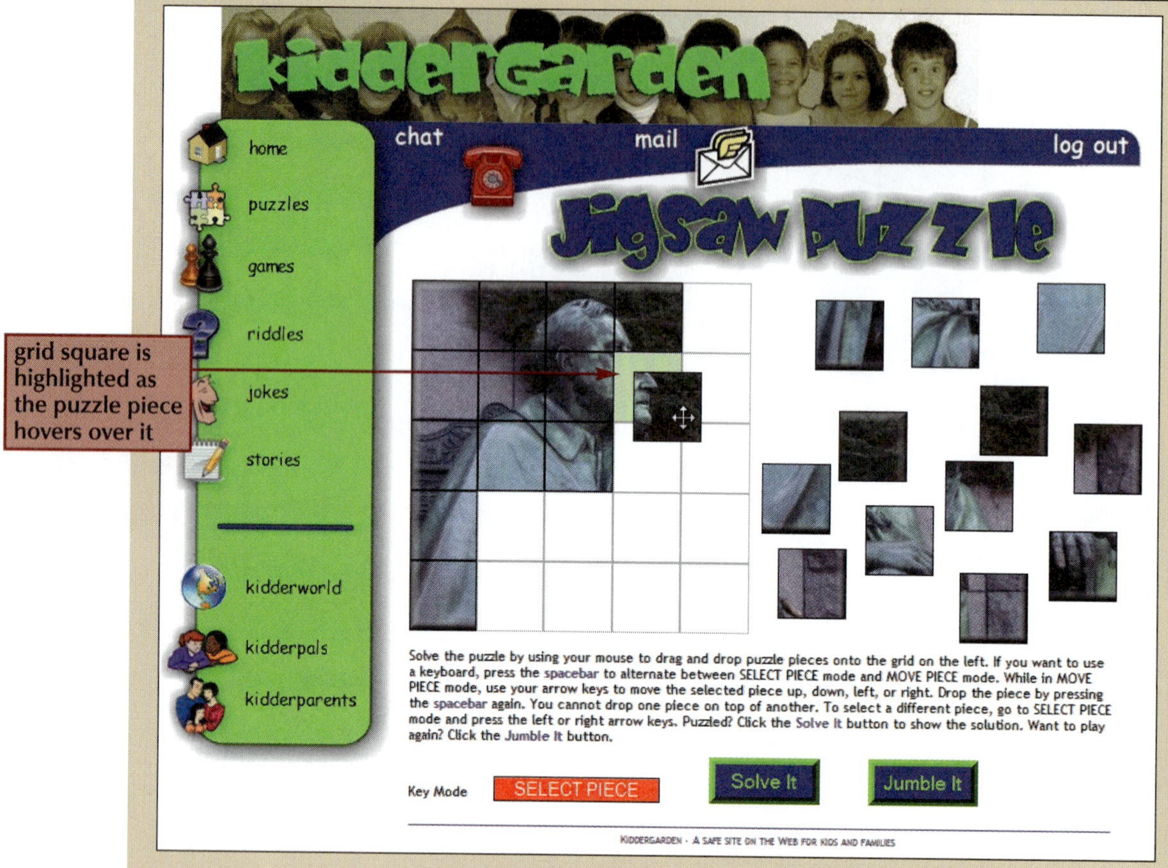

Pete is pleased with the addition of the mouse cursor style and the highlighted grid square. Both changes make it easier for users to interact with the jigsaw puzzle and avoid mistakes.

Specifying Mouse Buttons in Scripts | InSight

In writing code for the mouse actions in the jigsaw puzzle, you implicitly assumed that the user was pressing the left or primary mouse button. However, most mice have more than one button. Both the IE and the W3C event models provide support for three mouse buttons (left, middle, and right). You can determine which button was pressed using the button property

```
evt.button
```

where *evt* is the event object in either of the event models. The event models differ in the values returned by this property. In the W3C event model, the button values are 0 = left, 1 = middle, and 2 = right. In the IE event model, these values are 1 = left, 2 = right, and 4 = middle. Rarely will you write a script for the right and middle buttons because they often have default actions associated with them. For example, the right mouse button usually displays a shortcut menu for the highlighted object. You may not wish to interfere with these default actions.

The IE event model has an advantage over the W3C event model in that it allows for multiple buttons to be pressed. If the user clicks two or more buttons simultaneously, the sum of the button values is returned by the button property. So a user who presses both the right and middle buttons simultaneously will send the value 6 (2 + 4) to the event handler. Thus, under the IE event model, you can write scripts that involve two or more buttons being pressed simultaneously. The W3C event model does not support more than one button being pressed at time.

Working with Keyboard Events

Pete wants the site to be accessible to as many people as possible. He knows that some users have disabilities that make it difficult or even impossible for them to use a computer mouse. So, Pete wants users to also be able to play with the jigsaw puzzle using only the keyboard.

He sees keyboard activity working in two possible modes, as Figure 15-38 demonstrates. In Move Piece mode, the user moves a selected puzzle piece around the Web page by pressing any of the four keyboard arrow keys. In Select Piece mode, those same arrow keys are used to select different pieces from the puzzle. As you can see, what the arrow keys do depends on what mode is active.

Figure 15-38 Keyboard keys used in the jigsaw puzzle

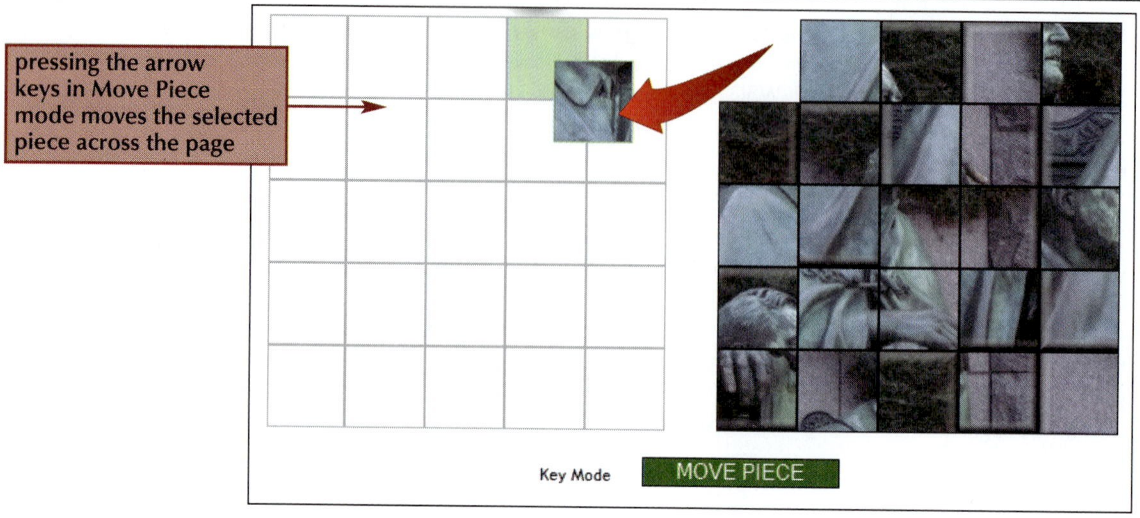
pressing the arrow keys in Move Piece mode moves the selected piece across the page
Key Mode
MOVE PIECE

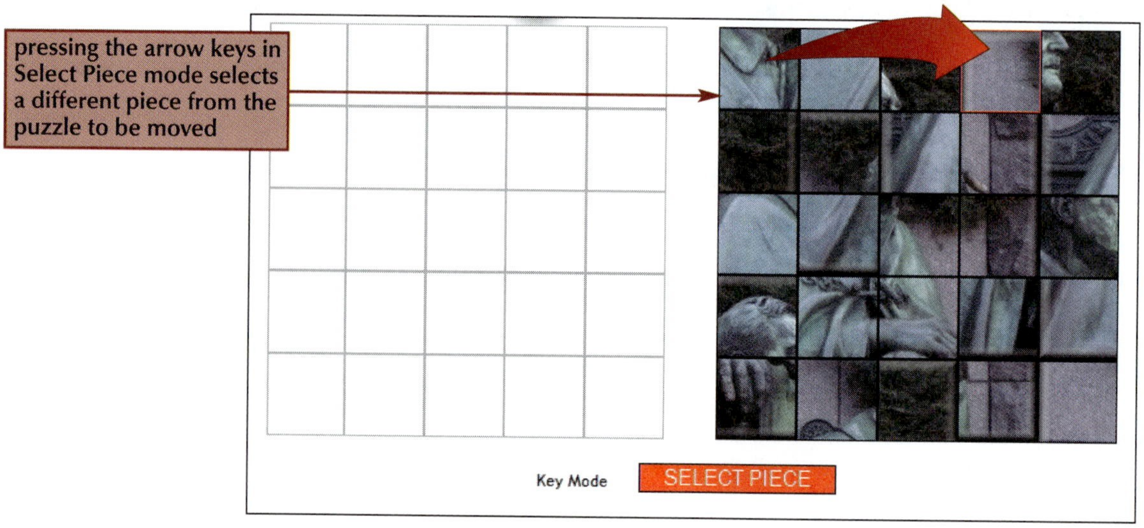
pressing the arrow keys in Select Piece mode selects a different piece from the puzzle to be moved
Key Mode
SELECT PIECE

Pete wants users to be able to switch between the two modes by pressing the Spacebar. If the user is in Move Piece mode, pressing the Spacebar has the added effect of dropping the piece in place on the Web page. To create the code for the two modes, you have to work with keyboard events.

Reviewing Keyboard Events

To make his program work, Pete wants to capture the action of a user pressing a keyboard key. Three distinct events occur in rapid succession when the user presses a key. These are:

1. **keydown** in which the user presses the key down
2. **keypress** which follows immediately after the onkeydown event
3. **keyup** which occurs after the key has been released by the user

The keydown and keypress events appear to be very similar; the difference between them lies in the difference between keyboard keys and the characters they generate. The keydown and keyup events occur as a result of a press and release of a physical keyboard key. The keypress event occurs very soon after the keydown event, at the moment when the computer generates a character in response to a keyboard action. Browsers treat the distinction between the keydown and keypress events somewhat inconsistently, which can be a source of frustration for programmers trying to create cross-browser compatible scripts. In DOM Level 3 (still to be adopted by most browsers), the keypress event has been replaced by the textinput event, which occurs whenever text is input by the user (by keyboard or not).

Tip

To capture the key the user pressed, use the onkeydown event. To work with the character produced by pressing the key, use the onkeypress event.

For the jigsaw puzzle, you want to capture the user action on the Spacebar and the four arrow keys, but not the characters that these keys generate (the four arrow keys usually do not generate characters anyway). So you'll create an event handler in response to the keydown event. Keyboard events usually occur in HTML elements that accept text entries such as input boxes or text area fields. Other than data entry fields, the keyboard events are associated with the entire document. The jigsaw puzzle contains no data entry fields, so you'll apply the following event handler to any keydown event occurring within the document:

```
document.onkeydown = keyGrab;
```

Under this event handler, whenever a user presses a key, the browser will run the keyGrab() function (which you will create shortly). You'll add this event handler to the init() function in the jpuzzle.js file.

To create an event handler for the onkeydown event:

1. Return to the **jpuzzle.js** file in your text editor.
2. Scroll down to the init() function and at the bottom of the function, insert the following command, as shown in Figure 15-39:

   ```
   document.onkeydown = keyGrab;
   ```

Figure 15-39 Code to create an event handler for the keydown event

```
   for (var i = 0; i < grids.length; i++) {
      grids[i].style.top = getStyle(grids[i],"top");
      grids[i].style.left = getStyle(grids[i],"left");
      grids[i].style.width = getStyle(grids[i],"width");
      grids[i].style.height = getStyle(grids[i],"height");
   }

   document.onkeydown = keyGrab;
}
```

runs the keyGrab() function whenever the user presses a key

Keyboard Event Properties

Both the IE and the W3C event models support several properties that provide information about the key that was pressed or the character produced by the keyboard event. Figure 15-40 summarizes these different keyboard event properties.

Figure 15-40 **Keyboard event properties**

Property	Description	Event Model
evt.altKey	Returns a Boolean value indicating whether the Alt key was pressed during the event, where *evt* is the event object	IE, W3C
evt.ctrlKey	Returns a Boolean value indicating whether the Ctrl key was pressed	IE, W3C
evt.shiftKey	Returns a Boolean value indicating whether the Shift key was pressed	IE, W3C
evt.metaKey	Returns a Boolean value indicating whether any meta key was pressed	W3C
evt.keyCode	Returns a key code indicating which key was pressed during the keyup and keydown events	IE, W3C
evt.charCode	Returns the ASCII character code indicating which character was produced during the keypress event	W3C
evt.which	Returns the ASCII character code indicating which key was pressed during the keydown, keypress, and keyup events	W3C

For example, to determine which key the user pressed, you can apply the keyCode property

```
evt.keyCode
```

to the event object, where *evt* is the event object under either event model. The keyCode property returns a code number identifying the key pressed by the user. Although there is no W3C specification for key code values, browsers have adopted a common set of code numbers partly based on ASCII codes. Figure 15-41 lists some of the key code values for the different keyboard keys.

Figure 15-41 **Key code values**

Key(s)	Key Code(s)	Key(s)	Key Code(s)
[0 – 9]	48 – 57	page up	33
[a – z]	65 – 90	page down	34
backspace	8	end	35
tab	9	home	36
enter	13	left arrow	37
shift	16	up arrow	38
ctrl	17	right arrow	39
alt	18	down arrow	40
pause/break	19	insert	45
caps lock	20	delete	46
esc	27	[f1 – f12]	112 – 123
space	32	num lock	144

To test the keyCode property, you'll add the keyGrab() function to the jpuzzle.js file and use it to report the key code for whatever key the user presses.

To report key code values:

1. Directly below the init() function in the **jpuzzle.js** file, insert the following code, as shown in Figure 15-42:

```
function keyGrab(e) {
   var evt = e || window.event;
   alert("Key Code: " + evt.keyCode);
}
```

Figure 15-42 Code to display key code values

```
   document.onkeydown = keyGrab;

}

function keyGrab(e) {
   var evt = e || window.event;
   alert("Key Code: " + evt.keyCode);
}
```

2. Save your changes to the file, and then reload **jigsaw.htm** in your Web browser.
3. Press the **Spacebar** on your keyboard and verify that an alert box similar to that shown in Figure 15-43 appears in your browser.

Figure 15-43 Alert dialog box showing the Spacebar key code value

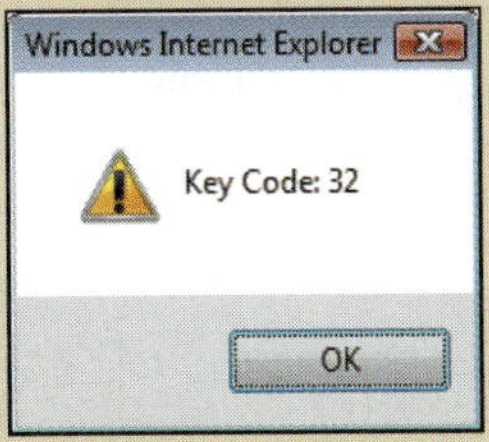

4. Continue pressing other keyboard keys to determine the key code values associated with each key.
5. Return to the **jpuzzle.js** file in your text editor, and then delete the line in the keyGrab() function that displays the alert box. You do not need the alert box for the program you will write.

Keyboard Events and Properties | Reference Window

- To run a command when the user presses down a key, use the onkeydown event handler.
- To run a command when the user releases a key, use the onkeyup event handler.
- To run a command when the user enters a character from the keyboard, use the onkeypress event handler.
- To retrieve the code of the key pressed by the user during the keydown or keyup event, use the property

  `evt.keyCode`

  where *evt* is the event object.

Toggling Between Modes in the Jigsaw Puzzle

Now that you've seen how to retrieve the code value of the key pressed by the user, you can use that information to add keyboard events to the jigsaw puzzle program. Users will require a visual clue as to which puzzle piece is the active piece—the one that will be affected by the actions of the keyboard. Pete suggests that the active piece should have a red border in Select Piece mode and a green border in Move Piece mode.

To keep track of the active piece, you'll create three global variables. The first, keyPiece, contains a reference to the currently active piece. The second variable, keyIndex, contains the index number of the current piece. The third global variable, selectMode, is a Boolean variable that indicates whether the user is in Select Piece mode or Move Piece mode. Its initial value should be set to true, indicating that the user is in Select Piece mode.

You'll add these three variables and set the initial appearance of the active puzzle piece.

To create the keyPiece, keyIndex, and selectMode variables:

1. Scroll to the top of the **jpuzzle.js** file and below the declaration of the mousePiece variable, insert the following global variables:

```
var keyPiece = null;
var keyIndex = null;
var selectMode = true;
```

2. Scroll down to the init() function and below the statement for the onkeydown event handler, insert the following global variables:

```
keyPiece = pieces[0];
keyIndex = 0;
keyPiece.style.borderColor = "red";
```

Figure 15-44 highlights the revised code.

Figure 15-44 Code to set global variables for the keyboard pieces

```
var grids = new Array();
var pieces = new Array();
var mousePiece = null;
var keyPiece = null;
var keyIndex = null;
var selectMode = true;
```

```
   document.onkeydown = keyGrab;
   keyPiece = pieces[0];
   keyIndex = 0;
   keyPiece.style.borderColor = "red";
}
```

sets the initial reference and appearance of keyPiece

3. Save your changes to the file, and then reload **jigsaw.htm** in your Web browser.
4. Verify that the first piece in the puzzle has a red border.

Recall that Pete wants users to be able to switch between Select Piece mode and Move Piece mode by pressing the Spacebar. When they switch modes, the border color of keyPiece should change between red and green. Another visual clue is that an input box on the Web page with the id attribute keyMode should change its text between SELECT PIECE and MOVE PIECE and change its background color between red and green. To accomplish this, you'll add the following function to the file:

```
function toggleMode() {
   selectMode = !selectMode;
   var modeBox = document.getElementById("keyMode");

   if (selectMode) {
      keyPiece.style.borderColor = "red";
      modeBox.value = "SELECT PIECE";
      modeBox.style.backgroundColor = "red";
   } else {
      keyPiece.style.borderColor = "rgb(151, 255, 151)";
      modeBox.value = "MOVE PIECE";
      modeBox.style.backgroundColor = "green";
   }
}
```

The toggleMode() function first switches the value of the selectMode variable. It then creates a reference to the keyMode box on the Web page. Based on the value of selectMode, it then changes the border color of keyPiece and the text and background color of the keyMode box.

You'll add this function to the jpuzzle.js file, and then run it in response to the user pressing the Spacebar.

To create the toggleMode() function:

1. Return to the **jpuzzle.js** file in your text editor, and then below the keyGrab() function, insert the following function:

```
function toggleMode() {
   selectMode = !selectMode;
   var modeBox = document.getElementById("keyMode");

   if (selectMode) {
      keyPiece.style.borderColor = "red";
      modeBox.value = "SELECT PIECE";
      modeBox.style.backgroundColor = "red";
   } else {
      keyPiece.style.borderColor = "rgb(151, 255, 151)";
      modeBox.value = "MOVE PIECE";
      modeBox.style.backgroundColor = "green";
   }
}
```

   Next you want to run the toggleMode() function whenever the user presses the Spacebar key, which has a key code value of 32.

2. Add the following line to the keyGrab() function, as shown in Figure 15-45:

```
if (evt.keyCode == 32) toggleMode();
```

Figure 15-45 **The initial toggleMode() function**

```
function keyGrab(e) {
   var evt = e || window.event;

   if (evt.keyCode == 32) toggleMode();
}

function toggleMode() {
   selectMode = !selectMode;
   var modeBox = document.getElementById("keyMode");

   if (selectMode) {
      keyPiece.style.borderColor = "red";
      modeBox.value = "SELECT PIECE";
      modeBox.style.backgroundColor = "red";
   } else {
      keyPiece.style.borderColor = "rgb(151, 255, 151)";
      modeBox.value = "MOVE PIECE";
      modeBox.style.backgroundColor = "green";
   }
}
```

runs the toggleMode() function whenever the user presses the Spacebar

switches between Select Piece and Move Piece modes

3. Save your changes to the file, and then reload **jigsaw.htm** in your Web browser.
4. Press the **Spacebar** key repeatedly and verify that the border color of the active puzzle piece and the text and color of the keyMode input box switch between Select Piece mode and Move Piece mode. See Figure 15-46.

Figure 15-46 **Select Piece and Move Piece modes**

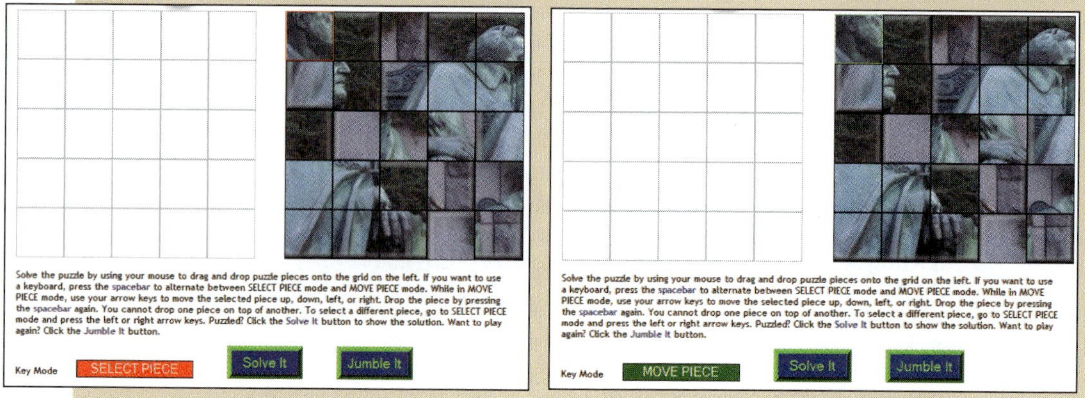

Select Piece mode | Move Piece mode

Now that you can toggle between the two modes, you can work on the actions of the keyboard within each mode. You'll start by writing a function to select a different puzzle piece by using the arrow keys.

Selecting a Piece with the Keyboard

Pete wants users to be able to select a different puzzle piece by pressing the Left and Right arrow keys. If the user presses the Left arrow key, the active piece should switch to the preceding puzzle piece. For example, if the active puzzle piece is piece23, pressing the Left arrow key should select piece22. If the user presses the Right arrow key, the next puzzle piece in the array should be selected. To keep track of the index number of the puzzle pieces, you've already created the keyIndex variable, setting its initial value to 0 (the first piece in the array). Thus, the function to select a piece is:

```
function selectPiece(diffIndex) {
   keyPiece.style.borderColor = "black";
   keyIndex = keyIndex + diffIndex;
```

```
   keyPiece = pieces[keyIndex];
   keyPiece.style.borderColor = "red";
}
```

The selectPiece() function has a single parameter, diffIndex, which stores the amount by which the keyIndex value will change. The first line of the function changes the border color of the currently active piece back to its default of black (because it will no longer be the active piece after the function is run). You then change the value of keyIndex by diffIndex. For the jigsaw puzzle application, you'll limit the values of diffIndex to either –1 or 1 so this function will either increase or decrease keyIndex by 1. The function then changes keyPiece to the item in the pieces array with an index value of keyIndex. The function concludes by setting the border color of the new keyPiece to red.

A problem with the current selectPiece() function is that it's possible to go beyond the boundary of the pieces array. For example, if keyPiece is the last item in the array, attempting to move beyond that item will result in an error message. A similar problem occurs if trying to move before the first item in the array. You can correct this problem with the following if condition:

```
if (keyIndex == -1) keyIndex = pieces.length - 1;
else if (keyIndex == pieces.length) keyIndex = 0;
```

This if condition tests whether the value of keyIndex equals –1. If so, it sets the keyIndex value to match the last item in the array, effectively moving the user from the first puzzle piece to the last puzzle piece. Similarly, if the keyIndex value has gone beyond the end of the array, it moves it back to the beginning. As a result, users can never move off the values in the array.

The selectPiece() function will be run in response to the user pressing either the Left or Right arrow key. If the user presses the Right arrow key, the function runs with a parameter value of 1 in the command

```
selectPiece(1)
```

causing the browser to select the next item in the pieces array as the keyPiece. Similarly, pressing the Left arrow key runs the function with a parameter value of –1 in the command

```
selectPiece(-1)
```

causing the browser to select the previous piece from the pieces index.

You'll add the selectPiece() function and event handlers for the Left and Right arrow keys to the jpuzzle.js file.

To create the selectPiece() function:

1. Return to the **jpuzzle.js** file in your text editor and directly below the keyGrab() function, insert the following function:

```
function selectPiece(diffIndex) {
   keyPiece.style.borderColor = "black";

   keyIndex = keyIndex + diffIndex;
   if (keyIndex == -1) keyIndex = pieces.length - 1;
   else if (keyIndex == pieces.length) keyIndex = 0;

   keyPiece = pieces[keyIndex];
   keyPiece.style.borderColor = "red";
}
```

2. Add the following two lines to the keyGrab() function, as shown in Figure 15-47:

```
else if (selectMode && evt.keyCode == 37) selectPiece(-1);
else if (selectMode && evt.KeyCode == 39) selectPiece(1);
```

Figure 15-47 Code to select a puzzle piece with the selectPiece() function

```
function keyGrab(e) {
   var evt = e || window.event;

   if (evt.keyCode == 32) toggleMode();
   else if (selectMode && evt.keyCode == 37) selectPiece(-1);
   else if (selectMode && evt.keyCode == 39) selectPiece(1);
}

function selectPiece(diffIndex) {
   keyPiece.style.borderColor = "black";

   keyIndex = keyIndex + diffIndex;
   if (keyIndex == -1) keyIndex = pieces.length - 1;
   else if (keyIndex == pieces.length) keyIndex = 0;

   keyPiece = pieces[keyIndex];
   keyPiece.style.borderColor = "red";
}
```

calls the selectPiece() function when the user presses the Left arrow or Right arrow key

changes the value of keyIndex

sets the new location of keyPiece

3. Save your changes to the file, and then reload **jigsaw.htm** in your Web browser.
4. With the puzzle still in Select Piece mode, repeatedly press the **Left arrow** key and then the **Right arrow** key, verifying that the identity of the active puzzle piece changes in response.

Moving a Piece with the Keyboard

Finally, you want users to be able to move a puzzle piece using only the Left, Right, Up, and Down arrow keys. To facilitate the movement of the keyPiece, you'll add the following function:

```
function keyMove(moveX, moveY) {
   keyPiece.style.left = parseInt(keyPiece.style.left) + moveX + "px";
   keyPiece.style.top = parseInt(keyPiece.style.top) + moveY + "px";
   highlightGrid(keyPiece);
}
```

The keyMove() function has two parameters, moveX and moveY, that indicate the number of pixels to move in the x and y directions. Positive values of moveX and moveY move the piece to the right and down; negative values move the piece to the left and up. The keyPiece is moved by modifying the value of its left and top style properties. As with the code to move the puzzle piece using the mouse, the keyMove() function will also highlight any grid square that the user moves the puzzle piece over.

Pete wants the selected puzzle piece to move 8 pixels at a time in any of four directions. To move the puzzle piece 8 pixels to the left when the user presses the Left arrow key (key code 37), you run the following command:

```
if (!selectMode && evt.keyCode == 37) keyMove(-8, 0);
```

The if condition also must confirm that the user is not in Select Piece mode before moving the puzzle piece. Commands to move the piece in the up, right, and down directions are similar:

```
if (!selectMode && evt.keyCode == 38) keyMove(0, -8);
if (!selectMode && evt.keyCode == 39) keyMove(8, 0);
if (!selectMode && evt.keyCode == 40) keyMove(0, 8);
```

You'll add the keyMove() function and the commands to run it in response to the keyboard events to the jpuzzle.js file.

To create the keyMove() function:

1. Return to the **jpuzzle.js** file in your text editor and then directly below the keyGrab() function, insert the following function:

```
function keyMove(moveX, moveY) {
   keyPiece.style.left = parseInt(keyPiece.style.left) +
moveX + "px";
   keyPiece.style.top = parseInt(keyPiece.style.top) + moveY
+ "px";
   highlightGrid(keyPiece);
}
```

2. Add the following four lines to the keyGrab() function, as shown in Figure 15-48:

```
else if (!selectMode && evt.keyCode == 37) keyMove(-8, 0);
else if (!selectMode && evt.keyCode == 38) keyMove(0, -8);
else if (!selectMode && evt.keyCode == 39) keyMove(8, 0);
else if (!selectMode && evt.keyCode == 40) keyMove(0, 8);
```

Code to move a keyboard piece with the movePiece() function — **Figure 15-48**

```
function keyGrab(e) {
   var evt = e || window.event;

   if (evt.keyCode == 32) toggleMode();
   else if (selectMode && evt.keyCode == 37) selectPiece(-1);
   else if (selectMode && evt.keyCode == 39) selectPiece(1);
   else if (!selectMode && evt.keyCode == 37) keyMove(-8, 0);
   else if (!selectMode && evt.keyCode == 38) keyMove(0, -8);
   else if (!selectMode && evt.keyCode == 39) keyMove(8, 0);
   else if (!selectMode && evt.keyCode == 40) keyMove(0, 8);
}

function keyMove(moveX, moveY) {
   keyPiece.style.left = parseInt(keyPiece.style.left) + moveX + "px";
   keyPiece.style.top = parseInt(keyPiece.style.top) + moveY + "px";
   highlightGrid(keyPiece);
}
```

- Left arrow key
- Up arrow key
- Right arrow key
- Down arrow key

3. Save your changes to the file, and then reload **jigsaw.htm** in your Web browser.
4. Press the **Spacebar** to switch to Move Piece mode. Then press and hold down any of the four arrow keys to move the selected puzzle piece across the page, verifying that when the piece is over a grid square, the square is highlighted.
5. Press the **Spacebar** to return to Select Piece mode, and then drop the active piece onto the Web page.
6. Continue to work with the Spacebar and the arrow keys to verify that you can select different pieces from the puzzle and move them using only the keyboard keys.

The keyboard interface still needs some fine-tuning. The active piece does not always appear on top of other pieces when it is being moved using the keyboard, and it doesn't snap into place when dropped onto the grid. You can fix these problems by inserting the same functions and variables you added when programming the puzzle for use with a mouse. The maxZ variable ensures that keyPiece is always on top of other pieces. The dropValid() and alignPiece() functions ensure that one piece doesn't drop on top of another piece, and that any dropped piece aligns with the puzzle grid.

Tip

Always look for ways to reuse variables and code in different parts of your programming rather than duplicating the code.

To complete the keyboard interface for the puzzle:

1. Return to the **jpuzzle.js** file in your text editor, and then scroll down to the toggleMode() function.

2. Insert the following expression at the beginning of the line to toggle the value of the selectMode variable to toggle the keyboard mode if the puzzle piece is located in a valid place to drop:

```
if (dropValid(keyPiece))
```

3. Directly after the command to set the border color of keyPiece to red, insert the following command to align any dropped piece to the grid:

```
alignPiece(keyPiece);
```

4. After the statement that sets the border color of keyPiece to the color value rgb(151, 255, 151), add the following command to keep keyPiece on top of all other objects when it is in motion by setting its zIndex value to maxZ:

```
maxZ++;
keyPiece.style.zIndex = maxZ;
```

Figure 15-49 highlights the new code inserted in the toggleMode() function.

Figure 15-49 Completed toggleMode() function

toggles the selectMode only when the puzzlepiece can be validly dropped

aligns dropped pieces with a grid square

keeps the selected moving piece on top of all other objects

```
function toggleMode() {
   if (dropValid(keyPiece)) selectMode = !selectMode;
   var modeBox = document.getElementById("keyMode");

   if (selectMode) {
      keyPiece.style.borderColor = "red";
      alignPiece(keyPiece);
      modeBox.value = "SELECT PIECE";
      modeBox.style.backgroundColor = "red";
   } else {
      keyPiece.style.borderColor = "rgb(151, 255, 151)";
      maxZ++;
      keyPiece.style.zIndex = maxZ;

      modeBox.value = "MOVE PIECE";
      modeBox.style.backgroundColor = "green";
   }
}
```

5. Save your changes to the file, and then reload **jigsaw.htm** in your Web browser.

6. Use your keyboard to select and move puzzle pieces, verifying that no moving piece is hidden behind another piece, that a piece cannot be dropped on top of another piece, and that pieces dropped onto the puzzle grid align with a grid square.

Understanding the keypress Event and Character Codes

The keydown event you used in the jigsaw puzzle program responds to the user pressing a key, but not necessarily typing a character. This distinction is important. A keyboard has a key for the letter A, but it makes no distinction between uppercase and lowercase letters. The keyCode property will indicate which letter key was pressed, but not whether the user typed A or a.

To determine what character the user typed, you use the keypress event along with the charCode property. The charCode property returns the character's ASCII code. The following expression returns the ASCII code of whatever character was typed by the user:

```
evt.charCode
```

where *evt* is the event object created from the keypress event. If the user typed a lowercase a, this expression will return a value 97, whereas typing an uppercase A will result in a value of 65. The charCode property should be used only with keys that actually produce characters. It should not be used with keys such as Shift or Ctrl, and the browser will usually return an undefined value for those keys. If you don't want to work with the ASCII codes, JavaScript allows you to convert these character codes into actual characters using the expression

```
String.fromCharCode(code)
```

where *code* is the ASCII code of the character.

One problem facing JavaScript programmers is that character codes are not handled equally by all browsers. Internet Explorer doesn't support the charCode property at all. Instead, the IE event model uses the keyCode property combined with the keypress event to determine the character typed by the user. This works for most browsers except Firefox, which returns a value of 0 if the keyCode property is used with the keypress event. Under Firefox, you use the which property to retrieve the character code of the pressed key.

This sounds confusing (and it is), but you can reconcile these differences in the following code which using object detection and values of the which property to determine which code value to use in determining the character typed by the user:

```
var evt = e || window.event;
if (evt.which == null)
   char = String.fromCharCode(evt.keyCode);
else if (evt.which > 0)
   char = String.fromCharCode(evt.which);
```

After these commands, the char variable will contain a text string representing the character entered by the keyboard under either event model and for any of the major browsers. The inconsistencies involved with characters and the keypress event are being dealt with in DOM Level 3 of the event model. How soon these changes are reflected in the browser market remains to be seen. However, for the jigsaw puzzle page, you're working with the only Spacebar and the four arrow keys, so you don't have to worry about interpreting the characters typed by the user.

Using Modifier Keys | InSight

In addition to keyboard characters, keyboards contain modifier keys. A **modifier key** is a keyboard key that is pressed along with a letter key to run special commands or to access program menus. For example, in many browsers, holding down the Ctrl key while pressing the P key runs the Print command. Most browsers support three modifier keys: Ctrl, Alt, and Shift. JavaScript uses these properties of the event object

```
evt.altKey;
evt.ctrlKey;
evt.shiftKey;
```

to determine the state of these keys, where *evt* is the event object for a keydown, keypress, or keyup event. Each of these properties returns a Boolean value that indicates whether the modifier key is being pressed during the event. By examining the keyCode and ctrlKey properties, you can determine whether the user is holding down the Ctrl key while pressing the P key. In addition to the three modifier keys, the W3C event model also supports the event object property

```
evt.metaKey;
```

to determine whether a Meta key is being pressed during a keyboard event. The Meta key is found on a UNIX workstation, and is usually equivalent to the Alt key on PC keyboards or the Command key on Macintosh keyboards.

Controlling and Canceling Events

Pete has been working with the keyboard interface to the jigsaw puzzle and he noticed one problem. In his browser, the arrow keys also control horizontal and vertical scrolling within the document window. Sometimes when Pete presses an arrow key to move a puzzle piece, the browser responds by both moving the piece and scrolling the window. He finds this distracting and wants you to suspend the default action of scrolling the browser window while the user is moving the piece.

Controlling Event Propagation

JavaScript supports several methods for controlling and canceling events occurring within a browser. At the most basic level, you can control how an event propagates through the object hierarchy. Because the two event models approach event propagation differently, they also use different methods to control that propagation.

You can cancel event bubbling under the IE event model by using the following cancelBubble property of IE's event object:

```
event.cancelBubble = true;
```

Once bubbling has been canceled, any objects higher up on the object tree will not receive the event. For example, in the following code, the browser calls the showLink() function whenever the user hovers the pointer over the first hypertext link in the document:

```
document.links[0].onmouseover = showLink;
function showLink() {
   commands
   event.cancelBubble = true;
}
```

The function runs some commands and then cancels event bubbling. This means that if the link has been nested within other elements on the page, none of the higher elements will "see" the mouseover event.

To turn event bubbling back on, you change the value of the cancelBubble property to false, using the following command:

```
event.cancelBubble = false;
```

Remember that because the IE event object is a global object, turning off event bubbling for one event turns it off for all events.

The corresponding property in the W3C event model is the method

```
evt.stopPropagation()
```

which stops an *evt* event object from propagating through the object tree. The stopPropagation() method is only applied during the bubbling phase. It cannot be applied during the capture phase. Unlike the cancelBubble property, the stopPropagation() method applies only to the current event being processed rather than all events in the document.

Canceling an Action

Many events have default actions associated with them. Hovering the pointer over a link changes the text of the window status bar; clicking a submit button in a Web form submits the contents of the form for processing. You've learned that you cancel form submission by having the onsubmit event handler return a value of false. This approach applies to other events as well. For example, you can disable a hypertext link by setting up an event handler that returns the value false when the link is clicked, as in the following code:

```
document.links[0].onclick = disableLink;
function disableLink() {
   return false;
}
```

You can also cancel a default action in the IE event model by setting the returnValue property of the event object to false, as in the following statement:

```
event.returnValue = false;
```

The corresponding command in the W3C event model uses the following preventDefault() method:

```
evt.preventDefault();
```

In most situations, it is easier to create a function that returns a false value, so the returnValue property and the preventDefault() method are rarely needed.

To restore the default action associated with an event, you change the return value back to true. For example, you can re-enable a blocked hypertext link by running the following commands:

```
document.links[0].onclick = enableLink;
function enableLink() {
   return true;
}
```

Canceling the default action associated with an event is most often used to substitute custom actions for the standard actions usually undertaken by the browser, which is what Pete wants to do with the default actions associated with the Spacebar and arrow keys.

To prevent the default actions associated with the Spacebar and arrow keys, you'll add the statement

```
return false;
```

to the commands of the keyGrab() function. Because you want to disable the default actions only for these keys and not others, you'll run the return false command only in response to the users pressing the Spacebar or an arrow key.

Tip

Use caution when canceling a default action. Users may not want their browser's default setting overruled by your program.

To cancel the default keyboard actions:

1. Return to the **jpuzzle.js** file in your text editor, and then scroll down to the keyGrab() function.
2. For each of the seven if conditions, enclose the results of the if statement within a command block within opening and closing curly braces and insert the following command:

   ```
   return false;
   ```

   Figure 15-50 highlights the new code added to the keyGrab() function.

Figure 15-50 Code to cancel keyboard events within the keyGrab() function

```
function keyGrab(e) {
   var evt = e || window.event;

   if (evt.keyCode == 32) {toggleMode(); return false}
   else if (selectMode && evt.keyCode == 37) {selectPiece(-1); return false}
   else if (selectMode && evt.keyCode == 39) {selectPiece(1); return false}
   else if (!selectMode && evt.keyCode == 37) {keyMove(-8, 0); return false}
   else if (!selectMode && evt.keyCode == 38) {keyMove(0, -8); return false}
   else if (!selectMode && evt.keyCode == 39) {keyMove(8, 0); return false}
   else if (!selectMode && evt.keyCode == 40) {keyMove(0, 8); return false}
}
```

cancels the default action associated with the spacebar

3. Save your changes to the file, and then reload **jigsaw.htm** in your Web browser.
4. Verify that when you press the Spacebar or any of the four arrow keys, the default action of the Web browser is canceled. (Canceling the scrolling action in this way is not supported under the Opera browser.)

The only task remaining on the jigsaw puzzle Web page is to give users the ability to re-jumble the puzzle or to have it solved for them. Pete already created functions to do these two tasks and added them earlier to the jpuzzle.js file. You will add an event handler to the init() function to run these functions when the user clicks the Jumble It and Solve It buttons on the Web page.

To complete the jigsaw puzzle program:

1. Return to the **jpuzzle.js** file in your text editor.
2. Within the init() function, add the following commands, as shown in Figure 15-51:

```
document.getElementById("jumble").onclick = jumbleIt;
document.getElementById("solve").onclick = solveIt;
```

Figure 15-51 Event handlers to run the jumbleIt() and solveIt() functions

```
   document.onkeydown = keyGrab;
   keyPiece = pieces[0];
   keyIndex = 0;
   keyPiece.style.borderColor = "red";

   document.getElementById("jumble").onclick = jumbleIt;
   document.getElementById("solve").onclick = solveIt;
}
```

jumbles the pieces of the puzzle again

shows the puzzle solution

3. Save your changes to the file, and then reload **jigsaw.htm** in your Web browser.
4. Click the **Solve It** button and verify that it shows the puzzle solution.
5. Click the **Jumble It** button and verify that it randomizes the puzzle again.

You have completed your work on the jigsaw puzzle page. As Kiddergarden continues to grow in popularity, Pete will be looking for other online games and puzzles to add to the Web site.

Session 15.3 Quick Check | Review

1. What style declaration displays an hourglass as the pointer? What is the equivalent JavaScript command to do this?
2. What property determines which mouse button was pressed during an event? Describe how the event models differ in their interpretations of the value returned by this property.
3. What event corresponds to a user pressing a keyboard key?
4. What is the difference between the keypress event and the keydown event?
5. What event object property determines which key was pressed by a user?
6. What key code value is generated when a user presses the Spacebar?
7. What event object property determines whether the user is pressing the Alt key?
8. What property or method halts event bubbling or propagation in the IE and W3C event models?
9. How do you cancel the default action of a browser?

Tutorial Summary | Review

In this tutorial, you learned how to work with the W3C and IE event models to capture and respond to mouse and keyboard events. The first session explored the two main event models, examining how events are propagated through the document tree. It also showed how to attach functions to events and how to enable multiple functions for the same event. The second session examined the properties of the event object under both the IE and W3C event models. It showed how to extract information about the event from the event object's properties, and how to use this information to create a drag-and-drop effect for a puzzle page. The third session continued to explore how to work with mouse events and mouse buttons. It showed how to modify the mouse cursor and how to determine which mouse button the user pressed. The third session then turned toward keyboard events, showing how to capture and respond to keyboard actions initiated by the user. The session concluded by examining how to halt the propagation of events through the object hierarchy, and how to override a browser's default response to an event.

Key Terms

anonymous function
bubbling phase
capture phase
event bubbling
event capturing
event model
event object
IE event model
keydown
keypress
keyup
modifier key
target phase
traditional binding
W3C event model

Practice | Review Assignments

Practice the skills you learned in the tutorial using the same case scenario.

Data Files needed for the Review Assignments: block0.jpg through block24.jpg, blockstxt.htm, kgmenu.jpg, kgtitle,jpg, libtxt.js, photo.jpg, sbblocks.css, sbtitle.jpg, slidetxt.js

Pete wants you to finish a Web page he has been working on that displays a sliding block puzzle. In a sliding block puzzle, the puzzle pieces are laid out in a grid with one blank space. Pieces adjacent to the blank space (either above, below, to the left, or to the right of the space) can be swapped with the space. The goal of the puzzle is to move the blocks into their correct positions on the grid. A preview of a partially finished puzzle page is shown in Figure 15-52.

Figure 15-52

The puzzle is divided into a 5 × 5 grid, with each block in the grid contained within a div element that is 60 pixels wide by 60 pixels high. The image on each block is set as the block's background image. Starting at the upper left of the grid and moving right and then down, the div elements have the ID names block0, block1, and so on. The blank space is also a div element, with the ID name blank. The image files for the blocks are named block0.jpg through block24.jpg.

Pete wants this puzzle to work with both the mouse and the keyboard. You need to program the following actions:

- If a user clicks a block to the left of, to the right of, above, or below the blank space, that block should swap positions with the blank space.

- Any block adjacent to the blank space should display the pointer cursor when the pointer hovers over it; all other blocks should display the default cursor.
- One block in the puzzle is highlighted with a red border. A user can highlight different blocks by pressing the arrow keys on the keyboard.
- If the highlighted block is adjacent to the blank space, a user can swap the highlighted block with the blank space by pressing the Spacebar on the keyboard.

Pete also provided several JavaScript files that contain functions you can use on the Web page. Figure 15-53 summarizes the functions that you'll use in this problem.

Figure 15-53

Function	Description
scrambleIt()	Reloads the current Web page, thus rearranging the puzzle blocks
solveIt()	Places the puzzle blocks in the correct order in the puzzle
getStyle(object, styleName)	Returns the computed style value for a specified styleName applied to an object
nextTo(object1, object)	Returns a Boolean value indicating whether object1 lies next to object2
withinIt(x, y, object2)	Returns a Boolean value indicating whether the coordinate (x, y) lies within the boundaries of object
swapObjects(object1, object2)	Swaps the page positions of object1 and object2
scrambleIntegers(size)	Returns an array of integers from 0 up to one less than size, sorted in random order with even parity observed in the sorting of the integers (to ensure that the sliding blocks puzzle is solvable)
randOrder()	Returns a random value between –0.5 and 0.5

Complete the following:

1. Use your text editor to open the **blockstxt.htm**, **libtxt.js**, and **slidetxt.js** files from the tutorial.15/review folder, enter ***your name*** and ***the date*** in the comment section of each file, and then save the files as **blocks.htm**, **library.js**, and **slideblocks.js**, respectively.
2. Go to **blocks.htm** in your text editor, review the contents of the file, link the file to the library.js and slideblocks.js external script files, and then close the file, saving your changes.
3. Go to **library.js** in your text editor, and then insert a function named **addEvent()** that provides cross-browser support for assigning event handlers to events. The function should have four parameters: **object** for the object in which the event occurs, **evName** for the name of the event, **fnName** for the name of the function, and **cap**, a Boolean value indicating whether the event handler is assigned during the capture phase or the bubbling phase.
4. Insert a function named **removeEvent()** that provides cross-browser support for removing event handlers to events and objects. Use the same parameters you used for the addEvent() function. Close the library.js file, saving your changes.

5. Go to the **slideblocks.js** file in your text editor. Pete already added a global variable named blocks that contains an array of the puzzle blocks on the page and a function named init() that initializes the page and the puzzle. Add the following two global variables: **blankBlock** and **keyBlock**. You do not have to assign an initial value to either variable.
6. Add the following commands to the init() function:
    a. Declare a variable named **randomIntegers** that is equal to the array returned by the scrambleIntegers() function. Use a value equal to one less than the length of the blocks array as the parameter value for the function.
    b. Loop through the contents of the blocks array from 0 up to *one less than* the length of the blocks array. For each block item in the loop, assign the background image file block*random[i]*.jpg, where *random[i]* is the corresponding random integer from the randomIntegers array.
    c. Within the loop, assign the following event handlers to each block item: (i) the swapWithBlank() function when the block item is clicked, (ii) the highlightBlank() function when the pointer hovers over the block, and (iii) the removeHighlight-Blank() function when the user moves the pointer out from the block. Use the addEvent() function you created earlier to assign each event handler.
    d. Set the value of blankBlock to the last entry in the blocks array. Set the value of keyBlock to the first entry in the blocks array.
    e. Use the addEvent() function to run the keyEvent() function when the user presses a keyboard key.
7. Create the **swapWithBlank()** function. The purpose of this function is to swap a block clicked by the user with the adjacent blank space (if the block is adjacent to the blank space). Add the following commands to the function:
    a. Create a variable named **evt** that points to the event object for the event, under either event model.
    b. Create a variable named **mouseBlock** that references the target or the source of the event.
    c. Use the nextTo() and swapObjects() function to test whether mouseBlock is next to blankBlock. If it is, then swap the position of the two objects.
8. Create a function named **highlightBlank()**. The purpose of this function is to highlight blocks adjacent to the blank space. To complete this function:
    a. Create a variable named **evt** that points to the event object, and create a variable named **mouseBlock** that references the target or source of the event.
    b. If mouseBlock is next to blankBlock, set the style of the mouse cursor to pointer.
9. Create a function named **removeHighlightBlank()**. The purpose of this function is to remove highlighting from blocks adjacent to the blank space. To complete this function:
    a. Create a variable named **evt** that points to the event object, and create a variable named **mouseBlock** that references the target or source of the event.
    b. If mouseBlock is next to blankBlock, set the style of the mouse cursor to default.
10. Create a function named **keySwapWithBlank()**. The purpose of this function is to swap the page positions of the keyBlock and blankBlock objects. Use the nextTo() and swapObjects() functions to test whether keyBlock is next to blankBlock. If it is, swap the positions of the two objects.

11. Create a function named **selectBlock()**. The purpose of this function is to move the keyBlock from its currently selected block on the puzzle to another block (either above, below, to the left of, or to the right of the current keyBlock). The function has two parameters named **diffX** and **diffY**. Add the following commands to the function:
    a. Declare a variable named **newX** equal to the left position of the keyBlock object plus the value of diffX. Use the parseInt method to extract only the numeric value from the left style value of keyBlock.
    b. Declare a variable named **newY** equal to the top position of the keyBlock object plus the value of diffY. Again, use the parseInt method to extract only the numeric value of the top style.
    c. Declare a variable named **oldKeyBlock** equal to keyBlock.
    d. Loop through all of the items in the blocks array. For each block item, use the withinIt() function to determine whether the coordinates indicated by (newX, newY) lie within the block item. If so: (i) set keyBlock to the block item, (ii) set the border color of keyBlock to red, (iii) set the border color of oldKeyBlock to black, and (iv) break off the for loop.
12. Create a function named **keyEvent()**. The purpose of this function is to respond to the event of the user pressing down the Spacebar or one of the four arrow keys on the keyboard. To complete this function:
    a. Create a variable named **evt** that points to the event object under either event model.
    b. If the user presses the Spacebar, run the keySwapWithBlank() function and return the value false.
    c. If the user presses the Left arrow key, run the selectBlock() function with parameter values of –30 and 0. Return the value false.
    d. If the user presses the Up arrow key, run the selectBlock() function with parameter values of 0 and –30. Return the value false.
    e. If the user presses the Right arrow key, run the selectBlock() function with parameter values of 90 and 0. Return the value false.
    f. If the user presses the Down arrow key, run the selectBlock() function with parameter values of 0 and 90. Return the value false.
13. Close the file, saving your changes.
14. Open **blocks.htm** in your Web browser. Verify that you can swap a block piece adjacent to the blank space with the blank space itself. Also verify that the style of the mouse cursor is pointer for blocks adjacent to the blank space, but default elsewhere.
15. Verify that (i) pressing the arrow keys moves the highlighting from one piece to another; and (ii) pressing the Spacebar when the highlighted piece is next to the blank space swaps the position of the two.
16. Submit the completed project to your instructor.

Apply | Case Problem 1

Use JavaScript to create a program that limits the amount of text entered into a text area box.

Data Files needed for this Case Problem: booktxt.htm, bw.css, bwlogo.jpg, comtxt.js, leftbar.jpg

Online BookWorms Helen Ungerstatz is a manager of the Online BookWorms Web site, which is dedicated to lovers of books and reading. One of Helen's tasks is to create a comments page where users can enter short comments about books they have read. To keep the comments short and to the point, Helen wants to limit each comment to 500 characters (another place on the Web site allows extended book reviews). Helen has designed a Web page where users can enter their comments into a text area box.

One problem that Helen has encountered is that the HTML textarea element does not support a maxlength attribute to limit the length of text users can enter. Helen asks you to write a JavaScript program to do this instead. Helen also wants your program to automatically count down the number of characters left before the user reaches the 500 character maximum. A preview of the page you'll create for Helen is shown in Figure 15-54.

Figure 15-54

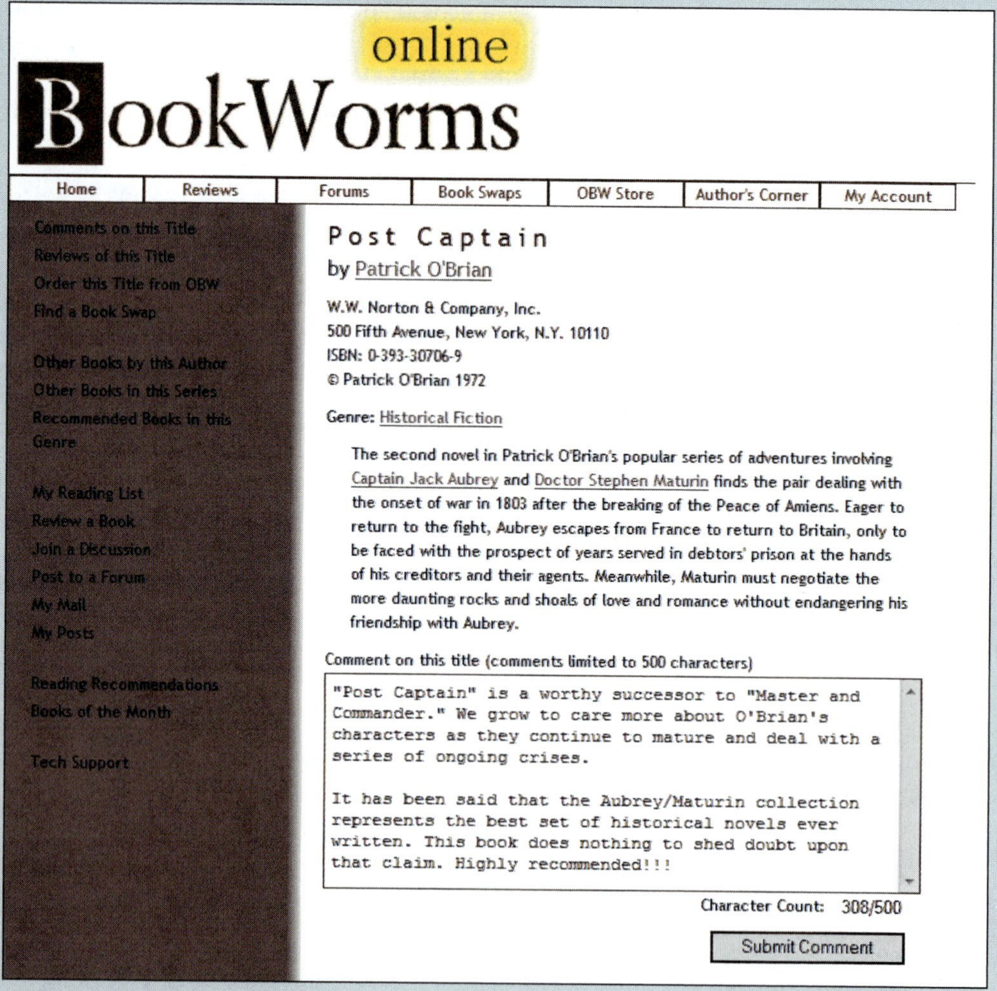

To create this application, the program needs to capture the keypress event so that you can check that space is still left in the text area box before accepting a character typed by the user, and it needs to capture the keyup event to update the count of characters in the comment box after the user has typed a character.

Complete the following:

1. Open the **booktxt.htm** and **comtxt.js** files from the tutorial.15/case1 folder in your text editor, enter ***your name*** and ***the date*** in the comment section of each file, and then save the files as **bookforum.htm** and **comments.js**, respectively.
2. Go to the **bookforum.htm** file in your text editor, study the contents and layout of the page, enter a link to the comments.js script file, and then close the file, saving your changes.
3. Go to the **comments.js** file in your text editor, declare a global variable named **maxLength** and set its value to 500, and then have the browser run the init() function when the page is loaded.
4. Create the **init()** function. The purpose of this function is to set up the event handlers for the Web page. Add the following commands to the function:
   a. Create a variable named **commentBox** that points to the textarea element with the ID comment.
   b. Create a variable named **countBox** that points to the input element with the ID wordcount.
   c. Set the value of countBox to the text string 0/*maxlength*, where *maxLength* is the value of the maxLength variable.
   d. Call the checkLength() function whenever the user presses the keyboard key within the commentBox object.
   e. Call the updateCount() function whenever the user releases a keyboard key within the commentBox object.
5. Create the **countText()** function. The purpose of this function is to return the number of non-white-space characters within the comment text area box. Add the following commands to the function:
   a. Declare a variable named **commentBox** that references the comment text area box.
   b. Store the regular expression /\s/g in the variable **commentregx**. This regular expression selects all of the white space characters within a specified text string.
   c. Use the regular expression replace() method to replace every occurrence of white space characters within the commentBox object with an empty text string, storing the resulting text string in a variable named **commentText**.
   d. Return the length of the commentText variable.
6. Create the **checkLength()** function. The purpose of this function is to confirm that users can enter a character into the comment text area box. Users can only enter a character if the number of characters currently in the box is less than the allowed maximum length, or if the keyboard key they press is either the Backspace key or the Delete key. Add the following commands to the function:
   a. Declare a variable named **evt** that points to the event object under either event model.
   b. Set an if statement with the following conditions: (i) If the value returned by the countText() function is less than maxlength, then return the value true; (ii) else if the user has typed the Backspace key or the Delete key, return the value true; (iii) otherwise, return the value false.

7. Create the **updateCount()** function. The purpose of this function is to update the character count after the user has typed characters. Add the following commands to the function:
   a. Declare the **countBox** variable that references the input element with the ID wordcount.
   b. Set the value of the **currentLength** variable returned by the countText() function.
   c. Set the value of the **countBox** object to the text string *currentLength/maxLength*, where *currentLength* is the value of the currentLength variable and *maxLength* is the value of the maxLength variable.
   d. If currentLength is less than maxLength, set the font color of the text in the countBox object to black with a background color of white; otherwise, set the font color to white on a red background.
8. Save your changes to the comments.js file.
9. Open **bookforum.htm** in your Web browser. Attempt to enter text into the comment text area box and verify that as you type non-white-space characters, the count of the characters listed for the box goes up. Also verify that if you attempt to exceed the 500-character limit, the browser prevents you from entering any characters—though it will accept input from the Backspace and Delete keys.
10. Submit your completed project to your instructor.

Apply | Case Problem 2

Use JavaScript to create a horizontal scroll bar for an image slide show.

Data Files needed for this Case Problem: back.jpg, badgertxt.htm, bar.jpg, corner.jpg, flibtxt.js, image0.jpg – image9.jpg, links.jpg, logo.jpg, slidetxt.js, styles.css

Badger Aviation Wayne Statz is the president and owner of Badger Aviation, an aviation company specializing in tours, charters, lessons, and shuttles in southern Wisconsin. He wants you to update the company's Web page. One of the pages you'll work with contains a slide show from one of Badger Aviation's tours of the area. Wayne wants you to create a horizontal scroll bar for the slide show that users can navigate with either the mouse or the keyboard. Figure 15-55 shows a preview of the page you'll create for Wayne.

Much of the layout is already done. Your job is to create the array of images for the slide show and program the operation of the scroll bar. The scroll button in the scroll bar has been stored in the Web page as a div element with the ID button. An external JavaScript file named functions.js contains two functions that you can use in completing this Web page: the placeIt() function places objects at specified coordinates on the page, and the getXCoord() function contains the x-coordinate of an object on the page. You'll have to create any other functions that you need.

Figure 15-55

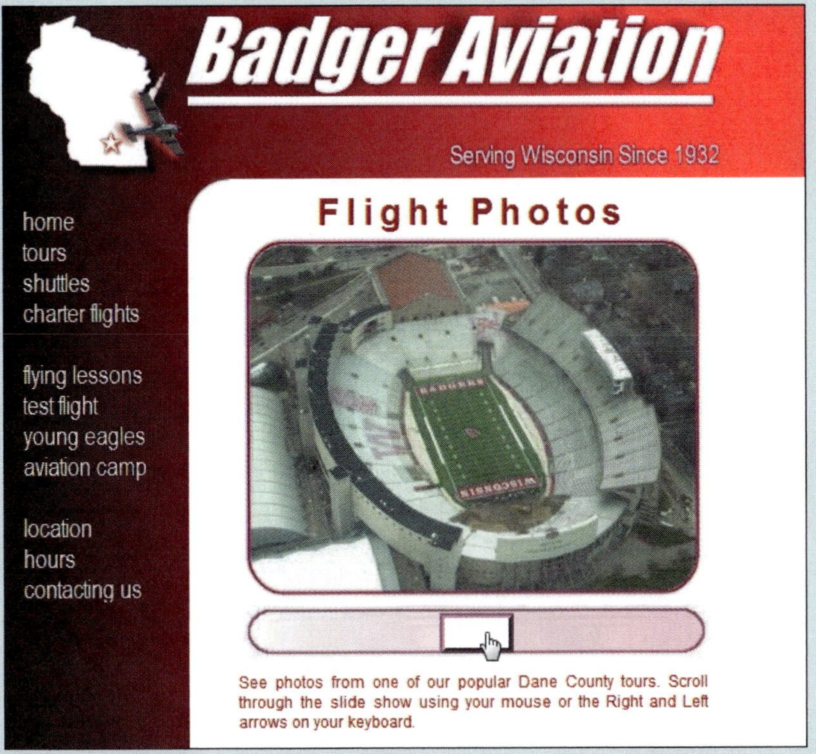

Complete the following:

1. Use your text editor to open the **badgertxt.htm**, **flibtxt.js**, and **slidetxt.js** files from the tutorial.15\case2 folder, enter ***your name*** and ***the date*** in the comment section of each file, and then save the files as **badger.htm**, **flibrary.js**, and **slideshow.js**, respectively.
2. Go to the **badger.htm** file in your text editor, study the contents of the file, and then add links to the external script files flibrary.js and slideshow.js. Close the file, saving your changes.
3. Go to **flibrary.js** in your text editor, and then insert a function named **addEvent()** that provides cross-browser support for assigning event handlers to events. The function should have four parameters: **object** for the object in which the event occurs, **evName** for the name of the event, **fnName** for the name of the function, and **cap**, a Boolean value indicating whether the event handler is assigned during the capture phase or the bubbling phase.
4. Insert a function named **removeEvent()** that provides cross-browser support for removing event handlers to events and objects. Use the same parameters you used for the addEvent() function. Close the flibrary.js file, saving your changes.

5. Go to the **slideshow.js** file in your text editor, and then declare a global variable named **scrollButton** and a global variable named **diffX**.
6. Have the browser run the function setup() when the page is loaded.
7. Insert the **setup()** function. The purpose of this function is to set up the Web and define the event handlers. Add the following commands to the function:
   a. Point the scrollButton object to the page element with the ID button.
   b. Retrieve and set the top style value of scrollButton, using the getStyle() function from the flibrary.js file.
   c. Retrieve and set the left style value of scrollButton, also using the getStyle() function.
   d. Define the cursor style of scrollButton to use the pointer cursor.
   e. Use the addEvent() function you created for the flibrary.js file to assign the grabIt() function (which you'll create shortly) to the mousedown event occurring within the scrollButton object. Assume that the event handler is assigned during the bubbling phase.
   f. Use the addEvent() function again to assign the keyShow() function to the Web document in response to the keydown event. Again, assume that the event handler occurs during the bubbling phase.
8. Create the **grabIt()** function. The purpose of this function is to "grab" the scroll button used in the slide show. Add the following commands to the function:
   a. Declare the **evt** variable, storing within it the event object under either event model.
   b. Declare a variable named **mouseX** that stores the clientX property of the event object.
   c. Set the value of the diffX variable equal to the numerical difference between the left coordinate of the scrollButton object and the value of the mouseX variable.
   d. Use the addEvent() method to assign the mousemove event handler to the scrollButton object, running the moveIt() function in response to that event. Assume that capture is done during the bubbling phase.
   e. Use the addEvent() method to assign the dropIt() function to the scrollButton object in response to the mouseup event. Again, assume that capture is done during the bubbling phase.
9. Create the **moveIt()** function. The purpose of this function is to move the scroll button in response to the movement of the pointer. Add the following commands to the function:
   a. Declare the **evt** variable, pointing to the event object under either event model.
   b. Declare the **mouseX** variable equal to the clientX property of the event object.
   c. Declare the **buttonPosX** variable. The purpose of this variable is to define the left coordinate of the scrolling button. Set its value equal to the sum of mouseX and diffX.
   d. Run the showSlide() function (which you'll create next), using the value of the buttonPosX variable as a parameter value.
10. Create the **showSlide()** function. The purpose of this function is to move the scroll button and determine what slide show image to display on the Web page. The function has a single parameter named **x** that represents the left coordinate of the scroll button. Add the following commands to the function:
   a. If x is less than 20, set the value of x equal to 20.
   b. If x is greater than 299, set the value of x equal to 299.
   c. Set the left coordinate of the scrollButton object equal to x.

   d. Declare a variable named **i** equal to (x – 20)/31 and then rounded down to the nearest integer. This converts the page coordinate to an index number. The value of the i variable is used to determine which of the nine image files to display in the slide show.
   e. Set the src property of the element with the ID, photo, equal to the image file image*i*.jpg, where *i* is the value of the i variable.
11. Create the **dropIt()** function. The purpose of this function is to stop moving the scroll button in response to movements of the mouse. Use the removeEvent() function you created for the flibrary.js file to move the event handler for the mousemove event from the scrollButton object.
12. Create the **keyShow()** function. The purpose of this function is to move the scroll button in response to the user pressing either the Left or Right arrow key. Add the following commands to the function:
   a. Declare the **evt** variable, pointing to the event object under either event model.
   b. Declare the **key** variable, setting it equal to the keyCode property of the event object.
   c. Declare the **buttonPosX** variable, setting it equal to the numeric value of the left position of the scrollButton object.
   d. If the user has pressed the Left arrow key, decrease the value of the buttonPosX variable by 31. If the user has pressed the Right arrow key, increase the value of the buttonPosX variable by 31.
   e. Run the showSlide() function using the value of the buttonPosX variable as the parameter value.
13. Save your changes to the file.
14. Open **badger.htm** in your Web browser. Verify that by dragging the scroll button on the Web page, you can move through the list of nine image files in the slide show. Press the Left and Right arrow keys on your keyboard and verify that you can move through the slide show using the keyboard.
15. Submit your completed project to your instructor.

Challenge | Case Problem 3

Explore how to use JavaScript events to create an online crossword puzzle.

Data Files needed for this Case Problem: across.gif, crosstxt.htm, down.gif, makepuzzle.js, parch.jpg, pcg.css, pcglogo.jpg, puzzle.css, runtxt.js

Park City Gazette The *Park City Gazette*, edited by Kevin Webber, is the weekly newspaper of Estes Park, Colorado. In addition to its print offerings, the newspaper has an online version for distribution on the Web. The paper is known for its puzzles and games, so recently Kevin decided to include a puzzle in the newspaper's online edition.

Kevin wants users to be able to type their answers directly into the puzzle. They should be able to navigate the puzzle by pressing the arrow keys on their keyboard, and typing a letter should move a user to the next cell. A user should also be able to toggle whether typing is entered vertically or horizontally by pressing the Spacebar on the keyboard.

Kevin wants the current cell in the puzzle to be displayed with a yellow background. If a user enters a correct letter into a cell, the background should change to light green. If a user enters an incorrect letter, a light red background should be displayed. Blank puzzle cells should be displayed with a white background. Figure 15-56 shows a preview of a partially completed puzzle with some correct and incorrect answers.

Figure 15-56

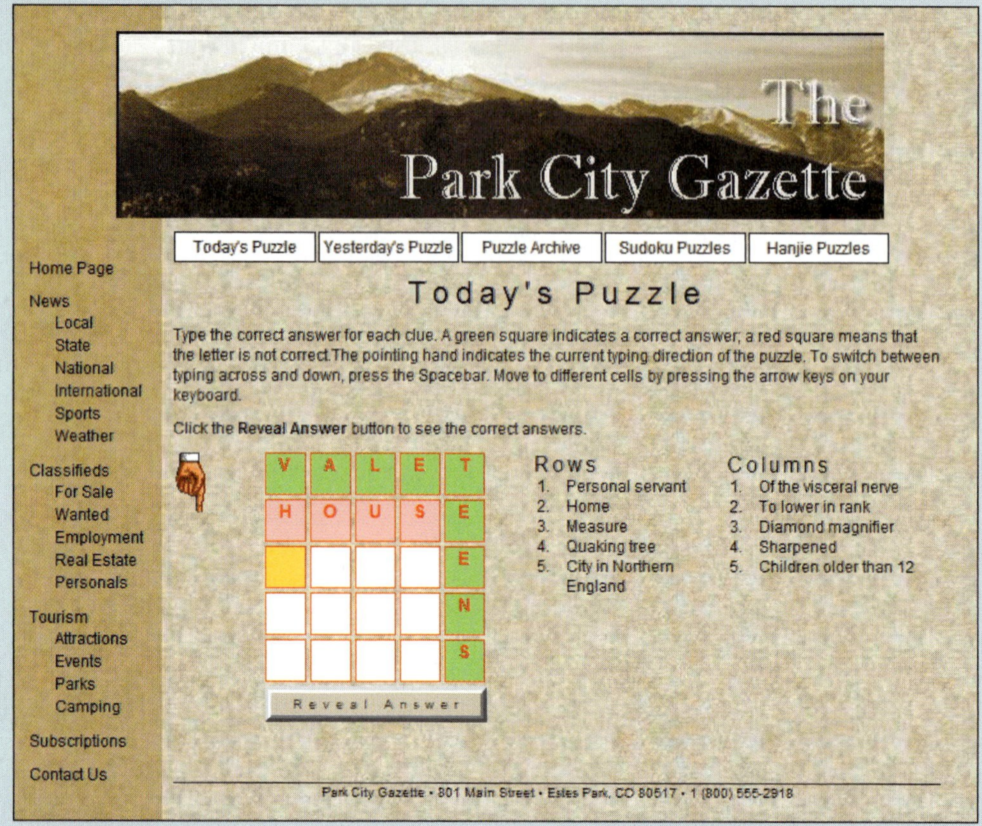

Each of the 25 cells in the puzzle is stored in a separate div element with the ID grid*xy*, where *x* represents the row number and *y* represents the column number. The row and column numbers start with 0 and go up to 4. Thus, the first cell in the puzzle has the ID grid00, the cell in the first row and second column has the ID grid01, and so on. The last cell in the puzzle has the ID grid44. You'll need to use this information to place the letters that users type in the correct cells in the puzzle.

One of Kevin's assistants already entered the HTML code for the puzzle page, and also produced some JavaScript code to generate the puzzle grid and its solution. Figure 15-57 describes the functions stored in the makepuzzle.js file.

Figure 15-57

Function	Description
writeClues()	Writes the puzzle clues onto the Web page where the puzzle clues are taken from two arrays named clues_across and clues_down
showAns()	Displays the puzzle answer; the text of the solution is contained in an array named words
writeText(object, text)	Writes the text string contained in the text parameter into the specified object

Complete the following:

1. Use your text editor to open the **crosstxt.htm** and **runtxt.js** files from the tutorial.15\case3 folder, enter ***your name*** and ***the date*** in the comment section of each file, and then save the files as **crossword.htm** and **runpuzzle.js**, respectively.
2. Go to the **crossword.htm** file in your text editor, study the contents of the file, and then add links to the external script files makepuzzle.js and runpuzzle.js. Close the file, saving your changes.
3. Go to the **runpuzzle.js** file in your text editor, and then add the following global variables to the file:
   a. **currentX** and **currentY**, representing the current column and row selected by the user from the puzzle. Set their initial values to 0.
   b. **currentCell** referencing the currently selected cell in the puzzle.
   c. **currentColor** storing the background color of the currently selected cell. Set its initial value to white.
   d. **across**, a Boolean variable indicating the direction in which data entry should occur. A value of true means that text is entered into the puzzle going across the cell. A value of false means that data entry goes down the cells. Set the initial value of the across variable to true.
   e. **keyNum**, a variable storing the keyCode value of whatever key is pressed by the user.
4. Have the browser run the init() function when the page is loaded.
5. Insert the **init()** function. The purpose of this function is to initialize the puzzle and set up the event handlers. Add the following commands to the function:
   a. Run the writeClues() function to write the puzzle clues into the Web page.
   b. Set the value of the currentCell variable to point to the grid00 cell.
   c. Set the background color of currentCell to yellow.
   d. When the user presses a keyboard key within the document, run the getKey() function.
   e. When the user clicks the Web element with the ID reveal, run the showAns() function.
   f. Change the cursor style of the reveal object to a pointer.
6. Insert the **getKey()** function. The purpose of this function is to respond to the keyboard key pressed by the user. Add the following commands to the function:
   a. Declare an event object named **evt** compatible with both event models.
   b. Store the key code of the event object in the **keyNum** variable.
   c. If the user has pressed the Spacebar key, run the toggleDirection() function and return the value false.
   d. If the user has pressed one of the arrow keys, run the moveCursor() function and return the value false.

EXPLORE

   e. If the user has pressed a letter from A to Z, run the writeGuess() function and return the value false.

7. Insert the **toggleDirection()** function. The purpose of this function is to toggle the direction in which text is typed into the puzzle. Add the following commands to the function:

EXPLORE

   a. If the value of the across variable is true, set the value of the across variable to false, and then change the source of the handimage inline image to the down.gif file.
   b. Otherwise, change the value of the across variable to true and change the source of the handimage inline image to the across.gif file.

8. Insert the **moveCell()** function. The purpose of this function is to change the row and column number of the selected cell in the crossword puzzle to a new cell. The function has two parameters named **diffX** and **diffY**. Add the following commands to the function:
   a. Increase the value of the currentX variable by diffX. Increase the value of the currentY variable by diffY.
   b. If currentX is less than 0, change its value to 4. If currentY is greater than 4, set its value to 0. Repeat this for the currentY variable.

9. Insert the **moveCursor()** function. The purpose of this function is to change the selected cell in the puzzle to a new row and/or column. Add the following commands to the function:
   a. Change the background color of the currentCell object to the value of the currentColor variable.
   b. If the user has pressed the Left arrow key, run the moveCell() function with parameter values of –1 and 0.
   c. If the user has pressed the Up arrow key, run the moveCell() function with parameter values of 0 and –1.
   d. If the user has pressed the Right arrow key, run the moveCell() function with parameter values of 1 and 0.
   e. If the user has pressed the Down arrow key, run the moveCell() function with parameter values of 0 and 1.
   f. Change the reference of the currentCell variable to point to the element with the ID grid*xy*, where *x* is the value of the currentX variable and *y* is the value of the currentY variable.
   g. Set the value of the currentColor variable to the background color of the current cell.
   h. Set the background color of the current cell to yellow.

10. Insert the **writeGuess()** function. The purpose of this function is to write the character that the user has typed into the current cell in the puzzle grid, and then to move to the next cell in the puzzle (either across or down). Add the following commands to the function:

EXPLORE

   a. Use the fromCharCode() method of the String object to store the character string represented by the keyNum variable in a variable named **outChar**.

EXPLORE

   b. Use the toUpperCase() method to change the text of the outChar variable to an uppercase letter.
   c. Call the writeText() function from the makepuzzle.js file to write the value of the outChar variable into the currentCell object.

d. If the text of outChar contains the correct letter for the cell, change the background color of the current cell to light green. (*Hint*: To test whether the outChar letter is correct, compare outChar's value to the value of the words array item words[*y* * 5 + *x*], where *y* is the value of the current column and *x* is the value of the current row.) If the value is not correct, change the background color of the current cell to pink.

e. If the value of the across variable is true, then move the location of the current cell to the right using the moveCell() function; otherwise, call the moveCell() function to move down.

f. Point the currentCell object to the element with the ID grid*xy*, where *x* is the value of the currentX variable and *y* is the value of the currentY variable. Store the background color of currentCell in the currentColor variable. Change the background color of currentCell to yellow.

11. Close the runpuzzle.js file, saving your changes.
12. Load **crossword.htm** in your Web browser. Verify that (i) when you type letters using the keyboard, those letters are displayed in the puzzle grid; (ii) the current cell is displayed with a yellow background; (iii) correct letters are displayed with a light green background; (iv) incorrect letters are displayed with a pink background; (v) pressing the arrow keys moves the current cell around the puzzle grid; (vi) pressing the Spacebar toggles the typing direction and swaps the pointing hand image; and (vii) clicking the **Reveal Answer** button reveals the puzzle solution. (*Note*: The Opera browser will intercept keystrokes for the H and P letters, and attempt to display the history list and printer dialog box. You can ignore these incidents and continue to type in the puzzle solution.)
13. Submit the completed project to your instructor.

Create | Case Problem 4

Create a drag-and-drop survey form for a presidential museum.

Data Files needed for this Case Problem: library.js, pm.txt, pmlogo.jpg, pres0.jpg – pres16.jpg

Presidential Mosaic Karen Xavier works at the Presidential Museum in Cleveland, Ohio. The museum features exhibits, talks, and displays that chronicle the history of the American presidency. One of Karen's goals is to provide interactive displays for museum patrons. She wants to establish a network of interactive kiosks scattered throughout the main floor of the museum. One of her ideas is to create interactive survey questions that patrons can answer as they tour the museum. Karen asks you to help create a Web page that contains a survey asking museum patrons who are the most popular presidents of the 20th century. Karen envisions a Web page with a list of the president names and portraits, which the museum patron can drag and drop onto a second list in the order of preference. To complete this survey page, you need to write a JavaScript program that does the following:

- Makes images of the 17 presidents from the 20th century into dragable objects
- Prevents users from dropping one presidential portrait upon another
- Includes a feature in which information about each president is displayed in a text area box when the user hovers the pointer over the presidential portrait

Karen has assembled the graphic images and the text required for the Web page. You'll use this material to create your final Web page. A preview of one possible solution to this project is shown in Figure 15-58, but you are encouraged to develop your own unique solution.

Figure 15-58

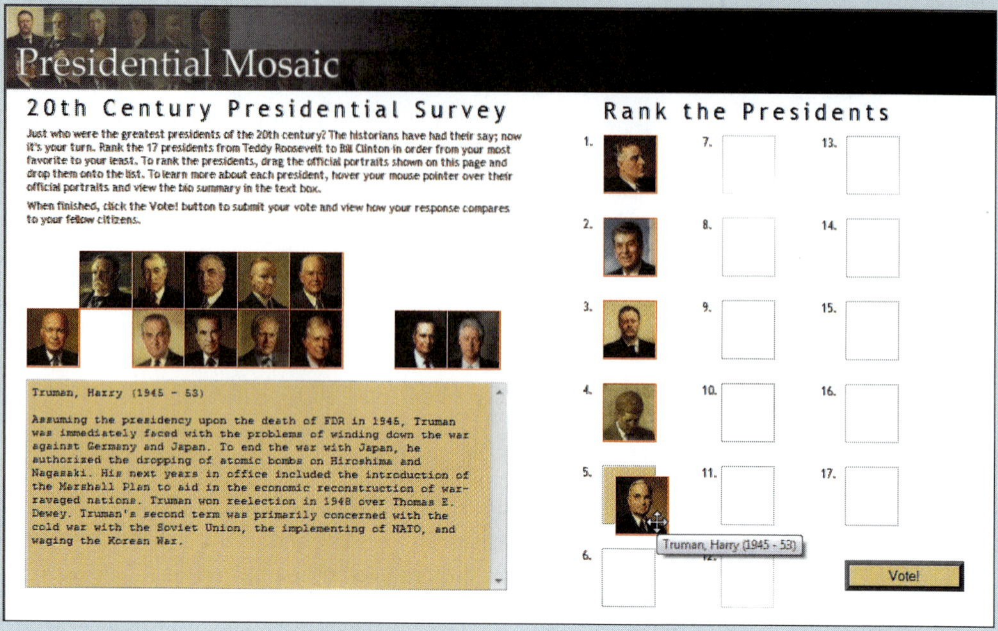

Complete the following:

1. Using the material found in the tutorial.15/case4 folder, create a Web page named **president.htm**. Include a comment section that describes the contents of your file and includes your name and the date. You may supplement the content provided for your Web page with any other content you think is appropriate for the task.
2. The design and layout of the page are up to you. Place the style definitions for your Web page in an external file named **pm.css**. Include a comment section in the file that documents its use and includes your name and the date. Link your Web page to this style sheet.
3. Create an external JavaScript file named **survey.js** that contains the code to enable users to drag and drop elements on the president.htm Web page. A few functions have been stored in the **library.js** file to help you with your program. The code should contain examples of the following features:
   a. Event handlers that involve event capturing supported under both event models
   b. Removing event handlers using a function that supports both event models
   c. Working with the properties of the event object under both event models
   d. Event handlers that respond to actions of the mouse
   e. Commands that modify the cursor style of an object
4. Link the Web page to the external JavaScript file and test the functionality of the page. Verify that you can drag and drop individual presidential portraits from their default location to their ranking on the list.
5. Submit the completed project to your instructor.

Review | **Quick Check Answers**

Session 15.1

1. `document.onclick = function () {alert("Click Detected");}`
2. From the bottom of the object hierarchy up to the top
3. `document.getElementById("Total").attachEvent("onclick", calcTotal);`
4. `document.getElementById("Total").detachEvent("onclick", calcTotal);`
5. Events are propagated from the top of the hierarchy during the capture phase, down to the event's target, and then back up the hierarchy during the bubbling phase.
6. `document.getElementById("Total").addEventListener("click", calcTotal, false)`
7. `document.getElementById("Total").removeEventListener("click", calcTotal, false)`

Session 15.2

1. IE event model: window.event
   W3C event model: the parameter of the event function
2. `type`
3. `screenX` and `screenY`
4. `clientX` and `clientY`
5. Increase the z-index of the object to be the maximum on the page.
6. Under the IE event model, the `this` keyword refers to the global object, which is the window itself. Under the W3C event model, the `this` keyword references whatever object is currently handling the event and calling the event function.
7. IE event model: `event.fromElement`
   W3C event model: `evt.relatedTarget`
8. IE event model: `event.toElement`
   W3C event model: `evt.relatedTarget`

Session 15.3

1. CSS: `cursor: wait`
   JavaScript: `object.style.cursor = "wait";`
2. Use the button property.
   The IE event model uses 1 = left, 2 = middle, 4 = right
   The W3C event model uses 0 = left, 1 = middle, 2 = right
3. `keydown`
4. The keydown event is fired when the user presses a keyboard key. The keypress event occurs immediately after the keydown event and indicates that a character has been sent to the browser from the act of pressing the key.
5. `keyCode`
6. 32
7. `altKey`
8. IE event model: `event.cancelBubble = true;`
   W3C event model: `evt.stopPropagation();`
9. Have the function handling the event return a value of false or run the following command:
   IE event model: `event.returnValue = false;`
   W3C event model: `evt.preventDefault();`

Ending Data Files

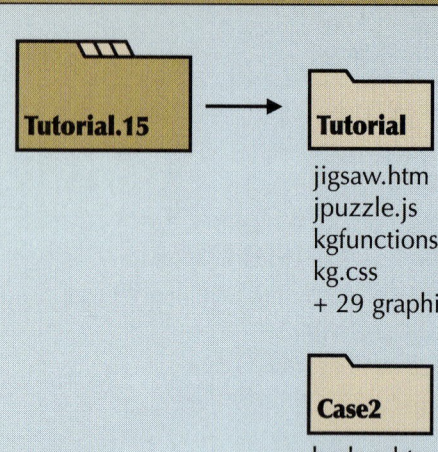

Tutorial.15 →

Tutorial
- jigsaw.htm
- jpuzzle.js
- kgfunctions.js
- kg.css
- + 29 graphic files

Review
- blocks.htm
- library.js
- slideblocks.js
- sbblocks.css
- + 29 graphic files

Case1
- bookforum.htm
- comment.js
- bw.css
- + 2 graphic files

Case2
- badger.htm
- flibrary.js
- slideshow.js
- styles.css
- + 15 graphic files

Case3
- crossword.htm
- makepuzzle.js
- runpuzzle.js
- pcg.css
- puzzle.css
- + 4 graphic files

Case4
- president.htm
- library.js
- survey.js
- pm.css
- + 18 graphic files

Working with Dynamic Content and Styles

Creating a Dynamic Table of Contents

Objectives

Session 16.1
- Learn how to create dynamic content under the IE DOM
- Understand the methods and properties of nodes and the node tree
- Learn to create element and text nodes
- Understand how to attach nodes to a Web page document

Session 16.2
- Apply node properties and styles to create dynamic content
- Work with the properties and methods of attribute nodes
- Work with element attributes

Session 16.3
- Hide and redisplay Web page objects
- Understand how to create recursive functions to navigate a node tree
- Learn to work with the properties and methods of style sheet objects

Case | Midwest University

Norene Somerville is a professor of history at Midwest University. One of her recent projects involves putting the text of important historic documents online for her students to download and study. The Web site she's creating will support a variety of different document formats, but Norene also wants each document to be available in HTML format on a single Web page. This format makes it easier for students to print out the complete text of a document without having to navigate an entire site or install word processing or document software. However, Norene is concerned that some of the documents are very long and would be difficult to manage if placed on a single page.

She believes that a table of contents that summarizes the different sections within a document and provides links to those sections would be a great aid to students. However, Norene doesn't have the time to create such a table of contents for each document in her online library. She wants a program to automatically generate these tables of contents, and she has asked you to develop such a utility.

Starting Data Files

Tutorial.16 →

Tutorial
treattxt.htm
usconsttxt.htm
switchtxt.js
toctxt.js
+ 3 CSS files
+ 3 graphic files

Review
fed10txt.htm
keytxt.js
stylestxt.js
fedpaper.css
print.css
hlogo.jpg

Case1
french5txt.htm
engfrtxt.js
french5.js
styles.css

Case2
camtxt.htm
filtertxt.js
cstyles.css
+ 3 graphic files

Case3
statstxt.htm
tabletxt.js
tstyles.css
+ 3 graphic files

Case4
temptxt.htm
scenetxt.js
plays.css
+ 6 graphic files

Session 16.1

Introducing Dynamic Content

You and Norene discuss the table of contents utility. She has created a sample document containing the text of the United States Constitution. She feels that this would pose an ideal challenge because the document is very long and divided into different topical sections.

To view Norene's Web page:

1. Use your text editor to open the **usconsttxt.htm** and **toctxt.js** files located in the tutorial.16/tutorial folder, enter ***your name*** and ***the date*** in the comment section of each file, then save the files as **usconst.htm** and **toc.js**, respectively.
2. Return to the **usconst.htm** file in your text editor, and study the contents and structure of the file. The document contains a div element with the ID toc, in which you'll place the table of contents. It also includes a div element with the ID doc, containing the text of the document upon which the table of contents will be based.
3. Open **usconst.htm** in your Web browser. See Figure 16-1. The table of contents will be placed in the blue box in the page's left margin.

Figure 16-1 The initial Constitution Web page

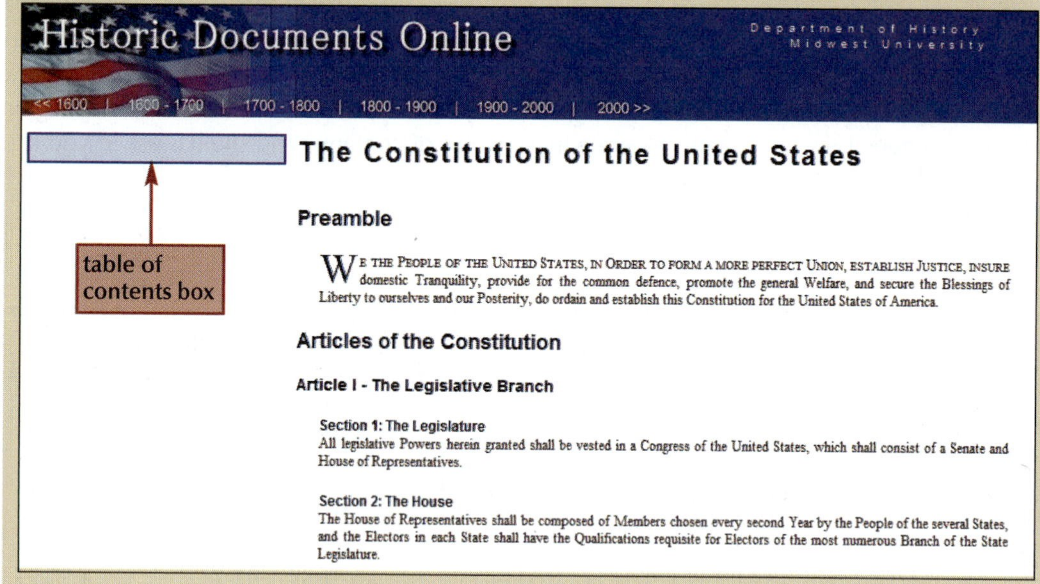
Historic Documents Online
Department of History
Midwest University
<< 1600 | 1600 - 1700 | 1700 - 1800 | 1800 - 1900 | 1900 - 2000 | 2000 >>
The Constitution of the United States
Preamble
We the People of the United States, in Order to form a more perfect Union, establish Justice, insure domestic Tranquility, provide for the common defence, promote the general Welfare, and secure the Blessings of Liberty to ourselves and our Posterity, do ordain and establish this Constitution for the United States of America.
Articles of the Constitution
Article I - The Legislative Branch
Section 1: The Legislature
All legislative Powers herein granted shall be vested in a Congress of the United States, which shall consist of a Senate and House of Representatives.
Section 2: The House
The House of Representatives shall be composed of Members chosen every second Year by the People of the several States, and the Electors in each State shall have the Qualifications requisite for Electors of the most numerous Branch of the State Legislature.
table of contents box

Examining the Table of Contents

Norene sketched her idea for the table of contents, as shown in Figure 16-2. Her idea is to create the table of contents as an ordered list, which is placed to the left of the source document. The table of contents utility should be automatically generated when the page is loaded by the browser, with minimal code added to the HTML document. Ideally, any table of contents application you create should be applicable to a wide selection of source documents.

Figure 16-2 Proposed table of contents layout

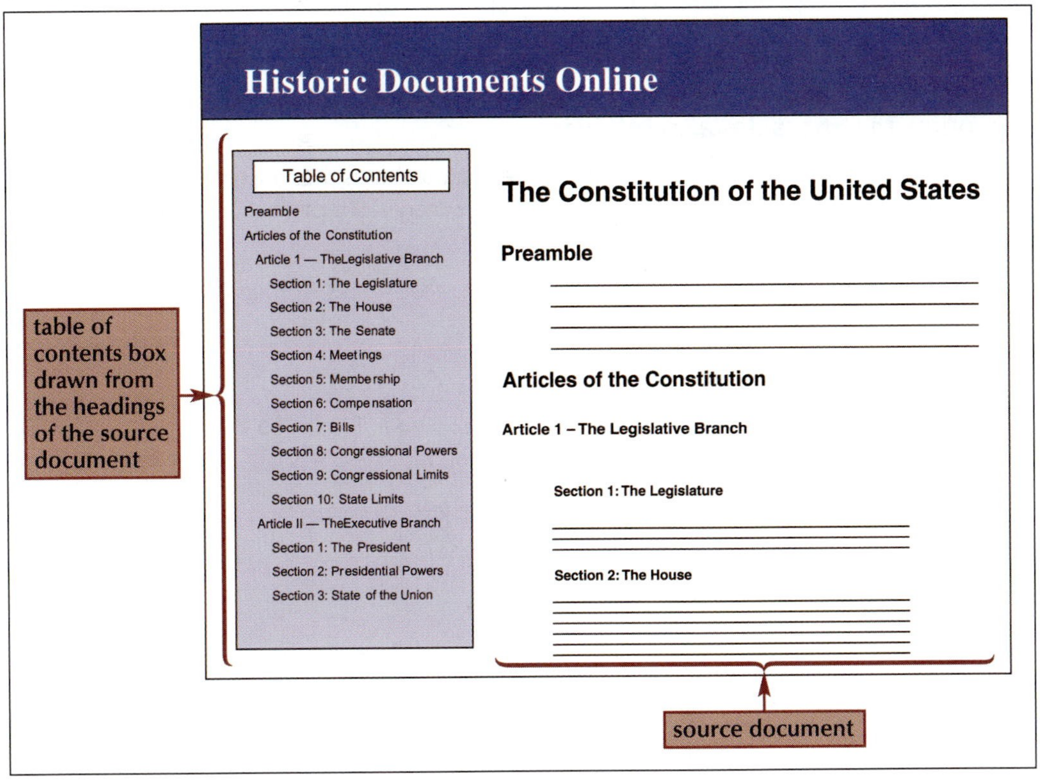

Norene suggests basing the table of contents on heading elements that are often used to break long HTML documents into topical sections. For example, the h1 heading usually marks a primary section in a document, h2 marks a secondary heading, and so on. Figure 16-3 shows the type of HTML code the table of contents application would generate. The utility would search the Web page for heading elements, copying the text of each heading into the table of contents. The table of contents would be organized as a nested ordered list with higher-level headings placed at the top of the list. For example, all h1 headings would be placed at the top level of the TOC, h2 headings would be listed within the h1 headings as the second level, and so on.

Figure 16-3 Document content converted into a table of contents

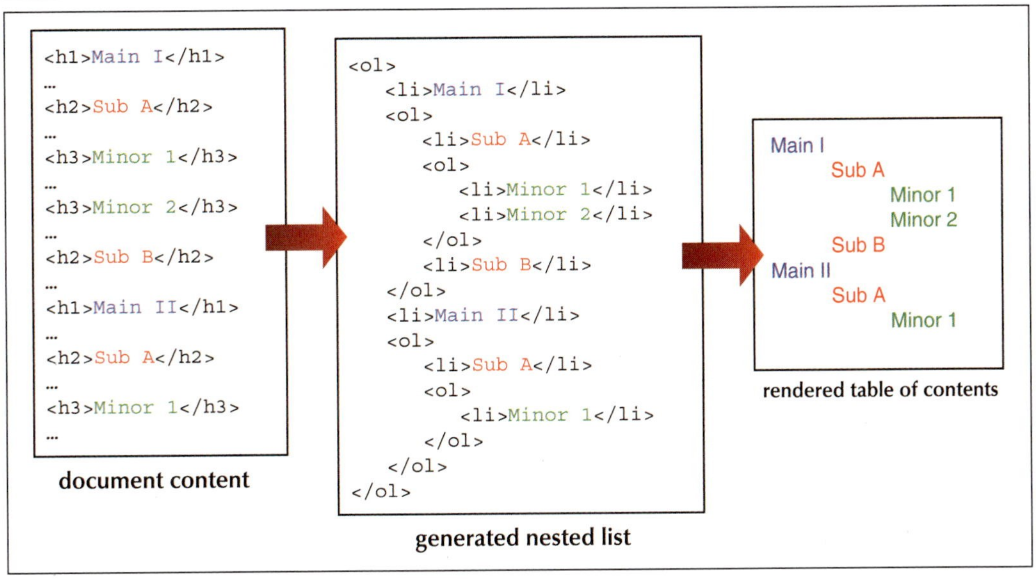

All of the JavaScript code that generates the table of contents will be located in an external file. This will allow Norene to easily apply the finished utility to other documents in her library. She created a file with some initial code, which you'll open now.

To open the toc.js JavaScript file:

1. Return to the **usconst.htm** file in your text editor, and then insert the following external script element to access the file in which you'll place the table of contents application:

```
<script src = "toc.js" type = "text/javascript"></script>
```

2. Close the file, saving your changes.
3. Return to the **toc.js** file in your text editor.
4. Add the following commands to the file, as shown in Figure 16-4, to run the makeTOC() function when the Web page is loaded:

```
addEvent(window, "load", makeTOC, false);

function makeTOC() {

}
```

Figure 16-4 Code to run the makeTOC() function when the page loads

```
function addEvent(object, evName, fnName, cap) {
   if (object.attachEvent)
       object.attachEvent("on" + evName, fnName);
   else if (object.addEventListener)
       object.addEventListener(evName, fnName, cap);
}

addEvent(window, "load", makeTOC, false);

function makeTOC() {

}
```

Note that this code uses the addEvent() function previously introduced to add the event under both the IE and W3C event models.

Inserting HTML Content into an Element

Generating a table of contents involves working with **dynamic content**, in which the content of the Web page is determined by the operation of a script running within the browser. Often, dynamic content is determined either by users' actions or by the content of other elements on the Web page or within the Web site. Noreen wants the table of contents to include the heading Table of Contents. One way of writing this heading into the table of contents box is to use the innerHTML property. The syntax of the innerHTML property is

```
object.innerHTML = content
```

where *object* is a Web page object and *content* is a text string containing HTML code to be written into that object. For example, to add an h1 heading to the toc element, you would run the following commands:

```
var TOC = document.getElementById("toc");
TOC.innerHTML = "<h1>Table of Contents</h1>";
```

You'll add these commands to the makeTOC() function.

To insert a heading into the TOC:

1. Within the toc.js file, go to the makeTOC() function and insert the following commands, as shown in Figure 16-5:

```
var TOC = document.getElementById("toc");
TOC.innerHTML = "<h1>Table of Contents</h1>";
```

HTML code added to the TOC object — **Figure 16-5**

```
function makeTOC() {
   var TOC = document.getElementById("toc");
   TOC.innerHTML = "<h1>Table of Contents</h1>";
}
```

2. Save your changes to the file, and then reload **usconst.htm** in your Web browser. The table of contents displays the new heading. See Figure 16-6.

Table of contents with the h1 heading inserted — **Figure 16-6**

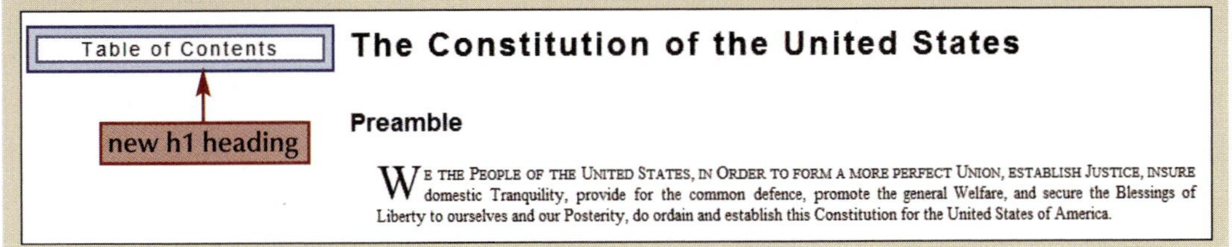
Table of Contents
new h1 heading
The Constitution of the United States
Preamble
We the People of the United States, in Order to form a more perfect Union, establish Justice, insure domestic Tranquility, provide for the common defence, promote the general Welfare, and secure the Blessings of Liberty to ourselves and our Posterity, do ordain and establish this Constitution for the United States of America.

The styles for the table of contents and the document are stored in the web.css style sheet. If you want to study the display styles that will appear as you create the table of contents throughout this tutorial, review the contents of this file.

Exploring innerText and textContent

The innerHTML property returns the HTML code found within an object, including any HTML tags, but it does not separate the text content from the text found in the markup tags. For example, if the document includes the tag

```
<div id = "doctitle">
   <h1>The Constitution of the <em>United States</em></h1>
</div>
```

the expression

```
document.getElementById("doctitle").innerHTML
```

returns

```
<h1>The Constitution of the <em>United States</em></h1>
```

In many cases, you're not interested in markup tags—only the text content of the element. Under the IE DOM, you can retrieve the text content, stripping out the HTML tags, by using the innerText property. Other browsers such as Firefox don't support this property, but instead support the textContent property, which returns the same results. You can use object detection to determine which property is supported by the user's browser, or combine the properties using the || (or) operator in the expression

```
object.innerText || object.textContent
```

where *object* is an object on the Web page. Applying this expression to content of the doctitle object described above yields the text string

```
The Constitution of the United States
```

without any markup tags from the original HTML fragment.

InSight | **Creating Dynamic Content in Internet Explorer**

The innerHTML property is not part of the official specifications for the W3C document object model, but it is part of the DOM for Internet Explorer. Because this property has proven valuable and simple to use, it is supported by all browsers. The IE DOM also supports other properties and methods to aid in the creation of dynamic content. However, these properties and methods are not as widely supported as the innerHTML property. One of these, the innerText property, has already been discussed. Another is the outerHTML property, which has the syntax

```
object.outerHTML = content;
```

where *object* is again the Web page object, but *content* is a text string of the HTML code for both the object and the content it contains. For example, if a Web page contains the element

```
<h1 id = "title">History Online</h1>
```

then the commands

```
var title = document.getElementById("title");
title.outerHTML = "<h2>Historic Documents</h2>";
```

are equivalent to replacing the h1 element with the following h2 element:

```
<h2>Historic Documents</h2>
```

Be aware that changing the element tags in addition to the element's content can result in unforeseen errors. For example, running the above code removes the title element from the document hierarchy because the ID attribute is not included in the new h2 element. Any subsequent part of the script that references the title element would result in an error. Use caution whenever you apply the outerHTML property to ensure that you don't change more of an element's content than you intended.

Working with Nodes

Although the innerHTML property writes HTML code into the document, it doesn't allow you to work with the newly inserted pieces of content as objects in their own right. A different approach is to use JavaScript to create nodes. A **node** represents an object within the Web page or Web browser. Anything in the document can be treated as a node, including every HTML tag and all of a tag's attributes. Even the tags in a document's head section, comment tags, and the <html> tag itself can be treated as nodes. The text within an HTML tag can also be treated as a node. For example, the tag

```
<h1>Table of Contents</h1>
```

consists of two nodes: one node for the h1 element and one node for the text string, Table of Contents, contained within that element.

Using a Node Tree

Nodes are arranged into a hierarchal structure called a **node tree**, which indicates the relationship between each of the nodes. Figure 16-7 shows a representation of a node tree for a simple HTML document. In the node tree, each element is treated as a separate node and the text within each element is treated as a node as well.

A document node tree — **Figure 16-7**

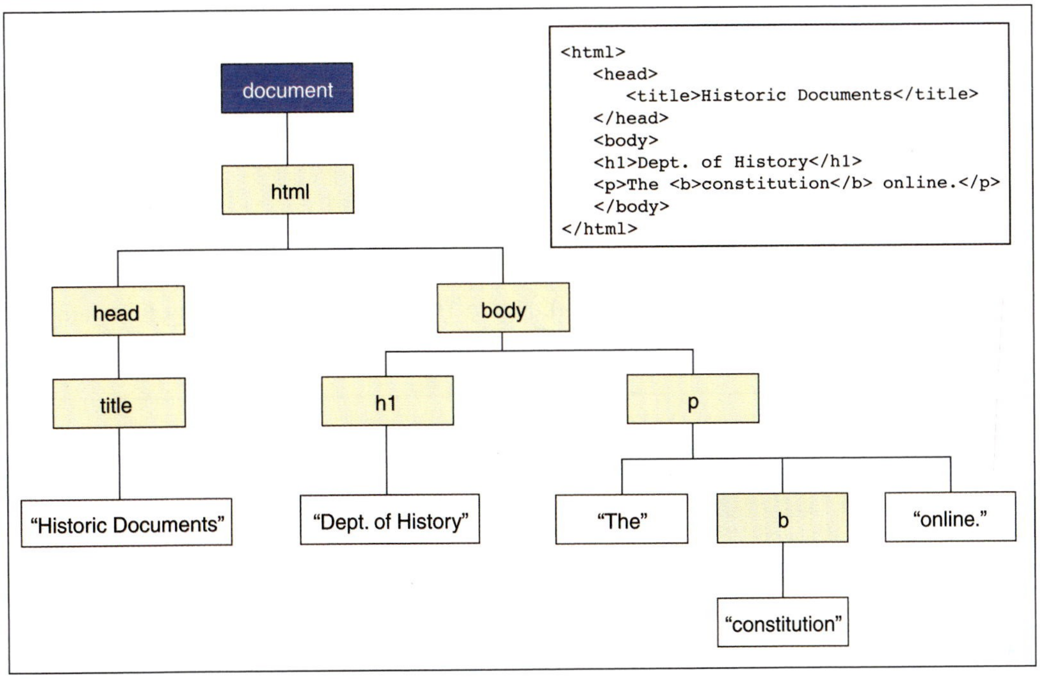

<html>
<head>
<title>Historic Documents</title>
</head>
<body>
<h1>Dept. of History</h1>
<p>The <b>constitution</b> online.</p>
</body>
</html>
document
html
head
body
title
h1
p
"Historic Documents"
"Dept. of History"
"The"
b
"online."
"constitution"

Nodes in a node tree have a familial relationship—each node can be a parent, child, and/or sibling of other nodes. To reference a node based on its relationship with the current node, use the expression

```
node.relationship
```

where *node* is the currently selected node or object and *relationship* is the relationship of another node to the current node. For example, the expression

```
node.parentNode
```

refers to the parent of *node*. In the node tree shown in Figure 16-7, the parent of the body node is the html node, and the parent of the html node is the document node. The parent of all nodes within a document is the **root node**. For HTML or XHTML documents, the root node is the html element. The root node is itself a child of the document node, which represents the entire document.

Each node can contain one or more child nodes. To reference the first child of the current node, use the following expression:

```
node.firstChild
```

In the node tree shown in Figure 16-7, the h1 node is the first child of the body node, and the text node "Dept. of History" is its first (and only) child. All of the child nodes are organized into the following object collection:

```
node.childNodes
```

Tip

A document's root node can also be referenced using the documentElement object.

As with other object collections, you can reference a particular object from this collection using the item's index number, as follows

```
node.childNodes[i]
```

where *i* is the index number of the child node. For example, to reference the first child of the current node, you could use either of the following expressions:

```
node.firstChild
```

or

```
node.childNodes[0]
```

Tip

With Web documents, the order of the child nodes matches the order of the elements as they appear in the HTML or XHTML file.

To determine the total number of child nodes for a given node, you use the following length property:

```
node.childNodes.length
```

The length of the childNodes collection for the paragraph element in Figure 16-7 is 3 (the two text nodes and the bold element). Figure 16-8 summarizes the rest of the familial relationships in the node tree.

Figure 16-8 **Node relationships**

Expression	Description
node.firstChild	Returns the first child of *node*
node.lastChild	Returns the last child of *node*
node.childNodes	Returns a collection containing the children of *node*
node.previousSibling	Returns the sibling prior to *node*
node.nextSibling	Returns the sibling after *node*
node.ownerDocument	Returns the root node of the document
node.parentNode	Returns the parent of *node*

Reference Window | Determining Node Relationships

- To access the parent of a node object, use the reference
  `node.parentNode`
  where *node* is a node object in the node tree.
- To reference the first and last child of a node, use the following reference:
  `node.firstChild`
  `node.lastChild`
- To reference the collection of all child nodes, use the following reference:
  `node.childNodes`
- To reference the previous and next sibling, use the following reference:
  `node.previousSibling`
  `node.nextSibling`

Determining Node Types, Names, and Values

The two document object models interpret white space in an HTML file differently. The W3C DOM calls for all occurrences of white space to be treated as text nodes. For example, the HTML code

```
<h1>Table of Contents</h1>
<h2>U.S. Constitution</h2>
```

contains five nodes: one node for the h1 element, one node for the h2 element, two nodes for the text contained within those two elements, and one node for the white space separating the h1 and h2 elements. The IE DOM does not treat occurrences of white space as text nodes. So under Internet Explorer, the above code contains only four nodes.

The difference between the two DOMs in how they handle white space may affect your program, so it's a good idea to determine whether a given node represents a text node, an element node, or some other type of node. The following properties provide information about a node's type, name, and value:

```
node.nodeType
node.nodeName
node.nodeValue
```

Tip

The nodeName property always returns element names in uppercase letters, so that an h1 element has the nodeName property value of H1.

The nodeType property is an integer indicating whether the node refers to an element, a text string, a comment, an attribute, and so on. The nodeName property returns the name of the node within the document. The nodeValue property returns the node's value. Figure 16-9 displays some of the values of these three properties for the different types of nodes you'll typically encounter in a Web page document.

Node types, names, and values **Figure 16-9**

Node	.nodeType	.nodeName	.nodeValue
Element	1	*ELEMENT NAME*	null
Attribute	2	*attribute name*	*attribute value*
Text	3	#text	*text string*
Comment	8	#comment	*comment text*
Document	9	#document	null

To see how these properties compare to a node tree, Figure 16-10 displays the nodeType, nodeName, and nodeValue property values for each of the nodes from Figure 16-7.

Nodes from the sample node tree **Figure 16-10**

Node	.nodeType	.nodeName	.nodeValue
Document	9	#document	null
html	1	HTML	null
head	1	HEAD	null
body	1	BODY	null
title	1	TITLE	null
"Historic Documents"	3	#text	Historic Documents
h1	1	H1	null
"Dept. of History"	3	#text	Dept. of History
p	1	P	null
"The "	3	#text	The
b	1	B	null
"constitution"	3	#text	constitution
" online"	3	#text	online

Nodes from the Sample Node Tree

Element nodes have no value. It might seem that an element node's value should be the content it contains, but that content is already its own node. If you want to change the text contained within an element, you must modify the value of that element's text node. For example, the title element contains the following text:

```
<h1 id = "title">History Online</h1>
```

To change the text of the title to "Historic Documents Online," you could run the following code under the W3C DOM:

```
var title = document.getElementById("title");
title.firstChild.nodeValue = "Historic Documents Online";
```

This code sample uses the firstChild reference because the text node is the first (and only) child of the title element.

Reference Window | Determining Node Properties

- To determine the type of object a node represents, use the property
  `node.nodeType`
  where *node* is a node object in the node tree. The nodeType property returns the value 1 for elements, 2 for attributes, and 3 for text nodes.
- To return the value of a node, use the following property:
  `node.nodeValue`
  For elements, the value of the nodeValue property is null. For attributes, the value represents the attribute's value. For text nodes, the value represents the text string contained in the node.
- To return the name of a node, use the following property:
  `node.nodeName`
  For elements, the name of the node matches the name of the element in uppercase letters. For attributes, the node name matches the attribute name. For text nodes, the node name is #text.

Creating and Attaching Nodes

To create the dynamic table of contents, you have to add new content to the Web page. The W3C DOM supports several methods to create new nodes, which are listed in Figure 16-11.

Figure 16-11 Methods to create nodes

Method	Description
`document.createAttribute(`*`att`*`)`	Creates an attribute node with the name *att*.
`document.createComment(`*`text`*`)`	Creates a comment node containing the comment text string *text*.
`document.createElement(`*`elem`*`)`	Creates an element node with the name *elem*.
`document.createTextNode(`*`text`*`)`	Creates a text node containing the text string *text*.
`node``.cloneNode(`*`deep`*`)`	Creates a copy of *node*. If the Boolean parameter *deep* is true, the copy extends to all descendants of the node object; otherwise, only *node* is copied.

Using these methods, you can create a wide variety of objects that can be used in a Web page document. For example, you would use the following expression to create a text node containing the text "Historic Documents Online":

```
document.createTextNode("Historic Documents Online")
```

All of the methods described in Figure 16-11 create single nodes, with the exception of the cloneNode() method. The cloneNode() method is useful when you need to create a copy of an existing node, including any descendants of that node. The command

```
newtitle = title.cloneNode(true)
```

creates a copy of the title node, including any descendants of that node. The cloneNode() method provides a quick and easy way of creating elements and their content without having to create each node individually.

Creating Nodes

| Reference Window

- To create an element node, use the method
  `document.createElement(`*`text`*`)`
  where *text* is the name of the element.
- To create an attribute node, use the method
  `document.createAttribute(`*`text`*`)`
  where *text* is the name of the attribute.
- To create a text node, use the method
  `document.createTextNode(`*`text`*`)`
  where *text* is the text string of the text node.
- To create a comment node, use the method
  `document.createComment(`*`text`*`)`
  where *text* is the text of the comment.
- To copy a preexisting node, use the method
  `node``.cloneNode(`*`deep`*`)`
  where *node* is the preexisting node and *deep* is a Boolean value indicating whether to copy all descendants of the node (true) or only the node itself (false).

Once a node has been created, it still must be attached to another node in the document's node tree to be part of the document. Unattached nodes and node trees are known as **document fragments** and exist only in a browser's memory. They are not rendered on the Web page, although you can still access document fragments and work with them in your program. Figure 16-12 describes several methods for attaching one node to another.

Figure 16-12 **Methods to attach or remove nodes**

Method	Description
`node.appendChild(new)`	Appends a *new* child node to *node*, attaching it as the last child node
`node.insertBefore(new, child)`	Inserts a *new* child node into *node*, placing it before the *child* node; if no *child* is specified the *new* child node is added as the last child node
`node.normalized()`	Traverses all child nodes of *node*; any adjacent text nodes are merged into a single text node
`node.removeChild(old)`	Removes the child node *old* from *node*
`node.replaceChild(new, old)`	Replaces the child node *old* with the child node *new*

Using the properties and methods described in Figures 16-11 and 16-12, you can create elaborate node trees that contain several levels of different nodes. Figure 16-13 describes the process by which you would create the following HTML fragment using those methods:

```
<p><i>Historic</i> Documents</p>
```

Figure 16-13 **Process to create and attach nodes**

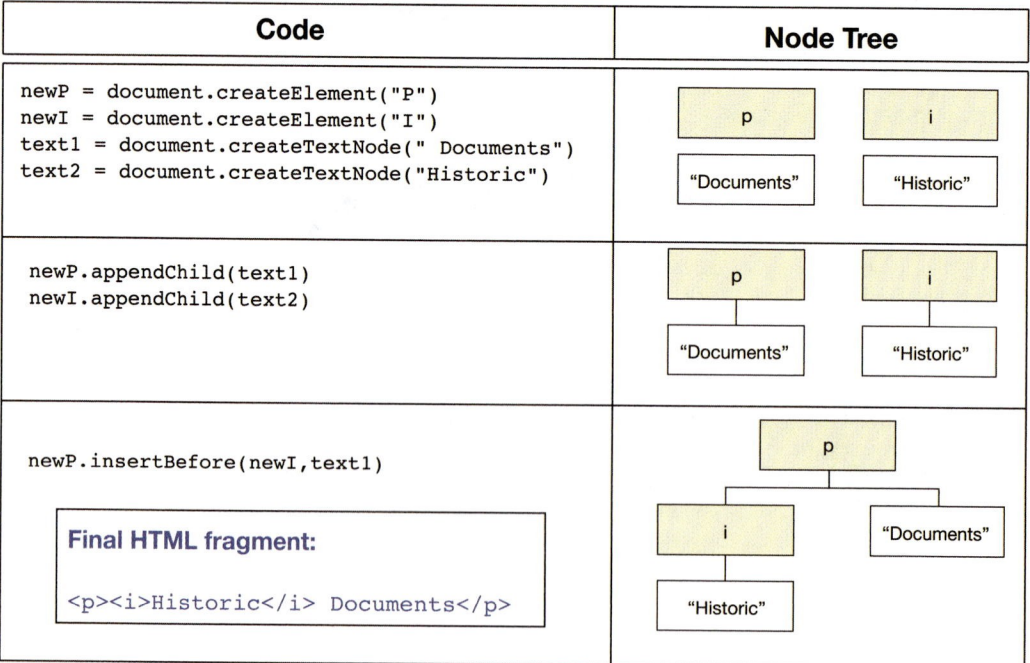

Code | **Node Tree**

```
newP = document.createElement("P")
newI = document.createElement("I")
text1 = document.createTextNode(" Documents")
text2 = document.createTextNode("Historic")
```

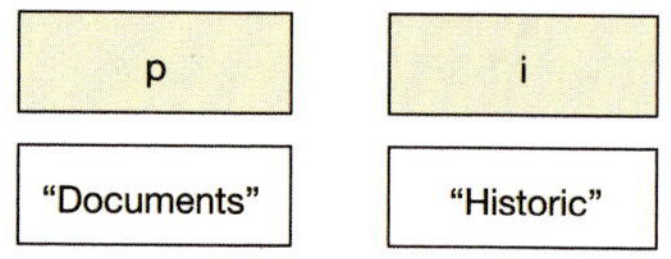


```
newP.appendChild(text1)
newI.appendChild(text2)
```

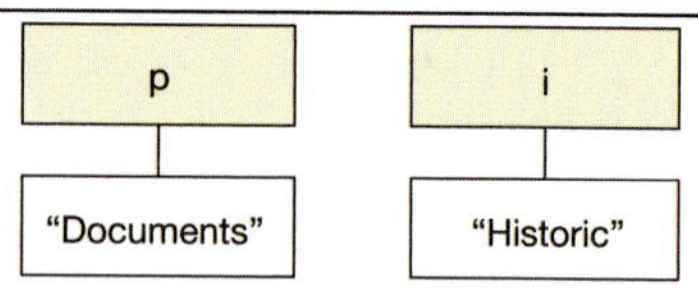


```
newP.insertBefore(newI,text1)
```

Final HTML fragment:

```
<p><i>Historic</i> Documents</p>
```

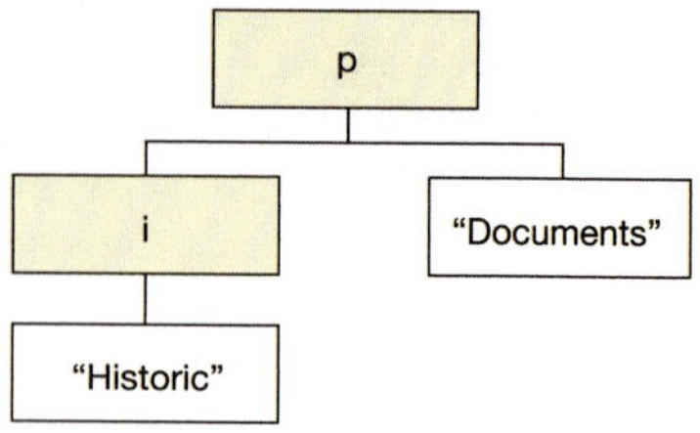

The approach shown in Figure 16-13 first uses the createElement() and createTextNode() methods to create four nodes: an element node for a paragraph, an element node for italicized text, a text node containing the text string "Historic", and a text node containing the text " Documents". The appendChild() method is then employed to attach the text nodes to the element nodes. The last line of code uses the insertBefore() method to insert the italicized text before the second text node. Although at first glance this approach may seem more cumbersome than simply using the innerHTML method, the advantage of nodes is that you can work with individual elements and text strings with more detail and flexibility than is possible with other methods.

Tip

When applied to a node that is already part of the document, the appendChild() and insertBefore() methods move the node from its current location in the document tree to its new location as a child node.

Attaching and Removing Nodes | Reference Window

- To append a new node as a child of a preexisting node, use the method
  `node.appendChild(new)`
  where *node* is the preexisting node and *new* is the new child. The new child node is appended to the end of the child nodes collection. If *new* already exists as a node in the document object tree, it is moved from its current location to the new location.
- To insert a new node at a specific location in the child nodes collection, use the method
  `node.insertBefore(new, child)`
  where *child* is the child node that the new node should be placed in front of. If *new* already exists as a node in the document object tree, it is moved from its current location to the new location.
- To remove a child node, use the method
  `node.removeChild(old)`
  where *old* is the child node to be removed.
- To replace one child node with another, use the following method:
  `node.replaceChild(new, old)`

Now that you've seen how to create and attach nodes, you'll create a node for an ol (ordered list) element and attach it to the table of contents on Norene's Web page. Currently, the content of the toc element consists of the elements

```
<div id = "toc">
   <h1>Table of Contents</h1>
</div>
```

which you want to change to

```
<div id = "toc">
   <h1>Table of Contents</h1>
   <ol></ol>
</div>
```

The code to create the ol list element and attach it to the table of contents is

```
var TOCList = document.createElement("ol");
TOC.appendChild(TOCList);
```

You'll add this code to the toc.js file.

To append an ordered list element to the table of contents:

1. Within the makeTOC() function in the toc.js file, insert the following code, as shown in Figure 16-14:

```
var TOCList = document.createElement("ol");
TOC.appendChild(TOCList);
```

Figure 16-14 Code to create and attach the ol element to the table of contents

```
function makeTOC() {
   var TOC = document.getElementById("toc");
   TOC.innerHTML = "<h1>Table of Contents</h1>";
   var TOCList = document.createElement("ol");
   TOC.appendChild(TOCList);
}
```

creates an element node for the ol element

appends the ol element to the table of contents element

2. Save your changes to the file.

Creating a List of Heading Elements

The next task is to populate the ordered list with list items, where the text of each list item matches the text of a heading element in the Constitution document. The code needs to do the following:

- Examine the child nodes of the Constitution document.
- For each child node, test whether it represents a heading element.
- If it is a heading element, extract the element's text and create a list item containing that same text.
- Append the list item as a new child of the ordered list in the table of contents.

For simplicity's sake, assume that each heading element is a child of the doc element on Norene's Web page (rather than nested within other elements) and that the heading elements contain only text and no other content.

Looping Through a Child Node Collection

There are two ways of looping through a collection of child nodes. One approach uses a counter variable that starts with a value of 0 and increases by 1 for each node, up to the length of the childNodes collection. The general form of this loop is:

```
for (var i = 0; i < node.childNodes.length; i++) {
   commands for node.childNodes[i]
}
```

In this form, the child nodes in the for loop have the object reference

```
node.childNodes[i]
```

where *node* is the parent node of the child nodes collection and *i* is the value of the counter variable in the for loop. The second approach uses familial references, starting with the first child of the parent node and then moving to each subsequent sibling until no siblings remain. The general form of this for loop is:

```
for (var n = node.firstChild; n != null; n = n.nextSibling) {
   commands for n
}
```

In this form, the current child node in the loop has the following object reference:

```
n
```

When no next sibling is available, the value of n is equal to null and the loop stops. Although both approaches yield the same results, the use of familial references is generally preferred because it does not require a browser to calculate the total length of the child nodes collection. For large documents containing thousands of nodes, this can speed up the processing time for the program. This method also provides the flexibility to insert new nodes into a document during the for loop without having to recalculate the length of the child nodes collection.

You'll use familial references in the following function to create the list of heading elements. The initial code for the function is:

```
function createList(object, list) {
   for (var n = object.firstChild; n != null; n = n.nextSibling) {
   }
}
```

This function has two parameters. The object parameter is the Web page object from which you will extract the list headings, and the list parameter contains the actual list as it is created by the createList() function. The initial code for this function simply uses a for loop to move through all of the children of the object parameter, sibling by sibling.

You'll add this function to the toc.js file.

To insert the createList() function:

1. Below the makeTOC() function, insert the following code, as shown in Figure 16-15:

```
function createList(object, list) {
   for (var n = object.firstChild; n != null; n = n.nextSibling) {
      // loop through all of the nodes within object

   }
}
```

Figure 16-15 **The createList() function**

```
function makeTOC() {
   var TOC = document.getElementById("toc");
   TOC.innerHTML = "<h1>Table of Contents</h1>";
   var TOCList = document.createElement("ol");
   TOC.appendChild(TOCList);
}

function createList(object, list) {
   for (var n = object.firstChild; n != null; n = n.nextSibling) {
      // loop through all of the nodes within object

   }
}
```

creates the list items for the table of contents

2. Save your changes to the file.

Matching the Heading Elements

Next you have to determine whether any of the child nodes of the object match one of the section headings that Norene wants to use to build her table of contents list. Recall that Norene wants to create section headings based on heading elements. To do this, you will first create an array of the element names for heading elements in the following command:

```
var sections = new Array("h1","h2","h3","h4","h5","h6");
```

The sections array is ordered from the element representing the highest level in the TOC (the h1 element) down to the lowest (the h6 element). In the Constitution document, you need to use only elements h1 through h3. However, including the full range of headings allows you to generalize the makeTOC() function for other documents in Norene's library.

Tip

To create a table of contents based on sections marked by elements other than headings, simply change the element names list in the sections array.

Next, you want to create a function that determines whether a given node comes from one of those heading elements. The code for this function, which we'll call levelNum(), is:

```
function levelNum(node) {
   for (var i = 0; i < sections.length; i++) {
      if (node.nodeName == sections[i].toUpperCase()) return i;
   }
   return -1;
}
```

The levelNum() function uses the nodeName property to test whether a given node matches one of the elements listed in the sections array. Because element names in the nodeName property are returned in uppercase letters, you must use the toUpperCase()method to convert the element names in the section array to uppercase letters as well. The function goes through each item in the sections array and, if a match is found, returns the array index number. Thus, an h1 element returns the value 0 (indicating that it represents the highest level in the table of contents), an h2 element returns the value 1, and so on. If a node object doesn't represent a section heading, the function returns the value –1.

You'll add the sections array and the levelNum() function to the toc.js file.

To insert the sections array and the levelNum() function:

1. Directly above the makeTOC() function, insert the following global variable declaration:

```
var sections = new Array("h1","h2","h3","h4","h5","h6");
```

2. Directly below the makeTOC() function, insert the following function:

```
function levelNum(node) {
   for (var i = 0; i < sections.length; i++) {
      if (node.nodeName == sections[i].toUpperCase()) return i;
   }
   return -1; // node is not a section heading
}
```

Figure 16-16 highlights the new code in the file.

Figure 16-16 The sections array and the levelNum() function

```
var sections = new Array("h1", "h2", "h3", "h4", "h5", "h6");

function makeTOC() {
   var TOC = document.getElementById("toc");
   TOC.innerHTML = "<h1>Table of Contents</h1>";
   var TOCList = document.createElement("ol");
   TOC.appendChild(TOCList);
}

function levelNum(node) {
   for (var i = 0; i < sections.length; i++) {
      if (node.nodeName == sections[i].toUpperCase()) return i;
   }
   return -1; // node is not a section heading
}
```

list of elements that can act as section headings

returns the level number of the section heading or –1 if not a section heading

The levelNum() function provides a way to determine whether a particular element within the constitution document represents a heading. The following code shows how you would extract the level number for any node:

```
var nodeLevel = levelNum(n);
if (nodeLevel != -1) {
   node represents a heading element
}
```

If the level is not equal to –1, then the node has to come from one of the six possible heading elements listed in the sections array. You'll add this if condition to the createList() function.

To create the nodeLevel variable:

1. Scroll down to the createList() function you inserted earlier and within the for loop insert the following commands, as shown in Figure 16-17:

```
var nodeLevel = levelNum(n);
if (nodeLevel != -1) {
   // node represents a section heading
}
```

Figure 16-17 if condition added to the createList() function

```
function createList(object, list) {
   for (var n = object.firstChild; n! = null; n = n.nextSibling) {
      // loop through all of the nodes within object

      var nodeLevel = levelNum(n);
      if (nodeLevel != -1) {
         // node represents a section heading

      }
   }
}
```

locates the section headings within the object

2. Save your changes to the file.

Creating the List Item Elements

Next, you'll create list item elements based on the section headings. The text of the list item should be taken from the text of the heading element. You can do that using the innerHTML property. The code is:

```
var listItem = document.createElement("li");
listItem.innerHTML = n.innerHTML;
list.appendChild(listItem);
```

You'll place these commands within the for loop of the createList() function so that for every section heading found in the source document, a corresponding list item is created for use in the table of contents.

To create the listItem variable:

1. Directly below the comment in the for loop, insert the following code, as shown in Figure 16-18:

```
// create a list item to match
var listItem = document.createElement("li");
listItem.innerHTML = n.innerHTML;
list.appendChild(listItem);
```

Figure 16-18 Code to create a list item for every section heading found

```
function createList(object, list) {
   for (var n = object.firstChild; n! = null; n = n.nextSibling) {
      // loop through all of the nodes within object

      var nodeLevel = levelNum(n);
      if (nodeLevel != -1) {
         // node represents a section heading
         // create a list item to match
         var listItem = document.createElement("li");
         listItem.innerHTML = n.innerHTML;
         list.appendChild(listItem);
      }

   }
}
```

text of the list item comes from the text of the section heading

2. Save your changes to the file.

Finally, you will call the createList() function from the makeTOC() function, specifying the constitutional document as the source document on which the TOC is based and the TOCList object as the object in which to place all of the TOC list items. Because you will reference the source document throughout this application, you will define it using a global variable named sourceDoc.

To generate the initial TOC:

1. Directly above the makeTOC() function, insert the following global declaration to create the sourceDoc variable:

```
var sourceDoc; // document on which the TOC is based
```

2. Within the makeTOC() function, add the following commands:

```
sourceDoc = document.getElementById("doc");

// generate list items containing section headings
createList(sourceDoc, TOCList);
```

Figure 16-19 shows the revised code.

Figure 16-19 Code to call the createList() function to generate the list items

```
var sections = new Array("h1", "h2", "h3", "h4", "h5", "h6");
var sourceDoc; // document on which the TOC is based

function makeTOC() {
   var TOC = document.getElementById("toc");
   TOC.innerHTML = "<h1>Table of Contents</h1>";
   var TOCList = document.createElement("ol");
   TOC.appendChild(TOCList);

   sourceDoc = document.getElementById("doc");

   // generate list items containing section headings
   createList(sourceDoc, TOCList);
}
```

3. Save your changes to the toc.js file, and then reload **usconst.htm** in your Web browser. The table of contents contains list items whose text is taken from the section headings in the constitution document. The list items appear in uppercase letters because of a style set in the web.css file, not because of any command in the makeTOC() function. See Figure 16-20.

Figure 16-20 The initial table of contents

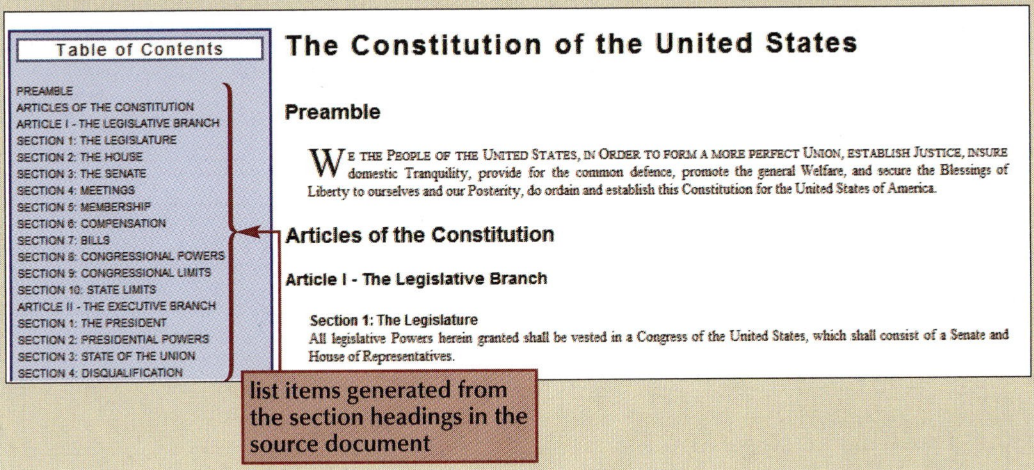

You've completed the initial work on the dynamic table of contents. By navigating through the node tree, you created list items matching every section heading in the constitution document. In the next session, you'll learn how to turn this table of contents list into a collection of nested lists based on the level of the different section headings.

Session 16.1 Quick Check | Review

1. What property can change the inner HTML content of an element?
2. What property extracts the text from an element, ignoring any markup tags? Provide an answer for both the IE and W3C DOMs.
3. What are nodes? What objects of an HTML file do they represent?
4. What property references the parent of a node?
5. What object references the third child node of an object?
6. For an element node representing a blockquote element, what values are returned by the nodeType, nodeName, and nodeValue properties?

7. What command creates a node containing the text string "U.S. Constitution"? Give the text string the variable name docText. What command creates an h2 element? Give the h2 element the variable name mainTitle.
8. What command places the text string you created in the previous question into the h2 element?

Session 16.2

Creating a Nested List

Norene reviewed the initial table of contents you created in the previous session. She is pleased that the table of contents extracts the text from all of the heading elements in the constitution document. However, it doesn't distinguish between main headings and subheadings. Norene wants you to revise the table of contents, making it a nested list in which lower-level headings are nested within upper-level headings. Figure 16-21 shows how the current HTML fragment generated by the createList() function needs to be modified to create a nested list of headings. All entries that match the h1 heading are placed at the top level of the table of contents, the entries for h2 headings are placed at the next lower level, and entries for h3 headings are placed at the lowest level.

Figure 16-21 **Current list being turned into a nested list**

Corresponding Level	
	h1 element
	h2 element
	h3 element

```
<ol>
   <li>Preamble</li>
   <li>Articles of the Constitution</li>
   <li>The Legislative Branch</li>
   <li>The Legislature</li>
   <li>The House</li>
   <li>The Senate</li>
...
   <li>The Executive Branch</li>
   <li>The President</li>
   <li>Presidential Powers</li>
...
   <li>Amendments</li>
   <li>I. Freedom of Expression</li>
   <li>II. Right to Bear Arms</li>
...
</ol>
```

current list

```
<ol>
   <li>Preamble</li>
   <li>Articles of the Constitution
      <ol>
         <li>The Legislative Branch>
            <ol>
               <li>The Legislature</li>
               <li>The House</li>
               <li>The Senate</li>
               ...
            </ol>
         </li>
         <li>The Executive Branch
            <ol>
               <li>The President</li>
               <li>Presidential Powers</li>
               ...
            </ol>
         </li>
      </ol>
   </li>
   ...
   <li>Amendments
      <ol>
         <li>I. Freedom of Expression</li>
         <li>II. Right to Bear Arms</li>
         ...
      </ol>
   </li>
</ol>
```

nested list

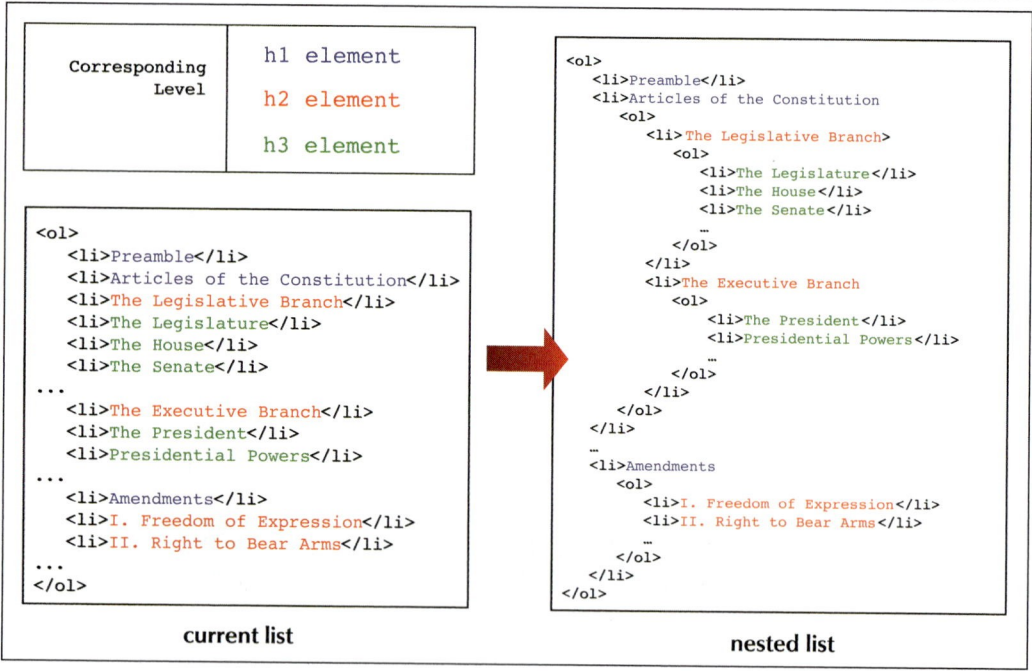

You need to modify the createList() function so that every time a list item is added to the TOC, the function determines whether to keep that item at the same level as the previous list item, to indent it as a new subheading, or to raise it up as coming from a previous main heading. To determine the level of each list item, you can use the information returned by the levelNum() function you created in the previous session. The levelNum() function returns a value of 0 for all h1 headings it encounters, 1 for all h2 headings, and

2 for all h3 headings. With that information, you can apply the following three rules to determine how a new list item should be placed in the table of contents:

1. If the level of the list item is unchanged from the level of the previous item, simply append it to the current list.
2. If the level number is higher than a previous item's level number (such as when an h3 heading follows an h2 heading), create a new nested list and append the list item to that new list.
3. If the level number is less than the previous item's level number (for example, when an h1 heading follows an h3 heading), append the list item to a list at a level higher up in the table of contents.

The key to these conditions is to record the previous item's level number. For that purpose, you'll create a new variable named prevLevel. You'll set the initial value of this variable to 0. The if condition to compare the value of prevLevel to the level of the current node has the general form:

```
if (nodeLevel == prevLevel)
   append the entry to the current list
else if (nodeLevel > prevLevel)
   append the entry to a new nested list
else if (nodeLevel < prevLevel)
   append the entry to a higher-level list
```

Recall that the nodeLevel variable contains the level of the current list item being added to the table of contents. You'll add these if conditions to the code of the createList() function.

To add the if conditions:

1. If you took a break after the previous session, make sure the toc.js file is open in a text editor and usconst.htm is loaded in your Web browser.
2. Return to the **toc.js** file in your text editor.
3. Scroll down to the createList() function, and then add the following command at the start of the function to declare and set the initial value of the prevLevel variable:

   ```
   var prevLevel = 0; // level of the previous TOC entry
   ```

4. Delete the following line:

   ```
   list.appendChild(listItem);
   ```

5. Add the following if statements in place of the line you just deleted:

   ```
   if (nodeLevel == prevLevel) {
      // append the entry to the current list
   }

   else if (nodeLevel > prevLevel) {
      // append the entry to a new nested list
   }

   else if (nodeLevel < prevLevel) {
      // append the entry to a higher-level list
   }
   ```

   Figure 16-22 shows new code in the createList() function.

Figure 16-22 if structure for the nested list

```
function createList(object, list) {

   var prevLevel = 0; // level of the previous TOC entry

   for (var n = object.firstChild; n!=null; n = n.nextSibling) {
      // loop through all of the nodes within object

      var nodeLevel = levelNum(n);
      if (nodeLevel != -1) {
         // node represents a section heading
         // create a list item to match
         var listItem = document.createElement("li");
         listItem.innerHTML = n.innerHTML;

         if (nodeLevel == prevLevel) {
            // append the entry to the current list
         }

         else if (nodeLevel > prevLevel) {
            // append the entry to a new nested list
         }

         else if (nodeLevel < prevLevel) {
            // append the entry to a higher-level list
         }
      }
   }
}
```

replaces the statement to append the list item

Next, you will enter the code for each if condition. If nodeLevel equals prevLevel, then the current node is at the same level as the previous entry and you simply need to append the new entry to the current list. Figure 16-23 shows how creating and appending this node to the node tree compares to inserting the code in an HTML fragment.

Figure 16-23 List item being added to a list

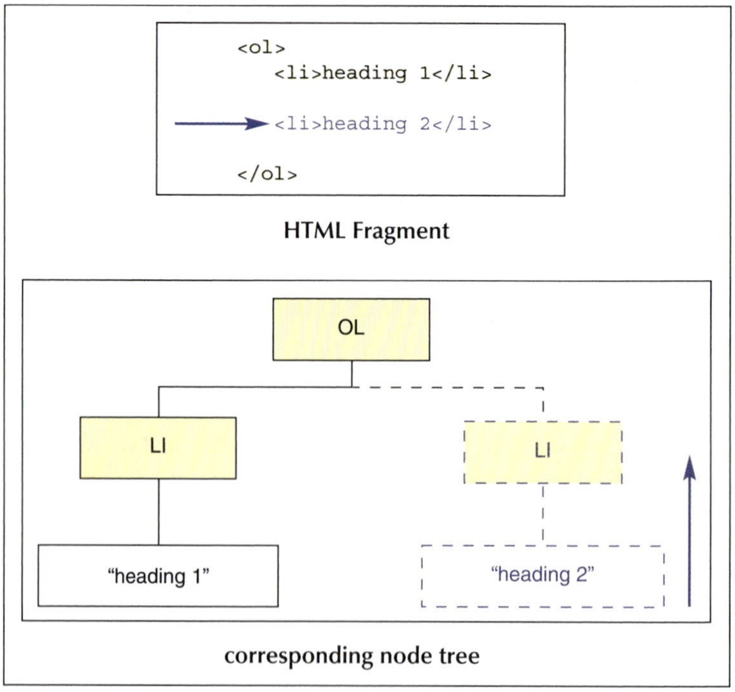

You'll add the command to insert the list item to the first condition in the createList() function.

To add the commands for the first condition:

1. Add the following command to the first if condition, as shown in Figure 16-24.

```
list.appendChild(listItem);
```

Figure 16-24 List item appended under the first condition

```
if (nodeLevel == prevLevel) {
   // append the entry to the current list
   list.appendChild(listItem);
}
```

2. Save your changes to the file, and then reload **usconst.htm** in your Web browser. The table of contents shows only the three h1 headings because they are the headings with a level value of 0 (h1 headings). No other headings are shown because the value of the prevLevel variable was set to 0 and was not changed by the code. See Figure 16-25.

Figure 16-25 Table of contents displays only the top level headings

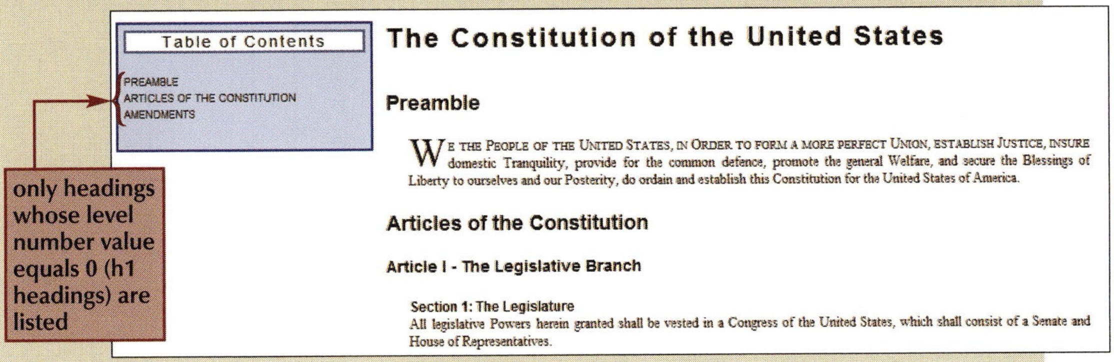
Table of Contents
PREAMBLE
ARTICLES OF THE CONSTITUTION
AMENDMENTS
only headings whose level number value equals 0 (h1 headings) are listed
The Constitution of the United States
Preamble
WE THE PEOPLE OF THE UNITED STATES, IN ORDER TO FORM A MORE PERFECT UNION, ESTABLISH JUSTICE, INSURE domestic Tranquility, provide for the common defence, promote the general Welfare, and secure the Blessings of Liberty to ourselves and our Posterity, do ordain and establish this Constitution for the United States of America.
Articles of the Constitution
Article I - The Legislative Branch
Section 1: The Legislature
All legislative Powers herein granted shall be vested in a Congress of the United States, which shall consist of a Senate and House of Representatives.

The next if condition involves the situation where the section heading is of a lower level than the one found for the previous entry (such as when an h2 heading follows an h1 heading). In that case, you want to insert the entry within a new list, nested within the previous entry. Figure 16-26 shows the HTML fragment and node tree of the new content in the table of contents.

Figure 16-26 **Nested list appended to the node tree**

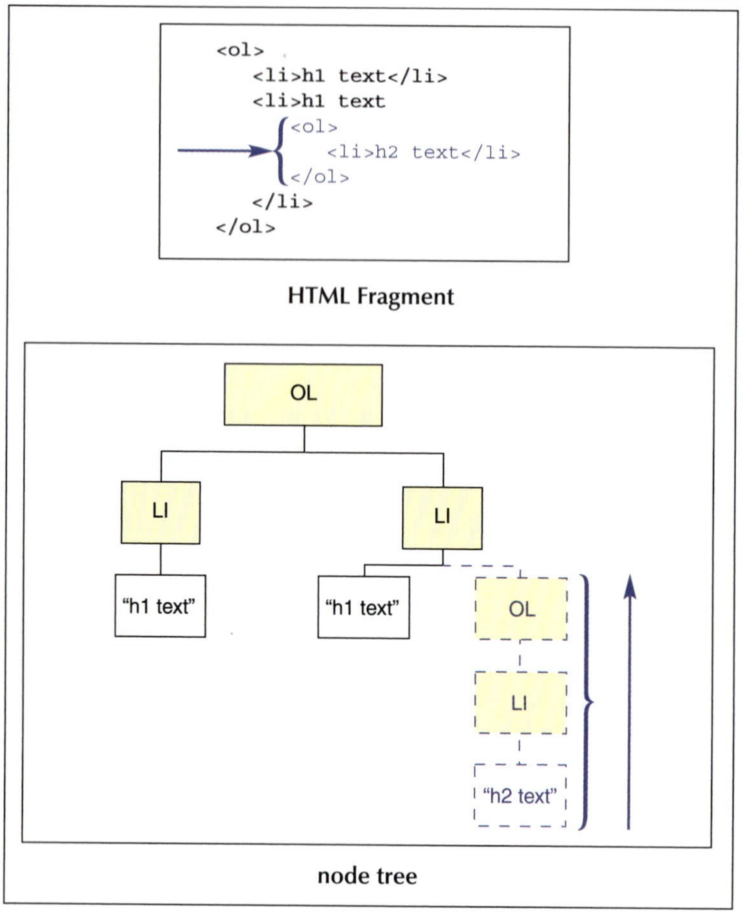

To do this in JavaScript, you create a new ordered list and then append the list item to it, using the following commands:

```
var nestedList = document.createElement("ol");
nestedList.appendChild(listItem);
```

The new list is then appended as a child of the previous—and last—entry in the current list, which can be done using the following command:

```
list.lastChild.appendChild(nestedList);
```

Finally, you need to make the nested list the new current list of the table of contents and set the value of the prevLevel variable to the level of the new entry. The commands to do this are:

```
list = nestedList;
prevLevel = nodeLevel;
```

You'll add these commands to the second if condition in the createList() function.

To add the commands for the second if condition:

1. Return to the **toc.js** file in your text editor.
2. Within the second if condition, insert the following code, as shown in Figure 16-27:

```
var nestedList = document.createElement("ol");
nestedList.appendChild(listItem);

list.lastChild.appendChild(nestedList);

list = nestedList;
prevLevel = nodeLevel;
```

Nested list appended under the second condition — **Figure 16-27**

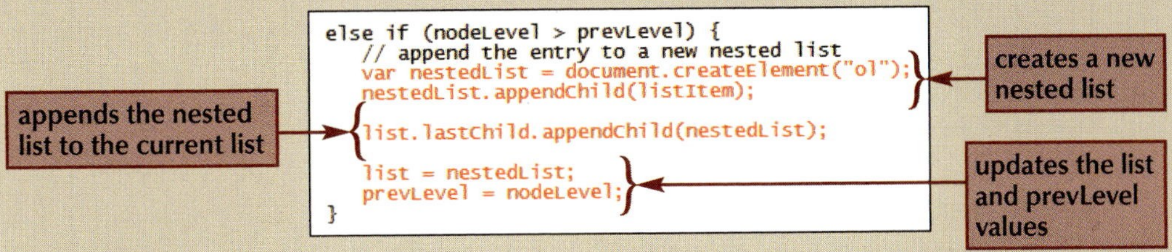

3. Save your changes to the file, and then reload **usconst.htm** in your Web browser. Figure 16-28 shows the current list of items in the table of contents with lower-level items nested within upper-level items.

Nested table of contents — **Figure 16-28**

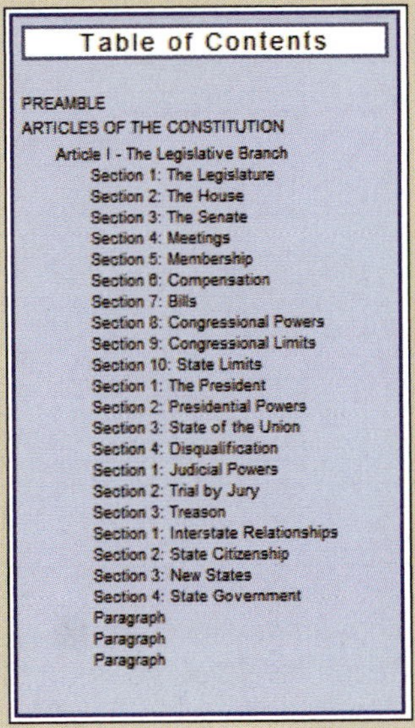

Don't worry that the other headings are missing from the table of contents. At this point, the createList() function only works going across the current level or down to the next level of headings. There are no commands to go up the nested list of items to higher-level headings. You'll add commands to handle that condition now.

When moving up one or more levels in the table of contents, you simply append the new list item to the correct list. Figure 16-29 shows an HTML fragment and the corresponding node tree for adding a new list item to a higher-level list.

Figure 16-29 List item appended to a higher level list

```
<ol>
   <li>h1 text</li>
   <li>h1 text
      <ol>
         <li>h2 text</li>
         <li>h2 text
            <ol>
               <li>h3 text</li>
               <li>h3 text</li>
               <li>h3 text</li>
            </ol>
         </li>
      </ol>
   </li>
   <li>h1 text</li>
</ol>
```

HTML fragment

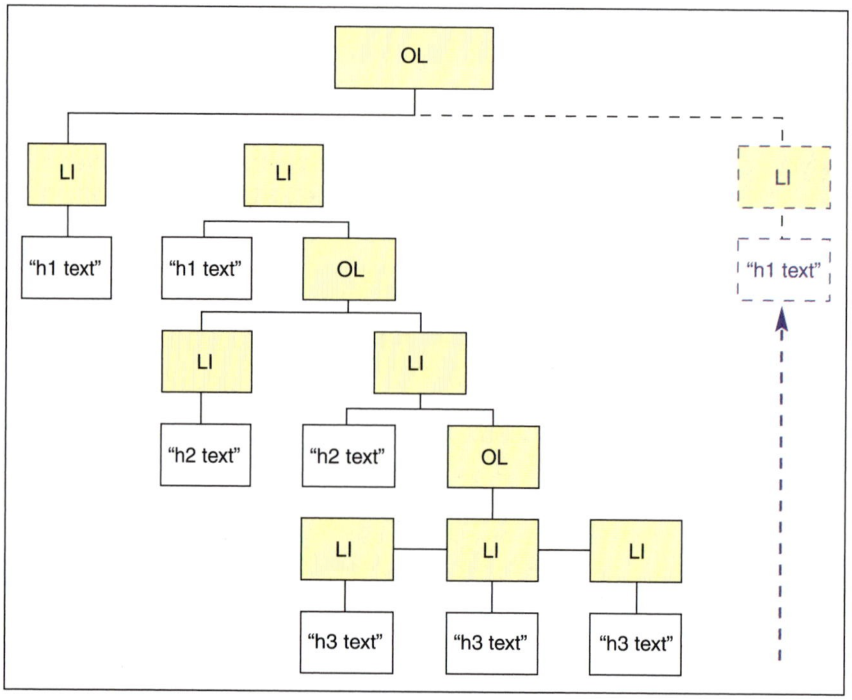

node tree

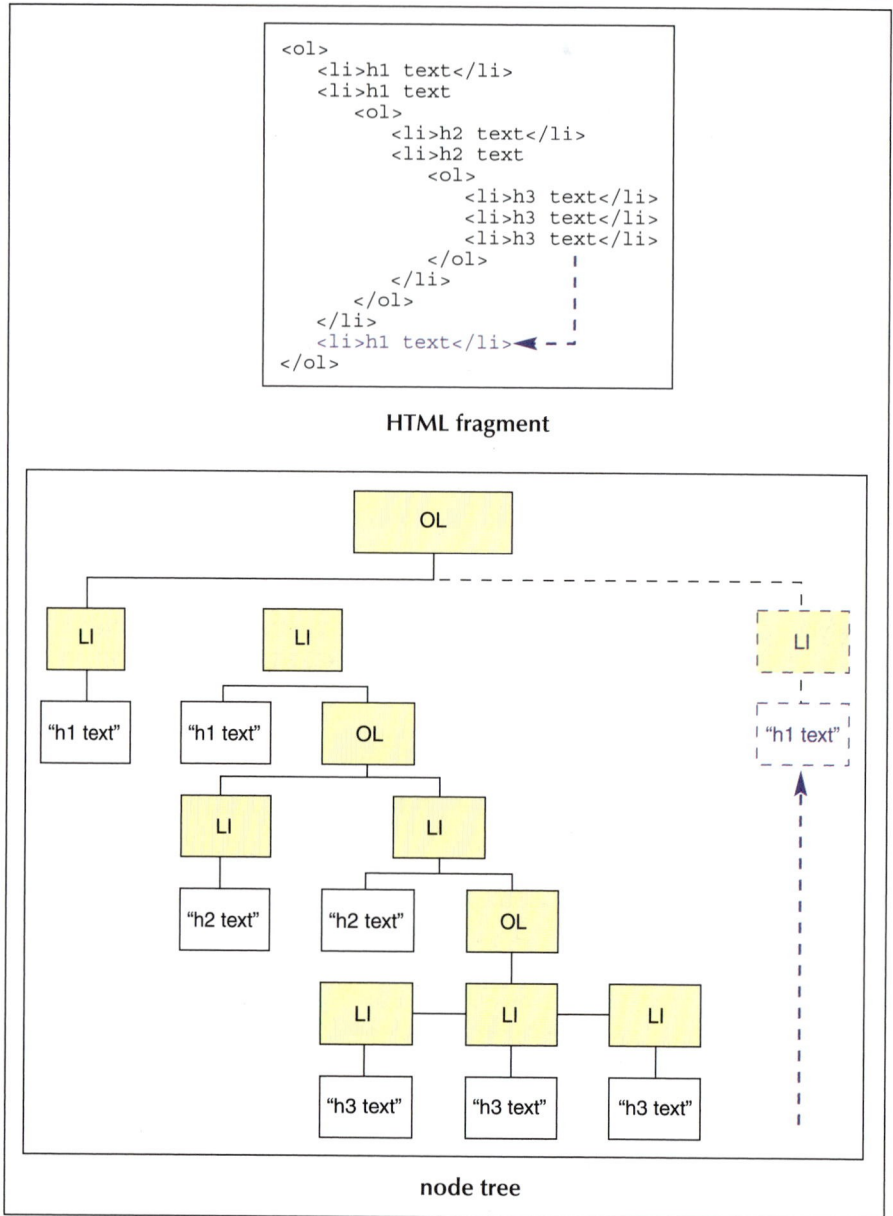

One challenge is figuring out how many levels to go up in the node tree. Examine Figure 16-29 and notice that for each level you go up in the section headings, you go up *two* levels in the node tree. For example, to go from h3 headings back up to h1 headings, you go up four levels in the node tree. Thus, to go up the node tree, you first calculate the difference between the current level headings and the level of the new entry, which is simply the difference between the prevLevel variable and the nodeLevel variable. You can store that difference in the following levelUp variable:

```
var levelUp = prevLevel - nodeLevel;
```

To move up the node tree, you apply the parentNode property twice, for each difference in level between the two headings. That approach can be placed in the following for loop:

```
for (var i = 1; i <= levelUp; i++) {list = list.parentNode.parentNode;}
```

On each iteration, the for loop points the list object to the TOC list two levels up on the node tree. The loop stops when it has gone up the correct number of levels as indicated by the levelUp variable. Once you're at the correct level, the remaining task is to append the list item and update the value of the prevLevel variable, using the following code:

```
list.appendChild(listItem);
prevLevel = nodeLevel;
```

You'll add these commands to the third if condition in the changeList() function.

To add the commands for the third condition:

1. Return to the **toc.js** file in your text editor.
2. Within the third if condition, insert the following code, as shown in Figure 16-30:

```
var levelUp = prevLevel - nodeLevel;
for (var i = 1; i <= levelUp; i++) {list = list.parentNode.parentNode;}

list.appendChild(listItem);
prevLevel = nodeLevel;
```

Figure 16-30 List item appended under the third condition

```
else if (nodeLevel < prevLevel) {
   // append the entry to a higher-level list
   var levelUp = prevLevel - nodeLevel;
   for (var i = 1; i <= levelUp; i++) {list = list.parentNode.parentNode;}

   list.appendChild(listItem);
   prevLevel = nodeLevel;
}
```

moves up two levels in the node tree

3. Save your changes to the file, and then reload **usconst.htm** in your Web browser. The table of contents shows all three levels of headings with the h1 headings represented at the highest level of the list, followed by the h2 headings, and then followed by the h3 headings. See Figure 16-31.

Figure 16-31 Table of contents as a nested list

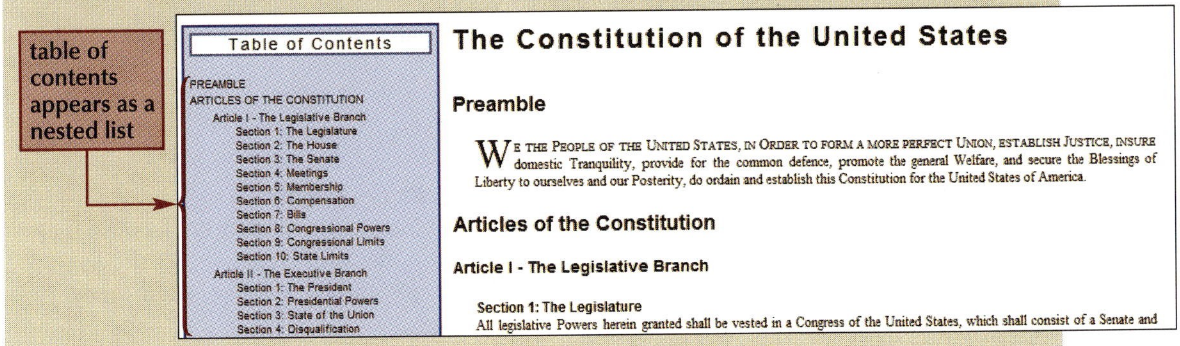

Working with Attributes

Norene is pleased with the table of contents your script generated for her document. Because this is a hypertext document, she wonders whether the entries in the table of contents could contain links to the section headings they represent.

Again, it is useful to write out the HTML code for the proposed change, even if you cannot view those markup tags in your document. Making this change involves two steps, which are illustrated in Figure 16-32:

1. Add an id attribute to each section heading (if it doesn't already have one) to mark its location on the Web page.
2. Change the content of each list item to a link pointing to the corresponding section heading.

Figure 16-32 **HTML fragment linking table of contents entries to section headings**

```
<ol>
   <li><a href = "#head1">Preamble</a></li>
   <li><a href = "#head2">Articles of the Constitution</a></li>
   <ol>
      <li><a href="#head3">Legislative Branch</a></li>
      <ol>
         <li><a href = "#head4">Section 1: The Legislature</a></li>
         <li><a href = "#head5">Section 2: The House</a></li>
         <li><a href = "#head6">Section 3: The Senate</a></li>
...
```

table of contents with links

```
<h1 id = "head1">Preamble</h1>
...
<h1 id = "head2">Articles of the Constitution</h1>
...
<h2 id = "head3">Legislative Branch</h2>
...
<h3 id = "head4">Section 1: The Legislature</h3>
...
<h3 id = "head5">Section 2: The House</h3>
...
<h3 id = "head6">Section 3: The Senate</h3>
....
```

section headings with id values

Before you can create and add the id and href attributes, you must understand how to work with attributes in the W3C DOM.

Creating Attribute Nodes

Attributes and their values are considered nodes and can be attached to element nodes. Unlike element and text nodes, attribute nodes are not part of the node tree because they are not counted as children of element nodes like text nodes are. Figure 16-33 shows how to represent the relationship between attribute nodes and the element nodes they are associated with.

Figure 16-33 **Attribute nodes**

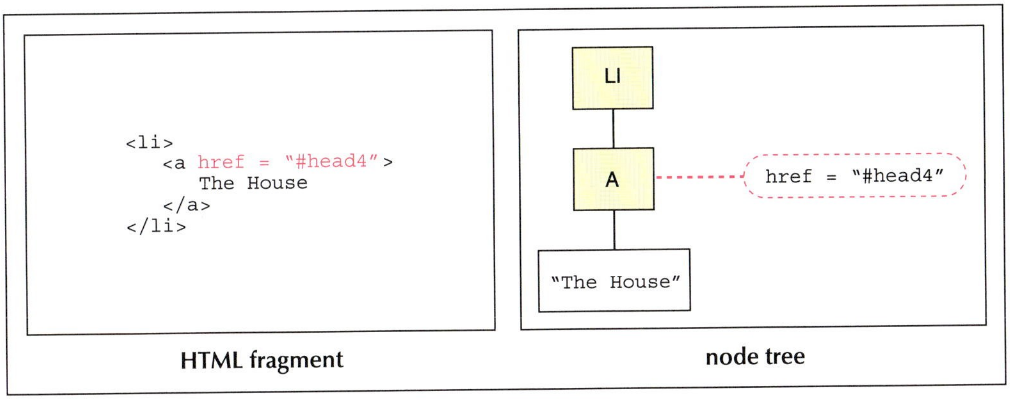

As you can see, attribute nodes have no familial relation with any node in the node tree. The W3C DOM supports several methods to create, attach, and set the values of attributes. Some of these are listed in Figure 16-34.

Figure 16-34 **Methods of attribute nodes**

Method	Description
`document.createAttribute(`*att*`)`	Creates an attribute node with the name *att*
node`.getAttribute(`*att*`)`	Returns the value of an attribute *att* from a *node* to which it has been attached
node`.hasAttribute(`*att*`)`	Returns a Boolean value indicating whether *node* has the attribute *att*
node`.removeAttribute(`*att*`)`	Removes the attribute *att* from *node*
node`.removeAttributeNode(`*att*`)`	Removes an attribute node *att* from *node*
node`.setAttribute(`*att*`,` *value*`)`	Creates or changes the *value* of the attribute *att* of *node*

To create or set an attribute for an element, you use the setAttribute() method. The following code creates a list item element and then uses the setAttribute() method to set the ID value of the list item to the text string TOChead1:

```
listItem = document.createElement("li");
listItem.setAttribute("id","TOChead1");
```

The net effect of these two commands is to create the following HTML fragment:

```
<li id = "TOChead1"></li>
```

In some cases, you need to determine whether an element has a particular attribute, such as the id attribute. In these situations, you use the hasAttribute() method, which returns the Boolean value true if the element contains the attribute. For example, the expression

```
listItem.hasAttribute("id")
```

would return the value true if the list item had an id attribute, and would return false if otherwise.

For Web page elements, the simplest approach to set an attribute value is to apply the HTML attribute as a property of the object using the syntax

```
object.attr = value;
```

Tip

Attribute nodes are usually reserved for working with elements that are not part of the body of the Web page, or for use with non-HTML content such as XML data sources.

where *object* is an object reference to the HTML page element, *attr* is the name of an HTML attribute associated with the element, and *value* is the value you want to assign to the attribute.

Setting the Section Heading IDs

Now that you've learned how to work with attributes, you'll turn to the next task, which is to insert IDs into all of the section headings in the constitution document. You'll name each of the section headings

```
headi
```

where *i* is a variable that equals 1 for the first section heading, 2 for the second heading, and so on. Refer back to Figure 16-32 for an example of how the IDs of the first six section headings will be numbered. You need to be careful not to overwrite any preexisting IDs because Norene might have already placed IDs in some of the <h1> through <h3> tags. You'll first test whether an ID attribute already exists for the element and insert an ID only if it doesn't already have one. As you create section IDs, you'll store each ID in a variable named sectionId; you'll use this variable later in the code to create the hypertext references for the links. The code to insert the section heading IDs for a particular node, n, is:

```
headNum++;
if (n.id == "") {n.id = "head" + headNum;}
```

Here, headNum is a counter variable that is increased each time the code encounters a section element in the constitution document. If the element has no ID, the counter variable creates one for it.

You'll add these commands to the createList() function.

To insert the section IDs:

1. Return to the **toc.js** file in your text editor.
2. Directly below the line that declares the prevLevel variable, insert the following line to declare the headNum variable, setting its initial value to 0:

   ```
   var headNum = 0; // running count of section headings
   ```

3. At the top of the for loop within the createList() function, insert the following commands, as shown in Figure 16-35:

   ```
   // insert id for the section heading if necessary
   headNum++;
   if (n.id == "") {n.id = "head" + headNum;}
   ```

Figure 16-35 Code to insert section IDs

```
function createList(object, list) {

   var prevLevel = 0; // level of the previous TOC entry
   var headNum = 0;   // running count of section headings

   for (var n = object.firstChild; n!=null; n = n.nextSibling) {
      // loop through all of the nodes within object

      var nodeLevel = levelNum(n);
      if (nodeLevel != -1) {
         // node represents a section heading

         // insert id for the section heading if necessary
         headNum++;
         if (n.id == "") {n.id = "head" + headNum;}

         // create a list item to match
         var listItem = document.createElement("li");
         listItem.innerHTML = n.innerHTML;
```

adds IDs to section headings that don't already have one

Tip

To avoid conflict with other possible ID values in the source document, you can use a JavaScript function to generate a completely random ID value.

Inserting Links

Next, you need to revise the structure of the TOC node tree to link each list item with its corresponding section in the constitution document. The href value for each link will be

```
#id
```

where *id* is the ID assigned to the section heading. You'll also set the ID of each list element to

```
TOCid
```

where *id* is again the ID of the corresponding heading element in the constitution document. This will allow you to easily match list items in the table of contents with their corresponding section headings. You'll need this information for some of the tasks you'll do in the next session. Figure 16-36 shows the node structure of the list items with and without the links.

List item being changed into a hypertext link | **Figure 16-36**

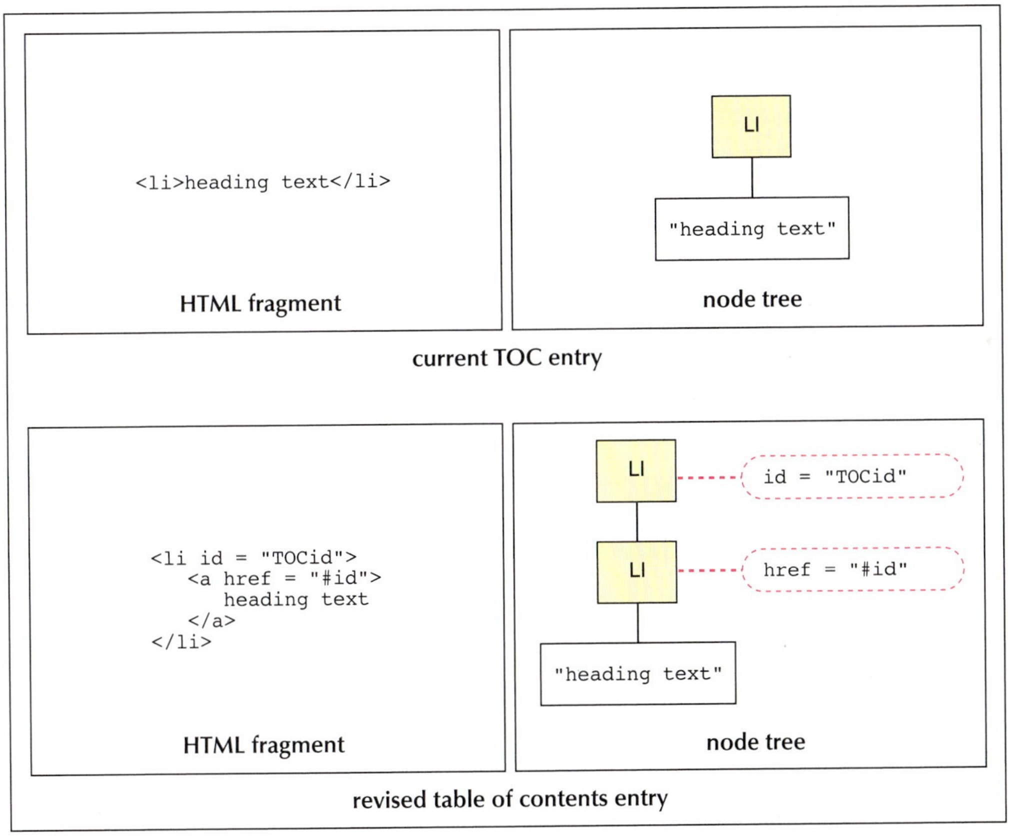

To create the new node structure, you'll replace the old commands that inserted the text of the link item with new code that inserts the item text as a hyperlink. First, you'll define an ID value for the list item, using the following command:

```
listItem.id = "TOC" + n.id;
```

Then, you'll create a hypertext link containing the text of the section head and an href attribute that points to the section head, using the following code:

```
var linkItem = document.createElement("a");
linkItem.innerHTML = n.innerHTML;
linkItem.href = "#" + n.id;
```

Finally, you'll append the hypertext link to the list item, using the following command:

```
listItem.appendChild(linkItem);
```

You'll insert these commands into the createList() function and then test the links in the table of contents.

To turn the list items into hypertext links:

1. Within the createList() function, delete the following line:

```
listItem.innerHTML = n.innerHTML;
```

2. Replace the deleted line with the following code, as shown in Figure 16-37:

```
listItem.id = "TOC" + n.id;

// Create a hypertext link to the section heading
var linkItem = document.createElement("a");
linkItem.innerHTML = n.innerHTML;
linkItem.href = "#" + n.id;

// Append the hypertext link to the list entry
listItem.appendChild(linkItem);
```

Figure 16-37 Code to insert hypertext links for each list item

```
var nodeLevel = levelNum(n);
if (nodeLevel != -1) {
   // node represents a section heading

   // insert id for the section heading if  necessary
   headNum++;
   if (n.id == "") {n.id = "head" + headNum;}

   // create a list item to match
   var listItem = document.createElement("li");
   listItem.id = "TOC" + n.id;

   // Create a hypertext link to the section heading
   var linkItem = document.createElement("a");
   linkItem.innerHTML = n.innerHTML;
   linkItem.href = "#" + n.id;

   // Append the hypertext link to the list entry
   listItem.appendChild(linkItem);

   if (nodeLevel == prevLevel) {
      // append the entry to the current list
      list.appendChild(listItem);
   }
```

delete the line to place the heading content into the list item

creates the hypertext link

appends the link to the list item

3. Save your changes to the file.
4. Reload **usconst.htm** in your Web browser. Each entry in the table of contents is a hypertext link. See Figure 16-38.

Table of contents as a list of links | **Figure 16-38**

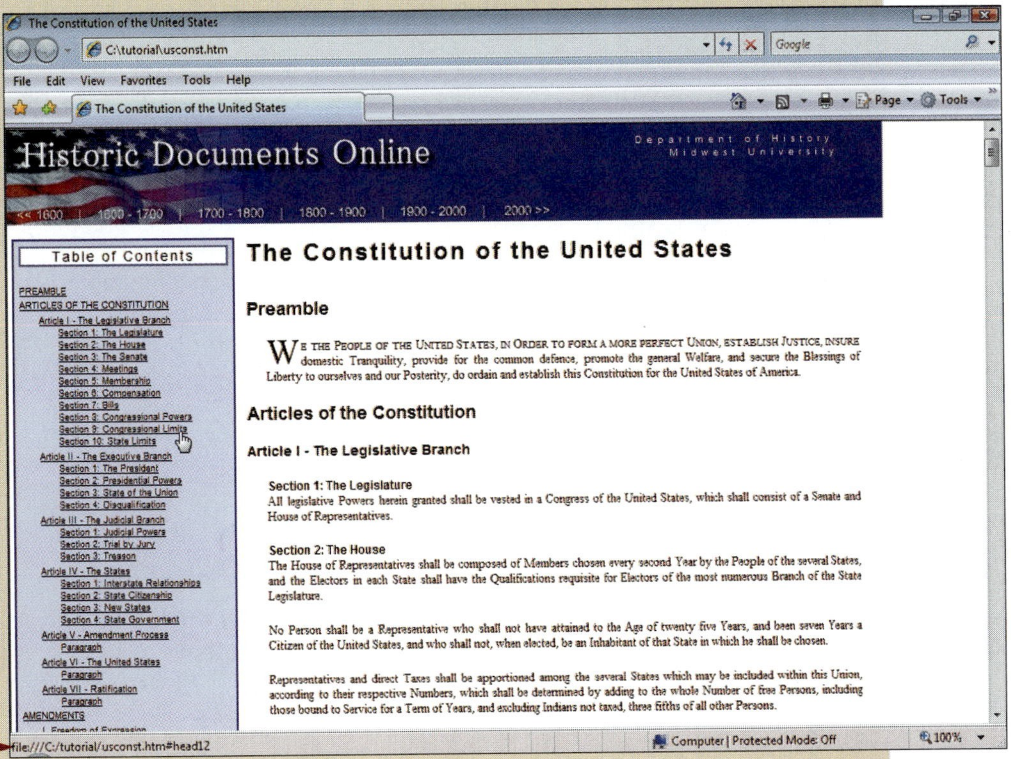
The Constitution of the United States
C:\tutorial\usconst.htm
File Edit View Favorites Tools Help
Historic Documents Online
Department of History
Midwest University
<< 1600 | 1600 - 1700 | 1700 - 1800 | 1800 - 1900 | 1900 - 2000 | 2000 >>
Table of Contents
PREAMBLE
ARTICLES OF THE CONSTITUTION
Article I - The Legislative Branch
Section 1: The Legislature
Section 2: The House
Section 3: The Senate
Section 4: Meetings
Section 5: Membership
Section 6: Compensation
Section 7: Bills
Section 8: Congressional Powers
Section 9: Congressional Limits
Section 10: State Limits
Article II - The Executive Branch
Section 1: The President
Section 2: Presidential Powers
Section 3: State of the Union
Section 4: Disqualification
Article III - The Judicial Branch
Section 1: Judicial Powers
Section 2: Trial by Jury
Section 3: Treason
Article IV - The States
Section 1: Interstate Relationships
Section 2: State Citizenship
Section 3: New States
Section 4: State Government
Article V - Amendment Process
Paragraph
Article VI - The United States
Paragraph
Article VII - Ratification
Paragraph
AMENDMENTS
The Constitution of the United States
Preamble
We the People of the United States, in Order to form a more perfect Union, establish Justice, insure domestic Tranquility, provide for the common defence, promote the general Welfare, and secure the Blessings of Liberty to ourselves and our Posterity, do ordain and establish this Constitution for the United States of America.
Articles of the Constitution
Article I - The Legislative Branch
Section 1: The Legislature
All legislative Powers herein granted shall be vested in a Congress of the United States, which shall consist of a Senate and House of Representatives.
Section 2: The House
The House of Representatives shall be composed of Members chosen every second Year by the People of the several States, and the Electors in each State shall have the Qualifications requisite for Electors of the most numerous Branch of the State Legislature.
No Person shall be a Representative who shall not have attained to the Age of twenty five Years, and been seven Years a Citizen of the United States, and who shall not, when elected, be an Inhabitant of that State in which he shall be chosen.
Representatives and direct Taxes shall be apportioned among the several States which may be included within this Union, according to their respective Numbers, which shall be determined by adding to the whole Number of free Persons, including those bound to Service for a Term of Years, and excluding Indians not taxed, three fifths of all other Persons.
file:///C:/tutorial/usconst.htm#head12
Computer | Protected Mode: Off
100%

target of the linked text

5. Click the different links in the table of contents and verify that the browser jumps to the corresponding section of the document.

InSight | Inserting Element Text Under the IE DOM

If you are supporting only the Internet Explorer browser, you can use methods in the IE DOM to insert elements at specific locations within the document tree. The syntax of these methods is

```
object.insertAdjacentHTML(position, content);
object.insertAdjacentText(position, content);
```

where *position* is a text string specifying the position in which the new HTML code or text is to be inserted relative to *object*, and *content* is the content to be inserted. The *position* parameter has four possible values:

- BeforeBegin inserts the content before the object's opening tag.
- AfterBegin inserts the content directly after the object's opening tag.
- BeforeEnd inserts the content directly before the object's closing tag.
- AfterEnd inserts the content after the object's closing tag.

For example, to insert the word Online at the end of the HTML fragment

```
<h1 id = "title">Historic Documents</h1>
```

you could run the command

```
title.insertAdjacentHTML("BeforeEnd"," Online");
```

which would change the code of the title element to

```
<h1 id = "title">Historic Documents Online</h1>
```

Keep in mind that these methods are supported only under the IE DOM. If you need to create a cross-browser Web site, use the node objects and methods to insert new text into the document.

You've completed the work for making the table of contents into a nested list of hypertext links. In the next session, you'll add more features to the table of contents, including the ability to contract and expand the table of contents and the constitution document.

Review | Session 16.2 Quick Check

1. What code creates two ul list elements, one nested inside of the other? Use the variable name topList for the upper list element and the variable name bottomList for the bottom list element.
2. In the previous question, what is the node reference to the topList object from a list item found in the bottom list?
3. Why are attribute nodes not part of the document node tree?
4. What node method determines whether an element contains the type attribute?
5. What command creates an input element with the variable name CBox and a type attribute value of checkbox? Use an attribute node method in your answer.
6. What commands would you add to the previous question to create the type attribute using a property rather than an attribute node method?
7. What expression would you use in the previous question to determine whether the CBox input element has a type attribute?

Session 16.3

Expanding and Collapsing a Document

Norene reviews the table of contents application. She has seen other lists in which the nested entries can be alternately hidden or displayed by clicking a plus/minus box. In a **plus/minus box**, a + symbol in the box indicates that content is hidden and a – symbol indicates that all the items are displayed. Clicking the + box reveals the hidden content and clicking the – box hides them, as shown in Figure 16-39.

Plus/minus box expands and collapses a list **Figure 16-39**

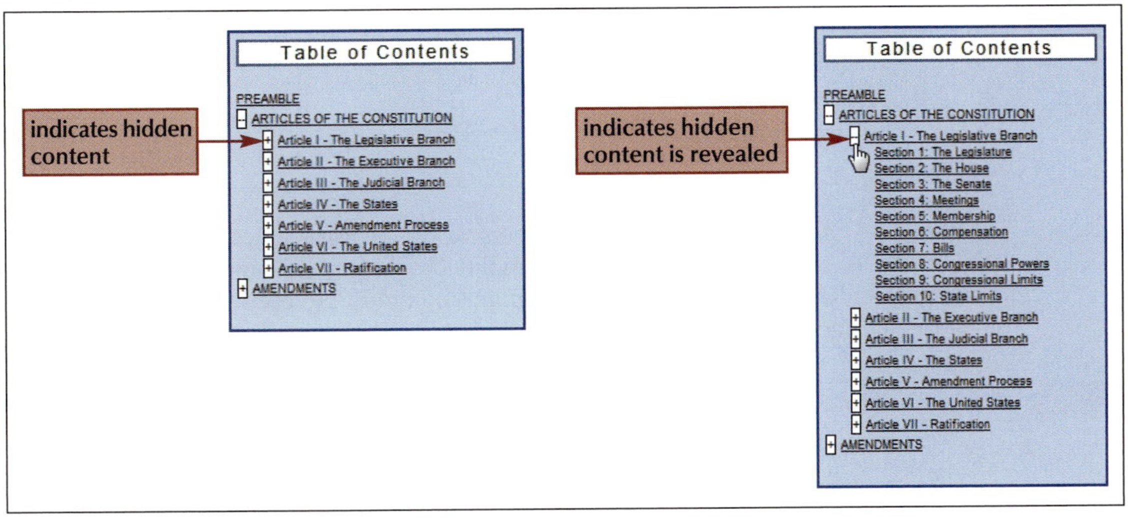

Norene wants you to add this feature to the table of contents so that users can expand or collapse the list. She also wants the contents of the document to mimic the appearance of the table of contents, so that as items are hidden in the table of contents, they are also hidden within the document. Creating this kind of dynamic content involves several of the tools and techniques you've learned in previous tutorials, including working with event objects and object styles.

Creating a Plus/Minus Box

First, you'll add the plus/minus boxes to the table of contents. Because you want to treat each plus/minus box as a distinct object, you'll place the text of the plus/minus box within a span element. Initially, the plus/minus box will display the -- symbol because the TOC will open with all list items displayed to users. The following commands create the plus/minus box:

```
plusMinusBox = document.createElement("span");
plusMinusBox.innerHTML = "--";
```

Next, you must determine where to place the plus/minus boxes in Norene's table of contents. Because the boxes are designed to alternately hide and display nested lists, they should be placed before the nested list in the node tree. Figure 16-40 shows where you would place the plus/minus box if you were writing the HTML tags directly, and how it would be rendered on the Web page. Notice that the styles for the span element, including the background color and border, have already been placed in the web.css file. This means you don't have to worry about formatting the plus/minus boxes for the Web page, but you can instead focus on inserting the content.

Figure 16-40 **Plus/minus box placed before the nested list**

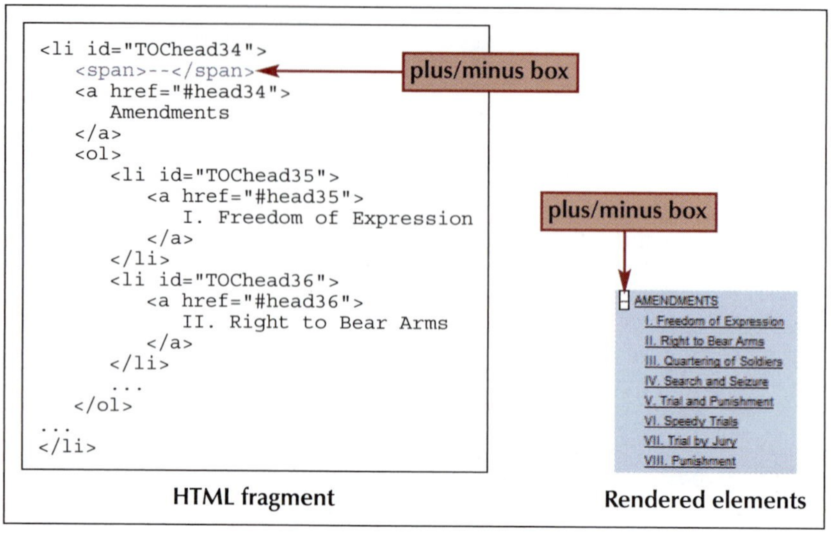

Figure 16-41 shows how this HTML fragment would be represented in the node tree (attribute nodes are not shown in order to simplify the diagram). As indicated in the HTML fragment and the node tree, the plus/minus box must be inserted as the first child of the last list item entry.

Figure 16-41 **Plus/minus box added to the node tree**

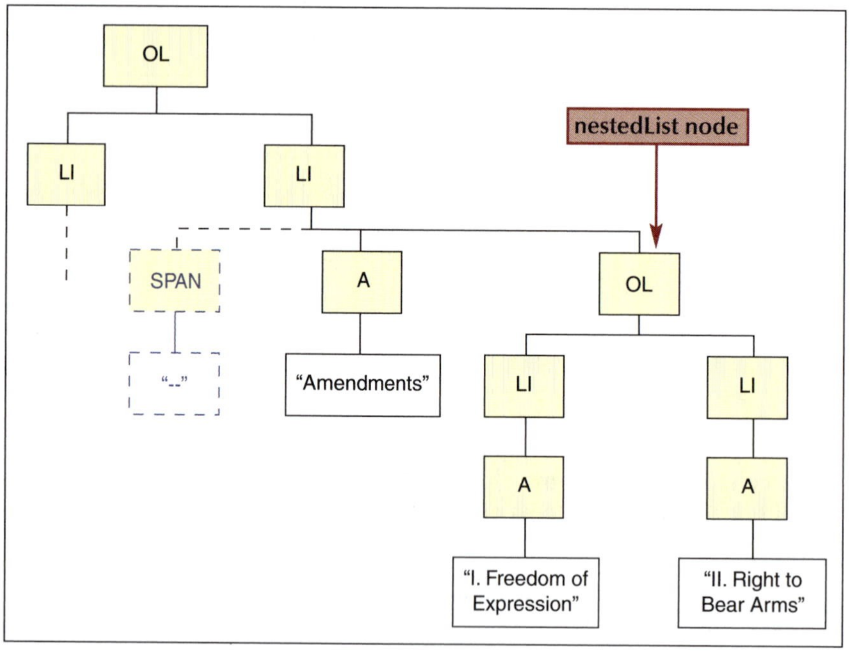

You can insert the plus/minus box using the insertBefore() method, which inserts new child nodes anywhere within a parent node. Recall that the general syntax of the insert-Before() method is

```
node.insertBefore(new, child)
```

where *node* is the parent node, *new* is a new node to be added as child of the parent, and *child* is the child node that the new node should be inserted in front of. To insert a plus/minus box, you'll use the following object reference for *node*

```
nestedList.parentNode
```

because that reference points to the parent of the nestedList object. The *child* node in front of which you want to place the plus/minus box is the <a> tag and can be referenced by:

```
nestedList.previousSibling
```

Thus, to insert the plus/minus box, you would run the following command:

```
nestedList.parentNode.insertBefore(plusMinusBox, nestedList.
previousSibling)
```

Compare this expression to the node tree diagram shown earlier in Figure16-41 to see how the use of familiar references makes it easier to move around the contents of the node tree. You will add the commands to create the plus/minus box to the createList() function.

To create and place the plus/minus box:

1. If you took a break after the previous session, make sure the toc.js file is open in a text editor and usconst.htm is loaded in your Web browser.
2. Return to the **toc.js** file in your text editor.
3. Go to the createList() function and insert the following code within the second if condition, as shown in Figure 16-42:

```
// Add plus/minus box before the text of the nested list
var plusMinusBox = document.createElement("span");
plusMinusBox.innerHTML = "--";
nestedList.parentNode.insertBefore(plusMinusBox,
nestedList.previousSibling);
```

Figure 16-42 Code to create and place the plus/minus boxes

```
else if (nodeLevel > prevLevel) {
   // append the entry to a new nested list
   var nestedList = document.createElement("ol");
   nestedList.appendChild(listItem);

   list.lastChild.appendChild(nestedList);

   // Add plus/minus box before the text of the nested list
   var plusMinusBox = document.createElement("span");
   plusMinusBox.innerHTML = "--";
   nestedList.parentNode.insertBefore(plusMinusBox, nestedList.previousSibling);

   list = nestedList;
   prevLevel = nodeLevel;
}
```

places a plus/minus box before each nested list

4. Save your changes to the file, and then reload **usconst.htm** in your Web browser. Plus/minus boxes appear before the nested list titles in the table of contents. See Figure 16-43.

Tip

You cannot view the HTML fragments generated by code, but you can view the node tree generated by your code under the Firefox browser by adding the DOM Inspector add-on from the Firefox Web site.

Figure 16-43 Table of contents with plus/minus boxes

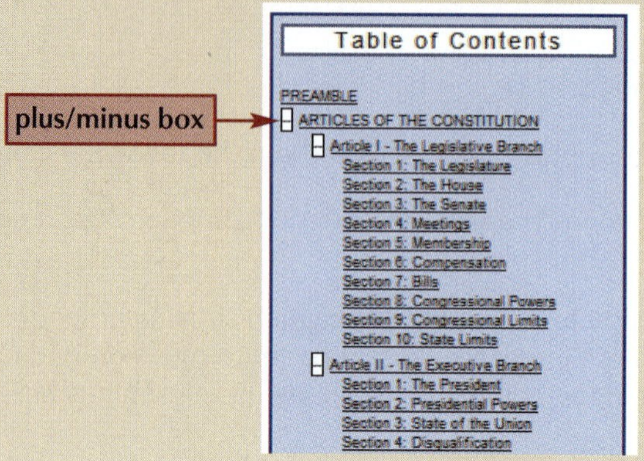

Adding an Event Handler to the Plus/Minus Boxes

You want users to be able to toggle between a plus sign and a minus sign in the plus/minus box by clicking the box. You'll use the addEvent() function already placed in the toc.js file to apply a cross-browser event handler to the plus/minus boxes. The code is:

```
addEvent(plusMinusBox, "click", expandCollapse, false);
```

The browser will run the expandCollapse() function whenever the user clicks a plus/minus box. The code of the expandCollapse() function is:

```
function expandCollapse(e) {
   var plusMinusBox = e.target || event.srcElement;

   if (plusMinusBox.innerHTML == "--") plusMinusBox.innerHTML = "+"
   else plusMinusBox.innerHTML = "--";
}
```

Each time the function is run, the text of the plus/minus box switches between a minus symbol and a plus symbol. The function uses an event object along with the target or srcElement properties to determine the box that the user clicked.

You'll add these commands to the toc.js file, and then test your code in the browser.

To insert the event handler for the plus/minus boxes:

1. Return to the **toc.js** file in your text editor.
2. Go to the createList() function and below the command to set the innerHTML property of the plus/minus box, insert the following function:

```
addEvent(plusMinusBox, "click", expandCollapse, false);
```

3. Below the createList() function, add the following function, as shown in Figure 16-44:

```
function expandCollapse(e) {
   var plusMinusBox = e.target || event.srcElement;

   // Toggle the plus and minus symbol
   if (plusMinusBox.innerHTML == "--") plusMinusBox.innerHTML = "+"
   else plusMinusBox.innerHTML = "--";
}
```

The expandCollapse() function **Figure 16-44**

```
         else if (nodeLevel > prevLevel) {
            // append the entry to a new nested list
            var nestedList = document.createElement("ol");
            nestedList.appendChild(listItem);

            list.lastChild.appendChild(nestedList);

            // Add plus/minus box before the text of the nested list
            var plusMinusBox = document.createElement("span");
            plusMinusBox.innerHTML = "--";
            addEvent(plusMinusBox, "click", expandCollapse, false);
            nestedList.parentNode.insertBefore(plusMinusBox, nestedList.previousSibling);

            list = nestedList;
            prevLevel = nodeLevel;
         }

         else if (nodeLevel < prevLevel) {
            // append the entry to a higher-level list
            var levelUp = prevLevel - nodeLevel;
            for (var i = 1; i <= levelUp; i++) {list = list.parentNode.parentNode;}

            list.appendChild(listItem);
            prevLevel = nodeLevel;
         }
      }
   }
}

function expandCollapse(e) {
   var plusMinusBox = e.target || event.srcElement;

   // Toggle the plus and minus symbol
   if (plusMinusBox.innerHTML == "--") plusMinusBox.innerHTML = "+"
   else plusMinusBox.innerHTML = "--";
}
```

runs the expandCollapse() function when the user clicks a plus/minus box

4. Save your changes to the file.

5. Reload **usconst.htm** in your Web browser and verify that clicking each plus/minus box toggles its symbol between a plus sign and a minus sign.

Hiding and Displaying the Nested Lists

The next action of the expandCollapse() function is to alternately hide or display the nested list associated with each plus/minus box. As shown in Figure 16-45, each nested list is placed two siblings away from the plus/minus box. You can reference the nested list using the following expression:

```
var nestedList = plusMinusBox.nextSibling.nextSibling
```

Figure 16-45 Position of the nested list relative to the plus/minus box

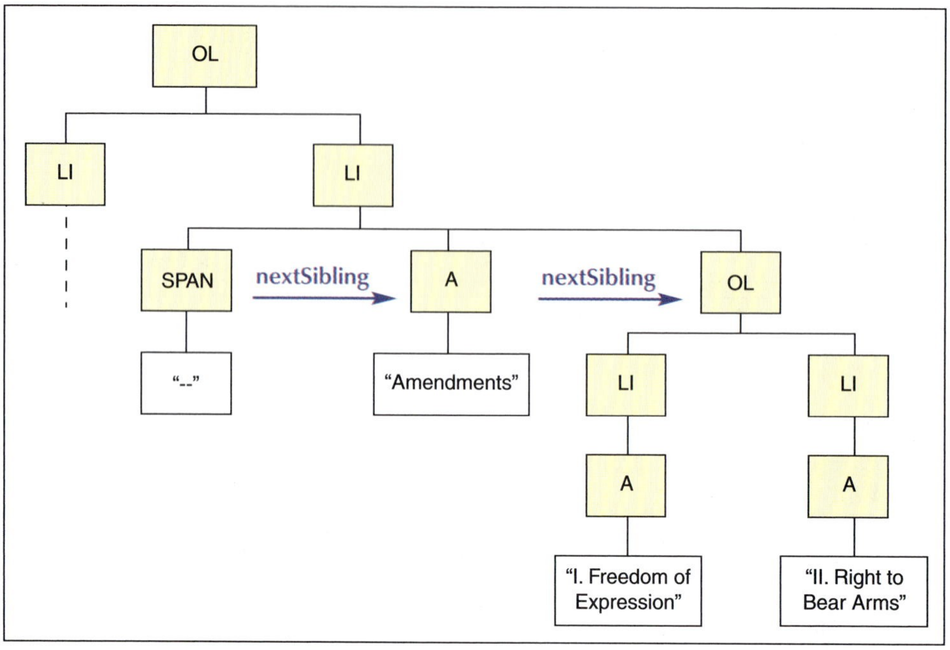

To hide the nestedList object, apply the style

```
nestedList.style.display = "none";
```

and to redisplay the object use

```
nestedList.style.display = "";
```

By not specifying a value for the display style from the object, the browser will apply whatever display style is appropriate for the object and its descendants. As with the plus and minus symbols, clicking a plus/minus box toggles the display style of the nested list between these two conditions.

You'll add commands to toggle the display style to the expandCollapse() function.

To expand and collapse the nested lists in the table of contents:

1. Return to the **toc.js** file in your text editor.
2. Scroll down to the expandCollapse() function and add the following statement after the declaration for the plusMinusBox variable:

```
var nestedList = plusMinusBox.nextSibling.nextSibling;
```

3. Add the following if statement at the end of the expandCollapse() function, as shown in Figure 16-46:

```
// Toggle the display style of the nested list
if (nestedList.style.display == "none") nestedList.style.display = ""
else nestedList.style.display = "none";
```

Figure 16-46 Code to expand and collapse the nested lists

```
function expandCollapse(e) {
   var plusMinusBox = e.target || event.srcElement;
   var nestedList = plusMinusBox.nextSibling.nextSibling;

   // Toggle the plus and minus symbol
   if (plusMinusBox.innerHTML == "--") plusMinusBox.innerHTML = "+"
   else plusMinusBox.innerHTML = "--";

   // Toggle the display style of the nested list
   if (nestedList.style.display == "none") nestedList.style.display = ""
   else nestedList.style.display = "none";

}
```

4. Save your changes to the file.
5. Reload **usconst.htm** in your Web browser and verify that as you click the plus/minus boxes in the table of contents, the nested lists within the table of contents are alternately hidden and redisplayed. Figure 16-47 shows the table of contents with a mixture of hidden and displayed nested lists.

Figure 16-47 Table of contents with hidden and displayed lists

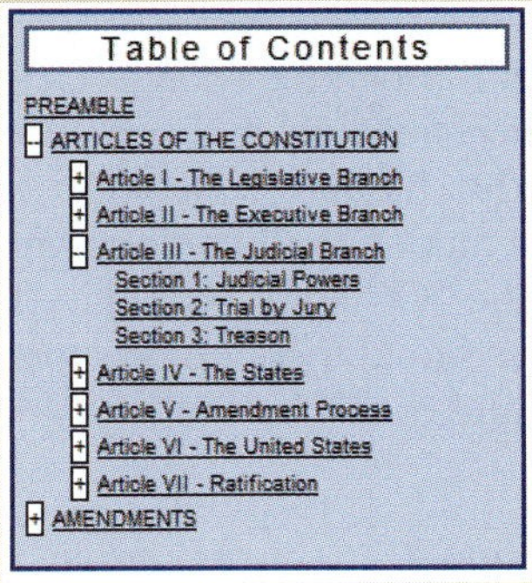

Expanding and Collapsing the Source Document

The final piece of the dynamic table of contents is to expand and collapse the document itself so that it mimics the actions of the table of contents. One problem is that the structure of the table of contents is markedly different from the structure of the source document. In the table of contents, different sections are nested within one another. By contrast, in the source document all sections are siblings, with only the section headings indicating when a section begins and ends, and the element names indicating what level each section represents. See Figure 16-48.

Figure 16-48 **Structure of the table of contents list and the document elements**

```
<ol>
   <li>Main Head
      <ol>
         <li>Subhead
            <ol>
               <li>Minor Subhead</li>
               <li>Minor Subhead</li>
            </ol>
         </li>
         <li>Subhead</li>
      </ol>
   </li>
   <li>Main Head
      <ol>
         <li>Subhead
            <ol>
               <li>Minor Subhead</li>
            </ol>
         </li>
      </ol>
   </li>
</ol>
```

nested list

```
<h1>Main Head</h1>
<p>Text</p>
<h2>Subhead</h2>
<p>Text</p>
<h3>Minor Subhead</h3>
<p>Text</p>
<h3>Minor Subhead</h3>
<p>Text</p>
<p>Text</p>
<h2>Subhead</h2>
<p>Text</p>
<p>Text</p>
<h1>Main Head</h1>
<p>Text</p>
<h2>Subhead</h2>
<p>Text</p>
<h3>Minor Subhead</h3>
<p>Text</p>
```

document elements

Your approach will be to loop through the source document, one node at a time. Each time the loop encounters a section heading, it checks whether the corresponding entry in the table of contents is displayed or hidden. If the entry is hidden, that section heading and all subsequent elements are hidden until the loop encounters another section heading. On the other hand, if the TOC entry is displayed, that section heading and all subsequent elements are displayed until the loop gets to another heading. The following code provides the general structure of this for loop:

```
var displayStatus = "";
for (var n = sourceDoc.firstChild; n != null; n = n.nextSibling) {
   var nodeLevel = levelNum(n);

   if (nodeLevel != -1) {
      // determine the display status of the TOC entry
   }
   if (n.nodeType == 1) { // node represents a page element
      // apply the current display status to the node
   }
}
```

This code starts by storing the display status in the displayStatus variable. The initial value is an empty text string indicating that the default display status of the objects will be applied by the browser. The for loop then goes through the nodes in the source document starting with the first child node and moving to the next sibling until no siblings are left. For each node, it tests whether the node is a heading element using the levelNum() function. If the value returned by the levelNum() function is not equal to –1 (indicating that the node represents one of the section headings), the code determines the display status of the TOC entry for that section heading. Also, each time through the loop, the display status is applied to the current node—but only if that node represents a Web page element.

Tip

Before changing the display style of a node, always confirm that the node represents a Web page element by testing that the value of the nodeType property equals 1.

You'll add this for loop and these if conditions to a function named expandCollapseDoc().

To insert the expandCollapseDoc() function:

1. Return to the **toc.js** file in your text editor.
2. At the bottom of the file, insert the following code, as shown in Figure 16-49:

```
function expandCollapseDoc() {
   var displayStatus = "";
   for (var n = sourceDoc.firstChild; n != null; n = n.nextSibling) {
      var nodeLevel = levelNum(n);

      if (nodeLevel != -1) {
         // determine the display status of the TOC entry
      }

      if (n.nodeType == 1) { // node represents a page element
         // apply the current display status to the node
      }

   }
}
```

Figure 16-49 The expandCollapseDoc() function

```
function expandCollapse(e) {
   var plusMinusBox = e.target || event.srcElement;
   var nestedList = plusMinusBox.nextSibling.nextSibling;

   // Toggle the plus and minus symbol
   if (plusMinusBox.innerHTML == "--") plusMinusBox.innerHTML = "+"
   else plusMinusBox.innerHTML = "--";

   // Toggle the display style of the nested list
   if (nestedList.style.display == "none") nestedList.style.display = ""
   else nestedList.style.display = "none";

}

function expandCollapseDoc() {
   var displayStatus = "";
   for (var n = sourceDoc.firstChild; n != null; n = n.nextSibling) {
      var nodeLevel = levelNum(n);

      if (nodeLevel != -1) {
         // determine the display status of the TOC entry
      }

      if (n.nodeType == 1) { // node represents a page element
         // apply the current display status to the node
      }
   }
}
```

3. Save your changes to the file.

You need to determine whether the corresponding entry in the table of contents is displayed. The problem is that the display status of an object cannot be determined by looking at its display style alone. This is because under CSS, display styles cascade down from objects higher up in the object hierarchy. So, for example, if an ol element is hidden on the Web page, all of the list items within that element are also hidden. The only way to determine whether an object is hidden is to move up the object hierarchy, testing each parent of the object until you arrive at the body element itself. If *any one of those parent objects* is hidden, then the object itself will be hidden. The following function provides code for moving up the object hierarchy in this way:

```
function isHidden(object) {
   for (var n = object; n.nodeName != "BODY"; n = n.parentNode) {
      if (n.style.display == "none") return true;
   }
   return false;
}
```

The isHidden() function starts with the current object and using the parentNode property moves up the object tree until it reaches the body element. At each step along the way, the function tests the display style of the current node in the loop. If the display style is set to none, the function immediately returns a value of true, indicating that the object is hidden. On the other hand, if the browser goes all the way up the object hierarchy without encountering one hidden parent, the object itself is not hidden and the function returns the value false.

You'll add the isHidden() function to the toc.js file.

To insert the isHidden() function:

1. Directly below the expandCollapseDoc() function, insert the following code, as shown in Figure 16-50:

```
function isHidden(object) {

   for (var n = object; n.nodeName != "BODY"; n = n.parentNode) {
      if (n.style.display == "none") return true;
   }

   return false;
}
```

Figure 16-50 The isHidden() function

```
function expandCollapseDoc() {
   var displayStatus = "";
   for (var n = sourceDoc.firstChild; n != null; n = n.nextSibling) {
      var nodeLevel = levelNum(n);

      if (nodeLevel != -1) {
         // determine the display status of the TOC entry
      }

      if (n.nodeType == 1) { // node represents a page element
         // apply the current display status to the node
      }
   }
}

function isHidden(object) {

   for (var n = object; n.nodeName != "BODY"; n = n.parentNode) {
      if (n.style.display == "none") return true;
   }

   return false;
}
```

returns a value of true if object is not visible on the Web page

2. Save your changes to the file.

You use the isHidden() function to determine the display status of any entry in the table of contents. Recall that in the previous session, each entry was given an ID based on the ID of a section heading. If the section heading has the ID *sectionId*, then the list item has the ID TOC*sectionId*. You can use the getElementById() method to locate the list item for each section heading as follows:

```
var TOCentry = document.getElementById("TOC" + n.id);
```

To set the display status of the section heading, you then call the isHidden() function as follows:

```
if (isHidden(TOCentry)) displayStatus = "none"
else displayStatus = "";
```

Finally, you apply the value of the displayStatus variable to the current node in the source document using the following command:

```
n.style.display = displayStatus;
```

You'll add these commands to the expandCollapseDoc() function, and then call the function from within the expandCollapse() function so that the source document is expanded and collapsed simultaneously with the table of contents.

To complete the expandCollapseDoc() function:

1. Scroll up the toc.js file to the expandCollapseDoc() function and insert the following commands below the first if condition:

```
var TOCentry = document.getElementById("TOC" + n.id);
if (isHidden(TOCentry)) displayStatus = "none"
else displayStatus = "";
```

2. Add the following command to the second if condition:

```
n.style.display = displayStatus;
```

3. Scroll up to the expandCollapse() function and add the following statements to the end of the function:

```
// expand and collapse the source document to match the TOC
expandCollapseDoc();
```

Figure 16-51 highlights the revised code in both functions.

Figure 16-51 **Completed expandCollapse functions**

```
function expandCollapse(e) {
   var plusMinusBox = e.target || event.srcElement;
   var nestedList = plusMinusBox.nextSibling.nextSibling;

   // Toggle the plus and minus symbol
   if (plusMinusBox.innerHTML == "--") plusMinusBox.innerHTML = "+"
   else plusMinusBox.innerHTML = "--";

   // Toggle the display style of the nested list
   if (nestedList.style.display == "none") nestedList.style.display = ""
   else nestedList.style.display = "none";

   // expand and collapse the source document to match the TOC
   expandCollapseDoc();
}

function expandCollapseDoc() {
   var displayStatus = "";
   for (var n = sourceDoc.firstChild; n != null; n = n.nextSibling) {
      var nodeLevel = levelNum(n);

      if (nodeLevel != -1) {
         // determine the display status of the TOC entry
         var TOCentry = document.getElementById("TOC" + n.id);
         if (isHidden(TOCentry)) displayStatus = "none"
         else displayStatus = "";
      }

      if (n.nodeType == 1) { // node represents a page element
         // apply the current display status to the node
         n.style.display = displayStatus;
      }
   }
}
```

expands and collapses the source document to match the TOC

determines whether the TOC entry is visible

applies the display status to the current node in the source document

4. Close the file, saving your changes.

5. Reload the **usconst.htm** file in your Web browser, and then click **plus/minus** boxes in the table of contents, verifying that the content displayed in the constitution document mimics the contents displayed in the table of contents. See Figure 16-52.

Figure 16-52 Documents expanded and collapsed

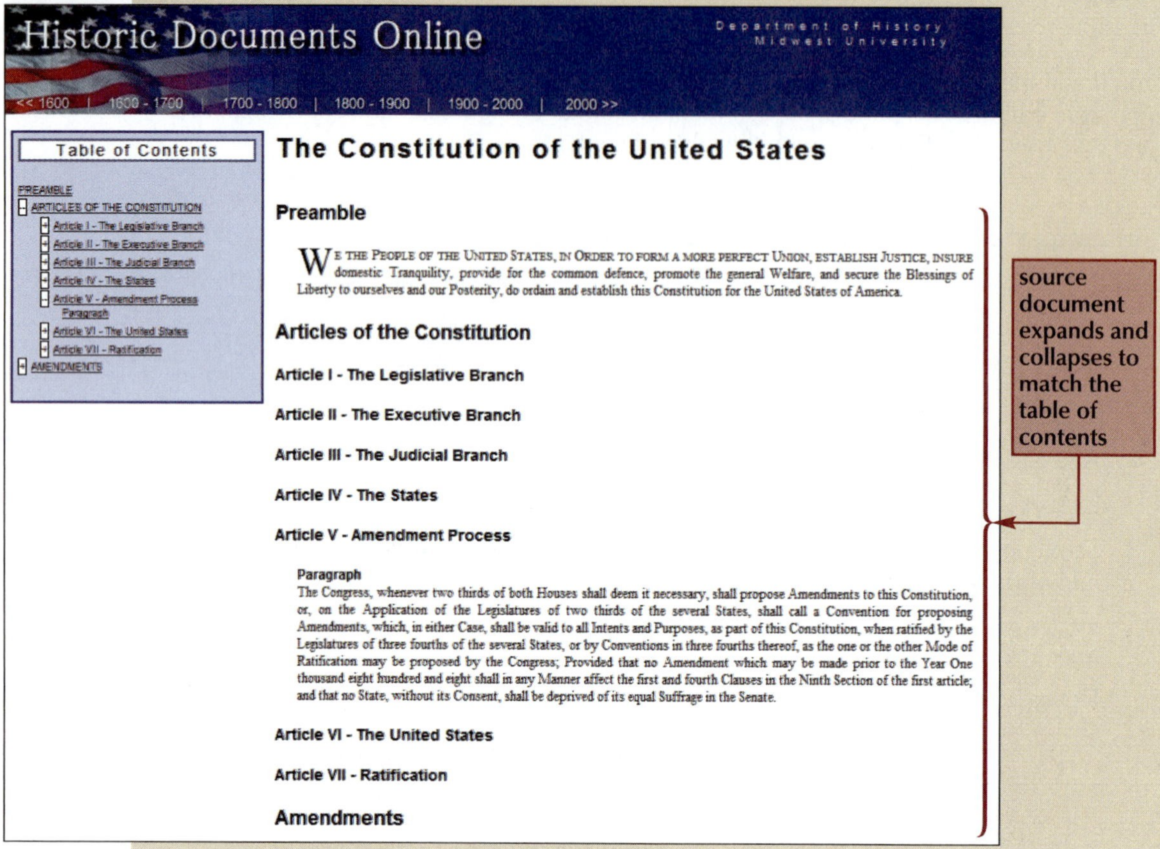

Testing the Dynamic Table of Contents

You show the dynamic table of contents application to Norene. She is pleased with the final product. She asks whether your work can be applied to other documents in her library. You test this by applying the application to a document containing the text of a 1790 peace treaty between the United States government and the Creek Indians.

To test the dynamic table of contents on a new document:

1. Use your text editor to open the **treattxt.htm** file from the tutorial.16/tutorial folder, enter ***your name*** and ***the date*** in the comment section, and then save the file as **treaty.htm**.
2. Above the closing </head> tag, insert the following script element to link the treaty file to the programs in the toc.js file:

```
<script src = "toc.js" type = "text/javascript"></script>
```

3. Insert the following div element directly below the <body> tag to hold the dynamic table of contents:

```
<div id = "toc"></div>
```

4. Add the following opening tag directly before the Preamble h1 element:

```
<div id = "doc">
```

5. Directly before the </body> tag at the bottom of the file, insert the closing **</div>** tag to enclose the content of the document within a div element. Figure 16-53 highlights the code added in the file.

Figure 16-53 **Revised treaty document**

```
    <title>Treaty with the Creek Indians: 1790</title>
    <link href="web.css" rel="stylesheet" type="text/css" />
    <script  src = "toc.js" type = "text/javascript"></script>
</head>

<body>
    <div id = "toc"></div>

    <div id="logo"><img src="hlogo.jpg" alt="Historic Documents" /></div>
    <div id="logosub">Department of History<br />Midwest University</div>
    <div id="doctitle"><h1>Treaty with the Creek Indians: 1790</h1></div>

    <div id = "doc">
       <h1>Preamble</h1>
       <p>THE parties being desirous of establishing permanent peace and
          friendship between the United States and the said Creek Nation, and
          the citizens and members thereof, and to remove the causes of war by
          ascertaining their limits, and making other necessary, just and
          friendly arrangements: The President of the United States, by Henry
          Knox, Secretary for the Department of War, whom he hath constituted with
          full powers for these purposes, by and with the advice and consent of
          the Senate of the United States, and the Creek Nation, by the
          undersigned Kings, Chiefs and Warriors, representing the said nation,
          have agreed to the following articles. </p>

    </div>

</body>
</html>
```

6. Close the **treaty.htm** file, saving your changes, and then open the file in your Web browser. The dynamic table of contents is displayed in the left margin. See Figure 16-54.

Figure 16-54 **Treaty document with the dynamic table of contents**

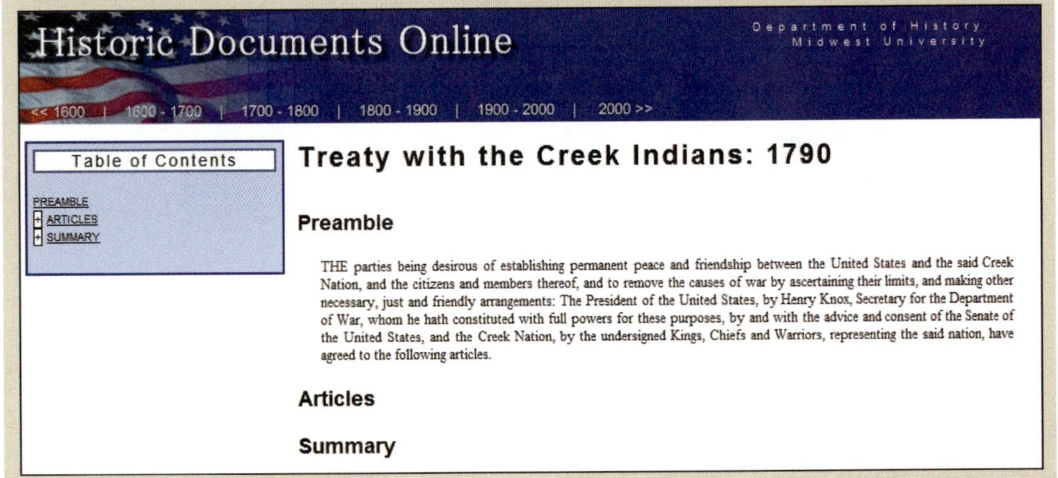

7. Click the **plus/minus** boxes to collapse and expand the document contents, and then click table of contents entries to move to the corresponding sections in the treaty.

InSight | Traversing the Node Tree with Recursion

In creating the dynamic table of contents, you made several simplifying assumptions. One was that all of the section headings in each historic document would be siblings and children of the source document. You did not allow for the possibility that a section heading would be further nested within another element. However, some applications that involve working with the node tree require a script to traverse the entire tree, touching each node. One way of doing this is through recursion. **Recursion** is a programming technique in which a function calls itself repeatedly until a stopping condition is met. The following is an example of a recursive function that counts the number of child nodes within a given node:

```
function countNodes(node, nodeCount) {
   for (var n = node.firstChild; n != null; n = n.nextSibling) {
      nodeCount++;
      countNodes(n, nodeCount);
   }
   return nodeCount;
}
```

Notice that the countNodes() function includes a for loop that loops through every child node of the given node object. For each child node the function finds, it increases the value of the nodeCount parameter by 1 and then calls *itself* to add to that total the number of children of that child node. Then, for each child node in *that set,* it calls the countNodes() function again to count the number of children in the next lower level. This process of drilling down the node tree continues until no descendant nodes remain in the node tree.

Every recursive function needs a starting point. If you wanted to count all of the nodes in Norene's source document, you would point the node parameter to the sourceDoc object and set the initial value of the nodeCount variable to 0. The expression to count all of the nodes would be:

```
countNodes(sourceDoc, 0)
```

If you apply this command to Norene's U.S. Constitution document, you would discover that the document contains 441 nodes under the W3C DOM. The IE DOM reports only 220 nodes, but that is due to the difference in how the DOMs treat white space nodes.

Switching Between Style Sheets

Norene is pleased with all of the work you have done on the dynamic table of contents. She has one last problem. Norene wants to give users the ability to easily switch their view of the documents stored on her Web site between the default Web page view you've been using, a page view more suitable for printing, and another page view that supports a larger text font. Figure 16-55 shows the document under each of these views.

Figure 16-55 Three views of the constitution document

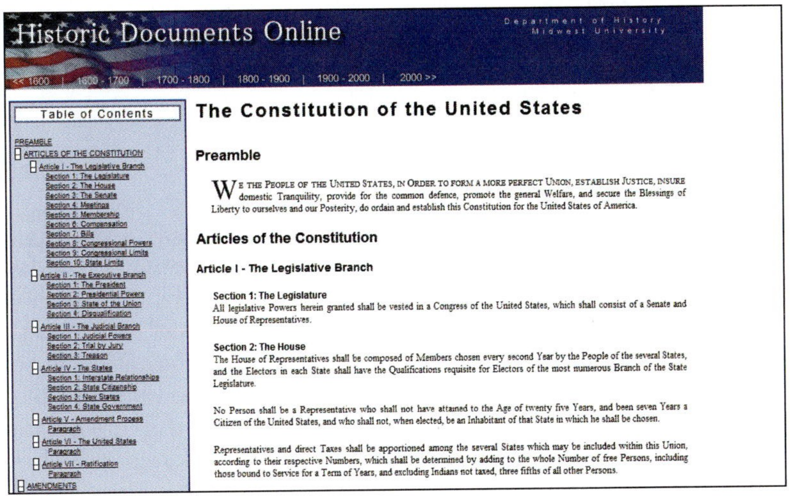

Web view

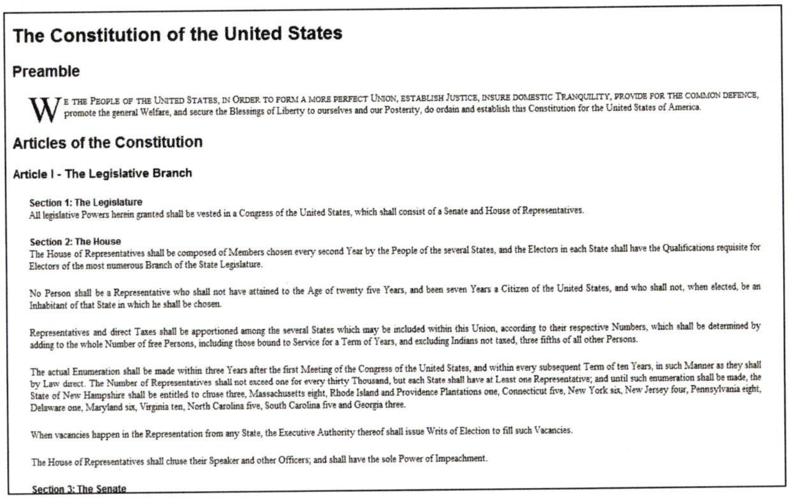

print view

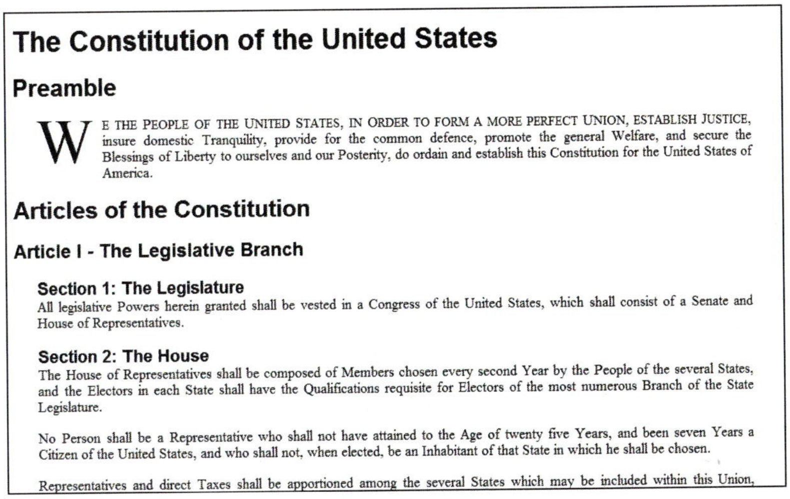

large text view

Norene already created three style sheets for the three views shown in Figure 16-55 and linked to them in the usconst.htm file. The following is the code for the three <style> tags:

```
<link type = "text/css" title = "Web" href = "web.css"
      rel = "stylesheet" />
<link type = "text/css" title = "Print" href = "print.css"
      rel = "alternate stylesheet" />
<link type = "text/css" title = "Large Text" href = "largetext.css"
      rel = "alternate stylesheet" />
```

Style sheets can be classified as persistent, preferred, and alternate. A **persistent style sheet** is a style sheet that is always active. It has a rel attribute value of stylesheet and does not have a title attribute. Persistent style sheets are loaded by the Web browser by default. A **preferred style sheet** is similar to a persistent style sheet except that it contains a title. Preferred style sheets are also turned on by default, but they also can be turned off by actions of the user. An **alternate style sheet** has a rel attribute value of alternate stylesheet and is identified by its title attribute. Alternate style sheets are not turned on by default, but the user can switch to them as alternates to the preferred style sheet.

For the usconst.htm file, Norene has created one preferred style sheet with the title Web based on the web.css file. You've been using this style sheet throughout this tutorial. The file also contains two alternate style sheets with the titles Print and Large Text, pointing to the print.css and largetext.css files, respectively. So far, those style sheets have not been activated for use in the constitution document.

Alternate style sheets can be activated in some browsers by selecting them from a menu of style sheet options. Opera has a built-in command to allow users to select their style sheet option. Firefox, on the other hand, provides an add-on to enable this functionality. Other browsers, such as Internet Explorer, do not provide a method for choosing alternate style sheets in placed or preferred sheets.

Norene wants you to provide this capability through a JavaScript program so that users running browsers other than Opera or Firefox can switch easily between style sheets. Norene envisions a program that will automatically create input buttons for each preferred or alternate style sheet listed in the HTML file. Users can then switch between the style sheets by clicking one of the input buttons on the Web page. Figure 16-56 shows a preview of this effect.

Input buttons to switch style sheets — **Figure 16-56**

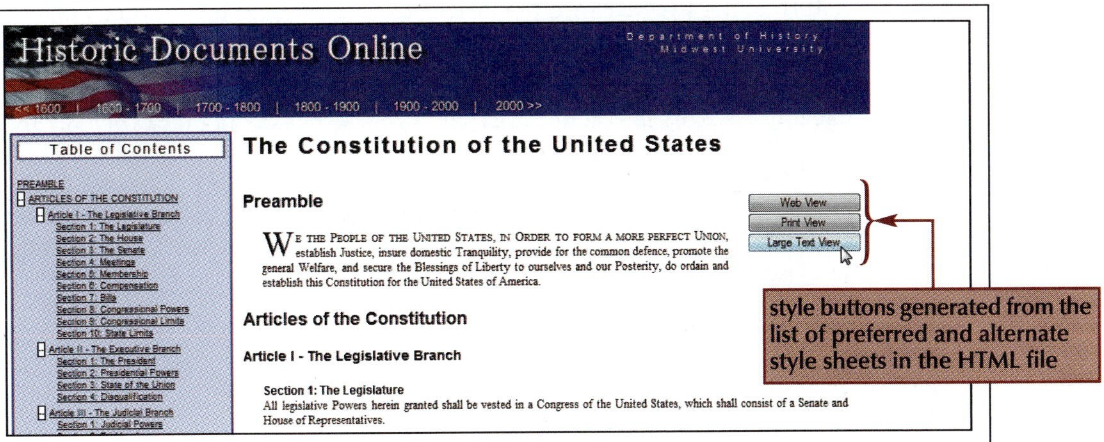

Clicking a style button ...

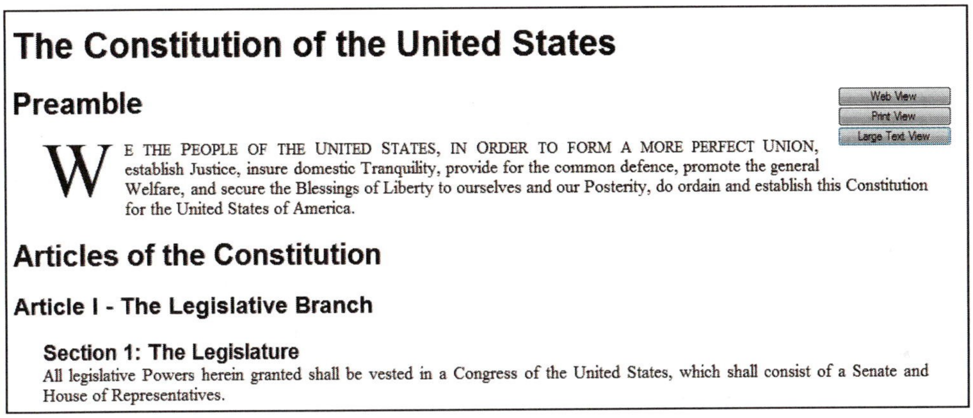

... activates the specified style sheet

You'll insert the code to create these input buttons in an external file named switchstyle.js and then link it to the usconst.htm file.

To create the switchstyle.js file:

1. Return to the **usconst.htm** file in your text editor, and then directly below the <script> tag to access the toc.js file, insert the following script element to access the switchstyle.js file:

```
<script src = "switchstyle.js" type = "text/javascript"></script>
```

2. Save your changes to the file.
3. Use your text editor to open the **switchtxt.js** file from the tutorial.16/tutorial folder, enter ***your name*** and ***the date*** in the comment section of the file, and then save the file as **switchstyle.js**.

   When the page is loaded by the browser, you'll run a function named makeStyle-Buttons() to generate the style buttons.

4. Add the following code to the bottom of the file:

```
addEvent(window, "load", makeStyleButtons, false);

function makeStyleButtons() {

}
```

You used the addEvent() function to provide a cross-browser solution to adding an event handler to the load event. As discussed in the previous tutorial, by adding the event handler in this way, you are not interfering with the event handler you've already created to generate the dynamic table of contents.

Working with the Link Element

So far, you've worked only with elements found in the body of a Web page. You can also access and modify elements found in the document's head. You can view the collection of all <link> tags in the current document using the following object reference:

```
document.getElementsByTagName("link")
```

From this collection of links, you want to extract only those links used for preferred or alternate style sheets. To do this, the link element needs to fulfill the following:

- Its rel attribute must equal either stylesheet or alternate stylesheet.
- It must have a style sheet title.

You'll store the link elements that fulfill these two criteria in an array named allStyles, which you'll create in the switchstyle.js file.

To create the allLinks variable:

1. Directly above the makeStyleButtons() function in the switchstyle.js file, insert the following global variable declaration:

```
var allStyles = new Array();
```

2. Within the makeStyleButtons() function, insert the following code to populate the allStyles array, as shown in Figure 16-57:

```
var allLinks = document.getElementsByTagName("link");

// Create an array of preferred or alternate style sheets
for (var i = 0; i < allLinks.length; i++) {
   if ((allLinks[i].rel == "stylesheet" ||
        allLinks[i].rel == "alternate stylesheet") &&
        allLinks[i].title != "") {
      allStyles.push(allLinks[i]);
   }
}
```

Figure 16-57 Code to populate the allStyles array

```
addEvent(window, "load", makeStyleButtons, false);

var allStyles = new Array();

function makeStyleButtons() {
   var allLinks = document.getElementsByTagName("link");

   // Create an array of preferred or alternate style sheets
   for (var i = 0; i < allLinks.length; i++) {
      if ((allLinks[i].rel == "stylesheet" || allLinks[i].rel == "alternate stylesheet")
         && allLinks[i].title != "") {
         allStyles.push(allLinks[i]);
      }
   }
}
```

allStyles array contains all link elements created for preferred or alternate style sheets

To create the buttons for each style sheet, you'll loop through all of the items in the allStyles array, creating one input button for each style sheet. The text displayed in each button will be "*style* view", where *style* is the title of the style sheet. You'll also set the title of each button to match the title of the style sheet to associate each button with its style sheet. You'll append each input button as a child of a new div element named styleBox.

You'll add this code to the makeStyleButtons() function.

To create input buttons for each titled link element in the document:

1. Directly below the for loop you just created, insert the following code, as shown in Figure 16-58:

```
// Create buttons for each preferred or alternate style sheet
var styleBox = document.createElement("div");

for (var i = 0; i < allStyles.length; i++) {
   styleButton = document.createElement("input");
   styleButton.type = "button";
   styleButton.value = allStyles[i].title + " view";
   styleButton.title = allStyles[i].title;

   styleBox.appendChild(styleButton);
}
```

Figure 16-58 Code to create form buttons for each style sheet

```
   // Create an array of preferred or alternate style sheets
   for (var i = 0; i < allLinks.length; i++) {
      if ((allLinks[i].rel == "stylesheet" || allLinks[i].rel == "alternate stylesheet")
         && allLinks[i].title != "") {
         allStyles.push(allLinks[i]);
      }
   }

   // Create buttons for each preferred or alternate style sheet
   var styleBox = document.createElement("div");

   for (var i = 0; i < allStyles.length; i++) {
     styleButton = document.createElement("input");
     styleButton.type = "button";
     styleButton.value = allStyles[i].title + " view";
     styleButton.title = allStyles[i].title;

     styleBox.appendChild(styleButton);
   }
}
```

box containing the style buttons

creates an input button for each style sheet

appends each button to the style box

2. Save your changes to the file.

Next, you have to define the appearance of the style buttons and the style box. The style buttons will each be 120 pixels wide and the font size of the button text will be 12 pixels. The box containing the buttons will be 125 pixels wide, with top and right margins of 5 pixels and bottom and left margins of 10 pixels. The box itself will be floated on the right margin of the page. Note that the IE and W3C DOMs use different properties to apply the float style. Under the IE DOM, the property is

```
object.style.styleFloat = position;
```

where *object* is the object to be floated on the page and *position* is the margin on which the object is floated (left, right, or none). Under the W3C DOM, the float style is applied using the following property:

```
object.style.cssFloat = position;
```

To work across all browsers, you can run both commands in your script. The browser will apply the property it recognizes and ignore the one that it doesn't.

To design the appearance of the style buttons and style box:

1. Directly above the command that appends each style button to the style box, insert the following lines:

```
// Define the styles of each button
styleButton.style.width = "120px";
styleButton.style.fontSize = "12px";
```

2. At the bottom of the makeStyleButtons() function, insert the following lines:

```
// Define the styles of the box containing the buttons
styleBox.style.width = "125px";
styleBox.style.cssFloat = "right";
styleBox.style.styleFloat = "right";
styleBox.style.margin = "5px 5px 10px 10px";
```

Figure 16-59 shows the inserted code.

Figure 16-59 Design styles applied to the style buttons and box

```
  for (var i = 0; i < allStyles.length; i++) {
    styleButton = document.createElement("input");
    styleButton.type = "button";
    styleButton.value = allStyles[i].title + " view";
    styleButton.title = allStyles[i].title;

    // Define the styles of each button
    styleButton.style.width = "120px";
    styleButton.style.fontSize = "12px";

    styleBox.appendChild(styleButton);
  }

  // Define the styles of the box containing the buttons
  styleBox.style.width = "125px";
  styleBox.style.cssFloat = "right";
  styleBox.style.styleFloat = "right";
  styleBox.style.margin = "5px 5px 10px 10px";
}
```

styles for each button

floats the style box on the right page margin

Finally, you'll attach the style box to the source document on Norene's page, placing it as the first child of that object.

To insert the style box on the Web page:

1. At the bottom of the makeStyleButtons() function, insert the following lines, as shown in Figure 16-60:

```
// Add the style box to the source document
var sourceDoc = document.getElementById("doc");
sourceDoc.insertBefore(styleBox, sourceDoc.firstChild);
```

Figure 16-60 Style box appended to the source document

```
  // Define the styles of the box containing the buttons
  styleBox.style.width = "125px";
  styleBox.style.cssFloat = "right";
  styleBox.style.styleFloat = "right";
  styleBox.style.margin = "5px 5px 10px 10px";

  // Add the style box to the source document
  var sourceDoc = document.getElementById("doc");
  sourceDoc.insertBefore(styleBox, sourceDoc.firstChild);
}
```

2. Save your changes to the file, and then reload **usconst.htm** in your Web browser. Three input buttons have been added to the Web page, each matching one of the preferred or alternate style sheets defined in the document. See Figure 16-61.

Figure 16-61 Style buttons for each preferred and alternate style sheet

The Constitution of the United States
Preamble
We the People of the United States, in Order to form a more perfect Union, establish Justice, insure domestic Tranquility, provide for the common defence, promote the general Welfare, and secure the Blessings of Liberty to ourselves and our Posterity, do ordain and establish this Constitution for the United States of America.
Web view
Print view
Large Text view

Initializing the Style Sheets

With the style buttons in place, you now must enable and disable the different style sheets. You can disable a style sheet using the command

```
styleSheet.disabled = true
```

and enable it with the command

```
styleSheet.disabled = false
```

where *styleSheet* is a preferred or alternate style sheet attached to the document. For Norene's application, you'll initially enable any preferred style sheet and disable any alternate style sheet. To do this, you'll add the following if statement to the for loop that creates the style buttons:

```
if (allStyles[i].rel == "stylesheet") {
   allStyles[i].disabled = false;
} else {
   allStyles[i].disabled = true;
}
```

You'll add this command to the switchstyle.js file.

To initialize the style sheets:

1. Return to the **switchstyle.js** file in your text editor.
2. Within the for loop to create the style buttons, insert the following code, as shown in Figure 16-62:

```
// Initialize the style sheets
if (allStyles[i].rel == "stylesheet") {
   allStyles[i].disabled = false;
} else {
   allStyles[i].disabled = true;
}
```

Code to initialize the style sheets Figure 16-62

```
// Create buttons for each preferred or alternate style sheet
var styleBox = document.createElement("div");

for (var i = 0; i < allStyles.length; i++) {

   // Initialize the style sheets
   if (allStyles[i].rel == "stylesheet") {
      allStyles[i].disabled = false;
   } else {
      allStyles[i].disabled = true;
   }

   styleButton = document.createElement("input");
   styleButton.type = "button";
   styleButton.value = allStyles[i].title + " view";
   styleButton.title = allStyles[i].title;
```

Switching Between Style Sheets

The last task in your program is to enable users to enable and disable the different style sheets by clicking one of the style buttons inserted into the Web page. Because the buttons and the style sheets share the same title, you can loop through all of the style sheets contained in the allStyles array, enabling the one style sheet that matches the title and disabling the others. The code for the loop is:

```
for (var i = 0; i < allStyles.length; i++) {
   if (allStyles[i].title == this.title) {
      allStyles[i].disabled = false;
   } else {
      allStyles[i].disabled = true;
   }
}
```

This for loop uses the `this` keyword to reference the button clicked by the user. You'll add this for loop to a function named changeStyle(), and then add an event handler to call this function whenever one of the style buttons is clicked.

To create event handlers for the style buttons:

1. Scroll to the bottom of the switchstyle.js file and insert the following function:

```
function changeStyle() {
   for (var i = 0; i < allStyles.length; i++) {
      if (allStyles[i].title == this.title) {
         allStyles[i].disabled = false;
      } else {
         allStyles[i].disabled = true;
      }
   }
}
```

2. Scroll up the file and insert the following code within the makeStyleButton() function, directly above the line that appends a styleButton to the styleBox:

```
// Apply an event handler to the style button
styleButton.onclick = changeStyle;
```

Figure 16-63 shows the newly inserted code.

Figure 16-63 **The changeStyle() function to switch the style sheets**

```
      // Apply an event handler to the style button
      styleButton.onclick = changeStyle;

      styleBox.appendChild(styleButton);
   }

   // Define the styles of the box containing the buttons
   styleBox.style.width = "125px";
   styleBox.style.cssFloat = "right";
   styleBox.style.styleFloat = "right";
   styleBox.style.margin = "5px 5px 10px 10px";

   // Add the style box to the source document
   var sourceDoc = document.getElementById("doc");
   sourceDoc.insertBefore(styleBox, sourceDoc.firstChild);
}

function changeStyle() {
   for (var i = 0; i < allStyles.length; i++) {
      if (allStyles[i].title == this.title) {
         allStyles[i].disabled = false;
      } else {
         allStyles[i].disabled = true;
      }
   }
}
```

runs the changeStyle() function whenever a style button is clicked

loops through all of the style sheets and enables only the one corresponding to the style button

3. Close the file, saving your changes.

4. Reload **usconst.htm** in your Web browser, and then verify that you can switch between the three style sheets by clicking the three style buttons on the Web page.

Working with the Style Sheets Object Collection

To complete the style sheet switcher, you had to examine the attributes of the link element. However, the link element can be used for objects other than style sheets. Instead of using the link element, you can also reference style sheets directly using the styleSheets object collection, which has the syntax

```
document.styleSheets[i]
```

where *i* is the index number of the style sheet. The first style sheet that a browser encounters has an index value of 0, the second has an index value of 1, and so on. Figure 16-64 lists the properties of the style sheet object. Some of these properties are specific to one DOM, and some properties are read-only and cannot be modified by the browser.

Properties of the style sheet object Figure 16-64

Property	Description
styleSheet.cssText	The text of the declarations in the style sheet (IE DOM)
styleSheet.disabled	Returns a Boolean value indicating whether the style sheet has been disabled (true) or has been enabled (false)
styleSheet.href	The url of the style sheet; for embedded style sheets, the href value is an empty text string [read-only]
styleSheet.media	A text string containing the list of media types associated with the style sheet [read-only]
styleSheet.rules	Returns the collection of rules within the style sheet (IE DOM)
styleSheet.cssRules	Returns the collection of rules within the style sheet (W3C DOM)
styleSheet.title	The title of the style sheet [read-only]
styleSheet.type	The MIME type of the style sheet [read-only]

Most browsers support the styleSheets object collection, but some do not. If you need a complete cross-browser solution, it is best to modify the attributes of the link element instead of working with the styleSheets collection.

Working with Style Sheet Rules | InSight

The style sheet object also contains an object collection that references the rules within the style sheet. In the W3C DOM, the object reference to the rules collection is

```
styleSheet.cssRules
```

where *styleSheet* is a styleSheet object. For example, if the first style sheet on a Web page contains the declarations

```
<style type = "text/css">
    h1 {color: red}
    h2 {color: blue}
 </style>
```

then the object reference

```
document.styleSheets[0].cssRules[0]
```

refers to the style sheet declaration h1 {color: red}. In the IE DOM, style sheet rules are referenced using the following object collection:

```
styleSheet.rules
```

You can add and remove rules from a style sheet under both DOMs. The IE DOM uses the addRule() and removeRule() methods. The equivalent methods under the W3C DOM are insertRule() and deleteRule().

Norene appreciates the work you've done adding a style switcher to her Web page. She will continue to apply the work you've done to her history site.

Review | Session 16.3 Quick Check

1. What command creates an inline image node named imgObj and then appends it as the first child of a node named listItem?
2. What command hides and removes from the page flow a page element with the ID imgObj?
3. What is recursion?
4. What are preferred and alternate style sheets? What is a persistent style sheet?
5. What are two ways of referencing style sheet objects linked to a document?
6. What command enables a *styleSheet* object? What command disables the same object?
7. What expression references the second rule from the document's third style sheet? Provide answers for both the IE and W3C DOMs.

Review | Tutorial Summary

In this tutorial, you learned how to create and manage dynamic content and styles to develop a dynamic table of contents application that could be applied to a wide variety of documents. In the first session, you learned how to apply the innerHTML property to insert new content into a page element. The first session also introduced the node tree, exploring how to navigate through a node tree, create new nodes, and attach them to a Web page document. Using this information, you created a list of section headings from a document. In the second session, you applied what you learned about node properties and methods to create a nested list of section headings. The second session also demonstrated how to work with attribute nodes and how to work with element attributes. In the third session, you created an expandable/collapsible document by applying the display style to elements within the dynamic table of contents and within the sample document. The third session also discussed how to access different style sheets created for a Web page document, showing how to create a style sheet switch to enable users to select the style sheet they want to apply to the document.

Key Terms

alternate style sheet
document fragment
dynamic content
node
node tree
persistent style sheet
plus/minus box
preferred style sheet
recursion
root node

Practice | Review Assignments

Practice the skills you learned in the tutorial using the same case scenario.

Data Files needed for the Review Assignments: fed10txt.htm, fedpaper.css, hlogo.jpg, keytxt.js, print.css, stylestxt.js

Norene has another application for you to add to her library of historic documents. Some documents are not broken into sections, so creating a table of contents would not be appropriate. For those documents, Norene wants the Web page to display a box containing a sorted list of keywords and phrases found in the document. Each keyword or phrase has been marked in the documents with a dfn (definition) element. The entries in the keyword list need to search the current historic document for the presence of these dfn elements and create links between the keyword list entries and the keywords in the document. Norene also wants the page to have a Web version and a print version, and she wants users to be able to easily switch between the two.

Figure 16-65 shows a preview of the page created for the tenth Federalist paper written by James Madison in 1787 on the danger of factions to the republic.

Figure 16-65

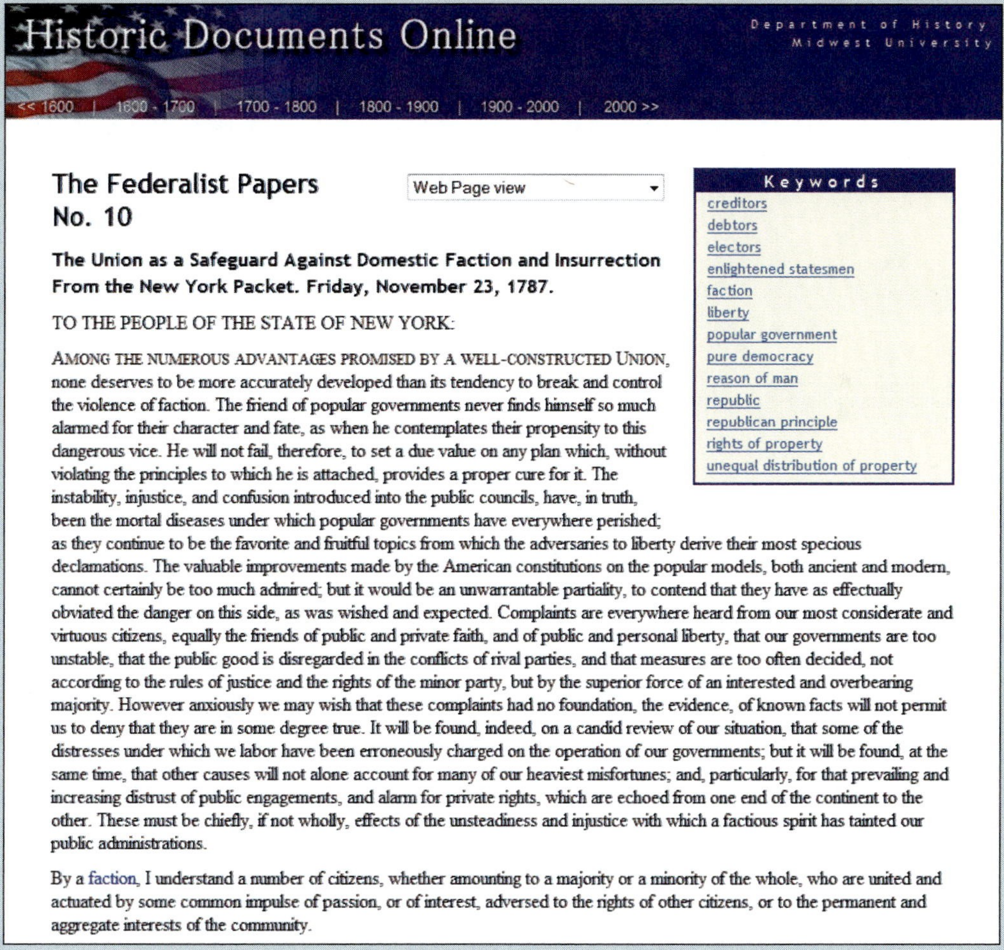

Norene has already provided the source document and external style sheets that format the appearance of the document and the keyword list for both the Web and the printer. You'll have to write the application that creates the content of the keyword list.

Complete the following:

1. Use your text editor to open the **fed10txt.htm**, **keytxt.js**, and **stylestxt.js** files from the tutorial.16/review folder, enter ***your name*** and ***the date*** in the comment section of each file, and then save the files as **fed10.htm**, **keywords.js**, and **styles.js**, respectively.
2. Go to the **fed10.htm** file in your text editor and study the contents of the file, paying attention to titles of the style sheets assigned to this document and the structure of the page contents. Add script elements to attach this document to the keywords.js and styles.js files, and then close the file, saving your changes.
3. Go to the **keywords.js** file in your text editor. Create a function named **makeElemList()**. The purpose of this function is to return an array containing a sorted list of the contents of elements with a common tag name. You'll use this function later to create a list of the keywords in the document. The function has a single parameter named **elem** that contains the text of the tag name. Add the following commands to the function:
   a. Store the collection of elements whose tag name equals the elem parameter in a variable named **elemList**. (*Hint:* Use the document.getElementsByTagName() method.)
   b. Declare a new array named **elemTextArr**.
   c. Create a for loop that goes through each of the objects in the elemList object collection. For each object, change the text to lowercase letters and store the content of the element in the corresponding elemTextArr array item. (*Hint*: Use the toLowerCase() String method to change the content of the object to lowercase letters.)
   d. Sort the entries in the elemTextArr array in ascending alphabetical order.
   e. Return the contents of the elemTextArr array.
4. Create a function named **setElemId()**. The purpose of this function is to create and return ID values for elements in the document that match a specific tag name and element content. You'll use this function later to insert matching ID values between the items in the keyword list and the keywords found in the document. The function has two parameters: **elem**, which contains the text of the tag name, and **elemText**, which contains the text of the element content. Add the following commands to the function:
   a. Store the collection of elements whose tag name equals the elem parameter in a variable named **elemList**.
   b. Create a for loop that goes through each of the objects in the elemList object collection.
   c. Within the for loop, test whether the content of the current elemList object, converted to lowercase letters, equals the value of the elemText parameter. If it does, test whether the ID of the object is equal to an empty text string. If the ID is missing, create a variable named **elemId** equal to the text string keyword*i*, where *i* is the value of the counter variable in the for loop, and set the ID of the object to the value of the elemId variable. If the ID is not missing, set the value of the elemId variable to the value of the ID attribute of the object.
   d. After the for loop has finished, return the value of the elemId variable. This is the ID that has been assigned to the element in the document.

5. Create a function named **makeKeyWordBox()**. The purpose of this function is to create a list of keywords drawn from the dfn elements in the historic document. There are no parameters for this function. Add the following commands:
   a. Declare a variable named **historyDoc** that references the element with the ID doc.
   b. Create an element node named **keywordBox** for a div element. Set the ID of the keywordBox to "keywords".
   c. Create an element node named **keywordBoxTitle** containing an h1 element. Set the content of the h1 element to the text string Keywords.
   d. Append keywordBoxTitle to the keywordBox node as a child.
   e. Create an element node named **ulList** containing a ul element. Append ulList as a second child of the keywordBox node. This unordered list will store the list of keywords in the document.
   f. Call the makeElemList() function using the text string dfn as the parameter value. Store the array returned by the function in a variable named keywords.
   g. Write a for loop that loops through all of the items in the keywords array that you just created. The purpose of this for loop is to create an unordered list of keywords, each one linked to a specific keyword in the document. For each item in the array, do the following: (i) Create an element node named **newListItem** that contains a list item element; (ii) Create an element node named **newLink** that contains a hypertext element; (iii) Set the content of newLink to the value of the current item in the keywords array (*Hint*: Use the reference keywords[*i*] where *i* is the value of the counter variable in the for loop.); (iv) Create a variable named **linkId** whose value is equal to the value returned by the setElemId() function using dfn and keywords[*i*] as the parameter values; (v) Change the href attribute of newLink to #*id* where *id* is the value of the linkId variable; (vi) Append newLink to newListItem and append newListItem to ulList.
   h. After the for loop has completed, append keywordBox as the first child of the historyDoc node.
6. Use the addEvent() function previously added to the file to run the makeKeyWordBox() function when the page is loaded by the browser.
7. Save your changes to the file, and then load **fed10.htm** in your Web browser. Verify that a box containing a list of keywords is displayed on the Web page with each entry in the list linked to a specific keyword within the historic document.
8. Return to the **styles.js** file in your text editor. Add a line to the bottom of the file to declare the global variable styleList as a new, empty array.
9. Use the addEvent() function to run the makeStyleListBox() function when the page is loaded by the browser.
10. Add the **makeStyleListBox()** function. The purpose of this function is to create a selection list whose entries match the list of style sheets present in the source document. Within this function, declare the variable **allLinks** matching all elements in the document with the tag name link.
11. Within the makeStyleListBox() function, add a for loop to loop through all of the entries in the allLinks object collection. If the rel attribute of the entry equals stylesheet or alternate stylesheet and the title attribute is nonempty, add the entry to the styleList array.
12. Create the selection list containing the list of style sheets by adding the following code to the makeStyleListBox() function:
    a. Create a select element node named **styleSelect**.

b. Loop through all of the entries in the styleList array. If the value of the rel attribute of the entry is not equal to stylesheet, disable the style sheet; otherwise, enable the style sheet. Also, for each entry in the array, create an option element node named **styleOption**. Set the value of the option element to the title value of the style sheet. Set the text contained within the option to "*stylesheet* view" where *stylesheet* is the title of the style sheet. Finally, append the option element to the styleSelect node.
c. After the for loop has completed, define the styles for the styleSelect element node. Set the width of the selection list to 220 pixels and float the selection list on the right margin. Set the margins around the selection list to 5 pixels above and to the right, and 10 pixels below and to the left.

13. Within the makeStyleListBox() function, add an event handler to the styleSelect object to run the changeStyle() function when the value of the selection is changed.
14. Complete the makeStyleListBox() function by declaring a variable named **sourceDoc** referencing the element with the ID doctitle. Append the styleSelect object as the first child of the sourceDoc object.
15. Create the **changeStyle()** function. The purpose of this function is to switch the style sheets employed by browser based on the choice of the user. Add the following commands to the function:
    a. Create a variable named **selectedItem** that contains the index number of the selected option from the selection list of style sheets. (*Hint:* You can reference the selection list using either the `this` keyword if you used traditional event binding, or the event object if you used the addEvent() function to create the event handler.)
    b. Create a variable named **styleOption** equal to the value of the selected option in the style sheet selection list.
    c. Loop through all of the entries in the styleList array. If the title of the style sheet equals the value of styleOption, enable the style sheet; otherwise, disable the style sheet.
16. Save your changes to the file, and then reload **fed10.htm** in your Web browser. Click the selection list generated by the code in the styles.js file, and verify that you can switch styles between the Web Page and Printer views.
17. Submit the completed project to your instructor.

Apply | Case Problem 1

Use the skills you learned to create an English-to-French translation page.

Data Files needed for this Case Problem: engfrtxt.js, french5.js, french5txt.htm, styles.css

French 101 Professor Eve Granger teaches French 101 at a local university. She is working on a Web site containing French phrases that she wants her students to review for the weekly quiz. She's asked you to help her create the Web site. She wants a student to be able to press the mouse button down on a French phrase in the site and have the English translation appear. When the student releases the mouse button, the French phrase should reappear. Figure 16-66 shows a preview of the Web page you'll create for Professor Granger.

Figure 16-66

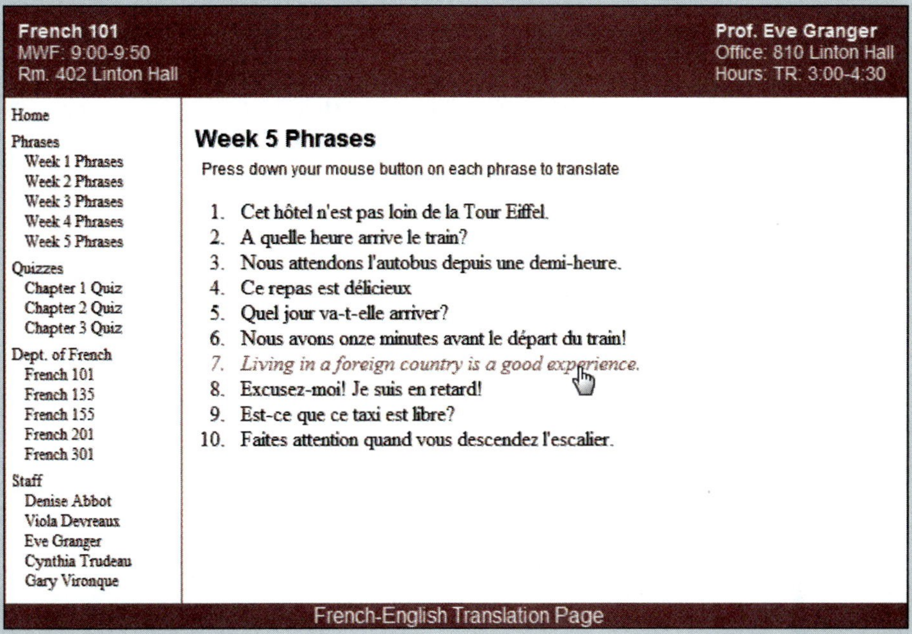

As a test case, Professor Granger has already created an external script file named french5.js that contains two arrays. The french array contains 10 French phrases. The english array contains the 10 English translations of those phrases. You'll use these arrays to insert the French phrases and their translations into the Web page. If your program works, you can then start to create similar pages that contain hundreds of translated phrases—but this is a good start.

Complete the following:

1. Use your text editor to open the **french5txt.htm** and **engfrtxt.js** files from the tutorial.16/case1 folder, enter ***your name*** and ***the date*** in the comment section of each file, and then save the files as **french5.htm** and **engfr.js**, respectively.
2. Go to the **french5.htm** file in your text editor and review the contents and structure of the file. Add two script elements that attach the french5.htm file to the french5.js and engfr.js script files. Close the french5.htm file, saving your changes.
3. Go to the **engfr.js** file in your text editor. Add a command to have the browser run the setUp() function when the page is loaded.
4. Create the **setUp()** function. The purpose of this function is to insert an ordered list of French phrases taken from the french array in the french5.js file and to add event handlers to switch these phrases to their English counterparts. Add the following commands to the setUp() function:
   a. Declare a variable named **transDoc** that references the element with the ID doc. It is within this element that you'll place the list of French phrases.
   b. Create an element node named **olElem** containing the ol element.

c. Loop through all of the items in the french array. For each item in the array, create an element node named **newLI** containing a list item element. Set the text contained within newLI to the text of the current item in the french array. Set the ID of the newLI element to *i*phrase, where *i* is the value of the index number in the array. Set the cursor style of the list item to pointer. Have the browser run the swapFE() function when the user presses the mouse button down on the list item, and run the swapEF() function when the mouse button is released. Finally, append the newLI element as a child of the olElem object.
d. After the loop has finished, append the olElem object to the transDoc object.

5. Create the **swapFE()** function. The purpose of this function is to display the English phrase in place of the French phrase selected by the user. Add the following commands to the function:
   a. The swapFE() function is only run in response to the mousedown event. Store the object in which the mousedown event occurred in a variable named **phrase**.
   b. If the node name of the phrase object indicates that the phrase object is a text node, point the phrase object to the parent of that text node. This is done to ensure that the object being examined is the list item element containing the phrase, and not simply the text of the phrase itself.
   c. Declare a variable named **phraseNum** that returns the index number of the phrase being selected. You can extract the index number by applying the parseInt() method to contents of the ID attribute of the phrase object.
   d. Change the inner HTML of the phrase object to the item in the english array with an index equal to the phraseNum variable.
   e. Change the font style of the phrase object to italic and the font color to the color value (155, 102, 102).

EXPLORE

6. Create the **swapEF()** function. The purpose of this function is to display the French translation of the phrase selected by the user. The code of the function should be identical to that used in the swapFE() function, except that it should use the french array rather than the english array and the phrase text should be displayed in a normal black font.
7. Close the file, saving your changes.
8. Open **french5.htm** in your Web browser. Verify that a list of 10 French phrases appears on the Web page. Also, verify that as you press the mouse button on each phrase, the English translation appears. When you release the mouse button, the French phrase should reappear.
9. Submit the completed project to your instructor.

Challenge | Case Problem 2

Explore table objects to create a data table filter.

Data Files needed for this Case Problem: cstyles.css, dc500.jpg, linksbg.jpg, logo.jpg, camtxt.htm, filtertxt.js

MicroCity David Forrest works at MicroCity, an online store for computers and electronics. One of his jobs is to create a table listing the different digital cameras sold by MicroCity. The company carries hundreds of digital camera models, and David thinks that the data table will be too long for customers to easily view it. He wants to give customers the ability to filter the data table, showing only those models that match certain criteria. Customers should be able to select the criteria from a drop-down list box. Figure 16-67 shows a preview of a prototype for a Web page that David wants you to help him create.

Figure 16-67

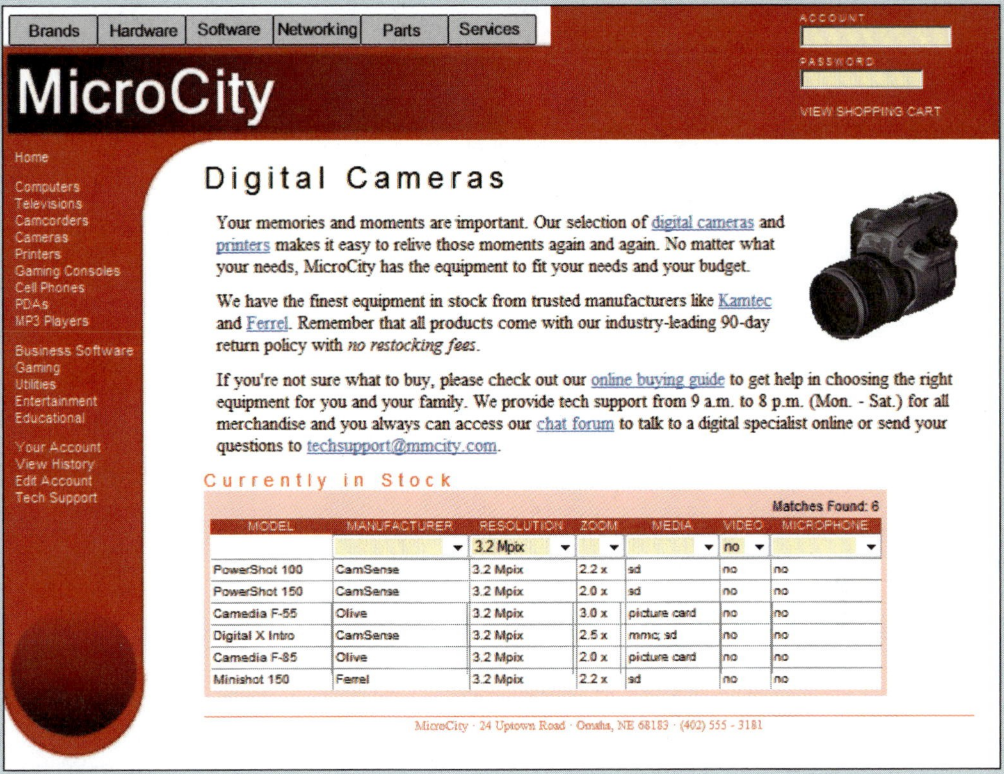

The data table shown in Figure 16-67 contains seven columns, indicating each camera's model name, manufacturer, resolution, zoom capability, storage media, and support for video, as well as whether it contains a microphone. The drop-down list boxes above the last six of those columns contain the unique values from each corresponding column. If a customer selects a zoom value of 3.0 x from the drop-down list box, only those cameras with that zoom feature should be displayed in the data table. Customers should be able to select more than one filter, and only those cameras satisfying all filter values should be shown.

The application that you'll create for Dave needs to be easily ported to other data tables on other Web pages. So any changes you make to the table need to be made using a JavaScript program, not by modifying the HTML tags in the Web page file. The application should do the following:

- Create selection list boxes for columns of values that will act as filters for the table.
- Populate each selection list with a list of unique values in the column, sorted in alphabetical order.
- Place the selection list boxes in cells in a new row of the table header.
- Filter the table in response to the user selecting a filter value from one of the selection list boxes.

This project will involve working with the structure and contents of a Web table. Web tables are organized into a hierarchy of row groups, rows, and cells within rows. The table header section of a Web table is referenced using the expression

```
table.tHead
```

where *table* is a reference to the Web table. Because Web tables can contain several tbody sections, the table bodies are referenced using the following object collection:

```
table.tBodies
```

Rows within a row group are referenced using the rows collection, and cells within a table row are referenced using the cells collection. The expression

```
table.tBodies[0].rows[2].cells[1]
```

references the second cell in the third row of the first tbody section in the Web table. You can determine the number of cells in a row or rows within a row group using the length attribute. The number of cells in the third row is

```
table.tBodies[0].rows[2].cells.length
```

and the number of rows in the row group is

```
table.tBodies[0].rows.length
```

JavaScript and HTML do not support direct object references to table columns. But if the table contains a column group, you can reference columns in that group using the expression

```
table.getElementsByTagName("col")
```

and JavaScript will return an object collection containing the col elements within the table. Once you create a column group, you can apply some of the properties of the col elements within the column group to columns within the Web table.

You'll use all of this information regarding the structure of Web table objects to complete this assignment and the next.

Complete the following:

1. Use your text editor to open the **camtxt.htm** and **filtertxt.js** files from the tutorial.16/case2 folder, enter ***your name*** and ***the date*** in the comment section of each file, and then save the files as **cameras.htm** and **filter.js**, respectively.
2. Go to the **cameras.htm** file in your text editor and review the contents and structure of the file. Pay careful attention to the structure and contents of the Web table describing the camera products sold by MicroCity. Note that David has included a colgroup element containing seven columns: one for each column in the data table. Also notice that each col element in the colgroup contains a class attribute that is equal to filter or nofilter. The columns from the nofilter class will not have selection filters added to them, while columns belonging to the filter class will have selection lists. Create a link between this document and the external script file, filter.js, and then close the file, saving your changes.
3. Go to the **filter.js** file in your text editor. Declare the following global variables but do not set their initial values yet:
   - **filterTable** which will reference the Web table containing the camera data
   - **filterCols** which will reference the col elements within that table
   - **filterHead** which will reference the head section of filterTable
   - **filterBody** which will reference the first (and only) tbody element in filterTable
4. Use the **addEvent()** function to add an event handler that runs the init() function when the page is loaded by the browser.

5. Create the **init()** function. The purpose of the init() function is to set up the data table filters and initialize the event handler in the document. Add the following commands to the function:
   a. Set the value of filterTable to the Web table with the ID filterTable.
   b. Have the filterCols variable reference all of the col elements within filterTable.
   c. Have filterHead reference the head row group of filterTable.
   d. Have filterBody reference the first entry in the tBodies row group within filterTable.
   e. Run the addTotalsRow() function.
6. Create the **countRecords()** function. The purpose of this function is to count the number of visible rows in the table body and then enter that information into the first row of the table header. Add the following commands to the function:
   a. Declare the **rowCount** variable, setting its initial value to 0.
   b. Loop through all of the rows in the filterBody row group. If the display style of a row is equal to "", then increase the value of rowCount by 1.
   c. Return the value of the rowCount variable.
7. Create the **addTotalsRow()** function. The purpose of this function is to insert a table row that displays a count of the number of rows in the table body section of the filter table. Add the following commands to the function:
   a. Declare a variable named **newRow** that contains an element node for the tr element. Declare a variable named **newCell** that contains an element node for the td element.
   b. Set the value of the colspan attribute for newCell equal to the number of cells in the first row of the filterHead row group. (*Note:* Because of a bug in the Internet Explorer browser, you must enter the colspan attribute using the property name colSpan, not colspan.)
   c. Set the inner HTML of newCell to the text string Matches Found: *countRecords* where *countRecords* is the value returned by the countRecords() function.
   d. Append newCell to newRow.
   e. Insert newRow before the first row in the filterHead row group.
8. Save your changes to the file, and then load **cameras.htm** in your Web browser. Verify that the table now contains a new header row displaying the text "Matches Found: 24".
9. Return to **filter.js** in your text editor. Next you'll create the code that adds selection lists to table cells in a new row appended to the head section of the table. Return to the init() function, and at the bottom of the function declare a variable named **newRow** that contains a tr element node.
10. Below that command within the init() function, insert a for loop to generate cells for the new table row. The for loop loops through the entries in the filterCols object collection, creating a new table cell for each column. Each time through the loop, do the following:
    a. Create an element node named **newCell** containing a th (table heading) element.
    b. Set the style of newCell so that its contents are left-aligned and displayed in a black font on a white background.
    c. If the current item in the filterCols object collection has a class name equal to filter, then you must create a selection list for the cell. Within the command block for the if statement, do the following: (i) Declare a variable named **newSelect** and set it equal to the object returned by the createSelectionList() function. The createSelectionList() function has a single parameter value equal to *i* where *i* is the index counter used in the for loop. (ii) Append the newSelect object to newCell.

   d. After the command block for the if statement, append newCell to newRow.
   e. After the for loop has finished, append newRow to the filterHead row group.
11. Create the **createSelectionList()** function. The purpose of this function is to create a selection containing the unique values found within a specified column in the table. The function has a single parameter, **colIndex**, which identifies the column from which the unique values are drawn. Add the following commands to the function:
   a. Declare an element node for the select element. Name the node **newSelect**.
   b. EXPLORE Create a custom property for newSelect named **cIndex**. Set the value of the cIndex property to colIndex.
   c. Create an element node named **blankOption** that contains an option element. Set the inner HTML of this node to the empty string "". Append the blankOption node to the newSelect node.
   d. Call the function addUniqueOptions() using parameter values newSelect and colIndex. The addUniqueOptions() function (which you'll create next) adds the remaining option elements to the newSelect selection list.
   e. Set the width style value of newSelect to 100% so that it fills up its table cell.
   f. Return the newSelect object.
12. Create the **addUniqueOptions()** function. The purpose of this function is to fill up the selection list with unique values found in a table column. The function has two parameters: selectionList and colIndex. The **selectionList** parameter points to an element node containing a selection list. The **colIndex** parameter indicates the index number of the column containing the data values. Add the following commands to this function:
   a. Declare a new array named **uniqueList**.
   b. Add a for loop that loops through the rows in the filterBody row group.
   c. Within the for loop, declare a variable named **rowCell** that points to the cell in the current row from the table column. (*Hint*: Use the object reference filterBody.rows[*i*].cells[*index*] where *i* is the value of the counter variable in the for loop and *index* is the value of the colIndex parameter in the function.)
   d. EXPLORE Extract the text of the cell, using either the innerText property (for the IE DOM) or the textContent property (for the W3C DOM). Store the text string in a variable named **cellValue**.
   e. Call the isUnique() function using cellValue and uniqueList as parameter values. If the function returns a value of true, then use the push() method to push the value of the cellValue variable into the uniqueList array. (*Hint:* The isUnique() function is provided for you. The function has a single purpose: It compares a given value to all of the values in a specified array. If the value is not matched in the array, the isUnique() function returns a value of true; otherwise, it returns a value of false.)
   f. At this point, the uniqueList array should contain all of the unique values in the data column. Sort the array to place the values in alphabetical order.
   g. Loop through all of the entries in the uniqueList array. For each item in the array, create an option element node. Set the inner HTML of the option element to the item value and then append the option element to the selectionList node.
13. Save your changes to the file, and then reload **cameras.htm** in your Web browser. The Web table should now contain a new header row with six selection lists for the six filterable columns. Click each selection list and verify that it contains a list of the unique values in the column, sorted in alphabetical order.

14. Return to the **filter.js** file in your text editor. At this point, you must program the selection lists to filter the data values in the Web table. Go to the createSelectionList() function. Directly above the statement to return the newSelect variable (the last statement in the function), insert a statement that assigns an event handler to the newSelect variable, running the doFilter() function whenever the value of the selection list changes.
15. Create the **resetTable()** function. The purpose of this function is to reset the Web table, allowing all rows in the tbody to be displayed. To complete the function, insert a for loop that loops through all of the rows in the filterBody object, setting the display style of each row to the empty text string "".
16. Create the **doFilter()** function. The purpose of this function is to loop through all of the selection lists containing the filter values, and then call a function to hide table rows that match those filter values. Add the following commands to this function:
    a. Call the resetTable()function to temporarily display all rows in the Web table.
    b. Declare a variable named **allSelects** that contains the object collection of all the select elements located in the filterHead row group. (*Hint:* Use the getElementsByTagName() method to locate the selection list elements with tag names of <select>.)

    EXPLORE

    c. Loop through all of the selection list items in the allSelects object collection. For each item, store the index of the selected option in the filterIndex variable and the text of that option in the filterText variable. Store the value of the custom cIndex property you created earlier in a variable named **colIndex**.
    d. The filterText variable tells you the filter value from the selection list, and the colIndex variable tells you the column to apply the filter to. Still within the for loop, test whether filterText is equal to the empty text string "". If it is not, call the filterColumn() function using the colIndex and filterText variables as parameter values.
    e. After the for loop has run, display the text Matches Found: *countRecords* in the first cell of the first row in the filterHead row group, where *countRecords* is the value returned by the countRecords() function.
17. Create the **filterColumn()** function. The purpose of this function is to hide rows in the data table whose cells do not match a specified filter value. The function has two parameters named colIndex and fText. The **colIndex** parameter indicates the table column on which to test the filter. The **fText** parameter contains the filter text. Add the following commands to the function:
    a. Loop through all of the rows in the filterBody row group. For each entry in the loop, create a variable named **rowCell** that references a cell in the current row from the column specified by the colIndex parameter.
    b. Within the loop, create a variable named **rowCellText** that uses either the innerText property (for the IE DOM) or the textContent property (for the W3C DOM) to extract the text stored in the rowCell object.
    c. Still within the loop, test whether rowCellText equals fText. If it does not, set the display style of the current row to none.
18. Save your changes to the file, and then reload **cameras.htm** in your Web browser. Click the different selection filters in the Web table and verify that selecting different filter values limits the rows displayed in the table to only those rows that match the filters. Also, verify that the table header displays the correct number of rows in the table. Finally, verify that you can unhide a hidden row by selecting an empty string from the filter selection list.
19. Submit your completed project to your instructor.

Challenge | Case Problem 3

Explore table objects to create a sortable Web table.

Data Files needed for this Case Problem: gradient.png, gradient2.png, sasrlogo.png, statstxt.htm, tabletxt.js, tstyles.css

Sporting Abstract and Statistical Review Walter Delacreaux is the owner and operator of the Sporting Abstract and Statistical Review, a new blog and forum to report on and analyze data from the world of sports. Walter wants to fill his Web site with useful tables that other people who share his enthusiasm for statistics can review and study. He wants these tables to be as interactive as possible. One feature he wants to add to his tables is the ability to sort them in a different order by clicking a column heading. Figure 16-68 shows a preview of the Web page you'll create for Walter.

Figure 16-68

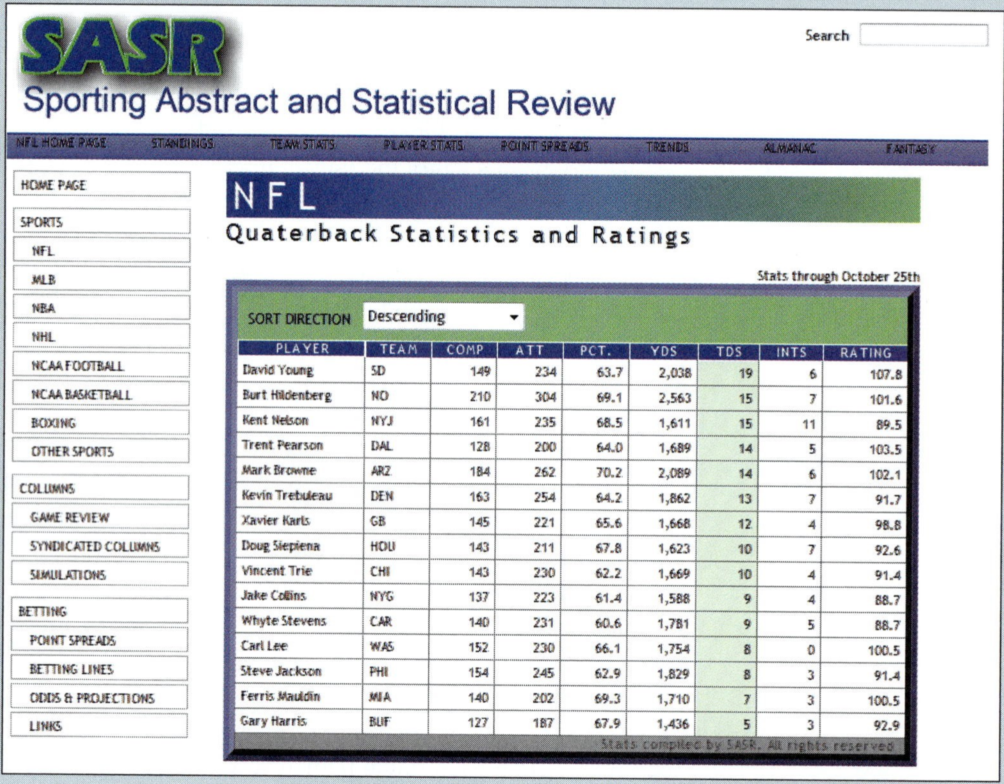

PLAYER	TEAM	COMP	ATT	PCT.	YDS	TDS	INTS	RATING
David Young	SD	149	234	63.7	2,038	19	6	107.8
Burt Hildenberg	NO	210	304	69.1	2,563	15	7	101.6
Kent Nelson	NYJ	161	235	68.5	1,611	15	11	89.5
Trent Pearson	DAL	128	200	64.0	1,689	14	5	103.5
Mark Browne	ARZ	184	262	70.2	2,089	14	6	102.1
Kevin Trebuleau	DEN	163	254	64.2	1,862	13	7	91.7
Xavier Karls	GB	145	221	65.6	1,668	12	4	98.8
Doug Siepiena	HOU	143	211	67.8	1,623	10	7	92.6
Vincent Trie	CHI	143	230	62.2	1,669	10	4	91.4
Jake Collins	NYG	137	223	61.4	1,588	9	4	88.7
Whyte Stevens	CAR	140	231	60.6	1,781	9	5	88.7
Carl Lee	WAS	152	230	66.1	1,754	8	0	100.5
Steve Jackson	PHI	154	245	62.9	1,829	8	3	91.4
Ferris Mauldin	MIA	140	202	69.3	1,710	7	3	100.5
Gary Harris	BUF	127	187	67.9	1,436	5	3	92.9

To create this application, you'll have to work with some of the objects found in Web tables. Information about these objects is provided in the introduction to Case Problem 2. You'll also have to work with some custom properties and functions. Some of these functions have been provided for you. Walter has already entered a sample table for you to work on and created the style sheet for the Web page. You will complete the project by writing the JavaScript code to enable users to sort the table with a click of the mouse button.

Complete the following:

1. Use your text editor to open the **statstxt.htm** and **tabletxt.js** files from the tutorial.16/case3 folder, enter ***your name*** and ***the date*** in the comment section of each file, and then save the files as **stats.htm** and **tablesort.js**, respectively.
2. Go to the **stats.htm** file in your text editor and review the document's content and structure. The table of QB stats includes a column group listing the nine columns in the table. The class value associated with each col element indicates whether the column data should be treated and sorted as alphabetic characters (asort) or numeric values (numsort). Add a script element to the document, linking the file to the tablesort.js file. Close the file, saving your changes.
3. Go to the **tablesort.js** file in your text editor. Declare the following global variables but do not set their initial values yet:
   - **sortTable** which will reference the Web table containing the QB statistics
   - **sortBody** which will reference the table body within sortTable
   - **sortHead** which will reference the head section of sortTable
   - **sortCols** which will reference the col elements within the sortTable
   - **sortDirection** which indicates the direction of sorting done in the table; set its initial value to descending
   - **sortIndex** which will indicate the index number of the column on which the sorting is done; do not set an initial value for the variable
4. Use the **addEvent()** function to add an event handler that runs the setupTable() function when the page is loaded by the browser.
5. Create the **setupTable()** function. The purpose of the setupTable() function is to set up the Web table for sorting. Add the following commands to the function:
   a. Point the sortTable variable to the Web table with the ID qbstats.
   b. Have the sortCols variable reference all of the col elements within sortTable.
   c. Have sortHead reference the heading row group of sortTable.
   d. Have sortBody reference the first entry in the tBodies collection within sortTable.
   e. Create a for loop that loops through all of the cells in the first row of the sortHead row group. For each cell in the row, create an event handler that runs the sortCol() function when the cell is clicked. Also, set the cursor style of the cell to pointer. Finally, add a customer property named **colIndex** to each cell, setting the property value to the value of the counter variable used in the for loop.
   f. After the for loop is completed, run the function addSortDirection().
6. Create the **addSortDirection()** function. The purpose of this function is to insert a new table row into the head of the table with a single cell containing a drop-down selection list. The drop-down selection will be used to allow users to easily switch the direction of sorting done in the table. Add the following commands to the function:
   a. Declare variables named **newRow** and **newCell** containing element nodes for the tr and th elements, respectively.

b. Set the inner HTML of newCell to the following HTML fragment:

```
<label for = 'sortdir'>Sort Direction</label>
```

EXPLORE

c. Use the setAttribute() method to add the colSpan attribute to the newCell node. Set the value of the colSpan attribute to the length of the sortCols object collection. (*Hint:* To support Internet Explorer, you must specify the attribute as colSpan, not colspan.)

d. Set the value of the className property for newCell to sortHeader.

7. Next you must create the selection list for the new cell you just created. Continue working in the addSortDirection() function by adding the following commands:
   a. Create a select element node named **sortSelect**.
   b. Add an event handler to the sortSelect to run the toggleSort() function when the value of sortSelect is changed by the user.
   c. Create and append two option buttons to sortSelect. The first should contain the inner HTML text Descending; the second should contain inner HTML equal to the text string Ascending.
   d. Append sortSelect to the newCell node, and then append newCell to the newRow node.
   e. Insert newRow as the first child of the sortHead row group.
8. Create the **toggleSort()** function. The purpose of this function is to toggle the value of sortDirection between descending and ascending. Insert an if condition that toggles the variable between these two possible values. After the if condition, insert a command to run the runSort() function, which you'll create shortly.
9. Save your changes to the file, and then load **stats.htm** in your Web browser. Verify that the table contains a new header row containing a drop-down selection list with the entries Descending and Ascending.
10. Return to **tablesort.js** in your text editor. Go to the empty **sortCol()** function, located directly below the alphaCompare() function. The purpose of this function is to set the value of the sortIndex variable and run the sort on the table. Add the following commands to the function:
    a. Set the value of **sortIndex** to the value of the colIndex property from the table heading cell clicked by the user. (*Hint:* Use either an event object or the `this` keyword to determine the element that called the sortCol() function.)
    b. Call the runSort() function.
11. Create the **runSort()** function. The purpose of this function is to sort the table by reordering the table rows within the table body. Because you'll be sorting the entire table based on the values on one column, you'll have to create an array containing those column values and then sort it either alphabetically or numerically. In the first line of the function, declare an empty array named **sortCells**. This array will contain the data to be sorted.
12. Next you have to loop through the rows in the table body, extracting values from the column on which the sort is based. Add a for loop to the runSort() function that loops through all of the rows in the table body. Within the for loop, do the following:
    a. Declare a variable named **sortCell** that points to the cell in the current row belonging to the column to be sorted. (*Hint:* Use the object reference sortBody.rows[*i*].cells[*sortIndex*] where *i* is the value of the counter variable used in the for loop and *sortIndex* is the value of the sortIndex variable.)

EXPLORE

b. Ignore any markup tags found within the table cells when sorting. Declare a variable named **celltxt** that is equal to the text contained within sortCell. Use either the innerText property (for the IE DOM) or the textContent property (for the W3C DOM).

c. Some numeric values contain non-numeric characters such as commas and dollar symbols. Create a variable named **regx** that contains the regular expression
`/(\,|\$)/g`
and then apply this regular expression using the replace() method to celltxt in order to strip out all occurrences of commas and dollar symbols, and replace them with empty text strings.

EXPLORE

d. Add some custom properties to sortCell. The sortCell variable contains an array of values, but you also want it to be able to reference the text value in the celltxt variable and the table row from which that value came from.

To do so is beyond the scope of this tutorial, but a custom function has been supplied for you in the file to allow you to do this. Call the addProps() function using sortCells[*i*] for the first parameter value, celltxt for the second parameter value, and sortBody.rows[*i*] for the third parameter value, where *i* is the counter variable used in your for loop. Store the value returned by the function in sortCells[*i*].

After calling this function, sortCells[*i*] will have two custom properties. The first, sortCells[*i*].value, will contain the value celltxt, and the second, sortCells[*i*].row, will reference the row from which celltxt came.

13. After the for loop has finished in the runSort() function, you will have an array, sortCells, that contains all of the values in the column to be sorted and references to the rows that those cells came from. Next, you have to add commands to the function to sort that array. Add the following commands to the function:

    a. Declare a variable named **sortType** that is equal to the className value of the *i*th entry in the sortCols object collection, where *i* is the value of the sortIndex variable.

EXPLORE

    b. If sortType equals asort, sort the sortCells array using alphaCompare() as the comparison function that determines the sorting order. If sortType equals numsort, sort the sortCells array using numCompare() as the comparison function for the sorting.

    c. If sortDirection equals ascending, then apply the reverse() method to the sortCells array to reverse the order of the array values.

    d. Loop through all of the items in the sortCells array. For each item, append the object sortCells[*i*].row to the sortBody row group, where *i* is the counter variable used in the for loop.

    e. Run the colorColumns()function.

14. Create the **colorColumns()** function. The purpose of this function is to highlight the column upon which the table has been sorted. Add the following commands to the function:

    a. Loop through all of the items in the sortCols object collection. For each item, set the backgroundColor style to white.

    b. After the loop, change the backgroundColor style of the item in the sortCols object collection whose index value equals sortIndex to the color value (232, 255, 232).

15. Close the file, saving your changes, and then reload **stats.htm** in your Web browser. Verify that you can sort the entire table by clicking the column headings for each column. Also, verify that you can sort the direction by clicking the selection list in the first header row. Finally, verify that the column upon which the sorting is based is highlighted in the table.
16. Submit the completed project to your instructor.

Challenge | Case Problem 4

Create a JavaScript utility to extract lines from an online play.

Data Files needed for this Case Problem: bio_out.jpg, globe_out.jpg, plays.css, plays_out.jpg, scenetxt.js, son_out.jpg, strat_out.jpg, tempest.jpg, temptxt.htm

The World of Shakespeare Clare Daynes, a professor of English literature at Midwest University, is working on a Web site of Shakespeare's works. She would like to give students who are doing textual analysis of the plays the ability to display only those lines spoken by selected characters. She has asked you to create a utility that generates a drop-down list containing all of the characters from a particular scene, listed in alphabetical order. When a student selects a character from the list, only those lines spoken by that character should be displayed. Figure 16-69 shows a preview of a Web page that fulfills Professor Daynes' request.

Figure 16-69

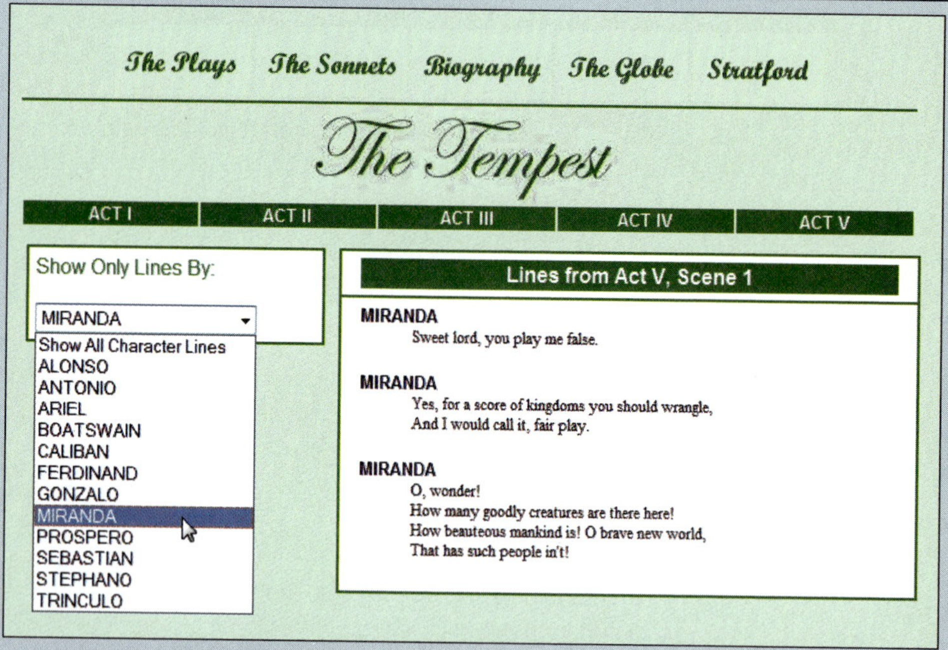

Professor Daynes has already created a Web page containing the text from the last act of *The Tempest*. The play text has been placed within a div element with the ID scene. The character names have been placed in h3 headings within that div element, with their lines following immediately after in blockquote elements. She has also created a div element with the ID characterList in which she wants the drop-down list box to be placed

She wants the content to be automatically generated by your utility. The HTML content of the list box should be

```
<p>Show Only Lines By:</p>
<select id = "cList">
   <option>Show All Character Lines</option>
   <option>Character 1</option>
   <option>Character 2</option>
...
</select>
```

where *Character 1* is the name of the first character in alphabetical order, *Character 2* is the name of the second character, and so on. To create a list of the characters from the scene, the following function has been provided for you:

```
uniqueElemText(elemName)
```

This function returns an array containing the unique text from HTML tags whose name equals *elemName*, sorted in order. For example, running the command

```
characterNames = uniqueElemText("h3")
```

creates an array named characterNames containing all of the unique character names found in h3 heading elements, sorted in alphabetical order.

Complete the following:

1. Use your text editor to open the **temptxt.htm** file from the tutorial.16/case4 folder, enter ***your name*** and ***the date*** in the comment section, and then save the file as **tempest.htm**. Create a link in the file to an external script file named **scene.js**.
2. Open the **scenetxt.js** file in your text editor, enter ***your name*** and ***the date*** in the comment section, and then save the file as **scene.js**.
3. Write a function that creates the contents of the character list box. Run the function when this page is loaded by the browser.
4. Add an event handler to the selection list you generated that runs a function to filter the contents of the scene whenever the user changes the selected character from the list.
5. Modify the function to filter the play so that it shows only the character name and succeeding lines for the selected character. All lines from other characters should be hidden. If the user selects Show All Character Lines, the entire scene should be displayed.
6. Test your Web page in your browser. Verify that only the lines from the selected character are displayed on the Web page, and that the entire scene is displayed if Show All Character Lines is selected.
7. Submit your completed Web site to your instructor.

Review | Quick Check Answers

Session 16.1

1. `innerHTML`
2. IE DOM: `innerText`
   W3C DOM: `textContent`
3. A node is part of the document object model that represents a particular type of content. Nodes can represent any element or object, including text strings, attributes, and HTML elements placed in either the head or body section of the document.
4. `parentNode`
5. `childNodes[2]`
6. The nodeType property returns the value 1. The nodeName property returns BLOCKQUOTE. The nodeValue property returns a null value.
7.
```
docText = document.createTextNode("U.S. Constitution");
mainTitle = document.createElement("h2");
```
8. `mainTitle.appendChild(docText);`

Session 16.2

1.
```
topList = document.createElement("ul");
bottomList = document.createElement("ul");
top.List.appendChild(bottomList);
```
2. `listItem.parentNode.parentNode;`
3. because they are not considered child nodes of the node to which the attribute has been applied
4. `hasAttribute("type")`
5.
```
CBox = document.createElement("input");
CBox.setAttribute("type", "checkbox");
```
6. `CBox.type = "checkbox";`
7. `(CBox.type == "")`

Session 16.3

1. `listItem.insertBefore(imgObj, listItem.firstChild);`
2. `imgObj.style.display = "none";`
3. Recursion is a programming technique in which a function calls itself repeatedly until a stopping condition is met.
4. A preferred style sheet is a style sheet that has a rel attribute value of stylesheet and has been assigned a title. An alternate style sheet has a title but the rel attribute is alternate stylesheet. A persistent style sheet has the rel attribute of stylesheet but no title. Persistent styles are always loaded by the browser.

5. Use the object collection stylesheets, or reference the link element using the reference
   `document.getElementsByTagName("link")`
6. To enable the style sheet: `styleSheet.disabled = false;`

   To disable the style sheet: `styleSheet.disabled = true;`
7. W3C DOM: `document.styleSheets[2].cssRules[1]`
   IE DOM: `document.styleSheets[2].rules[1]`

Ending Data Files

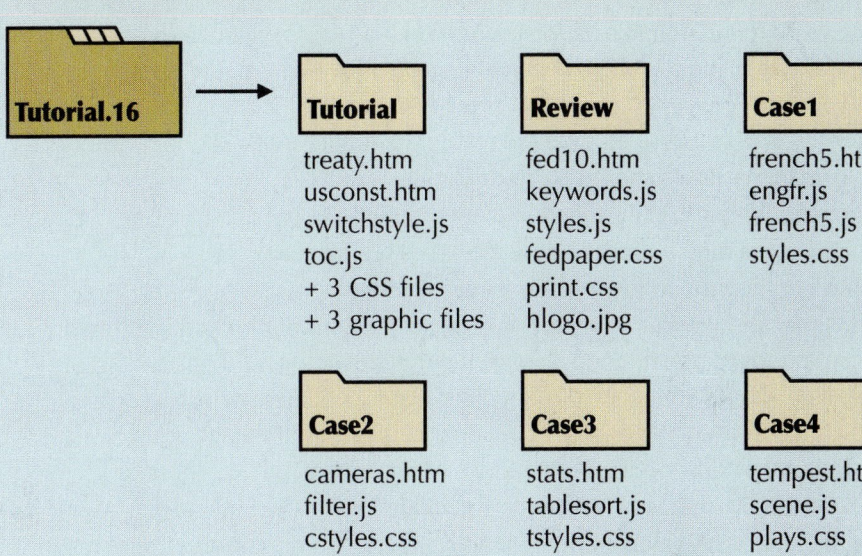

Tutorial.16 →

Tutorial
treaty.htm
usconst.htm
switchstyle.js
toc.js
+ 3 CSS files
+ 3 graphic files

Review
fed10.htm
keywords.js
styles.js
fedpaper.css
print.css
hlogo.jpg

Case1
french5.htm
engfr.js
french5.js
styles.css

Case2
cameras.htm
filter.js
cstyles.css
+ 3 graphic files

Case3
stats.htm
tablesort.js
tstyles.css
+ 3 graphic files

Case4
tempest.htm
scene.js
plays.css
+ 6 graphic files

Reality Check

JavaScript is a powerful tool for creating interesting and dynamic Web pages. Because of JavaScript's popularity, hundreds of sites are available on the Web with programming tips, sample scripts, and downloadable apps to assist you in writing your own JavaScript applications.

In this exercise, you will use JavaScript to write your own code, using the skills and features presented in Tutorials 11 through 16. Use the following steps as a guide to completing your code.

1. Using the applications found from the various frameworks available on the Web or by writing your own code, create a Web page containing a typing test form. The design and layout of the Web page is up to you, but it should contain the following features:
   a. A Web form in which users can type the text in the typing exam
   b. A typing sample that users should try to duplicate
   c. A start and stop button to start and stop the typing exam
   d. An input box containing a timer to time the user's typing exam
2. Use JavaScript to program the following actions on your typing exam page:
   a. The typing timer should start when the user clicks the Start button and use timed interval commands to update the value on the timer every second.
   b. Event handlers should intercept the keypress events initiated by the user and display each typed character in a div container element on the page.
   c. The Stop button should stop the typing timer when pressed.
3. Score the typing exam by writing scripts to do the following:
   a. Compare the typed characters to the characters in the typing sample. Count the number of typing errors.
   b. Highlight the mistyped characters on the Web page.
   c. Use regular expressions to loop through the number of words in the typing sample. Count up the number of words in the sample.
   d. Loop through the words typed in the typing exam. Count the number of misspelled words.
   e. Subtract the number of misspelled words from the total number of words. Divide the difference by the length of time (in minutes) needed to complete the typing exam. Report on the user's typing speed in terms of correct words per minute.
4. Share your typing exam with your classmates and colleagues. Evaluate each other's typing speed and level of accuracy. Report on the results of your typing tests.
5. Web sites load quicker and JavaScript programs are more responsive when the code is small and compact. Several applications are available on the Web to reduce the size of JavaScript files. Use a Web search engine to investigate these tools including the programs Squish, jscompact, JSMin, and Packers. How do these programs affect the format of a JavaScript file during the compacting process? How should you write your code to prepare it for compression?

Reality Check

6. Many Web sites contain prepackaged JavaScript tools also known as frameworks. Some of the more popular frameworks are Dojo, Prototype, Rico, qooxdoo, script.aculo.us, Yahoo! User Interface Library (YUI), and MooTools. Rather than creating your own programs to generate online calendars, pull-down menus, and so on, explore some of the applications available in these toolkits. What code in your typing exam program could be replaced by using a built-in script from one of these frameworks?
7. Document your code and describe what you've learned from creating this typing test form.
8. Submit the completed project to your instructor.

Color Names and Color Values

Appendix A

Both HTML and XHTML allow you to define colors using either color names or color values. HTML and XHTML support a list of 16 basic color names. Most browsers also support an extended list of color names, which are listed in the following table along with their RGB and hexadecimal values. The 16 color names supported by HTML and XHTML appear highlighted in the table. Web-safe colors appear in a bold font.

If you want to use only Web-safe colors, limit your RGB values to 0, 51, 153, 204, and 255 (or limit your hexadecimal values to 00, 33, 66, 99, CC, and FF). For example, an RGB color value of (255, 51, 204) would be Web safe, while an RGB color value of (255, 192, 128) would not.

Starting Data Files

There are no starting Data Files needed for this appendix.

Color Name	RGB Value	Hexadecimal Value
aliceblue	(240,248,255)	#F0F8FF
antiquewhite	(250,235,215)	#FAEBD7
aqua	**(0,255,255)**	**#00FFFF**
aquamarine	(127,255,212)	#7FFFD4
azure	(240,255,255)	#F0FFFF
beige	(245,245,220)	#F5F5DC
bisque	(255,228,196)	#FFE4C4
black	**(0,0,0)**	**#000000**
blanchedalmond	(255,235,205)	#FFEBCD
blue	**(0,0,255)**	**#0000FF**
blueviolet	(138,43,226)	#8A2BE2
brown	(165,42,42)	#A52A2A
burlywood	(222,184,135)	#DEB887
cadetblue	(95,158,160)	#5F9EA0
chartreuse	(127,255,0)	#7FFF00
chocolate	(210,105,30)	#D2691E
coral	(255,127,80)	#FF7F50
cornflowerblue	(100,149,237)	#6495ED
cornsilk	(255,248,220)	#FFF8DC
crimson	(220,20,54)	#DC1436
cyan	**(0,255,255)**	**#00FFFF**
darkblue	(0,0,139)	#00008B
darkcyan	(0,139,139)	#008B8B
darkgoldenrod	(184,134,11)	#B8860B
darkgray	(169,169,169)	#A9A9A9
darkgreen	(0,100,0)	#006400

Color Name	RGB Value	Hexadecimal Value
darkkhaki	(189,183,107)	#BDB76B
darkmagenta	(139,0,139)	#8B008B
darkolivegreen	(85,107,47)	#556B2F
darkorange	(255,140,0)	#FF8C00
darkorchid	(153,50,204)	#9932CC
darkred	(139,0,0)	#8B0000
darksalmon	(233,150,122)	#E9967A
darkseagreen	(143,188,143)	#8FBC8F
darkslateblue	(72,61,139)	#483D8B
darkslategray	(47,79,79)	#2F4F4F
darkturquoise	(0,206,209)	#00CED1
darkviolet	(148,0,211)	#9400D3
deeppink	(255,20,147)	#FF1493
deepskyblue	(0,191,255)	#00BFFF
dimgray	(105,105,105)	#696969
dodgerblue	(30,144,255)	#1E90FF
firebrick	(178,34,34)	#B22222
floralwhite	(255,250,240)	#FFFAF0
forestgreen	(34,139,34)	#228B22
fuchsia	**(255,0,255)**	**#FF00FF**
gainsboro	(220,220,220)	#DCDCDC
ghostwhite	(248,248,255)	#F8F8FF
gold	(255,215,0)	#FFD700
goldenrod	(218,165,32)	#DAA520
gray	(128,128,128)	#808080
green	(0,128,0)	#008000
greenyellow	(173,255,47)	#ADFF2F
honeydew	(240,255,240)	#F0FFF0
hotpink	(255,105,180)	#FF69B4

Color Name	RGB Value	Hexadecimal Value
indianred	(205,92,92)	#CD5C5C
indigo	(75,0,130)	#4B0082
ivory	(255,255,240)	#FFFFF0
khaki	(240,230,140)	#F0E68C
lavender	(230,230,250)	#E6E6FA
lavenderblush	(255,240,245)	#FFF0F5
lawngreen	(124,252,0)	#7CFC00
lemonchiffon	(255,250,205)	#FFFACD
lightblue	(173,216,230)	#ADD8E6
lightcoral	(240,128,128)	#F08080
lightcyan	(224,255,255)	#E0FFFF
lightgoldenrodyellow	(250,250,210)	#FAFAD2
lightgreen	(144,238,144)	#90EE90
lightgrey	(211,211,211)	#D3D3D3
lightpink	(255,182,193)	#FFB6C1
lightsalmon	(255,160,122)	#FFA07A
lightseagreen	(32,178,170)	#20B2AA
lightskyblue	(135,206,250)	#87CEFA
lightslategray	(119,136,153)	#778899
lightsteelblue	(176,196,222)	#B0C4DE
lightyellow	(255,255,224)	#FFFFE0
lime	**(0,255,0)**	**#00FF00**
limegreen	(50,205,50)	#32CD32
linen	(250,240,230)	#FAF0E6
magenta	**(255,0,255)**	**#FF00FF**
maroon	(128,0,0)	#800000
mediumaquamarine	(102,205,170)	#66CDAA
mediumblue	(0,0,205)	#0000CD
mediumorchid	(186,85,211)	#BA55D3

Color Name	RGB Value	Hexadecimal Value
mediumpurple	(147,112,219)	#9370DB
mediumseagreen	(60,179,113)	#3CB371
mediumslateblue	(123,104,238)	#7B68EE
mediumspringgreen	(0,250,154)	#00FA9A
mediumturquoise	(72,209,204)	#48D1CC
mediumvioletred	(199,21,133)	#C71585
midnightblue	(25,25,112)	#191970
mintcream	(245,255,250)	#F5FFFA
mistyrose	(255,228,225)	#FFE4E1
moccasin	(255,228,181)	#FFE4B5
navajowhite	(255,222,173)	#FFDEAD
navy	**(0,0,128)**	**#000080**
oldlace	(253,245,230)	#FDF5E6
olive	(128,128,0)	#808000
olivedrab	(107,142,35)	#6B8E23
orange	(255,165,0)	#FFA500
orangered	(255,69,0)	#FF4500
orchid	(218,112,214)	#DA70D6
palegoldenrod	(238,232,170)	#EEE8AA
palegreen	(152,251,152)	#98FB98
paleturquoise	(175,238,238)	#AFEEEE
palevioletred	(219,112,147)	#DB7093
papayawhip	(255,239,213)	#FFEFD5
peachpuff	(255,218,185)	#FFDAB9
peru	(205,133,63)	#CD853F
pink	(255,192,203)	#FFC0CB
plum	(221,160,221)	#DDA0DD
powderblue	(176,224,230)	#B0E0E6
purple	**(128,0,128)**	**#808080**

Color Name	RGB Value	Hexadecimal Value
red	**(255,0,0)**	**#FF0000**
rosybrown	(188,143,143)	#BC8F8F
royalblue	(65,105,0)	#4169E1
saddlebrown	(139,69,19)	#8B4513
salmon	(250,128,114)	#FA8072
sandybrown	(244,164,96)	#F4A460
seagreen	(46,139,87)	#2E8B57
seashell	(255,245,238)	#FFF5EE
sienna	(160,82,45)	#A0522D
silver	(192,192,192)	#C0C0C0
skyblue	(135,206,235)	#87CEEB
slateblue	(106,90,205)	#6A5ACD
slategray	(112,128,144)	#708090
snow	(255,250,250)	#FFFAFA
springgreen	(0,255,127)	#00FF7F
steelblue	(70,130,180)	#4682B4
tan	(210,180,140)	#D2B48C
teal	(0,128,128)	#008080
thistle	(216,191,216)	#D8BFD8
tomato	(255,99,71)	#FF6347
turquoise	(64,224,208)	#40E0D0
violet	(238,130,238)	#EE82EE
wheat	(245,222,179)	#F5DEB3
white	**(255,255,255)**	**#FFFFFF**
whitesmoke	(245,245,245)	#F5F5F5
yellow	**(255,255,0)**	**#FFFF00**
yellowgreen	(154,205,50)	#9ACD32

HTML Character Entities

Appendix B

The following table lists the extended character set for HTML, also known as the ISO Latin-1 Character Set. You can specify characters by name or by numeric value. For example, you can use either ® or ® to specify the registered trademark symbol, ®.

Not all browsers recognize all code names. Some older browsers that support only the HTML 2.0 standard do not recognize × as a code name, for instance. Code names that older browsers may not recognize are marked with an asterisk in the following table.

Starting Data Files

There are no starting Data Files needed for this appendix.

CHARACTER	CODE	CODE NAME	DESCRIPTION
			Tab
	Line feed
			Space
!	!		Exclamation mark
"	"	"	Double quotation mark
#	#		Pound sign
$	$		Dollar sign
%	%		Percent sign
&	&	&	Ampersand
'	'		Apostrophe
(	(		Left parenthesis
)	)		Right parenthesis
*	*		Asterisk
+	+		Plus sign
,	,		Comma
-	-		Hyphen
.	.		Period
/	/		Forward slash
0 - 9	0–9		Numbers 0–9
:	:		Colon
;	;		Semicolon
<	<	<	Less than sign

CHARACTER	CODE	CODE NAME	DESCRIPTION
=	=		Equal sign
>	>	>	Greater than sign
?	?		Question mark
@	@		Commercial at sign
A - Z	A–Z		Letters A–Z
[	[		Left square bracket
\	\		Back slash
]	]		Right square bracket
^	^		Caret
_	_		Horizontal bar (underscore)
`	`		Grave accent
a - z	a–z		Letters a–z
{	{		Left curly brace
|				Vertical bar
}	}		Right curly brace
~	~		Tilde
,	‚		Comma
ƒ	ƒ		Function sign (florin)
"	„		Double quotation mark
…	…		Ellipsis
†	†		Dagger
‡	‡		Double dagger
ˆ	ˆ		Circumflex

CHARACTER	CODE	CODE NAME	DESCRIPTION
‰	‰		Permil
Š	Š		Capital S with hacek
‹	‹		Left single angle
Œ	Œ		Capital OE ligature
	–		Unused
‘	‘		Single beginning quotation mark
’	’		Single ending quotation mark
“	“		Double beginning quotation mark
”	”		Double ending quotation mark
•	•		Bullet
–	–		En dash
—	—		Em dash
˜	˜		Tilde
™	™	™*	Trademark symbol
š	š		Small s with hacek
›	›		Right single angle
œ	œ		Lowercase oe ligature
Ÿ	Ÿ		Capital Y with umlaut
		*	Non-breaking space
¡	¡	¡*	Inverted exclamation mark
¢	¢	¢*	Cent sign
£	£	£*	Pound sterling
¤	¤	¤*	General currency symbol

CHARACTER	CODE	CODE NAME	DESCRIPTION
¥	¥	¥*	Yen sign
¦	¦	¦*	Broken vertical bar
§	§	§*	Section sign
¨	¨	¨*	Umlaut
©	©	©*	Copyright symbol
ª	ª	ª*	Feminine ordinal
«	«	«*	Left angle quotation mark
¬	¬	¬*	Not sign
–		*	Soft hyphen
®	®	®*	Registered trademark
¯	¯	¯*	Macron
°	°	°*	Degree sign
±	±	±*	Plus/minus symbol
^{2}	²	²*	Superscript 2
^{3}	³	³*	Superscript 3
´	´	´*	Acute accent
µ	µ	µ*	Micro sign
¶	¶	¶*	Paragraph sign
·	·	·*	Middle dot
ç	¸	¸*	Cedilla
^{1}	¹	¹*	Superscript 1
º	º	º*	Masculine ordinal
»	»	»*	Right angle quotation mark

CHARACTER	CODE	CODE NAME	DESCRIPTION
¼	¼	¼*	Fraction one-quarter
½	½	½*	Fraction one-half
¾	¾	¾*	Fraction three-quarters
¿	¿	¿*	Inverted question mark
À	À	À	Capital A, grave accent
Á	Á	Á	Capital A, acute accent
Â	Â	Â	Capital A, circumflex accent
Ã	Ã	Ã	Capital A, tilde
Ä	Ä	Ä	Capital A, umlaut
Å	Å	Å	Capital A, ring
Æ	Æ	&Aelig;	Capital AE ligature
Ç	Ç	Ç	Capital C, cedilla
È	È	È	Capital E, grave accent
É	É	É	Capital E, acute accent
Ê	Ê	Ê	Capital E, circumflex accent
Ë	Ë	Ë	Capital E, umlaut
Ì	Ì	Ì	Capital I, grave accent
Í	Í	Í	Capital I, acute accent
Î	Î	Î	Capital I, circumflex accent
Ï	Ï	Ï	Capital I, umlaut
F	Ð	Ð*	Capital ETH, Icelandic
Ñ	Ñ	Ñ	Capital N, tilde
Ò	Ò	Ò	Capital O, grave accent

CHARACTER	CODE	CODE NAME	DESCRIPTION
Ó	Ó	Ó	Capital O, acute accent
Ô	Ô	Ô	Capital O, circumflex accent
Õ	Õ	Õ	Capital O, tilde
Ö	Ö	Ö	Capital O, umlaut
×	×	×*	Multiplication sign
Ø	Ø	Ø	Capital O slash
Ù	Ù	Ù	Capital U, grave accent
Ú	Ú	Ú	Capital U, acute accent
Û	Û	Û	Capital U, circumflex accent
Ü	Ü	Ü	Capital U, umlaut
Ý	Ý	Ý	Capital Y, acute accent
Þ	Þ	Þ	Capital THORN, Icelandic
ß	ß	ß	Small sz ligature
à	à	à	Small a, grave accent
á	á	á	Small a, acute accent
â	â	â	Small a, circumflex accent
ã	ã	ã	Small a, tilde
ä	ä	ä	Small a, umlaut
å	å	å	Small a, ring
æ	æ	æ	Small ae ligature
ç	ç	ç	Small c, cedilla
è	è	è	Small e, grave accent
é	é	é	Small e, acute accent

CHARACTER	CODE	CODE NAME	DESCRIPTION
ê	ê	ê	Small e, circumflex accent
ë	ë	ë	Small e, umlaut
ì	ì	ì	Small i, grave accent
í	í	í	Small i, acute accent
î	î	î	Small i, circumflex accent
ï	ï	ï	Small i, umlaut
ð	ð	ð	Small eth, Icelandic
ñ	ñ	ñ	Small n, tilde
ò	ò	ò	Small o, grave accent
ó	ó	ó	Small o, acute accent
ô	ô	ô	Small o, circumflex accent
õ	õ	õ	Small o, tilde
ö	ö	ö	Small o, umlaut
÷	÷	÷*	Division sign
ø	ø	ø	Small o slash
ù	ù	ù	Small u, grave accent
ú	ú	ú	Small u, acute accent
û	û	û	Small u, circumflex accent
ü	ü	ü	Small u, umlaut
ý	ý	ý	Small y, acute accent
þ	þ	þ	Small thorn, Icelandic
ÿ	ÿ	ÿ	Small y, umlaut

Placing a Document on the World Wide Web

Appendix C

Once you complete work on a Web page, you're probably ready to place it on the World Wide Web for others to see. To make a file available on the World Wide Web, it must be located on a computer connected to the Web called a **Web server**.

Your **Internet Service Provider (ISP)**—the company or institution through which you have Internet access—probably has a Web server available for your use. Because each Internet Service Provider has a different procedure for storing Web pages, you should contact your ISP to learn its policies and procedures. Generally you should be prepared to do the following:

- Extensively test your files with a variety of browsers and under different display conditions. Eliminate any errors and design problems before you place the page on the Web.
- Check the links and inline objects in each of your documents to verify that they point to the correct filenames. Verify your filename capitalization—some Web servers distinguish between a file named "Image.gif" and one named "image.gif." To be safe, use only lowercase letters in all your filenames.
- If your links use absolute pathnames, change them to relative pathnames.
- Find out from your ISP the name of the folder into which you'll be placing your HTML documents. You may also need a special user name and password to access this folder.
- Use FTP, an Internet protocol for transferring files, or e-mail to place your pages in the appropriate folder on your ISP's Web server. This capability is built in to some Web browsers, including Internet Explorer and Netscape, allowing you to easily transfer files to your Web server.
- Decide on a name for your Web site (such as "http://www.jackson_electronics.com"). Choose a name that will be easy for customers and interested parties to remember and return to.
- If you select a special name for your Web site, you may have to register it. Registration information can be found at http://www.internic.net. Your ISP may also provide this service for a fee. Registration is necessary to ensure that any name you give to your site is unique and not already in use. Usually you will have to pay a yearly fee to use a special name for your Web site.

Once you've completed these steps, your work will be available on the World Wide Web in a form that is easy for users to access.

Starting Data Files

There are no starting Data Files needed for this appendix.

Making the Web More Accessible

Appendix D

Studies indicate that about 20% of the population has some type of disability. Many of these disabilities do not affect an individual's ability to interact with the Web. However, other disabilities can severely affect an individual's ability to participate in the Web community. For example, on a news Web site, a blind user could not see the latest headlines. A deaf user would not be able to hear a news clip embedded in the site's main page. A user with motor disabilities might not be able to move a mouse pointer to activate important links featured on the site's home page.

Disabilities that inhibit an individual's ability to use the Web fall into four main categories:

- **Visual disability:** A visual disability can include complete blindness, color-blindness, or an untreatable visual impairment.
- **Hearing disability:** A hearing disability can include complete deafness or the inability to distinguish sounds of certain frequencies.
- **Motor disability:** A motor disability can include the inability to use a mouse, to exhibit fine motor control, or to respond in a timely manner to computer prompts and queries.
- **Cognitive disability:** A cognitive disability can include a learning disability, attention deficit disorder, or the inability to focus on large amounts of information.

While the Web includes some significant obstacles to full use by disabled people, it also offers the potential for contact with a great amount of information that is not otherwise cheaply or easily accessible. For example, before the Web, in order to read a newspaper, a blind person was constrained by the expense of Braille printouts and audio tapes, as well as the limited availability of sighted people willing to read the news out loud. As a result, blind people would often only be able to read newspapers after the news was no longer new. The Web, however, makes news available in an electronic format and in real-time. A blind user can use a browser that converts electronic text into speech, known as a **screen reader**, to read a newspaper Web site. Combined with the Web, screen readers provide access to a broader array of information than was possible through Braille publications alone.

> "The power of the Web is in its universality. Access by everyone regardless of disability is an essential aspect."
>
> — Tim Berners-Lee, W3C Director and inventor of the World Wide Web

Starting Data Files

There are no starting Data Files needed for this appendix.

In addition to screen readers, many other programs and devices—known collectively as assistive technology or adaptive technology—are available to enable people with different disabilities to use the Web. The challenge for the Web designer, then, is to create Web pages that are accessible to everyone, including (and perhaps especially) to people with disabilities. In addition to being a design challenge, for some designers, Web accessibility is the law.

Working with Section 508 Guidelines

In 1973, Congress passed the Rehabilitation Act, which aimed to foster economic independence for people with disabilities. Congress amended the act in 1998 to reflect the latest changes in information technology. Part of the amendment, **Section 508**, requires that any electronic information developed, procured, maintained, or used by the federal government be accessible to people with disabilities. Because the Web is one of the main sources of electronic information, Section 508 has had a profound impact on how Web pages are designed and how Web code is written. Note that the standards apply to federal Web sites, but not to private sector Web sites; however, if a site is provided under contract to a federal agency, the Web site or portion covered by the contract has to comply. Required or not, though, you should follow the Section 508 guidelines not only to make your Web site more accessible, but also to make your HTML code more consistent and reliable. The Section 508 guidelines are of interest not just to Web designers who work for the federal government, but to all Web designers.

The Section 508 guidelines encompass a wide range of topics, covering several types of disabilities. The part of Section 508 that impacts Web design is sub-section 1194.22, titled

§ 1194.22 Web-based intranet and internet information and applications.

Within this section are 15 paragraphs, numbered (a) through (p), which describe how each facet of a Web site should be designed so as to maximize accessibility. Let's examine each of these paragraphs in detail.

Graphics and Images

The first paragraph in sub-section 1194.22 deals with graphic images. The standard for the use of graphic images is that

§1194.22 (a) A text equivalent for every nontext element shall be provided (e.g., via "alt", "longdesc", or in element content).

In other words, any graphic image that contains page content needs to include a text alternative to make the page accessible to visually impaired people. One of the simplest ways to do this is to use the alt attribute with every inline image that displays page content. For example, in Figure D-1, the alt attribute provides the text of a graphical logo for users who can't see the graphic.

Figure D-1 **Using the alt attribute**

```
<img src="jkson.jpg" alt="Jackson Electronics" />
```

Not every graphic image requires a text alternative. For example, a decorative image such as a bullet does not need a text equivalent. In those cases, you should include the alt attribute, but set its value to an empty text string. You should never neglect to include the alt attribute. If you are writing XHTML-compliant code, the alt attribute is required. In other cases, screen readers and other nonvisual browsers will recite the filename of a graphic image file if no value is specified for the alt attribute. Since the filename is usually of no interest to the end-user, this results in needless irritation.

The alt attribute is best used for short descriptions that involve five words or less. It is less effective for images that require long descriptive text. You can instead link these images to a document containing a more detailed description. One way to do this is with the longdesc attribute, which uses the syntax

```
<img src="url" longdesc="url" />
```

where *url* for the longdesc attribute points to a document containing a detailed description of the image. Figure D-2 shows an example that uses the longdesc attribute to point to a Web page containing a detailed description of a sales chart.

Using the alt attribute **Figure D-2**

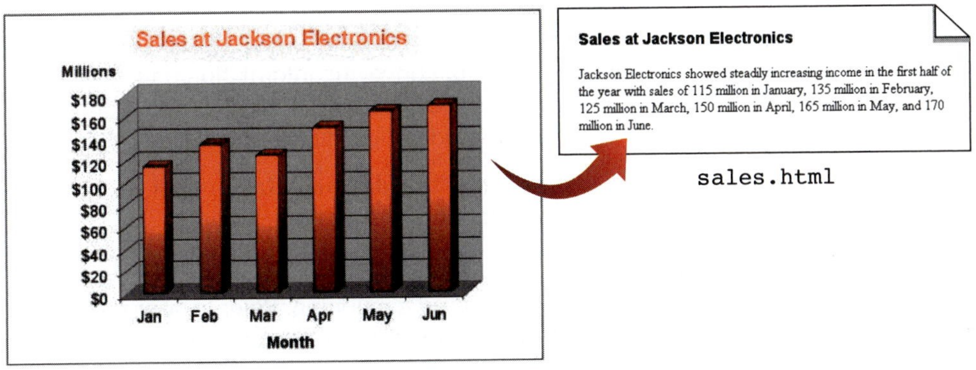


```
<img src="chart.jpg" alt="Sales Chart"
     longdesc="sales.html" />
```

In browsers that support the longdesc attribute, the attribute's value is presented as a link to the specified document. However, since many browsers do not yet support this attribute, many Web designers currently use a D-link. A **D-link** is an unobtrusive "D" placed next to the image on the page, which is linked to an external document containing a fuller description of the image. Figure D-3 shows how the sales chart data can be presented using a D-link.

Figure D-3 Using a D-link

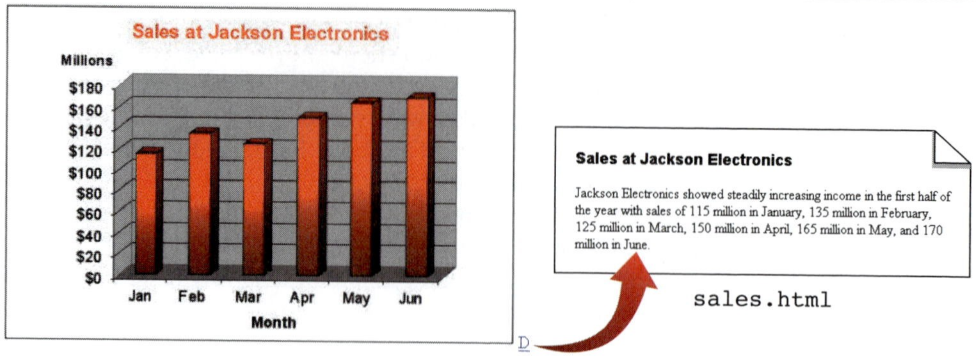


```
<img src="chart.jpg" alt="Sales Chart" />
<a href="sales.html">D</a>
```

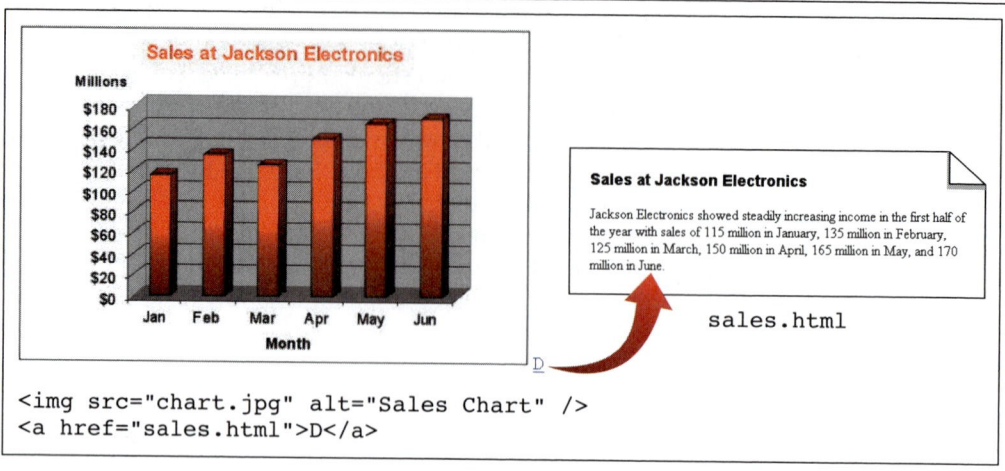

To make your page accessible to visually-impaired users, you will probably use a combination of alternative text and linked documents.

Multimedia

Audio and video have become important ways of conveying information on the Web. However, creators of multimedia presentations should also consider the needs of deaf users and users who are hard of hearing. The standard for multimedia accessibility is

§1194.22 (b) Equivalent alternatives for any multimedia presentation shall be synchronized with the presentation.

This means that any audio clip needs to be accompanied by a transcript of the audio's content, and any video clip needs to include closed captioning. Refer to your multimedia software's documentation on creating closed captioning and transcripts for your video and audio clips.

Color

Color is useful for emphasis and conveying information, but when color becomes an essential part of the site's content, you run the risk of shutting out people who are color blind. For this reason the third Section 508 standard states that

§1194.22 (c) Web pages shall be designed so that all information conveyed with color is also available without color, for example from context or markup.

About 8% of men and 0.5% of women are afflicted with some type of color blindness. The most serious forms of color blindness are:

- **deuteranopia**: an absence of green sensitivity; deuteranopia is one example of red-green color blindness, in which the colors red and green cannot be easily distinguished.
- **protanopia**: an absence of red sensitivity; protanopia is another example of red-green color blindness.
- **tritanopia**: an absence of blue sensitivity. People with tritanopia have much less loss of color sensitivity than other types of color blindness.
- **achromatopsia**: absence of any color sensitivity.

The most common form of serious color blindness is red-green color blindness. Figure D-4 shows how each type of serious color blindness would affect a person's view of a basic color wheel.

Types of color blindness **Figure D-4**

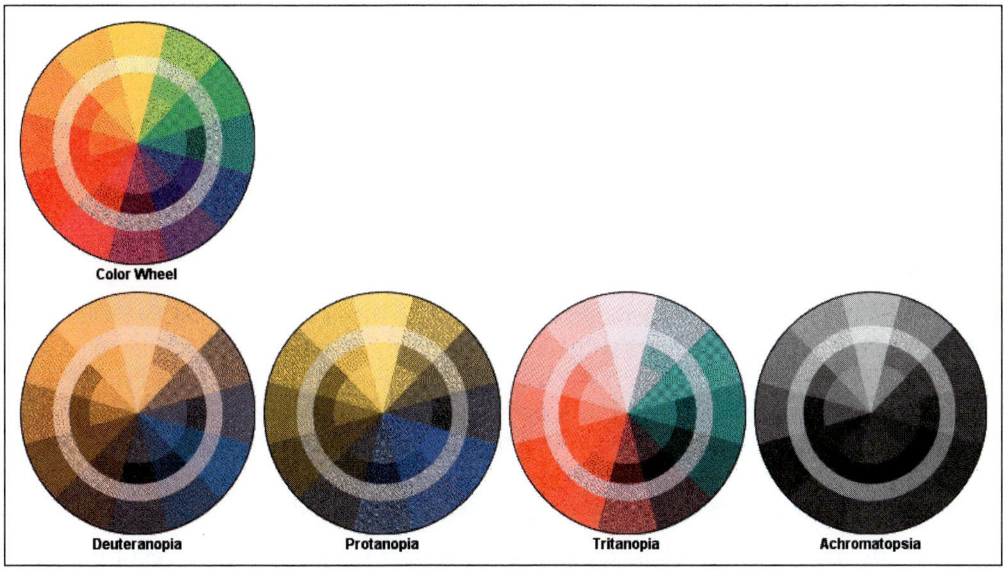

Color combinations that are easily readable for most people may be totally unreadable for users with certain types of color blindness. Figure D-5 demonstrates the accessibility problems that can occur with a graphical logo that contains green text on a red background. For people who have deuteranopia, protanopia, or achromatopsia, the logo is much more difficult to read.

The effect of color blindness on graphical content **Figure D-5**

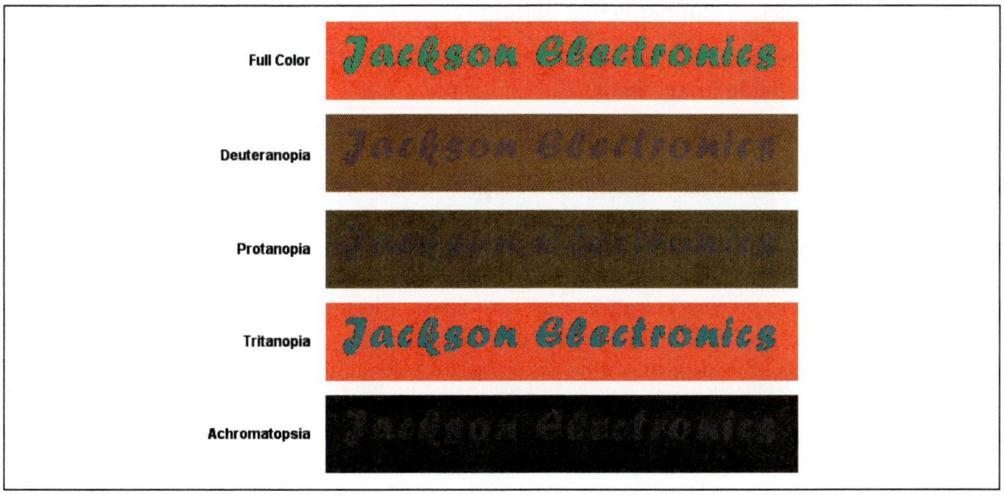

To make your page more accessible to people with color blindness, you can do the following:

- Provide noncolor clues to access your page's content. For example, some Web forms indicate required entry fields by displaying the field names in a red font. You can supplement this for color blind users by marking required fields with a red font *and* with an asterisk or other special symbol.
- Avoid explicit references to color. Don't instruct your users to click a red button in a Web form when some users are unable to distinguish red from other colors.
- Avoid known areas of color difficulty. Since most color blindness involves red-green color blindness, you should avoid red and green text combinations.

- Use bright colors, which are the easiest for color blind users to distinguish.
- Provide a grayscale or black and white alternative for your color blind users, and be sure that your link to that page is easily viewable.

Several sites on the Web include tools you can use to test your Web site for color blind accessibility. You can also load color palettes into your graphics software to see how your images will appear to users with different types of color blindness.

Style Sheets

By controlling how a page is rendered in a browser, style sheets play an important role in making the Web accessible to users with disabilities. Many browsers, such as Internet Explorer, allow a user to apply their own customized style sheet in place of the style sheet specified by a Web page's designer. This is particularly useful for visually impaired users who need to display text in extra large fonts with a high contrast between the text and the background color (yellow text on a black background is a common color scheme for such users). In order to make your pages accessible to those users, Section 508 guidelines state that

§1194.22 (d) Documents shall be organized so they are readable without requiring an associated style sheet.

To test whether your site fulfills this guideline, you should view the site without the style sheet. Some browsers allow you to turn off style sheets; alternately, you can redirect a page to an empty style sheet. You should modify any page that is unreadable without its style sheet to conform with this guideline.

Image Maps

Section 508 provides two standards that pertain to image maps:

§1194.22 (e) Redundant text links shall be provided for each active region of a server-side image map.

and

§1194.22 (f) Client-side image maps shall be provided instead of server-side image maps except where the regions cannot be defined with an available geometric shape.

In other words, the *preferred* image map is a client-side image map, unless the map uses a shape that cannot be defined on the client side. Since client-side image maps allow for polygonal shapes, this should not be an issue; however if you must use a server-side image map, you need to provide a text alternative for each of the map's links. Because server-side image maps provide only map coordinates to the server, this text is necessary in order to provide link information that is accessible to blind or visually impaired users. Figure D-6 shows a server-side image map that satisfies the Section 508 guidelines by repeating the graphical links in the image map with text links placed below the image.

Figure D-6 **Making a server-side image map accessible**

Client-side image maps do not have the same limitations as server-side maps because they allow you to specify alternate text for each hotspot within the map. For example, if the image map shown in Figure D-6 were a client-side map, you could make it accessible using the following HTML code:

```
<img src="servermap.jpg" alt="Jackson Electronics"
usemap="#links" />
<map name="links">
<area shape="rect" href="home.html" alt="home"
coords="21,69,123,117" />
<area shape="rect" href="products.html" alt="products"
coords="156,69,258,117" />
<area shape="rect" href="stores.html" alt="stores"
coords="302,69,404,117" />
<area shape="rect" href="support.html" alt="support"
coords="445,69,547,117" />
</map>
```

Screen readers or other nonvisual browsers use the value of the alt attribute within each <area /> tag to give users access to each area. However, because some older browsers cannot work with the alt attribute in this way, you should also include the text alternative used for server-side image maps.

Tables

Tables can present a challenge for disabled users, in particular those who employ screen readers or other nonvisual browsers. To render a Web page, these browsers employ a technique called **linearizing**, which processes Web page content using a few general rules:

1. Convert all images to their alternative text.
2. Present the contents of each table one cell at a time, working from left to right across each row before moving down to the next row.
3. If a cell contains a nested table, that table is linearized before proceeding to the next cell.

Figure D-7 shows how a nonvisual browser might linearize a sample table.

Figure D-7 Linearizing a table

table

Desktop PCs	Model	Processor	Memory	DVD Burner	Modem	Network Adapter
	Paragon 2.4	Intel 2.4GHz	256MB	No	Yes	No
	Paragon 3.7	Intel 3.7GHz	512MB	Yes	Yes	No
	Paragon 5.9	Intel 5.9GHz	1024MB	Yes	Yes	Yes

linearized content

Desktop PCs
Model
Processor
Memory
DVD Burner
Modem
Network Adapter
Paragon 2.4
Intel 2.4 GHz
256MB
No
Yes
No
Paragon 3.7
Intel 3.7GHz
512MB
Yes
Yes
No
Paragon 5.9
Intel 5.9GHz
1024MB
Yes
Yes
Yes

One way of dealing with the challenge of linearizing is to structure your tables so that they are easily interpreted even when linearized. However, this is not always possible, especially for tables that have several rows and columns or may contain several levels of nested tables. The Section 508 guidelines for table creation state that

§1194.22 (g) Row and column headers shall be identified for data tables.

and

§1194.22 (h) Markup shall be used to associate data cells and header cells for data tables that have two or more logical levels of row or column headers.

To fulfill the 1194.22 (g) guideline, you should use the <th> tag for any table cell that contains a row or column header. By default, header text appears in a bold centered font; however, you can override this format using a style sheet. Many nonvisual browsers can search for header cells. Also, as a user moves from cell to cell in a table, these browsers can announce the row and column headers associated with each cell. So, using the <th> tag can significantly reduce some of the problems associated with linearizing.

You can also use the scope attribute to explicitly associate a header with a row, column, row group, or column group. The syntax of the scope attribute is

```
<th scope="type"> … </th>
```

where *type* is either row, column, rowgroup, or colgroup. Figure D-8 shows how to use the scope attribute to associate the headers with the rows and columns of a table.

Figure D-8 Using the scope attribute

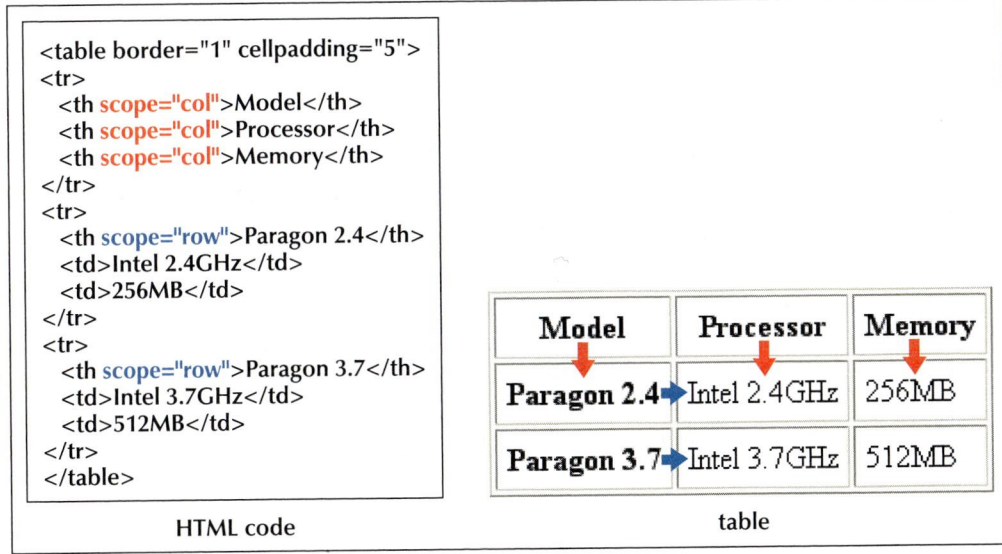

```
<table border="1" cellpadding="5">
<tr>
  <th scope="col">Model</th>
  <th scope="col">Processor</th>
  <th scope="col">Memory</th>
</tr>
<tr>
  <th scope="row">Paragon 2.4</th>
  <td>Intel 2.4GHz</td>
  <td>256MB</td>
</tr>
<tr>
  <th scope="row">Paragon 3.7</th>
  <td>Intel 3.7GHz</td>
  <td>512MB</td>
</tr>
</table>
```

HTML code

Model	Processor	Memory
Paragon 2.4	Intel 2.4GHz	256MB
Paragon 3.7	Intel 3.7GHz	512MB

table

A nonvisual browser that encounters the table in Figure D-8 can indicate to users which rows and columns are associated with each data cell. For example, the browser could indicate that the cell value, "512MB" is associated with the Memory column and the Paragon 3.7 row.

For more explicit references, HTML also supports the headers attribute, which specifies the cell or cells that contain header information for a particular cell. The syntax of the headers attribute is

```
<td headers="ids"> … </td>
```

where *ids* is a list of id values associated with header cells in the table. Figure D-9 demonstrates how to use the headers attribute.

Figure D-9 Using the headers attribute

```
<table>
<tr>
  <th id="c1">Model</th>
  <th id="c2">Processor</th>
  <th id="c3">Memory</th>
</tr>
<tr>
  <th id="r1" headers="c1">Paragon 2.4</th>
  <td headers="r1 c2">Intel 2.4GHz</td>
  <td headers="r1 c3">256MB</td>
</tr>
<tr>
  <th id="r2" headers="c1">Paragon 3.7</th>
  <td headers="r2 c2">Intel 3.7GHz</td>
  <td headers="r2 c3">512MB</td>
</tr>
</table>
```

HTML code

Model	Processor	Memory
Paragon 2.4	Intel 2.4GHz	256MB
Paragon 3.7	Intel 3.7GHz	512MB

table

Note that some older browsers do not support the scope and headers attributes. For this reason, it can be useful to supplement your tables with caption and summary attributes in order to provide even more information to blind and visually impaired users. See Tutorial 4 for a more detailed discussion of these elements and attributes.

Frame Sites

When a nonvisual browser opens a frame site, it can render the contents of only one frame at a time. Users are given a choice of which frame to open. So, it's important that the name given to a frame indicate the frame's content. For this reason, the Section 508 guideline for frames states that

§1194.22 (i) Frames shall be titled with text that facilitates frame identification and navigation.

Frames can be identified using either the title attribute or the name attribute, and different nonvisual browsers use different attributes. For example, the Lynx browser uses the name attribute, while the IBM Home Page Reader uses the title attribute. For this reason, you should use both attributes in your framed sites. If you don't include a title or name attribute in the frame element, some nonvisual browsers retrieve the document specified as the frame's source and then use that page's title as the name for the frame.

The following code demonstrates how to make a frame site accessible to users with disabilities.

```
<frameset cols="25%, *">
   <frame src="title.htm" title="banner" name="banner" />
   <frameset rows="100, *">
      <frame src="links.htm" title="links" name="links" />
      <frame src="home.htm" title="documents" name="documents" />
   </frameset>
</frameset>
```

Naturally, you should make sure that any document displayed in a frame follows the Section 508 guidelines.

Animation and Scrolling Text

Animated GIFs, scrolling marquees, and other special features can be a source of irritation for any Web user; however, they can cause serious problems for certain users. For example, people with photosensitive epilepsy can experience seizures when exposed to a screen or portion of a screen that flickers or flashes within the range of 2 to 55 flashes per second (2 to 55 Hertz). For this reason, the Section 508 guidelines state that

§1194.22 (j) Pages shall be designed to avoid causing the screen to flicker with a frequency greater than 2 Hz and lower than 55 Hz.

In addition to problems associated with photosensitive epilepsy, users with cognitive or visual disabilities may find it difficult to read moving text, and most screen readers are unable to read moving text. Therefore, if you decide to use animated elements, you must ensure that each element's flickering and flashing is outside of the prohibited range, and you should not place essential page content within these elements.

Scripts, Applets and Plug-ins

Scripts, applets, and plug-ins are widely used to make Web pages more dynamic and interesting. The Section 508 guidelines for scripts state that

§1194.22 (l) When pages utilize scripting languages to display content, or to create interface elements, the information provided by the script shall be identified with functional text that can be read by adaptive technology.

Scripts are used for a wide variety of purposes. The following list describes some of the more popular uses of scripts and how to modify them for accessibility:

- **Pull-down menus**: Many Web designers use scripts to save screen space by inserting pull-down menus containing links to other pages in the site. Pull-down menus are usually accessed with a mouse. To assist users who cannot manipulate a mouse, include keyboard shortcuts to all pull-down menus. In addition, the links in a pull-down menu should be repeated elsewhere on the page or on the site in a text format.
- **Image rollovers**: Image rollovers are used to highlight linked elements. However, since image rollovers rely on the ability to use a mouse, pages should be designed so that rollover effects are not essential for navigating a site or for understanding a page's content.
- **Dynamic content**: Scripts can be used to insert new text and page content. Because some browsers designed for users with disabilities have scripting turned off by default, you should either not include any crucial content in dynamic text, or you should provide an alternate method for users with disabilities to access that information.

Applets and plug-ins are programs external to a Web page or browser that add special features to a Web site. The Section 508 guideline for applets and plug-ins is

§1194.22 (m) **When a Web page requires that an applet, plug-in or other application be present on the client system to interpret page content, the page must provide a link to a plug-in or applet that complies with §1994.21(a) through (i).**

This guideline means that any applet or plug-in used with your Web site must be compliant with sections §1994.21(a) through (i) of the Section 508 accessibility law, which deal with accessibility issues for software applications and operating systems. If the default applet or plug-in does not comply with Section 508, you need to provide a link to a version of that applet or plug-in which does. For example, a Web page containing a Real Audio clip should have a link to a source for the necessary player. This places the responsibility on the Web page designer to know that a compliant application is available before requiring the clip to work with the page.

Web Forms

The Section 508 standard for Web page forms states that

§1194.22 (n) **When electronic forms are designed to be completed on-line, the form shall allow people using assistive technology to access the information, field elements, and functionality required for completion and submission of the form, including all directions and cues.**

This is a general statement that instructs designers to make forms accessible, but it doesn't supply any specific instructions. The following techniques can help you make Web forms that comply with Section 508:

- **Push buttons** should always include value attributes. The value attribute contains the text displayed on a button, and is rendered by different types of assistive technology.
- **Image buttons** should always include alternate text that can be rendered by nonvisual browsers.
- **Labels** should be associated with any input box, text area box, option button, checkbox, or selection list. The labels should be placed in close proximity to the input field and should be linked to the field using the label element.
- **Input boxes** and **text area boxes** should, when appropriate, include either default text or a prompt that indicates to the user what text to enter into the input box.
- **Interactive form elements** should be triggered by either the mouse or the keyboard.

The other parts of a Web form should comply with other Section 508 standards. For example, if you use a table to lay out the elements of a form, make sure that the form still makes sense when the table is linearized.

Links

It is common for Web designers to place links at the top, bottom, and sides of every page in their Web sites. This is generally a good idea, because those links enable users to move quickly and easily through a site. However, this technique can make it difficult to navigate a page using a screen reader, because screen readers move through a page from the top to bottom, reading each line of text. Users of screen readers may have to wait several minutes before they even get to the main body of a page, and the use of repetitive links forces such users to reread the same links on each page as they move through a site. To address this problem, the Section 508 guidelines state that

§1194.22 (o) A method shall be provided that permits users to skip repetitive navigation links.

One way of complying with this rule is to place a link at the very top of each page that allows users to jump to the page's main content. In order to make the link unobtrusive, it can be attached to a transparent image that is one pixel wide by one pixel high. For example, the following code lets users of screen readers jump to the main content of the page without needing to go through the content navigation links on the page; however, the image itself is invisible to other users and so does not affect the page's layout or appearance.

```
<a href="#main">
   <img src="spacer.gif" height="1" width="1" alt="Skip to main
content" />
</a>

...

<a name="main"> </a>
page content goes here ...
```

One advantage to this approach is that a template can be easily written to add this code to each page of the Web site.

Timed Responses

For security reasons, the login pages of some Web sites automatically log users out after a period of inactivity, or if users are unable to log in quickly. Because disabilities may prevent some users from being able to complete a login procedure within the prescribed time limit, the Section 508 guidelines state that

§1194.22 (p) When a timed response is required, the user shall be alerted and given sufficient time to indicate that more time is required.

The guideline does not suggest a time interval. To satisfy Section 508, your page should notify users when a process is about to time out and prompt users whether additional time is needed before proceeding.

Providing a Text-Only Equivalent

If you cannot modify a page to match the previous accessibility guidelines, as a last resort you can create a text-only page:

§1194.22 (k) A text-only page, with equivalent information or functionality, shall be provided to make a Web site comply with the provisions of this part, when compliance cannot be accomplished in any other way. The content of the text-only pages shall be updated whenever the primary page changes.

To satisfy this requirement, you should:

- Provide an easily accessible link to the text-only page.
- Make sure that the text-only page satisfies the Section 508 guidelines.
- Duplicate the essential content of the original page.
- Update the alternate page when you update the original page.

By using the Section 508 guidelines, you can work towards making your Web site accessible to everyone, regardless of disabilities.

Understanding the Web Accessibility Initiative

In 1999, the World Wide Web Consortium (W3C) developed its own set of guidelines for Web accessibility called the **Web Accessibility Initiative (WAI)**. The WAI covers many of the same points as the Section 508 rules, and expands on them to cover basic Web site design issues. The overall goal of the WAI is to facilitate the creation of Web sites that are accessible to all, and to encourage designers to implement HTML in a consistent way.

The WAI sets forth 14 guidelines for Web designers. Within each guideline is a collection of checkpoints indicating how to apply the guideline to specific features of a Web site. Each checkpoint is also given a priority score that indicates how important the guideline is for proper Web design:

- **Priority 1:** A Web content developer **must** satisfy this checkpoint. Otherwise, one or more groups will find it impossible to access information in the document. Satisfying this checkpoint is a basic requirement for some groups to be able to use Web documents.
- **Priority 2:** A Web content developer **should** satisfy this checkpoint. Otherwise, one or more groups will find it difficult to access information in the document. Satisfying this checkpoint will remove significant barriers to accessing Web documents.
- **Priority 3:** A Web content developer **may** address this checkpoint. Otherwise, one or more groups will find it somewhat difficult to access information in the document. Satisfying this checkpoint will improve access to Web documents.

The following table lists WAI guidelines with each checkpoint and its corresponding priority value. You can learn more about the WAI guidelines and how to implement them by going to the World Wide Web Consortium Web site at *www.w3.org*.

WAI Guidelines	Priority
1. Provide equivalent alternatives to auditory and visual content	
1.1 Provide a text equivalent for every nontext element (e.g., via "alt", "longdesc", or in element content). *This includes:* images, graphical representations of text (including symbols), image map regions, animations (e.g., animated GIFs), applets and programmatic objects, ascii art, frames, scripts, images used as list bullets, spacers, graphical buttons, sounds (played with or without user interaction), stand-alone audio files, audio tracks of video, and video.	1
1.2 Provide redundant text links for each active region of a server-side image map.	1
1.3 Until user agents can automatically read aloud the text equivalent of a visual track, provide an auditory description of the important information of the visual track of a multimedia presentation.	1
1.4 For any time-based multimedia presentation (e.g., a movie or animation), synchronize equivalent alternatives (e.g., captions or auditory descriptions of the visual track) with the presentation.	1
1.5 Until user agents render text equivalents for client-side image map links, provide redundant text links for each active region of a client-side image map.	3
2. Don't rely on color alone	
2.1 Ensure that all information conveyed with color is also available without color, for example from context or markup.	1
2.2 Ensure that foreground and background color combinations provide sufficient contrast when viewed by someone having color deficits or when viewed on a black and white screen. [Priority 2 for images, Priority 3 for text].	2
3. Use markup and style sheets and do so properly	
3.1 When an appropriate markup language exists, use markup rather than images to convey information.	2
3.2 Create documents that validate to published formal grammars.	2
3.3 Use style sheets to control layout and presentation.	2
3.4 Use relative rather than absolute units in markup language attribute values and style sheet property values.	2
3.5 Use header elements to convey document structure and use them according to specification.	2
3.6 Mark up lists and list items properly.	2
3.7 Mark up quotations. Do not use quotation markup for formatting effects such as indentation.	2
4. Clarify natural language usage	
4.1 Clearly identify changes in the natural language of a document's text and any text equivalents (e.g., captions).	1
4.2 Specify the expansion of each abbreviation or acronym in a document where it first occurs.	3
4.3 Identify the primary natural language of a document.	3
5. Create tables that transform gracefully	
5.1 For data tables, identify row and column headers.	1
5.2 For data tables that have two or more logical levels of row or column headers, use markup to associate data cells and header cells.	1
5.3 Do not use a table for layout unless the table makes sense when linearized. If a table does not make sense, provide an alternative equivalent (which may be a linearized version).	2
5.4 If a table is used for layout, do not use any structural markup for the purpose of visual formatting.	2
5.5 Provide summaries for tables.	3
5.6 Provide abbreviations for header labels.	3

WAI Guidelines	Priority
6. Ensure that pages featuring new technologies transform gracefully	
6.1 Organize documents so they may be read without style sheets. For example, when an HTML document is rendered without associated style sheets, it must still be possible to read the document.	1
6.2 Ensure that equivalents for dynamic content are updated when the dynamic content changes.	1
6.3 Ensure that pages are usable when scripts, applets, or other programmatic objects are turned off or not supported. If this is not possible, then provide equivalent information on an alternative accessible page.	1
6.4 For scripts and applets, ensure that event handlers are input device-independent.	2
6.5 Ensure that dynamic content is accessible or provide an alternative presentation or page.	2
7. Ensure user control of time-sensitive content changes	
7.1 Until user agents allow users to control flickering, avoid causing the screen to flicker.	1
7.2 Until user agents allow users to control blinking, avoid causing content to blink (i.e., change presentation at a regular rate, such as turning on and off).	2
7.3 Until user agents allow users to freeze moving content, avoid movement in pages.	2
7.4 Until user agents provide the ability to stop the refresh, do not create periodically auto-refreshing pages.	2
7.5 Until user agents provide the ability to stop auto-redirect, do not use markup to redirect pages automatically. Instead, configure the server to perform redirects.	2
8. Ensure direct accessibility of embedded user interfaces	
8.1 Make programmatic elements such as scripts and applets directly accessible or compatible with assistive technologies [Priority 1 if functionality is important and not presented elsewhere, otherwise Priority 2.]	2
9. Design for device-independence	
9.1 Provide client-side image maps instead of server-side image maps except where the regions cannot be defined with an available geometric shape.	1
9.2 Ensure that any element with its own interface can be operated in a device-independent manner.	2
9.3 For scripts, specify logical event handlers rather than device-dependent event handlers.	2
9.4 Create a logical tab order through links, form controls, and objects.	3
9.5 Provide keyboard shortcuts to important links (including those in client-side image maps), form controls, and groups of form controls.	3
10. Use interim solutions	
10.1 Until user agents allow users to turn off spawned windows, do not cause pop-ups or other windows to appear and do not change the current window without informing the user.	2
10.2 Until user agents support explicit associations between labels and form controls, ensure that labels are properly positioned for all form controls with implicitly associated labels.	2
10.3 Until user agents (including assistive technologies) render side-by-side text correctly, provide a linear text alternative (on the current page or some other) for *all* tables that lay out text in parallel, word-wrapped columns.	3
10.4 Until user agents handle empty controls correctly, include default, place-holding characters in edit boxes and text areas.	3
10.5 Until user agents (including assistive technologies) render adjacent links distinctly, include nonlink, printable characters (surrounded by spaces) between adjacent links.	3
11. Use W3C technologies and guidelines	
11.1 Use W3C technologies when they are available and appropriate for a task and use the latest versions when supported.	2
11.2 Avoid deprecated features of W3C technologies.	2
11.3 Provide information so that users may receive documents according to their preferences (e.g., language, content type, etc.)	3
11.4 If, after best efforts, you cannot create an accessible page, provide a link to an alternative page that uses W3C technologies, is accessible, has equivalent information (or functionality), and is updated as often as the inaccessible (original) page.	1

WAI Guidelines	Priority
12. Provide context and orientation information	
12.1 Title each frame to facilitate frame identification and navigation.	1
12.2 Describe the purpose of frames and how frames relate to each other if this is not obvious from frame titles alone.	2
12.3 Divide large blocks of information into more manageable groups where natural and appropriate.	2
12.4 Associate labels explicitly with their controls.	2
13. Provide clear navigation mechanisms	
13.1 Clearly identify the target of each link.	2
13.2 Provide metadata to add semantic information to pages and sites.	2
13.3 Provide information about the general layout of a site (e.g., a site map or table of contents).	2
13.4 Use navigation mechanisms in a consistent manner.	2
13.5 Provide navigation bars to highlight and give access to the navigation mechanism.	3
13.6 Group related links, identify the group (for user agents), and, until user agents do so, provide a way to bypass the group.	3
13.7 If search functions are provided, enable different types of searches for different skill levels and preferences.	3
13.8 Place distinguishing information at the beginning of headings, paragraphs, lists, etc.	3
13.9 Provide information about document collections (i.e., documents comprising multiple pages).	3
13.10 Provide a means to skip over multiline ASCII art.	3
14. Ensure that documents are clear and simple	
14.1 Use the clearest and simplest language appropriate for a site's content.	1
14.2 Supplement text with graphic or auditory presentations where they will facilitate comprehension of the page.	3
14.3 Create a style of presentation that is consistent across pages.	3

Checking Your Web Site for Accessibility

As you develop your Web site, you should periodically check it for accessibility. In addition to reviewing the Section 508 and WAI guidelines, you can do several things to verify that your site is accessible to everyone:

- Set up your browser to suppress the display of images. Does each page still convey all of the necessary information?
- Set your browser to display pages in extra large fonts and with a different color scheme. Are your pages still readable under these conditions?
- Try to navigate your pages using only your keyboard. Can you access all of the links and form elements?
- View your page in a text-only browser. (You can use the Lynx browser for this task, located at *www.lynx.browser.org*.)
- Open your page in a screen reader or other nonvisual browser. (The W3C Web site contains links to several alternative browsers that you can download as freeware or on a short-term trial basis in order to evaluate your site.)
- Use tools that test your site for accessibility. (The WAI pages at the W3C Web site contains links to a wide variety of tools that report on how well your site complies with the WAI and Section 508 guidelines.)

Following the accessibility guidelines laid out by Section 508 and the WAI will result in a Web site that is not only more accessible to a wider audience, but whose design is also cleaner, easier to work with, and easier to maintain.

HTML and XHTML Elements and Attributes

Appendix E

This appendix provides descriptions of the major elements and attributes of HTML and XHTML. The elements and attributes represent the specifications of the W3C; therefore, they might not all be supported by the major browsers. Also, in some cases, an element or attribute is not part of the W3C specifications, but instead is an extension offered by a particular browser. Where this is the case, the element or attribute is listed with the supporting browser indicated in parentheses. Likewise, many elements and attributes have been deprecated by the W3C. Deprecated elements and attributes are supported by most browsers, but their use is discouraged.

Where appropriate, the appendix lists the version number in which each element and attribute was introduced. For example, an HTML version number of 2.0 for the <base /> tag means that it is supported by HTML 2.0 *and above*. Version numbers for XHTML refer to the support under the XHTML strict DTD. An asterisk next to the XHTML version number means that the element or attribute is supported under the XHTML transitional or frameset DTD, but not the strict DTD.

The following data types are used throughout this appendix:

• *char*	A single text character
• *char code*	A character encoding
• *color*	An HTML color name or hexadecimal color value
• *date*	A date and time in the format: *yyyy-mm-dd*T*hh:mm:ss*TIMEZONE
• *integer*	An integer value
• *mime-type*	A MIME data type, such as "text/css", "audio/wav", or "video/x-msvideo"
• *mime-type list*	A comma-separated list of mime-types
• ***option1***|*option2*| ...	The value is limited to the specified list of *options*; a default value, if it exists, is displayed in **bold**
• *script*	A script or a reference to a script
• *styles*	A list of style declarations
• *text*	A text string
• *text list*	A comma-separated list of text strings
• *url*	The URL for a Web page or file
• *value*	A numeric value
• *value list*	A comma-separated list of numeric values

Starting Data Files

There are no starting Data Files needed for this appendix.

General Attributes

Several attributes are common to many page elements. Rather than repeating this information each time it occurs, the following tables summarize these attributes.

Core Attributes

The following four attributes, which are laid out in the specifications for HTML and XHTML, apply to all page elements and are supported by most browser versions.

Attribute	Description	HTML	XHTML
class="*text*"	Specifies the class or group to which an element belongs	4.0	1.0
id="*text*"	Specifies a unique identifier to be associated with the element	4.0	1.0
style="*styles*"	Defines an inline style for the element	4.0	1.0
title="*text*"	Provides an advisory title for the element	2.0	1.0

Language Attributes

The Web is designed to be universal and has to be adaptable to languages other than English. So, another set of attributes provides language support. This set of attributes is not as widely supported by browsers as the core attributes are. As with the core attributes, they can be applied to most page elements.

Attribute	Description	HTML	XHTML
dir="**ltr**|rtl"	Indicates the text direction as related to the lang attribute; a value of ltr displays text from left to right; a value of rtl displays text from right to left	4.0	1.0
lang="*text*"	Identifies the language used in the page content	4.0	1.0

Form Attributes

The following attributes can be applied to most form elements or to a Web form itself, but not to other page elements.

Attribute	Description	HTML	XHTML
accesskey="*char*"	Indicates the keyboard character that can be pressed along with the accelerator key to access a form element	4.0	1.0
disabled="disabled"	Disables a form field for input	4.0	1.0
tabindex="*integer*"	Specifies a form element's position in a document's tabbing order	4.0	1.0

Internet Explorer Attributes

Internet Explorer supports a collection of attributes that can be applied to almost all page elements. Other browsers do not support these attributes or support them only for a more limited collection of elements.

<table>
<tr><th>Attribute</th><th>Description</th></tr>
<tr><td>accesskey="char"</td><td>Indicates the keyboard character that can be pressed along with the accelerator key to access the page element</td></tr>
<tr><td>contenteditable="true|false|inherit"</td><td>Specifies whether the element's content can be modified online by the user</td></tr>
<tr><td>disabled="disabled"</td><td>Disables the page element for input</td></tr>
<tr><td>hidefocus="true|false"</td><td>Controls whether the element provides a visual indication of whether the element is in focus</td></tr>
<tr><td>tabindex="integer"</td><td>Specifies the position of the page element in the tabbing order of the document</td></tr>
<tr><td>unselectable="on|off"</td><td>Specifies whether the element can be selected by the user</td></tr>
</table>

Event Attributes

To make Web pages more dynamic, HTML and XHTML support event attributes that identify scripts to be run in response to an event occurring within an element. For example, clicking a main heading with a mouse can cause a browser to run a program that hides or expands a table of contents. Each event attribute has the form

```
event = "script"
```

where ***event*** is the name of the event attribute and ***script*** is the name of the script or command to be run by the browser in response to the occurrence of the event within the element.

Core Events

The general event attributes are part of the specifications for HTML and XHTML. They apply to almost all page elements.

Attribute	Description	HTML	XHTML
onclick	The mouse button is clicked.	4.0	1.0
ondblclick	The mouse button is double-clicked.	4.0	1.0
onkeydown	A key is pressed down.	4.0	1.0
onkeypress	A key is initially pressed.	4.0	1.0
onkeyup	A key is released.	4.0	1.0
onmousedown	The mouse button is pressed down.	4.0	1.0
onmousemove	The mouse pointer is moved within the element's boundaries.	4.0	1.0
onmouseout	The mouse pointer is moved out of the element's boundaries.	4.0	1.0
onmouseover	The mouse pointer hovers over the element.	4.0	1.0
onmouseup	The mouse button is released.	4.0	1.0

Document Events

The following list of event attributes applies not to individual elements within the page, but to the entire document as it is displayed within the browser window or frame.

Attribute	Description	HTML	XHTML
onafterprint	The document has finished printing (IE only).		
onbeforeprint	The document is about to be printed (IE only).		
onload	The page is finished being loaded.	4.0	1.0
onunload	The page is finished unloading.	4.0	1.0

Form Events

The following list of event attributes applies either to the entire Web form or fields within the form.

Attribute	Description	HTML	XHTML
onblur	The form field has lost the focus.	4.0	1.0
onchange	The value of the form field has been changed.	4.0	1.0
onfocus	The form field has received the focus.	4.0	1.0
onreset	The form has been reset.	4.0	1.0
onselect	Text content has been selected in the form field.	4.0	1.0
onsubmit	The form has been submitted for processing.	4.0	1.0

Internet Explorer Data Events

The following list of event attributes applies to elements within the Web page capable of data binding. Note that these events are supported only by the Internet Explorer browser.

Attribute	Description
oncellchange	Data has changed in the data source.
ondataavailable	Data has arrived from the data source.
ondatasetchange	The data in the data source has changed.
ondatasetcomplete	All data from the data source has been loaded.
onrowenter	The current row in the data source has changed.
onrowexit	The current row is about to be changed in the data source.
onrowsdelete	Rows have been deleted from the data source.
onrowsinserted	Rows have been inserted into the data source.

Internet Explorer Events

The Internet Explorer browser supports a wide collection of customized event attributes. Unless otherwise noted, these event attributes can be applied to any page element and are not supported by other browsers or included in the HTML or XHTML specifications.

Attribute	Description
onactive	The element is set to an active state.
onafterupdate	Data has been transferred from the element to a data source.
onbeforeactivate	The element is about to be set to an active state.
onbeforecopy	A selection from the element is about to be copied to the Clipboard.
onbeforecut	A selection from the element is about to be cut to the Clipboard.
onbeforedeactivate	The element is about to be deactivated.
onbeforeeditfocus	The element is about to become active.
onbeforepaste	Data from the Clipboard is about to be pasted into the element.
onbeforeunload	The page is about to be unloaded.
onbeforeupdate	The element's data is about to be updated.
onblur	The element has lost the focus.
oncontextmenu	The right mouse button is activated.
oncontrolselect	Selection using a modifier key (Ctrl for Windows, Command for Macintosh) has begun within the element.
oncopy	Data from the element has been copied to the Clipboard.
oncut	Data from the element has been cut to the Clipboard.
ondrag	The element is being dragged.
ondragdrop	The element has been dropped into the window or frame.
ondragend	The element is no longer being dragged.
ondragenter	The dragged element has entered a target area.
ondragleave	The dragged element has left a target area.
ondragover	The dragged element is over a target area.
ondragstart	The element has begun to be dragged.
ondrop	The dragged element has been dropped.
onerrorupdate	The data transfer to the element has been cancelled.
onfocus	The element has received the focus.
onfocusin	The element is about to receive the focus.
onfocusout	The form element has just lost the focus.
onhelp	The user has selected online help from the browser.
oninput	Text has just been entered into the form field.
onlosecapture	The element has been captured by the mouse selection.
onmouseenter	The mouse pointer enters the element's boundaries.
onmouseleave	The mouse pointer leaves the element's boundaries.
onmousewheel	The mouse wheel is moved.
onmove	The browser window or element has been moved by the user.
onmoveend	Movement of the element has ended.
onmovestart	The element has begun to move.
onpaste	Data has been pasted from the Clipboard into the element.

Attribute	Description
onpropertychange	One or more of the element's properties has changed.
onreadystatechange	The element has changed its ready state.
onresize	The browser window or element has been resized by the user.
onscroll	The scroll bar position within the element has been changed (also supported by other browsers).
onselectstart	Selection has begun within the element.
onstop	The page is finished loading.

HTML and XHTML Elements and Attributes

The following table contains an alphabetic listing of the elements and attributes supported by HTML, XHTML, and the major browsers. Some attributes are not listed in this table, but are described instead in the general attributes tables presented in the previous section of this appendix.

Element/Attribute	Description	HTML	XHTML
`<!-- text -->`	Inserts a comment into the document (comments are not displayed in therendered page)	2.0	1.0
`<!doctype>`	Specifies the Document Type Definition for a document	2.0	1.0
`<a> </a>`	Marks the beginning and end of a link	2.0	1.0
accesskey="*char*"	Indicates the keyboard character that can be pressed along with the accelerator key to activate the link	4.0	1.0
charset="*text*"	Specifies the character encoding of the linked document	4.0	1.0
coords="*value list*"	Specifies the coordinates of a hotspot in a client-side image map; the value list depends on the shape of the hotspot: shape="rect" "*left, right, top, bottom*"shape="circle" "*x_center, y_center, radius*"shape="poly" "*x1, y1, x2, y2, x3, y3, ...*"	4.0	1.0
href="*url*"	Specifies the URL of the link	3.2	1.0
hreflang="*text*"	Specifies the language of the linked document	4.0	1.0
name="*text*"	Specifies a name for the enclosed text, allowing it to be a link target	2.0	1.0
rel="*text*"	Specifies the relationship between the current page and the link specified by the href attribute	2.0	1.0
rev="*text*"	Specifies the reverse relationship between the current page and the linkspecified by the href attribute	2.0	1.0
shape="rect|circle|polygon"	Specifies the shape of the hotspot	4.0	1.0
title="*text*"	Specifies the pop-up text for the link	2.0	1.0
target="*text*"	Specifies the target window or frame for the link	4.0	1.0
type="*mime-type*"	Specifies the data type of the linked document	4.0	1.0
`<abbr> </abbr>`	Marks abbreviated text	4.0	1.0
`<acronym> </acronym>`	Marks acronym text	3.0	1.0
`<address> </address>`	Marks address text	2.0	1.0

Element/Attribute	Description	HTML	XHTML
`<applet> </applet>`	Embeds an applet into the browser (deprecated)	3.2	1.0*
align="absmiddle | absbottom | baseline | bottom | center | left | middle | right | texttop | top"	Specifies the alignment of the applet with the surrounding text	3.2	1.0*
alt="*text*"	Specifies alternate text for the applet (deprecated)	3.2	1.0*
archive="*url*"	Specifies the URL of an archive containing classes and other resources to be used with the applet (deprecated)	4.0	1.0*
code="*url*"	Specifies the URL of the applet's code/class (deprecated)	3.2	1.0*
codebase="*url*"	Specifies the URL of all class files for the applet (deprecated)	3.2	1.0*
datafld="*text*"	Specifies the data source that supplies bound data for use with the applet	4.0	
datasrc="*text*"	Specifies the ID or URL of the applet's data source	4.0	
height="*integer*"	Specifies the height of the applet in pixels	3.2	1.0*
hspace="*integer*"	Specifies the horizontal space around the applet in pixels (deprecated)	3.2	1.0*
mayscript="mayscript"	Permits access to the applet by programs embedded in the document		
name="*text*"	Specifies the name assigned to the applet (deprecated)	3.2	1.0*
object="*text*"	Specifies the name of the resource that contains a serialized representation of the applet (deprecated)	4.0	1.0*
src="*url*"	Specifies an external URL reference to the applet		
vspace="*integer*"	Specifies the vertical space around the applet in pixels (deprecated)	3.2	1.0*
width="*integer*"	Specifies the width of the applet in pixels (deprecated)	3.2	1.0*
`<area />`	Marks an image map hotspot	3.2	1.0
alt="*text*"	Specifies alternate text for the hotspot	3.2	1.0
coords="*value list*"	Specifies the coordinates of the hotspot; the value list depends on the shape of the hotspot: shape="rect" "*left, right, top, bottom*" shape="circle" "*x_center, y_center, radius*" shape="poly" "*x1, y1, x2, y2, x3, y3, ...*"	3.2	1.0
href="*url*"	Specifies the URL of the document to which the hotspot points	3.2	1.0
nohref="nohref"	Specifies that the hotspot does not point to a link	3.2	1.0
shape="rect | circle | polygon"	Specifies the shape of the hotspot	3.2	1.0
target="*text*"	Specifies the target window or frame for the link	3.2	1.0*
`<b> </b>`	Marks text as bold	2.0	1.0
`<base />`	Specifies global reference information for the document	2.0	1.0
href="*url*"	Specifies the URL from which all relative links in the document are based	2.0	1.0
target="*text*"	Specifies the target window or frame for links in the document	2.0	1.0*
`<basefont />`	Specifies the font setting for the document text (deprecated)	3.2	1.0*
color="*color*"	Specifies the text color (deprecated)	3.2	1.0*
face="*text list*"	Specifies a list of fonts to be applied to the text (deprecated)	3.2	1.0*
size="*integer*"	Specifies the size of the font range from 1 (smallest) to 7 (largest) (deprecated)	3.2	1.0*

Element/Attribute	Description	HTML	XHTML
<bdo> </bdo>	Indicates that the enclosed text should be rendered with the direction specified by the dir attribute	4.0	1.0
<bgsound />	Plays a background sound clip when the page is opened (IE and Opera only)		
balance="*integer*"	Specifies the balance of the volume between the left and right speakers where balance ranges from -10,000 to 10,000 (IE and Opera only)		
loop="*integer* | infinite"	Specifies the number of times the clip will be played (a positive integeror infinite) (IE and Opera only)		
src="*url*"	Specifies the URL of the sound clip file (IE and Opera only)		
volume="*integer*"	Specifies the volume of the sound clip, where the volume ranges from -10,000 to 0 (IE and Opera only)		
<big> </big>	Increases the size of the enclosed text relative to the default font size	3.0	1.0
<blink> </blink>	Blinks the enclosed text on and off		
<blockquote> </blockquote>	Marks content as quoted from another source	2.0	1.0
align="**left** | center | right"	Specifies the horizontal alignment of the content		
cite="url"	Provides the source URL of the quoted content	4.0	1.0
clear="**none** | left | right | all"	Prevents content from rendering until the specified margin is clear	3.0*	
<body> </body>	Marks the page content to be rendered by the browser	2.0	1.0
alink="*color*"	Specifies the color of activated links in the document (deprecated)	3.2	1.0*
background="*url*"	Specifies the background image file used for the page (deprecated)	3.0	1.0*
bgcolor="*color*"	Specifies the background color of the page (deprecated)	3.2	1.0*
bgproperties="*fixed*"	Fixes the background image in the browser window (IE only)		
bottommargin="*integer*"	Specifies the size of the bottom margin in pixels (IE only)		
leftmargin="*integer*"	Specifies the size of the left margin in pixels		
link="*color*"	Specifies the color of unvisited links (deprecated)	3.2	1.0*
marginheight="*integer*"	Specifies the size of the margin above and below the page (Netscape 4 only)		
marginwidth="*integer*"	Specifies the size of the margin to the left and right of the page (Netscape 4 only)		
nowrap="**false** | true"	Specifies whether the content wraps using normal HTML line-wrapping conventions (IE only)		
rightmargin="*integer*"	Specifies the size of the right margin in pixels (IE only)		
scroll="**yes** | no"	Specifies whether to display a scroll bar (IE only)		
text="*color*"	Specifies the color of page text (deprecated)	3.2	1.0*
topmargin="*integer*"	Specifies the size of the top page margin in pixels (IE only)		
vlink="*color*"	Specifies the color of previously visited links (deprecated)	3.2	1.0*
 	Inserts a line break into the page	2.0	1.0
clear="**none** | left | right | all"	Displays the line break only when the specified margin is clear (deprecated)	3.2	1.0*
<button> </button>	Creates a form button	4.0	1.0
datafld="*text*"	Specifies the column from a data source that supplies bound data for the button (IE only)		
dataformatas="html | plaintext | text"	Specifies the format of the data in the data source bound with the button (IE only)		

Element/Attribute	Description	HTML	XHTML
datasrc="*url*"	Specifies the URL or ID of the data source bound with the button (IE only)		
name="*text*"	Provides the name assigned to the form button	4.0	1.0
type="**submit**|reset|button"	Specifies the type of form button	4.0	1.0
value="*text*"	Provides the value associated with the form button	4.0	1.0
<caption> </caption>	Creates a table caption	3.0	1.0
align="bottom|center|left|right|**top**"	Specifies the alignment of the caption (deprecated)	3.0	1.0*
valign="top|bottom"	Specifies the vertical alignment of the caption		
<center> </center>	Centers content horizontally on the page (deprecated)	3.2	1.0*
<cite> </cite>	Marks citation text	2.0	1.0
<code> </code>	Marks text used for code samples	2.0	1.0
<col> </col>	Defines the settings for a column or group of columns	4.0	1.0
align="left|right|center"	Specifies the alignment of the content of the column(s)	4.0	1.0
bgcolor="*color*"	Specifies the background color of the column(s)		
char="*char*"	Specifies a character in the column used to align column values	4.0	1.0
charoff="*integer*"	Specifies the offset in pixels from the alignment character specified in the char attribute	4.0	1.0
span="*integer*"	Specifies the number of columns in the group	4.0	1.0
valign="top|middle|bottom|baseline"	Specifies the vertical alignment of the content in the column(s)	4.0	1.0
width="*integer*"	Specifies the width of the column(s) in pixels	4.0	1.0
<colgroup> </colgroup>	Creates a container for a group of columns	4.0	1.0
align="left|right center"	Specifies the alignment of the content of the column group	4.0	1.0
bgcolor="*color*"	Specifies the background color of the column group		
char="*char*"	Specifies a character in the column used to align column group values	4.0	1.0
charoff="*integer*"	Specifies the offset in pixels from the alignment character specified in the char attribute	4.0	1.0
span="*integer*"	Specifies the number of columns in the group	4.0	1.0
valign="top|middle|bottom|baseline"	Specifies the vertical alignment of the content in the column group	4.0	1.0
width="*integer*"	Specifies the width of the columns in the group in pixels	4.0	1.0
<dd> </dd>	Marks text as a definition within a definition list	2.0	1.0
<del> </del>	Marks text as deleted from the document	3.0	1.0
cite="*url*"	Provides the URL for the document that has additional information about the deleted text	3.0	1.0
datetime="*date*"	Specifies the date and time of the text deletion	3.0	1.0
<dfn> </dfn>	Marks the defining instance of a term	3.0	1.0
<dir> </dir>	Contains a directory listing (deprecated)	2.0	1.0*
compact="compact"	Permits use of compact rendering, if available (deprecated)	2.0	1.0*

Element/Attribute	Description	HTML	XHTML
<div> </div>	Creates a generic block-level element	3.0	1.0
align="left|center right|justify"	Specifies the horizontal alignment of the content (deprecated)	3.0	1.0*
datafld="*text*"	Indicates the column from a data source that supplies bound data for the block (IE only)		
dataformatas="html |plaintext|text"	Specifies the format of the data in the data source bound with the block (IE only)		
datasrc="*url*"	Provides the URL or ID of the data source bound with the block (IE only)		
nowrap="nowrap"	Specifies whether the content wraps using normal HTML line-wrapping conventions	3.0*	
<dl> </dl>	Encloses a definition list using the dd and dt elements	2.0	1.0
compact="compact"	Permits use of compact rendering, if available (deprecated)	2.0	1.0*
<dt> </dt>	Marks a definition term in a definition list	2.0	1.0
nowrap="nowrap"	Specifies whether the content wraps using normal HTML line-wrapping conventions		
<em> </em>	Marks emphasized text	2.0	1.0
<embed> </embed>	Places an embedded object into the page (not part of the W3C specifications, but supported by most major browsers)		
align="bottom|left |right|top"	Specifies the alignment of the object with the surrounding content		
autostart="true |false"	Starts the embedded object automatically when the page is loaded		
height="*integer*"	Specifies the height of the object in pixels		
hidden="true|false"	Hides the object on the page		
hspace="*integer*"	Specifies the horizontal space around the object in pixels		
name="*text*"	Provides the name of the embedded object		
pluginspage="*url*"	Provides the URL of the page containing information on the object		
pluginurl="*url*"	Provides the URL of the page for directly installing the object		
src="*url*"	Provides the location of the file containing the object		
type="*mime-type*"	Specifies the mime-type of the embedded object		
units="*text*"	Specifies the measurement units of the object		
vspace="*integer*"	Specifies the vertical space around the object in pixels		
width="*integer*"	Specifies the width of the object in pixels		
<fieldset> </fieldset>	Places form fields in a common group	4.0	1.0
align="left|center |right"	Specifies the alignment of the contents of the field set (IE only)		
datafld="*text*"	Indicates the column from a data source that supplies bound data for the field set (IE only)		
dataformatas="html| plaintext|text"	Specifies the format of the data in the data source bound with the field set (IE only)		
datasrc="*url*"	Provides the URL or ID of the data source bound with the field set (IE only)		
<font> </font>	Formats the enclosed text (deprecated)	3.2	1.0*
color="color"	Specifies the color of the enclosed text (deprecated)	3.2	1.0*
face="text list"	Specifies the font face(s) of the enclosed text (deprecated)	3.2	1.0*
size="integer"	Specifies the size of the enclosed text, with values ranging from 1 (smallest) to 7 (largest); a value of +integer increases the font size relative to the font size specified in the basefont element (deprecated)	3.2	1.0*

Element/Attribute	Description	HTML	XHTML
<form> </form>	Encloses the contents of a Web form	2.0	1.0
accept="*mime-type list*"	Lists mime-types that the server processing the form will handle	4.0	1.0
accept-charset="*char code*"	Specifies the character encoding that the server processing the form will handle	4.0	1.0
action="*url*"	Provides the URL to which the form values are to be sent	2.0	1.0
autocomplete="on|off"	Enables automatic insertion of information in fields in which the user has previously entered data (IE only)		
enctype="*mime-type*"	Specifies the mime-type of the data to be sent to the server for processing; the default is "application/x-www-form-urlencoded"	2.0	1.0
method="**get**|post"	Specifies the method of accessing the URL specified in the action attribute	2.0	1.0
name="*text*"	Specifies the name of the form	2.0	1.0
target="*text*"	Specifies the frame or window in which output from the form should appear	4.0	1.0
<frame> </frame>	Marks a single frame within a set of frames	4.0	1.0*
border="*integer*"	Specifies the thickness of the frame border in pixels (Netscape 4 only)		
bordercolor="*color*"	Specifies the color of the frame border		
frameborder="**1**|0"	Determines whether the frame border is visible (1) or invisible (0); Netscape also supports values of yes or no	4.0	1.0*
longdesc="*url*"	Provides the URL of a document containing a long description of the frame's contents	4.0	1.0*
marginheight="*integer*"	Specifies the space above and below the frame object and the frame's borders, in pixels	4.0	1.0*
marginwidth="*integer*"	Specifies the space to the left and right of the frame object and the frame's borders, in pixels	4.0	1.0*
name="*text*"	Specifies the name of the frame	4.0	1.0*
noresize="noresize"	Prevents users from resizing the frame	4.0	1.0*
scrolling="**auto**|yes|no"	Specifies whether the browser will display a scroll bar with the frame	4.0	1.0*
src="*url*"	Provides the URL of the document to be displayed in the frame	4.0	1.0*
<frameset> </frameset>	Creates a collection of frames	4.0	1.0*
border="*integer*"	Specifies the thickness of the frame borders in the frameset in pixels (not part of the W3C specifications, but supported by most browsers)		
bordercolor="*color*"	Specifies the color of the frame borders		
cols="*value list*"	Arranges the frames in columns with the width of each column expressed either in pixels, as a percentage, or using an asterisk (to allow the browser to choose the width)	4.0	1.0*
frameborder="**1**|0"	Determines whether frame borders are visible (1) or invisible (0); (not part of the W3C specifications, but supported by most browsers; Netscape also supports values of yes or no)		
framespacing="*integer*"	Specifies the amount of space between frames in pixels (IE only)		
rows="*value list*"	Arranges the frames in rows with the height of each column expressed either in pixels, as a percentage, or using an asterisk (to allow the browser to choose the height)	4.0	1.0*

<table>
<tr><th>Element/Attribute</th><th>Description</th><th>HTML</th><th>XHTML</th></tr>
<tr><td><hi> </hi></td><td>Marks the enclosed text as a heading, where i is an integer from 1 (the largest heading) to 6 (the smallest heading)</td><td>2.0</td><td>1.0</td></tr>
<tr><td>align="left|center|right|justify"</td><td>Specifies the alignment of the heading text (deprecated)</td><td>3.0</td><td>1.0*</td></tr>
<tr><td><head> </head></td><td>Encloses the document head, containing information about the document</td><td>2.0</td><td>1.0</td></tr>
<tr><td>profile="url"</td><td>Provides the location of metadata about the document</td><td>4.0</td><td>1.0</td></tr>
<tr><td><hr /></td><td>Draws a horizontal line (rule) in the rendered page</td><td>2.0</td><td>1.0</td></tr>
<tr><td>align="left|center|right"</td><td>Specifies the horizontal alignment of the line (deprecated)</td><td>3.2</td><td>1.0*</td></tr>
<tr><td>color="color"</td><td>Specifies the color of the line</td><td></td><td></td></tr>
<tr><td>noshade="noshade"</td><td>Removes 3-D shading from the line (deprecated)</td><td>3.2</td><td>1.0*</td></tr>
<tr><td>size="integer"</td><td>Specifies the height of the line in pixels or as a percentage of the enclosing element's height (deprecated)</td><td>3.2</td><td>1.0*</td></tr>
<tr><td>width="integer"</td><td>Specifies the width of the line in pixels or as a percentage of the enclosing element's width (deprecated)</td><td>3.2</td><td>1.0*</td></tr>
<tr><td><html> </html></td><td>Encloses the entire content of the HTML document</td><td>2.0</td><td>1.0</td></tr>
<tr><td>version="text"</td><td>Specifies the version of HTML being used</td><td>2.0</td><td>1.1</td></tr>
<tr><td>xmlns="text"</td><td>Specifies the namespace prefix for the document</td><td></td><td>1.0</td></tr>
<tr><td><i> </i></td><td>Displays the enclosed text in italics</td><td>2.0</td><td>1.0</td></tr>
<tr><td><iframe> </iframe></td><td>Creates an inline frame in the document</td><td>4.0</td><td>1.0*</td></tr>
<tr><td>align="bottom|left|middle|top|right"</td><td>Specifies the horizontal alignment of the frame with the surrounding content (deprecated)</td><td>4.0</td><td>1.0*</td></tr>
<tr><td>datafld="text"</td><td>Indicates the column from a data source that supplies bound data for the inline frame (IE only)</td><td></td><td>4.0</td></tr>
<tr><td>dataformatas="html|plaintext|text"</td><td>Specifies the format of the data in the data source bound with the inline frame (IE only)</td><td></td><td>4.0</td></tr>
<tr><td>datasrc="url"</td><td>Provides the URL or ID of the data source bound with the inline frame (IE only)</td><td></td><td>4.0</td></tr>
<tr><td>frameborder="1|0"</td><td>Specifies whether to display a frame border (1) or not (0)</td><td>4.0</td><td>1.0*</td></tr>
<tr><td>height="integer"</td><td>Specifies the height of the frame in pixels</td><td>4.0</td><td>1.0*</td></tr>
<tr><td>hspace="integer"</td><td>Specifies the space to the left and right of the frame in pixels</td><td>4.0</td><td>1.0*</td></tr>
<tr><td>longdesc="url"</td><td>Indicates the document containing a long description of the frame's content</td><td>4.0</td><td>1.0*</td></tr>
<tr><td>marginheight="integer"</td><td>Specifies the space above and below the frame object and the frame's borders, in pixels</td><td>4.0</td><td>1.0*</td></tr>
<tr><td>marginwidth="integer"</td><td>Specifies the space to the left and right of the frame object and the frame's borders, in pixels</td><td>4.0</td><td>1.0*</td></tr>
<tr><td>name="text"</td><td>Specifies the name of the frame</td><td>4.0</td><td>1.0*</td></tr>
<tr><td>scrolling="auto|yes|no"</td><td>Determines whether the browser displays a scroll bar with the frame</td><td>4.0</td><td>1.0*</td></tr>
<tr><td>src="url"</td><td>Indicates the document displayed within the frame</td><td>4.0</td><td>1.0*</td></tr>
<tr><td>vspace="integer"</td><td>Specifies the space to the top and bottom of the frame in pixels</td><td>4.0</td><td>1.0*</td></tr>
<tr><td>width="integer"</td><td>Specifies the width of the frame in pixels</td><td>4.0</td><td>1.0*</td></tr>
</table>

<table>
<tr><th>Element/Attribute</th><th>Description</th><th>HTML</th><th>XHTML</th></tr>
<tr><td><ilayer> </ilayer></td><td>Creates an inline layer used to display the content of an external document (Netscape 4 only)</td><td></td><td></td></tr>
<tr><td>above="text"</td><td>Specifies the name of the layer displayed above the current layer (IE only)</td><td></td><td></td></tr>
<tr><td>background="url"</td><td>Provides the URL of the file containing the background image (IE only)</td><td></td><td></td></tr>
<tr><td>below="text"</td><td>Specifies the name of the layer displayed below the current layer (IE only)</td><td></td><td></td></tr>
<tr><td>bgcolor="color"</td><td>Specifies the layer's background color (IE only)</td><td></td><td></td></tr>
<tr><td>clip="top, left, bottom, right"</td><td>Specifies the coordinates of the viewable region of the layer (IE only)</td><td></td><td></td></tr>
<tr><td>height="integer"</td><td>Specifies the height of the layer in pixels (IE only)</td><td></td><td></td></tr>
<tr><td>left="integer"</td><td>Specifies the horizontal offset of the layer in pixels (IE only)</td><td></td><td></td></tr>
<tr><td>pagex="integer"</td><td>Specifies the horizontal position of the layer in pixels (IE only)</td><td></td><td></td></tr>
<tr><td>pagey="integer"</td><td>Specifies the vertical position of the layer in pixels (IE only)</td><td></td><td></td></tr>
<tr><td>src="url"</td><td>Provides the URL of the document displayed in the layer (IE only)</td><td></td><td></td></tr>
<tr><td>top="integer"</td><td>Specifies the vertical offset of the layer in pixels (IE only)</td><td></td><td></td></tr>
<tr><td>visibility="hide|inherit|show"</td><td>Specifies the visibility of the layer (IE only)</td><td></td><td></td></tr>
<tr><td>width="integer"</td><td>Specifies the width of the layer in pixels (IE only)</td><td></td><td></td></tr>
<tr><td>z-index="integer"</td><td>Specifies the stacking order of the layer (IE only)</td><td></td><td></td></tr>
<tr><td><img> </img></td><td>Inserts an inline image into the document</td><td>2.0</td><td>1.0</td></tr>
<tr><td>align="left|right|top|texttop|middle|absmiddle|baselines|bottom|absbottom"</td><td>Specifies the alignment of the image with the surrounding content (deprecated)</td><td>2.0</td><td>1.0*</td></tr>
<tr><td>alt="text"</td><td>Specifies alternate text to be displayed in place of the image</td><td>2.0</td><td>1.0</td></tr>
<tr><td>border="integer"</td><td>Specifies the width of the image border (deprecated)</td><td>3.2</td><td>1.0*</td></tr>
<tr><td>controls="control"</td><td>For video images, displays a playback control below the image (IE only)</td><td></td><td></td></tr>
<tr><td>datafld="text"</td><td>Names the column from a data source that supplies bound data for the image (IE only)</td><td></td><td></td></tr>
<tr><td>dataformatas="html|plaintext|text"</td><td>Specifies the format of the data in the data source bound with the image (IE only)</td><td></td><td></td></tr>
<tr><td>datasrc="url"</td><td>Provides the URL or ID of the data source bound with the image (IE only)</td><td></td><td></td></tr>
<tr><td>dynsrc="url"</td><td>Provides the URL of a video or VRML file (IE and Opera only)</td><td></td><td></td></tr>
<tr><td>height="integer"</td><td>Specifies the height of the image in pixels</td><td>3.0</td><td>1.0</td></tr>
<tr><td>hspace="integer"</td><td>Specifies the horizontal space around the image in pixels (deprecated)</td><td>3.0</td><td>1.0*</td></tr>
<tr><td>ismap="ismap"</td><td>Indicates that the image can be used as a server-side image map</td><td>2.0</td><td>1.0</td></tr>
<tr><td>longdesc="url"</td><td>Provides the URL of a document containing a long description of the image</td><td>4.0</td><td>1.0</td></tr>
<tr><td>loop="integer"</td><td>Specifies the number of times the video will play (IE and Opera only)</td><td></td><td></td></tr>
<tr><td>lowsrc="url"</td><td>Provides the URL of the low-resolution version of the image (IE and Netscape only)</td><td></td><td></td></tr>
<tr><td>name="text"</td><td>Specifies the image name</td><td>4.0</td><td>1.0*</td></tr>
</table>

Element/Attribute	Description	HTML	XHTML
src="*url*"	Specifies the image source file	2.0	1.0
start="fileopen|mouseover"	Indicates when to start the video clip (either when the file is opened or when the mouse hovers over the image) (IE and Opera only)		
suppress="true|false"	Suppresses the display of the alternate text and the placeholder icon until the image file is located (Netscape 4 only)		
usemap="*url*"	Provides the location of a client-side image associated with the image (not well-supported when the URL points to an external file)	3.2	1.0
vspace="*integer*"	Specifies the vertical space around the image in pixels (deprecated)	3.2	1.0*
width="*integer*"	Specifies the width of the image in pixels	3.0	1.0
<input> </input>	Marks an input field in a Web form	2.0	1.0
align="left|right|top|texttop|middle|absmiddle|baseline|bottom|absbottom"	Specifies the alignment of the input field with the surrounding content (deprecated)	2.0	1.0*
alt="*text*"	Specifies alternate text for image buttons and image input fields	4.0	1.0
checked="checked"	Specifies that the input check box or input radio button is selected	2.0	1.0
datafld="*text*"	Indicates the column from a data source that supplies bound data for the input field	4.0	
dataformatas="html|plaintext|text"	Specifies the format of the data in the data source bound with the input field	4.0	
datasrc="*url*"	Provides the URL or ID of the data source bound with the input field	4.0	
height="*integer*"	Specifies the height of the image input field in pixels (not part of the W3C specifications, but supported by many browsers)		
hspace="*integer*"	Specifies the horizontal space around the image input field in pixels (not part of the W3C specifications, but supported by many browsers)		
ismap="ismap"	Enables the image input field to be used as a server-side image map	4.0	1.1
maxlength="*integer*"	Specifies the maximum number of characters that can be inserted into a text input field	2.0	1.0
name="text"	Specifies the name of the input field	2.0	1.0
readonly="readonly"	Prevents the value of the input field from being modified	2.0	1.0
size="*integer*"	Specifies the number of characters that can be displayed at one time in an input text field	2.0	1.0
src="*url*"	Indicates the source file of an input image field	2.0	1.0
type="button|checkbox|file|hidden|image|password|radio|reset|submit|text"	Specifies the type of input field	2.0	1.0
usemap="url"	Provides the location of a client-side image associated with the image input field (not well-supported when the URL points to an external file)	4.0	1.0
value="*text*"	Specifies the default value of the input field	2.0	1.0
vspace="*integer*"	Specifies the vertical space around the image input field in pixels (not part of the W3C specifications, but supported by many browsers)		
width="*integer*"	Specifies the width of an image input field in pixels (not part of the W3C specifications, but supported by many browsers)		

Element/Attribute	Description	HTML	XHTML
`<ins> </ins>`	Marks inserted text	3.0	1.0
cite="*url*"	Provides the URL for the document that has additional information about the inserted text	3.0	1.0
datetime="*date*"	Specifies the date and time of the text insertion	3.0	1.0
`<isindex />`	Inserts an input field into the document for search queries (deprecated)	2.0	1.0*
action="*url*"	Provides the URL of the script used to process the sindex data		1.0
prompt="*text*"	Specifies the text to be used for the input prompt (deprecated)	3.0	1.0*
`<kbd> </kbd>`	Marks keyboard-style text	2.0	1.0
`<label> </label>`	Associates the enclosed content with a form field	4.0	1.0
datafld="text"	Indicates the column from a data source that supplies bound data for the label (IE only)		
dataformatas="html|plaintext|text"	Specifies the format of the data in the data source bound with the label (IE only)		
datasrc="*url*"	Provides the URL or ID of the data source bound with the label (IE only)		
for="text"	Provides the ID of the field associated with the label	4.0	1.0
`<layer> </layer>`	Creates a layer used to display the content of external documents; unlike the ilayer element, layer elements are absolutely positioned in the page (Netscape 4 only)		
above="*text*"	Specifies the name of the layer displayed above the current layer (Netscape 4 only)		
background="*url*"	Provides the URL of the file containing the background image (Netscape 4 only)		
below="*text*"	Specifies the name of the layer displayed below the current layer (Netscape 4 only)		
bgcolor="*color*"	Specifies the layer's background color (Netscape 4 only)		
clip="*top, left, bottom, right*"	Specifies the coordinates of the viewable region of the layer (Netscape 4 only)		
height="*integer*"	Specifies the height of the layer in pixels (Netscape 4 only)		
left="*integer*"	Specifies the horizontal offset of the layer in pixels (Netscape 4 only)		
pagex="*integer*"	Specifies the horizontal position of the layer in pixels (Netscape 4 only)		
pagey="*integer*"	Specifies the vertical position of the layer in pixels (Netscape 4 only)		
src="*url*"	Provides the URL of the document displayed in the layer (Netscape 4 only)		
top="*integer*"	Specifies the vertical offset of the layer in pixels (Netscape 4 only)		
visibility="hide|inherit|show"	Specifies the visibility of the layer (Netscape 4 only)		
width="*integer*"	Specifies the width of the layer in pixels (Netscape 4 only)		
z-index="*integer*"	Specifies the stacking order of the layer (Netscape 4 only)		
`<legend> </legend>`	Marks the enclosed text as a caption for a field set	4.0	1.0
align="bottom|left|top|right"	Specifies the alignment of the legend with the field set; Internet Explorer also supports the center option (deprecated)	4.0	1.0*

Element/Attribute	Description	HTML	XHTML
<li> </li>	Marks an item in an ordered (ol), unordered (ul), menu (menu), or directory (dir) list	2.0	1.0
type="A|a|I|i|1|disc|square|circle"	Specifies the bullet type associated with the list item: a value of "1" is the default for ordered list; a value of "disc" is the default for unordered list (deprecated)	3.2	1.0*
value="*integer*"	Sets the value for the current list item in an ordered list; subsequent list items are numbered from that value (deprecated)	3.2	1.0*
<link />	Creates an element in the document head that establishes the relationship between the current document and external documents or objects	2.0	1.0
charset="*char code*"	Specifies the character encoding of the external document	4.0	1.0
href="*url*"	Provides the URL of the external document	2.0	1.0
hreflang="text"	Indicates the language of the external document	4.0	1.0
media="all|aural|braille|handheld|print|projection|screen|tty|tv"	Indicates the media in which the external document is presented	4.0	1.0
name="*text*"	Specifies the name of the link		
rel="*text*"	Specifies the relationship between the current page and the link specified by the href attribute	2.0	
rev="*text*"	Specifies the reverse relationship between the current page and the link specified by the href attribute	2.0	1.0
target="*text*"	Specifies the target window or frame for the link	4.0	1.0*
title="*text*"	Specifies the title of the external document	2.0	1.0
type="*mime-type*"	Specifies the mime-type of the external document	4.0	1.0
<map> </map>	Creates an element that contains client-side image map hotspots	3.2	1.0
name="text"	Specifies the name of the image map	3.2	1.0*
<marquee> </marquee>	Displays the enclosed text as a scrolling marquee (not part of the W3C specifications, but supported by most browsers)		
behavior="alternate|scroll|slide"	Specifies how the marquee should move		
bgcolor="*color*"	Specifies the background color of the marquee		
datafld="*text*"	Indicates the column from a data source that supplies bound data for the marquee		
dataformatas="html|plaintext|text"	Indicates the format of the data in the data source bound with the marquee		
datasrc="*url*"	Provides the URL or ID of the data source bound with the marquee		
direction="down|left|right|up"	Specifies the direction of the marquee		
height="*integer*"	Specifies the height of the marquee in pixels		
hspace="*integer*"	Specifies the horizontal space around the marquee in pixels		
loop="*integer*|infinite"	Specifies the number of times the marquee motion is repeated		
scrollamount="*integer*"	Specifies the amount of space, in pixels, between successive draws of the marquee text		
scrolldelay="*integer*"	Specifies the amount of time, in milliseconds, between marquee actions		
truespeed="truespeed"	Indicates whether the scrolldelay value should be set to its exact value; otherwise any value less than 60 milliseconds is rounded up		

Element/Attribute	Description	HTML	XHTML
vspace="*integer*"	Specifies the vertical space around the marquee in pixels		
width="*integer*"	Specifies the width of the marquee in pixels		
<menu> </menu>	Contains a menu list (deprecated)	2.0	1.0*
compact="compact"	Reduces the space between menu items (deprecated)	2.0	1.0*
start="*integer*"	Specifies the starting value of the items in the menu list		
type="A|a|I|i |1|disc|square| circle|none"	Specifies the bullet type associated with the list items	3.2	1.0*
<meta> </meta>	Creates an element in the document's head section that contains information and special instructions for processing the document	2.0	1.0
content="*text*"	Provides information associated with the name or http-equiv attributes	2.0	1.0
http-equiv="*text*"	Provides instructions to the browser to request the server to perform different http operations	2.0	1.0
name="*text*"	Specifies the type of information specified in the content attribute	2.0	1.0
scheme="*text*"	Supplies additional information about the scheme used to interpret the content attribute	4.0	1.0
<nobr> </nobr>	Disables line wrapping for the enclosed content (not part of the W3C specifications, but supported by most browsers)		
<noembed> </noembed>	Encloses alternate content for browsers that do not support the embed element (not part of the W3C specifications, but supported by most browsers)		
<noframe> </noframe>	Encloses alternate content for browsers that do not support frames	4.0	1.0*
<nolayer> </nolayer>	Encloses alternate content for browsers that do not support the layer or ilayer elements (Netscape 4 only)		
<noscript> </noscript>	Encloses alternate content for browsers that do not support client-side scripts	4.0	1.0
<object> </object>	Places an embedded object (image, applet, sound clip, video clip, etc.) into the page	4.0	1.0
archive="url"	Specifies the URL of an archive containing classes and other resources preloaded for use with the object	4.0	1.0
align="absbottom| absmiddle|baseline |bottom|left| middle|right| texttop|top"	Aligns the object with the surrounding content (deprecated)	4.0	1.0*
border="*integer*"	Specifies the width of the border around the object (deprecated)	4.0	1.0*
classid="*url*"	Provides the URL of the object	4.0	1.0
codebase="*url*"	Specifies the base path used to resolve relative references within the embedded object	4.0	1.0
codetype="*mime-type*"	Indicates the mime-type of the embedded object's code	4.0	1.0
data="*url*"	Provides the URL of the object's data file	4.0	1.0
datafld="*text*"	Identifies the column from a data source that supplies bound data for the embedded object	4.0	
dataformatas="html| plaintext|text"	Specifies the format of the data in the data source bound with the embedded object	4.0	
datasrc="*url*"	Provides the URL or ID of the data source bound with the embedded object	4.0	

Element/Attribute	Description	HTML	XHTML
declare="declare"	Declares the object without embedding it on the page	4.0	1.0
height="*integer*"	Specifies the height of the object in pixels	4.0	1.0
hspace="*integer*"	Specifies the horizontal space around the image in pixels	4.0	1.0
name="*text*"	Specifies the name of the embedded object	4.0	1.0
standby="*text*"	Specifies the message displayed by the browser while loading the embedded object	4.0	1.0
type="*mime-type*"	Indicates the mime-type of the embedded object	4.0	1.0
vspace="*integer*"	Specifies the vertical space around the embedded object	4.0	1.0
width="*integer*"	Specifies the width of the object in pixels	4.0	1.0
<ol> </ol>	Contains an ordered list of items	2.0	1.0
compact="compact"	Reduces the space between ordered list items (deprecated)	2.0	1.0*
start="*integer*"	Specifies the starting value in the list (deprecated)	3.2	1.0
type="A|a|I|i|1"	Specifies the bullet type associated with the list items (deprecated)	3.2	1.0*
<optgroup> </optgroup>	Contains a group of option elements in a selection field	4.0	1.0
label="*text*"	Specifies the label for the option group	4.0	1.0
<option> </option>	Formats an option within a selection field	2.0	1.0
label="*text*"	Supplies the text label associated with the option	4.0	1.0
selected="selected"	Selects the option by default	2.0	1.0
value="*text*"	Specifies the value associated with the option	2.0	1.0
<p> </p>	Marks the enclosed content as a paragraph	2.0	1.0
align="**left**|center|right|justify"	Horizontally aligns the contents of the paragraph (deprecated)	3.0	1.0*
<param> </param>	Marks parameter values sent to an object element or an applet element	3.2	1.0
name="*text*"	Specifies the parameter name	3.2	1.0
type="*mime-type*"	Specifies the mime-type of the resource indicated by the value attribute	4.0	1.0
value="*text*"	Specifies the parameter value	3.2	1.0
valuetype="**data**|ref|object"	Specifies the data type of the value attribute	4.0	1.0
<plaintext> </plaintext>	Marks the enclosed text as plain text (not part of the W3C specifications, but supported by most browsers)		
<pre> </pre>	Marks the enclosed text as preformatted text, retaining white space from the document	2.0	1.0
width="*integer*"	Specifies the width of preformatted text, in number of characters (deprecated)	2.0	1.0*
<q> </q>	Marks the enclosed text as a quotation	3.0	1.0
cite="*url*"	Provides the source URL of the quoted content	4.0	1.0
<s> </s>	Marks the enclosed text as strikethrough text (deprecated)	3.0	1.0*
<samp> </samp>	Marks the enclosed text as a sequence of literal characters	2.0	1.0
<script> </script>	Encloses client-side scripts within the document; this element can be placed within the head or the body element or it can refer to an external script file	3.2	1.0
charset="*char code*"	Specifies the character encoding of the script	4.0	1.0
defer="defer"	Defers execution of the script	4.0	1.0
event="*text*"	Specifies the event that the script should be run in response to	4.0	

Element/Attribute	Description	HTML	XHTML
for="*text*"	Indicates the name or ID of the element to which the event attribute refers to	4.0	
language="*text*"	Specifies the language of the script (deprecated)	4.0	1.0*
src="*url*"	Provides the URL of an external script file	4.0	1.0
type="*mime-type*"	Specifies the mime-type of the script	4.0	1.0
<select> </select>	Creates a selection field (drop-down list box) in a Web form	2.0	1.0
align="left|right|top|texttop|middle|absmiddle|baseline|bottom|absbottom"	Specifies the alignment of the selection field with the surrounding content (deprecated)	3.0*	
datafld="*text*"	Identifies the column from a data source that supplies bound data for the selection field	4.0	
dataformatas="html|plaintext|text"	Specifies the format of the data in the data source bound with the selection field	4.0	
datasrc="*url*"	Provides the URL or ID of the data source bound with the selection field	4.0	
multiple="multiple"	Allows multiple sections from the field	2.0	1.0
name="*text*"	Specifies the selection field name	2.0	1.0
size="*integer*"	Specifies the number of visible items in the selection list	2.0	1.0
<small> </small>	Decreases the size of the enclosed text relative to the default font size	3.0	1.0
<span> </span>	Creates a generic inline element	3.0	1.0
datafld="*text*"	Identifies the column from a data source that supplies bound data for the inline element (IE only)		
dataformatas="html|plaintext|text"	Specifies the format of the data in the data source bound with the inline element (IE only)		
datasrc="*url*"	Provides the URL or ID of the data source bound with the inline element (IE only)		
<strike> </strike>	Marks the enclosed text as strikethrough text (deprecated)	3.0	1.0*
<strong> </strong>	Marks the enclosed text as strongly emphasized text	2.0	1.0
<style> </style>	Encloses global style declarations for the document	3.0	1.0
media="all|aural|braille|handheld|print|projection|screen|tty|tv|"	Indicates the media of the enclosed style definitions	4.0	1.0
title="*text*"	Specifies the style of the style definitions	4.0	1.0
type="mime-type"	Specifies the mime-type of the style definitions	4.0	1.0
****	Marks the enclosed text as subscript text	3.0	1.0
****	Marks the enclosed text as superscript text	3.0	1.0
<table> </table>	Encloses the contents of a Web table	3.0	1.0
align="left|center|right"	Aligns the table with the surrounding content (deprecated)	3.0	1.0*
background="*url*"	Provides the URL of the table's background image (not part of the W3C specifications, but supported by most browsers)		
bgcolor="*color*"	Specifies the background color of the table (deprecated)	4.0	1.0*
border="*integer*"	Specifies the width of the table border in pixels	3.0	1.0
bordercolor="*color*"	Specifies the table border color (IE and Netscape 4 only)		

Element/Attribute	Description	HTML	XHTML
bordercolordark="*color*"	Specifies the color of the table border's shaded edge (IE only)		
bordercolorlight="*color*"	Specifies the color of the table border's unshaded edge (IE only)		
cellpadding="*integer*"	Specifies the space between the table data and the cell borders in pixels	3.2	1.0
cellspacing="*integer*"	Specifies the space between table cells in pixels	3.2	1.0
cols="*integer*"	Specifies the number of columns in the table		
datafld="*text*"	Indicates the column from a data source that supplies bound data for the table	4.0	
dataformatas="html|plaintext|text"	Specifies the format of the data in the data source bound with the table	4.0	
datapagesize="*integer*"	Sets the number of records displayed within the table	4.0	1.1
datasrc="*url*"	Provides the URL or ID of the data source bound with the table	4.0	
frame="above|below|**border**|box|hsides|lhs|rhs|void|vside"	Specifies the format of the borders around the table	4.0	1.0
height="*integer*"	Specifies the height of the table in pixels (not part of the W3C specifications, but supported by most browsers)		
hspace="*integer*"	Specifies the horizontal space around the table in pixels (not part of the W3C specifications, but supported by most browsers)		
rules="**all**|cols|groups|none|rows"	Specifies the format of the table's internal borders or gridlines	4.0	1.0
summary="*text*"	Supplies a text summary of the table's content	4.0	1.0
vspace="*integer*"	Specifies the vertical space around the table in pixels		
width="*integer*"	Specifies the width of the table in pixels	3.0	1.0
<tbody> </tbody>	Encloses the content of the Web table body	4.0	1.0
align="left|center|right|justify|char"	Specifies the alignment of the contents in the cells of the table body	4.0	1.0
bgcolor="*color*"	Specifies the background color of the table body		
char="*char*"	Specifies the character used for aligning the table body contents when the align attribute is set to "char"	4.0	1.0
charoff="*integer*"	Specifies the offset in pixels from the alignment character specified in the char attribute	4.0	1.0
valign="baseline|bottom|middle|top"	Specifies the vertical alignment of the contents in the cells of the table body	4.0	1.0
<td> </td>	Encloses the data of a table cell	3.0	1.0
abbr="*text*"	Supplies an abbreviated version of the contents of the table cell	4.0	1.0
align="**left**|center|right"	Specifies the horizontal alignment of the table cell data	3.0	1.0
background="*url*"	Provides the URL of the background image file		
bgcolor="*color*"	Specifies the background color of the table cell (deprecated)	4.0	1.0*
bordercolor="*color*"	Specifies the color of the table cell border (IE only)		
bordercolordark="*color*"	Specifies the color of the table cell border's shaded edge (IE only)		

<table>
<tr><th>Element/Attribute</th><th>Description</th><th>HTML</th><th>XHTML</th></tr>
<tr><td>bordercolorlight="color"</td><td>Specifies the color of the table cell border's unshaded edge (IE only)</td><td></td><td></td></tr>
<tr><td>char="char"</td><td>Specifies the character used for aligning the table cell contents when the align attribute is set to "char"</td><td>4.0</td><td>1.0</td></tr>
<tr><td>charoff="integer"</td><td>Specifies the offset in pixels from the alignment character specified in the char attribute</td><td>4.0</td><td>1.0</td></tr>
<tr><td>colspan="integer"</td><td>Specifies the number of columns the table cell spans</td><td>3.0</td><td>1.0</td></tr>
<tr><td>headers="text"</td><td>Supplies a space-separated list of table headers associated with the table cell</td><td>4.0</td><td>1.0</td></tr>
<tr><td>height="integer"</td><td>Specifies the height of the table cell in pixels (deprecated)</td><td>3.2</td><td>1.0*</td></tr>
<tr><td>nowrap="nowrap"</td><td>Disables line-wrapping within the table cell (deprecated)</td><td>3.0</td><td>1.0*</td></tr>
<tr><td>rowspan="integer"</td><td>Specifies the number of rows the table cell spans</td><td>3.0</td><td>1.0</td></tr>
<tr><td>scope="col|colgroup|row|rowgroup"</td><td>Specifies the scope of the table for which the cell provides data</td><td>4.0</td><td>1.0</td></tr>
<tr><td>valign="top|middle|bottom"</td><td>Specifies the vertical alignment of the contents of the table cell</td><td>3.0</td><td>1.0</td></tr>
<tr><td>width="integer"</td><td>Specifies the width of the cell in pixels (deprecated)</td><td>3.2</td><td>1.0*</td></tr>
<tr><td><textarea> </textarea></td><td>Marks the enclosed text as a text area input box in a Web form</td><td>2.0</td><td>1.0</td></tr>
<tr><td>datafld="text"</td><td>Specifies the column from a data source that supplies bound data for the text area box</td><td>4.0</td><td></td></tr>
<tr><td>dataformatas="html|plaintext|text"</td><td>Specifies the format of the data in the data source bound with the text area box</td><td>4.0</td><td></td></tr>
<tr><td>datasrc="url"</td><td>Provides the URL or ID of the data source bound with the text area box</td><td>4.0</td><td></td></tr>
<tr><td>cols="integer"</td><td>Specifies the width of the text area box in characters</td><td>2.0</td><td>1.0</td></tr>
<tr><td>name="text"</td><td>Specifies the name of the text area box</td><td>2.0</td><td>1.0</td></tr>
<tr><td>readonly="readonly"</td><td>Specifies the value of the text area box, cannot be modified</td><td>4.0</td><td>1.0</td></tr>
<tr><td>rows="integer"</td><td>Specifies the number of visible rows in the text area box</td><td>2.0</td><td>1.0</td></tr>
<tr><td>wrap="off|soft|hard"</td><td>Specifies how text is wrapped within the text area box and how that text-wrapping information is sent to the server-side program; in earlier versions of Netscape Navigator, the default value is "off" (Netscape accepts the values "off," "virtual," and "physical.")</td><td></td><td></td></tr>
<tr><td><tfoot> </tfoot></td><td>Encloses the content of the Web table footer</td><td>4.0</td><td>1.0</td></tr>
<tr><td>align="left|center|right|justify|char"</td><td>Specifies the alignment of the contents in the cells of the table footer</td><td>4.0</td><td>1.0</td></tr>
<tr><td>bgcolor="color"</td><td>Specifies the background color of the table body (not part of the W3C specifications, but supported by many browsers)</td><td></td><td></td></tr>
<tr><td>char="char"</td><td>Specifies the character used for aligning the table footer contents when the align attribute is set to "char"</td><td>4.0</td><td>1.0</td></tr>
<tr><td>charoff="integer"</td><td>Specifies the offset in pixels from the alignment character specified in the char attribute</td><td>4.0</td><td>1.0</td></tr>
<tr><td>valign="baseline|bottom|middle|top"</td><td>Specifies the vertical alignment of the contents in the cells of the table footer</td><td>4.0</td><td>1.0</td></tr>
<tr><td><th> </th></td><td>Encloses the data of a table header cell</td><td>3.0</td><td>1.0</td></tr>
<tr><td>abbr="text"</td><td>Supplies an abbreviated version of the contents of the table cell</td><td>4.0</td><td>1.0</td></tr>
<tr><td>align="left|center|right"</td><td>Specifies the horizontal alignment of the table cell data</td><td>3.0</td><td>1.0</td></tr>
<tr><td>axis="text list"</td><td>Provides a list of table categories that can be mapped to a table hierarchy</td><td>3.0</td><td>1.0</td></tr>
</table>

Element/Attribute	Description	HTML	XHTML
background="*url*"	Provides the URL of the background image file (not part of the W3C specifications, but supported by many browsers)		
bgcolor="*color*"	Specifies the background color of the table cell (deprecated)	4.0	1.0*
bordercolor="*color*"	Specifies the color of the table cell border (IE only)		
bordercolordark="*color*"	Specifies the color of the table cell border's shaded edge (IE only)		
bordercolorlight= "*color*"	Specifies the color of the table cell border's unshaded edge (IE only)		
char="*char*"	Specifies the character used for aligning the table cell contents when the align attribute is set to "char"	4.0	1.0
charoff="*integer*"	Specifies the offset in pixels from the alignment character specified in the char attribute	4.0	1.0
colspan="*integer*"	Specifies the number of columns the table cell spans	3.0	1.0
headers="*text*"	A space-separated list of table headers associated with the table cell	4.0	1.0
height="*integer*"	Specifies the height of the table cell in pixels (deprecated)	3.2	1.0*
nowrap="nowrap"	Disables line-wrapping within the table cell (deprecated)	3.0	1.0*
rowspan="*integer*"	Specifies the number of rows the table cell spans	3.0	1.0
scope="col|colgroup|row|rowgroup"	Specifies the scope of the table for which the cell provides data	4.0	1.0
valign="top|**middle**|bottom"	Specifies the vertical alignment of the contents of the table cell	3.0	1.0
width="*integer*"	Specifies the width of the cell in pixels (deprecated)	3.2	1.0*
<thead> </thead>	Encloses the content of the Web table header	4.0	1.0
align="left|center|right|justify|char"	Specifies the alignment of the contents in the cells of the table header	4.0	1.0
bgcolor="*color*"	Specifies the background color of the table body		
char="*char*"	Specifies the character used for aligning the table header contents when the align attribute is set to "char"	4.0	1.0
charoff="*integer*"	Specifies the offset in pixels from the alignment character specified in the char attribute	4.0	1.0
valign="baseline|bottom|middle|top"	Specifies the vertical alignment of the contents in the cells of the table header	4.0	1.0
<title> </title>	Specifies the title of the document, placed in the head section of the document	2.0	1.0
<tr> </tr>	Encloses the content of a row within a Web table	3.0	1.0
align="left|center|right"	Specifies the horizontal alignment of the data in the row's cells	3.0	1.0
background="*url*"	Provides the URL of the background image file for the row		
bgcolor="*color*"	Specifies the background color of the row (deprecated)	4.0	1.0*
bordercolor="*color*"	Specifies the color of the table row border (IE only)		
bordercolordark="*color*"	Specifies the color of the table row border's shaded edge (IE only)		
bordercolorlight= "*color*"	Specifies the color of the table row border's unshaded edge (IE only)		
char="*char*"	Specifies the character used for aligning the table row contents when the align attribute is set to "char"	4.0	1.0
charoff="*integer*"	Specifies the offset in pixels from the alignment character specified in the char attribute	4.0	1.0

Element/Attribute	Description	HTML	XHTML
height="*integer*"	Specifies the height of the table row in pixels		
valign="baseline|bottom|*middle*|top"	Specifies the vertical alignment of the contents of the table row	3.0	1.0
<tt> </tt>	Marks the enclosed text as teletype or monospaced text	2.0	1.0
<u> </u>	Marks the enclosed text as underlined text (deprecated)	3.0	1.0*
<ul> </ul>	Contains an unordered list of items	2.0	1.0
compact="compact"	Reduces the space between unordered list items (deprecated)	2.0	1.0*
type="**disc**|square|circle"	Specifies the bullet type associated with the list items (deprecated)	3.2	1.0*
<var> </var>	Marks the enclosed text as containing a variable name	2.0	1.0
<wbr />	Forces a line-break in the rendered page (not part of the W3C specifications, but supported by many browsers)		
<xml> </xml>	Encloses XML content (also referred to as a "data island") or references an external XML document (IE only)		
ns="*url*"	Provides the URL of the XML data island (IE only)		
prefix="*text*"	Specifies the namespace prefix of the XML content (IE only)		
src="*url*"	Provides the URL of an external XML document (IE only)		
<xmp> </xmp>	Marks the enclosed text as preformatted text, preserving the white space of the source document; replaced by the pre element (deprecated)	2.0	

Cascading Style Sheets

Appendix F

This appendix describes the selectors, units, and attributes supported by Cascading Style Sheets (CSS). Version numbers indicate the lowest version that supports the given selector, unit, or attribute. This appendix focuses on CSS1 and CSS2 styles. It does not include all of the CSS3 styles due to the state of CSS3's development and current level of browser support for CSS3. You should always check your code against different browsers and browser versions to ensure that your page is being rendered correctly. Additional information about CSS can be found at the World Wide Web Consortium Web site at *www.w3.org*.

Starting Data Files

There are no starting Data Files needed for this appendix.

Selectors

The general form of a style declaration is:

selector {*attribute1*:*value1*; *attribute2*:*value2*; ...}

where *selector* is the selection of elements within the document to which the style will be applied; *attribute1*, *attribute2*, etc. are the different style attributes; and *value1*, *value2*, etc. are values associated with those styles. The following table shows some of the different forms that a selector can take.

Selector	Matches	CSS
`*`	All elements in the document	2.0
e	An element, *e*, in the document	1.0
e1, *e2*, *e3*, ...	A group of elements, *e1*, *e2*, *e3*, in the document	1.0
e1 e2	An element *e2* nested within the parent element, *e1*	1.0
e1 > *e2*	An element *e2* that is a child of the parent element, *e1*	2.0
e1+*e2*	An element, *e2*, that is adjacent to element *e1*	2.0
e1.*class*	An element, *e1*, belonging to the *class* class	1.0
.*class*	Any element belonging to the *class* class	1.0
#*id*	An element with the id value *id*	1.0
[*att*]	The element contains the *att* attribute	2.0
[*att*="*val*"]	The element's *att* attribute equals "*val*"	2.0
[*att*~="*val*"]	The element's *att* attribute value is a space-separated list of "words," one of which is exactly "*val*"	2.0
[*att*|="*val*"]	The element's *att* attribute value is a hyphen-separated list of "words" beginning with "val"	3.0
[*att*^="*val*"]	The element's *att* attribute begins with "*val*"	3.0
[*att*$="*val*"]	The element's *att* attribute ends with "*val*"	3.0
[*att**="*val*"]	The element's *att* attribute contains the value "*val*"	3.0
[*ns*|*att*]	References all *att* attributes in the *ns* namespace	3.0

Pseudo-Elements and Pseudo-Classes

Pseudo-elements are elements that do not exist in HTML code but whose attributes can be set with CSS. Many pseudo-elements were introduced in CSS2.

Pseudo-Element	Matches	CSS
e:after {content: "*text*"}	Text content, *text*, that is inserted at the end of an element, *e*	2.0
e:before {content: "*text*"}	Text content, *text*, that is inserted at the beginning of an element, *e*	2.0
e:first-letter	The first letter in the element, *e*	1.0
e:first-line	The first line in the element, *e*	1.0

Pseudo-classes are classes of HTML elements that define the condition or state of the element in the Web page. Many pseudo-classes were introduced in CSS2.

Pseudo-Class	Matches	CSS
`:canvas`	The rendering canvas of the document	
`:first`	The first printed page of the document (used only with print styles created with the @print rule)	2.0
`:last`	The last printed page of the document (used only with print styles created with the @print rule)	2.0
`:left`	The left side of a two-sided printout (used only with print styles created with the @print rule)	2.0
`:right`	The right side of a two-sided printout (used only with print styles created with the @print rule)	2.0
`:root`	The root element of the document (the html element in HTML and XHTML documents)	
`:scrolled-content`	The content that is scrolled in the rendering viewport (Netscape only)	
`:viewport`	The rendering viewport of the document (Netscape only)	
`:viewport-scroll`	The rendering viewport of the document plus the scroll bar region (Netscape only)	
`e:active`	The element, *e*, is being activated by the user (usually applies only to hyperlinks)	1.0
`e:empty`	The element, *e*, has no content (Netscape only)	
`e:first-child`	The element, *e*, which is the first child of its parent element	2.0
`e:first-node`	The first occurrence of the element, *e*, in the document tree	
`e:focus`	The element, *e*, has received the focus of the cursor (usually applies only to Web form elements)	2.0
`e:hover`	The mouse pointer is hovering over the element, *e* (usually applies only to hyperlinks)	2.0
`e:lang(text)`	Sets the language, *text*, associated with the element, *e*	2.0
`e:last-child`	The element, *e*, that is the last child of its parent element	2.0
`e:last-node`	The last occurrence of the element, *e*, in the document tree (Netscape only)	
`e:link`	The element, *e*, has not been visited yet by the user (applies only to hyperlinks)	1.0
`e:not`	Negate the selector rule for the element, *e*, applying the style to all *e* elements that do not match the selector rules (Netscape only)	
`e:visited`	The element, *e*, has been already visited by the user (to only the hyperlinks)	1.0

@ Rules

CSS supports different "@ rules" designed to run commands within a style sheet. These commands can be used to import other styles, download font definitions, or define the format of printed output.

@ Rule	Description	CSS
`@charset "encoding"`	Defines the character set encoding used in the style sheet (this must be the very first line in the style sheet document)	2.0
`@import url(url) media`	Imports an external style sheet document into the current style sheet, where *url* is the location of the external style sheet and *media* is a comma-separated list of media types (optional)	1.0
`@media media {style declaration}`	Defines the media for the styles in the *style declaration* block, where *media* is a comma-separated list of media types	2.0
`@namespace prefix url(url)`	Defines the namespace used by selectors in the style sheet, where *prefix* is the local namespace prefix (optional) and *url* is the unique namespace identifier; the @namespace rule must come before all CSS selectors (Netscape only)	
`@page label pseudo-class {styles}`	Defines the properties of a printed page, where *label* is a label given to the page (optional), *pseudo-class* is one of the CSS pseudo-classes designed for printed pages, and *styles* are the styles associated with the page	2.0

Miscellaneous Syntax

The following syntax elements do not fit into the previous categories but are useful in constructing CSS style sheets.

Item	Description	CSS
`style !important`	Places high importance on the preceding *style*, overriding the usual rules for inheritance and cascading	1.0
`/* comment */`	Attaches a *comment* to the style sheet	1.0

Units

Many style attribute values use units of measurement to indicate color, length, angles, time, and frequencies. The following table describes the measuring units used in CSS.

Units	Description	CSS
Color	**Units of color**	
name	A color name; all browsers recognize 16 base color names: aqua, black, blue, fuchsia, gray, green, lime, maroon, navy, olive, purple, red, silver, teal, white, and yellow	1.0
#*rrggbb*	The hexadecimal color value, where *rr* is the red value, *gg* is the green value, and *bb* is the blue value	1.0
#*rgb*	A compressed hexadecimal value, where the *r*, *g*, and *b* values are doubled so that, for example, #A2F = #AA22FF	1.0
rgb(*red*, *green*, *blue*)	The decimal color value, where *red* is the red value, *green* is the green value, and *blue* is the blue value	1.0
rgb(*red*%, *green*%, *blue*%)	The color value percentage, where *red*% is the percent of maximum red, *green*% is the percent of maximum green, and *blue*% is the percent of maximum blue	1.0
Length	**Units of length**	
auto	Keyword which allows the browser to automatically determine the size of the length	1.0
em	A relative unit indicating the width and the height of the capital "M" character for the browser's default font	1.0
ex	A relative unit indicating the height of the small "x" character for the browser's default font	1.0
px	A pixel, representing the smallest unit of length on the output device	1.0
in	An inch	1.0
cm	A centimeter	1.0
mm	A millimeter	1.0
pt	A point, approximately 1/72 inch	1.0
pc	A pica, approximately 1/12 inch	1.0
%	A percent of the width or height of the parent element	1.0
xx-small	Keyword representing an extremely small font size	1.0
x-small	Keyword representing a very small font size	1.0
small	Keyword representing a small font size	1.0
medium	Keyword representing a medium-sized font	1.0
large	Keyword representing a large font	1.0
x-large	Keyword representing a very large font	1.0
xx-large	Keyword representing an extremely large font	1.0
Angle	**Units of angles**	
deg	The angle in degrees	2.0
grad	The angle in gradients	2.0
rad	The angle in radians	2.0

Units	Description	CSS
Time	**Units of time**	
ms	Time in milliseconds	2.0
s	Time in seconds	2.0
Frequency	**Units of frequency**	
hz	The frequency in hertz	2.0
khz	The frequency in kilohertz	2.0

Attributes and Values

The following table describes the attributes and values for different types of elements. The attributes are grouped into categories to help you locate the features relevant to your particular design task.

Attribute	Description	CSS
Aural	**Styles for Aural Browsers**	
azimuth: *location*	Defines the location of the sound, where *location* is left-side, far-left, left, center-left, center, center-right, right, far-right, right-side, leftward, rightward, or an angle value	2.0
cue: url(*url1*) url(*url2*)	Adds a sound to an element: if a single value is present, the sound is played before and after the element; if two values are present, the first is played before and the second is played after	2.0
cue-after: url(*url*)	Specifies a sound to be played immediately after an element	2.0
cue-before: url(*url*)	Specifies a sound to be played immediately before an element	2.0
elevation: *location*	Defines the vertical location of the sound, where *location* is below, level, above, lower, higher, or an angle value	2.0
pause: *time1 time2*	Adds a pause to an element: if a single value is present, the pause occurs before and after the element; if two values are present, the first pause occurs before and the second occurs after	2.0
pause-after: *time*	Adds a pause after an element	2.0
pause-before: *time*	Adds a pause before an element	2.0
pitch: *value*	Defines the pitch of a speaking voice, where *value* is x-low, low, medium, high, x-high, or a frequency value	2.0
pitch-range: *value*	Defines the pitch range for a speaking voice, where *value* ranges from 0 to 100; a low pitch range results in a monotone voice, whereas a high pitch range sounds very animated	2.0
play-during: url(*url*) mix repeat *type*	Defines a sound to be played behind an element, where *url* is the URL of the sound file; mix overlays the sound file with the sound of the parent element; repeat causes the sound to be repeated, filling up the available time; and *type* is auto to play the sound only once, none to play nothing but the sound file, or inherit	2.0
richness: *value*	Specifies the richness of the speaking voice, where *value* ranges from 0 to 100; a low value indicates a softer voice, whereas a high value indicates a brighter voice	2.0
speak: *type*	Defines how element content is to be spoken, where *type* is normal (for normal punctuation rules), spell-out (to pronounce one character at a time), none (to suppress the aural rendering), or inherit	2.0

Attribute	Description	CSS
`speak-numeral:` *`type`*	Defines how numeric content should be spoken, where *type* is digits (to pronounce one digit at a time), continuous (to pronounce the full number), or inherit	2.0
`speak-punctuation:` *`type`*	Defines how punctuation characters are spoken, where *type* is code (to speak the punctuation literally), none (to not speak the punctuation), or inherit	2.0
`speech-rate:` *`value`*	Defines the rate of speech, where *value* is x-slow, slow, medium, fast, x-fast, slower, faster, or a value in words per minute	2.0
`stress:` *`value`*	Defines the maximum pitch, where *value* ranges from 0 to 100; a value of 50 is normal stress for a speaking voice	2.0
`voice-family:` *`text`*	Defines the name of the speaking voice, where *text* is male, female, child, or a text string indicating a specific speaking voice	2.0
`volume:` *`value`*	Defines the volume of a voice, where *value* is silent, x-soft, soft, medium, loud, x-loud, or a number from 0 (lowest) to 100 (highest)	2.0
Backgrounds	**Styles applied to an element's background**	
`background:` *`color`* `url(`*`url`*`)` *`repeat attachment position`*	Defines the background of the element, where *color* is a CSS color name or value, *url* is the location of an image file, *repeat* defines how the background image should be repeated, *attachment* defines how the background image should be attached, and *position* defines the position of the background image	1.0
`background-attachment:` *`type`*	Specifies how the background image is attached, where *type* is inherit, scroll (move the image with the page content), or fixed (fix the image and not scroll)	1.0
`background-color:` *`color`*	Defines the color of the background, where *color* is a CSS color name or value; the keyword "inherit" can be used to inherit the background color of the parent element, or "transparent" can be used to allow the parent element background image to show through	1.0
`background-image: url(`*`url`*`)`	Specifies the image file used for the element's background, where *url* is the URL of the image file	1.0
`background-position:` *`x y`*	Sets the position of a background image, where *x* is the horizontal location in pixels, as a percentage of the width of the parent element, or the keyword "left", "center", or "right", *y* is the vertical location in pixels, as a percentage of the height and of the parent element, or the keyword, "top", "center", or "bottom"	1.0
`background-repeat:` *`type`*	Defines the method for repeating the background image, where *type* is no-repeat, repeat (to tile the image in both directions), repeat-x (to tile the image in the horizontal direction only), or repeat-y (to tile the image in the vertical direction only)	1.0
Block-Level Styles	**Styles applied to block-level elements**	
`border:` *`length style color`*	Defines the border style of the element, where *length* is the border width, *style* is the border design, and *color* is the border color	1.0
`border-bottom:` *`length style color`*	Defines the border style of the bottom edge of the element	1.0
`border-left:` *`length style color`*	Defines the border style of the left edge of the element	1.0
`border-right:` *`length style color`*	Defines the border style of the right edge of the element	1.0
`border-top:` *`length style color`*	Defines the border style of the top edge of the element	1.0

Attribute	Description	CSS
`border-color:` *color*	Defines the color applied to the element's border using a CSS color unit	1.0
`border-bottom-color:` *color*	Defines the color applied to the bottom edge of the element	1.0
`border-left-color:` *color*	Defines the color applied to the left edge of the element	1.0
`border-right-color:` *color*	Defines the color applied to the right edge of the element	1.0
`border-top-color:` *color*	Defines the color applied to the top edge of the element	1.0
`border-style:` *style*	Specifies the design of the element's border (dashed, dotted, double, groove, inset, none, outset, ridge, or solid)	1.0
`border-style-bottom:` *style*	Specifies the design of the element's bottom edge	1.0
`border-style-left:` *style*	Specifies the design of the element's left edge	1.0
`border-style-right:` *style*	Specifies the design of the element's right edge	1.0
`border-style-top:` *style*	Specifies the design of the element's top edge	1.0
`border-width:` *length*	Defines the width of the element's border, in a unit of measure or using the keyword "thick", "medium", or "thin"	1.0
`border-width-bottom:` *length*	Defines the width of the element's bottom edge	1.0
`border-width-left:` *length*	Defines the width of the element's left edge	1.0
`border-width-right:` *length*	Defines the width of the element's right edge	1.0
`border-width-top:` *length*	Defines the width of the element's top edge	1.0
`margin:` *top right bottom left*	Defines the size of the margins around the top, right, bottom, and left edges of the element, in one of the CSS units of length	1.0
`margin-bottom:` *length*	Defines the size of the element's bottom margin	1.0
`margin-left:` *length*	Defines the size of the element's left margin	1.0
`margin-right:` *length*	Defines the size of the element's right margin	1.0
`margin-top:` *length*	Defines the size of the element's top margin	1.0
`padding:` *top right bottom left*	Defines the size of the padding space within the top, right, bottom, and left edges of the element, in one of the CSS units of length	1.0
`padding-bottom:` *length*	Defines the size of the element's bottom padding	1.0
`padding-left:` *length*	Defines the size of the element's left padding	1.0
`padding-right:` *length*	Defines the size of the element's right padding	1.0
`padding-top:` *length*	Defines the size of the element's top padding	1.0

Attribute	Description	CSS
Content	**Styles to attach additional content to elements**	
`content: text`	Generates a text string to attach to the content of the element	2.0
`content: attr(attr)`	Returns the value of the *attr* attribute from the element	2.0
`content: close-quote`	Attaches a close quote using the characters specified in the quotes style	2.0
`content: counter(text)`	Generates a counter using the text string *text* attached to the content (most often used with list items)	2.0
`content: counters(text)`	Generates a string of counters using the comma-separated text string *text* attached to the content (most often used with list items)	2.0
`content: no-close-quote`	Prevents the attachment of a close quote to an element	2.0
`content: no-open-quote`	Prevents the attachment of an open quote to an element	2.0
`content: open-quote`	Attaches an open quote using the characters specified in the quotes style	2.0
`content: url(url)`	Attaches the content of an external file indicated in the *url* to the element	2.0
`counter-increment: id integer`	Defines the element to be automatically incremented and the amount by which it is to be incremented, where *id* is an identifier of the element and *integer* defines by how much	2.0
`counter-reset: id integer`	Defines the element whose counter is to be reset and the amount by which it is to be reset, where *id* is an identifier of the element and *integer* defines by how much	2.0
`quotes: text1 text2`	Defines the text strings for the open quotes (*text1*) and the close quotes (*text2*)	2.0
Display Styles	**Styles that control the display of the element's content**	
`clip: rect(top, right, bottom, left)`	Defines what portion of the content is displayed, where *top*, *right*, *bottom*, and *left* are distances of the top, right, bottom, and left edges from the element's top-left corner; use a value of auto to allow the browser to determine the clipping region	2.0
`display: type`	Specifies the display type of the element, where *type* is one of the following: block, inline, inline-block, inherit, list-item, none, run-in, table, inline-table, table-caption, table-column, table-cell, table-column-group, table-header-group, table-footer-group, table-row, or table-row-group	1.0

Attribute	Description	CSS
`height:` *length*	Specifies the height of the element in one of the CSS units of length	1.0
`min-height:` *length*	Specifies the minimum height of the element	2.0
`min-width:` *length*	Specifies the minimum width of the element	2.0
`max-height:` *length*	Specifies the maximum height of the element	2.0
`max-width:` *length*	Specifies the maximum width of the element	2.0
`overflow:` *type*	Instructs the browser how to handle content that overflows the dimensions of the element, where *type* is auto, inherit, visible, hidden, or scroll	2.0
`overflow-x:` *type*	Instructs the browser how to handle content that overflows the element's width, where *type* is auto, inherit, visible, hidden, or scroll (IE only)	
`overflow-y:` *type*	Instructs the browser on how to handle content that overflows the element's height, where *type* is auto, inherit, visible, hidden, or scroll (IE only)	
`text-overflow:` *type*	Instructs the browser on how to handle text overflow, where *type* is clip (to hide the overflow text) or ellipsis (to display the ... text string) (IE only)	
`visibility:` *type*	Defines the element's visibility, where *type* is hidden, visible, or inherit	2.0
`width:` *length*	Specifies the width of the element in one of the CSS units of length	1.0
Fonts and Text	**Styles that format the appearance of fonts and text**	
`color:` *color*	Specifies the color of the element's foreground (usually the font color)	1.0
`font:` *style variant weight size/line-height family*	Defines the appearance of the font, where *style* is the font's style, *variant* is the font variant, *weight* is the weight of the font, *size* is the size of the font, *line-height* is the height of the lines, and *family* is the font face; the only required attributes are *size* and *family*	1.0
`font-family:` *family*	Specifies the font face used to display text, where *family* is sans-serif, serif, fantasy, monospace, cursive, or the name of an installed font	1.0
`font-size:` *value*	Specifies the size of the font in one of the CSS units of length	1.0
`font-size-adjust:` *value*	Specifies the aspect *value* (which is the ratio of the font size to the font's ex unit height)	2.0
`font-stretch:` *type*	Expands or contracts the font, where *type* is narrower, wider, ultra-condensed, extra-condensed, condensed, semi-condensed, normal, semi-expanded, extra-expanded, or ultra-expanded	2.0
`font-style:` *type*	Specifies a style applied to the font, where *type* is normal, italic, or oblique	1.0
`font-variant:` *type*	Specifies a variant of the font, where *type* is inherit, normal, or small-caps	1.0
`font-weight:` *value*	Defines the weight of the font, where *value* is 100, 200, 300, 400, 500, 600, 700, 800, 900, normal, lighter, bolder, or bold	1.0
`letter-spacing:` *value*	Specifies the space between letters, where *value* is a unit of length or the keyword "normal"	1.0
`line-height:` *value*	Specifies the height of the lines, where *value* is a unit of length or the keyword, "normal"	1.0

Attribute	Description	CSS
`text-align:` *type*	Specifies the horizontal alignment of text within the element, where *type* is inherit, left, right, center, or justify	1.0
`text-decoration:` *type*	Specifies the decoration applied to the text, where *type* is blink, line-through, none, overline, or underline	1.0
`text-indent:` *length*	Specifies the amount of indentation in the first line of the text, where *length* is a CSS unit of length	1.0
`text-shadow:` *color x y blur*	Applies a shadow effect to the text, where *color* is the color of the shadow, *x* is the horizontal offset in pixels, *y* is the vertical offset in pixels, and *blur* is the size of the blur radius (optional); multiple shadows can be added with shadow effects separated by commas	2.0
`text-transform:` *type*	Defines a transformation applied to the text, where *type* is capitalize, lowercase, none, or uppercase	1.0
`vertical-align:` *type*	Specifies how to vertically align the text with the surrounding content, where *type* is baseline, middle, top, bottom, text-top, text-bottom, super, sub, or one of the CSS units of length	1.0
`white-space:` *type*	Specifies the handling of white space (blank spaces, tabs, and new lines), where *type* is inherit, normal, pre (to treat the text as preformatted text), or nowrap (to prevent line-wrapping)	1.0
`word-spacing:` *length*	Specifies the amount of space between words in the text, where *length* is either a CSS unit of length or the keyword "normal" to use normal word spacing	1.0
Layout	**Styles that define the layout of elements**	
`bottom:` *y*	Defines the vertical offset of the element's bottom edge, where *y* is either a CSS unit of length or the keyword "auto" or "inherit"	2.0
`clear:` *type*	Places the element only after the specified margin is clear of floating elements, where *type* is inherit, none, left, right, or both	1.0
`float:` *type*	Floats the element on the specified margin with subsequent content wrapping around the element, where *type* is inherit, none, left, right, or both	1.0
`left:` *x*	Defines the horizontal offset of the element's left edge, where *x* is either a CSS unit of length or the keyword "auto" or "inherit"	2.0
`position:` *type*	Defines how the element is positioned on the page, where *type* is absolute, relative, fixed, static, and inherit	1.0
`right:` *x*	Defines the horizontal offset of the element's right edge, where *x* is either a CSS unit of length or the keyword "auto" or "inherit"	2.0
`top:` *y*	Defines the vertical offset of the element's top edge, where *y* is a CSS unit of length or the keyword "auto" or "inherit"	2.0
`z-index:` *value*	Defines how overlapping elements are stacked, where *value* is either the stacking number (elements with higher stacking numbers are placed on top) or the keyword "auto" to allow the browser to determine the stacking order	2.0
Lists	**Styles that format lists**	
`list-style:` *type image position*	Defines the appearance of a list item, where *type* is the marker type, *image* is the URL of the location of an image file used for the marker, and *position* is the position of the marker	1.0
`list-style-image: url(`*url*`)`	Defines image used for the list marker, where *url* is the location of the image file	1.0

Attribute	Description	CSS
`list-style-type: type`	Defines the marker type used in the list, where *type* is disc, circle, square, decimal, decimal-leading-zero, lower-roman, upper-roman, lower-alpha, upper-alpha, or none	1.0
`list-style-position: type`	Defines the location of the list marker, where *type* is inside or outside	1.0
`marker-offset: length`	Defines the distance between the marker and the enclosing list box, where *length* is either a CSS unit of length or the keyword "auto" or "inherit"	2.0
Outlines	**Styles to create and format outlines**	
`outline: color style width`	Creates an outline around the element content, where *color* is the color of the outline, *style* is the outline style, and *width* is the width of the outline	2.0
`outline-color: color`	Defines the color of the outline	2.0
`outline-style: type`	Defines the style of the outline, where *type* is dashed, dotted, double, groove, inset, none, outset, ridge, solid, or inherit	2.0
`outline-width: length`	Defines the width of the outline, where *length* is expressed in a CSS unit of length	2.0
Printing	**Styles for printed output**	
`page: label`	Specifies the page design to apply, where *label* is a page design created with the @page rule	2.0
`page-break-after: type`	Defines how to control page breaks after the element, where *type* is avoid (to avoid page breaks), left (to insert a page break until a left page is displayed), right (to insert a page break until a right page is displayed), always (to always insert a page break), auto, or inherit	2.0
`page-break-before: type`	Defines how to control page breaks before the element, where *type* is avoid left, always, auto, or inherit	2.0
`page-break-inside: type`	Defines how to control page breaks within the element, where *type* is avoid, auto, or inherit	2.0
`marks: type`	Defines how to display crop marks, where *type* is crop, cross, none, or inherit	2.0
`size: width height orientation`	Defines the size of the page, where *width* and *height* are the width and the height of the page and *orientation* is the orientation of the page (portrait or landscape)	2.0
`orphans: value`	Defines how to handle orphaned text, where *value* is the number of lines that must appear within the element before a page break is inserted	2.0
`widows: value`	Defines how to handle widowed text, where *value* is the number of lines that must appear within the element after a page break is inserted	2.0
Scrollbars and Cursors	**Styles to format the appearance of scrollbars and cursors**	
`cursor: type`	Defines the cursor image used, where *type* is n-resize, ne-resize, e-resize, se-resize, s-resize, sw-resize, w-resize, nw-resize, crosshair, pointer, move, text, wait, help, auto, default, inherit, or a URL pointing to an image file; individual browsers also support dozens of other cursor types	2.0
`scrollbar-3dlight-color: color`	Defines the *color* of the outer top and left edge of the slider (IE only)	
`scrollbar-arrow-color: color`	Defines the *color* of the scroll bar directional arrows (IE only)	

Attribute	Description	CSS
`scrollbar-base-color:` *`color`*	Defines the *color* of the scroll bar button face, arrow, slider, and slider tray (IE only)	
`scrollbar-darkshadow-color:` *`color`*	Defines the *color* of the outer bottom and right edges of the slider (IE only)	
`scrollbar-face-color:` *`color`*	Defines the *color* of the button face of the scroll bar arrow and slider (IE only)	
`scrollbar-highlight-color:` *`color`*	Defines the *color* of the inner top and left edges of the slider (IE only)	
`scrollbar-shadow-color:` *`color`*	Defines the *color* of the inner bottom and right edges of the slider (IE only)	
Special Effects	**Styles to create special visual effects**	
`filter:` *`type parameters`*	Applies transition and filter effects to elements, where *type* is the type of filter and *parameters* are parameter values specific to the filter (IE only)	
Tables	**Styles to format the appearance of tables**	
`border-collapse:` *`type`*	Determines whether table cell borders are separate or collapsed into a single border, where *type* is separate, collapse, or inherit	2.0
`border-spacing:` *`length`*	If separate borders are used for table cells, defines the distance between borders, where *length* is a CSS unit of length or inherit	2.0
`caption-side:` *`type`*	Defines the position of the caption element, where *type* is bottom, left, right, top, or inherit	2.0
`empty-cells:` *`type`*	If separate borders are used for table cells, defines whether to display borders for empty cells, where *type* is hide, show, or inherit	2.0
`speak-header:` *`type`*	Defines how table headers are spoken in relation to the data cells, where *type* is always, once, or inherit	2.0
`table-layout:` *`type`*	Defines the algorithm used for the table layout, where *type* is auto (to define the layout once all table cells have been read), fixed (to define the layout after the first table row has been read), or inherit	2.0

JavaScript Objects, Properties, Methods, and Event Handlers

Appendix G

This appendix defines some of the important JavaScript objects, properties, methods, and event handlers. The JavaScript object is listed first, followed by any properties, methods, and event handlers associated with it.

Where a particular object, property, method, or event handler is supported only in a specific browser, this fact is noted in the table.

As always, you should test your code against a variety of browsers to ensure support.

JavaScript Elements	Description
`Anchor`	`An anchor in the document (use the anchor name)`
Properties	
accessKey	The hotkey that gives the element focus
charset	The character set of the linked document
coords	The coordinates of the object, used with the shape attribute
hreflang	The language code of the linked resource
name	The name of the anchor
nameProp	The string holding the filename portion of the URL in the href
shape	The string defining the shape of the object
tabIndex	The numeric value that indicates the tab order for the object
text	The anchor text
type	Specifies the media type in the form of a MIME type for the link target
Methods	
blur( )	Removes focus from the element
handleEvent (*event*)	Causes the Event instance *event* to be processed
focus( )	Gives the element focus
`Applet`	`A Java applet in the document`
Properties	
align	Specifies alignment, for example, "left
alt	Specifies alternative text for the applet
altHTML	Specifies alternative text for the applet
archive	A list of URLs
code	The URL for the applet class file
codeBase	The base URL for the applet
height	The height of the object in pixels
hspace	The horizontal margin to the left and the right of the applet
name	The name of the applet
object	The name of the resource that contains a serialized representation of the applet
vspace	The vertical margin above and below the applet
width	The width of the object in pixels
`Area`	`An area defined in an image map`
Properties	
accessKey	The hotkey that gives the element focus
alt	Alternative text to the graphic
cords	Defines the coordinates of the object
hash	The anchor name from the URL
host	The host and domain names from the URL
hostname	The hostname from the URL
href	The entire URL
pathname	The pathname from the URL

JavaScript Elements	Description
port	The port number from the URL
protocol	The protocol from the URL
search	The query portion from the URL
shape	The shape of the object, for example, "default", "rect", "circle", or "poly"
tabIndex	Numeric value that indicates the tab order for the object
target	The target attribute of the <area> tag
Methods	
getSelection()	Returns the value of the current selection3.0
Event Handlers	
onDblClick()	Runs when the area is double-clicked
onMouseOut()	Runs when the mouse leaves the area
onMouseOver()	Runs when the mouse enters the area
`Array`	`An array object`
Properties	
index	For an array created by a regular expression match, the zero-based index of the match in the string
input	Reflects the original string against which the regular expression was matched
length	The next empty index at the end of the array
prototype	A mechanism to add properties to an array object
Methods	
concat(*array*)	Combines two arrays and stores the result in a third array named *array*
join(*string*)	Stores each element in a text string named *string*
pop( )	"Pops" the last element of the array and reduces the length of the array by 1
push(*arg1, arg2, ...*)	"Pushes" the elements in the list to the end of the array and returns the new length
reverse( )	Reverses the order of the elements in the array
shift( )	Removes the first element from an array, returns that element, and shifts all other elements down one index
slice(*array, begin,end*)	Extracts a portion of the array, starting at the index number *begin* and ending at the index number *end*; the elements are then stored in *array*
sort(*function*)	Sorts the array based on the function named *function*; if *function* is omitted, the sort applies dictionary order to the array
splice(*start,howMany, [,item1[,item2 [,...]]]*)	Removes *howMany* elements from the array, beginning at index *start* and replaces the removed elements with the *itemN* arguments (if passed); returns an array of the deleted elements
toString( )	Returns a string of the comma-separated values of the array
unshift([Item1 [,item2[,...]]])	Inserts the items to the front of an array and returns the new length of the array
`Button`	`A push button in an HTML form (use the button's name)`
Properties	
accessKey	Indicates the hotkey that gives the element focus
align	Specifies the alignment of the element, for example, "right"
disabled	A Boolean indicating whether the element is disabled

JavaScript Elements	Description
enabled	Indicates whether the button has been enabled
form	The name of the form containing the button
name	The name of the button element
size	Indicates the width of the button in pixels
tabIndex	Indicates the tab order for the object
type	The value of the type attribute for the <button> tag
value	The value of the button element
Methods	
blur()	Removes focus from the button
click()	Emulates the action of clicking the button
focus()	Gives focus to the button
Event Handlers	
onBlur	Runs when the button loses the focus
onClick	Runs when the button is clicked
onFocus	Runs when the button receives the focus
onMouseDown	Runs when the mouse button is pressed
onMouseUp	Runs when the mouse button is released
Checkbox	A check box in an HTML form
Properties	
accessKey	Indicates the hotkey that gives the element focus
align	Specifies the alignment of the element, for example, "right"
checked	Indicates whether the check box is checked
defaultChecked	Indicates whether the check box is checked by default
disabled	Boolean indicating whether the element is disabled
enabled	Indicates whether the check box is enabled
form	The name of the form containing the check box
name	The name of the check box element
size	Indicates the width of the check box in pixels0
status	Boolean indicating whether the check box is currently selected
tabIndex	Indicates the tab order for the object
type	The value of the type attribute for the <input> tag
value	The value of the check box element
Methods	
blur()	Removes the focus from the check box
click()	Emulates the action of clicking on the check box
focus()	Gives focus to the check box
Event Handlers	
onBlur	Runs when the check box loses the focus
onClick	Runs when the check box is clicked
onFocus	Runs when the check box receives the focus

JavaScript Elements	Description
`Date`	`An object containing information about a specific date or the current date; dates are expressed either in local time or in UTC (Universal Time Coordinates), otherwise known as Greenwich Mean Time`
Methods	
getDate()	Returns the day of the month, from 1 to 31
getDay()	Returns the day of the week, from 0 to 6 (Sunday = 0, Monday = 1, etc.)
getFullYear()	Returns the year portion of the date in four-digit format
getHours()	Returns the hour in military time, from 0 to 23
getMilliseconds()	Returns the number of milliseconds
getMinutes()	Returns the minute, from 0 to 59
getMonth()	Returns the value of the month, from 0 to 11 (January = 0, February = 1, etc.)
getSeconds()	Returns the seconds
getTime()	Returns the date as an integer representing the number of milliseconds since December 31, 1969, at 18:00:00
getTimezoneOffset()	Returns the difference between the local time and Greenwich Mean Time in minutes
getYear()	Deprecated. Returns the number of years since 1900; for example, 1996 is represented by '96'—this value method is inconsistently applied after the year 1999
getUTCDate()	Returns the UTC getDate() value
getUTCDay()	Returns the UTC getDay() value
getUTCFullYear()	Returns the UTC getFullYear() value
getUTCHours()	Returns the UTC getHours() value
getUTCMilliseconds()	Returns the UTC getMilliseconds() value
getUTCMinutes()	Returns the UTC getMinutes() value
getUTCMonth()	Returns the UTC getMonth() value
getUTCSeconds()	Returns the UTC getSeconds() value
getUTCTime()	Returns the UTC getTime() value
getUTCYear()	Returns the UTC getYear() value
setDate(*date*)	Sets the day of the month to the value specified in *date*
setFullYear(*year*)	Sets the year to the four-digit value specified in *year*
setHours(*hour*)	Sets the hour to the value specified in *hour*
setMilliseconds(*milliseconds*)	Sets the millisecond value to *milliseconds*
setMinutes(*minutes*)	Sets the minute to the value specified in *minutes*
setMonth(*month*)	Sets the month to the value specified in *month*
setSeconds(*seconds*)	Sets the second to the value specified in *seconds*
setTime(*time*)	Sets the time using the value specified in *time*, where *time* is a variable containing the number of milliseconds since December 31, 1969, at 18:00:00
setYear(*year*)	Sets the year to the value specified in *year*
toDateString()	Returns a date as a string value
toLocaleDateString()	Returns a date as a string value
toTimeString()	Returns a time as a string value

JavaScript Elements	Description
toGMTString()	Converts the current date to a text string in Greenwich Mean Time
toLocaleString()	Converts a date object's date to a text string, using the date format the Web browser is set up to use
toSource	String representing the source code of the object
toString()	String representation of a Date object
toUTCString()	Date converted to string using UTC
UTC()	Milliseconds since December 31, 18:00:00, using UTC
UTC(*date*)	Returns *date* in the form of the number of milliseconds since December 31, 1969, at 18:00:00 for Universal Coordinated Time
setUTCDate(*date*)	Applies the setDate() method in UTC time
setUTCFullYear(*year*)	Applies the setFullYear() method in UTC time
setUTCHours(*hour*)	Applies the setHours() method in UTC time
setUTCMilliseconds (*milliseconds*)	Applies the setMilliseconds() method in UTC time
setUTCMinutes(*minutes*)	Applies the setMinutes() method in UTC time
setUTCMonth(*month*)	Applies the setMonth() method in UTC time
setUTCSeconds(*seconds*)	Applies the setSeconds() method in UTC time
setUTCTime(*time*)	Applies the setTime() method in UTC time
setUTCYear(*year*)	Applies the setYear() method in UTC time
`dir`	`A directory listing element in the document`
Properties	
compact	A Boolean indicating whether the listing should be compacted
`div`	`A <div> (block container) element in the document`
Properties	
align	Alignment of the element
`document`	`An HTML document (child of Window)`
Properties	
alinkColor	The color of active hypertext links in the document
all[ ]	An array of each of the HTML tags in the document
anchors[ ]	An array of the anchors in the document
applets[ ]	An array of the applets in the document
attributes[ ]	A collection of attributes for the element
bgColor	The background color of the document
body	Reference to the <body> element object of the document
charset	A string containing the character set of the document
characterSet	A string containing the character set of the document
childNodes[ ]	A collection of child nodes of the object
classes.*class.tag.style*	Deprecated; the *style* associated with the element in the document with the class name *class* and the tag name *tag*
cookie	A text string containing the document's cookie values

JavaScript Elements	Description
designMode	Specifies whether design mode is on or off
dir	A string holding the text direction of text enclosed in the document
doctype	Reference to the DocumentType object for the document
documentElement	Reference to the root node of the document object hierarchy
domain	The domain of the document
embeds	An array of the embedded objects in the document
expando	A Boolean dictating whether instance properties can be added to the object (*IE only*)
fgColor	The text color used in the document
firstChild	Reference to the first child node of the element, if one exists
form	A form within the document (the form itself is also an object)
forms	An array of the forms in the document
implementation	An object with method *hasFeature(feature, level)* that returns a Boolean indicating if the browser supports the feature given in the string *feature* at the DOM level passed in the string *level*
lastChild	Reference to the last child node of the element, if one exists
lastModified	The date the document was last modified
layers	An array of layer objects
linkColor	The color of hypertext links in the document
links	An array of the links within the document
localName	A string indicating the "local" XML name for the object
location	The URL of the document
media	The media for which the document is intended
nextSibling	Reference to next sibling of the node
nodeName	A string containing the name of the node, the name of the tag to which the object corresponds
nodeValue	A string containing value within the node
ownerDocument	Reference to the document in which the element is contained
parentNode	Reference to the parent of the object
parentWindow	Reference to the window that contains the document
previousSibling	Reference to the previous sibling of the node
protocol	A string containing the protocol used to retrieve the document—its full name
referrer	The URL of the document containing the link that the user accessed to get to the current document
security	A string that contains information about the document's certificate
styleSheets[ ]	Collection of style sheets in the document
title	The title of the document
URL	The URL of the document
vlinkColor	The color of followed hypertext links
XMLDocument	Reference to the top-level node of the XML DOM exposed by the document
XSLDocument	Reference to the top-level node of the XSL DOM exposed by the document

JavaScript Elements	Description
Methods	
addEventListener (whichEvent, handler, direction)	Instructs the object to execute the function *handler* whenever an event of the type stated in *whichEvent* occurs; *direction* is a Boolean telling which phase to fire; use true for capture and false for bubbling
appendChild(newChild)	Appends *newChild* to the end of the node's childNodes[ ] list
attachEvent(whichHandler, theFunction)	Attaches the function *theFunction* as a handler specified by the string *whichHandler*
clear()	Clears the contents of the document window
cloneNode(cloneChildren)	Clones the node and returns the new clone
close()	Closes the document stream
createAttribute(name)	Returns a new attribute node of a name given by string *name*
createComment(data)	Returns a new comment node with the text given by *data*
createElement(tagName)	Returns a new element object that corresponds to *tagName*
createEventObject ([eventObj])	Creates and returns a new Event instance to pass to *fireEvent()*
createStyleSheet ([url [,index]])	Creates a new styleSheet object from the Stylesheet at the URL in the string *url* and inserts it into the document at index *index*
createTextNode(data)	Returns a new text node with value given by *data*
detachEvent(whichHandler, theFunction)	Instructs the object to stop executing *theFunction* as a handler given the string *whichHandler*
dispatchEvent(event)	Causes *event* to be processed by the appropriate handler; is used to redirect events
fireEvent(handler [, event])	Fires the event handler given by *handler*
focus()	Gives focus to the document and fires *onfocus* handler
getElementById(id)	Returns the element with *id* (or *name*) that is equal to *id*
getElementByName(name)	Gets a collection of elements with *id* (or *name*) that is equal to *name*
getElementByTagName (tagname)	Gets a collection of elements corresponding to *tagname*
getSelection()	Returns the selected text from the document
hasAttributes()	Returns a Boolean showing if any attributes are defined for the node
hasChildNodes()	Returns a Boolean showing if the node has children
insertBefore(newChild, refChild)	Inserts the node *newChild* in front of *refChild* in the *childNodes*[ ] list of *refChild's* parent node
isSupported(feature [, version])	Returns a Boolean showing which feature and version identified in the arguments is supported
normalize()	Merges adjacent text nodes in the subtree rooted at this element
open()	Opens the document stream
recalc([forceAll])	If *forceAll* is *true*, all dynamic properties are reevaluated
removeChild(oldChild)	Removes *oldChild* from the node's children and returns a reference to the removed node
removeEventListener (whichEvent, handler, direction)	Removes the function *handler* for the event declared in *whichEvent* for the phase stated in the Boolean *direction*

JavaScript Elements	Description
replaceChild(newChild, oldChild)	Replaces the node's child node *oldChild* with the node *newChild*
setActive()	Sets the document as the current element but does not give it focus
write()	Writes to the document window
writeln()	Writes to the document window on a single line (used only with preformatted text)
Event Handlers	
onClick	Runs when the document is clicked
onDblClick	Runs when the document is double-clicked
onKeyDown	Runs when a key is pressed down
onKeyPress	Runs when a key is initially pressed
onKeyUp	Runs when a key is released
onLoad	Runs when the document is initially loaded
onMouseDown	Runs when the mouse button is pressed down
onMouseUp	Runs when the mouse button is released
onUnLoad	Runs when the document is unloaded
`Error`	`This object gives information about the error that occurred during runtime`
Properties	
description	Describes the nature of the error
lineNumber	The line number that generated the error
number	The numeric value of the Microsoft-specific error number
`File, FileUpload`	`A file upload element in an HTML form (use the FileUpload box's name)`
Properties	
accessKey	Indicates the hotkey that gives the element focus
disabled	A Boolean signifying if the element is disabled
form	The form object containing the FileUpload box
name	The name of the FileUpload box
size	The width in pixels
tabIndex	A numeric value of the width in pixels
type	The type attribute of the FileUpload box
value	The pathname of the selected file in the FileUpload box
Methods	
blur()	Removes the focus from the FileUpload box
focus()	Gives the focus to the FileUpload box
handleEvent(*event*)	Invokes the event handler for the specified *event*
select()	Selects the input area of the FileUpload box
Event Handlers	
onBlur	Runs when the focus leaves the FileUpload box
onChange	Runs when the value in the FileUpload box is changed
onFocus	Runs when the focus is given to the FileUpload box

JavaScript Elements	Description
`Form`	`An HTML form (use the form's name)`
Properties	
acceptCharset	Specifies a list of character encodings for input data to be accepted by the server processing the form
action	The location of the CGI script that receives the form values
autocomplete	Specifies whether form autocompletion is on or off
elements[ ]	An array of elements within the form
encoding	The type of encoding used in the form
enctype	Specifies the MIME type of submitted data
length	The number of elements in the form
method	The type of method used when submitting the form
name	The name of the form
target	The name of the window into which CGI output should be directed
Methods	
handleEvent(*event*)	Invokes the event handler for the specified *event*
reset()	Resets the form
submit()	Submits the form to the CGI script
urns(*urn*)	Retrieves a collection of all elements to which the behavior of string *urn* is attached
Event Handlers	
onReset	Runs when the form is reset
onSubmit	Runs when the form is submitted
`Frame`	`A frame window (use the frame's name)`
Properties	
document	The current document in the frame window
frames	An array of frames within the frame window
length	The length of the frames array
name	The name of the frame
parent	The name of the window that contains the frame
self	The name of the current frame window
top	The name of the topmost window in the hierarchy of frame windows
window	The name of the current frame window
Methods	
alert(*message*)	Displays an Alert box with the text string *message*
blur()	Removes the focus from the frame
clearInterval(*ID*)	Cancels the repeated execution
clearTimeout(*ID*)	Cancels the delayed execution *ID*
confirm(*message*)	Displays a Confirm box with the text string *message*
open(*URL, name, features*)	Opens a URL in the frame with the name *name* and a feature list indicated by *features*
print()	Displays the Print dialog box

JavaScript Elements	Description
prompt(*message, response*)	Displays a Prompt dialog box with the text string *message* and the default value *response*
setInterval(*expression, time*)	Runs an *expression* after *time* milliseconds
setTimeout(*expression, time*)	Runs an *expression* every *time* milliseconds
Event Handlers	
onBlur	Runs when the focus is removed from the frame
onFocus	Runs when the frame receives the focus
onMove	Runs when the frame is moved
onResize	Runs when the frame is resized
h1…h6	Heading level element in the document
Properties	
align	The alignment of the element, for example, "right"
head	Corresponds to the <head> element in the document
Properties	
profile	A list of the URLs for data properties and legal values
hidden	A hidden field on an HTML form (use the name of the hidden field)
Properties	
form	The name of the form containing the hidden field
name	The name of the hidden field
type	The type of the hidden field
value	The value of the hidden field
history	An object containing information about the Web browser's history list
Properties	
current	The current URL in the history list
length	The number of items in the history list
next	The next item in the history list
previous	The previous item in the history list
Methods	
back()	Navigates back to the previous item in the history list
forward()	Navigates forward to the next item in the history list
go(*location*)	Navigates to the item in the history list specified by the value of *location*; the *location* variable can be either an integer or the name of the Web page
hr	A horizontal rule element in the document
Properties	
align	Alignment of the object, for example, "right"
color	The color of the rule
noShade	A Boolean indicating that the rule is not to be shaded
size	The size (height) of the rule in pixels
width	The width of the rule in pixels

JavaScript Elements	Description
html	Corresponds to the <html> element in the document
Properties	
version	The DTD version for the document
iframe	An inline frame element in the document
Properties	
align	The alignment of the object, for example, "right"
allowTransparency	A Boolean specifying whether the background of the frame can be transparent
border	The width of the border around the frame
contentDocument	The document that corresponds to the content of this frame
contentWindow	The window that corresponds to this frame
frameBorder	String of "0" (no border) or "1" (show border)
height	The height of the frame in pixels
longdesc	The URL of a long description for the frame
marginHeight	Vertical margins in pixels
marginWidth	Horizontal margins in pixels
name	The name of the frame
width	The width of the frame in pixels
image	An inline image (use the name assigned to the image)
Properties	
align	Specifies the alignment of the object, for example, "left", "right", or "center"
alt	A string containing alternative text for the image
border	The width of the image border in pixels
complete	A Boolean value indicating whether the image has been completely loaded by the browser
height	The height of the image in pixels
hspace	The horizontal space around the image in pixels
isMap	A Boolean indicating whether the image is a server-sid image map
longDesc	The URL for a more detailed description of the image
loop	An integer indicating how many times the image is to loop when activated
lowSrc	Specifies a URL for a lower-resolution image to display
lowsrc	The value of the lowsrc property of the <img> tag
name	The name of the image
nameProp	Indicates the name of the file given in the *src* attribute of the <img> tag
src	The URL of the image
style	Reference to the inline *Style* object for the element
useMap	Contains a URL to use as a client-side image map
vspace	The vertical space around the image in pixels
width	The width of the image in pixels
Methods	
handleEvent(*event*)	Invokes the event handler for the specified *event*

JavaScript Elements	Description
Event Handlers	
onAbort	Runs when the image load is aborted
onError	Runs when an error occurs while loading the image
onKeyDown	Runs when a key is pressed down
onKeyPress	Runs when a key is pressed
onKeyUp	Runs when a key is released
onLoad	Runs when the image is loaded
implementation	Information about the DOM technologies the browser supports (child of Document)
Methods	
hasFeature(feature [, version])	A Boolean indicating if the browser supports the feature at the DOM level given in version
label	A form field label in the document
Properties	
accessKey	Indicates the hotkey that gives the element focus
form	The form that encloses the label
layer	A document layer (use the name of the layer); deprecated in favor of the standard <div> element *(NS 4.0 only)*
Properties	
above	The layer above the current layer (*NS 4.0 only*)
background	The background image of the layer (*NS 4.0 only*)
below	The layer below the current layer (*NS 4.0 only*)
bgColor	The background color of the layer (*NS 4.0 only*)
clip.bottom, clip.height, clip.left, clip.right, clip.top, clip.width	The size and position of the layer's clipping area (*NS 4.0 only*)
document	The document containing the layer (*NS 4.0 only*)
name	The value of the *name* or *id* attribute for the layer (*NS 4.0 only*)
left	The *x*-coordinate of the layer (*NS 4.0 only*)
pageX	The *x*-coordinate relative to the document (*NS 4.0 only*)
pageY	The *y*-coordinate relative to the document (*NS 4.0 only*)
parentLayer	The containing layer (*NS 4.0 only*)
siblingAbove	The layer above in the zIndex (*NS 4.0 only*)
siblingBelow	The layer below in the zIndex (*NS 4.0 only*)
src	The URL of the layer document (*NS 4.0 only*)
top	The *y*-coordinate of the layer (*NS 4.0 only*)
visibility	The state of the layer's visibility (*NS 4.0 only*)
zIndex	The zIndex value of the layer (*NS 4.0 only*)
Methods	
handleEvent(*event*)	Invokes the event handler for the specified *event* (*NS 4.0 only*)
load(*source, width*)	Loads a new URL into the layer from *source* with the specified *width* (*NS 4.0 only*)

JavaScript Elements	Description
moveAbove(*layer*)	Moves the layer above *layer (NS 4.0 only)*
moveBelow(*layer*)	Moves the layer below *layer (NS 4.0 only)*
moveBy(*x, y*)	Moves the *x* pixels in the *x*-direction, and the *y* pixels in the *y*-direction (*NS 4.0 only*)
moveTo(*x, y*)	Moves the upper-left corner of the layer to the specified0 (*x, y*) coordinate (*NS 4.0 only*)
moveToAbsolute(*x, y*)	Moves the layer to the specified coordinate (*x, y*) within the page (*NS 4.0 only*)
resizeBy(*width, height*)	Resizes the layer by the specified *width* and *height* (*NS 4.0 only*)
resizeTo(*width, height*)	Resizes the layer to the specified *height* and *width* (*NS 4.0 only*)
Event Handlers	
onBlur	Runs when the focus leaves the layer (*NS 4.0 only*)
onFocus	Runs when the layer receives the focus (*NS 4.0 only*)
onLoad	Runs when the layer is loaded (*NS 4.0 only*)
onMouseOut	Runs when the mouse leaves the layer (*NS 4.0 only*)
onMouseOver	Runs when the mouse hovers over the layer (*NS 4.0 only*)
legend	A <legend> (fieldset caption) element in the document
Properties	
accessKey	Indicates the hotkey
align	Specifies the alignment of the element, for example, "right"
form	The form in which the element is enclosed
link	A link within an HTML document (use the name of the link)
Properties	
accessKey	Indicates the hotkey that gives the element focus
charset	The character set of the linked document
coords	Defines the coordinates of the object
disabled	A Boolean indicating whether the element is disabled
hash	The anchor name from the link's URL
host	The host from the link's URL
hostname	The hostname from the link's URL
href	The link's URL
hreflang	Indicates the language code of the linked resource
media	The media the linked document is intended for
nameProp	Holds the filename portion of the URL in the *href*
pathname	The path portion of the link's URL
port	The port number of the link's URL
protocol	The protocol used with the link's URL
search	The search portion of the link's URL
target	The target window of the hyperlinks
text	The text used to create the link
type	Specifies the media type in the form of a MIME type for the ink target
Methods	
handleEvent(*event*)	Invokes the event handler for the specified *event*

JavaScript Elements	Description
Event Handlers	
onClick	Runs when the link is clicked
onDblClick	Runs when the link is double-clicked
onKeyDown	Runs when a key is pressed down
onKeyPress	Runs when a key is initially pressed
onKeyUp	Runs when a key is released
onMouseDown	Runs when the mouse button is pressed down on the link
onMouseOut	Runs when mouse moves away from the link
onMouseOver	Runs when the mouse hovers over the link
onMouseUp	Runs when the mouse button is released
`location`	`The location of the document`
Properties	
hash	The location's anchor name
host	The location's hostname and port number
href	The location's URL
pathname	The path portion of the location's URL
port	The port number of the location's URL
protocol	The protocol used with the location's URL
Methods	
Assign(*url*)	Assigns the URL in the string *url* to the object
reload()	Reloads the location
replace(*url*)	Loads a new location with the address *url*
`map`	`Corresponds to a <map> (client-side image map)element in the document`
Properties	
Areas[ ]	A collection of *areas* enclosed by the object
Name	String holding the name of the image map
`Math`	`An object used for advanced mathematical calculations`
Properties	
E	The value of the base of natural logarithms (2.7182...)
LN10	The value of the natural logarithm of 10
LN2	The value of the natural logarithm of 2
LOG10E	The base 10 logarithm of E
LOG2E	The base 2 logarithm of E
PI	The value of pi (3.1416...)
SQRT1_2	The square root of ½
SQRT2	The square root of 2
Methods	
abs(*number*)	Returns the absolute value of *number*
acos(*number*)	Returns the arc cosine of *number* in radians
asin(*number*)	Returns the arc sine of *number* in radians

JavaScript Elements	Description
atan(*number*)	Returns the arc tangent of *number* in radians
atan2()	Returns the arc tangent of the quotient of its arguments
ceil(*number*)	Rounds *number* up to the next-highest integer
cos(*number*)	Returns the cosine of *number*, where *number* is an angle expressed in radians
exp(*number*)	Raises the value of E (2.7182...) to the value of *number*
floor(*number*)	Rounds *number* down to the next-lowest integer
log(*number*)	Returns the natural logarithm of *number*
max(*number1, number2*)	Returns the greater of *number1* and *number2*
min(*number1, number2*)	Returns the lesser of *number1* and *number2*
pow(*number1, number2*)	Returns the value of *number1* raised to the power of *number2*
random()	Returns a random number between 0 and 1
round(*number*)	Rounds *number* to the closest integer
sin(*number*)	Returns the sine of *number*, where *number* is an angle expressed in radians
sqrt(*number*)	Returns the square root of *number*
tan(*number*)	Returns the tangent of *number*, where *number* is an angle expressed in radians
toString(*number*)	Converts *number* to a text string
menu	A <menu> (menu list) element in the document
Properties	
compact	A Boolean signifying whether the list should be compacted
navigator	An object representing the browser currently in use
Properties	
appCodeName	The code name of the browser
appName	The name of the browser
appVersion	The version of the browser
cookieEnabled	A Boolean signifying whether persistent cookies are enabled
language	The language of the browser
mimeTypes	An array of the MIME types supported by the browser
oscpu	A string containing the operating system
platform	The platform on which the browser is running
plugins	An array of the plug-ins installed on the browser
preference	Allows a signed script to get and set certain Navigator preferences (*NS 4.0 only*)
userAgent	The user-agent text string sent from the client to the Web serve
Methods	
javaEnabled()	Indicates whether the browser supports Java
plugins.refresh()	Checks for newly installed plug-ins
taintEnabled()	Specifies whether data tainting is enabled
Option	An option from a selection list (use the name of the option or the index value from the options array)
Properties	
defaultSelected	A Boolean indicating whether the option is selected by default
disabled	A Boolean indicating whether the element is disabled
index	The index value of the option
label	Alternate text for the option as specified in the *label* attribute

JavaScript Elements	Description
selected	A Boolean indicating whether the option is currently selected
text	The text of the option as it appears on the Web page
value	The value of the option
param	Corresponds to an occurrence of a <param> element in the document
Properties	
name	The name of the parameter
type	The type of the value when *valueType* is "ref"
value	The value of the parameter
valueType	Provides more information about how to interpret value; usually "data", "ref", or "object"
Password	A password field in an HTML form (use the name of the password field)
Properties	
defaultValue	The default password
name	The name of the password field
type	The type value of the password field
value	The value of the password field
Methods	
focus()	Gives the password field the focus
blur()	Leaves the password field
select()	Selects the password field
Event Handlers	
onBlur	Runs when the focus leaves the password field
onFocus	Runs when the password field receives the focus
plugin	A plug-in object in the Web page
Properties	
description	The description of the plug-in
filename	The plug-in filename
length	The number of MIME types supported by the plug-in
name	The name of the plug-in
popup	A popup window object created by using the createPopup() method in IE (*IE only*)
Properties	
document	Reference to the window's document (*IE only*)
isOpen	A Boolean indicating if the window is open (*IE only*)
Radio	A radio button in an HTML form (use the radio button's name)
PropertiesZ	
accessKey	Indicates the hotkey that gives the element focus
align	A string specifying the alignment of the element, for example, "right"
alt	Alternative text for the button

JavaScript Elements	Description
checked	A Boolean indicating whether a specific radio button has been checked
defaultChecked	A Boolean indicating whether a specific radio button is checked by default
defaultValue	The initial value of the button's *value* attribute
disabled	A Boolean indicating whether the element is disabled
form	The name of the form containing the radio button
name	The name of the radio button
type	The type value of the radio button
value	The value of the radio button
Methods	
blur()	Removes the focus from the radio button
click()	Clicks the radio button
focus()	Gives focus to the radio button
handleEvent(*event*)	Invokes the event handler for the specified *event*
Event Handlers	
onBlur	Runs when the focus leaves the radio button
onClick	Runs when the radio button is clicked
onFocus	Runs when the radio button receives the focus
RegExp	An object used for searching regular expressions
Properties	
global	Specifies whether to use a global pattern match
ignoreCase	Specifies whether to ignore case in the search string
input	The search string
lastIndex	Specifies the index at which to start matching the next string
lastMatch	The last matched characters
lastParen	The last parenthesized substring match
leftContext	The substring preceding the most recent match
multiline	Specifies whether to search on multiple lines
rightContext	The substring following the most recent match
source	The string pattern
Methods	
compile()	Compiles a regular search expression
exec(*string*)	Executes the search for a match to *string*
test(*string*)	Tests for a match to *string*
Reset	A reset button in an HTML form (use the name of the reset button)
Properties	
accessKey	Indicates the hotkey that gives the element focus
align	Specifies the alignment of the element, for example, "right"
alt	Alternative text for the button

JavaScript Elements	Description
defaultValue	Contains the initial value of the button
disabled	A Boolean indicating whether the element is disabled
form	The name of the form containing the reset button
name	The name of the reset button
type	The type value of the reset button
value	The value of the reset button
Methods	
blur()	Removes the focus from the reset button
click()	Clicks the reset button
focus()	Gives the focus to the reset button
handleEvent(*event*)	Invokes the event handler for the specified *event*
Event Handlers	
onBlur	Runs when the focus leaves the reset button
onClick	Runs when the reset button is clicked
onFocus	Runs when the reset button receives the focus
screen	An object representing the user's screen
Properties	
availHeight	The height of the screen, minus toolbars or any other permanent objects
availWidth	The width of the screen, minus toolbars or any other permanent objects
colorDepth	The number of possible colors in the screen
height	The height of the screen
pixelDepth	The number of bits per pixel in the screen
width	The width of the screen
Script	Corresponds to a <script> element in the document
Properties	
charset	The character set used to encode the script
defer	A Boolean indicating whether script execution may be deferred
src	The URL of the external script
text	The contents of the script
type	The value of the type attribute
Select	A selection list in an HTML form (use the name of the selection list)
Properties	
disabled	A Boolean indicating whether the element is disabled
form	The name of the form containing the selection list
length	The number of *options* in the selection list
multiple	A Boolean indicating whether multiple *options* may be selected
name	The name of the selection list
options[ ]	An array of options within the selection list; see the options object for more information on working with individual selection list options
selectedIndex	The index value of the selected option from the selection list

JavaScript Elements	Description
size	The number of options that are visible at one time
tabIndex	Numeric value that indicates the tab order for the object
type	The type value of the selection list
value	The *value* of the currently selected option
Methods	
add(element, before)	Adds the *option* referenced by the *element* to the list of options before the *option* referenced by *before*; if *before* is null, it is added at the end
blur()	Removes the focus from the selection list
focus()	Gives the focus to the selection list
handleEvent(*event*)	Invokes the event handler for the specified *event*
remove(index)	Removes the option at index *index* from the list of *options*
Event Handlers	
onBlur	Runs when the focus leaves the selection list
onChange	Runs when the focus leaves the selection list and the value of the selection list is changed
onFocus	Runs when the selection list receives the focus
`String`	`An object representing a text string`
Properties	
length	The number of characters in the string
Methods	
anchor(*name*)	Converts the string into a hypertext link anchor with the name *name*
big()	Displays the string using the <big> tag
blink()	Displays the string using the <blink> tag
bold()	Displays the string using the <b> tag
charAt(*index*)	Returns the character in the string at the location specified by *index*
charCodeAt(position)	Returns an unsigned integer of the Unicode value of the haracter at index *position*
concat(*string2*)	Concatenates the string with the second text string *string2*
fixed()	Displays the string using the <tt> tag
fontColor(*color*)	Sets the color attribute of the string
fontSize(*value*)	Sets the size attribute of the string
indexOf(*string, start*)	Searches the string, beginning at the *start* character, and returns the index value of the first occurrence of the string *string*
italics()	Displays the string using the <i> tag
lastIndexOf(*string, start*)	Searches the string, beginning at the *start* character, and locates the index value of the last occurrence of the string *string*
link(*href*)	Converts the string into a hypertext link pointing to the URL *href*
match(*expression*)	Returns an array containing the matches based on the regular expression *expression*
replace(*expression, new*)	Performs a search based on the regular expression *expression* and replaces the text with *new*
search(*expression*)	Performs a search based on the regular expression *expression* and returns the index number

JavaScript Elements	Description
slice(*begin, end*)	Returns a substring between the *begin* and the *end* index values; the *end* index value is optional
small()	Displays the string using the <small> tag
split(*separator*)	Splits the string into an array of strings at every occurrence of the *separator* character
strike()	Displays the string using the <strike> tag
sub()	Displays the string using the <sub> tag
substr(*begin, length*)	Returns a substring starting at the *begin* index value and continuing for *length* characters; the *length* parameter is optional
substring(*begin, end*)	Returns a substring between the *begin* and the *end* index values; the *end* index value is optional
sup()	Displays the string using the <sup> tag
toLowerCase()	Converts the string to lowercase
toUpperCase()	Converts the string to uppercase
style	This corresponds to an instance of a <style> element in the page
Properties	
disabled	A Boolean indicating whether the element is disabled
sheet	The styleSheet object corresponding to the element
styleSheet	The styleSheet object corresponding to the element
type	The value of the *type* attribute for the style sheet
Submit	A submit button in an HTML form (use the name of the submit button)
Properties	
accessKey	String indicating the hotkey that gives the element focus
alt	Alternative text for the button
defaultValue	The initial value of the button's *value* attribute
disabled	A Boolean indicating whether the element is disabled
form	The name of the form containing the submit button
name	The name of the submit button
tabIndex	Numeric value that indicates the tab order for the object
type	The type value of the submit button
value	The value of the submit button
Methods	
blur()	Removes the focus from the submit button
click()	Clicks the submit button
focus()	Gives the focus to the submit button
handleEvent(*event*)	Invokes the event handler for the specified *event*
Event Handlers	
onBlur	Runs when the focus leaves the submit button
onClick	Runs when the submit button is clicked
onFocus	Runs when the submit button receives the focus

JavaScript Elements	Description
`Text`	`An input box from an HTML form (use the name of the input box)`
Properties	
accessKey	A string indicating the hotkey that gives the element focus
defaultValue	The default value of the input box
disabled	A Boolean indicating whether the element is disabled
form	The form containing the input box
maxLength	The maximum number of characters the field can contain
name	The name of the input box
size	The width of the field in characters
tabIndex	The numeric value that indicates t1he tab order for the object
type	The type value of the input box
value	The value of the input bo
Methods	
blur()	Removes the focus from the input box
focus()	Gives the focus to the input box
handleEvent(*event*)	Invokes the event handler for the specified *event*
select()	Selects the input box
Event Handlers	
onBlur	Runs when the focus leaves the input box
onChange	Runs when the focus leaves the input box and the input box value changes
onFocus	Runs when the input box receives the focus
onSelect	Runs when some of the text in the input box is selected
`Textarea`	`A text area box in an HTML form (use the name of the text area box)`
Properties	
accessKey	Indicates the hotkey that gives the element focus
cols	The number of columns of the input area
defaultValue	The default value of the text area box
enabled	Indicates whether a text area field is enabled using a Boolean
form	The form containing the text area box
name	The name of the text area box
rows	The number of rows of the input area
tabIndex	Numeric value that indicates the tab order for the object
type	The type value of the text area box
value	The value of the text area box
Methods	
blur()	Removes the focus from the text area box
focus()	Gives the focus to the text area box
handleEvent(*event*)	Invokes the event handler for the specified *event*
select()	Selects the text area box
Event Handlers	
onBlur	Runs when the focus leaves the text area box
onChange	Runs when the focus leaves the text area box and the text area box value changes
onFocus	Runs when the text area box receives the focus
onKeyDown	Runs when a user presses a key
onKeyPress	Runs when a user presses or holds down a key
onKeyUp	Runs when a user releases a key
onSelect	Runs when some of the text in the text area box is selected

JavaScript Elements	Description
`window`	`The document window`
Properties	
clipboardData	Provides access to the OS's clipboard
defaultStatus	The default message shown in the window's status bar
directories	A Boolean specifying whether the Netscape 6 "directories" button is visible.
document	The document displayed in the window
frameElement	The *Frame* in which the window is enclosed
frames	An array of frames within the window (see the frames object for properties and methods applied to individual frames)
history	A list of visited URLs
innerHeight	The height of the window's display area
innerWidth	The width of the widow's display area
length	The number of frames in the window
location	The URL loaded into the window
locationbar.visible	A Boolean indicating the visibility of the window's location bar
menubar.visible	A Boolean indicating the visibility of the window's menu bar
name	The name of the window
opener	The name of the window that opened the current window
outerHeight	The height of the outer area of the window
outerWidth	The width of the outer area of the window
pageXOffset	The *x*-coordinate of the window
pageYOffset	The *y*-coordinate of the window
parent	The name of the window containing this particular window
personalbar.visible	A Boolean indicating the visibility of the window's personal bar
screen	The browser's *screen* object
screenLeft	The *x*-coordinate in pixels of the left edge of the client area of the browser window
screenTop	The *y*-coordinate in pixels of the top edge of the client area of the browser window
scrollbars.visible	A Boolean indicating the visibility of the window's scroll bars
scrollX	How far the window is scrolled to the right
scrollY	How far the window is scrolled down
self	The current window
status	The message shown in the window's status bar
statusbar.visible	A Boolean indicating the visibility of the window's status bar
toolbar.visible	A Boolean indicating the visibility of the window's toolbar
top	The name of the topmost window in a hierarchy of windows
window	The current window
Methods	
alert(*message*)	Displays the text contained in *message* in a dialog box
back()	Loads the previous page in the window
blur()	Removes the focus from the window
captureEvents()	Sets the window to capture all events of a specified type
clearInterval(*ID*)	Clears the interval for *ID*, set with the SetInterval method
clearTimeout()	Clears the timeout, set with the setTimeout method
close()	Closes the window
confirm(*message*)	Displays a confirmation dialog box with the text *message*
createPopup(*arg*)	Creates a popup window and returns a reference to the new popup object
disableExternalCapture	Disables external event capturing
enableExternalCapture	Enables external event capturing

JavaScript Elements	Description
find(*string, case, direction*)	Displays a Find dialog box, where *string* is the text to find in the window, *case* is a Boolean indicating whether the find is case-sensitive, and *direction* is a Boolean indicating whether the find goes in the backward direction (all of the parameters are optional)
focus()	Gives focus to the window
forward()	Loads the next page in the window
handleEvent(*event*)	Invokes the event handler for the specified *event*
moveBy(*horizontal, vertical*)	Moves the window by the specified amount in the *horizontal* and *vertical* directions
moveTo(*x, y*)	Moves the window to the *x*- and *y*-coordinates
open()	Opens the window
print()	Displays the Print dialog box
prompt(*message, default_text*)	Displays a Prompt dialog box with the text *message* (the default message is *default_text*)
releaseEvents(*event*)	Releases the captured events of a specified *event*
resizeBy(*horizontal, vertical*)	Resizes the window by the amount in the *horizontal* and *vertical* directions
resizeTo(*width, height*)	Resizes the window to the specified *width* and *height*
routeEvent(*event*)	Passes the *event* to be handled natively
scroll(*x, y*)	Scrolls the window to the *x, y* coordinate
scrollBy(*x, y*)	Scrolls the window by *x* pixels in the *x*-direction and *y* pixels in the *y*-direction
scrollTo(*x, y*)	Scrolls the window to the *x, y* coordinate
setActive( )	Sets the window to be active but does not give it the focus
setCursor(*type*)	Changes the cursor to *type*
setInterval(*expression, time*)	Evaluates the *expression* every *time* milliseconds have passed
setTimeout(*expression, time*)	Evaluates the *expression* after *time* milliseconds have passed
sizeToContent( )	Resizes the window so all contents are visible
stop()	Stops the window from loading
Event Handlers	
onBlur	Runs when the window loses the focus
onDragDrop	Runs when the user drops an object on or within the window
onError	Runs when an error occurs while loading the page
onFocus	Runs when the window receives the focus
onLoad	Runs when the window finishes loading
onMove	Runs when the window is moved
onResize	Runs when the window is resized
onUnload	Runs when the window is unloaded

JavaScript Operators, Keywords, and Syntactical Elements

Appendix H

The following table lists some of the important JavaScript operators, keywords, and syntactical elements. The first operators listed in the table are the assignment operators, used to assign values to variables and to document objects. The next operators are the arithmetic operators, used for performing arithmetic calculations on variables (addition, subtraction, multiplication, and division). The comparison operators are next and are used primarily in conditional expressions and in program loops. The JavaScript keywords listed in the table are special names reserved by JavaScript. The logical operators are used for evaluating whether an expression is true or false, and are primarily used in conditional expressions and in program loops. The last part of the table contains special syntax elements for marking the end of a program or for inserting a JavaScript comment.

Operators	Description
Assignment	**Operators used to assign values to variables**
=	Assigns the value of the variable on the right to the variable on the left (*x* = *y*)
+=	Adds the two variables and assigns the result to the variable on the left (*x* += *y* is equivalent to *x* = *x* + *y*)
-=	Subtracts the variable on the right from the variable on the left and assigns the result to the variable on the left (*x*- = *y* is equivalent to *x* = *x* - *y*)
*=	Multiplies the two variables together and assigns the result to the variable on the left (*x* *= *y* is equivalent to *x* = *x* * *y*)
/=	Divides the variable on the left by the variable on the right and assigns the result to the variable on the left (*x* /= *y* is equivalent to *x* = *x* / *y*)
&=	Combines two expressions into a single expression (x &= y is equivalent to *x* = *x* & *y*)
%=	Divides the variable on the left by the variable on the right and assigns the remainder to the variable on the left (*x* %= *y* is equivalent to *x* = *x* % *y*)
Arithmetic	**Operators used for arithmetic functions**
+	Adds two variables together (*x* + *y*)
-	Subtracts the variable on the right from the variable on the left (*x* - y)
*	Multiplies two variables together (*x* * *y*)
/	Divides the variable the left by the variable on the right (*x* / *y*)
%	Calculates the remainder after dividing the variable on the left by the variable on the right (*x* % *y*)
++	Increases the value of a variable by 1 (*x* ++ is equivalent to *x* = *x* + 1)
&	Combines two expressions (*x* & *y*) Decreases the value of variable by 1 (*x* -- is equivalent to *x* = *x* - 1)
-	Changes the sign of a variable (- *x*)
Comparison	**Operators used for comparing expressions**
==	Returns true when the two expressions are equal (*x* == y)
!=	Returns true when the two expressions are not equal (*x* != *y*)
!==	Returns true when the values of the two expressions are equal (*x* !== *y*)
>	Returns true when the expression on the left is greater than the expression on the right (*x* > *y*)
<	Returns true when the expression on the left is less than the expression on the right (*x* < *y*)
>=	Returns true when the expression on the left is greater than or equal to the expression on the right (*x* >= *y*)
<=	Returns true when the expression on the left is less than or equal to the expression on the right (*x* <= *y*)

Operators	Description
Conditional	**Operators used to determine values based on conditions that are either true or false**
(condition) ? value1 : value2	If *condition* is true, then this expression equals *value1*; otherwise it equals *value2*
Keywords	**JavaScript keywords are reserved by JavaScript**
infinity	Represents positive infinity (often used with comparison operators)
this	Refers to the current object
var	Declares a variable
with	Allows the declaration of all the properties for an object without directly referencing the object each time
Logical	**Operators used for evaluating true and false expressions**
^	The XOR (exclusive OR) operator
!	Reverses the Boolean value of the expression
&&	Returns true only if both expressions are true (also known as an AND operator)
||	Returns true when either expression is true (also known as an OR operator)
|	Returns true if the expression is false and false if the expression is true (also known as a NEGATION operator)
Syntax	**Syntactical elements**
;	Indicates the end of a command line
/ comments */*	Used for inserting *comments* within a JavaScript command line
// comments	Used to create a line of *comments*

Working with Cookies

Appendix I

Introducing Cookies

A **cookie** is a piece of information stored in a text file that a Web browser places on a user's computer. Typically, cookies contain data to be accessed the next time a user visits a particular Web site. For example, many online stores use cookies to store users' addresses and credit card information. This enables a store to access previously entered information from a cookie the next time a repeat user makes a purchase, freeing the user from reentering this material.

Where a browser places a cookie file depends on the browser. Netscape stores cookies in a single text file named cookie.txt. Internet Explorer stores cookies in a separate text file, typically in the Windows/Cookies folder. Browsers limit each cookie to 4 kilobytes in size, and a computer can generally not store more than 300 cookies at one time. If a browser tries to store more than 300 cookies, the oldest cookies are deleted to make room.

Cookies, the Web Server, and CGI Scripts

The first implementation of cookies was with a CGI script running on a Web server. A CGI script can retrieve the cookie information and perform some action based on the information in the file. The process works as follows:

1. A user accesses the Web site and sends a request to the CGI script on the Web server, either by filling out an order form or by some other process that calls the CGI script.
2. The CGI script determines whether a cookie for the user exists.
3. If no cookie is detected, the Web server sends a form, or page, for a user to enter the information needed by the cookie. This information is then sent to the CGI script for processing.
4. If a cookie is found, the CGI script retrieves that information and creates a new page, or modifies the current page, based on the information contained in the cookie.

Information is exchanged using the same Hypertext Transfer Protocol (HTTP) used for retrieving the contents of the Web page. This is because each transfer includes a header section that contains information about the document (such as its MIME data type) and allows for general information in the form:

```
field-name: field-value
```

These field-name/field-value pairs contain information that can be stored in a user's cookie.

To store this information on a Web server, a Web programmer must add the Set-Cookie statement to the header section of the CGI script. The Set-Cookie statement is used the first time the user accesses the Web page. Four parameters are often set with cookies: name, expires, path, and domain. The syntax is:

```
Set-Cookie: name=text; expires=date; path=text; domain=text; secure
```

The name parameter defines the name of the cookie, and its value cannot contain spaces, commas, or semicolons. The expire parameter indicates the date the information expires; if no expire parameter is included, the cookie expires when the user's browsing session ends. The path parameter indicates the URL path portion to which that cookie applies; setting this value to "/" allows the cookie to be accessed from any folder within the Web site. The domain parameter specifies the URL domain portion to which the cookie applies (usually the domain name of the current document). Finally, the secure parameter indicates that the data should be transferred over a secure link—one that uses file encryption.

Once the initial cookie is created, the browser sends the Cookie statement in the header section of the transfer the next time the user accesses the Web page. The syntax of this statement is

```
Cookie: name1:value1; name2:value2; ...
```

where *name1* is the first field name (whatever that might be) and *value1* is the value of the first field. The statement can contain as many field/value pairs as needed by the Web page so long as the total size of the cookie doesn't exceed 4 kilobytes.

Once the Web server retrieves the cookie field names and values, the CGI script processes them. Because CGI programming is beyond the scope of this book, you will focus on working with cookies on the client side with JavaScript.

Working with the Cookie Property

JavaScript uses the cookie property of the document object to retrieve and update cookie information. The cookie property is simply a text string containing all of the field/value pairs used by the cookie, with each pair separated by a semicolon. To set a value for a cookie, you would use the document.cookie property with the form

```
document.cookie='cookie1=OrderForm; expires=Mon, 08-Apr-
2006 12:00:00 GMT; path="/"; secure';
```

where the cookie contains the cookie1 field with the value OrderForm. This particular cookie expires at noon on Monday, April 8, 2006. Because the path value equals "/", this cookie is accessible from any folder within the Web site. The secure property has been set, so any transfer of information involving this cookie must use file encryption. Note that this is a long text string, with the string value enclosed in single quotation marks.

If your Web page had an online form named "Orders", you could create additional field/value pairs using the form names and values as follows:

```
document.cookie='cookie1=OrderForm; name='+document.Orders.Name.
value+'; custid=+'document.Orders.CustId.value;
```

Here, two additional fields have been added to the cookie: name and custid. The values for these fields are taken respectively from the Name field and the CustId field in the Orders form.

Reading a Cookie

One of the challenges of working with cookies in JavaScript is reading the cookie information. To do this you need to extract the appropriate information from the cookie's text string and place that information in the appropriate JavaScript variables. You can use several of JavaScript's string functions to help with this task. To start, create a function named "readCookie(fname)", where "fname" is the name of the field whose value you want to retrieve. The initial code looks like

```
function readCookie(fname) {
    var cookies=document.cookie;
}
```

where the text string of the cookie is stored in the cookies variable. In the text string, each field name is followed by an equal sign, so you can use the indexOf( ) method (see Appendix G) to locate the occurrence of the text string *"fname="*, where *fname* is the field name you want to retrieve. You'll store this location in a variable named startname. The command is:

```
startname=cookies.indexOf(fname+"=");
```

For example, if fname="custid" in the text string below, startname would have a value of 33, because custid starts with the thirty-third character in the text string.

```
cookie1=OrderForm; name=Brooks; custid=20010; type=clothes
```

What if the field name is not found in the cookie? In this case, startname has a value of -1, and you can create an If...Else conditional statement to handle this contingency. To simplify things for this example, you'll assume that this is not a concern, and continue.

Next you need to locate the field's value. This value is placed after the equal sign and continues until you reach a semicolon indicating the end of the field's value, or until you reach the end of the text string. The field's value then starts one space after the first equal sign after the field's name. You'll locate the beginning of the field value, using the same indexOf( ) method, and store that location in the startvalue variable. The command is:

```
startvalue=cookies.indexOf("=", startname)+1;
```

Here, you locate the text string "=", starting at the point startname in the cookies text string. You add one to whatever value is returned by the indexOf() method. In the text string

```
cookie1=OrderForm; name=Brooks; custid=20010; type=clothes
```

the value of the startvalue variable is 40, because the "2" in "20010" is the fortieth character in the string.

Next you locate the end of the field's value, which is the first semicolon after the startvalue character. If the field is the last value in the text string, there is no semicolon at the end, so the indexOf( ) method returns a value of -1. If that occurs, you'll use the length of the text string to locate the value's end. Once again, using the indexOf( ) method, you'll store this value in the endvalue variable. The JavaScript command is:

```
endvalue=cookies.indexOf(";",startvalue);
if(endvalue==-1) {
   endvalue=cookies.length;
}
```

In the text string below, the value of the endvalue variable for the custid field is 45.

```
cookie1=OrderForm; name=Brooks; custid=20010; type=clothes
```

To extract the field's value and store it in a variable named fvalue, use the substring( ) method

```
fvalue=cookies.substring(startvalue, endvalue);
```

where the startvalue indicates the start of the substring and the endvalue marks the substring's end. The complete readCookie(fname) function looks as follows:

```
function readCookie(fname) {
   var cookies=document.cookie;
   var startname=cookies.indexOf(fname+"=");
   var startvalue=cookies.indexOf("=", startname)+1;
   var endvalue=cookies.indexOf(";",startvalue);
   if(endvalue==-1) {
     endvalue=cookies.length;
   }
   var fvalue=cookies.substring(startvalue, endvalue);
return fvalue;
}
```

In a JavaScript program, calling the function

```
readCookie("custid");
```

would return a value of 20010, which is the customer id value stored in the cookie file. You should review this example carefully, paying close attention to the use of the indexOf( ) method and the substring( ) method.

Encoding Cookies

Values in the cookie text string cannot contain spaces, semicolons, or commas. This can be a problem if you are trying to store phrases or sentences. The solution to this problem is to encode the value, using the same type of encoding scheme that is used in URLs (which also cannot contain spaces, commas, and semicolons) or in the mailto action. JavaScript includes the escape( ) method for encoding your text strings. Encoding replaces blank spaces, semicolons, and commas with special characters. For example, if you want to insert an Address field in your cookie that contains a street number and an address, you could use the following JavaScript command:

```
document.cookie='Address='+escape(document.Orders.Address.value);
```

To read a text string that has been encoded, you use JavaScript's unescape( ) method. For example, you could replace the command that stores the field value in the fvalue variable in the readCookie( ) function with the following command:

```
var fvalue=unescape(cookies.substring(startvalue, endvalue));
```

This command removes any encoding characters and replaces them with the appropriate spaces, semicolons, commas, and so forth.

Exploring Filters and Transitions

Appendix J

If you are supporting only the Internet Explorer browser, you can take advantage of an IE-only style known as the filter. A **filter** is an effect that is applied to an object or page to change its appearance. Using Internet Explorer filters, you can make text or images appear partially transparent, add a drop shadow, or make an object appear to glow. Filters were introduced in Internet Explorer version 4.0 and are not supported by other browsers, so you have to use them with caution. Filters can be applied to any element with a defined height and width.

A filter is applied either by adding a filter style to the Web page's style sheet or by running a JavaScript command that applies the filter style to an object in the document. Let's first look at how to create a filter using styles.

Starting Data Files

There are no starting Data Files needed for this appendix.

Applying Filters Using CSS Styles

The syntax that Internet Explorer uses to employ the filter style differs between earlier versions of Internet Explorer and current versions of the browser. In IE version 4.0, the filter style is expressed as

```
filter: filter_name(params)
```

where *filter_name* is the name of one of the many Internet Explorer 4.0 filters, and *params* are the parameter values (if any) that apply to the filter. The syntax for filter styles employed in Internet Explorer 5.5 and above is:

```
filter: progid:DXImageTransform.Microsoft.filter_name(params)
```

In addition to the syntactical differences between the two versions, there are some differences in how different versions of Internet Explorer apply the filter style. In Internet Explorer 4.0, the filter effect is clipped when it is set too close to an object's boundary; with Internet Explorer 5.5 and above, the filter effect extends beyond an object's boundary.

Figure J-1 lists some of the filter names and parameters supported by Internet Explorer 5.5 and above.

Figure J-1 **Internet Explorer filters**

Filter Name	Parameters	Description
Alpha	style=0, 1, 2, 3 opacity=1–100 finishOpacity=1–100 startX=1–100 finishX=1–100 startY=1–100 finishY=1–100	Applies a transparency filter. A low opacity value makes the object transparent, while a high value makes the object opaque. The style parameter is used to indicate the direction of the transparency effect. The rest of the parameters control where in element the transparency is applied
BasicImage	rotation=0, 1, 2, 3 opacity=0–1 mirror=0, 1 invert=0, 1 xRay=0, 1 grayscale=0,1	Modifies the appearance of the object. The rotation parameter rotates the object (0=0 deg., 1=90 deg., 2=180 deg., 3=270 deg.). The opacity parameter sets the opacity of the object. The remaining parameters, if their values are set to "1," create a mirror image, invert the object, apply an "x-ray" effect, or display the object in grayscale
Blur	pixelRadius=*value* makeShadow =true,false shadowOpacity=0–1	Blurs the object. The pixelRadius parameter determines the amount of the blurring. The makeShadow and shadowOpacity parameters apply shadowing to the blur effect
Chroma	color=*#rrggbb*	Makes a specified color in the object transparent
DropShadow	color=*#rrggbb* offX=*value* offY=*value*	Creates a drop shadow of the specified color with a length of offX in the x-direction and offY in the y-direction
Emboss		Applies an embossing effect to the object
Engrave		Applies an engraving effect to the object
Glow	color=*#rrggbb* strength=1–255	Applies a glowing border around the object with the size of the glow determined by the strength parameter and the glow's color determined by the color parameter

Filter Name	Parameters	Description
Gradient	gradientType=0, 1 startColorStr=*#rrggbb* endColorStr=*#rrggbb*	Applies a color gradient to the object. The gradientType parameter determines the direction of the gradient, either vertical (0) or horizontal (1). The startColorStr and endColorStr parameters indicate the starting and ending colors. Intermediate colors are supplied by the filter
MotionBlur	direction=*angle* strength=1–255	Applies a motion blur effect. The direction parameter provides the angle of the motion, and the strength parameter indicates the length of the motion lines
Pixelate	maxSquare=*value*	Pixelates the object, where maxSquare is the size of the pixel
Shadow	direction=angle color=*#rrggbb* strength=1–255	Applies a simple drop shadow to the object with the angle of the shadow specified by the direction parameter, the color by the color parameter, and the size of the shadow determined by the strength parameter
Wave	freq=*value* lightStrength=*value* phase=*value* strength=*value*	Applies a sine-wave distortion to the object; the appearance of the wave is determined by the four parameters

For example, to apply a drop shadow filter in Internet Explorer 5.5 or above, you would add the following filter style to the element:

```
filter: progid:DXImageTransform.Microsoft.dropShadow (color=#FF0000,
offX=5, offY=10)
```

which places a red drop shadow (the hexadecimal color value of red is #FF0000) around the image with an offset of 5 pixels to the right and 10 pixels down. Figure J-2 shows some examples of other IE filter styles applied to an inline image.

Examples of IE filters **Figure J-2**

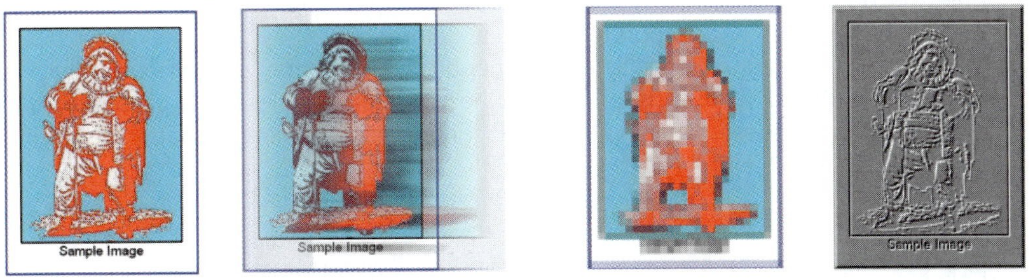

original image | MotionBlur (direction = 90, strength = 100) | Pixelate (maxSquare = 10) | Engrave()

Internet Explorer supports both the 4.0 and 5.5 filter styles, and you may find the 4.0 styles easier to work with in some situations. Figure J-3 describes how some of the version 4.0 filters are matched with their 5.5 counterparts.

Figure J-3 **Internet Explorer 4.0 and 5.5 filters**

IE 4.0 Filter	IE 5.5 Filter
Alpha	progid:DXImageTransform.Microsoft.Alpha
Blur	progid:DXImageTransform.Microsoft.MotionBlur
Chroma	progid:DXImageTransform.Microsoft.Chroma
DropShadow	progid:DXImageTransform.Microsoft.dropShadow
FlipH	progid:DXImageTransform.Microsoft.BasicImage(rotation=2, mirror=1)
FlipV	progid:DXImageTransform.Microsoft.BasicImage(mirror=1)
Glow	progid:DXImageTransform.Microsoft.Glow
Gray	progid:DXImageTransform.Microsoft.BasicImage(grayscale=1)
Invert	progid:DXImageTransform.Microsoft.BasicImage(invert=1)
Light	progid:DXImageTransform.Microsoft.Light
Mask	progid:DXImageTransform.Microsoft.MaskFilter
Shadow	progid:DXImageTransform.Microsoft.Shadow
Wave	progid:DXImageTransform.Microsoft.Wave
Xray	progid:DXImageTransform.Microsoft.BasicImage(xray=1)

Filters can also be combined to create interesting visual effects. The effects are added in the order in which they are entered into the style declaration. To combine the alpha filter with a drop shadow, for example, you would enter the following set of filters:

```
filter: progid:DXImageTransform.Microsoft.Shadow(direction=135,
color=#0000FF strength=5)
progid:DXImageTransform.Microsoft.Alpha(style=0, opacity=30)
```

This code applies a drop shadow to the object, and then changes the opacity value to 30. If you switch the order of the filters, the drop shadow is added after the object is made transparent, meaning that the shadow itself is not made transparent. You can also apply the same filter several times. For example, you can add two drop shadows to the same object by applying two shadow filters.

Most browsers do not support the Internet Explorer filter styles, and they are not part of the official specifications for CSS. When other browsers encounter a style sheet that employs the filter style, they usually ignore those particular styles while processing the other styles in the sheet. You can also use IE conditional comments to apply the filter styles only to select IE browsers.

Applying a Filter Style with JavaScript

As with other style attributes, the filter style can be applied in JavaScript using the style property. The syntax for applying a filter style is

```
object.style.filter = filter_text
```

where *object* is an object in the Web page, and *filter_text* is the text of the filters applied to the object. As in a style sheet, the text string can contain multiple filters separated by spaces. For example, to apply the alpha filter to the first inline image in a document, you could use the following JavaScript command:

```
document.images[0].style.filter = "progid:DXImageTransform.Microsoft.
Alpha(style=0, opacity=30)";
```

Internet Explorer's version of JavaScript also recognizes the **filter collection**, which is the collection of all filters associated with a particular object. The reference syntax of the filter collection is

```
object.filters[idref]
```

where *object* is an object that has some filters applied to it, and *idref* is either the index number or the name of a filter within that collection. As with other arrays, the index numbering starts at 0. For example, the expression

```
document.images[0].filters[1]
```

references the second filter associated with the first inline image in the document. If you want to reference the filter by its name, you would use a reference such as

```
document.images[0].filters["DXImageTransform.Microsoft.Alpha"]
```

where Internet Explorer's Alpha filter is one of the filters applied to the first inline image in the document. One of the purposes of using JavaScript to work with filter styles is to modify the parameter values. You can reference specific parameters within each filter using the syntax

```
filter.param
```

where *filter* is a specific filter in an object's filters collection, and *param* is the name of a parameter associated with the filter. For example, to change the opacity value of the Alpha filter for the first inline image, you could run the following expression:

```
document.images[0].filters["DXImageTransform.Microsoft.Alpha"]
.opacity = 25;
```

This command works only if the Alpha filter has already been defined for the inline image.

Using a Light Filter

Another popular filter that can add visual interest to Web pages is the Light filter, which creates the illusion of a light (or multiple lights) illuminating an object. Much like a drop shadow, adding a light source can give page elements a dynamic 3D effect. The style to create a Light filter in Internet Explorer 4.0 is:

```
filter: Light()
```

In Internet Explorer 5.5 and above, the style is:

```
filter: progid:DXImageTransform.Microsoft.Light()
```

Once you've created the Light filter, the next step is to define a light source for the object. This is done not with a style declaration, but with a JavaScript command. The three methods for creating a light source are: addAmbient(), addPoint(), and addCone(). The addAmbient() method applies an overall or ambient light to the object. The syntax of the method is

```
object.filters.Light.addAmbient(red, green, blue, strength)
```

where *object* is the object being illuminated; *red*, *green*, and *blue* are the RGB color values of the light; and *strength* is the strength of the light source, expressed as a number from 0 to 100. For example, the following statement adds a red light source at highest intensity on the document's first inline image:

```
document.images[0].filters.Light.addAmbient(255,0,0,100)
```

The addAmbient() method doesn't assume a specific location for the light source. To specify a location for the light, you can use the addPoint() method, which creates a point light source hovering above the object. The syntax to add a point light source to the Light filter is

```
object.filters.Light.addPoint(x, y, z, red, green, blue, strength)
```

where *x* and *y* are the horizontal and vertical coordinates of the light source, and *z* is the height, in pixels, of the light source above the object. For example, to create a high-intensity red light source 50 pixels "above" the object at the (x,y) coordinates (50, 75), you would use the following expression:

```
document.images[0].filters.Light.addPoint(50,75,50,255,0,0,100)
```

The addPoint() method assumes that the light is shone directly down on the object. If you want the light source to shine at an angle, you need to use the addCone() method. The syntax of the addCone() method is

```
object.filters.Light.addCone(x, y, z, x2, y2, red, green, blue,
strength, spread)
```

where *x*, *y*, *z* are once again the coordinates of the light source and *x2*, *y2* are the coordinates of the focus of the light—where the light actually "hits" the object. The spread parameter indicates the angle (or spread) of the light between the light source and the surface of the object. The spread parameter varies from 0 to 90 degrees. The other parameters have the same meanings as those used with the addAmbient() and addPoint() methods.

You can create up to 10 light sources to illuminate a particular object. Internet Explorer assigns each light source a number. The first light source you define has a light number of 0; the second light source has a value of 1, and so on. Once a light source has been created, Internet Explorer provides several methods to manipulate it. You can move the light source to a new location, change its color, change its intensity, or remove the light altogether. To move the light source to another location, use the method

```
object.filters.Light.moveLight(light, x, y, z, absolute)
```

where *light* is the light source's light number; *x*,*y*, and *z* are the new coordinates of the light source; and *absolute* is a Boolean value that has the value true when the new coordinates are expressed in absolute terms, and has the value false when the coordinates are expressed relative to the present coordinates of the light source. To change the color of the light, use the method

```
object.filters.Light.changeColor(light, red, green, blue, absolute)
```

where *red*, *green*, and *blue* are the new RGB color values of the light source; and *absolute* is a Boolean value that is true when the color values are expressed as absolute values, and false when the color values are to be added to the light source's current color values. You can use negative color values if the absolute parameter is set to false.

To change the intensity of the light source, use the method

```
object.filters.Light.changeStrength(light, strength, absolute)
```

where *strength* is the new strength of the light source, and *absolute* is a Boolean value that is set to true if the strength parameter is expressed in absolute terms, and false if the value of the strength parameter is to be added to the light source's current strength. Once again, the strength parameter can be negative if the value of the absolute parameter is set to false.

As you create light sources, you can remove the effect of a particular light source by setting its strength parameter back to 0. You can remove all of the light sources applied to a particular object by using the following method:

```
object.filters.Light.clear()
```

Internet Explorer does not provide a method of removing a specific light source while keeping all of the others.

By combining various filter styles including the different light filters with JavaScript, you can create wonderful visual effects with very little extra programming and no need to install specialized add-ins. However, remember these effects will be visible only to users of Internet Explorer.

Introducing Transitions

A second type of special effect supported by Internet Explorer is the transition. A **transition** is a visual effect that is applied to an object over an interval of time. For example, instead of having a pop-up menu disappear instantaneously, you can apply a transition that makes the pop-up menu appear to gradually blend into the background until it disappears. Transition styles are applied using the same format you use with filter styles. The transition styles first introduced with IE 4.0, are entered as

```
filter: filter_name(params)
```

and transitions introduced with IE 5.5 are entered as

```
filter: progid:DXImageTransform.Microsoft.filter_name(params)
```

where *filter_name* is the name of a transition style and params are parameters used by that transition. Internet Explorer 4.0 supports two possible transition values for *filter_name*: blend and reveal. In IE 4.0, a **blend transition** is a transition in which one object is blended into another. The style to create a blend transition is

```
filter: blendTrans(duration = value)
```

where *value* is the amount of time, in seconds, for the blending transition to take place. Two separate objects need not be used. You can apply a blend transition on a single object by initially making the object invisible (using the visibility style) and then applying the blendTrans() filter to move it to a visible state. A **reveal transition** is a more general transition in which a visual effect is applied as one object is changed into another. The style for the reveal transition under IE 4.0 is

```
filter: revealTrans(duration = value, transition = type)
```

where *type* is a number from 0 to 23, specifying the transition effect. The various transition effects and their numeric values are listed in Figure J-4.

Figure J-4 **Internet Explorer 4.0 transition styles**

Transition	Type Number	Transition	Type Number
Box In	0	Random Dissolve	12
Box Out	1	Split Vertical In	13
Circle In	2	Split Vertical Out	14
Circle Out	3	Split Horizontal In	15
Wipe Up	4	Split Horizontal Out	16
Wipe Down	5	Strips Left Down	17
Wipe Right	6	Strips Left Up	18
Wipe Left	7	Strips Right Down	19
Vertical Blinds	8	Strips Right Up	20
Horizontal Blinds	9	Random Bars Horizontal	21
Checkerboard Across	10	Random Bars Vertical	22
Checkerboard Down	11	Random	23

Figure J-5 shows an example of the circle out transition (with transition type number equal to 3) that transitions the inline image from one image file to another.

Figure J-5 **IE 4.0 circle out transition**

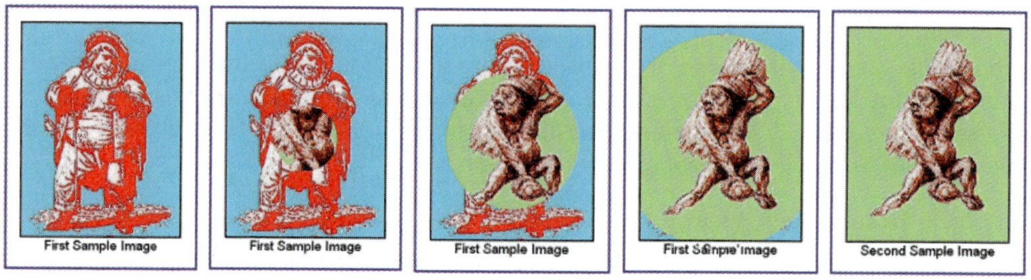

initial image revealTrans(duration = 10, transition = 3) final image

In Internet Explorer 5.5, the blendTrans() and revealTrans() transitions were replaced by a whole library of transition effects. Figure J-6 describes some of the Internet Explorer 5.5 transitions and their parameters. In addition to the parameters listed in Figure J-6, each transition also supports the duration parameter, which indicates how many seconds the transition lasts.

Internet Explorer 5.5 transition styles **Figure J-6**

Transition Name	Parameters	Description
Barn	motion=out, in orientation=horizontal, vertical	Applies a "barn door" transition
Blinds	bands=*value* direction=up, down, left, right	Applies a "window blinds" effect
Checkboard	direction=up, down, left, right squaresX=*value* squaresY=*value*	Creates a checkboard transition. The size of the checkboard is determined by the squaresX and squaresY parameters
Fade	overlap=0–1	Fades one object into another. The overlap parameter controls the degree of overlap as the fade occurs
GradientWipe	gradientSize=0–1 wipeStyle=0, 1 motion=forward, reverse	Wipes one object into another. The gradientSize parameter controls the blurring effect. The wipeStyle parameter indicates whether to wipe left to right (0) or up to down (1)
Inset		Applies an inset transition
Iris	irisStyle=*multiple* motion=out, in	Applies an iris-opening transition effect.The style of the iris is determined by the irisStyle parameter
Pixelate	maxSquare=*value*	Applies a pixelate transition, where maxSquare is the size of the pixel
RadialWipe	wipeStyle=clock, wedge, radial	Applies a radial wipe transition
RandomBars	orientation=horizontal, vertical	Applies a random bars transition
RandomDissolve	duration=*value*	Dissolves one object into another. The duration parameter indicates the dissolve time in seconds
Slide	slideStyle=hide, push, swap bands=value	Slides one object over or into another
Spiral	gridSizeX=*value* gridSizeY=*value*	Spirals one object into another
Stretch	stretchStyle=hide, push, spin	Stretches one object into another
Strips	motion=left-up, left-down, right-up, right-down	Wipes one object over another in a diagonal direction
Wheel	spokes=*value*	Applies a wheel transition
ZigZag	gridSizeX=*value* gridSizeY=*value*	Applies a zig-zag transition

Figure J-7 shows an example of applying the IE 5.5 stretch transition to replace one inline image with another.

Figure J-7 **IE 5.5 stretch style transition**

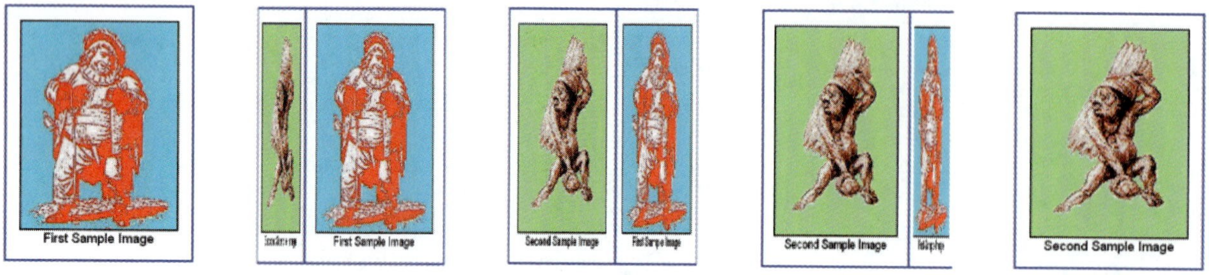

initial image

stretch (stretchStyle = push)

final image

Scripting a Transition

The code for scripting a transition follows the same syntax described earlier for filters. For example, the code to apply the RadialWipe transition with a WipeStyle value of "clock" to an object is

```
object.style.filter =
"progId:DXImageTransform.Microsoft.RadialWipe(WipeStyle=clock)"
```

where *object* is the object receiving the transition style. You can also use the filters collection to modify the parameter value of a selected transition. The following code sets the WipeStyle parameter of the RadialWipe transition to a value, of "clock":

```
object.filters["DXImageTransform.Microsoft.RadialWipe"].WipeStyle="clock";
```

Again, if you use a filters collection, you must define a filter style in the style sheet for the object.

Running a Transition

If you want to see the effect of a transition style on your object, you have to run it using a series of JavaScript commands. Running a transition involves four steps:

1. Setting the initial state of the object
2. Applying a transition to the object
3. Specifying the final state of the object
4. Playing the transition

The initial state of the object is the status of the object before the transition. This includes such things as the visibility property of the object, the source of an inline image, or any HTML code applied to the object. Once the initial state of the object has been determined, you apply the transition by using the apply() method

```
object.filters[idref].apply();
```

where *object* is the object that you want to apply the transition and idref is either the index number or the text of the transition name. Applying the transition does not actually run the transition, because the final state of the object has not been determined yet. At this point, it simply "freezes" the object in its initial state. Once the transition has been applied, you can write code to modify the appearance of the object, but because the object is frozen, these changes will not appear in the Web page.

After you've defined the final state of the object, you use the play() method to "unfreeze" the object and run the transition effect, moving the object from its initial state to its final state. The syntax for playing a transition is

```
object.filters[idref].play(duration);
```

where *duration* is the time, in seconds, for the transition to run. Note that for IE 4.0 transitions, the duration of the transition is entered as a parameter of the transition. The following code demonstrates how to create a transition between two sources for an inline image.

```
<style type="text/css">
   #Img1 {filter: progid:DXImageTransform.Microsoft.Slide(slideStyle =
push, Bands = 1)}
</style>
<script type="text/javascript">
var img = document.getElementById("Img1");
img.onclick = transitionImage;

function transitionImage() {
   img.filters[0].apply();
   img.src = "slide2.jpg";
   img.filters[0].play(2);
}
</script>
```

This code applies the transition to an inline image file whose ID attribute is equal to "Img1". When a user clicks the inline image, the transitionImage() function is called. The apply() method applies the Slide transition to the image and freezes it. The source of the inline image is changed to the slide2.jpg file. The play() method is then invoked, running the Slide transition for two seconds. After the transition is complete, the Img1 object is left displaying a new inline image.

The IE transitions can be applied to any HTML object. The following code shows how to apply a Fade-out transition to a div element containing a quote from Hamlet:

```
<style type="text/css">
   #Hamlet {visibility: visible; position: absolute}
   #Hamlet {filter: progid:DXImageTransform.Microsoft.Fade(overlap = 1)}
</style>
<script type="text/javascript">
var Hamlet = document.getElementById("Hamlet");
Hamlet.onclick = fadeOut;
```

```
function fadeOut() {
   Hamlet.filters[0].apply();
   Hamlet.style.visibility = "hidden";
   Hamlet.filters[0].play();
}
</script>
<div id="Hamlet" onclick="fadeOut()">
   <h1>The Rest is Silence</h1>
</div>
```

In this example, the text string will fade out when the user clicks it, changing its state from visible to hidden. Because this is a div element, you must define an absolute position before the transition can be applied. The span element has a similar requirement.

Using Interpage Transitions

Internet Explorer also allows you to create transitions between one Web page and another. These transitions, known as **interpage transitions**, involve effects applied to a page when a browser either enters or exits the page. Interpage transitions are created using the meta element within the head section of the HTML file. The meta element specifies the type of transition, the duration, and whether it's applied on entering or exiting the page. The four types of transitions occur when a user initially enters the Web page, exits the page, enters the Web site, or exits the site. The syntax for the four different interpage transitions are

```
<meta http-equiv = "Page-Enter" content = "type" />

<meta http-equiv = "Page-Exit" content = "type" />

<meta http-equiv = "Site-Enter" content = "type" />

<meta http-equiv = "Site-Exit" content = "type" />
```

where *type* is one of the transitions supported by Internet Explorer and the http-equiv attribute specifies when the transition should be applied. The syntax for the transition type is the same for interpage transitions as it is for an object within a page. These transitions appear only when you go from one page to another or from one Web site to another. A user does not see a Page-Enter transition if the page is the first file the user opens when starting a Web browser.

For example, to display an inset transition with a duration of 3 seconds when a user enters the page, you would apply the following meta element:

```
<meta http-equiv="Page-Enter"
content="progid:DXImageTransform.Microsoft.Inset(duration=3)" />
```

To apply a 2-second Wheel transition upon exiting the page, you would add the following meta element to the page head:

```
<meta http-equiv="Page-Exit"
content="progid:DXImageTransform.Microsoft.Wheel(Spokes=8, duration=2)" />
```

If a browser other than Internet Explorer encounters these meta elements, it will open or exit the page as usual without attempting to apply the transition style. So, do not rely on these transitions if you plan on supporting non–IE browsers.

Review | Appendix Summary

This appendix examined the Internet Explorer-only styles to create filters and transitions. It showed how to use filters to add drop shadows, blurs, light illumination and other special effects to document objects. It also examined how to apply graphic transitions between one document object and another. The appendix then examined how to work with these styles under both CSS and JavaScript. The appendix concluded by examining how to use the meta element to create interpage transitions.

Key Terms

blend transition	filter collection	reveal transition
filter	interpage transition	transition

Exploring AJAX

Appendix K

Asynchronous JavaScript and XML, otherwise known as **AJAX**, is a collection on interrelated Web technologies designed to create interactive Web and Internet applications. AJAX applications involve the following features and technology:

- Asynchronous—A Web page can request information from the Web server without having to halt its other activities as it awaits a response.
- JavaScript—JavaScript is used to make requests to the server and to present the response from the server to the user.
- XML—The data received from the server can be packaged as a snippet of XML, allowing it to be easily processed by JavaScript.

Jesse James Garrett was the first person to coin the AJAX acronym in the Web article AJAX: A New Approach to Web Applications, posted in February 2005 on the Web site for the Adaptive Path consulting firm, shown in Figure K-1. However, neither Garrett nor Adaptive Path invented AJAX. When Garrett wrote his article, AJAX-style applications such as Google Suggest, Google Maps, and GMail had already been developed by Google. Flickr was just coming out, providing a source for digital photo sharing. America Online's AIM Mail, another service that used AJAX principles, was about to come out. The Garrett article instead focused attention on this new approach to Web interactivity.

Starting Data Files

There are no starting Data Files needed for this appendix.

Figure K-1 **Original AJAX article**

adaptive path

blog | about us | services | events | **ideas** | contact | home

ideas

blog | reports | latest essay | newsletter | **essay archives** | reading list

Ajax: A New Approach to Web Applications

by Jesse James Garrett

February 18, 2005

If anything about current interaction design can be called "glamorous," it's creating Web applications. After all, when was the last time you heard someone rave about the interaction design of a product that wasn't on the Web? (Okay, besides the iPod.) All the cool, innovative new projects are online.

Despite this, Web interaction designers can't help but feel a little envious of our colleagues who create desktop software. Desktop applications have a richness and responsiveness that has seemed out of reach on the Web. The same simplicity that enabled the Web's rapid proliferation also creates a gap between the experiences we can provide and the experiences users can get from a desktop application.

That gap is closing. Take a look at Google Suggest. Watch the way the suggested terms update as you type, almost instantly. Now look at Google Maps. Zoom in. Use your cursor to grab the map and scroll

Jesse James Garrett is President and a founder of Adaptive Path. He is the author of the widely-referenced book The Elements of User Experience. Jesse's other essays include The Nine Pillars

Recent Essays

Project Management for Creative Teams: Art and Science
April 2, 2008

Kate Discusses the Role of Design in Business with Nathan Shedroff
March 18, 2008

Secil Watson Tells Jesse James Garrett About Experience Design at Wells Fargo
March 12, 2008

Stephen Anderson Tells Todd About Implementing Visionary Ideas
February 28, 2008

Indi Young Tells Kate About Mental Models & Her New Book

To better appreciate the difference between AJAX-style applications and other Web applications, let's examine the paradigm that predominated before AJAX.

Synchronous Communication

In the **classic Web application model** shown in Figure K-2, users interact with a Web server through a Web page running on their browser. The Web page might be a Web form in which a user enters some specific pieces of information such as a purchase order or a message. To send this information to the Web server for processing, the user might click a Submit button or use another method. The user's action triggers an HTTP request that is sent back to the Web server. The server processes this information, perhaps by running a Web server script or accessing a database program. If a response is required, data is sent back to the user, usually in the form of another Web page. So the level of information under the classic Web application model is chunked in pages: one page to request information; another page to report on the results of that request.

Classic Web application model **Figure K-2**

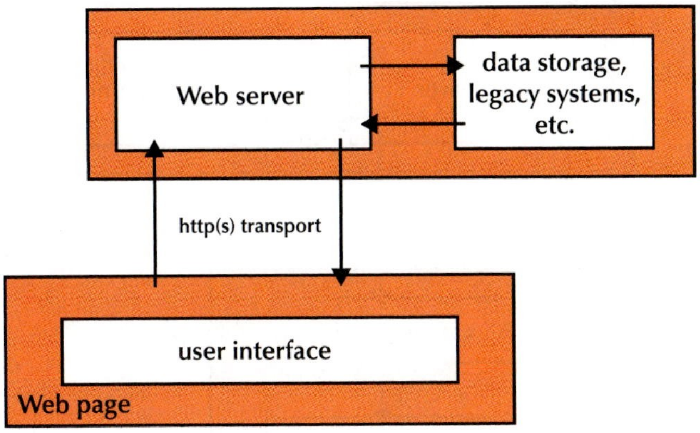

For example, the original version of the Google search page included a form in which users entered a search term, and then pressed a Google Search button to submit the search term to a database application running on the Google Web server. After a short delay, Google returned a collection of Web pages containing links to pages related to the search term.

One problem with the classic Web application model is that the whole communication is by its nature synchronous which means that the Web client or browser must wait on the response from the Web server before it can continue. As shown in Figure K-3, the user sends a request and then must wait for a response from the server before proceeding. While the user is waiting for a response in the form of a new Web page, the current Web page is unavailable for any work.

Synchronous communications in the classic Web application model **Figure K-3**

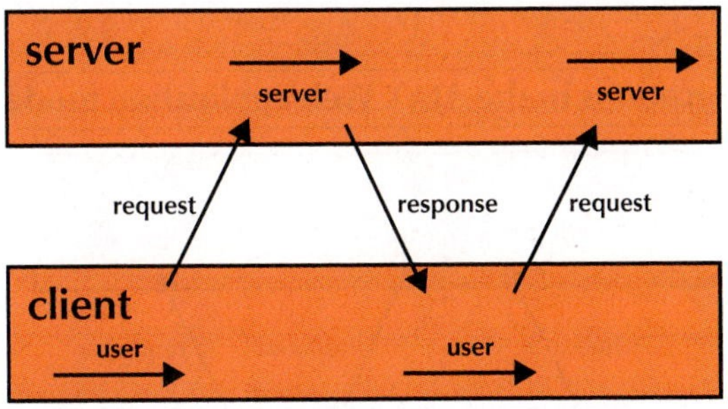

Asynchronous Communication

Under AJAX, an intermediary is added between the user and the server-side system, called the **AJAX engine**. As shown in Figure K-4, the AJAX engine is responsible for communicating with the server and for representing any information from the server to the user interface. The user interface interacts with the AJAX engine using code written in JavaScript, but the engine communicates with the server using the same HTTP requests that the classic Web application model employs.

Figure K-4 AJAX Web application model

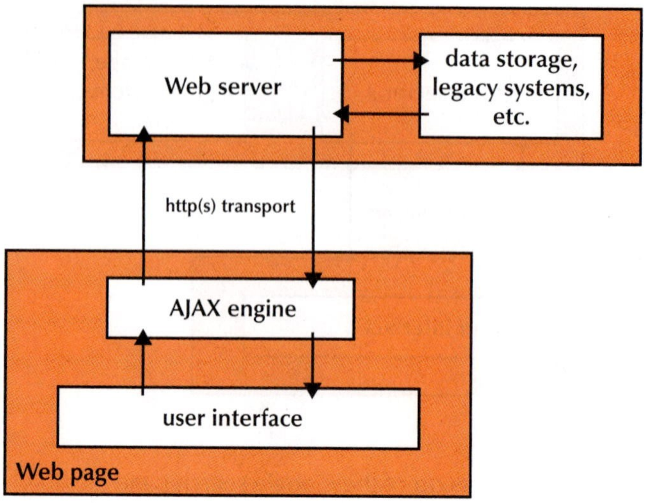

One important difference between the two models is the AJAX engine can be placed within a portion of the Web page, such as within an inline frame. This means that instead of having to transfer information by unloading old pages and loading new ones, only that section of the current Web page must be updated and changed. As shown in Figure K-5, from the user's point of view, this communication is **asynchronous**, which means that the communication between the AJAX engine and the server can occur independently from events occurring in the Web page. Because the AJAX engine is making requests to the server and receiving the response, the user is free to interact with the rest of the browser client. Also, because the server is not dealing with generating an entire Web page in its response, but only responding with specific and probably smaller, chunks of information, the load on the server is lessened.

Figure K-5 Asynchronous communications in the AJAX Web application model

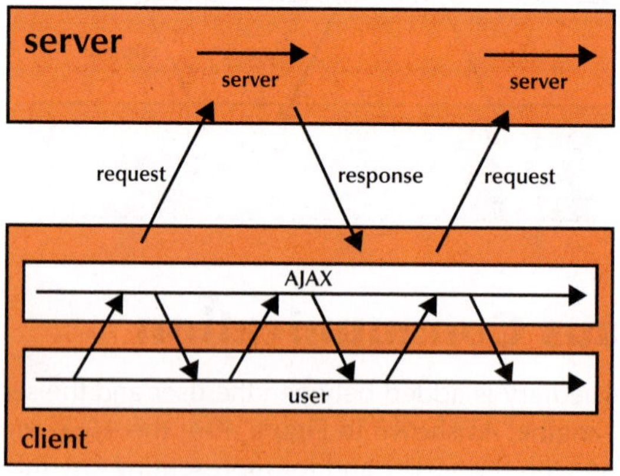

Figure K-6 shows how the AJAX engine operates within the Google search page. As the user types a search phrase in the input box, an AJAX engine is working behind the scenes to make a request to the Web server and download the response in the form of a set of suggestions based on the text the user is currently typing. The user has immediate interactivity with the server without losing access to the rest of the Web page.

Figure K-6 AJAX results on the Google search page

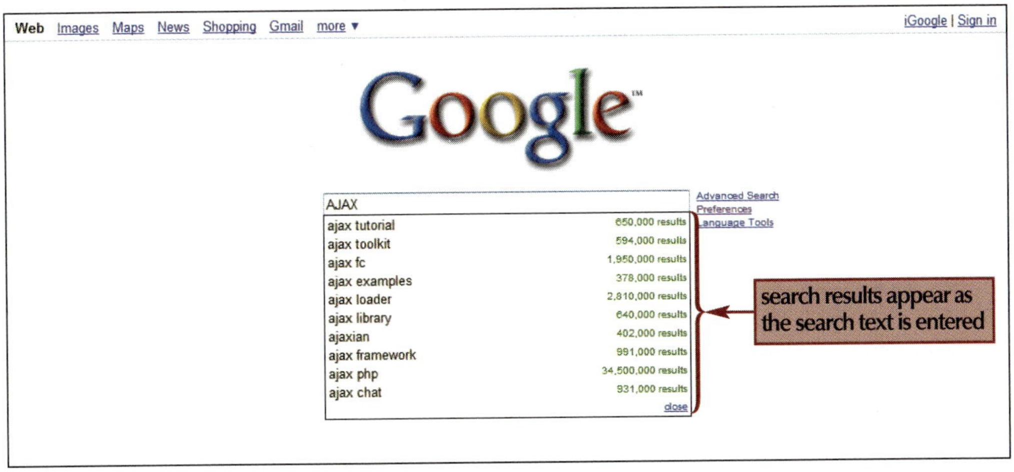

Exploring the XMLHttpRequest Object

To make an HTTP request to the server using JavaScript, you need an object class that provides the ability to do requests under the HTTP communications protocol. This class was originally introduced in Internet Explorer 5 as an ActiveX object. You can create the ActiveX object using the statement

```
request = new ActiveXObject("Microsoft.XMLHTTP");
```

or the statement

```
request = new ActiveXObject(Msxml2.XMLHTTP");
```

where *request* is a variable to store the request object. Non–Internet Explorer browsers support the following object class:

```
request = new XMLHttpRequest();
```

Although the XMLHttpRequest object is not part of the W3C DOM, it has become the de facto standard due to its near universal support in current versions of all major browsers. The request object is an abstract object, that does not appear on the Web page, but that supports a variety of methods and properties to facilitate the exchange of information with the server. There are several ways of creating an XMLHttpRequest object that is cross-browser compatible. The following code uses a series of try/catch statements to generate request object named req:

```
//native XMLHttpRequest object
if (window.XMLHttpRequest) {
   try {
      var req = XMLHttpRequest();
   } catch(e) {
      var req = false;
   }
//IE XMLHttpRequest object
} else if (window.ActiveXObject) {
   try {
```

```
        var req = new ActiveXObject("Microsoft.XMLHTTP");
    } catch(e) {
        var req = false;
    }
}
```

Once the XMLHttpRequest object has been created, the objects and properties applicable to it are essentially the same across browsers. This is the only cross-browser code that you must worry about in an AJAX application.

XMLHttpRequest Methods

Figure K-7 summarizes some of the methods associated with the XMLHttpRequest object.

Figure K-7 Methods of the XMLHttpRequest object

Method	Description
abort()	Stops the current request
getAllResponseHeaders()	Returns complete set of headers (labels and values) as a string
getResponseHeader(*headerLabel*)	Returns the string value of a single header label
open(*method, url, async, user, pwd*)	Assigns a method, destination URL, and optional attributes of the pending request
send(*content*)	Transmits the request, optionally postable string or DOM object data
setRequestHeader(*label, value*)	Assigns a label/value pair to the header to be sent with a request

To facilitate asynchronous communication between the Web browser and the Web server, you use the open() and send() methods in any AJAX application. The open() method initializes the connection to the server and has the following syntax:

```
open(method, url, async, user, pwd)
```

The first argument, *method*, specifies the method of communication with the server. The most common values for the *method* argument are GET and POST. Use GET on operations that are primarily data retrieval requests; use POST on operations that both send data to and receive data from the server. The second argument, *url*, specifies the URL of the page or service being requested. For security reasons, you cannot call pages on third-party domains; you can only use the same domain as the one that serves up the page containing the script. This means that client-side scripts cannot fetch Web service data from other data sources. Everything must come from the same domain. Nor can you access pages on the local machine. All AJAX requests must be sent to a server. The *async* argument is a Boolean value that indicates whether the request is asynchronous. If this argument is set to true (the default value), the execution of the JavaScript function will still continue while waiting for a response from the server. Finally, the *user* and *pwd* arguments specify a username and password, if these are required to communicate with the server. The *async*, *user*, and *pwd* arguments are all optional. The following examples apply the open() method:

```
request.open("GET", "http://www.store.com/accounts.xml", true);

request.open("GET", "reports.html", false);

request.open("POST", "show-accounts.php", true, "davis", "GRxu32");
```

where *request* is an XMLHttpRequest object. In the first example, communication with an XML document on the server is opened using the GET method. The connection is asynchronous. The second example uses the GET method to open a connection to the reports.html Web page. The URL is local so the server assumes that the current Web page is part of the same domain as reports.html. The connection is synchronous so that the function calling this XMLHttpRequest object halts until some response is received from the object. Finally, the third example shows how to use the POST method to access a PHP script running on the local domain. The connection is asynchronous and in this case a username and a password are required to make the connection.

Once communication with the server has been opened, you can send a request to the server using the method

```
send(content)
```

where *content* is the content to be sent to the server. The send() method can contain any data that you want to send to the server, if you POST the request. The data can be sent in the form of a query string, as in the example

```
request.send(username=RobertDavis&account=318912);
```

which sends a query with values set for the username and account fields. You might not need to send data to the server, but you still must apply the send() method as part of initiating the connection. If there is no data to send, you can specify a value of null in the send() method, as follows:

```
request.send(null);
```

XMLHttpRequest Properties

Once the request object has been created, opened, and sent, you can work with the properties of the request object to determine what kind of response has been received from the server. Figure K-8 summarizes some of the properties of the XMLHttpRequest object.

Properties of the XMLHttpRequest object **Figure K-8**

Property	Description
onreadystatechange	Event handler for an event that fires at every state change
readyState	A numeric value from 0 to 4 indicating the state of the request object
responseText	String version of data returned by the server process
responseXML	DOM-compatible document object of data returned from server
status	Numeric code returned by server, such as 404 for "Not Found" or 200 for "OK"
statusText	String message accompanying the status code

An important property is the onreadystatechange property, which is used to associate an event handler with a request object. The event handler runs whenever the readyState of the request object changes. The request object has the five possible states described in Figure K-9.

Figure K-9 **Values of the readyState property**

readyState	Description
0	The request is uninitialized with no connection having been made between the request object and the server
1	The request object is being loaded
2	The request object has finished loading
3	The request object is interacting with the server
4	The transaction between the request object and the server is complete

The following code shows how to use the onreadystatechange property to set up and handle the connection with the server and the response the server returns to the AJAX application.

```
request.onreadystatechange = ajaxAlert;
request.open("GET", "accounts.xml", true);
request.send(null);
function ajaxAlert() {
   commands when readyState changes in request object
   if (request.readyState == 4) {
   commands to run after the process is complete
   }
}
```

This code first assigns an event handler to the request object that runs whenever the state of the request object changes. The next two commands open the request object to connect to the accounts.xml file using the GET method under asynchronous communication. No data is sent to the server. The request object then goes through several states as the request is processed. The ajaxAlert() function is run whenever the status of the request object changes as it goes from being initialized through the completion of the transaction with the accounts.xml file.

Once the transaction is complete, you should check the status of the transaction using the status property; after all, the transaction may have failed. Figure K-10 lists the value of the status property. Note that if the status code is equal to 200, then the transaction has completed successfully. Anything else indicates that either the process is still running or has completed unsuccessfully.

Figure K-10 Values of the status property

Status Code	Description
100	Continue
200	OK
302	Found
400	Bad request
404	Not Found
408	Request timeout
500	Internal Server Error

Once you receive a response and the transaction has been completed successfully, you can examine the content sent from the server to the AJAX application. The request object has two properties that you can use to view this information. One is the following responseText property, which returns the information as a text string:

```
request.responseText
```

The other is the responseXML property

```
request.responseXML
```

which returns the information as an XML document. One advantage of the responseXML property is that you can use the document object model to view, navigate and manipulate the contents of the XML document. After all, the X in AJAX stands for XML. In either case, you can use JavaScript to extract information from the request object and display that information in the Web page without having to reload the Web page or refresh the browser window.

Exploring the Disadvantages of AJAX

AJAX has provided dynamic and interesting interactive content for thousands of Web sites. However, it is not without its critics. Among the problems and limitations of AJAX, keep in mind the following:

- AJAX can break the behavior of the browser's Back button because you cannot use the Back button to go backward on the information supplied by the request object. There are workarounds and tools to overcome this problem, including the use of invisible inline frames.
- You cannot easily bookmark a particular state of an AJAX application.
- If the AJAX connection to the server is slow, the delay in response may confuse users (one way to avoid this problem is to preload useful data).
- JavaScript must be enabled to use AJAX. Many users turn off JavaScript, also turning off the ability to use an AJAX application.
- AJAX applications may violate Section 502C guidelines, making it difficult for users with disabilities to interact with AJAX applications.

Still, AJAX has grown in popularity and has spawned thousands of new tools that can be easily incorporated into Web sites. If you intend on using AJAX in a Web site, you need to be familiar with both its great potential and its limitations.

Review | **Appendix Summary**

This appendix explored Asynchronous JavaScript and XML, otherwise known as AJAX. It compared the classic Web application model, which used synchronous communication, to the asynchronous communication used by the AJAX engine. The appendix also reviewed the XMLHttpRequest object, methods, and properties. Finally, the appendix reviewed some of the problems and limitations of AJAX.

Key Terms

AJAX
AJAX engine
asynchronous
Asynchronous JavaScript and XML (AJAX)
classic Web application model
synchronous

Glossary/Index

Note: Boldface entries include definitions.

Special Characters

A

counter variable A variable in a For loop that is used to track the number of times a set of commands is run. HTML 685–687

credit card number
- Lun formula for testing, HTML 839–841
- removing blank spaces, HTML 836–837
- validating patterns, HTML 837–839

CSS. *See* Cascading Style Sheets (CSS)

CSS clip style, animating pull-down menus, HTML 756–760

CSS style
- applying filters using, HTML J2–J4
- object properties, HTML 741–742
- retrieving style sheet values, HTML 763

CSS1 The first version of CSS, introduced in 1996, but not fully implemented by any browser for another three years. HTML 125

CSS2 The second version of CSS, introduced in 1998, which expanded the language to support styles for positioning, visual formatting, media types, and interfaces. HTML 125

CSS 2.1 An update to CSS2, introduced 2002, which did not add any new features to the language, but cleaned up minor errors that were introduced in the original specification. HTML 125

CSS3 The next version of CSS, still in development as of this writing; will add styles for user interfaces, accessibility, columnar layout, international features, mobile devices, and scalable vector graphics. HTML 125
- rounded boxes, HTML 330

CSS-P. *See* CSS-Positioning

CSS-Positioning (CSS-P) The collection of various positioning styles, added to CSS2. HTML 226

curly braces ()
- command blocks, HTML 686
- escape sequences, HTML 828
- repetition characters, HTML 827

cursor, setting style, HTML 895–897

custom object, HTML 732, HTML 763–766
- creating, HTML 765–766
- defining customized properties, HTML 764
- new operator, HTML 763–764
- running object constructors, HTML 764–765

customized object An object created by the user. HTML 732

D

data cell In a table, a cell used for any content that is not considered a heading. HTML 275–276

data rate The amount of data that has to be processed by a video player each second to play a video clip. HTML 431

data type Refers to the type of information stored in a variable. HTML 580–583

date method A method you can use to retrieve information from a date object or to change a date object's value. HTML 624–625

date object An object that contains information about a specified date and time. HTML 623–629
- creating date and time function, HTML 627–629
- creating date and time variables, HTML 623
- retrieving date, month, and hour values, HTML 624–625
- retrieving hour, minute, and second values, HTML 625–626
- setting date and time values, HTML 626–627

daylight savings time, HTML 627

debugging The process of searching code to locate a source of trouble. HTML 597–603
- common mistakes in JavaScript programs, HTML 599
- tools and techniques, HTML 599–603

declaring The process of telling the JavaScript interpreter to reserve memory space for a variable. HTML 578

decrement operator The unary operator that decreases the operand's value by 1, indicated by the — symbol. HTML 631, HTML 632

default action, canceling, HTML 914–915

default namespace The namespace that is assumed to be applied to the root element and any element within it-which includes, by default, any element within the document. HTML 540

defaultChecked property, option button, HTML 794

definition list A type of list that contains a list of terms, each followed by the term's description. HTML 25–27

delimiter A text string that marks the break between one substring and another. HTML 811–812

deprecated Refers to a feature of HTML or XHTML that is being phased out by the W3C and which might not be supported by future browsers. HTML 6

device-independent Documents, such as those written in SGML, that can in theory be used on almost any type of device. HTML 526

dialog, definition lists to mark, HTML 26

digital audio, HTML 413–417
- background sound, HTML 429
- file formats, HTML 416–417

digital video, HTML 431–434
- data rates and video quality, HTML 431–432
- file formats, HTML 432–433
- Flash. *See* Flash
- media players, HTML 434–446
- QuickTime video, HTML 439–443
- Windows Media Player, HTML 443–445

display style, HTML 180–183
- tables, HTML 311–312

displaying
- HTML documents, HTML 14–15
- nested lists, HTML 973–975
- scroll bars, HTML 490–491

div container A generic block-level element that you can resize and float to create different page layouts. HTML 174–180, HTML 326–330
- creating, HTML 175–176, HTML 178
- CSS3, HTML 330
- nesting, HTML 326–329
- style, crating, HTML 179
- width, setting, HTML 176–177

DOCTYPE declaration, HTML 538–539
- changing, HTML 547

document fragment An unattached node or node tree that exists only in a browser's memory. HTML 946

document object An object that references elements and features of the Web document or Web browser. HTML 732

document object model (DOM) The structure of all the objects within documents and browsers that are organized in a systematic way. HTML 733–735. *See also* DOM *entries*
- basic model, HTML 733–734
- document tree, HTML 735
- IE, node types, HTML 943
- IE, object references, HTML 739
- order of event ascent and descent through objects, HTML 872
- W3C, node types, HTML 942–943

document tree The hierarchy that each document object model organizes objects into. HTML 735

document type definition (DTD) A collection of rules used to specify what the correct content and structure is for a document. HTML 533–537
- attributes, HTML 535–537
- frameset, HTML 533, HTML 534
- setting, HTML 539
- strict, HTML 533, HTML 534–536, HTML 550
- transitional, HTML 533–534

document.writeln() method, HTML 573–575

document.write() method, HTML 573–575

dollar sign ($)
- escape sequences, HTML 828
- regular expressions, HTML 821

DOM. *See* document object model (DOM)

DOM Level 0. *See* basic model

DOM Level 1 The first specification, released in October 1998, provided support for all elements contained within HTML and XML documents. HTML 734

DOM Level 2 The second specification, released in November 2000, enhanced the document object model by providing an event model that specified how events are captured as they progress through the objects in a Web browser. DOM Level 2 also extended the style sheet model to work with CSS style sheets and provided a range model to allow programmers to manipulate sections of text within a document. HTML 734

DOM Level 3 The most recent specification, released in April 2004, provides a framework for working with document loading and saving, as well as for working with

F

G

H

I

J

Java A programming language used for applications on the Internet. HTML 454–464
- applets. *See* Java Virtual Machine (JVM)

Java Virtual Machine (JVM) A software program that runs the Java code and returns the results to the user's computer. HTML 454

JavaScript A subscript of Java, meant to be easy for nonprogrammers to use. HTML 563–604
- accessing external JavaScript files, HTML 590–594
- applying filter styles, HTML J4–J5
- commending JavaScript code, HTML 594–596
- conditional statements. *See* conditional statement
- creating date and time variables, HTML 623
- debugging, HTML 597–603
- development, HTML 568–569
- functions, HTML 583–589
- non-JavaScript browsers, HTML 577
- numeric values, HTML 643–646
- program loops. *See* program loop
- running commands as hypertext links, HTML 622
- script element, HTML 569–571
- statements, HTML 571
- syntax, HTML 575–576
- variables, HTML 578–583
- writing output to Web documents, HTML 571–575

jigsaw layout A table layout that involves breaking up page content into separate table cells that are then joined together like pieces in a jigsaw puzzle. HTML 314–321
- rounded border, HTML 320–321
- structure, defining, HTML 315–320

jigsaw puzzle
- dropping puzzle pieces, HTML 888–889
- highlighting grid square, HTML 897–900
- keeping dragged items on top, HTML 889–890
- moving pieces with keyboard, HTML 910–911
- preventing hidden pieces, HTML 890–892
- selecting pieces with keyboard, HTML 908–910
- setting up, HTML 862–867
- snapping pieces to puzzle grid, HTML 892–893
- toggling between modes, HTML 906–908, HTML 911–912

Joint Photographic Experts Group (JPEG) One of the main image file formats for Web pages; in the JPEG format, you can create images that use all 16.7 million colors available in the color palette. HTML 155–156

JPEG. *See* Joint Photographic Experts Group (JPEG)

Jscript A slightly different version of JavaScript, supported by Internet Explorer. HTML 569

JVM. *See* Java Virtual Machine (JVM)

K

kerning A typographic feature that refers to the amount of space between characters. HTML 146–147

keyboard, canceling default actions, HTML 914–915

keyboard event, HTML 901–913
- key code values, HTML 904–905
- keypress event and character codes, HTML 912–913
- modifier keys, HTML 913
- moving puzzle pieces, HTML 910–912
- properties, HTML 903–905
- selecting puzzle pieces, HTML 908–910
- toggling between modes, HTML 906–908

keydown The keyboard event in which the user presses the key down. HTML 902, HTML 903

keyMove() function, HTML 910–911

keypress The keyboard event that follows immediately after the onkeydown event. HTML 902, HTML 903
- character codes, HTML 912–913

keyup The keyboard event that occurs after the key has been released by the user. HTML 902, HTML 903

L

label statement, HTML 710–711

LAN. *See* Local Area Network (LAN)

language
- compiled, HTML 568
- interpreted, HTML 568
- strongly typed, HTML 581
- weakly typed, HTML 581

Latin-1 An extended character set of 255 characters that can be used by most languages that employ the Latin alphabet, including English, French, Spanish, and Italian; also called ISO-8859-1. HTML 43

layout
- lists, HTML 212–123
- page. *See* page layout

leading A typographic feature that refers to the amount of space between words. HTML 147–148

length of arrays, HTML 678–679

less than operator (<), HTML 647, HTML 648

less than or equal to operator (<=), HTML 648

Light filter, HTML J4, HTML J5–J7

linear structure A structure for a Web site in which each page is linked with the pages that follow and precede it. HTML 63

link An element in a hypertext document that allows you to jump from one topic or document to another, usually by clicking it with a mouse button. HTML 3
- creating, HTML 67–69
- between documents, HTML 78–80
- within documents, HTML 74–80
- effective, HTML 88
- frames, HTML 494–502
- id attribute, HTML 76–77
- inserting, HTML 965–967
- linking to Internet resources. *See* linking to Internet resources
- rollover effect, HTML 217–218
- running JavaScript commands as hypertext links, HTML 622
- semantic, HTML 101–102
- specifying folder path, HTML 69–73

link element, HTML 102–103
- style sheets, HTML 986–990

linking to external style sheets, HTML 129–130

linking to Internet resources, HTML 89–98
- e-mail addresses, HTML 94–98
- FTP servers, HTML 92–93
- local files, HTML 93–94
- URLs, HTML 89–90
- Web sites, HTML 90–92

list, HTML 22–27, HTML 207–213
- changing between vertical and horizontal lists, HTML 213
- defining position and layout, HTML 211–213
- definition, HTML 25–27
- marking, HTML 24
- nested, creating, HTML 954–961
- nesting, HTML 24–25
- ordered, HTML 22. *See* ordered list
- style, HTML 207–210, HTML 211
- unordered, HTML 23–24, HTML 26–27

load-time error An error that occurs when a script is first loaded by the browser. HTML 597

local area network (LAN) A network confined to a small geographic area, such as within a building or department. HTML 2

local file, linking to, HTML 93–94

local namespace A namespace for elements that do not belong to the default namespace. HTML 541

local scope Describes a variable created within a JavaScript function that can be referenced only within that function. HTML 589

local variable A variable with local scope. HTML 589

logical element An element that describes the nature of the enclosed content but not necessarily how that content should appear. HTML 33

logical error An error that doesn't involve syntax and structural mistakes, but results in incorrect results. HTML 598

logical operator An operator that allows you to connect two or more Boolean expressions. HTML 648–651

looping through child node collection, HTML 948–949

Luhn Formula A formula developed by a group of mathematicians in the 1960s to provide a quick validation check on an account number by adding up the digits in the number. HTML 839–841

M

mailto action, HTML 393

margin In the box model, the space between an element and other page content. HTML 166–167

N

plug-in An extra component added to a program (such as a Web browser) to provide a feature or capability not included in the program. HTML 413
- parameters, HTML 421–424

plus sign (+)
- addition assignment operator, HTML 632–633
- addition operator, HTML 631
- escape sequences, HTML 828
- increment operator, HTML 631–632
- repetition character, HTML 827

plus/minus box An object that can alternately hide or display nested entries; a + symbol in the box indicates that content is hidden and a — symbol indicates that all the items are displayed. HTML 969–973
- adding event handlers, HTML 972–973
- creating, HTML 969–972
- placing, HTML 971–972

PNG (PNG). *See* Portable Network Graphics

pop-up menu A menu in which a user clicks an object on the page and the menu appears, sometimes elsewhere on the page. HTML 760

Portable Network Graphics (PNG) A third graphic format gaining wider acceptance; PNG files include most of the same features as GIFs, but also provide file compression and the full 16.7 million colors available with JPEGs. HTML 156

position, lists, HTML 211

positioning objects with CSS, HTML 222–234
- callouts, HTML 223–226
- fixed positioning, HTML 231–232
- inherited positioning, HTML 231–232
- positioning styles, HTML 226–227

positioning objects with CSS
- absolute positioning HTML 227–230
- relative positioning, HTML 230–231

post method One of two possible values for the method attribute; sends form data in a separate data stream, allowing the Web server to receive the data through what is called standard input; because it is more flexible and safer, most Web designers prefer the post method for sending data to a server. HTML 391

preferred style sheet A style sheet that is similar to a persistent style sheet except that it contains a value for the title attribute. HTML 984

preformatted text Text that is displayed by the browser with the same spacing and line breaks that you enter. HTML 291

presentational attribute An attribute that specifically describes how an element should be rendered; almost all presentational attributes are now deprecated in favor of styles. HTML 37

primary color, HTML 135

print server A network node that provides printing services to the network. HTML 2

print style, HTML 252–255

program loop A set of commands that it is executed repeatedly until a stopping condition has been met. HTML 684–691. *See also specific loops*
- creating, HTML 691
- jumping to next iteration, HTML 709–710
- statement labels, HTML 710–711
- terminating, HTML 709

prolog, XML, HTML 530

property A description of an object's appearance, purpose, or behavior. HTML 732, HTML 733, HTML 740–743
- arrays of menus, HTML 742–743
- classes versus style object, HTML 742
- CSS styles, HTML 741–742
- event objects, HTML 878, HTML 879
- HTML attributes, HTML 740–743
- keyboard events, HTML 903–905
- nodes, HTML 944
- read-only, HTML 741

protected structure A structure for a Web site in which portions of the site are off-limits except to users with passwords (usually subscribers and registered customers). HTML 66–67

protocol A set of rules defining how information is passed between two devices. HTML 89–90

pseudo-class A classification of an element based on its current status, position, or use in the document. HTML 215–218
- page pseudo-classes, HTML 248–249

pseudo-element An element that is not part of the document tree, but is instead abstracted from what we know of an element's content, use, or position in the document. HTML 219–222
- drop caps, HTML 219–220
- generating text, HTML 221–222

publishing a Web page, HTML 48

pull-down menu A menu in which a menu title is always visible to the user, identifying the entries in the menu. When a user clicks the title or in some cases moves the pointer over the title, the rest of the menu is displayed, often accompanied by the effect of a menu being "pulled down" from the title. HTML 729–760
- animating, HTML 756–760
- objects. *See* object
- overview, HTML 730–732
- programming, HTML 747–755

Q

question mark (?)
- escape sequences, HTML 828
- repetition character, HTML 827

QuickTime, HTML 439–443
- parameters, HTML 422, HTML 441–443

quirks mode One of the two modes a browser can work in; in quirks mode, the browser applies its own interpretation of the box model and other features of CSS. HTML 173

R

r, escape sequences, HTML 828

RadialWipe transition, HTML J9

radio button. *See* option button

Random Bars Horizontal transition, HTML J8

Random Bars Vertical transition, HTML J8

Random Dissolve transition, HTML J8

random numbers, generating, HTML 638

Random transition, HTML J8

RandomBars transition, HTML J9

RandomDissolve transition, HTML J9

read-only property A property you cannot change, which has a fixed value. HTML 741

RealAudio file format, HTML 416

recursion A programming technique in which program code calls itself repeatedly until a stopping condition is met. HTML 982

regular expression A text string that defines a character pattern. HTML 818–835
- creating, HTML 818–819
- defining character positions, HTML 821–823
- defining character types and character classes, HTML 823–826
- escape sequences, HTML 828–829
- matching substrings, HTML 819–820
- methods, HTML 831–833
- object constructor, HTML 831
- setting flags, HTML 820–821
- spaces, HTML 820
- specifying alternate patterns and grouping, HTML 829–830
- specifying repeating characters, HTML 826–828
- validating financial data, HTML 835–841
- validating zip codes, HTML 834–835

regular expression literal The syntax for creating regular expressions. HTML 818

relative path A path that specifies a file's location in relation to the location of the current document. HTML 71–72

relative positioning Positioning that is used to move an element relative to its default position on the page. HTML 230–231

relative unit Units expressed relative to the size of other objects within a Web page. HTML 144

remainder assignment operator (%=), HTML 633

removeEvent() function, HTML 874–875

removing events, HTML 874–876

reserved target name A special name that can be used in place of a frame name as a target. HTML 498–502

reset button A control element that resets a form, changing all field values to their original default values and deleting any values that the user might have entered into the form. HTML 385–387

resetting forms, HTML 805–806